Lecture Notes in Computer Science 6406

Commenced Publication in 1973
Founding and Former Series Editors:
Gerhard Goos, Juris Hartmanis, and Jan van Leeuwen

Zhiwen Yu Ramiro Liscano
Guanling Chen Daqing Zhang
Xingshe Zhou (Eds.)

Ubiquitous Intelligence and Computing

7th International Conference, UIC 2010
Xi'an, China, October 26-29, 2010
Proceedings

Springer

Volume Editors

Zhiwen Yu
Northwestern Polytechnical University, School of Computer Science
Xi'an 710072, China
E-mail: zhiwenyu@nwpu.edu.cn

Ramiro Liscano
University of Ontario, Institute of Technology
Faculty of Engineering and Applied Science
Oshawa, ON L1H 7K4, Canada
E-mail: Ramiro.Liscano@uoit.ca

Guanling Chen
University of Massachusetts Lowell, Department of Computer Science
Lowell, MA 01854, USA
E-mail: glchen@cs.uml.edu

Daqing Zhang
Institute TELECOM SudParis
Telecommunication Network and Services Department
9 rue Charles Fourier, 91011 Evry Cedex, France
E-mail: Daqing.Zhang@it-sudparis.eu

Xingshe Zhou
Northwestern Polytechnical University, School of Computer Science
Xi'an 710072, China
E-mail: zhouxs@nwpu.edu.cn

Library of Congress Control Number: 2010935943

CR Subject Classification (1998): C.2, I.2, H.5, C.2.4, I.2.11, J.4

LNCS Sublibrary: SL 3 – Information Systems and Application, incl. Internet/Web and HCI

ISSN 0302-9743
ISBN-10 3-642-16354-8 Springer Berlin Heidelberg New York
ISBN-13 978-3-642-16354-8 Springer Berlin Heidelberg New York

springer.com

Printed in Germany

Typesetting: Camera-ready by author, data conversion by Scientific Publishing Services, Chennai, India
Printed on acid-free paper 06/3180

Preface

Ubiquitous sensors, devices, networks and information are paving the way toward a smart world in which computational intelligence is distributed throughout the physical environment to provide reliable and relevant services to people. This ubiquitous intelligence will change the computing landscape because it will enable new breeds of applications and systems to be developed, and the realm of computing possibilities will be significantly extended. By enhancing everyday objects with intelligence, many tasks and processes could be simplified, the physical spaces where people interact, like workplaces and homes, could become more efficient, safer and more enjoyable. Ubiquitous computing, or pervasive computing, uses these many "smart things" or "u-things" to create smart environments, services and applications.

A smart thing can be endowed with different levels of intelligence, and may be context-aware, active, interactive, reactive, proactive, assistive, adaptive, automated, sentient, perceptual, cognitive, autonomic and/or thinking. Research on ubiquitous intelligence is an emerging research field covering many disciplines. A series of grand challenges exists to move from the current level of computing services to the smart world of adaptive and intelligent services. Started in 2005, the series of UIC conferences has been held in Taipei, Nagasaki, Three Gorges (China), Hong Kong, Oslo and Brisbane.

The proceedings contain the papers presented at the 7th International Conference on Ubiquitous Intelligence and Computing (UIC 2010), held in Xi'an, China, October 26–29, 2010. The conference was accompanied by six vibrant workshops on a variety of research challenges within the area of ubiquitous intelligence and computing.

This year, the main conference received 128 submissions of which 36 were accepted as regular papers, corresponding to an acceptance rate of 28%. It had three keynote speeches from Sumi Helal, Kenji Mase, and Christian Becker. Also included were one invited paper, six special session papers, and five PSC (Pervasive Social Computing) special-track papers this year.

We would like to thank all the researchers and practitioners who submitted their work to UIC 2010, organized a workshop, or helped in any other way to make the conference a success. Special thanks go to the Program Vice Chairs, Program Committee members and external reviewers for all their work evaluating the papers, which is highly appreciated and absolutely vital to ensure the high quality of the conference. We offer our sincere thanks to the Steering Committee Chairs Jianhua Ma and Laurence T. Yang for their scientific suggestions and strong support. We appreciate the Publicity Co-chairs for advertising the conference. Many thanks also go to the Local Arrangement Chair, Yuying Wang, and Web Administration Chair, Haipeng Wang, for taking on much miscellaneous work.

Finally, we gratefully acknowledge the support by Northwestern Polytechnical University, Nokia, and the Aviation Industry Corporation of China (AVIC), as well as the technical sponsorships by IEEE, IEEE CS and the IEEE Technical Committee of Scalable Computing (TCSC).

August 2010

Zhiwen Yu
Ramiro Liscano
Guanling Chen
Daqing Zhang
Xingshe Zhou

UIC 2010 Conference Organization

Honorary Chairs

Yaoxue Zhang	Tsinghua University, China
Stephen S. Yau	Arizona State University, USA
Lionel M. Ni	Hong Kong University of Science and Technology, China

General Chairs

Daqing Zhang	Institute TELECOM SudParis, France
Xingshe Zhou	Northwestern Polytechnical University, China
Sajal Das	University of Texas at Arlington, USA

Program Chairs

Zhiwen Yu	Northwestern Polytechnical University, China
Ramiro Liscano	University of Ontario, Institute of Technology, Canada
Guanling Chen	University of Massachusetts, USA

Program Vice Chairs

Waltenegus Dargie	Technical University of Dresden, Germany
Tatsuya Yamazaki	NICT, Japan
Yu Chen	Tsinghua University, China

Advisory Committee Chairs

Norio Shiratori	Tohoku University, Japan
Mohan Kumar	University of Texas at Arlington, USA
Max Muehlhaeuser	Darmstadt University of Technology, Germany

Workshop Chairs

Robert C. Hsu	Chung Hua University, Taiwan
Mieso Denko	University of Guelph, Canada

Publicity Chairs

Bessam Abdulrazak	University Sherbrooke, Canada
Sung-Bae Cho	Yonsei University, South Korea
Wenbin Jiang	Huazhong University of Science & Technology, China
Artur Lugmayr	Tampere University of Technology, Finland
Hongbo Ni	Northwestern Polytechnical University, China
Evi Syukur	University of New South Wales, Australia

Panel Chairs

Christian Becker	University of Mannheim, Germany
Ren-Hung Huang	National Chung Cheng University, Taiwan

Demo/Exhibition Chairs

Gang Pan	Zhejiang University, China
Xing Xie	Microsoft Research Asia, China

Award Chairs

Frode Eika Sandnes	Oslo University College, Norway
Jiannong Cao	Hong Kong Polytechnic University, China

Special Track Chairs

Zheng Yan	Nokia Research Center, Finland
Yan Wang	Macquarie University, Australia

International Liaison Chairs

Marius Portmann	University of Queensland, Australia
Yo-Ping Huang	National Taipei University of Technology, Taiwan
Bernady O. Apduhan	Kyushu Sangyo University, Japan
Tao Mei	Chinese Academy of Sciences, China
Jong Hyuk Park	Seoul National University of Technology, South Korea
Judith Symonds	Auckland University of Technology, New Zealand

Industrial Liaison Chairs

Wei Han	China Aeronautical Computing Institute, China
Nagula Sangary	RIM, Canada
Yan Zhang	Simula Research Laboratory and University of Oslo, Norway

Local Arrangement Chair

Yuying Wang	Northwestern Polytechnical University, China

Web Administration Chair

Haipeng Wang	Northwestern Polytechnical University, China

Steering Committee

Jianhua Ma (Chair)	Hosei University, Japan
Laurence T. Yang (Chair)	St. Francis Xavier University, Canada
Hai Jin	Huazhong University of Science & Technology, China
Theo Ungerer	University of Augsburg, Germany
Jadwiga Indulska	University of Queensland, Australia
Jeffrey J.P. Tsai	University of Illinois at Chicago, USA

Advisory Committee

Norio Shiratori	Tohoku University, Japan
Mohan Kumar	University of Texas at Arlington, USA
Max Muehlhaeuser	Darmstadt University of Technology, Germany
Yuanchun Shi	Tsinghua University, China
Zhaohui Wu	Zhejiang University, China
Ahhwee Tan	Nanyang Technological University, Singapore

Program Committee

Sasitharan Balasubramaniam	WIT, Ireland
Martin Bauer	NEC Heidelberg, Germany
Neil Bergmann	University of Queensland, Australia
Yue-Shan Chang	National Taipei University, Taiwan
Liming Chen	University of Ulster, UK
Min Chen	Seoul National University, South Korea
Yiqiang Chen	ICT/Chinese Academy of Sciences, China
Doreen Cheng	Samsung R&D Center, USA
Antonio Coronato	ICAR-CNR, Italy
Domenico Cotroneo	Università di Napoli Federico II, Italy
Anand Dersingh	University of Ontario Institute of Technology, Canada
Babak Esfandiari	Carleton University, Canada
Dingyi Fang	Northwestern University, China
Kaori Fujinami	Tokyo University of Agriculture and Technology, Japan
Hongliang Gu	Shanghai Jiao Tong University, China

Lin Gu	HKUST, China
Tao Gu	University of Southern Denmark, Denmark
Bin Guo	Institute TELECOM SudParis, France
Jinhua Guo	University of Michigan at Dearborn, USA
Song Guo	The University of Aizu, Japan
Marcus Handte	Universität Bonn, Germany
Jessica Heesen	University of Freiburg, Germany
Didier Hoareau	University of La Réunion, France
Hui-Huang Hsu	Tamkang University, Taiwan
Bin Hu	Lanzhou University, China
Peizhao Hu	NICTA, Australia
Chung-Ming Huang	National Cheng Kung University, Taiwan
Runhe Huang	Hosei University, Japan
Yu Huang	Nanjing University, China
Sajid Hussain	Acadia University, Canada
Fuyuki Ishikawa	National Institute of Informatics, Japan
Beihong Jin	Institute of Software/Chinese Academy of Sciences, China
Ahmed Karmouch	University of Ottawa, Canada
Yasuharu Katsuno	IBM Tokyo Research Laboratory, Japan
Shonali Krishnaswamy	Monash University, Australia
Noriaki Kuwahara	Kyoto Institute of Technology, Japan
Shin'ichi Konomi	Tokyo Denki University, Japan
Yoshihiro Kawahara	The University of Tokyo, Japan
Choonhwa Lee	Hanyang University, Korea
Vili Lehdonvirta	Helsinki Institute for Information Technology, Finland
Frédéric Le Mouël	INSA Lyon, France
Gabriele Lenzini	University of Luxembourg, Luxembourg
Shijian Li	Zhejiang University, China
Zhuowei Li	Microsoft Corporation, USA
Antonio Liotta	Eindhoven University of Technology, The Netherlands
Ying Liu	Hong Kong Polytechnic University, China
Sanglu Lu	Nanjing University, China
René Meier	Trinity College, Dublin, Ireland
Kazuhiro Minami	University of Illinois at Urbana-Champaign, USA
Max Ott	NICTA, Australia
Susanna Pirttikangas	Oulu University, Finland
Neeli Prasad	Aalborg University, Denmark
Fano Ramparany	France Telecom, France
Anand Ranganathan	IBM, USA
Michael Rohs	TU Berlin, Germany
Gregor Schiele	Universität Mannheim, Germany
Alexander Schill	Technical University of Dresden, Germany
Lei Shu	Osaka University, Japan
Francois Siewe	De Montfort University, UK

Stephan Sigg	University of Braunschweig, Germany
Isabelle Simplot-Ryl	University Lille, France
Yue Suo	Tsinghua University, China
Chiu C. Tan	College of William and Mary, USA
Yan Tang	Vrije University Brussels, Belgium
Pin Tao	Tsinghua University, China
Jilei Tian	Nokia Research Center, China
Jean-Yves Tigli	University of Nice Sophia Antipolis, France
Anand Tripathi	The University of Minnesota, USA
Daoshun Wang	Tsinghua University, China
Sheng-De Wang	National Taiwan University, Taiwan
Athanasios Vasilakos	University of Western Macedonia, Greece
Agustinus Borgy Waluyo	Monash University, Australia
Hao Wang	Nokia Research Center, China
Yi Wang	Université catholique de Louvain, Belgium
Yufeng Wang	National Institute of Information and Communications Technology, Japan
Woontack Woo	Gwangju Institute of Science and Technology, South Korea
Zhijun Wang	Hong Kong Polytechnic University, China
Hirozumi Yamaguchi	Osaka University, Japan
Takuro Yonezawa	Keio University, Japan
Tomoko Yonezawa	ATR, Japan
Zainab Zaidi	NICTA, Australia
Justin Zhan	CMU, USA
Bofeng Zhang	Shanghai University, China
Jun Zhang	Dalian Maritime University, China
Yu Zheng	Microsoft Research Asia, China
Bosheng Zhou	Queen's University, UK
Jiehan Zhou	University of Oulu, Finland
Junyang Zhou	Hong Kong Baptist University, China

External Reviewers

Abdellatif Ben Rabaa, Alessandro Testa, Alvin Chin, Archi Delphinanto, Catello Di Martino, Cheng Zeng, Choonsung Shin, Christian Esposito, Christophe Debruyne, David Fotue, Enhong Chen, George Okeyo, Georgios Exarchakos, Giovanna Sannino, Hirotake Yamazoe, Hongbo Ni, Hyoseok Yoon, Imad Abdeljaouad, Ismaeel Al Ridhawi, John Khalil, Junfa Liu, Kai Dong, Kai Han, Majed Alhaisoni, Mikko Perttunen, Quan Qian, Ren-Hung Hwang, Roberto Pietrantuono, Stenio Fernandes, Vinit Padhye, Vlado Menkovski, Wonwoo Lee, Yichuan Jiang, Youdong Ding, Youngho Lee, Youngjung Suh, Youngmin Park, Yousif AL Ridhawi, Yu Yu, Yuki Arase, Zhenqiang Gong, Nidal Qwasmi.

Organized by

Northwestern Polytechnical University, China

Sponsored by

Northwestern Polytechnical University, China

Nokia Research Center, China

China Aeronautical Computing Institute, China

Table of Contents

Keynote Speeches

Invited Paper

Activity, Localization, and User Identification

Ubiquitous Services and Applications

Sensor Networks

Infrastructure, Middleware and Context-Awareness

Distributed Systems and Services

Wireless and Mobile Ad hoc Networks

Special Session: Ubiquitous Intelligence and Services

Special Track: Pervasive Social Computing

Programming Pervasive Spaces

Sumi Helal

Computer & Information Science & Engineering Department, University of Florida,
Gainesville, FL 32611, USA
helal@cise.ufl.edu

Abstract. In principle, the entire world can exploit ubiquitous and pervasive systems to great societal benefits. In practice, however, there is as yet no fundamental basis or widely accepted programming models for such systems. There is also no established curriculum for teaching pervasive and sensor-based computing. In this talk, I will present our ongoing research efforts in defining and supporting programmable pervasive spaces. I will start by presenting our experience and lessons learnt in building "assistive environments" for the elderly, to demonstrate the need for space programmability and to define critical new requirements particular to pervasive spaces. I will then present ATLAS, a middleware architecture and a sensor platform that supports self-integration and enables SODA – a service-oriented programming model. I will show how ATLAS was used as the foundation on which we built and programmed the Gator Tech Smart House, and how it enabled pervasive application development, and scalable data collection and analysis. I will then delineate the limitations of SODA and present programming model extensions that address space and user safety as well as reliability and scalability. Finally, I will present our views of a possible ecosystem within which our programming models and system support can be used to promote the proliferation of programmable and manageable pervasive systems.

Keywords: Pervasive spaces; programming model, assistive environments.

Z. Yu et al. (Eds.): UIC 2010, LNCS 6406, p. 1, 2010.

Ubiquitous Experience Media

Kenji Mase

Graduate School of Information Science, Nagoya University, Japan
mase@nagoya-u.jp

Abstract. Our daily activity in the future society will be facilitated by recording personal and joint experiences in the real and cyber world with a ubiquitous computing environment. We can exploit the recorded activity as a good source of human-human and human-computer communication for sharing experience, memory and knowledge. We are interested in audio-visual, ubiquitous, and/or wearable experience-capturing technology as an interaction-grounded lifelog tool. The talk addresses the advanced technologies of non-cumbersome indexed-recording, abstracting, and summarizing of experiences as well as sharing these experiences among people. We have developed several devices, algorithms and tools, such as a wearable interaction tracker and a multipoint-view Peg-Scope Viewer, which facilitate indexing the personal and joint experiences. Indexing experiences is a key technology for realizing usable future computational media, which we call ubiquitous experience media (UEM).

Keywords: Ubiquitous computing; personal experience.

Z. Yu et al. (Eds.): UIC 2010, LNCS 6406, p. 2, 2010.

The Operating System for the Computer of the 21st Century

Christian Becker

Chair for Information Systems II, Mannheim University, Germany
christian.becker@uni-mannheim.de

Abstract. Weiser's vision of Ubiquitous Computing has inspired many researchers and an active research community has been established in the past years. Various aspects have been investigated from novel user interfaces, applications to specialized hardware devices and system software helping application developers utilizing the capabilities of a smart world. In my talk I want to address the challenges researchers have addressed in the past. Based on a number of products and prototypes I will identify the problems where concepts and solutions exist and will also highlight open research challenges with a focus on adaptation and self-organization.

Keywords: Ubiquitous computing; operating system, adaptation.

Z. Yu et al. (Eds.): UIC 2010, LNCS 6406, p. 3, 2010.

Extracting Social and Community Intelligence from Digital Footprints: An Emerging Research Area

Daqing Zhang[1], Bin Guo[1], Bin Li[1], and Zhiwen Yu[2]

[1] Institut TELECOM SudParis, France
{daqing.zhang,bin.guo,bin.li}@it-sudparis.eu
[2] School of Computer Science, Northwestern Polytechnical University, P.R. China
zhiwenyu@nwpu.edu.cn

Abstract. As a result of the recent explosion of sensor-equipped mobile phone market, the phenomenal growth of Internet and social network users, and the large deployment of sensor network in public facilities, private buildings and outdoor environments, the "digital footprints" left by people while interacting with cyber-physical spaces are accumulating with an unprecedented breadth, depth and scale. The technology trend towards pervasive sensing and large-scale social and community computing is making "social and community intelligence (SCI)", a new research area take shape, that aims at mining the "digital footprints" to reveal the patterns of individual, group and societal behaviours. It is believed that the SCI technology has the potential to revolutionize the field of context-aware computing. The aim of this position paper is to identify this emerging research area, present the research background and some references to the relevant research fields, define the general system framework, predict some potential application areas, and propose some initial thoughts about the future research issues and challenges in social and community intelligence.

Keywords: Social and community intelligence; digital footprints; pervasive sensing.

1 Introduction

With the technological advances in sensing, computing, storage, communication and Internet, a lot of research areas have emerged such as sensor network, pervasive computing, Internet of Things, social network, to name just a few. From those emerging areas, there is a clear trend to augment the physical devices/objects with sensing, computing and communication capabilities, connect them together to form a network, and make use of the collective effect of networked things. As a result of the recent explosion of sensor-equipped mobile phone market, the phenomenal growth of Internet and social network users, and the large deployment of sensor network in public facilities, private buildings and outdoor environments, the digital traces left by people while interacting with cyber-physical spaces are accumulating at an unprecedented breadth, depth and scale, and we call all those traces left by people the "digital footprints". By 2009, four billions of mobile devices [1] were carried and used by people

Z. Yu et al. (Eds.): UIC 2010, LNCS 6406, pp. 4–18, 2010.

in the world everyday, which are recording individuals' digital traces using various built-in sensors and generating huge amount of "digital footprints" [2]. According to the 'World GPS Market Forecast to 2013', a 2010 market research report by RNCOS (http://www.rncos.com/), millions of cars and taxis are being equipped with GPS each year and the mobile location technologies market is expected to grow at a CAGR (Compound Annual Growth Rate) of about 20% to cross US$ 70 Billion by 2013, being another data source about the facets of individual, family and city. In addition, Internet services like e-mails, instant messaging, etc. and social networks like Facebook, MySpace, Twitter and LinkedIn record information about people's relationship and preferences; indoor and outdoor sensor network data provide more insights about people's environmental context.

Leveraging the capacity to collect and analyze the "digital footprints" at community scale, a new research field called "**social and community intelligence (SCI)**" is emerging that aims at revealing the patterns of individual, group and societal behaviours. The scale and heterogeneity of the multimodal, mixed data sources present us an opportunity to compile the digital footprints into a comprehensive picture of individual's daily life facets, radically change the way we build computational models of human behaviour, and enable completely innovative services in areas like human health, public safety, city resource management, environment monitoring, and transportation management.

Different from other closely related research areas such as sensor-based activity recognition, the unique characteristics of this new SCI research area can be embodied in the following aspects:

1. **Infrastructure:** The scale of the SCI system goes beyond single smart space and reaches the level of a community. Real-life, real-time data sensing and inference is a key system feature. An infrastructure is required to integrate large-scale and heterogeneous devices, software, and spaces, and provide systematic support for rapid application development, deployment, and evaluation.
2. **Data:** The data sources are multi-modal and heterogeneous. The social and community intelligence can be inferred from three main data sources: the mobile/wearable sensor data about the individual and moving space, the infrastructure-bound sensor data about the environment, and the social data about the individual's preference and relationship with others from social network and Internet interaction services. While each data source can independently shows one facet of the user's daily life, the combination of the three data sources can reveal unforeseen social behaviours.
3. **Technology:** The core technologies for SCI are data mining, machine learning and AI. And the objective of data processing and inference goes from recognizing the individual's physical activity and environmental context to extracting higher-level community and social behaviours (from talking to meeting; from driving slowly to traffic jam, there exist semantic gaps between individual activities and social/community behaviours).
4. **Application:** It aims to enable innovative services in society level like community healthcare, public safety, city resource management and transportation management.

Now let's use a simple use case in a university campus to illustrate the concrete ideas about social and community intelligence:

University campus is a typical high-density populated community (as shown in Fig. 1). Students often face the problem of finding partners doing sports in a certain free time slot, searching if there are free spaces available for exercises or study, etc. When a pandemic like H1N1 occurs, how to quickly identify who has been contacted by a suspect person, when and where the contact takes place is an important issue to avoid further spread of the disease. There are also queries like when will the next bus reaches the Bus Stop near Library, how many people are waiting in the bus stop, etc. In real-world environments, it is often difficult to answer these questions merely based on today's technologies. However, all those community services in university campus can be enabled by analyzing the pervasive data streams collected from personal mobile phone sensors, GPS from buses, WiFi or Bluetooth access points inside the building, social relationship from the web, etc. In the case of pandemic, for example, the distance and contact time with the suspect, the logical places for the meeting (e.g., office, bus), the relationship with the suspect (e.g., family, friend, colleague, unknown) are all important contexts affecting the probability of disease spread.

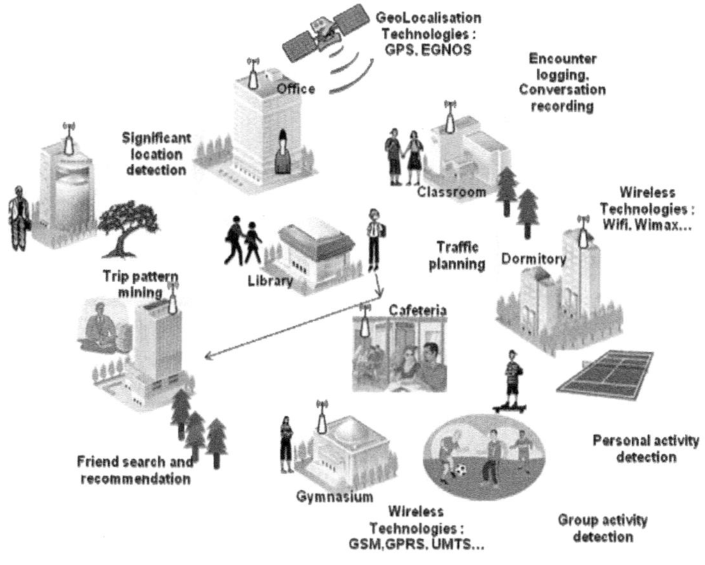

Fig. 1. Campus-scale community sensing and intelligence

The rest of this position paper is organized as follows. Section 2 presents the research background of social and community intelligence, followed by a general framework for SCI systems in Section 3. Then several potential applications of SCI and some initial thoughts about the open research issues in SCI are elaborated in Section 4 and 5, respectively. Finally, we conclude this paper by proposing some promising research directions.

2 Research Background

Research on social and community intelligence is at its early stage. However, as the result of convergence of several research disciplines such as sensor network, ubiquitous computing, mobile computing, machine learning, data mining, and social science, SCI has its deep roots in three recent fast-growing research fields according to the origin of data sources: 1) mobile/wearable sensor-based activity recognition, 2) context inference in smart spaces, and 3) social network analysis. While each of the three abovementioned research fields is an active, multi-disciplinary area itself with rich research challenges/applications, the "convergence" of these three fields is expected to be influenced by the advances of each one, and would present new challenges and opportunities as a result of "network effects". In the rest of this section, each of these three areas will be briefly introduced with some references.

2.1 Mobile/Wearable Sensor-Based Activity Recognition

The mobile/wearable sensor-based activity recognition research leverages the prevalence of wearable sensors and mobile sensors embedded into the mobile devices that are accompanying the users most of time, it aims at collecting the sensing data in the real life and predicting the daily activities of users at real-time. RFID (radio frequency identification), GPS (global position system), accelerometer are among the most popular sensors embedded in the mobile devices. Sensor-based activity recognition can be roughly divided into two categories based on where the sensors are deployed: human body or object. Wearable sensors attached to a human body can generate various signals when the user performs activities, which is effective to detect human physical movements, such as walking, running, scrubbing, and exercising. Object-based activity recognition is based on real-world observations that activities are characterised by the objects that are manipulated during their operation. Activities involving complex physical motions and complex interactions with the environment, e.g., grooming, cooking, phoning, toileting, washing hands, and so forth, can be recognised through this approach.

The key idea behind the sensor-based activity recognition is to build or learn a mathematical model of activity based on a series of observations which are represented by the sensor readings, then by feeding the real-time sensor readings to the model, the human activities are predicted. Take a well known work of RFID-based activity recognition for example [3]. Consider a household where each object (e.g., cups, spoons, and toothbrushes) is tagged with an RFID, if the subject wears a watch-like RFID reader on her wrist and performs her daily activities, then each object she touched during her performance can be tracked in real-time. By recording the sequence of the touched objects, machine learning and inference methods can then be applied to learn a model for recognizing daily activities ranging from simple ones like brushing teeth to critical ones like taking medication and cooking a meal (safety-related), etc. Most of the early work on sensor-based activity recognition was motivated by applications in elderly care [4], healthcare [5]. Some of them have also been applied to habitat monitoring with sensor networks [6], and tracking human interaction in offices [7].

Another line of research in sensor-based activity recognition is location-based activity recognition as a result of wide deployment GPS sensors. The earliest work in this line intended to detect the trip plan derivation based on GPS traces [8]. In the following years, a large body of work was reported, including significant location identification [9], transportation mode recognition and route prediction [10].

Recently with more and more mobile phones equipped with sensors, a few researchers initiated the research in individual/group behavior mining with mobile sensing data. For instance, MetroSense [2], a people-centric paradigm for urban sensing, explores sensor-embedded mobile phones to support personal and public sensing. By taking advantage of the data collected by mobile phones, Reality Mining project initiated at MIT intends to observe and characterize the social behaviour of individual users and organizations [11]. Another interesting study based on the monitoring of 100,000 mobile phone users, conducted by Northeastern Univ. in US, discovered that human trajectory has a high degree of spatial-temporal regularity, and humans follow simple reproducible patterns regardless of the diversity of travel history of individuals [12].

2.2 Context Inference in Smart Spaces

Earlier work on context inference mainly relies on static sensing infrastructure that is already deployed in smart spaces. One early project funded by the EPSRC in the UK was concerned with measuring crowd motion and density using cameras to detect potentially dangerous situations [13]. The Active Bats system uses ultrasonic sensors and the triangulation location-sensing technique to locate indoor objects [14]. Semantic Space builds an ontology-based infrastructure for extracting and querying contexts from smart spaces [15]. Yu et al. explore a set of static cameras and wearable sensors to mine semantic information like user attitudes in a smart meeting environment [16]. Sensor Andrew [17], a campus-wide static sensor network, is designed to host a wide range of applications including campus utility monitoring, social networking, and campus security surveillance.

2.3 Social Network Analysis

Humans are social by nature. People constantly participate in social activities to interact with others and form various communities. Social activities such as making new friends, forming an interest group to exchange ideas, sharing knowledge with others are constantly taking place in human society. The analysis of the social community interactions has been studied by social scientists and physicists for couple of decades [18]. An excellent introduction to the concepts and the mathematical tools for analyzing social networks can be referred to [19]. Early efforts on social network analysis are most based on the relational data obtained by survey.

During the last two decades, we have observed an explosive growth of Internet applications such as chatting, shopping, experience sharing, photo and video sharing, etc., which are now described as social software. These applications, along with the traditional e-mail, instant messaging, have changed the way that most of us used to communicate with each other and form social communities. Corresponding to this trend, a large body of work on social network analysis and knowledge discovery springs up, including Email communication networks [20], scientific collaboration and co-authorship network [21], etc..

More recently, as the internet stepped into the era of the Web 2.0, which advocates that users interact with each other as contributors to the web sites' content, researchers turned more attention to the online social utilities, such as Facebook, Twitter, and Blogs. For example, ArterMiner [22] seeks to harvest personal profile information from a user's homepage. Amit Sheth's research group has done much work on summarization of event info like space, time and theme from social web resources for building public services [23]. Twitter, a popular micro-blogging site, has been reported to support real-time mining of natural disasters such as earthquakes [24] and the moods of citizens [25].

3 A General Architecture

A general architecture for social and community intelligence system is shown in Fig. 2, which consists of five layers: *pervasive sensing layer*, *data anonymization layer, hybrid learning layer*, *semantic inference layer*, and *application layer*.

Layer 1: The large-scale pervasive sensing layer involves the three major information sources: mobile and wearable devices, static sensing infrastructure, social web and Internet services. The three sources have different attributes and strengths:

- Mobile devices and wearable sensors are always user-centric, thus great at sensing individual activities, interpersonal interactions, and significant locations.
- Static infrastructure, on the other hand, enables the detection of indoor user activities, group activities, and space context.
- Social Web is a major source to extract user profile info, significant relationship among users in a group activity. Extracted real-time event information (e.g., from Twitter) is also useful to recognize the ongoing group activity.

Due to the diverse features, aggregation and fusion of data from those three different sources provides unique opportunities to community intelligence extraction.

Layer 2: As privacy is a major concern for both private and organizational data sharing, our proposed framework incorporates an anonymization layer before the data releasing and processing. All the data released must be sufficiently anonymized, and different anonymization algorithms can be applied for privacy protection.

Layer 3: The hybrid learning layer applies diverse machine learning and data mining techniques to converting the low-level single-modality sensing data into high-level features or micro-context, the focus is to mine the frequent data patterns to derive the individual's behavior and single space context, before extracting the complete social and community intelligence.

Level 4: The semantic inference layer is needed when different features or micro-context need to be aggregated using logic-based inferences, it is complementary with statistical learning approach and often very effective to process the explicit rules describing the logical relationship between layer 3 outputs and expected SCI, based on expert's domain knowledge.

Layer 5: The application layer includes a variety of potential services that can be enabled by the availability of SCI. An application might be installed directly on the mobile device, or run on remote servers (such as a Web application) but communicate with the mobile device via wireless gateways.

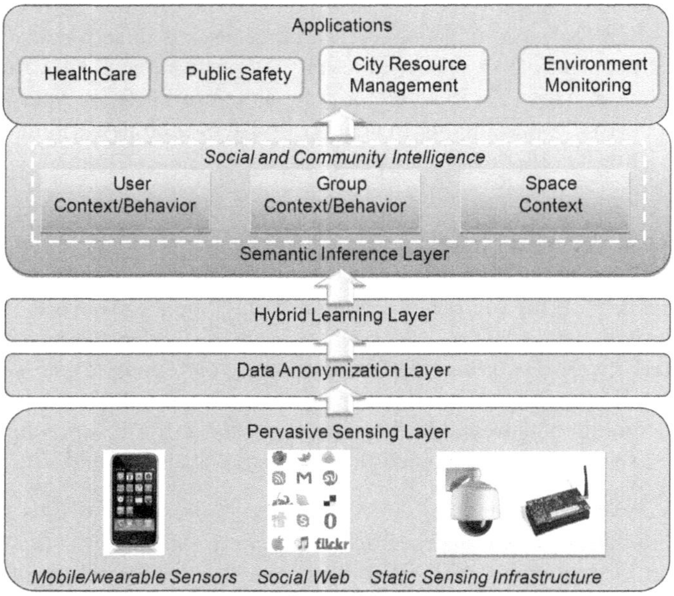

Fig. 2. A general architecture for community intelligence

4 Major Application Areas

SCI applications are mainly driven by the needs to (1) develop better social software to facilitate interaction and communication among groups of people; (2) predict the real-time change of real world to benefit human life. Here we can foresee at least the following six main SCI application areas:

4.1 Social Network Services

By logging various aspects of physical interactions among users (e.g., co-location, conversations) and mining user behavior patterns (e.g., place of interests), SCI nurtures the development of many social network services, such as friend recommendation and interpersonal interaction enhancement.

(1) Friend recommendation. By monitoring one's activities with mobile phones, including text messages, phone calls, and encounters, the FriendSensing application can recommend people to its users [26]. The Serendipity system calculates a similarity score by extracting the commonalities between two proximate users' profiles and behavioral data, and alerts the user that someone nearby might interest him/her [27].

(2) Interpersonal interaction enhancement. The CenseMe project exploits off-the-shelf smart phones to automatically infer people's presence (e.g., walking on the street, dancing at a party with friends) and then shares this presence through social network portals such as Facebook [28]. Koji et al. uses specially designed work badges to study the relationship between productivity and interpersonal interactions in a workplace. The badges contain infrared sensors, microphones, accelerometers, and location sensors to record the location and duration of conversations among workers, their physical distance apart, encounters, upper body motions, and so on [29].

4.2 Urban Sensing and City Resource Management

With wireless sensor platforms in the hands of masses, we can leverage community sensing to address urban-scale problems, such as city resource monitoring, traffic planning, and better use of public utilities.

Nericell is a system that can monitor road (e.g., potholed roads) and traffic conditions (e.g., chaotic traffic) using accelerometer, microphone, and GPS sensors in mobile phones [30]. MIT's Real Time Rome project (http://senseable.mit.edu/ realtimerome) uses aggregated data from cell phones, buses and taxis in Rome to better understand urban dynamics in real-time. The Biketastic project (http://biketastic.com) improves bike commuting in Los Angeles by combining local conditions with biker-contributed data (using mobile phones). It enables area bikers to plan routes with the least probability of traffic accidents and the best air quality. Zheng et al. extract interesting locations and travel sequences from multiple user's GPS trajectories, and enable travel recommendations for new visitors of a city [31].

4.3 Environment Monitoring

The nomadic, participatory, and in-situ experience nature of community sensing provides new opportunities for environment monitoring and natural resource protection.

(1) Nature preservation. With the help of human volunteers, the Great Backyard Bird Count project reports the cumulative counts of birdwatchers from across American in its website (http://www.birdsource.org/gbbc/). The MIT Owl project (http://web.mit.edu/newsoffice/2008/tracking-0822.html) is more interesting, which aims at leveraging the network of smart phones equipped with GPS, compasses, and directional microphones, to lessen human efforts in assessing owl populations.

(2) Pollution measurement. With the aid of portable pollution sensing devices, there have also been several projects targeting environment pollution measurement. The BikeNet application measures several metrics to give a holistic picture of the cyclist experience, including the $CO2$ level along the path. It facilitates public sensing and sharing by letting multiple users merge their individual data, for example, to create pollution and noise maps of their city [32]. In the PEIR project, GPS-enabled phones are used to detect user transportation mode (e.g., driving, walking), which is then used to assess an individual's environmental impact and exposure, like carbon footprints and exposure to air pollution [33].

(3) Disaster Reporting. The real-time user contributed data is helpful for emergent or dangerous event detection and reporting. For example, Twitter has been reported to support rapid response to the social or natural disasters such as terrorism attack in

Bombay [34] and earthquakes in Japan [24]. Comparing to traditional media, community sensing is more vigilant.

4.4 Human Health

SCI brings new opportunities for public health monitoring and personal well-being improvement.

(1) Public health. SCI can facilitate the anticipation and tracking of disease outbreaks across populations. For example, Epidemics of seasonal influenza are a major public health concern, causing tens of thousands of deaths worldwide each year. Its impact can be reduced by early detection of the disease activity. The Google researchers have shown that by mining indirect signals from millions of geographically localized health-related search queries, one can estimate the level of influenza-like illnesses in regions of the United States with a reporting lag of just 1 day [35]. It is faster than the estimates provided by government agencies, which publish regional data weekly based on virology and clinical statistics.

(2) Human well-being. With community sensing, we can log personal physical activity trajectory, track the food intake, sense the mental status in real-time, and record the social activities we attend each day, which can be used to improve human well-being management. For example, the Neat-o-Games system detects human movements (e.g., walking, running) by using a wearable accelerometer, and uses the computed quantity of motion to control the avatar of the user in a virtual community race game [36]. Playful Bottle is a mobile social persuasion system to motivate healthy water intake [37]. Nutrition Monitor, a mobile application, can track user food consumption and trends over time, and warn the user against unhealthy food choices [38].

4.5 Sentiment Applications

Sensing of user sentiments is important to context-aware computing, with which the applications can act accordingly. However, using physical sensors to directly sense personal sentiments is not an easy thing. Researchers have been exploring indirect ways to deal with this, one of which is to mine user-generated Web data. Some systems use a Web survey method. For example, Emotional City (http://www.emotionalcities.com/) and D-Tower (www.d-toren.nl) collect citizen moods through daily Web surveys, and display the emotions of the city through the change of light-colors of a building or a public sculpture. Others explore machine learning algorithms for sentiment mining. Bollen et al. proposes an extended Profile of Mood States (POMS) method to extract six dimensions of mood (e.g., tension, anger) from user posted tweets in Twitter [25].

4.6 Public Safety

Public safety involves the prevention of and protection from events that could endanger the safety of the general public, these events can be crimes or disasters. Public video surveillance systems have assisted a lot to city-wide event sensing and safety maintenance [39]. Recently, the Boston police department has embraced user contributed sensor data to assist in crime prevention [34].

5 Research Issues

We now turn our attention to key SCI research issues. To facilitate the development of SCI applications, one fundamental issue is gathering and management of heterogeneous data from different information sources. Other important issues are using machine learning algorithms to make sense of the "digital footprints" revealing the predefined patterns or unforeseen behaviors about individual, group and community, as well as the privacy concerns raised by sensing our daily lives.

5.1 Participatory or Opportunistic Sensing?

The first issue to be considered in sensing is what roles people should play in community sensing. For example, should they be interrupted to control the status (e.g., accept, stop) of a sensing task? There are two possible ways for sensing:

- *Participatory sensing*. It incorporates people into significant decision making process of the sensing system, deciding which application request to accept, what data to share, and to what extent privacy mechanisms should be allowed to impact data fidelity. That's to say, it allows participants to retain control over their raw data. The Personal Data Valut system is based on this idea, which seeks to provide easy-to-use toolkits to support data control [1].
- *Opportunistic sensing*. It shifts the burden of users by automatically determining when devices can be used to meet application's sensing requests. Instead of requiring human intervention to actively and consciously participate in the sensing, opportunistic sensing requests that a sensing device is automatically used whenever its state (location, user activity, and so on) matches an application's application requirements. This approach is proposed in [28].

Obviously there exists a tradeoff between participatory sensing and opportunistic sensing. Participatory sensing places demands on user involvement, which restricts the pool of willing participants, while opportunistic sensing takes on more resources for decision-making. More work needs be done to balance users' involvement and proper control while integrating proper protection mechanisms on data privacy (more discussions on privacy are given in Section 5.4).

5.2 Managing Heterogeneous and Multi-modal Data Sources

As in SCI system, the data producers can be very different in terms of modality (e.g., mobile phones, fixed cameras, Web services), their connectivity to the Internet (e.g., constant, intermittent, or affected by a firewall), their sharing willingness or privacy sensitivity, and resource capabilities for processing data locally. The information consumers are also heterogeneous in terms of running environments (applications that run locally or at community-level remotely), data needs (some might need only a high-level context information while others might need raw sensor data). The heterogeneity leads to several challenges on data management:

(1) Multi-modal. Different type of sensors have different attributes and capabilities, they might have different accuracy in sensing the physical and virtual world. Integrating information from diverse data sources adds difficulty to SCI mining. Raw data

from different sensor sources need to be transformed to the same metrics and represented by a shared vocabulary/ontology to facilitate the learning and inference process [15].

(2) Temporal and Continuous. The sensing data is recorded according to the time sequence, the system should consider multiple samples in the data stream while modeling the behaviors of individual and group, rather than consider each sensor reading in an isolated way. In addition, as the real world systems are all continuous, it's important to build models catering for the discrete, sampled sensor state.

(3) Inconsistency. The same sensor may sense the same event under different conditions (for example, sensing one's voice in a quiet office or noisy restaurant). However, for the same event, user context often leads to different inference results (good or poor). Due to environmental differences, a group of co-located sensors running the same classification algorithm and sensing the same event in time and space could compute different inference results, and thus leads to the issue of system inconsistency. Miluzzo *et al.* have proposed a collaborative approach to dealing with this inconsistency problem [40] and more solutions are needed.

(4) Difficult to label all data. Asking human to label large amount of data set is often difficult since it is extremely time consuming to perform real-life experiments to collect data, it takes even more time to label all the data properly. Thus it is highly desirable to learn system models from relatively small amount of labeled data [41].

5.3 Extracting High-Level SCI from Low-Level Sensing Data [41]

Social and community pattern mining considers the identification of a set of characteristics or behaviors associated with a social community based on the collection of intermediate-level individual activity/space context traces. Such social communities can be flexibly formed by those people in the same organization, at same places, with same behaviors, of same interests, etc., depending on different social application requirements [42]. By pooling individual user's context traces together and mining the underlying social patterns, different social or group behaviors can be extracted [43]. The extracted social context can be a social event such as an open concert, can be a social pattern in daily activity, can be a relationship among a group of people, and can be socially significant locations.

The key of the SCI pattern mining is to identify user similarity in the aforementioned social patterns with the objectives of offering social aware services. Unsupervised learning techniques, such as clustering, latent semantic analysis, matrix factorization, can be applied to achieve social context mining based on the user behavioral similarities. The process includes mining and discovery of common social contexts such as personal characteristics, cuisine preferences, eagerness of social participation, and also discovery of undefined social patterns for interest matching and social choice ranking.

In order to infer the social events based on the user context traces, the semantic gap between the low-level individual activities/spaces (e.g., walking/street, eating/restaurant, etc) and high-level social events (e.g., meeting, party, etc) should be bridged using some machine learning and inference techniques. As highlighted previously, the analysis of the latent relations between the basic human activities and semantic social events is the research focus of this module, with the goal of learning an ontology describing the relationship between the basic human activities and semantic social events.

5.4 Privacy and Trust

Sharing and revealing personal digital data could have a number of risks on user privacy. Compared with personal data (e.g., user profile, IDs), data gathered in community can reveal much more information about individual and organization's behaviours. For example, your location might reveal your interests; the health data about an organization might suggest environmental problems for the staff. The impact is obvious: if personal data cannot be anonymized and under the control of data owners, people may be less likely to share their data [28].

Privacy protection involves many elements, including identity (who is asking for the data?), granularity (how much does the data reveal about people? does it reveal one's identity?), and time (how long will the data be retained?) [1] There are two main research areas that deal with these needs: *data anonymization* [28, 43] and *user control* [1].

(1) Data anonymization techniques. The objective of *data anonymization* is not revealing the identity of users when they contribute their data. Several methods have been proposed. For instance, MetroSense uses k-anonymous method when users contribute location data to a server, where a user's position is generalized to a region containing at least k users [28]. Another promising approach based on secure multi-party computation allows mining data from many different organizations without ever aggregating these data into a central data repository. Each organization performs part of the computation based on its privately held data, and uses cryptography to encode intermediate results that must be communicated to other organizations performing other parts of the computation [43]. Other privacy-preserving methods are also being explored, such as sharing only statistical summaries of the individual data sets, and inserting random perturbations into individual data records before sharing them [43].

(2) Enhancing user control and decision making. User control is very important in personal data sharing as it is about what one wants to reveal and to whom one allows the system to reveal. For example, you might want to track your heart rate each day, but there is no reason to share that information with anyone but your doctor. Researchers in this field are exploiting methods that enable users to manage their data by tailoring access-control and data-management tools [1].

In addition to data privacy issue, trust of the data sources is another big thing. To mine social and community behaviors, we often need to import data from many anonymous participants. If there lacks the control to ensure the source is valid and information is accurate, this can lead to data trust issue. For example, Twitter data is sometimes unreliable due to the text's unmediated and casual nature; mobile phone users may send incorrect or even faked data to the data centre. Therefore, trust maintenance and abnormal detection methods should be developed to determine the trustworthiness and quality of collected data.

6 Conclusion

Social and Community Intelligence (SCI) represents a new interdisciplinary research and application field. With the rapid accumulation of "digital footprints" at community scale, we believe that the research scope of SCI will expand and its applications to multiply in next years to come. As we have discussed, the prevalence and development of SCI still face challenges ranging from multi-modal data gathering, heterogeneous data representation and management, to complex intelligence inference and privacy issues, which are expected to nurture a series of new research opportunities for academic researchers, industrial technologists, and business strategists as well. Even though the existing practices on social and community intelligence mainly consider single type of information sources – static sensor infrastructure, mobile and wearable sensors, or Internet and social web – we expect to see the explosion of the research on aggregated power of the three information sources as well as innovative applications enabled by SCI.

References

1. Shilton, K.: Four billion little brothers: Privacy, mobile phones, and ubiquitous data collection. Communications of the ACM 52(11), 48–53 (2009)
2. Campbell, A.T., Eisenman, S.B., Lane, N.D., Miluzzo, E., Peterson, R.A.: People-Centric Urban Sensing. In: Proc. of the 2nd Annual International Workshop on Wireless Internet (2006)
3. Philipose, M., Fishkin, K.P., Perkowitz, M., Patterson, D.J., Fox, D., Kautz, H., Hahnel, D.: Inferring activities from interactions with objects. IEEE Pervasive Computing 3(4), 50–57 (2004)
4. Pollack, M.E.: Intelligent technology for an aging population: The use of AI to assist elders with cognitive impairment. AI Magazine 26(2), 9–24 (2005)
5. Tentori, M., Favela, J.: Activity-aware computing for healthcare. IEEE Pervasive Computing 7(2), 51–57 (2008)
6. Szewczyk, R., Osterweil, E., Polastre, J., Hamilton, M., Mainwaring, A., Estrin, D.: Habitat monitoring with sensor networks. Communications of the ACM 47(6), 34–40 (2004)
7. Connolly, C.I., Burns, J.B., Bui, H.H.: Recovering social networks from massive track datasets. In: Proc. of the IEEE Workshop on Applications of Computer Vision, pp. 1–8 (2008)
8. Wolf, J., Guensler, R., Bachman, W.: Elimination of the travel diary: An experiment to derive trip purpose from GPS travel data. In: Proc. of the 80th Annual Meeting of the Transportation Research Board (2001)
9. Ashbrook, D., Starner, T.: Using GPS to learn significant locations and predict movement across multiple users. Personal and Ubiquitous Computing 7(5), 275–286 (2003)
10. Liao, L., Fox, D., Kautz, H.: Learning and inferring transportation routines. In: Proc. of the 19th AAAI Conf. on Artificial Intelligence, pp. 348–353 (2004)
11. Eagle, N., Pentland, A., Lazer, D.: Inferring Friendship Network Structure by using Mobile Phone Data. National Academy of Sciences (PNAS) 106(36), 15274–15278 (2009)
12. Gonzalez, M.C., Hidalgo, C.A., Barabasi, A.L.: Understanding individual human mobility patterns. Nature 453(5), 779–782 (2008)

13. Zhan, B., Monekosso, D.N., Remagnino, P., Velastin, S.A., Xu, L.: Crowd Analysis: a Survey in Machine Vision and Applications. Computer Science 19(5-6), 345–357 (2008)
14. Harter, A., Hopper, A., Steggles, P., Ward, A., Webster, P.: The Anatomy of a Context-aware Application. In: Proc. of MOBICOM 1999 (1999)
15. Wang, W., Zhang, D., Dong, J.S., Chin, C.Y., Hettiaarchchi, S.R.: Semantic Space: An Infrastructure for Smart Spaces. IEEE Pervasive Computing, 32–39 (2004)
16. Yu, Z.W., Yu, Z.Y., Aoyama, H., Ozeki, M., Nakamura, Y.: Capture, Recognition, and Visualization of Human Semantic Interactions in Meetings. In: Proc. of IEEE PerCom 2010, Mannheim, Germany, pp. 107–115 (2010)
17. Rowe, A., Berges, M., Bhatia, G., Goldman, E., Rajkumar, R., Soibelman, L., Garrett, J., Moura, J.: Sensor Andrew: Large-Scale Campus-Wide Sensing and Actuation. Carnegie Mellon University (2008)
18. Freeman, L.C.: The Development of Social Network Analysis: A Study in the Sociology of Science. Empirical Press (2004)
19. Wasserman, S., Faust, K.: Social Network Analysis: Methods and Applications. Cambridge University Press, Cambridge (1994)
20. McCallum, A., Wang, X., Corrada-Emmanuel, A.: Topic and role discovery in social networks with experiments on Enron and academic email. Journal of Artificial Intelligence Research 30(1), 249–272 (2007)
21. Barabasi, A.L., Jeong, H., Neda, Z., Ravasz, E., Schubert, A., Vicsek, T.: Evolution of the social network of scientific collaborations. Statistical Mechanics and its Applications 311(3-4), 590–614 (2002)
22. Tang, J., Jin, R.M., Zhang, J.: A Topic Modeling Approach and its Integration into the Random Walk Framework for Academic Search. In: Proc. of 2008 IEEE International Conference on Data Mining (ICDM 2008), pp. 1055–1060 (2008)
23. Sheth, A.: Computing for Human Experience – Semantics-Empowered Sensors, Services, and Social Computing on the Ubiquitous Web. IEEE Internet Computing 14(1), 88–97 (2010)
24. Sakaki, T., Okazaki, M., Matsuo, Y.: Earthquake Shakes Twitter Users: Real-time Event Detection by Social Sensors. In: Proc. of WWW 2010 Conference (2010)
25. Bollen, J., Pepe, A., Mao, H.: Modeling public mood and emotion: Twitter sentiment and socio-economic phenomena. In: Proc. of WWW 2009 Conference (2009)
26. Quercia, D., Ellis, J., Capra, L.: Nurturing Social Networks Using Mobile Phones. IEEE Pervasive Computing (2010)
27. Eagle, N., Pentland, A.: Social serendipity: Mobilizing social software. IEEE Pervasive Computing 4(2), 28–34 (2005)
28. Campbell, A.T., et al.: The Rise of People-Centric Sensing. IEEE Internet Computing 12(4), 12–21 (2008)
29. Ara, K., et al.: Sensible Organizations: Changing Our Business and Work Style through Sensor Data. Journal of Information Processing 16, 1–12 (2008)
30. Mohan, P., Padmanabhan, V.N., Ramjee, R.: Nericell: Rich Monitoring of Road and Traffic Conditions using Mobile Smart phones. In: Proc. of ACM SenSys 2008 (2008)
31. Zheng, Y., Xie, X., Ma, W.Y.: GeoLife: A Collaborative Social Networking Service among User, location and trajectory. IEEE Data Engineering Bulletin 33(2), 32–40 (2010)
32. Eisenman, S.B., et al.: The bikenet mobile sensing system for cyclist experience mapping. ACM SenSys 07, 87–101 (2007)
33. Mun, M., et al.: PEIR: the personal environmental impact report as a platform for participatory sensing systems research. In: Proc. of MobiSys 2009 (2009)

34. Sheth, A.: Citizen Sensing, Social Signals, and Enriching Human Experience. IEEE Internet Computing 13(4), 87–92 (2009)
35. Ferguson, N.M., et al.: Strategies for mitigating an influenza pandemic. Nature 442(7101), 448–452 (2006)
36. Fujiki, Y., Kazakos, K., Puri, C., Buddharaju, P., Pavlidis, I., Levine, J.: NEAT-o-Games: Blending Physical Activity and Fun in the Daily Routine. ACM Computers in Entertainment 6(2) (2008)
37. Chiu, M.C., et al.: Playful bottle: a mobile social persuasion system to motivate healthy water intake. In: Proc. of UbiComp 2009, pp. 185–194 (2009)
38. Dorman, K., et al.: Nutrition Monitor: A Food Purchase and Consumption Monitoring Mobile System. In: Proc. of MobiCASE 2009 (2009)
39. Hampapur, A., et al.: The IBM Smart Surveillance System. In: Proc. of IEEE Conference on Computer Vision and Pattern Recognition, Washington D.C. (2004)
40. Miluzzo, E., et al.: Darwin Phones: The Evolution of Sensing and Inference on Mobile Phones. In: Proc. of MobiSys 2010, San Francisco, CA, USA (2010)
41. Yang, Q.: Activity recognition: Linking low-level sensors to high-level intelligence. In: Proc. of the 21st Int'l Joint Conf. on Artificial Intelligence, pp. 20–25 (2009)
42. Pentland, A.: Socially aware computation and communication. IEEE Computer 38(3), 33–40 (2005)
43. Mitchell, T.M.: Mining Our Reality. Science 326(5960), 1644–1645 (2009)

Smart Itinerary Recommendation Based on User-Generated GPS Trajectories

Hyoseok Yoon[1], Yu Zheng[2], Xing Xie[2], and Woontack Woo[1]

[1] Gwangju Institute of Science and Technology, Gwangju 500-712, South Korea
{hyoon,wwoo}@gist.ac.kr
[2] Microsoft Research Asia, Beijing 100190, China
{yuzheng,xingx}@microsoft.com

Abstract. Traveling to unfamiliar regions require a significant effort from novice travelers to plan where to go within a limited duration. In this paper, we propose a smart recommendation for highly efficient and balanced itineraries based on multiple user-generated GPS trajectories. Users only need to provide a minimal query composed of a start point, an end point and travel duration to receive an itinerary recommendation. To differentiate good itinerary candidates from less fulfilling ones, we describe how we model and define itinerary in terms of several characteristics mined from user-generated GPS trajectories. Further, we evaluated the efficiency of our method based on 17,745 user-generated GPS trajectories contributed by 125 users in Beijing, China. Also we performed a user study where current residents of Beijing used our system to review and give ratings to itineraries generated by our algorithm and baseline algorithms for comparison.

Keywords: Spatio-temporal data mining, GPS trajectories, Itinerary recommendation.

1 Introduction

Traveling is one of the popular leisure activities people do in their free time. Nevertheless, travelers find it challenging to make the most out of the available yet limited time to have quality travels. Often, travelers do not have the luxury of 'trial-and-error' to find interesting locations and routes which could waste the available time once a wrong visit is made. This calls for the needs of good itinerary for travelers. In a series of attempts to ease the burden, many recommendations techniques are researched, especially for the tourism industry [1]. There are a few available options already. Commercial travel agencies provide a handful itineraries starting and ending in major locations with fixed duration of travel, which forces travelers to adapt to the itineraries, rather than receiving an itinerary based on their needs. Travelers also can ask residents in the region or refer to travel experts through travel web sites for recommendation. By intuition, inexperienced travelers can learn from experienced travel experts and active residents of the region to build a better travel plan.

Z. Yu et al. (Eds.): UIC 2010, LNCS 6406, pp. 19–34, 2010.

This is the exact intuition behind our approach to recommend itineraries, but through the data mining of user-generated GPS trajectories from travel experts and active residents of the region to be explored. The use of user-generated GPS trajectories enables many interesting applications. Figure 1 illustrates an application scenario of our work.

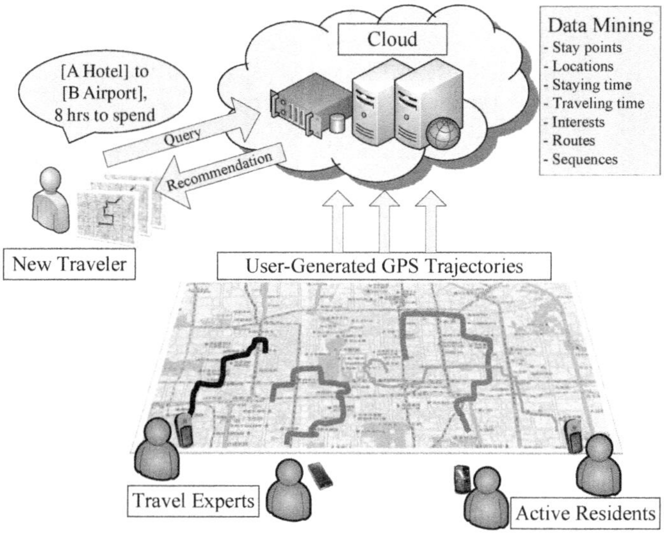

Fig. 1. Application scenario of smart itinerary recommender

As depicted in this application scenario, we recommend new travelers an itinerary that makes the efficient use of the given duration by considering multiple users' accumulated travel routes and experiences. If user-generated GPS trajectories stored on the cloud are accumulated as good examples for data mining, we can extract many features such as where to stay and how long to travel to aid new users in building an efficient travel itinerary.

Our contribution in this paper is as follows.

(1) We propose a *Location-Interest Graph* from multiple user-generated GPS trajectories to model typical user's routes in the area, including which locations are connected and the time relationship between locations.

(2) We model and define what a good itinerary is and how it can be evaluated in order to compare one itinerary to another one.

(3) We present a smart itinerary recommendation framework based on *Location-Interest Graph* generated offline and user query provided online to recommend highly efficient and balanced itinerary that outperforms baseline algorithms.

(4) We evaluate our method using a large GPS dataset collected from 125 users. Then we recommend itineraries from both a large set of simulated user queries and real user inputs to evaluate them according to several characteristics of itinerary and user ratings respectively.

The rest of the paper is organized as follows. Section 2 gives an overview of our system. Section 3 presents detail description of itinerary recommendation processes. In Section 4, we present experiment results and provide discussions. Section 5 reviews related works on itinerary recommendation and GPS data mining, followed by conclusion in Section 6.

2 Overview of Our System

In this section, we first define several terms used throughout the paper. Then we describe the architecture of smart itinerary recommender.

2.1 Preliminaries

Definition 1: Trajectory. A user's trajectory *Traj* is a sequence of time-stamped points, $Traj = \langle p_1, p_2, ..., p_k \rangle$. Points are represented by $p_i = (lat_i, lng_i, t_i)$, $(i = 1, 2, ..., k)$; t_i is a time stamp, $\forall 1 \leq i < k, t_i < t_{i+1}$ and (lat_i, lng_i) are GPS coordinates of points.

Definition 2: Distance and Interval. $Dist(p_i, p_j)$ denotes the geospatial distance between two points p_i and p_j, and $Int(p_i, p_j) = |p_i.t_i - p_j.t_j|$ is the time interval between two points.

Definition 3: Stay Point. A stay point s is a geographical region where a user stayed over a time threshold T_r within a distance threshold of D_r. In a user's trajectory, s is characterized by a set of consecutive points $P = \langle p_m, p_{m+1}, ..., p_n \rangle$, where $\forall m < i \leq n$, $Dist(p_m, p_i) \leq D_r$, $Dist(p_m, p_{n+1}) > D_r$ and $Int(p_m, p_n) \geq T_r$. Therefore, $s = (lat, lng, t_a, t_l)$, where

$$s.lat = \sum\nolimits_{i=m}^{n} p_i.lat/|P|, s.lng = \sum\nolimits_{i=m}^{n} p_i.lng/|P| \tag{1}$$

respectively stands for the average *lat* and *lng* coordinates of the collection P; $s.t_a = p_m.t_m$ is the user's arrival time on s and $s.t_l = p_n.t_n$ represents the user's leaving time.

Definition 4: Location History. An individual's location history h is represented as a sequence of stay points they visited with corresponding time of arrival: t_a, time of leave: t_l and time interval from s_i to s_j: $\Delta t_{i,j} = s_j.t_a - s_i.t_l$ where $\forall 1 < i < j \leq n$

$$h = \langle s_1 \xrightarrow{\Delta t_{1,2}} s_2 \xrightarrow{\Delta t_{2,3}} s_3, \ \dots \ , s_{n-1} \xrightarrow{\Delta t_{n-1,n}} s_n \rangle \tag{2}$$

We put together the stay points detected from all users' trajectories into a dataset $\boldsymbol{S}$, and employ a clustering algorithm to partition this dataset into some clusters. Thus, the similar stay points from various users will be assigned into the same cluster.

Definition 5: Locations. $L = \{l_1, l_2, ..., l_n\}$ is a collection of Locations, where $\forall 1 \le i \le n$, $l_i = \{s | s \in \boldsymbol{S}\}$ is a cluster of stay points detected from multiple users' trajectories: $i \ne j$, $l_i \cap l_j = \emptyset$. After the clustering operation, we can substitute a stay point in a user's location history with the cluster ID the stay point pertains to. Supposing $s_1 \in l_i, s_2 \in l_j, s_3 \in l_k, s_{n-1} \in l_l, s_n \in l_m$, Equation (2) can be replaced with

$$h = \langle l_i \overset{\Delta t_{i,j}}{\rightarrow} l_j \overset{\Delta t_{j,k}}{\rightarrow} l_k, \ \dots \ , l_l \overset{\Delta t_{l,m}}{\longrightarrow} l_m \rangle \tag{3}$$

Thus, different users' location histories become comparable and can be integrated to recommend a single location.

Definition 6: Typical Stay Time and Time Interval. For each location $l_i \in L$ with m stay points that pertain to this location, typical stay time t_s of location l_i is defined as median of stay time of stay point $s_k.t_s = s_k.t_l - s_k.t_a$ where $\forall s_k \in l_i$, $\forall 1 \le k \le m$.

$$l_i.t_s = Median(s_k.t_s) \tag{4}$$

For n location histories $(h_1, ..., h_n)$ with a sequence $l_i \overset{\Delta t_{i,j}}{\rightarrow} l_j$ where $l_i, l_j \in L$ and $l_i \ne l_j$, typical time interval $\Delta T_{i,j}$ from l_i to l_j is defined as in Equation (5) and all typical time intervals are put into a dataset $\boldsymbol{\Delta T}$ where $\forall 1 \le k \le n$.

$$\Delta T_{i,j} = Median(h_k.\Delta t_{i,j}) \tag{5}$$

Definition 7: Location Interest. I_j represents location interest at l_j which has a mutual reinforcement relationship with user travel experience [2]. The mutual relationship of location interest I_j and travel experience e_i are represented as Equation 6 and 7. An item r_{ij} stands for the times that user u_i has stayed in location l_j. Figure 2 depicts this relationship.

$$I_j = \sum\nolimits_{u_i \in U} r_{ji} \times e_i \tag{6}$$

$$e_i = \sum\nolimits_{l_j \in L} r_{ij} \times I_j \tag{7}$$

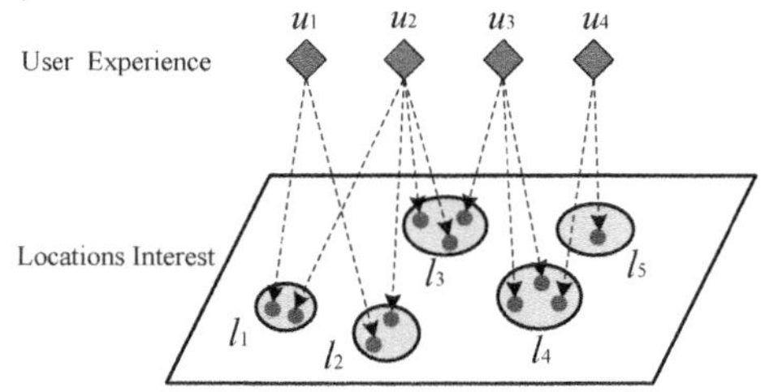

Fig. 2. Location interest and user experience

Definition 8: Trip. A trip $Trip$ is a sequence of locations with corresponding typical time intervals,

$$Trip = \langle l_1 \xrightarrow{\Delta T_{1,2}} l_2 \xrightarrow{\Delta T_{2,3}} l_3, \ \dots \ , \xrightarrow{\Delta T_{k-1,k}} l_k \rangle \tag{8}$$

where $\forall 1 \leq i < j \leq k$, $\Delta T_{i,j} \in \Delta T$ and $l_i, l_j \in L$ are locations. $Trip$ has four attributes, 1) the total staying time for visiting locations t_{stay}, 2) the total traveling time t_{trav}, 3) the duration of the trip t_{dur} and 4) the interest density of the trip i_{den} defined by the total sum of interest of locations divided by the number of locations.

$$t_{stay} = \sum_{i=1}^{k} l_i.t_s \tag{9}$$

$$t_{trav} = \sum_{i=1}^{k-1} \Delta T_{i,i+1} \tag{10}$$

$$t_{dur} = t_{stay} + t_{trav} \tag{11}$$

$$i_{den} = (\sum_{i=1}^{k} I_i)/k \tag{12}$$

Definition 9: Itinerary. An itinerary It is a recommended trip based on user's start point q_s and destination q_d constrained by trip duration threshold q_t in a query.

$$It = \langle q_s \in l_s \xrightarrow{\Delta T_{s,1}} l_1 \xrightarrow{\Delta T_{1,2}} l_2, \ \dots \ , l_{k-1} \xrightarrow{\Delta T_{k-1,k}} l_k \xrightarrow{\Delta T_{k,d}} q_d \in l_d \rangle \tag{13}$$

This means that the user will start a trip from q_s and end in q_d where the duration of trip t_{dur} does not exceed available q_t, $t_{dur} \leq q_t$.

Definition 10: User Query. A user-specified input with three attributes (start point, end point and duration) is defined as a user query, $Q = \{q_s, q_d, q_t\}$.

2.2 Architecture

For the itinerary recommendation, we configure our architecture into offline tasks for processing time-consuming and static information and online tasks for processing variable user queries as depicted in Figure 3. In offline processing, we analyze the user-generated GPS trajectories and build a *Location-Interest Graph* (G_r) with location and interest information, this is quite time consuming process which needs to be done once. Then G_r should be built again only after a significant amount of user-generated GPS trajectories are uploaded. In online processing, we use the G_r built in offline to recommend an itinerary based on a user-specified query.

Our recommendation method is consisted of the following six modular tasks. First two operations, (*Stay Points Extraction and Clustering*, *Location Interest and Sequence Mining*) are carried out in offline and the latter four operations (*Query Verification*, *Trip Candidate Selection*, *Trip Candidate Ranking*, *Re-ranking by Travel Sequence*) are performed online. Details are presented in Section 3.

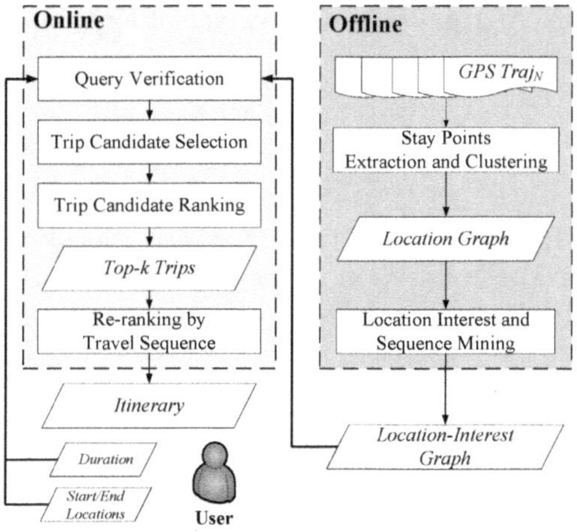

Fig. 3. Architecture of smart itinerary recommender

3 Itinerary Recommendation

In this section, we describe itinerary recommendation processes focusing more on the online processing part. We describe how we model itinerary, how G_r is utilized to generate itineraries and describe the involved selection and ranking algorithms.

3.1 Modeling Itinerary

Since an itinerary is limited by one's available time, known as duration of travel, we use duration as the first constraint in our algorithms. This constraint is very important for two reasons. First reason is that an itinerary with duration that exceeds user's requirement is of no use to users. Second reason is that it simplifies algorithmic complexity by providing a stopping condition. Additionally, we consider the following four factors to determine a good itinerary. We use the following first three characteristics to find trips that surpass some thresholds shown as a cube in Figure 4. The best ideal itinerary would have values equal to 1 in all three dimensions which is depicted as a black dot in Figure 4. The selected trips in the cube are re-ranked according to classical travel sequence to differentiate candidates further.

1) **Elapsed Time Ratio:** An itinerary that uses as much available time as possible is considered to be better, since time is a limited resource for any user, they want to utilize most of their available time.

2) **Stay Time Ratio:** People should spend more time on the locations rather than on the way traveling. An itinerary with less traveling time and more staying time on the site is considered to be a better choice.

3) **Interest Density Ratio:** Visitors to a new region would like to visit as many highly interesting locations as possible, i.e., popular locations and locations with cultural importance.

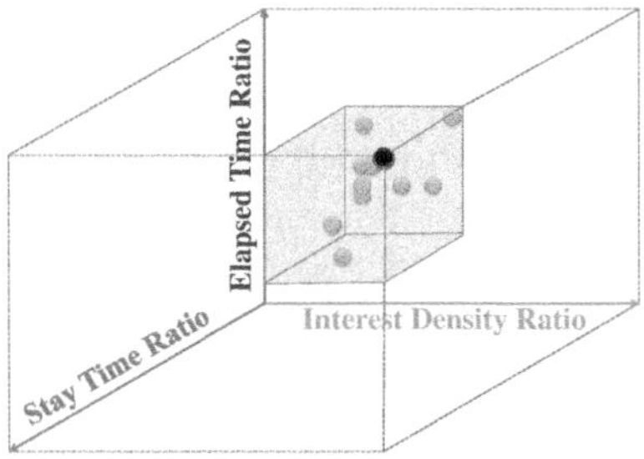

Fig. 4. Trip candidates for a good itinerary

4) **Classical Travel Sequence Ratio:** An itinerary that revisits travel sequences observed from classical travel sequence of previous users is considered to be better, since it reflects realistic routes taken by experts and local people in the region.

3.2 Location-Interest Graph

From multiple users' GPS trajectories, we detect stay points (Definition 3) and cluster them into locations (Definition 5). Further, location interest is calculated (Definition 7) and classical travel sequence is mined by considering hub scores, authority scores and probability of taking this specific sequence (See Section 4.5). Details of mining interesting locations and classical travel sequences are presented in [3]. With this information, we build G_r offline.

Definition 11: Location-Interest Graph (G_r). Formally, a G_r is a graph $G_r = (V, E)$. Vertex set V is Locations (Definition 5) L, $V = L = \{l_1, l_2, ..., l_k\}$. Edge set E is replaced by ΔT where $\Delta T_{i,j}$ stands for a travel sequence from l_i to l_j where $1 \leq i < j \leq k$ with typical time interval as its value. So if there exists an edge between l_i and l_j, then there is a non-zero travel time in corresponding $\Delta T_{i,j}$.

In summary, G_r contains information on 1) Location itself (interest, typical staying time) and 2) relationship between locations (typical traveling time, classical travel sequence).

3.3 Query Verification

In the online process, we first verify user query, $Q = \{q_s, q_d, q_t\}$ by calculating the distance between the start point and end point. There are two approaches we can estimate the distance, $Dist(q_s, q_d)$. First, we can use the harversine formula or the spherical law of cosines with the raw GPS coordinates of start point and end point. Alternatively, we can use Web service such as Bing Map to find traveling distance between two specified locations and traveling time. After confirming the calculated distance with duration in the query, we locate the start point and the end point in G_r by finding the nearest location. Next, the original query $Q = \{q_s, q_d, q_t\}$ is replaced with $Q\prime = \{l_s, l_d, q_t\}$ which is sent to the recommender.

3.4 Trip Candidate Selection

With the verified user query, we select trip candidates from the starting location l_s to the end location l_d. The only restriction we impose in this stage is time constraint so that the candidate trips do not exceed the given duration q_t. We first start from a path which includes the start location l_s as the sole location. Then we check other locations not in this path but are feasible to visit with the remaining duration iteratively. The constraint of duration and visited location information are used as heuristics to select the next location. As we add a new location for the path, we also keep a list of already added locations, so that this location is not checked in the next iteration. For each location added to the path, we subtract the stay time of the location and traveling time to the location to yield a new remaining time. Once the path reaches the end location, we add the generated path as a candidate trip. When all the candidates are added, we return n trip candidates as results.

3.5 Trip Candidate Ranking

Algorithm 1 shows trip candidate ranking algorithm. The algorithm returns an array of $top - k$ trips in decreasing order of the Euclidean distance value.

Algorithm 1. CandidateRanking(G_r,Tr_s,q_t)

Input: A Location-Interest Graph G_r, a set of trips Tr_s, and the duration q_t
Output: A set of top-k trips Tr_r, sorted by Euclidean distance

for all Trip $tr \in Tr_s$ **do**
  for all Location $loc \in tr$ **do**
    $t_{trav} \Leftarrow t_{trav} + G_r.\Delta T_{prevLoc,loc}$
    $t_{stay} \Leftarrow t_{stay} + loc.t_s$
    $i_{den} \Leftarrow i_{den} + I.loc$
    $prevLoc \Leftarrow loc$
  $tr.SetTime(t_{trav}, t_{stay})$
  if $tr.i_{den} > MaxI$ **then**
    $MaxI_d \Leftarrow tr.i_{den}$
  for all Trip $tr \in Tr_s$ **do**
    $tr.SetEucDist(tr.t_{dur}/q_t, tr.t_{stay}/q_t, tr.i_{den}/MaxI)$
$Tr_r \Leftarrow SortByEucDist(Tr_s)$
return Tr_r

After selecting n trip candidates from previous step, we rank each trip with factors from Section 3. The factors used to rank each trip $tr_i \in Tr_s$, $1 \leq i \leq k$ are,

1) *Elapsed Time Ratio (ETR)* $= tr_i.t_{dur}/q_t$
2) *Stay Time Ratio (STR)* $= tr_i.t_{stay}/q_t$
3) *Interest Density Ratio (IDR)* $= tr_i.i_{den}/Tr_s.MaxI$

Here, we can use some thresholds value to quickly reject undesirable candidates, i.e., reject candidates with elapsed time ratio less than 0.5. Then we find the Euclidean distance of each trip using these 3 dimensions as in Equation 14. Here

$Tr_s.MaxI$ refers to a maximum interest density value of all candidate trips which we use for normalization. We can assign different weight values for the factors by setting α_1, α_2, and α_3. For our system we treat three factors equally important by setting $\alpha_1 = \alpha_2 = \alpha_3 = 1$.

$$ED = \sqrt{\alpha_1(ETR)^2 + \alpha_2(STR)^2 + \alpha_3(IDR)^2} \tag{14}$$

3.6 Re-ranking by Travel Sequence

We have cut down the number of candidate trips from n to k. These k trips will likely have similar Euclidean distance values. So how can we differentiate between candidates, and recommend one over another? Our solution is to examine each trip's travel sequence and score them for any classical travel sequences.

The classical travel sequence integrates three aspects, the authority score of going in and out and the hub scores, to score travel sequences [3]. Figure 5 demonstrates the calculation of the classical score for a 2-length sequence $l_1 \Rightarrow l_3$. The connected edges represent people's transition sequence and the values on the edges show the times users have taken the sequence. Equation 15 shows the calculation based on the following parts. 1) The authority score of location l_1 (a_{l_1}) weighted by the probability of people moving out from this sequence (Out_{l_1,l_3}). In this demonstration, $Out_{l_1,l_3} = 5/7$. 2) The authority score of location l_3 (a_{l_3}) weighted by the probability of people's moving in by this sequence (In_{l_1,l_3}). 3) The hub scores h_b of the users (U_{l_1,l_3}) who have taken this sequence.

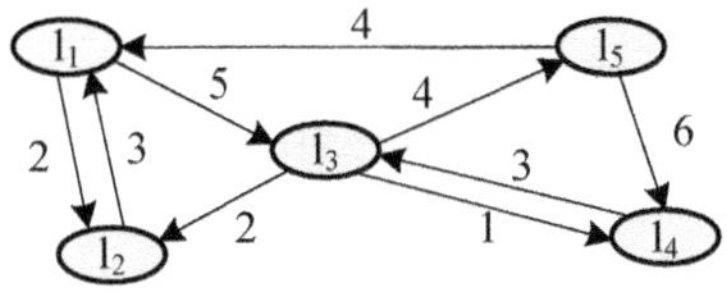

Fig. 5. Demonstration of classical travel sequence

Definition 12: Classical Travel Sequences

$$c_{l_1,l_3} = \sum_{u_k \in U_{l_1,l_2}} (a_{l_1} \times Out_{l_1,l_2} + a_{l_3} \times In_{l_1,l_3} + {h_b}^k) \tag{15}$$

So two trips might have similar value ranges in Euclidean distance after the first ranking, however they will have different classical travel sequence score. We give preference toward trips with higher classical travel sequence score, which means that we recommend trips to revisit previous users' practical travel sequences. Using the classical travel sequence matrix, we can score any travel sequence,

$$c(l_1 \rightarrow l_2 \rightarrow l_3) = c_{1,2} + c_{2,3} \tag{16}$$

Once we have classical travel sequence score of tr_i by calculating $c(tr_i)$, we normalize it by the maximum classical travel sequence score $MaxC$ found of all candidates.

Classical Travel Score Ratio (CTSR) $= c(tr_i)/MaxC$.
Then we once again use the Euclidean distance, this time including classical travel sequence score to re-rank k candidates. We use equal weights for all four factors as shown in Equation 17. The first itinerary with the highest Euclidean distance value is recommended to user, and the user can view alternative itineraries in the order of the Euclidean distance.

$$ED' = \sqrt{\alpha_1(ETR)^2 + \alpha_2(STR)^2 + \alpha_3(IDR)^2 + \alpha_4(CTSR)^2} \quad (17)$$

4 Experiments

In this section, we explain the experiment settings, evaluation approaches, and the experiment results.

4.1 Settings

To collect user-generated GPS trajectories, we have used stand-alone GPS receivers as well as GPS phones. With these devices, 125 users recorded 17,745 GPS trajectories in Beijing from May 2007 to Aug. 2009. In this experiment, time threshold T_r and distance threshold D_r are set to 20 minutes and 200 meters respectively. With these parameters, we detected 35,319 stay points from the dataset and excluded work/home spots. For clustering these stay points into unique locations, we used a density-based clustering algorithm OPTICS (Ordering Points To Identify the Clustering Structure) which resulted in 119 locations. Among these 119 locations, typical traveling time is assigned for the connected locations which serves as an edge set for G_r.

4.2 Evaluation Approaches

In the experiment, we use two evaluation approaches to evaluate our itinerary recommendation methods. First approach is based on a large amount of simulated user queries for the algorithmic level comparison. Using this synthetic data set, we evaluate the quality of the generated itineraries quantitatively compared to other baseline methods. Second approach is based on a user study where the generated itineraries by our method and baselines methods are evaluated by real users. In second approach, we observe how user's perceived quality of itineraries compare by different methods.

Simulation. We used simulation to generate a large quantity of user queries to evaluate the effectiveness of our method. For our simulation to cover most general cases of user input, we used four different levels for duration, 5 hours, 10 hours, 15 hours and 20 hours. Also the duration length seems reasonable for Beijing, China where all the user-generated GPS trajectories are exclusively collected, since it covers an area of about $16,000km^2$. For each duration level, we generated 1,000 queries. Since user query $Q = \{q_s, q_d, q_t\}$ is composed of two points, we generate two sets of GPS coordinates randomly. Here we put some constraints so that the generated queries follow normal distribution in terms of the distance between the start and end points.

User Study. In user study, we recruited 10 participants who are currently active residents and have lived in Beijing for preferably at least 3 years (average of 3.8 years), since our GPS logs are exclusively collected from the past three years. We asked each participant to use our system to generate itineraries by selecting a start location, an end location and duration of their choice. The recruited participants generated queries in their choice of locations where they were familiar with. Each user submitted 3 queries and gave ratings to 3 itineraries generated by our method and two other baseline methods. They carefully reviewed locations and sequences in the itinerary without knowing about the methods that produced results. Participants took about 30 minutes to completely review 3 sets of 3 itineraries where they were allowed to browse through 3 different itineraries for the query to give relative ratings after comparison. We asked participants following questions to give scores for each generated itinerary in different aspects (score of 1 being the lowest and 5 represents the highest score for better performance) as shown in Table 1.

Table 1. Questions for evaluation

Criteria	Question
Elapsed Time	How efficient is the itinerary in terms of the duration? (1-5)
Stay & Travel Time	How appropriate are staying time and traveling time? (1-5)
Interest	How interesting/representative are the included locations? (1-5)

Baselines. We compared the result of our recommendation with two baseline methods, Ranking-by-Time (RbT) and Ranking-by-Interest (RbI). RbT recommends the itinerary with the highest elapsed time usage. Ideally, it would recommend an itinerary with the elapsed time equal to the duration of the query, if there is such candidate exists. Similarly, RbI ranks the candidates in the order of total interest of locations included in the itinerary. So the candidate with the highest interest density ratio is recommended.

4.3 Results

Simulation. We generated 1,000 queries for each time level (5, 10, 15 and 20) and ran through 3 algorithms. For the duration of 5 hours, only 452 itinerary results were retrieved. For the duration of 10 hours, 15 hours and 20 hours, 935, 961, and 973 itinerary results are acquired respectively. There are three reasons that not all queries returned results. First reason is that simply there was not enough time to go from a start location to an end location. Even though the queries would pass initial query verification, there may be very few or no shorter directions to the end location while consuming the specified duration. Second reason is that there are areas with very few or no locations at all. So when the given time is short and the user starts from one of these sparse areas, the most of time is used up to go to a nearby location, yielding no results. Third reason is that user starts at a location which has very few outgoing edges, in that case, user might end up in a dead end early even though there are plenty of remaining time. For the recommended itineraries, we looked closely at the average of elapsed time, stay time, interest, classical sequence and Euclidean distance. Figure 6 shows the result for four different time levels. As expected, the baseline algorithm RbT and

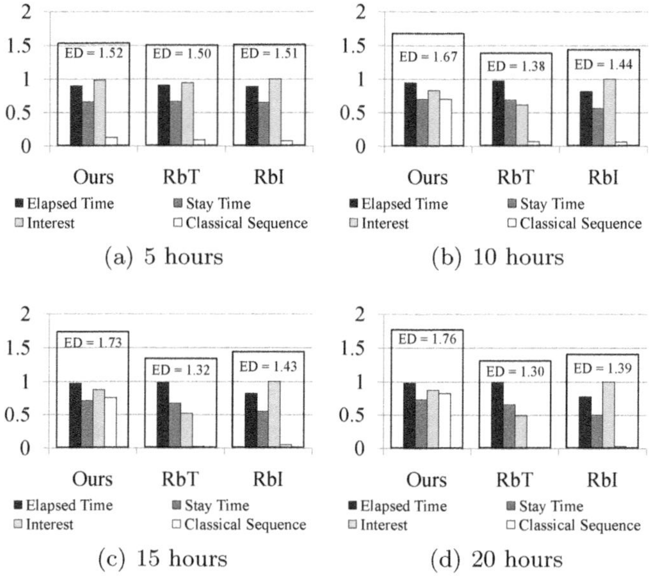

Fig. 6. Simulation results showing the average quality of itinerary generated by different methods

RbI yields best results in the aspect of elapsed time and interest respectively. However, the difference is minimal in the 5 hours level. All three algorithms produced similar quality results. If the duration is very short then there are not many candidates to consider and then many of them would overlap anyway. This explains almost identical graphs in Figure 6(a). The difference gets larger and noticeable as the duration gets longer. Still baseline algorithms successfully recommend itineraries that perform well in only one aspect. RbT has lower average of interest score compared to RbI and our algorithm. Also RbI has lower average of elapsed time compared to RbT and ours. Furthermore, both baseline algorithms produce itineraries that are poor in classical sequence aspect. So we can observe on the average, RbT and RbI will produce a biased or skewed itinerary focusing on only one attribute in a long term. On the other hand, our algorithm produces well-balanced itineraries in all four aspects. The Euclidean distance value gives a good indication that our algorithm produces balanced itinerary overall and even the recommended itineraries are comparable in other factors that are specialized by baseline algorithms. By looking at the Euclidean distance value, we observe that the performance of our algorithm increases with time whereas two baseline algorithms suffer from performance degradation.

User Study. For 10 participants' 30 queries over Beijing area, we observed the balance of different itinerary attributes in our algorithm compared to the baseline algorithms. As we observed from the simulation, our algorithm produces an itinerary that is well-balanced in the four attributes. So in this user study, we show that our algorithm produces results that are nearly equal to the baselines which specialize in a certain single attribute. For instance, we check how our result compares with RbT produced itinerary in terms of elapsed time. stay time and travel time. Since RbT produces results that maximize the time use, we wanted to check whether the difference user perceives is significant compare to our result which produces well-balanced and nearly close result. Table 2 shows the comparison between our algorithm and RbT in terms of time use. As the T-test reveals that there is no significant advantage in perceived elapsed time, stay time, and travel time from using RbT over ours. Similarly, we compared our result in terms of locations interest included in the itinerary as shown in Table 2. Here again the T-test reveals that there is no significant advantage in perceived interest from using RbI over ours.

Table 2. Comparison of temporal attributes and locations interest

Attribute(s)	Ours	Rank-by-Time	T-test
Elapsed Time	**3.97**	3.67	$p > 0.01$
Stay and Travel Time	**3.60**	3.27	$p > 0.01$
Attribute(s)	**Ours**	**Rank-by-Interest**	**T-test**
Interest	**3.27**	2.92	$p > 0.01$

4.4 Discussions

Temporal aspects. The length of duration is an interesting attribute to look at. Many participants used duration between 6 to 12 hours. It supports our initial assumption that people would not have such a long journey and keep them in a manageable size. For shorter duration, the measured quality of itineraries were less for our algorithm based on Euclidean distance of attributes. Conversely, two baseline algorithms produced the best quality at the shorter duration and recommended less efficient itineraries with longer duration. In extreme cases though, it was possible for baseline algorithms such as RbI to recommend an itinerary that only contains a couple of interesting locations without spending all available time. However, since duration was used as a stopping condition in selecting candidates, most recommended itineraries spend good ratio of available time in simulation and in real user queries alike.

Location interest and classical sequence. Our algorithm produced a balanced itinerary with higher classical sequence scores. In algorithmic level, our algorithm showed a great performance advantage in terms of the four attributes including classical travel sequence. However, in real queries by users it was difficult to measure location interest and classical travel sequences from the recommended itinerary. Even though an itinerary is composed of many locations and sequences, we only asked the participants to give ratings for the overall location interest and classical sequence. So they gave high score for classical travel sequences they could find, and gave lower score for any abnormal sequences that sometimes balances each other out. So this is different from our simulation where each location interest and classical travel sequences were accumulated to give the overall score. In our current algorithm, we only consider increment of score for location interest and any classical travel sequences found, yet in the real situation, we might need to decrease score or give penalties for totally uninteresting locations and awkward sequences.

5 Related Work

5.1 Itinerary Recommendation

Previously a number of itinerary generation and recommendation systems are introduced. There are interactive systems such as INTRIGUE [4] which provides an interface to browse different categories of location and select an area on a map. In this system, user needs to specify general constraints such as time constraints and user can interactively specify attraction items to be included in the itinerary. Another interactive system is TripTip [5] where a user selects first location to get recommendation on similar types of places using popular tags. Huang and Bian [6] build a travel recommendation system that integrates heterogeneous online travel information based on tourism ontology and recommends tourist attractions using travel preference estimated by the Bayesian network. Kumar et al., [7] present GIS-based Advanced Traveler Information System (ATIS) for Hyderabad City in India which includes a site-tour module based on the shortest distance. Compared to these works, we use simplified query composed of two points and duration where a complete set of itinerary is automatically generated based on real user-generated GPS trajectories. We also present the Euclidean distance based method to compare and measure the quality of itinerary.

5.2 GPS Data Mining Applications

The number of research and applications using GPS data is rapidly increasing. For example many researchers are finding patterns in GPS trajectory [8], convert raw GPS to routable road map [9], use GPS to find locations of interest [10] and combine with multimedia such geo-tagged photo for recommendation [11]. We also previously used GPS data to mine user similarity, interesting locations and travel sequences [2][3], recommend travels [12] and understand user's mobility on transportation mode [13] to understand user and build social networks in GeoLife [14]. Our work in this paper, extends location level recommendation to an itinerary level recommendation and proposes an efficient itinerary recommendation algorithm considering a multiple number of attributes in equally important weight. We also evaluate our method with a large set of real user-generated GPS trajectories in algorithmic level to the real use cases.

6 Conclusion

In this paper, user-generated GPS trajectories from 125 users were used to build *Location-Interest Graph* which contains useful location-related information (location, interest, stay time, travel time, classical travel sequence). Such information in a region, specifically Beijing, China is used to recommend an itinerary based on user query. An architecture for recommending an itinerary is proposed to handle user-generated GPS trajectories offline and user query processing online. Based on four popular attributes mined from our data set such as elapsed time, staying time, location interest and classical travel sequence, we proposed Euclidean distance based ranking to recommend an itinerary of good quality in all four aspects. We evaluated our method in algorithmic level by using 4,000 simulated user queries in four different time levels to confirm the performance gain in the overall quality over baseline algorithms. We achieved the best performance when it was used for the longer duration. Also active residents used our system to generate real queries and evaluated the resulting itinerary. As a result, we found that our algorithm recommends itineraries that are nearly as good for a single attribute focused baseline algorithms such as Rank-by-Time and Rank-by-Interest and better in overall quality.

Acknowledgments. This research was supported by Microsoft Research Asia and the MKE, Korea, under the ITRC (NIPA-2010-C1090-1011-0008).

References

1. Stabb, S., Werther, H., Ricci, F., Zipf, A., Gretzel, U., Fesenmaier, D., Paris, C., Knoblock, C.: Intelligent systems for tourism. IEEE Intelligent Systems 17(6), 53–66 (2002)
2. Zheng, Y., Zhang, L., Xie, X., Ma, W.Y.: Mining correlation between locations using human location history. In: GIS 2009, pp. 472–475 (2009)
3. Zheng, Y., Zhang, L., Xie, X., Ma, W.Y.: Mining interesting locations and travel sequences from gps trajectories. In: WWW 2009, pp. 791–800 (2009)
4. Ardissono, L., Goy, A., Petrone, G., Segnan, M.: A multi-agent infrastructure for developing personalized web-based systems. ACM Transactions on Internet Technology 5(1), 47–69 (2005)
5. Kim, J., Kim, H., Ryu, J.h.: Triptip: a trip planning service with tag-based recommendation. In: CHI EA 2009, pp. 3467–3472 (2009)
6. Huang, Y., Bian, L.: A Bayesian network and analytic hierarchy process based personalized recommendations for tourist attractions over the Internet. Expert Systems with Applications 36(1), 933–943 (2009)
7. Kumar, P., Singh, V., Reddy, D.: Advanced traveler information system for hyderabad city. IEEE Transactions on Intelligent Transportation Systems 6(1), 26–37 (2005)

8. Monreale, A., Pinelli, F., Trasarti, R., Giannotti, F.: Wherenext: a location predictor on trajectory pattern mining. In: KDD 2009, pp. 637–646 (2009)
9. Cao, L., Krumm, J.: From gps traces to a routable road map. In: GIS 2009, pp. 3–12 (2009)
10. Ashbrook, D., Starner, T.: Using GPS to learn significant locations and predict movement across multiple users. Personal and Ubiquitous Computing 7(5), 275–286 (2003)
11. Tai, C.H., Yang, D.N., Lin, L.T., Chen, M.S.: Recommending personalized scenic itinerary with geo-tagged photos. In: ICME 2008, pp. 1209–1212 (2008)
12. Zheng, Y., Xie, X.: Learning travel recommendation from user-generated gps trajectories. ACM Transaction on Intelligent Systems and Technology 1 (2010) (to be appeared)
13. Zheng, Y., Chen, Y., Li, Q., Xie, X., Ma, W.Y.: Understanding transportation modes based on gps data for web applications. ACM Transactions on the Web 4(1), 1–36 (2010)
14. Zheng, Y., Xie, X., Ma, W.Y.: Geolife: A collaborative social networking service among user, location and trajectory. IEEE Data Eng. Bull. 33(2), 32–39 (2010)

Inferring User Search Intention Based on Situation Analysis of the Physical World

Zhu Wang[1], Xingshe Zhou[1], Zhiwen Yu[1], Yanbin He[1], and Daqing Zhang[2]

[1] School of Computer Science, Northwestern Polytechnical University, P.R. China
[2] Institut TELECOM & Management SudParis, France
wangzhu@mail.nwpu.edu.cn

Abstract. Ubiquitous search of the physical world has recently received significant attention. In this paper, we investigate situation analysis based user intention recognition, which can be useful to retrieve information that may perfectly satisfy a user's needs. We first introduce a hierarchical user intention model based on CRFs (Conditional Random Fields). With the model, a BP (Belief Propagation) based inference method is proposed to recognize user search intention based on situation analysis. A variety of sensing mechanisms are adopted to collect context information of the physical world for robust and reliable situation analysis. We developed a prototype in a real home setting and experiments were performed to examine the effectiveness of the proposed approach.

Keywords: Situation analysis, search intention, CRFs, ubiquitous search.

1 Introduction

As the available information increases explosively, it becomes more and more difficult for human beings to find the information that meets their preferences. Therefore, theories and technologies of information searching have been studied, aiming at providing users with personalized information services. Currently, information searching mainly concerns the cyber world, and several search engines are available, such as Google, Yahoo and Bing. However, due to the rapid advances in embedded devices, wireless sensor networks, and mobile communication technologies, systems and devices that integrate sensing, computing and communication capabilities have been widely deployed, transforming the physical world into a ubiquitous computing platform. It is foreseeable that, in the near future, we will be offered the opportunities to access and search the information about physical objects directly, in a way much the same as searching the cyber world on the web using web searching engines.

Extending search from cyber world to physical world, i.e., *Ubiquitous Search* will provide us exciting services, especially fulfill our requirements of the physical world's real-time information. The key idea of ubiquitous search is to acquire, organize, and browse the desired information about objects in the physical world according to the user's needs, just like what we do in the web searching.

The existing ubiquitous search systems of the physical world mainly focus on the study of an intelligent physical object model, ubiquitous search system architecture,

Z. Yu et al. (Eds.): UIC 2010, LNCS 6406, pp. 35–51, 2010.

ubiquitous searching algorithms, security and privacy issues [1-9], whereas little research has been carried out on the human-centric perspective. Ubiquitous searching aims at providing users with real-time physical world information according to the users' needs, thus if the system is aware of the user's search intention, a much more personalized and attractive search service would be possible.

Traditionally, in the web search, users' query logs, browsing history and client side interaction information have been used to analyze users' search intention, and many user intention based search strategies have been proposed [10-16]. However, most web users are still unable to retrieve information corresponding to their search intention, because of the limited information available for real-time analysis of it. Fortunately, in a ubiquitous computing environment, as the large-scale deployment of sensing devices, much more real-time information is available for the accurate recognition of user intention, such as the user's current location, behavior or activity, ambient environmental context, etc. Therefore, it is possible to capture and infer the user's search intention in the ubiquitous computing environment.

In this study, we focus on inferring user search intention based on situation analysis of the physical world. A prototype system has been built for this purpose. With the belief that a user's search intention is tightly related to his or her current situation, we acquire users' intention based on situation analysis in the proposed system. Multiple sensors, such as UWB (Ultra Wideband) sensor, pressure sensor and environmental sensor, were employed to capture contextual information within a ubiquitous searching scenario. Specifically, a Conditional Random Fields (CRFs) model is adopted for the recognition of user intentions.

A lot of work has been done for the modeling, analyzing and recognizing of user intentions [17-20]. However, to the best of our knowledge, there is still no study about user intention based ubiquitous searching system. Our work may be regarded as an early attempt to investigate user intention in ubiquitous search of the physical world.

The rest of the paper is organized as follows. Section 2 discusses related work. Section 3 introduces the hierarchical user intention model. We present the user intention recognition algorithm based on situation analysis in Section 4. The inference techniques of CRFs are described in Section 5 and the experimental results are reported in Section 6. Finally, Section 7 concludes the paper.

2 Related Work

A number of ubiquitous searching systems have been developed in the past based on ubiquitous computing technologies. Snoogle [1-2] is developed as a search system suitable for small devices used in ubiquitous computing environments. With the perception that hardware resources of smart devices are generally quite limited, a space efficient algorithm has been proposed to perform top-k query on limited hardware resources, and compression schemes have been employed to reduce communication overhead. Snoogle also considers security and privacy protections for sensitive data. MAX [3] aims at facilitating human-centric search of the physical world. In the MAX system, all physical objects are tagged, and a hierarchical architecture consisting of tags, substations, and base-stations is adopted which enables the deployment of MAX not dependent on a specific physical space. MAX provides privacy protection mechanism both in the physical object level and the physical space level. Wang et al. [4] propose a ubiquitous searching architecture named USF (Ubiquitous Searching Framework) based on UIO (Ubiquitous Intelligent Object) model. USF adopts a cluster-based model with two tiers: the first tier is a mesh network consisting of all the UIOs, which are clustered into sub-systems, and the second tier is an overlay composed of the master UIOs of the subsystems. Home-Explorer [5] can help people search and find physical artifacts in a smart indoor environment where everyday artifacts are equipped with multiple sensors. The authors specially focus on the detection of hidden objects based on user-defined rules which are mainly abstracted from common sense knowledge and various physical relations among objects. Christian et al. [6] adopt a network of sensor-equipped mobile phones to construct a ubiquitous searching infrastructure. Mobile phones are used to distribute search queries and to report an object's location. A heuristics algorithm is proposed to determine the distribution scope of a search query. Several other studies [7-9] also take the mobile phone as an important type of sensor and investigate context searching and sharing mechanisms based on mobile phone networks and social networks, where context information such as location, weather condition and even view are shared.

The shared goal of these works is to build a ubiquitous searching architecture that provides real-time information of physical world objects using ubiquitous sensors and ubiquitous computing techniques. This differs from our study, which focuses on capturing the user's search intentions and providing adaptive information service.

Numerous studies have been specially conducted towards personalized Web search based on user intention. Kang & Kim [10] propose a user query classification scheme based on the difference of distribution, mutual information and the usage rate. User search intentions are inferred accordingly as query types, and different algorithms have been adopted to optimize the search results. Based on qualitative analysis of millions of user queries, Jansen et al. [11] identify characteristics of user queries based on three broad classifications of user intent (informational, navigational, and transactional) and propose a classification algorithm to automatically classify users' search queries. Teevan et al. [12] present search algorithms based on users' prior interactions for personalizing users' current Web search. The authors leverage implicit information about users' interests, such as previously issued queries and previously visited Web pages, to re-rank Web search results within a relevance feedback framework. Baeza-Yates et al. [13] propose a framework for the identification of user's interest based on the analysis of query logs. Both supervised and unsupervised learning are used to recognize the user's intention, where supervised learning are employed to identify the user interest given certain established goals and categories and unsupervised learning are adopted to validate the goals and categories used, refine them and select the most appropriate to the user's needs. An ontology-based framework is presented to automatically learn the user's search interests based on combined analysis of the user's past clicks and current queries [14]. Park et al. [15] put forward a framework to extract user intention by using machine learning methods based on HPVM (Hierarchical Phrase Vector Model). They propose a unique representation of user intention under different queries, contexts and users to improve information retrieval performance by filtering the results, recommending a new query, and distinguishing user's characteristics.

In general, the above-mentioned systems mainly focus on the usage of different information (such as users' query logs, browsing history and client side interaction data) to capture users' intention and optimize the Web search results; however, due to the limited sense ability of a Web search system, no context information of the user's current search situation has been adopted in the user intention analysis. Therefore, these works differ from our study, which focuses on capturing and employing the user's intention in a ubiquitous search system.

Quite few systems have attempted to use context information for the inference of user intention in the information searching area. Feng et al. [16] investigate the personalization of mobile search and propose an architecture to collect user's context information and derive user intention in given situations. A client-side context proxy is adopted to collect user information, analyze context information, and compile context profiles. An intelligent manager is used to identify ambiguous query, expand query, and reorder the result documents based on the compiled context profiles. However, this work is based on Web search system in the cyber world which is different from our work that concerns ubiquitous search of the physical world.

Several works have been done on the modeling, capturing and predicting of user intentions. Office Assistant [17] uses the approach of Bayesian Networks for analyzing and predicting the user goals. A temporal reasoning method is used for the changing of the user goals. Chen et al. [18] focus on modeling and predicting user intentions based on contextual features extracted from the user interaction. A Modified Naïve Bayes Classifier is used to support incremental learning in the intention modeling process. Armentano & Amandi [19] model user intentions based on Variable-Order Markov Model, and facilitate posterior detection of user intentions using the proposed model. Burghardt et al. [20] investigate user intention analysis based on the Hidden Markov Model in smart environment. In our work, a CRFs [21] model is adopted to capture and predict user intentions; as CRFs condition on the entire observation sequence, which avoids the need for independence assumptions between observations and vastly expands the set of features that can be incorporated into the model.

3 Hierarchical User Intention Model

The basic concept underlying our user intention model is shown in Figure 1. Each circle indicates an object such as a sensor reading, a situation, or a user intention. The edges illustrate probabilistic dependencies between these objects.

Sensor readings are the input to our model — which is temporally segmented into a sequence of cliques where each clique is the set of sensor readings at time t and would be used to reason the situation at time t. This sequence of cliques would generate a sequence of situation nodes at the next level of the model. This temporal segmentation is very compact and convenient for estimating high-level situations and enables our model to reason explicitly about the duration of a situation.

Situations are estimated for each clique of sensor readings, as illustrated in Figure 1. A situation is a pre-defined collection of contextual elements and is inferred based on current environmental context. In other words, our model labels a user's situation based on temporally segmented context information.

User intentions are dependent on situations which the user located in. Specifically, for a ubiquitous searching system, a user's information needs which defined as search intentions are closely related to his or her current situation. Therefore, it is reasonable to capture the user's search intention based on situation analysis.

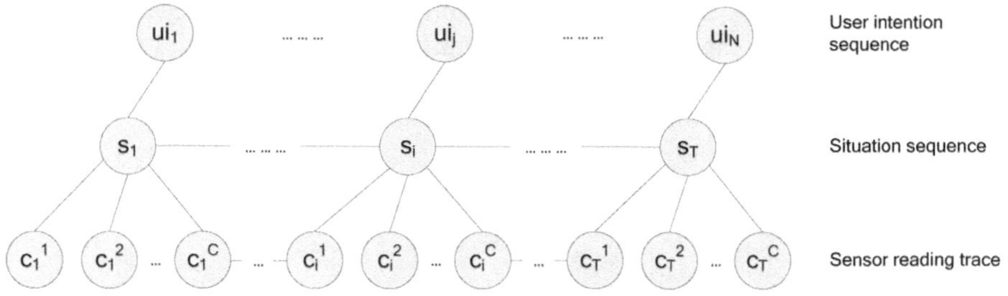

Fig. 1. The concept hierarchy for situation analysis based user intention recognition. For each day of data collection, the lowest level typically consists of thousands of context readings from multiple sensors.

Without loss of generality, we construct an instance of the above proposed user intention model in a home environment. A variety of sensors are deployed in an apartment where a UWB sensor is used to capture user location; a pressure sensor is adopted to determine whether a user is laying on the bed, sitting in a chair or not; a light sensor is applied to sense the light intensity; a smart unit embedded in an electrical household appliance is used to decide whether a appliance is on or not. Six familiar situations in home circumstances, such as sleeping, cooking, dining, reading, watching TV and surfing Internet, are investigated in this specific user intention model.

4 Conditional Random Fields for Situation Analysis

4.1 Preliminaries

Our goal is to develop a probabilistic temporal model that can extract high-level situations from sequences of sensor readings. Based on our previous discussion, the CRF model is selected for situation recognition.

CRFs are models for structured classification [21]. In particular, CRFs are undirected graphical models, where the structure of the graph encodes independence relationships between labels. The term conditional appears in the name of the model because CRFs are probabilistic models that condition on the observations. In other words, the structure of the graph encodes independence relationships between labels and not the observations. The model assumes no independence relationships between observations and, as a consequence, inference in CRFs remains tractable even when they incorporate complex and arbitrary features of the observations [22].

The nodes in CRFs represent a sequence of observations (e.g., sensor readings), denoted as $\mathbf{x} = (x_1, x_2, \ldots, x_T)$, and corresponding hidden states (e.g., situations), denoted as $\mathbf{y} = (y_1, y_2, \ldots, y_T)$. These nodes, along with the connectivity structure imposed by undirected edges between them, define the conditional distribution $p(\mathbf{y}|\mathbf{x})$

over the hidden states **y**. The fully connected sub-graphs of a CRF, called *cliques*, play a key role in the definition of the conditional distribution represented by a CRF. Let C be the set of all cliques in a given CRF. Then, a CRF factorizes the conditional distribution into a product of *clique potentials* $\phi_c(\mathbf{x}_c, \mathbf{y}_c)$, where every $c \in C$ is a clique of the graph and $\mathbf{x}_c$ and $\mathbf{y}_c$ are the observed and hidden nodes in such a clique. Clique potentials are functions that map variable configurations to non-negative numbers. Intuitively, a potential captures the "compatibility" among the variables in the clique: the larger the potential value, the more likely the configuration. Using clique potentials, the conditional distribution over the hidden state is written as:

$$P(y \mid x) = \frac{1}{Z(x)} \prod_{c \in C} \phi_c(x_c, y_c), \tag{1}$$

$$Z_x = \sum_y \prod_{c \in C} \phi_c(x_c, y_c), \tag{2}$$

where Z_x is the normalizing partition function. The computation of this partition function is exponential in the size of **y** since it requires summation over all possible configurations of hidden states **y**. Hence, exact inference is possible for a limited class of CRF models only.

Without loss of generality, potentials $\phi_c(\mathbf{x}_c, \mathbf{y}_c)$ are described by log-linear combinations of *feature functions* $f_c()$, *i.e.*,

$$\phi_c(x_c, y_c) = \exp(w_c^T \cdot f_c(x_c, y_c)), \tag{3}$$

where w_c^T is the transpose of a weight vector w_c, and $f_c(x_c, y_c)$ is a function that extracts a vector of features from the variable values. The feature functions, which are often binary or real valued, are typically designed by the user (combinations of such functions can be learned from data [23]). As we will show in the following Section, the weights are learned from labeled training data. Intuitively, the weights represent the importance of different features for correctly identifying the hidden states. The log-linear feature representation (3) is very compact and guarantees the non-negativeness of potential values. We can write the conditional distribution (1) as:

$$P(y \mid x) = \frac{1}{Z(x)} \prod_{c \in C} \exp\{w_c^T \cdot f_c(x_c, y_c)\}, \tag{4}$$

$$P(y \mid x) = \frac{1}{Z(x)} \exp\{\sum_{c \in C} w_c^T \cdot f_c(x_c, y_c)\}, \tag{5}$$

(5) follows by moving the products into the exponent. Before describing how to perform efficient inference and learning in CRFs, we will now show how CRFs can be used to implement our hierarchical user intention model.

4.2 Application of CRFs in Situation Recognition

Mapping from noisy, continuous sensor readings to discrete intention labels is a difficult task; therefore instead of using the raw sensor data, we typically transform the data via feature functions which map the sensor data into a form that is more useful for intention recognition. Conditional random fields, which are defined in terms of feature functions, are well suited to intention recognition from low-level sensor data.

Based on the temporal segmentation of sensor reading trace, we estimate the situation of each segment. To do so, we import a CRF that contains a hidden situation node for every segment extracted from the sensor reading trace.

This CRF consists of the two lower levels of the one shown in Figure 2. Each situation node is connected to various features, summarizing information resulting from the sensor reading segmentation. These features include:

Spatial information is important for discriminating different situations. Specifically, in a home circumstance, spatial information mainly refers to user's location, such as in the living room and in the study room. For example, when a user is cooking, he or she is most likely in a kitchen while extremely unlikely in a living room. Feature functions for the cliques connecting each situation node to one of the evidence nodes in the CRF shown in Figure 2 are binary indicator functions, one for each possible combination of spatial feature and situation. For instance, one such function returns 1 if the situation is cooking and the user is in the kitchen, while it should return 0 otherwise.

Temporal information, such as time of day and day of week, is discretized in order to allow more flexible feature functions. For example, time of day can be *Morning, Noon, Afternoon, Evening,* or *Night.* Similarly, feature functions for each possible combination of temporal feature and situation also are binary indicator ones. For instance, one such function returns 1 if the situation is sleeping and the time of day is night, while 0 otherwise.

Appliance information is another important context for discriminating situations, such as whether the TV set is on, whether the microwave oven is on, and whether the light is on. Again, we use indicator features to incorporate this information.

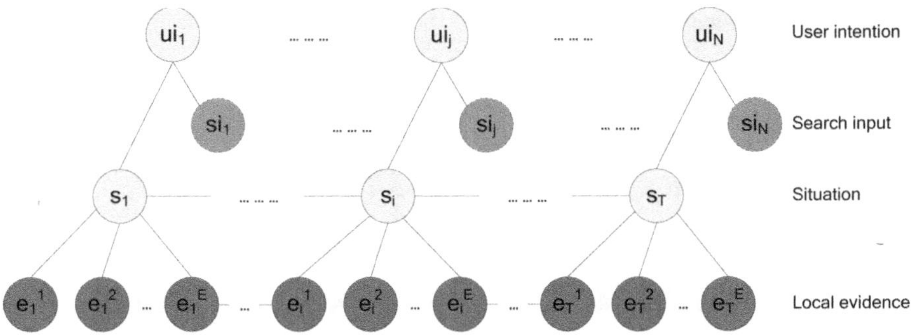

Fig. 2. CRF for labeling situations and user intentions. Situation nodes s_j range over situations and user intention nodes ui_j range over types of user intentions. Each situation node is connected to E observed local evidence nodes e_i^1 to e_i^E. Local evidence comprises information such as user location, device state, and time of day. User intention nodes are generated based on the situations inferred at the situation level and the user's corresponding search input.

The final object of the proposed model is to determine user intentions based on situation analysis. The situation in which a ubiquitous search is executed strongly indicates the type of the user's search intention. For example, in a cooking situation people tend to need information about cooking method of a specific dish, and in a reading situation people is most likely to perform a ubiquitous searching for information about a specific book. User's search input is another important factor that indicates user's search intention. Thus we firstly denote each user search intention as a two-tuples <si_i, s_i>, and then study the inference issues of user search intention based on the result of situation analysis.

4.3 Situation Inference

Algorithm 1 summarizes our algorithm for efficiently inferring situations.

Algorithm 1: Jointly inferring situations and user intentions

---

1. **Input:** Sensor reading trace $\{c_1^1, c_1^2, \ldots, c_1^C, \ldots, c_T^1, c_T^2, \ldots, c_T^C\}$
   i:=0
2. *// Generate situation segments and evidence by grouping sensor readings*
   $\{(s_1, s_2, \ldots, s_T), (e_1^1, e_1^2, \ldots, e_1^E, \ldots, e_T^1, e_T^2, \ldots, e_T^E)\} :=$
   Temporal_Segmentation $\{c_1^1, c_1^2, \ldots, c_1^C, \ldots, c_T^1, c_T^2, \ldots, c_T^C\}$
3. *// Generate CRF containing situation and local evidence nodes*
   CRF_0 := Instantiate_CRF(( ), $(s_1, s_2, \ldots, s_T)$,
   $(e_1^1, e_1^2, \ldots, e_1^E, \ldots, e_T^1, e_T^2, \ldots, e_T^E)$)
4. *// Determine MAP sequence of situations*
   $s_0^{*\prime}$:= MAP_Inference(CRF_0)
5. *// Merge the situation sequence*
   s_0^* :=Merge_Situations($s_0^{*\prime}$)
   do
   i:=i + 1
6. *// Generate user intentions by analyzing situations*
   $(ui_1, ui_2, \ldots, ui_N)_i$:= Generate_UserIntentions(s_{i-1}^*)
7. *// Generate complete CRF with instantiated user intentions*
   CRF_i := Instantiate_CRF($(ui_1, ui_2, \ldots, ui_N)_i$, $(s_1, s_2, \ldots, s_T)$,
   $(e_1^1, e_1^2, \ldots, e_1^E, \ldots, e_T^1, e_T^2, \ldots, e_T^E)$)
8. *// Perform MAP inference in complete CRF*
   (s_i^*, ui_i^*) := MAP_Inference(CRF_i)
9. **until** $s_i^* = s_{i-1}^*$
   Output: (s_i^*, ui_i^*)

The algorithm takes sensor reading trace as input. In Step 2, this trace is temporally segmented into local evidence nodes (e_i^1, e_i^2, ..., e_i^E). Each such node records a set of contextual information of the target circumstance in which a ubiquitous search may be carried out and would produce a situation node s_i. The situation nodes and their evidence are then used in Step 3 to generate a CRF such as the one shown in Figure 2. However, since user intentions are not yet known at this stage, CRF_0 contains no user intention nodes. MAP (Maximum a Posteriori) inference is then performed in this restricted CRF to determine the MAP situation sequence $s_0^{*\prime}$, which consists of a sequence of situations. As a situation may last some time, there would be neighboring situation nodes that actually belong to the same situation. Therefore, a merge operation is executed on sequence $s_0^{*\prime}$ in Step 5 which produces a reduced situation sequence s_0^*. At Step 6, such a situation sequence along with the user's search input sequence is used to extract user search intentions. This is done based on whether a specific user search intention is possible in the corresponding situation, under the given search input. Because a specific user intention might appear multiple times, we perform clustering to merge duplicate user intentions into one user intention node. This extraction is performed in Step 6, which returns a set of user intention nodes. These user intentions, along with (s_1, s_2, ..., s_T) and (e_1^1, e_1^2, ..., e_1^E, ..., e_T^1, e_T^2, ..., e_T^E) are used to generate a complete CRF in Step 7. Step 8 performs MAP estimation in this new CRF. Since this CRF has a different structure than the initial CRF_0, it might generate a different MAP situation sequence. If this is the case, then the algorithm returns to Step 6 and re-generates the set of user intentions using this improved situation sequence. This process is repeated until the situation sequence does not change, which is tested in Step 9. Finally, the algorithm returns the MAP situation sequence along with the set of user intentions.

5 Inference Techniques in CRFs

5.1 BP Based Inference in CRFs

In this section we will provide an introduction to the inference techniques of CRFs, where **x** is used to denote observations and **y** is used to denote hidden states. Given a set of observations, inference in a CRF may have two tasks: one is to estimate the marginal distribution of each hidden variable, and the other one is to estimate the most likely configuration of the hidden variables (*i.e.*, the MAP estimation). Both tasks can be solved under a framework called *belief propagation* (BP), which works by sending local messages through the graph structure of the model [24]. Therefore, we adopt BP based inference in this paper.

Without loss of generality, we mainly focus on describing the BP algorithm for pairwise CRFs, which are CRFs that only contain cliques of size two. Before running the inference algorithm in a pairwise CRF, it is possible to remove all observed nodes **x** by merging their values into the corresponding potentials; that is, a potential $\phi(\mathbf{x}, \mathbf{y})$ can be written as $\phi(\mathbf{y})$ because **x** is fixed to one value. Therefore, the only potentials in a pairwise CRF are local potentials $\phi(y_i)$, and pairwise potentials $\phi(y_i, y_i)$. Corresponding to the two types of inference problems, there are two types of BP algorithms: *sum-product* for marginal estimation and *max-product* for MAP estimation.

5.1.1 Sum-Product for Marginal Estimation

In the BP algorithm, we introduce a "message" $m_{ij}(y_j)$ for each pair of neighbors y_i and y_j, which is a distribution sent from node i to its neighbor j about which state variable y_j should be in. The messages propagate through the CRF graph until they (possibly) converge, and then the marginal distributions can be estimated from the stable messages. A complete BP algorithm defines how to initialize messages, how to update messages, how to schedule the message updates, and when to stop passing messages.

Message initialization: All messages $m_{ij}(y_j)$ are initialized as uniform distributions over y_j.

Message update rule: The message $m_{ij}(y_j)$ sent from node i to its neighbor j is updated based on local potentials $\phi(y_i)$, the pairwise potential $\phi(y_i, y_j)$, and all the messages to i received from i's neighbors other than j (denoted as $n(i) \setminus j$). More specifically, for sum-product, we have

$$m_{ij}(y_j) = \sum_{y_i} \phi(y_i)\phi(y_i, y_j) \prod_{k \in n(i) \setminus j} m_{ki}(y_i) \tag{6}$$

Message update order: The algorithm iterates the message update rule until it (possibly) converges. At each iteration, it usually updates each message once, where the update order might affect the convergence speed.

Convergence conditions: To test whether the algorithm converged, BP measures the difference between the previous messages and the updated ones. The convergence condition is met when all the differences are below a given threshold e.

In the sum-product algorithm, after all messages are converged, it is easy to calculate the marginals of each node and each pair of neighboring nodes as

$$b(y_i) \propto \phi(y_i) \prod_{j \in n(i)} m_{ji}(y_i) \tag{7}$$

$$b(y_i, y_j) \propto \phi(y_i)\phi(y_j)\phi(y_i, y_j) \prod_{k \in n(i) \setminus j} m_{ki}(y_i) \prod_{l \in n(j) \setminus i} m_{lj}(y_j). \tag{8}$$

The above algorithm can be applied to any topology of pairwise CRFs. When the network structure does not have a loop, the obtained marginals are guaranteed to be exact. When the structure has loops, the BP algorithm usually cannot obtain exact marginals, or it may even not converge. Fortunately, empirical experiments show that loopy belief propagation often converges to a good approximation of the correct posterior.

5.1.2 Max-Product for MAP Estimation

We denote the messages sent in the max-product algorithm as $m_{ij}^{max}(y_j)$. The whole algorithm of max-product is very similar to sum-product, except that in the message update rule summation is replaced by maximization. The new rule becomes

$$m_{ij}^{\max}(y_i) = \max_{y_i} \phi(y_i)\phi(y_i, y_j) \prod_{k \in n(i) \setminus j} m_{ki}^{\max}(y_i). \tag{9}$$

We run the max-product algorithm in the same way as for sum-product. After the algorithm converges, we calculate the MAP belief at each node y_i as

$$b(y_i) \propto \phi(y_i) \prod_{j \in n(i)} m_{ji}^{\max}(y_i). \tag{10}$$

If there is a unique MAP configuration $\mathbf{y}^*$, then the components of $\mathbf{y}^*$ are simply the most likely values according to the MAP belief (10).

We explained the two BP algorithms in the context of pairwise CRFs. For non-pairwise CRFs, there is a standard way to convert them to pairwise ones [25].

5.2 Parameter Learning

The goal of parameter learning is to determine the weights of the feature functions used in the conditional likelihood (see Equation 5). CRFs learn these weights *discriminatively,* that is, the weights are determined so as to maximize the conditional likelihood $p(\mathbf{y}|\mathbf{x})$ of labeled training data. This is in contrast to generative learning, which aims to learn a model of the joint probability $p(\mathbf{y}, \mathbf{x})$. In this paper, we adopt Maximum Pseudo-Likelihood (MPL) Estimation [24] and the experiments show that this type of learning is extremely efficient and consistently achieves good results.

6 Experimental Results

In this section, we evaluate the performance of our system in recognizing situations and user search intentions. As mentioned in Section 3, our experiment was conducted in a real home setting. We invited five volunteers to take part in the experiment, and each of them had spent one day in our rich sensor equipped apartment. Sensor data had been collected with one sample per minute during the experiment which produced five sensor reading traces for analysis. The volunteers were asked to write down the situation they were in and their estimate to the search result each time that they use the ubiquitous searching prototype system. Figure 3 shows some of the sensors we used in the experiment.

(a) (b)

Fig. 3. (a) UWB sensor and tag produced by Ubisense Limited that are used to capture a person's or a object's location. (b) Pressure sensor equipped chair and bed.

First, we manually labeled all situations and user search intentions in these traces. We used leave-one-out cross-validation for evaluation, that is, learning was performed based on the data collected from four volunteers and the learned model was evaluated on the fifth one. Pseudo-likelihood is used for learning and it converged in all our experiments. Loopy BP is used as the inference approach for evaluations. We used algorithm 1 for each evaluation, which extracted the MAP situations and user intentions from the sensor reading traces.

6.1 Example Analysis

The analysis result of one volunteer's sensor reading trace using algorithm 1 is illustrated in Figure 4.

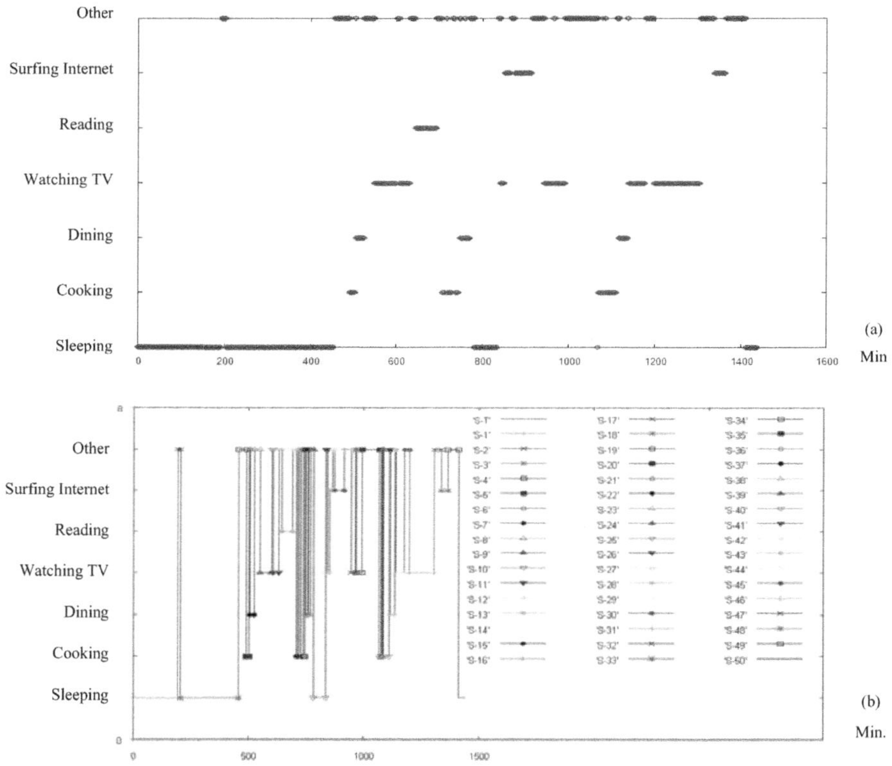

Fig. 4. (a) Situation sequence extracted from a volunteer's one day sensor reading trace. (b) Reduced situation sequence where S-1 to S-50 denote 50 different situation nodes and S-T denotes the transition between situations.

The sensor reading trace is firstly temporally segmented to 60×24 sensor reading sets, and each one would produce a set of local evidence. This is performed by Step 2 of algorithm 1. These local evidences then are used to generate the two lower-level of the user intention CRF using Step 3. MAP inference in this CRF determines one situation for each set of local evidence using the Step 4 of the algorithm, and the result is shown in Figure 4(a). Then the merge operation in Step 5 is executed to get a reduced situation sequence, which contains 50 situations as shown in Figure 4(b). Each search input, along with the corresponding situation, is used to generate one search intention node ui_i denoted as $<si_i, s_i>$ in a new CRF (Steps 7 and 8 of algorithm 1). MAP inference in this CRF provides labels for the recognized user intentions. The algorithm repeats generation of the CRFs until the MAP situation sequence does not change any more.

6.2 Labeling Situations Using Models Learnt from Others

Table 1 summarizes the results achieved with our experiments on the cross-validation data. The table shows the accuracy of our approach is quite high (above 90% accuracy for five situations, namely sleeping, cooking, dining, watching TV, and Reading, while accuracy rate for surfing Internet is 88.7%), especially when considering that the system was evaluated on only one day of data and was trained on only four days of data collected from different volunteers.

Table 1. Situation confusion matrix of cross-validation data

Truth	Inferred Labels							Total
	Sleeping	Cooking	Dining	Watching TV	Reading	Surfing Internet	Other	
Sleeping	502						23	525
Cooking		67	1				4	72
Dining		2	63				3	68
Watching TV				148			15	163
Reading					135	3	7	145
Surfing Internet					2	94	10	106
Other	3			17	4	9	328	361
Accuracy Rate (%)	95.6	93.1	92.6	90.8	93.1	88.7	90.1	92.8

6.3 Evaluation to the Prototype System

We developed a ubiquitous search prototype u-Search on a PDA (Personal Digital Assistant). Figure 5(a) shows the start-up interface of our prototype system, and Figure 5(b) illustrates the search result corresponding to user search intention <'Reading', 'Jane Eyre'>, where 'Reading' is the user's situation and 'Jane Eyre' is the user's search input.

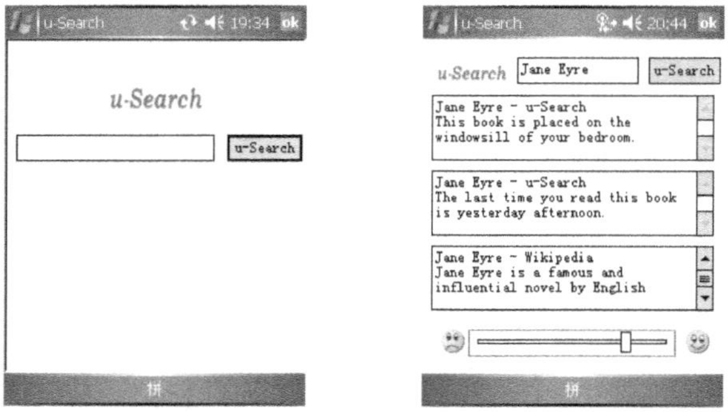

Fig. 5. (a) The start-up interface of our prototype system u-Search. (b) Search result corresponding to user search intention <'Reading', 'Jane Eyre'>, where 'Reading' is the user's situation and 'Jane Eyre' is the user's search input.

Figure 6(a) and (b) are the search results with search input 'Jane Eyre' when using Google and Bing on a PDA respectively. The results show that our situation analysis based ubiquitous searching system can provide more personal and more adaptive information.

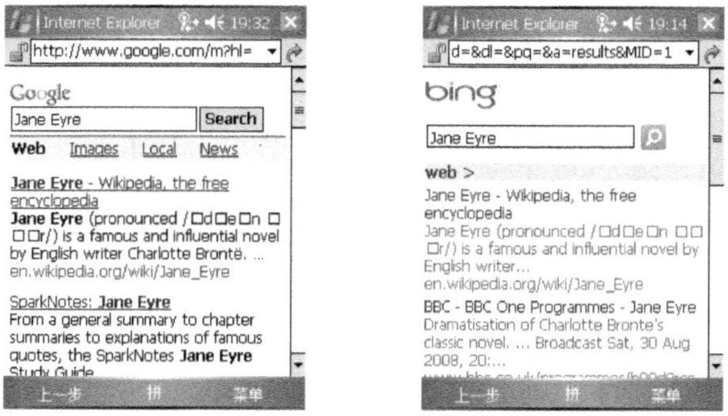

Fig. 6. (a) Search result with search input 'Jane Eyre' using Google. (b) Search result with search input 'Jane Eyre' using Bing.

In order to estimate user's satisfaction to our system, volunteers were asked to give a rating, ranging from 1 to 5, to the search result each time that they use the ubiquitous searching prototype system. During the experiment, five volunteers had altogether performed 42 ubiquitous searches and we got 38 valid ratings. The mean value of these 38 ratings is 4.05 and the average rating of each volunteer is shown in Figure 7, where V1 to V5 represent five volunteers.

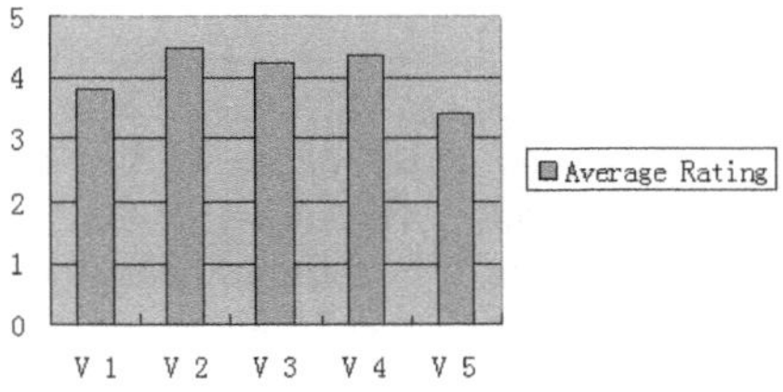

Fig. 7. The average rating of five volunteers

According to Figure 7, we can see that three volunteers' average rating are above 4, and the other two volunteers' average rating are above 3, illustrating that in most cases volunteers are satisfied with the search results of our prototype system.

7 Conclusions

We provided a novel approach to perform situation analysis of the physical world aiming at inferring user's search intention. In contrast to existing techniques, our approach uses one consistent framework for both low-level situation inference and the extraction of a user's search intentions. This is done by constructing a hierarchical conditional random field, where the upper level is generated based on MAP inference on the lower level. Our experiments based on traces of sensor readings show that situations can be accurately recognized and user intention based ubiquitous search can provide more personal and more adaptive information. We demonstrate that the proposed user intention model can be trained from a group of users and then applied successfully to a different user.

Currently six situations in home circumstance were involved in our system. We plan to investigate more situations: not only situations in home circumstance, but also situations in out-door circumstances. Furthermore, a rational classification mechanism for user's search intentions of the physical world has not been discussed in this paper, which should be quite useful for accurate ubiquitous search. This would be another direction for our future work.

Acknowledgments

This work was partially supported by the Natural Science Foundation of China (No. 60903125, 60803044), the National High Technology Research and Development Program of China (No. 2009AA011903), the Program for New Century Excellent

Talents in University (No. NCET-09-0079), the Natural Science Basic Research Plan in Shaanxi Province of China (No. 2010JM8033), and the Doctorate Foundation of Northwestern Polytechnical University (No. CX201018). The authors thank all the members of Ubiquitous Computing Lab of Northwestern Polytechnical University for their discussion and implementation of the system.

References

1. Tan, C.C., Sheng, B., Wang, H., Li, Q.: Microsearch: When Search Engines Meet Small Devices. In: Indulska, J., Patterson, D.J., Rodden, T., Ott, M. (eds.) PERVASIVE 2008. LNCS, vol. 5013, pp. 93–110. Springer, Heidelberg (2008)
2. Wang, H., Tan, C.C., Li, Q.: Snoogle: A Search Engine for the Physical World. In: The 27th IEEE Conference on Computer Communications, pp. 2056–2064 (2008)
3. Kiong, Y.K., Vikram, S., Mehul, M.: MAX: Wide Area Human-Centric Search of the Physical World. ACM Transactions on Sensor Networks 4(4), 26 (2008)
4. Wang, M., Cao, J., Sun, Y., Li, J.: Toward Ubiquitous Searching. In: The ICPADS 2007, pp. 1–8 (2007)
5. Guo, B., Satake, S., Imai, M.: Home-Explorer: Ontology-based Physical Artifact Search and Hidden Object Detection System. In: Mobile Information Systems, vol. 4, pp. 81–103. IOS Press, Amsterdam (2008)
6. Frank, C., Bolliger, P., Roduner, C., Kellerer, W.: Objects Calling Home: Locating Objects Using Mobile Phones. In: LaMarca, A., Langheinrich, M., Truong, K.N. (eds.) PERVASIVE 2007. LNCS, vol. 4480, pp. 351–368. Springer, Heidelberg (2007)
7. Koolwaaij, J., Tarlano, A., Luther, M., Nurmi, P., Mrohs, B., Battestini, A.: Context Watcher - Sharing Context Information in Everyday Life. In: The International Conference on Web Technologies, Applications, and Services (2006)
8. Gaonkar, S., Li, J., Choudhury, R.R., Cox, L., Schmidt, A.: Micro-Blog: Sharing and Querying Content through Mobile Phones and Social Participation. In: The 6th International Conference on Mobile Systems, pp. 174–186 (2008)
9. Dearman, D., Kellar, M., Truong, K.N.: An Examination of Daily Information Needs and Sharing Opportunities. In: The 21th International Conference on Computer Supported Cooperative Work, pp. 679–688 (2008)
10. Kang, I.-H., Kim, G.C.: Query Type Classification for Web Document Retrieval. In: 26th ACM SIGIR Conference on Research and Development in Information Retrieval, pp. 64–71. ACM Press, New York (2003)
11. Jansen, B.J., Booth, D.L., Spink, A.: Determining the User Intent of Web Search Engine Queries. In: The 16th International Conference on World Wide Web, pp. 1149–1150. ACM Press, New York (2007)
12. Teevan, J., Dumais, S.T., Horvitz, E.: Personalizing Search via Automated Analysis of Interests and Activities. In: 28th ACM SIGIR Conference on Research and Development in Informaion Retrieval, pp. 449–456. ACM Press, New York (2005)
13. Baeza-Yates, R., Calderón-Benavides, L., González-Caro, C.: The Intention behind Web Queries. In: Crestani, F., Ferragina, P., Sanderson, M. (eds.) SPIRE 2006. LNCS, vol. 4209, pp. 98–109. Springer, Heidelberg (2006)
14. Stamou, S., Ntoulas, A.: Search Personalization Through Query and Page Topical Analysis. In: User Modeling and User-Adapted Interaction, vol. 19(1-2), pp. 5–33. Kluwer Academic Publishers, Hingham (2009)

15. Park, G., Chae, J., Lee, D.H., Lee, S.: User Intention based Personalized Search: HPS(Hierarchical Phrase Serch). WSEAS Transactions on Circuits and Systems 7(4), 266–276 (2008)
16. Feng, G., Malek, A., Naphtali, R.: Personalized Approach for Mobile Search. In: The 2009 World Congress on Computer Science and Information Engineering, pp. 322–326. IEEE Computer Society, Washington (2009)
17. Horvitz, E., Breese, J., Heckerman, D., Hovel, D., Rommelse, K.: The Lumiere project: Bayesian user modeling for inferring the goals and needs of software users. In: The 14th Conference on Uncertainty in Artificial Intelligence, pp. 256–265 (1998)
18. Chen, Z., Lin, F., Liu, H., Liu, Y., Ma, W., Liu, W.: User Intention Modeling in Web Applications Using Data Mining. In: The World Wide Web: Internet and Web Information Systems, vol. 5(3), pp. 181–191. Kluwer Academic Publishers, Dordrecht (2002)
19. Armentano, M.G., Amandi, A.A.: Recognition of User Intentions for Interface Agents with Variable Order Markov Models. In: Houben, G.-J., McCalla, G., Pianesi, F., Zancanaro, M. (eds.) UMAP 2009. LNCS, vol. 5535, pp. 173–184. Springer, Heidelberg (2009)
20. Burghardt, C., Propp, S., Kirste, T., Forbrig, P.: Rapid Prototyping and Evaluation of Intention Analysis for Smart Environments. In: Tavanganan, D., Kirste, T., Timmermann, D., Lucke, U., Versick, D. (eds.) IMC 2009. CCIS, vol. 53, pp. 239–250. Springer, Heidelberg (2009)
21. Lafferty, J., McCallum, A., Pereira, F.: Conditional random fields: Probabilistic Models for Segmenting and Labeling Sequence Data. In: The 18th International Conference on Machine Learning, pp. 282–289. Morgan Kaufmann, San Francisco (2001)
22. Vail, D., Veloso, M., Lafferty, J.: Conditional Random Fields for Activity Recognition. In: The 6th International Joint Conference on Autonomous Agents and Multiagent Systems, pp. 1331–1338. ACM Press, New York (2007)
23. McCallum, A.: Efficiently Inducing Features of Conditional Random Fields. In: The 19th Conference on Uncertainty in Artificial Intelligence, UAI (2003)
24. Liao, L., Fox, D., Kautz, H.: Hierarchical Conditional Random Fields for GPS-Based Activity Recognition. Robotics Research 28, 478–506 (2007)
25. Yedidia, J., Freeman, W., Weiss, Y.: Understanding Belief Propagation and Its Generalizations: Exploring Artificial Intelligence in the New Millennium. Morgan Kaufmann Publishers, San Francisco (2001)

GPS Calibrated Ad-Hoc Localization for Geosocial Networking

Dexter H. Hu, Cho-Li Wang, and Yinfeng Wang

Department of Computer Science,
The University of Hong Kong,
Pokfulam Road, Hong Kong
{hyhu,clwang,yfwang}@cs.hku.hk

Abstract. Cost-effective localization for large-scale Geosocial networking service is a challenging issue in urban environment. This paper studies an ad-hoc localization technique which takes advantages of short-range interchanged location information for calibrating the location of mobile users carrying non-GPS mobile phones. We demonstrate by simulation that a small percentage of GPS-enabled mobile phones can greatly enable the localization of other non-GPS pedestrians in the urban environment. Based on the proposed localization technique, we implement a location-aware social networking tool called *Mobile Twitter*, similar to the microblogging service of Twitter, for fast propagation of social events happening in surroundings. Evaluation shows the our localization algorithm can achieve better accuracy of the location estimation and wider coverage as compared with the Amorphous algorithm and the Monte Carlo Localization (MCL) method. Moreover, we show that the Mobile Twitter implemented on an Android mobile phone is power-efficient in real-life usage scenarios.

1 Introduction

In recent years, Geosocial networking [4] has emerged as a new type of social networking application, by which various geographic services, such as nearby activity recommendation, event planning of friends in the same area, are provided to enable meaningful social dynamics in the real world. Mobile social networking has long be existing for years. However without location awareness, mobile social networking will be merely a simple extension to access social network websites [1, 2] from a mobile device. In fact there are many interesting geosocial events that are first discovered by ordinary mobile phone users, which are better off to be quickly informed to community, similarly to the social networking and microblogging service of Twitter [3], which gains popularity because it can deliver the freshest information quickly online. For example, Google Buzz [1] has quickly become one of most popular location-based service on the Internet, which allows users to see messages from nearby users. Therefore, localization is core building

[1] `http://www.google.com/buzz/help/privacy.html`

Z. Yu et al. (Eds.): UIC 2010, LNCS 6406, pp. 52–66, 2010.

block of these Location-Based Services (LBS). Without location information and the willingness of location information sharing, mobile social networking is not possible.

The most well-known and matured localization technique nowadays is the Global Positioning System (GPS) [2]. Due to the advancement of hardware manufacturing, more and more affordable mobile phones (e.g., iPhone 3G, Nexus One) come with a built-in GPS unit, which enables real-time tracking of user location. Many novel location-based services become a reality. According to ABI research [5], it is estimated that the number of mobile phone subscribers with GPS equipped devices will grow to 9% by the year 2011. So we could expect that only a small percentage of mobile phones have GPS functions in the near future, while the rest majority are without. This is one of the obstacles that hurdle the practicality of modern location-based services in people's daily life. One intuitive solution to this urban localization problem is allowing people with GPS to collaboratively help calibrate the localization of those without, by using ad hoc connectivity information in an urban district. Fortunately, ad hoc communication between mobile users can be done by Personal Area Network (PAN) wireless communication (e.g., ZigBee, Bluetooth).

In this paper, we first proposed a new GPS-calibrated ad-hoc localization algorithm named MobiAmorph, which takes advantages of short range interchanged information among mobile phones, so that many non-GPS mobile phone users will now be able to localize themselves based on information from nearby users. Second, we have done intensive experiments to show that MobiAmorph are superior than two typical distributed locations algorithms in urban environment. Third, we developed the *Mobile Twitter* application that are practical for real life usage and can encourage ad-hoc information sharing, so that mobile social applications will be more meaningful and location-aware (e.g., twitting social news with location information attached). With the help of GPS-enabled mobile users, localization is possible without the deployment of large infrastructure, hence, will boost its adoption. Also under certain mobility model, accurate GPS information can quickly propagate to non-GPS users, which is suitable for pedestrians in typical urban environment.

The rest of this paper is organized as follows. We review related work of localization approaches in Section 2. We explain the design of Mobile Twitter application in Section 3. Our proposed localization algorithm is explained in Section 4. We report the evaluation of algorithms under different experiment settings in Section 5. Section 7 concludes the paper with future work.

2 Related Work

Localization in general has long been a fundamental problem in Mobile Ad Hoc Networks (MANET) [6] and Wireless Sensor Networks (WSN) [7], on which many routing principles and applications rely. For instance, *geographic routing* in WSN needs location information as a priori to route message without

[2] `http://en.wikipedia.org/wiki/GPS`

knowledge of network topology. Many wireless applications that are related to monitoring and control, require accurate location information, such as wildlife habitat tracking, intrusion detection, disaster control, etc.

Existing distributed localization techniques can be divided into range-free and range-based approaches. Range-based approach makes use of additional hardware to obtain information like angle of arrival [8] and received signal strength [9], which may be affected by fading and introduce distance estimation error. This approach is generally expensive because of specially required hardware. Range-free localization approach, on the other hand, is a cost effective alternative, which uses location dissemination of seed with moderate to high density, and packet relaying of normal nodes, so that they can receive enough information to do self-localization. Our proposed algorithm falls in this category. MCL [10] and Amorphous [11] are two typical range-free localization algorithms, which are studied and compared in this paper.

The Monte Carlo Localization (MCL) technique represents the posterior distribution of a node's possible locations using a set of weighted samples. MCL internally maintains a set of N location samples in the deployment area, which are initially selected randomly from all possible locations. In the *Prediction* phase, it tries to compute a new possible location set based on the location set at the previous time step using maximum velocity. At the same time, MCL will get new information from seed nodes. MCL exchanges packets of seed with a maximum hop count value of two. *Filtering* step will eliminate those impossible predicted locations that are inconsistent with seed information. *Re-sampling* is performed to maintain enough N location samples after *Filtering*. Generally MCL is suitable for situation of nodes with high mobility, because a node cannot locate itself if there are no seeds within two hop distance and the algorithm can be very inaccurate in the beginning when it does not have enough samples to guess an accurate position.

Amorphous algorithm and its similar variant DV-HOP [12] are range-free localization algorithms based on hop-counting technique, which is similar to distance vector routing. Each seed broadcasts its location to neighbors and other nodes try to estimate their distance to seeds. The nodes will store the coordinates of enough number of seeds, which are propagated throughout the network and maintain the current minimum hop count to those seeds. Nodes calculate their position based on the received seed location information packets and corresponding hop count value, which is called the multilateration procedure. Amorphous algorithm has higher network coverage, (i.e. it can localize more nodes) and low requirement of the number of seed nodes. However, it can induce very high network traffic and too static for mobile situations in urban environment.

3 Mobile Twitter: Architecture Design

This section explains the *Mobile Twitter* application that uses "Ad Hoc Location Tracking" technique. Mobile Twitter is a geosocial networking software which motivates proactive social event propagation, and increase user incentive for location information sharing. It can be applied to many situations such as advertising, taxi call, ad hoc voting, and disaster/rescue systems. We have implemented it on Android [3] mobile platform in a street situation, where one user can quickly propagate a nearby news event attached with estimated location, allowing emergent or interesting social event to be shared quickly with others. It enables people with GPS-enabled phone to send instant messages with their GPS information to others through Bluetooth. Then the receiver can receive the GPS information and forward sender's message immediately. Mobile Twitter can calculate the current location and forward that message to others who are nearby and have switched on the same application. For the Non-GPS enabled phones, they can also create and send their new message to public through Bluetooth once their current location is calculated.

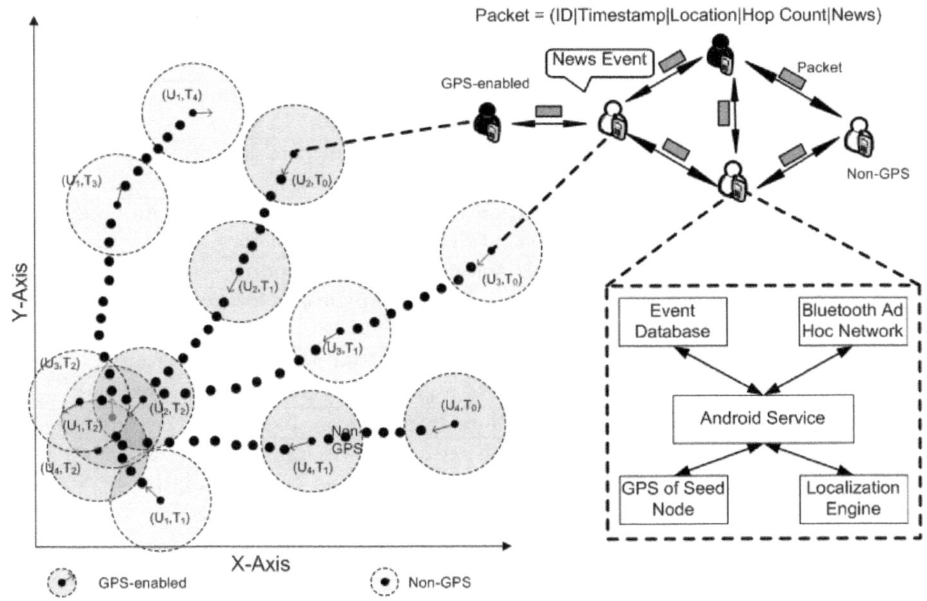

Fig. 1. Mobile Twitter Usage Scenario and Components

Figure 3 shows a typical usage scenario and different components within Mobile Twitter. The black mobile users have GPS enabled phones, while the white mobile user's phone does not have GPS function. All white mobile phones running Mobile Twitter application will be able to localize themselves upon receiving enough nearby location information packets, with the MobiAmorph algorithm explained in the next section. There is an *Android Service* process that accesses the *Localization Engine* of non-GPS nodes or directly get location information of GPS-enabled nodes. The *Bluetooth Ad Hoc Network* component will broadcast out user's (estimated) location or forward location packet received from nearby

[3] `http://developer.android.com/index.html`

nodes. It also broadcasts the application content (e.g. emergent news) stored in the *Event Database* to form a mobile social network. Mobile Twitter can visualize the news event on Google Maps with its estimated location attached by the first observer.

4 GPS Calibrated Ad Hoc Localization

We proposed a new GPS-calibrated localization algorithm, named MobiAmorph, based on the Amorphous algorithm [11], as shown in Algorithm 1. Table 1 summarizes common notations used in later discussion.

Table 1. Common Notations

Terminologies	**Explanations**
Node	user with Non-GPS mobile phone and willing to relay packets
Seed	user with GPS-enabled mobile phone and willing to share location information and relay packets
Hop Count	the number of hop unit that a packet need to travel between nodes there is a maximum hop count limit H_{max}
Accuracy	A.k.a Average Position Error (APE), the average of all node's (non-seed) location estimation errors in meters
Seed Ratio	Percentage of seeds among all nodes including seeds and nodes.
Packet Interval	Frequency at which each node broadcasts/forwards packet once every interval of t seconds
Coverage	Percentage of nodes within non-seed nodes with position estimation at the end of a packet interval t (i.e., localizable).
Density	Number of nodes within the $10000m^2$ area.
Node Speed	The speed of a node or seed in m/s,
Radio Range	The radius of a node's communication circle by ZigBee or Bluetooth (i.e., assuming no *degree of irregularity*)

The MobiAmorph algorithm addresses several weaknesses of Amorphous by relaxing trilateration criteria with additional historical data of past location estimates.

- Relaxed Trilateration: multilateration of Amorphous needs at least three reference points. Location estimating with overlapping circles can still have a decent estimation even there are only two reference points available. This will increase the chance of a node to calculate its position (i.e. increased coverage).
- Historical Data: it uses the last estimated location, to increase accuracy and coverage. Originally we cannot start calculation until there are at least three reference information received. Now, with last estimated location as a reference point, one can start estimating with only two reference information received. Together with relaxed trilateration, only one reference information

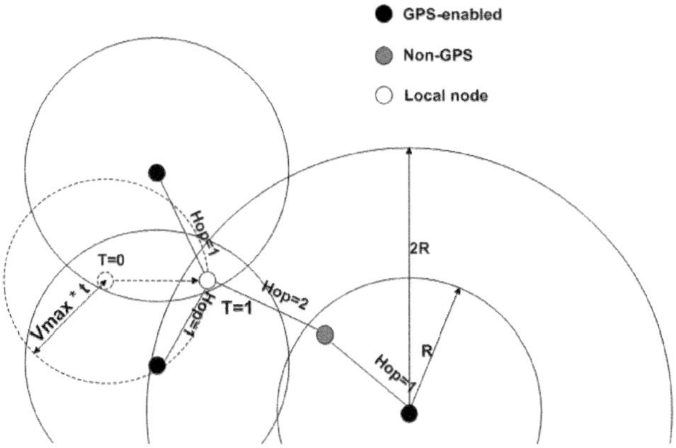

Fig. 2. Localization Considering Historical Data and Moving Velocity

is necessary to start estimation. For example, as shown in Figure 2, where T is the elapsed time from previous localized point and V_{max} is the maximum possible node speed. Originally, the estimated distance between seed and current location (radius r) equals to $h * \text{R}$ (radio range). Now we have another reference circle with radius $r = T * V_{max}$. This can overcome Amorphous's weakness of lack of mobility, as MobiAmorph now have a better estimation of current position base on historic data even when the user moves to a sparse area.

Algorithm 1. Skeleton of MobiAmorph Algorithm

1: /*The following steps are performed on node N every packet interval t.*/
2: **if** a node N is a Seed **then**
3:     broadcast current location packet l to neighbors at the end of t.
4: **else**
5:     receive packets, drop ones that exceeds H_{max} hop count, and update with smallest hop count if they are from the same node.
6:     **if** at the end of this interval phase t AND enough packets received **then**
7:         estimate location l by trilateration as in Figure 2.
8:         $N.localized \Leftarrow$ TRUE
9:         broadcast l to neighbors
10:     **else**
11:         $N.localized \Leftarrow$ FALSE
12:     **end if**
13: **end if**

MobiAmorph will accumulate packet during a packet interval (Line 5), and start trilateration if enough packet received at the end of that interval (Line 6). Line 8 and 11 record if a node is localizable in that interval and will be used to calculate coverage. It has a maximum hop count H_{max} of two, which can help avoid error accumulation and reduce the number of flooded packets.

5 Performance Evaluation and Analysis

We used a network simulator called MobiREAL [13] that can simulate the ad hoc network with realistic mobility of humans with mobile devices in the city. It can change their behavior depending on a given application context. We implemented the MobiAmorph algorithm in MobiREAL and report the detailed performance evaluation in this section. The goals of the evaluation are multi-fold:

1. compare coverage and accuracy of MobiAmorph with other well known ones under both street scenario and open area environments.
2. analyze MobiAmorph's coverage and accuracy affected by various factors, in order to get the recommended configuration for real life deployment.
3. evaluate the feasibility of the algorithm within the Mobile Twitter, considering power consumed by computation and communication on real devices.

5.1 Performance Comparison with Other Existing Algorithms

We evaluated three algorithms (namely, Amorphous, MCL, MobiAmorph) under both street area and open area scenarios. The street scenario is a $500m$ x $500m$ city area with buildings from TRACKIE [14] as in Figure 3(a), and the open area scenario is a $100m$ x $100m$ square as in Figure 3(b). The gray shapes are buildings, green dots are non-seed users (nodes), and red dots are GPS-enabled (seeds) users. The semitransparent area of each dot is the radio range, which is a perfect circle right now. The radio range of Bluetooth is around $10m$. We set the V_{max} to be $5m/s$, and the H_{max} to be 2. All nodes move in the street randomly and independently. We focus on tuning parameters of *seed ratio*, *packet interval* and *node speed*. The bold value in Table 2 is set as fixed parameter when testing other parameters.

Table 2. Parameter Settings on Street Scenario

Parameter	Value
Node Speed (m/s)	**1.5**, 3, 5
Radio Range (m)	**10**
Seed Ratio	0.2, **0.3**, 0.4, 0.5
Packet Interval	**5**, 15, 30, 60, 90
Density	**30**

Figure 4(a) and 4(b) illustrate the impact of packet interval to three algorithms under street scenario and open area environment respectively. MobiAmorph performs the best among the three. When the packet interval is between $5s$ - $90s$, Amorphous has the APE of $24m$ - $90m$, MCL has $22m$ - $89m$, while

MobiAmorph has $7m$ - $48m$ for street scenario. Similar results are also shown for open area environment. Higher packet interval will increase APE rapidly for all algorithms. Since larger transmission intervals may result in less information about neighbors. For Amorphous, with a longer packet interval, seed information packets cannot be exchanged frequently, nodes cannot receive useful information indirectly. For MCL, it is difficult for nodes to exchange the position information, as it randomly picked a sample location for position estimation and then negatively influenced the next step of position estimation.

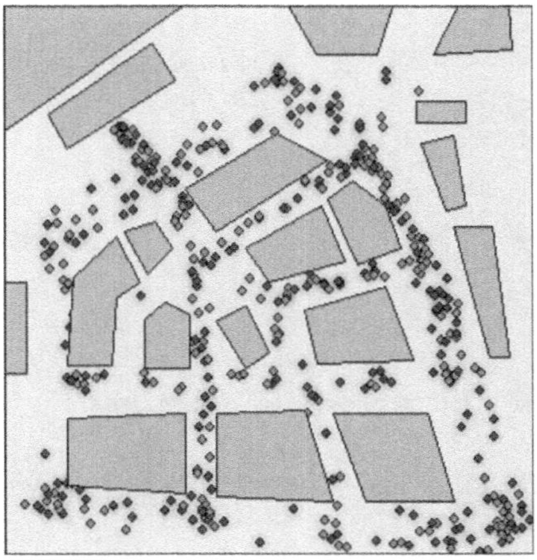

(a) Visualization of a $500m$ x $500m$ Street Area

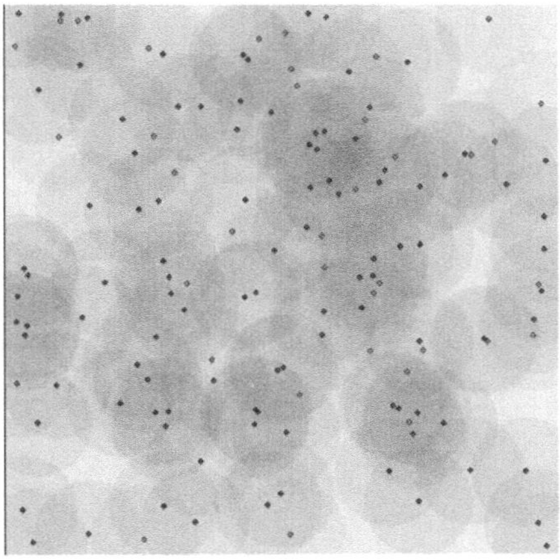

(b) Visualization of a $100m$ x $100m$ Open Area

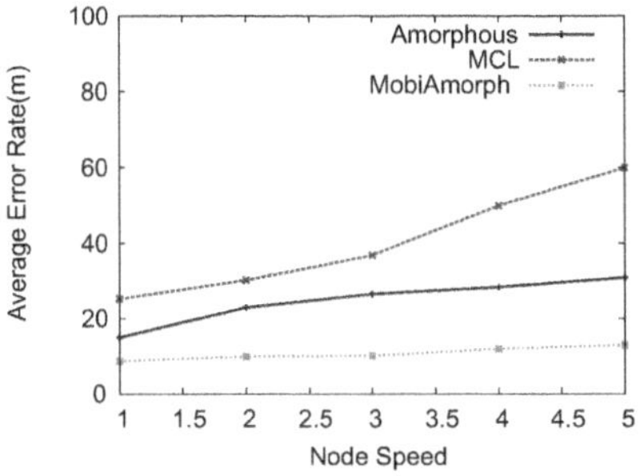

(c) APE vs. Node Speed in Street Scenario

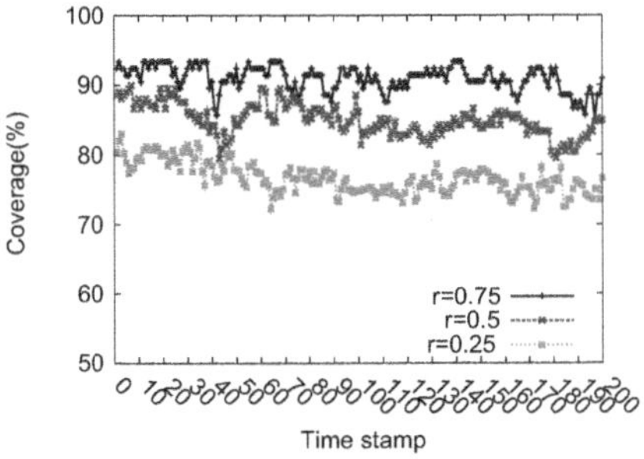

(d) Coverage vs. Seed Ratio over Time in Open Area

Fig. 3.

Figure 3(d) records the MobiAmorph's converge under different seed ratios in the open area environment. It shows that the higher the seed ratio, the higher the node coverage will consistently be over the time span of 200 seconds.

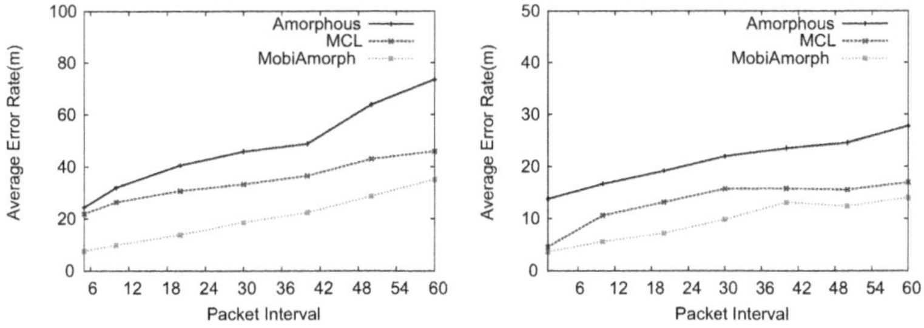

(a) APE vs. Packet Interval (Street) (b) APE vs. Packet Interval (Open Area)

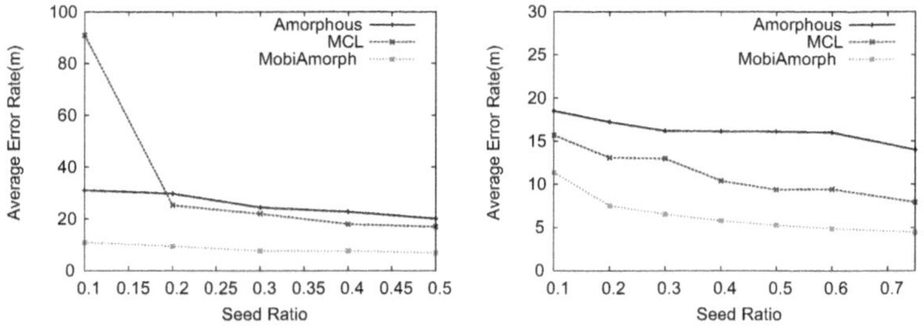

(c) APE vs. Seed Ratio (Street) (d) APE vs. Seed Ratio (Open Area)

Fig. 4. Effect of Packet Interval and Seed Ratio in Street Scenario and Open Area

Figure 4(c) and 4(d) illustrate the effects of the seed ratio in street scenario and open area environment respectively. We can see MCL is affected much more than others, because its nodes need to encounter enough mobile landmarks (e.g. N=15) to localize themselves. Amorphous needs to deploy more seeds to improve the accuracy because it needs stable ad-hoc networks where neighbors propagate seed position information. But it still has a relatively high error than MobiAmorph. If the seed ratio is very low (e.g., 0.2), nodes forward the packet received, after propagating certain hops, there will be large accumulated error. Moreover the calculation is based on the hop count information directly or indirectly received from the neighbor nodes, it prioritizes the seed information in the order of hop count.

Figure 3(c) illustrates the effects of node speed in street scenario. All algorithms have their APE increased with higher speed. MobiAmorph maintains low position error even when the node speed is high. Higher speed creates difficulties for receiving packets from neighbors. For MCL, APE is substantially increased from $22m$ at $1.5m/s$ to $60m$ at $5m/s$. This is because the uncertainty in the prediction phase becomes larger as node speed increases, which leads to wide range of position sample set and higher error. This is a side-effect of bad previous position sample set to current estimated position. Amorphous produces mild increase of average position error compared to MCL. Its error increases from $24.4m$ at $1.5m/s$ to $31m$ at $5m/s$. Amorphous is a localization technique that does not exploit historical information, and thus has less inaccurate influence.

All in all, we can see that our MobiAmorph algorithm achieves higher accuracy than the other two. For MCL, it cannot get many seed information because of the two maximum hop count limit; while our algorithm has a higher chance of getting more reference information. In addition, our algorithm makes use of previous estimate location as one of the reference point. For normal pedestrian model, it is obvious that will help reduce the possible location of the local node and hence increase the accuracy of the estimated location.

5.2 MobiAmorph Evaluation on Accuracy and Coverage

This section reports the simulation result of MobiAmorph algorithm in terms of Accuracy (APE) and coverage affected by node density and speed in the street scenario. Because we want to find the optimal algorithm configuration that fits a typical real life urban environment, where there are buildings and streets involved. Unless with explicit notice, the bold value in Table 3 will be fixed when evaluating other parameters in a figure.

Table 3. Parameters Settings in Street Scenario for MobiAmorph

Parameter	Value
Packet Interval (s)	5, **15**, 30, 60, 90
Seed Ratio	0.2, **0.3**, 0.4, 0.5
Speed (m/s)	**1.5**, 3, 5
Node Density (per $10000m^2$)	10, 20, **30**, 40
Radio Range (m)	**10**

Figure 5(a) shows the effect to accuracy by varying packet interval under different seed ratio. The algorithm reduces APE to $11m$, $7.9m$, $7m$ with packet interval at $15s$. So to have a reasonable average position error within $20m$, the packet interval should be less than 30 seconds. Figure 5(b) shows the effect to accuracy by node speed under various node densities. We can see that the higher the density, the smaller the APE. However, a higher speed of node will increase the APE.

Figure 5(c) illustrates the effects on coverage by density in area of $10000m^2$ under different seed ratio. The coverage is sensitive to node speed, because position calculation is related to packets exchange under suitable moving speed. Higher density also leads to higher chance of interchanging location information. At the same node speed, the higher node density, the higher coverage level. With speed at 1.5, 3, 5 m/s respectively, MobiAmorph increases coverage from 5%, 3%, 1% at low density of 10 to 54%, 27%, 10% at a higher density of 40. To achieve reasonable coverage of 40%, node speed $1.5m/s$ and density of more than 30 nodes in an area of $10000m^2$ are recommended.

Figure 5(d) illustrates the effects on coverage by packet interval under different seed ratios. Coverage is the percentage of localized non-seed nodes. MobiAmorph has high coverage when seed ratio is high, and packet interval is short, because

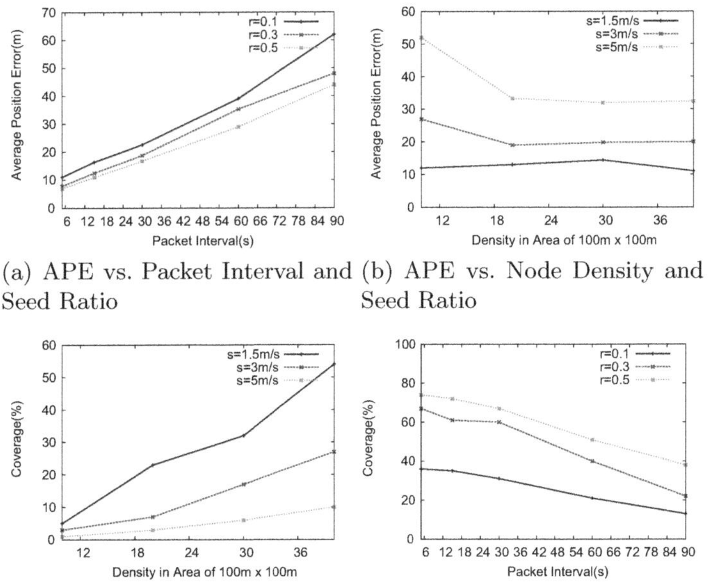

(a) APE vs. Packet Interval and Seed Ratio (b) APE vs. Node Density and Seed Ratio

(c) Coverage vs. Node Density and Seed Ratio (d) Coverage vs. Packet Interval and Seed Ratio

Fig. 5. MobiAmorph Algorithm Performance on Street Scenario

this situation provides higher opportunity for information exchange. With seed ratio at 0.1, 0.3, 0.5 respectively, MobiAmorph decreased coverage from 35%, 61%, 72% at packet interval $15s$ to 13%, 22%, 38% at packet interval of $90s$. To have a reasonable coverage of at least 40%, the packet interval should be less than $60s$, and the seed ratio should be at least 30%.

5.3 Traffic Overhead

To be fair, the communication traffic overhead is measured as the average number of message a node needs to send in each localization step. Although the actual size of traffic packets can vary slightly due to encoding and encryption. The Amorphous algorithm needs seeds to flood their information through out the network, and each node needs to relay and broadcast a specified number of seed location (e.g., 32). Both the MCL and MobiAmorph can share a node's location to their neighbors, which are relatively much less than Amorphous.

5.4 Mobile Twitter Deployment Evaluation

Basically we conducted two experiments to evaluate the Mobile Twitter on real phone. We are interested in power consumption by sending location packets over Bluetooth, and also application's longevity over time by monitoring CPU and memory consumption when running Mobile Twitter on an Android phone.

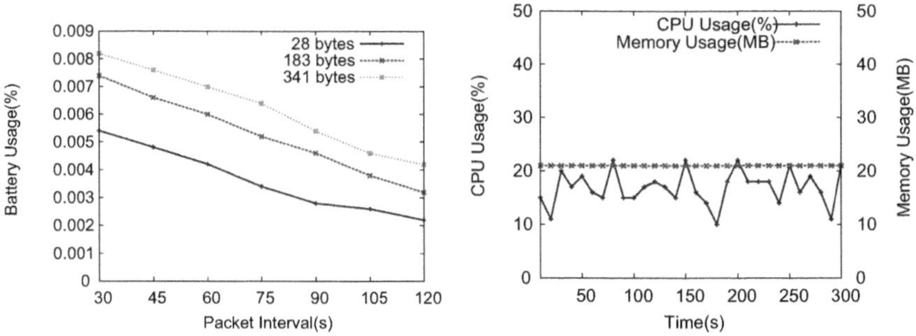

(a) Bluetooth Power Consumption (b) Memory and CPU Usage

Fig. 6. Evaluation of Mobile Twitter on Device

We used an HTC Hero phone with Android 2.1 OS to send packets to another one through Bluetooth with different packet interval and size. We recorded the voltages respectively before and after sending packets for 30 minutes at different packet intervals. Figure 6(a) shows that the Bluetooth power consumption is relatively small. With a fixed packet interval, smaller packet size consumes less battery and with a fixed packet size, larger packet interval consumes less battery. We also used the PowerManager class in Android API to see that the application can last for about 14 hours when running exclusively all the time, i.e. doing both the packet communication and localization computation. Figure 6(b) shows that CPU usage is constantly between 10% to 22% and the memory usage is under 21MB over a typical 5 minute usage span, which are acceptable on real mobile devices.

6 Discussion

6.1 Resolution Limitation

As shown by Radhika Nagpal et al [11], there is a theoretical limitation for localization techniques in range-free category using only connectivity information. Although the ranging precision limitation of ad hoc sensing capabilities posed serious challenges to MobiAmorph, our problem settings is for users in urban environment, where user scale and pedestrian mobility can be used to our advantage. With altruistic users' sharing of its accurate GPS location, our localization algorithm has higher coverage and accuracy than previous ones.

6.2 Privacy and Security for Adoption

To increase the adoption of Mobile Twitter, we need to have security extensions to our localization technique and encourage GPS information sharing among users. To be a secured localization technique, MobiAmorph needs to handle malicious seeds that will inject fake location information, and relay nodes that may corrupt the hop count and replay packets. Authentications by digital signatures are necessary to sign up seed's messages. Key establishments mechanisms like random key predistribution [15] can establish keys using symmetric cryptography, which is suitable for MobiAmorph algorithm as bidirectional verification is possible in our case. For relay attack, we can use defense techniques like synchronized clocks [16] with additional hardware.

MobiAmorph has good properties for security extension. First it is based on limited hop count and connectivity information when a user is moving around. So an attacker's damage is very temporary, as long as the user can receive authentic information in the future. This is the mobility issue to our benefits. So MobiAmorph is similar to MCL, both of which are less susceptible to malicious seeds than other static approaches. We also need to develop meaningful mobile social applications that encourage the sharing of location information among mobile users. But application message should be encrypted for privacy protection, while anonymized localization should be abstracted as an independent service among mobile users.

6.3 Pedestrian Mobility Model

Since we are targeting the usage of Mobile Twitter for geosocial networking application by mobile pedestrians in urban environment, users may carry a smart phone walking around with independent or group interest down the road. Realistic mobility model like Urban Pedestrian Flows (UPF) [17] can be applied to see the effects of various ad hoc localization algorithms.

7 Conclusion and Future Work

We studied the problem of ad hoc localization with the help of GPS information suitable for urban environment with pedestrians. We proposed the MobiAmorph algorithm that can localize non-GPS mobile users with location information propagated from GPS-enabled mobile devices. We compared it with other two distributed range-free localization algorithms. MobiAmorph is shown to be superior with high accuracy and coverage under various settings. In general, increasing the seed ratio among the same number of nodes or shortening the packet interval of location forwarding will improve accuracy and coverage, but the tradeoff need to be understood to determine appropriate deployment parameters.

The *Mobile Twitter* application is developed with the MobiAmorph algorithm on the Android mobile device, using Bluetooth, GPS and Google Maps. The application performance is satisfactory in real life situations. By analysis of the performance tradeoff, we figured out the recommended settings to *Mobile Twitter* that can perform with low power consumed by localization computation and

Bluetooth communication. Future works include evaluation of algorithms under irregular radio model, instead of perfect circle.

Acknowledgments. This research work is supported in part by HKU Seed Funding Program for Basic Research (Grant No. 10400018) and China 863 grant 2006AA01A111 (CNGrid). The authors thank Ip Chun Yin, Kwok Ka Ho, Kwok Wan Lai for their initial prototype implementation of this work.

References

1. Facebook, `http://www.facebook.com`
2. MySpace, `http://www.myspace.com`
3. Twitter, `http://twitter.com`
4. Geosocial networking, `http://en.wikipedia.org/wiki/Geosocial_networking`
5. GPS-Enabled, L.B.S.: Subscribers Will Total 315 Million in Five Years, `http://www.abiresearch.com/abiprdisplay.jsp?pressid=731`
6. Huang, R.: Probabilistic localization of mobile ad hoc networks. Phd Thesis, University of Texas Arlington (2006)
7. Savvides, A., Han, C.C., Strivastava, M.B.: Dynamic fine-grained localization in Ad-Hoc networks of sensors, pp. 166–179. ACM Press, New York (2001)
8. Niculescu, D., Nath, B.: Ad hoc positioning system (APS) using AOA. In: Twenty-Second Annual Joint Conference of the IEEE Computer and Communications(INFOCOM 2003), vol. 3, pp. 1734–1743. IEEE, Los Alamitos (2003)
9. Bahl, P., Padmanabhan, V.: RADAR: an in-building RF-based user location and tracking system. In: Nineteenth Annual Joint Conference of the IEEE Computer and Communications Societies (INFOCOM 2000), vol. 2, pp. 775–784. IEEE, Los Alamitos (2000)
10. Hu, L., Evans, D.: Localization for mobile sensor networks. In: 10th Annual international Conference on Mobile Computing and Networking, pp. 45–57. ACM, New York (2004)
11. Nagpal, R., Shrobe, H.E., Bachrach, J.: Organizing a Global Coordinate System from Local Information on an Ad Hoc Sensor Network. In: Zhao, F., Guibas, L.J. (eds.) IPSN 2003. LNCS, vol. 2634, pp. 333–348. Springer, Heidelberg (2003)
12. Niculescu, D., Nath, B.: DV Based Positioning in Ad Hoc Networks. Telecommunication Systems, 267–280 (2003)
13. Konishi, K., Maeda, K., Sato, K., Yamasaki, A., Yamaguchi, H., Higashino, T., Yasumoto, K.: MobiREAL Simulator Evaluating MANET Applications in Real Environments. In: 13th IEEE International Symposium on Modeling, Analysis, and Simulation of Computer and Telecommunication Systems, pp. 499–502. IEEE, Los Alamitos (2005)
14. Fujii, S., Uchiyama, A., Umedu, T., Yamaguchi, H., Higashino, T.: An Off-line Algorithm to Estimate Trajectories of Mobile Nodes Using Ad-hoc Communication (concise contribution). In: Sixth Annual IEEE International Conference on Pervasive Computing and Communications (PerCom 2008), pp. 117–124. IEEE, Los Alamitos (2008)
15. Eschenauer, L., Gligor, V.D.: A key-management scheme for distributed sensor networks. In: Conference on Computer and Communications Security, pp. 41–47. ACM, New York (2002)

16. Hu, Y.C., Perrig, A., Johnson, D.: Packet leashes: a defense against wormhole attacks in wireless networks. In: Twenty-Second Annual Joint Conference of the IEEE Computer and Communications (INFOCOM 2003), pp. 1976–1986. IEEE Societies, Los Alamitos (2003)
17. Maeda, K., Sato, K., Konishi, K., Yamasaki, A., Uchiyama, A., Yamaguchi, H., Yasumoto, K., Higashino, T.: Getting urban pedestrian flow from simple observation: realistic mobility generation in wireless network simulation, Montreal, Quebec, Canada, pp. 151–158. ACM, New York (2005)

Ontology-Enabled Activity Learning and Model Evolution in Smart Homes

George Okeyo*, Liming Chen, Hui Wang, and Roy Sterritt

Computer Science Research Institute
School of Computing and Mathematics, University of Ulster
BT37 0QB Newtownabbey, United Kingdom
okeyo-g@email.ulster.ac.uk,
{l.chen,h.wang,r.sterritt}@ulster.ac.uk

Abstract. Activity modelling plays a critical role in activity recognition and assistance in smart home based assisted living. Ontology-based activity modelling is able to leverage domain knowledge and heuristics to create Activities of Daily Living (ADL) models with rich semantics. However, they suffer from incompleteness, inflexibility, and lack of adaptation. In this paper, we propose a novel approach for learning and evolving activity models. The approach uses predefined "seed" ADL ontologies to identify activities from sensor activation streams. We develop algorithms that analyze logs of activity data to discover new activities as well as the conditions for evolving the seed ADL ontologies. We illustrate our approach through a scenario that shows how ADL models can be evolved to accommodate new ADL activities and preferences of individual smart home's inhabitants.

Keywords: Activity modelling, activity learning, ontology evolution, smart homes, ambient assisted living.

1 Introduction

Activity recognition allows ongoing ADL activities in a Smart Home (SH) [1] to be identified and therefore makes it possible to offer assisted living services to SH inhabitants. Typically, sensors are deployed in an SH to monitor an actor's behaviour and the situated environment. The collected sensor data are analysed to infer the ongoing activity. Activity recognition comprises many different tasks, namely behaviour and environment monitoring, data processing, activity modelling, and pattern recognition [2]. Central to activity recognition is activity modelling and representation, whereby computational activity models are built, and later used to reason on sensor data to infer ongoing activities.

An emerging approach to activity modelling is to explicitly model and represent ADLs using ontologies. ADL ontologies model activities as a hierarchy of classes and interrelationships, with each class described by a number of properties. Each property is used to characterise activity classes e.g. sensors, time,

* Corresponding author.

Z. Yu et al. (Eds.): UIC 2010, LNCS 6406, pp. 67–82, 2010.

and location. Given that there is a wide range of ADLs, and each ADL could be performed in a diversity of ways in terms of an individual's preferences and styles, it is quite common that some activities may not be originally anticipated, thus not being modelled by the seed ADL ontologies. This will make such activities impossible to be recognised. As a result they are flagged, during activity recognition, as *unknown* activities. Currently, the ontology-based approach has one major limitation i.e. the seed ontological activity models are static, unable to handle unforeseen activities and activity variants, without explicit manual revision. In addition, there is a lack of flexibility in handling different ways of performing activities by different users. This is relevant to the provision of personalised activity assistance.

In this paper, we present a novel approach, which is based on ontology evolution [3], to support continuous learning of ADL models. We create an initial ontology-driven knowledge base representing the ADL model and evolve it over time. For instance, given *unknown* activities or variations in performance of activities, the seed ontological activity models are changed through learning. In summary, the approach has the following strengths. Firstly, it uses common sense domain knowledge for representing activity models; hence activities can be identified in spite of sparse initial data. Secondly, it is open to new knowledge e.g. new kinds of activities and activity variants, making it capable of handling unforeseen activities. Thirdly, it leverages the strengths of *predefined* and *learnt* activity models to enable adaptability, flexibility and reusability. Through adaptability, it can dynamically handle changes in both the user environment and behaviour. Finally, through flexibility, it can offer both personalization and fine-grained activity recognition and assistance. We demonstrate, through a use scenario, how ontology evolution has been utilized to achieve activity model adaptation.

The remainder of the paper is organized as follows. Section 2 describes related work. Section 3 presents the proposed framework for adapting ontological activity models. Section 4 describes the method for activity learning and model evolution. Section 5 gives an illustrative scenario to demonstrate the framework. Finally, we conclude in Section 6.

2 Related Work

In the literature, two main approaches to activity modelling can be identified: data-driven and knowledge driven approaches. Data-driven approaches rely on probabilistic and statistical models to represent activities. Examples include Hidden Markov Models (HMMs) [4], dynamic and naive Bayes networks [5], support vector machines (SVMs) [6], graphical models [7] and multiple eigenspaces [8]. Individual activity models are obtained by training using large-scale data sets. The resulting activity models are then reasoned against sensor data to support activity recognition. Data-driven approaches are generally robust to noisy, uncertain and incomplete data but suffer from several drawbacks. They are not reusable since they need to be learnt for each activity and each individual. Secondly, they are not flexible to accommodate variations in individual's behaviour and the environment. Thirdly, they can be computationally expensive as each activity needs to be learnt separately. Finally, they require huge amounts of labelled training and test data to be available.

Knowledge-driven approaches, on the other hand, use artificial intelligence (AI) based knowledge representation formalisms for activity modelling. The core idea is to explore rich domain knowledge for activity modelling rather than to learn them from data as seen in data-driven approaches. One strand of work is to use logical formalisms to model and represent an activity as a sequence of events [9].Another strand uses ontologies to represent sensor data and activity models, e.g. [10], [11], [12], and [2]. For instance, [2] use ontologies to explicitly model ADLs and Description Logics (DL)-based reasoning for activity recognition. The strengths of the knowledge-based approach include: it captures clear semantics inherent in domain knowledge, allows domain knowledge and heuristics for activity models and data fusion to be incorporated, and supports knowledge based intelligent processing by being able to capture everyday common sense domain knowledge. The major weakness of the knowledge-driven approach is that the pre-defined activity models, derived from the expert's domain knowledge, are static and unable to adapt to user's behaviour changes. As a result, they cannot handle emergent activities or changes in the user's behaviour.

Our work belongs to the knowledge-driven approach but extends existing work [2] by allowing the adaptation of a predefined ADL activity model. Unlike [2], in our work the explicitly predefined ADL activity ontologies are used only as the seed activity models. The seed ontological activity model is evolved on the basis of newly discovered primitive activities or individual preferences. Since this may cause existing activities to be specialized further, our approach provides for consistent ontology change through ontology evolution [14].

3 Activity Learning and Model Evolution Framework

3.1 The Rationale

In an SH inhabitants perform ADLs in a given location, time and using specific objects. Collectively, these refer to context for the corresponding activity. This contextual information can be monitored and captured using sensors and be used to infer ongoing activities. In the ontology-based activity modelling, activity models that establish links between activities and their context can be created and represented as formal ADL ontologies. The resulting formal ADL ontologies typically depict an activity hierarchy in which each node, also called a class, denotes a type of ADL. Therefore, activity recognition amounts to constructing situations from sensor observations and reasoning with them against activity models represented by the ADL ontologies. Due to individual preferences and/or limitations, the performance of ADLs may vary. In some cases, even the same individual may carry out an activity in various ways and sequences. As such, activities can be modelled at multiple levels of abstraction, namely *generic, personalized and idiosyncratic* ADL models. Generic models capture available common sense domain knowledge that is common for most ADLs. Personalized models vary between individuals, while idiosyncratic models are special types of personalized models that capture the variations in how the same individual carries out ADLs.

The seed ADL ontology may not capture all possible ADL activities, including subtleties, due to differences among individuals and the idiosyncratic ways in which they carry out activities. The consequence is that the inference engine may fail to identify the ongoing activity. Consider the following scenarios - a labelled activity 'Make Tea' and an un-labelled one 'Make Milk'. A typical labelled activity, say *'Make Tea'*, may be performed in different ways. In addition, an individual may carry out the activity 'Make Milk', which is not modelled in the seed ADL ontology. It is important that the activity recognition system learns to recognize 'Make Milk' and the peculiarities of 'Make Tea' in order to provide reasonable and trustworthy ADL assistance.

To address this, the ADL ontology needs to be responsive and adaptable to individual inhabitants as well as to the different ways that an individual may complete activities. We capture information about ongoing activities as activity traces, which are logged for further analysis. In the captured information, we can distinguish between *labelled* and *un-labelled* activities. Labelled activities are those that are explicitly encoded with a term in the ADL ontology. They can be identified through ontological reasoning process. Unlabelled activities, on the other hand, are those activities carried out by the inhabitant but the reasoning engine cannot find a corresponding term in the ADL ontology. As a result the latter are logged with the label *'unknown'*. In the next sub-section, we describe a framework for adapting the ADL ontology in view of labelled and un-labelled activities.

3.2 The Architecture

We exploit ontology evolution [3] and integrate it with activity recognition and learning to give the generic framework shown in Fig. 1. The *ADL Ontology* creates an activity model that provides a semantic model of the Smart Home. The ADL ontology captures activities and contextual information e.g. time, location and actors and gives the semantics needed to support activity recognition. It uses classes to represent activities and their interrelationships and properties to connect activities with their context. The *Behaviour Ontology* captures repetitive patterns of behaviour (also called life habits) and associated semantic information. Due to lack of space, we will not describe how it is used. The *Activity Recognizer* is responsible for activity recognition and the recording of activity traces (AT). It receives sensor data as a sequence of sensor activations and reasons with these through Description Logics (DL)-based reasoning [15] against the ADL ontology to infer ongoing activities. It outputs activity data that includes inferred activities and activity traces; it records the latter in the Activity Log as instances of Trace Ontology.

The *Trace Ontology* provides the format of activity traces and allows metadata about the latter to be captured and stored. It describes information to be captured about each activity, e.g. sequences of sensors activations, temporal information and activity labels. Trace Ontology can be instantiated as individual activity traces in the Activity Log. *Activity Log* (AL) provides persistent storage of activity traces related to labelled and unlabelled activities. AL can be processed by the Ontology Evolution component to allow evolution of ADL and Behaviour ontologies. AL is represented in a suitable machine process-able format e.g. XML.

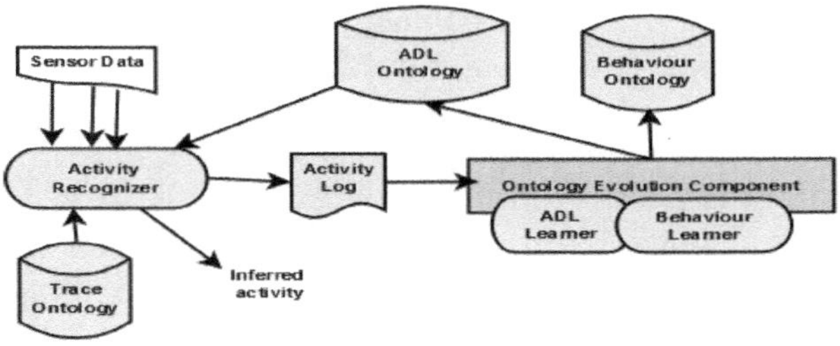

Fig. 1. The generic framework for activity model learning and evolution

To enhance the utility and responsiveness of the knowledge represented, we propose to evolve the ADL and Behaviour ontologies. We use ontology evolution to provide and formalize a systematic procedure for effecting ontology change and adopt the process described in [13]. As a consequence, we have central to our framework the *Ontology Evolution component* that is responsible for ontology evolution. The main function of this component is to evolve ADL and Behaviour ontologies while it maintains their consistency. It integrates two components, namely ADL Learner and Behaviour Learner, to analyze the Activity Log and perform evolution. The *ADL Learner* is responsible for evolving the ADL ontology. It determines whether to change the ADL ontology and the nature of change to make, e.g. whether to model new activities or variants of existing activities. To achieve this, it analyses the Activity Log using algorithms described in Section 4. The *Behaviour Learner* allows the Behaviour ontology to be evolved. It is responsible for discovering user behaviour (life habits) and changing the Behaviour ontology. Behaviours can be described as patterns of carrying out activities that appear repetitive.

In a nutshell, we separate the component used for learning from the component used for activity recognition. In this way learning only takes place later, after activity data has been collected for some time. The results of learning are enhanced ADL ontologies, and better recognition and decision support for activity assistance. This means that even before any learning can take place, it should still be possible to identify ongoing ADL activities. We describe a method for implementing the framework in the next section.

4 Activity Model Learning and Evolution Methods

In our approach, we propose to perform ADL adaptation by means of a formal Ontology Evolution process. The adopted process has six (6) phases [13]

namely: change capturing, change representation, semantics of change, change implementation, change propagation, and change validation. To perform ontology evolution, the first step is change *capturing phase* that entails a *change discovery* process. In this paper we focus on the change capturing phase. Change discovery aims to identify the changes that need to be made to the ontology of interest. According to [13] there are three broad approaches to change discovery, namely structure-driven, data-driven, and usage-driven discovery. For instance, in usage-driven change discovery, ontology usage data is analysed to discover problems with the ontology and conditions for evolving the ontology.

The types of changes related to labelled and unlabelled activities correspond to changes typically discovered through a *usage-driven change discovery* process. In our framework, this data is captured as activity traces, stored in the Activity Log. At present, a number of heuristics-based methods have been used for usage-driven change discovery. For instance, [16] uses the notion of semantic similarity that adopts ontology-matching techniques for discovery of new concepts. [13], describes statistical measures based on the ontology structure and its usage, e.g. navigation and querying. [17] has proposed the use of semantic similarity measure that uses background knowledge to compute similarity between terms. [18] specified Evolva, an ontology evolution framework, which only deals with the discovery of concepts.

Most existing methods deal with change discovery that leads to concept-related changes. Our work aims at the discovery of both instance- and concept-related changes. To this end, we propose a set of measures to formalize this discovery and then propagate them to the other phases in ontology evolution process. We use a combination of heuristic-based, statistical and semantic similarity measurements. The semantic similarity measures are capable of making comparisons among concepts, properties and instances and can be used to compare entities in both the Activity Log and the ADL ontology. In the next sub-sections, we describe the measures and the proposed algorithms for change discovery.

4.1 Preliminaries

In order to aid analysis and to apply the proposed measures, we adopt the following definition for ontology structure that the ADL Ontology and Trace Ontology must correspond to.

Definition 1 (Ontology Structure). *An ontology structure is a tuple* $O = \{C, P, R, A, I, H^C, H^R, H^A, Lit, domain, range\}$ *which consists of a set of concept symbols* C*, a set of relation symbols* R*, a set of attribute symbols* A*, a set of property symbols* $P = R \cup A$*, a set of instances* I*, and a concept hierarchy* $H^C \subseteq C \times C$*. Others are a relation hierarchy* H^R *, attribute hierarchy* H^A *and a set of literals* Lit. *The function* $dom : R \rightarrow C$ *gives the domain of* R *and function* $range : A \rightarrow Lit$ *gives the range of* A.

Further we define labelled and unlabelled activity traces, and corresponding sets for each.

Definition 2 (Labelled and Unlabelled Trace). *A labelled trace (LT) is a trace whose label has a corresponding term explicitly encoded in the seed ADL ontology (SO). An unlabelled trace (UT) is one associated with the label 'unknown'.*

Definition 3 (Unlabelled Activity Traces (UAT), Labelled Activity Traces (LAT)). *UAT is the set of all unlabelled activity traces in the Activity Log. LAT is the set of labelled activity traces.*

Suppose that the set of sensors in a Smart Home (SH) is denoted by S, and each sensor is identified by a sensor ID, s_x, this can be represented as $S : \{s_1, s_2, s_3, \cdots, s_n\}$. Similarly, given that a sensor activation is denoted by sa_y, a sequence of sensor activations over time can be denoted by SA and represented as $SA :< sa_1, sa_2, sa_3, \cdots, sa_k >$.Activity recognition involves reasoning with sensor activations against the seed ADL ontology. Typically, when the Activity Recognizer is given SA, it derives the relationship between SA and S denoted as a pair $< sa_y, s_x >$ that maps each sensor activation sa_y to a sensor s_x. It uses this information to infer ongoing activities as described in [2] by using Description Logics (DL)-based subsumption reasoning [19]. It generates activity traces over a given timeline and these can be recorded in the Activity Log.

The problem is to determine which labelled and unlabelled traces should cause the seed ADL ontology to be changed. In general, we can assume a total of N activity traces, made up of M labelled and L unlabelled traces. As the L unlabelled traces have no corresponding terms in the seed ADL ontology, it is necessary to set and implement the criteria to discover those traces that should lead to changes to the seed ADL ontology. We describe the learning and discovery process in Section 4.2. Similarly, from among the M labelled traces we need a method that discovers the traces that should cause changes to the structure of the seed ADL ontology. We describe the learning and discovery method in Section 4.3.

4.2 Learning Algorithm for Unlabelled Traces

In this section, we present an algorithm that analyzes unlabelled activity traces in order to propose changes to the seed ADL ontology. We define various heuristic-based measures and using these and various semantic similarity measures describe the process of analysis.

To determine the unlabelled traces that lead to seed ADL ontology change, we proceed by collecting all traces that have matching sensor activations into a set, $UAT_y \subseteq UAT$. Each UAT_y has traces with identical sensor activations.

$$UAT_y = \{UT_x | Sim_{act}(UT_i, UT_j) = 1\}, UAT_y \subseteq UAT, i \neq j, 1 \leq i, j, x, y \leq L . \tag{1}$$

We use semantic similarity measure $Sim_{act}(UT_i, UT_j)$ to determine matching traces. $Sim_{act}(UT_i, UT_j)$ is defined based on relation similarity measure $RS(UT_i, UT_j)$ derived from [20]. Sim_{act} calculates the similarity between two instances of activity traces on the basis of the relations defined in these instances.

In our method, it determines the similarity of activity traces based on the sensor activations involved. It is defined below:

$$Sim_{act}(UT_i, UT_j) = RS(UT_i, UT_j) \ . \tag{2}$$

We then collect all these UAT_y's into a set UAT, which is the union of all UAT_y as shown below:

$$UAT = UAT_1 \cup UAT_2 \cup \cdots UAT_y \ . \tag{3}$$

To determine how regular or frequent a given kind of trace is, we define the *ratio of occurrence* measure $RO_{trace}(UAT_y)$ for each UAT_y.

$$RO_{trace}(UAT_y) = \frac{\#\text{ of traces in } UAT_y}{L} \ . \tag{4}$$

In addition, we define a threshold value T_{RO} as the average ratio of occurrence for all distinct sets of unlabelled traces as shown below:

$$T_{RO}(UAT) = \frac{\sum_y RO_{trace}(UAT_y)}{m}, \text{m=\# of subsets in UAT} \ . \tag{5}$$

We set the condition that only those UAT_y whose ratio of occurrence is greater than or equal to the threshold can result in an ontology change. Using this condition, we determine these UAT_y's and pick only the first activity trace UT_{i1} into a set of candidate traces CT.

$$CT = \{UT_{i1} \,|UT_{i1} \in UAT_y, RO_{trace}(UAT_y) \geq T_{RO}(UAT)\} \ . \tag{6}$$

Let an instance of the seed ADL ontology be denoted by i_x^{SO}. For each activity trace $UT_k \in CT$, we use the sensor activations to create a temporary concept c_{temp} and a corresponding temporary instance i_{temp} in the ADL ontology, (i_{temp} is instance of c_{temp}) . We then compare the properties of i_{temp} with properties of i_x^{SO}. We define the semantic similarity measure $Sim_{property}\left(i_{temp}, i_x^{SO}\right)$ based on semantic matching measure $\overline{SM}$ derived from [21]. $Sim_{property}$ uses a measure of lexical similarity to calculate the similarity between two lexical entries, e.g. the similarity between two strings. $\overline{SM}$ uses string matching to compare lexical entries; in our case it compares the names of properties of i_{temp} and i_x^{SO}. $Sim_{property}$ returns 1 when there is a match, and a value greater than or equal to 0 otherwise, and it is defined below:

$$Sim_{property}\left(i_{temp}, i_x^{SO}\right) = \overline{SM}\left(i_{temp}, i_x^{SO}\right) \ . \tag{7}$$

When properties do not match, we recommend evolution based on concept related changes. On the other hand, we proceed to compare the property values for semantic similarity using $Sim_{property-value}\left(i_{temp}, i_x^{SO}\right)$. We recommend instance related changes if property values do not match, but do nothing otherwise.

$$Sim_{property-value}\left(i_{temp}, i_x^{SO}\right) = \frac{\left(\left(w_R * RS\left(i_{temp}, i_x^{SO}\right) + w_A * AS\left(i_{temp}, i_x^{SO}\right)\right)\right)}{(w_R + w_A)} . \tag{8}$$

RS and AS are relation and attribute similarity respectively and are defined in [20]. w_R and w_A are weights associated with each similarity measure. Fig. 2 shows the algorithm.

```
Def:
UAT_y = {UT_x | Sim_act(UT_i, UT_j) is equal to 1}
UAT := UAT_1 ∪ UAT_2 ∪ ... UAT_y
For Each UAT_y ⊆ UAT Do
        RO_trace(UAT_y) := (# of traces in UAT_y) / L
End
        T_RO(UAT) := (Σ_y RO_trace(UAT_y)) / m
Def:
CT := {UT_i1 | UT_i1 ∈ UAT_y, RO_trace(UAT_y) ≥ T_RO(UAT)}
I^SO ∈ SO //all instances of SO
For each UT_k ∈ CT Do
        Create c_temp and i_temp
For each i_x^SO ∈ I^SO Do
        If Sim_property(i_temp, i_x^SO) == 1 Then
                If Sim_property-value(i_temp, i_x^SO) == 1 Then
                        Action: make instance related change
                End
        Else
                Action: Make concept related change
        End
End
End
```

Fig. 2. Algorithm for unlabelled activity based change discovery

4.3 Learning Algorithm for Labelled Traces

In this section, we describe how to analyze labelled activity traces in order to propose changes related to individual inhabitants. We define various heuristic-based measures and show how these are used with semantic similarity measures to initiate ontology evolution.

By analysing the M labelled traces, we can extract the general information, e.g. 1) frequency of occurrence of each activity, 2) start time, duration and end-time of each activity, and 3) activity concepts associated with an activity trace. Take the case of a hypothetical activity 'Make Tea' as an example, and given that it occurs n- times ($n \leq M$) in the traces with differing sensors and/or sequence of sensors used. From the n, we can extract the following information: *1) frequency of occurrence of each sequence of activations 2) start time, duration and end-time of each activation 3) pattern(s) of activations and 4) predecessors of each activation.*

Using the results of the analysis, we can define measures that allow us to determine whether changes should be made to the seed ontology or not. We use a number of heuristics to guide this process, e.g., 1) the number of traces per activity; 2) the number of patterns of sensor activations per activity and their variability; and 3) whether coarse-grained or fine-grained recognition was possible. By using these heuristics , we define three measures: *ratio of occurrence, diversity* and *coarseness.* These are used in an algorithm to help decide when to effect changes to the seed ADL ontology.

The learning process can be described in the following. Given all labelled traces LAT, a subset LAT_z containing all traces with the label z (z corresponds to a term in the seed ADL ontology) can be denoted below.

$$LAT_z = \{LT_i \, | \text{all traces with the label z}\}, LAT_z \subseteq LAT, 1 \leq i \leq M \,. \quad (9)$$

We then collect all these LATz's into a set LAT, which is the union of all LAT_z

$$LAT = LAT_z \cup LAT_y \cup \cdots \cup LAT_m, \text{z,y,and m are labels} \,. \quad (10)$$

To determine whether an identified activity is coarse or fine, we define the measure coarseness. *Coarseness* determines how specific an activity associated with a given trace is and how definitive the recognition performance is. It is defined as a function of sub-concepts of the given activity and increases with increase in the number of sub-concepts involved. We then use non-zero values of coarseness to signify the need for concept related ontology change to the seed ADL ontology. This is aimed at refining the ontology structure, to enhance fine-grained activity recognition. *Coarseness* is calculated by the formula below:

$$coarseness\,(z) = 1 - \frac{1}{(numOfSubConcepts\,(z) + 1)} \,. \quad (11)$$

Subsequently, we determine how regular a given activity z occurs by defining ratio of occurrence. *Ratio of occurrence* (RO) determines how regular a given activity is identified in the traces. It is computed below:

$$RO_z\,(LAT_z) = \frac{\#\text{ of traces in } LAT_z}{M} \,. \quad (12)$$

In addition, we define a threshold value T_{RO} as the average ratio of occurrence for each $LAT_z \subseteq LAT$. We use the as:

$$T_{RO}\,(LAT) = \frac{\sum_z RO_z\,(LAT_z)}{n}, \text{n=\# of subsets in LAT} \,. \quad (13)$$

To determine how variable any LAT_z is, we define the measure *diversity*. Diversity defines how varied an activity z is, depending on the number of unique patterns of sensor activations that can be found in the set LAT_z. To determine the number of unique patterns, we compare the first activity trace $LT_1 \in LAT_z$ with subsequent activity traces $LT_i \in LAT_z$ and count each trace that is different from it using a variable *unique_patterns*. For each comparison, we use $Sim_{act}\,(LT_1, LT_i)$ defined based on relation similarity measure $RS\,(LT_1, LT_i)$ as specified in [20]. Sim_{act} is defined below:

$$Sim_{act}\,(LT_1, LT_i) = RS\,(LT_1, LT_i)\,, 1 < i \leq |LAT_z| \,. \quad (14)$$

Using the value for the number of unique patterns, we can define *diversity* as shown below.

$$diversity\,(LAT_z) = \begin{cases} 1 & unique\_patterns > 1 \\ 0 & \text{otherwise} \end{cases} \quad (15)$$

When diversity is 1 and the rate of occurrence is greater than or equal to the threshold value, we can recommend concept related change to the seed ADL ontology. This would enable the ontology to enhance personalization by accommodating idiosyncratic ways in which individuals carry out activities. Fig. 3 shows the algorithm.

```
Def:
    LAT_z := {LT_i | all traces with the label z}
    LAT := LAT_z ∪ LAT_y ∪ ... ∪ LAT_m
    For each LAT_z ⊆ LAT Do
        RO_z(LAT_z) := (# of traces in LAT_z) / M
        coarseness(z) := 1 − 1 / (numOfSubConcepts(z)+1)
        If  coarseness(z)! = 0 Then
            Action: Make concept related structure change
        End
    End
    T_RO(LAT) := (Σ_z RO_z(LAT_z)) / n
    For each LAT_z ⊆ LAT Do
            unique_patterns=0
            For each LT_i ∈ LAT_z Do
                    If Sim_act(LT_1,LT_i) ≠ 1 Then
                            unique_patterns = unique_patterns+1
                    End
            End
            If unique_patterns>1 Then
                    diversity (LAT_z) := 1
            Else diversity (LAT_z) := 0 End
            If diversity(LAT_z) = 1 and RO_z(LAT_z) ≥ T_RO(LAT) Then
                    Action: Make idiosyncratic change
            End
    End
```

Fig. 3. Algorithm for Labelled activity based Change Discovery

5 Illustration

We have prototyped the proposed framework. This includes the development of the underlying ontological models and the facilities to record and retrieve activity traces. We describe the protype and demonstrate its workings using typical use scenarios in subsections below.

5.1 Ontological Modeling and Representation

In a SH environment, inhabitants may carry out a variety of ADL activities. Typically, these are performed using certain objects and in predefined locations. For example, to make tea, the inhabitant may use a kettle, cup, tea bags, hot water, sugar and milk while located in the kitchen. This may occur in the morning, late afternoon and probably before going to bed. In a nutshell, each activity is carried out in some kind of context-where the context includes inhabitant, related activities, time, location and objects used. In addition, we can conceptualize ADLs at different levels of granularity: fine- and coarse-grained. Those ADLs with sub-activities or more specialized child activities are called coarse-grained ADLs. Specialized ADLs with no child activities are fine-grained and these identify very specific ADLs. The above constitute important common sense domain knowledge and heuristics to be modelled by creating ontology-based knowledge models.

We used the Web Ontology Language (OWL) [15], specifically OWL-DL, for ontological modelling and representation. As OWL-DL is based on the logical formalism Description Logics, ontological activity modelling can exploit DL-based reasoning for activity recognition. The core elements of the DL formalism are concepts, roles and individuals. These elements can be mapped to classes, properties and instances, respectively, in formal ontologies. We used Protege [22] to create ADL and Trace ontologies. We created the seed ADL ontology to represent the activity model used for activity recognition. The ADL ontology contains classes that allow us to explicitly model an aspect of the Smart Home and, together, they provide a semantic model for Smart Homes. Fig. 4 provides a fragment of ADL ontology for the Kitchen related ADLs. It shows direct and indirect subclasses of KitchenADL. We created the Trace Ontology that is used to instantiate activity traces in the Activity Log. We analyze the Activity Log in order to evolve the ADL ontology. It identifies the set of sensor activations (and therefore the sensors) involved, temporal information about the trace and the assigned label. In addition, it provides a list of likely activities given a particular series of sensor activations. Fig. 5 provides a visualization of the Trace Ontology using [23].

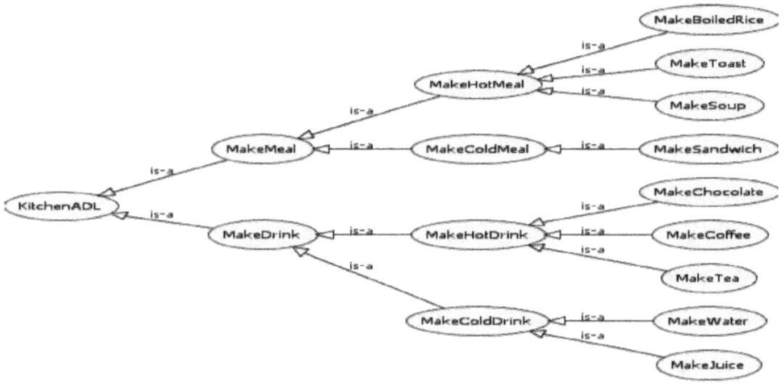

Fig. 4. The tree hierarchy of the Kitchen ADL classes

5.2 Inferring and Logging ADL Activities

The implemented system captures sensor activations and reasons with them to identify ongoing activities. When a sensor is activated, it is associated with properties in the ADL ontology and using these properties the Activity Recognizer attempts to identify the ongoing activity. It outputs a list of likely activities being performed or, if possible, the precise activity being performed. As an illustration, consider the following sequence of sensors being activated-*KitchenDoor, ChinaCup, ChineseTea, KitchenHotWater, WholeMilk* and *SandSugar*. The activity recognizer links these with properties defined in the ontology and by recognizing the classes involved and their relationships, it can identify the ongoing activity. Once the session is completed and the activity recognized, the information about the activated sensors and the activity are logged as instances of Trace Ontology.

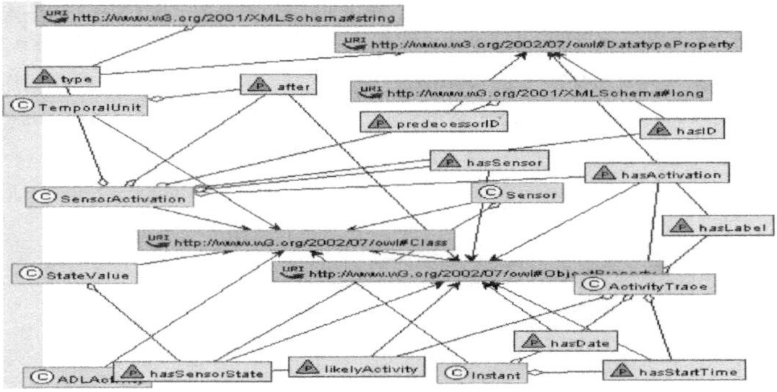

Fig. 5. The graphical representation of the Trace Ontology

5.3 Use Scenario

Consider a scenario whereby the system has monitored and collected fifty-three (53) activity traces. Among these nineteen (19) are unlabelled traces and thirty-four (34) are labeled traces. We can compare the 19 unlabelled traces using the semantic similarity measure Sim_{act}. From this comparison, it is determined that there are five (5) distinct patterns of activations-7 traces for first pattern, 2 traces each for second and third patterns, 5 for fourth pattern and 3 for the fifth pattern. We can compute the measures used by the algorithm described in Section 4.2 as shown in Table 1.

Table 1. Measures for Unlabelled Traces

Subsets of UAT	# of traces	RO_{trace}	T_{RO} (UAT)
UAT_1	7	0.368	0.2
UAT_2	2	0.105	
UAT_3	2	0.105	
UAT_4	5	0.263	
UAT_5	3	0.158	

Because the ratio of occurrence for UAT_1 and UAT_4 are greater than the threshold T_{RO}, we can recommend changes to the seed ADL ontology based on their traces. Due to space limitations, we do not show how to determine the specific kind of change to recommend.

Similarly we can analyze the thirty-four (34) labeled traces. We start by checking the label assigned to each trace and group traces that have the same label into individual subsets. Assume that we determine that the traces are associated with the labels Make Coffee, Make Tea and Make Meal. Further analysis discovers that ten (10) traces are labeled Make Coffee, thirteen (13) are Make Tea traces, and eleven (11) are Make Meal traces. We can compare traces in each subset, using Sim_{act}, to determine whether they have different sets of sensor activations or not. From this comparison, the Make Coffee and Make Meal traces are found to have only one (1) unique pattern each while Make Tea has three (3) distinct patterns. Therefore, we can compute the measures needed by the algorithm described in Section 4.3 as shown in Table 2 and Table 3.

Table 2. Coarseness for Activity Classes

Labels	# of Sub concepts	Coarseness
MakeTea	0	0
MakeCoffee	0	0
MakeMeal	6	0.86

Table 3. Diversity and Ratio of Occurrence for Labeled Traces

Subsets of LAT	# of Traces	Unique Patterns	Diversity	RO_z	$T_{RO}\,(LAT)$
$LAT_{MakeTea}$	13	3	1	0.382	0.323
$LAT_{MakeCoffee}$	9	1	0	0.265	
$LAT_{MakeMeal}$	11	1	0	0.324	

From Table 2 we are able to recommend a refinement to the Make Meal class in the seed ADL ontology due to its value of *coarseness*. In addition, from Table 3 we can recommend changes due to Make Tea. This is because it has non-zero diversity and the rate of occurrence is greater than the threshold. Due to space limitations, we do not show how to determine the specific kind of change to recommend.

6 Conclusions

It becomes evident that activity models are key to support reusable, adaptive and personalized activity recognition, and further the scalability and applicability of any assistive systems. This paper introduced an ontology-enabled framework for activity learning and model evolution in Smart Homes. We have proposed a system architecture and described its working mechanisms. We have developed algorithms for activity learning and activity model evolution through the analysis of ontology-based activity traces. We presented an initial implementation of an assistive system based on the proposed framework. We have outlined a use scenario to illustrate the operation of our framework. While full evaluation awaits further implementation and large-scale experiments, work so far has shown that this ontology-based approach is promising in the provision of quick-started, pragmatic and applicable real-world assistive systems.

References

1. Nehmer, J., Becker, M., Karshmer, A., Lamm, R.: Living assistance systems - an ambient intelligence approach. In: 28th International Conference on Software Engineering, pp. 43–50. ACM, New York (2006)
2. Chen, L., Nugent, C.D.: Ontology-based activity recognition in intelligent pervasive environments. Inter. J. of Web Info. Sys. 5, 410–430 (2009)
3. Haase, P., Sure, Y.: State-of-the-Art on Ontology Evolution. Technical report, Semantically Enabled Knowledge Technologies (2004)
4. Patterson, D.J., Fox, D., Kautz, H., Philipose, M.: Fine-grained activity recognition by aggregating abstract object usage. In: 9th IEEE Int. Symp. on Wearable Computers, pp. 44–51. IEEE Computer Society, Washington (2005)
5. Tapia, E.M., Intille, S.S., Haskell, W., Larson, K., Wright, J., King, A., Friedman, R.: Real-time recognition of physical activities and their intensities using wireless accelerometers and a heart rate monitor. In: 11th IEEE Int. Symp. on Wearable Computers, pp. 37–40. IEEE Computer Society, Washington (2007)
6. Huynh, T., Blanke, U., Schiele, B.: Scalable recognition of daily activities with wearable sensors. In: 3rd Int. Conf. on Location-and Context-Awareness, pp. 50–67. Springer, Heidelberg (2007)
7. Liao, L., Fox, D., Kautz, H.: Extracting places and activities from GPS traces using hierarchical conditional random fields. Int. J. Robotics Res. 26, 119–134 (2007)
8. Huynh, T., Schiele, B.: Unsupervised discovery of structure in activity data using multiple eigenspaces. In: Hazas, M., Krumm, J., Strang, T. (eds.) LoCA 2006. LNCS, vol. 3987, pp. 151–167. Springer, Heidelberg (2006)
9. Chua, S., Marsland, S., Guesgen, H.W.: Spatio-temporal and context reasoning in smart homes. In: Int. Conf. on Spatial Information Theory, pp. 9–20. Springer, Heidelberg (2009)
10. Lafti, F., Lefebvre, B., Descheneaux, C.: Ontology-Based Management of the Telehealth Smart Home, Dedicated to Elders in Loss of Cognitive Autonomy. In: 3rd Int. Workshop (2007)
11. Akdemir, U., Turaga, P., Chellappa, R.: An ontology based approach for activity recognition from video. In: 16th ACM Int. Conf. on Multimedia, pp. 709–712. ACM, New York (2008)
12. Yamada, N., Sakamoto, K., Kunito, G., Isoda, Y., Yamazaki, K., Tanaka, S.: Applying ontology and probabilistic model to human activity recognition from surrounding things. Trans. of the Info. Processing Soc. of Japan 48, 2823–2834 (2007)
13. Stojanovic, L.: Methods and Tools for Ontology Evolution, PhD Thesis, Research Center for Info. Technologies at the Uni. of Karslruhe (2004)
14. Flouris, G., Manakanatas, D., Kondylakis, H., Plexousakis, D., Antoniou, G.: Ontology change: classification and survey. Knowl. Eng. Rev. 23, 117–152 (2008)
15. Horrocks, I.: OWL: A description logic based ontology language. In: van Beek, P. (ed.) CP 2005. LNCS, vol. 3709, pp. 5–8. Springer, Heidelberg (2005)
16. Castano, S., Ferrara, A., Hess, G.: Discovery-Driven Ontology Evolution. In: 3rd Italian Semantic Web Workshop (2006)
17. Zablith, F., Sabou, M., d'Aquin, M., Motta, E.: Using Background Knowledge for Ontology Evolution. In: Int. Workshop on Ontology Dynamics (2008)
18. Zablith, F.: Ontology Evolution: A Practical Approach. In: Workshop on Matching and Meaning at Artificial Intelligence and Simulation of Behaviour (2009)
19. Horrocks, I., Sattler, U., Tobies, S.: Practical reasoning for expressive description logics. In: Ganzinger, H., McAllester, D., Voronkov, A. (eds.) LPAR 1999. LNCS, vol. 1705, pp. 161–180. Springer, Heidelberg (1999)

20. Maedche, A., Zacharias, V.: Clustering ontology-based metadata in the semantic web. In: 6th European Conf. on Principles and Practice of Knowledge Discovery in Databases, pp. 348–360. Springer, London (2002)
21. Maedche, A., Staab, S.: Measuring similarity between ontologies. In: Gómez-Pérez, A., Benjamins, V.R. (eds.) EKAW 2002. LNCS (LNAI), vol. 2473, pp. 251–263. Springer, Heidelberg (2002)
22. Protege, `http://protege.stanford.edu`
23. RDF-Graph-Visualization-Tool, `http://semweb.salzburgresearch.at/apps/rdf-gravity`

Support Vector Machines for Inhabitant Identification in Smart Houses

Rachid Kadouche, Hélène Pigot, Bessam Abdulrazak, and Sylvain Giroux

DOMUS Lab, Université de Sherbrooke
Sherbrooke, Québec, Canada
{Rachid.Kadouche}@usherbrooke.ca

Abstract. Authentication is the process by which a user establishes his identification when accessing a service. The use of password to identify the user has been a successful technique in conventional computers. However, in pervasive computing where computing resources exist everywhere, it is necessary to perform user identification through various means. This paper addresses the inhabitant identification issue in smart houses. It studies the optimum time and sensor set required to unobtrusively detect the house occupant. We use a supervised learning approach to address this issue by learning Support Vector Machines classifier (SVM), which predict the users by their daily life habits. We have analyzed the early morning routine with six users. From the very first minute, users can be recognized with an accuracy of more than 85%. Then we have applied an SVM feature selection algorithm to remove noisy and outlier features. Thus, this increases the accuracy to 88% using less then 10 sensors.

1 Introduction

Research in smart houses is becoming an important trend [1], [2], [3] . It is at the crossroad of research of many domains such as pervasive computing, machine learning, mobile computing, ect. The aim of smart houses research is to maximize comfort and productivity of the inhabitants while minimizing costs (installation, operation, and maintenance) and reducing the number of intrusive preventative devices. There are huge needs in health care to maintain at home people with special needs (PwSN[1]) and improve their quality of life using technology. However, PwSN have a large variability in their needs and levels of motor and/or cognitive handicap. Hence, they call for adapted services, especially when interacting with their environment. The task of environment personalization becomes more complicated in the case of multiple inhabitants in the house. According to [4], over half of the elderly live with their spouse, and one third live alone assisted by residential care. In both cases, the house should be able to correctly distinguish between multiple inhabitants before any other operation. The system should identify among a group of people who is currently

[1] PwSN: People with disabilities and elderly.

Z. Yu et al. (Eds.): UIC 2010, LNCS 6406, pp. 83–95, 2010.

present in the house in order to proceed with the environment adaptation and customization. For instance, predict the user's activities, and select some of their activities for automation. In addition, inhabitant identification allows detecting intrusions. For instance, if the system cannot recognize the occupant inside the house, anomalies can be triggered.

In case of PwSN, the identification system should take into account the omission errors of this population particularly when they are involved by themselves in the process (using a badge, introducing a password...). In this case, the risk of missing the identification task is high. Thus, the identification should be automatic. It should not intrude or disturb the user, but should quietly support them. In addition, several constraints should be considered to build such a system:

- Identification time should be short in order to proceed earlier to the environment personalization.
- Occupants' privacy have to be preserved. For instance, the use of video cameras and microphone are not recommended.
- The sensors used should be economic, designed to be quickly and ubiquitously installed and easy to dissimulate in the house to provide a familiar environment.
- Avoid the use of wearable tags. This reduces anxiety and the feeling of being constantly monitored.

In this paper, we have analyzed the inhabitant recognition issue in smart houses. Based on basic activities that people undertake each day, such as having breakfast, eating and using the bathroom. The particularity of our approach is the use of non intrusive sensors and devices to analyze the way, called habits, that each person performs these activities. Thus, it will be used to identify the user according to various criteria such as minimum time and the optimal set of sensors required, solution cost, number of house occupants, etc. We used Support Vector Machines (SVM) to learn the user's habits. Our approach does not require the users to wear any sensors, and the sensory system is completely hidden in the environment. Thus, in this paper we present our work which is divided into two phases. The first phase focussed on defining the minimum time needed to perform a high identification accuracy. In the second phase, using SVM features selection algorithm, we have studied the satisfactory sensors set required to unobtrusively detect the inhabitant. The second phase allows reducing the set of sensors used and eliminating those with little or no predictive information.

We mounted an experiment at DOMUS apartment [5] and tested our approach with six users. The tests showed very promising results.

2 Background and Related Work

Recent projects carried out by leading universities and companies have specifically addressed the sensors set minimization issues. Tapia et al., [6] use around 80 wireless accelerometers installed on objects in the house to detect around 30 activities. They report accuracies in many cases worse than 50%. Dalal et al., [7] showed a precision of 90% to detect meal preparation from 23 embedded sensors including motion sensors, switches and temperature sensors. Logan et al., [8] found that preparing and eating meal can be detected with an accuracy of 90% using 100 sensors whereas, using 8 sensors, accuracy of 82% was reported. These systems do not address the required optimum time for identification and focus only on users' activity detection in smart houses.

Existing identification systems in smart environments (companies, banks,..) mainly use invasive devices to detect the user, such as tags that are placed on the body (ex: RFID tags [9]) which contain the profile of the user. Other systems require the users to identify themselves by entering a password or by presenting a badge. These technics are not relevant in a house where the system is supposed to be less tiring to use and do not disturb the user.

Physiological measurements such us biometrics are often used for user identification in smart environments. They refer to automatic recognition of people based on their distinctive anatomical (e.g., face, fingerprint, hand shapes, iris, retina, hand geometry)[10,11]. These systems have not yet carried out automatic human recognition. They are sensitive to the environmental factors like shadow, light intensity and obstacles.

Other identification systems are based on Gait recognition. Gait-based methods use the modelling sequence of walking using cameras [12]. Continuous hidden Markov models [13] and eigenspace transformation combined with canonical space transformation [12] have been applied to identify a user from others. These technics suffer from occlusion, differences in background movements, and lighting conditions.

Floor sensor settings have been also used for user identification in smart environments. In [14] and [15], respectively use the nearest-neighbour and hidden Markov models (HMM) methods, for a footstep identification based on a small area of ground reaction force sensors. UbiFloor [16], based on neural network classifier, use binary type ON/OFF sensors to detect the characteristic walking styles of the user based on both single footsteps and walking from consecutive footsteps on the floor. In these systems, to perform a high resolution of the identification process, the house should be equipped with a large number of sensors. Thus, the cost of the identification should be high.

Although identification systems presented above present a flexible and natural way to identify the inhabitant without any wearable devices in smart environments, these solutions have many disadvantages. They are either costly or extracted features are sensitive to environmental factors and the recording devices are not always hidden from the user (ex, camera) which can compromise the individual's privacy. Our approach uses behavioral modelling based on users' habits inside the house. Our study, which have not yet been addressed in the literature, focus on analyzing the minimum time and the optimum sensors required to unobtrusively recognize the inhabitant. The key advantage of our approach is that it can uses any imbedded sensors already mounted in the smart house to detect the inhabitant.

3 Our Approach

This work deals with the inhabitant identification issue. It investigates the trade-offs when using various subsets of sensors. Of particular interest is whether a optimum time and sensors set can be used. We use supervised learning technics for predicting a person from inhabitant group (classification). This task predicts inhabitants after they have performed some activities inside the house. We follow a very standard procedure of data analysis. We first convert the disparate data provided by the apartment sensors into a series of vectors (matrix). Then we train SVM classifier to separate one user from others. The first phase of our work deals with the optimum time required for high identification accuracy and the second phase will choose the optimal sensors subset to perform a high precision by running a SVM future selection algorithm.

3.1 Support Vector Machines (SVM)

SVM are powerful classification systems based on regularization technics with excellent performances in many practical classification problems[17]. SVM deliver state-of-the-art performance in real-world applications such as text categorization, hand-written character recognition, biosequences analysis, image classification, etc. It is now established as one of the standard tools for machine learning and data mining. The SVM decision function is defined as follows:

$$f(y) = \sum_{i=1}^{N} \alpha_i K(x_i, y) + b \tag{1}$$

Here y is the unclassified tested vector, x_i are the support vectors and α_i their weights and b is a constant bias. $K(x, y)$ is the kernel function introduced into SVM to solve the nonlinear problems by performing implicit mapping into a high-dimensional feature space [18,19].

We have applied SVM to learn the user's activities inside the house. The SVM data input is a matrix defined by a set of vectors, each vector, called *pattern*, is composed of n components which we name *features*. Features are the apartment sensors' states. Patterns correspond to the user's activities and contains the state value of the involved sensors. Particulary in this paper, we have considered binary values (1 and 0). The value 1 (resp 0) means that the corresponding sensor state have been activated (resp not been activated). Each vector was labelled by the feature *Class* which defines the user who is performing the activity (see table 1).

Table 1 defines one user's pattern with 4 features. The vector presents the features' values corresponding to the activities that user $U1$ performed in the environment during a defined period p. Each sensor have two states. For instance the sensor *bedroom-lamp* have the states *open* and *close*. Thus, we can interpret this vector as followed: during the period p, the user *U1*, switched on the bedroom light (Lamp-Bedroom-Open), opened and closed the bedroom door(Door-Bedroom-Open, Door-Bedroom-Close). The objective of the first phase of our approach is to minimize the period p in order to have high identification accuracy.

Table 1. User's pattern example

Lamp-Bedroom-Open	Lamp-Bedroom–Close	Door-Bedroom-Open	Door-Bedroom-Close	Class
1	0	1	1	U1

We have to note that patterns do not give any temporal order of the actions performed by the user during the period p. Particulary in this work, the temporal constrain is not taken into account.

Multi Classes Classification. Various approaches are possible for constructing a multi class classifier for a multi class problem from basic binary SVM, e.g.[20]. The one we have found most successful is the pairwise classification (1 vs. 1)[21]. Where one classifier is trained for every possible pair of classes - resulting in $\frac{k\cdot(k-1)}{2}$ classifiers, where k is the number of inhabitant in our case.

3.2 Feature Selection

In the second phase of our approach we have used feature selection technics. It minimizes the feature set used for identification. Feature selection is one of the most important topics in machine learning. It can remove the irrelevant noisy and outlier features which may cause unexpected results. Thus, it improves the quality of the data set and the performance of learning systems. In our case, it allows also reducing the cost, computational speedup and storage of the inhabitant identification system. In this work, the SVM feature selection algorithm proposed in [22] for selecting relevant features have been applied. It evaluates the worth of feature by using an SVM classifier. features are ranked by the square of the weight assigned by the SVM. In multi class problems, features selection, is handled by ranking features for each class seperately using a one vs. all method and then dealing from the top of each pile to give a final ranking. This algorithm was proved in [23] to be better than others features selection algorithm.

4 Experimental Configuration

We conduct a series of experiments at DOMUS apartment. In this study, we focus only on the early morning habits. Particularly, we learn the SVM classifier to identify the apartment occupant. We assume that we are monitoring a group of people living together where the morning wake up time is different from one another. Each person at a time does the early morning routine alone in the apartment. This choice is due to being unable to detect the activity of one person among a group performing altogether activities inside the house.

Table 2. List of sensors used per zones

	Entrance hall	Living room	Dining room	Kitchen	Bathroom	Bedroom	Total
IR	0	1	1	3	0	0	5
Pressure Detector	1	0	0	0	0	0	1
Lamps	0	1	1	1	1	1	5
Door contacts	0	0	0	0	1	1	2
Switch contacts	0	0	0	19	0	0	19
Flow meters	0	0	0	0	2	2	4

4.1 DOMUS

The DOMUS laboratory [5] includes a standard apartment (kitchen, living room, dining room, bedroom and bathroom) located within the computer science department of the University of Sherbrooke and equipped with a set of infrared sensors, pressure detectors, smart light switches, electrical contacts on doors, audio and video systems, as well as smart tags (RFID) to obtain, in the apartment, the real-time position of the user and objects.

4.2 The Sensors

In this work we have considered 36 imbedded and unobtrusive sensors which are already mounted in DOMUS apartment, they allow us to cover a large space of potential sensors. Each sensor have two states (open and close) that makes a total of 72 features. Six zones are defined to cover the different apartment area (see figure 1). The number of installed sensors varies depending on the interested zone. Table 2 define their disposition per zone. The following list gives the details of each sensor.

- Infrared (IR) movement detectors: they provide the users' location in a zone. They cover a zone or a part of a zone. For example there is only one IR detector that covers the entire zone in the dining room and living room (salon), whereas three are installed in the kitchen covering oven, sink and toaster.
- Pressure detector: in form of tactile carpets placed on entrance hall, it detects the user moving between the bedroom and living room. The users can use two paths to move around these two zones are through the kitchen or through the entrance hall.
- Lamps Light switches: these sensors send an event every time the occupant turns the lights on or off.

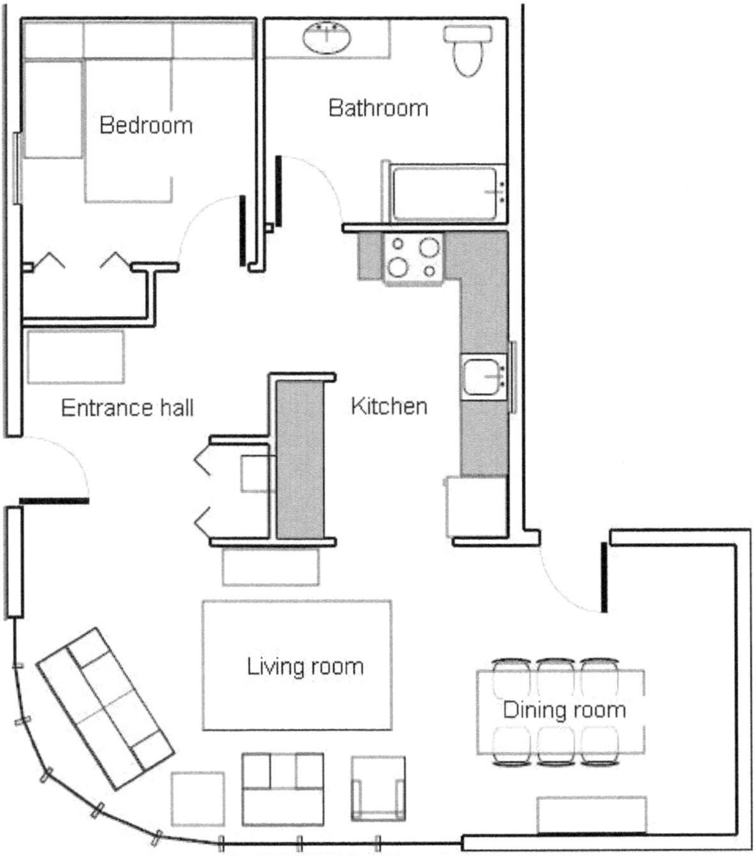

Fig. 1. Domus apartment

- Door contacts: these sensors are placed on the doors. They send an event related to the door state (open or close).
- Switches contacts: the same as door contact, they are placed on the lockers and fridge. They provide an event when their state is changed either opened or closed.
- Flow meter: they provide the taps and the flush toilet stats, two are mounted on the cold and hot water taps of the kitchen sink, one is mounted on the washbasins cold water tap and another in the flush toilet. They send an event when the tap is opened or closed and the flush toilet used.

5 Experimentation

5.1 The Experiment Scenario

Six adults have participated in the experiment; especially in this work we evaluated the early morning habits (wash up, having breakfast). The experience held in 2 times at DOMUS apartment. In the first time (serie 1), the user was asked to perform the early morning routine as he is used to do at home. In the second time (serie 2), he was asked to repeat the same routine where a constraint was introduced during the experiment. This constraint which joined another study conducted by colleagues in the DOMUS laboratory, consist on learning a tea recipe which takes at most 10 minutes. In serie 1 the user cames 10 times to the laboratory, ideally in two consecutive weeks. After 2 weeks break, the user start the serie 2, he was asked to come 5 days, ideally in one week. In both series, the user was free to use any equipment available in the apartment. The experiment time was about 45 minutes.

The experiment starts with the same apartment conditions for all the users, all doors closed and lights switched off. The user is asked to stay in the bedroom for one minute (time required to start data recording). Each user experiment define a sample data which represents a pattern, this makes a total of 60 samples for serie 1 and 30 samples for a serie 2.

5.2 Data Preprocessing

A preprocessing step is used to select, from the original values, the data subset that is used as input to the SVM classifier. We faced many problems during the experiment providing incorrect samples. This is due to technical (blackout during the experiment, server shutdown, ...) and experimental problems (user begins the experiment before start recording the data). We reported 16 incorrect samples which are eliminated in this phase. To recover this data, we need missing data technics [24] which is another issue that have not been addressed in this paper.

The data sampling are split into two subsets: A training set to learn a classifier and a test data set to estimate the performance of the classifier. The data of serie 1 are used as a training set, whereas both, data form serie 1 and serie 2 are used in test data set. Thus, in this experiment, two tests data sets are used:

– Training set (TS) with 54 samples obtained from serie 1 (100% serie 1). To estimate the classifiers performances we used the 10-fold cross-validation method [25].
– New set (NS) which is independent from the training set. It includes 20 samples from serie 2 (100 % serie 2).

6 Result and Discussion

Based on WEKA Framework [26], we have compared the effectiveness of SVM classifier among the following classifiers: Decision Tree, Random Forest, Bayesian Network, Neural Network. SVM classifier significantly achieves best performance among all of the classifiers. Its identification accuracy is over then 85%, where its under 84% for the other classifiers.

6.1 Minimum Identification Time (Phase 1)

We used normalized polynomial kernel [19] implemented in WEKA [26] and fixed the complexity parameter C to 100 to run the SVM identification system. In this phase, we studied the minimum time p required to perform the identification process. We trained the SVM classifier over TS data set and tested, first, with TS data set then with NS data set. Figure 2 shows the results of the SVM classifier accuracy over various experiment time periods p_1,p_2,...p_r . High identification precision was recorded at the very first minute of the experiment time (p= 1 minute). The SVM classifier accuracy is over then 85% for both test sets. The accuracy increases to 94.44% using TS data set. This is due to the test data set used (TS data set) which is the same set used to learn the SVM classifier.

In NS data set, the data are extracted from serie 2 where the user was asked to perform another activity (tea recipe). In this case, we expect that the user's behavior will change during the experiment and will be different from his behavior in serie 1. However, using NS set, as test data set, will increase the accuracy error. That is why in figure 2, the results are worse than 50% using NS set. But we observe that this value (50%)is recorded after the 20th minute of the experiment time using NS set. At the very first minute, the accuracy is equal to 90% . It means that, at the first minute of the early morning routine time, user mainly have the same behavior in both series 1 and 2 even if he performs the tea recipe in serie 2 (NS set) which is supposed to change his behavior. Thus, we conclude that the tea recipe is performed after the first minute of the early morning routine time for all the users.

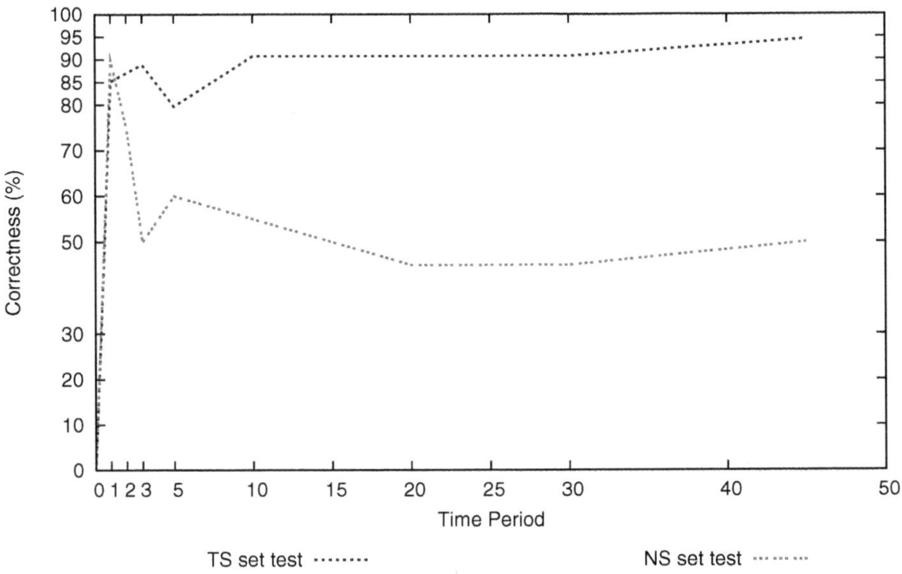

Fig. 2. SVM classification accuracy using TS and NS test sets

The results of the test using NS data set are interesting because it presents a situation which is close to our daily lives where different constraints can arise and change our behavior. Thus, we trained then tested the classifier with different data (series 1 and 2) involving different behaviors. The fact that having the same behavior during the first minute of the early morning routine time for both series, we assume that, for each user and for whatever he will do during the day, in the beginning of the morning routine he performs the same activities, called habits, that might make him distinguishable from others during this period.

In this phase we have proved that each user has his own manner to perform an activity (called habit). This prove is based on our ability to distinguish the six users between them.

6.2 Optimum Features Set (Phase 2)

In this phase, we studied the optimal features set required in the identification system. We applied a ranking SVM features selection algorithm over the 72 features used in this experiment. We have analyzed the accuracy of the SVM classifier for the first minute of the experiment time by varying the features set used. Based on their rank, the features list was reverse-sorted first, then, added one by one to the features set used. Thus, 72 feature sets were involved. We trained SVM classifier with the same parameters defined in section 6.1 over the 72 features sets. Then we used the two tests data sets defined above (TS and NS) to test the performance of the classifier. The predictive accuracies are shown in figure 3. We observe that, the results provided by the 10th ranked SVM features are the most significant using the two testing sets (TS and NS). The accuracy increases from 85.18% to 88.88% using the TS test set, whereas it remains almost constant (90%) using NS test set. Thus, SVM feature selection algorithm significantly reduces the classification error rate. This indicates that almost the original data sets have some noisy features, and these features hurt the performance of the SVM learning algorithm. However, in the real world applications, feature selection is needed before learning on all the data.

Table 3. 10th ranked SVM features

Sensor	Rank (%)
Fl01-TapColdWaterWashbasin-Bathroom-Close	71.6
5101-Lamp-Kitchen-Open	71
0215-Door-Bedroom-Close	70
0113-LockerC6-Kitchen-Open	68.1
0216-Door-Bathroom-Close	67.3
5105-Lamp-Bedroom-Close	65.9
5105-Lamp-Bedroom-Open	62.9
5103-Lamp-Livingroom-Open	62
5102-Lamp-Diningroom-Open	61.5
Fl04-TapColdWaterSink-Kitchen-Close	60.6

Table 3 defines the 10 highest ranked SVM features provided by the SVM feature selection algorithm. "Fl01" is a DOMUS sensor identifier, "TapColdWaterWashbasin" refer to the cold water tap of the washbasin, "Bathroom" is the localization zone of the sensor and "close" referring to the sensor state. The information provided by this sensor come from the flowmeter mounted on this tap. Not that the features "5103-Lamp-Livingroom-Open" and "5103-Lampe-Livingroom-Close" come from the same sensor livingroom lamp. Thus, the number of selected features is always less then the number of sensors involved. For instance, in our case, the ten features come form only nine sensors which are: tap cold water of the washbasin, kitchen lamp, bedroom door, locker kitchen (C6), bathroom door, bedroom lamp, livingroom lamp, diningroom lamp and tap cold water of the sink.

From table 3 we remark that the sensors chosen by the SVM feature selection algorithm provide the discriminant features. They reflect the user's habits that make him different from others during the first minute of the early morning routine. For instance, the lamps sensors are chosen because each user have his luminosity preference and the lights disposition at home. Thus, some of them switch on all the lamps of the house, other, switch on just the kitchen lamp, and so on.

This phase, by filtering the feature set, complements the first phase. It provides us the activity that makes the six users distinguishable between them.

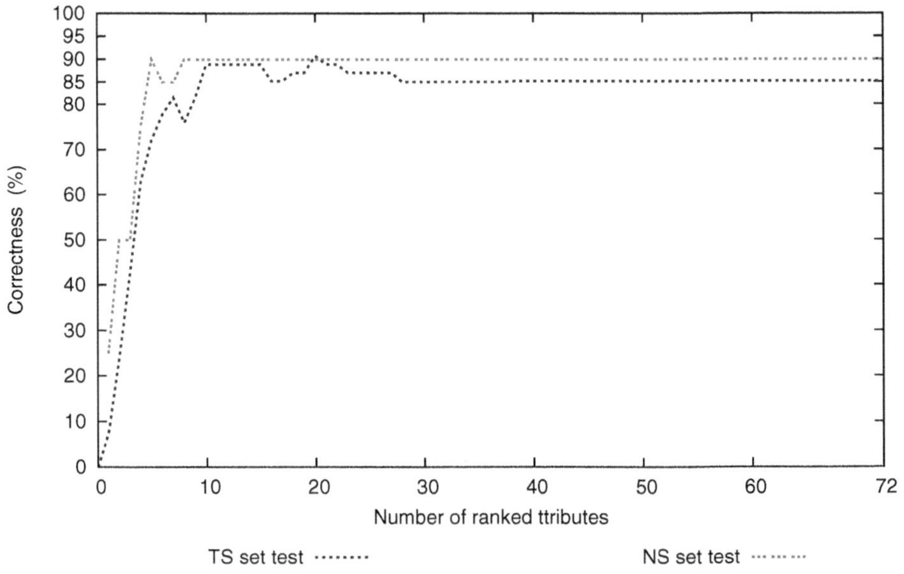

Fig. 3. SVM classification accuracy using SVM Ranked data

7 Conclusion

This paper deals with the inhabitant identification issue based on daily life habits in smart houses, we particulary studied the minimum time and the optimal sensors set required for the identification process. We used Support vector machines (SVM), to learn the user's habits for classification. We mounted an experiment with six users at DOMUS apartment to evaluate the users identification accuracy during the early morning routine through two phases. We found that from the very first minute of the experiment time, user can be identified with accuracy over 85% (phase 1). To define the optimum sensors set, we applied SVM features selection algorithm to eliminate the noisy features. We recorded an accuracy of 88% using less then 10 sensors (phase 2).

In phase 1 we proved that each user can have a habit that make him distinguishable from another, in phase 2 we provide an example of this habit. In a future work, we plan to vary the number of users involved in the results. In this paper, we have analyzed the behavior of six users living in the same house which is far from reality. Thus, we expect to find promising results if less then six users will be involved. We plan also to evaluate the identification process using another activity such as, preparing a meal, getting ready routine, etc. Finely, we are aiming at validating this concept in real environment involving PwSN by deploying this approach within pilot sites.

References

1. House_n: Mit house, `http://architecture.mit.edu/house_n/`
2. Pentland, A.: Smart rooms. Scientific American 274, 68–76 (1996)
3. AwareHome: Georgia tech aware home research initiative, `http://awarehome.imtc.gatech.edu`
4. Vierck, E., Hodges, K.: Aging: Lifestyles, Work and Money. Greenwood Press, Westport (2005)
5. DOMUS, `http://domus.usherbrooke.ca/`
6. Tapia, E.M., Intille, S.S., Larson, K.: Activity recognition in the home using simple and ubiquitous sensors. In: Ferscha, A., Mattern, F. (eds.) PERVASIVE 2004. LNCS, vol. 3001, pp. 158–175. Springer, Heidelberg (2004)
7. Dalal, S., Alwan, M., Seifrafi, R., Kell, S., Brown, D.: A rule-based approach to the analysis of elders' activity data: Detection of health and possible emergency conditions. In: AAAI Fall 2005 Symposium (2005)
8. Logan, B., Healey, J.: Sensors to detect the activities of daily living. In: 28th Annual International Conference of the IEEE, Engineering in Medicine and Biology Society, EMBS 2006, pp. 5362–5365 (2006)
9. Wolf, P., Schmidt, A., Klein, M.: Soprano: An extensible, open AAI platform for elderly peoplebased on semantical contracts. In: 3rd Workshop on Artificial Intelligence Techniques for Ambient Intelligence, AITAmI 2008 (2008)
10. Jain, A., Hong, L., Pankanti, S.: Biometric identification. ACM Commun. 43, 90–98 (2000)
11. Jain, A.K., Ross, A., Prabhakar, S.: An introduction to biometric recognition. IEEE Trans. on Circuits and Systems for Video Technology 14, 4–20 (2004)

12. Little, J., Boyd, J.E.: Recognizing people by their gait: The shape of motion. Videre 1, 1–32 (1998)
13. Cuntoor, K.R., Kale, A., Rajagopalan, A.N., Cuntoor, N., Krger, V.: Gait-based recognition of humans using continuous HMMS. In: Fifth IEEE International Conference on Automatic Face and Gesture Recognition, pp. 321–326 (2002)
14. Orr, R.J., Abowd, G.D.: The smart floor: a mechanism for natural user identification and tracking. In: Conference on Human Factors in Computing Systems, The Hague, The Netherlands, pp. 275–276. ACM, New York (2000)
15. Addlesee, M., Jones, A.H., Livesey, F., Samaria, F.S.: The orl active floor. IEEE Personal Communications 4, 35–41 (1997)
16. Yun, J.-S., Lee, S.-H., Woo, W.T., Ryu, J.H.: The user identification system using walking pattern over the ubifloor, Gyeongju, Korea, pp. 1046–1050 (2003)
17. Vapnik, V.: Statistical Learning Theory. Wiley-Interscience, Hoboken (1998)
18. Shawe-Taylor, J., Cristianini, N.: Kernel Methods for Pattern Analysis. Cambridge University Press, New York (2004)
19. Debnath, R., Takahashi, H.: Kernel selection for the support vector machine (biocybernetics, neurocomputing). IEICE Transactions on Information and Systems 87, 2903–2904 (2004)
20. Platt, J.C., Cristianini, N., Shawe-taylor, J.: Large margin dags for multiclass classification. In: Advances in Neural Information Processing Systems, pp. 547–553. MIT Press, Cambridge (2000)
21. Hastie, T., Tibshirani, R.: Classification by pairwise coupling. In: NIPS 1997: Proceedings of the 1997 Conference on Advances in Neural Information Processing Systems, vol. 10, pp. 507–513. MIT Press, Cambridge (1998)
22. Guyon, I., Weston, J., Barnhill, S., Vapnik, V.: Gene selection for cancer classification using support vector machines. Mach. Learn. 46, 389–422 (2002)
23. Rakotomamonjy, A.: Variable selection using svm based criteria. J. Mach. Learn. Res. 3, 1357–1370 (2003)
24. Little, R.J.A., Rubin, D.B.: Statistical analysis with missing data. John Wiley & Sons, Inc., New York (2002)
25. Devijver, P.A., Kittler, J.: Pattern recognition: A statistical approach. Prentice Hall, Englewood Cliffs (1982)
26. Witten, I.H., Frank, E.: Data Mining: Practical Machine Learning Tools and Techniques, 2nd edn. Morgan Kaufmann, San Francisco (2005)

Towards Non-intrusive Sleep Pattern Recognition in Elder Assistive Environment

Hongbo Ni[1,2], Bessam Abdulrazak[2], Daqing Zhang[3], Shu Wu[2], Zhiwen Yu[1], Xingshe Zhou[1], and Shengrui Wang[2]

[1] School of Computer Science, Northwestern Polytechnic University, China
{nihb,zhiwenyu,zhouxs}@nwpu.edu.cn
[2] Department of Computer, University of Sherbrooke, Canada
{Bessam.Abdulrazak,shu.wu,Shengrui.wang}@usherbrooke.ca
[3] Handicom Lab, Institut Telecom SudParis, France
Daqing.Zhang@it-sudparis.eu

Abstract. Quality of sleep is an important attribute of an elder's health state and its assessment is still a challenge. The sleep pattern is a significant aspect to evaluate the quality of sleep, and how to recognize elder's sleep pattern is an important issue for elder-care community. With the pressure sensor matrix to monitor the elder's sleep behavior in bed, this paper presents an unobtrusive sleep postures detection and pattern recognition approaches. Based on the proposed sleep monitoring system, the processing methods of experimental data and the classification algorithms for sleep pattern recognition are also discussed.

Keywords: Sleep pattern; elder-care; pressure sensor; naïve bayes; random forest.

1 Introduction

Sleep is indispensable to everybody. As have been reported in Ancoli-Israel and Roth [1] that is consistent with other national studies, about one-third of people had some kind of sleep problem. Hence, the study of sleep pattern, much of which is through sleep recordings, has consistently been a hot research topic. In fact, sleep disorder is more serious in elder community, In an aging study of over 9000 subjects aged 65 and older, more than 50% of older adults reported the frequent trouble falling asleep, difficult waking or waking too early, or needing to nap and not feeling rested[2].

Sleep disorders are under-recognized public health problems that have a cumulative effect on elders' physical and mental health, and usually put the older adult at greater risk for decreased physical functioning, problems with memory, increased risk of falls and mortality.

As the proportion of aged people in the population increases, a simple and minimally invasive detecting approach of the sleep behaviors in the bed should be developed to maintain the elders' health. Unfortunately, there are no convenient, unobtrusive and accurate ways to obtain elder's body behaviors during sleep outside of a clinic.

Z. Yu et al. (Eds.): UIC 2010, LNCS 6406, pp. 96–109, 2010.

Body movement is generally considered to be an important index in the analysis of sleep pattern shifts in sleep physiology [3]. The term 'body movements' can be described by body postures changing to/from a lying position, to turn from side to side, and to reposition the body while in bed. In the literature to analyze the distribution of behaviors during sleep [4-6], body movements were classified as minor movements (actogram signal or head leads artifact), major movements (actogram signal plus head leads artifact). Major movements usually are associated with changes in body posture, involving the head, arms, torso rotations, any combination of upper and lower limbs, and any combination of limbs and torso rotations. So, given a time interval, the sleep pattern can be detected by the body posture. In this paper, we will consider the 4 typical sleep postures, including left-lateral sleep (LLS), right-lateral sleep (RLS) and supine sleep (SS), prone sleep (PS) and these postures will be detected by a matrix of pellicle pressure sensors deployed in the bed. By detecting the sleep postures, the authors try to recognize the elder's sleep pattern in bed in a non-invasive means.

The key contributions in this paper include: i) Introducing pressure sensors into sleep detection; ii) Presenting the detailed design of sleep detection system; and iii) Proposing a sleep pattern recognition approach based on pressure data.

The rest of this paper is organized as follows: section 2 summarizes the related work in sleep detection; in section 3, we describe the design of sleep detection system with pellicle pressure sensors; section 4 proposes the experimental method for sleep posture detection; section 5 presents sleep pattern recognition approach based on the postures, and also discusses the experiments analysis and performance evaluation; finally section 6 presents the conclusion of this paper.

2 Related Work

Many sleep sensing approaches have been proposed for assessment of body behaviors in bed, in this section, we will describe some of the representative work on continuous sensing of body behaviors (movements) in bed.

The assessment of sleep-related motor disturbances is traditionally performed by overnight polysomnograph (PSG) to continuously record oractigraphy[7]. Although polysomnography, which includes EEG measurement, is a widely used and reliable method, the technique is rather complicated and both subject and examiner are seriously restricted [8]. With actigraphy, activity monitors are attached to a person's wrist or lower extremity [9, 10] to assess nocturnal activity. It is commonly used for long-term assessment and medical and behavior therapy in conditions such as insomnia and periodic limb movements during sleep (PLMS) [11]. Most of the actigraph models used in sleep studies can determine sleep and wake periods from the level of activity of the patient, but their algorithms only provide accurate sleep/wake periods if the patient provides bedtimes and get up times.

Besides, accelerometers and RFID can also be used to assess movement in bed [12][13], but they also place a burden on the subject because the patient has to wear them all the time.

Another important approach in this field is to assess sleep behaviors in bed in a continuous and unobtrusive way by instrumenting the bed itself. Tamura et al. [14] proposed a bed temperature measurement system for detection of body movement. The system detects torso and leg movements by placing arrays of 15 thermistors under the waist and under the legs. The system only reports the frequency of movements and time in bed, and does not classify the type of movement. Several authors [15-16] have employed the static charge sensitive bed (SCSB) for monitoring of motor activity. The SCSB is composed of two metal plates with a wooden plate in the middle that must be placed under a special foam plastic mattress, which will be difficult to build. Van der Loos also proposed a sensing system called SleepSmart, composed of a mattress pad with 54 force sensitive resistors and 54 resistive temperature devices, to estimate body center of mass and index of restlessness [17]. The system does not report the frequency and type of movements, and this large-size equipment is difficult to set up and can only be used in specific laboratories. Other sensing techniques, such as optical fibers and conductive fibers have also been used for monitoring body movement in bed. Tamura proposed a body movement monitoring system using optical fibers [18]. Kimura designed an unobtrusive vital signs detection system, which uses conductive fiber sensors to detect body position, respiration, and heart rate [19]. Technologically, the fiber sensors can be incorporated in a conventional bed sheet, but obviously it will be costly and not applicable for home use. The use of load cells is another approach to detect body movements in bed [20], in which load cells is placed at each corner of a bed. The detection of movements is based on short-term analysis of the mean-square differences of the load cell signals, and not applicable for specific sleep postures detecting.

As mentioned above, the previous solutions are not applicable for sleep detection in home in a non-invasive way, and this paper proposes an unobtrusive sleep posture detection system for elder-care, which is relatively cheap and easy to deploy in a common bed without any special alteration.

3 System Development

In this section, we will discuss our sleep detection system (SDS) in two aspects. On the one hand, we will address the framework and main components of SDS; on the other hand, we will also describe the FFS Matrix deployment.

3.1 The Framework of SDS

To date, we have implemented SDS in the first step, and the goal of SDS is to develop a low-cost, multi-sensor, modular, unobtrusive sleep sensing platform that accurately infers the sleep posture, discovers the sleep pattern and provides personalized suggestions in future. The framework of SDS can be seen in Fig.1, and there are four levels in it, including physical sense level, data acquisition level, posture detection level, and service provision level.

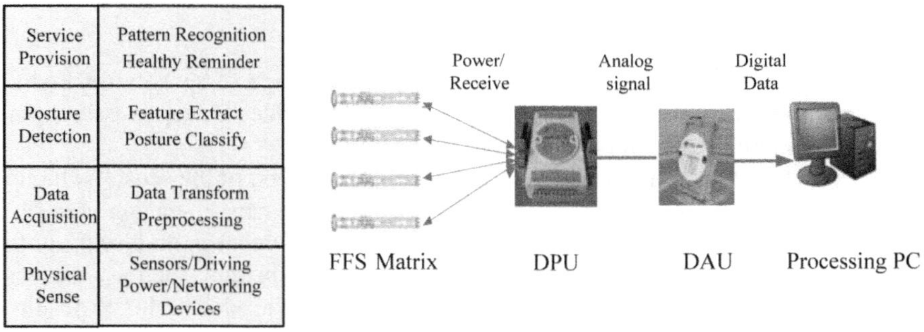

Fig. 1. The Framework and Main Components of SDS

Physical Sense: the level consists of a matrix of 32 pressure sensors and a Driving Power Unit (DPU) to sense the body pressure. In SDS, we chose a novel type of pressure sensor named FlexiForce. The Flexiforce sensor (FFS) is ultra-thin, low-cost and flexible. FFS is resistive-based technology and will produce an analog signal. FFS acts as a variable resistor in an electrical circuit. When the sensor is unloaded, its resistance is very high (greater than 5 Meg-ohm); when a force is applied to the sensor, the resistance decreases. To trigger the FFS-Matrix, we applied a direct-current low-voltage driving power unit (DPU). For ensuring the scalability of FFS, we customized a multi-channel port for DPU, and it can support 80 FFSs.

Data Acquisition: this level includes a Data Acquisition Unit (DAU) to process the analog signal. As seen in Fig. 1, DPU power the FFS-Matrix and transmits the analog signals as current, and then the DAU receives and transforms these signals into digital data. Concurrently, DAU will also connect with the Processing PC with the Standard MODBUS RTU protocol, and its output is a digitized data that is correlated to the applied pressure but is not an absolute measure of pressure.

Posture Detection: this level is modularized software residing in the Processing PC, including three parts: the receiving module is a soft port to receive real-time digitized data from the DAU; the forwarding module is to input the data into MySQL database for permanent storage and also feed the raw data into posture detection module, which is finally to preprocess the received data and analysis the elder's sleep posture using classification algorithms.

Service Provision: based on the sleep postures and their duration, we can infer the elderly user's sleep pattern, and evaluate the quality of sleep. On the one hand, the important healthy information will be fed back to the elder and his caregiver; on the other hand, the preferred sleep posture is usually recommended according to the elder's own disease [22], for example, an elder with coronary heart disease is generally suggested a right-lateral sleep posture, thus SDS will also provide necessary reminder to the elder when the sleep pattern is improper for his health. This part is under developing and we will report our progress in future.

3.2 Sensors Deployment

Besides the framework of SDS, we must meet the challenge of sensors deployment. Based on the investigation, we choose FFS to monitor the elder's sleep pressure in bed, which is 203mm long, 14 mm wide, and 0.208 mm thick.

As seen in Fig.2, there is an "active sensing area" at the end of the sensor, which is a 9.53mm diameter circle. The application of a force to the active sensing area of the sensor results in a change in the resistance of the sensing element in inverse proportion to the force applied. FFS is constructed of two layers of substrate, such as a polyester film [21]. Meanwhile, known from common sense that the elder's body posture is mainly relied on his trunk, hence the FFS Matrix was deployed as seen in Fig.2, and there are two arrays to monitor the body pressure of back and hip separately. To ensure the accuracy, these two FFS arrays are fixed onto a flexible and rigid pad, and which occupies 2M by 0.75M, with sensor elements spaced 10 CM apart. The pad is placed on the bed under the coverlet and on the top of normal mattress, without any special installation requirement. Please note, this is the first step of our implementation, and the normal width of this material is 0.75M (we have booked a customized king-size pad from the vendor). Moreover, the 10CM-distance between the FFSs is from our trial experiments, which is proper arrangement for detecting an adult's pressure. We will try more experiments and adjust the distance if the solution applied to child-care.

Since FFS is ultra-thin and non-invasive, the elder will not feel any uncomfortable for FFS Matrix and can be easy to accept the unobtrusive monitoring manner. Furthermore, we developed a 48-channel hub-like port to assemble so many wires connecting sensors, which is placed under the bed together with DPU and DAU.

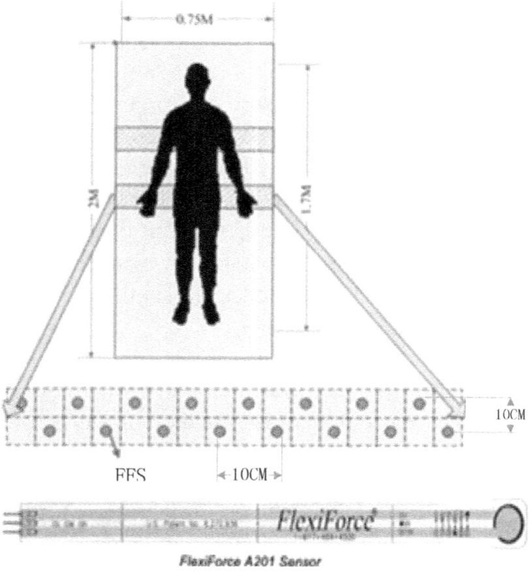

Fig. 2. The Deployment of FFS Matrix

4 Experiments Description

In this section, we will introduce the approach of collecting data from pressure sensors. In order to verify the usability of SDS, we selected 10 students (8 men, 2 women; ages 21 to 26 years) to participate in the study, whose body forms are very diverse.

As we known, the common possible sleep postures are left-lateral sleep (LLS), right-lateral sleep (RLS) and supine sleep (SS), prone sleep(PS), and from result of Reuters' research, the most unusual is flat on the stomach (just 6.5% of all sexes)[23]. So we first collected the sensors' data as follows: every subject slept on the SDS for 15 times in turn, and randomly lied in the LLS, RLS and SS for 5 times separately. Please note, the subjects' positions and respective gestures for sleep were not restricted, that is, they lied in the bed as they preferred. Although there are many subclasses of posture in real world, this paper is to report our primary work, and verify the reasonability of our solution.

When a subject sleeps on the SDS, there will be an event trigger for the Data Acquisition component, and the pressure value will be detected. To continuously monitor the user's sleeping procedure, the Data Acquisition component adopts the event-driven mechanism, and that is, when there is a posture transition, the pressure value will be updated in real-time.

After the experiments, 150 groups of raw data were obtained, and as mentioned in 3.1, the data was sent to MySQL database and the posture analysis module simultaneously. The format of row data can be seen in Fig.3, and the first is subject ID, the second is the data tag, the third is posture ID, and the next 32 are the real value of FFSs.

```
INSERT INTO `posture_rawdata` VALUES
(1,1202151858,1,182,182,182,188,188,182,188,200,572,188,277,200,176,176,182,182,211,199,2
05,211,199,199,205,211,533,199,1519,211,205,199,199,199);
INSERT INTO `posture_rawdata` VALUES
(1,1202151902,1,182,182,182,188,188,182,194,200,530,188,259,200,176,176,182,182,211,199,2
05,211,199,199,205,211,451,199,1507,211,205,199,199,199);
INSERT INTO `posture_rawdata` VALUES
(1,1202152002,0,182,182,182,188,188,188,188,430,1061,188,235,200,176,176,182,182,211,205,
205,217,199,199,205,217,1120,199,205,211,205,199,199,199);
INSERT INTO `posture_rawdata` VALUES
(1,1202152006,0,182,182,182,188,188,182,188,424,1214,188,194,200,176,176,182,182,211,199,
205,217,205,199,205,217,1202,199,205,211,205,199,199,199);
```

Fig. 3. Snapshot of Data-sheet from MySQL

5 Experiments Analysis and Pattern Recognition

5.1 Typical Three Postures Detection

To analyze the experimental data and detect the sleep postures, we adopt two classification methods to predict the sleep posture of a new observation based on the training sleep posture data set. The first one is Naïve Bayes. Since Naive Bayes classifier, which is a simple probabilistic classifier based on applying Bayes' theorem with attribute independence assumption [24], has worked quite well in many complex real-world situations, it is implemented on our data set. Meanwhile, since the sleep data set is a high-dimension data set, the different importance of dimensions may impact the result significantly. For this reason, we import the Random Forest method, which has advantage in estimating weight of dimensions and is suitable for high-dimension data set [25].

Two evaluated validations are involved into the analysis of the experimental results, 10-fold cross-validation and leave-one-out cross validation. In the 10-fold cross-validation, the sleep data set is randomly partitioned into 10 subsamples. In the 10 subsamples, one subsample is retained as the testing data, and the remaining 9 subsamples are used as training data. This cross-validation process is then repeated 10 times with each of the 10 subsamples used once as the test data. The predict accuracies of 10-fold cross-validation in the following tables are the average result of 10 tests from the folds. As the name suggests, leave-one-out involves using a single observation of the sleep data set as the test data, and the remaining observations as the training data. This is repeated such that each observation in the sample is used once as the validation data. The predict accuracy is the average predict result of 150 times tests.

As mentioned in section 4, the data set contains 150 observations belonging to 3 kinds of sleep postures, which are left-lateral sleep, right-lateral sleep and supine sleep. Before the data analysis, we have tried some typical pre-processes on the data set, for example, discretize, normalization, but the classification accuracy of the data set is decreased. Therefore, the classification methods are implemented on the raw data set. The results of two classification methods and two validation processes are list in the table below. The average value is the weighted average accuracy of LLS, SS and RLS. The SD represents the standard deviation.

Table 1. Predict Accuracy with Two Cross-Validations

	10-fold		Leave-one-out	
	Naïve Bayes	Random Forest	Naïve Bayes	Random Forest
LLS	0.6200	0.8600	0.6000	0.8800
SS	0.6600	0.8600	0.6800	0.8800
RLS	0.7600	0.8600	0.7800	0.8600
Average	0.6800	**0.8600**	0.6867	**0.8733**
SD	0.0721	**0.0000**	0.0902	**0.0115**

Comparing with 10-fold cross-validation, the leave-one-out cross-validation has more training observations than 10-fold, the predict accuracy of leave-one-out validation is slightly higher than 10-fold. The Average value of Table 1 also shows the Naïve Bayes and Random Forest both have a little improvement of predict accuracy on the leave-one-out validation test contrasting with the 10-fold.

We analyze the result in the leave-one-out validation. The Table 1 indicates that when we use the Random Forest as the classification method, it provides us almost 90% accuracy to predict the sleep postures, while the Naïve Bayes attains the accuracy about 69%. The Random Forest method performs over Naïve Bayes method in classifying this high-dimension data set. The table also indicates that the Random Forest method is a more stable method compared with Naïve Bayes. Since the SD value of Random Forest is smaller, it means the prediction accuracies of these three sleep postures have similar predict accuracies. While in the Naïve Bayes method, left-lateral sleep has the lowest predict accuracy 60%, while the highest predict accuracy is the right-lateral sleep 78%. Compared the results of these two methods, the Random Forest method has higher predict accuracy and attains more stable results than the Naïve Bayes method in our sleeping postures data set.

Table 2. Predict Accuracy of New Observations

Person Number	Number observation	Naïve Bayes	Random Forest
#1	52	0. 9038	0.8462
#6	44	0. 5454	0.7273
#7	123	0. 8292	0.8211
Average		0. 7900	**0.8082**
SD		0.1891	**0.0627**

We collect more sleep posture data to verify the validity of classification methods in predicting the sleep postures. Three subjects of the previous test (No.1, No.6, No.7) sleep on the bed all for one hour and sleep postures are collected for 52 times, 44 times and 123 times, in which all three sleep postures are contained. We implement 150 observations in the previous test as the training data set, and 219 observations of these three subjects are treated as test data. The characteristic of the test data and the detection accuracy are described in the Table 2. It shows two methods both obtain about 80% accuracy and Random Forest performs a little better than Naïve Bayes in this test data. When we compare the accuracies between different test subjects, the Random Forest method seems more stable than Naïve Bayes on different subjects, since the SD value of Random Forest is 0.0347, while the Naïve Bayes is 0.2046.

Table 3. Predict Accuracy of New Observations Based on Different Sleep Postures

Sleep Posture	Number observation	Naïve Bayes	Random Forest
LLS	51	0.5098	0.7647
SS	121	0.9091	0.8182
RLS	47	0.7872	0.8298
Average		0.7900	**0.8082**
SD		0.2046	**0.0347**

Then we summarize the results based on the sleep postures, LSS, SS and RLS. The number of three sleep postures and the summary prediction results are illustrated in Table 3. It indicates that the Naïve Bayes performs the best on SS sleep posture prediction about 90% accuracy and worst on LSS about 51%, while the Random Forest is also more stable on different postures detection with smaller SD value.

5.2 Five Postures Detection

In the previous section, we have implemented and analysis the Naïve Bayes and Random Forest method on three typical postures prediction. In order to confirm the effective of these two methods, we use them on data sets with more postures, which include prone sleep (PS) and getting up (GU) in addition. We collect two data sets, and the first one (Dataset1) is composited by 269 observations of three subjects, and another one (Dataset2) is with 269 observations of ten subjects. Two validations are applied as the test in the previous section. The prediction results are list in the following two tables.

Table 4. Prediction Accuracy of Dataset1

	10-fold		Leave-one-out	
	Naïve Bayes	Random Forest	Naïve Bayes	Random Forest
LLS	1.0000	0.9804	1.0000	0.9804
SS	0.9835	0.9917	0.9835	0.9917
RLS	0.8085	1.0000	0.8298	1.0000
PS	0.9545	0.9545	0.9545	0.9818
GU	0.0000	1.0000	0.0000	1.0000
Average	0.9294	**0.9851**	0.9331	**0.9814**
SD	0.4257	**0.0190**	0.4265	**0.0095**

Table 5. Prediction Accuracy of Dataset2

	10-fold		Leave-one-out	
	Naïve Bayes	Random Forest	Naïve Bayes	Random Forest
LLS	0.4752	0.8515	0.5050	0.8416
SS	0.6959	0.8713	0.6959	0.8713
RLS	0.8041	0.8351	0.7938	0.8454
PS	0.9773	0.9318	0.9773	0.9545
GU	0.0000	1.0000	0.0000	1.0000
Average	0.6874	**0.8663**	0.6921	**0.8687**
SD	0.3769	**0.0678**	0.3735	**0.0710**

Comparing with the two results, Naïve Bayes attains not bad prediction results of the data set with 3 subjects as seen in the Table 4. When the number of subjects increases from 3 to 10, we can see the prediction accuracy decreases greatly from 93% to 69%. Concurrently, the prediction accuracy of Random Forest also decreases, but it is less the decrease of Naïve Bayes.

Although the SD value of Naïve Bayes decreases and the SD value of Random Forest is increasing, when the number of subjects is increasing. The SD value of Random Forest is still much smaller than the SD value of Naïve Bayes. The result also indicates that the Random Forest method is more stable than Naïve Bayes.

There are just 6 observations of "getting up" posture. While the Naïve Bayes predicts them as prone sleep by mistake, the Random Forest correctly detected them all in our test. The Random Forest method seems more sensitive in dealing with the detection of small class.

5.3 Sleep and Turn-Over Patterns of One Subject

In this section, we collect sleep posture data set of one subject and analysis the sleep posture and turn over pattern of him. One person is treated as our test subject and we monitor his sleep behaviors in the bed with pressure sensor device for a relatively long time (e.g. one week). Since we implement the random forest method and use some data of this subject as training, the predict accuracy attains about 98% of this subject. Then, the time lengths and distributions of different sleep postures are collected. At the meanwhile, the time length and probability of different turn-over are attained and analysis in this section.

The following Table 6 is a part of sensor pressure data set collected in one night. The first column is the time when the sensor value is recorded. The S.1 to S.30 columns are the pressure values of the sensor 1 to sensor 30 in one record. The last column is the predicted sleep posture of this subject based on random forest method.

Table 6. Part of Sensor Pressure Data

Data-Time	S.1	S.2	S.3	...	S.8	S.9	S.10	...	S.30	Posture
100322234011	342	353	530	...	347	365	412	...	275	SS
100322234023	271	318	471	...	330	342	365	...	258	SS
100322234031	206	200	212	...	230	247	241	...	234	LLS
100322234103	206	200	212	...	601	241	235	...	234	LLS
100322234145	206	200	212	...	601	241	235	...	234	LLS
100322234357	206	200	212	...	648	454	224	...	234	PS
100322234406	212	206	224	...	843	235	230	...	240	RLS
100322234439	206	206	218	...	831	235	224	...	240	RLS
100322234441	206	206	212	...	837	235	224	...	240	RLS
100322234445	200	200	206	...	218	230	224	...	234	GetUP
...	...	...	...	...	...	...	...	...	...	...

From this time series data sets, we can calculate the time length of different sleep postures besides the Get up posture. The time length distributions of different sleep postures are demonstrated in following Fig.4. It indicates that RLS and SS is the major sleep posture of this subject, then is the LLS. The PS is the rare one among them.

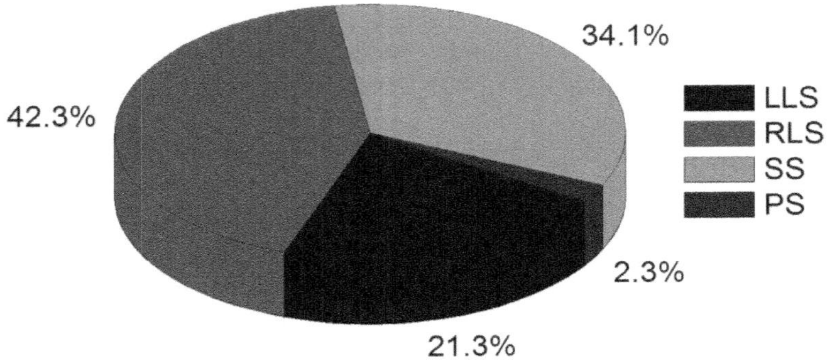

Fig. 4. Time Length Distribution of Different Postures

Now, we turn to analysis the turn-over action of this subject. Theoretical, there are eight kinds of different turn-over. In order to obtain the distribution of them, we simplify the time series data set of sleep posture firstly. When we remove the time factor in the above time series data, the data is simplified illustrated by the stream of different sleep postures. The same posture detected continually is used just one to represent it. For example, there are three continual LLS sleep posture in Table 6; just one of them is saved. The time series of sleep posture of Table 6 can be transferred to be the summarized one in the following Fig.5.

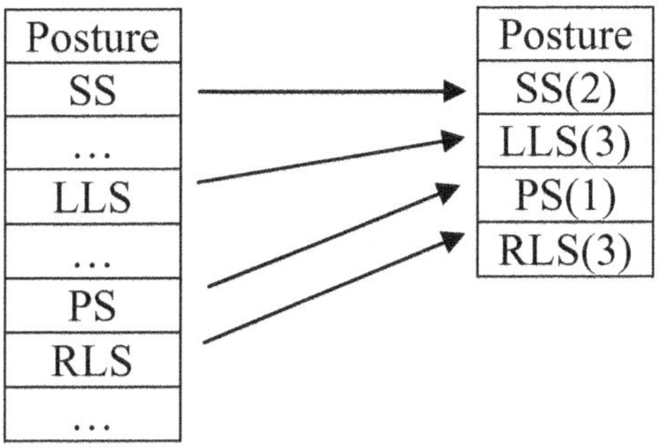

Fig. 5. Summarization of Different Postures

While the Get Up action is not taken into consideration, 4 different turn-over status can be obtained from the above table. They are SS->LLS, LLS->PS and PS->RLS. Collecting all the times of different turn-over, the different probabilities of eight turn over can be attained and denoted in the following Fig. 6.

It indicates the SS->LLS and LLS->SS are with the highest probabilities in all eight turn-over, and then is the RLS->SS followed by SS->RLS. The PS->RLS and LLS->PS are the rare turn-over of this subject. In addition, the PS->LLS and RLS->PS are never happened turn over action in data set of this subject.

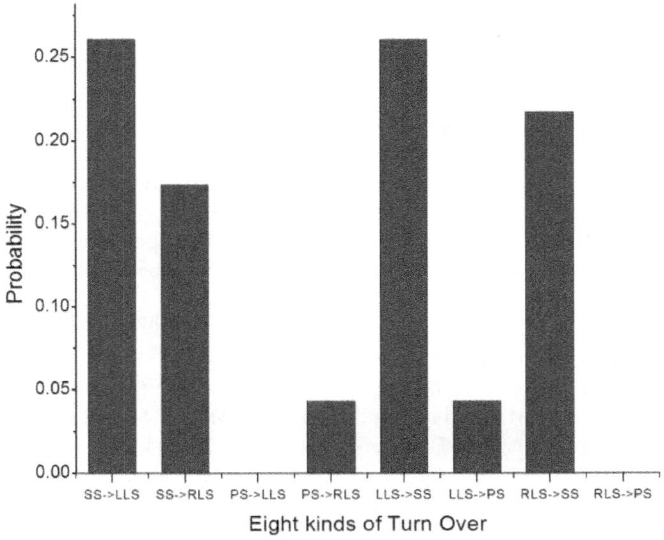

Fig. 6. The Probabilities of Eight Kinds of Turn-Over

Based on the normal sleep pattern of one subject, we can analysis the dynamic sleep posture and the anomaly sleep posture of this subject in our future work.

6 Conclusions and Future Work

This paper proposed an unobtrusive sleep pattern recognition system based on a kind of ultra-thin pressure sensor matrix. We presented the design of sensors deployment and the implementation of the sleep behaviors detection system. Moreover, based on the experiments, we discussed the data analysis and evaluation of the system and the result proved that the proposed solution is a promising way to monitor the elder's sleep postures and recognize his sleep pattern. In the near future, we will detect more specific postures in order for accurate sleep pattern recognition. Concurrently, the detection of the abnormal behaviors in bed will be another interesting direction and we also plan to invite some elders to evaluate the real benefice of the system.

Acknowledgment. This work is being supported by the Fond Nature of Technologies, MELS Program, Quebec, Canada, and partially supported by the National High Technology Research and Development Program of China under Grant No. 2009AA011903.

References

1. Foley, D.J., Monjan, A.A., Brown, S.L., et al.: Sleep complaints among elderly persons: an epidemiologic study of three communities. Sleep 18(6), 425–432 (1995)
2. Foley, D., Ancoli-Israel, S., Britz, P., Walsh, J.: Sleep disturbances and chronic disease in older adults: results of the 2003 National Sleep Foundation Sleep in America Survey. J. Psychosom. Res. 56, 497–502 (2004)

3. Aaronson, S.T., Rashed, S., Biber, M.P., Hobson, J.A.: Brain state and body posture: a time-lapse video study of sleep. Arch. Gen. Psychiatry 39, 330–335 (1982)
4. Muzet, A.: Dynamics of Body Movements in Normal Sleep. Presented at Eighth European Congress on Sleep Research, Szeged, Hungary (1986)
5. Aaronson, S.T., Rashed, S., Biber, M.P., Hobson, A.: Brain State and Body Posture. Archives of General Psychiatry 39, 330–335 (1982)
6. Wilde-Frenz, J., Schulz, H.: Rate and Distribution of Body Movements during Sleep in Humans. Perceptual and Motor Skills 56, 275–283 (1983)
7. Cheng, C.M., Hsu, Y.L., Young, C.M., Wu, C.H.: Development of a portable device for tele-monitoring of snoring and OSAS symptoms. In: Telemed e-Health 2008, vol. 14, pp. 55–68 (2008)
8. Wilde-Frenz, J., Schulz, H.: Rate and Distribution of Body Movements during Sleep in Humans. Perceptual and Motor Skills 56, 275–283 (1983)
9. Tuisku, K., Holi, M.M., Wahlbeck, K., Ahlgren, A.J., Lauerma, H.: Quantitative Rest Activity in Ambulatory Monitoring as a Physiological Marker of Restless Legs Syndrome: A Controlled Study. Movement Disorders 18, 442–448 (2002)
10. Shneerson, J.M., Smith, I.E.: The Validation of a New Actigraphy System for the Measurement of Period Leg Movements in Sleep. Sleep Medicine 6, 507–513 (2005)
11. Tryon, W.W.: Issues of Validity in Actigraphic Sleep Assessment. Sleep 27, 158–165 (2004)
12. Prill, T., Fahrenberg, J.: Simultaneous Assessment of Posture and Limb Movements (e.g., periodic leg movements) with Calibrated Multiple Accelerometry. Physiological Measurement, 47–53 (2007)
13. Occhiuzzi, C., Marrocco, G.: RFID Technology for the Neuroscience: Feasibility of Sleep Disease Monitoring. In: Proceedings of EuCAP 2009, Berlin (2009)
14. Tamura, T., Zhou, J., Mizukami, H., Togawa, T.: A System for Monitoring Temperature Distribution in Bed and Its Application to the Assessment of Body Movement. Physiological Measurements 14, 33–41 (1993)
15. Kaartinen, J., Kuhlman, I., Peura, P.: Long-term Monitoring of Movements in Bed and Their Relation to Subjective Sleep Quality. Sleep and Hypnosis 5(3), 145–153 (2003)
16. Rauhala, E., Erkinjuntti, M., Polo, O.: Detection of Periodic Leg Movements with a Static-Charge-Sensitive Bed. Journal of Sleep Research 5, 246–250 (1996)
17. Van der Loos, H.F.M., Ullrich, N., Kobayashi, H.E.R.: Development of sensate and robotic bed technologies for vital signs monitoring and sleep quality improvement. Autonomous Robots 15(1), 67–79 (2003)
18. Tamura, T., Nishigaichi, A., Nomura, T.: Monitoring of body movement during sleep in bed. In: Proceedings of the Annual International Conference of the IEEE Engineering in Medicine and Biology Society, pp. 1483–1484 (1992)
19. Kimura, H., Kobayashi, H., Kawabata, K., Van der Loos, H.F.: Development of an unobtrusive vital signs detection system using conductive fiber sensors. In: Proceedings 2004 IEEE/RSJ International Conference on Intelligent Robots and Systems, pp. 307–312 (2004)
20. Adami, A.M., Hayes, T.L., Pavel, M., Singer, C.M.: Detection and classification of movements in bed using load cells. In: IEEE 27th Annual International Conference of the Engineering in Medicine and Biology Society, pp. 589–592 (2005)
21. The website of Tekscan Int., `http://www.tekscan.com/flexiforce/flexiforce.html`
22. Simonceli, L., Bittar, R.S.M., Greters, M.E.: Posture restrictions do not interfere in the results of canalith repostureing maneuver. Braz. J. Otorhinolaryngol. 71, 55–59 (2005)

23. `http://maisonbisson.com/blog/post/10182/claim-sleep-position-personality/`
24. John, G.H., Langley, P.: Estimating Continuous Distributions in Bayesian Classifiers. In: Proceedings of the Eleventh Conference on Uncertainty in Artificial Intelligence, San Mateo, pp. 338–345 (1995)
25. Breiman, L.: Random Forests. Machine Learning 45(1), 5–32 (2001)

The Making of a Dataset for Smart Spaces

Eunju Kim, Sumi Helal, Jaewoong Lee, and Shantonu Hossain

Mobile and Pervasive Computing Laboratory,
The Department of Computer and Information Science and Engineering
University of Florida
{ejkim,helal,jwlee,shossain}@cise.ufl.edu

Abstract. In this paper we propose a two-phase methodology for designing datasets that can be used to test and evaluate activity recognition algorithms. The trade offs between time, cost and recognition performance is one challenge. The effectiveness of a dataset, which contrasts the incremental performance gain with the increase in time, efforts, and number and cost of sensors is another challenging area that is often overlooked. Our proposed methodology is iterative and adaptive and addresses issues of sensor use modality and its effect on overall performance. We present our methodology and provide an assessment for its effectiveness using both a simulation model and a real world deployment.

Keywords: Activity Dataset, Activity Dataset Design, Activity Recognition, Pervasive Space Simulation.

1 Introduction

Activity recognition technology is critical to many human-centric ubiquitous applications. Activity models, activity recognition algorithms, and activity recognition sensor platforms are active areas of research [1][4][5][6][8][10]. Experiments are necessary for validating novel ideas and collecting comprehensive datasets. Furthermore, a variety of experimental setups are required due to the diversity in human activities. However, building an experimental environment that closely mimics real-world applications requires significant effort and cost. As a solution, many research groups have shared their activity datasets [4][5][6][7][10]. However, since sensor technology is rapidly evolving, researchers often need to upgrade or replace an existing activity dataset. This demands new and efficient methods to create activity data. Yet, so far there has been little research done on effective creation of activity dataset using minimal cost, effort and time. In this paper, we propose a methodology for creating effective activity datasets using lesser resources compared to existing methods.

1.1 Motivation

Our motivation is developing processes and tools to create highly effective activity datasets. We observe that activity datasets, even in the same domain, may considerably

Z. Yu et al. (Eds.): UIC 2010, LNCS 6406, pp. 110–124, 2010.

differ due to the number of sensors, sensor types, and the way the sensors are used (sensor use modality). This variety implies that collecting an effective dataset requires solving several problems.

First of all, using more sensors may trade-off cost for achieving higher activity recognition performance. For example, if we use many sensors, it may be better to detect an activity. However, it is also more expensive. Therefore, it is necessary to find an effective number of sensors.

Secondly, finding the proper type of sensors is crucial to generate an effective dataset. For instance, although a sound sensor can be used to recognize *eating* activity, other type of sensors such as RFID or camera sensors may produce more accurate data to detect the *eating* activity when there is noise because people watch television while eating food.

Lastly, the effectiveness of a dataset can be achieved by a modality analysis of sensors such as install location (wearable, environment), size, and other constraints. In other words, sensor should be carefully fitted (and sometimes, conditioned) to best suite the intended purpose. For example, if we plan to install pressure sensors on a bed to detect a sleeping activity, we should carefully analyze and find the most appropriate location on bed and we should adjust the operational range of the sensor to better detect the weight of a person (e.g., use appropriate resistor to shift range of sensitivity).

As shown above, it is important to determine the effective number of sensors, type, and usage modality to accurately detect the target activity and to collect high quality corresponding datasets. Therefore, it is essential to develop a new methodology which allows discovering the most serious erroneous flows during the design phase, leaving only little errors and adjustments to be dealt with before actual deployment.

1.2 Proposed Approach

As a solution to the aforementioned problem, we propose a two phase activity dataset design approach. Our approach is composed of three steps: activity design, simulation, real-world instrumentation. Instead of building a real sensor setup immediately after activity design, we have a simulation step in the middle of the process. This approach has several advantages. First of all, it can help in discovering and selecting a most effective sensor set for a specific purpose. In many cases, the sensor setup relies on the knowledge and intuition of the researcher. If too few or too many sensors are used, the quality and effectiveness of the dataset could be questioned. By performing simulation, this risk will be reduced. Secondly, our approach can save time and cost since all investigations are performed in a tightly controlled environment. Finally, the activity dataset produced by our approach can be utilized as a standard dataset to verify the activity model under investigation along with its activity recognition algorithms.

The rest of this paper is organized as follows. In section 2, we will describe several related works. The proposed approach is explained in section 3. The experiments and results are discussed in section 4. Finally, section 5 concludes the paper.

2 Related Work

We will talk about experimentally obtained activity recognition dataset in real world and simulation based activity dataset.

2.1 Real-World Activity Recognition Datasets

Activity recognition datasets have been collected by several research groups. MIT provides three datasets called PLIA1 (PlaceLab Intensive Activity Dataset1), PLIA2, and PL Couple (PlaceLab Couple) [4][5][6]. In PLIA1, the researchers built a real experimental environment in a 1000 sq. ft. apartment and installed approximately 214 sensors such as temperature, humidity light, pressure, current, water and gas flow, object, accelerometer, camera, and microphone sensors [4]. They performed a set of common household activities during 4-hour period and collected sensor data of 89 activities [4]. In PLIA2, they introduced a portable wireless sensor platform named MITes [5]. The MITes platform includes five types of wearable sensors such as accelerometers, heart rate, ultra violet radiation exposure, an RFID reader in a wristband form factor, and location beacons [5]. It also includes six environmental sensor types such as light, temperature, switch, object, proximity, and current [5]. This PlaceLab dataset2 was recorded with a volunteer. He performed a set of common household activities during the four-hour period using a set of instructions [5]. The third dataset, PLCouple1, consisted of 100 hours of annotated data from a couple who lived in the PlaceLab [6]. This experiment is performed for 15 days with 900 sensor inputs including wired sensors, motion-detection sensors, and RFID tag.

Artificial Intelligence Laboratory, Washington State University provides several activity datasets for single resident and multiple-residents. The datasets are further specialized into normal activity, abnormal activity, interwoven activity respectively [7][8]. Human subjects lived in the laboratory-built smart apartment and the smart workplace [7]. The smart apartment had three bedrooms, a bathroom, a kitchen, and a living/dining room. Custom-built analog sensors were installed to monitor motion, water, burner, telephone, and item use. The smart workplace is a lab which is organized into four cubicles, a server area, a postdoc office, a meeting room, a lounge, and a kitchen. Motion sensor, power line controllers, and magnetic open/close sensors are installed in the space. This is used to recognize social interaction activities among people in the lab such as apart, coming, going, or joint together [7][8].

University of Amsterdam provides real world activities of daily living dataset (ADL) [10]. This data set records ADL performed by a 26-year-old man living in a three-bedroom apartment [10]. The researchers installed 14 state-change sensors in the house. Data has been recorded for 24 days. Sensors are installed in several places in the apartment including doors, cup-boards, refrigerator, and toilet flush.

The main focus of collecting datasets has been to closely represent actual activities in real environments. For instance, the PLIA datasets and University of Amsterdam dataset tried to overcome the limitations imposed by laboratory environments [4][10]. Washington State University dataset collected multiple residents and interwoven datasets because they better represent real-world situations [8]. Hence, these datasets are a step toward realizing real-world applications. Our research takes activity recognition a step forward by generating effective datasets. Collecting activity datasets requires not only high cost but also time and effort. Datasets having the same domain may differ due to different sensor types and numbers. Some sensors may be redundant while in some cases the number of sensors may be insufficient.

2.2 Simulation Based Activity Datasets

Useful sensory data from real world deployments of pervasive spaces is very scarce. This is due to the significant cost, and elaborate groundwork needed to create actual spaces. Given the aforementioned challenges, simulation is a promising and sensible alternative in practical ways to experiment with human activities in pervasive spaces. Simulation enables researchers to create focused synthetic replications of important events and activities under study. It can be easily changed and refined allowing the researchers to experiment, analyze and fine-tune their models and associated algorithms. Also, a simulation model that mimics an existing real world is most likely to answer more questions (generate much more data) than the actual space. This early stage simulation can help researchers evaluate their ideas and algorithms quickly and with reasonable accuracy [11].

There have been several approaches to introduce the simulation concepts and algorithms and to develop the simulating tools. SENSORIA [13], is a simulator focusing on traffic generation, energy consumption and inherent protocols of wireless sensor network (WSN). In [19], a detailed simulation model was presented which also focuses on accurate model for battery, processor power consumption and in network traffic. In [16], Discrete-Event system Specification (DEVS) was proposed to define asynchronous discrete-events to be simulated. Since these approaches suggest modeling simulation events occurring in WSN environment, routing and communication becomes non-trivial factors for them. However, the events and environments they are modeling could not be available to simulate human activities. They have lacks of specific and complex labeling which is necessary to describe human activities performed in pervasive environment.

DiaSim [15] simulator executes pervasive computing applications by creating an emulation layer and developing simulation logic using a programming framework. It describes a pervasive computing environment in terms of stimulus procedures (any change in the environment that can be consumed by sensors) and simulated services (sensors and actuators) in a specification language called DiaSpec. However, DiaSim simulates applications such as fire situations, intrusions, etc. to identify potential conflicts. It does not care much for human activities performed in pervasive spaces.

The human activities can be simulated through Persim [14][17] developed at University of Florida. It allows researchers to fine-tune simulation models until his/her satisfaction. Because costs in establishing a virtual pervasive space and simulating it are very low, researchers can design what they want to establish. However, these models and designs might not be realistic in terms of possibility that the designed spaces could be existed. In order to get much more reasonable yet still accurate simulation mode and its dataset, this paper proposes a heuristic way to design an effective space through fine-tuning experiments.

3 Two Phase Dataset Design Approach

We developed a two phase approach for activity dataset design as shown in Fig. 1. Phase 1 is concerned with generating activity dataset using simulation after activity design. The purpose of the activity design is looking at the nature of human activities and matching the activities with the most suitable sensor technology, and finding the specific use modalities that boost the effectiveness and the contributions of the sensor to the target activity. The activity design is followed by generation of activity dataset through simulation. Phase 1 goes through multiple iterations until the target dataset achieves high recognition performance. Once this is accomplished, we move to phase 2 in which we implement the actual sensor instrumentation and collect actual activity data in the real sensor environment. This real world activity dataset would be more effective and accurate compared to that of a single phase activity dataset.

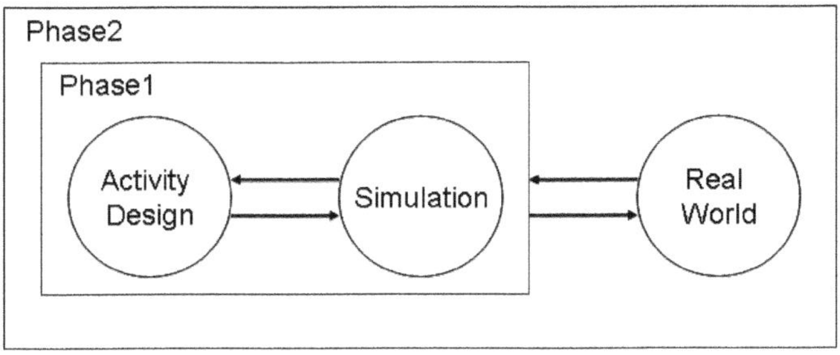

Fig. 1. Two phases activity dataset collection process

3.1 Activity Design

Designing activities is a detailed step in the making of a dataset. It consists of four sub-steps: Generic Activity Model Design, Selection of Target Activities, Functional Instrumentation, and Modality Analysis. We describe each of these sub-steps in the following sub-sections.

3.1.1 Generic Activity Model Design

A well-defined activity model is very important because other steps are directly influenced (limited or empowered) by the activity model. In [1], we proposed a generic multi-layer activity model that is shown in Fig. 2. The generic model was intended to provide clear separation between the sensors layer (observation sub-system) and the rest of the activity model (any model). The goal of this separation is to enable a more scalable approach to try and error research in which researchers are empowered to explore varieties of sensors until they arrive at the most "effective" sensor set. In this paper, we instantiate this generic model based on the activity design on hand. A brief description of each layer of the generic model is shown below. More detailed description is in [1].

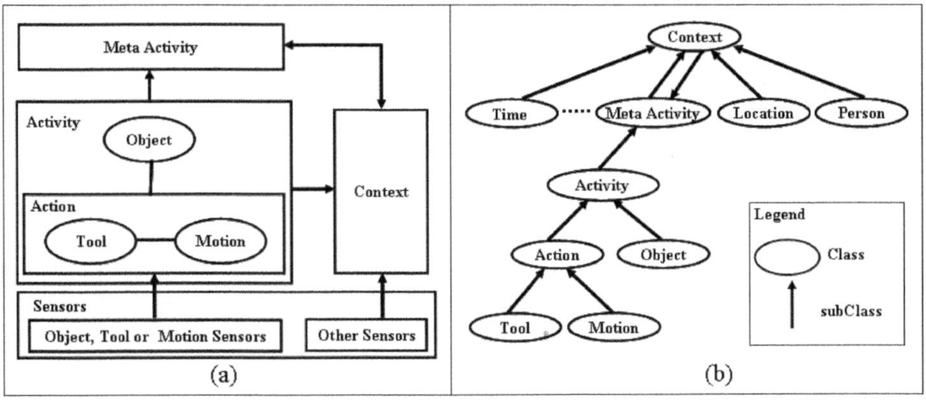

Fig. 2. Generic Activity Model, (a) block diagram of activity model (b) class hierarchy for activity ontology

Sensors. These are the installed sensors in the pervasive space (e.g. smart home). Sensor data is classified into four types: motion, tool, object, and context sensor data. Motion sensors measure movements of people such as raising an arm, turning the body, or folding legs. Both tool and object sensor data come from sensors attached to the artifacts. An artifact can be both a tool and an object since the same item may be used as a tool or an object. For example, spoons, forks and dishes are tools for *eating* but they are objects of *dish washing*. Therefore, it is important to distinguish between tools and objects to avoid misinterpretation of activities. For example, *washing a spoon* may be incorrectly interpreted as an *eating* activity.

Action. Action is a combination of tools and motion. For example, a *cutting* action is composed of hand motions and a knife [1].

Activity. Activity is a collection of combination of actions and objects. Activities may involve multiple actions that occur in a certain order. For example, "eating" activity is collection of actions such as *cutting, picking*, or *chewing*.

Meta activity. A meta activity contains several activities which are related to each other. For example, a meta activity *Having a meal* is collection of *eating* and *drinking* activities performed by same user at similar times.

Context. Context is the information used to determine the situation where an activity is performed [1]. Time, location, and temperature are contextual information.

3.1.2 Selection of the Target Activity

We need to decide the domain of activities. Activity domain is classified in many ways such as home, office, school, or kindergarten. For example, if we want to collect daily living activities at a home of an elderly person, then there would be several activities such as sleeping, eating, cooking, and etc [3]. Among all activities, we need to choose a subset and define the meta activities, activities, and actions according to our generic activity model.

3.1.3 Functional Instrumentation

After selecting the target activities, we need to find which information needs to be sensed. For example, for *eating* activity, there are many types of information such as eating sound, eating motion, the amount of food consumed, location of user. However, collecting all those information may not be necessary. Therefore; we should choose an effective combination of this information. After we determine the information to sense, we need to decide proper sensors according to its function. For instance, there are acoustic sensors for detecting sound and several types of motion sensors for sensing human motions. However, there will always be information that no available sensor can support. For instance, detecting nutrition information the elderly take is very helpful in tracking their health status. However, it may not be easy to find suitable sensors that can sense such nutrition information. Therefore, only effective and synergistic sets of information and sensors are chosen in this step.

3.1.4 Modality Analysis

Once we decide upon the information to be detected and sensors to be used, we should find how to utilize sensors to acquire information most effectively. This is a question of modality of use of the sensor. Modalities include the number of sensors to use, the way a sensor is worn or the location it is placed at, the feasibility of sensors such as size or performance. All such relevant modalities are analyzed in this step. For example, if *eating* is a target activity and if we want to detect *eating* motion, motion sensor will be chosen. If there is a very small motion sensor, *eating* activity can be detected by the motion sensors installed in spoon or fork. Otherwise, residents may need to wear motion sensor on their arm or hand, which is obviously a great inconvenience and therefore must be avoided. Also, the spoon and fork will need to be washed. So the sensors should be durable to withstand a wash cycle. Otherwise, alternative ways to detect the same activities must be explored. Hence, modality analysis is indeed very important in addressing all above issues.

3.1.5 Sample Design

We designed target activities based on a scenario in which Mrs. Smith, an 87 years old woman, lives alone in a smart house [3]. A detailed analysis of her daily life reveals 11 meta activities and 31 activities which we casted into our generic activity model as shown in Table 1.

Table 1. Meta activities, Activities, and Actions of Mrs. Smith's scenario

Meta Activity	Activity	Action
Rest	Sleeping, Relaxing	Lying down, Getup
Having a meal	Eating, Drinking	Cutting, Picking, Scooping, Serving, Lifting a cup
Getting out	Leaving & Arriving home	Open front door, Close front door, Standing on a door mat.

In the Functional Instrumentation step, we decided on information and sensors consistent with Table 1. The information for *sleeping* or *relaxing* activity recognition is pressure and vibration level of bed or sofa. For *eating* and *drinking* activity, usage of *eating* and *drinking* tools such as spoon, fork, knife, plate, or cup are chosen. To recognize the leaving and arriving activity, door status or the pressure of door mats (on both sides) will be used. Table 2 shows an example of the specific outcome of this step for *sleeping* and *eating* activity.

Table 2. Example of Activity and Sensor Designs for *sleeping* and *eating* activities

MetaActivity - Activity (Location)	Actions	Information & Modality (Possible place to install sensors)	Sensor (number of sensors)
Rest - Sleeping (Bedroom)	• Lying-down • Getup	• Pressure of mattress - Below a mattress • Vibration of mattress - Top of a mattress	• Vibration sensor (1) -Phidgets 1104 Vibration Sensor [9] • Force sensor sensor (1) -Phidgets 3102 8" FlexiForce sensor 0-100lb. Resistive Force sensor [9]
Having a meal - Eating (Dining room)	• Cutting • Picking • Scooping	• Usage of eating tools - Spoon, Fork, Knife	• RFID Reader (1) -Phidgets 1023 RFID reader [9] • RFID Tag (2) - Phidgets 3007 RFID tags [9]
	• Serving	• Weight of food - Below a dining mat - Dish or Bowl	• Pressure sensor -Phidgets 3105 Interlink Electronics 1.5" Square FSR [9]

In modality analysis, we analyzed the sensor technology available in the market and choose the most synergetic sensors that fit the target activities. Table 3 presents an example of sensor deployment for eating activity based on the modality analysis.

Table 3. Example of Modality Analysis for *eati*ng activity

Activities	Infrastructure Requirement	
Eating	• Integration Equipments - Phidget 1070 [9], Phidget SBC [9] or Portable device for networking (eg. Smart phone) • Integration Schema 	Modality Justification: 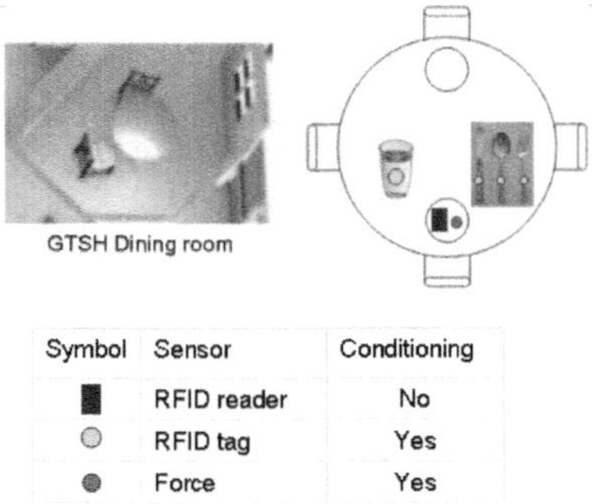

3.2 Activity Simulation

Now we move into the simulation step in Phase 1. The Persim simulator [14], which is an event-driven, human activity simulator was used. Persim is capable of capturing the physical elements of a space including its sensors, actuators and human activities. Persim users typically build a simulation "project" over multiple sessions before they are ready to generate data or make a multitude of changes to the sensory elements, the activities or even the structure of the output dataset. Data generated by Persim follows the Sensory Dataset Description Language (SDDL) proposed standard. This allows users to start a simulation project by uploading a dataset originally generated by another user (through Persim), modifying the design and fine-tuning the experiments to achieve a specific research-goal.

One powerful feature of Persim is its ability to weave simulated events into actual events in datasets represented in SDDL. This feature empowers the owner or any other user of an actual dataset to go back in time and explore slight variation in the actual space without actually repeating the experiments or collecting additional sensor data. Thus the simulator is intended to open a new dimension of collaborative research in the area of human activity recognition and other simulator applications.

3.2.1 Scenario-Based Simulation

In order to simulate activities, Persim needs a scenario which describes the target activities. The scenario includes where the activities happen and how they occur. Hence how well and how realistic the scenario is defined is the main key in obtaining meaningful simulation results. Daily activities in the morning could be one of the examples of scenarios. In the morning a human usually gets up, jogs, and then has breakfast. These activities occur in the bedroom, outside of the house and in the dining room. The sensors and RFIDs which are deployed or attached on objects in the areas generate data when they detect moves related to the activities.

3.2.2 Mapping Scenario to Simulation

There are four essential steps to map scenario to simulation. First, a space and its various areas are designed to create higher level of realism through the use of space templates such as single family home, apartment, etc. In the second step, sensor/actuator components provide sensors and actuators to be deployed in the designed space. Following the scenario, sensors and actuators are located at proper positions with the correct attributes such as the type of sensor, sensor event generator, and domain value generator. Note that these attributes also can be edited to get fine result of simulation. Thirdly, activities and actuation rules are added. Activities rules are defined with their own name and include behaviors such as walking from an area to another area or object interactions such as grabbing a spoon. Actuation rules specify the logic of the actuation based on sensor events and in terms of invoking actuator(s). In the fourth step, the user prescribes two important mappings: activities-to-sensors mapping. The former mapping specifies which sensors are relevant to the detection of each activity. For easy and convenient mapping, Persim provides a mapping table, shown Fig. 3.

In the latter mapping, each actuator is mapped twice, once to the set of sensors that could trigger it, and once again by the set of sensors that could be affected by the actuator when triggered. Persim also has a mapping table for sensors and actuators.

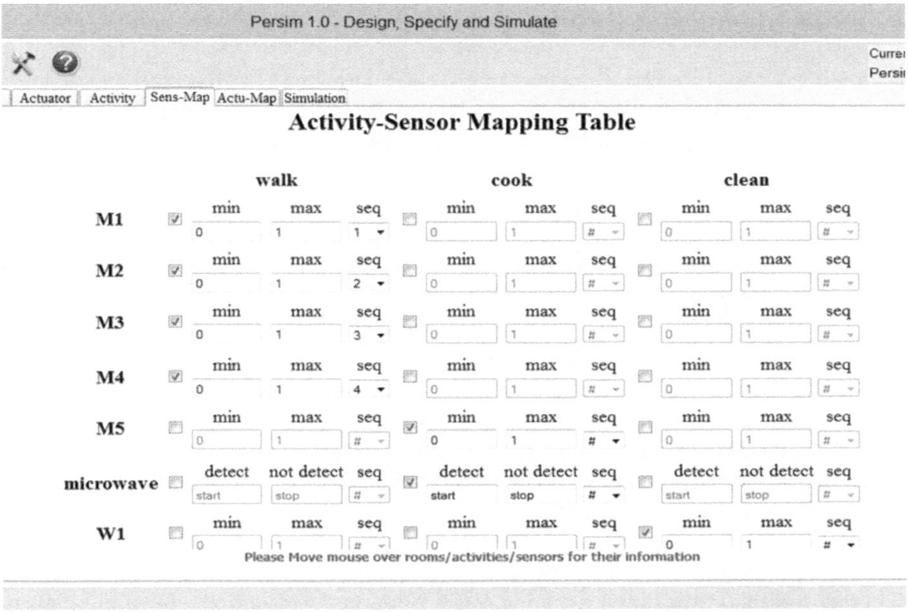

Fig. 3. Activity-sensor mapping table

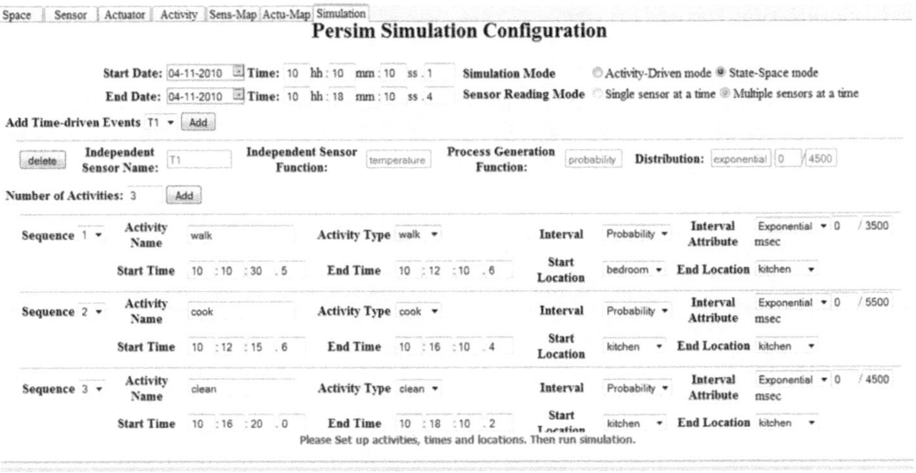

Fig. 4. Persim simulation configuration

In the last step, a user finalizes simulation configuration with proper parameters such as simulation time and process generating intervals. Fig. 4 shows the simulation configuration table. Finally, Persim is ready to simulate activities as defined in the scenario. Note that the user may repeatedly go over these five steps to make changes or fine-tune the simulation.

4 Experiments and Results

We validated our two phase dataset approach in terms of effectiveness and accuracy of the generated dataset through the experimentations. We performed both simulation and real sensor deployment/data collection. First, we designed a simulation model (e.g. parameters) of two designed activities. Next, we simulated the two activities with respect to the model and generated datasets. Then, we instrumented a space with real sensor configuration and collected sensor data of the performed activity. We compared the effectiveness and performance of the two datasets using an activity recognition algorithm/system.

If the effectiveness and accuracy of the simulation dataset are comparable to the real sensor dataset, we conclude that the two-phase dataset design approach is useful. To illustrate, in terms of effectiveness, both the simulation and real sensor dataset should have similar results because the simulation should be helpful to determine the most effective sensor set. However, the accuracy of the simulation dataset could be higher than real sensor dataset because certain unexpected situations that occur in real-world are not accounted for in the simulation model. For example, if we want to collect sleeping activity data for 20 minutes, simulation data will include sleeping activity data for this time. But real sensor dataset can miss some part of the activity data due to sensor noise and network delay. Section 4.1 describes the simulation parameters, and Section 4.2 provides experimental data collected from the real sensors along with a comparison with the simulation results.

4.1 Simulation Based Dataset

We considered five morning activities performed daily, which are: sleeping, getting out through a door, getting in through a door, relaxing on a couch and having breakfast. In each activity, we deployed three types of sensors – vibration sensor, force sensor, and RFID tags as shown in Table 4.

Table 4. Sensors and RFID tags for each activity

Activity	Vibration Sensor	Force Sensor	RFID Tags
Sleeping	V01, V02, V03	F01, F02	
Getting out/in		F03, F04	RFID_Door01
Relaxing	V04, V05, V06		
Eating		F05	RFID_Fork 01 & 02 RFID_Knife 01& 02 RFID_Spoon 01& 02

Table 4 provides a labeled list of all the sensors used in the simulation experiments. Since our goal is to determine the effective types and numbers of sensors, we considered several possible sensor combinations. In this experiment, all sensors have uniform distribution with 0 mean and a variance of 1. RFID tags generate only 0 or 1 values (1 when a tag is detected).

Table 5 shows simulation results for the *sleeping* activity. This activity is split into two actions: *Lying down* and *getting up*. Since *Lying down* is at most associated with 1 force sensor (F01) and 3 vibration sensors, we test 3 cases. Another force sensor, F02 detects a movement when a human subject gets up and puts his/her foot on the carpet that is attached to the sensor. Hence this sensor is used in every single case. The right-most column of Table 5 presents the simulation accuracy based on the activity recognition algorithm described previously. The algorithm [1] slices simulated events in a unit time (1 minute) so that the number of time slots the test case has been simulated can be determined. Then the algorithm can show how many time slots might be recognized among them. Therefore, their ratio, shown in the right-most column, indicates how many unit events are generated in a time window slot.

In these simulation experiments, we assume that the sensors for case 2 are deployed between the positions of sensors for case 3. Therefore sensors at the edges in case 3 might have greater distance between each other. We think it will reduce the probability of detecting *vibration on the bed*, and eventually the number of the recognized time slots is slightly less than the one in case 2. Hence, we might see that case 2 indicates higher efficiency than case 3, even though it has less vibration sensors than case 3. Also, case 2 will be efficient in terms of cost of devices.

Table 5. The *sleeping* activity simulation cases

Case #	Number of Vibration Sensors	Number of Force Sensors	Number of Detections	Number of 1 min. Slots	Number of Activities Recognized	Accuracy
1	1	2	46	20	14	70.0%
2	2	2	49	20	17	85.0%
3	3	2	37	20	16	80.0%

For *eating* activity results, we have four cases resulting from the combination of one force sensor and two RFID readers. Their simulation results are shown in Table 6. When only RFIDs are used to sense the activity, intuitively these cases cannot recognize the activity well because sensing some tableware does not always involve eating. In the worst case, for instance, a human may intends to eat and hence prepares utensils, but does not actually eat anything. A force sensor, F05 could help to detect the activity accurately, since it is triggered by change of force on the plate. For instance, when the user scoops mashed potato on the plate, the force sensor detects it and we could conclude that eating is happening with a spoon sensed by an RFID reader.

Table 6. The *eating* activity simulation cases

Case #	Number of RFID Readers	Number of RFID Tags	Number of Force Sensors	Number of Detection	Number of 1 min. Slots	Number of Activity Recognized	Accuracy
1	1	3	0	38	15	0	0.0%
2	2	3	0	50	15	0	0.0%
3	1	3	1	59	15	12	80.0%
4	2	3	1	102	15	13	86.7%

The test case with two RFID readers and one force sensor shows good accuracy, which is 86.7%. The accuracy does not drop by much (drops to only 80.0%) when we use only one RFID reader. Even though the first case has better performance, it costs almost twice as much as the case with a single RFID reader. Trading off little performance for significant cost reduction, the one RFID and one force sensor case could be most effective.

4.2 Verification by Real Sensor Deployment

In this section, we verify our two-phase approach by experiments with real sensors. The real sensor set is the same as that used for the simulation in Section 4.1. We implemented and executed an activity recognition algorithm to compare the performance of dataset. The real sensor dataset is compared to the simulation dataset.

In Table 7 the performance of sleeping datasets is shown. The datasets represent 20 minutes of sleeping activity. Both simulation and real dataset show that the second case is more effective than other cases. However, simulation dataset shows better performance than the real sensor dataset.

Table 7. Comparison of *sleeping* activity. It presents accuracy between simulation and real sensor datasets for *sleeping* activity.

Case #	Number of Vibration Sensor	Number of Force Sensor (Bed)	Number of Force Sensor (Floor)	Accuracy of Simulation Dataset	Accuracy of Real Sensors Dataset
1	1	1	1	70.0 %	65.0 %
2	2	1	1	85.0 %	80.0 %
3	3	1	1	80.0 %	75.0 %

Table 8 shows the *eating* activity datasets which are performed 15 minutes for each case. It compares the performance of simulation dataset with real sensor dataset. To filter out false *eating* activity, the activity recognition system does not consider the *eating* activity to be executed if there is only a single action in a specific time slot (e.g. one minute). For example, if there is only *serving* action or *cutting* in a time slot, it is unlikely that the person is actually eating the food. Both cases show that force sensor is crucial for detecting *eating* activity. Table 8 shows that the dataset of both cases exhibit better performance when the number of RFID readers increased. However, the effect of increasing the number of RFID readers is less than 7%.

Table 8. Comparison of *eating* activity datasets is shown. It presents accuracy between simulation and real sensor datasets for *sleeping* activity.

Case #	Number of RFID Readers	Number of RFID Tags	Number of Force Sensor (Plate)	Accuracy of Simulation Dataset	Accuracy of Real Sensors Dataset
1	1	3	0	0.0 %	0.0 %
2	2	3	0	0.0 %	0.0 %
3	1	3	1	80.0 %	93.3 %
4	2	3	1	86.7 %	100.0 %

In Table 7 and Table 8, we observe that *eating* activity dataset shows better performance than *sleeping* activity. It means *sleeping* is more difficult to detect than *eating*. This is because of the inherent features of the *sleeping* activity. To illustrate, when people sleep well, there is very little action that can be detected by a sensor. However, when people eat well, it usually translates into greater physical activity. Since activity is recognized depending on the performance of their actions, *eating* activity is easier to detect than *sleeping* activity.

Our two-phase approach thus requires less time and cost compared to one-phase approach. In the experiment, it took an average of 1 or 2 minutes for the simulator to create a dataset for each case in Table 7 and 8, while it took 15 or 20 minutes per case. The total simulation time for all cases was 14 minutes and recording time of an effective dataset was 35 minutes. Therefore, to collect an effective dataset, two-phase approach requires 49 minutes. On the other hand, for one-phase approach the subject of the selected activities participated for a total of 15 or 20 minutes per activity, totaling 2 hours of data recording. Therefore, one-phase approach took 2 hours in addition to the sensor installation time.

5 Conclusion

Activity recognition research requires availability of datasets for testing and evaluation of recognition algorithms and for better understanding of human activities. However, it is often difficult to acquire or establish suitable datasets because they may simply not exist or if they have to be constructed, they require a lot of effort, time, and cost. In order to alleviate this problem, we proposed a two-phase activity dataset design approach, which is composed of three steps. To validate our approach, we implemented both a simulator and a real sensor environment for *sleeping* and *eating* activities. We compared the simulation datasets with real sensor datasets and showed similar results in terms of performance and effectiveness of the sensor set chosen according to our design approach.

A major advantage of the proposed approach is that researchers can acquire the most effective sensor configuration through well-controlled simulations instead of repeated real-world sensor deployment/assessment loops. This allows researchers to test novel activity recognition algorithms and activity models quickly, cost-effectively and accurately. Therefore, this approach can potentially accelerate the research and development of activity recognition systems.

References

1. Helal, S., Kim, E.J., Hossain, S.: Scalable Approaches to Activity Recognition Research. In: 8th International Conference Pervasive 2010 Workshop (2010)
2. Kim, E.J., Helal, S., Cook, D.: Human Activity Recognition and Pattern Discovery. IEEE Pervasive Computing 9(1), 48–52 (2010)
3. Mann, W., Helal, S.: Smart Technology: A Bright Future for Independent Living. The Society for Certified Senior Advisors Journal 21, 15–20 (2003)

4. Intille, S.S., Larson, K., Tapia, E.M., Beaudin, J., Kaushik, P., Nawyn, J., Rockinson, R.: Using a live-in laboratory for ubiquitous computing research. In: Fishkin, K.P., Schiele, B., Nixon, P., Quigley, A. (eds.) PERVASIVE 2006. LNCS, vol. 3968, pp. 349–365. Springer, Heidelberg (2006)
5. Tapia, E.M., Intille, S.S., Lopez, L., Larson, K.: The design of a portable kit of wireless sensors for naturalistic data collection. In: Fishkin, K.P., Schiele, B., Nixon, P., Quigley, A. (eds.) PERVASIVE 2006. LNCS, vol. 3968, pp. 117–134. Springer, Heidelberg (2006)
6. Logan, B., Healey, J., Philipose, M., Tapia, E.M., Intille, S.S.: A long-term evaluation of sensing modalities for activity recognition. In: Krumm, J., Abowd, G.D., Seneviratne, A., Strang, T. (eds.) UbiComp 2007. LNCS, vol. 4717, pp. 483–500. Springer, Heidelberg (2007)
7. Washington State University Activity dataset, `http://ailab.eecs.wsu.edu/casas/datasets.html`
8. Crandall, A., Cook, D.: Coping with multiple residents in a smart environment. Journal of Ambient Intelligence and Smart Environments, 323–334
9. Phidgets plug & play sensors, `http://www.phidgets.com/`
10. Kasteren, T., Noulas, A., Englebienne, G., Krose, B.: Accurate Activity Recognition in a Home Setting. In: Proceedings of the Tenth International Conference on Ubiquitous Computing (Ubicomp 2008), Seoul, Korea, pp. 1–9 (2008)
11. Elfaham, A., Hagras, H., Helal, A., Hossain, S., Lee., J., Cook, D.: A Fuzzy Based Verification Agent for the PerSim Human Activity Simulator in Ambient Intelligent Environments. In: Proceedings of the IEEE World Congress on Computational Intelligence, Barcelona, Spain, July 18-23 (2010)
12. Helal, A., Mendez-Vazquez, A., Hossain, S.: Specification and Synthesis of Sensory Datasets in Pervasive Spaces. In: Proceedings of the IEEE Symposium on Computers and Communications (ISCC 2009), Sousse, Tunisia, July 5-8 (2009)
13. Al-Karaki, J.N., Al-Mashaqbeh, G.A.: SENSORIA: A New Simulation Platform for Wireless Sensor Networks. In: Proceedings of the 2007 International Conference on Sensor Technologies and Applications, pp. 424–429. IEEE Computer Society, Los Alamitos (October 2007)
14. Hossain, S., Helal, A., Lee, J.W., Hagras, H., Alfaham, A., Cook, D.: PerSim – A Simulator for Human Activities in Pervasive Spaces, University of Florida Technical Report number REP-2010-485 (January 2010)
15. Jouve, W., Bruneau, J., Consel, C.: DiaSim: A parameterized simulator for pervasive computing applications. In: PERCOM 2009: Proceedings of the 2009 IEEE International Conference on Pervasive Computing and Communications, pp. 1–3 (March 2009)
16. Antoine-Santoni, T., Santucci, J., Gentili, E.D., Costa, B.: Modelling & simulation oriented components of wireless sensor network using DEVS formalism. In: SpringSim 2007: Proceedings of the 2007 Spring Simulation Multiconference, pp. 299–306 (March 2007)
17. Persim – A simulator for human-activities in Pervasive Spaces. Project web site, `http://www.icta.ufl.edu/projects_persim`
18. SDDL – Sensory Dataset Description Language. Specifications and resources web site, `http://www.icta.ufl.edu/persim/sddl/`
19. Varshney, M., Bagrodia, R.: Detailed Models for Sensor Network Simulations and their Impact on Network Performance. In: Proceedings of the 7th ACM International Symposium on Modeling, Analysis and Simulation of Wireless and Mobile Systems, pp. 70–77. ACM, New York (October 2004)

Introduction to the Business Processes with Ambient Media - Challenges for Ubiquitous and Pervasive Systems

Artur Lugmayr

EMMi Lab., Department of Business Information Management and Logistics,
Tampere Univ. of Technology (TUT)
P.O. Box 541, Korkeakoulunkatu 8, FI-33101 Tampere, Finland
lartur@acm.org

Abstract. Ambient media (aka ubiquitous media) are around us since quite a while. First products and services are emerging in our daily lives. The connection between the physical environment and the digital overlay through smart sensor networks became reality. However, many believe that the application of ubiquitous technology in real commercial solutions is still far out in the future. Within the scope of this paper, we introduce the reader into the business opportunities of ambient media and give a technology roadmap how this new technology might be developing during the next years. The paper shows current shortcomings, technology trends, and existing business solutions and attempts to forecast it's potentials in the next decade. The reader is introduced into issues of supply chain management, application domains, ubiquitous technology in (e)commerce, standards, and business models based on ambient media. This paper shows the perspective from a telecom operator, content creator, consumer, device manufacturer, consumer, and domain specific value-chain participant. It shall act as starting point for further investigation of the business of ambient media.

Keywords: Ubiquitous computation, pervasive computation, ambient media, ambient intelligence, agent based computation, RFID.

1 Introduction

The revolution of ambient media took place silently during recent years. Much ambient technology emerged in consumer homes or into supply chains without actively noticing the underlying technology. There exist many examples, such as location based services on mobile phones, RFID technologies for supply chain management, and smart sensor networks in cars. Currently there is poor research work on the business aspects of ambient media, due to the fragmented nature of applications, services, technologies, and consumers. However, the main question of this publication is: ***How can ambient media improve businesses?***

To understand the business of ubiquitous media, we have to understand the different impact factors and parameters before analyzing existing literature. For the scope

Z. Yu et al. (Eds.): UIC 2010, LNCS 6406, pp. 125–137, 2010.

of this article, business developments around ambient media have been categorized according the following criteria:

1. global and macroeconomic trends;
2. technological enabler and base technologies;
3. integration of physical world and digital overlay; and
4. value-creation through additional services and application;

As the topic is rather wide, and many more than the covered aspects could be discussed, the following aspects have been emphasized:

- increased data quality, accuracy, and granularity;
- improved and optimized production processes;
- integration and harmonization of information management;
- characteristics of ambient media and the key-technologies;
- integration of value-chain and automation of the supply chain;
- etc.

As the basis of investigation and discussions, the article considers the following services and application for comparisons and examples of ambient media examples:

- Nokia's Ovi Maps and Google Maps as examples for navigation;
- Stress monitoring systems developed by Firstbeat Technologies (see [23]);
- Competition entries for the Nokia Ubimedia Awards organized by MindTrek Ry (see see [1]);
- Results from the SAME workshop series as organized by the Ambient Media Association (AMEA) (see [1]).

Currently there is a quite wide set of global and macroeconomic trends. These trends directly impact on business in general, however, as well as on the development of ambient media. In the following the most significant trends have are enumerated:

- Aging population vs. population growth
- Confusion on financial markets
- Global warming and climate change
- Regulation policies and government policy
- Globalization and internationalization
- Sustainable energies
- Consumer and society behavior
- Unions and other interest groups

From the technological side, many technical enablers led to the development of ambient media as they exist today. The most significant ones are:
There exist several technical enablers:

- RFID tags
- Sensor and actuator technologies

- Middleware and thin client technology
- Miniaturization of electronics

This publication is structured as follows: section 2 introduces ambient media as concept, and reviews it's most significant related works; section 3 presents how the physical world and the digital overlay can be integrated, and what the major technical components are; section 4 very briefly pinpoints to the major technological enables and basic technologies in relation to supply chain and value chain; section 5 provides a roadmap and discusses the results.

2 Very Brief Introduction to Ambient Media

Ubiquitous computation and pervasive computation had their starting points during the 90s, and their foundations have been laid in various publications (e.g. [24] [25]). Ubiquitous computation laid the foundation of technology leading to ambient technology. However, the idea rapidly evolved with the introduction of ambient intelligence, which improves the ideas by a more holarchistic viewpoint towards ubiquitous computation. With the introduction of ambient intelligence as European Framework around the year 2003, the foundation for a new concept has been laid [9] [8]. This new technology is the basis for investigation within this work as well as it is for ambient media technology. But this work introduces the concept of building a media environment on top of ambient technologies. However, any new introduced technology has implications on the form how content is presented. As e.g. film cameras introduced the medium motion pictures, also ambient technology introduces the medium ambient media. Many times ambient media are solely discussed as possibility

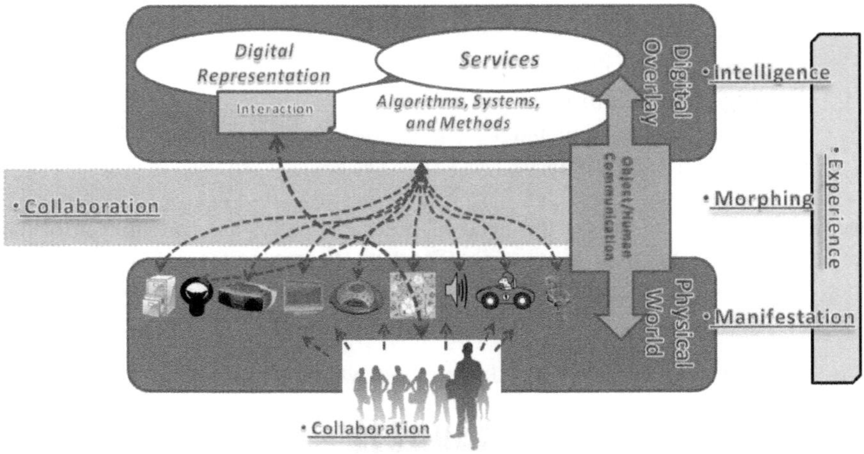

Fig. 1. Depicting the idea of ambient media as digital overlay over the physical world. The principles of ambient media (*manifestation, morphing, intelligence, experience,* and *collaboration*) are included (see e.g. [13]).

for advertising embedded throughout the natural environment. However, ambient media go much further, and embed a media environment into the natural human environment. This issue has especially been discussed in [13], [15], and [16].

Ambient media are characterized through the following principles [13]:

- **Manifestation:** they way how digital objects render through time and space throughout the natural environment (e.g. language output of a GPS based navigation system);
- **Morphing:** how the digital overlay is linked through communication channels to real-world physical objects (e.g. embedded computers sense their environment via data coming from sensor networks);
- **Experience:** knowledge and eventually wisdom based systems based on consumer experience (e.g. agent based systems or personalization systems turning data to knowledge);
- **Collaboration:** collaboration rather than interaction and interoperability are the key in ambient systems. Ambient system technology collaborates between themselves or the users collaborates with the system (e.g. language based input or automated interoperable systems);
- **Intelligence:** methods and algorithms to smartly interpret data and the environment (e.g. systems aggregate content rather than push/pull schemes).

3 Integration of Physical World and Digital Overlay (Morphing)

One principle of ambient media is the principle of morphing, where the physical world is connected to a digital overlay. A ubiquitous system 'sees' its environment through sensor networks, and reacts by utilizing actuators in the physical world. Especially in *Business Information Systems (BIS)*, we can identify several challenges which are relevant for realizing ubiquitous systems:

- information quality;
- integration of information systems;
- costs for realization; and
- information reporting.

Information quality addresses the need of precise, timely, and valuable information obtained through information systems. The key-attributes of such systems are presented in Fig. 2. As stated in [19], the attributes of information quality can be put to the following categories:

- *Time-attributes:* attributes dealing with when, freshness, how often, and for which time-span data is available;
- *Content-attributes*: attributes dealing with information error-freeness, relevancies in specific situations, sufficiency, and the message to be transmitted;
- *Form-attributes:* attributes dealing with information presentation, interaction, and the way how it is presented to the consumer;

In the case of ambient media systems, pervasive technology has several advantages in comparison to other technologies:

- increased timeliness of high quality information in 'real-time';
- automated aggregation of information rather than push/pull schemes;
- integration of information management systems and processes; and
- application of intelligent algorithms for information processing;
- information consumer experience orientation for presentation and interaction.

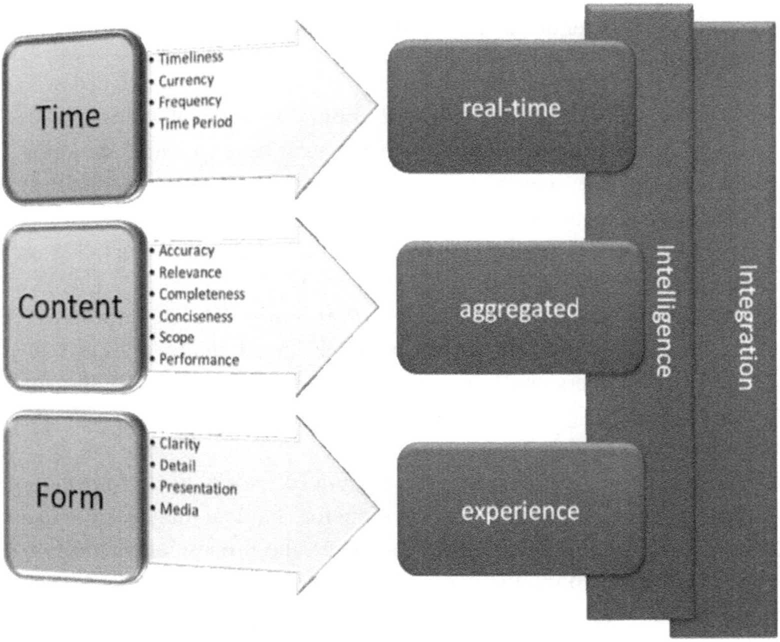

Fig. 2. Attributes of information quality in general (from [19]), and their application in ambient media systems through the attributes *real-time, complete,* and *interpreted*

3.1 Increased Timeliness of High Quality Information in 'Real-Time' (Real-Time)

In [6] a discussion about two essential factors concerning the increased timeliness of high quality information have been discussed: 1) advantages of applying ambient technologies for data gathering in comparison to manual based information gathering; and 2) affects of data quality in business environments that are based on ambient technologies.

Especially the mapping between the physical world and the digital overlay allows closing the tradeoff between the visions of the 'real-time' enterprise and the 'low data quality' enterprise. In a real-time company, ambient intelligent technology collects highly accurate information with a high frequency to be considered for further evaluation. However, currently the costs for realizing the 'real-time' enterprise are currently simply too high. Low quality data, gathered at lower frequencies is given preference, due to lower costs. One typical example is e.g. retail, where nowadays yearly inventories are preferred, rather than investments in improving the tracking of sales goods between retail shelves, storage space, and product distributors via RFID tags. For further reading, please refer to [6].

3.2 Automated Aggregation Information Rather Than Push/Pull Schemes (Aggregation)

Ambient media shift the responsibility of compiling content on system level. Nowadays people either pull the content from the web by explicitly searching for it via search engines – or they get the content pushed to their homes, without direct possibility to change the content, as e.g. in broadcasting. However, the future is aggregation, where the system compiles content in behalf of the consumer – contextualized, personalized, and individualized.

One excellent example is the *Portable Personality (P2)* software, which collects metadata from various sources. An engine mines the metadata to usage context on any device and provides personalized content from any source [14]. Other more prominent examples are Google news or location based services as currently provided e.g. by Nokia Maps and Google's mobile services.

One of the key issues is how data can be integrated into *Business Information Systems (BIS)*. Currently many client based solution for ambient media start to emerge on markets (e.g. location based services). However, the process of integration of data of ubiquitous systems still requires much development. Examples for a professional integration of data are e.g. integration of location information to film material during movie production. The challenge is the automation of the process.

Viewing the automation and smart integration of data from a media viewpoint, let's refer to Figure 3. Today's media landscape is dominated by participatory media (e.g. social media). However, the content model in the past evolved from content offerings to a mass market, niche media (e.g. themed TV channels), towards participatory media, where the consumer is the content creator. In the future, the media environment will be evolving towards a smart environment, where existing journalistic practices are shifting towards personalized context aware service spaces rather than single services. The key to enable smart media environments and integrated service spaces is context information.

Depicting the idea of ambient media as digital overlay over the physical world. The principles of ambient media (*manifestation, morphing, intelligence, experience,* and *collaboration*) are included (see e.g. [13]).

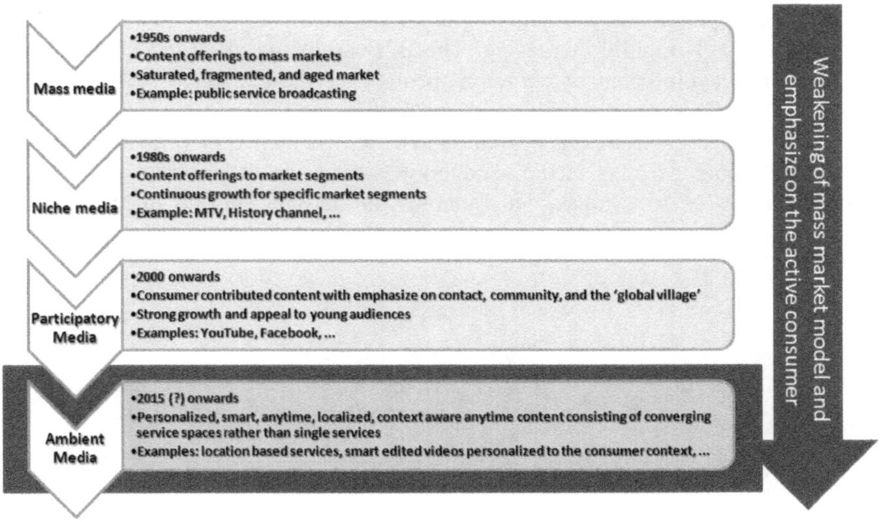

Fig. 3. Evolution of the content model – from mass media (to mass audiences), niche media (themed to market segments), participatory media (consumer contributed content), towards ambient media (smart media). Extended by ambient media and further descriptions from [12].

3.3 Integration of Information Management Systems and Processes (Integration)

The integration of information management systems and processes spans partners from the whole value chain. They require harmonizing their ways of exchanging either tangible or intangible goods. This is especially important in supply chain management. Supply chain management deals with "controls the flow of products and services from suppliers right through to the end consumer" [22]. Efficient and productive supply chain management is enabled through the integration of information management systems and processes. This can only happen through the development of common agreements how information exchange between business partners is taking place between information systems.

Considerable efforts have been done on the field of electronic commerce, which let as series of standards emerge that cover 1) identification; 2) tracking; 3) management; and 4) protection of either physical or digital goods. A compilation of standards normally utilized in electronic commerce has been discussed in [20]. The publication discusses a wide set of standards typically used in supply chain management such as e.g. bar codes, RFID tags, EPCglobal, and EAN.UCC. These standards are used to uniquely identify products and their application for supply chain management is common in today's world of eCommerce. However, the publication also pinpoints to other – more advanced – standards for the automation of the supply chain, such as ebXML. ebXML has been designed by the *Organization for the Advancement of Structured Information Standards (OASIS)* on the basis of XML. The standard enables among other possibilities the automation of *messaging, business processes,* and *exchange of trading partner profiles.*

Where the upper standards mostly focus on physical goods, the market for intangible digital goods is rapidly increasing. The B2B exchange of digital media is on the raise, and the development of common formats for the exchange of information is required. This trend is very visible e.g. in the film & TV industry, where standards such as the *Material eXchange Format (MXF)* are published [18]. MXF enables the exchange of content across media production houses via the Internet rather than on physical carriers such as tapes. This enables the automation and integration of the supply chain from production house to the final distributor and further to the consumer.

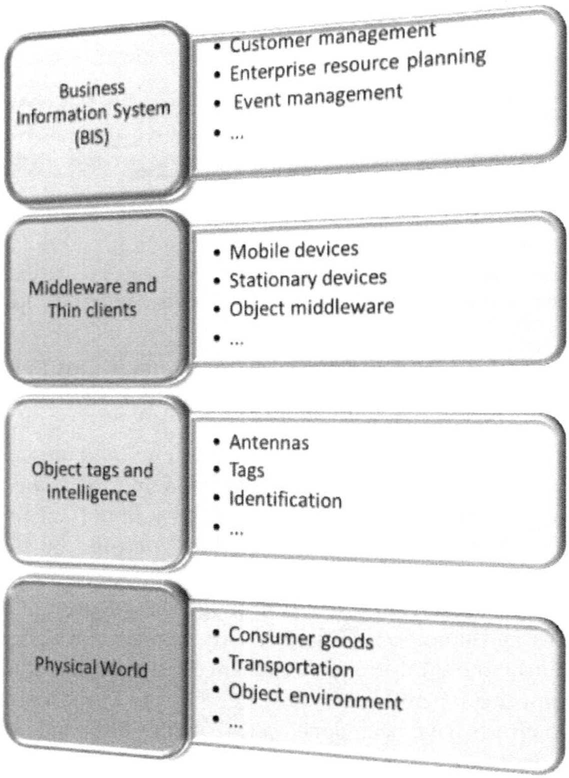

Fig. 4. Integration of information systems from *Business Information Systems (BIS)* down to objects in the physical world (extended from [7])

It is obvious, that with a rapid increase of ambient media technology, the automation of the supply chain is taking place. Currently there is still a trade-off between costs and benefits, but with the decline of costs of miniaturized technologies the gap will get closer. Ambient media allow a seamless integration of the value chain and speeding up the business processes, especially with the advent of more and more digital goods. However, the integration of information system happens vertically, from *Business Information System (BIS)* down to the physical world object level. This implies a harmonization of all the levels to enable full integration of several platforms (see Fig. 4). The vertical integration of the value chain and the need for harmonization has been discussed in [7]. One major issue is the integration of middleware from end-to-end. This issue has been discussed e.g. within the SAME workshop series in [21].

3.4 Application of Intelligent Algorithm for Information Processing (Intelligence)

Intelligent methods and algorithms for information processing are predominant in any ambient media system. One of the key-technology is agent based computation. Agent based computation currently provides one of the main solutions, where software reacts autonomously on external stimuli. One practical example is e.g. the 3APL-M platform, which provides the core technology for deploying smart software on mobile devices. Agents on mobile phones are e.g. capable of contextualizing sensory input in behalf of the consumer [11][10].

3.5 Consumer Experience Orientation for Information Presentation and Interaction (Experience)

The research field of consumer experience is hyping in today's IT services. However, the idea behind consumer experience goes far beyond the current though of simply improving user-interfaces and providing cool hardware designs. The idea of experience in ambient media is that experience means knowledge. Thus experience relate to how humans enjoy media and how humans "act or process directly perceiving events or reality" [17]. Thus, neither the product (e.g. hardware), nor the services attached to the hardware, and nor content is king. The experience as such, consisting of a service space as agglomeration of devices, services, and content is king. Interoperability is one of the technical key-factors to create such an experience.

There are quite a few examples that underlay this direction. One is 'The Cloud', where services are embedded into the Web and the consumer can access a full service cloud online. In ambient media, the vertical and horizontal integration of household equipment will lead to an integrated space, where many devices collaborate. The human becomes a collaborator rather than a user of the system.

4 Value Creation through New Applications and Services

Within the scope of creating value through new applications, content, and services, we have to distinguish between consumer applications, and the application of ambient technology throughout the supply chain. Currently much research is centered on consumer applications, as they are easier to introduce rather than to change existing business processes. Within the scope of this section, the topic 'value creation' for both business domains is discussed.

The main question concerning value creation through applications is, which challenges business are coping with, when adopting new technologies from the ubiquitous domain. A good starting point has been researched in [5], where four key challenges have been identified based on the theories of [2]:

- **Network challenge:** challenges related to the outbalancing of the value of new technology and cost benefit through the introduction of new technologies throughout the value chain. One example for this challenge is the introduction of RFID tags for retail chains, and who overtakes the costs (either the retailer or the distributor) (see e.g. [5]);
- **Constraints challenges:** challenges related to value chain exterior factors, such as regulations, privacy, or global macro-economic trends. One good example are privacy concerns of location aware services, context aware services, or the data of a smart home;
- **Implementation challenges:** challenges faced due to technological problems, resources, knowledge, and practicability of the planed system;
- **Valuation challenges:** challenges related to the tangible valuation either before investment or after investment.

Several of these challenges directly impact the introduction of new ambient media technology.

To understand the value creation through ambient media services, we have to understand the reason why industrial players should invest into new technologies. To understand the costs and benefits, especially to valuate the return on investment a suitable taxonomy has been developed in [4] entitled the "benefits ladder", which is illustrated in Table 1. In the following sections applied ambient media is discussed from the perspective of the Project Ladder focusing on two steps of the ladder: mandatory changes, and automation.

Table 1. Benefits Ladder of added value applications for corporations (compiled from [4])

Project Ladder	Meaning
Mandatory changes	Forced changes through competitive pressure, technological necessity, or regulatory/legal necessity
Automation	Cost reduction in production through decreasing production costs or increasing labor productivity
Direct Value-Added	Applications adding direct value to the product through the technical system as such
MIS/DSS Systems	Services improving management level planning, control, and decision making utilizing technology
Infrastructure	Improvements of the productivity of businesses through advanced infrastructure
Inter-organizational Systems	Systems improving cross-organization transactions of any kind
Strategic Systems	Infrastructure to improve competitive advantage, productivity, new ways of managing, and develop new types of businesses (see [3])
Business Transformations	Benefits through systems enabling transformation of business due to lack of success, change of economic environment, survival, weak success in competition, or poor management strategies

One of the most prominent ambient media services are location based services such as e.g. GPS based navigation. Google offered free access to navigation, through their service offering via Google Maps, which provided Google. With the development of a mobile client, also other consumer device manufactures were forced to keep up with the competitive advantage of Google's service to provide free navigation. This is a good example for adding value forced through competitive pressure, as e.g. Nokia had to cope with the competition through free offering of the Nokia Ovi Maps service. However, the later still allows the access to the navigation service offline, thus without Internet access, which makes enhances the competitiveness of Nokia Ovi Map's application.

A good example for automation as infrastructure for improving competitive advantage through new ways of managing and increasing productivity is FirstBeat Technologies [23]. The idea of the developed system is to decrease the stress level and increase productivity and motivation of employees. The developed system allows analyzing stress levels and recovering from stressful situations. The system can be considered as infrastructure increasing work motivation and productivity of employees, thus increasing labor productivity. This system could be also considered as strategic system, and introduce new ways of management by gaining additional productivity through a well-balanced working life.

5 Discussion and Roadmap

Nowadays many companies and business don't know the value of ambient media technologies. Slowly they understand the value for their businesses, and why investing in this technology will benefit their revenues. In the following, the levels of the development of ambient media as well as the key-conclusions of this publications are compiled together (see Fig. 5):

Level 1 (Technical Enabler and Base Technologies): at the beginning there is always a new technology and technical enablers allowing the possibility for the development of new systems for media. In the case of ambient media, it's mobile technology, emotional computation, smart algorithms, wireless technologies, and smart environments – just to mention a few. Many of these technologies are currently under development or found already their way into consumers' homes.

Level 2 (Gadgets & Consumer Electronics): as seen from other domains, this technology is used for gadgets or other household items (e.g. Tamagotchi). Currently location based services are shaping mobile services. We can describe ambient media as silent revolution, happening slowly and in the background, rather than in the foreground. Ambient media are already here, and all-present (e.g. interactive walls in cities).

Level 3 (Supply Chain Integration): a more problematic issue is the integration of the total supply chain with interoperable standards and smart data exchange mechanisms. This includes production, as well as the consumer side. Today we see e.g.

tracking systems for trucks as one example. However, the future will show which standards are emerging, and which technologies will be dominating markets.

Level 4 (Value Chain Integration): the next step is the value-chain integration, where various business partners are integrating their *Business Information Systems (BIS)* and develop semi-automated process to exchange content, consumer interaction, and services. This step will be the most crucial part.

Level 5 (Innovation of Models): as in any S-Curve model, each innovation requires the re-invention of it. Thus at the end of the various levels of development of ambient media, will be the re-innovation of ambient media through new services. However, this is far in the future and new computational models are required.

Fig. 5. Levels of development for ambient media systems – from technical enabler towards innovation of the model of ambient media

As conclusion, ambient media services are currently already widely deployed, despite the consumer might not be aware of it. However, what we still have to re-think is, what actually content means, and which impact ambient media will have on other aspects, such as the business supply chain. However, any new technology leads to new innovations, and we are just on the brink of emergence of ambient media.

References

1. Ambient media association (amea), `http://www.ambientmediaassociation.org`
2. Chircu, A.M., Kauffman, R.J.: Limits to value electronic commerce-related it investments. Journal of Management Information Systems 14(2), 59–80 (2000)
3. Earl, M.J.: Management Strategies for Information Technology. Prentice-Hall, Englewood Cliffs (1989)
4. Farbey, B., Land, F., Targett, D.: A taxonomy of information systems applications: The benefits ladder. European Journal of Information Systems 4, 41–50 (1995)
5. Fleisch, E., Tellkamp, C.: The challenge of identifying value-creating ubiquitous computing applications. In: Dey, A.K., Schmidt, A., McCarthy, J.F. (eds.) UbiComp 2003. LNCS, vol. 2864, Springer, Heidelberg (2003), `http://www.alexandria.unisg.ch/publications/21555`
6. Fleisch, E., Tellkamp, C.: The business value of ubiqutious computing technologies. In: Roussos, G. (ed.) Ubiquitous and Pervasive Commerce. Springer, London (2006)
7. Hackenbroich, G., Bornhoevd, C., Haller, S., Schaper, J.: Optimizing business processes by automatic data acquisition: Rfid technology and beyond. In: Roussos, G. (ed.) Ubiquitous and Pervasive Commerce. Springer, London (2006)

8. ISTAG: Scenarios for ambient intelligence in 2010 - final report (February 2001), http://www.cordis.lu/ist/istag.htm
9. ISTAG: Ambient intelligence: From vision to reality (2003)
10. Koch, F., Meyer, J.J.C., Dignum, F., Rahwan, I.: Programming deliberative agents for mobile services: the 3apl-m platform. In: Bordini, R.H., Dastani, M.M., Dix, J., El Fallah Seghrouchni, A. (eds.) PROMAS 2005. LNCS (LNAI), vol. 3862, pp. 222–235. Springer, Heidelberg (2006)
11. Koch, F.: 3apl-m: Platform for lightweight deliverative agents, http://www.cs.uu.nl/3apl-m/
12. Kueng, L.: Strategic Management in the Media - From Theory to Practice. Sage, London (2008)
13. Lugmayr, A.: Ambient media. Novatica 33(188), 35–39 (2007), http://www.ati.es/novatica/infonovatica_eng.html
14. Lugmayr, A., Reymann, S., Kemper, S., Dorsch, T., Roman, P.: Bits of personality everywhere: Implicit user-generated content in the age of ambient media. In: International Symposium on Parallel and Distributed Processing with Applications, ISPA 2008, pp. 516–521 (2008)
15. Lugmayr, A., Risse, T., Stockleben, B., Kaario, J., Laurila, K.: Special issue on semantic ambient media experiences. Multimedia Tools and Applications 44(3), 331–335 (2009), http://www.springerlink.com/content/w220782h1h508943
16. Lugmayr, A., Risse, T., Stockleben, B., Laurila, K., Kaario, J.: Semantic ambient media - an introduction. Multimedia Tools and Applications (2009), doi: 10.1007/s11042-009-0282-z, http://www.springerlink.com/content/5616q82741340375
17. Merriam-Webster: Merriam-webster dictionary, http://www.m-w.com/cgi-bin/dictionary
18. MXF: Material exchange format (mxf), http://www.mxf.org/
19. O'Brien, J.A.: Management Information Systems - Managing Information Technology in the Internetworked Enterprise, 4th edn. McGraw Hill, New York (1999)
20. Roussos, G.: Supply chain management standards in ubiqutious commerce. In: Roussos, G. (ed.) Ubiquitous and Pervasive Commerce. Springer, London (2006)
21. Singh, V.K., Pirsiavash, H., Rishabh, I., Jain, R.: Towards Environment-to-Environment (e2e) Multimedia Communication Systems (2008)
22. Slack, N., Chambers, S., Johnston, R., Betts, A.: Operations and Process Management. Prentice Hall, UK (2009)
23. Technologies, F.: http://www.firstbeat.fi/
24. Weiser, M.: The computer for the 21st century. Scientific American (1991), http://www.ubiq.com/hypertext/weiser/SciAmDraft3.html
25. Weiser, M.: The world is not a desktop. Interactions, 7–8 (1994)

A Steerable Tangible Interface and Its Evaluation

WooHyeon Kim[1], Jun Lee[1], HyungSeok Kim[2], MinGyu Lim[2], and Jee-In Kim[1,*]

[1] Department of Advanced Technology Fusion, Konkuk University, Seoul, Korea
[2] Department of Internet and Multimedia, Konkuk University, Seoul, Korea
{woohyuni,junlee,hyuskim,mlim,jnkm}@konkuk.ac.kr,
jnkm@konkuk.ac.kr

Abstract. A tabletop interface can provide multi-layered images and a see-through effect of multimedia contents in order for a user to explore contents effectively in a very convincing way. Using these techniques, we can provide adapted information in various useful ways, depending on the user's Region of Interest (ROI). Previous researches use indirect methods such as laser pointers and touch interactions to manipulate the ROI, but these methods are not intuitive to use. We propose an improved version of Steerable Tangible Interface (STI), with which users can manipulate contents more intuitively due to its tactile characteristic. Our experiments show that the proposed STI reduces the completion time of given tasks and improves user's memory of remembering content when they are compared with ordinary touch based interactions.

Keywords: Tangible User Interface, Tabletop Interface, Multi-layered Contents.

1 Introduction

Tabletop interfaces with more than 30-inch displays such as Microsoft Surface [1] come into wide use. While it is possible to represent multimedia contents on large tabletop interfaces, users are only interested in a small area at a time. Therefore, it is very important to use the ROI (Region of Interest) effectively on large screen displays.

There have been several ROI-based approaches for tabletop interfaces. Baudisch et al [2, 3] developed a Focus plus context technique using a multi-resolution approach, which provides more detailed and high-resolution images in a user's ROI. Hu et al [4] applied the Focus plus context technique on a tabletop interface. The technique enables users to see more detailed high-resolution information in their ROIs. However, this technique requires additional devices to display enhanced images such as projectors and mirrors for ROI in addition to ones for whole tabletop area. Spindler et al [5] and Lee et al [6] used the Magic Lenses technique [7] to imitate a see-through effect, as it shows information that is hidden behind the normal contents. However, they did not support simultaneous interactions of multiple users.

Hsiao et al [8] show that it is better to move the focus region rather than the context area in order to change the examined area. Staadt et al [9] use laser pointers for manipulating the focus region in an indirect way. Hu et al [4] change the ROI with touch interactions on a tabletop interface, which is a more direct way than the previous one.

* Corresponding author.

Z. Yu et al. (Eds.): UIC 2010, LNCS 6406, pp. 138–150, 2010.

Spindler et al [5] propose the Magic Lenses technique. They use a paper onto which the visual image of the ROI is projected by a projector hung on the ceiling. Lee et al [6] recognize STI (Steerable Tangible Interface) using a Wii-Remote [10] which is hung on the ceiling. However, both of them do not function well if the projector or STI is covered by the user's hand. Furthermore, they do not consider multiple ROIs even though a tabletop can be used by multiple users.

Brygg et al [11] propose physical "lens" as a tangible interface and it can be placed upon a tabletop interface or held by a hand. However, it is impossible to interact with the tangible interface by moving it around.

In this paper, we present an improved version of our previous ROI-based approach with STI [6]. The STI help users to explore multi-layered contents. Our previous version had an external recognition system for an STI and it was located on the ceiling. Since there was an occlusion problem, the recognition system was moved under the table in the improved version.

Our results from user studies for evaluation show that users can explore and navigate through the multi-layered contents on a tabletop interface effectively with STI, and that the STI helps users to memorize what they have learned.

2 Hardware

The proposed STI is combined with a tabletop interface. This section describes architecture of the STI and our tabletop interface in detail. We also discuss how a STI is applied to a tabletop interface to recognize a ROI.

2.1 Structure of Our Tabletop System

The tabletop system (called as 'u-Table' and shown in Figure 1) works as follows: When the infrared (IR) camera captures an image, it recognizes STI and fingertip input. The recognized information is sent to the application layer as XML data with which the application interacts with users. After all, a projector behind the tabletop system projects the information onto the screen. Figure 2 shows the data flow more specifically.

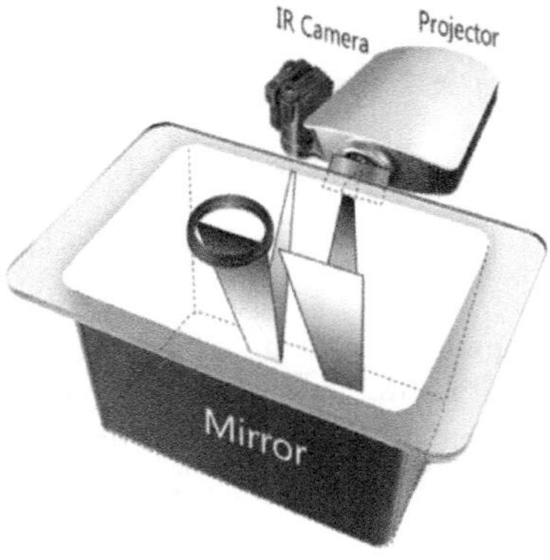

Fig. 1. u-Table - a tabletop interface system

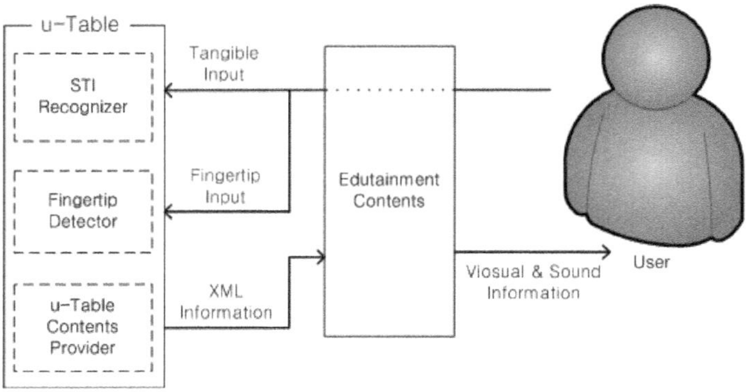

Fig. 2. Flow chart of the data stream in the tabletop system

2.2 Structure of the STI

Lee et al [6] developed ring-shaped tangible interface called STI [6] which had 2 LEDs in its outskirt. They used Wii-Remote which is hung on the ceiling to recognize the STI. The size parameters of a STI are shown in Table 1 and a picture is shown in Figure 3.

Table 1. Size parameters of a STI

item	size
diameter	7.1 inches
width	0.6 inches
height	0.4 inches

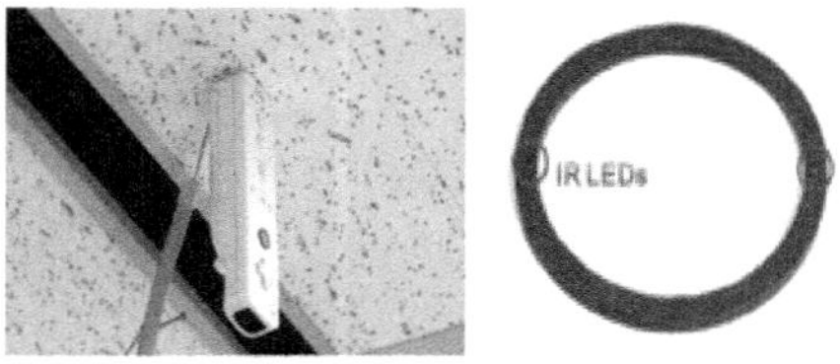

(a)Wii-Remote (b) STI

Fig. 3. A Wii-Remote and a STI

A problem of the previous version of the STI is that it cannot be recognized if the LEDs of the STI are covered by the user's hand. To remove such an occlusion problem, we eliminated the external Wii-Remote and turned the STI upside down. Without an external recognizer, the improved STI can now be recognized by the IR camera, which is under the tabletop interface.

Another problem of the previous version of the STI is that it could not detect multiple STI's. As shown in Figure 4(a), the system cannot recognize the correct position of two STIs which are placed close to each other. We solved the problem by adding one more LED to each STI, that is, three LED per STI (as shown in Figure 4(b)).

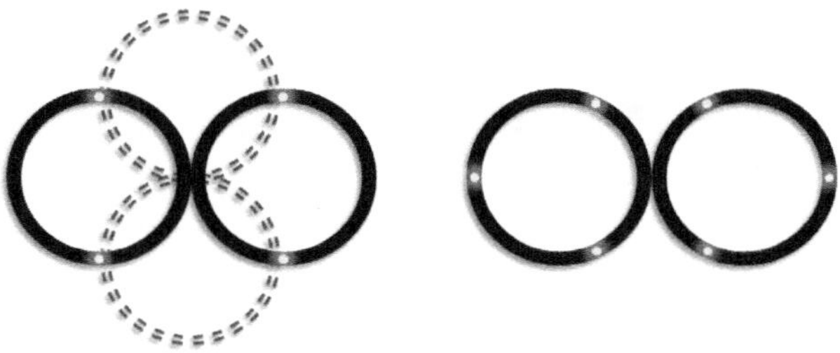

(a) Conflict with 2 LEDs (b) Improved STIs

Fig. 4. An improved STI

As shown in Figure 5, we detect a STI from its three LEDs inputs with the following steps:

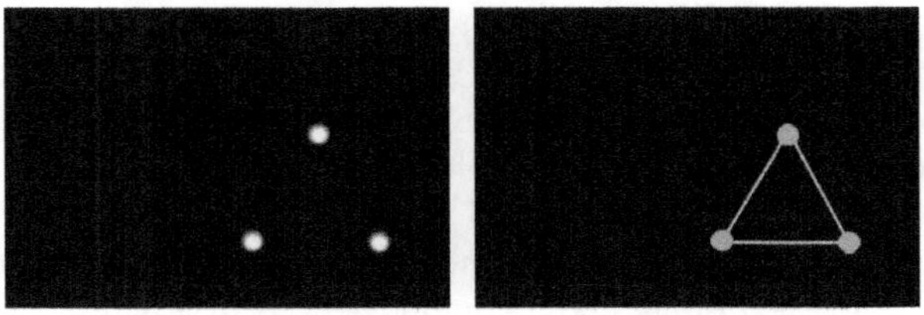

(a) Raw image (b) Detected STI

Fig. 5. Raw input image and the detected position of the STI after the recognition process

Step 1. Detect points whose intensity value is higher than a threshold value in the input image (Figure 5(a)).
Step 2. From the outermost points, search the point placed in given distance and connect them together.
Step 3. If there are three lights, they are recognized as a STI (Figure 5(b)).

Up to four STIs can be recognized by selecting an outermost light as the initial choice. If the initial choice is not the outermost light, three lights of the origin from two or even three different STIs could be mistaken to be labeled as one STI. In this case the remaining lights would not match for the other STIs, as the distance between some of the lights would not be the desired distance. Thus, the outermost point is selected as a seed to indentify STI.

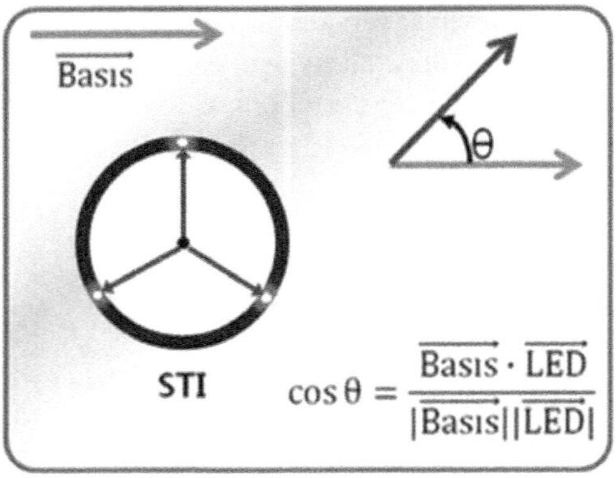

Fig. 6. Distinction rotation of STI

The center coordinates of a STI are calculated by the position of its three LEDs. The rotation of the STI can be detected by the following process:

Step 1. Calculate vectors from the center of the STI to the LEDs.
Step 2. Compare the vectors with their Basis vectors as shown in Figure 6.
Step 3. Accumulate their differences and call of the rotation event if necessary.

3 Content

The position and the rotation information of the STI calculated from the hardware layer are sent to the application layer by which the user can interact with the content.

We use anatomical charts for medical education as our experimental contest for STI. As the human body is three dimensional, the content has various three dimensional relations with each organ and a complicated layer structure. Accordingly, it is hard to represent an anatomical chart on a two dimensional tabletop screen. Thus, we divided the internal organs into four layers as shown in Figure 7. The internal organs of each layer are listed in Table 2.

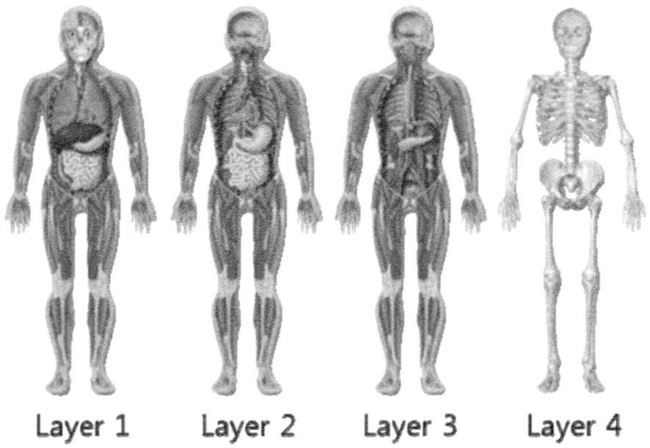

Fig. 7. Layered anatomical charts

Table 2. Components of each layer

Layer number	Detail items
Layer 1	Eyes, brain, lungs, liver, intestines
Layer 2	Heart, small intestine, bladder
Layer 3	Throat, kidney, pancreas, spleen, bladder
Layer 4	Skeleton structure

When this content is run on a tabletop interface, users can navigate through each layer by rotating the STI (as shown in Figure 8).

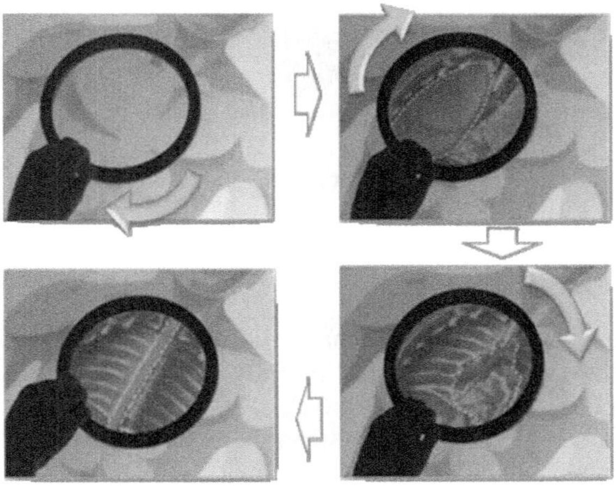

Fig. 8. Rotation interaction with the STI

Figure 9 shows a scene of the displayed images on the tabletop system when two users simultaneously use our system with two STIs. Figure 10 illustrates the overall structure of the contents.

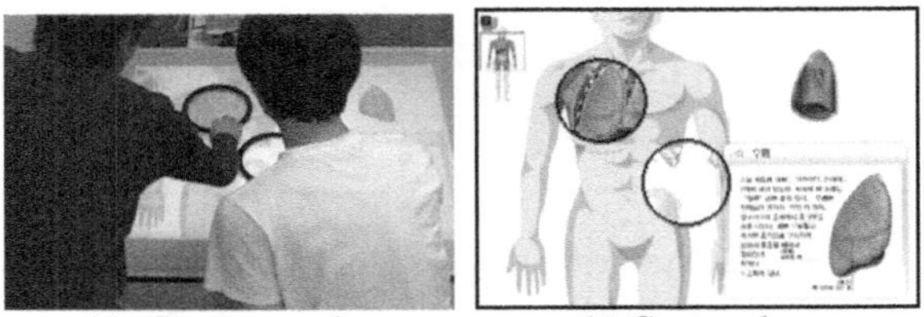

(a) Demonstration (b) Captured screen

Fig. 9. Application with multiple users

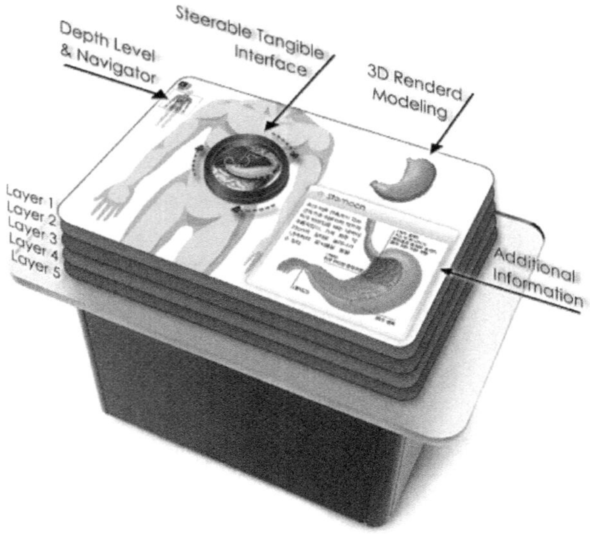

Fig. 10. Overall structure of the content

4 User Studies

The proposed STI is used to provide enhanced images for ROI of a user while s/he is exploring the layered anatomical charts. In order to evaluate the effectiveness of our system, we carried out two user studies. The first test was to evaluate whether our interface with STI can be more efficient than the usual touch interaction, when users explore the contents on a tabletop interface. We measured task completion time as an index to evaluate efficiency. The second test was to check whether our STI can be more helpful for user to memorize what they have learned. We check performances of our subjects in terms of their memorization capability depending on their interfaces.

4.1 Experiment 1: Task Completion Time

(Hypothesis 1) When users explore contents on a tabletop interface, the completion time using a STI is shorter than the completion time using touch interactions.

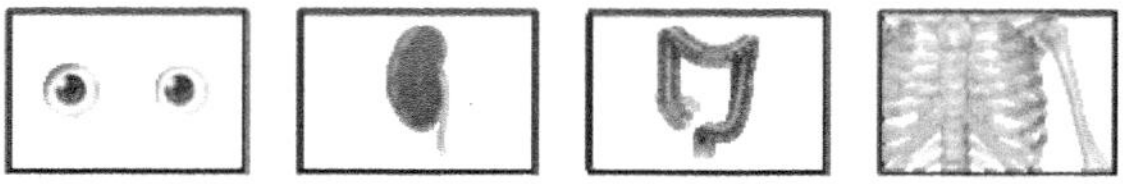

Fig. 11. Target organs to be explored for the first user study.

We measured how much time it takes for the users to discover the given internal organs shown in Figure 11. The number of the participants was 54 and we randomly separated them into two groups, each of which consists of 27 participants. The average age of the participants is 24.9 years old in the STI group whose members used STI for exploring the layered anatomical charts to find target organs in Figure 11. There are 6 females and 21 males. The Touch group does not use STI and the average age of its members is 26.1 years old. The group consists of 12 females and 15 males. The STI group members have used u-Table (our tabletop interface) for 4.7 months. On the other hand, the Touch group members have used u-Table for 5.5 months.

All the participants had to find the target internal organs (shown in Figure 11) in a fixed order, from left to right items of Figure 11. The organs are placed in the 1st, 3rd, 1st and 4th layer respectively, so that users cannot discover the next one without navigating through the layers.

In the STI group, a subject moves to another layer by rotating STI. And the layer is changed when the angle of the rotation is larger than 15 degrees. In the Touch group, a subject rotates his/her hand on the tabletop screen. And the layer is changed when the duration of the rotating hand gesture is longer than 0.5 seconds. In both cases, if the subject rotates clockwise, the content changes into a down layer ('zooming-in'). Otherwise, the content changes to upper layer by the counter-clockwise rotation ('zooming-out').

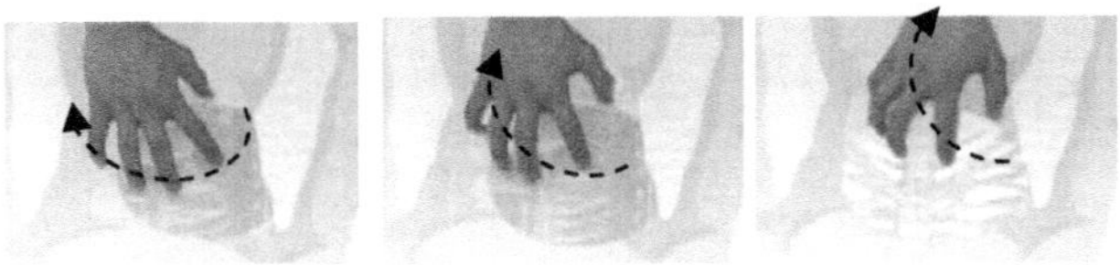

(a) (b) (c)

Fig. 12. Rotating ROI with the Touch based interaction technique

Results

The task completion time of the touch group was 58.4 seconds to find the given organs and that of the STI group was 44.1 seconds as shown in the graph in Figure 13. The STI group completed the task 14.3 seconds quicker than the touch group in average. It means that the STI approach helps users to improve their task completion time by 24%. We also measured the number of errors when the participants mistakenly jumped to wrong layers. The participants had to move to appropriate layer because the target organ was placed in the 1st, 3rd, 1st and 4th layers. If they visit an inappropriate layer, it is regarded as an error. The average number of error times was 1.5 in the STI group and 1.7 in the Touch group.

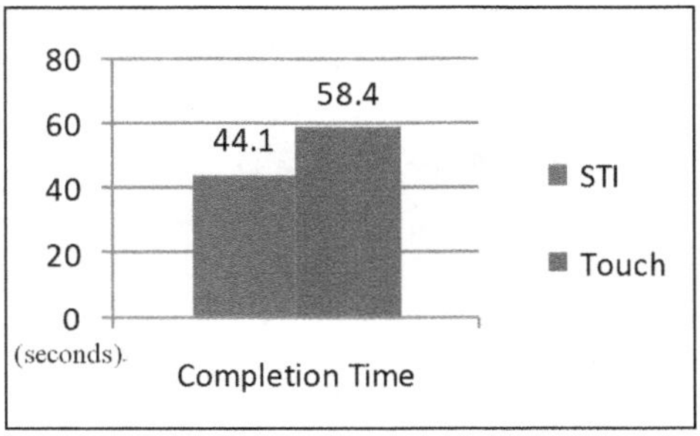

Fig. 13. Average task completion times of the test groups

Table 3 shows the result of the ANOVA test with the data from the 54 participants. It shows that the proposed STI based interaction is more efficient than the touch based interaction with the p-value 0.00274, which is smaller than 0.05.

Table 3. The result of the ANOVA test for Experiment 1

Difference	SS	F	P-value	F crit
14.3	17154.3	9.89162	0.00274	4.026631

4.2 Experiment 2-1: Short-Term Memory

(Hypothesis 2-1) When users manipulate the system with STI, their short-term memories receive more information through the ROI than it would do with the touch based interaction.

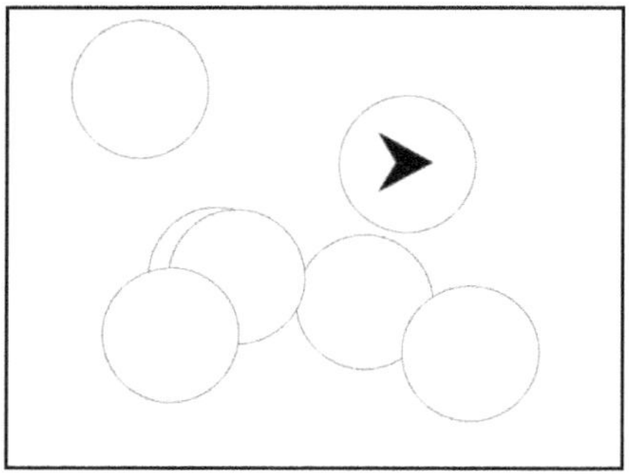

Fig. 14. Application for Experiment 2-1

In the application for Experiment 2-1 as shown in Figure 14, there are seven circles which move around on the screen. As the emergent angle of a circle bouncing off the wall is equal to its incident angle, a user can predict its further path. An icon is randomly selected from a set of icons in Figure 15 and displayed in the selected circle for 2 seconds. The selected circle disappears after the display time is up. The subjects are requested to capture the circles using STIs or fingertip gestures.

Fig. 15. The icons list: The users indicate the icons which they have seen from the list

The number of the subjects for this test was 28. We randomly divided the participants into 2 groups: the STI group and the Touch group. There were 7 females and 7 males in the STI group. Their average age was 25.8 years old. They experienced u-Table for 10.1 months in average. The Touch group included 4 females and 10 males. Their average age was 26.9 years old. Their average experiences with u-Table were 5.7 months. Right after the subjects removed all of the circles, they were asked to indicate the icons they have seen in the picture shown in Figure 15. The screen had been captured into movie clips during the experiment. And using the movie clips, we found out whether participants indicated correct icons.

Results

The average number of icons that the participants of the STI group remembered was 6.53. For the participants of the Touch group, it was 6.37. The difference was about 0.16, which means that the members of the STI group remembered slightly more icons than those of the Touch group. The result of the ANOVA test is shown in Table 4. The difference value is very small and the p-value is quite large (0.54039 > 0.05). It means that the STI does not provide a more efficient way to remember the information given through the ROI in the user's short-term memory.

Table 4. The Result of the ANOVA test for Experiment 2-1

Difference	SS	F	P-value	F crit
0.16	0.2647	0.38297	0.54039	4.14909

The difference value is very small and the p-value is greater than 0.05. It implies that STI does not provide a more efficient way to remember the information given through ROI in the user's short-term memory.

4.3 Experiment 2-2: Long-Term Memory

(Hypothesis 2-2) When the users manipulate the system with the STI, the long-term memory receives more information through the ROI than it would with the Touch interaction.

The participants were asked again to indicate which icons they had seen in the previous experiment after 24 hours from Experiment 2-1. The order of the icons in the list was shuffled from that in the previous list, lest the participants remember the positions of the icons in the list.

Results

The average number of icons that the STI group remembered was 5.65 and the participants in the touch group remembered 4.68 icons. The difference was 0.97 which showed that the amount of icons remembered by the STI group was 14% better than the amount remembered by the touch group members. The result of the ANOVA test about the 17 participants of each group is shown in Table 5. As the p-value is less than 0.05, the difference between the two groups is significant.

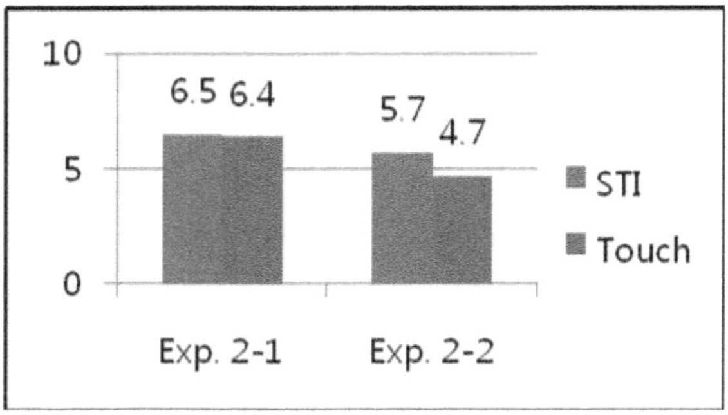

Fig. 16. Overall results of Experiment 2

Table 5. The Result of the ANOVA test for Experiment 2-2

Difference	SS	F	P-value	F crit
0.97	2741.6	9.89162	0.02364	4.026631

In summary, the proposed STI can help users to remember more of the examined content by utilizing the ROI.

In the research by Hu et al [4], high resolution information is given into the focus region and relatively low resolution information is given into the peripheral region. Even though we provide information with the same resolution into both regions, they are separated physically by the STI so that users can concentrate more on their ROI. Eventually, the information provided within the ROI that is confined with the STI seems to remain in the user's memory longer than that with the touch interaction.

According to the John Sweller's theory [14] about cognitive load, humans have a limited amount of capacity available in processing information. If too much information is given, a person cannot deal with it efficiently and will undergo a cognitive overload. In the proposed system, we divide the focus region and the peripheral region physically so that the information reaching the user's mental space is restricted by STI. It allows its user to gather only the information s/he is interested in and thus reduces the risk of having cognitive overload.

4.4 Qualitative Satisfaction

We evaluated qualitative satisfaction after completing Experiment 1. We surveyed the user's satisfaction information by using the computer usability satisfaction questionnaire (CUSQ) [15] which consists of 19 questions. It can be classified into 4 parts: usefulness, information, interface and overall satisfaction.

Table 6 shows the average results of CUSQ between the two user groups. In total, the STI group gets higher points than the Touch group (3.5 points). Especially, the satisfaction of the interface showed the most differences between the STI group and the Touch group (7.2 points).

Table 6. CUSQ Satisfaction scores

	STI	Touch	Difference
Total score	81.7	78.2	+3.5
Usefulness	81.9	78.6	+3.3
Quality of Information	82.1	79.2	+2.9
Interface	79.7	72.5	+7.2
Overall Satisfaction	83.1	82.7	+0.4

5 Conclusions

In this paper, we proposed an improved version of STI for focusing on a region and utilized it for intuitive manipulations for multi layered edutainment content. The STI is a ring-shaped device to enhance the visualization of the region inside of the ring, and to provide control of the visualization methods by rotating the ring. The proposed STI enhances the recognition performance by utilizing under-the-screen image capture and three LEDs. Our improvement is that the recognition system of STI is relocated under the table. With the proposed STI, we can utilize multiple STIs on a single tabletop. It is our second improvement. Our improved STI also allows recognizing moving STIs with less error. The STI is applicable to applications with multiple views, including one with multi-layered educational content. A user can move his/her area of interests by moving his/her STI. By rotating his/her STI, s/he can change the types or the layers of the content inside, while existing tangible interface can only provide single layered content.

To evaluate the performance of STI, we conducted a set of experiments. The experiments showed that the STI was effective when users manipulated multiple layers and selected positions on a tabletop interface. The users who manipulated the system with the STI remembered more of what they have learned than the users with the Touch interactions.

For the future works, we are planning to apply more complex interactions with STI. The STI currently provides only rotation interaction, but some of users hope to magnify contents with STI. In that case, rotating STI with a touching tabletop screen simultaneously would magnify the content. And we are planning to design other types of STI such rectangular and triangular shaped ones. A method to create a resizable and changeable STI is needed to provide users with a flexible way to change their ROI since the ROI is different for each user. In order to improve recognition algorithms for these various STIs, the visual tags [16] can be utilized instead of LED lights.

Acknowledgment

This work is financially supported by Korea Minister of Ministry of Land, Transport and Maritime Affairs(MLTM) as U-City Master and Doctor Course Grant Program and supported by the Seoul R&BD Program (10581).

References

1. Microsoft Surface (2007), `http://www.microsoft.com/surface/`
2. Baudisch, P., Good, N., Stewart, P.: Focus plus context screens: combining display technology with visualization techniques. In: Proc. of UIST 2001, pp. 31–40. ACM Press, New York (2001)
3. Baudisch, P., Good, N., Bellotti, V., Schraedley, P.: Keeping things in context: A comparative evaluation of focus plus context screens, overviews, and zooming. In: Proc. of CHI 2002, pp. 259–266. ACM Press, New York (2002)
4. Hu, T., Chia, Y., Chan, L., Hung, Y., Hsu, J.: i-m-Top: An interactive multi-resolution tabletop system accommodating to multi-resolution human vision. In: Proc. of IEEE Tabletop, pp. 177–180 (2008)
5. Spindler, M., Stellmach, S., Dachselt, R.: PaperLens: Advanced Magic Lense Interaction Above the Table top. In: Proc. of the ACM International Conference on Interactive Tabletops and Surfaces, pp. 77–84 (2009)
6. Lee, J., Roh, Y.T., Kim, J.I., Kim, W.H., Hong, S.P., Kim, H.S.: A Steerable Tangible Interface for Multi-Layered Contents played on a Tabletop Interface. In: ACM Interactive Tabletops and Surfaces (2009)
7. Bier, E.A., Stone, M.C., Pier, K., Buxton, W., DeRose, T.D.: Toolglass and Magic Lenses. In: Proc. Of SIGGRAPH 1993, pp. 73–80. ACM Press, New York (1993)
8. Hsiao, C., Chan, L., Hu, T., Chen, M., Hsu, J., Hung, Y.: To Move or Not to Move: A Comparison between Steerable versus Fixed Focus Region Paradigms in Multi-Resolution Tabletop Display Systems. In: Proc. of the 27th International Conference on Human Factors in Computing Systems, CHI 2009, pp. 153–162 (2009)
9. Ahlborn, B.A., Kreylos, O., Hamann, B., Staadt, O.: A Foveal Inset for large Display Environments. In: Proc. of the 2006 ACM International Conference on Virtual Reality Continuum and its Applications, pp. 281–288 (2006)
10. Nintendo Wii-Remote (2006), `http://wii.nintendo.com`
11. Ullmer, B., Ishii, H.: The metaDesk: Models and Prototypes for Tangible User Interfaces. In: Proc. of the 10th Annual ACM Symposium on User Interface Software and Technology, pp. 223–232 (1997)
12. Lee, J.H., Kim, J.I.: u-Table: A Tabletop Interface for Multiple Users. In: Gavrilova, M.L., Gervasi, O., Kumar, V., Tan, C.J.K., Taniar, D., Laganá, A., Mun, Y., Choo, H. (eds.) ICCSA 2006. LNCS, vol. 3980, pp. 983–992. Springer, Heidelberg (2006)
13. Lee, J.H., Lee, J., Kim, J.I., Kim, H.S.: Believable interaction with a quasi-tangible tabletop interface. In: Computer Animation and Virtual Worlds, pp. 121–132 (2007)
14. Sweller, J.: Cognitive load during problem solving: Effects on Learning. Cognitive Science 12, 257–285 (1988)
15. Lewis, J.R.: Psychometric evaluation of the CUSQ (Computer Usability Satisfaction Questionnaire) using data from five years of usability studies (Tech. Report 29.3418), NC: IBM Corp. (2001)
16. Bartindale, T., Harrison, C.: Stacks on the Surface: Resolving Physical Order using Fiducial Markers With Structured Transparency. In: ACM Interactive Tabletops and Surfaces, pp. 23–25 (2009)

Alerting Accidents with Ambiguity: A Tangible Tabletop Application for Safe and Independent Chemistry Experiments

Akifumi Sokan[1], Nobuhiro Inagawa[1], Kosuke Nishijo[1], Norihide Shinagawa[1], Hironori Egi[2], and Kaori Fujinami[1]

[1] Department of Computer and Information Sciences
[2] Information Media Center
Tokyo Universtiy of Agriculture and Technology, Japan
akifumi.sokan@gmail.com, fujinami@cc.tuat.ac.jp

Abstract. We propose a tangible learning system that facilitates chemistry experiments in a safe and independent manner. The system displays messages that alert a student to avoid a possible accident based on the experimental context. Here, we introduce the way of information presentation with three-dimensional ambiguity: semantic, spatial and temporal. Also, a prototype tabletop application named A^3 (A-CUBE) is presented, which extracts various contexts in a procedure of a chemistry experiment. Finally, we report on an evaluation experiment to measure its usability and to test the feasibility.

Keywords: Tangible learning, information presentation with ambiguity, avoidance of possible accidents, procedure-awareness, augmented reality, projector-camera system.

1 Introduction

A number of systems that aim to realize well-rounded education have been studied and developed with the recent advancement in Information Technology. For example, the u-learning [10] allows students to study at their own pace by utilizing terminals anytime anywhere and to have smooth communication with a teacher. In contrast to the increasing demands of the u-learning paradigm, it is reported that learning throughout extraordinary operations like a chemistry experiment, which constraints the activities of students at a specific time and place, is decreasing due to the risk of accidents [20].

A major cause of accidents during chemistry experiments in lower-level university classes is misuse of experimental apparatuses or materials, which often originates from inexperience or lack of knowledge and inadvertence due to habituation of their usage. In Japan, safety training that aims to decrease the risk of an accident caused by misuse in a chemistry experiment is basically done at the beginning of a semester as a classroom lecture, using materials such as videos and textbooks. This particular training style can accommodate a large number of students at a time; however, it may generate gaps between the safety procedures being learned and actual practice. This

Z. Yu et al. (Eds.): UIC 2010, LNCS 6406, pp. 151–166, 2010.

disparity may, in turn, impair the effect of the training, and thus failures of preventing accidents are caused by human error. Alternatively, a laboratory assistant can support students during experiments; however, to guide every student all the time is virtually impossible.

Therefore, we propose a system as a tangible user interface that has suitable learning characteristics [23] to support on-site safety training for chemistry experiments. The system presents a message related to an experiment at hand, where the message contains an alert to avoid a possible accident and to learn the situation for future use as well. One of the most important design issues to consider is to make the students independent of the system. If a safety-training system is too suggestive all of the time, it would certainly be helpful for a student only at that time, but it would deprive her of a chance to learn to avoid danger by herself. We believe that the system should be as calm as possible to make a chance of learning about safety, but at the same time it should prevent a student from facing danger. Keeping the balance between learning safety experiments and being safe is our major concern.

The rest of the paper is organized as follows: a conceptual framework for information presentation is introduced in Section 2. The design and implementation of a prototype system is presented in Section 3. Section 4 presents the evaluation regarding the usability and the feasibility of the prototype followed by discussion in Section 5. We examine related work in Section 6. Finally, we conclude the paper and show future work in Section 7.

2 Controlling Presentation Ambiguity

A human error occurs in case that people maintain non-centered or extreme nervousness [28]; people in non-centered repeatedly execute simple tasks but cannot notice a change into a critical situation, while, in extreme nervousness, they overlook an abnormal sign because an attention span becomes extremely short. We consider that presentation with appropriate levels of stimulus would contribute to avoid non-centered and extreme nervousness and propose controlling the ambiguity of the message being presented. Here, the term ambiguity means that there are multiple interpretations of a particular situation. The potential of multiple interpretations to facilitate reflection and increase awareness of related topics has been considered in other studies [8, 30]. As Sengers et al. reported with an example of a traffic system that has no traditional traffic instrument, engaging in a sense-making process infused with ambiguity would contribute to stretch out with her feeling/thinking and thus to make her safe [30]. We propose a three-dimensional space of ambiguity comprising semantic, spatial and temporal dimensions (Fig. 1).

– **Semantic Ambiguity**

Semantic ambiguity indicates that the presented information itself is ambiguous even if presented at the correct position and the precise time. During an initial stage of the present study, we roughly classified an image-based presentation into ambiguous (Fig. 1, upper row), and a textual message into unambiguous (Fig. 1, lower row). A textual message in this case consists of a desired action and the reason, e.g., "provide enough distance because it is flammable."

- **Spatial Ambiguity**
Spatial ambiguity is characterized by the presence of an association with a target object. The most unambiguous association is projecting information onto an object of interest so that a strong association between the information and the object is established. Intille et al. utilized the technique for learning foreign words [13]. The two images in the left column of Fig. 1 are examples of an unambiguous presentation, where messages are presented near target objects. By contrast, presenting information at a static position requires a person to identify the target by herself, thus being ambiguous. The right column in Fig. 1 shows this case, where messages are displayed in a dedicated area on the near side of the table. This came from an implication found in [26], which means the projection on an object with a display frame has a potential to make an association with information presentation and a target weaker.
- **Temporal Ambiguity**
Temporal ambiguity is represented by the temporal difference between the experimental procedure at the time of presentation and the procedures leading to a possible accident. If a message is presented a few steps prior to a part of the experimental protocol where there is potential for an accident to occur, it would not directly warn students of this possible accident. We consider that this particular situation would facilitate reflection on the association to resolve this disconnectedness.

Note that an accident that is not associated with a particular step of an experiment, e.g., dropping a glass beaker on the floor, would have low temporal ambiguity.

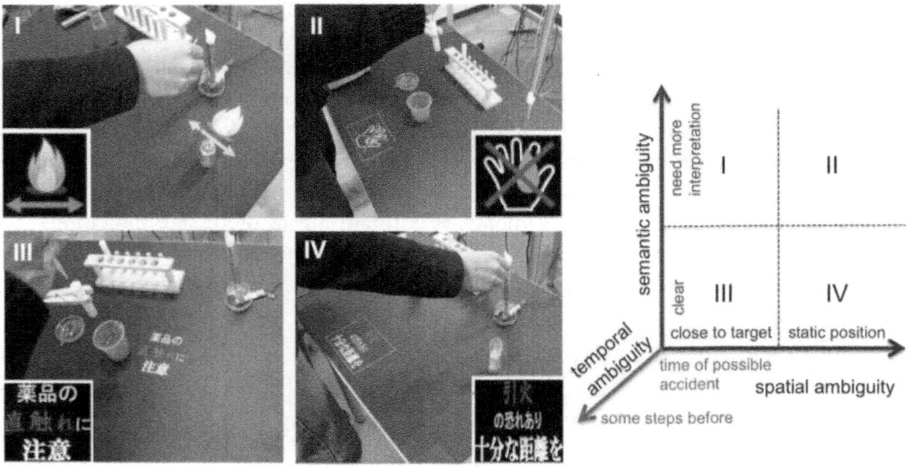

Fig. 1. Examples (left) and the concept (right) of the three-dimensional ambiguous space of the presentation. Note that the pair I-IV (II-III) indicates the same alert for a possible accident.

3 Prototype System: A^3

We developed a prototype tabletop application, "Alerting Accidents with Ambiguity" (A^3: A-CUBE), that supports safe and independent chemistry experiments. In this section, we describe the design and implementation of A^3.

3.1 Requirements

Based on interviews with experts in a chemistry experiment and analysis of a textbook of a chemistry experiment, we identified the following requirements for designing system functionalities:

1. **Presenting information near an object**
   A^3 should present information close to a target in order to realize less ambiguous presentation. Such a near-object presentation would facilitate a strong association of presented information with a target object. Note that presentation aimed at the real world may raise unexpected cognitive issues in case of presenting "onto" real-world objects [27].
2. **Little impact on a user and existing equipments**
   A^3 should minimize an impact on user's operations and be flexibly applied to existing equipments. The system should not let a user be aware of its presence too much lest a user should cause accidents. Also, it is important to deploy the system in an environment without replacing existing instruments since such instruments have inherent constraint, e.g. the inflammable material and the color (*black* for the ease of detection of powder/liquid on the surface) of a desk.
3. **Identifying a current phase in an experimental procedure**
   A chemistry experiment basically has a procedure, and an accident often occurs at a particular phase in a procedure. A system can take an appropriate action if it has a prior knowledge about accidents in an experimental procedure and can identify a phase in a procedure. We call such a procedure-dependent system's behavior "procedure-awareness".
4. **Identifying contexts for a wide variety of experimental material/apparatus**
   As a textbook for a chemistry experiment indicates, a procedure is defined by a set of operations, where particular experimental materials and/or apparatus are utilized. This indicates the information obtained from these physical objects could be utilized to recognize a current phase in a procedure. To make a system scalable to a wide variety of chemistry experiments, it is important to recognize the contexts of heterogeneous objects in an experiment. Such contexts include the identity, the position on a table, the state of content in an object, and the relationship with other objects or a user.

3.2 Design Issues

In this section, we describe the design issues and the approaches of A^3 from the points of view of display method and experimental context recognition.

– **Method of displaying**

We have three options in the method of displaying information near an object: 1) embedding an ordinal computer screen into a table, 2) super-imposing digital information with a physical image that is seen though a head mounted display (HMD), and 3) projecting information on the surface through a video projector. The method of displaying by a computer screen is not flexibly applied to an existing laboratory. A HMD can handle rich contents by showing 3D high digital information [1], while the presence of a display on the face would make a certain impact to prevent a user from engaging operations. In contrast, the projection-based approach is realized by simply attaching a downward-pointing video projector on a fixed stand or the ceiling. However, such a projection still has an issue that if the information is projected onto an object, the distortion of presentation occurs. Although every method has pros and cons, we determined adopting the projection-based approach in consideration of requirement (2).

– **Experimental Context Recognition**

To fulfill requirement (3) and (4), A^3 needs to extract the relationship of "an object and an object" or "an object and an operator" as context. Two ways of such context extraction are figured out: 1) tracking the body part of an operator by utilizing various sensors and 2) identifying the position of objects on a table and an operator. The system has to be able to present information at any position on a table to satisfy requirement (1). However, context extraction using body-worn sensors have difficulty in recognizing entire information like positional relationship of tabletop objects and an operator. On the other hand, as reported in [12], person's activity can be extracted based on three-dimensional position information. Therefore, we adopted the identification of 3D position of objects on a table to extract operational contexts.

– **Method to specify the position of objects**

For a method to specify the position of objects on a table, we have three options: 1) image segmentation and recognition by object's visual features (the pattern-recognition approach), 2) localization based on triangulation of a wireless tag and 3) visual marker-based identification. The pattern recognition approach needs an exclusive feature extraction method for each object. In case of direct tracking of the finger-tip [21], we must formulate complicated image recognition algorithm to extract features of the finger-tip like colors of skin and matching a feature-point. Additionally, this method needs a high-performance camera and careful control of it [5], and therefore it would be difficult to satisfy requirement (4). By contrast, the wireless tag-based localization and visual marker-based identification are able to identify various objects universally. The wireless tag-based approach, however, needs to make a special infrastructure to identify the position of objects on a table [12]. Without this process, the accuracy required for supporting a tabletop operation with wireless tag would not be enough [24]. Although there is a limitation that both methods need to attach a tag/marker to an object, we determined to apply the visual marker-based identification to fulfill requirement (1) and (2). Note that the visual marker-based approach does not extract contextual information of an object without any movement from only the identification of a tabletop object placement, e.g. the temperature and the pressure. To address this issue, we adopt an appropriate sensor.

3.3 System Overview

Fig. 2 shows the overall architecture of A^3. First, the condition of objects on a table and an operator is extracted as low-level context from a visual marker identification system or any other sensor. The extracted context is then sent to Procedure Manager consisting of Scene Transition Controller and Object Manager. Here, "scene" indicates a certain process in an experiment, and an overall procedure is expressed as a set of each scene. In other words, A^3 transits a procedure from the current scene to the next scene based on extracted context information and presents various types of information by each scene. Scene Transition Controller tracks a current scene and manages scene transition. Object Manager manages object information related to experimental apparatus/material like a visual marker ID and object state, e.g. "chemical X was poured into a beaker". Next, based on context information sent to Procedure Manager, Scene Transition Controller obtains the states of target objects stored in Object Manager and notifies Presentation Controller of scene transition. Contents Manager extracts scene specific information, e.g. a file path of a particular image, from a configuration file. In case of less ambiguous spatial presentation, Contents Renderer obtains current coordinate value of a presentation target from Object Manager. Finally, Contents Renderer presents information retrieved from a configuration file through a projector and a speaker.

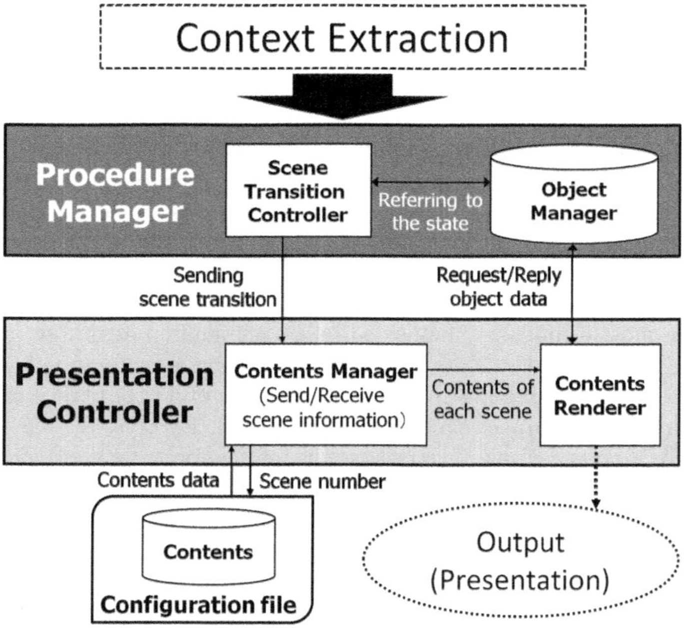

Fig. 2. The information flow of A^3

3.4 Controlling Presentation Contents with Three-Dimensional Ambiguity

The three-dimensional ambiguity in Section 2 is controlled in the following manner. In terms of semantic ambiguity, image-based presentation was utilized to represent "high semantic ambiguity", while a textual expression was utilized for "low semantic ambiguity", which we assumed an image and a text have large and small number of interpretations, respectively. The two types of presentation were controlled by switching a function that renders image and textual information. In terms of spatial ambiguity, presentation at a static position was utilized to represent "high spatial ambiguity".

A static position indicates a fixed part on tabletop (see Fig. 1 left-II and IV). On the other hand, presentation close to the target was utilized for "low spatial ambiguity" (see Fig. 1 left-I and III). The fixed-area presentation is realized by setting a coordinate parameter on fixed-value, while the side-by-side presentation is realized by projection near a target marker. In other words, Contents Renderer periodically requests the marker position from Object Manager. In terms of temporal ambiguity, the *step* of presentation in an experimental procedure is subject to control (Fig. 3); information is presented some steps prior to the step where an accident is likely to happen in order to represent "high temporal ambiguity". By contrast, presentation at just before a possible accident is for "low temporal ambiguity". Note that an accident that does not relate to a particular step in an experiment is alerted with "low temporal ambiguity", which includes "a beaker is put on the edge of a table", for example.

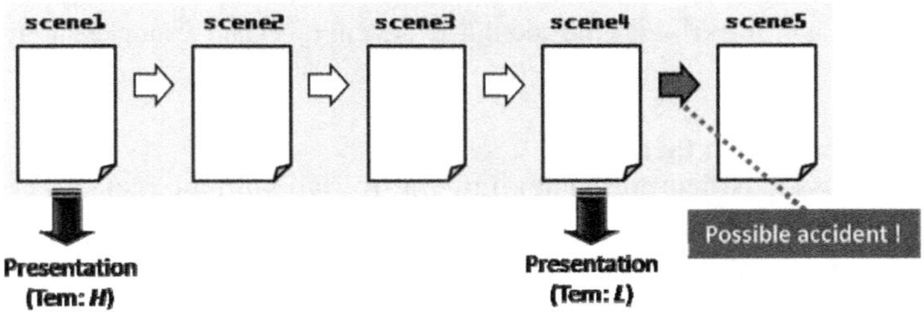

Fig. 3. Controlling temporal ambiguity. If a possible accident occurs between scene 4 and scene 5, presentation at scene 4 is considered as "low ambiguous presentation", while "high ambiguous presentation" can be done at scene 1, for example.

3.5 Relevant Functionalities in Information Presentation

In this section, we describe the issues and our solutions in presenting information. 1) Presentation out of a table and 2) presentation onto a target are the functionalities applied in case of presentation tracking close to a target, and 3) Audio-based alerting can make a user aware of presentation information more effectively.

– **Presentation out of a table**

In presenting information by marker tracking, we defined the central point of a marker as original point that corresponded to the upper left vertex of image/character rectangle information (Fig. 4, left). That means presentation is situated lower right direction in relation to central point of a marker. Information is projected out of a table frame in case that a marker is moved to too lower or right position on tabletop (Fig. 4, right). We addressed this issue by changing the direction of presentation based on the position in which a target object exists; at first, we place four markers on the four corners of a table (Fig. 5, left). Next, the system detects the position of a marker on "Table coordinate system" consisting of markers in four corners, and finally directs rendering contents in the direction where presentation is not out of a table (Fig. 5, right).

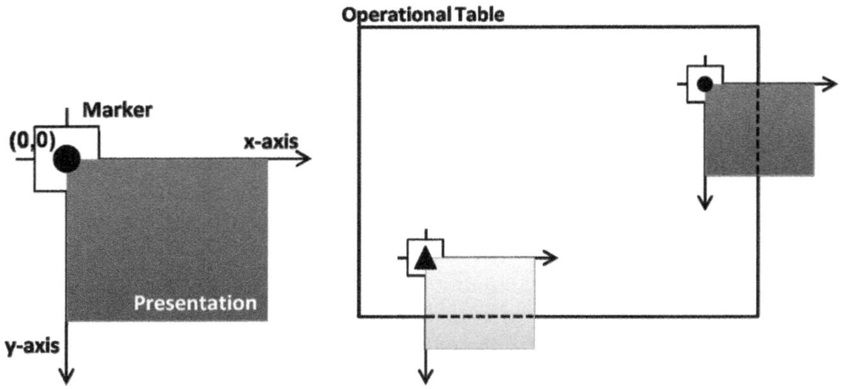

Fig. 4. Definition of marker-centered coordinate system (left) and examples of presentation out of a table (right)

– **Presentation onto a target**

An important issue is that presentation might overlap with a target object in case that the area of the base is large. We addressed the issue by utilizing the width and the depth of basal aspect. Therefore, Object Manager additionally stores "the area of base": in fact, the values of width and depth of basal aspect (Fig. 6).

– **Audio-based alerting**

A^3 is equipped with sound playback facility to support more effective on-site safety training. An operator can acquire information not only visually by a projector but also acoustically by alerting sound playback from a speaker. However, the omni-directional propagation of acoustic wave may become a weakness at the same time. In this case, bystanders may feel vexatiousness because the sound reaches to those who do not need to be alerted.

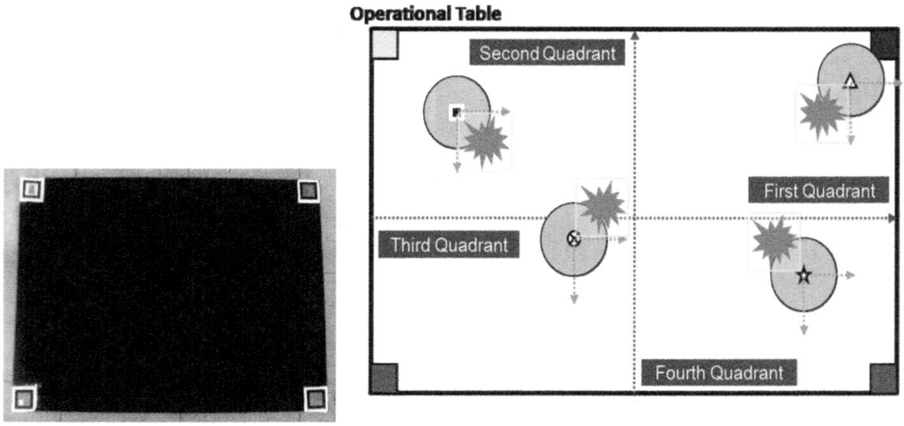

Fig. 5. Four markers in corners (left) and examples of coordinate adjustment (right). Four markers formulate "Table coordinate system" and the relative position of presentation depends on the quadrant of a marker to avoid being projected out of a table.

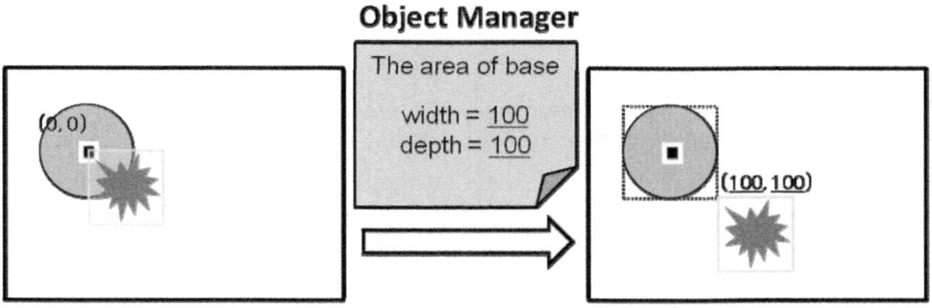

Fig. 6. Coordinate adjustment by the area of base. Value of width and depth of basal aspect is stored in Object Manager.

3.6 Implementation-Specific Information

To realize marker-based object's position identification, we applied ARToolkit (Augmented Reality Toolkit) [18] that could do the identification task relative easily and in a real-time manner. A web camera (Microsoft LifeCam Cinema (15FPS, 1280x720)) was set in front aspect of a projector (EPSON Offirio EB-1725 (XGA, 1024x768)). Both the web camera and the video projector were attached on a prop of 0.9 meters high from a tabletop. The size of a marker should be smaller so as not to interfere a user's operation. Therefore, it was 3.0 centimeters square due to the limitation of installation method mentioned above and camera performance. The tabletop area available for projection was 0.6m x 0.8m, which is standard size for a student individual experiment. Procedure Manager and Presentation Controller were implemented on the Java platform. In addition, Phidgets interface kit [11] is applied to recognize context that is difficult to extract from a visual marker-based approach such as an operation without moving a material/apparatus on tabletop.

4 Usability Evaluation

In this section, we describe the usability evaluation of A^3 as a supporting system for safety and independent experiments.

4.1 Subjects and Evaluation Method

Eight undergraduate and graduate students participated in the experiment. None of them were chemistry majors. They were asked to perform a chemistry experiment with imitation material/apparatus. We adopted a basic scenario found in a textbook of a chemistry experiment: "Examine whether another material is made when you heat iron and a mixture of the sulfur". The subjects filled in System Usability Scale (SUS) [2] of ten items with five phases of 0~4, which easily enables to evaluate system usability. The result of SUS is expressed with numerical value of 0~100. A system is superior in usability if the result numerical value is higher. Also, we had our original questionnaire-based survey with an interview session to investigate subjective opinions. The subjects filled in questions with five phases of 1~5 shown in Table 1. In addition to the feedback from potential users of the system, we asked two experts in chemistry experiments about feasibility of A^3.

Table 1. Contents of the original questionnaire. Q1, Q2 and Q3 are questions for usability of the system. Q4 and Q5 for the evaluation as a supporting system to provide safe and independent chemisty experiments.

Q01	Did you understand a target of presentation easily?
Q02	Did you feel the information was presented in synchronization with your action in real time?
Q03	Were you satisfied with the stability of the system?
Q04	Do you think this system enhances the prediction of possible danger?
Q05	Do you think this system decreases accidents in a chemistry experiment?

4.2 Experimental Settings

Table 2 shows the experimental setting utilized in the experiment. The number of scene was totally 23, in which the transition was realized by various operational contexts that were realized by 22 visual markers and one pressure sensor; the appearance of chemical X, the distance between chemical X and chemical Y, mixing chemical X with chemical Y and the movement of chemical X by visual marker-based extraction, and pushing of a dropper by a pressure sensor. The levels of the three types of ambiguity in the presentation were set up as Semantic: High and Low, Spatial: Low and Temporal: Low. Fig. 7 illustrates examples of information presentation. A^3 played alerting sound as well as visually presented information to encourage subjects to perceive presentations. The frequency and the duration of the alerting sound were determined based on Japanese Industrial Standards (JIS) to satisfy that it was easy-to-hear and straightforward [15,16].

Table 2. Data of various experimental environment in an evaluation experiment

The number of visual markers	22
The type of supplemental sensor	Pressure (force)
The number of scene	23
Extracted context	Visual marker-based: Appearance, Distance, Mixing and Movement Non-visual marker-based : Pressure
Ambiguity	Semantic: High and Low Spatial: Low Temporal: Low
Annunciation sound	4,000Hz twice briefly

Fig. 7. Two examples of information presentation: when a subject puts a mortar on a table (left), the system presents information with ambiguity; Sem: L, Spa: L and Tem: L. When heat a test tube (right), with ambiguity; Sem: H, Spa: L, Tem: L.

4.3 Result

Table 3 and Table 4 show the results of SUS and the original questionnaire per subject, respectively. The answer is more positive as the value gets large. The average score for all subjects in SUS questionnaire was 56.6, which was slightly higher than the full score (100.0). Regarding the average per question, the averages for S01, S03 and S04 are relatively-low score, and for S02, S06 and S07 are relatively-high score.

Table 3. The score of SUS questionnaire

Subject	A	B	C	D	E	F	G	H	**Average**
SUS	**62.5**	**40.0**	**85.0**	**37.5**	**50.0**	**40.0**	**70.0**	**67.5**	**56.6**
S01	0	2	4	0	1	1	3	2	1.6
S02	3	3	4	3	4	1	3	3	3.0
S03	3	0	3	1	1	1	3	3	1.9
S04	3	1	4	1	0	0	2	3	1.8
S05	3	1	3	1	3	2	2	2	2.1
S06	3	2	2	2	4	4	3	3	2.9
S07	3	1	4	4	3	2	3	4	3.0
S08	2	1	3	0	3	3	3	3	2.3
S09	3	3	3	1	1	1	3	1	2.0
S10	2	2	4	2	0	1	3	3	2.1

5 Discussion

5.1 Usability of A^3

The positive and negative answers presented in Table 3 and Table 4 are as follows. Note that we set a threshold to classify an answer of the SUS and the original questionnaire into "positive" or "negative", in which the score more than 2.5 in the SUS questionnaire and 3.0 in the original questionnaire was classified into "positive" .

Table 4. The score of the original questionnaire. Note that the questions are shown in Table 1.

Subject	A	B	C	D	E	F	G	H	**Average**
Q01	5	4	4	2	5	4	5	5	4.3
Q02	5	2	5	5	4	2	4	2	3.6
Q03	2	2	4	2	2	2	4	4	2.8
Q04	2	2	5	4	4	4	5	3	3.6
Q05	3	2	5	5	5	4	4	4	4.0

- Questions that the subjects answered *positively*
  S02: I found the system unnecessarity complex.
  S06: I thought there was too much inconsistency in this system.
  S07: I would imagine that most people would learn to use this system very quickly.
  Q01: Did you understand a target of presentation easily?
- Questions that the subjects answered *negatively*
  S01: I think that I would like to use this system frequently.
  S03: I thought the system was easy to use.
  S04: I think that I would need the support of technical person to be able to use this system.
  Q03: Were you satisfied with the stability of the system?

We found that A^3 had provided the subjects with the uncomplicated operation and presentation by the positive answer of S02, S06, S07 and Q01. On the contrary, A^3 failed in providing the subjects with a desire of frequent utilization due to the negative answer for S01. In fact, a marker was sometimes not recognized due to unexpected operation of a subject, which required the subjects to perform the activity repeatedly. We consider the reason for the comparatively low values in the average scores of S03, S04 and Q03 are also due to the malfunction of the marker recognition sub-system. However, by taking into account all factors together, we consider that the usability of A^3 is not low by any means. We need to improve the system to reduce the malfunctioning. Here, more robust context recognition is required. At the same time, we need to investigate an interaction technique to present information under mis-detection of an operational context.

5.2 A^3 as a System for Supporting Safe and Independent Experiments

As can be seen from the average scores for Q04 and Q05 in Table 4, most subjects considered A^3 as a system that would contribute to predict possible danger and keep them safe in a chemistry experiment. We also obtained the reasons for the positive response from an interview such that "I do not try to think about this and that without a presentation." and "I was thankful to this system for checking my knowledge about danger." We consider that the information presentation was a trigger for active thinking of an operator. Also, some subjects mentioned the capability of presentation with ambiguity such that "I remember image information, and it is bothersome to read and understand a mean of presentation each time" and "I think it is effective in terms of learnability if various presentations were projected close to a target". Thus, we consider the presentation with ambiguity facilitated active thinking of the subjects.

5.3 Evaluation by the Experts in Chemistry Experiments

The experts pointed that A^3 would help a student to become accustomed to the essential preparation in an experiment. For example, a student must wear safe goggles and heat-resistant glove, but sometimes they forget to follow the rules because of botheration. In such a case, automatic alerting is desirable because it is impossible for a teacher to pay attention to every student all the time. So, A^3 alerts students instead of a teacher by utilizing marker-based context-awareness such as identification of the position of safe goggles and a heat-resistant glove on tabletop and sensor-based context-awareness of human movement.

They evaluated A^3 that it would become feasible enough to apply as on-site safety training for actual chemistry experiments if we could meet the following two requirements: 1) the material of a marker should not be made of paper to avoid a fire accident and 2) a marker attached to a test tube should be smaller. For the first requirement, we can replace a paper-based marker with unburnable material, while, for the second request, we might set a camera on lower position above the table surface or attach it to test tube tongs.

We also got an opinion to change the presentation contents depending on the skill of a student. For example, the system could provide a beginner with explicit (low ambiguous) presentation in order to surely avoid an accident, while, to a skilled student, implicit presentation could be provided to facilitate thinking about information presentation. We need to have more concrete understanding of the relationship between a skill-level and an appropriate level of ambiguity.

5.4 Enhancement of Operational Context

As described in Section 3.2 A^3 was built on a software framework that allows a new type of a sensor to be incorporated into the system. In the experiment, a pressure

Fig. 8. By a dropper on which a pressure sensor is set, we can extract context that chemical liquid is tapped off from a beaker. Depended on the combination of a marker and a sensor, various contexts can be extracted.

(force-sensitive) sensor was utilized (Fig. 8). Other possible sensors are, for example, a thermo camera to detect the temperature of a beaker at the time of a chemical reaction, and an accelerometer/gyro sensor to detect the tilt of a material/apparatus and the movement of an operator. By these ways of the extraction, A^3 becomes able to alert an operator to various abnormal situations. Moreover, the underlying middleware of A^3 encapsulates the heterogeneity of sensor devices, which encourages a developer to adopt various sensors.

6 Related Work

In the field of ubiquitous computing, many products and studies have been proposed and developed, which aims to make a space smart [3,19] e.g. comfortable, effective and sensitive for the public. Our system also makes a space smart; however, it differs from previous study in the point of targets and purposes. We proposed our system in order to enhance the learnability of a safe way of chemistry experiments for the beginner to avoid danger through an on-site training.

Our system is a tangible learning system, an application domain of Tangible User Interfaces [14], that utilized Augmented Reality (AR) technologies in terms of information presentation in the real world and a user operation with physical objects. The comparison of tangible user interfaces with AR in learning physical molecular structure model has also been studied [4], which suggests the utility and the trend of preferred personality of AR and physical model. A few notable applications have been proposed and prototyped, which includes supporting to learn 1) molecular structure in a tangible manner [6,7] and 2) the appropriate way of a chemistry experiment and quantity of chemical materials [29]. These are systems that allow a student to learn scholarly contents like a molecular structure effectively by realizing highlighted presentation with 3D objects [9]. As mentioned above, our system is unique in the point that facilitates safety training over the course of an experiment.

Regarding the direct information presentation on a real object from a projector, Steering Projector Display [25] installed in the ceiling and PlayAnywhere [31] can also project information on any location. As the name suggests, these systems can project information on any positions, e.g. a cabinet. By utilizing these technologies in the presentation functionality of A^3, we can extend the space of on-site safety training to the entire experimental laboratory. Improvement of a projector has examined by another approach against the distortion of presentation. Pico projector [22] and a wearable projector [17] are mobile projectors that can also be applied to the information presentation that go beyond an operational table or a shelf without any spatial limitation. We will consider applying above-mentioned technologies to a chemistry laboratory, so that projection of information in A^3 would become more versatile to support safety training.

7 Conclusion

In this paper, we proposed and prototyped a tangible tabletop application (A^3) to support safe and independent chemistry experiments. The system presents information with three-dimensional ambiguity, i.e. spatial, temporal, and semantic ambiguities.

The results of a usability test with SUS indicate that the participants perceived roughly positive. The analysis by an additional questionnaire and an interview showed that a major concern in the usability was improper operation in the context recognition. We will improve A^3 based on the result of SUS, especially, robust visual marker-based context recognition.

In addition to the improvement, we need in-depth understanding of the effect of multiple interpretations, *ambiguity*, in learning a way of a chemistry experiment that is effective for future independent experiment while avoiding an accident during an ongoing experiment. Furthermore, we need to investigate the impacts of other factors, such as the personalities of students, the risk of dependency on the system, and the severity of possible accidents, which we assumed to be identical in the present study. Taking these factors into consideration would allow the system to determine suitable presentations based on students' attributes and possible accidents that are identified by the state-of-use of experimental apparatuses and materials.

Acknowledgements

We would like to thank Prof. Wuled Lenggoro and Dr. Mayumi Tsukada for helpful advice concerning accidents during chemistry experiments. This work has been supported by a MEXT fund for Grant-in-Aid for Scientific Research (C) No. 21500117.

References

1. Billinghurst, M., et al.: The magicbook: a transitional ar interface. Computers & Graphics 25, 745–753 (2001)
2. Brooke, J.: SUS: a "quick and dirty" usability scale. In: Brooke, J. (ed.) Usability Evaluation in Industry, p. 193. Taylor and Francis, Abington (1996)
3. Brumitt, B., et al.: EasyLiving: Technologies for Intelligent Environments. In: Thomas, P., Gellersen, H.-W. (eds.) HUC 2000. LNCS, vol. 1927, pp. 12–29. Springer, Heidelberg (2000)
4. Chen, Y.: A study of comparing the use of augmented reality and physical models in chemistry education. In: Proc. ACM 2006, pp. 369–372 (2006)
5. Cotting, D., et al.: Embedding Imperceptible Patterns into Projected Images for Simultaneous Acquisition and Display. In: Proc. ISMAR 2004, pp. 100–109 (2004)
6. Fjeld, M., et al.: Chemistry Education: A Tangible Interaction Approach. In: Proc. INTERACT 2003, pp. 287–294 (2003)
7. Fjeld, M., et al.: Tangible user interface for chemistry education: comparative evaluation and re-design. In: Proc. CHI 2007, pp. 805–808 (2007)
8. Gaver, H., et al.: The History Tablecloth: Illuminating Domestic Activity. In: Proc. DIS 2006, pp. 199–208 (2006)
9. Gläser, T., et al.: Chemieraum - Tangible Chemistry in Exhibition Space. In: Proc. TEI 2009, pp. 16–18 (2009)
10. Graschew, G., et al.: From e-learning towards u-learning: ICT-enabled ubiquitous learning & training. In: Proc. CATE 2007, pp. 141–146 (2007)
11. Greenberg, S., Fitchett, S.: Phidgets: easy development of physical interfaces through physical widgets. In: Proc. the 14th Annual ACM Symposium on User Interface Software and Technology, pp. 209–218 (2001)

12. Harter, A., et al.: The anatomy of a context-aware application. In: Proc. MobiCom 1999, pp. 59–68 (1999)
13. Intille, S.S., et al.: Ubiquitous Computing in the Living Room: Concept Sketches and an Implementation of a Persistent User Interface. In: Proc. UbiComp 2003, pp. 265–266 (2003)
14. Ishii, H., Ullmer, B.: Tangible Bits: Towards Seamless Interfaces between People, Bits and Atoms. In: Proc. CHI 1997, pp. 234–241 (1997)
15. JIS S 0013. Guidelines for the elderly and people with disabilities – Auditory signals on consumer products. JIS (2002)
16. JIS S 0014. Guidelines for the elderly and people with disabilities – Auditory signals on consumer products – Sound pressure levels of signals for the elderly and in noisy conditions. JIS (2003)
17. Karitsuka, T., Sato, K.: A Wearable Mixed Reality with an On-board Projector. In: Proc. ISMAR 2003, p. 321 (2003)
18. Kato, H., et al.: An Augmented Reality System and its Calibration based on Marker Tracking. TVRSJ 4(4), 607–616 (1999)
19. Kidd, C., et al.: The Aware Home: A Living Laboratory for Ubiquitous Computing Experience. In: Streitz, N.A., Hartkopf, V. (eds.) CoBuild 1999. LNCS, vol. 1670, pp. 191–198. Springer, Heidelberg (1999)
20. Kusuyama, Y., Yamakawa, Y.: Some Problems in the Chemical Education and the Development of Teaching Materials (4). Bulletin of the Center of Research and Instruction on Practical Education 5, 139–145 (1995) (in Japanese)
21. Lee, T., Höllerer, T.: Initializing Markerless Tracking Using a Simple Hand Gesture. In: Proc. ISMAR 2007, pp. 1–2 (2007)
22. Madden, D.: CES 2008: DLP shows off working Pico projector prototype (2008), http://www.pocketlint.co.uk/news/news.phtml/12082/13106/pico-projector-prototype-shown-off.phtml (accessed May 3, 2010)
23. Marshall, P.: Do tangible interfaces enhance learning? In: Proc. TEI 2007, pp. 163–170 (2007)
24. Ogino, A., et al.: Integrated Wireless LAN Access System: Study on Access Method based on Location Information. In: DICOMO 2003, pp. 569–572 (2003) (in Japanese)
25. Pinhanez, C.: The Everywhere Displays Projector: A Device to Create Ubiquitous Graphical Interfaces. In: Abowd, G.D., Brumitt, B., Shafer, S. (eds.) UbiComp 2001. LNCS, vol. 2201, pp. 315–331. Springer, Heidelberg (2001)
26. Pinhanez, C., Podlaseck, M.: To Frame or Not to Frame: The Role and Design of Frameless Displays in Ubiquitous Applications. In: Beigl, M., Intille, S.S., Rekimoto, J., Tokuda, H. (eds.) UbiComp 2005. LNCS, vol. 3660, pp. 340–357. Springer, Heidelberg (2005)
27. Podlaseck, M., et al.: On Interfaces Projected onto Real-World Objects. In: Proc. CHI 2003 Extended Abstracts on Human Factors in Computing Systems, pp. 802–803 (2003)
28. Reason, J.: Human error. Cambridge University Press, Cambridge (1990)
29. Sakamoto, M., Matsuishi, M.: Hands-on training for chemistry laboratory in a ubiquitous computing environment. In: Proc. SUTC 2008, pp. 561–563 (2008)
30. Sengers, P., et al.: Staying open to interpretation: engaging multiple meanings in design and evaluation. In: Proc. DIS 2006, pp. 99–108 (2006)
31. Wilson, A.: PlayAnywhere: a compact interactive tabletop projection-vision system. In: Proc. UIST 2005, pp. 83–92 (2005)

Dependency Relation Based Detection of Lexicalized User Goals

Ruixue Duan[1,2], Xiaojie Wang[1], Rile Hu[2], and Jilei Tian[2]

[1] Beijing University of Posts and Communications, Beijing, China
duanruixue@gmail.com, xjwang@bupt.edu.cn
[2] Nokia Research Center, Beijing, China
{rile.hu,jilei.tian}@nokia.com

Abstract. Understanding user goal has played an important role in improving the quality of the search engines. Many previous researches focus on finding prominent statistical features to classify the user goal into Border's taxonomy. But it is difficult to achieve high precision because of the weakness of taxonomy definition. This paper first gives a lexicalized taxonomy for user goal, and then proposes a dependency relation based algorithm to detect lexicalized user goals. To alleviate the sparseness of direct dependency relation, we extend our algorithm to include second order dependency relations. The experimental results show that our extended algorithm can achieve precision of 89% on correctness and 79% on relevance, and thus it outperforms previous related algorithm significantly.

Keywords: Second order dependency relation; user goal; lexicalized taxonomy.

1 Introduction

Search engines have become one of the most important tools for people to access desired information in Internet. The development of search engines has made a great progress in recent years, however, it nowadays suffers from critical challenges in dealing with short queries [1]. Understanding the user's goal behind the short queries is the key technical enabling to enhance the quality of search engines. For achieving it, researches have made some efforts in two ways. One is to give a taxonomy as labels of different user's goal. Another is to develop various approaches to label a given search query.

Border [2] classified user goal into three categories: navigational, informational and transactional(resources). Basing on user survey and query log analysis, he got the degree of the importance of each class. Rose et al. [3] revised the set of user goal taxonomy and proposed a hierarchical structure. The hierarchical structure was static and manually designed based on their experiences. But they did not mention how to classify user goal into their taxonomy. Baeza-Yates et al. [4] classified user goal into informational, not informational and ambiguous. And they manually labeled some queries to train SVM and PLSA classifiers. It

Z. Yu et al. (Eds.): UIC 2010, LNCS 6406, pp. 167–178, 2010.

is expensive and time consuming. Furthermore, it is hard to utilize the result of classification.

A lot of work is based on Border's taxonomy [5]. Kang and Kim [6] used queries' terms distribution, mutual information, anchor text, and POS information to classify the queries into Border's taxonomy. They used different strategies to retrieve documents according to whether a query is informational or navigational. Their experimental results showed that the classification of query's goal can improve the performance of search engines. Lee et al. [7] focused on clicks made by users to guide the classification. They used click distribution, anchor-link distribution and also combination of all features to train the model. However, it is hard to determine the threshold value in the distribution graph to distinguish navigational or informational goal. Joachims [8] used eye tracking to interpret click data as implicit feedback. Yuan et al. [9] proposed four entropy-based features extracted from anchor data and click-through data, and then combined multiple features to train an SVM model. The precision of the model reached to 97%. There is nearly no error in distinguishing navigational from informational goals, but distinguishing transactional from informational user goal is more difficult, for it is similar between those two categories.

Previous work has shown that Border's taxonomy is not so clear. Navigational and non-navigational goal are easy to distinguish, while for the border between informational and transactional goal is not easy to be drawn. Another problem is that granularity of the taxonomy is too coarse. Even though we known that the query is informational, we still cannot understand what the user exactly wants.

Some researchers selected a more complex taxonomy. They classified web query into topic categories, such as ACM KDD Cup'05 hierarchical taxonomy. However, web queries are usually short, it contains little information in query itself, so it is difficult to classify web query into topic category. They manually labeled some queries in KDD 05, but found that over 85% queries have multiple categories [10]. Recently, some other researchers added external web knowledge to enrich the queries [11]. Moreover, even we can classify web query into a specific topic, there are still many potential user goals for each query. Except for the granularity of the taxonomy, another more important problem for the taxonomy is that it is static. We still cannot detect user goal for each query respectively. In fact, each short query with only a noun can have both goals. But different queries may have word specific goal, for example, query "Michael Jackson"may have goals of "download his music"and "find his information", query "potato"may have goals of "buy potato"and "cook". According to Pustejovsky [12], it is telic role (co-occurred verbs of the noun)that reveal what is the noun for, namely what is the goal of the noun.

He [13,14] , although it did not start from Pustejovsky's idea of telic role, used verb and noun pair (Verb+Noun pair) to represent user goal dynamically and proposed a statistical model which can extract the potential user goals. Inspired by this and Pustejovsky's Generative Lexicon, we also focus on analyzing user goal employing the natural language processing (NLP) technique. In our approaches, dependency relation analysis is used to improve the effectiveness of Verb+Noun pair extraction.

The contributions of this paper are summarized as follows.

First of all, a dynamic hierarchical taxonomy is proposed to handle different kinds of queries basing on telic role in Generative Lexicon. It works better than the static taxonomy stated above.

Secondly, two novel algorithms are employed to detect the user goal. It is the first attempt to find user goal using dependency relation. The algorithms improve the effectiveness of user goal detection.

This paper is organized as follows. Section 1 gives a brief introduction and related work. We then present our taxonomy for the query goal detection in section 2, and introduce how to use dependency relation to detect user goal in section 3. Two methods DRVN(dependency relation for Verb+Noun pair) and EDRVN(Extended DRVN) are proposed for improving user goal detection. In section 4, the experiments show that both DRVN and EDRVN significantly outperform He's method. Finally, we conclude the paper and point out some future research directions in section 5.

2 Taxonomy of Query Goals

A dynamic hierarchical taxonomy for web queries proposed in this section. Web queries are firstly classified into navigational and non-navigational. The non-navigational queries are further classified into several subclasses which are dependent by queries themselves. Different queries may have different subclasses under non-navigational label.

Fig. 1 shows our hierarchical taxonomy of user goal. In top level, user goals are divided into navigational and non-navigational. Previous researches have shown that the differences between navigational and non-navigational queries are significant and can be distinguished easily.

A navigational query aims to find a home page of a portal web site or institution. It is easy to be distinguished from other query goals. Much previous work has been done on enhancing the identification of navigational goals. Some simple clues have been used to identify navigational goals. This type of queries often includes a keyword of web site URL. For example, query "yahoo"is to find a portal web site whose URL is http://www.yahoo.com. Click distribution analysis can also be helpful on navigational query detection. The accuracy of navigational goals identification has reached 97% [9].

For non-navigational part, it includes Border's informational and transactional query. We can find distinguishable difference from the definition of informational and transactional query. It is, however, hard to distinguish those two categories. Occasionally human cannot do it well. Take the query "Michael Jackson"as example, we are not sure whether users want to browse some news of Michael Jackson or to download his music. For clearing these two goals, queries should be something like "Michael Jackson news"and "Michael Jackson download". But for different objectives, in order to distinguish these two goals, queries should be extended in different ways. For example, when a user want to find basic information about a book "XXX", he or she may uses a query like "XXX introduction", while if he or she wants to download the book "XXX", the query may be "XXX download". Things will be more complex if the query word is ambiguous. For a query "apple", a extended query like "apple introduction" may bring users to both fruit apple and company apple. In this case, the user should extend his query with more words, like "apple fruit introduction", for making his goal clearer. It is not a good way to ask user to show his goal because it makes user to built a longer query themselves.

Unlike Rose's static hierarchical taxonomy, we classify the non-navigational query into several subclasses according to the query's semantics and propose a query word dependent way to solve the problem.

According to Pustejovsky [12], telic role of a noun (co-occurred verbs of the noun)is a good hint for intent identification. We make use of it for user goal indication. So, the subclass will be labeled by different verbs which can form a Verb+Noun pair with the word in given query. Fig. 1 shows that we use $g_i(i \in 1 \ldots n)$ to represent the subclass user goal for non-navigational query. Its number and content will dynamically changes with the word in given query. Different query has different user goal set instead of some predefined categories.

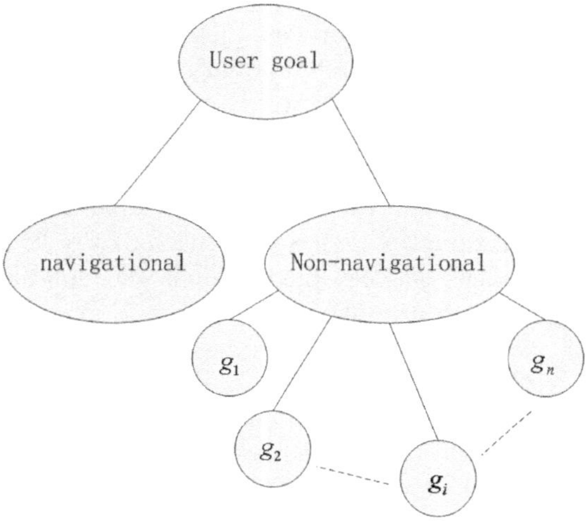

Fig. 1. Hierachical taxonomy of user goal

3 Identification of Query Goals Using Dependency Relation

As we have known, it is very efficient to distinguish non-navigational goal from navigational goal. Therefore, the remained problem is how to classify users' goals in non-navigational case. This section will present two progressive algorithms on how to classify the user goals dynamically according to users' queries.

Non-navigational goal is more complicated than that of navigational. We cannot judge what the user exactly means only using the short query. Search engine is a good assistant tool for solving the problem. Multiple query related snippets can be retrieved from search engine [15]. Those snippets are regarded as context of the query. Our assumption is that the context of the query can include some telic role (verbs) related to or the same as the user goal. We use the Verb+Noun pair to represent the potential user goal similar with that in He [13]. But unlike He [13,14] where all the queries are represented in Verb+Noun pairs, if user has already submit his need in Verb+Noun pairs, we suppose the query is non-ambiguous and do not need to find other proper Verb+Noun pairs to represent it. So we focus on the queries which contain only nouns or verbs.

A statistics based method can be used to find some Verb+Noun pairs [13,14], but it is not sure if those pairs keep some semantic relations.This paper will first find all Verb+Noun pairs by implementing dependency analysis on snippets, then select some of them to represent user goal.

After giving a brief introduction to dependency relation, we will then give two algorithms to progressively generate promising Verb+Noun pairs to represent users' possible goals.

3.1 Dependency Relation

A dependency relation [16] is an asymmetric binary relation between a word called head(or governor, parent), and another word called modifier(dependent, daughter). Normally the dependency relations form a directed graph that connects all the words in a sentence. An example dependency structure is show in Fig. 2. Where, each node contains a word. Two words linked by a directed arc which means they have a dependency relation along the direction of the arc. For example, "我"depends on "喜欢", "红"depends on "苹果". Labels on the arcs show the types of dependency relation. For example, the relation between "我"and "喜欢"is "SBV", and the relation between "红"and "苹果"is "ATT"in Fig. 2.

3.2 Using Dependency Relation to Get Verb+Noun Pair

Among different relations in dependency tree, we are interested in relation between verb and noun in sentences. We will use it for user goal classification.

We concern the queries which contain only nouns and verbs. Our algorithms will find Verb+Noun pairs for noun queries. The similar method can be used for verb queries. The details of the algorithm DRVN(Dependency Relation for Verb +Noun pair)is described as follows.

Firstly, for a given query, search engines are used to retrieve a lot of query related snippets. The snippets are context of the query. We will use only parts of the retrieved snippets since there is redundancy in retrieved snippets. Linked web pages are not used ,since it will introduce much computational complexity.

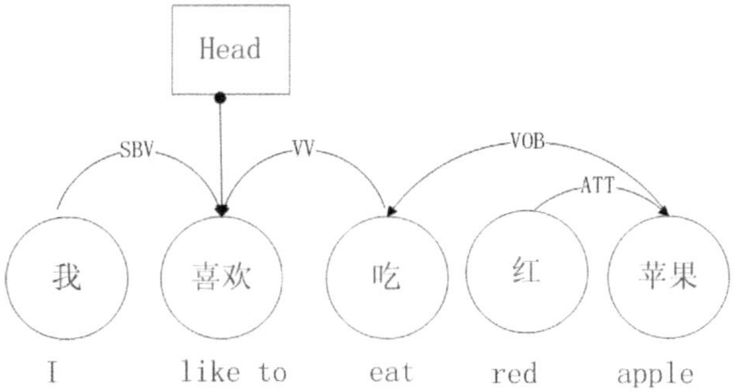

Fig. 2. Example of a dependency structure

We then use a dependency parser to parse all sentences that contain the query in selected snippets. In this way, we can get some dependency pairs. We only keep pairs which have form of Verb+Noun. Direction and type of relation of the dependency pairs are ignored, therefore Noun+Verb can be regarded as same as Verb+Noun. Of course, before dependency parsing, morphological analysis and POS tagging are needed for preprocessing. If it is used for Chinese, segmentation is also needed before POS tagging.

Finally, we sort all Verb+Noun pairs according to their numbers of occurrence, and select the top n Verb+Noun pairs as the potential user goals.

Comparing with He [13,14] , our approach concerns verbs and nouns which are directly related to the query instead of all verbs in the snippets. It makes our approach gets only query specific extension, and can achieve better precision, while He [13,14] often gets unrelated user goals. For example, when the query is "Michael Jordan", He [13] find some Verb+Noun pairs like "download address"which is unrelated to the query.

On the other hand, it can be regarded as a defect of DRVN. Since it only collects dependency relations including the query within a sentence, the amount of Verb+Noun pairs is very limited especially when it only uses parts of snippets. To alleviate this problem, we therefore propose an extension of DRVN.

3.3 EDRVN(Extended DRVN)

Reminding that all dependency relations in a sentence can be extracted by a dependency parser, we just use relations between verbs and nouns which including the query directly. In this section, we design a way to get more meaningful Verb+Noun structures by making use of other relations in dependency structures of sentences.

Let N_q be a noun in the query, two types of nodes which have dependency links with N_q are then extracted. One type is verb, the relation between N_q and each linked verb form a Verb+Noun pair, which has been introduced in above DRVN algorithm. Another type is noun. Let N_q_list denote the set of these nouns. The relation between N_q and each noun in N_q_list form a Noun+Noun pair. Each noun in N_q_list is then used to find verbs which have direct dependency relation with it. V_q_list denote the set of these verbs. More Verb+Noun are extracted. Furthermore, some second order dependency from N_q to these verbs(second order Verb+N_q) can also be derived through nouns in N_q_list. In principal, three and even higher order of Verb+Noun pair can be extracted according to above process. Considering higher order relations are not so reliable, we here only care second order relations. Fig. 3 gives a sketch map of this process.

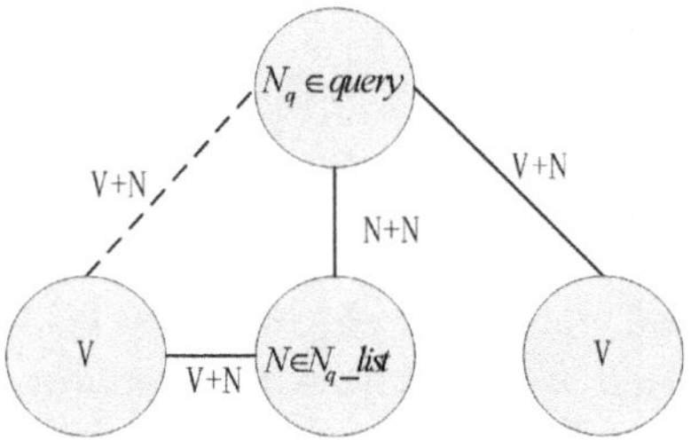

Fig. 3. Extend Verb+Noun pair

In this way, more Verb+Noun pairs are extracted from snippets. Like that in DRVN algorithm, we can then sort all Verb+Noun pairs according to their numbers of occurrence in all snippets, and select the top n Verb+Noun pairs as the potential goals representation of the query. But there are second order Verb+Noun relation. They should contribute differently with direct relation in representing user goals.

For giving our algorithm on making use of second order dependency relations, the problem is reformatted as follows. Suppose we have two direct dependency pairs $n_1 + n_2$(Noun+Noun relation,N+N for short) and $n_2 + v_2$(Verb+Noun relation, V+N for short), where n_1,n_2 are nouns, and v_2 is a verb. A second order dependency is then created, i.e. $v_2 + n_1$, as shown in Fig. 4 's dashed line which called $V + N^{(2)}$.

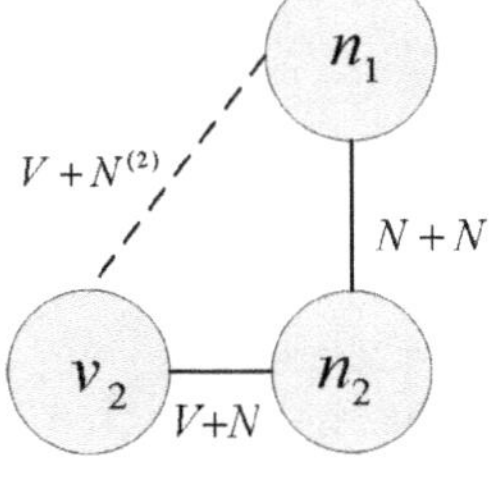

Fig. 4. $V + N^{(2)}$ pair

For directly linked Verb+Noun pair, we still count the occurrence of it as the weight of the relation like that in DRVN. Let $W^{(1)}(n_2, v_2)$ stands for the weight of the direct dependency relation $n_2 + v_2$.

For indirect relations, like v_2+n_1 in Fig. 4, we combine both weights of n_2+v_2 and $n_1 + n_2$ to get the weight of it. However, besides n_2, there are many other nodes connected v_2 and n_1. We must summary all the possible paths from v_2 to n_1 through middle nodes. Suppose each noun in N_1_list can be a middle node. Let $W^{(2)}(n_1, v_2)$ stands for the weight of $v_2 + n_1$, we calculate it using *equation*(1).

$$W^{(2)}(n_1, v_2) = \sum_{n_k \in N_1\_list} \left[F^{(1)}(n_1, n_k) \times F^{(1)}(n_k, v_2) \times W^{(1)}(n_k, v_2) \right]. \quad (1)$$

Where $F^{(1)}(n_1, n_k)$ is calculated by *equation*(2). The numerator count of the direct dependency relation $n_1 + n_k$, the denominator sums all the direct dependency relation pairs contained n_1. It represents the importance of n_k to n_1, ranged from 0 to 1. The same method is used to calculate $F^{(1)}(n_k, v_2)$ shown in *equation*(3).

$$F^{(1)}(n_1, n_k) = \frac{W^{(1)}(n_1, n_k)}{\sum_{n_j \in N_1\_list} W^{(1)}(n_1, n_j)}. \quad (2)$$

$$F^{(1)}(n_k, v_2) = \frac{W^{(1)}(n_k, v_2)}{\sum_{v_j \in V_k\_list} W^{(1)}(n_k, v_j)}. \quad (3)$$

After multiple $F^{(1)}(n_1, n_k)$ with $F^{(1)}(n_k, v_2)$, we can get the importance of v_2 to n_1 through node n_k, and then, multiple $W^{(1)}(n_k, v_2)$ to calculate the weight of indirect relations through node n_k.

Equation(4) stands for the weight of n_i and v_j. It sums the weights of direct and indirect dependency relation. α is a parameter to adjust the importance of $W^{(1)}(n_i, v_j)$and $W^{(2)}(n_i, v_j)$.

$$W(n_i, v_j) = W^{(1)}(n_i, v_j) + \alpha \times W^{(2)}(n_i, v_j). \quad (4)$$

4 Experiment

4.1 Experiment Steup

Data Set: 15 Chinese queries are used in our experiments. For each query, Top 500 snippets are downloaded from "baidu"search engine. The dependency parser [17] is used to parse these snippets. Top 100(sorted by frequency) Verb+Noun and Noun+Noun pairs are extracted. We set α to $m \times 0.2$ in experiences, m stands for the number of retrieved snippets, therefore, $\alpha = 100$ in experiences.

Evaluation Metric: Three participants(Chinese native speakers) are asked to vote whether a retrieved pair is correct and relevant for each query. Widely used

Precision at position n and Normalized Discounted Cumulative Gain are used to evaluate each algorithm on different aspects.

Precision at position n is listed in *equation*(5).It measures the correctness of the retrieved top n Verb+Noun pairs.

$$P@n = \frac{\#correct\ results}{n}. \tag{5}$$

It is worth to explain the meaning of correctness. As long as a Verb+Noun pair is a correct collocation, it is a correct answer no matter whether it is related to the query. For example, For query "乔丹"(Michael Jordan), suppose a retrieved pair is "发送+信息"(send+message). Although it is not relevant to the query, $P@n$ counts it as a correct answer because it is a correct collocation in Chinese. While "发送+喜欢"(send+like) is incorrect because it is not a correct collocation in Chinese. In a word, $P@n$ only evaluates if a Verb+Noun pair is a linguistically legal pair. We need this measure because only a correct Verb+Noun pair can efficiently reveal a goal of the noun by the verb.

Normalized Discount Cumulative Gain(NDCG) [18] is then used to measure whether a retrieved pair is related to a given query.

We define three ratings of relevance, i.e. "0=not relevant", "1=partially relevant"and "2=definitely relevant". Then the Discounted Cumulative Gain(DCG) accumulated at a particular ranking position p is defined as:

$$DCG_p = rel_1 + \sum_{i=2}^{p} \frac{rel_i}{\log_2 i}. \tag{6}$$

Where rel_i is the graded relevance of the result at position i.

User goals set vary in length depending on the query. Comparing the performance from one query to the next cannot be consistently achieved using DCG alone, so the cumulative gain at each position for a chosen value of p should be normalized across queries. This is done by sorting user goals list by relevance, producing an ideal DCG at position p ($IDCG_p$).The $NDCG_p$ is computed in equation (7):

$$NDCG_p = \frac{DCG_p}{IDCG_p}. \tag{7}$$

Note that $IDCG_p$ is the idea result of the DCG_p, in perfect ranking, the DCG_p will be the same as $IDCG_p$ producing an NDCG of 1.0. All NDCG calculations are then relative values on the interval 0.0 to 1.0 .

4.2 Experiment Result

Same data is used to implement DRVN, EDRVN algorithm, as well as He [14]'s algorithm. Fig. 5 shows the $P@n$ of the three algorithms at several positions. From Fig. 5 we can see that DRVN and EDRVN outperform He's algorithm at all positions. Averagely, DRVN outperforms He's algorithm by 11.58%, while

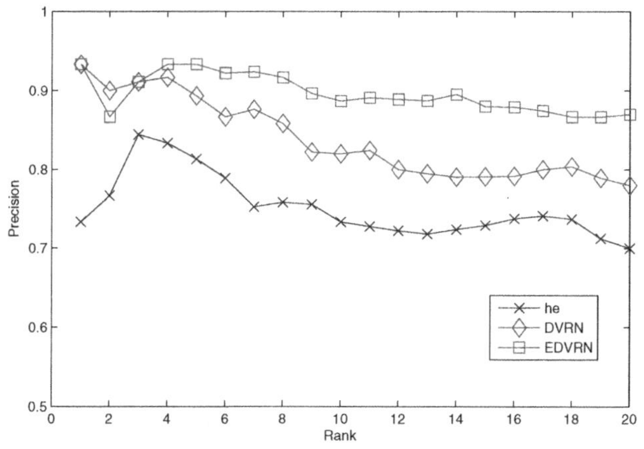

Fig. 5. P@n of three algorithms

EDRVN outperforms it much more(19.47%). It conforms that dependency relation is helpful on making the Verb+Noun pairs more reasonable. Although current performance of Chinese dependency analysis is not satisfied, it can give extra useful information.

Comparing with DRVN and EDRVN, we can find DRVN outperforms EDRVN when N<4, performs poorer than EDRVN when N≥4. DRVN algorithm only uses direct dependency relations. Those Verb+Noun pairs with higher frequencies(for example: top 3) are much possible to be correct collocations. As the number of N increases, the frequency of Nth retrieved Verb+Noun pair decreases inversely, the precision therefore decreases accordingly. By making use of second order dependency relations, EDRVN alleviates this problem. Precisions are kept on a much stable level in Fig. 5. The average precision of EDRVN is 89.61%, it outperforms DRVN by 7.16%.

Fig. 6 shows the results of NDCG. The curves of three algorithms show the situation similar to that in $P@n$. DRVN and EDRVN outperform He's algorithm by 26.44% and 40.16% respectively. EDRVN achieves better NDCG than DRVN at all ranking positions. Average NDCG of EDRVN is 79.70%, it outperforms DRVN by 10.87%.

Therefore, on both $P@n$(correctness) and NDCG (relevance), we have EDRVN > DRVN > He's algorithm. Table. 1 gives a example of top 10 possible user goals for Chinese query "绿茶"(green tea). It lists the results by both He's and EDRVN algorithm.

In Table. 1, each Verb+Noun can be considered to connect to a possible user goal. By re-organize web pages according to the Verb+Noun pairs it inlcudes, we can get user goal based web pages re-organization. It demonstrates examples of user goals for Chinese query "绿茶"(green tea)and lists the result of He and EDRVN. We can see He [14] get lots of result that not relevant to query, and EDRVN find more reasonable user goals.

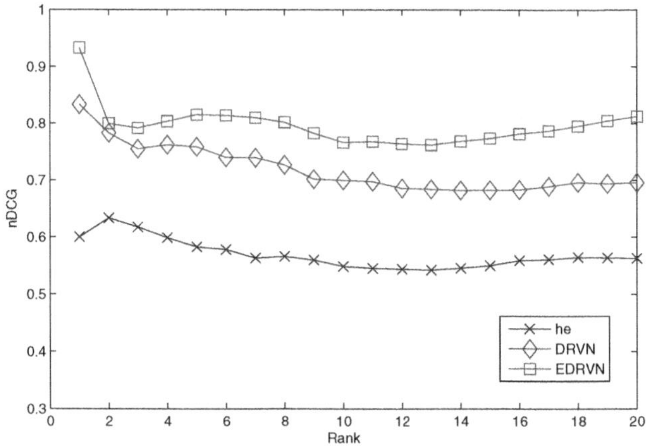

Fig. 6. NDCG of three algorithms

Table 1. Example of user goals

Rank	He user goals	EDRVN user goals
1	载入数据 (load data)	绿茶喝(drink green tea)
2	绿茶喝 (drink green tea)	喜欢绿茶 (like green tea)
3	喜欢绿茶 (like green tea)	泡绿茶(make green tea)
4	打印文章 (print paper)	茶发酵(ferment tea)
5	载入网 (load web)	生产绿茶(produce green tea)
6	载入中国(load China)	绿茶加 (add green tea)
7	测试绿茶 (test green tea)	称绿茶 (weigh green tea)
8	供应信阳 (supple xinyang)	绿茶飘香 (fragrance green tea)
9	研究绿茶 (research green tea)	绿茶免费 (free green tea)
10	说数据 (say data)	生产企业 (production company)

5 Conclusion and Future Work

In this paper, we provided a dynamic hierarchical taxonomy for user goals detection. We first classify user goals into navigational and non-navigational. And then for the non-navigational goals, we detect user goal according to each query. We use dependency relations to get more reasonable Verb+Noun pairs. To alleviate the problem of data sparseness, we make use of second order dependency relations. Experimental results show our EDRVN algorithm can achieve precision of 89.61% on correctness and 79.70% on relevance, outperform He's algorithm by 19.47% and 40.16% respectively.

Though our approach is effective for detecting user goals, there is still space to improve. Besides this, we have not clustered the similar user goals into a group yet. Each verb represent a user goal. In the future, verbs with similar meaning may be clustered into a single user goal.

Acknowledgements. This work was supported by joint research grant of Nokia-BUPT funding program. It was also partly supported by NSFC90920006 and RFDP20090005110005. Thanks to Harbin Institute of Technology for providing the dependency parser.

References

1. Cui, H., Wen, J.R., Nie, J.Y., Ma, W.Y.: Probabilistic Query Expansion Using Query Logs. In: Proceedings of the 11th International Conference on World Wide Web, pp. 325–332 (2002)
2. Border, A.: A taxonomy of web search. In: SIGIR 2002 Forum, vol. 36(2) (2002)
3. Rose, D.E., Levinson, D.: Understanding user goals in web search. In: Proceedings of the Thirteenth Int'l. WWW 2004 (2004)
4. Baeza-Yates, R., Calderon-Benavides, L., Gonzalez-Caro, C.: The Intention Behind Web Queries. In: Crestani, F., Ferragina, P., Sanderson, M. (eds.) SPIRE 2006. LNCS, vol. 4209, pp. 98–109. Springer, Heidelberg (2006)
5. Ashkan, A., Agichtein, E., et al.: Characterizing Query Intent From Sponsored Search Clickthrough Data. In: SIGIR-IRA 2008(2008)
6. Kang, I.H., Kim, G.: Query Type Classification for Web Document Retrieval. In: SIGIR 2003, pp. 64–71 (2003)
7. Lee, U., Liu, Z., Cho, J.: Automatic Identification of User Goals in Web Search. In: WWW 2005, pp. 391–400 (2005)
8. Joachims, T., Granka, L., Pan, B.: Accurately Interpreting Click through Data as Implicit Feedback. In: SIGIR 2005 (2005)
9. Yuan, X., Dou, Z., Liu, F.: Automatic User Goals Identification Based on Anchor Text and Click-Through Data. Wuhan University Journal of Natural Sciences (2008)
10. Shen, D., Sun, J.T., et al.: Building bridges for web query classification. In: SIGIR 2006, pp. 131–138 (2006)
11. Border, A.Z., et al.: Robust classiffication of rare queries using web knowledge. In: SIGIR 2007, pp. 231–238 (2007)
12. Pustejovsky, J.: The Generative Lexicon. MIT Press, Cambridge (1995)
13. Chang, Y.S., He, K.Y., et al.: Identifying User Goals from Web Search Results. In: WI 2006 (2006)
14. He, K.Y., Chang, Y.S., et al.: Improving Identification of Latent User Goals through Search-Result Snippet Classification. In: WI 2007 (2007)
15. Ferragina, P., Gulli, A.: A Personalized Search Engine Based on Web-Snippet Hierarchical Clustering. In: WWW 2005, pp. 801–810 (2005)
16. Hudson, R.: Word Grammar. Blackwell, Oxford (1984)
17. Liu, T., Ma, J., Zhu, H., et al.: Dependency parsing based on dynamic local optimization. In: Proceedings of Tenth Conference on Computational Natural Language Learning. CoNLL Shared Task, New York, pp. 111–115 (2006)
18. Jarvelin, K., Kehalainen, J.: Cumulated Gain-Based Evaluation of IR Techniques. ACM Transactions on Information Systems (2002)

Identification of Gait Patterns Related to Health Problems of Elderly

Bogdan Pogorelc[1,2] and Matjaž Gams[1,2]

[1] Jožef Stefan Institute, Department of Intelligent Systems, Jamova 39, Ljubljana, Slovenia
[2] Špica International d. o. o., Pot k sejmišču 33, Ljubljana, Slovenia
{bogdan.pogorelc,matjaz.gams}@ijs.si

Abstract. A system for automatic identification of gait patterns related to health problems of elderly for the purpose of supporting their independent living is proposed in this paper. The gait of the user is captured with the motion capture system, which consists of tags attached to the body and sensors situated in the apartment. Position of the tags is acquired by the sensors and the resulting time series of position coordinates are analyzed with machine learning algorithms in order to identify the specific health problem. We propose novel features for training a machine learning classifier that classifies the user's gait into: i) normal, ii) with hemiplegia, iii) with Parkinson's disease, iv) with pain in the back and v) with pain in the leg. Results show that naive Bayes needs more tags and less noise to reach classification accuracy of 98 % than random forest for 99 %.

Keywords: Health problems detection, human motion analysis, gait analysis, machine learning, data mining, human locomotion, ambient intelligence.

1 Introduction

Nowadays the amount of elderly in the developed countries is high and is increasing. Consequently the active population's capacity for taking care of its elderly members is decreasing. [1].

Moreover, elderly want to live at their homes for as long as possible. When living alone, nobody could detect the potential health problem of the elderly. To overcome this problem, we propose system for automatic ubiquitous elderly health care, for which we developed accurate techniques for recognition of common health problems manifesting in gait of elderly. In case the system would recognize the health problem, it would automatically notify the physician and show him/her the explanation of the automatic diagnose in form of visualization of the kinematic model. Therefore, elderly would get constant health care at their homes and physicians would be less (over)occupied with work, however they would still have the possibility to confirm/reject automatic diagnose. In this case elderly would gain constant (ubiquitous) support, providing them more safety and confidence in living at their homes.

The target health problems for automatic recognition are: hemiplegia (usually the result of stroke), Parkinson's disease, pain in the leg and pain in the back. The gait of the user is captured with the motion capture system, which consists of the tags attached to the body. The position of the tags is acquired by the sensors situated in the

Z. Yu et al. (Eds.): UIC 2010, LNCS 6406, pp. 179–191, 2010.

apartment and the resulting time series of position coordinates are analyzed with machine learning algorithms in order to recognize the specific health problem.

First objective of the research is to discover to what extent the automatic recognition of health problems with motion capture system is feasible. Second objective is to investigate the classification accuracy achievable using various numbers/placements of tags on the user's body and various amounts of noise in tag coordinates. Tag placement must achieve a trade-off between usability and technical requirements – the users prefer as few tags as possible, but too few tags cannot ensure sufficient accuracy. Both the finding regarding noise and tag placement can affect motion-capture system selection and further development and applications of care systems for elderly.

The paper is organized as follows. In Section 2 we present related work from the fields of movement recognition and sensor appliances used for the task of human behavior movement recognition. In Section 3 we propose our movement recognition system, which is based on the novel features which we describe in that section. We also define the machine learning setting, which we use for prediction of previously chosen health problems. In Section 4 we evaluate the performance of machine learning classifiers. In Section 5 we propose prototype application for the explanation of the interpreted health state. Section 6 concludes our paper and presents the potential further work in this field.

2 Related Work

Motion capture. For the automatic recognition of the movement (gait) pattern, the movement must first be captured. For this purpose many types of motion capture devices exist. Widely used are inertial sensors, nowadays usually in the form of MEMS (Micro-Electro-Mechanical Systems)-based inertial systems composed of accelerometers or gyro sensors [2-4]. The second widely used approach uses video-image processing for the reconstruction of the human body movement [21, 24]. The third approach uses cameras in combination with tags attached to the body. Usually infra-red (IR) cameras are used and the body posture is reconstructed from the position of the retroreflective tags [13], as in our approach.

There also exist some specific measurement devices for the recognition of tremor – a symptom in Parkinson's disease, but not in hemiplegia, pain in the leg and pain in the back. Tremor can be acquired with variety of measuring approaches, including sensors for a measurement of the angle of the joint deflection in tremor-type joint movements [5] and with electromyography [6].

We did not address the recognition of the activities of daily living, such as walking, sitting, lying, etc., and the detection of falling, which has already been solved [9, 16]. We were focused on solving a more challenging task, which is the recognition of gait-related health problems.

Recognition of health problems. In related work [10, 11, 12], physicians and physical therapists usually diagnose health problems which manifest in gait just by manually observing the user's gait. If they cannot decide for certain diagnose easily, they can use semiautomatic approach. In this approach, they capture the movement using motion capture system and then they analyze it by manual observing the time series of the movement (such as time series of angles of legs, etc.).

They use the same procedure for pre-rehabilitation planning (e.g. physical therapy) and after- rehabilitation evaluation to calculate the difference in movement between those states. They also use some special medical tests, e.g., test for assessment of balance. However, none of those approaches can provide constant real-time observation of the elderly at home, for fast recognition of changes in movement (gait), indicating some health problem or progress in at home rehabilitation.

The example of the semiautomatic approach is also [24], where a system for long-term monitoring of the gait in Parkinson's disease is presented. The characteristics of every stride taken were acquired using a lightweight ankle-mounted sensor array that saved the data into a small pocket PC. In comparison to our approach, the described approach was meant for the monitoring of progress of Parkinson's disease for the known Parkinson's disease patient and was not used for the early automatic recognition of health problems.

The work [5] presents sensors for the measurement of the angle of joint deflection in tremor-type joint movements, which can also be used to assess Parkinson's disease. However, the sensor systems are too big and would prevent users from doing the activities of daily living if the systems were to be worn all day. Just like the system described previously it has major drawback in comparison to our approach, because the system cannot automatically recognize Parkinson's disease or any other health problem.

Using similar motion-capture system as that in our approach, the automatic distinguishing between health problems such as hemiplegia and diplegia is presented in [15]. A classification accuracy of 92.5 % was reported. This was achieved with Self-Organizing Maps, whose features were wavelet-transformed gait characteristics such as walking speed and stride length.

To present the motion recognition field more generally, also fall detection and activity recognition will be mentioned here. The works are broken down by the choice of motion capture system.

Fall detection and activity recognition using inertial sensors. Fall detection with accelerometers and gyro sensors [21] is quite common, particularly when using simple threshold algorithms [14], achieving classification accuracies close to 100 %. With a more advanced approach using the One-Class SVM machine learning algorithm whose features were accelerations, changes in acceleration etc., an accuracy of 96.7 % was reported [23].

Accelerometers can also be used for activity recognition. Five tri-axial accelerometers distinguished 30 physical activities of various intensities with an accuracy of 94.9 % with person-dependent training and 56.3 % with person-independent training [20]. This was achieved with C4.5 decision trees using various time- and frequency-domain features.

Fall detection and activity recognition from video. Fall detection and activity recognition from video are also quite common. In an example of fall detection [21], objects in the video were first identified and then rules were applied to the aspect ratios of their bounding boxes, their horizontal and vertical gradients and angles, achieving an average accuracy of 83 %. In an example of activity recognition [24], ten states related to the activities of daily living were distinguished with an average accuracy of 74.1 %. This was achieved by first reconstructing the human body in the video and then matching its state against models defined using a specialized language.

Fall detection and activity recognition from video and tags. This work, using similar motion capture devices as ours [19], used 43 body tags sampled with 30 Hz to distinguish between seven activities related to military operations, reporting an accuracy of 76.9 %. This was achieved with the SVM machine learning algorithm whose features were the tag coordinates belonging to two postures separated by 1/3 of a second, reduced in number to 20 using Principal Component Analysis.

Another paper on activity recognition [18] used 41 body tags sampled with 120 Hz to distinguish between 21 dance gestures, reporting an accuracy of 99.3 %. The gestures were represented with Gaussian mixture models of joint angles. The high accuracy can in part be attributed to the high quality of the input data, the strictly defined gestures and the fact that testing was always done on the same dancer as the training.

Investigation of the optimal placement of motion capture devices. An important part of the research presented in this paper is the study of the impact of the placement of tags on the user's body and the amount of noise in tag coordinates on the classification accuracy. The closest work in this respect that we are aware of investigated the placement of accelerometers for fall detection [8, 14]. Their finding was that the head provides optimal accuracy, but is impractical, the wrist is not appropriate, and the waist is a good option.

3 Health Problem Recognition System

Targeted Health Problems. For the development of our health problem recognition system we focused on four health problems and normal walking as a reference in accordance with the suggestions received from the collaborating medical expert. The specific health problems for recognition were suggested based on the incidence in the elderly aged 65+, the medical significance and the feasibility of their recognition from the observed subjects' movements. The following four health problems were chosen as the most appropriate [10, 11, 12]: Parkinson's disease, hemiplegia, pain in the leg and pain in the back.

Construction of the Features for Machine Learning. A physician usually diagnoses target health problems while observing a patient's gait (i.e. posture and the walking pattern). Since the gaits of patients with the observed four health problems and normal gait look similar to each other, a physician needs to pay attention to many details that need to be transformed into computable quantities. In practice, the observed five health states can be detected by the distinctive walking patterns [10, 11, 12]. For the task of the automatic health- problem recognition we proposed and tested 13 features that are based on the tag locations, for 12 tags, placed on the shoulders, elbows, wrists, hips, knees and ankles of the elderly.

The proposed features are listed as follows:

I. Absolute difference between i) average distance between right elbow and right hip and ii) average distance between right wrist and left hip.

II. Average angle of the right elbow.
III. Quotient between maximal angle of the left knee and maximal angle of the right knee.
IV. Difference between maximal and minimal angle of the right knee.
V. Difference between maximal and minimal height of the left shoulder.
VI. Difference between maximal and minimal height of the right shoulder.
VII. Quotient between i) difference between maximal and minimal height of left ankle and ii) maximal and minimal height of right ankle.
VIII. Absolute difference between i) difference between maximal and minimal speed (magnitude of velocity) of the left ankle and ii) difference between maximal and minimal speed of the right ankle.
IX. Absolute difference between i) average distance between right shoulder and right elbow and ii) average distance between left shoulder and right wrist.
X. Average speed (magnitude of velocity) of the right wrist.
XI. Frequency of angle of the right elbow passing average angle of the right elbow.
XII. Average angle between i) vector between right shoulder and right hip and ii) vector between right shoulder and right wrist.
XIII. Difference between average height of the right shoulder and average height of the left shoulder.

The features for the identification of the chosen four health problems were designed with the help of a medical expert. They are afterwards used for modeling using the machine learning methods.

Modeling Target Health Problems using Machine Learning. To construct a predictive model which can be subsequently used to automatically recognize health problems in the subjects yet to be observed (our first objective from the Introduction), we employed supervised learning methods from the field of machine learning (sub-field of the artificial intelligence field). In supervised learning, a training data set of already labeled subjects (i.e. classified into one of the target five classes) is used to construct a model, which is later used to predict the class of the subjects for which we wish to detect the health problem.

Our task was therefore to classify the recordings of walking into five classes: four with selected health problems (classes *hemiplegia*, *parkinson*, *pain-leg*, *pain-back*) and one without it (*normal*).

Data for the evaluation of the proposed approach was collected by recording the gaits of test subjects with particular walking patterns, of which each subject was recorded 4-5 times. The final data set of 141 recordings consisted of:

- 25 recordings of normal walking,
- 45 recordings of walking with hemiplegia,
- 25 recordings of walking with Parkinson's disease,
- 25 recordings of walking with a limp due to a pain in the leg,
- 21 recordings of walking with a limp due to a pain in the back.

The recordings consisted of the position coordinates for the 12 tags worn on the body, sampled with 60 Hz. The tag coordinates were acquired with Smart IR motion capture system with 0.5 mm standard deviation of noise.

For each subject, the locations of the sensor tags were recorded in a session which lasted 5-8 seconds from which a vector of 13 proposed features was computed. These learning examples were labeled with the type of the representing health problem, yielding the final data on which the classifier was trained.

4 Experiments and Results

In our experimental work we focused on analyzing the classification accuracies of model, built using the machine learning methods. The experimental classification accuracies were obtained using stratified 10-fold cross validation. We compared naive Bayes and random forest machine learning algorithms implemented in Weka [22].

The 10-fold cross-validation resulted in classification accuracy of 97.2 % and 99.3 % for naive Bayes and random forest classifier, respectively.

Table 1. Confusion matrices of naive Bayes (left) and random forest classifier (right), where H=hemiplegia, L=pain in the leg, N=normal (healthy) walking, P=Parkinson's disease and B=Pain in the back. Numbers denote quantity of the classified examples.

		classified as				
		H	**L**	**N**	**P**	**B**
true class	**H**	42	2	1	0	0
	L	0	25	0	0	0
	N	1	0	24	0	0
	P	0	0	0	25	0
	B	0	0	0	0	21

		classified as				
		H	**L**	**N**	**P**	**B**
true class	**H**	45	0	0	0	0
	L	0	25	0	0	0
	N	0	0	25	0	0
	P	1	0	0	24	0
	B	0	0	0	0	21

Table 1 shows the confusion matrices, i.e. how many examples of a certain true class (in rows) are classified in one of possible five classes (in columns).

For the real world cases, we can use confusion matrices for three purposes:

- We can observe how many false positives (false alarms) can be expected using these classifiers. When in real world use the system would report false alarm, e.g., normal walking is classified as some health problem, ambulance could drive to pick up the elderly which would cause unnecessary costs. In case of naive Bayes, normal walking was in 1 of 25 examples erroneously classified as hemiplegia.
- We can see how many false negatives can be expected using these classifiers. False negatives could mean potentially risky situation for the elderly, as his/her health problem would not be recognized automatically. In case of naive Bayes, hemiplegia was in 1 of 45 examples erroneously classified as normal walking.
- We can identify between which health states (classes) the errors (misclassifications) occurs. Consequently, we can add additional features to help distinguish between those particular classes. The misclassifications happened very rarely.

The results show that in the proposed approach false positives/negatives are very rare, i.e., they would not cause much unnecessary ambulance costs. Since the method accurately classified most true health problems, it represents high confidence and safety for the potential use in elderly care.

4.1 Variation of Noise

To test the robustness of the approach, we added Gaussian noise with varying standard deviation (and zero mean) to the raw coordinates. The standard deviation of noise was varied from 0 mm to 50 mm in steps of 5 mm.

As a preprocessing step, a Kalman filter was used to smooth the potentially unrealistic difference between the positions of two consecutive time samples, caused by the addition of Gaussian noise to the captured positions [17]. The classification accuracies the classifiers, modeled on noisy data, are shown in Table 2.

Table 2. Classification accuracies (CA in [%]) of the naive Bayes (second row) and random forest classifier (third row) built on data with added noise. The table cells contain the classification accuracy and the significance level of the two-tailed paired t-test which was performed between the cross-validation folds of the initial setting (0 mm noise) and the corresponding amount of noise denoted by the table column. Dark shading denotes the experiments in which the classification accuracy significantly changed ($\alpha < 0.05$).

Noise [mm]	*0*	5	10	15	20	25	30	35	40	45	50
CA (NB)	*97.2*	97.9 $\alpha =$ 0.608	98.6 $\alpha =$ 0.168	97.2 $\alpha =$ 0.999	95.7 $\alpha =$ 0.443	95.7 $\alpha =$ 0.443	96.5 $\alpha =$ 0.654	95.7 $\alpha =$ 0.343	93.6 $\alpha =$ 0.096	92.2 $\alpha =$ 0.045	92.2 $\alpha =$ 0.068
CA (RF)	*99.3*	97.9 $\alpha =$ 0.168	99.3 $\alpha =$ 0.999	98.6 $\alpha =$ 0.591	99.3 $\alpha =$ 0.999	97.9 $\alpha =$ 0.168	97.9 $\alpha =$ 0.352	97.9 $\alpha =$ 0.343	96.5 $\alpha =$ 0.099	93.6 $\alpha =$ 0.053	94.3 $\alpha =$ 0.008

Table 2 shows the results of varying the amount of standard deviation of noise in the range 0 – 50 mm. The results indicate that only significant decrease in classification accuracy happened at 45 mm and 50 mm for naive Bayes and random forest, respectively. Both algorithms manage to retain their performance long while increasing the data noise.

Even with the highest amount of noise added, the classification accuracies of both classifiers were much higher than the accuracy of the majority class classifier with classification accuracy of 31.9 %. Majority class classifier defines the lowest acceptable classification accuracy, which can be trivially achieved by classifying all examples into the majority class, i.e., class with the largest number of training examples. Therefore, the models are robust to the addition of the noise.

4.2 Reduction of the Number of Tags

Since wearing the full complement of 12 tags may be annoying to the user, we investigated ways to reduce the number of tags. We started with all 12 tags and removed them in the order that retained the largest number of the features when decreasing the number of tags by one. Consequently, the "best" tag placement for each number of the 12 tags was obtained. The classification accuracies for the best tag placements for various numbers of tags and without addition of noise are shown in Table 3.

Table 3. The classification accuracies achieved with the best tag placements for each number of tags. The table cells contain the classification accuracy and the significance level of the two-tailed paired t-test which was performed between the initial setting (12 tags) and the corresponding number of tags. Dark shading denotes the experiments in which the classification accuracy decreased significantly ($\alpha < 0.05$).

Nr. of tags	*12*	11	10	9	8	7	6	5	4	3	2	1
CA (NB)	*97.2*	97.9 $\alpha =$ 0.343	98.6 $\alpha =$ 0.168	97.9 $\alpha =$ 0.343	97.2 $\alpha =$ 0.999	92.9 $\alpha =$ 0.052	96.5 $\alpha =$ 0.591	93.6 $\alpha =$ 0.052	92.9 $\alpha =$ 0.195	83.0 $\alpha =$ 0.001	68.8 $\alpha <$ 0.001	50.4 $\alpha <$ 0.001
CA (RF)	*99.3*	97.9 $\alpha =$ 0.573	99.3 $\alpha =$ 0.965	100.0 $\alpha =$ 0.343	100.0 $\alpha =$ 0.343	95.7 $\alpha =$ 0.053	98.6 $\alpha =$ 0.343	97.9 $\alpha =$ 0.168	95.7 $\alpha =$ 0.096	90.8 $\alpha =$ 0.009	73.8 $\alpha <$ 0.001	42.6 $\alpha <$ 0.001

The results show that decreasing the number of tags results in the decrease of classifier's performance. From Table 3 we can observe that 4 is the smallest number of tags for which the performance of classifiers is insignificantly different compared to the initial setting.

For recognizing target health states, the positions of tags from the most to the least appropriate are: shoulder, wrist, elbow, hip, ankle and knee.

4.3 Dependence of the Classification Accuracy on the Tag Placement and Noise Level

Besides experimenting with tag placement, for every placement we also varied the standard deviation of noise from 0 to 50 mm. Fig. 1 and Fig. 2 show the dependence of the classification accuracy (CA) on the tag placement and the noise level. We can observe a variation of the noise in the standard deviation from 0 to 50 mm on horizontal axis and the best tag placement for each number of tags from 12 to 1 tag on the vertical axis. Each curve of different color and shape (e.g. doted, dashed) connects points of the particular classification accuracy.

Fig. 1 illustrates that naive Bayes classifier never exceeded classification accuracy of 99 %. It (nearly) reached the classification accuracy of 98 % with 10-12 tags and 0-5 mm noise. At least 8 tags with 0-35 mm noise and precisely 6 tags with 0-40 mm noise were required to surpass the 95 % accuracy limit. At least 3 tags with 0-10 mm noise, 4 tags with 15-40 mm noise and 5 tags with 45-50 mm noise were needed to achieve the classification accuracy of over 80 %.

Fig. 2 shows the classification accuracies for the random forest classifier. It needed only 8 tags with noise 0-20 mm to reach the classification accuracy of over 99 % except for the "islands" of insignificantly lower accuracies. To reach the accuracy of over 95 %, 4 tags for 0-10 mm, 5 tags for 15-25 mm and 6 tags for 30-40 mm noise were required. To exceed the boundary of 90 %, 3 tags for 0 mm, 4 tags for 5-35 mm, 5 tags for 40 mm and 6 tags for 45-50 mm noise were needed. To exceed the accuracy of 80 %, at least 3 tags for 0-35 mm, 4 tags for 35-45 mm and 5 tags for 50 mm were required.

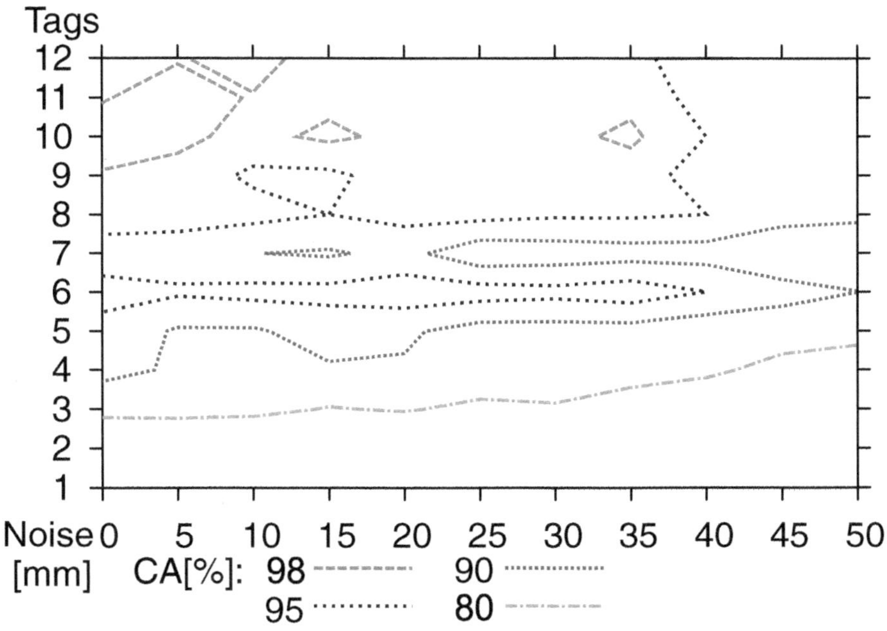

Fig. 1. Classification accuracy with respect to the number of tags and the noise level for the recognition of the target health problems using the naive Bayes classifier

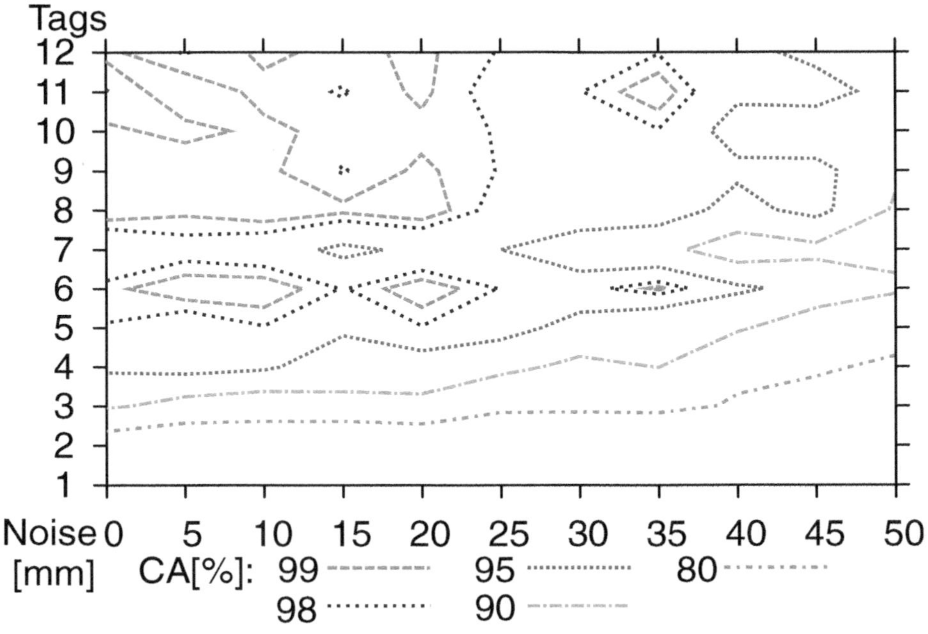

Fig. 2. Classification accuracy with respect to the number of tags and the noise level for the recognition of the target health problems using the random forest classifier

Although the classification accuracies of the random forest classifier are overall better than of naive Bayes, naive Bayes has important advantage in interpretability of the predictions. In case the system recognizes some health state it explains the reasons for classification to the physician.

5 Explanation of the Interpreted Health State

Because it is very important for the physician to obtain an explanation for the interpreted health state, we also paid a lot of attention to it and developed a control-panel prototype, which is intended to be used by physicians (shown in Fig. 3).

In the middle of the prototype screen, there is visualization of the kinematic model of the elderly moving through the room. In the upper-right-hand corner there are controls for saving and loading the captured movement. Underneath there are the time series of the calculated angles. In the lower-left-hand corner the time series of the x, y and z positions are shown for all 13 tags (the 13th tag is calculated from the positions of the nearest tags). When the health problem is recognized, the red alarm button appears in the left upper-left-hand corner with the necessary description of the recognized case for the relatives and for the medical center that has the control panel.

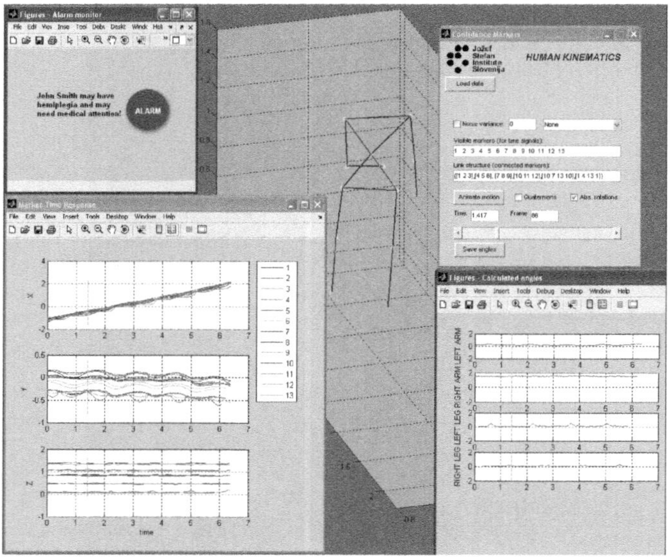

Fig. 3. Control panel prototype for the explanation of the interpreted health state

6 Conclusion

A system for the automatic identification of gait patterns related to health problems of elderly has been proposed in this research. Time series of the detected positions of the body parts from the motion-capture system are transformed into a form for supervised machine learning methods using novel features for recognition of health problems. Although the automatic recognition of health problems is rarely addressed in research, our results are promising.

First objective of the research was to discover to what extent the automatic recognition of health problems with motion capture system is feasible. The results show that in the initial setting (no noise, all tags) decision tree and random forest algorithm achieved an average classification accuracy of 97.2 % and 99.3 %, respectively. This is much higher than the 31.9 % of the reference majority class; consequently, achieved classification accuracies are high. In the experimental results of initial setting, there were a few false positives/negatives, thus they would not cause much unnecessary ambulance costs in implementation of our approach in practice. Since the system accurately classified the most true health problems, it represents high confidence and safety for the elderly in the potential use in elderly care. Therefore, the automatic recognition of health problems with motion capture system is feasible to a high extent.

Second objective was to investigate the classification accuracy achievable using machine learning approach and various numbers/placements of tags on the user's body and various amounts of noise in tag coordinates. Tag placement must achieve a trade-off between usability and technical requirements – the users prefer as few tags as possible, but too few tags cannot ensure sufficient accuracy. Both the finding regarding noise and tag placement can affect motion-capture system selection and further development and applications of care systems for elderly.

The results of varying the amount of noise indicate that only significant difference in classification accuracy occurred at 45 mm and 50 mm for naive Bayes and random forest, respectively. Both algorithms manage to retain their performance long while increasing the data noise. The approach is therefore robust to the addition of the noise. The results of decreasing the number of tags show that it causes the decreasing of classifier's performance. Four is the smallest number of tags for which the classification accuracies of classifiers are insignificantly different compared to the initial one.

The results of investigation of the dependence of the classification accuracy on the tag placement and noise level show that naive Bayes (nearly) reached the classification accuracy of 98 % with 10-12 tags and 0-5 mm noise, while random forest needed only 8 tags with noise 0-20 mm to reach the classification accuracy of over 99 %. Although the classification accuracies of the random forest classifier are overall better than of naive Bayes, naive Bayes has important advantage in interpretability of the predictions. In case the system recognizes some health state it explains the reasons for classification to the physician.

Because it is very important for the physician to obtain an explanation for the interpreted health state, we also paid a lot of attention to it and developed a control-panel prototype for the explanation of the interpreted health state, which is intended to be used by physicians. When the health problem is recognized, the alarm button appears with the necessary description of the recognized case for the relatives and for the medical center that has the control panel.

In future work, additional features to improve distinguishing between classes, where the confusion matrices showed misclassifications, can be added, although these misclassifications happened very rarely. Using wearable (e.g. inertial) motion capture system instead of infra-red one would allow recognition of health problems of elderly even outside of their homes. This would be possible with adaptation of our algorithms. Modification of the proposed recognition system could be used also for automatic evaluation of rehabilitation process (e.g. after stroke) at home.

Acknowledgments. This work is partially financed by the European Union, the European Social Fund. The authors thank Martin Tomšič, Bojan Nemec and Leon Žlajpah for their help with data acquisition, Anton Gradišek for his medical expertise and Zoran Bosnić and Mitja Luštrek for helpful discussions.

References

1. Toyne, S.: Ageing: Europe's growing problem. BBC News, `http://news.bbc.co.uk/2/hi/business/2248531.stm` 2009-01-19
2. Strle, D., Kempe, V.: MEMS-based inertial systems. Informacije MIDEM 37(4), 199–209 (2007)
3. Jurman, D., Jankovec, M., Kamnik, R., Topič, M.: Inertial and magnetic sensors: The calibration aspect. Informacije MIDEM 37(2), 67–72 (2007)
4. Dimic, F., Mušič, B., Osredkar, R.: An example of an integrated GPS and DR positioning system designed for archeological prospecting. Informacije MIDEM 38(2), 144–148 (2008)
5. Ribarič, S., Rozman, J.: Sensors for measurement of tremor type joint movements. Informacije MIDEM 37(2), 98–104 (2007)
6. Trontelj, J., Trontelj, J., Trontelj, L.: Safety Margin at mammalian neuromuscular junction – an example of the significance of fine time measurements in neurobiology. Informacije MIDEM 383(3), 155–160 (2008)
7. Bourke, A.K., Lyons, G.M.: A threshold-based fall-detection algorithm using a bi-axial gyroscope sensor. Medical Engineering & Physics 30(1), 84–90 (2006)
8. Bourke, A.K., Scanaill, C.N., Culhane, K.M., O'Brien, J.V., Lyons, G.M.: An optimum accelerometer configuration and simple algorithm for accurately detecting falls. In: Proc. BioMed 2006, pp. 156–160 (2006)
9. Confidence: Ubiquitous Care System to Support Independent Living, `http://www.confidence-eu.org`
10. Craik, R., Oatis, C.: Gait Analysis: Theory and Application. Mosby-Year Book (1995)
11. Harrison, R.D.: Harrison's principles of internal medicine, 14th edn. McGraw Hill, New York (1998)
12. Perry, J.: Gait Analysis: Normal and Pathological Function. McGraw-Hill, Inc., New York (1992)
13. eMotion. Smart motion capture system, `http://www.emotion3d.com/smart/smart.html`
14. Kangas, M., Konttila, A., Lindgren, P., Winblad, P., Jamsa, T.: Comparison of low-complexity fall detection algorithms for body attached accelerometers. Gait & Posture 28(2), 285–291 (2008)
15. Lakany, H.: Extracting a diagnostic gait signature. Pattern recognition 41, 1627–1637 (2008)
16. Luštrek, M., Kaluža, B.: Fall Detection and Activity Recognition with Machine Learning. Informatica (Slovenia) 33(2), 197–204 (2009)
17. Maybeck, P.S.: Stochastic models, estimation, and control. Mathematics in Science and Engineering 141 (1979)

18. Qian, G., Guo, F., Ingalls, T., Olson, L., James, J., Rikakis, T.: A gesture-driven multimodal interactive dance system. In: Proc. ICME 2004, pp. 1579–1582 (2004)
19. Sukthankar, G., Sycara, K.: A cost minimization approach to human behavior recognition. In: Proc. AAMAS 2005, pp. 1067–1074 (2005)
20. Tapia, E.M., Intille, S.S., Haskell, W., Larson, K., Wright, J., King, A., Friedman, R.: Real-time recognition of physical activities and their intensities using wireless accelerometers and a heart rate monitor. In: Proc. ISWC 2007, pp. 37–40 (2007)
21. Vishwakarma, V., Mandal, C., Sura, S.: Automatic detection of human fall in video. In: Ghosh, A., De, R.K., Pal, S.K. (eds.) PReMI 2007. LNCS, vol. 4815, pp. 616–623. Springer, Heidelberg (2007)
22. Witten, I.H., Frank, E.: Data Mining: Practical Machine Learning Tools and Techniques, 2nd edn. Morgan Kaufmann, San Francisco (2005)
23. Zhang, T., Wang, J., Liu, P., Hou, J.: Fall detection by wearable sensor and One-Class SVM algorithm. LNCIS, vol. 345, pp. 858–863 (1988)
24. Zouba, N., Boulay, B., Bremond, F., Thonnat, M.: Monitoring activities of daily living (ADLs) of elderly based on 3D key human postures. In: Proc. ICVW 2008, pp. 37–50 (2008)
25. Moore, S.T., et al.: Long-term monitoring of gait in Parkinson's disease. Gait Posture (2006) doi:10.1016/j.gaitpost.2006.09.011

An Energy Efficient Localization Strategy for Outdoor Objects Based on Intelligent Light-Intensity Sampling

Frode Eika Sandnes

Faculty of Engineering, Oslo University College, Oslo, Norway
frodes@hio.no

Abstract. A simple and low cost strategy for implementing pervasive objects that identify and track their own geographical location is proposed. The strategy, which is not reliant on any GIS infrastructure such as GPS, is realized using an electronic artifact with a built in clock, a light sensor, or low-cost digital camera, persistent storage such as flash and sufficient computational circuitry to make elementary trigonometric computations. The object monitors the lighting conditions and thereby detects and tracks the sunrise and sunset times. By the means of a simple celestial model an estimate of the geographical position of the object can be made. An intelligent light sampling method is proposed allowing the object to sleep most of the time and hence save battery power. The strategy is energy efficient and the speed of convergence can be adjusted as a function of the energy consumed. Objects employing the method can therefore operate for long times without recharging their batteries. The strategy has applications in mobile sensor networks where nodes need to log geographical information, sensing equipment such as floating buoyancies, or pervasive technologies in need of geospatial information such as digital cameras, mobile devices, etc.

Keywords: Intelligent objects, geo-location, object tracking.

1 Introduction

Geographical information is an important attribute of modern information systems, especially within the field of mobile, pervasive and ubiquitous computing systems [7]. For instance, geo-tagging is particularly useful for image tagging allowing more convenient organization and retrieval [3] of images. Current solutions usually rely on GPS which provides excellent accuracy. However, GPS devices are expensive, consume much electrical power and take a long time to lock onto overhead satellites. The most worrying aspect about the GPS technology is that this infrastructure is reaching the end of its lifetime and there is yet no realistic replacement available [5]. Several strategies that omit GPS technology have been proposed. For instance in sensor networks one may find the location of a sensor by triangulating according to range using the location of other neighboring anchor sensor whose location is known [18]. In the field of image recognition landmark recognition has been used to determine the location of the observer by identifying known landmarks [19]. Clearly, this is an ambitious strategy that both depends on powerful image processing algorithms

Z. Yu et al. (Eds.): UIC 2010, LNCS 6406, pp. 192–204, 2010.

and extensive landmark databases. Another branch of research is inspired by traditional navigation according to the celestial bodies including the sun, stars and the moon, and also the detection of time [6, 16]. Of these, geographical locations have been estimated based on direct sun observations, that is, observation of the sun elevation over the horizon by the means of a camera [4, 17]. Problems with these strategies are that they either require a wide angle lens or very low sun elevations. Instead, it has been proposed to measure the sun elevation indirectly using shadows [11, 14]. One problem with sun observations is that it will only work on sunny days. To combat this it has been proposed to measure the sun elevation indirectly using the overall light intensity of images as even on cloudy days the light intensity will vary with the hour of the day [12, 15]. Related research has the access to regular image sequences acquired by webcams and these can be used to detect the relative location of webcams [8, 9] or absolutely by identifying sunrise and sunsets [13].

2 Method

The method proposed herein can be reformulated as the problem of identifying and tracking the sunrise and sunset times. The strategy therefore has two major stages, namely initialization involving the identification of sunset and sunrise times and tracking involving detecting object motions by observing changes in the sunset and sunrise times. This paper first outlines hardware requirements. Next, the employed celestial model is presented. Finally, the initialization and tracking procedures are described.

2.1 Hardware Requirements

The method proposed herein is based on electronic objects with a built in clock which maintains a relatively accurate account of time and date. Digital clocks are built into most electronic hardware nowadays and can run for many years on one single battery with limited drift. It is therefore assumed that at any time the object can enquire the current time t and date d. It is assumed that the time is set to Universal Time (UTC) which makes the calculations presented herein simple and is represented in decimal form in the range from 0 to 24. Issues such as daylight saving time are thus avoided. Next, the date d is represented as the day of the year, where January 1st is day 1, etc. In this strategy the year information is not used.

Next, the strategy requires that the electronic object has some form of light sensor that is capable of measuring the lighting condition e. This can for instance be a simple and low cost exposure value meter such as those built into most low-cost digital cameras [1, 2, 10] or it could be a low cost camera (CCD-chip). In the cases of exposure values (EV) then e is a real value between 0 to approximately 20. If a camera is used a simple representation of exposure can be obtained simply using:

$$e = \frac{1}{X \cdot Y} \sum_{x=1}^{X} \sum_{y=1}^{Y} I_{x,y} \tag{1}$$

Where $I_{x,y}$ is the pixel intensity for the pixel located at x, y in the image and X and Y are the width and height of the image, respectively. To reduce computation a small subset of these points can be sampled throughout the image using some two dimensional sampling pattern.

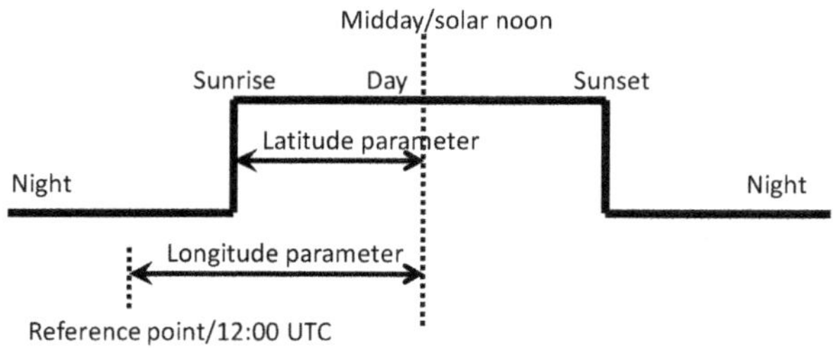

Fig. 1. Daylight parameters influenced by latitude and longitude

2.2 Celestial Model

The method described herein can be reduced to the problem of identifying and tracking the sunset and sunrise times. Given an accurate measurement of the sunrise time $t_{sunrise}$ and sunset time t_{sunset}, the solar noon t_{midday} is simply:

$$t_{midday} = \frac{t_{sunset} - t_{sunrise}}{2} \tag{2}$$

Note that it is assumed that the sunrise occurs before the sunset in the representation of time. If the sunset occurs "before" the sunrise then the computations wrap around so that they fit within the range of 0 to 24.

Next, the angular sunset a_{sunset} can be computed as follows:

$$a_{sunset} = \frac{\pi}{12}(t_{sunset} - t_{midday}) \tag{3}$$

Note that the sign should be inverted if the sunrise occurs after the sunset within the 24 hour UTC time window. Then, the latitude φ of the objects location can be found by numerically solving for latitude using the following equation:

$$\cos(a_{sunset}) = \frac{\sin(-0.83) - \sin(\varphi)\cdot\sin(\delta)}{\cos(\varphi)\cdot\cos(\delta)} \tag{4}$$

Where δ is the declination of the sun and can be approximated by

$$\delta = \text{-}0.4092797\cos\left(\frac{2\pi}{365}(d+10)\right) \tag{5}$$

Finally, the longitude of the object is simply found using:

$$\lambda = 2\pi \frac{12 - t_{midday}}{24} \tag{6}$$

These parameters are illustrated in Fig. 1.

2.3 Initialization

2.3.1 Brute Force

Initialization involves locating the time of the sunrise and sunset for an object when first switched on. The geographic location identified during the initialization is later used during tracking. Given a sufficient supply of electric power, for instance if the object has a steady power supply the initialization can be simply be performed using brute force by continuously sampling the lighting condition. If the light sensor is sampled at r samples per second, then this is the same as M samples for each 24 hour cycle, given by:

$$M = 24 \times 60 \times 60 \times r \tag{7}$$

The accuracy of the measurements will therefore be in the range of:

$$a = \frac{360}{M} \tag{8}$$

It will take maximum 24 hours to identify the location and the effort involved is defined by $E=Mp$ where p is the energy consumed to perform each sample and E is the total energy. This is the optimal solution in terms of speed and accuracy. However, for a power constrained device the strategy is unrealistic as a very simple device could run out of power after just a few hours or sooner. In the following a series of more energy efficient strategies will be explored.

2.3.2 Binary Subdivision

The strategy presented herein is based on iterative subdivision. Each 24 hour cycle defines one round, or one iteration, and the brute force method is simply based on performing the initialization in one round. Imagine instead that at each round only one sample is taken at a strategic location and that a pattern of the whereabouts of the sunrise an sunsets is established over time. In the first round two samples are taken, namely at 0 UTC and 12 UTC. This allows us to determine with 180 degree accuracy when it is night and when it is day. Next in the second round two more samples are taken at 6 UTC and 18 UTC. Then, one will be able to determine the location of the sunrise and sunset down to a sector of 90 degrees. Then for the third round the two sectors where the sunrise and sunset are located is further subdivided in two equal halves by sampling the midpoint. This procedure continues until the desired accuracy

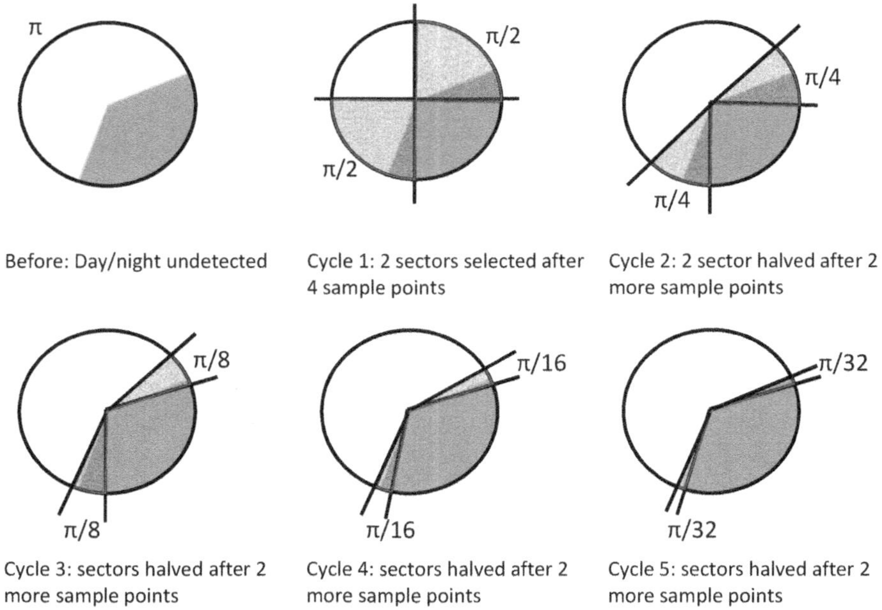

Fig. 2. Binary subdivision initialization

is acquired. In general, at round n the sunset and sunrise times are determined with an accuracy a of

$$a = \frac{360}{2^n} \tag{9}$$

Alternatively, the number of steps, that is, 24 hour cycles, it takes to achieve an accuracy of a with this strategy is:

$$n = \frac{\ln\left(\frac{360}{a}\right)}{\ln(2)} \tag{10}$$

The energy consumed is thus:

$$E = 2np \tag{11}$$

where p represents one unit of consumed power sampling the light intensity.

2.3.3 N-Way Subdivision

A problem with binary subdivision is that it can take quite a few days to get a good lock on the sunrise and sunset times. In the mean time the object might have moved or the changes in the season may have significantly affected the sunrise and sunset times because of changes in sun declination. In other situations it may be desirable to obtain a more instant geographical estimate of the location by investing more power. For this

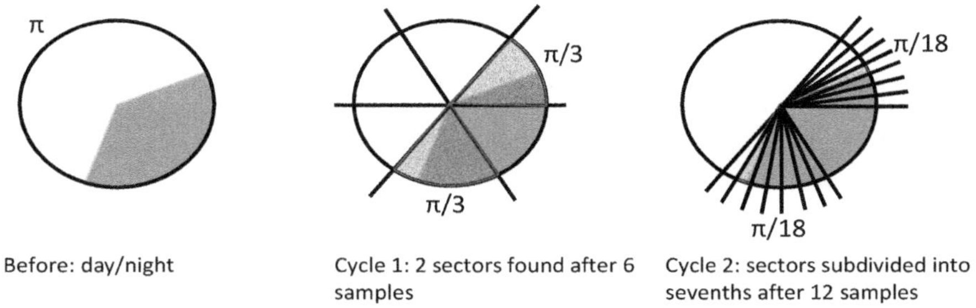

Fig. 3. N-way subdivision initialization

purpose an N-ary subdivision scheme may be employed. With the N-way subdivision scheme the 24 hour cycle is first split into four 90 degree sectors. Then, the two sectors where the sunrise and sunset may be present are further subdivided N-ways and so forth. After n steps the acquired accuracy is therefore

$$a = \begin{cases} \dfrac{360}{4N^{n-1}} & \text{if } N \leq 4 \\ \dfrac{360}{N^{n}} & \text{if } N > 4 \end{cases} \tag{12}$$

Alternatively, to achieve an accuracy of a with N subdivisions n steps are needed, namely:

$$n = \begin{cases} \dfrac{\ln\left(\dfrac{360}{4a}\right)}{\ln N} + 1 & \text{if } N \leq 4 \\ \dfrac{\ln\left(\dfrac{360}{a}\right)}{\ln N} & \text{if } N > 4 \end{cases} \tag{13}$$

And, the energy consumed is

$$E = \begin{cases} 4p + 2N(n-1)p & \text{if } N \leq 4 \\ 2Nnp & \text{if } N > 4 \end{cases} \tag{14}$$

2.3.4 Analysis

Table 1 lists the characteristics of the three initialization strategies for various accuracy requirements. According to these estimates an accuracy of 0.1 degrees is realistic as this relies on the sunset and sunrise to be detected with an accuracy of just below half a minute. For higher accuracies it may not be realistic under general conditions to obtain a sufficient accurate lighting condition measurement. Assuming that an accuracy of 0.1 degrees is the target, namely 1.1 km, the table reveals that with the binary methods this will take 12 days, and just 2 days with a 100-way strategy. However, the more rapid determination requires next to 2,000 % more energy than the binary method. A good balance is struck with the 4-way method which finds the location with the desired accuracy in half the time, namely in 6 days with just twice as much energy consumed, or in just 4 days with 4 times as much energy consumed. In comparison the brute force method would need to take 3,600 samples during one cycle to achieve an accuracy of 0.1 degrees and hence consume 3,600 units of energy which is nearly 10 times that of the 100-way strategy. However, the location would then be found in 24 hours in the worst case.

Table 1. Theoretical accuracy, convergence time, and energy consumption parameters for intelligent intensity light sampling

		binray		3-way		4-way	
Acc. (deg)	Acc. (time)	cycles	E	cycles	E	cycles	E
10	40 min	6	12	3	16	3	20
1	4 min	9	18	6	34	5	36
0,1	24 sec	12	24	8	46	6	44
0,01	2.4 sec	16	32	10	58	8	60
0,001	0.24 sec	19	38	12	70	10	76
0,0001	0.024 sec	22	44	14	82	11	84

		5-way		10-way		100-way	
Acc. (deg)	Acc. (time)	cycles	E	cycles	E	cycles	E
10	40 min	3	30	2	40	1	200
1	4 min	4	40	3	60	2	400
0,1	24 sec	6	60	4	80	2	400
0,01	2.4 sec	7	70	5	100	3	600
0,001	0.24 sec	8	80	6	120	3	600
0,0001	0.024 sec	10	100	7	140	4	800

2.4 Tracking

Once the geographical location of the object is detected one may wish to track the new position of the object if the object has moved. If the object is stationary then no tracking is needed. The degree to which an object is moving will depend on the specific application. Therefore, a dynamic strategy is proposed herein that can be used to adjust the tracking according the needs of the application.

2.4.1 Object Speed and Distance Travelled

First, one should define the maximum theoretical speed s of the object in meters per second. Given a maximum speed of s then the maximum possible distance in meters that can be travelled during one 24 hour cycle is $D = 24 \times 60 \times 60 \times s$. The potential distance travelled in a single 24 hour cycle is of particular interest as sunrise and sunset measurements can only be taken once each 24 hours. As there is 1,852 meters in one nautical mile, that is, one arc minute, the total distance in degrees *W* is therefore:

$$W = \frac{24 \times 60 \times s}{1852} \tag{15}$$

For example, imagine that the object is mounted on a road vehicle such as a car with a maximum speed of 100 km/hour, then, the maximum theoretical distance travelled in degrees during a 24 hour cycle is 21.5 degrees. However, the practical distance is likely to be much smaller if the vehicle is driven by a single person as a person is unable to drive for 24 hours. A more realistic number is in light of this is 7 degrees. Moreover, the driver may not drive in a straight line and will also be unable to maintain a speed of 100 km/hour and the net distance is therefore yet smaller.

Still, a maximum threshold of *W* may be used as a limit on the sunrise and sunset times if converted to hour angle t_W.

$$t_w = \frac{24}{360} W \tag{16}$$

2.4.2 Seasonal Changes

The declination of the sun affects the sunset and sunrise times according to Eq. (4). These changes are quite large on a daily basis close to the solstices. Given the previous longitude and latitude and the sun declination angle for the current cycle revised sunrise and sunset times can be computed using Eq. (4).

2.4.3 Dynamic Tracking

During each cycle a sample point is taken just before (pre-test) and after (post-test) the sunrise and the sunset times adjusted for seasonal changes due to the declination of the sun. These measurements are further separated *a* apart. Now, if say the second of the two tests fail, then this is an indication that the sunrise or sunset occur later and one therefore continues to sample points at regular interval separated by a until the test is true or, until the difference between the original test and the point is *W*. If the test is still false the next sample point is taken at a distance of *W*, then 2*W*, 4*W*, 8*W*, etc, until the test is true. Using this strategy the new position can be detected during the same cycle. The pre-test and post-test mechanism is stated in Table 2.

Table 2. Interpretation of pre-test and post-test results

Pre-test	Post-test	Type	Interpretation	Action
Day	Night	Sunset	Stationary	
Day	Day	Sunset	Later sunset	Sample more points
Night		Sunset	Earlier sunset	Sample earlier next cycle
Night	Day	Sunrise	Stationary	
Night	Night	Sunrise	Later sunrise	Sample more points
Day		Sunrise	Earlier sunrise	Sample earlier next cycle

If the first of the two tests fail, then this is an indication that the sunrise or sunset has already occurred. In this situation the new position needs to be detected during the next cycle. The strategy is therefore to take a sample at $-W$ before the failed test and at regular intervals separated by a until the test is true. If one reaches the same point in time as the previous cycle then the new sunrise or sunset has occurred before $-W$, and yet another cycle is needed. In the third cycle a sample is taken at $-W$. If this test is true then regular samples at separated by a are taken. If the test is false, another test at $-2W$ is taken during the next cycle, and so forth.

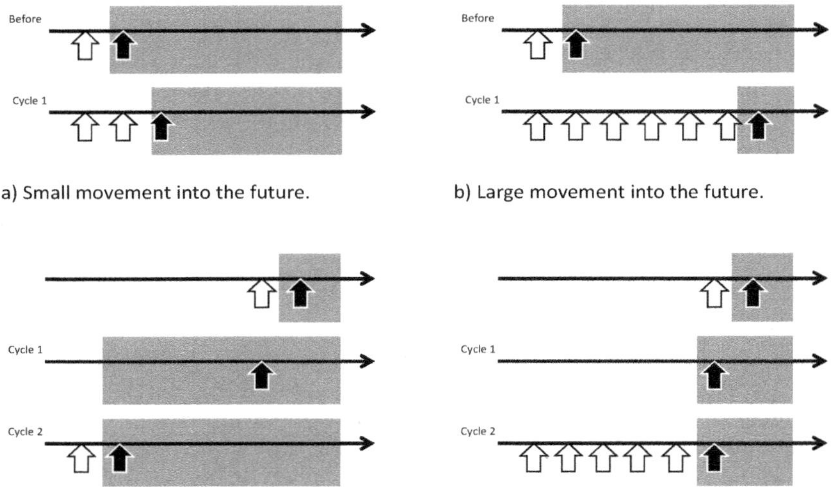

a) Small movement into the future.

b) Large movement into the future.

c) Large movement into the past.

d) Small movement into the past.

Fig. 4. Tracking sunset changes. White arrows signify tests that yields daylight and black arrows denote tests that return night. The gray box mark night. Time is represented left to right.

Fig. 4 illustrates the tracking procedure. Fig. 4 a) shows an example where the sunset is slightly delayed. This is detected in the 1st cycle as the second test yields daylight instead of night. Therefore, another sample is taken one time step later which then yields night and the new sunset time is detected. Fig. 4 b) shows a larger sunset change. Here, the second test again yields day and the test is repeated at regular intervals until the test returns night. In this example, another five tests are needed to successfully determine the magnitude of the change. Fig. 4 c) shows a large change into the past, that is, the sunset occurs much earlier than before. During the first cycle the first test returns night and the algorithm therefore knows that the sunset has already occurred. During the next cycle the tests start earlier according to the maximum threshold W, in this case six steps earlier. The first test yields day and the second test yields night and hence the new sunset time is successfully detected. In this instance the new sunset is found with very few additional tests, but it takes one more cycle to determine the new location compared to when the sunset is postponed. Finally, Fig. 4

d) shows a small change in sunset time towards an earlier time. Also, here the first test returns night and the algorithm know that the sunset has occurred earlier. During the subsequent cycle the testing begins six time units earlier and six tests are needed until the sunset is detected. In this instance slightly more effort is needed, but the change is successfully detected with the desired accuracy.

Table 3. Linguistic interpretations of changes in day length and solar noon. Here t_0 and t_1 denote the time of the solar noon in UTC for the previous and current cycle, respectively, and δt_0 and δt_1 denote the length of day at the previous and current cycle, respectively. Combinations are possible, for example north-east, south-west, etc.

solar noon	day length	season	movement
$t_1 = t_0$	$\delta t_1 = \delta t_0$		no movement
$t_1 > t_0$			west
$t_1 < t_0$			east
	$\delta t_1 > \delta t_0$	winter	south
	$\delta t_1 > \delta t_0$	summer	north
	$\delta t_1 < \delta t_0$	winter	north
	$\delta t_1 < \delta t_0$	summer	south

2.4.4 Analysis

The advantage of the outlined tracking procedure is that only 4 samples need to be taken every 24 hours when the object is not moving to confirm that the object is stationary. However, the strategy is able to instantly track small movements in either one or two cycles with limited number of additional samples. Next, the strategy is also able to track larger movements, but with lesser accuracy and in some cases it needs more cycles to detect the changes.

Movements towards the west can be detected during the same cycle irrespective of the magnitude, while movements towards the east will be detected during the next cycle if they are small or after a few more cycles if the movement is larger. A motion towards a pole during its hemispheres winter season will be detectable in the same cycle while a motion towards a pole during its hemispheres summer season is detected during the next cycle or later, depending on the magnitude of the movement. This is illustrated in Table 3.

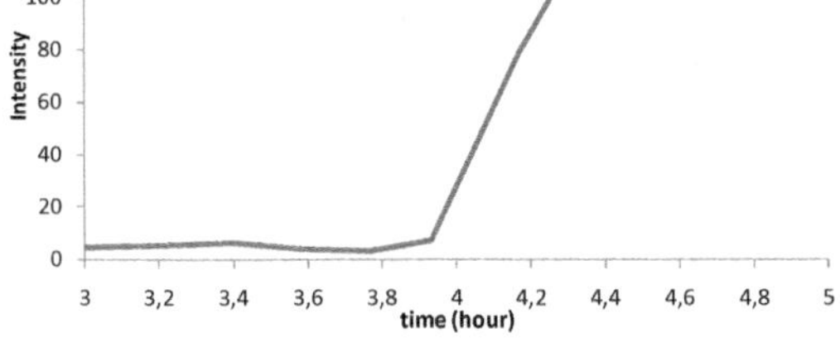

Fig. 5. Gradual increase in intensity towards sunset

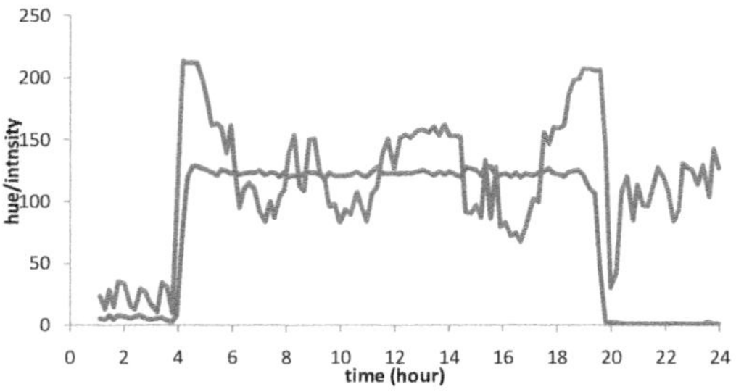

Fig. 6. Sudden hue changes predict sunrises and sunsets

2.4.5 Enhancements

Several theoretical enhancements are possible. Sunrises can be predicted if early measurements are taken. This is because the light intensity increases gradually over some time interval before one passes the threshold of 85% of full daylight intensity which is used in this study. If a light intensity measurement is taken that is above the night baseline value but yet below the threshold then this is a sign that a sunrise is approaching soon and the sample rate can be dynamically increased. This is illustrated by Fig. 5 which shows an authentic intensity plot obtained using a webcam. Clearly the intensity rises for about 20 minutes before the sun breaks.

However, it may be more difficult to get a pre warning of a sunset in this way as this will suddenly drop below the threshold value. One way to overcome this is to observe additional features. If the light sensor is capable of capturing color spectrum information then additional information can be exploited to better predict sunrises and sunsets. For instance, the CCD sensors in digital cameras are capable of detecting color as well as intensity. This is because sunsets and sunrises often are characterized by large changes in overall changes in hues which affect entire scenes. Such changes in hue occur prior to sunsets and thus a detection in hue change can be used to predict an upcoming sunset. This is illustrated in Fig. 6 which is an authentic 24 hour plot obtained using a webcam. The steady line shows the overall image intensity and the other line illustrates overall image hue. Clearly, the hue is changing dramatically just before the sunrise and sunset. In fact, these can be seen as the two peaks in the hue plot. However, the exploitation of such features is the topic of future research.

3 Limitations

There are several challenges associated with the proposed strategy. Firstly, the strategy assumes a relatively steady view of its surroundings. If the object is constantly moving about in various directions the light intensity may be affected and consequently lead to erroneous sunrise and sunset detections. Moreover, other effects such as weather conditions may impact the results. Although the strategy works on both cloudy and sunny days, days with extremely heavy blankets of clouds may introduce erroneous readings.

Another source of error could be the accuracy of the clock. It is natural for clocks to drift. Modern electric clocks are often driven by quartz crystals whose frequency varies with temperature. Objects submerged in environments with extreme temperatures, such as sensors in arctic climates, may be affected if equipped with low cost clock hardware.

4 Conclusions

A strategy for building low-cost and GPS-independent geo-awareness into ubiquitous objects was presented. The strategy is based on maintaining accurate time and irregularly sampling the outdoor lighting conditions, thereby detecting the sunrise and sunset times. The sunrise and sunset times are used with a celestial model to derive the estimated latitude and longitude of the object, and under optimal condition the method holds potential of achieving an accuracy of 0.1 degrees or about 11.1 km accuracy. The strategy is energy efficient and its energy consumption can be adjusted dynamically according to desired responsiveness. For objects that are very mobile, that is, travel great distances at high speeds more energy is needed to quickly detect the changes. However, for objects with very little motion a less aggressive sampling strategy can be employed.

References

1. ANSI, ANSI PH2.7-1973 American National Standard Photographic Exposure Guide, American National Standards Institute, New York (1973)
2. ANSI, ANSI PH2.7-1986. American National Standard for Photography - Photographic Exposure Guide, American National Standards Institute, New York (1986)
3. Carboni, D., Sanna, S., Zanarini, P.: GeoPix: image retrieval on the geo web, from camera click to mouse click. In: The Proceedings of the 8th Conference on Human-Computer Interaction with Mobile Devices and Services, pp. 169–172 (2006)
4. Cozman, F., Krotkov, E.: Robot localization using a computer vision sextant. In: Proceedings of IEEE International Conference on Robotics and Automation, pp. 106–111 (1995)
5. GAO, Global Positioning System: Significant Challenges in Sustaining and Upgrading Widely Used Capabilities, United States Government Accountability Office (2009)
6. Gongora, T.A., Stuart, R.: Holographic sundial. Applied Optics 29(32), 4751–4752 (1990)
7. Hightower, J., Borriello, G.: Location systems for ubiquitous computing. Computer 34(8), 57–66 (2001)
8. Jacobs, N., Roman, N., Pless, R.: Toward Fully Automatic Geo-Location and Geo-Orientation of Static Outdoor Cameras. In: The Proceedings of IEEE Workshop on Applications of Computer Vision, pp. 1–6 (2008)
9. Jacobs, N., Satkin, S., Roman, N., Speyer, R., Pless, R.: Geolocating Static Cameras. In: The Proceedings of IEEE 11th International Conference on Computer Vision (ICCV 2007), pp. 1–6 (2007)
10. Ray, S.F.: Camera Exposure Determination. In: Jacobson, R.E., Ray, S.F., Atteridge, G.G., Axford, N.R. (eds.) The Manual of Photography: Photographic and Digital Imaging, Focal Press (2000)
11. Sandnes, F.E.: Determining the Geographical Location of Image Scenes based on Object Shadow Lengths. Journal of Signal Processing Systems (2010)
12. Sandnes, F.E.: Geo-Spatial Tagging of Image Collections using Temporal Camera Usage Dynamics. In: The Proceedings of I-SPAN 2009, pp. 160–165 (2009)

13. Sandnes, F.E.: A Simple Content-Based Strategy for Estimating the Geographical Location of a Webcam. In: Qiu, G., Lam, K.M., Kiya, H., Xue, X.-Y., Kuo, C.-C.J., Lew, M.S. (eds.) PCM 2010. LNCS, vol. 6297, pp. 36–45. Springer, Heidelberg (2010)
14. Sandnes, F.E.: Sorting holiday photos without a GPS: What can we expect from contents-based geo-spatial image tagging? In: Muneesawang, P., Wu, F., Kumazawa, I., Roeksabutr, A., Liao, M., Tang, X. (eds.) PCM 2009. LNCS, vol. 5879, pp. 256–267. Springer, Heidelberg (2009)
15. Sandnes, F.E.: Where was that photo taken? Deriving geographical information from image collections based on temporal exposure attributes. Multimedia Systems (2010) (in press)
16. Stewart, I.: What in heaven is a digital sundial? Scientific American, 104–106 (1991)
17. Trebi-Ollennu, A., Huntsberger, T., Cheng, Y., Baumgartner, E.T.: Design and analysis of a sun sensor for planetary rover absolute heading detection. IEEE Transactions on Robotics and Automation 17(6), 939–947 (2001)
18. Venkatesh, S., Buehrera, R.M.: Multiple-access insights from bounds on sensor localization. Pervasive and Mobile Computing 4(1), 33–61 (2008)
19. Zheng, Y.-T., Ming, Z., Yang, S., Adam, H., Buddemeier, U., Bissacco, A., Brucher, F., Chua, T.-S., Neven, H.: Tour the world: Building a web-scale landmark recognition engine. In: The Proceedings of IEEE Conference on Computer Vision and Pattern Recognition (CVPR 2009), pp. 1085–1092 (2009)

RESS: A Data Dissemination Protocol Using Residual Energy and Signal Strength for Wireless Sensor Networks*

Sooyeon Park[1], Moonseong Kim[2], Euihoon Jeong[1], and Young-Cheol Bang[1]

[1] Department of Computer Engineering
Korea Polytechnic University, 429-703, Korea
{anisoo,ehjeong,ybang}@kpu.ac.kr
[2] Information and Communications Examination Bureau
Korean Intellectual Property Office, 302-701, Korea
moonseong@kipo.go.kr

Abstract. In this paper, a data dissemination protocol that transmits data collected for Wireless Sensor Networks (WSNs) is newly proposed, and the proposed proactive protocol takes into account energy consumption minimized and delay time disseminated. The well-known SPMS (Shortest Path Mined SPIN) forms the shortest path-based routing table obtained by Bellman Ford Algorithm (BFA) and disseminates data using a multi-hop path in order to minimize energy consumption. The mentioned properties of SPMS cause memory burden to create and maintain the routing tables. In addition, whenever BFA is executed, it is necessary to suffer from the energy consumption and traffic occurred. In order to overcome this problem, a proactive dissemination protocol using ***R****esidual* ***E****nergy and* ***S****ignal* ***S****trength*, called RESS, is proposed in this paper. Simulation results show RESS outperforms SPMS up to 7% and 84% in terms of the energy consumption and traffic messages, respectively.

Keywords: Proactive Dissemination Protocol, Wireless Sensor Networks, SPIN, SPMS.

1 Introduction

Wireless Sensor Networks (WSNs) are an important technology in smart home, ubiquitous computing, and military surveillance. In order to observe the environment accurately, sensor nodes must be initially deployed suitably [1]. Moreover, WSNs consist of a large number of sensor nodes distributed through a wide area, and a data dissemination protocol is an important issue for WSNs because each sensor node has to accurately collect and efficiently disseminate data [2]. Thus, two representative proactive dissemination schemes, that are a flooding and Sensor Protocols for Information via Negotiation (SPIN) [3], are introduced hereafter. Since each node just

* This work was supported by the IT R&D program of MKE/KEIT (KI002164, On the development of Sensing based Emotive Service Mobile Handheld Devices). Dr. Kim and Prof. Bang are the corresponding authors.

Z. Yu et al. (Eds.): UIC 2010, LNCS 6406, pp. 205–214, 2010.

considers broadcasting to all neighbor nodes whenever the node receives a data, the flooding is the simplest dissemination protocol. Although the fast dissemination could be guaranteed in the flooding, there is still an energy consumption problem due to duplicated transmissions. In SPIN, therefore, a data is transmitted after an exchange of information between neighbor nodes using a metadata in order to overcome the duplicated transmissions problem. However, SPIN never considers the energy status of nodes; thus, the energy consumption at each node increases because all data are transmitted using the same power level.

Since the energy consumption is generally proportional to a power of the distance between sensor nodes, Shortest Path Minded SPIN (SPMS [4]) that disseminates data collected using a multi-hop path reduces the energy consumption. The routing table should be created and maintained; therefore, SPMS cannot help maintaining the routing table for a zone, which is defined as the maximum power level of a node [5]. Namely, each node creates the routing table of the shortest paths obtained by distributed Bellman Ford Algorithm (BFA). However, though SPMS disseminates the data using the shortest path, if a node on the shortest path fails, the shortest path can no longer be used. Thus, backup nodes, PRONE and SCONE, are used in SPMS to overcome this problem. If a node does not receive a data, the node first requests the data from PRONE. And if the node also does not receive the data from PRONE, it requests the data from SCONE again. If the node does not receive a data from SCONE node finally, it directly requests the data from its source node. As a result, it is necessary to suffer from a memory problem and a lot of control packets to manage the routing tables.

In this paper, we propose a protocol using ***R***esidual ***E***nergy and ***S***ignal ***S***trength (RESS). The proposed RESS simultaneously takes into account the energy consumption minimized and delay time disseminated without routing table for WSNs. The remainder of this paper is organized as follows. Section 2 explains the operation and the problem about the previous dissemination protocols, SPIN and SPMS. Section 3 details the proposed protocol RESS. Section 4 evaluates our proposal and finally, Section 5 concludes this paper.

2 Related Work

2.1 SPIN: Sensor Protocols for Information via Negotiation

SPIN [3] solved the mentioned data duplication problem of the flooding by a 3-way handshake; that is, metadata are exchanged to each other, and it decides whether a sensor node has a data or not. The first step is the *advertisement step*; a sensor node with a data broadcasts an advertisement message, ADV, with metadata as shown in Fig. 1(a). The second step is the *request step*; a sensor node, which has received the ADV, checks the metadata and decides whether the data is necessary or not, as depicted in Fig. 1(b). If the data is necessary, the node could transmit the request message, REQ, to the sensor node that sent the ADV message. The third step is the *data transfer step*; a sensor node, which has received REQ message, transmits data to the sensor node that sent the message, as shown in Fig. 1(c).

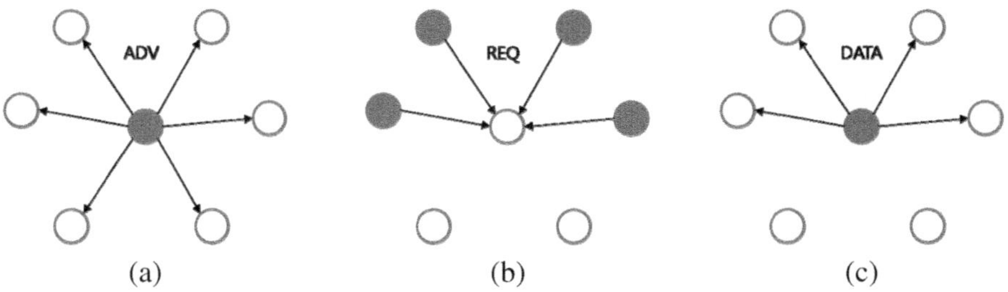

Fig. 1. The Operation of SPIN

SPIN disseminates a data to the whole area without duplicated data; hence, it could distribute about 50% more data per unit energy than that of the flooding, because the size of an advertisement message is smaller than that of the data sensed [6]. However, whenever a data is disseminated in SPIN, all data are transmitted using the same power level without consideration of the distance between its neighbors. Since the energy consumption is generally proportional to a power of the distance between nodes for WSNs, SPIN may not be capable of effective data transmission.

2.2 SPMS: Shortest Path Minded SPIN

SPMS uses a multi-hop model in order to reduce the energy consumption caused by the mentioned problem in SPIN [7]. SPMS has to know the destination nodes before transmitting a data; thus, a routing table should be created and maintained. Since WSNs generally comprise thousands of nodes, it is infeasible that each sensor node maintains its routing table for all nodes. Hence, each node maintains a routing table for a limited zone, which is defined as the maximum power level of each node, in order to reduce the creation and maintenance costs of the routing table. Here, each node creates a shortest path routing table using Bellman Ford Algorithm (BFA) in preparation for data transmission. The following is the operation of SPMS. First, the shortest path routing table is created using BFA. Second, the metadata are exchanged similarly to SPIN. A node with a transmitted data broadcasts ADV message in its zone. Finally, the third step is a request step. Foremost nodes received ADV message check the metadata, and then the node decides whether or not the data is necessary. If the data is necessary, REQ message is not transmitted directly to the node sent ADV message, REQ message could be transmitted using the shortest path. Therefore, if the source node is not the next hop neighbor node, the node received ADV message could wait for a time previously defined until the next hop neighbor node transmits ADV message. Namely, all nodes transmit the REQ message and receive the data through the multi-hop by the shortest path. If ADV message could not be received from the next hop neighbor node by the fixed time, REQ message is transmitted to PRONE or SCONE. The authors of [8] propose SPMS-Recursive (SPMS-Rec) that is an enhanced SPMS protocol designed to reduce energy consumption and delay. The operation of SPMS-Rec is generally identical to SPMS, yet the failure operation differs slightly. However, the routing table is also used as same with previous SPMS.

Due to the memory and other cost problems, even if each node just considers the routing information of the limited zone area, it is necessary to still suffer from the memory consumption in WSNs. Hence, the cost problem caused by the routing table should be improved, since the convergence time of BFA is $O(n^3)$ where, n is the number of edges. Furthermore, if a failure of node occurs, BFA could be re-executed; however the cost for re-execution is not also considered. Recently a transmission radius could become wider; that means there may be many sensor nodes in a zone, and the cost of the routing tables may become higher. Actually, the fundamental problem is from the consideration of the routing tables. The authors of [9] have compared with SPMS recently; however, in their proposed scheme EDAS, they have used the actual distance between nodes without any consideration for the routing tables. Since it is difficult to measure the real distance accurately, we use the signal strength instead of the actual distance; and, the performance results are only compared with SPMS.

3 RESS: A Protocol Using Residual Energy and Signal Strength

Much traffic and delay occur from BFA in SPMS. In addition, costs such as memory consumptions for the creation and maintenance of the routing table are burdensome. In this paper, a protocol using ***R**esidual **E**nergy and **S**ignal **S**trength*, called RESS, is proposed. The proposed RESS takes into account the low energy consumption and the transmission delay time without creation of the routing table.

3.1 Components

There are three message types (ADV, REQ, and ACK) and two timers (T_{Adv} and T_{Data}) in RESS. Each sensor node maintains information of two nodes; PRIMARY and SECONDARY. The descriptions of each message and timer are as follows:

(1) ADV

A node with a transmitted data broadcasts an ADV advertisement message. The source node inserts its own residual energy to the ADV message when the ADV message is broadcasted. Aside from the source node, each intermediate no de inserts its own residual energy; in addition, the residual energy of PRIMARY or SECONDARY is inserted to the ADV message. Here, the PRIMARY or SECONDARY has been used as a destination node for a REQ message recently.

(2) REQ

The REQ message is used to request data from its neighbor node.

(3) ACK

If a node receives the REQ message from its neighbor node, the ACK message is transmitted to the node that has transmitted the REQ message, for once; after that, every data transmission is begun continuously. When the ACK message is transmitted, its residual energy is also inserted in this message.

(4) $T^X{}_{Adv}$

After a node X receives the ADV message from its neighbor, the node X sets a timer $T^X{}_{Adv}$ instead of transmitting the REQ message. The timer $T^X{}_{Adv}$ could be set based on the signal strength in order to use the shortest path as possible. That is, if the signal strength is weak, then the value may be longer than that of strong signal strength. The timer $T^X{}_{Adv}$ is fixed to make sure whether or not there is a node that is closer than X to the node that has sent the ADV. If the node X cannot overhear the REQ that has been sent from other node until the timer T^{X}_{Adv} expire s, then the node X sends the REQ message to PRIMARY. If a node Y overhears REQ of other nodes before a timer T^{Y}_{Adv} expires, then the timer T^{Y}_{Adv} should be terminated.

(5) T_{Data}

This timer is assumed to guarantee to receive the requested data as the upper bound delay time; thus, the value is same with every node. A timer T_{Data} is set when REQ is transmitted. If the requested data is not received until the timer T_{Data} expires, REQ is retransmitted to SECONDARY on behalf of PRIMARY, and T_{Data} is reset. Otherwise, the timer T_{Data} is terminated automatically.

(6) PRIMARY and SECONDARY

The residual energies of PRIMARY and SECONDARY are compared with the information of ADV and ACK, whenever the messages are received. The node that has the highest residual energy of all values becomes PRIMARY, and another node that has the secondary one becomes SECONDARY. REQ is transmitted to PRIMARY and T_{Data} is set, if someone's REQ is not overheard until the timer T_{Adv} expires. In addition, if ACK for the sent REQ is not received from PRIMARY, then REQ is retransmitted to SECONDARY on behalf of PRIMARY and T_{Data} is reset.

3.2 The Operation of RESS

In Fig. 2, the operation of RESS is described, and an explanation of each step is as follows:

(1) The source node A broadcasts the advertisement message ADV with its residu al energy. (Fig. 2 (a))

(2) B, C, D, and E received ADV from A set a timer T_{Adv} based on the signal stren gth, and they register A with its residual energy as PRIMARY. (Fig. 2 (b))

(3) Since the timer T^{B}_{Adv} has expired before B receives REQ from other nodes, B transmits REQ to PRIMARY A, and B sets the timer T_{Data} simultaneously. (Fig. 2(c)). Due to REQ of B, every timer T_{Adv} is terminated.

(4) The node A transmits ACK with current residual energy to B sent REQ, for on ce. (Fig. 2(d)). After that, every data transmission is begun continuously.

(5) Since B receives ACK from A, the timer T_{Data} is terminated. At this time, B up dates the information of the residual energy of PRIMARY, A; then, B broadca sts ADV that has the received residual energy of A and its own residual energy as same with the mentioned step (1). (Fig. 2(e)). If ACK is not received from A until the timer T_{Data} expires, REQ is resent to SECONDARY on behalf of P RIMARY and the timer T_{Data} is also reset.

(6) C, D, and E received ADV from B make the timer T_{Adv} as same with the step (2). (Fig. 2(f)) Here, the residual energies of A (the previous node of B) and B i n ADV are compared with the residual energies of PRIMARY and SECONDA RY. The two nodes that have the largest two values of the four values become PRIMARY (the node with the maximum value) and SECONDARY (the node with the secondary value). The collected data is disseminated to all nodes based on the residual energy and signal strength by mentioned operation, repeatedly.

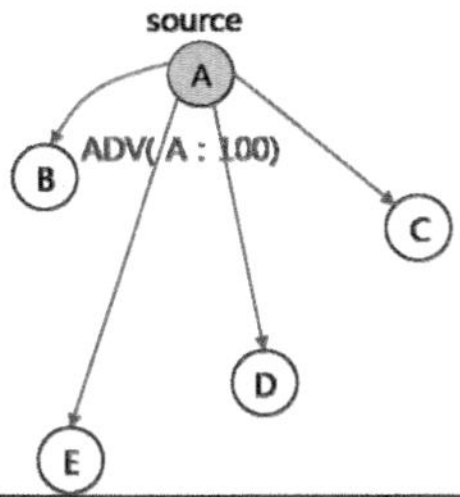

Node	Energy	Primary	Secondary
A	100		
B	100		
C	100		
D	100		
E	100		

(a)

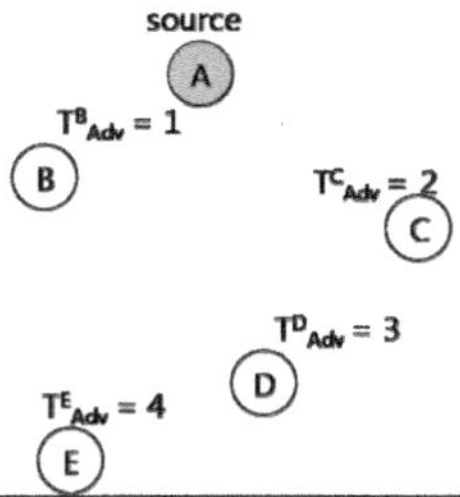

Node	Energy	Primary	Secondary
A	100		
B	100	A(100)	
C	100	A(100)	
D	100	A(100)	
E	100	A(100)	

(b)

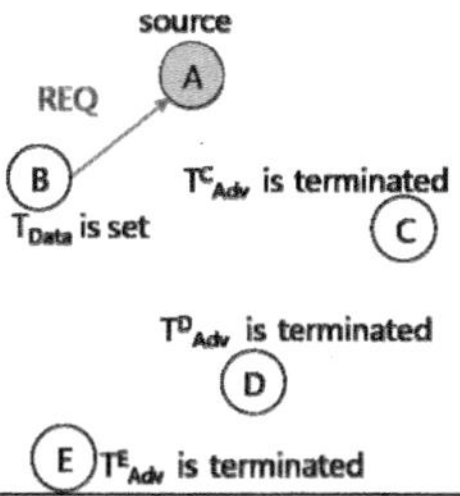

Node	Energy	Primary	Secondary
A	100		
B	100	A(100)	
C	100	A(100)	
D	100	A(100)	
E	100	A(100)	

(c)

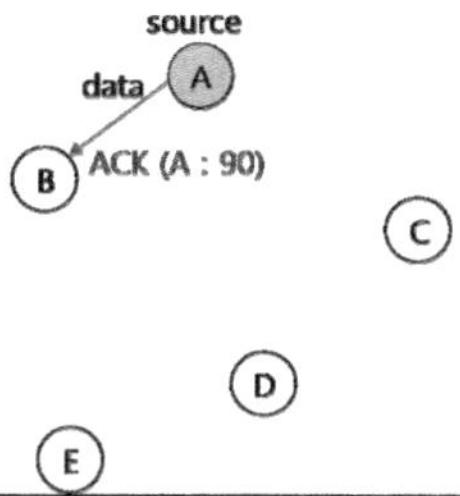

Node	Energy	Primary	Secondary
A	90		
B	100	A(100)	
C	100	A(100)	
D	100	A(100)	
E	100	A(100)	

(d)

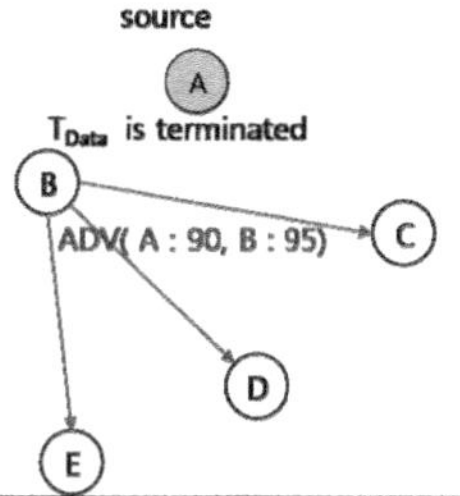

Node	Energy	Primary	Secondary
A	90		
B	95	A(90)	
C	100	A(100)	
D	100	A(100)	
E	100	A(100)	

(e)

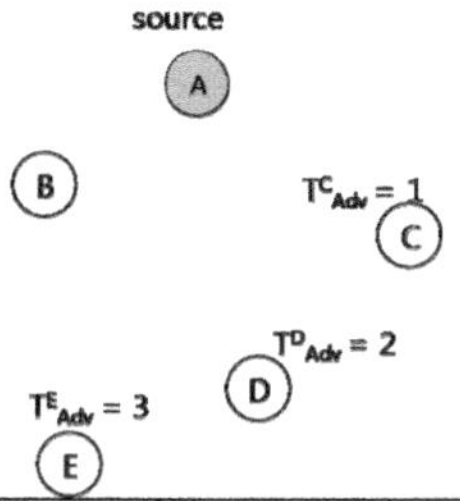

Node	Energy	Primary	Secondary
A	90		
B	95	A(90)	
C	100	B(95)	A(90)
D	100	B(95)	A(90)
E	100	B(95)	A(90)

(f)

Fig. 2. The operation of RESS; here, the amount of the residual energy is in the parenthesis

4 Performance Evaluations

We implement the proposed dissemination protocol RESS using Qualnet v4.5 [10] to evaluate the performance. The main parameters in the simulation configuration are listed in Table 1.

Table 1. Simulation Configuration

Network Area	150*m* x 150*m*
Initial Energy	1200 mJoule
Energy Model	MICA2 or MICA2DOT
Battery Model	Simple Linear Model
Radio Type	IEEE 802.11b Radio
Size of Data Packet	512bytes
Measure of BFA	Distance Vector
Number of data generated	1,000

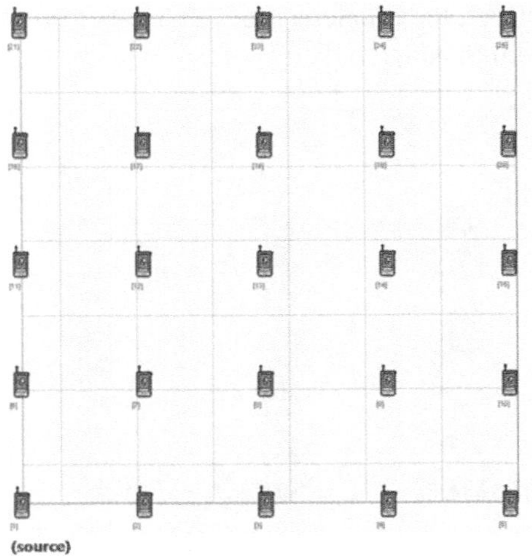

Fig. 3. A given network organized as 25 nodes

Fig. 3 describes a given network consisting of 25 nodes distributed in a grid over the area of 150*m* x 150*m*. The node in the left bottom corner is chosen as the source node with an event occurred. The initial energy value of each node is 1,200 *mJoule*, the energy model is "MICA2 or MICA2DOT", the battery model is Simple Linear Model, the radio type is IEEE 802.11b Radio, the measure of BFA is the distance vector, and the number of data generated is 1,000. RESS is compared with SPMS for the total energy consumption, the delay time, and the total number of data in terms of several nodes.

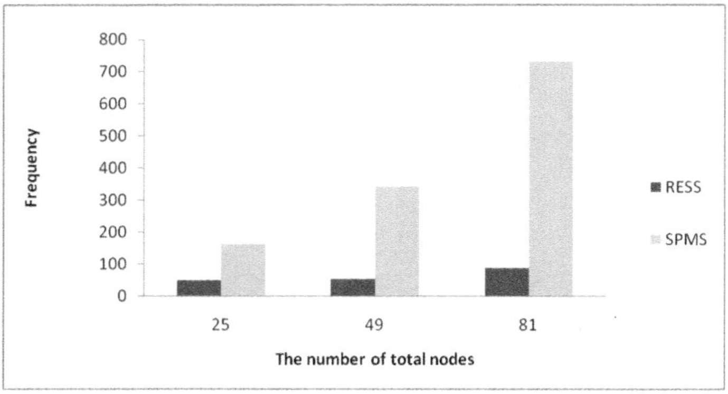

Fig. 4. The average numbers of the total control messages

Fig. 4 explains the average number of the total control messages for each number of total nodes. Here, the number is able to denote the node density for the given WSN. Many control packets are generated due to BFA in SPMS; however, because RESS does not need to use BFA, the efficiency for the number of messages increases up to 84% in comparison with SPMS.

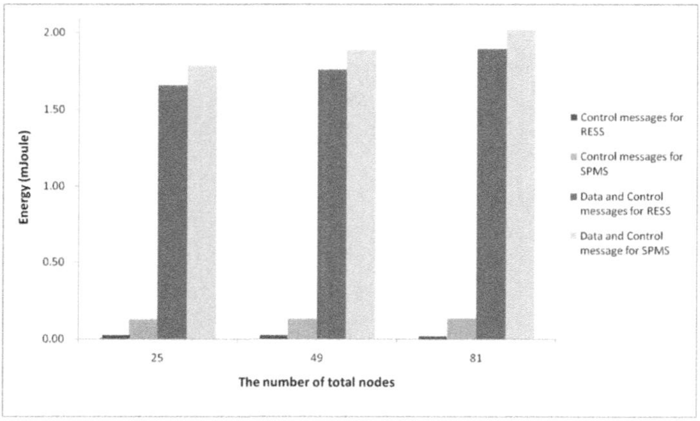

Fig. 5. The average energy consumption used to the control and data messages for each number of total nodes under 1,000 messages generated

Fig. 5 shows the average energy consumption used for the control and data messages. For the only control message, SPMS wastes approximately 0.13 *mJoule*; however, RESS consumes about 0.003 *mJoule*. We note that RESS reduces the energy consumption approximately 97% in comparison with SPMS. Since the energy used for BFA in SPMS may be high, the total energy consumption of SPMS could be higher than RESS. For the control and data messages, the average consumed energy of RESS decreases approximately 7% in comparison with SPMS.

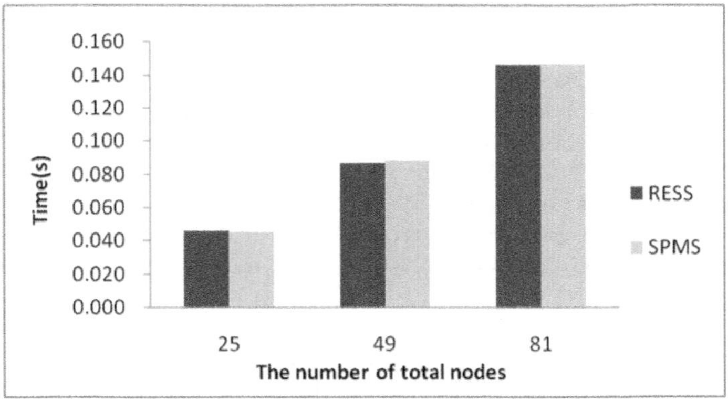

Fig. 6. The average delay time used to disseminate the data over the area

Finally, Fig. 6 shows the average delay time taken to disseminate data over the ent ire area. We note that the delay time of SPMS based on the shortest path is similar to t hat of RESS, which takes into account the residual energy and the signal strength.

5 Conclusion

In this paper, a proactive dissemination protocol RESS that simultaneously takes into account residual energy and signal strength for Wireless Sensor Networks is proposed. The proposed RESS has outperformed well-known SPMS up to 7% in terms of energy consumption. Even if SPMS considers the shortest path using Bellman Ford Algorithm (BFA), the delay time of SPMS is similar to that of RESS. In addition SPMS has the burdensome memory consumption to maintain the routing table obtained by BFA; however, RESS does not need such memory consumption. The reason is there is no routing table. Furthermore, since SPMS should manage the routing table, a lot of control packets occur; in contrast, RESS has reduced the number of messages than SPMS up to 84%.

References

1. Choi, W., Das, S.K.: A Novel Framework for Energy - Conserving Data Gathering in Wireless Sensor Networks. In: INFOCOM 2005, vol. 3, pp. 1985–1996. IEEE, Los Alamitos (2005)
2. Kim, M., Mutka, M.W., Cho, S.-H., Choo, H.: A Dissemination Protocol to Guarantee Data Accessibility within N-hops for Wireless Sensor Networks. In: Hawaii International Conference on System Sciences (HICSS-42), pp. 1–8. IEEE, Los Alamitos (2009)
3. Heinzelman, W.R., Kulik, J., Balakrishnan, H.: Adaptive Protocols for Information Dissemination in Wireless Sensor Networks. In: MOBICOM 1999, pp. 174–185. ACM/IEEE (1999)
4. Khanna, G., Bagchi, S., Wu, Y.-S.: Fault Tolerant Energy Aware Data Dissemination Protocol in Sensor Networks. In: International Conference on Dependable Systems and Networks (DSN 2004), pp. 795–804. IEEE, Los Alamitos (2004)

5. Haas, Z.J., Pearlman, M.R.: The performance of query control schemes for the zone routing protocol. IEEE/ACM Transactions on Networking 9(4), 427–438 (2001)
6. Heinzelman, W.B., Chandrakasan, A.P., Balakrishnan, H.: An application-specific protocol architecture for wireless microsensor networks. IEEE Transactions on Wireless Communication 1(4), 660–670 (2002)
7. Pottie, G.J., Kaiser, W.J.: Embedding the Internet: wireless integrated network sensors. Communications of the ACM 43(5), 51–58 (2000)
8. Khosla, R., Zhong, X., Khanna, G., Bagchi, S., Coyle, E.J.: Performance Comparison of SPIN based Push-Pull Protocols. In: WCNC 2007, pp. 3990–3995. IEEE, Los Alamitos (2007)
9. Seo, J., Kim, M., Choo, H., Mutka, M.W.: EDAS: Energy and Distance Aware Protocol Based on SPIN for Wireless Sensor Networks. In: LNCS Transactions on Computational Science VI, vol. 5730, pp. 115–130. Springer, Heidelberg (2009)
10. Scalable Network Technologies web site, `http://www.scalable-networks.com`

Design and Implementation of Mobile Sink Node in SDMA Applications

Xiwei Zhang[1,2], Jia Yu[3], and Guihai Chen[1]

[1] Department of Computer Science, Nanjing University, No 22, Hankou Road, Nanjing, China
[2] Department of Computer and Information, Hohai University, No 1, Xikang Road, Nanjing, China
[3] Administrative College of JiangSu Province, Nanjing, China
zxw@hhu.edu.cn, yuj@sdx.js.cn, gchen@nju.edu.cn

Abstract. Mobile nodes are used to solve the problems existing in static wireless sensor networks such as energy hole, overlapping and hot spot etc. Through data gathering and relaying, mobile nodes can reduce the amount of data transmitting between the static nodes, which can conserve the power of these nodes and therefore to prolong the lifetime of network. In this paper we describe the DataTruck, a new open-source sensing platform specifically designed to support our experimental research in mobile sensor networks, which is used to collect data from static sensors. The DataTruck node is designed around the LM3S1607 ARM Cortex-M3 series Microprocessor and the IEEE 802.15.4 compliant CC2430 radio from Chipcon. The new features include support for a large storage and a rapid moving speed. Furthermore, we integrated a smart antenna system to gather the data from multiple static nodes concurrently which transmitting data using the same frequency of channel. The experiments show that DataTruck can collect data efficiently and reduce the average data delay by using SDMA technology.

Keywords: Wireless sensor networks; mobile sink; SDMA; smart antenna.

1 Introduction

Wireless sensor networks can be used to monitor physical or environmental conditions, and collect and transmit sensed data. These networks can serve as an infrastructure for a number of applications including surveillance, medical monitoring, agricultural cultivation, facility monitoring, and entertainment. For a number of applications, sensor nodes could be deployed in a vast area or in harsh environments. Hence, they need to operate with a limited power source. To efficiently manage these limited resources, efficient resource allocation for sensing and communications is of great importance.

For many envisioned applications, a non-mobile wireless sensor network is usually adequate to meet the application requirements. However, this approach has several disadvantages. First, in order to satisfy coverage and connection demand, a large amount of sensor nodes are needed, it raises a serious over-detection problem in some

Z. Yu et al. (Eds.): UIC 2010, LNCS 6406, pp. 215–227, 2010.

areas. Second, stationary sensor networks cause "hot spot" problem, i.e., the energy of some sensor nodes will be depleted quickly due to frequently data relaying. Third, the lifetime of the networks is short for the nodes not only have to sense the physical events but also transmit the sensed data. In short, because of absence of mobility, a dense network may often be infeasible, due to financial constraints, or undesirable, due to the negative effects a dense network may have on the sensor field or the environment.

With recent advances in robotics and low power embedded systems, mobile nodes [3, 4, 5, 6, 7, 8, 10] are becoming a viable choice for the sensing applications mentioned above. These mobile nodes may be mobile data ferries, or mobile data relays, which responsible to collect data from the sensor nodes or relay data from the sensor nodes to base station. In this approach, a small number of mobile devices referred to as data ferry roam about sensing fields and collect data from sensors. As a result, significant network energy saving can be achieved by reducing or completely avoiding costly multi-hop wireless transmissions. On the other hand, if the mobile node has sense ability, called *mobile sensor*, it can cover more area than a stationary sensor over a period of time because it can move to anywhere to capture the event. Mobile nodes can promote the network performance efficiently. We know for a random deployment in static sensor networks, the sensor density should increase as $O(\log l + kloglogl)$ to provide k-coverage in a network with size of l. In [3], authors prove an all mobile sensor network can provide k-coverage over the field with a constant density of $O\left(K\right)$, independent of network size l.

Mobile Wireless Sensor Network (MWSN) can be mainly divided into two categories. One is all nodes in the network is mobile. However, these nodes only have limited mobility to maintain the steady of network [5]. The other category is widely researched that there are partly nodes in the network is mobile, and other nodes is static, so the network is called hybrid network. In this network, static nodes are responsible for sensing the data, and the mobile nodes move to them to collect the data or relay the data to base station. Figure 1 is a classical application of a hybrid network.

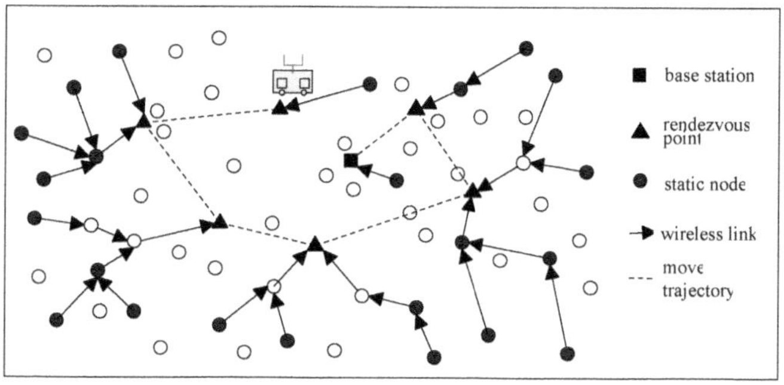

Fig. 1. In this hybrid network, in order to save the delay of data, static node send data to rendezvous points at first, mobile node only needs to visit the rendezvous points. So the move trajectory of mobile nodes is shorted.

In this paper, we design a mobile sink node named DataTruck. Mobile sink usually have no sense ability, so the main function of DataTruck is collect data from other static sensor and then return to base station. The DataTruck platform is a new sensor node platform designed to support mobility experiments in sensor networks. Although our design is driven by the research requirements of our group, extra effort was taken during the design phase to specify a feature set that is complimentary to existing platforms and can serve multiple aspects of research and education in sensor networks. The DataTruck platform is built around an LM3S1607 ARM Cortex-M3 series Microprocessor from Luminary Semiconductor and a CC2430 radio with a 250kbps raw data rate from Chipcon. The choice of the Cortex-M3 microcontroller provides a wealth of peripherals and flexible modes of operation. The Chipcon radio and its use with an IEEE 802.15.4 compliant MAC protocol, make our node interoperable with other sensor nodes available in the community such as Telos and Micaz.

Although the above schemes can perform data gathering in MWSN, there still exist inefficiencies in these schemes. When the DataTruck in the intersect area of communication range of several nodes, it should gather data one by one. In this paper, we will further improve the performance of data gathering in WSNs by considering two critical factors: *mobility* and *space-division multiple access* (SDMA) technique. To the best of our knowledge, this is the first work that introduces SDMA technique to mobile sink node design and explores the utility of a joint design of mobility and SDMA technique in data gathering schemes.

The rest of this paper is organized as follows. Section 2 introduces hardware design of DataTruck and the compare of other mobile nodes. In section 3, we design a dual-antennas system on DataTruck using smart antenna technology based on SDMA. Section 4 presents experiment and simulation results and section 5 concludes the paper.

2 Hardware Design of DataTruck

2.1 The Core Circuit Board

The DataTruck architecture is depicted in Figure 2. The main processing unit is an LM3S1607 ARM Cortex-M3 series microcontroller [13]. We found of this processor to be an appealing choice since it provides a rich set of peripherals, multiple power options and a suitable memory configuration. The LM3S1607 microcontroller is based on the ARM Cortex-M3 controller core operating at 50 MHz, with 128 KB single-cycle flash, 32 KB single-cycle SRAM, a 32-ch DMA, a 24-bit Systick Timer, an SSI / SPI controller, two I2C interfaces, 3 UARTs, a 10-bit analog-to-digital converter (ADC) with 8 input channels. The processor have plentiful peripheral interfaces, we can achieve an additional large storage (16Mbits) of external RAM through UART interface.

Operating System and Communication Protocol Stack: To make DataTruck interoperable with other devices, we ported Chipcons IEEE 802.15.4 compliant medium access control protocol which we operate inside the µC/OS-II operating system developed by Micrium[14].

The µC/OS-II is a portable, ROMable, scalable, preemptive, real-time deterministic multitasking kernel for microprocessors, microcontrollers and DSPs. Offering unprecedented ease-of-use, µC/OS-II is delivered with complete 100% ANSI C source code and in-depth documentation.

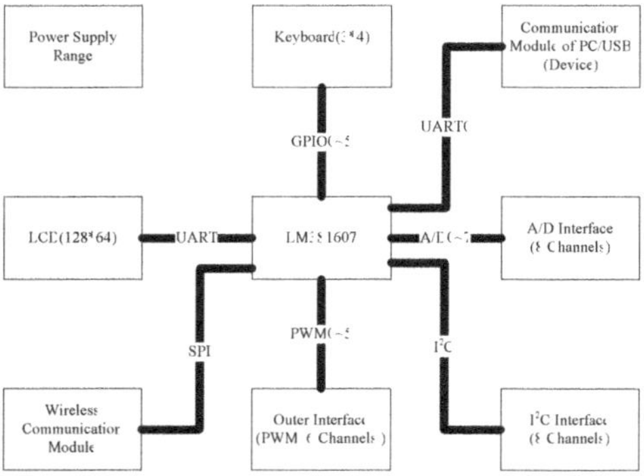

Fig. 2. The hardware design graph of main processing unit

μC/OS-II manages up to 250 application tasks. μC/OS-II includes: semaphores; event flags; mutual-exclusion semaphores that eliminate unbounded priority inversions; message mailboxes and queues; task, time and timer management; and fixed sized memory block management.

DataTruck Support API: To support the special features of DataTruck we implemented a specialized protocol that consists of the following modules:

Device Drivers Module. This component includes the low level interfaces to all the devices and the I/O peripherals on the DataTruck including the radio, the Real Time Clock, the ADC, the UART, the timers and the DMA controller. Using this module, applications can easily initialize, configure and use all the devices connected to the various I/O interfaces of the node.

Radio Manager Module. This module is responsible for configuring the communication subsystem. Applications can call this component to change the transmission power level of the radio and/or its security configuration.

Frequency Manager Module. The frequency manager is responsible for changing the operating clock frequency of the node while preserving the correct timing of the operating system, the Zigbee MAC layer and the application running on the node.

2.2 The Motor Drive Circuit

DataTruck uses L298P as motor circuit to drive its 4 linear motion actuators. The L298 is an integrated monolithic circuit in a 15-lead Multiwatt and PowerSO20 packages. It is a high voltage, high current dual full-bridge driver designed to accept standard TTL logic levels and drive inductive loads such as relays, solenoids, DC and stepping motors. Two enable inputs are provided to enable or disable the device independently of the input signals. The emitters of the lower transistors of each bridge are connected together and the corresponding external terminal can be used for the connection of an external sensing resistor. An additional supply input is provided so that the logic works at a lower voltage. The motor drive circuit is depicted in Fig.3.

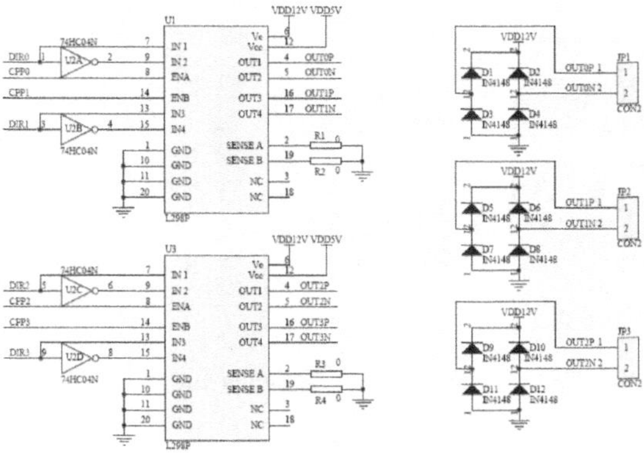

Fig. 3. The schematic of motor drive circuit

The speed of motor is calculated using formula (1), which is adjusted by controlling the PWM duty cycle through programming. Suppose V_{max} is maximum rotation speed of motor, duty cycle is$D$, the average speed of motor is V_d.

$$V_d = V_{max} \times D. \tag{1}$$

Where $D = t/T$ is duty cycle. T is a value of cycle of a timer, which is preset by the processor. t is the time of high level in the cycle which is set in the program, and is satisfied $t < T$.

2.3 Wireless RF Communication Circuit

DataTruck uses CC2430 (CHIPCON-CC2430, 2007) as the control chip of wireless communication circuit. The CC2430 is a true System-on-Chip (SoC) solution specifically tailored for IEEE 802.15.4 and ZigBee applications. It enables ZigBee nodes to be built with very low total bill-of material costs. The CC2430 combines the excellent performance of the leading CC2420 RF transceiver with an industry-standard enhanced 8051 MCU, 128 KB flash memory, 8 KB RAM and many other powerful features.

The CC2430 is highly suited for systems where ultra low power consumption is required. This is ensured by various operating modes. Short transition times between operating modes further ensure low power consumption. This is ensured by various operating modes. Short transition times between operating modes further ensure low power consumption. It need less than 0.6μA current consumption in standby mode, where external interrupts can wake up the system.

The picture of CC2430 is shown in Figure 4, and the schematic of wireless RF communication circuit used in our system is depicted in Figure 5.

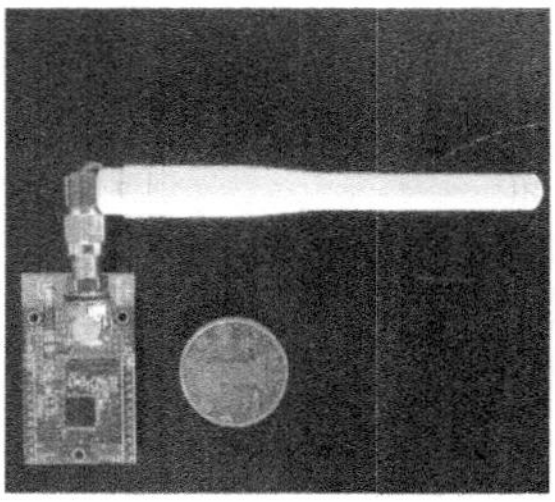

Fig. 4. Appearance of CC2430

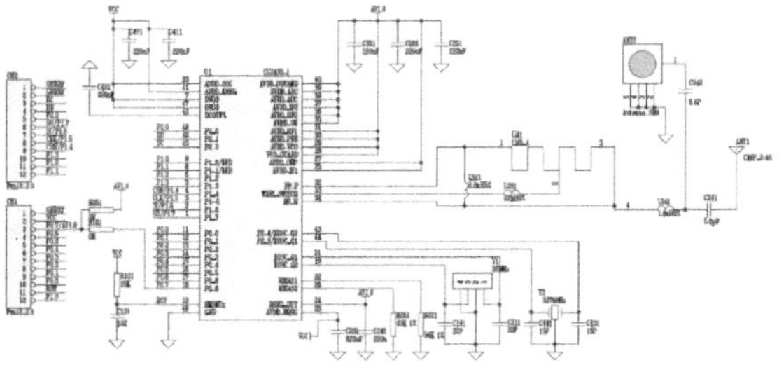

Fig.5. Schematic of CC2430 in DataTruck

2.4 Comparison of Other Mobile Nodes

The photo of DataTruck is depicted in Figure 6. The main advantages of DataTruck are listed as follows.

Strong computing and storage ability. We use LM3S1607 microcontroller which is a 32-bit embedded processor. Ana we achieve an additional large storage (16Mbits) of external RAM through UART interface.

Table 1. Comparison between DataTruck and other mobile nodes

Parameters	DataTruck	Robomote	XYZ
CPU	ARM7 LM3S1607	AVR Atmel 8535	ARM7 OKI ML67Q5002
Communication module	CC2431	UART	CC2420
Number of motors	4	2	①
Maximum speed(cm/s)	130-180	15-20	①
Storage(K)	128	1	32
External Storage(M)	16	0	2
Data uploading speed (kbps)	250	192	250
External A/D interfaces	yes	no	yes
Maximum running time(hr)	10	1	①
Operation system	uc/os-II	tinyos	SOS

①XYZ is a node move along a string, so it cannot be compared in these aspects.

Rapid move speed. DataTruck has 4 linear motion actuators and its maximum move speed reaches 1.8m/s.

Plentiful peripheral interfaces. DataTruck can connect multiple sensors to sense the environment through these interfaces although it has none sensors now.

Low cost. Total cost of all components of DataTruck is no more than 50 dollars.

The comparison between DataTruck and other mobile nodes (such as Robomote[7] and XYZ[8]) is listed in Table 1.

Fig. 6. A node of DataTruck

3 Design of Multi-antenna Array

3.1 SDMA

Space-Division Multiple Access (SDMA) is a channel access method based on creating parallel spatial pipes next to higher capacity pipes through spatial multiplexing and/or diversity, by which it is able to offer superior performance in radio multiple access communication systems.

The kernel part of SDMA is smart antenna. Smart antennas (also known as adaptive array antennas, multiple antennas and recently MIMO) are antenna arrays with smart signal processing algorithms used to identify spatial signal signature such as the direction of arrival (DOA) of the signal, and use it to calculate beamforming vectors, to track and locate the antenna beam on the mobile target.

In SDMA system the beams are like multiple space division channels. It provides a new domain, named space domain, expect other three domains (time domain, frequency domain and code domain). Although when the user is utilizing the same frequency and address code in the same time, they can use the space-division channels to promote the capacity of communication system. In Figure 7, there are 4 users provide communication through different space channels without interference.

3.2 Design of Dual-Antennas System

In this paper, we are mainly consider the case when the DataTruck is equipped with two antennas, because it is not hard to mount two antennas on the DataTruck, while it will likely become difficult and even infeasible to mount more antennas due to the constraint on the distances between antennas to ensure independent fading.

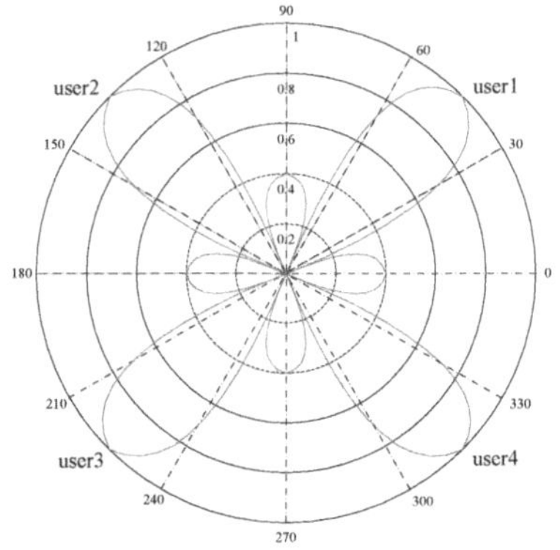

Fig. 7. SDMA creates spatial channel for each user

Now we will present the design of a smart antenna system with dual-antennas. Smart antennas have two main functions: DOA estimation and Beamforming. In this paper, smart antenna achieves DOA and identifies the directions of the received signals around the array antenna by the MUSIC (Multiple Signal Classification) algorithm [10]. We control the direction of the main beam by the LS-DRCMA (least squares-de-spread re-spread constant module algorithm) algorithm [11] and thus track the desired source signal, and at the same time generate deep nulls in the direction of interfering signals. Here we use dual FPGA and DSP chip to design the smart antenna system, which is shown in Figure 8.

In Figure 8, the CORRELATE module in FPGA-B uses the signal which is transmitted from FPGA-A after beamforming to synchronize all signal data. The synchronization point is delivered to DSP and the signal data is despreaded in DEMODULE module and then is transmitted to DSP to respread. The data after respreading is used to be the desired signal for weight solving of Cholesky-LS module. Another goal of these data is send to ERRORCODE_RATIO module for solving the error data rate which is the parameter of the state of system.

The sensing data from AD6645 were sent to DDC for wave tracking which means the signal frequency will be nulled from 40MHz after AD sampling. The signals will be orthogonalized and sent to X_DPRAM module and DBF module. X_DPRAM module translates these 4 line concurrent data to 32-bit serial data and sends these data to DSP for weight solving using EDMA mode through EMIFB interface.

The functions of DSP mainly include scheduling and computing. For instance, in DSP there are some modules which are used to control the synchronization state of system, and regenerate the desired signal after respreading, etc. The system needs initialization and the *ResetFPGA( )* function is called to set the parameters of FPGA. After initialization DSP reads synchronization point and respreading data from FPGA-A to determine whether the system is enter the synchronization state. Then the DSP recalculate the weight and update the weight value in the FPGA-B, and compute the error code rate at the same time.

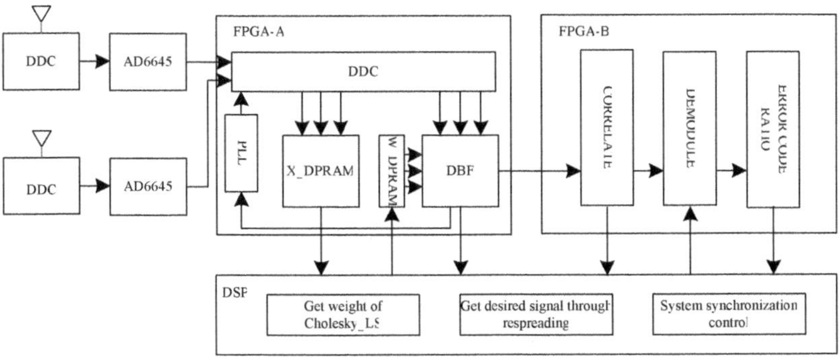

Fig. 8. The architecture of smart antennas system

3.3 Selection of Compatible Source Nodes

Due to the smart antenna cannot null the interference which in the same direction of desired signal, not any couple of sensor nodes can send data to DataTruck. In order to revert to the original data, the source couple of nodes should satisfy certain conditions, which we call this couple of nodes is compatible [12]. In this section, we use Linear Decorrelator Strategy (LDS) to analyze this problem.

To guarantee that the decorrelator operation is successful, we need to limit the number of simultaneous data streams to no more than the number of receive antennas. In other words, since the DataTruck is equipped with two receive antennas, at most two sensors can send data simultaneously to the DataTruck. Figure 9 shows the transceiver architecture of SDMA with the linear decorrelator. For simplicity, we will use h_i to denote $[h_{i1}, h_{i2}]^T$ which represents the complex channel coefficient vector (or called spatial signature) between sensor i and the two receive antennas of the DataTruck. h_1 and h_2 are the two columns of the channel coefficient matrix H. Suppose sensor 1 wants to send data z_1 and sensor 2 wants to send data z_2. The received vector at the DataTruck can be written as

$$y = h_1 z_1 + h_2 z_2 + n. \tag{2}$$

where n is channel noise.

We can see from Eq. (2) that each data stream faces an extra source of interference from the other data stream. An idea that can be used to remove this inter-stream interference from an interested sensor is to project the received signal y onto the subspace orthogonal to the one spanned by the other channel vector. That is, we choose e_1 and e_2 as the filter vectors for sensor 1 and sensor 2, respectively, which satisfies $e_1^* h_2 = 0$ and $e_2^* h_1 = 0$. Hence, the received signal can be decoded as

$$\begin{cases} z_{t1} = e_1^* y = e_1^* h_1 z_1 + e_1^* n \\ z_{t2} = e_2^* y = e_2^* h_2 z_2 + e_2^* n \end{cases}. \tag{3}$$

After processed this way, the inter-stream interference nulling can be achieved. e_1 can be any vector that lies in V_1 which is the space orthogonal to h_2, however, to maximize the received signal strength, e_1 should lie in the same direction as the projection of h_1 onto V_1. e_2 should be similarly chosen. e_1 and e_2 can be unit vectors because increasing the length of them will not increase the SNR. e_1 and e_2 can be expressed as follows

$$\begin{cases} e_1 = \frac{1}{\sqrt{|h_{22}|^2+|h_{21}|^2}}[h_{22}^*, -h_{21}^*]^T \\ e_2 = \frac{1}{\sqrt{|h_{12}|^2+|h_{11}|^2}}[h_{12}^*, -h_{11}^*]^T \end{cases}. \tag{4}$$

From Eq. (3), we can see that the signal part of $\hat{z}_1$ and $\hat{z}_2$ are $e_1^* h_1 z_1$ and $e_2^* h_2 z_2$, respectively. Since $\|e_1^* h_1\|^2 \leq \|h_1\|^2$ and $\|e_2^* h_2\|^2 \leq \|h_2\|^2$, we can further see that the projection operation always reduces the length of h_i unless h_i is already orthogonal to the spatial signature of the other data stream. This is the overhead for nulling out the interference. Hence, the effective channel for z_1 would be in deep fading whenever the projection of h_1 onto e_1 is small. A similar situation is also applicable to z_2. Therefore, for given transmission power of each sensor, not any two sensors can successfully transmit data to the DataTruck simultaneously. To ensure the DataTruck can successfully decode the received signal, the follow criteria should be satisfied

$$\begin{cases} Pr_1 = P_t \left|e_1^* h_1\right|^2 \geq \delta_0, SNR_1 = P_t \left|e_1^* h_1\right|^2 / \sigma^2 \geq \delta_1 \\ Pr_2 = P_t \left|e_2^* h_2\right|^2 \geq \delta_0, SNR_2 = P_t \left|e_2^* h_2\right|^2 / \sigma^2 \geq \delta_1 \end{cases}. \tag{5}$$

where Pr_1, Pr_2, SNR_1 and SNR_2 are received power and SNR of the received data from the two sensors, respectively, P_t is denoted as the transmission power of each sensor, and δ_0 is the receive sensitivity threshold while δ_1 is the SNR threshold for the DataTruck to correctly decode the received data. Any two sensors that satisfy this criteria can successfully make concurrent data uploading to the DataTruck. Such two sensors are said to be *compatible* [12].

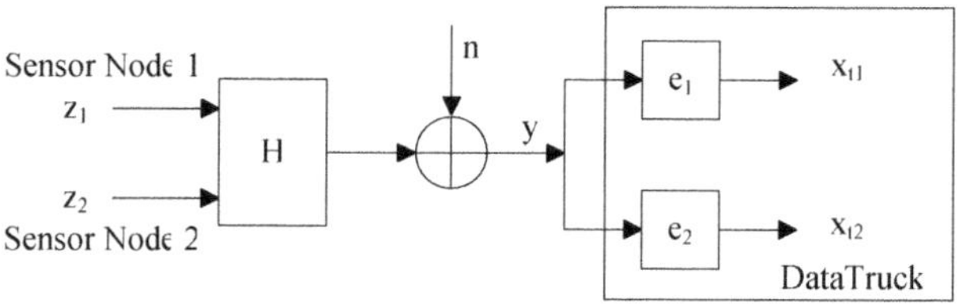

Fig. 9. Linear Decorrelator Strategy (LDS) in SDMA

Therefore, when we select the trajectory of DataTruck, the position of compatible nodes should be took into consideration to find the shortest path of DataTruck and collect maximum size of data.

4 Experiments and Simulations

To compare the proposed solution, we have made two kinds of experiments to test the performance of DataTruck.

In the real experiments, we use DataTruck (with single antenna) to gather data from static sensor nodes. There are 20 static nodes in the room, and DataTruck knows the position of each node. DataTruck visit all nodes along a fixed trajectory and each node is visited once in every round.

The DataTruck is equipped with an infrared ranging module which is used to avoid the barrier. When DataTruck find the barrier it will turn left or right with an angle of 30 degree, then it will go to the position along prior direction using the electronic compass module.

We compare the lifetime of network and the average data delay between using DataTruck and communicating directly with different sensing frequency of static nodes. The results are shown in Figure 10.

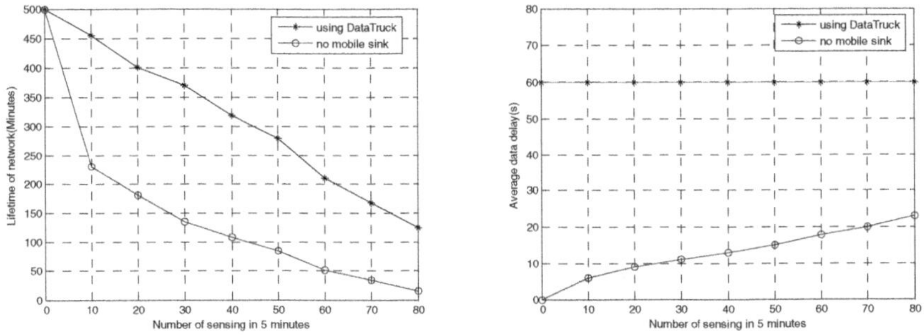

(a) sensing frequency VS. lifetime of network (b) sensing frequency VS. average data delay

Fig. 10. The relationship between sensing frequency and lifetime and data average

From Figure 10(a) we can see, while the frequency of data sensing increases, the lifetime of network is reduced rapidly with no mobile sink, because there are "hot spot" problem in this network, the nodes near base station will die quickly for relaying all data transmitted from other nodes. In Figure 10(b) the average delay is not changed when using DataTruck for data gathering, this is because the DataTruck pick up data from all nodes when it moving along the trajectory regardless of the frequency of data sensing.

We use simulations to verify the performance of DataTruck with dual antennas. Suppose a sensor network with 40 static nodes evenly distributed in 100×100 meter square field. There are 30 data rendezvous points on the trajectory of DataTruck which mean in these rendezvous points there is at least one pair of compatible nodes can send data to DataTruck. We suppose the communication range of nodes is 30 meter and the data amount of each node send to DataTruck is 1M bytes. We analyze the performance of DataTruck through adjusting the moving speed of DataTruck and the transmitting rate between static sensor nodes and DataTruck, which is showed in Figure 11.

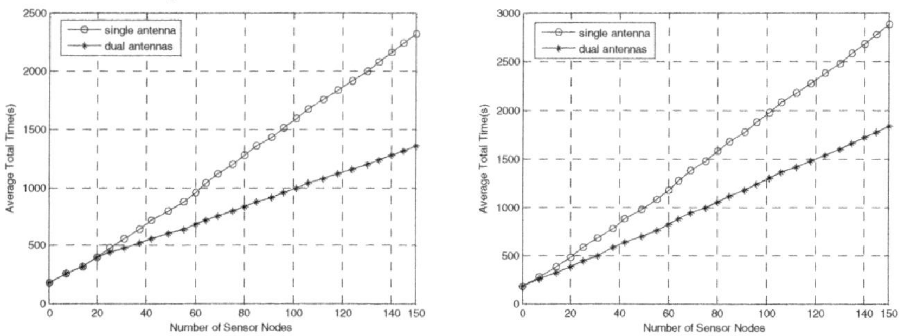

(a) moving speed is 0.5m/s; transmitting rate is 90Kbps

(b) moving speed is 1m/s; transmitting rate is 50Kbps

Fig. 11. The relationship between number of sensors and average data delay when Datatruck with single antenna or dual antennas

From Figure 11 we can see that with the increasing number of static sensor nodes, the data delay is reduced apparently using dual antennas. This means DataTruck with dual antennas is suitable for data gathering when the density of sensor nodes is high. The figure shows if there are 100 sensor nodes in the field, the data delay is reduced 40% when the DataTruck using dual antennas than single antenna.

5 Conclusions

In this paper, we have introduced the design and implementation of DataTruck, a mobile sink node for data gathering which has a high performance. We have shown the software and hardware design of DataTruck, and for the purpose of gathering data efficiently, we design a smart antenna system on DataTruck. Through experiments we can see that the mobile sink can save the energy of the network, and with the dual antennas, it reduces the average data delay apparently.

Acknowledgments. The work is partly supported by China NSF grants (60573131, 60673154, 60721002, 60825205), Jiangsu High-Tech Research Project of China (BG2007039), China 973 project (2006CB303000) and Hohai Science Fund grant (2008428511) and the Fundamental Research Funds for the Central Universities.

References

1. Tolle, G., Polastre, J., Szewczyk, R., Culler, D., et al.: Amacroscope in the redwoods. In: ACM SenSys, pp. 51–63 (2005)
2. Mayer, K., Ellis, K., Taylor, K.: Cattle health mon-itoring using wireless sensor networks. In: IASTEDCCN (2004)
3. Srinivasan, W.W.V., Chua, K.-C.: Trade-offs between mobility and density for coverage in wireless sensor networks. In: MobiCom (2007)
4. Wang, G., Cao, G., Porta, T.L.: Movement-assisted sensor deployment. In: 23rd Annual IEEE Conference on Computer Communications (INFOCOM), pp. 2469–2479 (2004)

5. Chellappan, S., Gu, W., Bai, X., Xuan, D., Ma, B., Zhang, K.: Deploying wireless sensor networks under limited mobility constraints. IEEE Transactions on Mobile Computing 6(10) (2007)
6. Xing, G., Wang, T., Jia, W., Li, M.: Rendezvous design algorithms for wireless sensor networks with a mobile base station. In: MobiHoc (2008)
7. Dantu, K., Rahimi, M., Shah, H., Babel, S., Dhariwal, A., Sukhatme, G.S.: Robomote: enabling mobility in sensor networks. In: IPSN (2005)
8. Lymberopoulos, D., Savvides, A.: Xyz: a motion-enabled, power aware sensor node platform for distributed sensor network applications. In: IPSN (2005)
9. Gandham, S.R., Dawande, M., Prakash, R., Venkatesan, S.: Energy efficient schemes for wireless sensor networks with multiple mobile base stations. In: Globecom (2003)
10. Wei, L., li, L., jin, Z.: Smart An tenna Design Ba sed on MUS IC and LMS Algorithms. Electronic Sci. & Tech./ (January15 2009)
11. Renbiao, W., Xiao, K., Lunlong, Z., Tieqiao, H.: Design and Realization of Smart Antenna Based on DSP+FPGA. Journal of Civil Aviation University of China 27(1) (February 2009)
12. Zhao, M., Ma, M., Yang, Y.: Mobile Data Gathering with Space-Division Multiple Access in Wireless Sensor Networks. In: 27rd Annual IEEE Conference on Computer Communications, INFOCOM (2008)
13. Introduction of LM3S1607 microprocessor. Texas Instruments, LuminaryMicro, `http://www.luminarymicro.com/products/LM3S1607.html`
14. µC/OS-II Kernel, `http://www.micrium.com/page/products/rtos/os-ii`
15. Intel mote (*i*Mote), `http://www.intel.com/research/exploratory/motes.htm`

RCO: A Multi-channel MAC Protocol with Random Cooperation for Sensor Networks

Jinbao Li and Desheng Zhang

School of Computer Science and Technology, Heilongjiang University, Harbin, Heilongjiang, China, 150080
Key Laboratory of Database and Parallel Computing of Heilongjiang Province, Harbin, Heilongjiang, China, 150080
jbli@hlju.edu.cn, zhang.de.sheng@qq.com

Abstract. To handle triple hidden terminal problems, this paper proposes RCO, an asynchronous multi-channel MAC protocol with random cooperation for sensor networks. By adopting a probability-based random cooperation, RCO effectively alleviates, if not eliminates, triple hidden terminal problems. More importantly, RCO is fully distributed with no requirements of time synchronization or multi-radio. Therefore, it is very easy to implement RCO in resource-constrained wireless sensor nodes. The simulation and real testbed experimental results show that RCO achieves significant improvement in energy efficiency with increasing benefit when the number of channels and traffic loads increase, while maintaining higher throughput.

Keywords: WSNs; MAC protocols; Multi-channel; Random cooperation.

1 Introduction

Emerging as one of the dominant technology trends, wireless sensor networks (WSNs) have a wide range of potential applications [1]. Recently, some multi-channel MAC protocols (mcMAC) have been proposed to support these applications via parallel transmissions, *e.g.*, MMSN [2], Y-MAC [3], and PMC [4]. These mcMACs have several advantages. *First*, because generally mcMACs employ one channel to send control information and multiple channels to send data, the overall channel utilization increases. *Second*, multiple node-pairs can simultaneously commence communications on different orthogonal channels, which can achieve higher network throughput and shorter latency. *Third*, mcMACs involve no extra hardware cost due to that current off-the-shelf WSNs radios such as CC2420 [19] already offer multiple orthogonal channels for parallel communications.

A mcMAC mainly consists of *channel selection* and *media access*. Channel selection decides how to select idle channels for all the nodes efficiently in order to optimize the performance of WSNs; access whereas, media decides when and how all the nodes access channels that have been selected for them to avoid data packet collisions. Based on the scheme used to access media, existing media access schemes generally fall in two basic categories: *Time Division Multiple Access* (*TDMA*) and

Z. Yu et al. (Eds.): UIC 2010, LNCS 6406, pp. 228–242, 2010.

Carrier Sense Multiple Access (*CSMA*). In TDMA [2][3][5][6], time is divided up into discrete time slots, which have equal or unequal lengths based on different protocols. The time slots are allocated to all the nodes in the network where the nodes are scheduled to send or to receive packets based on different schemes. However, TDMA requires time synchronization, which involves considerable overhead. Whereas, in CSMA [4][12][13][14], all nodes poll channels and initiate a handshake with their receivers when they have packets to send. This scheme is a natural way for nodes to access shared media. However, CSMA may bring more collisions than TDMA, since all nodes in the network may begin to transmit packets simultaneously.

According to how frequently channel selection schemes are performed, channel selection schemes can be generally classified as *static* and *dynamic* ones. Under static schemes [2], every node chooses its own dedicated channel to receive data, and switches to other channels to send data. To avoid collisions, static schemes have to guarantee to select different channels for different nodes within two-hop neighborhood, so the number of channels required in static schemes is *at least* as large as the number of two-hop nodes. To remedy this drawback, dynamic schemes [4][5] dynamically select channels for communicating node-pairs on demand. Therefore, channels are occupied by busy node-pairs only. Thus, the number of channels required is *at most* half of the number of two-hop nodes plus the number of Control Channel (CC), which is typically set to one and used to reserve Data Channels (DC).

Dynamic channel selection and CSMA with duty cycling are jointly considered as suitable schemes for WSNs because of three reasons as follows. *First*, dynamic channel selection schemes require less number of channels than static schemes. *Second*, CSMA involves no overhead of time synchronization required by TDMA. *Third*, duty cycling is a scheme to address the idle listening problem in WSNs, which is considered as one of the largest sources of energy consumption in WSNs [1]. However, these combined schemes sometimes fail to offer satisfactory performance since *Triple Hidden Terminals problems* (THT) undermine performance of mcMACs, which are defined in Section 3.

In this paper, aiming at THT, an asynchronous mcMAC protocol with Random CoOperation is proposed, called RCO. Involving no overhead of time synchronization and multi-radio, RCO is tailored to handle THT. The key novelty of this work is that all the neighbors of a transmitting node-pair can randomly send cooperative packets based on a dynamic probability to invalidate the channel selection made by this node-pair, when they assume that the node-pair selects a busy channel for transmission.

This paper hopes to contribute in the following ways: (1) makes the first attempt to apply a probability-based random cooperation scheme to handle triple hidden terminals problems; (2) proposes a duty cycle based multi-channel MAC protocol, which exploits dynamic channel selection and asynchronous media access scheme to improve network throughput; (3) evaluates the performance of ROC by both simulation and real testbed experiments.

The rest of this paper is organized as follows. Section 2 surveys related mcMACs. Section 3 describes the motivation behind this work and the definition of triple hidden terminals problems. Section 4 introduces the design of RCO, followed by its evaluation in Section 5. Section 6 concludes the paper.

2 Related Work

In this section, related mcMACs are surveyed from two categories: *synchronous* and *asynchronous*, respectively.

2.1 Synchronous mcMACs

Zhou *et al.* [2] propose MMSN which is the first mcMAC that takes into account the restrictions imposed by WSNs. Senders in MMSN switch their current channels to channels of intended receivers at the beginning of every slot when they have packets to send. Salajegheh *et al.* [6] propose HyMAC for WSNs where the communication period consists of a number of frames, which are divided up into scheduled slots and contention slots. The base station allocates specific time slots and channels to all nodes for communication. Jovanovic *et al.* [7] propose TFMAC for WSNs where a frame consists of a contention period and a contention-free period that contains some equal sized time slots. It works similarly with HyMAC except that the schedules are made by all nodes rather than the base station. Kim *et al.* [3] propose Y-MAC for WSNs where time is divided up into several fixed-length frames. The frames are composed of a broadcast period and a unicast period. The difference between Y-MAC and above mcMACs is that Y-MAC schedules receivers rather than senders to achieve low energy consumption to extend the lifetime of WSNs.

So *et al.* [5] propose MMAC for *ad hoc* networks by dividing up time into multiple slots, where all nodes exchange control information on the CC for reservations of DCs at the front of each slot and switch to DCs for data communication at the rest of the slot. Chen *et al.* [8] propose MAP for *ad hoc* networks. MAP works in the same way to MMAC but has variable-size data time slots, so it avoids the problem that data slot has to be set according to the maximum data packet size. Tzamaloukas *et al.* [9] propose CHAT for *ad hoc* networks using channel hopping scheme. Under CHAT, all idle nodes switch among all channels using a common hopping sequence. Moreover, both the sender and its receiver will stop hopping when they are aware of that they have to communicate with each other. Bahl *et al.* [10] propose SSCH for *ad hoc* networks, which works in a different way to CHAT by adopting multiple hopping sequences for different nodes. Under SSCH, a data communication starts when two nodes hop on the same channel. Tzamaloukas *et al.* [11] propose RICH-DP based on channel hopping for wireless networks, which differentiate itself with a receiver-initiated collision-avoidance scheme.

To sum up, above studies design protocols by time synchronization where let all control information or data be sent in some well-known slots and channels. For larger scale WSNs, however, synchronization itself remains an open issue that is not completely solved on low cost sensor nodes with cheap faulty clocks that are prone to drift. One common solution is to send SYNC packets periodically, but these SYNC packets can induce considerable overhead, which consumes more energy and makes channels more crowded.

2.2 Asynchronous mcMACs

Wu *et al.* [12] propose DCA for *ad hoc* networks, which uses two radios, one for control information exchanging and the other for data communication. Adya *et al.* [13] propose MUP for wireless networks. MUP employs two radios like DCA, but it allows both radios to send control information and data interchangeably. Jain *et al.* [14] propose RBCS for wireless networks with a dedicated radio for control information exchanges. However, this protocol utilizes a receiver-based channel selection scheme via SNR comparisons at receivers. Nasipuri *et al.* [19] propose a multi-radio MAC protocol for wireless networks. It distinguishes itself by a "soft" channel reservation scheme as it gives the preference to the channel that was used for the last successful communication.

Above four protocols are based on multi-radio scheme. Exploiting multi-radio can simplify the design of protocols by dedicating one radio on the CC to overhear the control information exchanging consistently. However, multi-radio schemes lead to not only larger node size but also more energy consumption. More importantly, increasing hardware cost makes the multi-radio schemes unrealistic for large scale WSNs.

Luo *et al.* [16] exploit Distributed Information SHaring mechanism (DISH) and propose CAM-MAC for *ad hoc* networks. In CAM-MAC, when a node-pair performs a channel reservation on the CC, all neighbors may send cooperative packets to invalidate the reservation if they aware of that the selected DC or receiver is unavailable. Luo *et al.* [17] propose ALTU based on altruistic cooperation, which introduces some specialized nodes called altruists whose only role is to acquire and share channel usage information.

These two mcMACs are based on DISH. Nevertheless, in every channel reservation, all the idle neighbors of the sender and its receiver will send packets for invalidation if they assume that this reservation is invalid. This scheme involves more packet transmission than necessary and easily results in cooperative packet collisions, since many cooperative packets can be sent simultaneously. Thereby, this scheme will consume considerable energy under large-scale WSNs context.

Le *et al.* [4] propose PMC which utilizes a control theory approach to dynamically add available channel in a distributed method. In PMC, nodes work on current available channels by CSMA, and decide whether to switch to the next available channel based on certain parameters, which vary with channel utilization from time to time. However, computing methods of these parameters need further discussion. Sun *et al.* [18] propose RI-MAC which is a receiver-initiated single-channel MAC protocol for WSNs. It attempts to minimize the time that a sender and its receiver occupy the wireless medium to find a rendezvous time for exchanging data. Wu *et al.* [19] propose TMCP which is a multi-channel protocol that does not require time synchronization among nodes. However, this protocol is more like a topology control protocol than a MAC protocol. Zhou *et al.* [20] present CUMAC using cooperation for underwater WSNs, but it requires a tone device on each node to notify collisions, which increases the cost of WSNs.

2.3 Summary

All mcMACs mentioned have at least one limitation below: (1) multi-radio hardware requirement; (2) fine-granular synchronization; (3) considerable cooperation cost. However, the design of RCO avoids all these limitation. RCO only uses one single radio and is fully asynchronous. Even though RCO is based on cooperation either, its probability-based random cooperation greatly reduces the probability that multiple neighbors send cooperative packets simultaneously.

3 Definition of Triple Hidden Terminal Problems (THT)

Triple hidden terminals include three kinds of hidden terminal as follows: **(1)** *multi-hop hidden terminal* which is the traditional hidden terminal in *multi-hop* networks; **(2)** *multi-channel hidden terminal* which is a new kind of hidden terminals in *multi-channel* networks [5]; **(3)** *sleep hidden terminal* which is the latest kind of hidden terminals defined by this paper in *duty cycle based* networks. Since WSNs *jointly* involves multi-hop, multi-channel and duty cycling together, it will suffer from all triple hidden terminal problems.

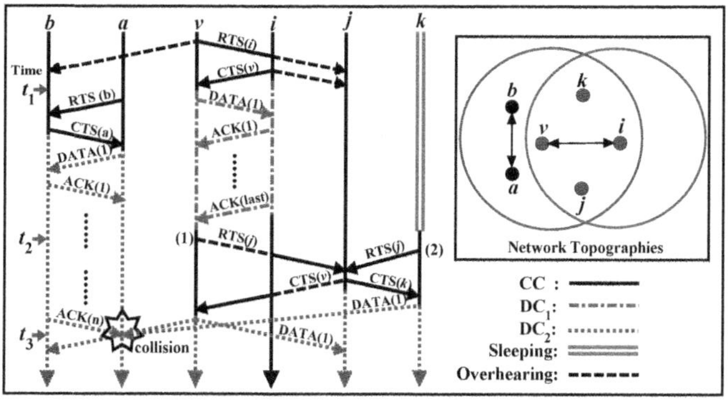

Fig. 1. The illustration of THT

An illustration of THT is given in Fig.1, which involves one CC and two DCs. Node a, b, v, i, and j are awake and k is sleeping. When v has data for i, v randomly selects an idle DC such as DC_1 and puts the reservation information (*e.g.*, who will occupy which channel for how long) into a RTS and sends to i on the CC. Then, i sends a CTS back to v to confirm this RTS. Next, v and i switch their channels to DC_1 around time t_1. The awake neighbors of v and i (*e.g.*, a, b and j) update their channel usage information by overhearing on the CC; whereas, the sleeping neighbors (*e.g.*, k) still assume that DC_1 is idle. During $(t_1,\ t_2)$, a has data for b. a randomly selects an idle DC such as DC_2 and then switches to DC_2 with b after a reservation. Because v and i as well as k are not overhearing on CC during $(t_1,\ t_2)$, v, i and k still assume that DC_2 is idle. Around time t_3, two situations can cause packet collisions at a or b. **(1)** When v finishes sending data to i, v has data for j. If v also selects DC_2 that a and b are still occupying, then a collision can happens. In this case, v is called the *multi-channel hidden terminal* of a and b. **(2)** When k wakes up, k has data for j. If k also selects DC_2 that a and b are still occupying, then a collision can happens as well. In this case, k is called the *sleep hidden terminal* of a and b. RCO handles THT with a *probability-based random cooperation.*

4 Design of RCO

Before RCO is described in detail, two assumptions are made as follows. (1) Wireless bandwidth is equally divided into one dedicated CC for control packet exchanging and K DCs for data communication. In addition, every channel is orthogonal to the others. (2) Each sensor is equipped with a same single switchable half-duplex radio.

4.1 Overview of RCO

RCO is a dynamic duty cycle based asynchronous mcMAC with random cooperation. Three features of RCO are described as following. *Firstly*, RCO utilizes a sender centric coordination to wake up its receiver by a series of reservation packets (RTS), according to predetermined duty cycle. In addition, each idle node periodically turns its radio on and off based on its own duty cycle to conserve energy and to prolong the lifetime of WSNs. *Secondly*, the independent sleeping schedule of each node reflects the asynchronization of RCO. *Thirdly*, in RCO, every node randomly cooperates with the transmitting neighbor to select an idle DC for it.

In RCO, all the nodes take five actions as follows. Overhearing: When an active node is idle, it monitors the CC to overhear control information exchanging to update its Channel Usage Information (CUI) for next channel reservation. Reserving: When it has packets to send, it uses a handshake scheme with its receiver on the CC to negotiate a DC for data communication. Communicating: After reserving, this node and its receiver employ media access scheme for communication on the DC they reserved. Random Cooperation: When a node overhears its neighbors reserving a busy DC, it computes a probability p, and then it sends a cooperative packet with p to inform its neighbor that it should select again, or it continues to overhear with $1-p$. Duty cycling: When being idle for a certain length of time decided by the duty cycle, the node turns off its radio and enters sleeping period for a certain length of time, which also decided by the duty cycle.

In this paper, the upper bound of probability p, denoted as p^*, with which all neighbors on the CC can send a cooperative packet is given by

$$p^* = \min(1, \frac{1}{ENC}),$$

where ENC is the expected number of neighbors of the receiver on the CC, which can be obtained by the CUI of the node. During every cooperation phase, all neighbors of the receiver *uniformly* choose p in interval $(0, p^*)$, and send operative packets with p or continue to overhear with $1-p$. The reason that a node cooperates with its neighbor with p is to make the expectation of number of cooperative nodes is equal to or less than 1. Therefore, RCO can greatly alleviate, if not totally eliminate, collisions between cooperative packets themselves as well as between cooperative packets and reservation packets.

4.2 Channel Selection of RCO

The channel selection of RCO is a dynamic scheme, and its objective is to avoid THT. When a sender has packets to send, it uses its CUI to obtain the Assumed Idle DCs (AIDC). Next, this sender makes these AIDCs into a list, called AIDC List (***AIDCL***), and then sends *AIDCL* to its receiver. When this *AIDCL* is received, its receiver does the same actions to obtain its *AIDCL*, and computes the intersection of *AIDCL*s, called Final *AIDCL*(***AIDCL***), and then randomly choose an AIDC from *FAIDCL*, and finally broadcast the ID number of that AIDC to all neighbors in an ANnounCement packet (***ANC***). If neighbors of the receiver overhear this *ANC* and find that this AIDC is actually busy, then its neighbors computes a probability p based on the condition of network, and then send a cooperative packet (***COP***) to the receiver with probability p. A *COP* includes the CUI of a neighbor of the receiver. Therefore, the receiver can update its *FAIDCL* to choose a new AIDC, and sends another *ANC* to make a announcement. When no *COP* is received, the receiver notifies the sender to switch that AIDC for transmission.

Algorithm 1. Media Access of RCO

```
If (upper layer message coming) { put message into packet buffer; set up sending timer;}
If (sleeping timer fired) { turn off radio; set up active timer by the duty cycle;}
If (active timer fired)  { turn on radio; set up sleeping timer by the duty cycle ;}
If (CTS timer fired)  { send the ID number of AIDC selected in CTS to S;}
If (sending timer fired){
   check whether R is on the DC by CUI; use CCA to sense the CC;
   If (R is on DC || CC is busy){
      back off for a while and tries to send later;}
   Else {obtain AIDCL by CUI; send it in RTS to R;}};
If (receiving a packet){
   If (packet is RTS){ //as a receiver
      obtain AIDCL by CUI; obtain FAIDCL; randomly select an AIDC in FAIDCL;
      broadcast ID number of that AIDC in ANC within one hop; set up CTS timer;}
   If (packet is ANC){ //as a neighbor
      If (AIDC in ANC is busy){
      compute probability p; send its CUI in COP to R with p;}}
   If (packet is COP){ //as a receiver
      obtain a new AIDCL by CUI in COP; randomly select an AIDC in FAIDCL;
      broadcast ID number of that AIDC in ANC within one hop; set up CTS timer;}
   If (packet is CTS){ //as a sender
      switch to AIDC in the CTS; send DATAs to R;}
   If (packet is DATA){ //as a receiver
      relay to the upper layer;}
};
```

4.3 Media Access of RCO

Two new kinds of packet are included in CSMA-based RCO, which are ***ANC*** (used to announce the AIDC that the receiver tries to use) and ***COP*** (used to inform the receiver that it needs to update its $FAIDCL$ for reselecting a new AIDC). The media access of RCO is given in Algorithm 1 where S and R represent a sender and its receiver. In RCO, a node-pair precedes an actually message communications with a cooperative handshake scheme ($RTS/ANC/COP/CTS$). The cooperative handshake scheme is used to negotiate an AIDC by this node-pair and their neighbors.

4.4 An Illustration of RCO

An illustration of RCO is shown in Fig.2, which involves one CC and three DCs. Three node-pairs, *i.e.*, AB, CD and EF, are communicating on DC_2, DC_2 and DC_1, respectively. G is a neighbor of S, and H is a neighbor of R. Both S and R overheard the channel announcements of AB and CD, but missed that of EF due to sleeping. Nevertheless, both G and H overheard the channel announcements of EF. When S has packets for R, three phases must be accomplished as follows.

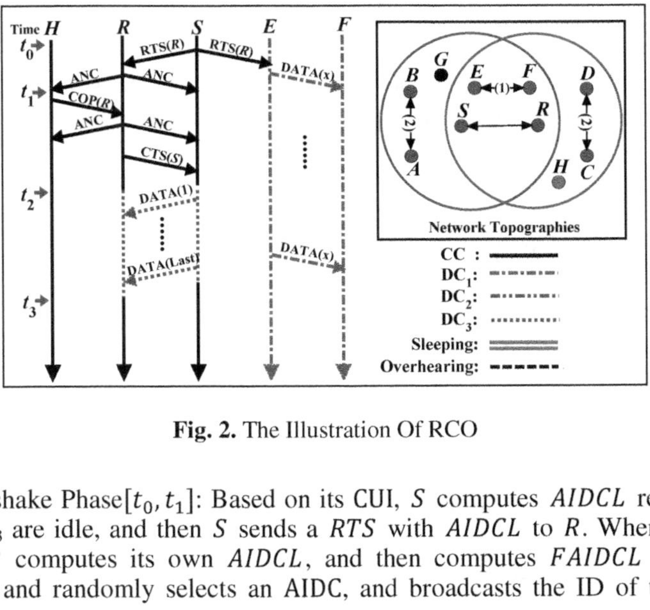

Fig. 2. The Illustration Of RCO

(1) Handshake Phase$[t_0, t_1]$: Based on its CUI, S computes $AIDCL$ recording that DC_1 and DC_3 are idle, and then S sends a RTS with $AIDCL$ to R. When R receives this RTS, R computes its own $AIDCL$, and then computes $FAIDCL$ via $AIDCL$s of R and S, and randomly selects an AIDC, and broadcasts the ID of this AIDC in an ANC.

(2) Cooperative Phase$[t_1, t_2]$: Assume DC_1 is the AIDC selected by R, and then H and G receive this ANC correctly. Because DC_1 is occupied by EF, both H and G should send a COP to R with probability p they computed. Assume H actually sends a COP and G does not. Therefore, R continue to select a new AIDC, say DC_3, and sends its ID in a new ANC. After a length of time, no COP is received by R, and then R sends the number of DC_3 in a CTS to S. Neighbors of R update their CUI via this CTS.

(3) Data Communication Phase$[t_2, t_3]$: After S receives this CTS, S and R switch to DC_3 and communicate with each other.

5 Performance Evaluation

We conduct both simulation and real testbed experiments to examine the performance of RCO in Section 5.1 and Section 5.2, respectively.

5.1 Simulation Experiments

A homemade simulator is involved for performance comparisons. 289 nodes, whose radio communication ranges are set to 40m, are uniformly deployed in a square area of size 200m × 200m with a node density of 38 (*i.e.*, a node that is not at the edge of the network has 37 neighbors). The traffic model where all packets are delivered from many sources to many destinations is used. The payload size is set to 32 Bytes, and the channel bandwidth is set to 250 Kbps. The duty cycle is set to 50%.

To investigate values of random cooperation, we compare RCO with 4 protocols: (1) CSMA\CA that is a classic single channel MAC protocol; (2) MMSN [2] that is a typical synchronous mcMAC with a static channel selection for WSNs; (3) PMC [4] that is an asynchronous mcMAC for WSNs with a dynamic channel selection; (4) CAM-MAC [16] that is a synchronous mcMAC for ad hoc networks with DISH.

Four groups of simulations are conducted to examine four metrics as follows: aggregate throughput, packet delivery ratio, communication latency and energy consumption. Different total number of channels and loads are considered. The total number of channels involves the CC and all DCs, and loads are varied by the change of the number of CBR (Constant Bit Rate) streams in the network.

5.1.1 Evaluation on throughput

The aggregate throughput is computed as the total amount of all useful data packets successful delivered via the MAC layer in the network per unit time.

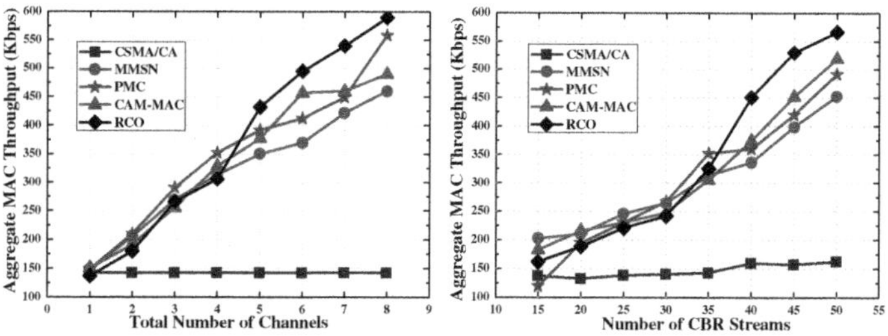

(a)Throughput vs. Number of Channels (b) Throughput vs. Loads

Fig. 3. Throughput evaluation

When the total number of channels is increased, the throughput changes are shown in Fig.3 (a). 35 CBR streams are used in this simulation. Compared with others, RCO has lower throughput when the total number of channels is relatively small. Beside the duty cycling scheme, this is also due to that under random cooperation of RCO, where all neighbors cooperates with receivers probabilistically. This scheme will pay a considerable cost if the total number of channels is small. When more channels are available, RCO, CAM-MAC and PMC allow more nodes to communicate on different DCs simultaneously. This is because they employ the dynamic channel selections, and thus outperform CSMA\CA and MMSN. However, when the total number of channels becomes larger, RCO performs a little better than CAM-MAC and PMC. This is because CAM-MAC suffers from collisions of cooperative packets and PMC suffers from THT, whereas RCO greatly alleviates collisions of cooperative packet and tackles THT effectively, so achieves higher throughput.

The aggregate throughput is explored when different network loads are used in Fig.3 (b). The total number of channels is set to 4. It is observed that the throughputs of all protocols rise with the number of CBR streams. This is because if more node-pairs are involved in communications, more parallel transmissions will occur on the DCs. Under light loads, RCO is suboptimal to other protocols. However, the results show that under heavy loads, RCO performs progressively better than others, which shows that RCO significantly benefits from the random cooperation when the degree of THT increases with loads, even though it is still duty cycling.

5.1.2 Evaluation on Packet Delivery Ratio

The Packet Delivery Ratio (PDR) is computed as the ratio of the total number of packets that MAC layer successful delivered, and the total number of packets that the upper-layer requests MAC layer to deliver.

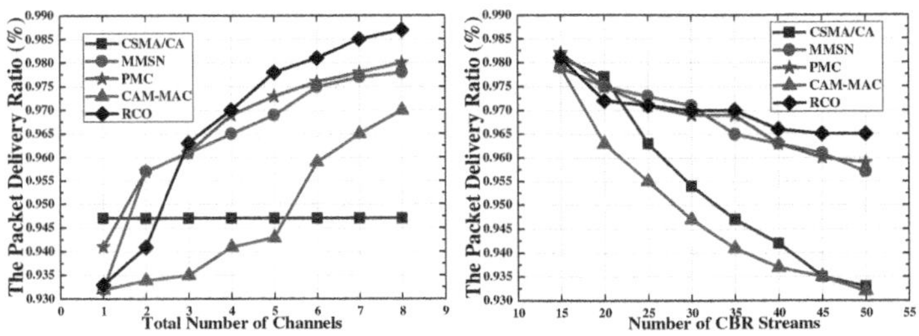

(a) PDR vs. Number of Channels (b) PDR vs. Loads

Fig. 4. Packet delivery ratio evaluation

When total number of channels is increasing, PDR changes are observed in Fig.4 (a). CBR streams are set to 35 in this simulation. The results show that the PDR goes up with the rise of the total number of channels. When total number of channels is smaller than 4, MMSN and PMC achieve better performances than CAM-MAC and

RCO. One possible reason is that schemes of CAM-MAC and RCO to handle THT undermine the PDR. However, when the total number of channels is larger than 5, RCO performs better than others due to that RCO copes with THT that becomes more severe when the total number of channels becomes larger.

The PDR is measured via varying the network loads. The total number of channels is set to 4. In Fig.4 (b), all PDRs generally drop when the loads are heavier except that of RCO, which maintains stable. This is because that under random cooperation, node-pairs more likely find an idle DC for communication in time before the packets are dropped by the sender due to exceeding their lifetime.

5.1.3 Evaluation on Latency

The communication latency reflects time delay that a data packet from the upper-layer waits for a channel reservation until this packet is sent.

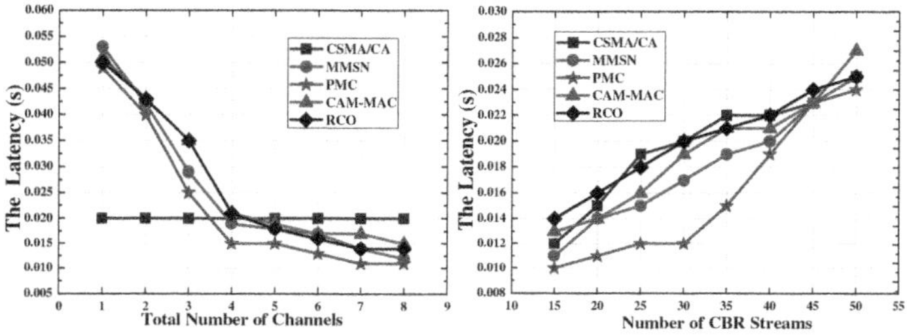

(a) Latency vs. Number of Channels (b) Latency vs. Loads

Fig. 5. Latency evaluation

When the total number of channels is increasing, latency changes are observed in Fig.5 (a). The number of CBR streams is set to 35. The results show that compared with others, RCO has a similar or larger latency when the total number of channels is smaller than 3. However, as it increasingly steps up, the difference on latency becomes negligible, because others suffer the retransmission resulted from THT.

The latency is explored in Fig.5 (b), when different loads are used. The total number of channels is set to 4. It is observed that when the loads are light, RCO has a larger latency than most of other protocols. However, when THT becomes severer as the loads are heavier, the gap between RCO and other protocols on latency becomes narrower, because RCO effectively addresses THT.

5.1.4 Evaluation on Energy Consumption

In this study, the energy consumption for all protocols is computed as the energy consumed to successfully deliver a useful data byte. RCO is expected to achieve energy efficiency via its random cooperation and avoiding the energy consumption for time synchronization and the retransmission caused by THT.

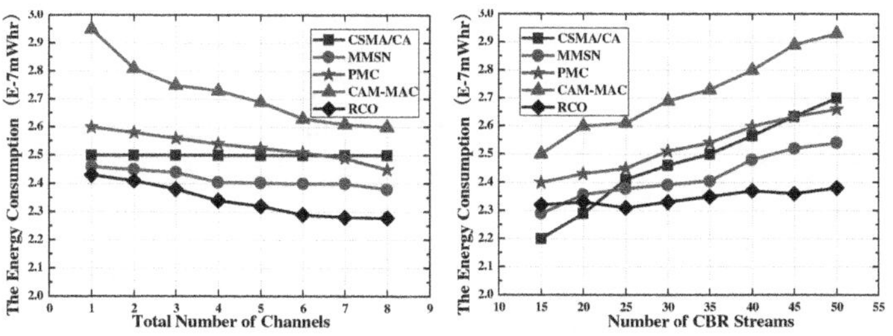

(a) Energy vs. Number of Channels (b) Energy vs. Loads

Fig. 6. Energy consumption evaluation

As the total number of channels increases, the energy consumption changes are observed in Fig.6 (a). The number of CBR streams is set to 35. The results show that the energy consumptions of all protocols decrease with the rise of the total number of channels, but RCO outperforms others all the time. This means that RCO conserves more energy to prolong the lifetime of WSNs by avoiding time synchronization of MMSN and continuously channel switching of PMC. Whereas, CAM-MAC consumes higher energy than others all the time due to its collisions of cooperative packets, which undermines many communications when THT is less serious.

The energy consumption is measured by varying the loads. The total number of channels is set to 4. In Fig.6 (b), all energy consumptions increase when the loads rise. RCO maintains lower energy consumption when the number of CBR streams is larger than 20. This is because the other protocols suffer from certain problems. MMSN consumes much energy to maintain time synchronization among all the nodes when loads are heavy; PMC has many collisions on the current channel when the loads are heavy; CAM-MAC seriously suffers from collisions between cooperative packets and reservation packets when more node-pairs communicate simultaneously.

5.2 Testbed Experiments

We implement RCO on a real sensor node platform and conduct experiments to evaluate the real performance of RCO. RCO is evaluated in the μC/OS [20] on the hawk node, which is a sensor node platform developed by Heilongjiang University. The hawk node is equipped with nRF905 radio and MSP430 processor, and a picture of hawk node is shown in Fig.7 (a). For visualization purposes, we use the three LEDs (red, green, and yellow) on each node to indicate specific events. For example, that the red LED is on indicates the node is communicating on a DC. Meanwhile the green and the yellow LED indicate the specific number of DC (a maximum of 2^2=4 DCs can be represented), *e.g.*, in Fig.7 (b) the red and yellow LEDs of node 2 and 9 are on, which indicates they are communicating on the DC_3. Whereas, that the red LED is off and the yellow and green LEDs are on indicate the node is overhearing on the CC. That all LED are off indicates the node is sleeping.

(a) Hawk node (b) A snapshot in the testbed experiment

Fig. 7. Testbed experiments

The testbed consists of 10 hawk nodes deployed within one hop as in Fig.7 (b) for throughput comparisons. By this setting, all nodes are within the communication range of each other, which was also used by Lou *et al.* [16]. The size of packets is set to 32 Byte, and the transmission rate is set to 100 Kbps. All nodes choose a neighbor at random to enable a unicast communication. The experiment repeats for 10 times, and when it is over, all nodes send their total amount of data received to a sink one by one, which is a special node connected to a desktop computer, and thus throughput can be obtained.

Due to synchronization of MMSN and complexity of PMC for parameter computations, we only implemented RCO and CAM-MAC, and compare them with two varieties of RCO. First variety is called RCO-30%, which works similarly with RCO except that it utilizes a static cooperation probability of 30%; second variety is called RCO-50%, which utilizes a static cooperation probability of 50%.

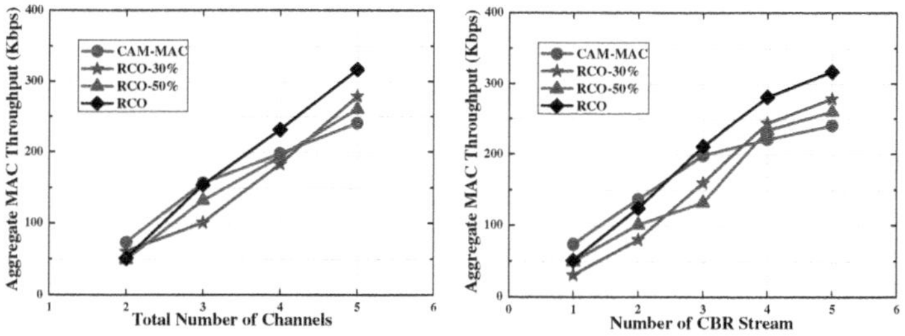

(a) Throughput vs. Number of Channels (b) Throughput vs. Loads

Fig. 8. Testbed evaluation on throughput

The throughput is explored as the different total number of channel is used. The number of CBR streams is set to 5. From Fig.8 (a), it is observed that CAM-MAC has higher throughput than RCO and its two varieties, when the total number of channels is less than 4. CAM-MAC does not have to enable duty cycling, which compromises the throughput of RCO, when THT is less serious. However, RCO achieve better throughput as the total number of channel is larger than or equal to 4. The explanation of this improvement is that when more DCs are available, THT becomes more serious, and RCO tackles it with less cost than CAM-MAC. This is consistent with the simulation comparisons shown in Fig.3 (a). In addition, RCO has similar throughput with RCO-30% and RCO-50% when the total number of channels is small, whereas it outperforms them when the total number of channels is larger than 3. The results further justify the values of random cooperation.

When the number of channels is set to 5 and the loads are varying, throughputs are observed in Fig.8 (b). It shows that RCO and its two varieties have lower throughput than CAM-MAC, when loads are small. This is due to when fewer nodes are communicating, DISH of CAM-MAC works better in tackling THT than random cooperation of RCO. However, when loads are heavy, more collisions happen between cooperative packets under CAM-MAC. Therefore, RCO outperforms CAM-MAC when the number of CBR Stream is equal to or larger than 3. Note that RCO works better than RCO-30% and RCO-50%, which shows that dynamic random cooperation actually improve the throughput of RCO than static random cooperation.

6 Conclusion

Triple hidden terminal problems are major causes of energy wastage in WSNs. To address these problems, in this paper, an asynchronous multi-channel duty cycle MAC protocol called RCO is proposed. RCO exploits random cooperation to effectively handle the triple hidden terminal problems. Being fully distributed with no requirements of time synchronization or multi-radio, RCO is very easy to be implemented in resource-constrained sensor nodes. Meanwhile, RCO achieves energy efficiency by decoupling duty cycling as well. The simulation and real testbed experiments show that RCO handles triple hidden terminals effectively, and achieves significant improvement in energy efficiency with increasing benefit when traffic loads and the number of available channels increase, while maintaining higher throughput.

Acknowledgments. This work is partly supported by the Key Scientific and Technological Research Project of Heilongjiang Province of China (No. GC09A109), the Graduate Innovative Research Project of Heilongjiang Province of China (No, YJSCX2010-019HLJ), the Innovative Research Project of Heilongjiang University (No. 2010208) and the Innovative Laboratory Project of Heilongjiang University (No.2010046).

References

1. David, E.C., Deborah, E., Mani, S.: Overview of Sensor Networks. In: IEEE Computer, Special Issue on Sensor Networks (2004)
2. Gang, Z., Chengdu, H., Ting, Y., Tian, H., John, A.S., Tarek, F.B.: MMSN: Multi-Frequency Media Access Control for Wireless Sensor Networks. In: The 25th Conference on Computer Communications (2006)
3. Youngmin, K., Hyojeong, S., Hojung, C.: Y-MAC: An Energy-efficient Multi-Channel MAC Protocol for Dense Wireless Sensor Networks. In: ACM/IEEE International Conference on Information Processing in Sensor Networks (2008)

4. Hieu, K.L., Dan, H., Tarek, A.: A Practical Multi-Channel Media Access Control Protocol for Wireless Sensor Networks. In: ACM/IEEE International Conference on Information Processing in Sensor Networks (2008)
5. Jungmin, S., Nitin, V.: Multi-Channel MAC for Ad Hoc Networks: Handling Multi-Channel Hidden Terminals Using a Single Transceiver. In: The Fifth ACM International Symposium on Mobile Hoc Networking and Computing (2004)
6. Mastooreh, S., Hamed, S., Antonis, K.: HyMAC: Hybrid TDMA/ FDMA Medium Access Control Protocol for Wireless Sensor Networks. In: IEEE 18th International Symposium on Personal, Indoor and Mobile Radio Communications (2007)
7. Milica, D.J., Goran, L.D.: TFMAC: Multi-Channel MAC Protocol for Wireless Sensor Networks. In: 8th International Conference on Telecommunications in Modern Satellite, Cable and Broadcasting Services (2007)
8. Jenhui, C., Shiann-Tsong, S., Chin-An, Y.: A New Multichannel Access Protocol for IEEE 802.11 Ad Hoc Wireless LANs. In: The 14th IEEE International Symposium on Personal, Indoor and Mobile Radio Communications (2003)
9. Asimakis, T., Garcia-Luna-Aceves, J.J.: Channel-Hopping Multiple Access with Packet Trains for Ad Hoc Networks. In: Mobile Multimedia Communications (2000)
10. Paramvir, B., Ranveer, C., John, D.: SSCH: Slotted Seeded Channel Hopping for Capacity Improvement in IEEE 802.11 Ad-Hoc Wireless Networks. In: The Tenth Annual International Conference on Mobile Computing and Networking (2004)
11. Asimakis, T., Garcia-Luna-Aceves, J.J.: A Receiver-Initiated Collision-Avoidance Protocol for Multi-Channel Networks. In: Twentieth Annual Joint Conference of the IEEE Computer and Communications Societies (2001)
12. Shih-Lin, W., Chih-Yu, L., Yu-Chee, T., Jang-Ping, S.: A New Multi-Channel MAC Protocol with On-Demand Channel Assignment for Multi-Hop Mobile Ad Hoc Networks. In: 5th International Symposium on Parallel Architectures, Algorithms and Networks (2000)
13. Atul, A., Paramvir, B., Jitendra, P., Alec, W., Lidong, Z.: A Multi-Radio Unification Protocol for IEEE 802.11 Wireless Networks. In: 1st International Conference on Broadband Networks (2004)
14. Nitin, J., Samir, R.D., Asis, N.: A Multichannel CSMA MAC Protocol with Receiver-Based Channel Selection for Multihop Wireless Networks. In: 10th International Conference on Computer Communications and Networks (2001)
15. Asis, N., Jun, Z., Samir, R.D.: A Multichannel CSMA MAC Protocol for Multihop Wireless Networks. In: IEEE Wireless Communications and Networking Conference (1999)
16. Tie, L., Mehul, M., Vikram, S.: Cooperative Asynchronous Multichannel MAC: Design, Analysis, and Implementation. IEEE Transactions on Mobile Computing 8(3) (2009)
17. Tie, L., Mehul, M., Vikram, S.: Extended Abstract: Altruistic Cooperation for Energy-Efficient Multi-Channel MAC protocols. In: The Thirteenth Annual International Conference on Mobile Computing and Networking (2007)
18. Yanjun, S., Omer, G., David, B.J.: A Receiver Initiated Asynchronous Duty Cycle MAC Protocol for Dynamic Traffic Loads in Wireless Sensor Networks. In: The 6th ACM Conference on Embedded Networked Sensor Systems (2008)
19. Yafeng, W., John, A.S., Tian, H., Jiakang, L., Shan, L.: Realistic and Efficient Multi-Channel Communications in Wireless Sensor Networks. In: The 27th Conference on Computer Communications (2008)
20. Zhong, Z., Zheng, P., Jun-Hong, C., Zaihan, J.: Handling Triple Hidden Terminal Problems for Multi-Channel MAC in Long-Delay Underwater Sensor Networks. In: The 29th Conference on Computer Communications (2010)

Power and Bandwidth Efficiency of IEEE 802.15.4 Wireless Sensor Networks

Xiaodong Zhao[1], Wan Zhang[2], Wensheng Niu[1], Yadi Zhang[1], and Liqiang Zhao[2]

[1] Aeronautical Computing Technique Research Institute, Xi'an, Shaanxi, 710068, China
[2] State Key Laboratory of Integrated Services Networks, Xidian University, Xi'an, Shaanxi, 710071, China
cindyzhao63116@sina.com

Abstract. In WSNs, energy conservation is the primary goal, while throughput and delay are less important. This results in a tradeoff between performance (e.g., throughput, delay, jitter, and packet-loss-rate) and energy consumption. In this paper, to jointly optimize performance and energy consumption, firstly, we carry out a comprehensive analysis of bandwidth and power efficiency of IEEE 802.15.4 WSNs. Secondly, a power-efficient MAC protocol, PeMAC, and a bandwith-efficient MAC protocol, BeMAC, are presented in this paper. In PeMAC and BeMAC, based on power and bandwidth efficiency criterion respectively, each node independently adjusts its contention parameters (e.g., the minimum backoff period) to the estimated system state (e.g., the number of competing nodes). Simulation results show that PeMAC and BeMAC can increase the power and bandwidth efficiency respectively while still maintaining reasonable system performance.

Keywords: Wireless Sensor Network, Bandwidth Efficiency, Power Efficiency.

1 Introduction

As an emerging technology, wireless sensor networks (WSNs) have a wide range of potential applications including environment monitoring, smart spaces, medical systems and robotic exploration. Performance analysis and optimization of WSNs, especially its medium access control (MAC) protocols, have attracted much research interests. Traditional MAC protocols for wireless ad hoc networks are designed to maximize throughput and minimize delay. As sensor nodes are generally battery-operated, to design a good MAC protocol for WSNs, the first attribute that has to be considered is energy saving [1]. Other important attributes (such as throughput and delay) are generally the primary concerns in traditional wireless ad hoc networks, but in WSNs they are secondary.

IEEE 802.15.4 is one of the most influential WSN standards, and its basic MAC protocol is based on Carrier Sense Multiple Access with Collision Avoidance (CSMA/CA) [2]. Moreover, each node periodically sleeps, wakes up, listens to the channel, and then returns to sleep. During the sleeping period, the node turns off its radio to preserve energy. During the active period, it can communicate with its neighbors. Although this periodic active/sleep mechanism performs effectively for

Z. Yu et al. (Eds.): UIC 2010, LNCS 6406, pp. 243–251, 2010.

saving energy, throughput is reduced because only the active period is used for communication, and delay increases because a message-generating event may occur during the sleeping period. In that case, the message will be queued until the start of the next active period.

To handle load variations in time and location, T-MAC (timeout MAC) dynamically ends the active period [3]. Based on Aloha with preamble sampling specifically designed for infrastructure WSNs [4], WiseMAC (wireless sensor MAC) provides lower power consumption for the same delay than IEEE 802.15.4. To achieve a low power operation, B-MAC (Berkeley MAC) employs an adaptive preamble sampling scheme to reduce duty cycle and minimize idle listening [5]. DSMAC (dynamic S-MAC) dynamically changes the sleeping interval with fixed listening interval length and therefore the duty cycle of sensors is adjusted according to the current traffic condition [6].

As there is an increasing demand for WSNs to support real-time traffic, which has certain requirements on throughput and delay, the future WSNs should achieve all the goals, energy saving, throughput, and delay at the same time. Hence, the future MAC protocols of WSNs aim at increasing the b/s/W power efficiency, i.e., increasing performance while still maintaining reasonable energy consumption.

Hence, firstly, in section 2 we carry out a comprehensive analysis of radio efficiency of WSNs. As much investment in WSNs aims at improving the bandwidth efficiency [7] or power efficiency [8], the bandwidth and power efficiency of IEEE 802.15.4 WSNs are analyzed in detail. Secondly, in section 3, based on the power and bandwidth efficiency criteria, we present a heuristic approach for WSNs to improve the bandwidth efficiency in b/s and the power efficiency in b/s/W respectively. Thirdly, in section 4, simulation studies are carried out to evaluate the performance of the proposed approaches. Finally, the concluding remarks are given in Section 5.

2 Bandwidth and Power Effieicncy of IEEE 802.15.4 WMNs

2.1 Definition of Radio Efficiency

By definition, efficiency is the ratio of the attained utility and the consumed resources [9]. In wireless communications, a user aims at transmitting its packets successfully under its quality-of-service (QoS) requirements. Hence, the radio utility metrics should include the successfully packets in bit, and QoS metrics (such as bandwidth in b/s, delay and packet loss rate). On the other hand, available radio resources up to now can be classified into six categories, time, frequency, space, code, power and user in six different domains. Hence, a novel concept of radio efficiency is presented in this paper, which is defined as the number of successfully transmitted bits per resource category in a domain, corresponding to bit-per-second-per-Hz-per-antenna-per-code-per-Watt-per-user (b/s/Hz/antenna/code/W/user), under given QoS constraints. In view of the time and power, two major resource categories in WSNs, we consider the b/s bandwidth efficiency and b/s/W power efficiency respectively as the principal efficiency criterion in this paper. Obviously, the bandwidth and power efficiency are two special cases of the above radio efficiency.

2.2 Description of IEEE 802.15.4

In 802.15.4, before each new transmission attempt, a node generates a random slotted backoff interval, and the number of the backoff slots is uniformly chosen in the range [0, W_0-1]. The minimum backoff period, W_0, is set equal to a value 2^{MinBE}-1, where *MinBE* is the minimum value of the backoff exponential. The backoff counter value decrements at every slot without sensing the channel. Once the backoff counter reaches zero, the node performs the first clear channel assessment (CCA). If the channel is idle, it will perform the second CCA. And if the channel is idle again, the node will transmit its frame. If the channel is busy during either the first or the second CCA, *BE* is added to 1 until up to the maximum backoff exponential (aMaxBE) period is reached. Once BE reaches aMaxBE , it will remain at the value until the packet is transmitted successfully or the retransmission time (*m*) reaches retry limit. While the limit is reached, retransmission attempts will cease and the packet will be discarded.

2.3 Bandwidth and Power Efficiency of IEEE 802.15.4 WSNs

In this subsection, starting from the model proposed in [11-13], we derive a formula that explicitly relates the b/s/W power efficiency and the b/s bandwidth efficiency to the transmission probability, which is also related to the number of competing nodes and contention parameters (e.g., W_0, and *m*).

Following [11-13], we consider a scenario composed of a fixed number *n* of competing nodes, each operating in saturation conditions [11], i.e., whose transmission queue always contains at least a packet ready for transmission, under an ideal channel condition (no hidden terminals and capture).

Let γ be the probability that a node transmits in a randomly chosen slot, and W_{Tx}, W_{Rx}, and W_{idle} be the average transmission, receiving and idle power respectively. And then the probability P_{tr} that there is at least one transmission in the considered time slot can be expressed as:

$$P_{tr} = 1 - (1-\gamma)^n \, , \tag{1}$$

and the probability P_s that exactly one node transmits on the channel upon at least one node's transmitting can be expressed as:

$$P_s = \frac{n\gamma(1-\gamma)^{n-1}}{P_{tr}} \, . \tag{2}$$

With regard to the status of packet transmission in a given slot, there are three possibilities [12-13]. Firstly, there is a successful transmission with the probability, $P_{suc} = P_{tr}P_s$, whose time length is $T_s = T_l + T_{ack} + \delta$, where T_l, T_{ack} and δ are time durations for transmitting a data frame, receiving an Acknowledgement (ACK) control frame and waiting for the ACK frame respectively. And the average consumed energy is

$E_s = (W_{Tx}+W_{Rx})T_s+(n-1)W_{idle}$. Secondly, there is collision if more than one node transmits simultaneously, with the probability, $P_{fail} = P_{tr}(1-P_s)$, whose time length is $T_c = T_l$. And the average consumed energy is $E_c = (n_c W_{Tx}+W_{Rx})T_c+(n- n_c)W_{idle}$. Finally, the channel is idle when all the nodes are in the backoff states, which happens with probability $P_{idle} = 1-P_{tr}$, whose time length is δ. And then the average consumed energy is $E_{idle} = n\delta W_{idle}+\delta W_{Rx}$.

We are now able to express the b/s/W power efficiency and b/s bandwidth efficiency as:

$$\eta_{power} = \frac{\text{Average payload successfully transmitted in a slot}}{\text{Average consumed energy in a slot}} = \frac{\overline{P}P_{suc}}{P_{suc}E_s + P_{fail}E_c + P_{idle}E_{idle}}, \tag{3}$$

and

$$\eta_{Bandwith} = \frac{\text{Average payload successfully transmitted in a slot}}{\text{a slot time}} = \frac{\overline{P}P_{suc}}{P_{suc}T_s + P_{fail}T_c + P_{idle}\sigma}, \tag{4}$$

where $\overline{P}$ is the average payload size in bit.

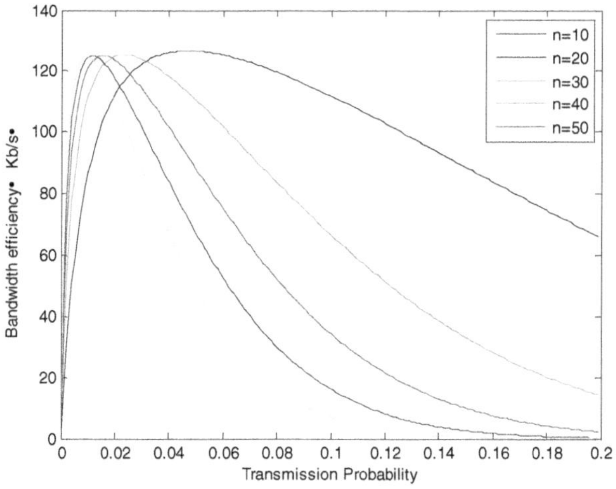

Fig. 1. Bandwidth efficiency versus the transmission probability

We can plot the figure about the bandwidth and power efficiency versus the transmission probability γ, as shown in Figure 1 and 2.

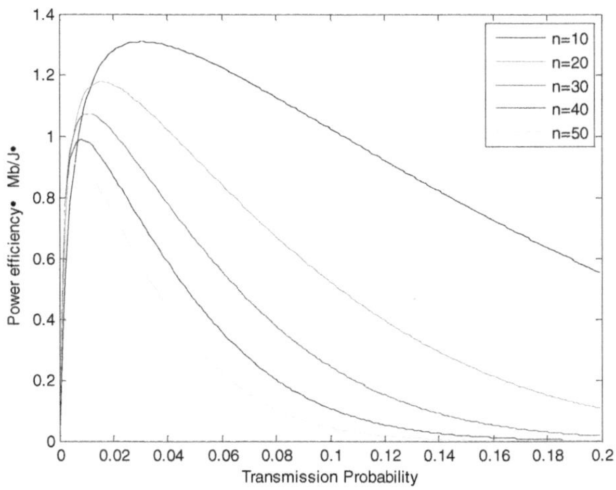

Fig. 2. Power efficiency versus the transmission probability

3 Bandwidth and Power Efficient MAC Protocols for WMNs

In this section, we present a bandwidth and power efficient MAC protocol, BeMAC and PeMAC, to achieve the b/s bandwidth efficiency and b/s/W power efficiency respectively by tuning the contention parameters (e.g., the minimum backoff period) upon estimating the system state (e.g., the number of competing nodes).

[13] shows that γ depends on the network size and the contention parameters (e.g., W_0 and m), as follows:

$$\gamma = \frac{2(1-2p)(1-p)(1-p^{(m+1)})}{W_0(1-p)^2[1-(2p)^{(m+1)}]+(1-2p)(3-\alpha)(1-p^{(m+1)})(1-p)+L(1-2p)(1-p)^2(1-p^{(m+1)})}, \tag{5}$$

where

$$p = \alpha + \beta - \alpha\beta, \tag{6}$$

and α and β are the probability of the channel being busy for the first and the second CCA respectively, which are discussed in detail in [12-13].

Based on equation (5) and (6), we can explicitly compute the optimal transmission probability that each node should adopt in order to achieve the maximum power or bandwidth efficiency within a considered network scenario, i.e., the number of competing nodes n.

As n is not a directly controlled variable, the only way to achieve optimal performance is to employ adaptive techniques to tune the values of contention parameters (e.g., W_0) upon estimating the value of n.

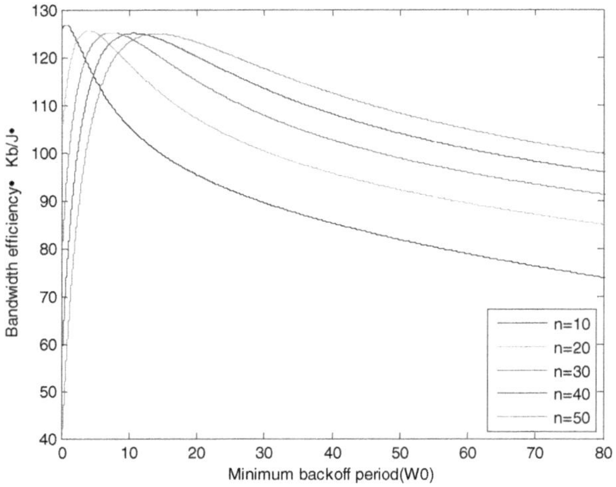

Fig. 3. Bandwidth efficiency versus the minimum backoff period

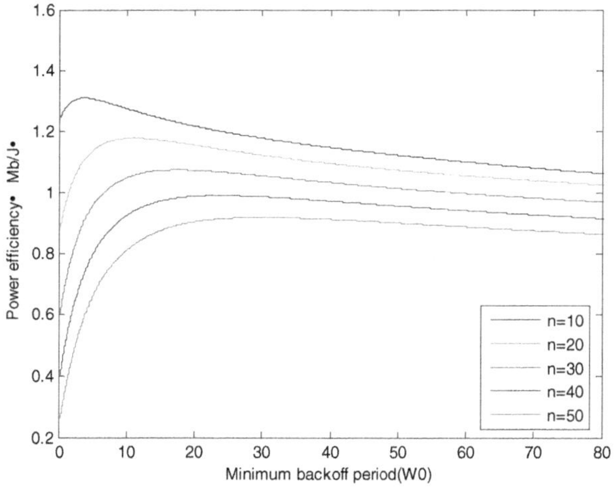

Fig. 4. Power efficiency versus the minimum backoff period

Based on the above analysis, we implement a look-up table, in order to calculate the optimal values of minimum backoff periods from the number of competing nodes, as shown in Table 1.

Moreover, in order to estimate the number of competing nodes in IEEE 802.11 WLANs, [14] provided two run-time estimation mechanisms, i.e., auto regressive moving average (ARMA) and Kalman Filters, and we also developed a frame-analytic estimation mechanism [15]. All the estimation mechanisms are also valid in IEEE 802.15.4 WSNs. For simplicity, we assume that each node knows the number of competing nodes. Hence, in BeMAC and PeMAC, to achieve the maximum bandwidth efficiency and power efficiency respectively, each node adjusts its minimum backoff period by looking up Table 1.

Table 1. Max. bandwidth and power efficiency versus the transmission probability and W_0

Number of competing nodes (n)	Transmission Probability (γ)	Min. backoff period (W0)	Max. Bandwidth efficiency (Kb/s)	Max. Power efficiency (Mb/J)
10	0.0471	2	126.7	
10	0.0306	3		1.31
20	0.0232	4	125.6	
20	0.0157	8		1.18
30	0.0154	8	125.2	
30	0.0107	12		1.08
40	0.0115	11	125	
40	0.0083	17		0.99
50	0.0092	14	124.9	
50	0.0068	21		0.92

4 Performance Evaluation

To evaluate the proposed protocols, we performed the following simulations. The values of the parameters used to obtain numerical results for the above analysis and the following simulations are specified in IEEE 802.15.4. We set a star topology with one coordinator and many devices, where the number of devices increases from 10 to 50 at a step of 5. Each device generates new fixed size packets under a Poisson process and transmits them to the access point. The packet arrival rate is always in the saturation case.

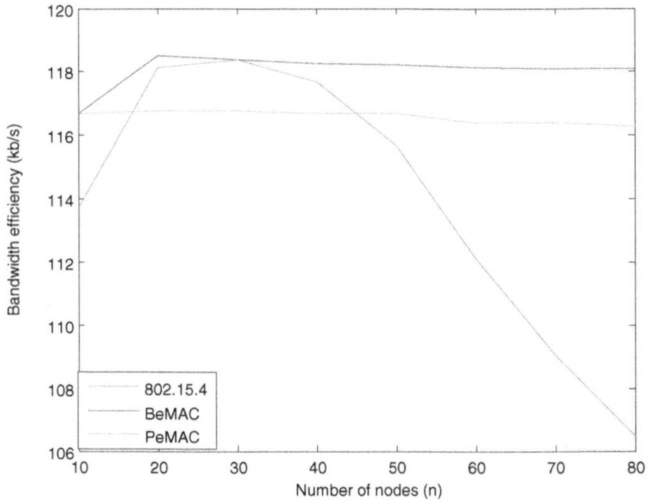

Fig. 5. Bandwidth efficiency

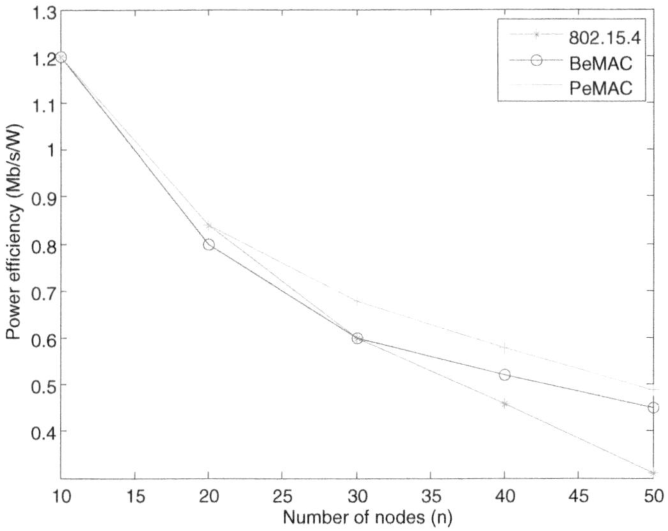

Fig. 6. Power efficiency

Fig. 5-6 shows that the bandwidth efficiency of BeMAC and the power efficiency in PeMAC are higher than that of IEEE 802.15.4 especially for large number of nodes. In IEEE 802.15.4, when node transmits a packet, the initial backoff period is chosen from a fixed value. A node obtains the suitable backoff period always after several collisions. But in BeMAC and PeMAC, it can be chosen according to the number of competing nodes. So the two protocols can avoid many collisions and decrease the energy consumed on the collisions. Based on two different criterions, the b/s bandwidth and b/s/W power efficiency, BeMAC and PeMAC can achieve the maximum bandwidth and power efficiency of WSNs respectively.

5 Conclusion and Further Work

In this paper, firstly, after introducing a novel concept of radio efficiency, a comprehensive analysis of bandwidth and power efficiency is presented for IEEE 802.15.4 WSNs. Secondly, based on the analytical results, the optimal values of transmission probability and the minimum backoff period are obtained to achieve the maximum bandwidth or power efficiency. Thirdly, the BeMAC and PeMAC protocol are presented to achieve the maximum bandwidth and power efficiency respectively, where each node adjusts its minimum backoff period to the estimated number of competing nodes. Finally the simulation results show that BeMAC and PeMAC improve the bandwidth and power efficiency respectively while still maintaining reasonable system performance.

Acknowledgments. This work is supported by the 111 Project (B08038), State Key Laboratory of Integrated Services Networks (ISN090105), Program for New Century Excellent Talents in University (NCET-08-0810), National Natural Science Foundation of China (No. 60772137), and UK-China Science Bridges: R&D on (B)4G Wireless Mobile Communications.

References

1. Akyildiz, I.F., Su, W., Sankarasubramaniam, Y., Cayirci, E.: Wireless sensor networks: a survey. Computer Networks 38, 393–422 (2002)
2. IEEE Standard 802.15.4: Wireless Medium Access Control (MAC) and Physical Layer (PHY) Specification for Low-Rate Wireless Personal Area Networks
3. Dam, T., Langendoen, K.: An adaptive energy-efficient MAC protocol for wireless sensor networks. In: SenSys, pp. 171–180 (2003)
4. El-Hoiydi, A., Decotignie, J.D.: WiseMAC: An Ultra Low Power MAC Protocol for the Downlink of Infrastructure Wireless Sensor Networks. In: ISCC, pp. 244–251 (2004)
5. Polastre, J., Hill, J., Celler, D.: Versatile Low Power Media Access for Wireless Sensor Networks. In: SenSys, pp. 95–107 (2004)
6. Lin, P., Qiao, C., Wang, X.: Medium Access Control with Dynamic Duty Cycle For Sensor Networks. In: WCNC, pp. 1534–1539 (2004)
7. Goldsmith, A., Chua, S.G.: Variable-rate variable-power MQAM for fading channels. IEEE Transaction on Communication 45, 1218–1230 (1997)
8. Verdu, S.: Spectral efficiency in the wideband regime. IEEE Transactions on Information Theory 48, 1319–1343 (2002)
9. Gow, G., Smith, R.: Mobile and Wireless Communications: An Introduction. Open University Press/McGraw-Hill (2005)
10. Zheng, J., Lee, M.L.: A Comprehensive Performance Study of IEEE 802.15.4 Sensor Network Operation, pp. 218–237. IEEE Press, Los Alamitos (2006)
11. Park, T.R., Kim, T.H., Choi, J.Y., Kwon, W.H.: Throughput and energy consumption analysis of IEEE 802.15.4 slotted CSMA/CA. IEEE Electronics Letters 41, 1017–1019 (2005)
12. Arindam, K.D., Sumit, R.: Analysis of the contention access period of IEEE 802.15.4 MAC. ACM Trans. Sensor Networks 3, 1–29 (2007)
13. Wen, H., Lin, C., Chen, Z.J., Yin, H., He, T., Eryk, D.: An Improve Markov Model for IEEE 802.15.4 Slotted CSMA/CA Mechanism. J. Computer Science and Technology 24, 495–504 (2009)
14. Bianchi, G., Tinnirello, I.: Kalman Filter Estimation of the Number of Competing Terminals in an IEEE 802.11 network. In: INFOCOM, pp. 844–851 (2003)
15. Zhao, L., Zou, X., Ding, W., Zhang, H., Zhang, J.: Game-theoretic Cross-layer Design in WLANs. In: IEEE International Wireless Communications and Mobile Computing Conference (IWCMC), pp. 570–575 (2008)

Protecting Source Location Privacy in Wireless Sensor Networks with Data Aggregation

Wenbo Yang and Wen Tao Zhu

State Key Laboratory of Information Security
Graduate University of Chinese Academy of Sciences
P. O. Box 4588, Beijing 100049, P.R. China
wbyang@is.ac.cn, wtzhu@ieee.org

Abstract. Many efforts have been made to protect sensor networks against attacks, and standard mechanisms such as encryption are widely used to provide security services. However, the wireless transmission of a message itself may reveal to the adversary the origin of a sensed event, i.e., the source location of the message. Providing such position privacy in sensor networks is a challenging task. Traditional anonymity techniques are inappropriate for resource-constrained sensor networks, but an adversary may easily monitor the network communications. In this work, we focus on protecting source location privacy in the global attack model, where an adversary may have a global view of the communications in a sensor network and employ traffic analysis to locate the message sources. A flexible and effective countermeasure based on secure data aggregation is proposed to prevent the leakage of source location information. Both theoretical analysis and simulations are presented to validate the proposed scheme.

Keywords: Wireless sensor networks, information security, location privacy, anonymity, data aggregation.

1 Introduction

As an emerging network technology, wireless sensor networks (WSNs) are regarded as a promising solution to monitoring the physical world in unattended, unreachable, and even dangerous environments. Sensor networks that consist of many small and cheap sensors can be used in many industrial and civilian application areas, such as environment and habitat monitoring, military surveillance, smart health care, and target tracking. Because these applications often require sensor networks to be deployed in harsh environments, they are confronted with a lot of security issues.

Many efforts have been made to protect sensor networks from hostile attacks. Traditional technologies such as encryption and authentication are widely used to provide security services. However, due to the broadcast nature of wireless communications, the transmission of an encrypted message itself will leak some valuable information to the adversary. Consider an example of panda monitoring

Z. Yu et al. (Eds.): UIC 2010, LNCS 6406, pp. 252–266, 2010.

introduced in [1]. When a sensor node, called the *reporter node* in this article, detects the appearance of a panda, it may report in a confidential manner when and where the panda is found to the sink node (i.e., the base station) along a multi-hop route. Nevertheless, even without knowing the encryption key(s) employed by the reporter node(s), an adversary can still trace back hop by hop to the source location of the detected event by eavesdropping on the communications. Then the position of the panda is revealed to the adversary, and something unexpected may happen. It is important to guarantee location privacy of reporter nodes in many similar monitoring applications.

Providing source location privacy in sensor networks is a challenging task. Due to limited node power supply and computational resources, traditional anonymity techniques are not appropriate to sensor networks. On the other hand, an adversary can easily detect the message transmission in the WSN, and perform traffic analysis or even inject malicious packets.

Several source location privacy protection schemes have been proposed for sensor networks [2]. Most of them [1, 3, 4, 5] assume that the adversary has only a limited local view of the network traffic, that is, only message transmissions within his overhearing radius can be detected by the adversary. Thus the adversary must trace back step by step, typically starting from the sink node, to find the original message source. Particularly, the adversary is likely to identify the location of the reporter node when the event of interest is reported multiple times (e.g., periodically), even if the reporter node changes (e.g., the panda being detected moves within the sensor network deployment field). All these schemes [1, 3, 4, 5] will fail when the adversary has a global view of the network traffic [6], even if the detection is only reported once instead of multiple rounds. The point lies in that the adversary may easily locate the message source by observing which sensor node starts sending the first packet in this circumstance.

In this work, we focus on protecting source location privacy in a *global attack model*, where an adversary has a global view of the whole network traffic and is able to use traffic analysis techniques to determine the location of the message source. We propose a flexible and effective aggregation-based scheme to hide the reporter node so as to prevent the leakage of its location information. The major features of our solution are summarized below:

- The reporter mask mechanism can be adjusted to achieve different levels of security depending on the requirements of the sensor network application involved.
- The network structure in our scheme is self-organized, so it can easily adapt to network changes such as node addition and revocation. We do not require sensors to be placed at the exact predetermined positions as [6] does.
- Depending on different situations, the system parameters can be tuned to balance the energy consumption and the event reporting latency but without sacrificing privacy.

The rest of this paper is organized as follows. In section 2 we discuss related work. In section 3 we present the network and threat model. In section 4 we propose our aggregation-based source location protection scheme. In section 5 we evaluate the proposal with both theoretical analysis and simulations. Section 6 concludes this paper.

2 Related Work

A number of source location privacy-preserving algorithms have been proposed in recent years [2]. Most of them were based on the assumption that the adversary overhears only local network traffic, so the adversary must trace back step by step from the base station to discover the message source. The privacy conservation level is measured by the number of messages the reporter node has sent before it is found (referred to as the *safety period* [1]). The commonly used strategy to increase the safety period is increasing the number of steps required to reach the reporter node from the base station.

In [1, 3], a flooding routing strategy called *phantom routing* is proposed to defend against an adversary who wants to trace back to the reporter node by eavesdropping on the network traffic. Phantom routing consists of two stages. At the first stage, the packet starts a random (or directed) walk, ends at a node which we call the *phantom source*. At the second stage, the packet is delivered through flooding from the phantom source to the sink. A later work [4] demonstrates an attack against the flooding-based phantom routing introduced in [1,3], and proposes a new routing strategy GROW (Greedy Random Walk). GROW uses a two-way random walk to construct the route and thus reduces the chance an eavesdropper can collect the location information. The random walk is initiated from both the source and the sink until the two paths intersect. A Bloom filter is used by each node to store its neighbors that have already participated in the random walk to avoid backtracking of the random path.

In CEM (Cyclic Entrapment Method [5]), several loops are established after the deployment of the WSN. Real messages can be routed through these loops easily, but an adversary who is not aware of these loops will be entrapped by the cycling of fake messages. Therefore the expected time required for the adversary to locate the reporter node is increased. As the length of loops increases, the privacy provided by CEM also increases, but at the cost of more energy consumption.

However, if the adversary has a global knowledge of the network traffic, the above schemes [1, 3, 4, 5] will fail because the adversary can easily locate the reporter node by observing which node starts the communication with the base station [7]. Two techniques are proposed in [7] for privacy-preserving routing in the global attack model, a *periodic collection* method and a *source simulation* method. The periodic collection method has each node send packets (real or dummy) periodically regardless of whether there are real data or not. It provides the optimal location privacy but can only be applied to applications that collect data at a low rate and do not have strict requirements on message latency. The source simulation method simulates the movement pattern of real objects and creates multiple candidate traces in the network to hide the traffic triggered by real objects, so the energy consumption is reduced at the cost of sacrificing some privacy.

In many schemes that rely on dummy traffic to hide real message transmissions, messages are sent out following some statistical pattern to avoid leaking information. Real messages must be postponed to satisfy the statistical pattern, which causes a high event reporting latency. A FitProbRate scheme is proposed in [8] to reduce the real event reporting latency while keeping a statistically strong source anonymity.

The overhead caused by the dummy traffic generated to hide real message transmissions is usually high. To avoid the explosion of network traffic, [6] uses some special nodes called *proxy nodes* to drop dummy messages on their way to the base station, and proposes a heuristics local search algorithm to solve the optimal proxy placement problem. Two schemes are proposed in [6], a proxy-based filtering scheme (PFS) and a tree-based filtering scheme (TFS). The proxy placement algorithm requires all sensors to be placed at the exact positions that are predetermined in the network planning phase. But this requirement may not be satisfied in reality due to the hostility, inaccessibility, and unpredictability at the deployment site. Moreover, the traffic at a proxy node will be heavily congested if events happen intensively in the area covered by its associated sensor nodes. It will result in large message delay and dropping ratio.

3 Network and Threat Model

3.1 Network Model

We assume that the sensor network consists of a large number of sensor nodes which have roughly the same computing capabilities, power resources, and expected lifetime. Each sensor node is equipped with a wireless transceiver which can be used to communicate with the sensor nodes within its transmission range. All sensor nodes are deployed in a target field to monitor some event occurrences. We do not require sensors to be placed at the exact predetermined locations as [6] does. Thus the sensor network can be deployed easily by dropping from an air-plane or other means.

3.2 Threat Model

Though many existing schemes assume the adversary has only a limited local view of the network traffic, we adopt the *passive global attack model* following [6, 7]. We assume that the adversary has the ability to monitor and analyze all the communications in the network. However, to avoid being detected, the adversary does not interfere with the proper functioning of the network, i.e., he will not conduct active attacks such as malicious packets injection, jamming, and denial of service attack. To illustrate the threat model clearly, we use the Panda-Hunter game [1] as an example.

In the Panda-Hunter game, a large number of wireless sensor nodes are deployed in the natural habitat of giant pandas to monitor the activities of them. When a panda is detected by a sensor node, it will report data (e.g. time and location) periodically to the base station. There exists a hunter acting as the adversary who wants to poach the panda. Since all packets are sent over the air, the hunter may eavesdrop on the communications to obtain the location information of pandas in this area. He does not wish to be noticed by the owner of the sensor network. So he will not conduct active attacks which can be easily detected by the network controller.

In the global attack model, the adversary has the ability to learn all the communications in the entire sensor network. The hunter can achieve this ability by using an array of targeted antennae, or deploying his own sensor network in this area to monitor the target network [7]. In the later case, the size of a sensor network to monitor wireless radio signals can be much smaller than the size of a sensor network to sense animal activities. Though it is still expensive, it is worth the cost considering the value of the location information of pandas [7].

We assume the adversary can use some advanced traffic analysis techniques such as *rate monitoring* and *time correlation* [6]. In a rate monitoring attack, the adversary monitors the packet sending rate of nodes and pays more attention to the nodes that have a higher packet sending rate. In a time correlation attack, the adversary observes the correlation in sending time between neighbor nodes and attempts to deduce a forwarding path.

4 Aggregation-Based Source Location Protection Scheme

In this section, we describe our aggregation-based source location protection scheme (ASLP) and discuss some related issues.

4.1 Scheme Overview

In our scheme, we adopt a cluster-tree hierarchical network topology model which is widely used in many sensor network communication protocols [9, 10, 11, 12]. Each cluster is configured with two parameters: λ and τ. The meaning of each parameter is described bellow:

- λ : Every sensor node in the cluster sends out messages with intervals following an exponential distribution with a parameter of λ. We can change the value of λ to control the message generation rate.
- τ : The cluster head reports an aggregation result to the base station every τ time units.

We use dummy traffic to prevent the adversary from locating the reporter nodes. Each sensor node sends out encrypted real or dummy messages periodically to defend against traffic analysis. The time intervals between these messages follow an exponential distribution $Exp(1/\lambda)$. We employ in-cluster data aggregation to reduce the message overhead caused by dummy traffic. If message filtering is enabled, the aggregated messages will be further filtered along the route based on their contents. Next, we present the details of our scheme.

4.2 Scheme Details

Clustering and Building the Routing Tree. In the initial phase, we divide the sensor network into clusters to perform data aggregation. The cluster heads are organized into a tree structure rooted at the base station, which is called the *routing tree.* Many algorithms [9,10,11,12] have been proposed to cluster sensor networks and build the routing tree. Our scheme does not rely on any particular clustering or routing tree construction algorithm, so we merely assume that the cluster-tree structure can be built in the initial phase and the cluster head can be re-elected when needed to prolong the network lifetime. Each cluster is assigned a unique cluster id *cid* and each sensor in the cluster is assigned a unique in-cluster sensor id *sid*. Thus we can identify a single sensor node by (cid, sid). It is assumed that each sensor node can establish pairwise keys with its cluster head and parent node.

Setting Cluster Parameters. After the construction of the cluster-tree structure, the base station sends the values of λ and τ to each cluster head. The parameters for different clusters may be different. Upon receiving the parameter pair (λ, τ), the cluster head broadcasts λ to all sensor members in the cluster. τ is not broadcasted because it is only useful to the cluster head. This procedure will be repeated when the cluster parameters need to be reconfigured.

Sensor Node Operations. After knowing the value of λ, each sensor node can generate exponentially distributed time intervals with a random number generator [13]. If a sensor detects an event, it will generate a report message and send it out at the next probabilistic interval. Otherwise, it will generate a dummy message at the next interval.

The format of a report message depends on the further aggregation algorithm to be used. Next, we take a simple additive aggregation algorithm as an example to illustrate our idea. In this case, a message consists of three parts as shown bellow:

$$\{\ id \mid body \mid time\ \}.$$

The *id* is a *sid* or a *cid* depending on who sends it. The *body* part stores the data. The *time* denotes the time stamp of this message.

We assume that the sensor network monitors only a specific event. So we can use 1 or 0 to denote an event happens or not. Each sensor in the cluster takes one bit in the message body to store its observation. For example, if the cluster size is 10, and a sensor with $sid = 5$ detects an event at time t, the report message to be sent at the next interval will be:

$$\{0101|E_{k_s}(0000100000)|t\},$$

where k_s is the session key deduced from the pairwise key shared between the sensor and its cluster head. If no event is detected in a time interval, the sensor will send a dummy message with a fake t at the next time interval:

$$\{0101|E_{k_s}(0000000000)|t\}.$$

In-cluster Data Aggregation. After receiving a message, the cluster head decrypts it and puts it into an aggregation buffer. When an interval of τ time units passed, the cluster head aggregates messages in the buffer, then sends the aggregated message to the base station following the routing tree.

Many functions, such as SUM, AVERAGE, MAX, and MIN, can be used in data aggregation. Based on our assumption, we use two aggregation functions: SUM on message bodies and AVERAGE on message time stamps. Assume after a τ period, 4 messages from different sensors have been put into the aggregation buffer:

$$M_1 : \{0001|0000000000|t_1\}$$
$$M_4 : \{0100|0000000000|t_4\}$$
$$M_5 : \{0101|0000100000|t_5\}$$
$$M_7 : \{0111|0010000000|t_7\}$$

First, the cluster head adds the message bodies together, which yields 0010100000. Second, it calculates the average of time stamps of real messages (M_5 and M_7 in this case), that gives $t_{cid} = (t_5 + t_7)/2$. Finally the aggregated message will be:

$$\{cid|0010100000|t_{cid}\}.$$

It will be sent hop by hop to the base station confidentially following the routing tree.

Though averaging time stamps of real messages sacrifices some accuracy, it is a trade-off between time accuracy and reporting latency. In each aggregation round, only one message from each cluster member can be stored in the aggregation buffer. If a sensor node reports more than once in a τ interval, we only store the latest real message. The sending time intervals of a sensor node have a mean of $1/\lambda$, so the average number of messages generated by it in τ time units is $\tau \cdot \lambda$. We can reduce the occurrences of message overlapping by carefully selecting the values of τ and λ.

The additive aggregation is performed on plain-text in the above example, which makes it vulnerable to node compromise attacks. Though compromising reporter nodes could not gain much information, compromising a cluster head will reveal all messages aggregated or forwarded by it. To defend against node compromise attack, we can use a secure additive data aggregation scheme (such as CPDA [11], O-ASP [14], and the one proposed in [15]) to aggregate the message bodies directly without decrypting them. However, message filtering along the route must be disabled because the forwarder node cannot distinguish real messages from dummy ones if a secure aggregation algorithm is used.

Message Filtering Along the Routing Tree. Aggregated messages are transmitted following the routing tree. If message filtering is enabled, dummy messages will be filtered out along the route. After receiving a message from a child, the parent node decrypts it. If the aggregated message contains at least one real event report, the parent node re-encrypts it and pushes it into a routing queue to wait for sending at the next τ interval. Otherwise, the message will be dropped. If the routing queue is empty at the next τ interval, a dummy message will be sent out.

4.3 System Parameters

System parameters λ and τ play critical roles in our scheme. λ determines how often events are reported. If λ is too large, dummy messages will be generated at an unnecessarily high rate and cause high message overhead; if λ is too small, events will be reported at a very low rate and then the reporting latency of a real event is increased. The value of τ determines the message transmission latency. A greater τ will increase the message delay but reduce the message overhead, while a smaller τ does the opposite.

It is hard to determine fixed values for λ and τ. First, before the sensor network is deployed, we have little knowledge about what the event occurrence rate will be. Second, the event occurrence rate may vary greatly in different conditions. Take the Panda-Hunter game [1] for example. The activities of pandas may be totally different in day and night, sunny and rainy days. So the values of λ and τ in our scheme can be tuned during network operation to reduce the energy consumption. The proper values of λ and τ for each cluster are calculated by the base station based on different situations, and broadcasted or unicasted to cluster heads. Because the base station has sufficient computational and energy resources, it will not be an issue to redistribute these parameters.

4.4 Security Analysis

Privacy is the first concern in our analysis. In our scheme, the adversary can observe messages being sent by each sensor with intervals following a certain probabilistic distribution. However, as the message are encrypted and of the same length, the attacker cannot distinguish the real ones from the dummy ones. The cluster head aggregates these messages, and sends the aggregated messages following the routing tree to the base station every τ time unit. Each intermediate node along the route delays and sends out real or dummy messages periodically too. So the attacker cannot gain any additional information on real events in our scheme. The occurrence of a real event is independent of the attacker's observation. Therefore, according to [6], our scheme has the property of *event source unobservability*, which means that any event happening in the system is unobservable to the attacker.

One feature of our scheme is that secure data aggregation algorithms can be employed to defend against node compromise attack. Cluster heads play critical roles in our scheme. If some of the cluster heads, especially those which are near the sink, are compromised, all the messages from their child clusters will be leaked to the attacker. A secure data aggregation scheme [15,11,14] can aggregate the encrypted messages directly without knowing the real content. Thus the attacker could not gain any additional information from the compromising of cluster heads.

5 Evaluation and Simulations

5.1 Performance Evaluation

In our scheme, real messages are postponed following some statistical patterns to avoid being differentiated from dummy ones, which introduces delay to the event report. We assume the processing and transmission time of messages can be ignored. Then the delay of a real message consists of three parts: the sending delay d_s at reporter node, the in-cluster aggregation delay d_c, and the queueing delay d_q along the routing tree.

We assume that the event occurrences at a sensor node can be modeled by a Poisson process. Given a cluster c with parameters (λ_c, τ_c), the message sending intervals of a sensor node in c follow the exponential distribution $Exp(1/\lambda_c)$. According to the PASTA (Poisson Arrivals See Time Averages [16]) property, the average sending delay should be

$$E(d_s) = \frac{1}{\lambda_c}. \tag{1}$$

The cluster head H_c sends out an aggregated message every τ_c time units. Let N denote the number of member nodes in cluster c. Since the minimum of exponential random variables is also exponentially distributed [17], the time intervals between all messages arriving at H_c also follow an exponential distribution with a rate of $N\lambda_c$. We further assume the fraction f_c^{real} of the messages arriving at H_c is real and consider real messages only. If we define the *service time* of a message as the time between when it arrives at the aggregation buffer and when it is sent out, we can view H_c as an $M/G/\infty$ queueing system because the message arrival process is Poisson with a rate $\lambda_c^{real} = N\lambda_c f_c^{real}$. Since every message starts to be served immediately after arriving, according to the queueing theory [18], here the sojourn time of a message in H_c is equal to its service time. Since the service time of a message in H_c follows a uniform distribution $U[0, \tau_c]$, the expected time that a real message spends on waiting for aggregation is

$$E(d_c) = \frac{\tau_c}{2}. \tag{2}$$

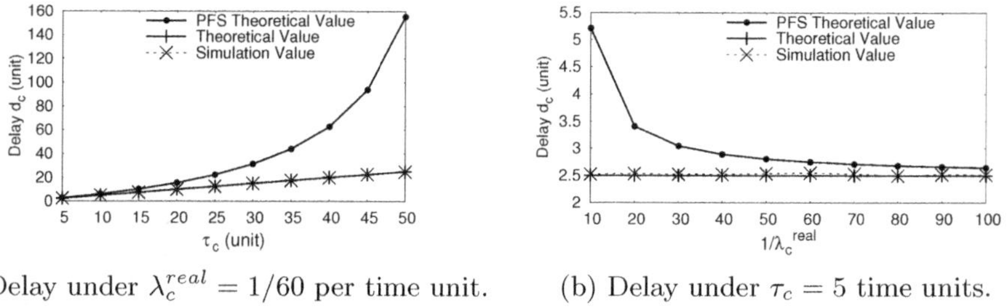

(a) Delay under $\lambda_c^{real} = 1/60$ per time unit. (b) Delay under $\tau_c = 5$ time units.

Fig. 1. Delay of real messages at the cluster head

We use simulations to verify our theoretical analysis about d_c and compare it with PFS [6]. For the PFS scheme, we view a proxy $\mathcal{P}$ as a cluster head and its associated sensor nodes as its cluster members. So the buffering interval T_{proxy} in PFS is equivalent to τ_c in our scheme and we set the rate parameter $\lambda_{\mathcal{P}}^{real} = \lambda_c^{real}$ for PFS. The simulation results are shown in Figure 1a and Figure 1b. From these figures, we can find that the simulation value matches well with our theoretical analysis. The average delay in our scheme is much lower than that of PFS, especially when τ_c is large or λ_c^{real} is high. It is reasonable because the real messages are packed together through aggregation in our scheme, and thus they have no need to wait for the next interval to be transmitted. The aggregation delay in our scheme has no relationship with the message generation rate λ_c. So our scheme can better cope with the situation where the real message generation rate changes greatly during time.

If a secure aggregation algorithm is used, message filtering is disabled. In this circumstance, the parent node must have the ability to handle all the messages from its child nodes. It means that the outgoing data rate of the parent node H_p must be greater than or equal to the incoming rate of messages from its child nodes. This gives us the inequality constraint

$$\frac{1}{\tau_p} \geq \sum_{i \in P} \frac{1}{\tau_i} \Rightarrow \tau_p \leq \frac{1}{\sum_{i \in P} \frac{1}{\tau_i}} \tag{3}$$

where P is the set of clusters whose heads are children of H_p. Let M denote the number of child nodes H_p has, i.e. $M = |P|$. Because messages are received and sent in fix intervals, the waiting time is determined after all child nodes send out the first message. If the first sending time of each node is evenly distributed in $[0, \tau_p]$, the expected queueing delay d_{q_p} at node H_p should be

$$E(d_{q_p}) \approx \frac{\tau_p}{2}, \quad \tau_p \leq \frac{1}{\sum_{i \in P} \frac{1}{\tau_i}}. \tag{4}$$

We use simulations to verify our analysis of d_{q_p}. In the simulation setup, H_p has three child nodes with identical $\tau_c = 50$. The value of τ_p changes from 1 to $16(\lfloor 50/3 \rfloor)$. From Figure 2 we can see that if the start sending times of child

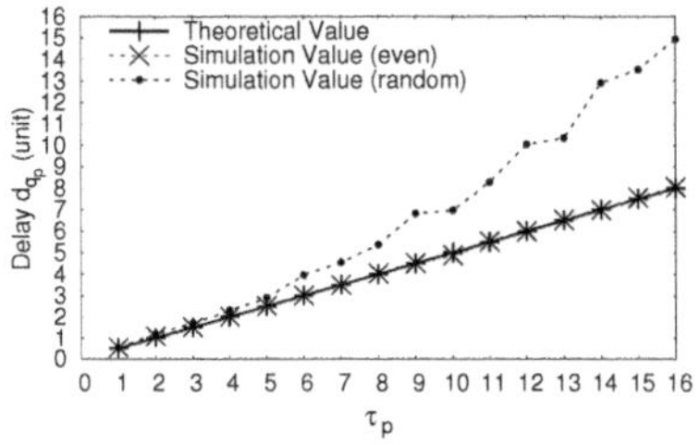

Fig. 2. Queueing delay of real messages at H_p without message filtering ($M = 3$, $\tau_c = 50$)

nodes are evenly distributed in $[0, 50]$, we can obtain a queueing delay of $\tau_p/2$. If the start sending times are randomly distributed in $[0, 50]$, the queueing delay gets larger than we expected.

If message filtering is enabled, the parent H_p can examine the content of an aggregated message and distinguish real messages from dummy ones. Recall that the fraction f_c^{real} of the messages arriving at H_c is real, then H_c will send out a real aggregated message with probability f_c^{real}. Thus the time intervals between the real messages sent by H_c are geometrically distributed with a success probability of f_c^{real}. So H_p will have M geometrically distributed message inputs. It seems that H_p is a queueing system with bulk arrivals. However, we cannot use a discrete queueing system to model H_p because (i) the arrival time slot τ_c may not be equal to the departure time slot τ_p and (ii) the arriving time of messages from its child nodes may not be at the same time slot edges. Since the message incoming rate of H_p is $\lambda_p^{real} = \sum_{i \in P} \frac{f_i^{real}}{\tau_i}$, we use a Poisson process with a rate of λ_p^{real} to approximate the message arrival process of H_p. Then H_p can be viewed as a classic $M/G/1$ queueing system [6]. The service time s_p represents the time difference between when a message arrives at the front of the queue and when it is sent out. Following a similar analysis as in [6], we have

$$E(s_p) = \frac{\tau_p}{2 - \lambda_p^{real} \tau_p} \tag{5}$$

$$E(s_p^2) = (1 - \lambda_p^{real} E(s_p)) \frac{\tau_p^2}{3} + \lambda_p^{real} E(s_p) \tau_p^2 \tag{6}$$

Then the expected queueing delay at the parent node H_p is given by the average sojourn time of the $M/G/1$ queueing system [18],

$$E(d_{q_p}) = E(s_p) + \frac{\lambda_p^{real} E(s_p^2)}{2(1 - \lambda_p^{real} E(s_p))}. \tag{7}$$

We use simulations to verify our theoretical analysis about d_{q_p}. The number of child nodes of H_p is set to 3. For simplicity, we assume that the values of τ_c and f_c^{real} for all child nodes are identical. In the first simulation, we set $f_c^{real} = 1/60$

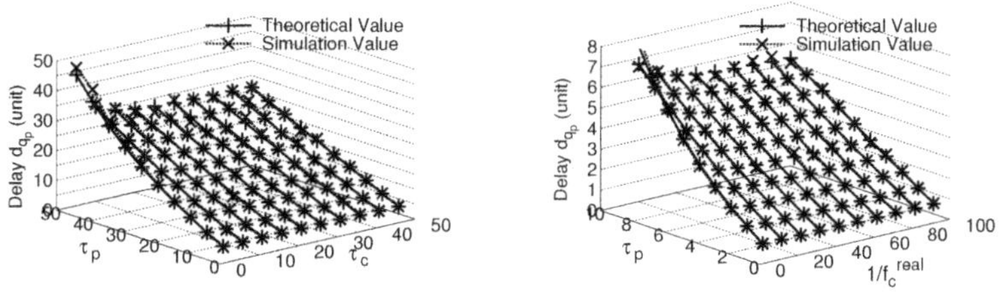

(a) Queueing delay under $f_c^{real} = 1/60$. (b) Queueing delay under $\tau_c = 5$.

Fig. 3. Queueing delay of real messages at H_p with message filtering ($M = 3$)

(so $\lambda_p^{real} = 3/(60\tau_c)$) and change τ_c and τ_p from 5 to 50. From Figure 3a we can see that d_{q_p} increases as τ_p increases. When τ_c increases, the message arrival rate λ_p^{real} decreases, so d_{q_p} decreases a little accordingly. In Figure 3b, we fix τ_c and demonstrate the effect of changes of f_p^{real}. Simulations show that d_{q_p} decreases as f_p^{real} decreases because the message arrival rate becomes smaller.

5.2 System Simulations

We conduct some simulations comparing the proposed scheme with a baseline scheme and a TFS-like scheme. In the baseline scheme, every sensor sends real or dummy messages with intervals following the same statistical distribution as in our ASLP scheme. The messages are forwarded step by step through the routing tree without aggregation, filtering, and intentionally postponing. The TFS-like scheme differs with the TFS scheme [6] only on the proxy selecting method. In the TFS-like scheme, cluster heads are selected as the proxy nodes in TFS to cope with our cluster-tree network topology model. If the routing queue of intermediate node is full, subsequent messages will be dropped in all schemes.

Simulation Setup. In the simulations, we deploy 640 sensor nodes in a $1000m \times 1000m$ square field. The base station is placed at the center of the field. Each sensor has a maximum transmission range of $50m$. The sensor network is organized into 85 clusters. The cluster sizes range from 3 to 14. The maximum routing tree level is 4.

We set the aggregation buffer size to the corresponding cluster size for each cluster head, and set the routing queue size to 8 for all tree nodes. Though λ and τ (r_{source} and T_{proxy} in the TFS-like scheme, respectively) can be configured separately in ASLP, we use the same values for all clusters in the simulations to be compatible with the TFS-like scheme. The value of τ is set to $5s$, and $1/\lambda$ (the mean of message generation intervals) changes from $1s$ to $10s$. We assume a sensor can process and transmit 20 messages in $1s$ reliably. So the message loss is caused only by message dropping along the route.

We observe that different types of event have different occurrence patterns. Taking habitat monitoring for example, solitary animals live alone while social animals show in groups. So we simulate the event occurrences in two different modes, a *random mode* and a *group mode*. In the random mode, five sensor nodes are randomly selected to generate real messages while others generate dummy messages. In the group mode, a group of five sensor nodes located in a radius of $50m$ is randomly selected to generate real messages. The real event occurrence rate is set to one per ten seconds. In addition, each simulation has been run for 2,000 seconds and repeated 100 times.

We evaluate the performances of different schemes in three metrics: *message overhead*, *event detection ratio* and *event reporting delay*. Message overhead is defined as the number of dummy messages that have been generated or forwarded in the network. Event detection ratio is the ratio of events detected by the base station. Event reporting delay is the time difference between the time when an event happens and when the base station receives the event report.

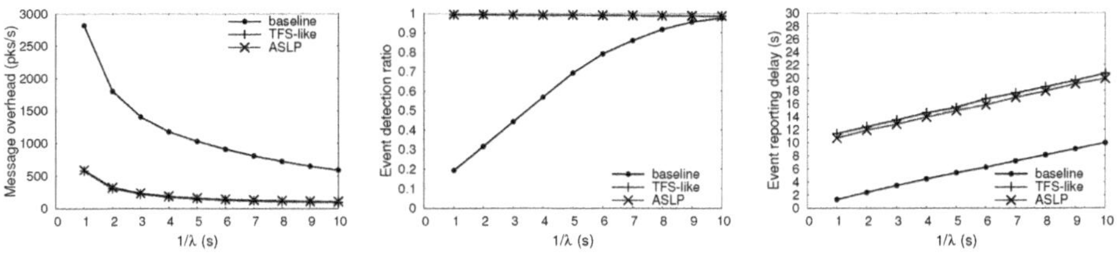

(a) Message overhead (b) Event detection ratio (c) Event reporting delay

Fig. 4. Performance of schemes in random mode

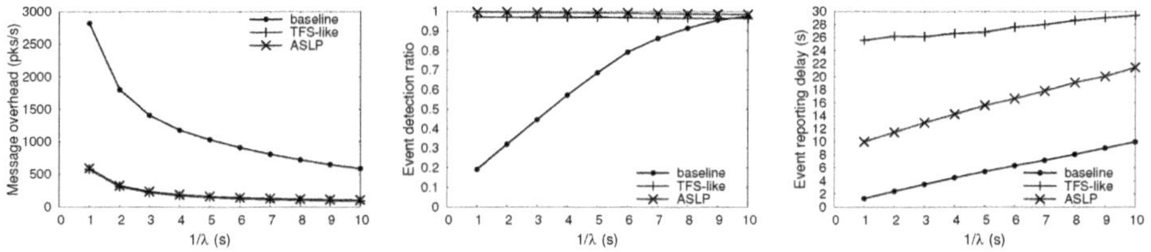

(a) Message overhead (b) Event detection ratio (c) Event reporting delay

Fig. 5. Performance of schemes in group mode

Simulation Results. Figure 4 and Figure 5 show the performance of schemes in random mode and group mode, respectively. From Figure 4a and Figure 5a we can see that as the message generation rate λ increases ($1/\lambda$ decreases), the message overhead increases. However, compared with the baseline scheme, the message overhead of TFS-like and ASLP increases much slower. TFS-like and ASLP have roughly the same message overhead because they have the same configuration on message generation rates of reporter nodes and cluster heads.

Figure 4b and Figure 5b illustrate the ratio of events detected by the base station. We can see that the event detection ratios of the baseline scheme increase when λ decreases. This is because the decrease of dummy messages generation rate alleviates the traffic congestion at cluster heads, therefore less messages are dropped. The event detection ratios of ASLP slightly decrease when λ decreases because a larger sending interval increases the possibility that an event happens more than once in the same interval, which is only reported once. Comparing Figure 4b with Figure 5b, we can see that the event detection ratio of TFS-like in group mode are less than that in random mode. The reason is that in group mode events happen intensively in a local part of the network, so traffic gets more congested in that area and real messages are dropped with a larger probability than in random mode. However, due to message aggregation, ASLP has similar event detection ratios close to 1 in both modes.

Figure 4c and Figure 5c show the average reporting delay of event occurrences. The baseline scheme has the smallest event reporting delay, because in the baseline scheme messages are transmitted without intentionally postponing as we do in TFS-like and ASLP. Since the queueing delay d_q is too small, the event reporting delay of the baseline scheme is dominated by the sending delay d_s and the simulation result matches well with our theoretical analysis of d_s in Formula (1). The TFS-like scheme has a much larger delay in the group mode than in the random mode. This result is not surprising. Recall that in the group mode, events happen intensively in a local part of the network. The fraction of real messages arriving at a cluster head in that area is larger than that in the random mode, so the queueing delay is getting larger according to our previous analysis. However, the in-cluster data aggregation in ASLP reduces the number of real messages to be forwarded. Figure 4c and Figure 5c show that the event reporting delay of ASLP is much less affected by different modes. Because events happen sparsely in the random mode, the data aggregation in ASLP provides little help on reducing the number of real messages. So we can observe that in Figure 4c, TFS-like and ASLP have similar event reporting delay.

In summary, compared with the baseline scheme, TFS-like and ASLP can both significantly reduce message overhead and improve event detection ratio at a cost of increased latency. However, ASLP shows a much better performance than TFS-like in group mode where events happen intensively in a local part of the network.

6 Conclusion and Future Work

In this paper, we investigate the leakage of source location information in sensor networks in a global attack model. A flexible and effective scheme based on secure data aggregation is proposed to protect source location privacy in sensor networks. Different configurations can be selected to meet the requirements on security, event reporting delay, and network lifetime. We perform theoretical analysis on event reporting delay and use simulations to validate the analysis. Simulation results demonstrate that our scheme has a better performance than the baseline scheme and the TFS [6]-like scheme. Optimal choices of system parameters to best balance between message overhead, event detection ratio, and reporting delay are part of our future work.

Acknowledgement

This work was supported by the National Natural Science Foundation of China under Grant 60970138.

References

1. Ozturk, C., Zhang, Y., Trappe, W.: Source-location privacy in energy-constrained sensor network routing. In: Proc. 2nd ACM workshop on Security of Ad hoc and Sensor Networks, pp. 88–93 (2004)
2. Li, N., Zhang, N., Das, S.K., Thuraisingham, B.: Privacy preservation in wireless sensor networks: a state-of-the-art survey. Ad. Hoc. Netw. 7(8), 1501–1514 (2009)

3. Kamat, P., Zhang, Y., Trappe, W., Ozturk, C.: Enhancing source-location privacy in sensor network routing. In: Proc. 25th IEEE International Conference on Distributed Computing Systems, pp. 599–608 (2005)
4. Xi, Y., Schwiebert, L., Shi, W.: Preserving source location privacy in monitoring-based wireless sensor networks. In: Proc. 20th International Parallel and Distributed Processing Symposium, pp. 425–432 (2006)
5. Ouyang, Y., Le, X., Chen, G., Ford, J., Makedon, F.: Entrapping adversaries for source protection in sensor networks. In: Proc. International Symposium on a World of Wireless, Mobile and Multimedia Networks, pp. 10–34 (2006)
6. Yang, Y., Shao, M., Zhu, S., Urgaonkar, B., Cao, G.: Towards event source unobservability with minimum network traffic in sensor networks. In: Proc. 1st ACM Conference on Wireless Network Security, pp. 77–88 (2008)
7. Mehta, K., Liu, D., Wright, M.: Location privacy in sensor networks against a global eavesdropper. In: Proc. IEEE International Conference on Network Protocols, pp. 314–323 (2007)
8. Shao, M., Yang, Y., Zhu, S., Cao, G.: Towards statistically strong source anonymity for sensor networks. In: Proc. 27th IEEE International Conference on Computer Communications, pp. 466–474 (2008)
9. Heinzelman, W.R., Chandrakasan, A., Balakrishnan, H.: Energy-efficient communication protocol for wireless microsensor networks. In: Proc. 33rd Hawaii International Conference on System Sciences, pp. 3005–3014 (2000)
10. Younis, O., Fahmy, S.: HEED: a hybrid, energy-efficient, distributed clustering approach for ad hoc sensor networks. IEEE Trans. on Mob. Comput. 3(4), 366–379 (2004)
11. He, W., Liu, X., Nguyen, H., Nahrstedt, K., Abdelzaher, T.T.: PDA: Privacy-preserving data aggregation in wireless sensor networks. In: Proc. 26th IEEE International Conference on Computer Communications, pp. 2045–2053 (2007)
12. Madden, S., Franklin, M.J., Hellerstein, J.M., Hong, W.: TAG: A tiny aggregation service for ad-hoc sensor networks. In: Proc. 5th Symposium on Operating Systems Design and Implementation, pp. 131–146 (2002)
13. Knuth, D.E.: 3.4. In: The Art of Computer Programming, 3rd edn. Seminumerical Algorithms, vol. 2, pp. 132–133. Addison Wesley Longman, Amsterdam (1998)
14. Feng, T., Wang, C., Zhang, W., Ruan, L.: Confidentiality protection for distributed sensor data aggregation. In: Proc. 27th IEEE International Conference on Computer Communications, pp. 475–483 (2008)
15. Castelluccia, C., Chan, A.C.F., Mykletun, E., Tsudik, G.: Efficient and provably secure aggregation of encrypted data in wireless sensor networks. ACM Trans. on Sens. Netw. 5(3), 1–36 (2009)
16. Wolff, R.W.: Possion arrivals see time averages. Operations Research 30(2), 223–231 (1982)
17. Mood, A.M., Graybill, F.A., Boes, D.C.: 5.3.2. In: Introduction to The Theory of Statistics, pp. 182–185. McGraw-Hill, New York (1974)
18. Kleinrock, L.: Queueing Systems. Theory, vol. 1. John Wiley and Sons, Inc., Chichester (1975)

A Middleware for Intelligent Environments and the Internet of Things

Luis Roalter, Matthias Kranz, and Andreas Möller

Technische Universität München
Arcisstr. 21, 80333 Munich, Germany
roalter@tum.de, matthias.kranz@tum.de, andreas.moeller@tum.de

Abstract. Interdisciplinary research from the domains of pervasive computing or ubiquitous computing, computer-human-interaction and computer science has led to the development of many intelligent environments, either on lab scale or as live in laboratories. While several middleware have been developed in this field, no standard middleware for intelligent environments or ubiquitous computing has evolved yet.

We consider the lack of a de-facto standard middleware for distributed sensor-actuator environments as one of the key issues limiting research on intelligent environment and the proliferation of intelligent environments from research environments to their deployment in our everyday lives. In addition, we expect the advent of personal robotics for health care and ambient assisted living scenarios in the context of ubiquitous computing in the close future.

In this paper, we report on the successful application of a robotic middleware as glue between sensors, actuators and services and its application in a deployed example scenario. Thereby, we verify by examples the applicability of robotic middleware for complex ubiquitous computing environments.

To foster re-use and potential community-adoption, we share our source code, documentation and data sets (in the future) via `https://vmi.lmt.ei.tum.de/ros/`.

Keywords: Middleware, Internet of Things, Ubiquitous Computing, Intelligent Environments, Sensors, Actuators, Services.

1 Introduction

While novel information and communication technologies are widely available, bandwidth, processing power and storage are no longer restricting factors, so is currently the lack of a common middleware to interconnect heterogeneous distributed systems. While many middleware have been proposed, none has been accepted by the community as standard yet. The availability of a suitable middleware though would allow to focus on the applications and services intelligent environments can provide to humans and to bootstrap the development of distributed ubiquitous computing systems.

Z. Yu et al. (Eds.): UIC 2010, LNCS 6406, pp. 267–281, 2010.

The paper is structured as follows. In Sec. 2 we discuss selected middleware from the domain of ubiquitous computing and general requirements for middleware in the field of intelligent environments. In Sec. 3 we report on an example for an intelligent environment using a middleware from the robotics domain and discuss the applicability of this middleware for intelligent environments against the previously identified criteria. We share our experiences with this middleware, the demonstration scenario, and demonstrate its suitability for intelligent environments. We thereby hope to enable other researchers to accelerate their research on applications and services, instead of focusing on middleware development. Our experiences are summarized in Sec. 4. We conclude our paper in Sec. 5 by giving a short overview on future work.

2 Related Work

Yau et al. [1] divide ubiquitous computing middleware by the way of communication and data exchange in two categories: either data is exchanged by applications communicating via a shared space (such as a Blackboard or Tuple Space) or by an RPC or service-style oriented manner by calling functions and receiving processed information. Yau et al. also extend the notion of middleware from connecting heterogeneous distributed sensors and actuators (we subsume anything that "(re-)acts" on information, such as agents, displays, etc., as actuators) to context-awareness. While context-awareness requires more than the mere connection of inputs and outputs, and more application scenarios do require more specialized middleware, the basic problem of meaningfully interconnecting devices and applications so far has not been concludingly addressed. As Nakajima et al. [2] describe their middleware, they state that most middleware does not "offer generic services for building ubiquitous computing applications. They support to develop applications for specific domains to realize ubiquitous computing visions". A one size fits all solution will most probably not exist, though we think that for *most* scenarios a common basis, as we will later introduce in our example scenario, could be beneficial. The urge of a suitable middleware becomes more pressing as the Internet of Things [3] also demands for a middleware that allows both data management and for interaction with the Internet of Things [4].

The main requirements, characteristics and design issues for middleware in intelligent environments have been discussed extensively in the literature [2,1,5, 6,7,8,9,10]. Summarizing the selected requirements by high-level keywords, an ideal of a middleware would allow for

- abstraction over heterogeneous input and output hardware devices
- abstraction over hardware and software interfaces
- abstraction over data streams (continuous or discrete data or events) and data types
- abstraction over physicality (location, context)
- abstraction over the development process (time of integration of services or devices)

While specific issues have been addressed in various research efforts, no standard middleware for intelligent environments has yet evolved in the area of ubiquitous computing.

Different middleware systems, such as GAIA [10] and MundoCore [9], have been proposed and used in the relatively young research field of pervasive and ubiquitous computing. The challenges of distributed multimodal information processing, connecting heterogeneous input and output technologies have very different demands towards middleware systems. Unfortunately, reuse and finally development in this domain is limited usually to the initial developers of a respective middleware and no community yet evolved to pursue the ambitious goal of a unified middleware.

This vicious circle of no or only limited reuse (both in more projects and by more researchers) and thus the lack of necessary extensions or drivers finally leads to the neglection of available middleware again. Existing middleware also have not been designed to have a long development life cycle beyond the end of the research project and to allow for future integration of demands and upcoming technologies.

We therefore investigated the available middleware especially with a focus on community support, maturity, extent of supported hardware and software, and data management architecture.

As promising candidates we identified two middleware systems from the robotics domain, Player/Stage [11] and ROS (Robot Operating System) [12]. Key factors supporting the idea of using a middleware from the robotics domain are:

- The challenges with respect to the heterogeneous devices and interfaces in robotics seem very similar to those found in the context of intelligent environments.
- Player as example has reached a large the maturity - this middleware is used, supported and further developed in the robotics community for more than 10 years by now.
- Conceptually an intelligent environment is very similar to a static, non-movable robot, a so-called “ImmoBot” [13].

Player so far has already been reported to have been used in the context of intelligent environments [14,15]. As ROS is intended to be a successor of Player and also is downward compatible, we opted to assess the potential of ROS in the use case presented in Sec. 3.

Therefore, we took the view of a robotic systems developer and investigated the potential of a robotic middleware for distributed, heterogeneous, sensor-actuator-based, communicating intelligent environments. As ROS is downward compatible w.r.t. existing drivers and components, and includes many modern concepts of distributed architectures, we decided to explore the potentials of ROS in more details.

The data management architecture includes decentralized peer-to-peer network concepts, publish-subscribe information distribution or bi-directional services between components. The middleware not only allows for inclusion of an immense variety of sensing and actuation systems, but also to visualize and simulate, both the information flow and the physical space using e.g. OGRE (open source 3D Graphics Engine, `http://www.ogre3d.org`) and ODE (Open Dynamics Engine, `http://www.ode.org`) open source engines. This allows designing 3D objects in a CAD style manner, such as the different service cores, investigating their interaction and sending the very same information as the deployed sensor-actuator system would do - well before any physical prototyping is done. This reduces the time needed for iterative development and refinement and also costs. Additionally, the physical paths a human would have to take in such an environment can be predicted, calculated and optimized already during the development phase in the middleware. This also has an impact on the prediction of the interaction times with the different digital systems. The inclusion for real world simulation capabilities originates from e.g. robotic SLAM where algorithms have to be re-tested often but a real experiment is quite expensive and thus cannot be re-conducted for each run of a test.

3 Cognitive Office - An Open Test Bed for Ubiquitous Computing Research

We will now report on the application of the chosen robotic middleware ROS in the context of an intelligent environment, the Cognitive Office. This environment is a normal office room in our faculty that has been transformed into an 'intelligent environment'. The room is a one person office space and actively inhabited and use for all kinds of office and research work and thus a "normal" environment. As physical entity in space, the office is considered to be an ImmoBot [13].

Following Mark Weiser's philosophy at Xerox PARC of "Build what you use, and use what you build" this environment serves as live in lab [16]. The 3D Gazebo model of the office space, as seen from the center of the room, is shown in Fig. 1 and Fig. 2.

As for most intelligent environments, a "final" set of devices and services is unlikely to be known in advance and also most probably will never exist, it was important that sensors, actuators, interfaces and services can be added at any point of time in the development phase.

We were interested in integrating a large variety of different hardware devices – from industry components such as an IP networked power switch to research hardware as Phidgets (`http://www.phidgets.com`) to end user prototyping micro-controller-based systems as Arduino (`http://www.arduino.com`). From software side, we wanted to be able to integrate external web based services such as RSS news feeds or social networking platforms such as Twitter. Our intention here was to connect physical and virtual worlds, especially regarding community based services to allow the intelligent environment to share its digital data with human users in a more convenient manner.

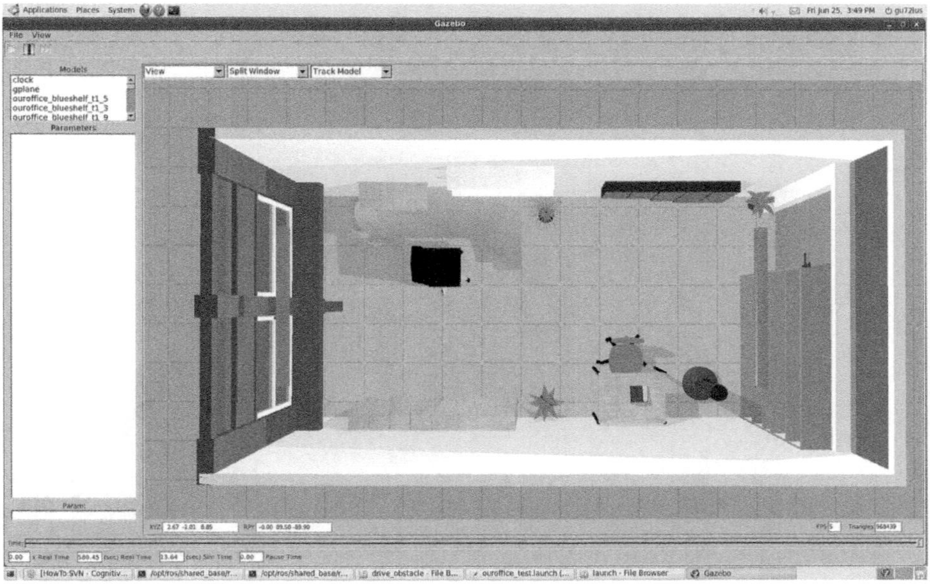

Fig. 1. The Cognitive Office visualized in the Gazebo viewer running on top of the ROS middleware. The ceiling has been made transparent, several light sources have been placed inside the room model. The model should look as realistic as possible.

3.1 Sensors and Actuators

For our example to be realistic, we tried to be as inclusive as possible regarding the set of sensors, devices, actuators, and services and to include what has been used in most comparable intelligent environments. As of now, we have connected the following sensors and actuators via various interfaces to the robotic middleware:

- ultrasonic and PIR sensors for movement detection via Arduino boards
- reed contact switches on the door, windows, and drawers via Phidgets Interface Kit boards
- light and temperature sensors via ZigBee
- RFID sensors via a dedicated web service
- instant messaging data (mood, activity) via plugins
- social networking data (Twitter) via web service
- IP power switches via a HTTP web server
- traffic and weather information via RSS news feeds
- web cam via USB
- moisture, temperature and light sensors for office plants via Twitter (Fig. 3)
- ...

This list could be continued, but already gives an idea of the complexity and diversity of the developed intelligent environment. We have shown that many commonly found devices and systems in ubiquitous computing environments are easily integratable with the ROS middleware. So could an environmental-based

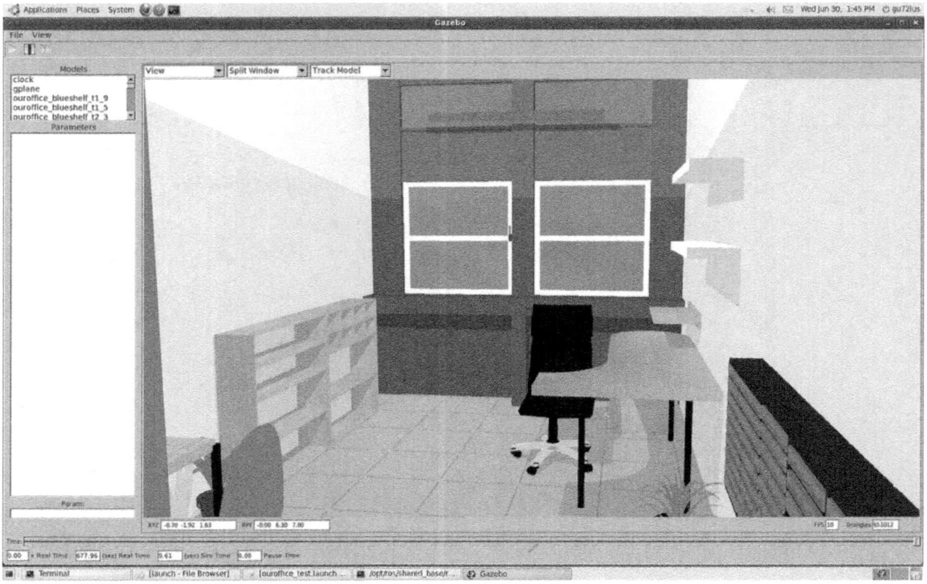

Fig. 2. Part 2 of the Cognitive Office: the workplace with shelves. The 3D model is a 1:1 match of the physical real-world office. All elements – drawers, windows – can be controlled by physical controllers, detecting and visualizing the state of the real, physical world.

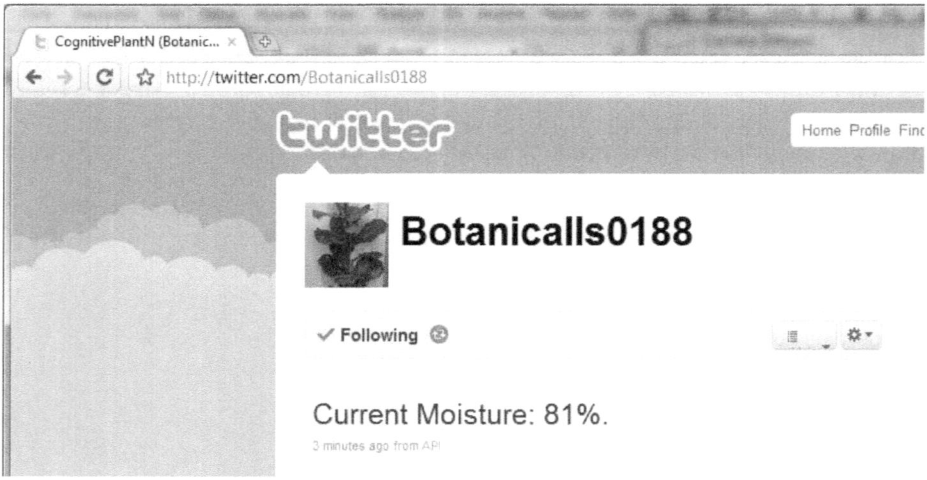

Fig. 3. The "Botanicalls" (http://www.botanicalls.com) device directly publishes e.g. moisture information to Twitter. This data is imported via a web service using the Twitter API into the ROS middleware and published to the plant care controller.

Thracker [17] be added for detecting pick and place tasks in the shelf, or an tangible user interface for instant messaging [18] be easily added to the ecology of devices commonly found in modern office spaces.

We have proven by constructing examples that ROS makes an interesting candidate middleware for further investigation in the context of ubiquitous and pervasive computing. Future work will e.g. include a comparison on e.g. the lines of code to integrate systems in different middleware or how a complex task it is to support new systems in ROS.

3.2 Event and Service-Based Data Exchange

Data from various sources and heterogeneous sensor and actuator devices is centrally managed by a ROS middleware server instance located in the Cognitive Office. As ROS allows to "connect" several servers, we deployed a second system in another office in another building where co-workers are located. Data from both servers then is available to data consumers, e.g. on a mobile Linux based device for services such as location information. Location information is visualized through our university's visitor service (see Fig. 5).

Part of the above mentioned sensors deliver event-based data which are then published to registered listeners. This blackboard-like publish/subscribe architectures allows to connect an arbitrary number of information producers and consumers. A naming service allows to "search" for topics of interest, such as location information.

Other information is exchanged via request/response services, using dedicated message exchange formats. Examples in our intelligent environment are for example the day length calculation to obtain the amount of daylight. The service sends the date information and receives an answer containing the time information. This information is used by the plant care service that ensures that the plant receives enough daylight to support optimal growing. This is only computed once a day.

While being a simple service and implementation, it still proves the support of services in general and of closed control loops across different distributed heterogeneous devices and systems in the ROS middleware for intelligent environments as they are commonly found in ubiquitous computing.

3.3 Context Services

As Schmidt et al. [19] state, there is more to context than location. We have implemented a rudimentary set of context inference services on top of the middleware to provide convenient services to the office user. The following list gives an idea of currently implemented context services:

- length of day
- date and time
- weather information
- appointments and calendar information
- status information
- disruptabilty
- ...

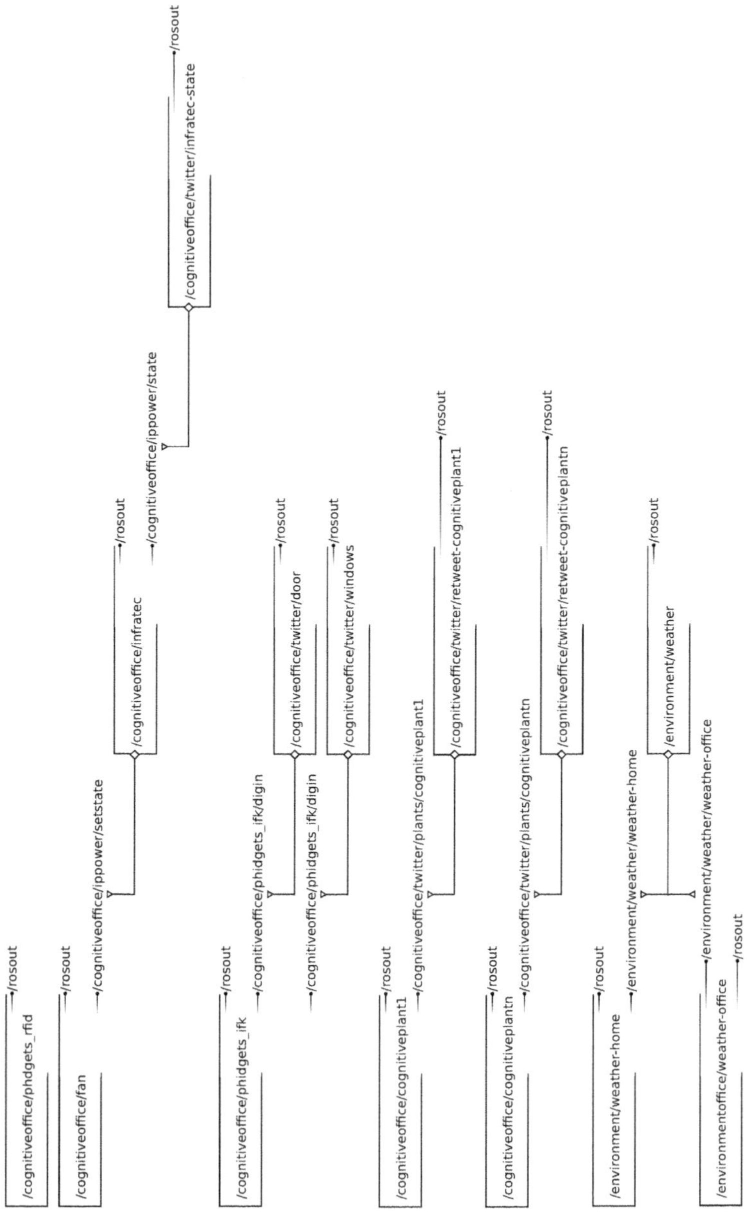

Fig. 4. Event-based data is made available via a publish/subscribe data management mechanism. Examples are open/close events of doors and windows acquired by local sensors or traffic information acquired by remote RSS news feeds.

As location is an important cue to activity and context information, both for the middleware and e.g. office visitors such as students, the computed location information is shared on a public display outside the office. A privacy filter ensures that only abstracted and public information is displayed, e.g. the general information "away for today" or "in lecture". The latter is augmented with a map of the lecture room using a university map service (see Fig. 5).

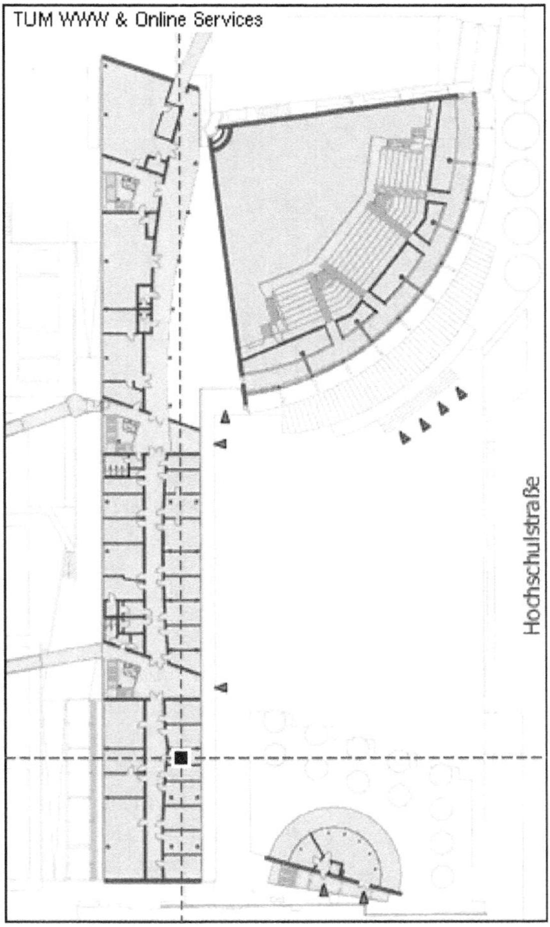

Fig. 5. Context information, such as the location of the office user, are obtained by the Cognitive Office's custom services. The location information is then visualized, e.g. to visitors, on a wireless picture frame outside the office room. The location is, after computation, fed into the university's room service system, the resulting image downloaded and automatically made available to the picture frame via an UPNP media server connected to the ROS middleware or via a RSS news feed.

As you may have noticed, the room-precision of the point can only be reached if you already know the room where the person is located. This will be automated soon when the annotation tools as shown in Fig. 6 will be finished. We will provide multiple ways for the indoor localization, such as WLAN and DECT [20].

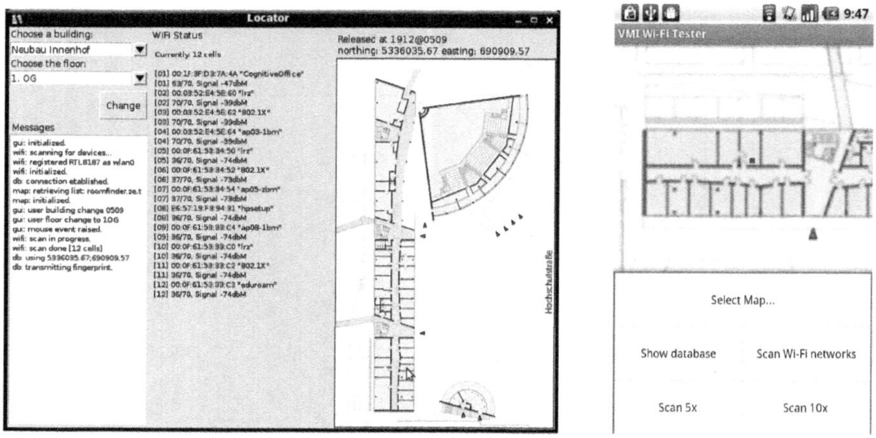

(a) Linux Fingerprinting Application (b) Android Fingerprinting App

Fig. 6. Creating precise annotation from WLAN fingerprints to obtain the current location of the user. This picture shows the user interface which is used to annotate the WLAN fingerprints on a laptop around the building (a). The locating application will run without a complex UI on an iPhone or Android Smart Phone as well (b).

3.4 End User Services

Other example services, besides location information for colleagues, are travel information. Using data from the user's personal calendar the travel times to meetings and for the drive home are estimated. Depending on the targets (in campus, off campus, conference, ...) and the preferred travel methods (foot, car, ...), a prediction on the time necessary to go from A to B is made, including latest information such as RSS news feeds on the current traffic situation. This is presented to the user, e.g. to notify him to start traveling home earlier as a traffic jam on his route is to be expected.

Simpler services are responsible for automatic lightning of the individual work spaces where presence is detected e.g. by the usage of a computer or by ultrasonic distance sensors. The lights are then automatically switched on via an IP power switch to provide convenient lightning. A last example for a personalized service is the "cold coffee warning". As the office user sometime is busier than expected, a fresh coffee can get cold. To prevent the user to take a sip of an ice cold coffee, an intelligent coffee cup is used. The idea of the cup is similar to Beigl et al. [21]. Our version features temperature sensors inside the cup, presence information is acquired using an RFID augmented cup place holder (see Fig. 7).

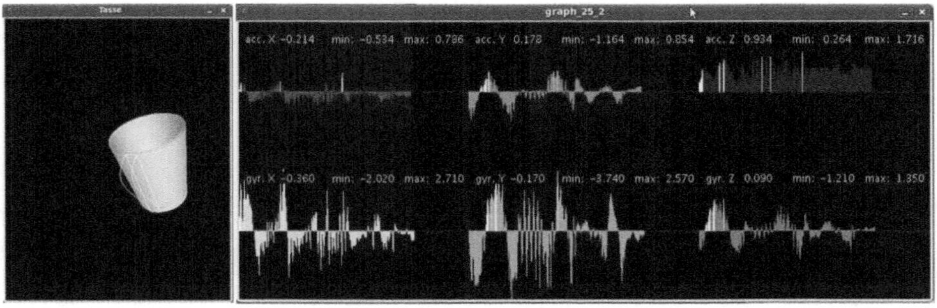

Fig. 7. The Cognitive Cup features an ATMEL microcontroller, a ZigBee RF transceiver, a 6 DOF IMU (3D acceleration and 3D gear rates), a temperature sensor and an embedded RFID tag. The figure shows the orientation information in 3D space calculated from its embedded IMU. The data is wirelessly communicated to the middleware and in case of cold coffee, a warning is displayed on the user's screen when a RFID reader detects the "leave" event equaling to the take event of the cup.

The set of services is currently focused on automated building control, e.g. a temperature and climate control service has been implemented. Future services will also focus on multimodal computer-human interaction.

To achieve a better integration of the digital information available in the technical system of the middleware, we connected all event based outputs (excluding video and audio streams) to a social networking platform. While ROS directly allows for convenient visualization of and direct interaction with all sensors and actuators, we feel that this way of visualization is not appropriate to "normal" users. We here think of using ROS in the context of an independent living project [22] and a care giver wishing to access the data. A development tool will not be appropriate in this scenario.

As Twitter has recently be used e.g. during clinical operations to inform relatives about the progress (`http://scienceroll.com/2009/01/19/twitter-live-surgery-sugarstats-and-100-ways-for-hospitals/`), we chose to also use Twitter and finally make use of the rich set of visualization tools on top of Twitter (see Fig. 8).

A public information display presents selected information to office visitors, such as the current location (e.g. when lecturing) or the next consultation hours. Data is acquired from many sources, text and images are generated using standard Linux tools such as "convert", and this data is finally published on a connected UPNP media server and displayed on a WLAN picture frame outside the office.

4 Experiences

As our overall experiences were positive, we will begin with the negative impressions and conclude with our positive experiences.

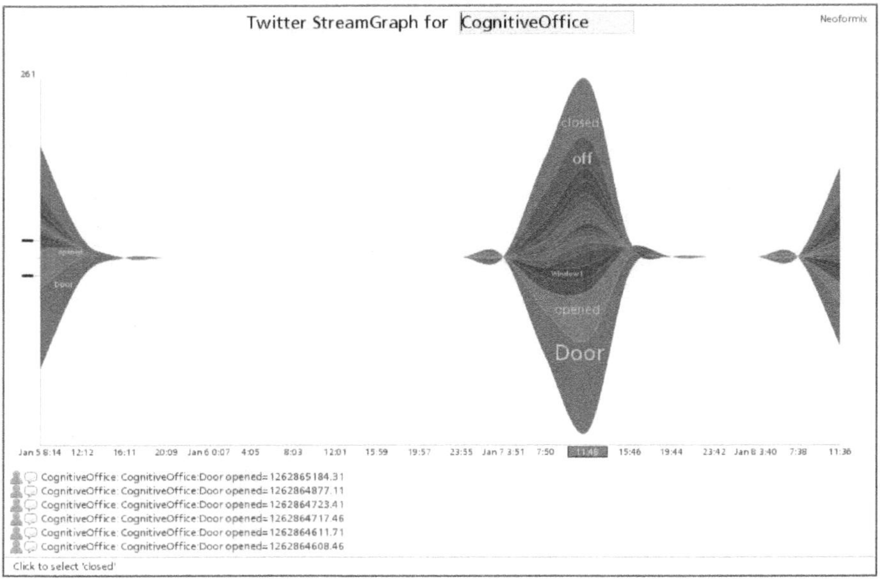

Fig. 8. Visualization of sensor and actuator event data published to a social networking platform. The data here was experimentally sent to a Twitter account and later visualized using Neofomix StreamGraph web-based tool. A normal user can easily see e.g. which events occurred at what time and what information was acquired and processed in the middleware.

The documentation of the middleware is, in parts, in an early state, but fast and constantly improving. This can be attributed to the youth of ROS as successor of Player. The search results of the ROS website often did not contain valuable information and we had to look at the code in order to complete some parts. Though, now tutorials and additional documentation are added at a high rate.

As the middleware is, in our view, very capable and impressive, the initial way into the structure and features was sometimes hard. Initial tutorials exist and provide very valuable starting points but are really required reading to be able to use ROS.

The built system (we used ROS with Ubuntu Linux) was very convenient – missing Linux system packages are downloaded on demand and dependencies with other ROS packages are automatically resolved. The rosmake build tool allows easy compilation of the packages. The middleware, examples and tutorials work out of the box and allow adoption for initial own interfaces. After two weeks the first real interfaces and parts where working, allowing us to dig deeper inside the middleware. A to do for future work for us will include a comparison e.g. of development tools, speed and lines of code of ROS and other ubiquitous computing middleware.

The development tools, besides the build system, include tools for listing available topics and services and to visualize them. Fig. 4 is the output of the rxgraph tool. Complex sets of topics and services can be stored in configuration files (.launch files), the addition and removal of services is possible at runtime. Logging and playback of all data is possible and support faster algorithm development. The (2D/3D) visualization of the physical sensors and actuators further speeds up the development process. The visualization tool (Gazebo) also includes the possibility of triggering sensor events by clicking – e.g. to click on the door (Fig. 1) and generate the "open" event. For intelligent environments this implicates that services and applications can already be prototyped long before an intelligent home would be build as virtual and real events generate the same data.

The possibility of interconnecting several ROS servers, allowing to partition computation, easily supports developers of intelligent environment to build a more complex system in a Lego brick manner.

We developed software using C, C++, Java and Python to implement the presented environment. This choice of languages allowed us to develop efficient code (in C) where necessary and to quickly prototype (in Python) novel ideas.

From first hand experiences with other middleware systems such as the EITool Kit [23] for computer-human interaction in distributed environments or with wireless sensor node based environments featuring Particles or Crossbow hardware, Player and ROS, as well as from discussions with colleagues, we feel that ROS is a very interesting candidate middleware for intelligent environments.

5 Conclusions and Future Work

After the investigation of available middleware systems for intelligent environments, we chose an open source, community-supported middleware from the robotics domain to develop a distributed sensor-actuator-system. We explored the potentials of the ROS middleware in the context of the use case of an intelligent office environment. We connected a diverse set of heterogeneous devices via different physical media and implemented a set of initial services.

We shared our experiences gathered during the incremental development process of the presented intelligent office environment.

Our experiences so are very positive and we therefore think that this development experience report can be of great value for researchers and developers of intelligent environments.

To foster research, we invite researchers to use our scenario as starting point for using ROS as middleware in ubiquitous computing. Therefore, we share our 3D models and code at `https://vmi.lmt.ei.tum.de/ros/`. We – in addition to the available documentation of ROS at `http://www.ros.org` – share our data, code and documents with the UbiComp community.

Resources

Open source code, documentation and data sets (in the future) are shared via `https://vmi.lmt.ei.tum.de/ros/`.

Acknowledgments

This work has been funded in parts from the German DFG funded Cluster of Excellence 'CoTeSys – Cognition for Technical Systems'.

We also acknowledge the individual contributions of our students and wish to thank them for all their efforts.

References

1. Yau, S.S., Karim, F., Wang, Y., Wang, B., Gupta, S.K.S.: Reconfigurable context-sensitive middleware for pervasive computing. IEEE Pervasive Computing 1(3), 33–40 (2002)
2. Nakajima, T., Fujinami, K., Tokunaga, E., Ishikawa, H.: Middleware design issues for ubiquitous computing. In: MUM 2004: Proceedings of the 3rd International Conference on Mobile and Ubiquitous Multimedia, pp. 55–62. ACM, New York (2004)
3. Floerkemeier, C., Langheinrich, M., Fleisch, E., Mattern, F., Sarma, S.E. (eds.): IOT 2008. LNCS, vol. 4952. Springer, Heidelberg (2008)
4. Kranz, M., Holleis, P., Schmidt, A.: Embedded interaction: Interacting with the internet of things. IEEE Internet Computing 14, 46–53 (2010)
5. Landay, J.A., Borriello, G.: Design patterns for ubiquitous computing. Computer 36(8), 93–95 (2003)
6. Aiken, R.J., Abramski, A., Bates, J., Blackadar, T.: Middleware for Ubiquitous Computing. In: Gellersen, H.-W. (ed.) HUC 1999. LNCS, vol. 1707, pp. 301–303. Springer, Heidelberg (1999)
7. Nakajima, T.: Case study of middleware infrastructure for ambient intelligence environments. In: Nakashima, H., Aghajan, H., Augusto, J.C. (eds.) Handbook of Ambient Intelligence and Smart Environments, pp. 229–256. Springer, New York (2010)
8. Su, H., Fu, X., Li, Z., Yang, Q., Teng, S.: A Service-oriented Middleware for Pervasive Computing Environments. In: 1st International Symposium on Pervasive Computing and Applications, pp. 36–41 (2006)
9. Aitenbichler, E., Kangasharju, J., Mühlhäuser, M.: Mundocore: A light-weight infrastructure for pervasive computing. Pervasive Mob. Comput. 3(4), 332–361 (2007)
10. Román, M., Hess, C., Cerqueira, R., Ranganathan, A., Campbell, R.H., Nahrstedt, K.: A middleware infrastructure for active spaces. IEEE Pervasive Computing 1(4), 74–83 (2002)
11. Collett, T.H., MacDonald, B.A., Gerkey, B.P.: Player 2.0: Toward a practical robot programming framework. In: Proc. of the Australasian Conf. on Robotics and Automation (ACRA), Sydney, Australia (2005)
12. Quigley, M., Conley, K., Gerkey, B., Faust, J., Foote, T.B., Leibs, J., Wheeler, R., Ng, A.Y.: Ros: an open-source robot operating system. In: ICRA Workshop on Open Source Software (2009)
13. Goldman, R.P., Baral, C.: Robots, softbots, immobots: The 1997 aaai workshop on theories of action, planning and control. Knowl. Eng. Rev. 13(2), 179–184 (1998)
14. Kranz, M., Schmidt, A., Rusu, R., Maldonado, A., Beetz, M., Hornler, B., Rigoll, G.: Sensing technologies and the player-middleware for context-awareness in kitchen environments. In: Fourth International Conference on Networked Sensing Systems, INSS 2007, pp. 179–186 (June 2007)

15. Kranz, M., Schmidt, A., Maldonado, A., Rusu, R.B., Beetz, M., Hörnler, B., Rigoll, G.: Context-aware kitchen utilities. In: TEI 2007: Proceedings of the 1st International Conference on Tangible and Embedded Interaction, pp. 213–214. ACM, New York (2007)
16. Intille, S.S., Larson, K., Tapia, E.M., Beaudin, J., Kaushik, P., Nawyn, J., Rockinson, R.: Using a live-in laboratory for ubiquitous computing research. In: Fishkin, K.P., Schiele, B., Nixon, P., Quigley, A. (eds.) PERVASIVE 2006. LNCS, vol. 3968, pp. 349–365. Springer, Heidelberg (2006)
17. Wimmer, R., Holleis, P., Kranz, M., Schmidt, A.: Thracker - using capacitive sensing for gesture recognition. In: Proceedings of the 26th IEEE International Conference Workshops on Distributed Computing Systems, ICDCSW 2006, p. 64. IEEE Computer Society, Washington (2006)
18. Kranz, M., Holleis, P., Schmidt, A.: Ubiquitous presence systems. In: Proceedings of the 2006 ACM Symposium on Applied Computing, SAC 2006, pp. 1902–1909. ACM, New York (2006)
19. Schmidt, A., Beigl, M., Gellersen, H.-W.: There is more to context than location. Computers and Graphics 23(6), 893–901 (1999), `http://citeseer.ist.psu.edu/schmidt98there.html`
20. Kranz, M., Fischer, C., Schmidt, A.: A comparative study of dect and wlan signals for indoor localization. In: PerCom., pp. 235–243. IEEE Computer Society, Los Alamitos (2010)
21. Gellersen, H.-W., Beigl, M., Krull, H.: The mediacup: Awareness technology embedded in a everyday object. In: Gellersen, H.-W. (ed.) HUC 1999. LNCS, vol. 1707, pp. 308–310. Springer, Heidelberg (1999)
22. Kranz, M., Linner, T., Ellmann, B., Bittner, A., Roalter, L.: Robotic service cores for ambient assisted living. In: 4th International Conference on-NO PERMISSIONS, Pervasive Computing Technologies for Healthcare (Pervasive Health), pp. 1–8 (22-25, 2010)
23. Holleis, P., Schmidt, A., Paasovaara, S., Puikkonen, A., Häkkilä, J.: Evaluating capacitive touch input on clothes. In: ter Hofte, G.H., Mulder, I., de Ruyter, B.E.R. (eds.) ACM International Conference Proceeding Series, pp. 81–90. ACM, New York (2008)

An Infrastructure for Real Objects Augmentation with Additional Personalized Information Services

Rui Neves Madeira[1,2] and Nuno Correia[2]

[1] Escola Superior de Tecnologia de Setúbal, IPS, Setúbal, Portugal
rui.madeira@estsetubal.ips.pt
[2] Interactive Multimedia Group, DI/FCT/New University of Lisbon, Mt. Caparica, Portugal
nmc@di.fct.unl.pt

Abstract. In recent years, the research in the area of Ubiquitous Computing has intensified, with many technological advances occurring, but the current scenario is still far away from an everyday life fulfilled with seamless ubiquitous systems. Within this context, a proposal of an infrastructure is studied and presented. It is based on a set of guiding principles and a generic architecture, having a well focused application goal inside the area. It is directed at supporting the implementation of systems that augments physical objects present in a daily life environment. Initially, the augmentation is made with the main target of presenting additional personalized information, although it can support other services. Developed prototypes allowed testing the integration of mature and recognized technologies, also serving as proof of the infrastructure's viability.

Keywords: Intelligent environments, smart objects, personalization, bluetooth, mobile devices, public displays.

1 Introduction

Ubiquitous Computing (Ubicomp) [1] has the main goal of building computer systems that support and facilitate the daily lives of users, but being the least intrusive possible. The paradigm of Ubicomp is very broad and integrates many others paradigms, with the implementation of, almost totally, ubiquitous systems not being simple and straightforward. The lack of a common general infrastructure serving as supporting basis has been considered, for several years, as being one of the key obstacles to the implementation of robust and generic Ubicomp systems [2, 3]. The characteristics of each space and application scenario require the most diverse approaches.

Some reference projects, developed for several years (e.g., MIT Oxygen [4], HP Cooltown of HP Labs [5], Aura at CMU [6] and Gaia at University of Illinois [7]), take the risk of implementing ambitious and complex systems, intending to support a large number of daily tasks. However, we consider that instead of developing systems that answer completely to all the issues of Ubicomp, i.e., physical environments interconnected with each other to implement the vision of Weiser in its entirety, for now, we must follow a prudent iterative path, starting by identifying platforms (concepts,

Z. Yu et al. (Eds.): UIC 2010, LNCS 6406, pp. 282–296, 2010.

hardware, software, applications) with which is possible to perform a consistent work [8].

Ubicomp systems represent a major opportunity to enhance the experience of users in physical spaces, whether private or public, by effective means that support their located activities, which may have a personalized support. A well defined application scenario is the enhancement of users experience by augmenting the physical objects of their everyday life, presenting additional information and services. It is important that solutions follow an approach combining, in a non intrusive way, activities taking place in a physical space with a new functionality of augmentation.

Therefore, this paper presents a work that follows a cautious and iterative approach to the vision of Ubicomp, with a well focused goal. A proposal of an infrastructure is presented with a high level of abstraction allowing an easy and fast development of systems that augment physical objects present in an environment, which may be even itself seen as a large physical object (e.g., a business building).

The augmentation of the objects should be done by:

1. Initially, presenting additional personalized contextual information (it can support other related services) on public displays placed, preferably, close to the augmented objects. This way, the presentation of the information is made where and when is needed (embedded on it), being as unobtrusive as possible, and with passive interaction from the users.
2. Additionally, allowing an active interaction through mobile devices, as long as requested by users.

First, in Section 2, we present the problem's requirements and generic scenario followed by a set of guiding principles for the correct infrastructure design. Then, as main contribution, we propose a generic and modular architecture that was designed to implement the desired computing infrastructure in any physical space (in Section 3). We have developed prototypes based on the infrastructure, using mature technologies for detection and communication, e.g., Bluetooth (BT) and RFID The paper also presents the latter one, with relevance to architecture instantiation issues and used technologies (in Section 4). A set of related works, having points in common with our proposal, is discussed in Section 5. Finally, we present contributions and future work as conclusions in Section 6.

2 Requirements and Guiding Principles

In this section, we identify and describe guiding principles for a proper specification of the desired infrastructure, but first we summarize the requirements behind them.

The infrastructure definition is based on the detection of people involved in their everyday life activities, which have passive interactions that might be considered incidental with the augmented objects. In a first scenario of application, the basic aim is to ensure that only the detection of the user's co-presence near the object will activate the presentation of additional contextual information in a public display. There is a one to one relationship between an object, or part of it, and a public display. An object can be considered a physical, inanimate and easily viewed entity, or can even be considered as an institution or another user with activity in the environment of the application. In any of these cases, we are augmenting objects by providing embedded contextual information, not available by just looking at them.

A second level of interaction should be considered by the infrastructure design. Though triggered by a passive interaction, even "incidental", coming from the co-presence of the user in the environment, there can be an active interaction with the object/display pair, using for this purpose ordinary personal handheld mobile devices. These devices also allow the provision of additional information in a private mode.

Fig. 1 shows the generic scenario resulting from the requirements formulation.

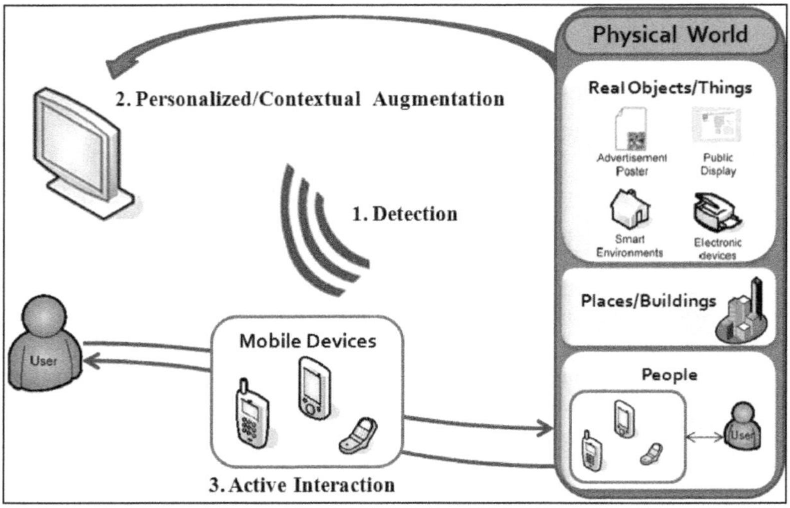

Fig. 1. Generic scenario: user detection, object augmentation and active interactions

2.1 Guiding Principles Description

Ambient Information System Concept. Although, initially, we did not have the concern to implement Ambient Information Systems (AIS), we think that the infrastructure should follow, as much as possible, the requirements and characteristics of these systems. Considered a sub-domain of Ubicomp, the concept of AIS has the main goal of presenting information through smooth and integrated changes in the environment, allowing that users are not distracted from their regular tasks, but being able to receive and be aware of non critical additional information [9].

Incidental Interactions with Co-Presence Notion. The notion of "incidental interactions" was proposed by Alan Dix to describe actions that are co-opted by a system to serve a purpose other than the one initially thought [10]. An incidental interaction can be seen as a situation where actions executed for another purpose are interpreted in order to improve future interactions in everyday life. This notion is important for us since the normal user interaction with an object will start its augmentation, without an obvious additional effort by the user. Related with these interactions is the detection of people that allow the computation of co-presence to be embodied within the real–world [11]. The notion of space is also crucial for the establishment of the interaction style and information presentation format. We considered the space types proposed in [12], like public, private, or transient space.

Public Situated Displays. These devices, also categorized as "boards" and preferably large, exist in various forms and scales (e.g., street displays, projection displays, kiosks, small screens next to objects). The infrastructure takes into account the integration of these stationary devices in a system, since they offer great opportunities for collaboration and a better resolution for combination of information. In a first approach, the goal is to have the information that augments an object displayed next to it, with the display being a direct extension of the object. Thus, the action to augment the object becomes, initially, contained and dependent on the user approximation, being less intrusive and not forcing the user to take an active interaction. According to their availability and access modality, the infrastructure's displays are categorized as [13]: public, shared, proactive and even interactive.

Embedded Personalized Contextual Information. The aim with the use of situated displays is to provide contextual information at decision points, which are where the objects are placed or exist. Situated displays provide additional information integrated, embedded, in the context of application. This process can be seen, merely, as a simple action of getting more and better information about an object, but also as an aid to make better decisions regarding the activities to be performed in an augmented space. The mobile devices displays can also be used as they can be embedded in the context. Following this principle, the information presentation is made where and when is needed, being as unobtrusive as possible, and with passive interaction [14]. Finally, the information should be contextual and personalized, based on the object, its specific location, the scenario and the detected user profile and data.

Mobile Devices Ubiquity. Nowadays, mobile devices (e.g., mobile phones, PDAs) are essential tools for our daily living, being almost universally connectable and found in almost all locations, situations. Therefore, the proposed work should take into account the mobile devices ubiquity. Depending on the context and type of application, the devices may be valuable tools when used for the detection of users. Thus, the space or the objects can feel the co-presence of a user in a natural and non-intrusive way. The user does not need to carry an extra identifier to be recognized in an application scenario. To accomplish this, using personal devices, it is assumed that there is a one to one relation between a user and her personal mobile device. In a complementary view, these devices can also be used to add active interactions and more private and personalized information, since mobile small screens are better for mobility and personalization flexibility purposes [15].

3 Infrastructure's Generic Architecture

The architecture must be comprehensive covering various types of scenarios and allowing a faster implementation of different systems. A generic modular architecture allows maximizing its reuse, adapting to the needs of each application.

3.1 General Overview

The proposed architecture is based on three main components that are on the augmented object side (Fig. 2), considering the fundamental principle of pro-activity of the object/display pair in relation to the user. The components are the following:

- Tracking – It is a mechanism for detection and identification of the Tag (or User), being responsible for "sensing" the co-presence of the user in a smart object area. It includes an interface for short-range communication with the user.
- Application Core - This one is the responsible for implementing the business logic of the application. It must be able to analyze and process the information given by the Tracking component, crossing it with contextual information related to the object and user profile.
- Display Interface – This component includes specific modules to smoothly integrate the situated displays as principle in the infrastructure.

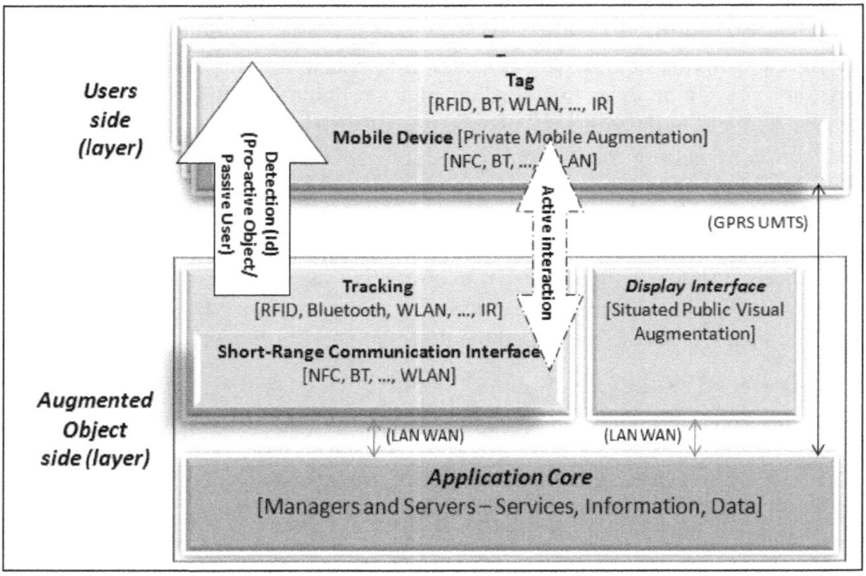

Fig. 2. General overview of the generic architecture

The user side can be seen as a simple Tag (e.g., RFID, BT-enabled mobile phone), which has a passive interaction resulting from her natural presence in the scenario. For active interactions, the architecture integrates a component for the object mobile augmentation with the use of mobile devices (can be personal). This augmentation enables the communication with the object through short-range technologies, or via GPRS/UMTS, and allows the visualization of private information.

Furthermore, the proposal can be seen as typical client/server architecture. Both the Tag component and the object's Display Interface component are considered as clients. On the other side, the user is detected by the Tracking component server that requests a service to the Application Core servers. Depending on the application scenario, the Application Core can be shared (applicable) by several objects, with several users with mobile devices behaving as clients of each object.

3.2 Details of the Architecture

Fig. 3 presents a detailed architecture of both the user and the augmented object side.

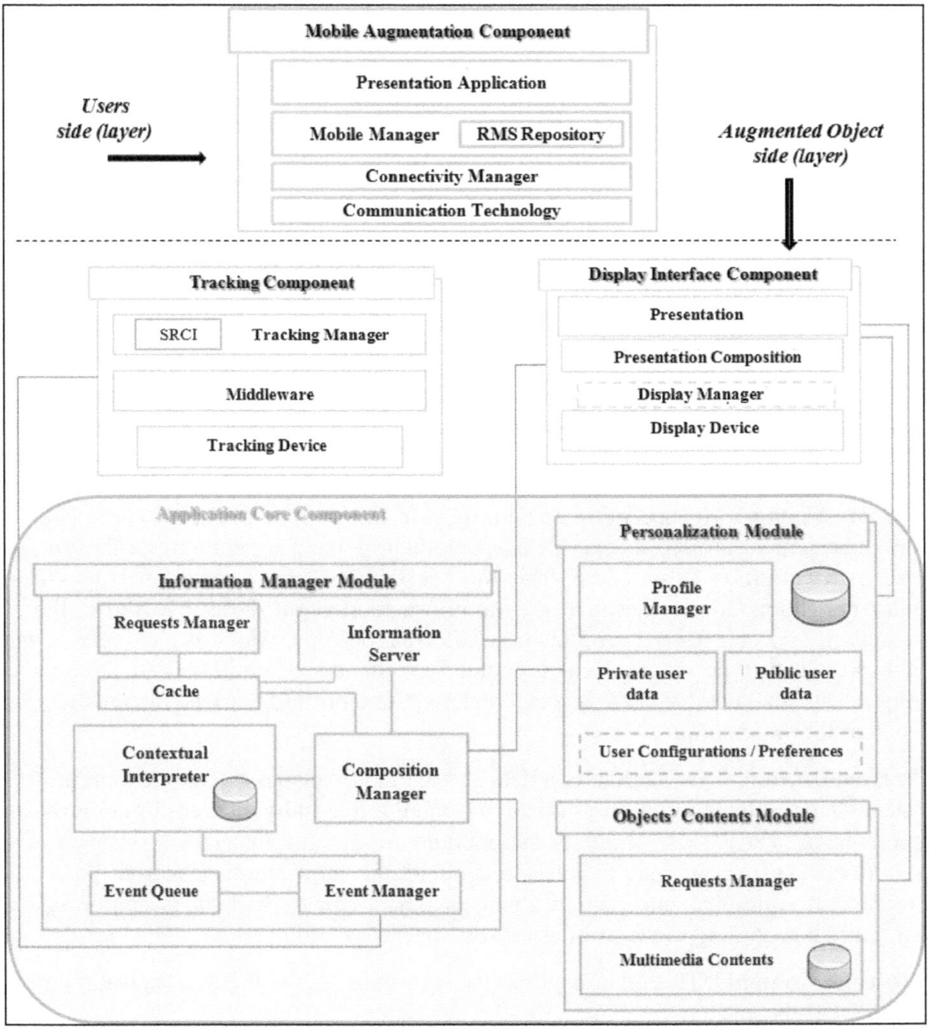

Fig. 3. Detailed architecture with all the main modules

Mobile Augmentation. This component provides to the user an additional object augmentation, which can go outside the environment of application. It allows the direct communication with the Tracking component via short-range technology. It has a *Connectivity Manager* that provides an abstraction in relation to the used technology. This makes the programming of the application (*Mobile Manager/Presentation)* independent of used technology. The *Mobile Manager* includes an optional sub-module for management services, providing facilities in the process of enhancing the object, but being dependent on used technology thus presenting programming issues. As an alternative to the near active interaction, there is a long distance communication option (e.g., via GPRS) with the Information Manager module (Information Server).

Tracking. Through this component, it is possible to know how much time a user spent in the pre-defined object area. There are several technologies that can be used with this module (e.g., RFID, BT). So, it is advisable to create an abstraction layer – *Tracking Manager* – to work as output interface, providing, transparently and uniformly, all data to the application core. Also noteworthy is the *Middleware* layer, which is dependent on chosen technology for a specific project development. This layer makes the abstraction of the *Tracking Devices* (hardware) used in the implementation, being essential for the top layer, which thus only has to integrate the interface(s) provided by the *Middleware.* A SRCI (Short-Range Communication Interface) sub-module permits the manager to be aware of other devices that want to communicate with him, adding the option of active interactions by the users.

Display Interface. It is the real output module of an implemented system, being responsible for the final *Presentation* of the additional information about an object, but it can be programmed to provide other services. The application scenario and number of users are crucial to the *Display Device* choice. An abstraction/management layer - *Display Manager* – is needed in certain use cases, i.e., to create uniform protocols for the management of used display devices, facilitating the programming of the *Presentation Composition* sub-module. This module requests and receives messages from the Application Core server that provide information about those involved in the interaction, i.e., object, user, and also the information type, which is the element that indicates what type of graphical user interface should be built/used. It also makes requests to the Personalization and Object's Contents modules to obtain the final content for presentation.

Personalization. This module is a data service that manages the application profiles and user data, integrating an optional sub-module for individual configurations and preferences. The *Profile Manager* sub-module defines and manages a set of profiles based on preferences and interests related to the application scenario. Since the amount of additional information about an object can be high, it is appropriate to structure it according to the profiles created for the scenario.

Objects' Contents. This other data service is responsible for the data repository about the scenario's objects.

Information Manager. Each time the user changes her status, i.e., being, or ceasing to be, detected next to an object, an event occurs and a related handler ensures the application status update. Therefore, the *Event Manager* receives and controls the inputs generated by the Tracking component. The *Event Queue* must be implemented in certain applications with a great number of parallel events being triggered.

The module core is composed of a *Contextual Interpreter* (CI) and a *Composition Manager* (CM). After getting information from the Tracking module, the CI is responsible for correlating the detected user, which has a specific profile, with the detected object to obtain the corresponding additional information (see model in Fig. 4). As a next step, it sends a message (document) to the CM, giving knowledge about the executed interpretation. The CM sub-module combines this information with data gathered from data servers, producing another document to send to the *Information Server*. The document must also be produced according to the detection or request origin. If the CM has received a message from the CI, then the produced document must contain a minimum of information, because it is directed to the Display Interface module. In case of a request from a mobile device (in an active interaction context), then the document must be a final one containing all the expected information. Depending on the scenario of application, the CM takes into account, for example, the local settings, user preferences and object location. This composition module is the responsible for selecting, composing and structuring the information to be displayed. Therefore, the CM is dependent on the application scenario, but the CI is clearly an independent API, with a model prepared to any object augmentation scenario (Fig. 4).

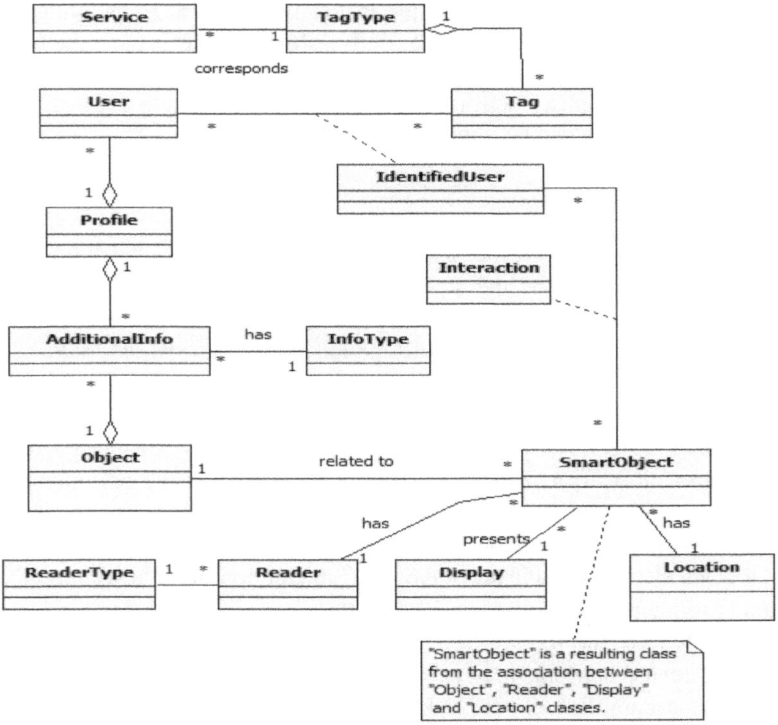

Fig. 4. Contextual Interpreter's model (architecture)

The CI model works for a scenario composed of multiple objects, such as a museum room, but also in cases where a conceptual large object is considered, such as an institution. It allows the association of multiple displays to one object, being useful in institutions scenarios. It should be noted that: a "SmartObject" corresponds to an "Object" to augment, a "Location", and is associated with a "Reader" to detect users, and a "Display"; “AdditionalInfo" indicates which object data should be combined taking into account a certain user "Profile"; "InfoType" is important for the CM module, because it indicates what types of multimedia information are represented in the object's "AdditionalInfo"; an "IdentifiedUser" corresponds to a "User" with a "Tag" (e.g., a BT enhanced mobile device) for a certain period of time; a "User" has always a "Profile" (even if the generic one); and whenever a user is detected by a "SmartObject", the data of a new "Interaction" is stored to help determining the interaction type (passive, active, etc).

Finally, the *Information Server* provides the final documents, created by the CM, for both the Display Interface and the requests made by mobile devices. As for the *Requests Manager*, it manages and transmits the information to the Tracking component, which is needed by the SRCI for active interactions with mobile devices.

4 directInfo2u, a Bluetooth Based System Prototype

The directInfo2u was implemented at the installations of Yang's Martial Arts Association Portugal (YMAAP), as a case study, although the same system could be applied to other institutions and scenarios or spaces. On the other hand, different infrastructure-based systems, such as the divingForPearls system [16] and the UbiSmartWheel project [17], can be implemented with success.

4.1 Scenario Main Issues

The main idea was to convert the institution into a large object “visited” by multiple users/clients. Users could be the students, instructors, or visitors wanting to know something more about YMAAP. The idea was to naturally detect users and augment the YMAAP object with additional information. This information could be generic, for any kind of user, or personalized and directed to registered users.

The system is composed of a public shared display, a server and the mobile devices of the YMAAP's users. For a simple installation, the display was placed at the lobby with the server close to it. Bluetooth (BT) was adopted as the communication and detection technology and the modules were developed in Java. We can find almost a BT sensor attached to any person, through the mobile devices. A person going to the YMAAP academy would have an “incidental” interaction with the system, having the opportunity to interact actively with the directInfo2u system. For this, a client application was created for the mobile devices registered in the system (Fig. 5). When an unregistered device appears, it is asked to register and to install the application to maximize the capabilities of the system. However, it is not necessary to have the client application installed to be registered.

For security purposes, the user will need to make a mobile authentication in order to make a direct communication with the server. These communications can have as objective: a) making available additional information (which may be more extensive) to the user's personal device, to read it later; b) sending private information to the user; c) sending questionnaires to the user; or d) information requested by the user.

Finally, an important point in conflicts resolution is that the public presentation duration of a piece of additional information should be inversely proportionate to the number of users simultaneously detected in the space. From a determined number of users, the additional information will only be general.

a) b)

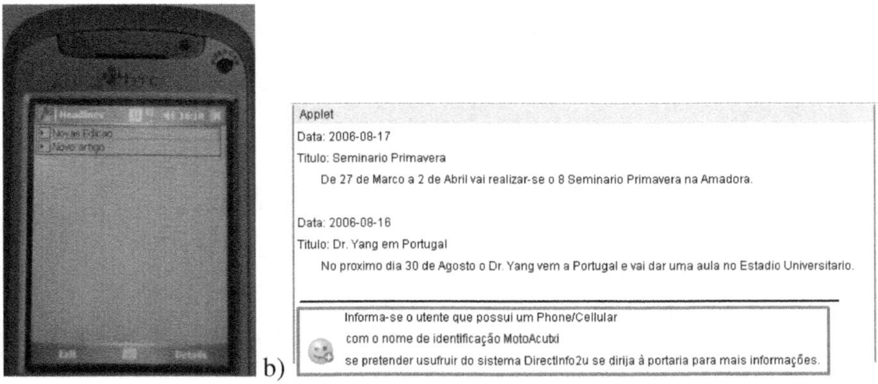

Fig. 5. a) A mobile application screen and b) Situated display with information for a known user and for a detected unregistered client (*in portuguese*)

4.2 Personalization

We defined six user profiles for this prototype as a simple approach and while working on a context-aware recommendation system to reach more complex scenarios. The profiles are associated with YMAA preferences and users choose them at the registration moment.

The generic profile 0 is dedicated to all users who prefer not to choose preferences. Furthermore, the profiles 1-4 are for those who want to receive a larger amount of information in a few seconds (while passing through the lobby), information about the area of major concern. The last of the profiles is for all "visitors" which, although not being registered, are users considered "official" as they have BT-enabled devices that are detected. Therefore, these users can see few lines of advertising on the institution.

4.3 Key-Points of Architecture Instantiation

The architecture instantiation with relations between modules is described in Fig.6.

Regarding the Tracking Device, a USB BT dongle connected to the server transforms it in a BT-enabled device, being able to detect and to communicate with BT-enabled mobile devices. The Middleware module integrates three layers, with focus on the JSR-82 API. The JSR-82 hides the complexity of the BT protocols stack, providing a simple set of API's for Java development. As initially the JSR-82 API was only implemented for mobile devices, it was needed to use the BlueCove implementation of it for J2SE. The Tracking Manager uses the BlueCove API and creates a XML document that is sent by TCP whenever a detection event occurs, indicating: the time-stamp when a device (tag) is observed or is lost; the device identification; and the identified reader that triggered the event. In this case, it interfaces directly with an Event Manager in the Application Core. This module has to manage the XML messages received from the previous module, filtering and organizing them for the Contextual Interpreter (CI).

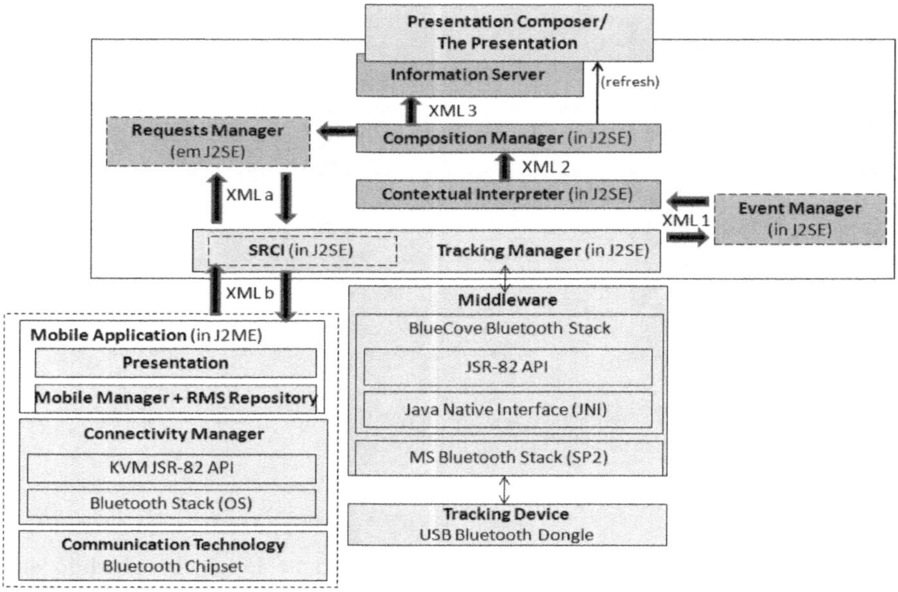

Fig. 6. Architecture instantiation of the directInfo2U system

The CI module is the system's "decision maker", processing data received from the *Tracking Manager*. Upon receiving a XML document with a detection indication, it makes an immediate processing, followed by the update of its contextual information database. Thus, knowing the object (only one in this case), next to which is the user, will determine what additional information to display and where to do it. With the contextual data determined, a second XML document (XML 2) is created and passed to the CM module. This one is responsible for placing a third document (XML 3) in the right folder of the *Information Server* (IS). A folder for each object/display pair was created in the IS, with names according to the corresponding displays names. This is how the CM module knows where to place the generated XML document. Before doing so, it processes the XML document passed by the previous module. It questions the Personalization module to retrieve some data about the detected user and the Objects' Content module to retrieve a portion of information that is essentially text. An "InfoType" element (see CI model in Fig.4) in XML 2 indicates if the additional information has text in its composition, beyond the generic summary that is already included. Content such as image or video will be retrieved from the database only by the *Presentation Composition* sub-module. Finally, the module automatically refreshes an XHTML file that is in the folder where the XML 3 document was previously placed. The CM has one more task, the creation of XML documents with information to be accessed by mobile devices. The document is made available to the *Requests Manager*, thus, being available to be requested by a mobile device. In case a mobile device does not implement the API JSR-82, it may be placed in the *Information Server*. The server also has a folder for each mobile device, which may request through GPRS the most recent document.

The SRCI module was implemented to complement the Tracking Manager. It can start communicating with one of the discovered devices, but for this application it was programmed only to accept RFCOMM communication requests coming from users. When the mobile application requests a communication, the SRCI queries the Requests Manager database to obtain the XML document that refers to the device.

The *Mobile Application* client is developed in Java (J2ME) for devices that support the MID profile. It has two main modules: one with services to interact with the server via Bluetooth (*Connectivity Manager* with two layers); and another one to manage the possible information received from the system (*Mobile Manager*). Not all the mobile devices can run the first module to interact directly with the system. To accomplish that, the device must be embedded with the JSR-82 API. If a device does not embed the API, the solution is the direct communication with the Information Server, where the object has an URL address to be accessed through WAP. In this way, the user will be able to receive XML documents to consult later and to store them in the client repository, a Record Management System (RMS).

5 Related Work

This section presents a representative selection of works that share principles and architecture points with the proposed infrastructure or that are similar to our prototypes. In [18] we can find a survey about context-aware middleware that includes important works, but mostly with very different goals from ours.

Table 1 summarizes the related work in terms of principles and implementation main factors. The Table is self-explanatory in relation to the comparison between these works and our proposal, showing that the latter adds significant different points.

A very ambitious work is the AWARE project [19], which has the goal to implement a context-aware space in a section of a hospital environment. The system is essentially composed of a tracking module for clinics and patients, an infrastructure for acquisition, management and distribution of contextual information, and tools like a situated display and mobile phones, both used only by clinics.

In [20] is specified the ActivitySpot infrastructure, which is used to support located activities by occasional visitors of the application spaces. Users are directed to actively interact with the implemented system by personal mobile devices, public displays, and other technologies. Depending on the action, the system can also present personalized information targeted to the user profile. Another system, BluScreen [21], uses BT-enabled mobile devices to influence a public display by detecting the audience around it. Users are used to influence the content of a public display only by their detection, thus having a passive interaction with the system. The user's passive interaction with the screen is co-opted to incidentally provide feedback and thereby change the content a user receives in the future. The DiABlu project [22] is an infrastructure, also based on BT technology and personal mobile devices, for the detection of people in an environment. Several answers to the detection type can be created in the form of arts applications presented in a public display.

Table 1. Comparative table of related work

Issue / Project	A.I.S.	Co-Presence notion	Public Display	Mobile Device Use	Information About...	Personalized Information	Active interaction device	Supporting Technology	With Arch. proposal
magicmirror	X	X	X		Obj.	x	Touch-screen	RFID	
ActivitySpot		x	X	X	Obj.	X	Mobile device	various	X
Rememberer		x		X	Obj.		other	IR, camera	X
Wi-Art		X		X	Obj.			RFID	
AWARE	X	X	X	X	Obj.		Mobile device	BT	X
DIABlu	X	X	X	X	arts		Mobile device	BT	X
A. Knight's Castle	X	X		X	Obj.		Mobile device	RFID	x
BluScreen	x	X	X	X	Obj.			BT	
Proposed Work	x	X	X	X	Obj.	X	Mobile device	RFID, BT, ...	X

The magicmirror system [23] is a commercial solution that is interesting because it integrates a mirror with a touch screen function. The system includes a computer, a RFID reader and a Wi-Fi transceiver and has the elementary function of presenting additional information about cloth articles, when tried by clients in the fitting room of a clothes store. Therefore, this system augments objects by providing information in a situated display and using RFID technology for an unobtrusive identification of users. In Italy, La Sapienza University, through its RFID Lab center, has developed an RFID based solution for the Museo delle Origini, with the name of Wi-Art [24]. The system lets the users to receive, in a PDA device, additional information about a piece every time they go closer to the objects. The most relevant data about the pieces are stored in the respective RFID tags that mark them. With the PDA, a user can read a tag and extract data to her device, thus, being able to visualize additional information in the PDA display. One of the first projects related to museum visits was Rememberer [25], which is based on the Cooltown project [5]. It works as a tool to capture personal experiences while visiting a museum, allowing the construction of a visit record composed by web pages about the visited exhibitions. It includes annotations and photographs taken during the visit. Initial tests were carried out with the use of cameras, RFID technology and PDAs with Wi-Fi communication.

Finally, the Augmented Knight's Castle project also bases its infrastructure in RFID technology, pointing the pervasive augmentation to a Playmobil playset named "Knight's Empire Castle" [26]. The scenario of the game is educationally enriched and augmented by audio contents and does not use displays with additional information. Some pieces of the set were marked with RFID tags and it also integrates mobile devices equipped with RFID for the users' active interaction.

6 Conclusions and Future Work

The development of Ubicomp systems is still a time consuming, costly and error prone process, often leading to sub-optimal results. The presented infrastructure addresses this issue, providing a generic and modular architecture that can be used for the development of systems that should follow the set of guiding principles that were gathered and described to augment real objects. The applicability and maturity of the infrastructure is shown through its usage for the development of different prototypes. The specified components, which were implemented for the prototypes, can be directly reused, as API's, or easily adapted to suit similar projects, demonstrating the extension feasibility of the proposal.

With the prototypes is possible to confirm the utility of RFID and BT, which have confirmed as good choices for systems like the proposed. For some applications it may be interesting to combine the two, RFID and BT, as Salminen et al. did in [27].

For future work, we have plans to enhance our platform and to deploy and test other technologies and physical spaces. Regarding interaction with users, we are using the developed prototypes to conduct thorough HCI and personalization studies. We intend to present contributions about the personalization issue in a short period of time as we are deeply working on it.

References

1. Weiser, M.: The Computer for the 21st Century. Scientific American 265(3), 66–75 (1991)
2. Kindberg, T., Fox, A.: System Software for ubiquitous Computing. IEEE Pervasive Computing 1(2), 1268–1536 (2002)
3. Storz, O., Friday, A., Davies, N.: Towards 'Ubiquitous' Ubiquitous Computing: an alliance with 'the Grid'. In: System Support for Ubiquitous Computing Workshop at UbiCOMP 2003 (October 2003)
4. MIT Project Oxygen Team: MIT Project Oxygen Overview (June 2004), `http://www.oxygen.lcs.mit.edu/Overview.html`
5. Barton, J., Kindberg, T.: The CoolTown User Experience. In: Technical Report 2001-22, HP Laboratories, Palo Alto, California (2001)
6. Sousa, J.P., Garlan, D.: Aura: An Architectural Framework for User Mobility in Ubiquitous Computing Environments. In: Proc. 3rd IEEE/IFIP Conf. on Software Architecture, pp. 29–43. Kluwer Academic Publishers, Dordrecht (August 2002)
7. Román, M., Hess, C.K., Cerqueira, R., Ranganathan, A., Campbell, R.H., Nahrstedt, K.: Gaia: A Middleware Infrastructure to Enable Active Spaces. IEEE Pervasive Computing 1(4), 74–83 (2002)
8. Ravi, N., Iftode, L.: A Note On Pervasive Computing. In: LaMarca, A., Langheinrich, M., Truong, K.N. (eds.) Pervasive 2007. LNCS, vol. 4480. Springer, Heidelberg (2007)

9. Pousman, Z., Stasko, J.: A taxonomy of ambient information systems: four patterns of design. In: Proc. AVI 2006: Working Conference on Advanced Visual Interfaces, pp. 67–74 (2006)
10. Dix, A.: Beyond intention - pushing boundaries with incidental interaction. In: Proc. Building Bridges: Interdisciplinary Context-Sensitive Computing, Glasgow University (2002)
11. Dourish, P.: Where the Action Is. MIT Press, Cambridge (2001)
12. Mitchell, K., Race, N., Suggitt, M.: iCapture: Facilitating Spontaneous User-Interaction with Pervasive Displays using Smart Devices. In: Proc. Pervasive Mobile Interaction Devices (PERMID 2006) - Mobile Devices as Pervasive User Interfaces and Interaction Devices (at Pervasive 2006) (May 2006)
13. Koch, M.: Supporting Community Awareness with Public Shared Displays. In: Proc. of 18th Bled eConference "eIntegration in Action" (2005)
14. Schmidt, A., Kranz, M., Holleis, P.: Embedded Information. In: Workshop Ubiquitous Display Environments on UbiComp 2004 (September 2004)
15. Agamanolis, S.: Designing displays for Human Connectedness (book chapter). In: O'Hara, K., Perry, M., Churchill, E., Russell, D. (eds.) Public and Situated Displays: Social and Interactional Aspects of Shared Display Technologies. Kluwer, Dordrecht (2003)
16. Madeira, R.N., Correia, N.: divingForPearls: A System with RFID based on a Ubiquitous Infrastructure. In: Proc. 4th International Conference on Ubiquitous Information Technologies & Applications (ICUT 2009), IEEE Computer Society Press, Los Alamitos (December 2009)
17. Postolache, O., Madeira, R.N., Correia, N., Girão, P.: UbiSmartWheel – A Ubiquitous System with Unobtrusive Services Embedded on a Wheelchair. In: Proc. ACM 2nd International Conference on PErvasive Technologies Related to Assistive Environments (PETRA 2009), pp. 1–4. ACM press, New York (June 2009)
18. Kjær, K.E.: A survey of context-aware middleware. In: Proc. of the 25th Conf. on IASTED int. Multi-Conference: Software Engineering, pp. 148–155. ACTA Press (February 2007)
19. Bardram, J.E., Hansen, T.R., Mogensen, M., Sogaard, M.: Experiences from real-world deployment of context-aware technologies in a hospital environment. In: Dourish, P., Friday, A. (eds.) UbiComp 2006. LNCS, vol. 4206, pp. 369–386. Springer, Heidelberg (2006)
20. Pinto, H., Jose, R., Campos, J.C.: An Interaction Model and Infrastructure for Localized Activities in Pervasive Computing Environments. In: Proc. ICPS 2007: IEEE International Conference on Pervasive Services, perser, pp. 232–241 (July 2007)
21. Sharifi, M., Payne, T., David, E.: Public Display Advertising Based on Bluetooth Device Presence. In: Proc. Mobile Interaction with the Real World Workshop, pp. 52–55 (2006)
22. Cardoso, J.: Enabling user interaction in installation art using mobile devices. British HCI Group Interfaces Magazine 58, 6–9 (2006)
23. Thebigspace: The magicmirror system, `http://www.thebigspace.com`
24. Holloway, S.: RFID in museums and galleries. In: IT-DIRECTOR.COM (September 2007), `http://www.it-director.com/business/content.php?cid=9838`
25. Fleck, M., Frid, M., Kindberg, T., O'Brien-Strain, E., Rajani, R., Spasojevic, M.: Rememberer: A Tool for Capturing Museum Visits. In: Borriello, G., Holmquist, L.E. (eds.) UbiComp 2002. LNCS, vol. 2498, pp. 48–55. Springer, Heidelberg (2002)
26. Lampe, M., Hinske, S.: Integrating Interactive Learning Experiences into Augmented Toy Environments. In: Pervasive Learning 2007: Design Challenges and Requirements Workshop At Pervasive2007, vol. 4480. Springer, Heidelberg (May 2007)
27. Salminen, T., Hosio, S., Riekki, J.: Enhancing Bluetooth Connectivity with RFID. In: Proc. of PerCom 2006, pp. 36–41. IEEE Computer Society, Los Alamitos (2006)

A Low-Cost Ubiquitous Family Healthcare Framework

Yongqiang Lu[1], Lei Zhang[1], Yu Chen[1], Yingjie Ren[1], Jing Liu[2], Weikang Yang[1], and Yuanchun Shi[1]

[1] Research Insititute of Information Technology, Tsinghua Univ.
[2] Department of Biomedical Engineering, Tsinghua Univ.
{luyq,yuchen}@tsinghua.edu.cn

Abstract. This paper proposes a low-cost ubiquitous healthcare framework for home-based health and medical care systems. This framework mainly resolves the problem of bio-data gathering and preprocessing at home through 1) the hierarchical data flow model and 2) the networking and structured models. The framework is compatible for most of communication methods and medical appliances commonly used, and it is able to be extended to vast space and mobile scenes. This framework is economic to use based on current techniques. A reference implementation is also given to validate the framework.

Keywords: Ubiquitous healthcare, family healthcare, sensor network, unobtrusive measurement.

1 Introduction

Family healthcare is an extension of the family medicine perception which emerged in 1960s and advocates continuous human-centric medical services over homes, communities and hospitals [1]. It focuses not only on the patients but also on the rest, family members in health or in sub-health, transforming and renewing the discipline of family medicine to meet the needs of patients in changing medical environment [2] and even helping recognize the abnormal health state and making relative health services accessible for average people at home.

Ubiquitous healthcare or pervasive healthcare is a conception of the healthcare to anyone, anytime, and anywhere by removing location, time and other constraints while increasing both the coverage and the quality [3]. Recently pretty some successful applications have appeared over all of the world, such as the TeCaRob [4] of University of Florida which builds a system that allows caregivers to provide assistance and services remotely, the uHouse [5] of Seoul National University which developed a comprehensive home health monitoring system for patients, and the Ubimon [6] of Imperial College of London which develops a patient monitoring environment with lower-power sensor network. All of such applications cover the known four important aspects of ubiquitous healthcare, namely the pervasive health monitoring, intelligent emergency management system, pervasive healthcare data access, and ubiquitous mobile telemedicine [3], based on which many industrial companies have also set up

Z. Yu et al. (Eds.): UIC 2010, LNCS 6406, pp. 297–306, 2010.

business about remote health recording/monitoring system [7], [8], living reminder and emergency assistance [9], and telemedicine [10], [11].

Due to the initiation of ubiquitous healthcare, home becomes a key environment of employing it. How to resolve the application interfaces and make services more convenient at home is a long-keeping issue in this field. Although related research and business focuses on different aspects, the key problem they are all faced with is the data problem, i.e. how to fetch, how to model, how to transfer, how to analyze, how to use, etc. Following such a principle, the authors propose a low-cost compact and extendable ubiquitous healthcare framework available for applications based on home. By sticking to such a framework, different bio-signal processing sensor-integrated devices can work together, different bio-data can formulate together, different medical applications can deploy together. The reference implementation and protocols would also be validated behind to make this framework feasible and applicable for different organizations, vendors and service providers.

The remainder of the paper is organized as follows. Section 2 will describe the hierarchical data flow; section 3 will describe the framework architecture and the basic models and methods used in it, and the section 4 will give an initial reference implementation based on this framework.

2 Hierarchical Data Flow

All ubiquitous healthcare applications are data-centric. They manipulate all kinds of bio-data and provide their services upon them. The framework should give the data model for developers to position their objective and align with other service providers within the home healthcare domain since it will firstly resolve the data problem. A systematic standard family healthcare deployment can be illustrated as Fig. 1(a), which connects different social units (such as homes, communities and hospitals) and different services (tele-systems and mobile systems) tightly together, distributes the traditional medical care jobs over deeper levels, and shares the public critical medical resources with higher efficiency.

Fig. 1(b) shows the data-centric flow diagram which describes our methodology in resolving the ubiquitous healthcare problem by data perspective. This flow consists of three data manipulation levels two of which are deep-resolution levels and one of which is a coarsening higher-level application level. With the two deep levels handling the data-fetching and data-modeling, any applications of application level can run upon them with free and easy data interfaces and protocols within home-domain healthcare perception.

Another advantage using this hierarchical data flow model is that application developers and medical device vendors do not need to face each other directly any more, and all the field is hence open to anyone who cares about it. After corresponding protocols or common data APIs defined in data-level models, anyone can join developing services and devices, and to offer a systematic solution is not a monopolistic game any longer.

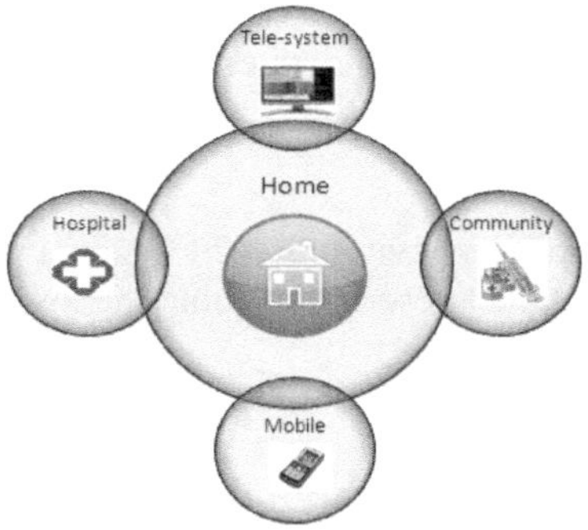

(a) Family healthcare deployment in medical system

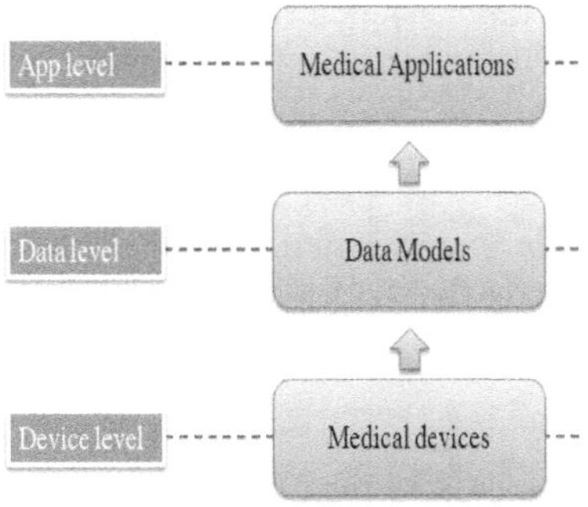

(b) The hierarchical data flow

Fig. 1. Family healthcare is the most bottom data unit of the entire social medical system. In (a), the tele-system stands for those telemedicine/remote monitoring systems and so on; the mobile stands for those movable health services and systems; the hospital stands for the professional medical organizations and the community stands for any intermediate medical levels. In (b), a hierarchical data flow can separate the bottom data-fetch from the higher-level medical applications.

This hierarchical data flow model can also make sure the extendibility of our framework. All original device-level data processing such as bio-signal collecting, translating, and so on could be packaged into the device-level models and all device vendors need only to take care of the protocols, standards of this level. In the meantime, the models in this level also make sure the extendibility to any-type medical instruments and devices for various bio-information gathering. In addition, all application-oriented data preprocess, preparation and APIs could be packaged into the data model level, which is also responsible for data verification, validation and maintenance. This level acts as a connecting component between the low-level devices and the high-level applications. Above them two, the application level represents all applications needing bio-data. Actually, this level often needs to be resolved further, e.g. data storage and mining applications should be placed in front of the even-higher applications like professional systems and tele-diagnosing systems. Nevertheless, the hierarchical data model here leaves the extending space of this level, and those extensions would not affect the correctness and efficiency of the hierarchical model and the framework in this work. This framework has good compatibility with current techniques and good extendibility for all kinds of users, and therefore is very low-cost for both the development and the deployment.

3 The Framework and the General-Purpose Data Models

As the hierarchical data flow model suggests, the key part of the data models would be lying in the two lower levels, i.e. the device and data levels. This section will describe the corresponding models set up in the two lower data levels for general purpose. The device-level model is a sensor network model covering all kinds of current main-stream bio-signal types and gathering methods including both healthcare and clinical standard; the data-level model is a bio-information oriented data structure supporting all data from device level; it also includes a data maintenance model.

3.1 The Framework Architecture

Firstly, in order to introduce the backgrounds and the environment of the data models more easily, the framework architecture with detailed description about the lower data levels will be illustrated in Fig. 2.

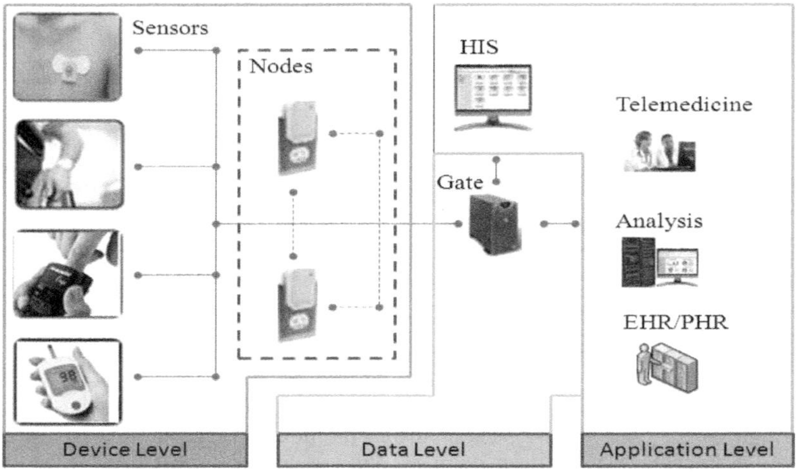

Fig. 2. The architecture of the family healthcare framework. The most left-side shows the *sensors*; the appliances in the dashed rectangle are the *nodes* which are optional; the following important part of this architecture is a computing-machine *gate*; the most right-side objects in solid rectangle are the example medical and healthcare applications based on the data models exported at the gate.

This framework architecture in Fig. 2 consolidates the hierarchical data model and the corresponding network and deployment in the entire architecture. The device-level model is formulated as a sensor network since all bio-information gathering methods of the current state of the art are nearly sensor based, especially those could be used in home domain. The data-level model resolves the device-level data, manage them and export APIs, which is resident on the gate. The applications run based on the APIs of the data level exported at the gate and fulfill the real medical and healthcare services. The related data models in the lower two levels will be described in detail respectively in the following two sections.

3.2 Device-Level Sensor Network Based Data Model

The data model of this level comprises of two parts, one is the networking model and the other is the data interface. The goal is to handle the data-gathering issue, independent of the network topology, communication method and protocols.

The Networking Model. The networking model, as Fig. 2 shows, should be a loose-topology model which is compatible for any current mainstream communication methods, such as Wifi, Bluetooth, Zigbee and so on. Of course, if wired communication methods are preferred, the corresponding sensors and nodes could also be similarly customized to meet this requirement without changing this model at all.

As Fig. 2 shows, the sensors are responsible for gathering the original bio-signal or the extracted bio-information, say, the blood pressure at some time. The nodes are optional for the data model, which means they actually act as data relays, data transfer units or access points for the extendibility of the model, for example, if the sensors are deployed sparsely in a vast indoor area and the communication capability could not meet, or users are in a outdoor scene with just a mobile phone, some relay units or data transfer units (e.g. installed on a mobile phone) might be needed. The gate is an important intelligent data processing unit, which should have basic capability of data storage, data preprocessing and data fusion. At the same time, the data API for high-level applications are also resident here. The applications in Fig. 2 represent all medical and healthcare systems which are almost data-centric and need the original end-user bio-information.

It should be noted that the data model is sensor network based, which means the system is original bio-signal oriented and is not covering the situation when users are using big ultrasonic or CT, MRI machines. However, this situation actually is easier to handle because there are only some images or files to store or transfer, but it is not reasonable to be considered in such a home-domain framework. If such requirements are really necessary in real applications, we should add them into the data-level modeling part above this level.

The Device Data Interface. Firstly, devices should register themselves when they access the network. The register data message format should contain the information in Table 1, which describes the data format in the first row and gives an example in the second row.

Table 1. Device register message format of necessary information

Device ID	Device Type (classification)	Register Time
Universal ID string	Standard type code string	hh:mm:ss, yyyy/mm/dd
UI01001EF	DT01SC00 (e.g. for ECG)	10:05:05, 2010/03/01

After devices registered, the data transferring could be started. The general-purpose data message format for data-transferring should contain the information in Table 2. This message is not presented as package format and it is at user's desire to divide the message into packages on transferring. The data body could be defined and extended according to the corresponding data format standard based on the device types and data types in implementation of the framework.

Table 2. Data transferring message format of necessary information

Start Tag	Data	Time	End Tag
Message start string	Data body	Gathering time	Message end string
AA00	Blood pressure data	10:10:00, 2010/03/01	5555

It should be noted that the mapping of the data message to the source device should be taken care of in real implementation according to the communication protocol and the scene where the framework is used.

The data interface only has one-way communication. This is specially designed for the compatibility to the devices of weak computing capability and does not affect the correctness and the extendibility of the framework. The corresponding extension to the powerful embedded devices could be added to fulfill the mutual-way commands or operations such as state-query, error-diagnose and response-at-request, etc.

3.3 Data-Level Data Modeling and APIs

As the hierarchical data flow model mentioned, the data level mainly handle the generalized bio-data modeling, maintenance and APIs. The entire model of this level is sketched in Fig. 3 and each individual part will be described respectively.

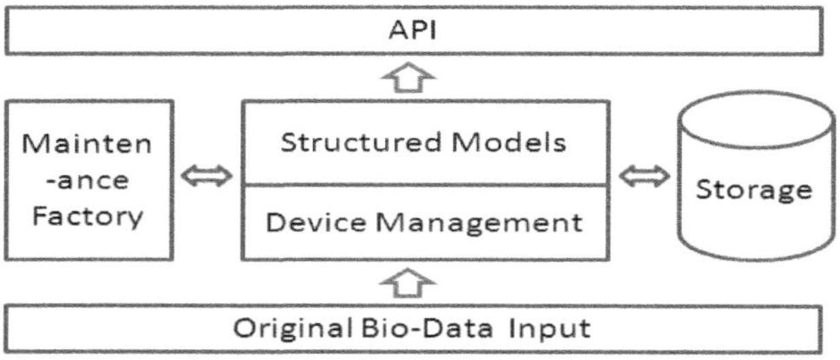

Fig. 3. The data-level modeling architecture. This level maintains structured bio-data models with a data input from lower device level and a data output interface for high-level users. The maintenance factory contains data preprocessing, verifying, validating and other maintenance algorithms. The storage offers the data archive and IO interfaces. The device management module is also needed to manage the device resources and the possible data mapping.

Bio-Data Input and Device Management. The data input interface gets the data from devices via certain communication protocols. Some conversion and translation might be needed to formulate the basic structured data. The device management module is also needed to help maintain the device information and the data mapping since there would be multiple medical devices used in the framework.

Structured Bio-Data Models and Storage. According to the main human bio-signals current medical appliances and devices could achieve, the data model covers nearly all the data type we could care about in home-domain usages as Table 3 shows. The reasons why the structured model is used are that 1) device-level data is structured, 2) structured data is easy to port via APIs and easy to be archived via either XML or database 3) structured content is easy to be defined as guidelines or standards.

Table 3. Structured bio data

User ID	Data type	Value	Time
Data owner ID string	0-255 integer	The data value	Gathering time
001 (someone)	1 (temperature)	36.5 (℃)	10:10:00, 2010/03/01

The structured data listed in Table 3 is somewhat redundant and essential to be extended to any archive method. This data structure is also easy to be extended to cover discrete or continuous data from devices. The data volume could be compressed on archiving or on transferring by some extraction method like functions or fitting methods.

Maintenance Factory. In order to improve the robustness of the framework, the data variation, error and noise must be taken into account. The data pool of the structured models should have a maintenance factory to guarantee this. The factory is an algorithm set which could handle the data verification, correctness and pruning. For example, some data might be not precise due to the device warm-up or preparation problems; even some data is wrong or from wrong users; or some data is changed to another new gathering methods and so on. Users are promised to have unobtrusive measurement [5], and they of course should be free of any complex data maintenance assistance, which should be accomplished by the maintenance factory. The algorithms could be used in this module are mostly the data fusion related algorithms, such as Bayes, neutral networks, wavelet analysis and so on.

APIs. The application programming interface exported to high-level applications is another key component of the data level, which could make the framework really valued by real service providers. The APIs should contain the following functions as Table 4 lists.

Table 4. APIs for high-level applications

Name	Description
getSpotValue	Get some value of certain devices on certain time-stamp
getAvgValue	Get the average value over certain time periods
getStructuredPara	Get extracted information on the certain data range of a certain device, e.g. get the heart rhythm from blood pressure data, get the intervals of QT waves from ECG, or get the breath from temperature data, etc. The corresponding structured extraction type should be defined in advance.
getArchiveData	Get the archived data for a certain time range on a certain device or data type. Standard or conventional format should be returned.

4 The Reference Implementation

In order to validate the framework, we implement a reference system based on it. The *sensor* parts in the device level are mapped to real medical appliances we can buy and revised based on Bluetooth 2.0. Currently one Bluetooth ECG, one Bluetooth blood pressure monitor and one Bluetooth oximeter are accomplished. They are only revised by adding a Bluetooth module to the formal well-constructed RS232 data interfaces. The *nodes* are omitted and the *gate* is deployed on a PC. Two simple APIs that offering spot and average values are used and simple monitoring reminders are validated on the home server which has internet access capability. The deployment sketch is shown in Fig. 4. Most of jobs are done by software, and the cost is very low.

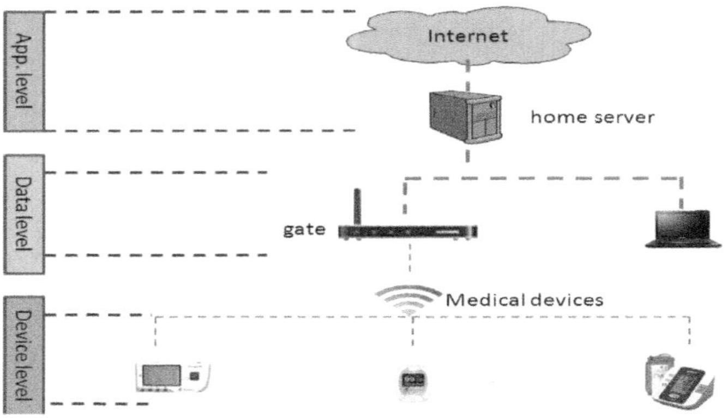

Fig. 4. The network deployment sketch. In our experiment, we have now implemented Bluetooth based ECG, blood pressure and oximeter. They are integrated together towards an intelligent gate which is connected to home-domain network.

The general device revision flow is very simple. There are normally RS232 data interfaces on the chips of the traditional digital medical devices, such as ECG or blood pressure. We just easily feed the data out from those interfaces to the Bluetooth modules, (we use CSR Bluetooth chips), and setup the corresponding wireless operation behaviors by AT instructions. Finally we use a mapped computer serial port to manipulate the data populated from the Bluetooth devices.

In this implementation, we setup the data transferring format under the framework of that described in Section 3.2, the detailed ECG format is listed in Table 5, the blood pressure format is listed in Table 6, and the oximeter is listed in Table 7.

Table 5. Data transferring format of ECG. We use 128-byte sampling data per second

Start Tag	Data	Time	End Tag
2 Bytes	Sampling data in 1 sec	6 Bytes	2 Bytes
AAAA	Fixed-length Data	In seconds	5555

Table 6. Data transferring format of BP (Blood Pressure), totally 8 Bytes

Start Tag	Data	Time	End Tag
2 Bytes	4 Bytes	NA	2 Bytes
AA00	2 for systolic, 1 for dias., 1 for pulse	Handled in server	5555

Table 7. Data transferring format of oximeter

Start Tag	Length	Data Type	Data	Time	End Tag
2 Bytes	2 Bytes	1 byte	Length bytes	NA	2 Bytes
55AA	Data length	0 or 1	Data body	In server	5555

From the tables form 5 to 7, we can see that there are some interesting points reflecting the flexibility of this framework: a) Some data is fixed-length but some is variable; b) some devices support time-fetching but some don't and need to be handled at data-gathering servers, e.g. BP and oximeter; c) some packets may handle different kinds of data types, e.g. the oximeter handles pulse waveform (type 0) and blood oxygen saturation (type 1).

Furthermore, the device management module illustrated in Section 3.3 is triggered upon the first packet of the message achieved. In this implementation the different devices are mapped to different computer serial ports and some manual manipulation is needed to validate the map due to the limitation of the low-level Bluetooth adaption software we use currently. In order to support automatic device discovery, either the Bluetooth adaption software should be customized or other communication means and protocols should be employed.

Fig.5 gives the actual experimental results in this implementation. This result includes ECG, blood pressure, blood oxygen saturation, and the pulse waveform which is achieved via the oximeter. Meanwhile, the pulse number can be calculated by both blood pressure monitor and oximeter, which might have some little error between them due to device variation.

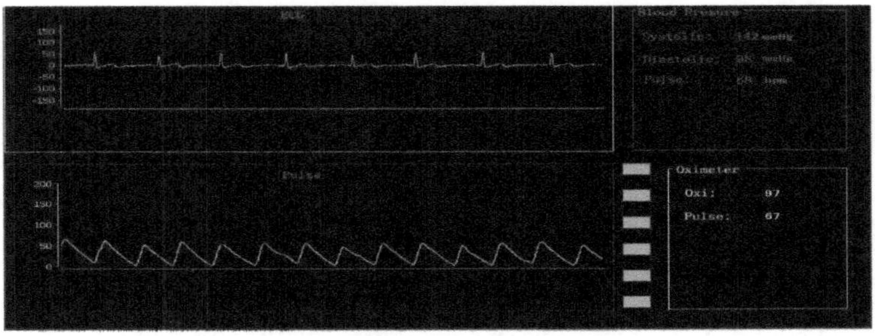

Fig. 5. The ECG, blood pressure and oximeter results which also include a pulse waveform. The pulse waveform is achieved from the oximeter.

In the meantime, in order to validate the applications based on this framework, we implement a remote ECG monitoring system which gets those wireless gathering data via this home-domain network and displays at remote desktops. Fig. 6 shows the details.

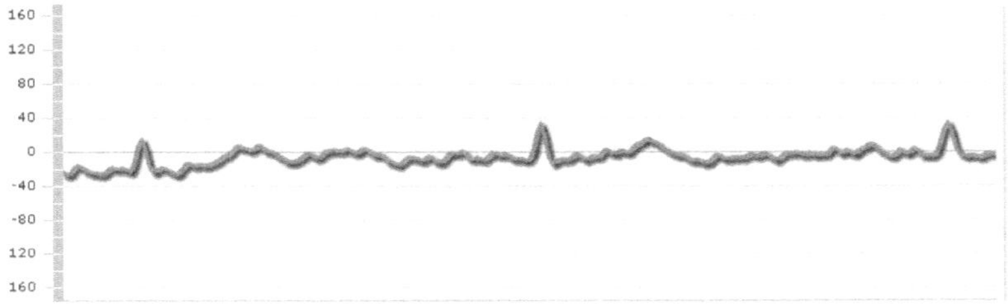

Fig. 6. The remote ECG monitoring verification for the application interfaces

It should be pointed out that in this remote application an XML-based data interface is used corresponding to those APIs defined in Table 4. The detailed XML description is omitted here.

5 Conclusion and Future Work

This paper presents a low-cost ubiquitous family healthcare framework which handles heterogeneous sensing bio-data via a general bio-date model, compatible for both dynamic waveforms and spot values and feasible for both APIs and XML/database. A reference implementation based on revising current ECG, BP monitor and oximeter that could be bought on markets is presented to validate the framework. The devices are easily modified by adding Bluetooth modules and handled by a commonly-used computer serial port mapping. Final prototype experimental results are also shown. In future work, more portable application interfaces such as Web Services should be added to this framework to validate it to more vast applications. At the same time, more reliable and robust wireless bio-data gathering devices and wireless communication methods should be developed or used.

Acknowledgements

This work is supported by National High-Tech Research and Development Plan of China under Grant No. 2009AA011906 and National Core-High-Base Major Project of China under Grant No. 2009ZX01036-002-3.

References

1. Gu, L.: The Interfection of the Rising of General Medicine from the View of the Post-Modern Philosophy. J. of Medicine and Philosophy 26(10), 7–9 (2005)
2. Martin, J.C., Avant, R.F., et al.: The Future of Family Medicine: A Collaborative Project of the Family Medicine Community. Ann. Fam. Med. 2 (Suppl. 1), s3–s32 (2004)
3. Varshney, U.: Pervasive Healthcare and Wireless Health Monitoring. Mobile Networks and Applications 12(2-3) (2007)
4. Helal, A., Abdulrazak, B.: TeCaRob: Tele-Care using Telepresence and Robotic Technology for Assisting People with Special Needs. International Journal of Human-friendly Welfare Robotic Systems 7(3) (2006)
5. Seo, J.W., Park, K.: The development of a ubiquitous health house in South Korea. In: Davies, N., Mynatt, E.D., Siio, I. (eds.) UbiComp 2004. LNCS, vol. 3205. Springer, Heidelberg (2004)
6. Ng, J.W.P., Lo, B.P.L., et al.: Ubiquitous Monitoring Environment for Wearable and Implantable Sensors (UbiMon). In: The International Conference on Ubiquitous Computing (Ubicomp), Nottingham, England (2004)
7. Catherine, M., DesRoches Dr., P.H., et al.: Electronic Health Records in Ambulatory Care — A National Survey of Physicians. The New England Journal of Medicine 359(1), 50–60 (2008)
8. Google Health, `https://www.google.com/health`
9. BianQueFeiJiu: the Mobile Health Management and Rescue Service System, `http://www.mhealthservices.com`
10. EU ehealth news, `http://www.ehealthnews.eu`
11. HinaCom, Enterprise PACS, `http://www.hinacom.com`

A Lattice-Theoretic Approach to Runtime Property Detection for Pervasive Context

Tingting Hua[1,2], Yu Huang [1,2,⋆], Jiannong Cao[3], and Xianping Tao[1,2]

[1]State Key Laboratory for Novel Software Technology
Nanjing University, Nanjing, China, 210093
[2]Department of Computer Science and Technology
Nanjing University, Nanjing, China, 210093
huatingting0820@gmail.com, {yuhuang,txp}@nju.edu.cn
[3]Internet and Mobile Computing Lab, Department of Computing
Hong Kong Polytechnic University, Hong Kong, China
csjcao@comp.polyu.edu.hk

Abstract. Runtime detection of contextual properties is one of the primary approaches to enabling context-awareness. Existing property detection schemes implicitly assume that contexts under detection belong to the same snapshot of time. However, this assumption does not necessarily hold in the asynchronous pervasive computing environments. To cope with the asynchrony, we first model environment behavior based on logical time. One key notion of our model is that all meaningful observations of the environment have the lattice structure. Then we propose the LAT algorithm, which maintains the lattice of meaningful observations at runtime. We also propose the LATPD algorithm, which achieves detection of contextual properties at runtime. We implement algorithms over the open-source context-aware middleware MIPA, and simulations are conducted. The evaluation results show that LAT and LATPD support effective detection of contextual properties in asynchronous environments.

Keywords: Lattice, Property detection, Asynchronous environment, Context-awareness.

1 Introduction

Pervasive computing aims at building a computing paradigm in which computations are carried out in a non-intrusive manner [11,22,14]. Pervasive applications are typically context-aware [7,12,25]. To achieve context-awareness, applications need to detect whether contexts bear specified properties, thus adapting their behavior accordingly. For example, in a smart office scenario, the user may specify that: "the user is in the office and the temperature is higher than 30℃". Thus the application can adaptively turn on/off the air-conditioner.

Existing property detection schemes implicitly assume that contexts being checked belong to the same snapshot of time [4,13,25]. However, this assumption

⋆ Corresponding author.

Z. Yu et al. (Eds.): UIC 2010, LNCS 6406, pp. 307–321, 2010.

does not necessarily hold in pervasive computing environments [7,23,15,16,18]. Specifically, context collecting devices may not have synchronized clocks and may run at different speeds. They heavily rely on wireless communications, which suffer from finite but arbitrary delay [15,16]. Moreover, due to resource constraints, context collecting devices often adaptively schedule the dissemination of context data, which also results in asynchrony [23].

To cope with the intrinsic asynchrony in pervasive computing environments, we argue that the concept of time needs to be re-examined [20,15]. Instead of assuming the availability of global time or synchronized interaction, we introduce logical time [19]. Based on the notion of logical time, the set of all meaningful observations of the computing environment has the lattice structure [2]. This lattice structure serves as the basis for detection of contextual properties in asynchronous environments. Specifically,

- We reinterpret the problem of specification and detection of contextual properties based on logical time.
- We propose the LAT algorithm which constructs the lattice of all meaningful observations at runtime.
- We propose the LATPD algorithm, which achieves online detection of contextual properties based on the lattice of meaningful observations.

The LAT and LATPD algorithms are implemented over the open source context-aware middleware - MIPA [1], and simulations are conducted. The evaluation results show that, LAT and LATPD achieve effective detection of contextual properties, even when faced with dynamic changes in frequency of context data update, message delay and number of context collecting devices.

The rest of this paper is organized as follows. Section 2 discusses our model of environment behavior. Section 3 and 4 present the LAT and LATPD algorithms respectively. Section 5 presents the experimental evaluation. Section 6 reviews the related work. In Section 7, we conclude the paper with a summary and the future work.

2 Property Detection for Pervasive Context in Asynchronous Environments

In this section, we first describe how we model behavior of the asynchronous pervasive computing environment. Then we show the lattice structure among meaningful observations of the environment. Finally we discuss the specification and detection of contextual properties. Notations used in the model are listed in Table 1.

2.1 System Model

Detection of contextual properties assumes the availability of an underlying context-aware middleware [25] (see more discussions in Section 5.1). The middleware accepts contextual properties specified by the application and detects these

Table 1. Notations used in model of the environment behavior

Notation	Explanation
n	number of non-checker processes
$P^{(k)}$	the kth non-checker process
$s_i^{(k)}, e_i^{(k)}$	the ith state or event on $P^{(k)}$
P_{che}	the checker process
$\mathcal{G}$	global state (either consistent or inconsistent)
$\mathcal{C}$	consistent global state
$\phi, \phi^{(k)}$	CGS predicate ϕ, which is conjunction of all local predicate $\phi^{(k)}$

properties at runtime. Specifically, a collection of *non-checker processes* (denoted by $P^{(1)}, P^{(2)}, \cdots, P^{(n)}$) are deployed to detect states of specific regions of the environment. Examples of non-checker processes are sensor agents manipulating physical sensors. One *checker process* P_{che} collects environment information from non-checker processes, and achieves runtime detection of contextual properties. P_{che} is usually a third-party service deployed on the context-aware middleware.

We model all processes involved in property detection as a loosely-coupled message passing system, without any global clock or shared memory. Communications suffer from finite but arbitrary delay. Dissemination of context data may also be delayed due to resource constraints. We re-interpret the notion of time based on the classical Lamport's definition of the *happen-before* (denoted by '$\rightarrow$') relation resulting from message passing [19], and its "on-the-fly" coding given by Mattern and Fidge's vector clocks [21,8].

2.2 Consistent Global State (CGS) and the Lattice of CGSs

In a run of the system, each $P^{(k)}$ generates its trace, which consists of a series of *local states* connected by *contextual events* [1]:$s_0^{(k)}, e_0^{(k)}, s_1^{(k)}, e_1^{(k)}, s_2^{(k)}, e_2^{(k)} \cdots$. A *global state* $\mathcal{G} = [s^{(1)}, s^{(2)}, \cdots, s^{(n)}]$ is defined as a vector of local states from each $P^{(k)} (1 \leq k \leq n)$. One key notion in describing state of the environment is the *Consistent Global State* (CGS). If the constituent local states of a global state $\mathcal{C}$ are pairwise concurrent, $\mathcal{C}$ is a CGS, i.e. $\mathcal{C} = [s^{(1)}, s^{(2)}, \cdots, s^{(n)}], \forall\, i \neq j, \neg(s^{(i)} \rightarrow s^{(j)})$. The CGS denotes a meaningful observation of the environment [2].

It is intuitive to define the *precede* (denoted by '$\prec$') relation between two CGSs: $\mathcal{C} \prec \mathcal{C}'$ if $\mathcal{C}'$ is obtained via advancing $\mathcal{C}$ by exactly one step on one non-checker process. The *lead-to* relation (denoted by '$\leadsto$') between two CGSs is defined as the transitive closure of '$\prec$'. The set of all CGSs with the '$\leadsto$' relation define a lattice[3,2]. Fig. 1 shows an example of a two-dimensional lattice (meanings of the labels 'T' and 'F' will be explained in Section 4.2). The lattice structure among all CGSs serves as a key notion in the specification and detection of contextual properties in this work. P_{che} observes that the system advances

[1] For the ease of interpretation, we omit events and only use states in discussions below.

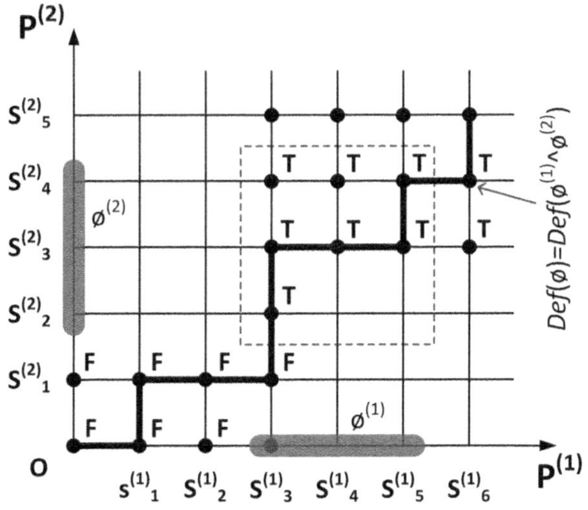

Fig. 1. Lattice structure and the $Def(\phi)$ detection based on Lattice

from one CGS to the next. This observed sequence of CGSs is defined as the *Linear Extension* (LE) of the lattice.

2.3 Specification of Contextual Properties

Contextual properties are delineated via logical predicates specified under our model of environment behavior. Specifically,

- *Local predicates* are specified over local states on some $P^{(k)}$. The value of a local predicate only depends on local information with respect to $P^{(k)}$. Local predicates delineate properties of specific region of the environment.
- *Global predicates* are specified over CGSs to delineate global properties of the environment. As CGSs are combined from local states from each non-checker process, CGS predicates are combined with local predicates connected by logical connectors $\wedge, \vee$ and $\Rightarrow$ (imply).
- *Predicate transformers* $Def(\cdot)$ and $Pos(\cdot)$ are applied over CGS predicates [5,2]. The predicate transformers are necessary because the asynchronous environment is intrinsically nondeterministic. The system can proceed along multiple possible paths (sequence of CGSs connected by '$\prec$') in the lattice. Thus, global predicates alone do not make any sense. $Def(\cdot)$ means that the predicate holds on every possible paths of system execution, while $Pos(\cdot)$ means that the predicate holds on at least one of the paths.

In this work, we study how to check conjunctive predicate

$$Def(\phi) = Def(\phi^{(1)} \wedge \phi^{(2)} \wedge \cdots \wedge \phi^{(n)})$$

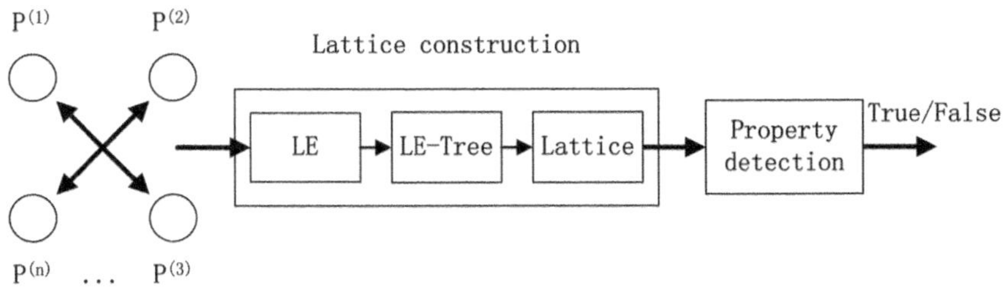

Fig. 2. The general process of property detection based on lattice

We focus on conjunctive predicates, because other logical connectors can be easily detected if we can detect conjunctive predicates [10,9]. In pervasive computing environments, since context data is intrinsically noisy, we focus on $Def(\cdot)$, which enables the application to ensure that the context bears user-specified properties.

2.4 Detection of Contextual Properties

The general process of property detection is shown in Fig. 2. The non-checker processes send *control messages* among each other to establish the happen-before relations required by the property detection. Non-checker processes also send *checking messages* to P_{che} for further detection of the specified property.

P_{che} employs the LAT algorithm to construct the lattice at runtime. It also employs the *Lattice-based Property Detection* (LATPD) algorithm to detect specified contextual properties at runtime. Each time P_{che} receives checking messages from non-checker processes, the LAT algorithm is invoked to construct the lattice incrementally. Once new CGSs are built into the lattice, the LATPD algorithm is invoked to detect specified properties. In the following Section 3 and 4, we describe the design of LAT and LATPD in detail.

During the detection of contextual properties, we assume that no messages are lost, altered, or spuriously introduced. We do not make any assumptions about FIFO nature of channels. The checker needs to use message numbers to guarantee that it receives the checking messages from one single non-checker process in a FIFO manner [10,9].

3 Lattice Construction

In this section, we discuss how the lattice of CGSs is constructed at runtime. The lattice is constructed in three phases:

- *Obtaining the Linear Extension (LE).* Due to the asynchrony in pervasive computing environments, local information sent earlier may arrive at P_{che} later. LAT first needs to obtain the CGS from all local states it collects and then obtain the LE, which consists of CGSs connected by '$\prec$'.

Algorithm 1. Obtaining the LE

```
Upon a new local state s of P^(k) arrives
Que^(k).enque(s);
i := k ; /* i is the index of P^(k) */
while i ⩽ n do
    s := Que^(k).head();
    if for the last CGS C in LE, s||C[j], (1 ⩽ j ⩽ n, j ≠ k) then
        s and C[j] forms a new CGS C', and C' is appended to LE;
        delete_head(Que^(k));
        i := 1;
    else
        i++;
    end if
end while
```

- *Constructing the LE-Tree.* Local states involved in the LE can be further combined to obtain all possible CGSs. These CGSs are constructed from CGSs in the LE and form the LE-Tree.
- *Obtaining the lattice.* The LE-Tree is a subgraph of the lattice. The lattice among all CGSs is obtained by adding the precede relations (between CGSs) which are not present in the LE-Tree.

3.1 Obtaining the LE

To obtain the LE, P_{che} first needs to identify the pair-wise concurrent local states and obtain the constituent CGSs. P_{che} maintains a queue $Que^{(k)}$ of local states for each $P^{(k)}(1 \leq k \leq n)$ and keeps the latest CGS $\mathcal{C}$ of LE. Upon the arrival of a new local state s on $P^{(k)}$, P_{che} first appends s to $Que^{(k)}$, and then scans the head elements of all queues. If s is concurrent with all other local states of $\mathcal{C}$, a new CGS $\mathcal{C}'$ is obtained, and P_{che} deletes s from $Que^{(k)}$. P_{che} iteratively checks CGS and delete head elements until no CGS can be obtained. The CGS obtained in turn forms the LE. Pseudo codes for obtaining the LE are listed in Algorithm 1.

3.2 Constructing the LE-Tree

The LE obtained above is only one of all the possible paths of system execution. We can obtain all other possible CGSs by combining local states involved in the LE. CGSs are gradually constructed from the LE and all possible CGSs form the LE-Tree. Specifically, when a new CGS is appended to the end of LE, P_{che} takes the new CGS as root, sets the previous LE-Tree as one of its subtree and generates other subtrees. CGSs in the new subtrees are obtained by combining newly arrived local states with local states on other non-checker processes. Construction of the LE-tree is inspired by [17] and the pseudo codes are listed in Algorithm 2.

Algorithm 2. Constructing the LE-Tree

Upon a new CGS $\mathcal{C}$ is appended to LE
link old tree's root CGS $\mathcal{R}$ to $\mathcal{C}$;
$\mathcal{R} := \mathcal{C}$;
construct_branch($\mathcal{R}$);

construct_branch($\mathcal{R}$)
$set_{CGS} = \{ \mathcal{C} \mid$ the CGSs precedes $\mathcal{R} \}$
for each $\mathcal{C}$ in set_{CGS} **do**
  if $\mathcal{C}$ has existed **then**
    continue;
  else
    link $\mathcal{C}$ to $\mathcal{R}$;
    $\mathcal{R} := \mathcal{C}$;
    construct_branch($\mathcal{R}$);
  end if
end for

Algorithm 3. obtaining the lattice

$set_{CGS} = \{ \mathcal{C} \mid$ the CGSs precedes $\mathcal{R} \}$
for each $\mathcal{C}$ in set_{CGS} **do**
  $set_{brother} = \{ \mathcal{C}' \mid$ the CGSs precedes $\mathcal{R}$ except $\mathcal{C} \}$;
  for each $\mathcal{C}'$ in $set_{brother}$ **do**
    $set_{pre} = \{\mathcal{C}_{pre} \mid$ the CGSs precedes $\mathcal{C}' \}$
    for each $\mathcal{C}_{pre}$ in set_{pre} **do**
      if $\mathcal{C}_{pre}$ precedes $\mathcal{C}$ **then**
        link $\mathcal{C}_{pre}$ to $\mathcal{C}$;
      end if
    end for
  end for
  obtaining_the_lattice($\mathcal{C}$);
end for

3.3 Obtaining the Lattice

The LE-Tree contains all possible CGSs and it is a subgraph of the lattice of CGSs. We complete construction of the lattice by generating all the possible edges which are not present in the LE-Tree. Specifically, a DFS traversal is conducted over the LE-Tree. In the lattice, the precede relation only exists from the CGS on the $(i-1)^{th}$ level to CGS on the ith level. Thus we just need to check the CGSs that are on the lower level of the current CGS. Pseudo codes for obtaining the lattice from LE-tree are listed in Algorithm 3.

4 Runtime Detection of Contextual Properties

In section 3, we discussed how LAT constructs the lattice of CGSs at runtime. In this section, we present how the LATPD algorithm detects user-specified

Algorithm 4. LATPD on the non-checker process side

Upon LP_k becomes true
send control-msg to other non-checker processes;
$VC^{(k)}[k] + +$;
Upon LP_k becomes false
$VC^{(k)}[k] + +$;
Upon Recv control-msg
$VC^{(k)} = max\{VC_{recv}, VC^{(k)}\}$;
Upon $P^{(k)}$ proceeds to a new local sate $s^{(k)}$
send $s^{(k)}$ to checker process;

contextual properties based on the lattice. Detection of contextual properties runs on both non-checker and checker process sides.

4.1 Property Detection on the Non-checker Process Side

Each $P^{(k)}$ maintains its logical vector clock $VC^{(k)}$. In order to establish the happen-before relation required for property detection, non-checker processes send control messages among each other. When local predicate changes from false to true, $P^{(k)}$ sends control messages to other non-checker processes. When local predicate value changes from true to false, $P^{(k)}$ just increases $VC^{(k)}[k]$. Whenever $P^{(k)}$ proceeds to a new local state, it sends a checking message to P_{che} for further detection of contextual properties. Pseudo codes of LATPD on the non-checker process side are listed in Algorithm 4.

4.2 Property Detection on the Checker Process Side

P_{che} keeps listening to the non-checker processes and detects specified contextual properties based on the lattice of CGSs constructed by the LAT algorithm (Section 3). The property detection process is incremental, i.e., when new CGSs are added to the lattice, P_{che} checks whether these newly added CGSs makes $Def(\phi)$ hold.

In the detection of $Def(\phi)$, we use *path_flag* to record information about the predicate detection. $\mathcal{C}_{cur}.path\_flag$ is true if and only if every path from initial CGS $\mathcal{C}_{ini}$ to current CGS $\mathcal{C}_{cur}$ contains at least one CGS on which ϕ is true. To compute $\mathcal{C}_{cur}.path\_flag$, we need the ϕ value on $\mathcal{C}_{cur}$ and the *path_flag*s of all the predecessors of $\mathcal{C}_{cur}$. If ϕ is true on $\mathcal{C}_{cur}$, then $\mathcal{C}_{cur}.path\_flag$ is true. If ϕ is false on $\mathcal{C}_{cur}$ while the *path_flag*s of all the predecessors of $\mathcal{C}_{cur}$ are true, $\mathcal{C}_{cur}.path\_flag$ is also true. Otherwise, $\mathcal{C}_{cur}.path\_flag$ is false.

Based on the *path_flag*, we detect $Def(\phi)$ if $\mathcal{C}_{cur}$ satisfies the following three requirements:

- $\mathcal{C}_{cur}.path\_flag$ is true. Then every path from $\mathcal{C}_{ini}$ to $\mathcal{C}_{cur}$ has at least one CGS that satisfies $Def(\phi)$.
- $\mathcal{C}_{cur}.\phi$ is false. This ensure that the ϕ is true on all paths not the same last CGS.

Algorithm 5. detecting $Def(\phi)$

set_{CGS} ={ $\mathcal{C}$ | the CGSs precedes $\mathcal{C}_{cur}$ }
for each $\mathcal{C}$ in set_{CGS} **do**
    if $\mathcal{C}.path\_flag$ is uncomputed **then**
        $detecting\_Def(\phi)(\mathcal{C})$;
    end if
end for
compute $\mathcal{C}_{cur}.path\_flag$;
if $\mathcal{C}_{cur}.path\_flag = true$ **then**
    if $\mathcal{C}_{cur}.\phi$ is false **then**
        if $\mathcal{C}_{cur}$ is on the LE **then**
            $Def(\phi)$ is true;
            $\mathcal{C}_{cur}.path\_flag := false$;
        end if
    end if
end if

- $\mathcal{C}_{cur}$ is on the LE. We only need to check the CGSs on LE to avoid redundant detection.

Fig. 1 shows an example of detecting $Def(\phi)$ on the lattice. The local predicates $\phi^{(1)}$ and $\phi^{(2)}$ are true on the local states with shadows. The T or F note on each CGS node is the value of *path_flag*. We detect the $Def(\phi)$ on $\mathcal{C} = [s_6^{(1)}, s_4^{(2)}]$ as $\mathcal{C}$ satisfies the three requirements. Whenever detecting the $Def(\phi)$ on a $\mathcal{C}$, P_{che} set $\mathcal{C}_{cur}.path\_flag$ false. Pseudo codes for the detection of $Def(\phi)$ are listed in Algorithm 5.

4.3 Discussion

On the non-checker process side, the number of message activities is $O(p)$, where p is the upper bound of length for each queue of non-checker processes. On the checker process side, the main space cost is for the lattice. We regard the space for a single CGS as one unit. The worst-case space cost is $O(p^n)$ when the lattice contains all possible CGSs. However, usually many of the global states are not consistent, thus not appearing in the lattice. The comparisons for adding one CGS into lattice is $O(n^3)$. In the next section, we further study the performance of LAT and LATPD via simulations.

5 Experimental Evaluation

In this section, we study whether LAT and LATPD effectively detect contextual properties by simulations. We first describe implementation of both algorithms. Then we describe the experiment setup. Finally we discuss the evaluation results.

5.1 Implementation

The detection of contextual properties assumes the availability of an underlying context-aware middleware. We have implemented the middleware based on one of our research projects - *Middleware infrastructure for Predicate detection in Asynchronous Environments* (MIPA) [1]. From MIPA's point of view, a pervasive computing environment is composed of an application layer, a property detection layer and a context source layer, as shown in Fig. 3.The context source layer persistently collects contexts of concern. The property detection layer receives contexts from multiple decentralized and asynchronous context sources, and detects specified contextual properties at runtime. The application achieves context-awareness by specifying contextual properties of its interest to MIPA. The checker process in charge of the property detection is implemented as a third-party service, plugged into MIPA. Non-checker processes are deployed to manipulate context collecting devices, monitoring different parts of the environment.

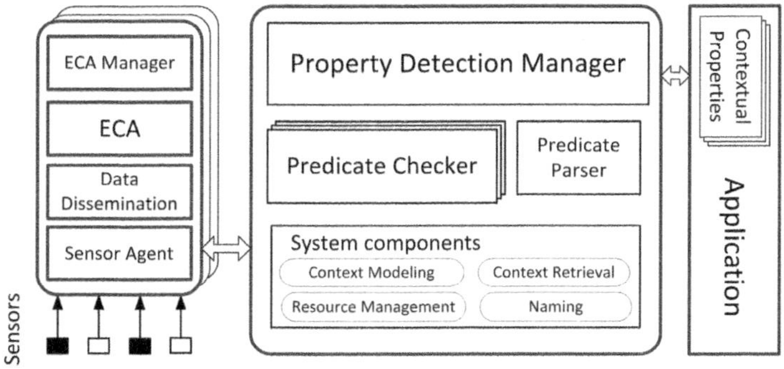

Fig. 3. System architecture of MIPA

5.2 Experiment Setup

We simulate a smart office scenario, in which a context-aware application intelligently controls the air-conditioner. Specifically, the application specifies $Def(\phi) = Def(\phi^{(1)} \wedge \phi^{(2)})$. Here, $\phi^{(1)}$ = "the user is in the office" and $\phi^{(2)}$ = "temperature inside the office is higher than 30℃". The user's location is detected when its smart phone connects to the access point inside the office. The temperature is detected by the temperature sensor in the office. The smart phone and the sensor node do not necessarily have synchronized clocks. They may also delay the update of context data to save energy. The duration of user's stay in an office follows the exponential distribution. The average durations the user stays inside and outside the office is 25 and 5 minutes respectively. The temperature also follows the exponential distribution. The temperature is above 30℃ for 5 minutes every 30 minutes.

In the evaluation, we study the probability that LATPD correctly detects the specified contextual property. We also study the time and space cost of LAT for maintaining the lattice. We first study the impact of asynchrony of the environment. Specifically we study the message delay and the interval between update of the context data. Then we study the impact of the number of non-checker processes. To study the performance of LATPD when faced with asynchrony, we get the probability of correct detection by calculating the ratio of $\frac{Num_{LATPD}}{Num_{phy}}$. Here, Num_{LATPD} stands for the number of times when LATPD detects specified contextual property, and Num_{phy} stands for the actual number of times specified property holds (according to physical time).

5.3 Effects of Asynchrony of the Environment

In this simulation, we first change the average message delay and investigate its impact on LATPD. As shown in Fig. 4, the probability of correct detection decreases linearly by 11.25% as the average message delay increases from 0s to 60s. The probability decreases because, as the message delay increases, the uncertainty of the environment increases. The application is thus faced with more meaningful observations (CGSs). Then LATPD has less chances to detect $Def(\phi)$.

Then we change the interval between context updates. As shown in Fig. 5, the probability of correct detection decreases slowly as the data update interval increases. When the update increases to around 20m, the decrease slows down. The update interval affects the probability similarly as the message delay does, since it also increases the uncertainty of the environment and makes LATPD faced with more CGSs.

The evaluation results show the impact of the asynchrony and justify our work for asynchronous environments.

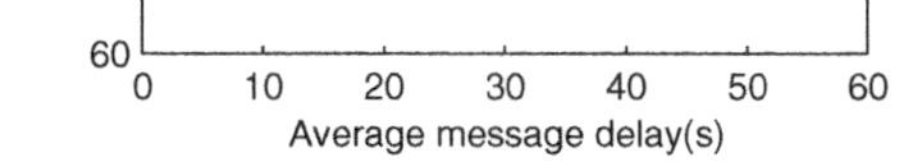

Fig. 4. Effects of tuning message delay

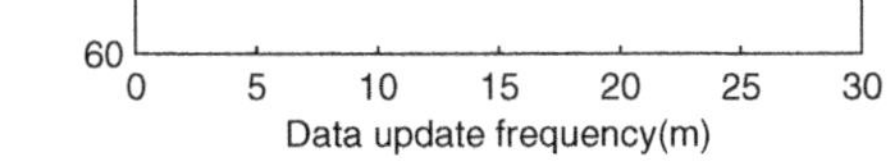

Fig. 5. Effects of tuning data update interval

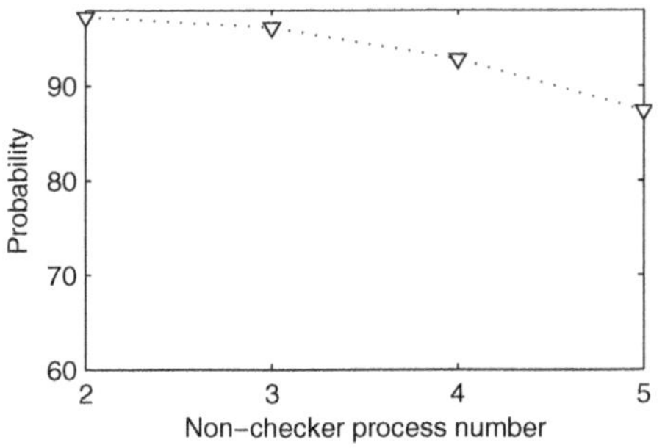

Fig. 6. Correct detection probability of increasing non-checker process number

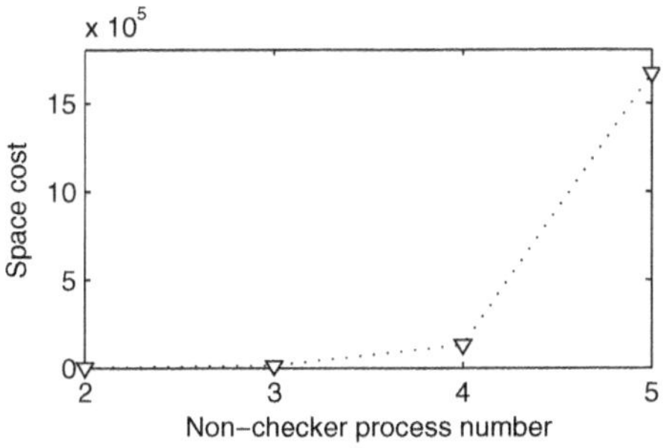

Fig. 7. Space cost for increasing non-checker process number

5.4 Effects of Tuning the Number of Non-checker Processes

In this simulation, we study how the number of non-checker processes impacts the cost of the LAT algorithm. We set the average message delay to 5s and the data update interval to 3m. Then we change the number of non-checker processes from 2 to 5. We find in the simulation that the probability of correct detection decreases as the number of non-checker processes increases, as shown in Fig. 6. This is mainly because when the number of non-checker processes increases, there are more chances that they do not concurrently hold. Thus $Def(\phi)$ has more chances not to hold.

Concerning the cost for lattice construction, we find that size of the lattice is greatly affected by the number of non-checker processes. As the number of non-checker process increases, the space cost increases exponentially, as shown in Fig. 7. This is in accordance with the analysis in section 4.3. A potential approach to reducing the space cost is to delete online part of the lattice, which will not affect further detection of contextual properties. We leave investigations on this issue to our future work.

The response time is relatively stable. The response time for each message from the non-checker process is within 1s. As the number of non-checker processes increases, there is no significant increase in the delay for detecting the contextual properties. This is also in agreement with the analysis in section 4.3.

6 Related Work

Various schemes have been proposed for contextual property detection. In [24], properties were modeled by tuples, and property detection was based on comparison among elements in the tuples. In [25], property constraints were expressed in first-order logic, and an incremental property detection algorithm was proposed. In [13], a probabilistic approach was proposed to further improve the effectiveness of property detection. However, existing schemes do not sufficiently consider the asynchrony in pervasive computing environments. It is implicity assumed that the contexts under detection belong to the same snapshot of time. Such limitations make these schemes do not work in asynchronous pervasive computing environments.

In asynchronous systems, the concept of time must be carefully reexamined. In [19], the causality resulting from message passing is used to define the *happen-before* relation. Based on the happen-before relation, logic clocks for asynchronous systems can be devised [8,21]. In [6], Cooper et al. introduce the checking of general constraints expressed by logic predicates. In [10,9], conjunctive predicates have shown its power of specifying contextual properties. These predicate detection schemes do not sufficiently utilize the lattice structure of asynchronous computations. In[17], the ideal tree is used to give a linear space algorithm for detection of $Pos(\Phi)$. However, the ideal tree does not contain sufficient information of the asynchronous computation and may not support detection of predicates other than $Pos(\Phi)$. Moreover, existing schemes are mainly designed for debugging of distributed programs. They only passively detect predicates. Our LAT and LATPD algorithms are proposed for achieving context-awareness based on property detection. LATPD requires the non-checker processes to proactively send messages among each other to build the temporal ordering required for property detection.

7 Conclusion and Future Work

In this paper, we study the problem of runtime property detection for pervasive context in asynchronous pervasive computing environments. Toward this objective, our contributions can be described as follows: i) we propose a lattice-theoretic framework for detection of contextual propreties; ii) we propose the LAT algorithm which constructs the lattice of CGSs at runtime. We also propose the LATPD algorithm which achieves online detection of contextual properties; iii) we implement both algorithms over the open-source context-aware middleware - MIPA. Simulations are conducted to evaluate the performance of LAT and LATPD.

In our future work, we will study the detection of dynamic properties delineating the behavior patterns of the pervasive computing environment. We also need to study how to reduce the space cost for maintaining the lattice of CGSs.

Acknowledgments

This work is supported by the National Natural Science Foundation of China (No. 60903024, 60736015, 60721002), the National 973 Program of China (2009CB 320702), the National 863 Program of China (2009AA01Z117) and the National Special Program for Grand Science and Technology Challenges of China (2009ZX 01043-001-06).

References

1. MIPA - Middleware Infrastructure for Predicate detection in Asynchronous environments, `http://mipa.googlecode.com/`
2. Babaoğlu, O., Fromentin, E., Raynal, M.: A unified framework for the specification and run-time detection of dynamic properties in distributed computations. J. Syst. Softw. 33(3), 287–298 (1996)
3. Babaoğlu, O., Raynal, M.: Specification and verification of dynamic properties in distributed computations. J. Parallel Distrib. Comput. 28(2), 173–185 (1995)
4. Bu, Y., Gu, T., Tao, X., Li, J., Chen, S., Lu, J.: Managing quality of context in pervasive computing. In: Proc. International Conference on Quality Software (QSIC 2006), Beijing, China, pp. 193–200 (2006)
5. Charron-Bost, B., Delporte-Gallet, C., Fauconnier, H.: Local and temporal predicates in distributed systems. ACM Trans. Program. Lang. Syst. 17(1), 157–179 (1995)
6. Cooper, R., Marzullo, K.: Consistent detection of global predicates. In: Proc. ACM/ONR Workshop on Parallel and Distributed Debugging, New York, NY, USA, pp. 167–174 (1991)
7. Dey, A.: Providing architectural support for building context-aware applications. Ph.D. Thesis, Georgia Institute of Technology (2000)
8. Fidge, C.J.: Partial orders for parallel debugging. In: Proc. ACM SIGPLAN and SIGOPS Workshop on Parallel and Distributed Debugging, Madison, Wisconsin, US, pp. 183–194 (1988)
9. Garg, V.K., Waldecker, B.: Detection of strong unstable predicates in distributed programs. IEEE Transactions on Parallel and Distributed Systems 7, 1323–1333 (1996)
10. Garg, V., Waldecker, B.: Detection of weak unstable predicates in distributed programs. IEEE Transactions on Parallel and Distributed Systems 5, 299–307 (1994)
11. Garlan, D., Siewiorek, D., Smailagic, A., Steenkiste, P.: Project aura: Toward distraction-free pervasive computing. IEEE Pervasive Computing 1(2), 22–31 (2002)
12. Henricksen, K., Indulska, J.: A software engineering framework for context-aware pervasive computing. In: Proc. IEEE International Conference on Pervasive Computing and Communications (PERCOM 2004), Orlando, Florida, USA, pp. 77–86 (2004)
13. Huang, Y., Ma, X., Tao, X., Cao, J., Lu, J.: A probabilistic approach to consistency checking for pervasive context. In: Proc. IEEE/IFIP International Conference on Embedded and Ubiquitous Computing (EUC 2008), Shanghai, China, pp. 387–393 (2008)
14. Huang, Y., Cao, J., Jin, B., Tao, X., Lu, J., Feng, Y.: Flexible cache consistency maintenance over wireless ad hoc networks. IEEE Trans. Parallel Distrib. Syst. 21(8), 1150–1161 (2010)
15. Huang, Y., Ma, X., Cao, J., Tao, X., Lu, J.: Concurrent event detection for asynchronous consistency checking of pervasive context. In: Proc. IEEE International Conference on Pervasive Computing and Communications (PERCOM 2009), Galveston, Texas, USA (2009)
16. Huang, Y., Yu, J., Cao, J., Ma, X., Tao, X., Lu, J.: Checking behavioral consistency constraints for pervasive context in asynchronous environments. In: Technical Report, Institute of Computer Software. Nanjing University (2009), `http://arxiv.org/abs/0911.0136`

17. Jegou, R., Medina, R., et al.: Linear space algorithm for on-line detection of global predicates. In: Proc. International Workshop on Structures in Concurrency Theory (STRICT 1995), pp. 175–189. Springer, Heidelberg (1995)
18. Kaveti, L., Pulluri, S., Singh, G.: Event ordering in pervasive sensor networks. In: Proc. IEEE International Conference on Pervasive Computing and Communications Workshops (PERCOMW 2009), Galveston, US, pp. 604–609 (2009)
19. Lamport, L.: Time, clocks, and the ordering of events in a distributed system. ACM Commun. 21(7), 558–565 (1978)
20. Lee, E.A.: Cyber-physical systems - are computing foundations adequate? In: NSF Workshop on Cyber-physical Systems: Research motivation, Techniques and Roadmap, Position Paper, Austin, Texas, USA (2006)
21. Mattern, F.: Virtual time and global states of distributed systems. In: Proc. International Workshop on Parallel and Distributed Algorithms, Holland, pp. 215–226 (1989)
22. Roman, M., Hess, C., Cerqueira, R., Ranganathan, A., Campbell, R.H., Nahrstedt, K.: A middleware infrastructure for active spaces. IEEE Pervasive Computing 1(4), 74–83 (2002)
23. Sama, M., Rosenblum, D.S., Wang, Z., Elbaum, S.: Model-based fault detection in context-aware adaptive applications. In: Proceedings of the 16th ACM SIGSOFT International Symposium on Foundations of Software Engineering (SIGSOFT 2008/FSE-16), pp. 261–271. ACM, New York (2008)
24. Xu, C., Cheung, S.C.: Inconsistency detection and resolution for context-aware middleware support. In: Proc. ACM SIGSOFT International Symposium on Foundations of Software Engineering (FSE 2005), Lisbon, Portugal, pp. 336–345 (2005)
25. Xu, C., Cheung, S.C., Chan, W.K., Ye, C.: Partial constraint checking for context consistency in pervasive computing. ACM Trans. Softw. Eng. Methodol. 19(3), 1–61 (2010)

Modeling Files with Context Streams

Qunjie Qiu, Gang Pan, and Shijian Li

Department of Computer Science, Zhejiang University, China
{qbark,gpan,shijianli}@zju.edu.cn

Abstract. Files are fundamental for information storage in computer operating systems. This paper explores user and environment context to improve personal file management. We focus on the user-oriented files in a computer operating system, which are usually operated manually, such as document files, image and video files. We formalize the dynamics of contexts to sequential signals, called context streams. Each context stream is a one-dimensional function of time. With the model of context stream, files can be reorganized using a set of discretely sampled streams based on file operation such as file creating, editing, and deleting. We proposed and implemented a file system with context streams, named ScudFile. Three applications of the ScudFile, file browsing, file searching, and file recommendation, are introduced. The evaluation of time and usability demonstrates the effectiveness of the ScudFile system.

Keywords: Context-stream, context file system.

1 Introduction

Files are very important units to store data in computer operating systems. However, the increasing number of personal files makes users difficult to manage and access. In the past few years, the storage capacity of hard disks is increasing rapidly. People now do not worry about where to save the data any more. Nevertheless, the challenge is arising that how can we manage millions of personal files in a convenient manner.

Nowadays, the mainstream operation systems, such as Windows, Linux, and MacOS, basically use directory, a tree structure, to organize and manage files. In this way, each file has a unique file path, user can use this path to access a file. The advantage is that user can create a semantic file path to help find files, for example, we can create a directory of "publication" in the OS and put all the published papers in this directory. But with the growing number of files, tree directory exposed many shortcomings:

a) *File classification*: to create a semantic file path, users have to classify a file to a category, such as “music”, “movie”. However, in practice, so many files are difficult to be classified to a specific category, they often suitable for variety of categories while user classify.
b) *Access depth*: the more detailed classification, the deeper file stores in the tree directory structure, such as “F:/Music/Ch/Male/Pop/2000/fly.mp3”, users have to go deep five subdirectory to access the file of "fly.mp3". It is inconvenient for users to access a file with so long path.

Z. Yu et al. (Eds.): UIC 2010, LNCS 6406, pp. 322–336, 2010.

c) *Locating files*: users have to manually specify a path to locate files. However it is a huge burden for users to remember hundreds of thousands of files. It also causes a huge burden for users to give each directory a meaningful name.

Many efforts have been made to tackle these problems. Virtual file directory is a major solution, which uses various information to describe files, and then creates a similar directory access mechanism according to the description. Thus, user can use the traditional file access method to access files which they want, but the file path is made from file's description information. Context file system and semantic file system are examples of virtual file directory. Context file system uses the context information to describe files, and semantic file system uses semantic information [1,2]. They both facilitate the work of file search, but they don't alleviate the burden of file management. For either context or semantics as description information, users need to participate in creating description.

In this paper, we propose a context organization model-context stream to organize context information for files. It helps users find files quickly by automated description and analysis information. We focus on the files which users will access directly, that means system files are not under our consideration. We divide the files into two categories: user-oriented files and system-oriented files. User-oriented files are those users will operate manually, such as documents, audio, images, and video; System-oriented files are those an operating system needed and users usually do not need to know about, such as temporary files and binary program files. This paper is for the user-oriented files.

The paper is organized as follows. In Section 2, we describe the relative work. Section 3 describes the concept of context stream and show how to model files with context stream. A file system with context stream, named ScudFile, is presented and implemented in Section 4. In Section 5, we give three applications of the ScudFile system. Section 6 presents the evaluation, and Section 7 concludes the paper.

2 Related Work

Nowadays, file system is one of the basic modules in an operation system. Files are one of the most important storage forms [17]. In the ordinary PCs, the numbers of files almost reach millions. The growing file number makes users difficult to manage and access. How to manage the users' file? How to find the needed file quickly? These become very important.

Semantic file system [2] uses the key words and property information to describe files and directories. Based on the information, the file system creates virtual file directory to help users find the files which they want. To access a file, the file path will be parsed and translated to attribute-based queries. For example "User:Tony/Type:PPT/Name:lecture/" will be translated to the queries of "Query(User=Tony) and

Query(Type=PPT), Query(Name=lecture)" [4]. This approach makes the sequence of attributes insignificant. Semantic file system is potential to improve file search, but the process of description increases users' burden. Traditionally, semantic information comes from two sources: content analysis and manual configuration. Most users are unwilling to perform the tedious and time-consuming job. In addition, the manual job will bring unpredictable errors. Content analysis obtains the semantic information by analyzing the file path and keywords of file content. The disadvantage of this approach is that the information obtains from content analysis is often misunderstood by users. Even users are sometimes confused with what is the correct value.

Context file system uses the context such as time, location as description information and uses virtual file directory to access files. The ParcTab [13] project is to integrate context with file access. ParcTab associates files with location information. When users move between different locations, the file browser will change the file list. However, the ParcTab only uses location information to associate files. It has no effect for the files which are not sensitive to locations. The context file system in the Gaia [1,2,9] project uses several of context information to associate files. In the file system, users associate files and directories with scenarios, which are the combination of context information. When a user enters a pervasive computing environment, the context information from physical devices is compared with the description information of scenarios for preparing the eligible files and directory. Gaia uses context to organize information so that it is easier for users to find desirable material for launched or long-running applications. But it needs users to decide when the files will be used and manually adds to describe file. OmniStore [5,6] is a file system that automatically associates the context information to files. OmniStore needs the support of physical device to collect all the available context information. When a file is created, OmniStore uses the collected context information to describe the file. It collects context information at regular intervals. In the whole process, users have not any burden, and can find the files by the context of file creation.

Google file system (GFS) [17] is a scalable distributed file system for large distributed data. It provides fault tolerance while running on inexpensive hardware. And it delivers high aggregate performance to a large number of clients. There are many products and technologies of Google are based on GFS, such as Google Search and Google mail. GFS adopts one single master node which maintains all file system metadata and multiple chunkservers in one cluster. The client application implements the file system API and communicates with the master and chunkservers to write or read data.

Connections[7] is a file system search tool that provides fast file search. It combines traditional content-based search with context information gathered from user activity. Connections identify temporal relationships between files by tracing file system calls, and use the relationships to expand and reorder traditional content search results. This is similar to the data prefetching of the operation system, which use the relevance of files to accelerate searching.

3 Modeling Files with Context Streams

3.1 Context Stream: Dynamics of Contexts

Different from the traditional computing systems, ubiquitous computing systems use context information to allow applications to adapt to user's environment [10,12]. In order to organize and analyze the context information associated with files better, we propose a context organization model, called Context Stream, in which, each dynamic context has a context stream. The *i*th context stream is defined by a continuous sequential signal as function of time.

$$\mathcal{C}_i = c_i(t)$$

This concept is similar to character stream, audio stream, and video stream. The discrete data, arranged through a certain way, form a continuous stream of data set. Time is a special kind of context. Many contexts are dependent on it. Thus we use time as the marking of information organization. For example, the location context stream of a person can be denoted with C_L:

$$C_L = c_{L_1} c_{L_2} c_{L_3} c_{L_4} \ldots\ldots$$

Fig. 1 illustrates an example of the location context stream. It shows the location change of a person in a day.

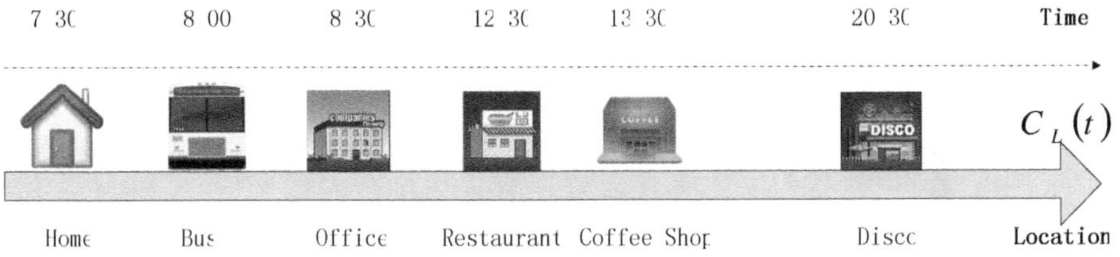

Fig. 1. Illustration of the location context stream

Usually we only need to analyze a part of context information in some discrete samples of context stream. Here we define the concept of *Context Substream*. The substream of the *i*-th context is defined as follows, which is a discrete signal sampled from a continuous context stream:

$$\Lambda_i = \{c_i(t_j^i)\}_{j=1}^{N_i}$$

It is a subset of a context stream. For example, in the context stream of location, we may only focus on the locations where a user has made file operations.

3.2 Modeling Files with Context Streams

Two aspects are concerned when integrating context information with files: 1) when is a file connected with context; 2) which context information is used to describe files.

In order to implement file description automatically, we choose the file operation as the trigger for updating file description and use the context of operation as description information.

We hope to use context streams to automatically describe files. The different categories of description information develop different modes of file description. If the context information of which job the file belongs to is used as the description, users often have to manually specify the job a file associated, e.g., the Gaia context file system [9]. Because nobody else knows exactly what the files are for, it is hard to get the context automatically. Semantic file system uses the semantic information as description which is from directory analysis and content analysis. We choose file operation as the trigger to associate the file with context information, which makes the process of labeling files automatic and temporal. A file operation can be detected by the application from file system. Compared with tedious file path, the context of file operation may be easier for users to remember.

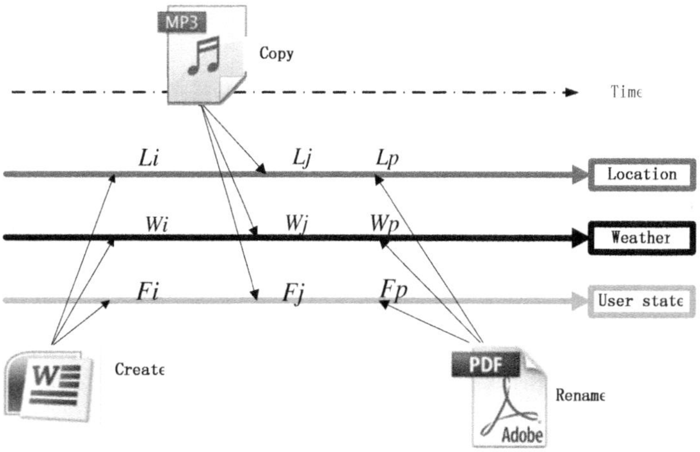

Fig. 2. Attaching files onto context streams at points of file operations. Here we show three context streams: location, weather, and user state.

As shown in Fig. 2, when a file operation happened, the target file will be "hung" on the context streams. Because the environment where users stay contains many kinds of context information, such as location, weather, and user state, the file will be described by multiple context information. From the perspective of context stream, the target file is hung on multiple context streams. The PDF file in the Fig. 2 is operated at the time of p, it is hung on the context streams of location, weather and user state at the point of time p simultaneously.

From Fig. 2 we can see that, the context stream can be considered as collection of the points hung with files and that without association with any file. The points hung with files form a context substream. The time point i, j and p on the location context stream, arranged in the temporal order, can make up of a context substream, where the file operations happen.

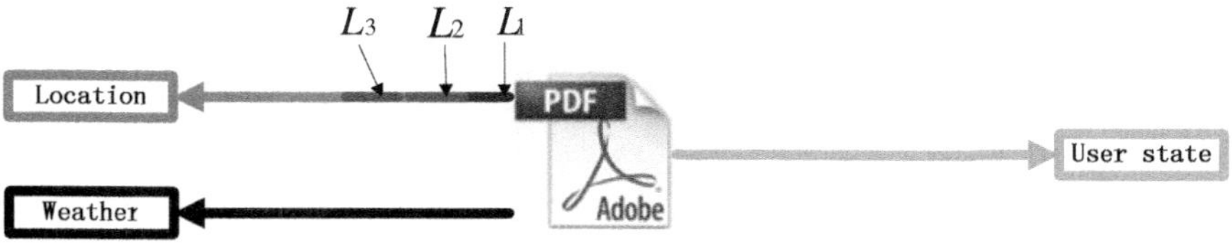

Fig. 3. Illustration of context substreams of a single file

Each single file s attached by several context substreams, in which we recoded all operations of the target file. As shown in Fig. 3, each substream for a specific context, contains the file operation history, i.e. the file has been operated in which location, under what weather, what the user state, and when the user operated:

$$des(t) = \begin{cases} C_L(t) \\ C_s(t) \\ C_W(t) \end{cases}$$

4 ScudFile: A File System with Context Streams

In the current operation systems, users locate files in two ways: 1) to locate files by browsing in the tree structure "folder/directory"; 2) to search files by keywords. However, both methods are inefficient when the amount of files becomes large. We consider a context-aware solution to associate files with context information such as time, location, and then use this information to help users to manage the files. In this section, we first describe ScudFile, a file system with context streams, then its implementation. ScudFile achieves to associate context streams with files automatically by tracing system calls when users operate on the files. The context streams are used to organize appropriate files for user applications.

4.1 Architecture of the ScudFile

Fig. 4 illustrates the architecture of ScudFile. It builds upon traditional file systems such as NTFS, FAT32 and EXT2. From a user's perspective, ScudFile is a kind of file managers like the Total Commander. Internally, ScudFile traces user's files operations and automatically associates files with context streams, and then help with file management. Its architecture is composed of five modules: Tracer, Context Acquisition, Context Description, Context Analysis and Context Management.

Tracer: this module sits between application and the file system, monitoring the file operations. Because our system focuses on the file operations which only from users, but not that from the system, the Tracer needs to distinguish the user-oriented files and the system-oriented files. Tracer is the trigger point when the ScudFile starts to update context streams of files.

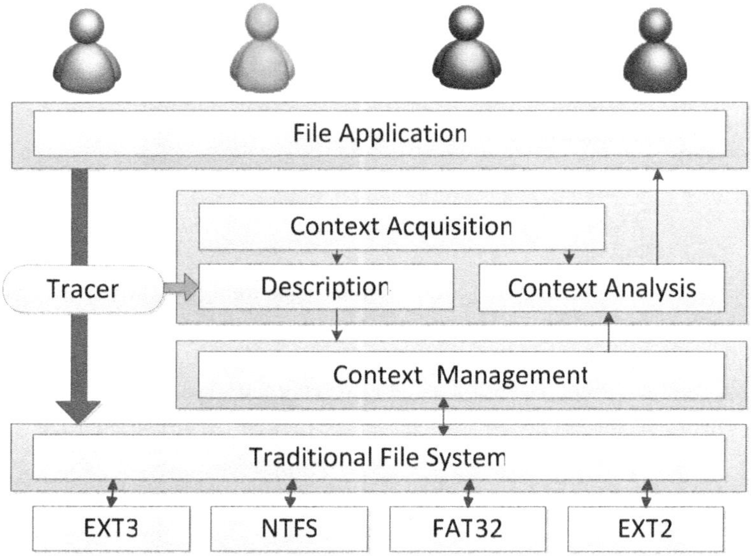

Fig. 4. ScudFile Architecture

Context Acquisition: this module is responsible for getting context information. In our system, we describe the file with context information at each point of file operation. This module needs to provide context information in nearly real-time manner since outdated information will affect the accuracy of context streams for files. Some context could be acquired from the operation system, such as time and file type. Others could be gathered from sensors or devices connected the operating systems such as location and velocity. It also could be obtained from Internet, such as weather.

Context Description: this module transforms the context information got from Context Acquisition into context description. We define a XML-specification format to describe file. The context description of a file holds the whole operation history of this file.

Context Analysis: this module is not in the process of context description. It is application-oriented. According to different application, using various algorithms, obtain the file list which is useful in the current context.

Context Management: context information in the file description will be rebuilt into context stream in this module. It manages relationship between files and context streams.

4.2 A MS-Windows-Based Implementation

We implement ScudFile on MS-Windows platform for its popularity. There exist three main issues for our implementation.

- **How to intercept the file operations**

The tracer component of the ScudFile watches user activities and traces all the file system calls. We use the hook technology to intercept each file system call. We choose the Detours library released by Microsoft, which can detect most of Win32 function calls. We intercept the Win32 functions concerning file operations by re-writing the in-memory code for target functions. Unlike static redirection or DLL re-linking, the interception techniques used in the Detours library are guaranteed to work to locate the target function regardless of the method used by application or system code.

```
// give a nick name of system call.
DETOUR_TRAMPOLINE(
BOOL WINAPI Trampoline_CopyFile(   LPCTSTR  lpExistingFileName,
                                   LPCTSTR lpNewFileName, BOOL bFailIfExists),
                                  CopyFile);
...............
////start replace system functions
DetourFunctionWithTrampoline( (PBYTE)Trampoline_CopyFile,
                              (PBYTE)Shadow_CopyFile);
..................
////stop replace system functions
DetourRemoveWithTrampoline( (PBYTE)Trampoline_CopyFile,
                            (PBYTE)Shadow_CopyFile);
```

There are two important functions: DetourFunctionWithTrampoline, which is used to replace system functions, and DetourRemoveWithTrampoline, which is used to remove the replace. As shown above, the first step to use the macro of DETOUR_TRAMPOLINE to give the system API a nick name, because we should call the function to do the real file operation after our extra work. In the example, we use "Trampoline_CopyFile" as the nick name of CopyFile which is the system function for copy files. Then use the DetourFunctionWithTrampoline to replace the target function with our function. Now all the system call of CopyFile becomes to call the function of Shadow_CopyFile. In Shadow_CopyFile, we do the task of context acquisition and updating file description. Before the function returns, we call the Trampoline_CopyFile to do the real work of file copy. From the system function, we can get the file name of target file. Because we only focus on the user-oriented files, after getting the operation information, we determine whether the target file is user-oriented or not.

- **How to semantically describe files**

We need to describe two kinds of information for files: file information and operation information. File information which usually keeps unchanged contains some static information such as file name and file path, which usually keeps unchanged. The operation information contains contexts such as operate type, operate time. In our system, we record the whole history of file operations for data analysis. The example shown below demonstrates an operation of file creation. For each operation, there will be a node of "SF:Action" to record the operation information. Sometimes, the target file will be operated frequently, such as action of file saving. For these frequent actions with a short time interval, we merge them into one action.

```
<SF:File>
    <SF:FileUser>qbark</SF:FileUser>>
    <SF:FileName>Lecture</SF:FileName>
    <SF:FilePath>F:\Work\</SF:FilePath>
    <SF:FileType>PPT</SF:FileType>

<SF:FileKeyWord>Meeting</SF:FileKeyWord>
    <SF:Action>
        <SF:OpType>Create</SF:OpType>
        <SF:Time>201002131224</SF:Time>
        <SF:Location>442</SF:location>
        <SF:Weather>Sun</SF:Weather>
    </SF:Action>
<SF:File>
```

- **How to hasten the processing of file context streams**

The extra work introduced by ScudFile will increase the computation cost. We use the technology of *multithreading* programming to reduce the negative effect. For all the file operations, we create a thread to do the task of context acquisition and file description when a file operation event is detected. In the function of *Shadow_CopyFile,* the extra work includes three aspects: 1) estimate if the target file is user-oriented or not; 2) get the current context information; 3) describe target file with context stream.

```
...............
DWORD ThreadId;
m_hThread = CreateThread( NULL,0,Routine,this,0,&ThreadId );
if( NULL == m_hThread )
{
        CloseHandle( m_hDir );
        m_hDir = INVALID_HANDLE_VALUE;
}
................
```

5 Applications

Here we introduce three applications based on ScudFile. These applications use the context streams of files to help users find files which may needed for data analysis.

5.1 File Browsing with Context Streams

Most of the current file systems use tree directory form to organize users' files. Users have to go deeper layer by layer to access a file they want. With the increase of file number, it becomes a boring job. We implement a file browsing based on ScudFile in terms of context streams to show files in the form of virtual directory.

In our implementation, files are mounted in the context stream according to the context of file operation. From the perspective of a context stream, files are arranged according to the operation time. The file list is not static, but varying with users' file operations. The file accessed recently will appear on the top of the file list.

As shown in Fig. 5, files are accessed by choosing the context stream. The leftmost buttons represent the different types of context streams. By clicking the buttons, we can choose a context stream and the system will give a detail information about the context stream. After a context is selected, for example, "home", the list of files which satisfy conditions will be shown in the right with virtual directory. All the files listed were ever operated by the user at home.

5.2 File Searching with Context Streams

Different from files searching based on keywords in traditional file managers, ScudFile enables the context information to help user's searching. For searching using keywords of file name or file content, user needs to keep in mind some information of target file. With the number of file increasing, it is a burden for users to remember so much information. Users may be easy to remember the operation contexts better than the miscellaneous file names, e.g. where the file was modified.

ScudFile has recorded the context of operations. Thus, user can search the target file through the context of operations, for example, weather and location. This application extends the function of content-based search.

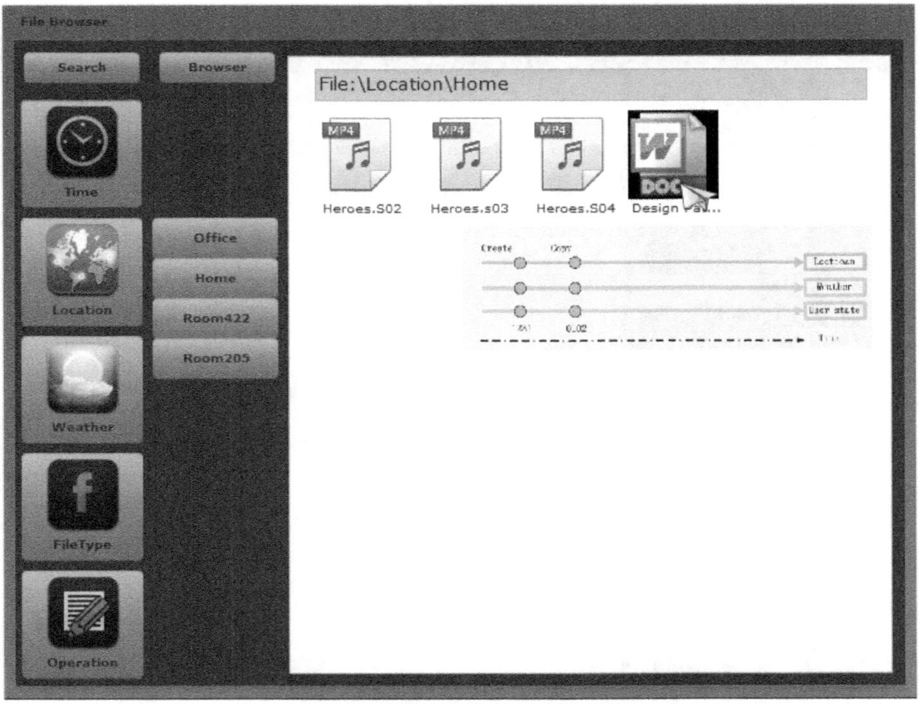

Fig. 5. The interface of the ScudFile browser. The leftmost lists contexts.

5.3 File Recommending with Context Streams

Some user behaviors are regular, so do file operations. User often has similar pattern of file accesses in the similar environment. For example, a user is accustomed to hearing music after dinner, so in that context, he often needs to browse music media files. We could provide these files to the user in advance, enabling users to quickly access. ScudFile has recorded the history of file operations, from the information of context stream, we can find the connection between contexts and file access.

We choose those contexts useful for representing the characteristics of operation to integrate in similarity measure, such as location, time, and file type. Location and time give us the most important environmental information, others such as weather or temperature is not related to file operation closely. File type and other file attribute give us which category file belongs to. We define the similarity between a context and a file using history information.

$$r = \frac{\sum_i^n x}{\sum_i^n y}$$

Where "n" is the number of the "similar" intervals on the context stream (a similar interval means a maximum continuous segment where all the context values are close

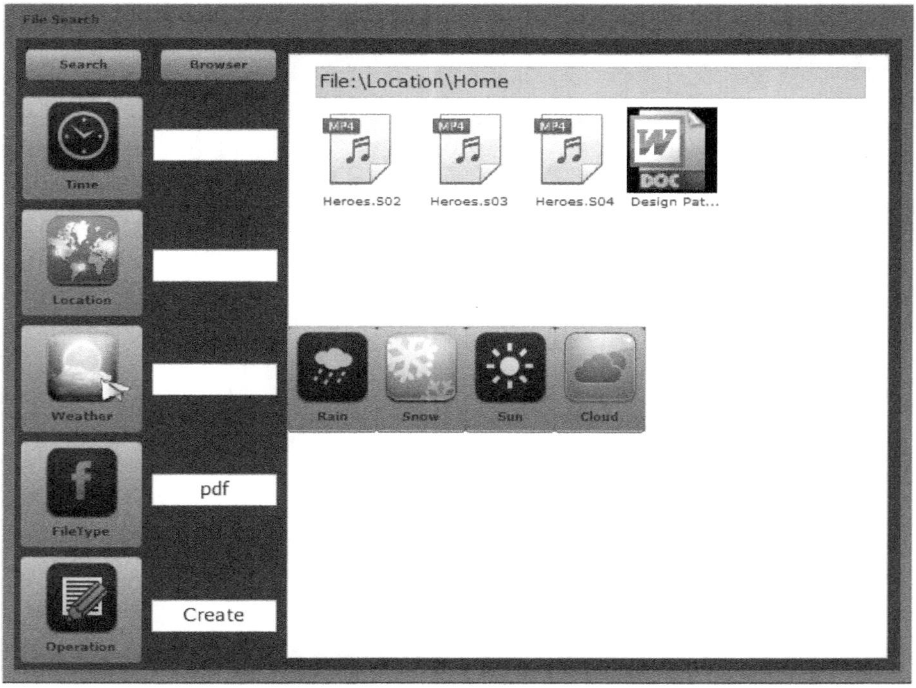

Fig. 6. The interface of file search in ScudFile. User is choosing the weather context stream as searching condition.

to the current context), "y" is the number of file operations in the last *i* similar intervals, and "x" is the number of file operations for a certain file type in the last *i* similar intervals. Therefore, the result represents the correlation between the context and file type. Then, to enhance the experience of file recommendation, we merge together the results of correlated file type, latest accessing time, and the neighbors of high correlated files to make a recommendation list.

6 Evaluation

In the section, we present two experiments for evaluation of our systems. The first one is time cost of file operations compared with the original Windows 7. The second evaluation is the usability test of the system.

1. Generation of similar intervals and get: *n*
2. Search file operations in these intervals on the context stream.
3. Count file operations in the first *i* similar intervals, and get the number pairs: (x, y)
4. Compute the *r*
5. Merge the results from file type, access time, and neighboring rule.
6. Output recommendation file list.

Fig. 7. File recommendation algorithm in ScudFile

6.1 Time Cost

The current implementation of ScudFile uses the hook technique to detect users' file operations, and add context information to the description file. It causes extra computational cost besides file operations. In order to evaluate the difference of time cost between the ScudFile and the original in Windows 7, we carried out four types of file operations, create, copy, rename, and delete, with 20,000 times for each operation. The hardware configuration of desktop computer used in the experiment is Intel Dual Core CPU E5200, 2.5GHz with 4G DRAM. The operating system used is Microsoft Windows 7. The result is shown in Fig. 8.

From the experimental results, we can see the extra time cost caused by our system is not significant, just couples of milliseconds for each time of operation. That means the extra time will not affect users when using the ScudFile. The good performance is mainly attributed to the employment of multithreading technology. When we want to update file description, we create a new thread.

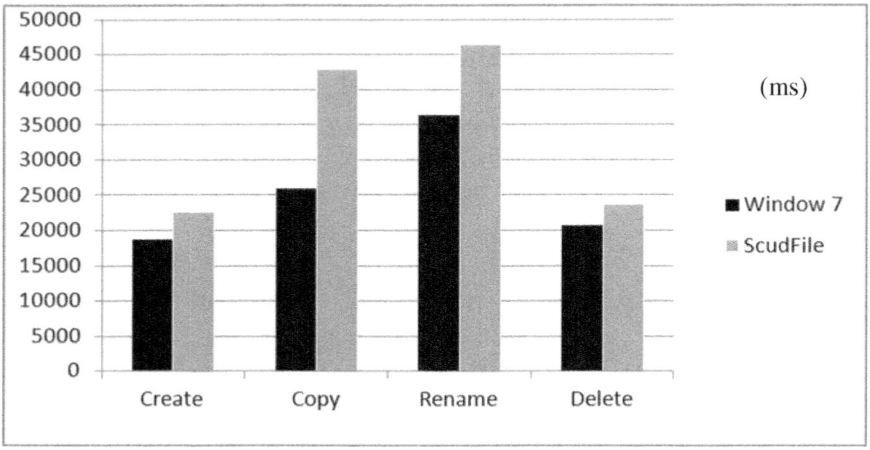

Fig. 8. Time cost comparison in the case of 20,000 operations

6.2 Usability Test

To evaluate the user experience of our system, we employed five volunteers to use our system. After one week of usage, we interviewed them to ascertain their opinions and observations on our system. All the five users were provided the following questionnaire in order to get their opinions.

Question 1 I find the system is easy to use.
1 … 2 … 3 … 4 … 5
Question 2 I find the system is efficient to locate files
1 … 2 … 3 … 4 … 5
Question 3 I find the system is easy to learn.
1 … 2 … 3 … 4 … 5
Question 4 I find the system has no effect for file operation speed.
1 … 2 … 3 … 4 … 5
Question 5 My overall impression of the ScudFile system.
Very negative 1 … 2 … 3 … 4 … 5 Very positive

The Table 1 shows the quantitative evaluation results of the five questions. All the users complete the use experiment, and give their opinions of the usability. From the

Table 1. Quantitative evaluation of the usability (Qn = Question n)

Volunteer	Q1	Q2	Q3	Q4	Q5
A	4	4	5	4	4
B	3	4	4	5	4
C	4	4	4	4	3
D	4	3	5	5	4
E	5	3	4	5	4
Average	4	3.6	4.4	4.6	3.8

result, we can learn that the ScudFile has little effect to speed of file operations, and is easy to use for most of people. The result of Q2 shows that the accuracy of locating files is still a challenge in our system. This would be our main work in the future.

7 Conclusions

As individual data files grow, organizational and search tools for file management grow increasingly important. How to integrate context with files, how to enhance users' convenience without increasing the burden on users become new issues. In this paper, we presents context stream to organize files, and build a ScudFile file system integrated with context stream. It can automatically connect contexts with files by tracing the file system calls. We also implement three applications: file browsing, file searching, file recommendation. The evaluation result demonstrates that the ScudFile is effective to help personal file management. The idea of association of files with context streams is expected to be integrated into traditional files systems to improve users' experience of personal file management.

Acknowledgements

This work is supported in part by the National High-Tech Research and Development (863) Program of China (No. 2008AA01Z149, 2009AA011900), the HGJ Program (2009ZX01039-001-002-004), and Zhejiang Provincial NSF (No.Y1090690). The corresponding author is Dr. Gang Pan. The authors would thank anonymous reviewers for their valuable comments.

References

1. Hess, C.K., Campbell, R.H.: A Context-aware Data Management System for Ubiquitous Computing Applications. In: Proceedings of the 23rd International Conference on Distributed Computing System, Providence, RI, May 19-22 (2003)
2. Gifford, D.K., Jouvelot, P., Sheldon, M.A., O'Toole Jr., J.W.: Semantic File System. In: ACM Symposium on Operating System Principles, pp. 16–25. ACM Press, New York (1991)
3. Gopal, B., Manber, U.: Integrating content- based access mechanisms with hierarchical file system. In: Sysposium on Operating Systems Design and Implementation, pp. 265–278. ACM, New York (1999)
4. Hess, C.K., Campbell, R.H.: An application of a context-aware file system. Person Ubiquit. Comput. 7(6), 339–352 (2003)
5. Karypidis, A., Lalis, S.: OmniStore: Automating data management in a personal system comprising several portable devices. Pervasive and Mobile Computing Journal 3(5) (October 2007)
6. Karypidis, A., Lalis, S.: OmniStore: A system for ubiquitous personal storage management. In: Fourth IEEE International Conference on Pervasive Computing and Communications (PerCom 2006), Pisa, Italy, March 13-17 (2006)
7. Soules, C.A.N., Ganger, G.R.: Connections: Using context to enhance file search. In: Proceedings of the 20th ACM Symposium on Operating Systems Principles (2005)

8. Clifford Neuman, B.: The Prospero File System: A Global File System Based on the Virtual System Model. Computing Systems 5(4), 407–432 (1992)
9. Roman, M., Hess, C.K., Cerqueira, R., Ranganat, A., Campbell, R.H., Nahrstedt, K.: Gaia: A Middleware Infrastructure for Active Space. IEEE Pervasive Computing, 74–83 (October-December 2002)
10. Dey, A.K.: Understanding and suing context. Personal Ubiquitous Comput. 5(1), 4–7 (2001)
11. Satyanarayanan, M., Kistler, J., Kumar, P., Okasaki, M., Siegel, E., Steere, D.: Coda: A Hignly Available File System For a Distributed Workstation Environment. IEEE Trans. Computers 39(4), 447–459 (1990)
12. Dey, A.K., Abowd, G.D.: Towards a beter understanding of context and context-awareness. Technical report FIT-GVU-99-22, Georigia Institute of Technology (1999)
13. Schilit, B.N., Adams, N., Want, R.: Context-Aware Computing Applications. In: IEEE Workshop on Mobile Computing Systems and Application, pp. 85–90 (1994)
14. Amer, A., Long, D., Paris, J.-F., Burns, R.: File access prediction with adjustable accuracy. In: International Conference on Performance, Computers and Communication (2002)
15. Song, Y., Choi, Y., Lee, H., Kim, D., Park, D.: Searchable virtual file system: Toward an intelligent ubiquitous storage. In: Chung, Y.-C., Moreira, J.E. (eds.) GPC 2006. LNCS, vol. 3947, pp. 395–404. Springer, Heidelberg (2006)
16. Lei, H., Duchamp, D.: An analytical approach to le prefetching. USENIX Annual Technical Conference. In: USENIX Association (1997)
17. Ghemawat, S., Gobioff, H., Leung, S.-T.: The google file system. In: SOPSP 2003: Proceedings of the Nineteenth ACM Symposium on Operating Systems Principles, pp. 29–43 (2003)
18. Google, http://www.google.com/

CASPER: Mining Personalized Services

Jeongkyu Park and Keung Hae Lee

Hanggongdae gil 100, Hwajeon-dong, Deogyang-gu, Goyang-city,
Gyeonggi-do, 412-791, South Korea
{fcopark,khlee}@kau.ac.kr

Abstract. Context-aware computing has brought a new style of human computer interaction. Computing is moved into the background of the user's environment. Devices collaborate to exhibit smart behaviors for the user. Despite much progress in research on context-aware services, few studies have addressed the issue of creating new context-aware services catered to a person. This paper presents CASPER, a novel method of constructing personal context-aware services. CASPER observes the behavior of the user in the service domain and identifies the patterns that can be mapped to useful context-aware services for him/her. We discuss the CASPER model and an experiment that we conducted as a proof of concept. The result of the experiment shows that CASPER is able to discover personal context-aware services from the living data of the user.

Keywords: Context-awareness, Context-aware Service, Pattern Analysis, Personalized Service.

1 Introduction

Context-aware computing has created a new style of human computer interaction. In context-aware computing, computers go behind the scene and appear when necessary. The user can enjoy a service that is automatically launched by the underlying computing system when he/she needs it. As the spectrum of computing services widens and the number of available services grows, the user faces an increasingly complex task of knowing about right services. Context-aware computing can alleviate this difficulty by moving the burden of decision from the user to the computing system, which oversees the user's situation and finds a service appropriate for the situation. Context-aware computing will make our lives more convenient. Despite much progress in context-aware computing research, few researchers address the issue of how to create useful context-aware services.

1.1 Personal Context-Aware Service

Most context-aware services are designed for general purposes. For example, a location-based map service showing nearby gas stations and shopping centers is a service targeted for general users. A service that turns on the light when someone enters a meeting room doesn't distinguish who the person is. Although these types of common

Z. Yu et al. (Eds.): UIC 2010, LNCS 6406, pp. 337–351, 2010.

services are powerful and beneficial to every user, their designs are based on a common denominator approach and inherently weak in dealing with personal needs.

Useful context-aware services change from person to person. A useful service for a person may turn out not so useful to another [10]. Personal context-aware services are the services targeted for a specific user. We believe that personal context-aware services can extend the benefit of context-aware computing beyond what common service approaches alone can offer. Although a common service approach can support personalization to some extent through parameterization of user preferences, it obviously cannot match a wide variety of personal needs. One's personal service needs can be handled better if services are built from personal requirements to begin with.

1.2 CASPER

Context-aware services are usually defined using service definition tools and specification languages. In general, these tools and languages are intended for developers and require programming knowledge that transcends the end user. Context-aware services would be best described by the user, who will actually use them. However, the user may not know about all the useful services that can make her life easier. A considerable amount of human activities are iterated in trivial rounds of daily life. Continuously iterated activities tend to occur unconsciously. For this reason, some regularly repeated behaviors with which the user can be helped often go unnoticed.

CASPER is a method of defining personal context-aware services and represents our effort for offsetting the shortcomings of common service approaches. In the daily life, a person takes actions based on his/her situations. We can view a person's life as a series of events observed in the service domain where she resides. It is our hypothesis that if we can identify behavior patterns of a user, we can create useful context-aware services which are personalized for the particular user. CASPER carefully observes a user's life and deduces behavior patterns embedded in it to externalize them as context-aware services. CASPER performs this task with minimal human intervention. We believe that CASPER can serve as a means of defining context-aware services complementary to common service approaches.

2 Related Work

Earlier works on context-aware services may be divided into two categories: studies on service infrastructures [1][2][3][4][5] and those on service definition [6][7][8][9][10]. This paper focuses on the latter, context-aware service definition. Works on context-aware service definition can be further divided into two subgroups depending on who defines the service. A group of studies assumes that context-aware services are defined by the developer or skilled engineers [6][7][8]. The other group believes that services should be defined by the end-user, who knows better about what he/she wants [9][10]. Both approaches have strengths and weaknesses. Developer-defined services would be more appropriate for common services that are intended for general users compared with those defined by end users. On the other hand, end user-oriented service definition methods offer a more effective means of facilitating the development of personalized context-aware services; it is the end user who knows best about useful services for his/her own life. However, even a simple specification method involves a certain level of technical knowledge and experience which may overwhelm the end user.

Well-known specification languages for context-aware services are ECA-DL [7] and SOCAM[6]. ECA-DL (Event-Condition-Action Domain Specific Language) is a specification language that allows a context-aware service to be defined by specifying events, conditions, and actions. ECA-DL supports clauses for scoping, selection, and iteration. It also supports various operators, wild card expressions and events. These programming language constructs give ECA-DL a strong expressive power. However, the complexity of the language makes ECA-DL unreachable for most end users. SOCAM is another language for defining context-aware services. It expresses a context-aware service using simpler logical operators such as "and" and "or." The SOCAM language is relatively simpler and easier to use than ECA-DL. However, end users may still find it highly technical and difficult to use.

JIGSAW supports a method of defining a context-aware service by the end-user[9]. It introduces puzzle pieces, each of which represents an event that may occur in the service domain. An end user defines a context-aware service for herself by simply arranging JIGSAW pieces in a row. For example, the user can define a context-aware service that can be put as "Turn on the light of the living room when a person enters the house." by placing a JIGSAW piece describing the user entering a house and then another with a living room light on. While JIGSAW is simple to use, its limited expressive power makes it difficult to describe more general situations. Moreover, as the number of situations and events grows, the definition process will easily get convoluted.

Another notable research known as 'a CAPpella'[10] describes a demonstration-based context-aware service definition method. It can train the context-aware system through demonstration of a desired behavior. If a user wants to create a context-aware service like "Turn on the office light when a person enters the office," the user instructs 'a CAPpella' to start recording of the situation. The user then actually demonstrates the desired context-aware behavior by entering the office, turning on the light, and finally, informing the system of the end of the situation. The sensor-enabled computing system records the events observed during the demonstration. Then, the user can review recorded events and define the desired behavior by marking a situation and corresponding actions using the user interface system of 'a CAPpella'. In our view, it is a shortcoming of 'a CAPpella' to require demonstrations on purpose and the editing of recorded events to mark a situation and actions.

Brdiczka et al. explains another interesting service definition method based on image-processing[11]. The user defines specific situations with their images and related actions for the situations. For instance, suppose that when someone lies down, the light should be dimmed. If the system detects a situation of someone's lying down, it launches the action "dim the light." This method assumes image-processing and machine-learning capabilities. We view that it would be difficult to support situations involving concepts without matching images such as humidity, temperature, time and so on.

From our perspective, the above methods share a common limitation. None of them address the issue of how we can create context-aware services that are useful to the user. We believe that it is a difficult but important issue that needs to be addressed. Casper can be viewed as an interface agent described by Lieberman [17]. This paper's contribution to the field is the dynamic creation of context-aware services based on the observation of the user in real life.

3 The CASPER Model

CASPER is a method for creating personal context-aware services. New computing services come to existence in two ways. First, although very difficult, some computing services are invented. More often, services are designed based on the user requirements and experiences. CASPER is unique in that it derives services from user experiences.

CASPER's focus is on making useful services pertinent to a particular user. CASPER attains this goal with an algorithmic procedure which searches for potential context-aware services in the user's actual living data. CASPER first draws out user's behavior patterns manifested in her living data. Selected behaviors are transformed into context-aware services. The process of CASPER's service definition can be automated, human intervention being minimized.

We believe that CASPER can be used in many different smart environment settings such as homes, offices, hospitals, schools, etc. For the scope of this paper, we will confine our discussion to a smart home environment. While majority of current home devices are yet used individually, a plenty of sensor-equipped, instrumented, and networked devices will be put to work together to create smart services thanks to home networking and standardization efforts[12][13][15]. We first define the data model for CASPER as below:

[Event]
Time: $\mathbb{N}$

EventOccurrence

e:Event
t: Time

EventList

el : seq EventOccurrence

$\forall i,j : \mathbb{N} \bullet i < j \Rightarrow el[i].t <= el[j].t$

___*Service*___________________________

condition, action : Event
UserLivingData: EventList

3.1 Event List

For the purpose of creating personal context-aware services for a user, we model the behavior of a human who lives in a smart home as a sequence of recorded events such as "door opened," "light turned on," etc. that occurred in the service domain of the user over a period of interest. We will call this collection of data *User Living Data*. An *Event* denotes any action that causes a state transition on a device found in the service domain. An *Event Occurrence* is an event occurred at a specific time. An *Event List* is a set of collected events arranged in a temporal order. Formally, an event list is a sequence of ordered pairs of the form (e, t), where e and t denotes an event and the time it occurred, respectively. CASPER represents a user's living data for processing as an event list.

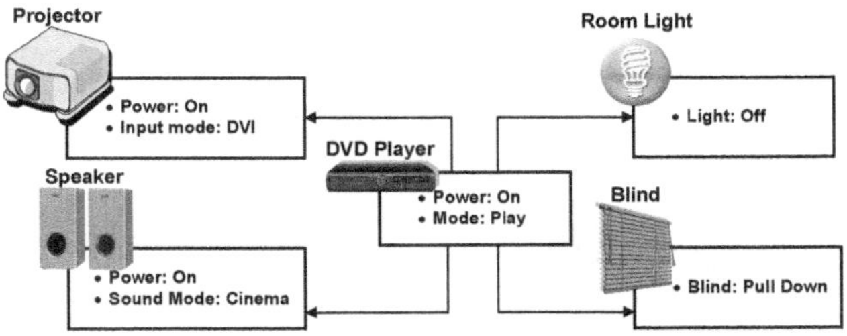

Fig. 1. A Home Theater Scenario

The events associated with a user's living give a clue to her preferences. It is our observation that we can make personal context-aware services by exploiting this information present in the living data of the user. To explain it further, let's take a look at a typical home theater scenario shown in Figure 1. In this scenario, a user wants to watch a movie with a DVD player on a big screen using a high resolution projector and a hi-fi stereo system. He first turns on the DVD player to play a movie. He then starts the projector and changes its input mode to "DVI." He also turns on the speaker and put its sound mode to "Cinema." Finally, he turns off the room light and pulls the blind down to be immersed in the movie. Each action taken in the course of controlling the devices is an event. In CASPER, an event plays dual roles, namely, *Condition* (a firing condition) and *Action*. When an event is interpreted as a condition, its occurrence may trigger an action, which is also an event. For example, the event of starting a movie can be viewed as the context for launching a service being set, which leads to take actions for preparing the equipment such as the projector, the speaker, the room light, and the blind. CASPER reasons context-aware services from a series of events recorded in the event list.

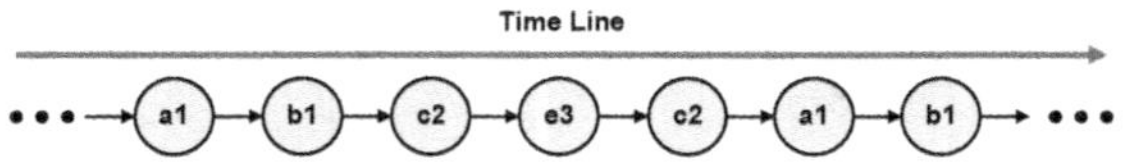

Fig. 2. An Example of Event List

Figure 2 shows an example event list. In this figure, a circle represents an event. Events on the left of an arrow precede in time those on its right. We define a context-aware service as a pair of events, namely, an execution condition and an action to be taken. A context-aware service consisting of events *x* and *y* is denoted by <x,y> and is interpreted as when *x* occurs, *y* follows.

We now explain how CASPER creates personal context-aware services from user living data. The CASPER method consists of four steps, namely, cutoff, decomposition, selection and implementation. While some of these steps can be merged with others, we keep this structure for the benefit of explanation.

CASPER takes a user's living data as the input and processes them to produce a set of context-aware services for the user. In order to do this, the cutoff step first identifies proximate events that occurred relatively close in time. The decomposition step extracts service candidates from cutoff lists. The selection step reaps qualified candidates as final services, which can be translated into a form executable on the target context-aware platform. The selection step can be refined by an additional step of filtering anomalous scenarios. We now explain each of the steps in more detail.

3.2 Cutoff

The *cutoff* procedure groups a series of proximate events to analyze causality among them. As mentioned above, a context-aware service is modeled as a pair of an execution condition and an action. We suspect that if an action is triggered by a previous event, the two events will appear not too far apart in time. In general, an event that triggers an action is more likely found in a recent past than at a distant point in time. This is because when there is a large time gap, an earlier action may be superseded by a more recent one. It is even possible that the whole situation changes. Suppose, for example, that having finished watching a movie in the living room, the user enters another room and starts reading a book. The events that occur from this point on will hardly have causal relationship with those that occurred during the movie watching. For this reason, CASPER looks for events that appeared near when making a context-aware service out of an event list.

Figure 3 demonstrates the cutoff process. Iterating on each event of the event list, we group all the events existing within a time interval, which we call *cutoff time*. Initially, event a1 is grouped with events b1 and c2, which exist within the distance of cutoff time *T*.

In effect, we are grouping actions of which a1 may have been the cause. In other words, events b1 and c2 are action candidates in our search for pairs of cause and action. A white circle denotes an execution condition, a dark circle being an action triggered by the condition. Upon the next round, b1, the next event, is grouped with c2, e3, and c2. In this fashion, CASPER creates a set of cutoff lists for the given event list.

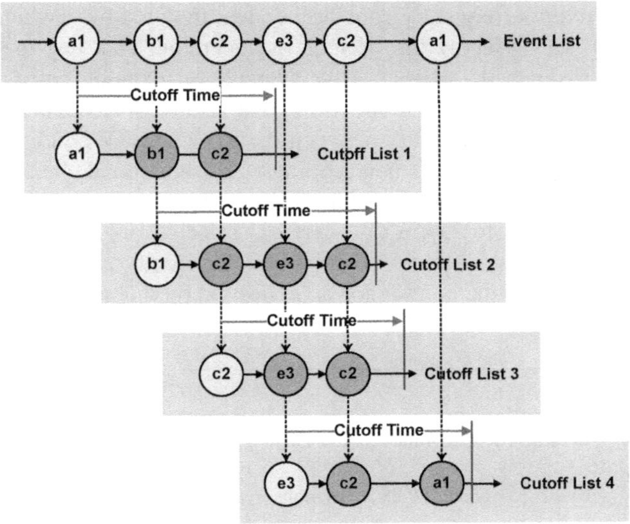

Fig. 3. A Cutoff Example

3.3 Decomposition

Decomposition is a process of identifying which event is actually related to which action. In the decomposition step, a cutoff list is broken into a set of *CA*'s, where a CA (Condition-Action) is a pair of a condition and an action, whose causality is yet to be examined. Figure 4 shows an example of a decomposition process.

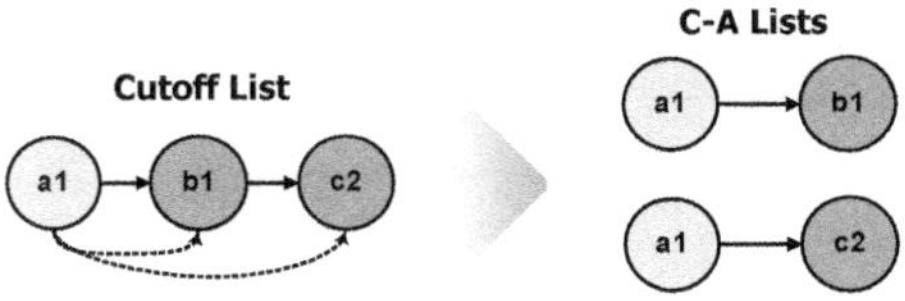

Fig. 4. An Example of Decomposition

In the cutoff list, events b1 and c2 occurred near event a1. It suggests that they may have occurred as a consequence of event a1. For example, if a1 is always followed by b1, we may be able to conclude that a1 triggered b1. Performing decomposition on all cutoff lists, we get a collection of CA's, which are service candidates. Later, CASPER will check the causality of each CA to make final choices.

3.4 Service Selection

In this step, we select viable CA's. Each CA we obtained during decomposition is examined to be selected or discarded based on two criteria. First, we discard any event that occurred not frequently enough, i.e., less than *m* times, where *m* is the minimum frequency value set by the user or the operator. This test prevents spurious CA's from being selected as services. With *m*=2, for example, all CA pairs whose condition was observed less than two times are removed. Second, we screen a CA further with a measure of causality between its two events. We judge causality using the probability of the first event's being followed by the second one as observed in the event list. The service selection procedure requires the causality to be greater than *p*, a threshold value. That is to say, a CA <x,y> is selected only if it is observed often enough. Here, the threshold values *m* and *p* are empirically chosen constants and can be adjusted according to the confidence level desired by the user. We will discuss this later with our experiment again.

```
Input:
  CA_set candidates;      // the set of CA pairs
Output:
  CA_set viableServices;  // the set of viable services

   const int m=m0;                  // Minimum Occurrences
   const float p=p0;                // Probability Threshold
   int coutnEvent(Event a);         // returns frequency of an event
   int couuntCAPair(CA_pair a);     // returns frequency of a CA pair

Service Selection
for x ∈ candidates do {
      if countEvent(x.left) >= m
      if (countCAPair(x)/countEvent(x.first) >= p
            insert x to viableServices;
   }
```

Fig. 5. The Selection Algorithm

The screening based on the above two tests assures that any CA <x,y> chosen have been seen often enough, and whenever event x occurs, it is likely to be responded by y within the cutoff time. The service selection process discussed above is summarized as an algorithm in Figure 5. The algorithm takes *candidates*, the set of all CA's generated in the decomposition process as the input and outputs *viableServices*, the set of CA's that passed the two tests discussed above. *m* is the minimum frequency while *p* is the probability threshold. Iterating on each member of *candidates*, the procedure checks if its first event occurred at least *m* times. The function call countEvent(x.first) returns the frequency of the first event of x. The function call countPair(x) returns the frequency of x itself, where x is a CA. These functions can easily compute the requested values using frequency tables which are constructed during the decomposition process. Each CA that satisfies the minimum frequency requirement is checked again for causality. Causality is computed to see if it is at least *p*, the minimum value required. A CA that meets both criteria is inserted to *viableServices*.

3.5 An Example Analysis

Figure 6 shows an example which illustrates an application of the CASPER algorithm to an event list. Starting with the given event list, CASPER performs cutoff and decomposition. The result is also shown in the figure. The initial event list consists of nine event occurrences out of five different event types. The time of occurrence for each event is indicated by a number above it.

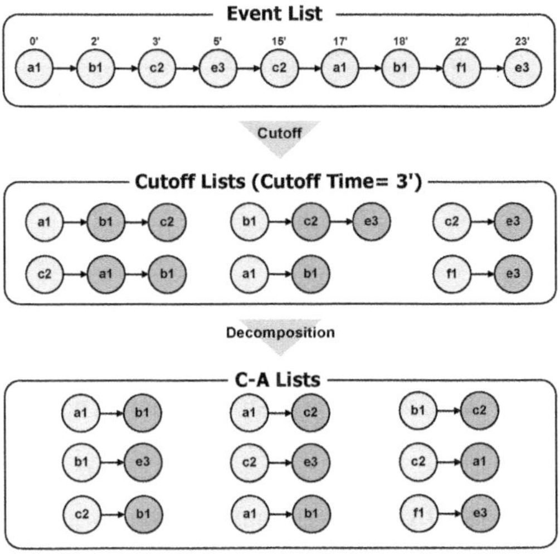

Fig. 6. An Example of Cutoff and Decomposition

In this example, the cutoff was done with three seconds as the cutoff time. Six cutoff lists were generated. The number of events in a cutoff list may vary depending on how frequently events arrived within three seconds. For example, the first cutoff list contains three events while the last one contains only two. After cutoff, The decomposition step breaks each cutoff list into a group of CA's of the form <x,y>, where x and y comes from the head and tail of the cutoff list, respectively. For example, the first cutoff list "a1→b1→c2" is decomposed into {<a1,b1>, <a1,c2>}. At the completion of the decomposition step, we get nine CA's as shown in the figure.

Table 1 summarizes the result of the cutoff and decomposition. It also shows the process of selecting services. For this example, we used 2 and 0.9 as the value of *m* and *p*, respectively. The frequency of event a1 is 2 as it occurred twice in the event list. The CA set of Figure 6 shows that this event has two CA's associated with it, namely, <a1,b1> and <a1,c2>. Similarly, we can get frequencies and associated CA's for other events. The probability of <a1,b1> is 1, which is calculated by the expression 2/2 according to the algorithm in Figure 5. CASPER uses this probability as the measure of causality in choosing services as explained earlier.

The causality of <a1,c2> is 1/2=0.5. Since it is less than the probability threshold, 0.9, this CA is discarded while <a1,b1> survives the test. If we raise the values of *m* and *p*, the confidence on the result of selection increases while the number of selected services decreases, and vice versa.

Table 1. Service Selection of Figure 6

Event	Event Frequency	Related CA	CA Frequency	Causality
a1	2	<a1,b1>	2	1.0
		<a1,c2>	1	0.5
b1	2	<b1,c2>	1	0.5
		<b1,e3>	1	0.5
c2	2	<c2,e3>	1	0.33
		<c2,a1>	1	0.33
		<c2,b1>	1	0.33
f1	1	<f1,e3>	1	1.0

3.6 Refinement

Each candidate that survived the service selection process would be included in the final list of services. However, the experiment showed that two types of abnormal services could arise. We address this problem by modifying the selection step with filtering processes: *repetition* and *collision*. For repetition, consider a service, for example, "If the bathroom light is turned on, it will be turned off soon." With such a service around, the bathroom light will go out prematurely as soon as the user turns it on. We remove repetition by discarding a CA whose execution condition and action are associated with the same object.

Collision occurs when two services with the same execution condition have different actions on the same object. For example, consider a user who always washes her hands when she comes home. Observing her behavior, CASPER retrieves two conflicting services, "If the front door is opened, the bathroom light is turned on soon", "If the front door is opened, the bathroom light is off soon." Collision can be handled by discarding CA's causing it. Another way of handling the collision problem is to pass this information to the user for selection. In our experiment, we simply discarded CA's with collision.

3.7 Implementation

In this step, we define selected CA's using a service specification language. Services need be defined as a form that can be executed on the underlying context-aware platform (also known as context-aware service middleware). In general, services are defined using a context-aware service specification language. As our interest for this paper exist in exploring how we can make personal context-aware services, we will assume that a language such as ECA-DL and SOCAM will be used for this purpose and avoid further discussion in this direction.

4 Experiment and Evaluation

In order to verify the usefulness of the CASPER method, we designed and performed an experiment. One of the problems we faced when we tried to assess the usefulness of CASPER was the lack of human living data to start with. Actual living data were necessary but collecting such data itself was a difficult task. We believe that smart homes in the future will be studded with devices that are sensor-enabled, instrumented, and networked [5][12][13][14][15] [16]. The computer-based logging of user living data will become available in such an environment.

Table 2. The Events Used for the Experiment

Appliance	Event	Event ID
Front Door	Open	a1
Living Room Light	On	b1
	Off	b2
Air Conditioner	On	c1
	Off	c2
	Timer Set	c3
Television	On	d1
	Off	d2
	Mute	d3
	Sound	d4
Telephone	Answer	e1
	Call	e2
	Hang Up	e3
Bathroom Light	On	f1
	Off	f2
Water Heater	On	g1
	Off	g2
DVD Player	On	h1
	Pause	h2
	Play	h3
	Off	h4
Car	Start Up	i1

In our experiment, we had to collect living data manually due to the lack of the hardware environment which would collect user living data automatically. For this purpose, a subject was hired and asked to record all of the information associated with his living to the extent relevant to CASPER. Although it was arduous, he made every effort to keep a record of events that occurred on the devices and equipments located at his home over a ten day period. Then, we applied the CASPER method to the collected data in order to see how well CASPER can derive useful context-aware services for him. While collected manually, the data set were useful enough for our purpose of demonstrating the usefulness of the CASPER algorithm. Table 2 shows the devices that exist in his smart home environment and the events associated with them.

The details of collected data are not shown due to space limit. Total 348 event occurrences were observed on 9 devices for the period of 15,574 minutes (259 hours).

Table 3. Useful Services

Time Block	Useful Service ID	Meaning
1	b1→c1	Living Room Light On → AC On
	b1→d1	Living Room Light On → TV On
	b1→f1	Living Room Light On → Bathroom Light
	b1→g1	Living Room Light On → Boiler On
	c1→f1	AC On → Bathroom Light On
	c1→g1	AC On → Boiler On
	e1→h2	Telephone Incoming → DVD Pause
	e2→d3	Telephone Outgoing → TV Mute
	e3→d4	Telephone Hang Up → TV Mute Off
	g1→f1	Boiler On → Bathroom Light On
	h4→d1	DVD Off → TV On
2	a1→b1	Front Door Open → Living Room Light On
	a1→c1	Front Door Open → AC On
	a1→d1	Front Door Open → TV On
	a1→f1	Front Door Open → Bathroom Light On
	a1→g1	Front Door Open → Boiler On
	d1→f1	TV On → Bathroom Light On
	d1→g1	TV On → Boiler On
	d2→h1	TV Off → DVD On
	f2→g2	Bathroom Light Off → Boiler Off
3	d2→h1	TV Off → DVD On
4	d2→c3	TV Off → AC Set Timer
5	a1→i1	Front Door Open → Car Start Up
	c2→a1	AC Off → Front Door Open
	...	...
	c2→i1	AC Off → Car Start Up
	d2→i1	TV Off → Car Start Up
	f2→g2	Bathroom Light Off → Boiler Off

Time Block - 1: all day, 2: 8pm-10pm, 3: 10pm-0am, 4: 12am-2am, 5: 8am-10am.

The living data were divided into five two-hour blocks besides 8pm-10am, the block of the whole period: 8pm-10pm, 10pm-12am, 12am-2am, and 8-10am. In order to measure the effectiveness of CASPER, we analyzed the full list of possible services and selected the services that we felt useful (Table 3). CASPER's answer was graded against this selection. There were total 32 services that were found useful. In more detail, there are eleven useful services for block 1, nine for block 2, one for each of block 3 and 4, and finally ten for block 5. We regarded these services as the correct answer which CASPER should match. The performance of CASPER was measured by its hit ratio defined as

$$Hit\ Ratio = \frac{\#Correct\ Service - \#Incorrect\ Service}{\#User - preferred\ Service}$$

The hit ratio is calculated as the ratio between the number of correct services produced by CASPER and the number of the services that we chose for all time blocks. If the set of services produced by CASPER exactly match all of the selected services, the hit ratio would become one, the perfect score. On the other hand, if CASPER generates no matching services, hit ratio becomes 0.

CASPER can make two kinds of errors. One is to fail to produce a correct service that exists. This is reflected in the first term of the numerator. The other is to produce an incorrect service, that is, a service which was not desired by the user. In the case that CASPER produces incorrect services, hit ratio is adjusted by deducting the number of incorrect answers from that of correct answers. While the selection of desired services was made by both authors to increase the objectivity of the evaluation, the opinion of the subject can be important. We agreed on most of the selected services but found some of them arguable like "Start heating the water for bath when the door is opened at seven o'clock." In such a case, the subject's opinion was valued higher than ours.

Table 4. Hit Ratios of CASPER

T	*m*	*p*			
		0.7	**0.8**	**0.9**	**1.0**
5	**5**	0.56 (20, 2)	0.56 (19, 1)	0.53 (17, 0)	0.31 (10, 0)
	10	0.53 (17, 0)	0.47 (16, 1)	0.50 (16, 0)	0.28 (9, 0)
15	**5**	0.78 (29, 4)	0.59 (22, 3)	0.59 (21, 2)	0.47 (17, 2)
	10	0.78 (26, 1)	0.56 (19, 1)	0.53 (18, 1)	0.44 (14, 0)
30	**5**	0.22 (20, 13)	0.41 (25, 12)	0.69 (28, 6)	0.44 (16,2)
	10	0.38 (16, 7)	0.56 (24, 6)	0.69 (27, 5)	0.44 (15, 1)

Legend - *T*: Cutoff Time (sec.), *m*: Min. Occurrence, *p*: Min. Probability.

The CASPER algorithm was implemented in Java 1.6. We ran the program on Windows XP for 24 times varying the values of three parameters, viz. cutoff time(T), minimum frequency(m), and probability threshold(p). Table 4 shows a summary of the result obtained from the experiment. In the table, a decimal fraction denotes a hit ratio. The first and second integer value in parentheses is the number of correct services and incorrect services, respectively. For example, with T=5, m=10, p=0.9, CASPER generated 16 correct services and no incorrect services. Hit ratios ranged from 0.28 to 0.78. For this user, the highest hit ratio 0.78 was observed when T=15 and p=0.7. While hit ratio is a measure of the effectiveness of CASPER, we also pay attention to the number of correct services it produced. When m=5, there were 29 correct answers and 4 mistakes while for m=10, there were 26 correct answers and only one mistake. The hit ratio turned out relatively low at p=1.0, when we only accepted those pairs of events which appeared together all the time.

Two interesting observations are in order. Note that when T=30, m=10, the number of correct services and the hit ratio increase as p increases. It was contrary to our expectation that the number of selected services would decrease as p increases. For example, the number was 16 at p=0.7 and 27 at p=0.9 and. This seems anomalous since we seem to be getting more services when we tightened the probability requirement. A similar behavior can be observed on the number of correct services when we vary cutoff time T from 5 to 30. With p fixed at 0.7, the highest hit ratio 0.78 came when T=15 while the lowest 0.22 occurred when T=30. This unusual behavior of CASPER was found due to the effect of the refinement that we discussed in Section 3.4. As we lower the probability threshold, we get not only more CA's but also more conflicting CA's. Similarly, while a wider cutoff window lets more CA's pass through, the possibility of repetition and collision rise. The elimination of such problematic cases resulted in a reduction on the set of final choices. We view that CASPER's performance is meaningful. CASPER was able to garner up to 29 useful services out of 32 (91%) from the user's living data. CASPER's performance will be improved with more experiments and evolutions on its algorithm. Our contribution for this paper is that we have shown that it is possible to derive personal context-aware services from user living data.

5 Conclusion and Future Works

We introduced CASPER, a model of constructing personal context-aware services based on observed user behaviors. We discussed CASPER's method of automatically deriving context-aware services from living data in detail. Its effectiveness was demonstrated with a case study. An experiment on a user and his actual living environment showed that CASPER successfully derived up to 91% of the total context-aware services that the authors and the subject himself deemed useful. CASPER can be used in two ways for building personal context-aware services. First, CASPER may be used as a service recommendation system. It is tedious to analyzing one's own behavior only relying on memory. For example, the problem of finding all of the useful context-aware services for a user may not be an easy task. CASPER can help in this situation by recommending a large part of them. CASPER can also be used as an automatic context-aware service definition method. As the probability threshold and minimum occurrence are tightened, the possibility that CASPER produces false services will become extremely low. The services produced at p=1.0 may be immediately defined as context-aware services. This paper only considered CA's whose execution conditions are atomic. In general, the execution condition of a context-aware service may be a composition of multiple conditions. We plan to investigate extending CASPER's capability to cover N-to-1 relationships as well in the future.

Acknowledgements

This research was supported by the National Research Foundation of Korea grant funded by Korea government in 2009. The authors would like to thank the referees for their excellent comments which contributed to improving the quality of this paper.

References

1. Pinto, R.P., Cardozo, E., Guimaraes, E.G.: A Component Framework for Context-Awareness. In: 2008 International Wireless Communications and Mobile Computing, August 6-8, pp. 315–320 (2008)
2. Xiaosheng, T., Qinghua, S., Ping, Z.: A Distributed Context Aware Model for Pervasive Service Environment. In: 1st International Symposium on Wireless Pervasive Computing, January 16-18 (2006)
3. da Silva, L.O.B., van Wijnen, R.P., Vink, P.: A Service-Oriented Middleware for Context-Aware Applications. In: 5th International Workshop on Middleware for Pervasive and Ad-Hoc Computing, pp. 37–42 (2007)
4. Park, I., Choi, H., Shin, K.-Y., Kim, J., Park, S.: GAS2: Context Awareness Service System based on Wireless Sensor Networks. In: 2006 Advanced Communication Technology, February 20-22, vol. 2, pp. 1231–1234 (2006)
5. Thayer, S.M., Steenkiste, P.: An Architecture for the Integration of Physical and Information Spaces. Personal and Ubiquitous Computing 7(2) (July 2003)
6. Gu, T., Pung, H.K., Zhang, D.Q.: A service-oriented middleware for building context-aware services. Journal of Network and Computer Applications 28(1) (January 2005)
7. da Silva Santos, L.O.B., Ramparany, F., Costa, P.D., Vink, P., Etter, R., Broens, T.: A Service Architecture for Context Awareness and Reaction Provisioning. In: 2007 IEEE Congress on Services, July 9-13, pp. 25–32 (2007)
8. Corradi, A., Montanari, R., Tibaldi, D.: Context-based Access Control for Ubiquitous Service Provisioning. In: 2004 Computer Software and Applications Conference, September 28-30, vol. 1, pp. 444–451 (2004)
9. Rodden, T., Crabtree, A., Hemmings, T., Koleva, B., Humble, J., Akesson, K.-P., Hansson, P.: Configuring the Ubiquitous Home. In: The 6th International Conference on Designing Cooperative Systems, May 11-14 (2004)
10. Dey, A.K., Hamid, R., Beckmann, C., Li, I., Hsu, D.: A CAPpella: Programming by Demonstration of Context-aware Applications. In: The SIGCHI Conference on Human factors in Computing Systems, April 24-29, pp. 33–40 (2004)
11. Brdiczka, O., Crowley, J.L., Reignier, P.: Learning Situation Models in a Smart Home. IEEE Transactions on Systems, Man, and Cybernetics—Part B: Cybernetics 39(1) (February 2009)
12. Gupta, R., Sumeet, T., Agrawal, D.P.: Jini Home Networking: A Step toward Pervasive Computing. IEEE Computer 35(8), 34–40 (2002)
13. UPnP Forum, Understanding of universal plug and play (June 2000), `http://www.upnp.org/resources/whitepapers.asp`
14. Nakajima, T.: Pervasive Servers: A framework for creating a society of appliances. ACM Personal and Ubiquitous Computing 7(3-4) (July 2003)
15. OSGi Alliance, OSGI Service Platform Service Compendium (April 2007)
16. Duquennoy, S., Grimaud, G., Vandewalle, J.-J.: The Web of Things: interconnecting devices with high usability and performance. In: 6th International Conference on Embedded Software and Systems (ICESS 2009), HangZhou, Zhejiang, China (2009)
17. Lieberman, H.: Autonomous interface agents. In: The SIGCHI Conference on Human Factors in Computing Systems, pp. 67–74 (1997)

A Simple Public-Goods Game Based Incentive Mechanism for Resource Provision in P2P Networks

Yufeng Wang[1], Akihiro Nakao[1,2], and Jianhua Ma[3]

[1] National Institute of Information and Communications Technology (NICT), Tokyo 184-8795, Japan
wfwang@nict.go.jp
[2] University of Tokyo, Tokyo 113-0033, Japan
nakao@iii.u-tokyo.ac.jp
[3] Hosei University, Tokyo 184-8584, Japan
jianhua@hosei.ac.jp

Abstract. P2P networks can be thought as common goods in that they rely on voluntary provision of resources from individual peers (storage space or bandwidth, etc.) to support the creation and operation of service in P2P network. But, there exist social dilemma in P2P resource provision: Cooperators produce a valuable common good at some cost to themselves while defectors attempt to exploit the resource without contributing. Thus groups of cooperators are better off than groups of defectors. However, in any mixed group, defectors outperform cooperators and hence the dilemma. In this paper, we propose a P2P resource provision mechanism based on public goods game. The key point of this scheme lies in that: small entry fee is set for all peers, and peers can voluntarily join P2P resource provision system. After entering, each peer can independently choose to provide resource or freeride. Furthermore, some specific cooperators (so-called punishers) can voluntarily punish those defectors, which will bring small punishment cost to those punishers. For evolutionary dynamics, each peer simply imitates the strategy of peer with better utility. Theoretical analysis and experimental results show that the proposed mechanism can incentivize peers to contribute resource, and the whole P2P network will almost converge to the state of punisher.

Keywords: P2P networks, Incentive mechanism, Public goods game.

1 Introduction

Peer-to-Peer (P2P) systems are self-organizing, distributed resource-sharing networks. By pooling together the resources of many autonomous machines, they are able to provide an inexpensive platform for distributed computing, storage, or data-sharing that is highly scalable. Note that there are two different cases in resource management: resource allocation (allocation of the existing resource) and resource provision (provision of resource shared by all participants). In the first case, the designer should decide whether and what percentage of a good (with given capacity) each peer should

Z. Yu et al. (Eds.): UIC 2010, LNCS 6406, pp. 352–365, 2010.

consume. In the second case, the designer's task is to entice independent participant to provide resource (with its right share). In this paper, we focus on the latter case.

In P2P systems, it is imperative for each peer to voluntarily contribute resources (e.g., storage, bandwidth, and contents, etc.) However, intuitively, each peer would prefer to "free ride" on the contribution of other peers by consuming available resources and services without contributing anything, and thus avoid the corresponding costs. It was reported that nearly 70% of Gnutella users shared nothing with other users (these users simply free-ride on other users who share information), and nearly 50% of all file search responses come from the top 1% of information sharing nodes [1]. In following-up study (five years later), it was found that 85% of users share nothing [2], which implies the free-riding problem had got worse in the intervening years. Generally, lack of cooperation is one of the key problems that confront today's P2P systems. Incentive mechanisms play a crucial role to encourage cooperation among autonomous nodes. Recent researches at the intersection of economics and computer science are overviewed, and some open questions related to free-riding in P2P systems are also discussed [3~5].

Considering the rationality of each participant in P2P resource provision scheme, game theory is an appropriate tool to analyze and design the incentive mechanism in P2P systems. Specifically, a differential service based incentive mechanism for P2P systems was proposed to eliminate free riding and increase overall availability of the system [6]. A simple fixed-contribution scheme was proposed to alleviate the free-riding [7], in which each peer merely pays the same fixed fee toward the total cost, and peers unwilling to do so are excluded. Our paper significantly differs from the above fixed-contribution scheme: instead that the fixed contribution is set as specific value, which is calculated based on global information in network, the entry fee in our paper can be set as any arbitrary small value, and small entry fee plus voluntary principle will drive rational peers into punishers, which not only cooperate, but also punish the freeriders. It is found that imposing penalty on all users that join the system is effective under many scenarios, and, in particular, system performance degrades significantly only when the turnover rate among users is high [8]. Ref. [9] develops a model of the interaction of rational peers in a P2P network that has its heart in altruism, an intrinsic parameter reflecting peers' inherent willingness to contribute. The authors find that, under the effects of altruism, a substantial fraction of peers will contribute when altruism levels are within certain intervals, even though no incentive mechanism is used. Our paper does not assume any altruistic feature at all, and illustrates that, through exerting small entry cost and respecting each peer's rationality, the P2P network can still work toward reciprocation state.

Basically, the above work are all inspired from the classical game theory, and particular, adopt some non-cooperative games to model peer's rationality: each wants to maximize his utility, which depends on his benefit (the resources of the system he can use) and his cost (his contribution). However, those schemes can not completely characterize the evolutionary dynamics of strategies as a whole population. Moreover, they assume forward-looking model of perfect rationality of participants, which works on the principle of utility optimization (assume that each peer has the knowledge about the global information of system, and selects strategy to best response to current system's state). The above perfect rationality brings great burden to peer's cognitive ability, and in most cases, it is unfeasible. On the contrary, our paper adopts EGT-inspired

(Evolutionary Game Theory) approach in which individuals attempt to optimize their utilities by imitating the behaviors of peers with better payoff. This stochastic learning is a backward-looking approach, and thus assumes much lighter cognitive capabilities on the part of individuals than does traditional rationality.

Generally, the classical game-theoretical approach focused on the determination of optimal strategic behaviors of rational individuals in a static setting. EGT places this framework into a dynamical context, and describes how successful strategies spread in a population. Specifically, such approach generally includes three phases: interaction phase, evolution phase and mutation phase [10~12]. Interaction phase specifies some rules by which entities interact. Interactions among individuals are always modeled as some specific game like Prisoner's Dilemma (PD) game or coordination game, etc. [13]. In evolution (reproduction) phase, each agent differentially reproduces children based on its utility. The reproduction can be genetic (entities actually reproduce next generation) or cultural (entities are seen as behaviors or ideas that can replicate horizontally among peers within a generation). The above interpretation of cultural reproduction gives us a clue as to how evolutionary models can be used in modeling of P2P incentive mechanisms. Mutation phase means that, in the evolution, with very small probability, agents change their strategies to incorporate innovation. In our framework, the small mutation can be intuitively interpreted as mistake or curiosity when peers imitate others' strategies.

In this paper, we design simple incentive mechanism which fully respects peers' rationality, and can encourage peers to provide resource. In particular, the small entry fee is set for peers who want to join the resource provision and sharing scheme. And all behaviors are all voluntarily conducted by each rational peer: each peer can choose whether to join the resource provision scheme or not (peers who do not to join, are risk averse and do not bear the entry fee, so-called loners); after joining, each peer can choose to contribute resource (cooperative) or to freeride (defect); some cooperative peers, so-called punishers, can voluntarily punish defectors, which will bring those punishers some cost. Through analyzing the evolutionary dynamics, we show that the simple mechanism can stimulate peers to contribute resource, and the whole peers will converge to the punisher.

The paper is organized as follows: section 2 describes the public goods model used in this paper, and schematically illustrates the proposed incentive mechanism. The evolutionary dynamics of the proposed public-goods based incentive mechanism is theoretically analyzed in section 3. The simulation results are provided in section 4, which investigate the effect of various parameters on the evolutionary dynamics of P2P system. Finally, we briefly conclude this paper.

2 Model and Assumptions

Inherently, there exists social dilemma in P2P resource provision: cooperators (denoted as 'C') produce a valuable common good at some cost to themselves while defectors (represented as 'D') attempt to exploit the resource without contributing. Thus groups of cooperators are better off than groups of defectors. However, in any mixed group, defectors outperform cooperators and hence the dilemma. In order to restrain the defect behavior, some cooperators (so-called punishers, 'P') would like to punish those defectors, which will bring small punishment cost to those punishers themselves. But, if there only exist three types of peers, C, D and P, then P2P systems will finally converge to D. Because, for small mutation, cooperators obtain the same payoff as punishers, and can thus invade and replace publishers through neutral drift. Once cooperators have taken over the whole system, defectors are advantageous and take over. Furthermore, P and D are bistable, which means that each strategy is a best response to itself. That is, a small percentage of P mutants could not successfully invade the population of D. Thus, the evolutionary end state will converge to D [14][15]. Naturally, the question is how to build incentives to make selfish people contribute to the system, e. g. provide disk space, CPU cycles or network bandwidth. Recently, the costly punishment has been shown to invade when a rare percentage of individuals are allowed to opt out of cooperative ventures [16].

Basically, the vast majority of models on the cooperation evolution consider pair-wise interactions (that is, model the interactions as PD-like games). An important generalization consists of extending the PD to interactions among more than two players. The resulting *N*-player games are traditionally called Public Goods Game. In a typical Public Goods experiment, a group of, e.g., six players get an endowment of $10 each. Every player then has the option to invest part or all of their money into a common pool knowing that the experimenter is going to triple the amount in the pool and divide it equally among all players regardless of their contribution. If everybody invests their money, each player ends up with $30. However, each invested dollar only yields a return of 50 cents to the investor. Therefore, if everybody plays rationally, no one will invest, and hence the group of players will forgo the benefits of the public good.

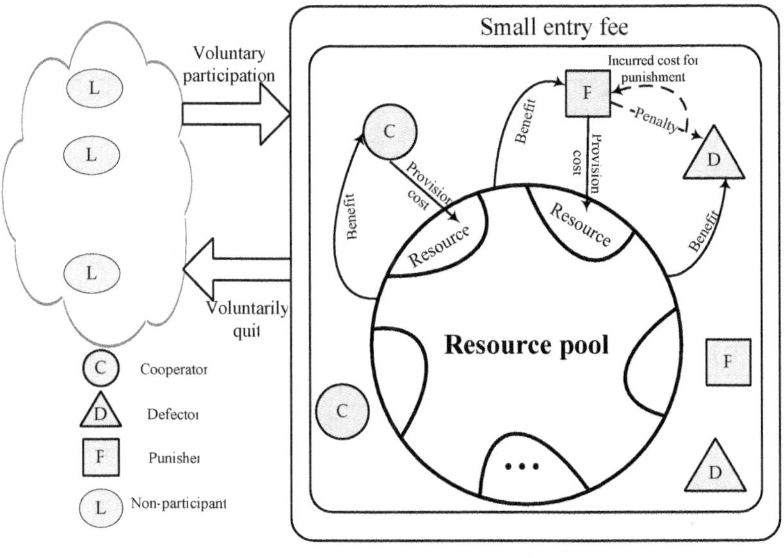

Fig. 1. The schematic illustration of public-goods based incentive mechanism

Our incentive mechanism scheme is greatly inspired from the above simple public goods game. In particular, for P2P resource provision, we consider a well-mixed population of peers with constant size *M*. For general case, *N* individuals are randomly selected and offered with the option to participate in a risky, but potentially profitable, resource provision scheme. Note that *N*=*M* is the specific case. Fig.1 schematically illustrated the public-goods game-based incentive mechanism scheme. Basically, there exist four types of users in P2P systems: The non-participants, denoted as 'L', represent individuals who, by default, do not join the public enterprise, and thus do not pay the entry cost; defectors, 'D', who participate, but do not contribute; cooperators 'C' who contribute but do not punish the defectors; and punishers, 'P', who not only contribute to the commonwealth but also punish the defectors. As shown in Fig. 1, L peers can voluntarily join the resource provision scheme, and all participants can voluntary quit the scheme. For simplicity, we assume that each 'C' (and 'P') peer will provide benefit α to resource pool, and bear service-providing cost c_s, and $\alpha>c_s$. Each P peer will impose penalty c_p, on a defector, and similarly incur punishment cost c_u for the punishment behavior. Considering the inherent dynamics of peers' behaviors, we assume that each peer simply imitates the strategy of peer with better utility. Note that, for theoretical analysis, our paper assumes extremely simple and ideal model for P2P resource provision. Actually, in real-world situation, costs and benefits should be carefully defined and measured empirically. But, even though the model is very simplified, it still illuminates some interesting results.

In brief, to help in the description of the public-goods game based incentive scheme, table 1 provides a list of symbols and their definitions used in this paper. For clarity, we let the number 1, 2, 3 and 4 to respectively denote the strategies of C, D, P, and L.

Table 1. Symbols and their definitions used in the paper

Symbol	Definition
M	The total number of peers in P2P system
N	The average number of peers in each group
μ	The strategy mutation probability in evolutionary phase
β	The intensity of selection
α	The benefit that cooperators (and punishers) contribute to the public goods by providing resource
c_s	The cost that cooperators (and punishers) incur by provision of resource, without loss of generality, let c_s=1
c_e	The entry fee set for peers who join the resource provision scheme
c_p	The penalty that punishers impose on defectors
c_u	The incurred cost for punishers who conduct the punishment behaviors
i_G, i_B, i_P, i_L	The respective number of cooperators, defectors, punishers and non-participants existing in the P2P system

3 Theoretical Analysis of Public-Goods Based Incentive Scheme

The theoretical analysis of the stochastic dynamics in public-goods game based incentive mechanism can be greatly simplified in the limiting case: the mutation probability is near to zero, for in the above case, the whole P2P system almost always consists of one or two types at most. This holds because, when the mutation probability is zero, the four monomorphic states are absorbing, and for sufficient small mutation probability, the fate of a mutant (i.e. its elimination or fixation) is settled before the next mutant appears. Thus, the transitions between pair of the four pure states, C, D, L and P, occur, when a mutant appears and spreads to fixation. Note that, in experiments, because of the following facts: in some cases, groups are naturally mixed, including more than two strategies of peers, and the number of simulation rounds is limited, there exist gaps between theoretical calculations and experimental values in some simulations.

Specifically, in finite population, the groups engaging in a public goods game are given by multivariate hypergeometric sampling. For transitions between two pure states, this reduces to sampling (without replacement) from a hypergeometric distribution. In a population of size M with m_i individuals of type i and $(M\text{-}m_i)$ of type j, the probability of selecting k individuals of type i and $(N\text{-}k)$ individuals of type j in N trails, is given as follows:

$$H(k,N,m_i,M)=\frac{\binom{m_i}{k}\binom{M-m_i}{N-k}}{\binom{M}{N}} \tag{1}$$

Obviously, for equation (1), the following two equation hold:

$$\sum_{k=0}^{N} H(k,N,m_i,M)=1;\ \sum_{k=0}^{N} k\cdot H(k,N,m_i,M)=\frac{N}{M}m_i$$

Thus, in a population of i_G cooperators and $(M\text{-}i_G)$ defectors, the average payoff to cooperators, P_{12}, and defector, P_{21} can be respectively denoted as follows:

$$\begin{aligned}P_{12}(i_G)&=\sum_{k=0}^{N-1} H(k,N-1,i_G-1,M-1)\left(\frac{k+1}{N}\alpha-c_s-c_e\right)\\&=\frac{\alpha}{N}\left(1+\frac{N-1}{M-1}(i_G-1)\right)-c_s-c_e\end{aligned} \tag{2}$$

$$P_{21}(i_G)=\sum_{k=0}^{N-1} H(k,N-1,i_G,M-1)\left(\frac{k}{N}\alpha-c_e\right)=\frac{\alpha}{N}\cdot\frac{N-1}{M-1}\cdot i_G-c_e \tag{3}$$

Note that, in P_{12}, the focal peer is C peers, so the total number of other C peers is denoted as $(i_G\text{-}1)$.

Similarly, we can get: $P_{13}=P_{31}=\alpha-c_s-c_e$ (4)

$$P_{14}(i_L)=P_{34}(i_L)=(1-\binom{i_L}{N-1}\Big/\binom{M-1}{N-1})\cdot(\alpha-c_s-c_e)-\binom{i_L}{N-1}\Big/\binom{M-1}{N-1}\cdot c_e \tag{5}$$

$$P_{23}(i_P)=\frac{(N-1)}{(M-1)}\left(\frac{\alpha}{N}-c_p\right)i_P-c_e \tag{6}$$

$$P_{24}(i_L) = -c_e \tag{7}$$

$$P_{32}(i_P) = \frac{\alpha}{N} - c_s - c_e - (N-1)c_u + \frac{(N-1)}{(M-1)}\left(\frac{\alpha}{N} + c_u\right)(i_P - 1) \tag{8}$$

$$P_{41} = P_{42} = P_{43} = 0 \tag{9}$$

Reproduction can be genetic or cultural. Here, we adopt the pairwise comparison rule, which has been recently shown to provide a convenient framework of game dynamics at all intensities of selection. According to this rule, two peers from the P2P system, *i*-strategy and *j*-strategy are randomly selected for update (only the selection of mixed pair can change the composition of the population). The strategy of *i* will replace that of *j* with a probability given by the Fermi function:

$$p = \frac{1}{1 + e^{-\beta(P_{ij} - P_{ji})}} \tag{10}$$

The quantity β, which in physics corresponds to an inverse temperature, controls the intensity of selection. When β is large, the individual with the lower payoff will always adopt the strategy of the other individual. For $\beta \ll 1$, we recover the weak selection limit of the frequency dependent Moran process, which can be viewed as a high temperature expansion of the dynamics [17]. Note that, instead of the weak selection always used in biological and social systems (the weak selection assumption could be justified as follows: First, most real life situations are involved in many different games, and each particular game only makes a small contribution to the overall performance; Second, in most case, only weak selection is analytical), but, for technological network, strong selection is more feasible than weak selection. Hereby, we put emphasis on the strong selection. Then, the probability to increase the number of *i*-strategy peers from l to $l+1$, and the probability to decrease the number of *i*-strategy peers from l to l-1, are represented as:

$$T_l^{\pm} = \frac{l}{M}\frac{M-l}{M}\frac{1}{1 + e^{\mp\beta(P_{ij}(l) - P_{ji}(l))}} \tag{11}$$

The quantity of interest in finite population dynamics is the fixation probability ρ_{ij}, which is the probability that a population of *j*-strategy peers invaded by a single *i*-strategy peer evolves with mutations to a population of all *i*-strategy peers. The probability depends only on the ratio $\alpha_l = T_j^- / T_j^+$. For the pairwise comparison process, the ratio reduces to $\alpha_l = \exp[-\beta(P_{ij}(l) - P_{ji}(l))]$. Finally, the fixation probability of ρ_{ij} is given as follows [17]:

$$\rho_{ij} = \frac{1}{\sum_{k=0}^{M-1}\prod_{l=1}^{k}\alpha_l} \tag{12}$$

The fixation probability ρ_{ij} define the transition probabilities of a Markov process among the four different homogeneous states of the population. The transition matrix is shown as the following matrix (13), and the stationary distribution can be easily calculated [16], which approximately indicates the probability to find the system in one of the four homogeneous states. That is, the normalized right eigenvector to the largest eigenvalue (which is 1 for the matrix (13)) determines the stationary distribution, i.e., indicates the probability to find the system in one of the four homogenous states.

$$\begin{array}{c} \\ C \\ D \\ P \\ L \end{array}\begin{array}{c} \begin{array}{cccc} \quad C \quad & \quad D \quad & \quad R \quad & \quad L \quad \end{array} \\ \begin{pmatrix} 1-(\rho_{21}+\rho_{31}+\rho_{41})/3 & \rho_{12}/3 & \rho_{13}/3 & \rho_{14}/3 \\ \rho_{21}/3 & 1-(\rho_{12}+\rho_{32}+\rho_{42})/3 & \rho_{23}/3 & \rho_{24}/3 \\ \rho_{31}/3 & \rho_{32}/3 & 1-(\rho_{13}+\rho_{23}+\rho_{43})/3 & \rho_{34}/3 \\ \rho_{41}/3 & \rho_{42}/3 & \rho_{43}/3 & 1-(\rho_{14}+\rho_{24}+\rho_{34})/3 \end{pmatrix} \end{array} \tag{13}$$

4 Simulations

In this section, we thoroughly investigate the effect of various parameters in the proposed public goods game-based incentive mechanism on the cooperation evolution. Due to the lasting dynamics of imitating and mutating process in our scheme, in our simulations, we define the homogeneous state of each strategy as follows: whenever more than 90% of the peers opt for one strategy, then it is counted as being in the respective homogeneous state. Then, based on the number of homogeneous states, we calculate the ratio of time average for each strategy (so-called, experimental time average), and compare with the stationary distribution of matrix (13). In our paper, the latter is named as theoretical time average. Note that we also use other value, like 95% as threshold, and get very similar results.

4.1 Illustration of Strategy Frequencies with Entry Fee and without Entry Fee

Fig. 2 a) shows the changes of strategy frequencies, as evolutionary rounds go by. The strategy frequency denotes how many percentages of peers with specific strategy are the whole P2P network. In longer runs, their regime can occasionally break down as a

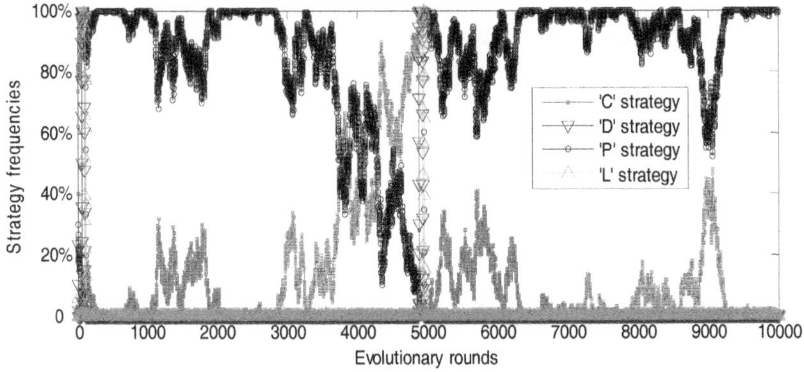

The scenario: M=500, N=50, μ=0.0005, β=10, α=10, c_s=1, c_e=0.1, c_p=0.2, c_u=0.1.

Fig. 2. a) Illustration of strategy frequencies (with entry fee c_e=0.1)

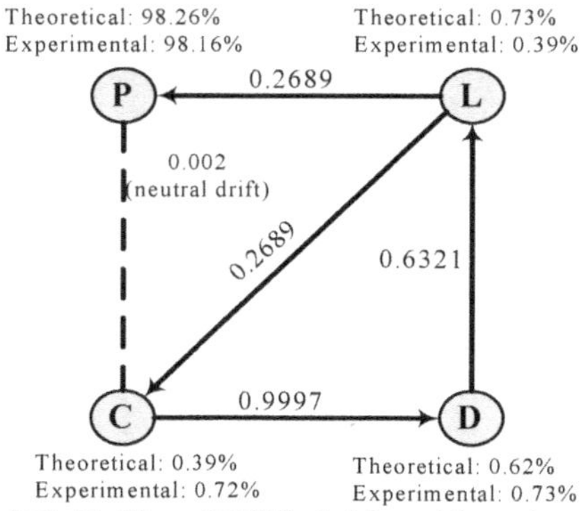

The scenario: M=500, N=50, μ=0.0005, β=10, α=10, c_s=1, c_e=0.1, c_p=0.2, c_u=0.1.

Fig. 2. b) Stationary probability distributions and transition probabilities (with entry fee c_e=0.1)

result of C peers invading by neutral drift, but, after another series of oscillations among C, D, and L peers (rock-paper-scissors-like succession), P peers dominate the whole network again.

The graphical phenomenon in Fig. 2 a) can be explained by transition probabilities among those four strategies, shown in Fig. 2 b). First, P and D are bistable, which means that, choosing between P and D, each strategy is a best response to itself. That is, small percentage of P mutants could not successfully invade the population of D, and vice versa. Thus, there exist no transition between P and D. Then, the transition probabilities from L to C, from C to D, from D to L, and, and from L to P are relatively large. And furthermore, when there exist only P and C peers in P2P system, all peers' utilities are same. Thus, the transition probability between P and C is neutral drift, $1/M$, which is extremely small. Naturally, most of time should be spent in the P state. Fig. 2 b) also shows the consistence between theoretical time average and experimental time average (Note that the experimental values in Fig. 2 b) is the result after 10^5 evolutionary rounds).

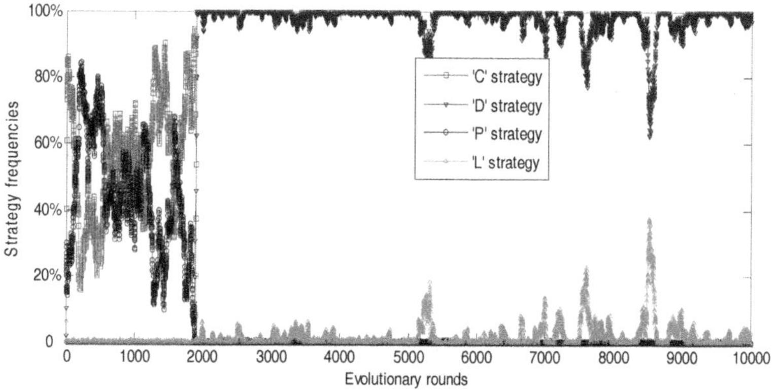

The scenario is: M=500, N=50, μ=0.0005, β=10, α=10, c_s=1, c_e=0, c_p=0.2, c_u=0.1.

Fig. 3. a) Illustration of strategy frequencies (without entry fee)

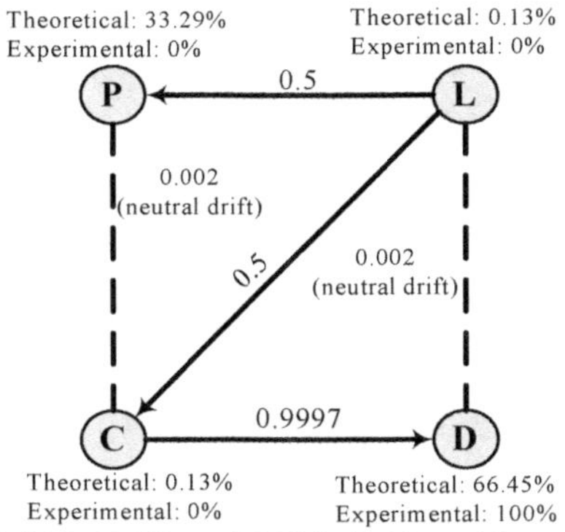

The scenario is: M=500; N=50; μ=0.0005; β=10, α=10, c_s=1, c_e=0, c_p=0.2, c_u=0.1.

Fig. 3. b) Stationary probability distributions and transition probabilities (without entry fee)

Fig. 3 a) and Fig. 3 b) respectively illustrate the strategy frequencies, and the stationary probability distributions as well as transition probabilities under the condition of zero entry fee. Note that, when entry fee is zero, if there only exist L and D peers in the P2P system, then their utilities are all same, which lead to the neutral drift between L and D. In Fig. 3 a), obviously, for zero entry fee, The P2P system is almost occupied by D state. Interestingly, even though the theoretical analysis predicts that almost 33% of homogenous states (according to our definition) belong to P, but, actually, experimental result shows that only D strategy can reach the 90% threshold, and can be regarded as the homogenous state (note that the experimental values in Fig. 3 b) is the result after 10^5 evolutionary rounds). We think the Fig. 3 a) can give partial reason: in real experiments, once the whole P2P networks located in D state, then, through small mutation, the L peers appear, and after long evolutionary rounds, the percentage of L peers will be large, but not large to reach the 90% threshold. Then L peers will be quickly replaced by C and P peers (for the transition probabilities from L to C, and from L to D is relatively large), but, meanwhile, there still exist some D peers (because the transition between L and D is neutral drift, which is extremely small). In a sense, the above scenario is more or less similar to the P2P system which includes C, D, and P peers, and naturally, it is impossible (or very difficult) for P strategy to reach the 90%. Briefly, when entry fee is zero, the neutral drift between D and L will cause the difficulty for the transition from whole D to whole L state. Probably, for extreme small mutation probability and a huge number of evolutionary rounds (like one billion), the experimental values would converge to the theoretical values.

The above phenomenon also implies that, for strong selection, even though the entry fee is very small, it is indispensable for the emergence of cooperative behavior in P2P resource provision. Otherwise, the P2P resource provision and sharing system would be mostly occupied by D peers, and, actually, the experimental result is worse than theoretically expected result.

4.2 Impact of Selection Intensity on the Time Averages

Fig.4 a) illustrates, when entry fee is imposed, the effect of selection intensity on the time average of various strategies. Obviously, when selection intensity is zero, that is, the evolutionary dynamics of P2P network is completely determined by neutral drift, thus, in the long runs, probability to find the system in one of the four homogenous states should be identical for each strategy. As the selection intensity gradually increases, the P strategy quickly dominates all other strategies. But, as shown in Fig.4 b), when there exist no entry fee, the P2P system is mostly spent in the D state, even though the selection intensity is only slightly larger than zero.

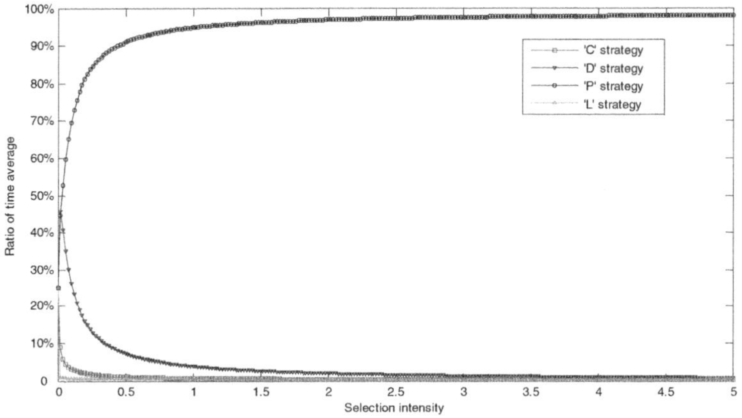

The scenario: M=500, N=50, μ=0.0005, α=10, c_s=1, c_e=0.1, c_p=0.2, c_u=0.1.

Fig. 4. a) The effect of selection intensity on the time average (with entry fee c_e=0.1)

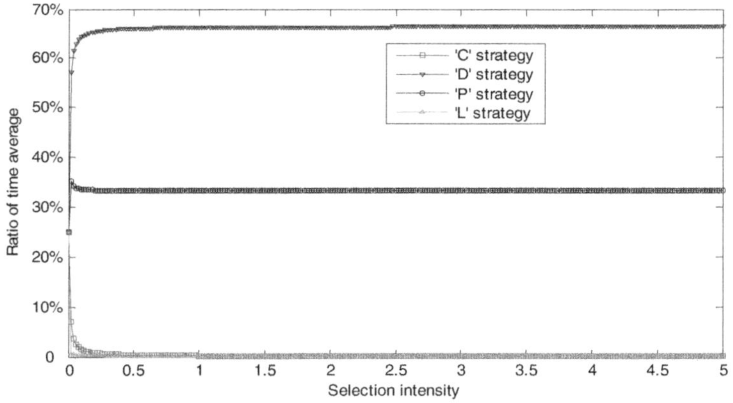

The scenario: M=500, N=50, μ=0.0005, α=10, c_s=1, c_e=0, c_p=0.2, c_u=0.1.

Fig. 4. b) The effect of selection intensity on the time average (without entry fee)

4.3 Impact of Entry Fee and Punishment Cost on the Time Averages

Fig. 5 shows the theoretical and experimental time average of various strategies, with the change of entry fee. Note that each point is the result after 10^5 evolutionary rounds. We can see that, the theoretical values are consistent with the experimental value, and the small entry fee can facilitate the emergence of almost whole P state. Interestingly, it does not mean that the larger entry fee is, the more time the system would stay in the P state. On the contrary, intuitively, if the entry fee was too large, it would prevent more peers from joining the resource provision venture, that is, more peers will select the L strategy. The theoretical time average of L strategy in Fig. 5 slightly shows the above trend.

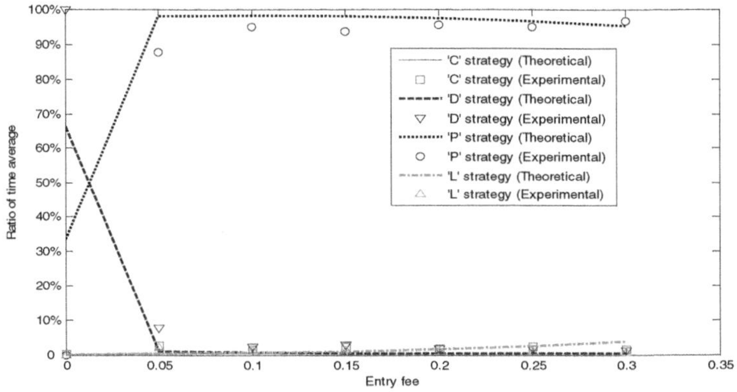

The scenario: M=500, N=50, μ=0.0005, β=10, α=10, c_s=1, c_p=0.2, c_u=0.1

Fig. 5. The effect of entry fee on the time average (Theoretical and Experimental)

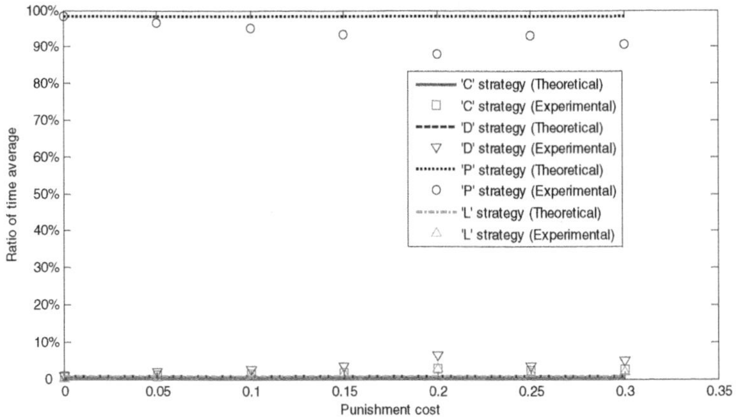

The scenario: M=500, N=50, μ=0.0005, β=10, α=10, c_s=1, c_e=0.1, c_p=0.2

Fig. 6. The effect of punishment cost on the time average (Theoretical and Experimental)

Fig. 6 shows the theoretical and experimental time average of various strategies, with the change of punishment cost. Generally, in all experiments, P strategy dominates all other strategies in P2P system. On the other hand, we can see that, when the punishment cost is relatively small, the theoretical values are consistent with the experimental value. As punishment cost increases, the gap between theoretical values and experimental values became large. The reason lies in that, theoretical analysis only ideally considers the transition between pair of strategies and calculates the transition probabilities between pair of strategies, and furthermore, for strong selection, the transition probabilities from L to C, from C to D, from D to L, and from L to P almost keep constant with the small change of punishment cost. However, in real experiments, sometimes, there exist mixed strategies (more than two strategies), thus, relatively large punishment cost will decrease P peers' utilities too much, which make it not easy for P peers to dominate the P2P system (in comparison with small punishment cost).

5 Conclusion

It is argued that P2P networking environments are heterogeneous, dynamic and distributed environments managed by multiple administrative authorities, shared by users with different and competing interests, or even autonomously provided by independent and rational users. The distinguished feature in P2P networks is that each player determines its behaviors autonomously. Thus, "Design for choice" [18] is the fundamental principle for P2P networks. Under the prerequisite that designer should fully respect peers' rational behaviors, this paper designs simple public-goods game based incentive mechanism, to encourage peers to provide resource. Specifically, we model the resource provision as that of creating a public good: a commodity from which all nodes benefit, and apply evolutionary game theory model to formally analyze its dynamics. The theoretical and experimental results show that small entry fee will drive the P2P system into almost full of punishers: time will mostly be spent on the state of punisher, which no only contribute resource, but voluntarily punish defectors. Briefly, our paper shows that it is feasible to construct an effective resource provision mechanism without assuming altruism or resorting to external mechanisms.

Acknowledgments. This research is partially support by the 973 Program 2007CB310607, 863 Project 2007AA01Z206 and 2006AA01Z235, NSFC Grants 60802022 and 60772062.

References

1. Adar, E., Huberman, B.: Free Riding on Gnutella. First Monday Online Journal (2000)
2. Hughes, D., Coulson, G., Walkerdine, J.: Free Riding on Gnutella Revisited: the Bell Tolls? IEEE Distributed Systems Online 6 (2005)
3. Chuang, J.: Designing Incentive Mechanisms for Peer-to-Peer Systems. In: 1st IEEE Workshop on Grid Economics and Business Models (2004)
4. Sami, R., Katabi, D., Faratin, P., Wroclawski, J.: Practice and Theory of Incentives in Networked Systems (PINS): Workshop Report. In: ACM SIGCOMM Workshop on Practice and Theory of Incentives in Networked Systems (2004)

5. Feldman, M., Chuang, J.: Overcoming Free-Riding Behavior in Peer-to-Peer Systems. ACM SIGecom Exchanges 5(4), 41–50 (2005)
6. Buragohain, C., Agrawal, D., Suri, S.: A Game Theoretic Framework for Incentives in P2P Systems. In: 3rd International Conference on Peer-to-Peer Computing (2003)
7. Courcoubetis, C., Weber, R.: Incentives for Large Peer-to-Peer Systems. IEEE Journal on Selected Areas in Communications 24(5) (2006)
8. Feldman, M., Papadimitriou, C., Chuang, J., Stoica, I.: Free-Riding and Whitewashing in Peer-to-Peer Systems. IEEE Journal on Selected Areas in Communications 24(5) (2006)
9. Vassilakis, D.K., Vassalos, V.: An Analysis of Peer-to-Peer Networks with Altruistic Peers. Peer-to-Peer Networking and Applications 2(2) (2009)
10. An, B., Vasilakos, A.V., Lesser, V.: Evolutionary Stable Resource Pricing Strategies. In: ACM SIGCOMM (2009)
11. Lee, C., Suzuki, J., Vasilakos, A.V.: iNet-EGT: An Evolutionarily Stable Adaptation Framework for Network Applications. In: 4th BIONETICS (2009)
12. Wang, Y.F., Nakao, A.: On Cooperative and Efficient Overlay Network Evolution based on Group Selection Pattern. IEEE Trans. on Systems, Man and Cybernetics - Part B (Cybenetics) 40(3) (2010)
13. Nisan, N., Roughgarden, T., Tardos, E., Vazirani, V.V.: Algorithmic Game Theory. Cambridge University Press, Cambridge (2007)
14. Hauert, C., et al.: Exploration Dynamics in Evolutionary Games. Proceedings of the National Academy of Sciences 106(3), 709–712 (2009)
15. Wang, Y.F., Nakao, A., Vasilakos, A.V., Ma, J.H.: P2P Soft Security: On Evolutionary Dynamics of P2P Incentive Mechanism. Elsevier Computer Communications (2010) (in press), `http://dx.doi.org/10.1016/j.comcom.2010.01.021`
16. Hauert, C., et al.: Via Freedom to Coercion: the Emergence of Costly Punishment. Science 316(5833), 1905–1907 (2007)
17. Traulsen, A., Nowak, M.A., Pacheco, J.M.: Stochastic Dynamics of Invasion and Fixation. Phys. Rev. E 74 (2006)
18. Clark, D.D., Wroclawski, J., Sollins, K.R., Braden, R.: Tussle in Cyberspace: Defining Tomorrow's Internet. IEEE/ACM Transactions on Networking (TON) 13(3) (2005)

A Novel Framework for Service Description and Operations

Yu Bai[1], Yaoxue Zhang[1], Yuezhi Zhou[1], Laurance T. Yang[2], Linkai Weng[1], and Hao Liu[1]

[1] Key Laboratory of Pervasive Computing, Ministry of Education, Tsinghua National Laboratory for Information Science and Technology, Department of Computer Science and Technology, Tsinghua University, Beijing 100084, China
baiyu85@gmail.com, zyx@moe.edu.cn, zhouyz@mail.tsinghua.edu.cn, wlk02@mails.tsinghua.edu.cn, liuhao.buaa@gmail.com

[2] Department of Computer Science, St .Francis Xavier University, Antigonish, Canada
ltyang@gmail.com

Abstract. Along with the increase in users' demands for service functions, single services or simple functions cannot satisfy users' requirements any more. Therefore, we need service composition to provide customized services or compound functions to meet users' needs. However, existing methods cannot describe customized services or guarantee the safety of service composition, so we propose a novel framework for service description and operations in this paper. Our framework is composed of a new format for service description and a set of service operations. The former is used to describe the structure of customized services and to be the foundation of service operations, while the latter is used to represents the dependency relationships between services and to verify the safety of service composition. Compared to the existing service description languages, our method can be used to describe customized services and to be the basis for achieving the automation of service composition. An example is given to demonstrate that our approach can provide better service description and safe service composition.

Keywords: Service description, service operations, safe service composition.

1 Introduction

To facilitate efficient development, deployment, maintenance and usage of software functions, the concept *service* has been put at a significant position in several emerging computing paradigms, such as Ubiquitous Computing [8], Software as a Service (SaaS) [7], and Cloud Computing [6]. *Service* does not only draw great attention from academia communities, but it has also become a hot issue in industry. As important

Z. Yu et al. (Eds.): UIC 2010, LNCS 6406, pp. 366–381, 2010.

applications, *services* are regarded as high value-added products and there have been millions of services released on the Internet for users [17].

Nowadays, in order to meet users' diverse demands quickly and flexibly, single services or simple functions should be composed together to provide customized services or compound services [16], since users may often need to add subservices into existing service to obtain a composite service which can provide additional functions, or remove part of subservices to get a simplified service which is convenient to use. Nevertheless, considering the fact that services are usually developed and deployed by different groups, in different languages, and with interoperability constraints, it makes the universal and standardized service description framework essentially important for automatic service composition.

However, existing service description languages always describe single services or simple functions from certain aspects and they are insufficient for automatic service composition. Web Service Description Language (WSDL) [1] is used to give syntactic description of name and parameters of a service, but it does not support automatic service discovery or service composition since it cannot provide any semantic supports [4, 5]. Web Ontology Language (OWL) [2] allows formal conceptual modeling via logical ontologies, but it may bring semantic aliasing problems [4]. Although Web Ontology Language for Service (OWL-S) [3] adds industry specific ontologies to OWL, it cannot infer what functions that a service can actually provide [5]. Universal Service-Semantics Description Language (USDL) [4] can provide semantic information based on WSDL and OWL, but it cannot verify the process of safe service composition, because it lacks description for service operations. On the other hand, existing standard executable language for specifying interactions with Web Services such as Business Process Execution Language (BPEL) [18] etc. are difficult to guarantee efficient composition verification.

To overcome the deficiencies of existing methods mentioned above and to provide customized services for users automatically, we propose a novel service description framework, which contains two main parts: a new format for service description and a set of service operations. The former is used to describe the structure of customized services and to be the foundation for supporting service operations, while the latter is used to represent the dependency relationships between services and verify the safety of service composition. According to the study of service definitions, we describe service as a 7-tuple based on WSDL, which is a standard to specify service syntax. The service 7-tuple can be used as semantic information and the basis for service publication and service discovery. After combining syntax and semantics together, to describe service dependency relationships more intuitively and precisely, we define three service operations, which can be used to guarantee safe service composition and simplify the formula derivation of service composition.

This paper is organized as following. In Section 2, we describe service as a 7-tuple and illustrate the different roles played by the seven elements. Section 3 presents the operations between subservices and services. We use an example to explain how to use our framework to describe service and guarantee the safety of service composition in Section 4. Finally we address conclusions and future work in the last section.

2 A New Format for Service Description

Through the study of service definitions [10, 11, 12, 13, 14, 15], we found *service* has some characteristics such as reusability, spatio-temporal characteristic, substitutability, etc. To encompass these characteristics, we describe *service* as a 7-tuple (see Fig.1), which can represent most characteristics of a service well. Service 7-tuple is based on WSDL, which is nature for describing service syntax, and we borrow the ideas of two main parts (portType and message) in WSDL to describe service structure. In addition, we add semantic information such as *Space*, *Time*, *Function* and *Quality* into service 7-tuple to support the automation of service discovery, service substitution and service composition. Therefore, service 7-tuple can be regarded as semantic complement to WSDL. Service 7-tuple can be used as the basis to describe the structure of customized services and the foundation to support service operations.

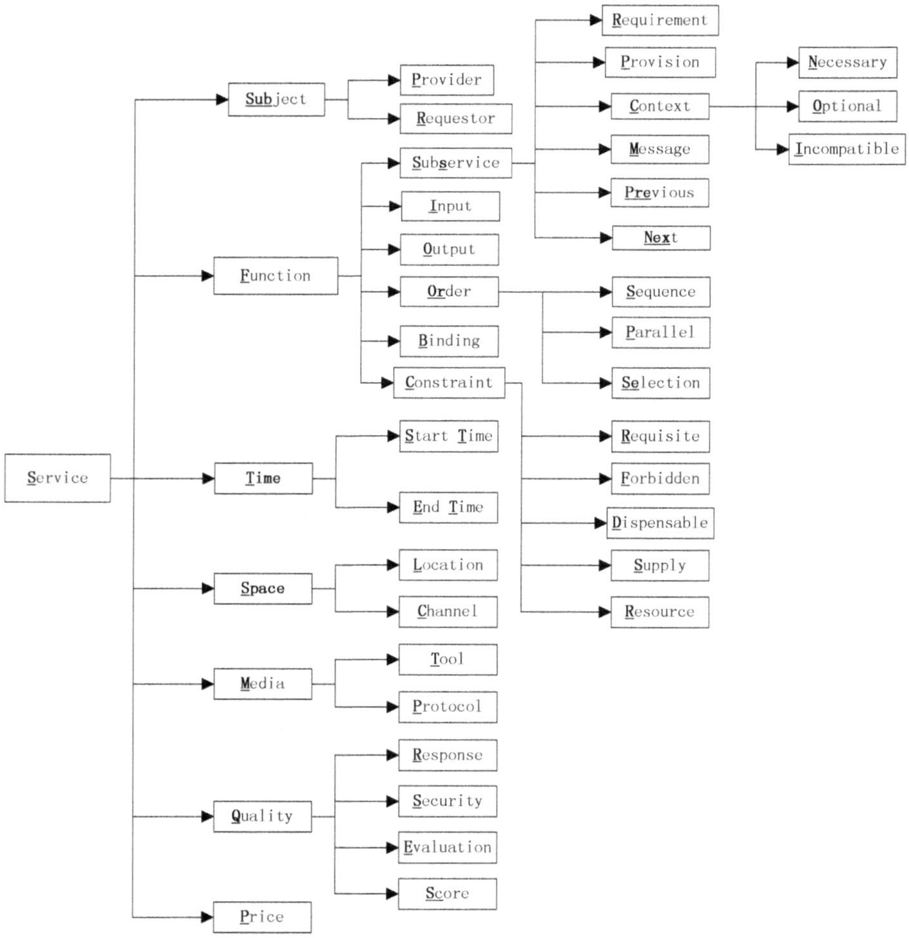

Fig. 1. Service 7-Tuple

Definition 1 (Service). *Service* is an interactive process between subjects which satisfies spatio-temporal characteristics through a specific communication media.

$$\text{Service} := (\mathbf{Sub}\text{ject}, \mathbf{F}\text{unction}, \mathbf{T}\text{ime}, \mathbf{S}\text{pace}, \mathbf{M}\text{edia}, \mathbf{Q}\text{uality}, \mathbf{P}\text{rice})$$

Each element of service 7-tuple can be identified by their first letter and our framework supports dot operation to display the hierarchy of service.

Definition 2 (Subject). *Subject* represents both sides of the given service, which is composed of *Provider* (service render) and *Requestor* (service user).

$$\mathbf{Sub}\text{ject} := < \mathbf{P}\text{rovider}, \mathbf{R}\text{equestor} >$$

Definition 3 (Function). *Function* represents service functions and the relationships between services.

$$\text{Function} := < \mathbf{S}\text{ub}\mathbf{s}\text{ervice}, \mathbf{I}\text{nput}, \mathbf{O}\text{utput}, \mathbf{Or}\text{der}, \mathbf{B}\text{inding}, \mathbf{C}\text{onstraint} >$$

1) **SS (Subservice):** *Subservice* and *Service* are the same concept, although they present different tuples to the outside. In fact, *Subservice* and *Service* have same structure and some of their tuples are equivalent. For example, *Subservice Requirement* corresponds to *Service Input*, *Subservice Provision* corresponds to *Service Output* and *Subservice Context* corresponds to *Service Constraint.* Concept *Service* and *Subservice* are used in different scenarios: the former is used to provide functions for users (outside) and the latter is used when service composition happens (inside). One *Service* can be regarded as one *Subservice* when it is added into an existing *Service* to generate composite service.

$$\mathbf{SS} :=< \mathbf{R}\text{equirement}, \mathbf{P}\text{rovision}, \mathbf{C}\text{ontext}, \mathbf{M}\text{essage}, \mathbf{Prev}\text{ious}, \mathbf{Next} >$$

- **R (Requirement)** represents all functions of the given subservice needed to be provided by other subservices.
$$\mathbf{R} := \{r_1, r_2, r_3, \dots \dots, r_n\}$$
- **P (Provision)** represents all functions of the given subservice can provide to other subservices.
$$\mathbf{P} := \{p_1, p_2, p_3, \dots \dots, p_n\}$$
- **C (Context)** represents dependency relationship of the given subservice.
$$\mathbf{C} := < \mathbf{N}\text{ecessary}, \mathbf{O}\text{ptional}, \mathbf{I}\text{ncompatible} >$$
  - **N (Necessary)** specifies the minimal set of necessary requirements of the given subservice. If *Necessary* cannot be satisfied, this subservice cannot be installed into the existing service. It is represented by a solid line in illustration. There are two kinds of *Necessary*, which are provided by *Resource* (nr_i) or provided by other subservices (np_j).
$$\mathbf{N} = \{nr_1, nr_2, \dots \dots, nr_i, np_1, np_2, \dots \dots, np_j\}$$
  - **O (Optional)** specifies the indispensable requirements of the given subservice. *Optional* will not prevent the subservice from installing if it

cannot be provided. Optional requirements can provide extra functions and it is represented by a dotted line in the illustration.

$$\mathbf{O} = \{o_1, o_2, \dots \dots, o_n\}$$

- **I (Incompatible)** specifies the conflicted requirements of the given subservice. *Incompatible* may conflict with the requirements of the given subservice or even disrupt the whole system. It is represented by negation in the illustration.

$$\mathbf{I} = \{i_1, i_2, \dots \dots, i_n\}$$

- **M (Message)** represents communication information between subservices, whose meaning is different from that of *message* in WSDL.
- **Pre (Previous)** represents the previous subservice(s) of the given subservice.
- **Nex (Next)** represents the next subservice(s) of the given subservice.

2) **I (Input)** represents input parameter and is the only input source of the given service. Different input parameters can obtain different output results.

$$\mathbf{I} := \{par_1, par_2, \dots \dots, par_n\}$$

3) **O(Output)** represents *Return Value* when input is valid, otherwise *Error Message.*

$$\mathbf{O} := < \mathrm{RV}, \mathrm{EM} >$$

4) **Or (Order)** represents the assembly orders of a *service*. There are three main assembly orders of service composition, which are *Sequence Assembly* (Seq, $SS_i \rightarrow SS_j$), *Parallel Assembly* (Par, $SS_i \uparrow_a SS_j$), and *Selection Assembly* (Sel, $SS_i || SS_j$), where SS_i, SS_j, SS_k and SS_l are four arbitrary subservices.

Order

$$\text{Seq:}\ \frac{SS_i.\mathrm{Nex} = SS_j, SS_j.\mathrm{Pre} = SS_i, SS_j \subseteq_S SS_i}{SS_i \rightarrow SS_j} \qquad \text{Sel:}\ \frac{\text{if } S.F.C \vdash a, \text{then } SS_i, \text{eles } SS_j}{SS_i \uparrow_a SS_j}$$

$$\text{Par:}\ \frac{(SS_i \vee_R SS_j \subseteq_S SS_k) \text{ and } (SS_l \subseteq_S SS_i \vee_P SS_j)}{SS_i || SS_j}$$

Three formulas mentioned above mean that if the conditions which are above the line can be satisfied, the corresponding assembly sequence which is below the line will be obtained. We take *Sequence Assembly* as an example to explain the details of service *Order*. If the *Next* subservice of SS_i is SS_j, the *Previous* subservice of SS_j is SS_i and $SS_j \subseteq_S SS_i$, we say the *Order* between SS_i and SS_j is *Sequence Assembly*, which is denoted by $SS_i \rightarrow SS_j$. The unknown expressions in *Order* such as $SS_j \subseteq_S SS_i$, $SS_i \vee_R SS_j$, $SS_i \vee_P SS_j$, etc will be discussed in Section 3.

5) **B (Binding)** represents mapping information between *Service* and *Subservices*. It records which subservices' requirements will be bound with the input of service and which subservices' provisions will be bound with the output of service.
6) **C (Constraint)** is composed of *Context* of all subservices. If service S_1 is composed of subservice SS_i, i=1~n, then $S_1.F.C = SS_1.C + SS_2.C + \dots \dots + SS_n.C$. *Constraint* is composed of *Requisite*, *Dispensable*, *Forbidden*, *Supply* and

Resource. In our framework for service description, all service expressions begin with S or SS, which represents Service or Subservice respectively. For example, Service.Function.Constraint is abbreviated to $\mathrm{S.F.C}$ for convenience and SS.C.N means Subservice.Context.Necessary.

$$\mathbf{C} := < \mathbf{R}\text{equisite}, \mathbf{D}\text{ispensable}, \mathbf{F}\text{orbidden}, \mathbf{S}\text{upply}, \mathbf{Res}\text{ource} >$$

- **R (Requisite)** is composed of the *Necessary* of all subservices.
- **D (Dispensable)** is composed of the *Optional* of all subservices.
- **F (Forbidden)** is composed of the *Incompatible* of all subservices.
- **S (Supply)** is composed of the *Provisions* of all subservices.
- **Res (Resource)** represents system resource, such as CPU, memory size and hard disk size. For example, if $\mathrm{SS_n}$ needs 500M memory ($\mathrm{nr_1}$), and *Resource* can provide 1G memory, we say $\mathrm{nr_1}$ is satisfied by ($\propto$) *Resource*, denoted by

$$\mathrm{nr_1} \propto \mathrm{Resource}$$

If all requirements of $\mathrm{SS_n}$ can be satisfied by the *Resource* of $\mathrm{S_1}$, denoted by

$$\mathrm{SS_n.C.N} \propto \mathrm{S_1.F.C.Res}$$

When $\mathrm{SS_n}$ is added into/removed from $\mathrm{S_{old}}$ to obtain a new service $\mathrm{S_{new}}$, we should modify the *Resource* of $\mathrm{S_{old}}$, which is denoted by

$$\mathrm{S_{old}.F.C.Res} \Rightarrow_{\mathrm{SS_n}} \mathrm{S_{new}.F.C.Res}$$

Constraint is used when service adds or removes one or several subservices, which will be discussed in Section 3. After adding/removing subservice $\mathrm{SS_n}$ to/from service $\mathrm{S_{old}}$ to obtain service $\mathrm{S_{new}}$, we need to *Update Constraint*

$$\mathrm{S_{new}.F.C} = \mathrm{S_{old}.F.C} + \mathrm{SS_n.C}$$

where

$$\mathrm{S_{new}.F.C.R} = \mathrm{S_{old}.F.C.R} + \mathrm{SS_n.C.N}$$
$$\mathrm{S_{new}.F.C.F} = \mathrm{S_{old}.F.C.F} + \mathrm{SS_n.C.I}$$
$$\mathrm{S_{new}.F.C.D} = \mathrm{S_{old}.F.C.D} + \mathrm{SS_n.C.O}$$
$$\mathrm{S_{new}.F.C.S} = \mathrm{S_{old}.F.C.S} + \mathrm{SS_n.P}$$

Definition 4 (Time). *Time* represents the temporal characteristics of the given service and it is a part of *Service Input*. It is composed of *Start Time* and *End Time*.

$$\mathbf{T} := < \mathbf{S}\text{tart }\mathbf{T}\text{ime}, \mathbf{E}\text{nd }\mathbf{T}\text{ime} >$$

Definition 5 (Space). *Space* represents the spatial characteristics of the given service and it is a part of *Service Input*. It is composed of *Location* and *Channel*.

$$\mathbf{S} := < \mathbf{L}\text{ocation}, \mathbf{C}\text{hannel} >$$

We use an example to explain the meaning of *Time* and *Space*. If we want to send a mail from China to America (*Space* Characteristics), we have three services for choice which are ordinary mail (7 days), UPS (2 days) and E-mail (5 seconds). If we want to get the mail in 3 days, we can choose UPS or E-mail. But if we must get the mail in 1 day, Email is the only choice. If service S_1 can satisfy *Time* or *Space* of *Input*, which is denoted by

$$S_1.T/S_1.S \propto S_1.\text{Input}$$

Definition 6 (Media). *Media* represents the *Tool* and *Protocol* during using service.

$$\mathbf{M} := <\text{Tool}, \text{Protocol}>$$

Definition 7 (Quality). *Quality* represents the quality of given service. It is composed of *Response*, *Security*, *Evaluation* and *Score*.

$$\textbf{Quality} = <\textbf{R}\text{esponse}, \textbf{S}\text{ecurity}, \textbf{E}\text{valuation}, \textbf{Sc}\text{ore}>$$

1) **R (Response)** represents the score of service response and it is a relative value of existing results. Based on the Mail-Sending example, the ranking result for Response is {Email=9, UPS=7, letters = 3}.
2) **S (Security)** the scoring process is similar to that of *Response*.
3) **E (Evaluation)** is given by users and scoring process is similar to that of *Response*.
4) **Sc (Score)** is the comprehensive evaluation of the given service. It is the criteria for people to choose service. People can adjust the weight of *Response*, *Security* and *Evaluation* according to their requirements. If service S_1 can satisfy the *Quality Score* of *Service Input*, which is denoted by

$$S_1.Q.Sc \propto S_1.\text{Input}$$

Definition 8(Price). *Price* represents the cost of using given service.

3 Operations between Subservices and Services

Based on semantic information defined in Section 2, we discuss the operations between subservices and services in this section. To describe the operations more conveniently, we at first define five basic relationships between subservices. The last three relationships can also be represented by *Inclusion Relationships*.

1. **Union of Requirements $SS_i \vee_R SS_j$.**

$$SS_i \vee_R SS_j \triangleq \{np|np \in SS_i.C.N \text{ or } np \in SS_j.C.N\}$$

2. **Union of Provisions $SS_i \vee_P SS_j$.**

$$SS_i \vee_P SS_j \triangleq \{p \mid p \in SS_i.P \text{ or } p \in SS_j.P\}$$

3. **Requirement Inclusion (RI) $SS_i \subseteq_R SS_j$.**

$$SS_i \subseteq_R SS_j \triangleq \{\forall np_i \in SS_i.C.N, \text{then } np_i \in SS_j.C.N\}$$

4. **Provision Inclusion (PI) $SS_i \subseteq_P SS_j$.**

$$SS_i \subseteq_P SS_j \triangleq \{\forall p_i \in SS_i.P, \text{then } p_i \in SS_j.P\}$$

5. **Satisfaction Inclusion (SI) $SS_i \subseteq_S SS_j$.**

$$SS_i \subseteq_S SS_j \triangleq \{\forall np_i \in SS_i.C.N, \text{then } np_i \in SS_j.P\}$$

Inclusion Relationships

$$RI: \frac{\forall np_i \in SS_i.C.N, \text{then } np_i \in SS_j.C.N}{SS_i \subseteq_R SS_j} \qquad PI: \frac{\forall p_i \in SS_i.P, \text{then } p_i \in SS_j.P}{SS_i \subseteq_P SS_j}$$

$$SI: \frac{\forall np_i \in SS_i.C.N, \text{then } np_i \in SS_j.P}{SS_i \subseteq_S SS_j}$$

Next, we discuss the details of operations between subservices and services. There are three main operations between subservices and services: *Subservice Addition/Removal*, *Subservice Substitution* and *Service Combination*.

3.1 Subservice Addition/ Removal

Subservice Addition and *Subservice Removal* are important operations in service composition, because users may often need to add subservices into existing service to obtain a composite service which can provide additional functions, or remove part of subservices to get a simplified service which is convenient to use. Because the processes of these two operations are similar, we take *Subservice Addition* as an example to explain the details of these two operations. In this example, we add subservice SS_n into existing service S_{old} to obtain a new service S_{new}.

The process of *Subservice Addition* can be divided into two main stages: *Addition Check* and *Information Update*. Fig.2 illustrates the process mentioned above. This process can be performed iteratively in *Service Combination*.

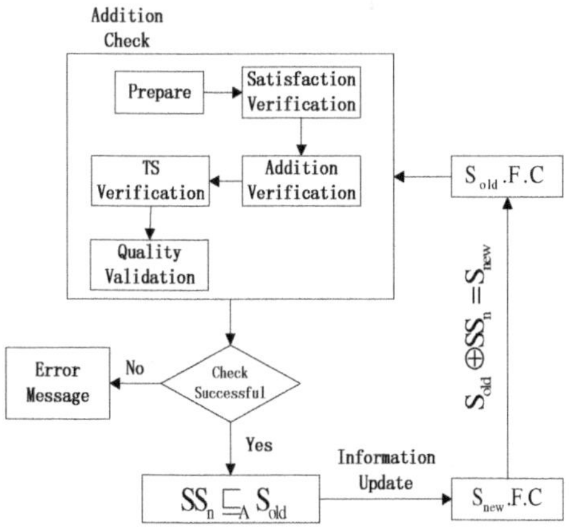

Fig. 2. Subservice Addition

Addition Check

1. Prepare. Determine *Order* of S_{new} and the insertion position of SS_n ($SS_i \rightarrow SS_n \rightarrow SS_j$). Find out previous subservice SS_i and following subservice SS_j of SS_n.

2. Satisfaction Verification. The requirements of SS_n should be satisfied by the provisions of SS_i, and the requirements of SS_j should be satisfied by the provisions of SS_n, that is $SS_n \subseteq_S SS_i$ and $SS_j \subseteq_S SS_n$.

3. Addition Verification. SS_n does not need the functions which are forbidden in S_{old}, SS_n cannot provide the functions which are forbidden in S_{old}, and all resource requirements of SS_n can be satisfied by *Resource* of S_{old}, that is,

$$\forall np_i, nr_i \in SS_n.C.N, np_i, nr_i \notin S_{old}.F.C.F \Leftrightarrow SS_n.C.N \cap S_{old}.F.C.F = \emptyset,$$
$$\forall p_i \in SS_n.P, p_i \notin S_{old}.F.C.F \Leftrightarrow SS_n.P \cap S_{old}.F.C.F = \emptyset,$$
$$\text{and } SS_n.C.N \propto S_{old}.F.C.Res$$

4. TS Verification. Check temporal-spatial characteristics of the subservice, that is

$$S_{new}.T/S_{new}.S \propto S_{new}.Input$$

5. Quality Validation. The addition of subservice SS_n should make $Q.Sc$ higher than users' requirement.

$$S_{new}.Q.Sc \propto S_{new}.Input$$

If SS_n can satisfy the five requirements above, we say SS_n *addition-satisfy* ($\sqsubseteq_A$) S_{old}, which is denoted by $SS_n \sqsubseteq_A S_{old}$.

Information Updates

$$S_{new}.F.C = S_{old}.F.C + SS_n.C$$

Then update the previous and following subservice of subservice SS_n

$$SS_n.Pre = SS_i, \quad SS_n.Nex = SS_j$$
$$SS_i.Nex = SS_n, \quad SS_j.Pre = SS_n$$

At last modify the *Resource* of S_{old}

$$S_{old}.F.C.Res \Rightarrow_{SS_n} S_{new}.F.C.Res$$

The complete process of *Subservice Addition* ($\oplus$) can be described as:

$$(SS_n \sqsubseteq_A S_{old}) \vdash (S_{old} \oplus SS_n = S_{new})$$

3.2 Subservice Substitution

Subservice Substitution happens when we want to use subservice SS_{new} to substitute subservice SS_{old} which has already been in service S_{old} to obtain a new service S_{new}. We define two kinds of substitution, one is used to address substitutability independent of service constraints (*Strict Substitution*) and the other is based on particular service constraints (*Context-based Substitution*).

Strict Substitution. Subservice SS_{new} can substitute SS_{old} in all *Service Constraints*, which is denoted by $SS_{new} \asymp SS_{old}$.
Context-based Substitution. Subservice SS_{new} can substitute SS_{old} in given *Service Constraints* (C_{temp}), which is denoted by $SS_{new} \asymp_{C_{temp}} SS_{old}$.

Strict Substitution rarely happens, so we will focus on *Context-based Substitution*. *Context-based Substitution* can be divided into two main stages, which are *Context-based Substitution Check* and *Information Update*.

Context -based Substitution Check

1. Prepare. We know SS_{old} is substituted by SS_{new}, so we can find out the previous subservice SS_i and the following subservice SS_j of SS_{new} by *Service Order*.
2. Satisfaction Verification. The requirements of SS_{new} should be satisfied by the provisions of SS_i, and the requirements of SS_j should be satisfied by the provisions of SS_{new}, that is $SS_{new} \subseteq_S SS_i$ and $SS_j \subseteq_S SS_{new}$.
3. Substitution Verification. All new functions which are in SS_{new} but not in SS_{old} provided by SS_{new} can not conflict with existed functions in S_{old}, and all functions which are in SS_{old} but not in SS_{new} provided by SS_{old} are dispensable, and all resource requirements of SS_{new} can be satisfied by *Resource* of S_{old},that is

$$\forall p_i \in SS_{new}.P, \text{and } p_i \notin SS_{old}.P, \exists p_i \notin S_{old}.F.C.F$$

$$\forall p_i \in SS_{old}.P, \text{and } p_i \notin SS_{new}.P, \exists p_i \in S_{old}.F.C.D$$

$$\text{and } SS_{new}.C.N \propto S_{old}.F.C.Res$$

4. TS Verification. Check temporal-spatial characteristics of the subservice, that is

$$S_{new}.T/S_{new}.S \propto S_{new}.\text{Input}$$

5. Quality Validation. The substitution of SS_{old} should make the $S_{new}.Q.Sc$ higher than users' requirement.

$$S_{new}.Q.Sc \propto S_{new}.\text{Input}$$

If SS_{new} can satisfy the five requirements above, we say SS_n *Context-Based Substitute* ($\asymp_{C_{temp}}$) SS_{old}, which is denoted by $SS_{new} \asymp_{C_{temp}} SS_{old}$, where $C_{temp} = S_{old}.F.C - SS_{old}.C$.

Information Update

The process of *Information Update* is similar to that of *Subservice Addition*. The complete process of *Context-based Substitution* can be described as

$$(SS_{new} \asymp_{C_{temp}} SS_{old}) \vdash (S_{old} - SS_{old} + SS_{new} = S_{new})$$

3.3 Service Combination

In fact, *Service Combination* is not a concrete operation but rather a complete process of generating service. It begins with *Service Initialization* and ends with *Service Publication*. Different users' requirements may bring different steps of service composition. The more subservices are to be composed, the more complicated the process is. *Subservice Addition* is the main part of *Service Combination* and it may be used iteratively to add new subservices into existing service to obtain required service.

Fig.3 illustrates a simple instance for *Service Combination*. First, by analyzing users' requirements, we find three subservices SS_1, SS_2 and SS_3 which can provide all functions to meet users' needs. Then we calculate the dependency relationships between these three subservices and get the service assembly sequence $(SS_1||SS_2) \rightarrow SS_3$. At last, we compose these subservices together to obtain a new service S_{new}.

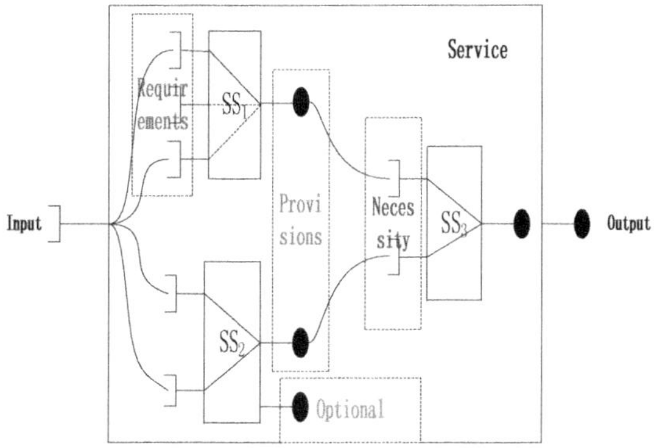

Fig. 3. Subservice Composition

1. Service Initialization. Through analyzing function dependencies of these three subservices, we determine *Order* as $(SS_1||SS_2) \rightarrow SS_3$ and calculate the *Quality Score* as $S_{new}.Q.Sc >= 9.0$ according to users' requirements. Then we create an empty service S_{new} and use *Order, Score* and *Resource* to finish initialization.
2. Addition Check. Check whether SS_1 and SS_2 can be added into S_{new}, that is $SS_1 \sqsubseteq_A S_{new}$ and $SS_2 \sqsubseteq_A S_{new}$.
3. Information Update. After adding SS_1 and SS_2 into S_{new}, we get

$$S_{new}.F.C = SS_1.C + SS_2.C$$

4. Satisfaction Check. Check whether the provisions of SS_1 and SS_2 can satisfy the requirements of SS_3, that is $SS_3 \subseteq_S SS_1 \vee_P SS_2$.
5. Subservice Communicate. Build communication information between subservices and modify *Binding* between service and subservices.
6. Service Publication. S_{new} can satisfy users' requirements and we will store it as a subservice in order to reuse next time.

4 Case Study

In this section, we will use an example to summarize our novel framework for service description and operations. First, we will use service 7-tuple to describe two subservices respectively. Second, we will use three operations defined in Section 3 to prove that these two subservices can be composed together safely. Then we will represent the result of service composition. At last we will make a comparison between our method and existing service description languages.

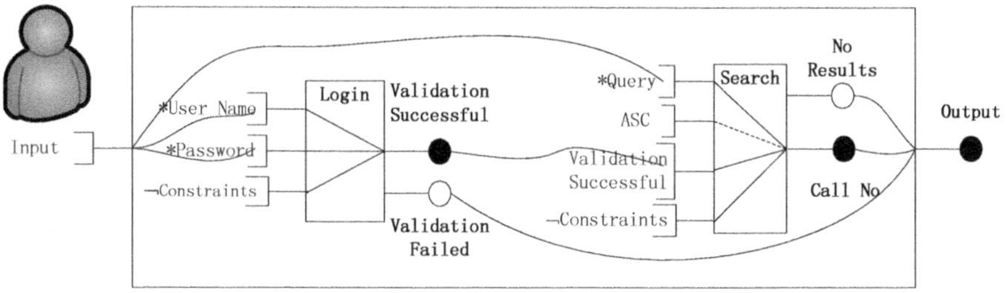

Fig. 4. Book-Borrowing Service

A Simple Book-Borrowing Service: Fig.4 describes a simplified Book-Borrowing Service which is an interactive process between the users and the library. Book-Borrowing Service consists of two subservices which are *Login* and *Search*. It takes in User Name (UN), Password (PW) and Query as input and Advanced Search Condition (ASC) as optional requirement. It also has some *Constraints* to limit the *Input* of the service, such as the length of PW is between 6 to 10 and UN cannot contain characters such as "?, \, /, *, :". There are three kinds of *Output* which are Validation Failed (invalid user name or password), Call No. (users can get the book they want) or No Results (the book is not in the library).

Fig.5 represents the description of two subservice *Login* (left) and *Search* (right) by service 7-tuple. It can not only describe the syntactic information such as *Requirements* and *Provisions* which are the main task of WSDL, but it can also record some service semantic information such as *Context*, *Previous* and *Next*.

<definition>	<definition>
……	……
<portType Subservice = Login>	<portType Subservice= Search>
<Requirements>	<Requirements>
<r1 = User Name>	<r1 = Query>
<r2 = PW>	<r2 = VS>
</Requirements>	</Requirements>
<Provisions>	<Provisions>
<p1 = Validation Successful>	<p1 = Call No>
<p2 = Validation Failed>	<p2 = No Results>
</Provisions>	</Provisions>
<Context>	<Context>
<np1 = User Name>	<np1 = Query>
<np2 = PW>	<np2 = Validation Successful>

<i1 = 6 ≤ #PW ≤ 10>	<o1 = ASC>
<i2 = {? \ / *:} ∉ User Name>	<i1 = 0 < #Query ≤ 30>
</Context>	</Context>
<Previous>	<Previous>
<p1 = service input>	<p1 = Login>
</Previous>	</Previous>
<Next>	<Next>
<n1 = Search>	<n1 = service output>
</Next>	</Next>
</portType>	</portType>
</definition>	</definition>

Fig. 5. Description for Subservice Login and Search

After the description for subservices *Login* and *Search*, we use operations between subservices and services defined in Section 3 to prove safe service composition. This process is based on service semantics while existing description languages cannot guarantee the safety of this process.

Service Composition:

$$\frac{\{\text{User Name}, \text{PW}\} \subset \text{Input} \qquad \dfrac{\text{User Name} = \text{"user1"}}{\text{"?}\backslash/*\text{:"} \notin \text{UserName}} \qquad \dfrac{\text{PW} = \text{"123456"}}{6 \le \#\text{PW} \le 10}}{\text{SS}_1 \sqsubseteq_S \text{Input}}$$

$$\frac{\dfrac{\text{SS}_1 \sqsubseteq_S \text{Input}}{\text{Validation Successful}}}{\text{SS}_1.\text{P} = \{\text{Validation Successful}\}}$$

$$\frac{\dfrac{\text{Query} = \text{"UIC"}}{0 < \#\text{Query} \le 30} \qquad \text{ASC} = \text{"by author"} \qquad \text{VS} \in \text{SS}_1.\text{P} \qquad \{\text{Query}\} \subset \text{Input}}{\text{SS}_2 \sqsubseteq_S \text{Input} \vee_P \text{SS}_1}$$

$$\frac{\dfrac{\text{SS}_2 \sqsubseteq_S \text{Input} \vee_P \text{SS}_1}{\text{Call No} \qquad \text{SS}_2 \sqsubseteq_A \text{S}_{\text{old}}}}{\text{S}_{\text{old}} \oplus \text{SS}_2 = \text{S}_{\text{new}}}$$

Information Update:

$$\frac{\dfrac{\text{SS}_2 \sqsubseteq_A \text{S}_1}{\text{S}_{\text{old}} \oplus \text{SS}_2 = \text{S}_{\text{new}}}}{\text{SS}_1.\text{Pre} = \text{Input} \qquad \text{SS}_2.\text{Pre} = \text{SS}_1 \qquad \text{SS}_1.\text{Nex} = \text{SS}_2 \qquad \text{SS}_2.\text{Nex} = \text{Output}}$$

$$\frac{\text{User Name}, \text{PW} \in \text{SS}_1.\text{C.N} \qquad \text{VS}, \text{Query} \in \text{SS}_2.\text{C.N}}{\text{S}_2.\text{F.C.R} = \{\text{User Name}, \text{PW}, \text{VS}, \text{Query}\}}$$

$$\frac{\text{ASC}}{\text{S}_2.\text{F.C.D} = \{\text{ASC}\}}$$

$$\frac{\text{"?}\backslash/*\text{:"} \notin \text{UserName} \qquad 6 \le \#\text{PW} \le 10 \qquad 0 < \#\text{Query} \le 30}{\text{S}_2.\text{F.C.F} = \{(\text{"?}\backslash/*\text{:"} \notin \text{UserName}), (11 \le \#\text{PW or}\#\text{PW} \le 5), (30 < \#\text{Query})\}}$$

Fig. 6. Derivation of Safe Service Composition

In the derivation of safe service composition, we check the global constraints such as $"?\backslash/*:" \notin \text{UserName}$ and $6 \le \#PW \le 10$. We also verify the *Optional* requirement ASC to check whether the service can provide additional functions. Then we use *Information Update* to update service *Resource*. At last, we obtain a new service *Book-Borrowing* (see Fig.7), which is composed of subservices *Login* and *Search*. Service *Book-Borrowing* can be stored as a subservice for reusing next time.

Service Description

```
<definition>
......
  <portType Service = Book Borrow>
    <Subjects>
      <p = library>
      <r = user1>
    </Subjects>
    <Functions>
      <Subservice>
        <SS1= Login>
        <SS2= Search>
      </Subservice>
      <Input>
        <i1= User Name>
        <i2= PW>
        <i3=Query>
      </Input>
      <Output>
        <rv =Call No.>
        <em1=Validation Failed>
        <em2=No Results>
      </Output>
      <Order>
        <I → SS1 → SS2 → O>
      </Order>
      <Binding>
        <b1=bind I with SS1, SS2>
        <b2=bind O with SS1, SS2>
      </Binding>
      <Constraints>
        <r1 = User Name>
        <r2 = PW>
        <r3 = Query>
        <d1 = ASC>
        <f1 = "?\/*:" ∉ UN>
        <f2 = 11 ≤ #PW , #PW ≤ 5>
        <f3 = 30 < #Query >
        <p1 = Call No. >
        <res1 = computer >
        <res2 = Internet >
      </Constraints>
    </Functions>
    <Time>
      <st = 2010-3-25 pm 3:35:01>
      <et = 2010-3-25 pm 3:45:01>
      <d = 10mins>
    </Time>
    <Space>
      <l = library>
      <c = Internet>
    </Space>
    <Media>
      <t = PC>
      <p = HTTP>
    </Media>
    <Quality>
      <t = 8.5>
      <s = 9.5>
      <e = 9>
      <sc = 9>
    </Quality>
    <Price>
      <p = to register a username>
    </Price>
  </portType>
</definition>
```

Fig. 7. Description for Book-Borrowing Service

Finally, we present a comparison between our framework and other popular approaches such as WSDL, OWL-S and USDL. First, while WSDL is used to give syntactic description of the name and parameters of a service, our framework provides service 7-tuple in order to make service directly semantically searchable and assembled. For example, we introduce semantic information such as Constraints, Order and Quality to realize the automation of service discovery, service substitution and service composition. In addition, we use the concept Function to represent what the service actually does and this task cannot be described directly in OWL-S. At last, our framework supports the derivation of service operations which are defined in Section 3 and our method can verify the safety of service composition which is still an open question for USDL.

5 Conclusions and Future Work

In this paper, we propose a novel framework for service description and operations, which is based on semantics while respects to syntax. The framework is composed of service 7-tuple and a set of service operations. Through the summary and the conclusion of service definition and service characteristics, we describe service as a 7-tuple, and it is regarded as semantic information and the basis to support service operations. Furthermore, based on service 7-tuple, we define three operations to express the dependency relationships between subservices and to prove the safety of service composition. Finally, an example is introduced to explain how to use our framework to describe customized service and guarantee the safety of service composition. As a part of the future work, we will use our framework to generate subservice dependency relationship graph automatically and verify the validity of web service composition by programming.

Acknowledgments

This work has been supported in part by the National High Technology Research and Development Program of China (Grant No.: 2009AA011906) and National Core-High-Base Major Project of China (Grant No.: 2009ZX01036-002-3). We would like to thank the anonymous reviewers for their helpful comments on this paper.

References

1. Web Service Description Language, `http://www.w3.org/TR/wsdl`
2. Web Ontology Language, `http://www.w3.org/TR/2004/REC-owl-guide-20040210/`
3. OWL-S, `http://www.daml.org/services/owl-s/1.0/owl-s.html`
4. Bansal, A., Kona, S., Simon, L., Hite, T.D.: A Universal Service-Semantics Description Language. In: Proceedings of the Third European Conference on Web Services, pp. 214–225. IEEE Computer Society, Washington (2005)
5. Le, D., Nguyen, V., Goh, A.: Matching WSDL and OWL-S Web Services. In: Proceedings of the 2009 IEEE International Conference on Semantic Computing, pp. 197–202. IEEE Computer Society, Washington (2009)
6. Armbrust, M., Fox, A., Griffith, R., Joseph, A.D., Katz, R., Konwinski, A., Lee, G., Patterson, D., Rabkin, A., Stoica, I., Zaharia, M.: Above the Clouds: A Berkeley View of Cloud Computing. Technical report, UCB/EECS-2009-28 (2009)

7. Papazoglou, M.P.: Service-Oriented Computing: Concepts, Characteristics and Directions. In: Proceedings of the Fourth International Conference on Web Information Systems Engineering (2003)
8. Weiser, M.: Some Computer Science Issues in Ubiquitous Computing. Communications of the ACM 36(7), 75–84 (1993)
9. Cambronero, M.E., Díaz, G., Martínez, E., Valero, V.: A Comparative Study between WSCI, WS-CDL, and OWL-S. In: Proceedings of the 2009 IEEE International Conference on e-Business Engineering, pp. 377–382. IEEE Computer Society, Washington (2009)
10. O'Sullivan, J., Edmond, D., Hofstede, A.T.: What's in a Service? Distributed and Parallel Databases 12(2-3), 117–133 (2002)
11. Piccinelli, G., Mokrushin, L.: Dynamic Service Aggregation in Electronic Marketplaces. Computer Networks: The International Journal of Computer and Telecommunications Networking (2001)
12. Sahai, A., Machiraju, V., Wurster, K.: Managing Next Generation E-Services. Technical report, HPL (2000)
13. Kuebler, D., Eibach, W.: Metering and accounting for Web services (July 2001), `http://www.ibm.com/developerworks/library/ws-maws/?n-ws-7191`
14. Lewis, R.C., Booms, B.H.: The Marketing Aspects of Service Quality. In: Berry, L., Shostack, G., Upah, G. (eds.) Emerging Perspectives in Services Marketing, pp. 99–104. American Marketing Association, Chicago (1983)
15. Chen, H., Chakraborty, D., Xu, L., Joshi, A., Finin, T.: Service discovery in the future electronic market. In: Workshop on Knowledge-Based Electronic Markets (KBEM 2000)—Proceedings of the 17th National Conference on Artificial Intelligence (AAAI 2000), pp. 1–6. AAAI Press/ MIT Press, Austin, Texas, USA (2000)
16. Yaoxue, Z., Cunhao, F.: Active Service: Concept, Architecture and Implementation. Thomson Learning (2005) ISBN: 7030145763
17. Abe, T.: What is Service Science. Research Report. The Fujitsu Research Institute Economic Research Center, Tokyo, Japan, No.246 (2005)
18. Fu, X., Bultan, T., Su, J.: Analysis of Interacting BPEL Web Services. In: WWW 2004, New York, USA, May 17-22 (2004)

A Self-Adaptive Hardware/Software System Architecture for Ubiquitous Computing Applications

Chun-Hsian Huang, Jih-Sheng Shen, and Pao-Ann Hsiung

Department of Computer Science and Information Engineering,
National Chung Cheng University, Chiayi, Taiwan−621, ROC
{huang,sjs92,pahsiung}@cs.ccu.edu.tw

Abstract. Within ubiquitous computing environments, services and devices can be dynamically adapted to changing conditions, and thus adaptivity becomes a key requirement in providing possibly better system performance. Most existing ubiquitous computing systems either support only software adaptation or manage reconfigurable hardware functions as conventional hardware devices. As a result, system adaptation and performance improvement are still restricted. To provide more robust system adaptation, we propose a self-adaptive hardware/software system architecture (SAHA) that consists of service suppliers, a hardware adapter, a system manager, an observer, and a reconfigurable hardware architecture. Further, SAHA supports both hardware preemption and hardware virtualization within a complete self-aware system adaptation mechanism such that the utilization of system resources is enhanced and better performance is provided for ubiquitous computing applications. Experiments with a ubiquitous computing service for information encryption demonstrate that SAHA can reduce the turnaround time by at least 11.9% of that required by using the conventional method.

Keywords: Hardware/Software Adaptation, Ubiquitous Computing Applications.

1 Introduction

With the increase in user requirements, ubiquitous computing provides human being with a more perfect life. Under natural interaction, ubiquitous computing enables information processing to be thoroughly integrated into everyday living. In such a ubiquitous computing environment, not only services and devices can be dynamically adapted to changing environments, but contexts and preferences of users can be also switched seamlessly.

To support dynamically changing and unpredictable ubiquitous computing applications, adaptivity becomes a key requirement in providing better system performance. Most existing dynamic adaptive approaches to ubiquitous computing [1, 3, 10] focus on adapting software services and applications, while hardware devices only passively support the changing software applications. In

Z. Yu et al. (Eds.): UIC 2010, LNCS 6406, pp. 382–396, 2010.

such a hardware architecture, hardware functions can be only configured once at design-time so that new hardware functions cannot be reconfigured at run-time, which leads to the inefficient use of hardware resources. Further, this restricts the adaptivity of ubiquitous computing system to changing environment conditions, and system performance is thus restricted by the underlying hardware. Though several research works [2, 7] have adopted the dynamic reconfiguration capability of FPGA [12] to support hardware adaptation, the hardware functions in these approaches [2, 7] are still managed as conventional hardware devices. This means that once the device node of a hardware function has been opened by a software application, the hardware function cannot be accessed by other software applications at the same time, though it is not always accessed by the software application that opens its device node. As a result, the utilization of reconfigurable hardware resources and the enhancement of system performance are still limited. To be able to not only adapt on-demand hardware/software functionalities but also provide better *Quality-of-Service* (QoS), ubiquitous computing applications require a more robust and effective infrastructure that can autonomously adapt its software and hardware functions to meet the dynamic requirements of various environmental situations.

In this work, we try to solve the above adaptivity and performance problems in the current existing ubiquitous computing systems [1–3, 7, 10] by proposing a *Self-Adaptive Hardware/software system Architecture* (SAHA). Figure 1 gives an example for illustrating the practicability of the proposed SAHA. In this ubiquitous computing environment, each family member can use his/her own electronic devices to monitor the house, watch the live television programs, and listen to the voice messages recorded in the home telephone via SAHA. To ensure the QoS and the information security, all data will be compressed, encrypted, or both in SAHA and then transferred to family members. Computing-intensive functions, such as *Discrete Cosine Transform* (DCT), cryptographic, and hash functions are implemented as hardware devices to provide better performance. Further, SAHA can adapt on-demand its hardware and software functionalities to different service requirements, based on the network services and electronic products used by family members.

Figure 1 shows an ideal blueprint to apply SAHA to ubiquitous computing environments. However, it must solve several issues related to ubiquitous computing, including 1) how to make hardware functionalities adaptable? 2) how to make hardware adaptation more efficient? 3) how can the utilization of hardware devices be maximized to serve more users? 4) when must hardware functionalities be adapted to different user requirements?

To make hardware functionalities adaptable, the dynamic partial reconfiguration technology [12] of FPGA devices is adopted in SAHA to perform computing-intensive functions. Hardware functions can be dynamically configured on-demand into the FPGA device, thus making the utilization of hardware logics in a FPGA device more efficient. To make hardware adaptation efficient, SAHA integrates our previously proposed hardware preemption technology [4], as a result of which high-priority hardware functions can interrupt low-priority hardware functions that

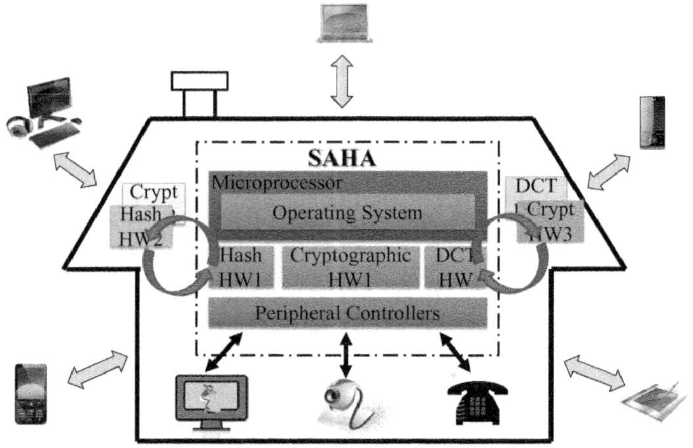

Fig. 1. Ubiquitous Computing Environment

have been configured in the FPGA. Thus, the utilization of hardware logic resources can be significantly enhanced. To maximize the utilization of hardware devices to serve more users, SAHA also integrates our previously proposed hardware virtualization technology [5], and thus a hardware device is virtualized such that it can be accessed by more than one user at the same time. To determine when the hardware functionalities must be adapted, SAHA provides a robust ubiquitous computing infrastructure. It includes service suppliers to interact with users, a hardware adapter to manage hardware functionalities on an FPGA device, an observer to be aware of the characteristics of user applications, and a system manager to manage all system adaptations. With the changes in environment conditions and user requirements, SAHA can effectively and autonomously adapt its hardware/software functions to support better performance.

Our previous works [4, 5] have introduced the detailed designs of hardware preemption and virtualization mechanisms, respectively, and this work will focus on the design of SAHA for ubiquitous computing applications. The rest of the article is organized as follows. Section 2 discusses the related research works. Section 3 introduces the design of SAHA, while Section 4 introduces how the hardware virtualization and preemption techniques can be realized in SAHA to support system adaptation. The experimental evaluation and analyses are given in Section 5. Finally, Section 6 concludes this work.

2 Related Work

Within a ubiquitous computing environment, computing devices are aware of changes in their environment, and thus they need to automatically adapt to environmental changes for satisfying user requirements. Odyssey [8] was a typical ubiquitous computing approach that supported application-aware adaptation to adjust the quality of accessed data to match available resources. However, due to the lack of support for coordination between the adaptation policies, its notification approach may lead to inefficient solutions. To more efficiently support the capability of adaptation, Efstratious et al. [1] proposed an architecture that could support adaptive context-aware applications. However, a main constraint in the approach was that the infrastructure only notified applications about the environmental changes, and then application themselves needed to trigger the adaptive mechanism. Instead of the passive application adaptation, Ghim et al. [3] proposed a reflective approach to dynamic adaptation that could perform adaptation operation triggered by changes in the policy and context, while users and applications could trigger adaptation using policy documents. However, hardware functions in the existing research works [1, 3, 8] cannot be adapted to different requirements, which thus restricts system adaptation and performance enhancement.

To support hardware adaptation, Danek et al. [2] proposed self-adaptive networked entities (SANE) to build pervasive computing architectures. The SANE design included an observer to monitor computation process. Furthermore, a computing engine could be on-demand reconfigured as different hardware functions at runtime to adapt to different system requirements, by using the partial dynamic reconfiguration technology [12]. Lagger et al. [7] also proposed a self-reconfigurable pervasive platform for cryptographic applications. They compared a full-software design with a coprocessor design that had an FPGA device which could be partially configured with different cryptographic hardware cores. Compared to the former, the performance of the latter was significantly enhanced due to dynamic reconfiguration techniques. However, these existing approaches to hardware adaptation [2, 7] still managed reconfigurable hardware functions as conventional hardware devices. As a result, the enhancement of system performance using partial reconfiguration technology is still limited, which makes the utilization of reconfigurable hardware functions inefficient.

In this work, SAHA provides a robust ubiquitous computing infrastructure that includes service suppliers, a hardware adapter, an observer, a system manager, a reconfigurable hardware architecture. Instead of focusing on only software adaptation [1, 3, 8], SAHA further supports hardware adaptation by adopting the partial reconfiguration technology. Different from the existing approaches to hardware adaptation [2, 7] that manage reconfigurable hardware functions as conventional hardware devices, SAHA integrates hardware preemption [4] and hardware virtualization [5] for providing more efficient system adaptation to changing ubiquitous computing applications. At the same time, system performance can be further enhanced through system adaptation.

3 Self-Adaptive Hardware/Software System Architecture

To realize hardware adaptation, we implement the hardware architecture of SAHA in an FPGA device, instead of an ASIC device. In general, not all hardware functions are always accessed by the software applications. Using the FPGA

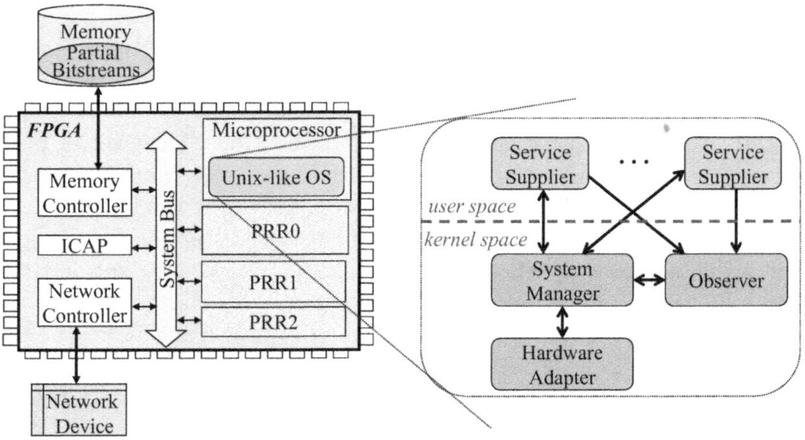

Fig. 2. Self-Adaptive Hardware/Software System Architecture

devices, hardware functions can be configured on-demand at runtime, without integrating them into the system at design time. As a result, though the total amount of logic resources required by all hardware functions exceeds that available in the FPGA, SAHA can still support a larger number of hardware functions by using the capability of hardware adaptation. Furthermore, because a large part of computing-intensive functions in the current SAHA implementation are cryptographic and hash functions, the parameter-specific architecture of the FPGA device also enables SAHA to provide better performance [11].

The SAHA design consists of a microprocessor, an FPGA device, a network device, and an off-chip memory, as shown in Figure 2. The hardware architecture of SAHA is implemented by using the *Early Access Partial Reconfiguration* (EA PR) design flow [12], in which several *Partial Reconfigurable Regions* (PRRs), such as `PRR0`, `PRR1`, and `PRR2` as shown in Figure 2, are implemented in the FPGA. They can be dynamically reconfigured as different hardware functions to meet the requirements for different service suppliers. All reconfigurable hardware functions are encapsulated as partial bitstreams and stored in an off-chip memory. Further, the hardware architecture of SAHA contains an *Internal Configuration Access Port* (ICAP) controller to configure the partial bitstreams into the FPGA.

The microprocessor runs a unix-like *Operating System* (OS) that includes service suppliers, a hardware adapter, a system manager, and an observer. Their detailed introductions are given in the following sections.

3.1 Service Supplier

The service supplier is a software application that interacts with a user, while it interacts with hardware functions for data capture and processing. Each service supplier has a priority, and thus the system manager can decide when it starts

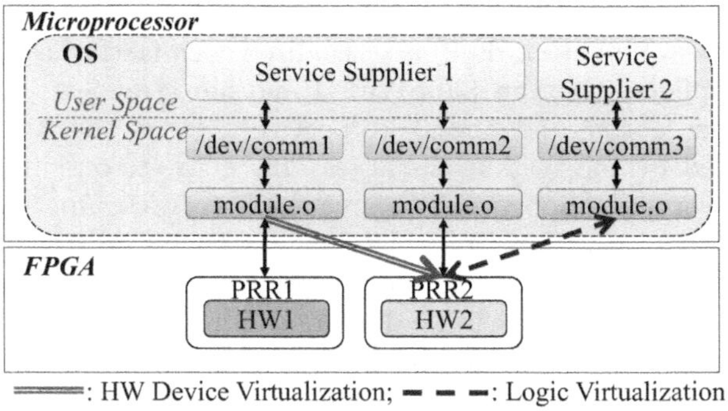

Fig. 3. Hardware Virtualization Mechanism

to serve its user, based on the current ubiquitous computing environmental conditions. Further, similar to the interactions between software applications and hardware devices in a conventional embedded OS, service suppliers in SAHA also interact with reconfigurable hardware functions through the device nodes. As a result, though SAHA supports system adaptation, the generality in accessing the hardware device design is still not sacrificed. Further, because all software and hardware adaptations in SAHA are performed underlying the kernel level, service suppliers can serve their users in a natural interaction method, without any adjustment in them.

3.2 Hardware Adapter

The hardware adapter is used to manage the reconfigurable hardware architecture. When a service supplier requests a hardware function that is not configured in the FPGA, the hardware adapter thus loads the corresponding partial bitstream to the ICAP controller for configuring the required hardware function into the FPGA. The hardware adapter also records which hardware functions are now configured in the PRRs and which service suppliers are accessing them. As a result, the system manager can inquire about the information to estimate which system adaptation, such as hardware reconfiguration, hardware virtualization, and hardware preemption, is better for all ubiquitous computing applications. Further, the hardware adapter needs to support the system manager for performing the hardware preemption mechanism. The details of the hardware preemption mechanism in SAHA will be introduced in the next section.

3.3 System Manager

The system manager is the core of SAHA that coordinates all system adaptations. It not only manages all data transfers within the SAHA design, but also supports the hardware virtualization and preemption techniques.

Two types of hardware virtualizations, namely logic virtualization and hardware device virtualization, are supported by the system manager, as described in the following. 1) In the many-to-one logic virtualization as shown in Figure 3, a required hardware function (`HW2`) is virtualized such that it can be accessed by two service suppliers, `Service Supplier 1` and `Service Supplier 2`, through the device nodes `comm2` and `comm3`, respectively. Here, the data synchronization is controlled by the system manager. This many-to-one mapping between more than one service supplier and a configured hardware function increases the utilization of a hardware function. 2) In the hardware device virtualization as illustrated in Figure 3, the kernel module that is linked to and drives a specific hardware function (`HW1`) can be dynamically re-linked to another hardware function `HW2`. Without unnecessarily copying data between the *user space* and *kernel space*, the processing results of `HW1` can be directly transferred to `HW2` through the kernel module. This one-to-many mapping is a seamless reconfiguration of the underlying hardware, without any change to the software. Thus, using the hardware virtualization technique, multiple service suppliers can serve their users under the illusion of full access to the same reconfigurable hardware function through their own device nodes, while a service supplier can also access two or more reconfigurable hardware functions. Therefore, for changing ubiquitous computing environments, SAHA can adapt to more user requirements, while it can provide better performance.

Though the partial reconfiguration technique enables parts of an FPGA device to be reconfigured as different hardware functions at runtime, the occupied logic resources of a configured hardware function can be released only after it finishes its execution. This would incur significant time overhead, and thus degrade system performance. However, for ubiquitous computing applications, the support for seamless services is very important. As a result, SAHA integrates the hardware preemption technique to further enhance the utilization of hardware logic resources per unit time. When the hardware preemption mechanism is triggered, the system manager requests the hardware adapter to send a swap-out signal to a hardware function that is being accessed by a service supplier with lower priority. After all the context data of the swap-out hardware function are saved in an off-chip memory, the hardware adapter reconfigures the required hardware function into the corresponding PRR. Then, it notifies the system manager that the hardware function can be accessed. Here, the context data are the collections of the state registers and data registers. When the swap-out hardware function is reconfigured into the FPGA and all its context data are restored, it can continue execution from the state in which it was swapped out.

As for the determination of when hardware virtualization and preemption mechanisms are used due to system adaptation, the system manager needs to collaborate with the observer. The detailed introduction will be given in the next section.

3.4 Observer

Both the system manager and the hardware adapter provide the capability of system adaptivity for SAHA. As to when system adaptation is triggered, it mainly depends on the observer. Thus, the observer plays a key role to make

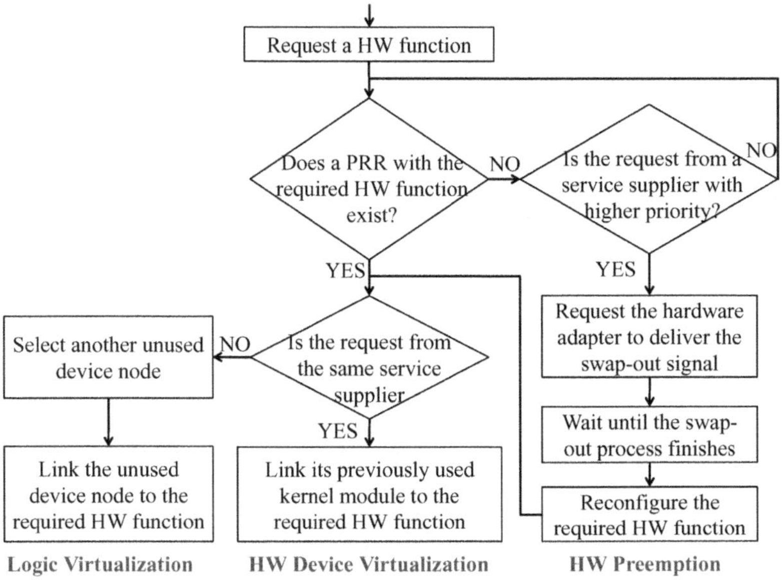

Fig. 4. Self-Aware System Adaptation

SAHA self-aware to adapt to ubiquitous computing environments. The observer is aware of the characteristics of currently running applications. As shown in Figure 4, it collaborates with the system manager to decide which of the three proposed techniques, namely logic virtualization, hardware device virtualization, and hardware preemption.

When a service supplier requests for a hardware function, the observer first asks the system manager whether the required hardware function has been configured in a PRR. If not, the observer determines what the priority level of the service supplier is, and then it queries the system manager whether the priority of this service supplier is higher than any service supplier that is accessing reconfigurable hardware functions. In our current implementation of SAHA, the priority levels of all service suppliers need to be preset during system initialization by users. Otherwise, SAHA is based on a first-come-first-served basis. If the service supplier does not have higher priority, it will wait until the required hardware function is configured into the FPGA. Otherwise, the hardware preemption mechanism is invoked, such that the system manager requests the hardware adapter to start the swap-out process. After the swap-out process finishes, the required hardware can be configured into the FPGA. Then, the observer continues to collaborate with the system manager to decide which hardware virtualization technique will be used.

When the required hardware function is already configured, the observer checks whether the request is received from the same service supplier. If not, the system manager invokes the logic virtualization to dynamically link another unused device node to the required hardware function. Otherwise, the system manager invokes the hardware device virtualization to dynamically link the previously used kernel module to the PRR with the required hardware function, and thus the processing results of the previous hardware function can be directly transferred to the requested hardware function. Note that, using the hardware device virtualization, when a pair of device node and kernel module is linked to only one hardware function, the final processing results are thus transferred back to the service supplier.

Through the cooperation between the service suppliers, the hardware adapter, the system manager, and the observer, SAHA can provide a robust infrastructure that is capable of self-aware adaptation to ubiquitous computing applications. As to what types of ubiquitous computing applications are suited to SAHA, the related analysis will be given in Section 5.1.

4 Implementation of Hardware/Software Adaptation

Besides the support of reconfigurable hardware architecture as introduced in Section 3, this section will introduce how the hardware virtualization and preemption techniques can be realized in SAHA to support system adaptation.

To support the hardware virtualization mechanism, both the interfaces of device drivers and reconfigurable hardware functions in SAHA must be unified, such that service suppliers and reconfigurable hardware functions can be many-to-one and one-to-many mapped. Therefore, we further propose a unified communication mechanism in SAHA to standardize the hardware/software communication interface, as shown in Figure 5. To minimize user design efforts, in our design environment, a user-designed hardware function can be integrated with a 3-tier interface, including (a) a partially reconfigurable (PR) template, (b) a reusable wrapper design, and (c) a communication interface component.

The PR template consists of eight 32-bit input data signals, one 32-bit input control signal, four 32-bit output data signals, and one 32-bit output control signal. It also contains an optional *Data Transformation Component* (DTC) for unpacking incoming data and packing outgoing data based on the I/O registers sizes in the hardware functions, and a reusable wrapper design to support hardware preemption technique. The wrapper architecture in Figure 5 mainly consists of a context buffer (`CB`) to store context data and a swap controller (`SC`) to manage the swap-out and swap-in activities.

Two types of reusable wrapper designs, namely *Last Interruptible State Swap* (LISS) wrapper and *Next Interruptible State Swap* (NISS) wrapper, are supported by SAHA, as described in the following. 1) The LISS wrapper stores the hardware context at each interruptible state, thus the hardware function can be swapped out from the last interruptible state whenever there is a swap request. It can be used for hardware functions whose context data size is less than that of the context buffer, as a result of which all context data can be stored in the context buffer using a single data transfer. 2) The NISS wrapper requires the hardware function to execute until the next interruptible state, store the context, and then swap out. It can be used when the context data size is larger

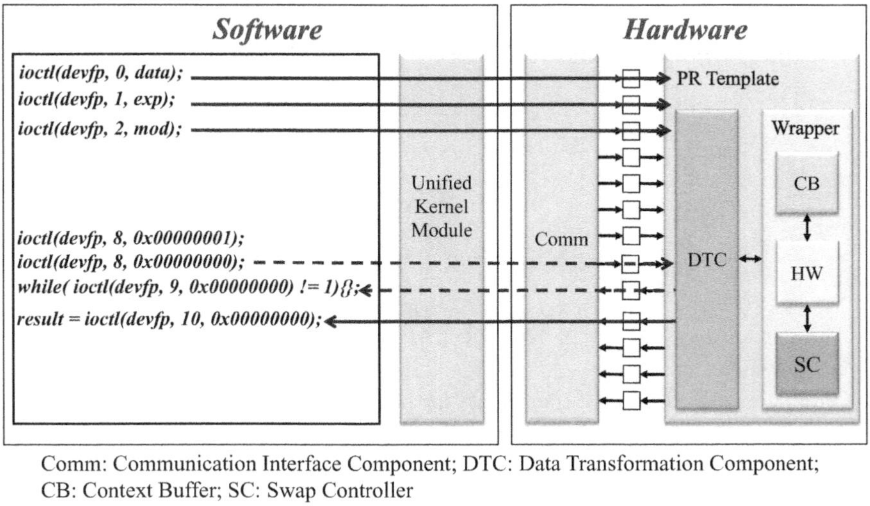

Fig. 5. Unified Communication Mechanism

than that of the context buffer, where the process of storing the context data into buffer and reading into memory is repeated and controlled by the hardware adapter. The communication interface component is used to connect the PR template to the system bus. Further, the processing results can be buffered in the communication interface component until the service supplier reads them.

Within the software part, different from the traditional device driver designed for a specific hardware function, a unified kernel module is designed to only interact with the fourteen 32-bit signals of the PR template. All the interactions between service suppliers and reconfigurable hardware functions are through the `ioctl` system calls of the unified kernel module and implemented in a hardware control library. Thus, a new user-designed hardware function needs to be only integrated with a PR template and included its control methods into the hardware control library. As a result, SAHA can be easily extended to support more types of ubiquitous computing applications, without being only restricted to our current implemented applications.

5 Experimental Evaluation

The current SAHA design was implemented on the Xilinx ML310 platform [13] with a Virtex II Pro FPGA device, in which the PetaLinux embedded OS [9] ran on a Xilinx MicroBlaze soft-core processor. Due to the resource limitations of our current implementation, only two different sized PRRs were implemented in the FPGA. In this section, we will first analyze the impact on system performance using the hardware preemption and preemption techniques in SAHA, and then give a case study that SAHA itself adapts to ubiquitous computing applications using both hardware preemption and hardware virtualization.

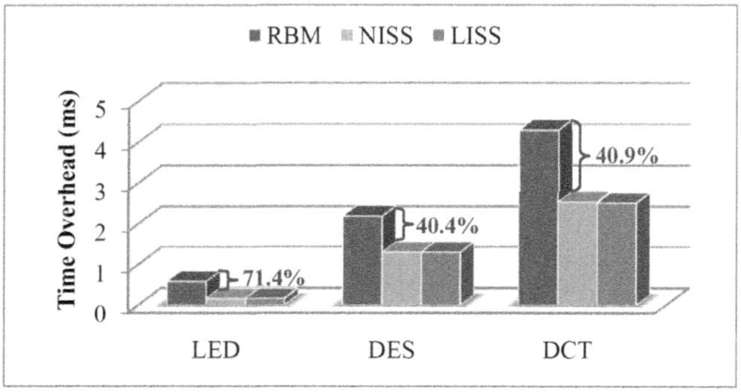

Fig. 6. Experiments on Hardware Preemption

5.1 Performance Analysis

Hardware Preemption. In our current implementation, the software processing time is much more than the hardware processing time. To clearly show the contribution to hardware preemption in SAHA, we directly compared it with another reconfiguration-based method (RBM) [6]. Here, RBM requires readback support from the reconfigurable logic such as state extraction from the readback stream and manipulation of the bitstreams for context restoring.

Figure 6 shows the time overheads in swapping out and swapping in for the LED controller, the *Data Encryption Standard* (DES), and DCT hardware functions. We can observe that the hardware preemption mechanism in SAHA performs better than RBM. From the experimental results, our method can reduce the swap time by 71.4%, 40.4%, and 40.9% of that required by RBM for the LED, DES and DCT hardware functions, respectively. We are thus saving much time, which is very important for supporting seamless ubiquitous computing services. Even though additional reconfiguration time is required, the hardware preemption mechanism in SAHA would enable more service suppliers to adapt to changing environmental conditions and achieve higher system performance.

Hardware Virtualization. To analyze the impact on system performance using hardware virtualization in SAHA, we first measure the time required for each of the following basic operations. The average amounts of time to insert a kernel module, to open a device node and to close it are 830, 0.253, and 0.048 milliseconds, respectively. The average amounts of time to write a 32-bit data to and to read a 32-bit data from the kernel space are 0.022 and 0.022 milliseconds, respectively. The average computing time for processing a 128 $\times$ 64 pixel image using the RSA32, RSA64, RSA128, RC6, CRC32, CRC64, and CRC128 hardware functions is 0.026 milliseconds, while the average time to read a 32-bit data from a hardware function and then write it to another hardware function through the unified kernel module is 0.0028 milliseconds.

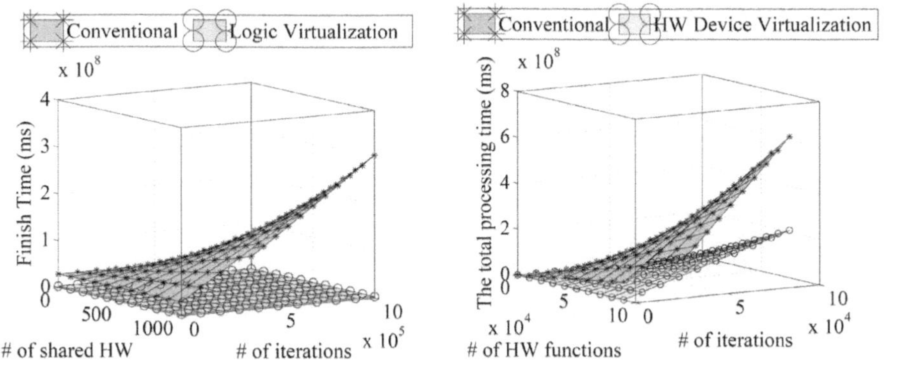

(a) Logic Virtualization and Conventional Method

(b) HW Device Virtualization and Conventional Method

Fig. 7. Comparison between Hardware Virtualization and Conventional Method

As introduced in Section 3.3, through logic virtualization, a service supplier can access a hardware function that has been accessed by another previous service supplier, as long as the previous service supplier is not using it, irrespective of whether it is released or not. Without logic virtualization, the hardware function cannot be accessed until the previous service supplier releases it. Thus, using the conventional method in the best case, the waiting time would be equal to the total processing time of the shared hardware functions in the previous service supplier. Based on our measurement of the time required by each basic operation, Figure 7(a) compares logic virtualization and the conventional access method by looking at the finish time of a service supplier that has some hardware functions previously accessed by another service supplier. Here, the numbers of shared hardware functions and iterations to access the shared hardware functions in the previous service supplier are set ranging from 0 to 1,000 and from 0 to 1,000,000, respectively. We can observe that the time required by using the logic virtualization becomes lesser and lesser compared to the time required by using the conventional access method, when the numbers of shared hardware functions and iterations to access the shared hardware functions in the previous service supplier gradually increases. This is because logic virtualization reduces significantly the waiting time for the shared hardware functions. Thus, performance improvement using the logic virtualization becomes more and more prominent with an increase in the total processing time of shared hardware functions in the previous service supplier.

Using hardware device virtualization, the processing results (data) of a hardware function can be directly transferred to another hardware function through the unified kernel module. Thus, hardware device virtualization is used to save time by avoiding repeated data transfers between the OS kernel and the user level. Based on our measurement of the time required by each basic operation, Figure 7(b) shows the total processing time of a service supplier using the hardware device virtualization technique and the conventional method. Here, the number of hardware functions to be sequentially accessed by the service supplier and the number of iterations to access the hardware functions are both set ranging from 0 to 100,000. We can observe that the time required by using the hardware device virtualization technique becomes lesser and lesser compared to the time required by using the conventional method, when the numbers of hardware functions and iterations to access the hardware functions gradually increase.

From the above results, we can clearly observe that the hardware virtualization technique allows greater performance improvement, compared to the conventional method, when a service supplier requires more and more iterations to access hardware functions. This also shows that the hardware virtualization technique will play a key role to help system adaptation and provide better performance, especially for ubiquitous computing applications, such as multimedia applications and the cryptographic applications, that usually must process a larger amount of information and data.

5.2 Case Study Using Both HW Preemption and Virtualization

In this experiment, SAHA will serve two ubiquitous computing applications, including a monitoring service and a live television service. Note that this experiment does not use the stream buffering technology and mainly shows performance improvement in SAHA, and thus the amounts of time to capture data from the peripherals and transfer data to users on the network are omitted. As shown in Figure 8, the live television service requests for processing fifty images using the RC6 and CRC32 hardware functions with a QoS requirement of total 90 seconds. However, the DCT and CRC32 hardware functions are now configured in `PRR1` and `PRR2`, respectively, where the DCT function required by the low-priority monitoring service has already executed for 50 ms and `PRR1` is selected to configure the required RC6 function.

Without the hardware preemption technique, the RC6 hardware function will be configured in `PRR1` only after the DCT function finishes. According to our experimental results, it needs 527.2099 ms exclusive of the previous execution time of 50 ms to finish the current DCT execution and 177 ms to configure the RC6 function. Note that here we assume that the current monitoring service (with requirement for the DCT hardware function) can also be preempted after one DCT execution. If this is not the case, a much greater delay will be incurred without the hardware and software preemption. However, using the hardware preemption technique, it needs only 1.2687 ms for the NISS wrapper or 1.2552 ms for the LISS wrapper to swap out the DCT function, and 177 ms to configure the RC6 function. The latency in starting to serve the live television service without and with the hardware preemption technique is around 0.704 seconds and 0.178 seconds, respectively.

After hardware and software preemption, the required RC6 hardware function is configured into `PRR1`. Using the conventional method, the live television service must now wait until the currently executing monitoring service closes the device node `comm1` that is linked to `PRR1`, and then the live television service opens the same device node `comm1` to access `PRR1` with the RC6 hardware function.

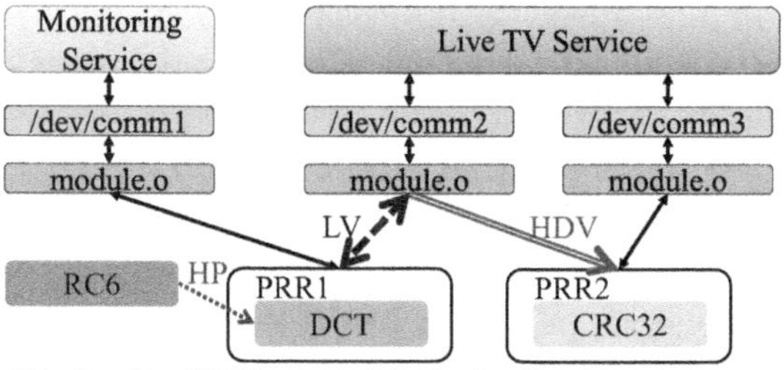

Fig. 8. Case Study using both Hardware Preemption and Virtualization

However, using the logic virtualization, another pair `comm2` of device node and kernel module can be simultaneously used to connect to `PRR1` and the live television service starts accessing `PRR1` with the RC6 hardware function more quickly. The time saved by not waiting for another monitoring service to close and open the device node `comm1`, namely logic virtualization, is around 0.301 seconds according to our experimental results.

Finally, using the hardware device virtualization, the processing results (output data) of the RC6 hardware function in `PRR1` can be directly transferred to the CRC32 hardware function in `PRR2` through the kernel module in the pair `comm2` of device node and kernel module without going back and forth between the OS kernel and the user levels, as introduced in Section 3.3. The total amounts of time required for performing the live television service without and with the hardware virtualization technique are 96.397 seconds and 85.336 seconds, respectively, for processing 50 images. As a result, if both the hardware preemption and virtualization techniques are not used, then the live television service needs 97.101 (0.704+96.397) seconds, which means the QoS requirement cannot be achieved. However, if both the hardware preemption and virtualization techniques are used, then the live television service needs only 85.514 (0.178+85.336) seconds, which means the QoS requirement can be achieved. SAHA can reduce around 11.9% of the time required by using the conventional method. The experimental results demonstrate that through system adaptation using both the hardware preemption and virtualization techniques, system performance can be significantly enhanced.

6 Conclusion

To provide a more robust ubiquitous computing infrastructure, we propose a self-adaptive hardware/software system architecture (SAHA) that solves the issues related to system adaptation, as described in Section 1. SAHA also integrates the hardware preemption and virtualization techniques and has a complete self-aware system adaptation mechanism to provide better performance for ubiquitous computing applications. Our experimental results also demonstrate that not only system resources can be effectively utilized, but system performance can be also improved significantly, when ubiquitous computing applications are served by SAHA.

Acknowledgments

This work was partially supported by the research project NSC98-2221-E-194-049-MY3, National Science Council, Taiwan.

References

1. Efstratiou, C., Cheverst, K., Davices, N., Friday, A.: An Architecture for the Effective Support of Adaptive Context-Aware Applications. In: Tan, K.-L., Franklin, M.J., Lui, J.C.-S. (eds.) MDM 2001. LNCS, vol. 1987, pp. 15–26. Springer, Heidelberg (2000)
2. Danek, M., Philippe, J.-M., Honzik, P., Gamrat, C., Bartosinski, R.: Self-Adaptive Networked Entities for Building Pervasive Computing Architectures. In: Hornby, G.S., Sekanina, L., Haddow, P.C. (eds.) ICES 2008. LNCS, vol. 5216, pp. 21–24. Springer, Heidelberg (2008)
3. Ghim, S.-J., Yoon, Y.-I., Choe, J.-W.: A Reflective Approach to Dynamic Adaptation in Ubiquitous Computing Environment. In: Kahng, H.-K., Goto, S. (eds.) ICOIN 2004. LNCS, vol. 3090, pp. 75–82. Springer, Heidelberg (2004)
4. Huang, C.-H., Hsiung, P.-A.: Software-Controlled Dynamically Swappable Hardware Design in Partially Reconfigurable Systems. EURASIP J. Embedded System Article ID 231940 (2008) doi:10.1155/2008/231940
5. Huang, C.-H., Hsiung, P.-A.: Hardware Resource Virtualization for Dynamically Partially Reconfigurable Systems. IEEE Embedded Systems Letters 1(1), 19–23 (2009), doi:10.1109/LES.2009.2028039
6. Kalte, H., Porrmann, M.: Context Saving and Restoring for Multitasking in Reconfigurable Systems. In: 15th IEEE International Conference on Field Programmable Logic and Applications (FPL), pp. 223–228. IEEE CS Press, Los Alamitos (August 2005)
7. Lagger, A., Upegui, A., Sanchez, E., Gonzalez, I.: Self-Reconfigurable Pervasive Platform for Cryptographic Application. In: 16th IEEE International Conference on Field Programmable Logic and Applications (FPL), pp. 777–780. IEEE CS Press, Los Alamitos (August 2006)
8. Noble, B.: System Support for Mobile, Adaptive Applications. IEEE Personal Communications 7(1), 44–49 (2000)
9. PetaLogix. PetaLinux, `http://www.petalogix.com`
10. Sun, J.-Z.: Adaptive Determination of Data Granularity for QoS-Constraint Data Gathering in Wireless Sensor Networks. In: 2009 Symposia and Workshops on Ubiquitous, Autonomic and Trusted Computing (UIC-ATC), pp. 401–405. IEEE Computer Society, Los Alamitos (June 2009)
11. Wollinger, T., Paar, C.: How Secure are FPGAs in Cryptographic Applications. In: Peter Cheung, Y.K., Constantinides, G.A. (eds.) FPL 2003. LNCS, vol. 2778, pp. 1–3. Springer, Heidelberg (2003)
12. Xilinx: Early Access Partial Reconfiguration User Guide - UG208 (2006)
13. Xilinx: ML310 User Guide (2007)

Toward Distributed Declarative Control of Networked Cyber-Physical Systems*

Mark-Oliver Stehr, Minyoung Kim, and Carolyn Talcott

SRI International
{stehr,mkim,clt}@csl.sri.com

Abstract. Networked Cyber-Physical Systems (NCPS) present many challenges that are not suitably addressed by existing distributed computing paradigms. They must be reactive and maintain an overall situation awareness that emerges from partial distributed knowledge. They must achieve system goals through local, asynchronous actions, using (distributed) control loops through which the environment provides essential feedback. Typical NCPS are open, dynamic, and heterogeneous in many dimensions, and often need to be rapidly instantiated and deployed for a given mission. To address these challenges, we pursue a declarative approach to provide an abstraction from the high complexity of NCPS and avoid error-prone and time-consuming low-level programming. A longer-term goal is to develop a distributed computational and logical foundation that supports a wide spectrum of system operation between autonomy and cooperation to adapt to resource constraints, in particular to limitations of computational, energy, and networking resources. Here, we present first steps toward a logical framework for NCPS that combines distributed reasoning and asynchronous control in space and time. The logical framework is based on partially ordered knowledge sharing, a distributed computing paradigm for loosely coupled systems that does not require continuous network connectivity. We illustrate our approach with a simulation prototype of our logical framework in the context of networked mobile robot teams that operate in an abstract instrumented cyber-physical space with sensors.

1 Introduction

A growing number and variety of devices can sense and affect their environment. Some are fairly simple, such as radio-frequency identification (RFID) access control, some quite sophisticated, such as mobile robots with localization and sensing capabilities. This opens up an opportunity for a new generation of *Networked Cyber-Physical Systems* (NCPS). Such systems can provide complex,

* Support from National Science Foundation Grant 0932397 (A Logical Framework for Self-Optimizing Networked Cyber-Physical Systems) and Office of Naval Research Grant N00014-10-1-0365 (Principles and Foundations for Fractionated Networked Cyber-Physcial Systems) is gratefully acknowledged. Any opinions, findings, and conclusions or recommendations expressed in this material are those of the author(s) and do not necessarily reflect the views of NSF or ONR.

Z. Yu et al. (Eds.): UIC 2010, LNCS 6406, pp. 397–413, 2010.

situation-aware, and often critical services in applications such as distributed surveillance, crisis response, medical systems, self-assembling structures or systems, networked space/satellite missions, or distributed critical infrastructure monitoring and control. General principles and tools are urgently needed for building robust, effective NCPS using individual cyber-physical devices as building blocks. In this paper, we present a declarative approach to NCPS based on a logical framework that supports distributed reasoning and can interact with the physical world asynchronously through observations and goal-oriented control.

Cyber-physical systems are often deployed in challenging environments with a wide spectrum of networking characteristics. They should be able to take advantage of opportunities for communication as they arise and must be robust in spite of delays and disruptions due to, for example, mobility, failures, or nodes entering and leaving the system. Topology changes (network partitioning in the extreme case) can happen continuously, so that even the common assumption of globally stable periods, which is crucial for many distributed algorithms, is not realistic. Hence, the logical framework is developed on top of a loosely coupled distributed computing model based on the *partially ordered knowledge-sharing* paradigm that has been used in our earlier work on disruption-tolerant networking [16]. Knowledge (as opposed to, say, a packet) is a semantically meaningful unit of information that can be stored, processed, aggregated, and communicated to other nodes. A unique feature of the knowledge-sharing model is that it is parameterized by an application-dependent partial order on knowledge that is available to all nodes and provides an abstraction of the knowledge semantics. In this model, the network topology can change continuously, communication can be unreliable, and no bounds are assumed on communication delays. As a consequence, any form of communication between nodes is acceptable. Similar to data mules for sensor networks [5] or message ferrying in delay- and disruption-tolerant networks [7], each node can cache knowledge for extended periods of time and hence can exploit the (possibly mobile) network dynamics to share knowledge without relying on an end-to-end path at any point in time.

The declarative view of NCPS enables us to recast information collection, control, and decision problems as logical problems that are primarily centered around the duality of two kinds of knowledge: facts and goals. Facts can represent sensor readings at specific locations and other information that is derived by possibly distributed computation. Goals can represent queries for information or requests to the system or individual components to perform certain actions. Although there are cases where a goal can be directly satisfied by a single action, it is more often the case that distributed actions are needed, sometimes in a coordinated manner that requires cooperation across multiple nodes. In our logical framework, both facts and goals will be treated on an equal footing together with corresponding reasoning rules. The distributed, dynamic, and interactive nature of the underlying systems is rarely considered in logical frameworks, which are traditionally designed as closed systems. Our framework is flexible enough to take into account the heterogeneous resources and capabilities at each node. Each node cooperates with its neighbors and interacts with its environment by sensing and affecting, driven by facts and goals. Overall system goals are refined to goals achievable by an individual node or device. Reasoning takes place locally at each node in the network as well as in cooperation (and competition) with other nodes. Seamless integration of cooperation and autonomy ensures that there is no need to rely on the existence or connectivity of other nodes, so that the local operation can always proceed, although possibly in a less optimal fashion. Solutions can be shared and composed oportunistically without being subject to any rigid or hierarchical flow constraints.

Recent applications of cognitive and more specifically declarative techniques in communication and networking, [4] being a noteworthy example, have attracted a lot of interest, but a declarative treatment of NCPS still remains a challenge. To study this problem we use *self-organizing mobile robots* as an example capturing many of the challenges of NCPS [5]. This example is inspired by previous work at SRI, in particular the Centibots project [14] that has developed a team-based hierarchical planning approach to accomplish a mission such as collaborative mapping, and the Commbots project [8], where the mission objective is to improve network connectivity by distributed control of robotic routers.

After presenting a simplified version of our distributed logical framework in Section 2, we illustrate in Section 3 the key ideas and a prototypical implementation by means of an abstract simulation of a networked mobile robot team operating in an instrumented cyber-physical space. Some related work will be summarized in Section 4.

2 Distributed Logic and Cyber-Inference

Declarative control aims at providing the user with a logical view of the cyber-physical system so that user objectives can be conveyed to the system, which then will make its best effort to realize those objectives. Such objectives are given in the context of the current system state (which is only approximately and partially observable). Furthermore, the user objectives can be part of a larger set of objectives (e.g., including system policies and objectives from other users), which we simply refer to as the system goal. Declarative control is the process of continuous adaptation of the system to transition to a state that satisfies the system goal, which in turn can continue to change based on feedback from the environment or because of new user requests.

The purpose of logic in this context is many-fold. First of all, it provides a language to express and communicate system goals. Dually, it allows expressing and communicating facts about the current system state. In both cases, communication includes communication with the users but also communication among the components of the system. At the level of an individual cyber-physical component, the logic provides a declarative interface for goal-oriented control and feedback through observations that are represented as logical facts. Finally, it provides a framework for inference and computation, which allows facts and goals to interact with each other and form new facts or goals.

Aiming at a solution to declarative control that covers the entire spectrum between cooperation and autonomy and makes opportunistic use of networking resources, it is clear that the logic needs to be inherently distributed. The opportunity to exchange knowledge with other nodes should lead to cooperation, and the absence of such opportunities should lead to more autonomous behavior. In the following we present a simple distributed inference system that accomplishes this goal. We use Horn clause logic to illustrate our approach, which we expect to generalize to more expressive logics.

For the following abstract logical treatment, we assume a networked cyber-physical system S with a finite set of cyber-nodes N. We assume a time-dependent network and environment model, in which two cyber-nodes have the capability to communicate (uni- or bidirectionally) whenever the network conditions admit it and where each cyber-node can have (not necessarily the same) sensors and actuators. The sensors can generate observations at arbitrary time points. The actuators are driven by goals, which they can either attempt to satisfy immediately or in a continuous asynchronous process with (partial) feedback provided through observations. Instead of imposing restrictive conditions on S we generally allow S to operate under arbitrary conditions. In the following, we use x and y to range over cyber-nodes and t to range over the time domain, for which we use natural numbers in this paper. For the following, we also assume a fixed signature Σ and a fixed finite theory Ω over Σ in Horn clause logic that is shared by all nodes of the cyber-physical system. We assume that Σ contains built-in constants for natural numbers and names of cyber-nodes. Additional *built-in functions*, and *built-in predicates* can be included in Σ. To account for the temporal and distributed character of cyber-physical systems, we assume that the signature Σ contains a distinguished set of predicates (distinct from built-ins) that we refer to as *cyber-predicates*, i.e., predicates that define the interface of the logic with the outside world (i.e., cyber-physical devices and users).

Using P and Q to range over atoms, we furthermore assume that all clauses in Ω are uniquely labeled and definite, i.e., of the form $l : P_1, \ldots, P_n \Rightarrow Q$ with a unique label l, where Q is not the application of a built-in predicate. For our proof system, we assume that $\Omega = \Omega_{\mathrm{f}} \cup \Omega_{\mathrm{b}}$, where Ω_{f} and Ω_{b} are sets of clauses that we refer to as *forward and backward clauses*, respectively.

The set of *facts* is simply defined as the set of all ground atoms. Hence, all predicates are allowed to occur in facts. The set of *goal predicates* is any set of predicates that includes at least the built-in predicates and all predicates that appear in the conclusion of a backward clause, i.e., a clause from Ω_{b}. Certain cyber-predicates can be included in this set if they are intended to form goals. For the purpose of this paper, the set of *goals* is simply the set of (not necessarily ground) atoms that are applications of goal predicates. A unit of *knowledge* can be either a fact or a goal. To simplify the presentation in this paper we assume that facts and goals can always be distinguished, even if they have the same underlying atom. Occasional conversions between a fact and a goal with the same atom should be clear from the context and will be left implicit. From now on, we will use K to range over units of knowledge and F and G to range over facts and goals, respectively.

A fact or goal that is the application of a built-in predicate is called a *built-in fact* or *built-in goal*, respectively. Given a built-in goal G, we say that $\sigma(G)$ is a *solution* of G iff there is a substitution σ such that $\sigma(G)$ is ground (hence can be viewed as a fact) and satisfied. All cyber-predicates p_c are explicitly time dependent and form atoms $p_c(t, \ldots)$, where t is a natural number denoting its timestamp, i.e., its time of creation at the creating node. A *cyber-fact* or *cyber-goal* is any fact or goal, respectively, of this form. Note that this does not preclude cyber-facts and cyber-goals from having additional temporal attributes or constraints that can be specified in the remaining arguments, e.g., the time of obervation in the case of a cyber-fact, or a deadline in the case of a cyber-goal.

To utilize the partially ordered knowledge-sharing model, we assume that the set of all knowledge units is equipped with a strict partial order $<$, called the *subsumption order*,[1] and a strict partial order $\prec$, called the *replacement order*, that extends $<$. The intended meaning of $K \prec K'$ is that K' replaces K, because K is semantically subsumed by K' (in this case we have $K < K'$), or because K is obsolete relative to K', e.g., out of date.

The logical state of a cyber-node is of the form $\Gamma \vdash \Delta$ @ t, x, where x is the unique name of the node, t is a natural number representing its local time, Γ is a finite set of facts, and Δ is a finite set of goals. It is worthwhile to point out that the interpretation of $\Gamma \vdash \Delta$ @ t, x is nonstandard, and quite different from sequent calculus even without t, x. Intuitively, Γ is a set of facts that is continuously growing through observations or by inference, while Δ is a set of goals that the system is trying to satisfy without necessarily aiming to satisfy all of them. To reflect the reality of cyber-physical systems, inference is a continuous typically nonterminating process, and goals and facts can change at any time due to environment and user interaction. Since reasoning is a distributed process in space and time and the world can change during this process, an approach quite different from traditional work in formal specification, logic programming, or automated deduction is needed. We will also see that a goal does not have to be solved to be useful, but as a cyber-goal can still have an impact on the environment, which may be observable through cyber-facts.

A configuration of a cyber-physical system S is a set of local states $\Gamma \vdash \Delta$ @ t, x, one for each cyber-node x of S. Given a configuration c containing $\Gamma \vdash \Delta$ @ t, x, we write $\mathcal{F}_x(c)$ and $\mathcal{G}_x(c)$ to denote Γ and Δ, respectively. The proof system in Figure 1 defines a labeled transition relation $\rightarrow$ on configurations of the cyber-physical system S in the following sense: For configurations c and c', we have $c \rightarrow_r c'$ iff there exists an instance r of a proof rule such that c contains the premises of r, and c' is obtained by an update of c with the conclusion, i.e., by replacing $\Gamma \vdash \Delta$ @ t, x by the conclusion $\Gamma' \vdash \Delta'$ @ t', x.

For readability, we have omitted an implicit side condition $t < t'$ in all proof rules ($t_x < t'_x$ in the communication rules), meaning that time increases monotonically at least by one unit in each step. Furthermore, we view each fact or goal as a singleton set and use the comma operator to denote set union. If the

[1] In the general model, the subsumption order is a quasi-order, but in this paper we identify knowledge units that are related by the induced equivalence relation.

comma operator is used in the premise of a proof rule, we always assume that it denotes the union of disjoint sets, i.e., Γ, K implies $K \notin \Gamma$ if it occurs in a premise. For a set $\mathcal{K}$ of knowledge units, we write $K \prec \mathcal{K}$ if there exist $K' \in \mathcal{K}$ such that $K \prec K'$, respectively. In the context of a proof rule that has a premise $\Gamma \vdash \Delta$ @ t, x we say that K is *fresh* (at x) if neither $K \in \Gamma, \Delta$ nor $K \prec \Gamma, \Delta$. In the condition of proof rules we use σ to range over all (not necessarily ground) substitutions that satisfy the condition of the proof rule. Some conditions in the reasoning rules will further restrict σ to most general substitutions.

To give some intuitive explanation of the proof rules in Figure 1, the control rule represents the addition of a new user-level objective to the set of system goals. The observation rule captures the generation of information from the environment. This can happen spontaneously or can be triggered by a goal that a cyber-device attempts to satisfy. The communication rules allow cyber-nodes to exchange facts or goals by means of asynchronous communication. The nature of communication, i.e., whether it is uni-/bidirectional, unicast, multicast, or broadcast remains unspecified. The replacement rules are used to overwrite subsumed and obsolete facts and goals. In this paper, we assume only a loose form of logical time synchronization that satisfies the minimal monotonicity requirement formulated in the communication rules. Of course, this does not preclude implementations with time synchronization that takes place even when no knowledge is exchanged. The forward and backward rules implement forward and backward reasoning. The first forward rule applies an instance of a Horn clause from the underlying theory if all conditions are available as facts, generating a new fact $\sigma(Q)$ corresponding to the conclusion in this process. The second forward rule covers the case where the available facts are not sufficient to apply the clause so that a new subgoal $\sigma(P_j)$ needs to be generated for a missing fact. The backward rules are analogous to the two forward rules, but apply a Horn clause in a goal-directed way, by first unifying the conclusion with an existing goal. Again, if the present facts are not sufficient to cover all conditions of a clause, a new subgoal is generated. In both forward and backward rules, the selection of facts, goals, and rules is entirely nondeterministic, and many strategies are sensible as long as they satisfy some local weak fairness requirements. Finally, the sleep rule allows the system to wait and hence slow down the reasoning for an arbitrary amount of time, e.g., to save energy, wait for new knowledge, or use the resources for other purposes.

The proof system is specifically designed to enable a distributed implementation using randomization techniques that can be used to satisfy the local fairness conditions with probability one. Facts and goals are represented as knowledge in the partially ordered knowledge-sharing model, where knowledge can be opportunistically exchanged across multiple hops and cached in the network until it is locally replaced by knowledge that is higher in the partial order. No global consistency is assumed or needed in this approach. There are several places in the proof system, where nondeterminism at a given node x can be implemented by a randomized choice. First, there is the selection of clauses in the four reasoning rules. Second, there is the selection of facts and/or goals to which the clause is

$$\frac{\Gamma \vdash \Delta \ @\ t, x}{\Gamma \vdash \Delta, G \ @\ t', x} \quad \text{if } G = p_c(t, \ldots) \text{ is a cyber-goal} \qquad \text{(Control)}$$

$$\frac{\Gamma \vdash \Delta \ @\ t, x}{\Gamma, F \vdash \Delta \ @\ t', x} \quad \text{if } F = p_c(t, \ldots) \text{ is a cyber-fact} \qquad \text{(Observation)}$$

$$\frac{\Gamma, F \vdash \Delta \ @\ t, x}{\Gamma \vdash \Delta \ @\ t', x} \quad \text{if } F \prec \Gamma, \Delta \qquad \text{(Replacement1)}$$

$$\frac{\Gamma \vdash \Delta, G \ @\ t, x}{\Gamma \vdash \Delta \ @\ t', x} \quad \text{if } G \prec \Gamma, \Delta \qquad \text{(Replacement2)}$$

$$\frac{\Gamma_x \vdash \Delta_x \ @\ t_x, x \quad \Gamma_y, F \vdash \Delta_y \ @\ t_y, y}{\Gamma_x, F \vdash \Delta_x \ @\ t'_x, x} \qquad \text{(Communication1)}$$
if $x \neq y$, $t'_x \geq t_y$, and F is fresh at x.

$$\frac{\Gamma_x \vdash \Delta_x \ @\ t_x, x \quad \Gamma_y \vdash \Delta_y, G \ @\ t_y, y}{\Gamma_x \vdash \Delta_x, G \ @\ t'_x, x} \qquad \text{(Communication2)}$$
if $x \neq y$, $t'_x \geq t_y$, and G is fresh at x

$$\frac{\Gamma \vdash \Delta, G \ @\ t, x}{\Gamma, \sigma(G) \vdash \Delta, G \ @\ t', x} \qquad \text{(Built-in)}$$
if G is a built-in goal with a solution $\sigma(G)$ such that $\sigma(G)$ is fresh.

$$\frac{\Gamma, \sigma(P_1), \ldots, \sigma(P_n) \vdash \Delta \ @\ t, x}{\Gamma, \sigma(P_1), \ldots, \sigma(P_n), \sigma(Q) \vdash \Delta \ @\ t', x} \qquad \text{(Forward1)}$$
if $l : P_1, \ldots, P_n \Rightarrow Q$ is a clause from Ω_f,
and $\sigma(Q)$ is a fresh fact.

$$\frac{\Gamma, \sigma(P_1), \ldots, \sigma(P_{j-1}) \vdash \Delta \ @\ t, x}{\Gamma, \sigma(P_1), \ldots, \sigma(P_{j-1}) \vdash \Delta, \sigma(P_j) \ @\ t', x} \qquad \text{(Forward2)}$$
if $l : P_1, \ldots, P_n \Rightarrow Q$ is a clause from Ω_f,
σ is a most general substitution, $\sigma(P_j)$ is a goal, and $\sigma(P_j)$ is fresh.

$$\frac{\Gamma, \sigma(P_1), \ldots, \sigma(P_n) \vdash \Delta, G' \ @\ t, x}{\Gamma, \sigma(P_1), \ldots, \sigma(P_n), \sigma(Q) \vdash \Delta, G' \ @\ t', x} \qquad \text{(Backward1)}$$
if $l : P_1, \ldots, P_n \Rightarrow Q$ is a clause from Ω_b,
$\sigma(Q) = \sigma(G')$ is a fresh fact.

$$\frac{\Gamma, \sigma(P_1), \ldots, \sigma(P_{j-1}) \vdash \Delta, G' \ @\ t, x}{\Gamma, \sigma(P_1), \ldots, \sigma(P_{j-1}) \vdash \Delta, G', \sigma(P_j) \ @\ t', x} \qquad \text{(Backward2)}$$
if $l : P_1, \ldots, P_n \Rightarrow Q$ is a clause from Ω_b,
$\sigma(P_j)$ is a fresh goal, σ is a most general substitution such that $\sigma(Q) = \sigma(G')$.

$$\frac{\Gamma \vdash \Delta \ @\ t, x}{\Gamma \vdash \Delta \ @\ t', x} \qquad \text{(Sleep)}$$

Fig. 1. Proof Rules of our Distributed Logical Framework for NCPS

applied. Third, there is the choice of the substitution and hence solution in the rule for built-ins. And finally, there is the sleep rule, which can be implemented by random waiting using a suitable distribution to make the reasoning process adaptive to resource constraints and network conditions.

3 Sample Application

To test our ideas we will focus on a specific application that we call *self-organizing mobile robots* as a special case of controllable networks that captures many interesting aspects of NCPS [5]. Consider a self-organizing network of mobile robots deployed in a building, e.g., to achieve situation awareness during an emergency. This is a challenging test case for various reasons. The network is highly dynamic, and temporary disconnections or failures are part of the normal operation and need to be compensated for by real-world actions. Parameters such as a robot's position can be controlled only indirectly via actions, and costs of changes (e.g., energy consumption) cannot be neglected.

As a concrete sample mission, we chose a primary goal such as delivery of the collected information (e.g., images) from a particular area to a specific node with some time constraints. We assume that each room in the building is equipped with acoustic sensors or motion sensors and the goal is to collect information in areas where noise or motion is detected. The mobile robots have camera devices that can capture a fullsight (i.e., 360-degree view) snapshot of a target area. The raw image may be directly sent to other nodes if the network supports it, or it can be preprocessed, e.g., by applying some form of compression or abstraction, and feature extraction (possibly at a different more powerful node), and then communicated to other nodes.

For the specific example, we assume that the primary goal is injected into the network by the user at a fixed root node around which initially the robots are randomly clustered. Goals and facts are opportunistically shared whenever connectivity exists. Each robot can compute its local solution based on its local knowledge. The solution assigns an approximate target region as a subgoal to each robot, which then starts to move in order to locally realize the goal. The distributed reasoning continues so that the local solutions are continuously recomputed and movements are adjusted correspondingly. In addition to the randomness due to network and environment, randomization techniques, e.g., random selection of clauses and goals, and random waiting, are used to desynchronize the robots. The movements are constrained by the floor plan, which could be opportunistically updated and shared, but is simply assumed to be given as part of the logical theory, which is available at all nodes, in our simple example. The network connectivity model can also be exploited to suppress position changes that would lead to disconnections. Still, temporary disruptions are possible due to system perturbations, failures, and uncertainty caused by delayed/incomplete knowledge.

3.1 Simulation Setup

Figure 2 shows knowledge sharing between three cyber-nodes and their devices. Each node is equipped with a knowledge manager, i.e., an implementation of the distributed knowledge-sharing model, a reasoner, i.e., an implementation of our logical framework, and attached devices that can be regarded as subnodes exhibiting a declarative knowledge-based interface. The devices are using the distributed knowledge-sharing model but are implemented using conventional code (simulation code in our case), i.e., outside the logical framework. Figure 2 contains two mobile robots, each with a positioning device and a camera device. It also contains a fixed sensor node, which can have attached noise or motion sensors or both. In our simulation, we experimented with one to five robots and used a root node that is similar to a robot but assumed to be at a fixed location and serves as a user access point to the cyber-physical system.

By definition, cyber-facts/goals have a form $p_c(t, e_1, ...e_n)$. However, in our example we leave the creation time t implicit in the case of cyber-goals, because it is not used in the theory.

To illustrate a simple operation, assume now that a user injects a goal such as $TakeSnapshot(t_T, t_T + \Delta t_{sd}, a, I)$ with $t_T = 0.0$ and $\Delta t_{sd} = 20.0$ into the root node. t_T and Δt_{sd} indicate the earliest time and the deadline to take the snapshot. The reasoner cannot solve this goal by means of the logical theory, but the local camera device may find that it can handle $TakeSnapshot(0.0, 20.0, a, I)$ by taking an image of the area a in the time interval 0.0, ..., 20.0. As a result it generates a fact $Snapshot(10.0, a, i)$, indicating that image i was taken at time 10.0 in area a, which is added to the local knowledge base and can in turn lead to further reasoning in the logical theory.

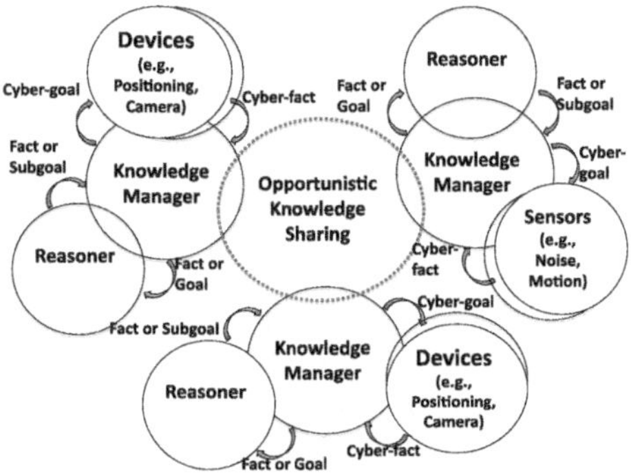

Fig. 2. Distributed Knowledge Sharing between two Robots and a Sensor in an Instrumented Cyber-Space

Knowledge (i.e., facts and goals) is opportunistically disseminated whenever connectivity exists among robots. In our experiments, we use an abstract topological *mobility model* instead of a model with actual coordinates. We assume that rooms in our scenario correspond to regions exhibiting similar connectivity, and the *network model* is defined so that links are up between robots when they reside in the same or adjacent rooms. For our experiments, we use a disruption-tolerant networking simulator [16] that abstracts from the underlying networking stack. It uses a simple graph-based dynamic network model, where each link has a state, e.g., up or down, and is characterized by its abstract features such as bandwidth, latency, and error rate. The floor plan restricts the mobility and will be reflected by a collection of adjacency facts as part of the theory.

3.2 Declarative Problem Formulation

Figure 3 shows the logical theory that is used to declaratively represent our sample application. The predicates are summarized in Table 1. Recall that a user wants the system to take an image whenever some trigger condition occurs, process it, and deliver it at the root node. The trigger conditions are specified as forward clauses $F1$ and $F2$, which can be applied at any time when the conditions are met.

Forward Clauses:

$F1: Noise(T, A) \Rightarrow Trigger(T, A).$
$F2: Motion(T, A) \Rightarrow Trigger(T, A).$
$F3: Adjacent(A, B) \Rightarrow Adjacent(B, A).$

Backward Clauses:

$B1: Interest(T_I, I, R) \Leftarrow Result(T_I, T_T, 0, I), Deliver(T_I, T_T, 1, I, R).$
$B2: Deliver(T_I, T_T, N_D, I, R) \Leftarrow Delivered(T_I, T_T, N_D, I, R).$
$B3: Deliver(T_I, T_T, N_D, I, R) \Leftarrow$
$\quad Position(T_P, R, A), Position(T'_P, R', A'), R' \neq R,$
$\quad MoveTo(T_I, T_T, N_D, 0, \infty, R', A), Deliver(T_I, T_T, N_D, I, R).$
$B4: Result(T_I, T_T, N_D, I') \Leftarrow CompImage(T_I, T_T, N_D, I), I' = Extract(I).$
$B5: CompImage(T_I, T_T, N_D, I') \Leftarrow RawImage(T_I, T_T, N_D, I), I' = Compress(I).$
$B6: RawImage(T_I, T_T, N_D, I) \Leftarrow Trigger(T_T, A), T_I \leq T_T,$
$\quad MoveTo(T_I, T_T, N_D, 0, T_T + \Delta t_{sd}, R, A),$
$\quad TakeSnapshot(T_I, T_T, N_D, T_T + \Delta t_{sd}, A, I).$
$B7: TakeSnapshot(T_I, T_T, N_D, D, A, I) \Leftarrow$
$\quad Snapshot(T_I, T_T, N_D, T_S, A, I), T_T \leq T_S, T_S \leq D.$
$B8: MoveTo(T_I, T_T, N_D, W', D, R, B) \Leftarrow Position(T_P, R, B), T_P \leq D.$
$B9: MoveTo(T_I, T_T, N_D, W', D, R, B) \Leftarrow Adjacent(A, B), W' > -b_w, W = W' - 1,$
$\quad MoveTo(T_I, T_T, N_D, W, D, R, A), Move(T_I, T_T, N_D, W', D, R, A, B).$

Replacement Ordering: (f denotes a fact and g a goal and x denotes either)

$O1: f: Position(t_P, r, \ldots) \prec f: Position(t'_P, r, \ldots)$ if $t_P < t'_P$.
$O2: x: X(t_I, \ldots) \prec g: Interest(t'_I, \ldots)$ if $t_I < t'_I$.
$O3: x: X(t_I, t_T, n_D, \ldots) \prec f: Result(t_I, t_T, n_D, \ldots)$ if $x: X \neq f: Result$.
$O4: x: X(t_I, t_D, n_D, \ldots) \prec f: Deliver(t_I, t_D, n_D, \ldots)$ if $x: X \neq f: Deliver$.

Variables: T: time, D: snapshot deadline, A and B: area, R: robot,
I: image or derived information, N: identifier, W: weight
Constants: Δt_{sd}: relative snapshot deadline (max. delay from trigger event),
b_w: bound for weight (diameter of the floor plan)

Fig. 3. Logical Theory for Distributed Surveilance by a Team of Mobile Robots

Like all knowledge, facts are disseminated in the network, hence compensating for heterogeneity in the node capabilities and other limitations, e.g., due to resources and sensor failures.

Different from forward clauses, backward clauses are evaluated only when a user or the reasoner injects a goal (or a new subgoal) that unifies with the conclusion of the clause. For example, the backward clause $B1$ is triggered by an *Interest* goal and generates a corresponding fact when successfully applied. In the case of $B2$ and $B3$, the reasoner attempts to check if the required image is delivered to the root node. If a corresponding *Delivered* fact is available, then the *Deliver* goal is satisfied by applying $B2$. Otherwise, $B3$ needs to be used to check the current position of the root node (via the *Position* fact) and to guide the robot toward the area where the root node is positioned (via the *MoveTo* subgoal). $B4$-$B6$ specify how we construct an image I. When one of trigger conditions, $F1$ or $F2$, is met, a robot needs to be located at the specific area

Table 1. Interpretation of Cyber-Predicates and Theory Predicates

Atom	Type	Realization	Meaning
$Adjacent(a, b)$	Fact	Theory	areas a and b are adjacent (represents floorplan)
$Noise(t, a)$	Cyber-Fact	Sensor	noise is detected in the area a at time t
$Motion(t, a)$	Cyber-Fact	Sensor	motion is detected in the area a at time t
$Trigger(t, a)$	Fact	Theory	triggering condition is met in the area a at time t
$Position(t, r, a)$	Cyber-Fact	Positioning	robot r is positioned in the area a at time t
$Interest(t_I, I, r)$	Cyber-Goal	Theory	user at root node r is interested in information I
$Result(t_I, t_T, n_D, I)$	Goal	Theory	an feature extraction I needs to be computed
$CompImage(t_I, t_T, n_D, I)$	Goal	Theory	an abstract image I needs to be computed
$RawImage(t_I, t_T, n_D, I)$	Goal	Theory	an image I needs to be generated
$MoveTo(t_I, t_T, n_D, w, t, R, b)$	Goal	Theory	robot R needs to move to the area b until time t
$Move(t_I, t_T, n_D, w, t, R, a, b)$	Cyber-Goal	Positioning	robot R needs to move from area a to area b until time t
$TakeSnapshot(t_I, t_T, n_D, t, a, I)$	Goal	Theory	a snapshot I needs to be taken in area a between time $t_T, ..., t$
$TakeSnapshot(t_I, t_T, n_D, t, a, I)$	Cyber-Goal	Camera	a snapshot I needs to be taken in area a between time $t_T, ..., t$
$Snapshot(t_I, t_T, n_D, t_s, a, i)$	Cyber-Fact	Camera	a snapshot i is taken in the area a at time t_s
$Deliver(t_I, t_T, n_D, i, r)$	Cyber-Goal	Root Node	request information i to be delivered to user at root node r
$Delivered(t_I, t_T, n_D, i, r)$	Cyber-Fact	Root Node	information i has been delivered to user at root node r

(the $MoveTo$ predicate should be satisfied for this purpose) to take a snapshot. Only after these two subgoals, $Trigger$ and $MoveTo$ in $B6$, are satisfied, the $TakeSnapshot$ goal can be realized by the device, which generates $Snapshot$ as a new fact. Now, a fact $RawImage$ can be generated as specified by $B6$ and $B7$.

The clauses $B4$ and $B5$ show the processing of a captured image, namely, compression and feature extraction. For example, in the condition of $B5$ the $Compress$ function takes an image I and assigns the compressed image to I'. Raw images are implemented as built-in objects with attributes such as time and area information, and image processing functions such as *Compress* and *Extract* do not alter that information.

The *Adjacent* predicate is used to represent the topological floor plan, which in turn determines the network connectivity among robots. $Adjacent(a, b)$ means areas a and b are adjacent rooms. The forward clause $F3$ captures the assumption that adjacency, and hence connectivity, is symmetric. The clause $B9$ also uses the *Adjacent* predicate to plan the robot movement, since a *Move* goal can be realized by the robot's positioning device only if the room is adjacent.

The *MoveTo* goal will generate a new *Position* fact when it is realized. For example, $MoveTo(T_I, T_T, N_D, 0, T_T + \Delta t_{sd}, R, A)$ is used in the condition as a subgoal of $B6$, and $Position(0.0, r, a)$ is a fact that the local device of robot r provides as its initial position. The clause $B9$ is of particular interest, since it initiates the position change of a robot. As we see from $B8$, if the current position of a robot is equal to its destination, then the *MoveTo* predicate is already satisfied. Otherwise, a robot plans to move toward the destination as specified in $B9$. We use W and the bound b_w to limit the depth of the *MoveTo* subgoal generation. The value W is also used to represent weighted goals to enable locally weight-adaptive goal selection, a first step toward combining distributed reasoning and optimization. When a positioning device has a local choice among several possible *MoveTo* goals, it favors a *MoveTo* goal with a higher weight W since higher weight indicates a goal closer to the final destination, 0 being the maximum. Generally, other factors can influence the local goal selection of cyber-physical devices, e.g., in this case, since R is unbound, robots closer to an area with sufficient resources may be more likely to select a corresponding goal if it is easier for them to realize.

In addition to forward and backward clauses, the replacement ordering is specified in Figure 3. Under $O1$ we specify that an old *Position* fact of a robot is replaced by a new *Position* fact based on their timestamps. In $O2$, an old *Interest* goal becomes obsolete in view of a new *Interest* goal based on the time t_I associated with the *Interest* goal. Under $O3$ and $O4$, we specify orderings so that a fact can cancel goals and facts (except itself) that have led to the generation of such a fact. To avoid canceling goals and facts that are not related to a specific fact, we assume that t_I, t_T, n_D can serve as unique identifiers. Specifically, t_I and t_T are intended to distinguish different interest goals and trigger conditions, respectively. We define t_I and t_T as the time when an interest goal is injected ($B1$) and when a trigger condition occurs ($B6$), respectively. The number n_D, which can be either 0 or 1, distinguishes between *Result* and *Deliver* stages in $B1$, and their corresponding subgoals and related facts.

3.3 Sketch of a Distributed Execution

Figure 4 shows duality of two kinds of knowledge: facts and goals. Facts can be derived from observations or by applying forward clauses. Goals can be injected by a user or refined by applying backward clauses. Forward reasoning derives facts from known facts. Backward reasoning refines a goal to a number of subgoals. Facts and goals are both disseminated in the network as shown in Figure 2.

A goal can be matched with a fact anywhere in the network as illustrated with dotted lines in Figure 4. For example, the goal $Trigger(T, A)$ can be matched with the fact $Trigger(0.0, a)$ as illustrated in Figure 5.

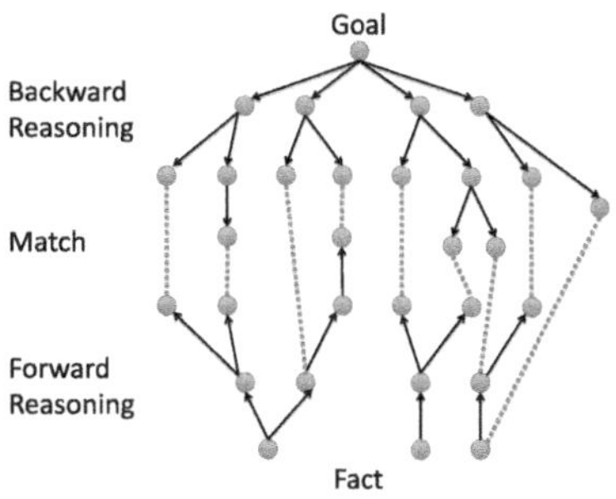

Fig. 4. Matching between Goals and Facts

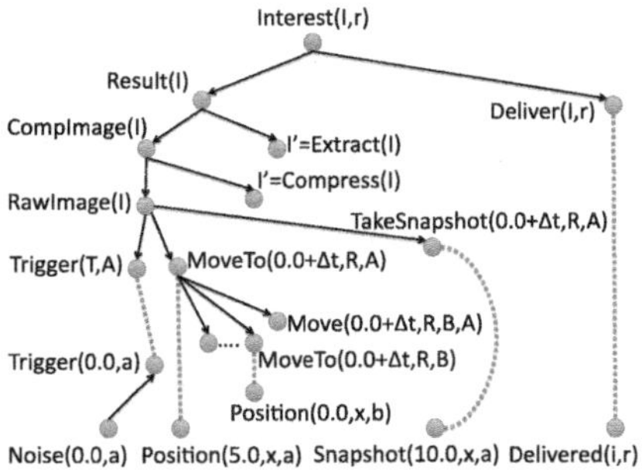

Fig. 5. Example of Distributed Execution

Figure 5 shows a more detailed view of a possible execution of the theory from Figure 3. For brevity, we have omitted some identifier arguments (e.g., T_I,T_T,N_D) in the figure and in the following description unless they are needed. At the top of Figure 5, the user injects a cyber-goal $Interest(I, r)$ at the root node r. At the bottom, a $Noise$ cyber-fact (representing an observation) leads to a fact $Trigger(0.0, a)$ by forward reasoning. In our framework, conditions are processed from left to right as we explained in Section 2. For example, the clause $B1$ in Figure 3 applied to the goal $Interest(I, r)$ attempts to solve $Result(I)$ before $Deliver(I, r)$, and $Result(I)$ fails at first, since a fact $Result(i)$ does not exist yet. The local reasoner feeds $Result(I)$ as a new subgoal into the local knowledge base. The knowledge base contains two goals at this point, $Interest(I, r)$ and $Result(I)$. Assume that $Result(I)$ is randomly selected from the local knowledge base. Subsequently, $CompImage(I)$ and then $RawImage(I)$ are fed into the knowledge base as new subgoals.

Clause $B6$ for $RawImage(I)$ has three subgoals involving $Trigger$, $MoveTo$, and $TakeSnapshot$. The leftmost subgoal can be finally matched with a fact $Trigger(0.0, a)$ that is derived from forward reasoning as depicted at the bottom of Figure 5. Next, the $MoveTo$ goal is further refined by applying $B8$ or $B9$. In case the root node r is positioned in the area a, it is able to detect its position and generate $Position(0.0, r, a)$ as a fact. Otherwise, backward clause $B9$ is used to plan for movement toward the desired area. The cyber-goal $Move(w, t + \Delta t, R, a, b)$ is realized by the local positioning device of a robot x when its current position is a and current time is before the deadline t. As a result, a new cyber-fact such as $Position(5.0, x, a)$ will be generated if the robot x indeed manages to move to a at the time 5.0 assuming a deadline $t + \Delta t = 20.0$. In a similar manner, the local camera device of robot x could take a snapshot of the area and have $Snapshot(10.0, a, i)$ generated to realize $TakeSnapshot(t, a, I)$, which eventually leads to the satisfaction of the $RawImage(I)$ goal.

The goals $CompImage(I)$ and $Result(I)$ can in turn be solved by the robot x, since it has a $RawImage(i)$ available as a fact in its local knowledge base. Alternatively, thanks to the fuly distributed nature of the reasoning process, $Compress$ or $Extract$ can be solved at other nodes (e.g., depending on resource availability) including the root node r, because $RawImage(i), CompImage(i)$, and $Result(i)$ are facts and disseminated through the network. The backward clause $B3$ is used to steer a robot toward the root node r unless backward clause $B2$ can be applied because the delivery has already been accomplished by means of other nodes or the robot can directly satisfy the delivery to the user (or to a higher-layer application). In the end, $Interest(I, r)$ is selected and satisfied by generating a fact $Delivered(i, r)$ at the root node r.

3.4 Discussion and Variations

The distributed nature of the framework improves the robustness of the system under intended or unintended perturbations. For instance, the system continues to operate correctly, i.e., within the scope of the logical theory, even after a human disables or replaces a robot or moves it to a different location. Complete failure of robots or some of their devices is covered as well. If the system is not already heterogeneous from the beginning, partial failures or resource limitations (e.g., battery charge of a robot) will eventually lead to a heterogeneous system which is why any assumption of homogeneity is avoided.

We have also experimented with several variations of the running example. For instance, the robot movement can be constrained by adding a condition $Movable(T, R, A)$ in $B9$ to check if a robot R can move away from an area A at time T. Now coverage, connectivity, or energy constraints can be formulated such as $Energy(T, R, E), E \geq e \Rightarrow Movable(T, R, A)$ to make sure that only robots with a sufficient amount of energy participate in position changes.
Our simple example assumes that the floor plan is given in advance. However, generalizing techniques such as SLAM (simultaneous localization and mapping) [3], which are well established in robotics, models could continuously adapt to the facts derived from observations, specifically the floor plan and the connectivity model. In the case of the floor plan, observations could be simply added as facts and SLAM could benefit from consequences generated based on a background theory. In the case of connectivity, the model parameters could be adapted to match the facts generated by neighbor discovery or even (distributed) signal strength measurements if available. SLAM could be generalized to a distributed mapping of signal strength or more generally the wireless spectrum for the purpose of network optimization [10]. An interesting direction would be to explore how such algorithms can be developed in a declarative framework.

4 Related Work

The idea of applying declarative techniques in communication and networking is not new. A large body of work exists in the areas of specification, analysis, and synthesis of networking policies and protocols, e.g., in the context of security, routing, or dynamic spectrum access.

Declarative querying of sensor networks has been studied through several approaches, for instance in [18], which composes services on the fly and in a goal-driven fashion using a concept of semantic streams. Declarative techniques to specify destinations have been used in disruption-tolerant networking [2]. A variant of Datalog has been applied to the declarative specification of peer-to-peer protocols in the P2 system [12]. Based on this work, [4] develops a very interesting approach to declarative sensor networks that can transmit generated facts to specific neighbors and can also utilize knowledge about neighbors to specify, e.g., routing algorithms. The promising idea of providing an abstraction that views a system as a single asset (an ensemble) rather then programming its individual components has been explored in several papers. Most interesting, the approach adapted in Meld [1] extends the ideas from declarative sensor networks to modular robots, i.e., ensembles of robots with inter-robot communication limited to immediate neighbors. As an example, the movement of a composite robot emerges as a result of the coordinated interaction between its homogeneous robot modules. An earlier functional approach to programming sensor networks is the Regiment macro-programming system [13], which uses a stream-based data-flow language. Most of the work focuses not on the theoretical foundations, but on the efficient compilation into a conventional programming language, which is one possible approach for practical deployment. Another approach, which we sometimes refer to as *embedded formal methods*, is the use of an effient reasoning engine in embedded systems such as software-defined radios [6] or routers [16] as explored in the context of disruption-tolerant networking.

In this paper, we have presented first steps toward combining forward and backward reasoning in a fully distributed fashion with knowledge that is transparently shared. A fixed or known neighborhood is not assumed in our more abstract approach, and the use and dissemination of both facts and goals aims at general cyber-physical systems with distributed actuation, and hence leads us beyond sensor networks, in particular to dynamic sensor/actuator networks that are, unlike ensembles, inherently heterogeneous.

5 Conclusions and Future Work

We have presented a distributed computational and logical foundation for declarative control of NCPS. Our approach is based on distributed knowledge sharing and supports a broad spectrum of operations between autonomy and cooperation with minimum assumptions on network connectivity. Specifically, we developed a distributed inference system based on Horn clause logic with built-ins and cyber-predicates that can capture the interaction with the physical world. In the underlying distributed computing model, facts and goals are represented as knowledge that can be shared opportunistically and guide the distributed reasoning process. The duality between facts and goals extends to the proof system, which treats forward and backward reasoning on an equal footing. Essential properties of our logical framework, such as soundness, completeness, and termination conditions, have been established under very general conditions, which will be the subject of a future paper.

A key feature of our distributed logical framework is its dynamic and interactive nature, meaning that facts represent observations, and goals can lead to changes in the environment that will manifest themselves as new facts flowing into the system. Whether an original local goal can be solved is often secondary, because the combined effect of a set of local goals on the cyber-physical system and its nondeterministic dynamics can lead to solutions of higher-level goals even without requiring solutions of all lower levels. To cope with system perturbations and unexpected failures, it is essential that local goals are not eliminated as soon as they are satisfied, because their main purpose, namely steering the system toward the satisfaction of a high-level property, may not have been achieved yet. Only after certain high-level goals are reached, auxiliary goals can be eliminated so that they do not have to comptete with new goals that steer the system toward the next high-level objective. Real-world systems are more complex, because such processes take place concurrently at multiple levels of abstraction and at different time scales. Our combination of a logic with an underlying partial order facilitates a new declarative specification style, which is particularly suitable for open distributed systems that can interact with a cooperative or uncooperative environment.

For experimentation, we have implemented a prototype of our logical framework that heavily relies on randomization techniques to achieve decoupling and implement locally fair nondeterminism that is used in our proof system to cover a broad range of possible implementations with different reasoning strategies. Our experiments with the simulation of an abstract networked multirobot system are a snapshot of ongoing work, but illustrate the application and the features of our framework in a simplified but nontrivial setting, and indicate possible directions for future work.

For realistic experiments, we plan to make use of existing robotic abstraction layers, such as the open-source Player/Stage/Gazebo Project [15]. Experiments in a real-world multirobot testbed similar to that of SRI's Centibots [14] and Commbots [8] projects are another possible direction. Beyond multirobot teams, we see opportunities to apply (extensions of) our framework to other unmanned autonomous vehicles, networks of pico-satellites [17], instrumented smart spaces [11], ad hoc social networking in a cyber-physical (instrumented) world, and next-generation adaptive networks and cognitive radios [9], where the devices exhibit a high degree of flexibility and the network can be morphed to adapt to user objectives and policies. Clearly, a lot of work remains ahead, because many of these applications require the combination of distributed reasoning with distributed optimization, and the use of weighted goals in our example is only a very first step in this direction.

References

1. Ashley-Rollman, M.P., Goldstein, S.C., Lee, P., Mowry, T.C., Pillai, P.: Meld: A declarative approach to programming ensembles. In: Proc. of the IEEE International Conference on Intelligent Robots and Systems (IROS 2007) (October 2007)

2. Basu, P., Krishnan, R., Brown, D.W.: Persistent delivery with deferred binding to descriptively named destinations. In: Proc. of IEEE Military Communications Conference (2008)
3. Choset, H., Nagatani, K.: Topological simultaneous localization and mapping (SLAM): Toward exact localization without explicit localization. IEEE Trans. on Robotics and Automation 17(1), 125–137 (2001)
4. Chu, D., Popa, L., Tavakoli, A., Hellerstein, J.M., Levis, P., Shenker, S., Stoica, I.: The design and implementation of a declarative sensor network system. In: SenSys 2007: Proc. of the 5th International Conference on Embedded Networked Sensor Systems, pp. 175–188 (2007)
5. Dressler, F.: Self-Organization in Sensor and Actor Networks. Wiley, Chichester (2008)
6. Elenius, D., Denker, G., Stehr, M.-O.: A semantic web reasoner for rules, equations and constraints. In: Calvanese, D., Lausen, G. (eds.) RR 2008. LNCS, vol. 5341, pp. 135–149. Springer, Heidelberg (2008)
7. Farrell, S., Cahill, V.: Delay- and Disruption-Tolerant Networking. Artech House, Inc., Norwood (2006)
8. Gerkey, B.P., Mailler, R., Morisset, B.: Commbots: Distributed control of mobile communication relays. In: Proc. of the AAAI Workshop on Auction Mechanisms for Robot Coordination (AuctionBots), pp. 51–57 (2006)
9. Troxel, G.D., et al.: Enabling open-source cognitively-controlled collaboration among software-defined radio nodes. Comput. Netw. 52(4), 898–911 (2008)
10. Grisetti, G., Stachniss, C., Burgard, W.: Nonlinear constraint network optimization for efficient map learning. Trans. Intell. Transport. Sys. 10(3), 428–439 (2009)
11. Kim, M., Massaguer, D., Dutt, N., Mehrotra, S., Ren, S., Stehr, M.-O., Talcott, C., Venkatasubramanian, N.: A semantic framework for reconfiguration of instrumented cyber physical spaces. In: Workshop on Event-based Semantics, CPS Week (2008)
12. Loo, B.T., Condie, T., Garofalakis, M., Gay, D.E., Hellerstein, J.M., Maniatis, P., Ramakrishnan, R., Roscoe, T., Stoica, I.: Declarative networking. ACM Commun. 52(11), 87–95 (2009)
13. Newton, R., Morrisett, G., Welsh, M.: The regiment macroprogramming system. In: IPSN 2007: Proc. of the 6th International Conference on Information Processing in Sensor Networks, pp. 489–498. ACM, New York (2007)
14. Ortiz, C.L., Vincent, R., Morisset, B.: Task inference and distributed task management in the Centibots robotic system. In: AAMAS 2005: Proc. of the Fourth International Joint Conference on Autonomous Agents and Multiagent Systems, pp. 860–867 (2005)
15. Rusu, R.B., Maldonado, A., Beetz, M., Gerkey, B.: Extending Player/Stage/Gazebo towards cognitive robots acting in ubiquitous sensor-equipped environments. In: ICRA '07: Proc. of the IEEE International Conference on Robotics and Automation Workshop for Network Robot Systems (2007)
16. Stehr, M.-O., Talcott, C.: Planning and learning algorithms for routing in disruption-tolerant networks. In: Proc. of IEEE Military Communications Conference (2008)
17. Toorian, S., Diaz, K., Lee, S.: The CubeSet approach to space access. In: IEEE Aerospace Conference (2008)
18. Whitehouse, K., Zhao, F., Liu, J.: Semantic streams: A framework for composable semantic interpretation of sensor data. In: Römer, K., Karl, H., Mattern, F. (eds.) EWSN 2006. LNCS, vol. 3868, pp. 5–20. Springer, Heidelberg (2006)

AdContRep: A Privacy Enhanced Reputation System for MANET Content Services

Zheng Yan[1] and Yu Chen[2]

[1] Nokia Research Center, Helsinki, Finland
zheng.z.yan@nokia.com
[2] Aalto University, Espoo, Finland
yu.chen.fifi@gmail.com

Abstract. Mobile ad hoc network (MANET) has become a practical platform for pervasive social networking. In such a system, various content information flows in terms of content query and response. To which extent should mobile users trust it, whilst user privacy can also be preserved? For solving this problem, we propose AdContRep, a privacy enhanced reputation system for MANET content services. We develop a novel hybrid trust model to evaluate node recommendation trust and content reputation in the context of frequent change of node pseudonyms. The evaluation is based on ephemeral node experiences and/or historical node recommendation behaviors. Our simulation results show the model's effectiveness with regard to unfair rating attack and on-off attack. A prototype implementation based on Nokia N810 tablets further proves the concept of AdContRep design.

1 Introduction

A mobile ad hoc network (MANET) is a collection of autonomous nodes that communicate with each other by forming a multi-hop radio network and maintaining connectivity in a decentralized manner. Nowadays, MANET has become a practical platform for social networking and computing. For example, a user could query people in vicinity using his/her mobile device about which shop is on sale, which movie is recommended to see, or which mobile application should be installed for tagging the locations of photos. The user's neighbors can respond these queries by providing their recommendations via MANET. This kind of social networking is very valuable for the mobile users, especially when fixed networks (e.g. Internet) or mobile networks are temporarily unavailable or costly to access.

In such a pervasive social networking system, various content information flows. Examples are a mobile application installation link, a URL of a service, a web page and a textual message typed by a user. How much should a user trust different content information received over the MANET? Meanwhile, in order to preserve personal privacy and avoid malicious tracking, the user generally would like to use an anonymous identity (ID) or pseudonym in the content recommendation query and response. All above introduces a demand to provide a practical privacy enhanced reputation system for MANET content services that could help the mobile user easily make a decision for content selection.

Z. Yu et al. (Eds.): UIC 2010, LNCS 6406, pp. 414–429, 2010.

This paper proposes AdContRep to satisfy this demand. We design a novel hybrid trust model to evaluate both MANET node recommendation trust (in short node trust) and content reputation (i.e. the public trust in content). It concerns both historical node recommendation behaviors accumulated by a trusted server (TS) who knows the nodes' real identities and ephemeral experiences collected by individual nodes using pseudonyms. On the basis of the hybrid trust model, we apply credible content reputation evaluation by weighting a node's votes on contents with its credibility. The credibility is generated based on the node trust and node-node social relationships. Particularly, the node trust is certified by the trusted server based on historical node recommendation behaviors. It is further evolved according to the node's voting quality at the individual nodes. And this process is iterative in AdContRep.

AdContRep provides credible content reputation evaluation in order to overcome unfair rating attacks [5, 17]. We adopt suitable decay on the contributions of past experiences and bad voting punishment to prevent on-off attacks [23]. In addition, AdContRep supports privacy enhancement in the system design. The paper contributes to the literature by solving the following questions:

- Which reputation system architecture is appropriate for MANET content services with user privacy preservation?
- Which trust model is practical for such a system in order to enhance privacy?
- Which trust/reputation evaluation algorithms are effective and robust, thus can be applied in the system?

The rest of the paper is organized as follows. Section 2 gives a brief overview of related work. Section 3 introduces AdContRep system design. The algorithms used for content reputation generation and node trust evaluation are described in Section 4, followed by experimental simulation results in Section 5. We further discuss the system implementation and privacy issues in Section 6. Finally, conclusions and future work are presented in the last section.

2 Related Work

Jøsang et al. classified reputation system architecture into two main types: centralized and distributed [1]. The system architecture determines how ratings and reputation scores are communicated between participants in a reputation system. In the literature, distributed trust evaluations have been studied in MANET, seldom the solutions support node privacy [2-4]. This could cause such potential attacks as bad mouthing attacks or unfair rating attacks targeting at a specific node [5]. Most existing systems maintain a statistical representation of reputation by borrowing tools from the realms of game theory (Confidant [31] and Core [7], and peer-to-peer networks [19]) and Bayesian analytics [30]. These systems try to counter selfish routing misbehavior of nodes by enforcing nodes to cooperate with each other and counter any arbitrary misbehavior of nodes. However, little work has paid attention to the content reputation issue in MANET with node privacy as a main concern. On the other hand, practical reputation systems generally apply a centralized server to collect feedback for reputation generation (e.g. eBay [14], Yahoo auctions [18], and Internet-based systems such as Keynote [24]). However, many existing systems (e.g. Amazon, eBay) lack considerations on the credibility of a user's rating. This greatly influences the quality of produced reputations. The usage of pseudonym and the ease of its change additionally complicate the picture by allowing participants to effectively erase their prior history. AdContRep adopts a hybrid reputation system architecture, where node trust and content reputation are evaluated in a distributed way, but with the support of a centralized trusted server.

In the literature, trust and reputation mechanisms have been widely studied in various fields of distributed systems, such as ad hoc networks, peer-to-peer (P2P) systems, Grid computing, pervasive computing and e-commerce [6]. Many mechanisms have been developed for supporting trusted communications and collaborations among computing nodes [2, 3, 8, 11, 12]. Examples are FuzzyTrust system [13], the eBay user feedback system [14], PeerTrust model [15], an objective trust management framework (OTMF) for MANET [12] and Credence - a robust and decentralized system for evaluating the reputation of files in a P2P system [16]. In these researches, trust can be modeled, calculated and thus expressed using a value. However, none of the above studies consider how to support privacy. Thus it is hard to directly apply them into AdContRep.

Recently, a number of reputation systems have been proposed in the context of digital contents and ad hoc networks [25]. For example, Thomas Adler and Alfaro proposed a content driven reputation system for Wikipedia authors solely on the basis of content evolution; but not on user-to-user comments or ratings [25]. The concept of data centric trust in volatile environments, such as ad hoc networks, was introduced in [4] to evaluate the node trust through the data reported by it.

Gupta, et al. proposed a partially distributed reputation system for P2P systems by introducing a reputation computation agent (RCA). Its system structure is similar to AdContRep. But this system does not concern the challenges caused by privacy enhancement. In addition, the RCA is applied only for calculating peer's reputation based on its contributions to the system. In AdContRep, we apply the trusted server to update both node recommendation trust and content reputation on the basis of long-term historical recommendation behaviors.

In most reputation systems in the ad hoc networks, the reputation of a node is shared globally in the network. The purpose is to make the reputation of a node known to all other nodes and decrease the detection time. Thus maintaining and disseminating indirect reputation information incur overhead at both the individual node and the network. OCEAN [27] discounts second-hand reputation exchange and only utilizes local reputation based on direct observations in order to achieve a reasonable performance. AdContRep concerns both local-aware and global-aware reputations by aggregating local experiences and global experiences together. By deploying the trusted server, the overhead of reputation maintenance and dissemination is eliminated among MANET nodes.

Inconsistent reputation problem (i.e. different nodes may have different reputation values for the same node) often occurs in the ad hoc networks due to subjective reason and/or different local experiences. This makes it hard to distinguish correct reputation ratings from reputation voting messages. LARS (Locally Aware Reputation System) [28] was proposed to deal with selfish behaviors and malicious behaviors (e.g. packet dropping and unfair rating). In LARS, the reputation of a node is derived from direct observation and exchange of second hand reputation information is disallowed. In AdContRep, we apply the trusted server to uniform node recommendation trust and content reputation based on local experiences reported by nodes. This trust/reputation information is issued to the node by the server. Serving as the initial value of trust, it is further evolved based on new experiences collected at the individual node. In addition, the above process is iterated. Thereby, we avoid the inconsistent reputation problem and eliminate node trust inaccuracy caused by multi-hop reputation dissemination. Trust/reputation evaluation is based on first-hand experiences and direct votes no matter at the TS or the node.

A reputation rating system based on past behavior of evaluators was proposed in [29]. Trust in the evaluator indexes its impact on the rating system. The trust value is dynamically adjusted based on past estimation performance. In AdContRep, the node trust is adjusted based on its past voting performance. It is evaluated by each individual node and at the TS based on ephemeral and historical experiences, respectively.

Nowadays, reputation systems may face the problem of unfair ratings by artificially inflating or deflating reputations [14, 18, 20, 21]. They are vulnerable to a number of potential attacks, such as Sybil attack, on-off attack, independent/collaborative bad mouthing attack, and conflict behavior attack [22, 23]. The usage of pseudonyms introduces new challenges since it makes hard to trace malicious behaviors. It also influences the accuracy of reputation. Sun et al. proposed a number of schemes to overcome some of the above attacks, but they did not consider the additional challenges caused by privacy preservation [5, 9].

3 AdContRep System Design

3.1 Application Scenarios and Research Requirements

We consider the following scenario as our target MANET content service. A MANET node A queries its neighbors about a mobile application for photo tagging, e.g. in a football auditorium. Its neighbors could further distribute this query to other nodes (via broadcast or multicast). Supposing that a set of nodes respond the query, node A processes all collected responses and calculates the reputation values of recommended contents in order to assist its user's decision. After consuming the content, node A could provide feedback to a trusted server (TS) by rating the content and reporting collected recommendations. Thus the TS can evaluate the reputation of involved contents based on all collected data. It can also evaluate all recommender nodes' trust based on recommendation behaviors by aggregating all information about the same node together (although they could use multiple pseudonyms). Periodically or by request, the server issues a new pseudonym with a valid node trust token to each node. The trust token contains the node latest recommendation trust value evaluated by the TS and a time stamp to indicate its valid period. A more interesting scenario is a node could view the trust values of other nodes in vicinity with the aid of the TS (e.g. via a location based service). Reputation visualization promotes honest and secure social networking.

A number of constraints and requirements are raised in the practical deployment of such a system. We summarize them as our research assumptions and basic requirements. First, the system is expected to support user privacy. The node's real identity should be hidden in MANET social networking. The user's pseudonym could be frequently changed in order to enhance privacy and avoid potential tracking; whilst the node's real identity is registered at the TS. Second, the nodes can connect to the trusted server periodically (e.g. 1 time per day) although real time connection is not always available. Finally, a small amount of transferring data is preferred among MANET node-to-node communications in order to achieve effective power consumption [26]. However, there is no such strict constraint with regard to message length for the node and TS communications [26]. Introducing the centralized TS has a number of practical advantages: a) avoid inconsistent reputation problem; b) support accurate node trust evaluation based on registered unique node ID even though the node's pseudonyms could be changed, thus overcome the Sybil attack; c) provide an economic approach to collect useful data from pervasive social networking that can further support other promising services (e.g. location based content recommendation services). Thereby, the design can potentially support some business models (e.g., Nokia Ovi). In adContRep, we assume that the TS is trustworthy enough to preserve user's private data.

In AdContRep, malicious nodes can provide dishonest recommendations on contents in order to frame good ones and/or boost bad ones. This attack, referred to as the bad mouthing or unfair rating attack is the most straightforward attack [5, 9]. Malicious nodes could also behave well and badly alternatively, hoping that they can remain undetected while causing damage [5, 9]. This attack is called as the on-off attack, which is also one type of conflict behaviour attack. AdContRep aims at overcoming at least the above two common attacks.

3.2 AdContRep System Structure

We can find both distributed and centralized reputation architecture in the literature. Both have advantages and disadvantages [1]. We attempt to utilize their advantages in AdContRep. Fig. 1 illustrates AdContRep's structure. It is a hybrid trust/reputation management infrastructure. At each node device, a network observer records recommendations. A content observer monitors the usage history of the contents in order to generate real usage behavior based trust cue [10]. A content voter provides a user interface for the node user to recommend and vote contents. A content query provides the node user an interface to send content recommendation request (the query) in MANET. A trust information disseminator reports the recommendation records to the TS. A trust evaluator evaluates the query responder nodes' recommendation trust, the reputation of recommended contents and provides the results to the user. A reputation extractor receives the trust tokens issued by the TS and a list of reputation values of different contents. Trust DataSet stores all data related to the above functional blocks in the node.

At the server side, a reputation generator calculates node trust values and content reputation values; meanwhile it identifies malicious nodes. A reputation distributor distributes the trust tokens, as well as content reputation values to each node periodically or by request. An ID manager handles node registration and issues new node pseudonyms (by request or periodically). A trust information receiver collects the records reported by the nodes and saves them into Reputation DataSet, which also saves the content reputation information, the trust token of each node and the nodes real IDs and their pseudonyms.

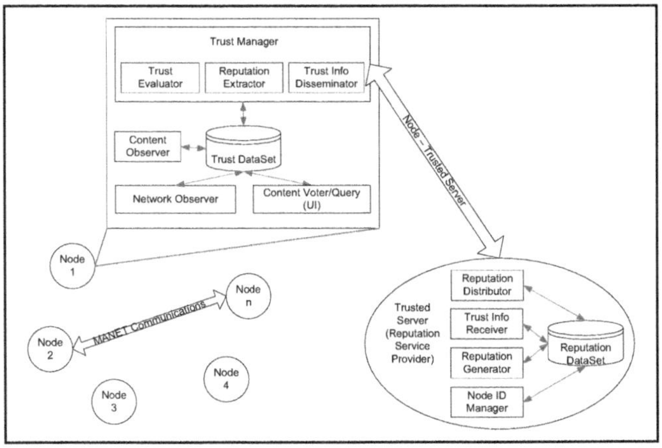

Fig. 1. AdContRep System Structure

3.3 AdContRep Trust Model

The way to calculate trust is often called the trust model [21]. Based on the above system design, we propose a hybrid trust model – AdContRep model to generate node trust and content reputation.

In AdContRep, the MANET node processes query response regarding content recommendations. The trust evaluator calculates the content reputation based on the votes provided by recommender nodes, the number of collected recommendations (i.e., content popularity) and the recommender nodes' trust values certified by the TS, which is further evolved based on local experiences. The evaluated content reputation will be displayed to help the node user make a selection decision. Herein, the trust value of a recommender node partially serves as the credibility of its recommendation. This trust value contains two parts: one is provided by the TS by assessing historical node recommendation behaviors. The other is the node's local evaluation on the recommender node based on its accumulated experiences. The local evaluation is evolved on the basis of the trust value issued by the TS. In our opinion, credibility provides a reason to trust. Recommendation credibility is essential for generating a reliable reputation value.

In order to preserve privacy, AdContRep applies the TS to issue and manage the pseudonyms of nodes. The TS can identify the real identities of nodes. It could frequently or periodically issue a new pseudonym to the node. Thus, the local experiences are accumulated only based on valid pseudonyms. For example, Node A would assume Node B as a different node once Node B uses a new pseudonym, even though they had interaction with each other before. Historical evaluation on the node's recommendation trust can only be conducted at the TS by considering all recommendation behaviors related to a concrete node possibly having multiple pseudonyms. Notably, a new trust token is always issued together with pseudonym change. However, the node may only request updating the trust value by issuing a new trust token without changing its pseudonym.

Particularly, the TS also collects direct votes on different contents and the statistical data of node interaction for the purpose of evaluating the node trust and content reputation. The node trust token (containing the node trust value) is issued by the TS with non-repudiation. Due to the usage of pseudonyms, only the TS can evaluate the node trust in an accurate way based on historical recommendation behaviors. Thus, introducing the TS can greatly improve the precision of trust/reputation evaluation. The TS is also responsible for issuing the blacklist of malicious nodes and the favourite list of honest nodes to the AdContRep nodes.

Meanwhile, the TS can generate the reputation of various contents based on the feedback and recommendation records reported by the query nodes. A content recommendation service based on content reputation can be provided. The evaluation of node trust and content reputation is iterative at both the node and TS based on newly accumulated experiences and information.

4 Algorithms

4.1 Trust/Reputation Evaluation at a Query Node

For generating content reputation at the query node, we consider all collected votes and recommender nodes' voting credibility, the content popularity and the content reputation value issued by the TS if any. The content popularity is reflected by the number of votes and its percentage with regard to the total votes. The more number and/or percentage of the recommendations, the more reputable the content is. The query node applies Algorithm 1 to calculate content reputation and node trust.

Suppose *K* notes respond node *q*'s query and K_m nodes of them recommend content C_m. Their votes are $V^{C_m} = \{V_1^{C_m}, V_2^{C_m}, ..., V_{K_m}^{C_m}\}$. Totally, *M* contents are recommended in the query response. We calculate the credibility of voting W_q^k for node *k* at node *q* as below according to interest similarities and *k*'s recommendation trust s_q^k :

$$W_q^k = Cred(\alpha, s_q^k) = \frac{\alpha * s_q^k}{Z} \tag{1}$$

where α is a community factor, we assume the credibility is high if two nodes fall into the same community with similar interests. If *q* and *k* are in the same community, $\alpha = \omega_s$, else $\alpha = \omega_d$; and $\omega_s > \omega_d$. In our simulation, we assume a query happens inside a community and set α as 1. s_q^k is the trust value held by node *q* on node *k*, which is upgraded based on the trust token issued by the TS and fine tuned according to node *q*'s local experiences. *Z* is a normalization factor to make $\sum_{k=1}^{K_m} W_q^k = 1$. Note that if the content reputation is available from the TS, we can treat it as the server's vote and set high credibility for it.

For content C_m with K_m votes, we have its reputation calculated as below by considering the popularity of content, the votes and their credibility.

$$T_{C_m} = \left\{1 - \exp\left(\frac{-K_m^{\ 2}}{2(\sigma+\varepsilon)^2}\right)\right\} \sum_{k=1}^{K_m} W_q^k V_k^{C_m} \tag{2}$$

Herein, we apply a revised Rayleigh cumulative distribution function $\left\{1-\exp(\frac{-K_m{}^2}{2(\sigma+\varepsilon)^2})\right\}$ to model the impact of K_m on content reputation. $\sigma > 0$, is a parameter that inversely controls how fast the number of recommenders impacts on T_{C_m}, which increases as K_m increases. σ can be set from 0 to theoretically ∞, to capture the characteristics of different scenarios (We set $\sigma = 1.01$ in our simulations). $\varepsilon = -K_m / K$ is the percentage of recommendations, which is a factor to indicate the users' preference on content C_m. We apply ε to further adjust K_m's influence.

The evaluation by node q on node k's recommendation trust is based on node k's trust token s^k and voting quality. s_q^k is reset to s^k each time when a new trust token is issued since the server's evaluation on node trust is more accurate. Then it is further evolved according to its recommendation performance experienced by node q using the following formulas:

$$\rho = \frac{1}{2}\left\{\max\left(V_k^{C_m}\right) - \min\left(V_k^{C_m}\right)\right\} \tag{3}$$

$$x = \rho - \left|T_{C_m} - V_k^{C_m}\right| \tag{4}$$

If $x = \rho - \left|T_c - V_k^{C_m}\right| < \varphi \quad (\varphi = 0)$, $\gamma{+}{+}$;

$$s_q^k = \begin{cases} s_q^k + \delta x & (\gamma < thr) \\ s_q^k + \delta x - \mu\gamma & (\gamma \geq thr) \end{cases} = \begin{cases} 1 & (s_q^k > 1) \\ 0 & (s_q^k < 0) \end{cases} \tag{5}$$

Where $\delta > 0$ is a parameter to control the adjustment of s_q^k. In order to detect on-off attackers, we further introduce a warning flag γ to record the number of bad recommendations. γ's initial value is 0. It is increased by 1 each time when a bad vote happens. thr is a threshold to indicate the on-off attack. $\mu > 0$ is a parameter to control bad voting punishment. $\max\left(V_k^{C_m}\right)$ is the maximum voting value, whilst $\min\left(V_k^{C_m}\right)$ the minimum voting value. φ is a parameter to decide the bad vote. We set $\delta = 0.05$, $\mu = 0.1$ in our simulations.

Algorithm 1. Trust/Reputation Evaluation at a Query Node *q*

1. Input:
2. - $\{V^{C_m}\}$ $V^{C_m} = \{V_1^{C_m}, V_2^{C_m}, \ldots\ldots, V_{K_m}^{C_m}\}$: K_m votes on content C_m; $m = (1, \ldots M)$
3. - K: the total number of query responders;
4. - α : a community factor;
5. - M: the number of contents recommended regarding a query;

6. **For** each recommender node k, **do**
7. Calculate the credibility of voting W_q^k based on (1);
8. **For** each recommended content, **do**
9. Content reputation generation based on (2);

10. Adjust s_q^k , **For** each node k, **do**
11. **For** each recommended content by node k, **do**
12. s_q^k adjustment based on (3), (4) and (5);

13. Output: T_{C_m} ($m=1,...,M$); s_q^k ($k=1,...,K$).

4.2 Trust/Reputation Evaluation at TS

The content reputation is generated at the TS by considering all collected node recommendation information, the nodes' trust values, and the content's popularity. Algorithm 2 is designed to calculate content reputation and node trust at the TS.

Suppose a total number of L nodes register into the AdContRep system with real IDs $N=\{n_1,n_2,......n_L\}$. Currently, there are M' contents involved in recommendations $C=\{C_1,C_2,......,C_{M'}\}$. K_m' nodes recommend content C_m with votes $V^{C_m}=\left\{\{V_1^{C_m}\},\{V_2^{C_m}\},......,\{V_{K_m}^{C_m}\}\right\}$. The total number of content recommenders is K'. Obviously, $L \ge K' \ge K_m'$.

In practice, node k could vote content C_m many times at different time t_i: $\{V_k^{C_m}\}=\{V_k^{C_m(t_i)}\}$. Considering the time's influence and the potential on-off attack, we pay more attention to the node's recent voting. $\overline{V_k^{C_m}}$ is the aggregated votes of node k on content C_m.

$$\overline{V_k^{C_m}}=\frac{1}{O}\sum_k V_k^{C_m(t_i)}e^{-\frac{|t-t_i|^2}{\beta}} \tag{6}$$

Where $O=\sum_{n_i} e^{-\frac{|t-t_i|^2}{\beta}}$; $V_k^{C_m(t_i)}$ is node k's vote on C_m at time t_i; t is the content reputation calculation time; β is a parameter to control time decaying ($\beta=2$ in our simulations).

Similar to (1), we generate node k's voting credibility W^k by considering its recommendation trust s^k. Differently, we also consider local evidence r^k (observed by the content observer in Fig.1) as one influence factor in W^k generation. For example, r^k is generated based on the content usage statistics in order to indicate the node user's preference on the content [10]. In this case, W^k is content-dependent (as $W_{C_m}^k$ shown in Line 9 of Algorithm 2). Thereby, we have:

$$W^k=\Psi\left(s^k,r^k\right)=\frac{s^k * r^k}{Z'} \tag{7}$$

Where s^k is the node k's trust value and r^k is the credibility/reliability value provided by node k (We set r^k =1 in our simulation supposed that it is not available). Z' is a normalization factor to make $\sum_{k=1}^{K} W^k=1$.

For content C_m, its reputation value can be calculated as below:

$$T'_{C_m} = f\left(K'_m\right)\sum_{k=1}^{K'_m} W^k \overline{V_k^{C_m}} \tag{8}$$

Where $f\left(K'_m\right)=\left\{1-\exp\left(\frac{-K_m'^{2}}{2(\sigma+\varepsilon)^2}\right)\right\}$ ($\varepsilon=-K'_m/K'$) is also the Rayleigh cumulative distribution function (We set $\sigma=5$ at the TS in our simulations).

At the node registration time, s^k is set with an initial value (e.g. 0.5 in our simulations). Then, it is further evolved based on node *k*'s voting performance on all involved contents.

$$\rho=\frac{1}{2}\left\{\max\left(V_k^{C_m}\right)-\min\left(V_k^{C_m}\right)\right\} \tag{9}$$

$$y=\rho-\left|T'_{C_m}-\overline{V_k^{C_m}}\right| \tag{10}$$

If $y<\varphi$ $(\varphi=0)$, $\gamma{+}{+}$;

$$s^k=\begin{cases} s^k+\delta y & (\gamma<thr) \\ s^k+\delta y-\mu\gamma & (\gamma\geq thr)\end{cases}=\begin{cases}1 & \left(s^k>1\right) \\ 0 & \left(s^k<0\right)\end{cases} \tag{11}$$

where δ, μ, thr, γ, φ, $\min\left(V_k^{C_m}\right)$ and $\max\left(V_k^{C_m}\right)$ have the same meanings as described in Section 4.1. Similar to (5), we design function (11) to adjust the node trust value at the TS.

Algorithm 2. Trust/Reputation Evaluation at the Trusted Server (TS)

1. Input:
2. - $C=\{C_1,C_2,\ldots\ldots,C_M\}$, $N=\{n_1,n_2,\ldots\ldots n_L\}$; s^k ($k=1,\ldots,L$);
3. - $\{V^{C_m}\}$, $V^{C_m}=\left\{\{V_1^{C_m}\},\{V_2^{C_m}\},\ldots\ldots,\{V_{K'_m}^{C_m}\}\right\}$: K'_m votes on content C_m;
4. - K': the total number of content recommenders;
5. Organize votes based on real node IDs n_l $(l=1,\ldots,L)$;
6. **For** each node k, **do**
7. **For** each recommended content C_m by *k*, **do**
8. Aggregate node k's votes on content C_m based on (6);
9. Calculate W^k (or $W_{C_m}^k$) based on (7);
10. **For** each content C_m, **do**
11. Content reputation generation based on (8);
12. Adjust s^k, **For** each node *k*, **do**
13. **For** each recommended content by node *k*, **do**
14. s^k adjustment based on (9), (10) and (11);
15. Output: T'_{C_m} ($m=1,\ldots,M$); s^k ($k=1,\ldots,L$).

---

5 Evaluation and Implementation

We design a number of simulations to first show the advantages of AdContRep in assisting users' decision, and then demonstrate the effects of unfair rating and on-off attacks on AdContRep. In our simulations with Matlab, $L = 50$, we randomly select a query node (from good nodes) and a random number of nodes to respond each query. We consider three contents ($M = 3$) with quality low ($T_{C_1} = 0.1$), medium ($T_{C_2} = 0.5$) and high ($T_{C_3} = 0.9$), respectively. For simulation simplification, we assume that ad hoc routing trust can be ensured.

5.1 Effects of AdContRep System

We test the performance of Algorithm 1 when the server connection is not available with four scenarios: 1) each query responding node randomly selects one content to vote honestly; 2) each responding node votes all contents honestly; 3) 5 fixed attackers in the network randomly vote one content dishonestly (e.g. deflate C_3 and inflate C_1 and C_2), whilst other responding nodes randomly vote one content honestly; 4) 5 fixed attackers vote all contents dishonestly, whilst other responding nodes vote all contents honestly. In all of above scenarios, we fix the query node and suppose that all node pseudonyms are not changed. Fig.2 shows this simulation result. We observe that 1) Algorithm 1 performs well when there is no any attack in the system, as shown in Fig.2 (a) and (b); 2) it can adjust the node recommendation trust to improve the content reputation evaluation, as shown in Fig.2 (c) and (d); 3) Algorithm 1 performs better if more recommendation information is collected locally (comparing Fig.2 (a) to Fig.2 (b) and Fig.2 (c) to Fig.2 (d)). Note that in Fig.2 (a) and (c), some reputation values of C_3 are very low, this is caused by a small number of recommendations since a random number of nodes are selected to respond the queries in this simulation.

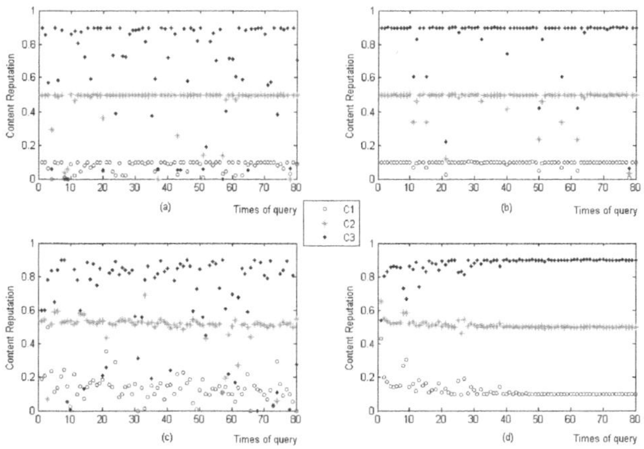

Fig. 2. Content reputations at a query node: (a) each recommender node votes one content honestly; (b) each recommender node votes all contents honestly; (c) 5 malicious nodes vote one content dishonestly; (d) 5 malicious nodes vote all contents dishonestly

We further test the performance of both Algorithms 1 and 2 when the server connection is available periodically with the same four scenarios. We randomly select a query node in each query. The query node reports the query results each time when it connects the server after a query. The node's pseudonym is changed if it has responded 3 queries. During the change, the server issues a new trust token attached to the new pseudonym. The simulation result is shown in Fig.3. Three observations are made. First, AdContRep performs very well at the TS when there is no attack in the system (Fig.3 (a) and (b)). Second, AdContRep can adjust the node recommendation trust to identify the malicious node and improve the content reputation evaluation efficiently even though the node pseudonyms could be changed frequently (Fig.3 (c.2, c.3) and (d.2, d.3)). Third, AdContRep performs better if more recommendation information is accumulated by the TS (comparing Fig.3 (a) to Fig.3 (b) and Fig.3 (c) to Fig.3 (d)). Finally, the TS can evaluate node trust and content reputation more accurately and efficiently than the nodes (comparing Fig.3 to Fig.2), thus it is significant to introduce the TS into AdContRep.

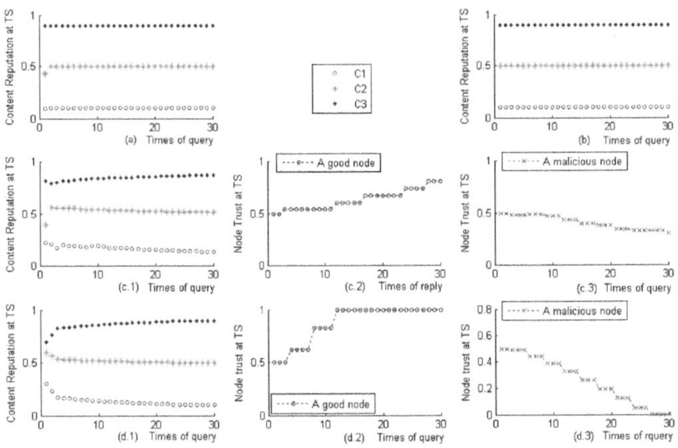

Fig. 3. Content reputations at TS: (a) each recommender node votes one content honestly; (b) each recommender node votes all contents honestly; (c) 5 malicious nodes vote one content dishonestly; (d) 5 malicious nodes vote all contents dishonestly

5.2 Unfair Rating Attack and On-Off Attack

We adopt commonly used metrics in information retrieval, Recall (*R*), Precision (*P*) and F measure (*F*) to describe the malicious node detection performance. For each good node *k*, the number of nodes that belong to Malicious Node (*MN*) and are indeed detected as *MN*, denoted as $x(k)$; the number of nodes that don't belong to *MN* but are added to *MN*, denoted as $y(k)$; the number of nodes that belong to *MN* but are not detected as *MN*, denoted as $z(k)$. With these data we do a precision-recall evaluation. We define:

$$R(k) = \frac{x(k)}{x(k) + z(k)} \tag{12}$$

$$P(k) = \frac{x(k)}{x(k) + y(k)} \tag{13}$$

$$F(k) = \frac{2P(k)R(k)}{P(k) + R(k)} \tag{14}$$

The node average F measure of the whole network is:

$F = \sum_{k=1}^{|G|} F(k)/|G|$, where $|G|$ is the number of good nodes in the network.

The influence of the unfair rating attack is demonstrated in Fig.4 (a). We test two scenarios: 1) 5 fixed attackers in the network randomly vote one content dishonestly, whilst other responding nodes randomly vote one content honestly; 2) increase the number of attackers to 10 nodes. We observe that the malicious node detection at the node is much slower than the TS due to the frequent change of node pseudonyms. Thus, introducing the TS can effectively improve the AdContRep's performance and at the same time enhance the node privacy. In addition, it takes a bit longer time for AdContRep to detect all unfair rating nodes if their percentage is higher.

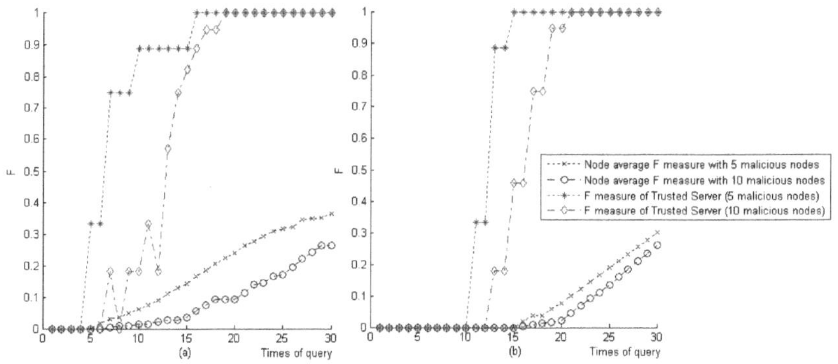

Fig. 4. F measure of nodes and TS regarding malicious node detection performance: (a) unfair rating attack (*thr* = 30); (b) on-off attack (*thr* = 5)

The influence of the on-off attack is demonstrated in Fig.4 (b). We test two scenarios: 1) 5 fixed attackers randomly vote one content with honest and dishonest recommendations alternatively, whilst other responding nodes randomly vote one content honestly; 2) increase the number of attackers to 10 nodes. We get similar results to Fig.4 (a). We also observe that the system can still achieve good performance with the help of the TS when the on-off attack happens. This is because we decay past recommendations at the TS. The influence of past good or bad behaviors is trivial on current content reputation generation. Additionally, bad voting punishment helps AdContRep easily find potential malicious nodes. For the purpose of node-server performance comparison, the TS does not issue the blacklist of malicious nodes to each node in the simulations.

5.3 Implementation

We have implemented an AdContRep prototype system using Nokia N810 tablets as the MANET nodes and an Apache server playing as the TS. The implementation satisfies all requirements as specified in Section 3.1. We attempt to achieve efficient power consumption by controlling the message length of node communication within 100 bytes and applying an Awareness ad hoc networking platform developed in [26] by the Nokia Research Center. The prototype system provides essential security protection on node-server communications with Open SSL and node-node communications by utilizing a community symmetric key.

6 Conclusions and Future Work

In this paper, we designed AdContRep for trust/reputation evaluation on both MANET nodes and contents recommended over MANET. We developed a novel trust model and a couple of algorithms to evaluate node recommendation trust and content reputation at both node side and the trusted server. Thus accurate long-term historical experiences accumulated by the trusted server and ephemeral experiences collected by the nodes can be aggregated for a more precise and reliable trust/reputation evaluation in MANET content services. We did simulation based evaluation. The results showed AdContRep's effectiveness with regard to the unfair rating attack and the on-off attack. We also implemented a prototype AdContRep based on Nokia N810 tablets. The system satisfies all specified requirements, thus proves the concept of AdContRep design and further illustrates its practical advantages. Regarding the future work, we will further improve the AdContRep system based on user studies and extend it to support new business scenarios.

References

1. Jøsang, A., Ismail, R., Boyd, C.: A Survey of Trust and Reputation Systems for Online Service Provision. Decision Support Systems 43(2), 618–644 (2007)
2. Sun, Y., Yu, W., Han, Z., Liu, K.J.R.: Information Theoretic Tramework of Trust Modeling and Evaluation for Ad Hoc Networks. IEEE Journal on Selected Area in Communications 24(2), 305–317 (2006)
3. Theodorakopoulos, G., Baras, J.S.: On Trust Models and Trust Evaluation Metrics for Ad Hoc Networks. IEEE Journal on Selected Areas in Communications 24(2), 318–328 (2006)
4. Raya, M., Papadimitratos, P., Gligory, V.D., Hubaux, J.-P.: On Data-Centric Trust Establishment in Ephemeral Ad Hoc Networks. In: IEEE INFOCOM, pp. 1912–1920 (2008)
5. Sun, Y., Han, Z., Liu, K.J.R.: Defense of Trust Management Vulnerabilities in Distributed Networks. IEEE Communications Magazine 46(2), 112–119 (2008)
6. Yan, Z., Holtmanns, S.: Trust Modeling and Management: from Social Trust to Digital Trust. In: Subramanian, R. (ed.) Computer Security, Privacy and Politics: Current Issues, Challenges and Solutions, pp. 290–323. Idea Group Inc., USA (2008)
7. Michiardi, P., Molva, R.: Core: A COllaborative REputation Mechanism to Enforce Node Cooperation in Mobile Ad Hoc Networks. In: Lioy, A., Mazzocchi, D. (eds.) CMS 2003. LNCS, vol. 2828, pp. 107–121. Springer, Heidelberg (2003)

8. Yan, Z.: Trust Management for Mobile Computing Platforms. Doctoral dissertation, Helsinki Univ. of Technology (2007) ISBN No. 9789512291205
9. Sun, Y., Han, Z., Yu, W., Liu, K.J.R.: A Trust Evaluation Framework in Distributed Networks: Vulnerability Analysis and Defense Against Attacks. In: INFOCOM, pp. 1–13 (2006)
10. Yan, Z., Yan, R.: Formalizing Trust Based on Usage Behaviors for Mobile Applications. In: González Nieto, J., Reif, W., Wang, G., Indulska, J. (eds.) ATC 2009. LNCS, vol. 5586, pp. 194–208. Springer, Heidelberg (2009)
11. Lin, C., Varadharajan, V., Wang, Y., Pruthi, V.: Enhancing Grid Security with Trust Management. In: Proc. of IEEE Int. Conf. on Services Computing, pp. 303–310 (2004)
12. Li, J., Li, R., Kato, J.: Future Trust Management Framework for Mobile Ad Hoc Networks. IEEE Communications Magazine 46(4), 108–115 (2008)
13. Song, S., Hwang, K., Zhou, R., Kwok, Y.K.: Trusted P2P Transactions with Fuzzy Reputation Aggregation. IEEE Internet Computing 9(6), 24–34 (2005)
14. Resnick, P., Zeckhauser, R.: Trust Among Strangers in Internet Transactions: Empirical Analysis of eBay's Reputation System. In: Baye, M. (ed.) Advances in Applied Microeconomics: The Economics of the Internet and E-Commerce, vol. 11, pp. 127–157. Elsevier, Amsterdam (2002)
15. Xiong, L., Liu, L.: PeerTrust: Supporting Reputation-Based Trust for Peer-to-Peer Electronic communities. IEEE Trans. on Knowledge and Data Engineering 16(7), 843–857 (2004)
16. Walsh, K., Sirer, E.G.: Fighting Peer-To-Peer SPAM and Decoys with Object Reputation. In: Proc. of P2PECON, pp. 138–143 (2005)
17. Dellarocas, C.: Immunizing Online Reputation Reporting Systems Against Unfair Ratings and Discriminatory Behavior. In: Proc. of 2nd ACM Conf. E-Commerce, pp. 150–157 (2000)
18. Resnick, P., Kuwabara, K., Zeckhauser, R., Friedman, E.: Reputation Systems. Communications of the ACM 43(12), 45–48 (2000)
19. Xiong, L., Liu, L.: A Reputation-Based Trust Model for Peer-To-Peer Ecommerce Communities. In: Proc. of the IEEE Conf. on E-Commerce, pp. 228–229 (2003)
20. Corritore, C.L., Kracher, B., Wiedenbeck, S.: On-line Trust: Concepts, Evolving Themes, a Model. Int. J. of Human-Computer Studies 58(6), 737–758 (2003)
21. Yang, Y., Sun, Y., Kay, S., Yang, Q.: Defending Online Reputation Systems Against Collaborative Unfair Raters Through Signal Modeling and Trust. In: SAC, pp. 1308–1315 (2009)
22. Douceur, J.R.: The Sybil Attack. In: Druschel, P., Kaashoek, M.F., Rowstron, A. (eds.) IPTPS 2002. LNCS, vol. 2429, pp. 251–260. Springer, Heidelberg (2002)
23. Liu, Z., Yau, S.S., Peng, D., Yin, Y.: A Flexible Trust Model for Distributed Service Infrastructures. In: Proc. of 11th IEEE Symposium on Object Oriented Real-Time Distributed Computing, pp. 108–115 (2008)
24. Blaze, M., Feigenbaum, J., Lacy, J.: Decentralized Trust Managament. In: Proc. of the IEEE Symposium on Security and Privacy (1996)
25. Adler, B.T., Alfaro, L.: A Content Driven Reputation System for the Wikipedia. In: WWW 2007, pp. 261–270 (2007)
26. Ahtiainen, A., Kalliojarvi, K., Kasslin, M., Leppanen, K., Richter, A., Ruuska, P., Wijting, C.: Awareness Networking in Wireless Environments: Means of Exchanging Information. IEEE Vehicular Technology Magazine 4(3), 48–54 (2009)
27. Bansal, S., Baker, M.: Observation-Based Cooperation Enforcement in Ad Hoc Networks. Technical Report, Stanford University, NI/0307012 (2003)

28. Hu, J., Burmester, M.: LARS: A locally Aware Reputation System for Mobile Ad Hoc Networks. In: Proc. of the 44th ACM Annual Southeast Regional Conf., pp. 119–123 (2006)
29. Kujimura, K., Nishihara, T.: Reputation Rating System Based on Past Behavior of Evaluators. In: Proc. of the 4th ACM Conf. on Electronic Commerce, pp. 246–247 (2003)
30. Buchegger, S., Boudec, J.Y.L.: The Effect of Rumor Spreading in Reputation Systems for Mobile Ad-Hoc Networks. In: Proc. of WiOpt Modeling and Optimization in Mobile, Ad Hoc and Wireless Networks (2003)
31. Buchegger, S., Boudec, J.L.: Performance Analysis of the CONFIDANT Protocol. In: Proc. of the ACM International Symposium on Mobile Ad Hoc Networking and Computing (MobiHoc), pp. 226–236 (2002)

Context-Awareness Handoff Planning in Heterogeneous Wireless Networks

Hsiao-Yun Huang[1], Chiung-Ying Wang[2], and Ren-Hung Hwang[1]

[1] Dept. of Computer Science and Information Engineering,
National Chung-Cheng University, Taiwan, R.O.C.
[2] Dept. of Information Management,
Transworld University, Taiwan, R.O.C.
yunmiaow@exodus.cs.ccu.edu.tw, {wjy,rhhwang}@cs.ccu.edu.tw

Abstract. This paper addresses a context-awareness handoff planning mechanism in heterogeneous wireless networks for seamless ubiquitous access. The proliferation of digital devices with communication capability heralds the era of ubiquitous computing, as predicted by Mark Weiser. Mobile devices with multi-mode interfaces can access heterogeneous wireless networks, such as wireless local area network (WLAN), worldwide interoperability for microwave access (WiMAX) network and third generation (3G) network. In heterogeneous wireless networks, different network provides different network capability, transmission range, data rate, access cost, security policy and quality of service. Therefore, a ubiquitous access aims to provide users intelligent human-centric context-aware handoff mechanism in heterogeneous wireless networks at anytime anywhere is gradually become an important issue. Optimal handoff planning in heterogeneous wireless networks considers the needs of users, accessing service and the surrounding context. However, most of existing handoff mechanisms only considered few contexts that lead to not able to select the most suitable network for individual user. In this paper, we propose a human-centric context-aware solution to access most appropriate network that satisfies individual user's requirement, fulfills seamless data transmission and reduces handoff delay. We develop two integrated approaches for context-awareness handoff planning mechanisms, namely MADM approach and GA approach. The MADM approach contains initial process and decision process. Initial process weights context by Analytic Hierarchy Process (AHP) method while decision process selects the most appropriate network by Technique for Order Preference by Similarity to Ideal Solution (TOPSIS). The GA approach uses Genetic Algorithm to minimize handoff under given QoS constraints. Performance of proposed mechanisms is evaluated under different services with different QoS considerations. Our simulation results show that both mechanisms are able to derive a proper network handoff plan which guarantees QoS requirements and reduces delay, jitter, and number of handoffs.

Keywords: Ubiquitous computing, human-centered computing, context-awareness, MADM, genetic algorithm, handoff, heterogeneous wireless networks.

Z. Yu et al. (Eds.): UIC 2010, LNCS 6406, pp. 430–444, 2010.

1 Introduction

The demand for optimal handoff in heterogeneous wireless networks has risen significantly in recent years, driven by the rapid development of wireless and communication technologies. Wireless services have been rapidly deployed everywhere, and digital devices with communication capability have become popular and pervasive. Ubiquitous network consists of different wireless networks, such as wireless local area network (WLAN), worldwide interoperability for microwave access (WiMAX) network and third generation (3G) network offering user different service and network capacity. However, most of the previous handoff mechanisms are computer-centric and lacking of consideration of various contexts and multiple networks and thus are unable to achieve the vision of Mark Weiser [1] of a ubiquitous environment with human-centric applications. Context-awareness is the key feature to human-centric applications. In order to guarantee the quality of service (QoS) of accessing internet and different services, the demand for context-awareness, intelligent, ubiquitous access and seamless handoff between heterogeneous wireless networks is a critical issue.

Heterogeneous wireless network consists of different networks, such as WLAN, WiMAX and 3G with different characters in network capability, transmission range, data rate, access cost, security policy and quality of service. IEEE 802.11 [2] is a popular and wildly used standard carrying out WLAN. WLAN connectivity is usually free and provides high data rate but only supports short transmission range. WiMAX is based on the IEEE 802.16 standard [3] with a wild transmission radius, high bandwidth and QoS support. 3G is the next generation of GSM network which provides higher data rates allowing 3G networks to offer multimedia services. One of the third-generation (3G) mobile telecommunications technologies is Universal Mobile Telecommunications System (UMTS). Recently, with the HSDPA protocol, 3G, or so called 3.5G, is able to provide a higher data rate at 7.2Mbps. Facing so many heterogeneous wireless networks in a ubiquitous environment, there is an increasing need to address the handoff decision problem.

To help address the problem and develop the solution, a scenario is described as following. Bob is taking a train from Taichung city to Taipei city and using his smart phone to watch major league baseball game while emailing a large file to his secretary. The smart phone faces the problem of selecting one of the available networks to connect to the streaming server and ftp server giving the constraint that different applications have different session duration time and QoS requirements, such as bandwidth, delay, and jitter. Therefore, giving a list of available networks, include WLAN, WiMAX and 3G networks, the smart phone needs a mechanism to select which network is the most appropriate network for satisfying application and user's requirements. The problem of selecting the most appropriate network may need to consider various contexts such as network availability, bandwidth, signal strength, timeless, reliability, access cost, quality of service (QoS) of the required service. The problem considered herein is formally defined as how to select the most appropriate network to handoff for an individual user based on his requirements and context of his surrounding environment, such as user preference, signal strength, access cost, network capability, bandwidth, access cost and quality of service (QoS).

Context-awareness is the key feature for human-centered services as it enables services adaptive to human needs. In this paper, the collected contexts are stored in a distributed context management server [4], referred as U-gate. In this paper, we assume that a user's moving path has been planned by context-aware path planning mechanism [5] provided by the context server.

In this paper, we aim to design a context-awareness handoff planning mechanism in heterogeneous wireless networks consisting of WLANs, WiMAX and 3G. The handoff problem consists of horizontal and vertical handoff. The design goals of the proposed mechanism include: (1) the mechanism should be scalable, and easy to implement in a distributed manner in ubiquitous environment. (2) based on various contexts, the solution should be able to automatically select the most appropriate target network that best fits user and service requirements. (3) the proposed mechanism has to monitor and guarantee the QoS of connectivity. Two mechanisms are proposed. Both of them uses Spatial Conceptual Map (SCM) [6] model the real-world map and the network and environmental context. Analytic Hierarchy Process (AHP) [7] and Technique for Order Preference by Similarity to Ideal Solution (TOPSIS) [8] are adopted in the Multiple-attribute decision making (MADM) mechanism to solve network selection mechanism. Specifically, the initial process of MADM decides the weight of each context by the AHP method while the decision process of MADM selects the most appropriate network by TOPSIS. In the GA mechanism, Genetic Algorithm (GA) [9] is used to obtain a list of appropriate handoff networks to handoff to achieve minimal handoff under QoS constraints on the pre-planned path [5]. Our simulation results show that both mechanisms are able to derive a proper network handoff plan which guarantees QoS requirements and reduces delay, jitter, and number of handoffs.

The remainder of this paper is organized as follows. Section 2 presents related works. Section 3 introduces the SCM model to transfer map information. The context-awareness handoff planning mechanism is described in Section 4. Experimental results are presented in Section 5. Conclusions are finally drawn in Section 6.

2 Related Works

In heterogeneous wireless network environment, handoff decision problems have been studied extensively in the past. However, most of early works [10-13] made their handoff decision based on limited parameters of AP/BS, such as RSSI. The RSSI-based approach leads to problems of heavy load for a specific AP/BS, low performance for mobile devices and ping pong effect. Therefore, more parameters need to be taken into account; especially the heterogeneous wireless networks have different characters.

Context-aware handoff has recently been studied. These approaches are the most related research to our work. In [14-21], the authors consider more parameters, such as service type, available bandwidth, power consumption, cost, throughput and delay to evaluate candidate networks and select the best network by decision method. In these approaches, quality of service (QoS) is provided and ping-pong effect is avoided. However, the use's preference is ignore which is important for context-awareness service for individual user. In our previous work [22][23], context-aware handoff mechanism considers various contexts, including user preference. However, it is designed for homogeneous wireless network only, namely the WLAN network.

Decision method is very important for handoff decision problem. Several works [21, 24, 25] use cost function to evaluate the cost of available networks. The network with minimal cost was selected as the target network to handoff. The TOPSIS [8] attempts to define the ideal solution and the negative ideal solution. In [16], TOPSIS is employed to make decision of ranking the available networks. Nevertheless, more contexts are considered in our scenario and the weight of context for different service and individual user is different. More advanced multiple criteria decision method is necessary to deal with this problem. The Analytic Hierarchy Process (AHP) [7] is a Multiple-attribute decision making (MADM) method for solving complicated problems with multiple optimizing criteria. MADM method is adopted to compare multiple contexts and obtain relative weights of criteria. AHP is widely used in [17-20]. In [15], AHP and TOPSIS are integrated to obtain relative weights of criteria and rank the network, respectively. However, [15] lacked a context management model that considers a wide variety of context. Therefore, the first context-awareness handoff planning mechanism combines the AHP and TOPSIS to obtain the optimal handoff planning.

Genetic algorithm (GA) [9] is a search method for solving large-scale optimization problems. Many researches use GA to solve handoff planning [23][26]. In our previous work [23], GA-based context-aware handoff mechanism (GA-based UbiHandoff) also uses GA to minimize handoff by finding appropriate APs. However, the proposed mechanism is designed for indoor and WLAN environment only. Algorithms proposed in [26] also adopt hybrid parallel fuzzy logic (FL)-based decision, multiple-criteria decision making (MCDM) systems, and genetic algorithms (GAs) to select appropriate access network. In these algorithms, network stability, resource utilization, user satisfaction, and quality of service (QoS) provisioning are considered. Therefore, the second context-awareness handoff planning mechanism adopts a GA to obtain the optimal handoff planning. Moreover, A distributed context server (U-gate) architecture provides complete context management is used in this work.

3 Spatial Conceptual Map Model

In order to represent the trajectory map and environment context, the Spatial Conceptual Map (SCM) model is used. The proposed approach provides a user with a SCM to draw a portion of heterogeneous networks composed of a set of landmark objects (*Oi*), a set of medium objects (*Wj*) and influence areas of those objects. The path in the map composed of a sequence Way elementary areas (WEAs) which are parts of the Ways of the SCM and are determined according the criteria [6]. For easy deployment and implement, the proposed mechanism was implemented in a 326-acre campus environment, Chung Cheng University (CCU) Campus, and its SCM representation is shown in Fig. 1. In addition to the information of landmark objects, a set of medium objects (*Wj*) and influence areas of those objects, the proposed mechanism relies on AP/BS contexts to plan handoff; therefore, the information of WLAN Access Point (AP), WiMax Base Station (WiMax_BS) and 3G Base Station (3G_BS) need to be considered in this paper. For an example of Matrix of Orientation and

Adjacency and Characteristic (MOAC) [27] representation of the map, the readers are referred to [22]. In order to identify the WEAs of SCM, we use a MOAC, contains relevant and characteristic information of each WEA and landmark object and displacement direction between two WEAs [22].

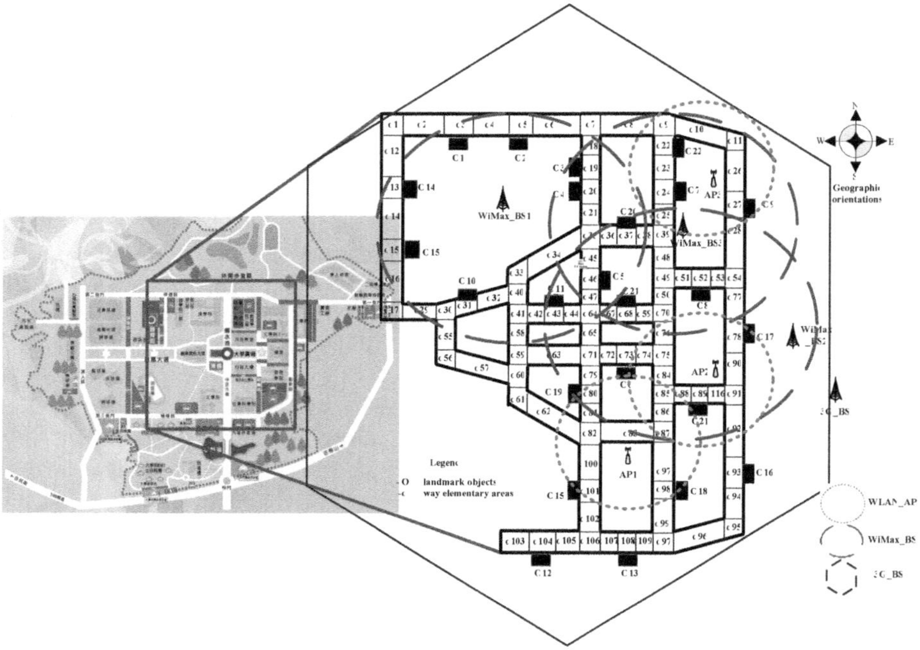

Fig. 1. Chung Cheng University (CCU) Campus Map and SCM representation

The AP/BS context is also describes in MOAC. Since state information of APs, WiMax_BSs, 3G_BSs is also considered in this work, each AP, WiMax_BS, 3G_BS is also associated with a characteristic function $Co(AP_i)$, $Co($WiMax_BS$_i)$ and $Co($3G_BS$_i)$, respectively. For example, WEA α_{19} is covered by two AP$_s$, two WiMax BSs and on 3G BS, the characteristic function of $Co(\alpha_{19})$ is then denoted by c1={AP_4, AP_5, WiMax_BS1, WiMax_BS2, 3G_BS}.

4 Context-Awareness Handoff Planning Mechanism

In this section, we present two context-awareness handoff planning mechanisms, including MADM and GA. Section 4.1 describes the initial process of weighting context by Analytic Hierarchy Process (AHP) method. Section 4.2 and 4.3 describes how to make decision of selecting network by MADM and GA, respectively.

4.1 Initial Process

The initial process determines weight of each context by AHP. AHP provides a decision hierarchy and requires pairwise comparison among criteria. The steps of AHP are described as follows: (1) built a hierarchical structure of objective, criteria, and alternatives; (2) construct a pair-wise comparison matrix by comparing contexts, calculate this pair-wise comparison matrix to gain the eigenvector as weight of each level; (3) integrate the weights of each level to determine the overall weight.

The first step of AHP is to construct the problem into a hierarchy structure. Since many contexts must be considered, contexts are decomposed into multiple levels. Fig. 2 shows the hierarchy structure of context used in the proposed AP/BS selection mechanism. The abbreviation and quantification of context attribute is shown in Table 1.

The second step is weighting the contexts. To construct a pair-wise comparison matrix of each level, contexts at the same level are compared with each other. The comparison is judged based on the relative importance scale [7]. The relative importance of comparison factors is indicated by a scale from 1 to 9. The matrix entries are also inversed with respect to the main diagonal, and the diagonal of comparison matrix represents the factor compared with itself. Hence, the value of all diagonals is 1.

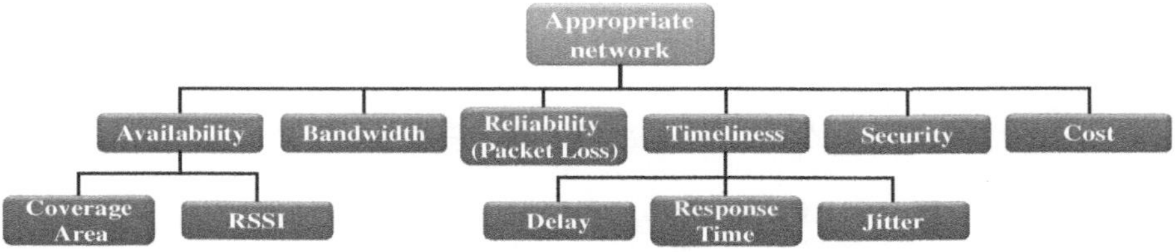

Fig. 2. Hierarchy structure of AP/BS selection

Table 1. Abbreviation and quantification of context attribute

Attribute	Description	Abbreviation	Quantification
Availability	Coverage Area	CA	i number
	Received signal strength	RSS	Weak ··· Strong 1 ⟺ 5
Bandwidth	Bandwidth	B	j Mbps
Timeliness	Delay	D	k ms
	Response time	RT	x ms
	Jitter	J	y ms
Reliability	Packet loss rate	L	z %
Security	Security	Sec	0, if security is provided by network
Cost	Cost	Cost	0, if transmit packet is free

The final step is calculating a pair-wise comparison matrix to obtain the eigenvector (priority vector). Equation $AW=\lambda_{max}W$ shows the weight of each level, where A is the pair-wise comparison matrix, λ_{max} is the eigen value, and W is the eigenvector. If the pair-wise comparison matrix is constructed by human experts, inconsistencies may occur. Therefore, eigen values are used to test consistency. Specifically, AHP uses consistency ratio (CR) to evaluate whether the comparison matrix is consistent. The CR value is gained from consistency index (CI) and random index (RI) ratio $CR=CI/RI$. If CR value is below 0.1, the comparison is consistent. RI [7], and the CI value is obtained by equation $CI=\lambda_{max}-n/n-1$ where variable n is the factor number. Finally, the overall weight is obtained by integrating the weight of each level.

4.2 Decision Process by MADM

The decision process provides efficient and seamless handoff plan to mobile devices. The TOPSIS [8] is adopted to make decision for ranking the network. The steps of TOPSIS are to determine the positive and negative ideal solution first and then find the alternative that is nearest the best solution and furthest from the worst solution.

4.2.1 Construct Context Matrix of Network

The first step constructs the context matrix of network. Based on the SCM model, several QoS attributes of network are considered to facilitate handoff planning. The attributes evaluated at each network are shown in equation (1). The values of QoS attributes are first acquired and stored in the context server then retrieved at the network selection phase. Assuming N networks and nine attributes, an Nx9 relative matrix is constructed as equation (2).

$$Network_i = [CA_i \ RSSI_i \ .B_i \ D_i \ RT_i \ J_i \ L_i \ Sec_i \ C_i] \tag{1}$$

$$Network = \begin{bmatrix} CA_1 & RSSI_1 & B_1 & D_1 & RT_1 & J_1 & C_1 \\ CA_2 & RSSI_2 & B_2 & D_2 & RT_2 & J_2 & C_2 \\ \cdot & \cdot & \cdot & \cdot & \cdot & \cdot & \cdot \\ \cdot & \cdot & \cdot & \cdot & \cdot & \cdot & \cdot \\ CA_N & RSSI_N & B_N & D_N & RT_N & J_N & C_N \end{bmatrix} \tag{2}$$

4.2.2 Normalize Context Matrix

The second step normalizes the context matrix. Context attributes must be normalized because they are not measured by the same scale or unit. After normalization, the value of each attribute lies within the interval [0, 1]. Normalization is performed using equation (3). The matrix $Network_{norm}$ is obtained after the normalization.

$$(Attribute_{norm})_i = \left(\frac{Attribute_i}{\sqrt{\sum_{j=1}^{N} Attribute_j^2}}\right)_i \tag{3}$$

4.2.3 Assign Attribute Weight

The third step weights each attribute in context matrix by the AHP model. Since applications may have different QoS requirements, the weight of each QoS attribute must be updated accordingly. The sum of weights obtained from AHP must be adjusted to 1 using equation (4). Matrix $Network_{w\text{-}norm}$ is obtained by multiplying attribute weight and normalized context matrix ($Network_{norm}$), as shown in equation (5).

$$W = W_{CA} + W_{RSSI} + W_B + W_D + W_{RT} + W_J + W_L + W_{Sec} + W_C = 1 \tag{4}$$

$$Network_{w\text{-norm}} = \begin{bmatrix} W_{CA}*(CA_{norm})_1 & W_{RSSI}*(RSSI_{norm})_1 & W_B*(B_{norm})_1 & W_D*(D_{norm})_1 & W_{RT}*(RT_{norm})_1 & W_J*(J_{norm})_1 & W_L*(L_{norm})_1 & W_{Sec}*(Sec_{norm})_1 & W_C*(C_{norm})_1 \\ W_{CA}*(CA_{norm})_2 & W_{RSSI}*(RSSI_{norm})_2 & W_B*(B_{norm})_2 & W_D*(D_{norm})_2 & W_{RT}*(RT_{norm})_2 & W_J*(J_{norm})_2 & W_L*(L_{norm})_2 & W_{Sec}*(Sec_{norm})_2 & W_C*(C_{norm})_2 \\ \cdot & \cdot & \cdot & \cdot & \cdot & \cdot & \cdot & \cdot & \cdot \\ \cdot & \cdot & \cdot & \cdot & \cdot & \cdot & \cdot & \cdot & \cdot \\ W_{CA}*(CA_{norm})_N & W_{RSSI}*(RSSI_{norm})_N & W_B*(B_{norm})_N & W_D*(D_{norm})_N & W_{RT}*(RT_{norm})_N & W_J*(J_{norm})_N & W_L*(L_{norm})_N & W_{Sec}*(Sec_{norm})_N & W_C*(C_{norm})_N \end{bmatrix} \quad (5)$$

4.2.4 Determine the Positive/Negative Ideal Solution

The fourth step determines the best and worst values for each attribute and measures the closeness/separation distance for the best and worst cases. The positive and negative ideal solution for each attribute usually corresponds to the maximum or the minimum value of the attribute. For example, for RSSI, bandwidth, and security level, the larger the value, the better the QoS. However, for attribute values such as delay, response time, jitter, packet loss and cost, the smaller the better. Equation (6) shows the best and the worst solution to each attribute. The distance from each alternative to the best and the worst solution is calculated using a Euclidean distance. In equation (7), $S_{i\text{-}Best}$ and $S_{i\text{-}Worst}$ represent the distance from the alternative to the best and worst solutions, respectively.

$$\begin{aligned} Attribute_{Best} &= \{(\max_i (Attribute_{W-norm})_i \mid j \in J),(\min_i (Attribute_{W-norm})_i \mid j \in J')\mid i = 1,2,\ldots,n\} \\ Attribute_{Worst} &= \{(\min_i (Attribute_{W-norm})_i \mid j \in J),(\max_i (Attribute_{W-norm})_i \mid j \in J')\mid i = 1,2,\ldots,n\} \end{aligned} \quad (6)$$

$$\begin{aligned} S_{i-Best} &= \sqrt{\begin{matrix} ((CA_{w-norm})_i - CA_{Best})^2 + ((RSSI_{w-norm})_i - RSSI_{Best})^2 + ((B_{w-norm})_i - B_{Best})^2 + ((D_{w-norm})_i - D_{Best})^2 + \\ ((RT_{w-norm})_i - RT_{Best})^2 + ((J_{w-norm})_i - J_{Best})^2 + ((L_{w-norm})_i - L_{Best})^2 + ((Sec_{w-norm})_i - Sec_{Best})^2 + ((C_{w-norm})_i - C_{Best})^2 \end{matrix}} \\ S_{i-Worst} &= \sqrt{\begin{matrix} ((CA_{w-norm})_i - CA_{Worst})^2 + ((RSSI_{w-norm})_i - RSSI_{Worst})^2 + ((B_{w-norm})_i - B_{Worst})^2 + ((D_{w-norm})_i - D_{Worst})^2 + \\ ((RT_{w-norm})_i - RT_{Worst})^2 + ((J_{w-norm})_i - J_{Worst})^2 + ((L_{w-norm})_i - L_{Worst})^2 + ((Sec_{w-norm})_i - Sec_{Worst})^2 + ((C_{w-norm})_i - C_{Worst})^2 \end{matrix}} \end{aligned} \quad (7)$$

4.2.5 Make Decision

The final step is selecting the solution that is nearest to the best solution and furthest from the worst solution. The AP/BS has the highest P_i value calculated from equation $P_i = S_{i\text{-}Worst} / (S_{i\text{-}Best} + S_{i\text{-}Worst})$ is the selected solution for MADM-based network selection, where P_i represents the relation of an alternative to the best and worst solution, and highest P_i represents the desired solution that is nearest to the best case and furthest from the worst cases.

4.3 Decision Process by GA

Genetic algorithm is an evolution algorithm solving optimization problem. A population of candidate solution is denoted as a chromosome. Fitness function is adopted to evaluate each chromosome and appropriate solutions are found through selection, crossover, and mutation operations.

Handoff planning problem can be considered as an optimization problem. The objective of handoff planning is minimizing the number of handoffs and satisfying QoS constraints. The objective function is shown in equation (8), where $F(\vec{p})$ represents the total number of handoffs on path $\vec{p}$, and HO_{ij} indicates whether a handoff is made when moving from location *i* to location *j*. If HO_{ij} equals 1, handoff is required; otherwise, HO_{ij} is set to 0. The QoS constraints are specified in equation (9), where

$RSSI(\vec{p})$ represents RSSI requirements at this path, and θ_x and θ_y are thresholds for RSSI, B, etc..

$$\mathrm{F}(\vec{p}) = \sum_{i,j\in\vec{p}} HO_{ij} \qquad HO_{ij} = \begin{cases} 1, & \text{if } Network_i \neq Network_j \\ 0, & \text{if } Network_i = Network_j \end{cases} \tag{8}$$

$$\begin{aligned} x(\alpha_i) \geq \theta_x \qquad & X = \{RSSI(\vec{p}), B(\vec{p})\} \qquad & x \in X \\ y(\alpha_i) \leq \theta_y \qquad & Y = \{RT(\vec{p}), D(\vec{p}), J(\vec{p}), L(\vec{p})\} \qquad & y \in Y \end{aligned} \tag{9}$$

4.3.1 Chromosome Representation and Population Initialization

In general, GA initially encodes chromosomes and generates the initial population. The encoding method proposed in [28] is used in this study. The chromosome is encoded in *n* positive integers where *n* is the number of WEAs, as Fig. **3** shows. Upper and lower sequences represent locus number and chromosome, respectively. Each number in the chromosome represents a gene, which represents the id of the desired network of the solution.

Locus number	1	2	3	4	5	6	7	8	9	10	11	12
Chromosome	3	3	1	1	1	3	3	3	6	6	6	6

Fig. 3. Example of chromosome encode

4.3.2 Fitness Evaluation

The fitness value of a chromosome is the value of the objective function for the solution (e.g., a handoff number) represented by the chromosome. The fitness function shown in equation (10) measures the handoff number of the path that satisfies all quality constraints. QoS constraints is handle by penalty function [29] as shown in equation (11).Note that end-to-end QoS attributes are evaluated, e.g., the delay represents the end-to-end delay of a path.

$$\mathrm{f_i} = \mathrm{F}(\vec{p}) \times (1 + \alpha \mathrm{P}(\vec{p})) \tag{10}$$

$$\begin{aligned} \mathrm{P}(\vec{p}) &= \sum_{x\in\{RSSI,B\}} f(x)_i + \sum_{y\in\{RT,D,J,L\}} g(y)_i \\ f(x)_i &= \begin{cases} 1, & \text{if } x < \theta_x \\ 0, & otherwise \end{cases} \qquad x \in \{RSSI, B\} \\ g(y)_i &= \begin{cases} 1, & \text{if } y > \theta_y \\ 0, & otherwise \end{cases} \qquad y \in \{RT, D, J, L\} \end{aligned} \tag{11}$$

4.3.3 Operation of Selection and Crossover

Two-tournament random selection [30] and single-point crossover are used to select chromosomes for selection and crossover operations. The proposed algorithm randomly selects the point at which the two parents have the same handoff AP. Two new offspring chromosomes are then generated by swapping the genes behind the cross-over point.

4.3.4 Mutation Operation

The mutation operation is one kind of random change in the chromosome to avoid local optimization. In this study, special consideration is adopted to enhance the convergence rate. The mutation operation occurs according to a given probability. In the first case, if the gene at the mutation point differs from the prior gene, and if the prior gene is still accessible at the mutation point, the gene at the mutation point changes to the prior gene. In the second case, if the first case is not confirmed, and if the next gene is accessible at this location, the gene at the mutation point changes to the next gene. Otherwise, the mutation occurs by random selection from the list of accessible networks.

5 Experimental Results

In this section, performance of the proposed mechanisms is evaluated by different service. For easy deployment and implement, the proposed mechanism was implemented in a small scope environment, Chung Cheng University (CCU) Campus, as shown in Fig. 1. It contains 3G network, three wimax BSs and three wlan APs in the environment. In this experiment scenario, a user moves from O4 at α 20 to O22 at α 22. The sketch of the AP/BS distribution of Fig. 1 and moving path is shown in Fig. 4.

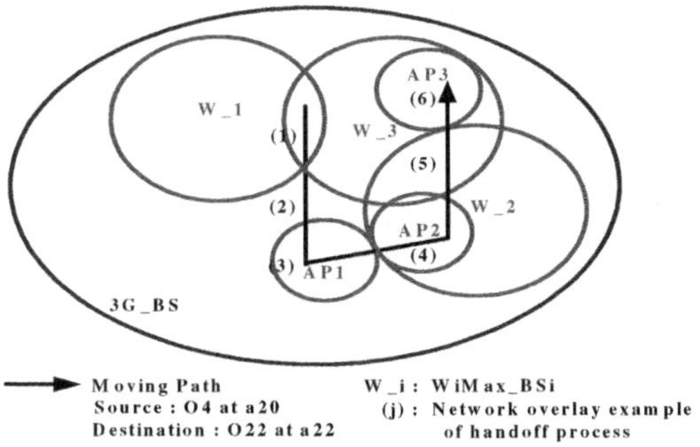

Fig. 4. The sketch of the network distribution and moving path

There are two cases, voice service and ftp service considered in the experiments. The moving path is passing through α 20→α 21 →α 35→ α 45→ α 46→ α 47→ α 64→ α 65→α 71→ α 79→ α 80→ α 81→ α 82→ α 83→ α 87→ α 86→ α 85→ α 88→ α 89→ α 116→ α 91→ α 90→ α 78→ α 77→ α 54→ α 28→ α 27→ α 26→ α 11→ α 10→ α 9→ α 22. In the first case, the user using the voice service while moving toward the destination. In the second case, ftp service is employed by the user to transmit a file while moving along the path.

The QoS parameters evaluated by AHP are shown in Table 2. From Table 2, we can observe that the weights of QoS parameters evaluated by AHP of two services are different. The rationale is that the requirement of voice and ftp services is different. The CR value of voice service is 0.074, and that of ftp service is 0.063. Both are below 0.1, which indicates that the weights calculated by AHP are consistent. Delay and jitter are heavily weighted in voice service while bandwidth and delay are heavily weighted in ftp service. Meanwhile, GA parameters are set as follows: population size = 100, generation number = 100, penalty parameter = 2, crossover probability = 0.8, mutation probability = 0.5 and runtime = 30.

Table 2. Weigh of context

Weight	**Availability**		**Bandwidth**	**Timeliness**		
	CA	RSSI	B	D	RT	J
Voice Service	0.1166		0.1166	0.4207		
	0.0389	0.0778		0.1912	0.0382	0.1912
FTP Service	0.1023		0.2380	0.2317		
	0.0340	0.0682		0.1390	0.0463	0.0463
Weight	**Reliability**	**Security**	**Cost**	**CR value**		
	L	Sec	Cost			
Voice Service	0.1025	0.0652	0.1784	0.0740		
fFTP Service	0.1153	0.0841	0.2286	0.0630		

While moving from O4 at α 20 to O22 at α 22, the user will meet different situation of network overlay. The network overlay examples of handoff process list as following and marks in Fig. 4.

(1) The user is under 3G network, WiMax_BS1 and WiMax_BS3.

(2) The user is leaving the coverage of WiMax_BS1 and WiMax_BS3, and only 3G network can be access.

(3) The user moves into the coverage of WLAN_AP1.

(4) The user leaves the coverage of WLAN_AP1, and moves into the coverage of WLAN_AP2 and WiMax_BS2.

(5) The user leaves the coverage of WLAN_AP2, and moves into the coverage of WiMax_BS3. WiMax_BS2 and 3G still can be accessed.

(6) The user leaves the coverage of WiMax_BS2, and moves into the coverage of WLAN_AP3. There are three network can be accessed, 3G, WiMax_BS3 and WLAN_AP3.

The AP/BS selection result of using voice service is shown in Fig. 5.1. Voice service requires lower delay and jitter. In example (1) of Fig. 4, the proposed mechanism selects WiMax_BS3 to serve voice service. Since the WiMax_BS3 has lower delay and jitter than WiMax_BS1. In example (4) of Fig. 4, WiMax_BS2 is selected because it has lower jitter than WLAN_AP2. In example (5) and (6) of Fig. 4, WiMax_BS3 is used to handoff because it has lower delay and jitter than WiMax_BS2 and WLAN_AP3. Therefore, in Fig. 5, the handoff planning result of voice service is WiMax_BS3->3G BS->WLAN_AP1-> WiMax_BS2-> WiMax_BS3. QoS performance of each network is shown in Table 3.

Table 3. QoS performance of each network

Network	Bandwidth	Timeliness			Packet Loss Rate	Security	Cost
		Delay	Response time	Jitter			
3G	5	35	35	35	0.04	1	5
WiMax_BS1	15	25	25	30	0.03	1	2
WiMax_BS2	15	25	25	25	0.03	1	2
WiMax_BS3	10	20	25	20	0.03	1	2
WLAN_AP1	25	25	25	25	0.03	1	0
WLAN_AP2	25	25	25	40	0.03	1	0
WLAN_AP3	25	25	30	40	0.03	1	0

The handoff planning result of ftp service is shown in Fig. 6. The second scenario considers ftp service, which requires higher bandwidth and lower delay. According to the QoS performance shown in Table 3, the network with higher bandwidth and lower delay is selected to serve ftp service. Therefore, in Fig. 6, the handoff planning result of ftp service is WiMax_BS1->3G BS->WLAN_AP1->WLAN_AP2-> WiMax_BS2-> WLAN_AP3.

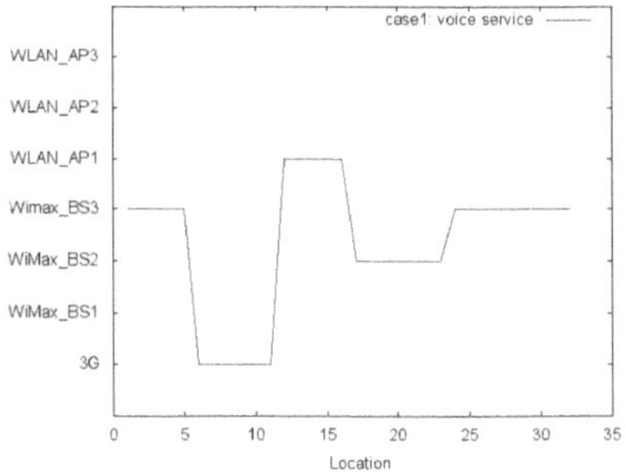

Fig. 5. AP/BS planning of voice service

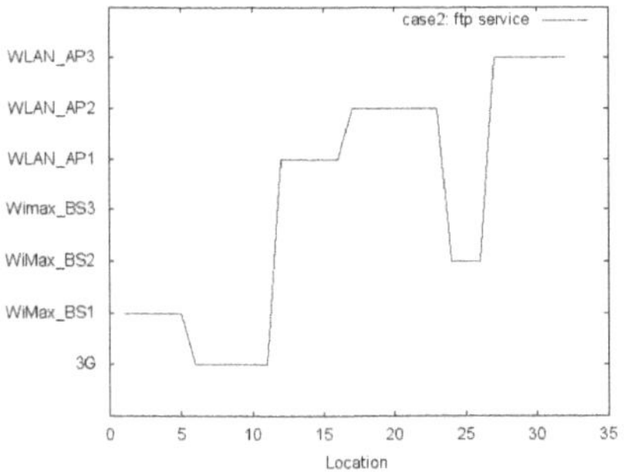

Fig. 6. AP/BS planning of ftp service

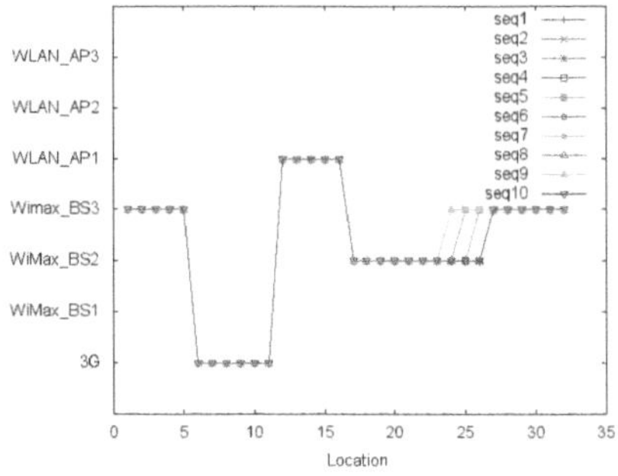

Fig. 7. Ten handoff AP/BS planning results of voice service obtained by GA

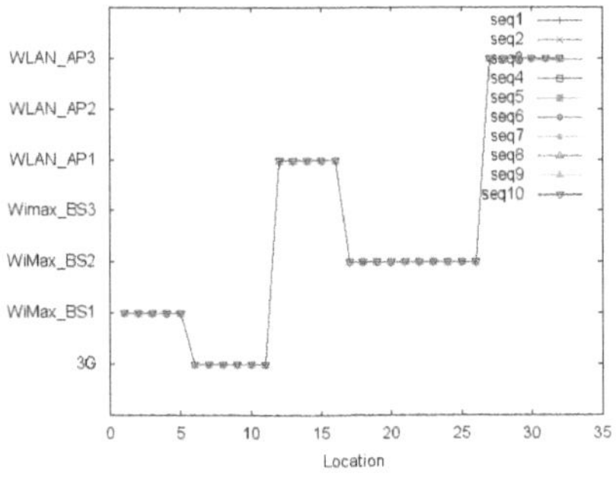

Fig. 8. Ten handoff AP/BS planning results of ftp service obtained by GA

Fig. 7 and Fig. 8 show handoff decisions made by GA. The ten best results using voice service and ftp service selected from 30 runs are presented. The sequence number in Fig. 7 and Fig. 8 indicate the rank of these ten results. Threshold of bandwidth, delay, and jitter is 10MB, 30ms and 30ms, respectively. According to the network status shown in Table 3, Qos constraint is satisfied. The number of handoffs of using voice and ftp services are the same, i.e., 4, which indicates that the proposed method reduces handoff number and guarantees QoS constraint.

6 Conclusion and Future Works

In this paper, we have proposed an intelligent and seamless service to achieve ubiquitous access. The design goal is to design a human-centric context-aware handoff planning mechanism in heterogeneous wireless networks. Specifically, the proposed mechanism takes into account multiple requirements and context of users and network when planning the most approximate network. The two proposed mechanisms adopted SCM, AHP, TOPSIS and GA to plan efficient and seamless network handoff mechanism. Experimental results show that the proposed mechanisms efficiently select the most approximate network which guarantees availability, bandwidth, signal strength, timeless, reliability, lower access cost, quality of service (QoS) simultaneously.

Future researches focus on further improvement the proposed mechanism. First, more kinds of context could be considered for decision making. Also we will consider more popular wireless networks available in our daily environment, such as Bluetooth and mobile communication systems (e.g. GPRS, CDMA, iDen). Resource reservation and allocation also need to be taken into account while performing handoff planning. Finally, future experiments will compare performance of the proposed mechanism with that of other existing works.

Acknowledgment

The research is supported by the NSC97-2221-E-194-011-MY3,NSC97-2221-E-194-012-MY3,NSC97-2221-E-194-027-MY2, National Science Council, ROC.

References

1. Weiser, M.: The Computer for the Twenty-First Century. Scientific American, 94–104 (1991)
2. IEEE 802.11: Wireless LAN Medium Access Control (MAC) and Physical Layer (PHY) Specifications (2007 revision), IEEE-SA (June 2007), http://standards.ieee.org/getieee802/download/802.11-2007.pdf
3. IEEE Std. 802.16e-2005, IEEE Standard for Local and Metropolitan Area Networks - Part 16: Air Interface for Fixed Broadband Wireless Access Systems -Amendment 2: Physical and Medium Access Control Layers for Combined Fixed and Mobile Operation in Licensed Bands (February 2006)
4. Lu, J.H., Wang, C.Y., Hwang, R.H.: Open Framework for Distributed Context Management in Ubiquitous Environments. has been accepted to IJAHUC Special Issue on Ubiquitous Multimedia Computing: Systems, Networking, and Applications

5. Wang, C.Y., Hwang, R.H.: Context-aware Path Planning in Ubiquitous Network. In: Zhang, D., Portmann, M., Tan, A.-H., Indulska, J. (eds.) UIC 2009. LNCS, vol. 5585, pp. 54–67. Springer, Heidelberg (2009)
6. Kettani, D., Moulin, B.: A Spatial Model Based on the Notions of Spatial Conceptual Map and of Object's Influence Areas. In: Freksa, C., Mark, D.M. (eds.) COSIT 1999. LNCS, vol. 1661, pp. 401–416. Springer, Heidelberg (1999)
7. Saaty, T.L.: How to Make a Decision: The Analytic Hierarchy Process. European Journal of Operational Research 48, 9–26 (1990)
8. Hwang, C.L., Yoon, K.P.: Multiple Attribute Decision Making: Methods and Applications. Springer, Heidelberg (1981)
9. Goldberg, D.E.: Genetic Algorithms in Search, Optimization, and Machine Learning. Addison-Wesley, Massachusetts (1989)
10. Zhang, N., Holtzman, J.M.: Analysis of handoff algorithms using both absolute and relative measurements. IEEE Transactions on Vehicular Technology 45(1), 174–179 (1996)
11. Marichamy, P., Chakrabarti, S., Maskara, S.L.: Performance evaluation of handoff detection schemes. In: IEEE Conference on Convergent Technologies for the Asia-Pacific 2003, vol. 2, pp. 643–646 (2003)
12. Pahlavan, K., Krishnamurthy, P., Hatami, A., Ylianttila, M., Makela, J.P., Pichna, R., Vallstron, J.: Handoff in hybrid mobile data networks. IEEE Pers. Commun. 7(2), 34–47 (2000)
13. Pollini, G.P.: Trends in handover design. IEEE Communication Magazine 34(3), 82–90 (1996)
14. Ma, D., Ma, M.: A QoS-Based Vertical Handoff Scheme for Interworking of WLAN and WiMAX. In: IEEE Global Communications Conference (GLOBECOM), pp.1–6 (December 2009)
15. Dhar, J., Kiran, S.R., Reddy, K.Y.: Network Selection in Heterogeneous Wireless Environment: A Ranking Algorithm. In: Third International Conference on Wireless Communication and Sensor Networks (WCSN 2007), pp. 41–44 (December 2007)
16. Bari, F., Victor, C.M.: Automated Network Selection in a Heterogeneous Wireless Network Environment. IEEE Network 21, 34–40 (2007)
17. Ahmed, T., Kyamakya, K., Ludwig, M.: A Context-Aware Vertical Handover Decision Algorithm for Multimode Mobile Terminals and Its Performance. In: IEEE/ACM Euro American Conference on Telematics and Information Systems (EATIS 2006), pp.19–28 (2006)
18. Song, Q., Jamalipour, A.: Network Selection in an Integrated Wireless LAN ans UMTS Environment Using Mathematical Modeling and Computing Techniques. IEEE Wireless Communications Magazine 12, 42–49 (2005)
19. Song, Q., Jamalipour, A.: An adaptive quality-of-service network selection mechanism for heterogeneous mobile networks. Wireless Communications and Mobile Computing 5, 697–708 (2005)
20. Balasubramaniam, S., Indulska, J.: Handovers between heterogeneous networks in pervasive systems. In: International Conference on Communications Technology (ICCT 2003), pp.1056–1059 (April 2003)
21. Wang, H., Katz, R., Giese, J.: Policy-Enabled Handoffs Across Heterogeneous Wireless Networks. In: Workshop on Mobile Computing Systems and Applications (WMCSA) pp. 51–60 (1999)
22. Huang, H.Y., Wang, C.Y., Hwang, R.H.: Context-awareness Handoff Planning in Ubiquitous Network. In: The 1st International Symposium on Cyber-Physical Intelligence (CPI 2009), Brisbane, Australia, pp. 7–9 (July 2009)

23. Wang, C.Y., Huang, H.Y., Hwang, R.H.: Mobility Management in Ubiquitous Environments. Personal and Ubiquitous Computing (April 2010) (accepted)
24. McNair, J., Zhu, F.: Vertical Handoffs in Fourth-generation Multinetwork Environments. IEEE Wireless Communications 11, 8–15 (2004)
25. Zhu, F., McNair, J.: Optimizations for vertical handoff decision algorithms. In: IEEE Wireless Communications and Networking Conference (WCNC), vol. 2, pp. 867–872 (2004)
26. Alkhawlani, M., Ayesh, A.: Access Network Selection Based on Fuzzy Logic and Genetic Algorithms. Advances in Artificial Intelligence, vol.2008, Article ID 793058 (2008)
27. Samaan, N., Karmouch, A.: A Mobility Prediction Architecture Based on Contextual Knowledge and Spatial Conceptual Maps. IEEE Transactions on Mobile Computing Utility-based Intelligent Network 4(6), 537–551 (2005)
28. Lei, L., Wang, H., Wu, Q.: Improved Genetic Algorithms Based Path planning of Mobile Robot Under Dynamic Unknown Environment. Mechatronics and Automation, 1728–1732 (2006)
29. Yeniay, Ö.: Penalty function methods for constrained optimization with genetic algorithms. Journal of Mathematical and Computation Application 10, 45–56 (2005)
30. Goldberg, D.E., Deb, K.: A comparative analysis of selection schemes used in genetic algorithms. In: Foundation of Genetic Algorithms, pp. 69–93 (1991)

On the Improving Strategies upon the Route Cache of DSR in MANETs

Jiaxu Chen[1], Yazhe Tang[1], Dian Fu[1], and Heng Chang[2]

[1] Dept of Computer Science & Technology, Xi'an JiaoTong University, Xi'an, People's Republic of China
cjx_squall@163.com, yztang@mail.xjtu.edu.cn, fd0511@163.com
[2] Huawei Technologies Co., Ltd.
changheng@huawei.com

Abstract. In MANETs, DSR has been extensively studied since proposed. One of the most significant strategies that improve DSR is the route cache. The route cache strategy is utilized to reduce overheads and peer-to-peer delay, which means in brief, allowing an intermediate node to reply a RREQ message. In this paper, we concentrate on the DSR protocol and the strategies which are proposed to improve its performance. We indicate that some of the strategies are so novel that they can be extracted as an individual protocol with a little complementarity. As a result, we establish a semi-proactive protocol composed of the Active Packets and RERR flooding, both of which are improving strategies on the route cache of DSR. Simulation results show that it can be used as a protocol under a certain circumstance and has a performance outperforms its source strategies and DSR on several metrics.

Keywords: Active Packets, DSR, route cache.

1 Introduction

Routing is an important proportion in the wireless ad hoc network, which is not only dynamically self-organizing and self-configuring, but also a temporary and infrastructureless network without fixed hosts (or base stations). In Mobile Ad Hoc Networks (MANETs) [1], nodes move arbitrarily, and each node operates both as a host and as a router at the same time. Packets are forwarded along multi-hop paths to other nodes that are out of the transmission range. The frequent change of the topology, caused by the mobility of nodes, makes the traditional Internet routing protocols not applicable any more.

So far, a number of routing protocols have been proposed for MANETs. They can be divided into two types, namely proactive and on-demand according to the route discovery mechanisms. In proactive protocols, paths are established beforehand and most of the overheads come from maintaining the paths. While in on-demand routing, paths are created right before the source node wants to send a packet. These proposed protocols include DSDV [2], DSR [3], AODV [4], ZRP [5], and TORA [6]. Among them, DSR is a typical on-demand routing protocol.

Z. Yu et al. (Eds.): UIC 2010, LNCS 6406, pp. 445–458, 2010.

We will give a brief introduction of DSR in Sect. 2. By introducing route cache, DSR successfully reduces the overheads and the peer-to-peer delay. While on the other side, the route reply storm and the stale links brought by the route cache strategy degrade the performance of the protocol. In this paper, we concentrate on the DSR protocol and its strategies on route cache. We find that some of the strategies are so novel that they can be extracted individually with a little complementarity. Consequently, we establish a semi-proactive protocol based on the Active Packets and RERR flooding, both of which are two improving strategies of route cache in DSR.

The rest of the paper is organized as follows. In Sect. 2, we make recommendations for DSR and the strategies proposed to improve its performance. We associate two of the strategies, Active Packets and RERR flooding, together in Sect. 3 and establish our TAP protocol. Section 4 describes the simulation and gives an analysis of the simulation results. Finally, a conclusion is summarized in Sect. 5.

2 Related Works

The Dynamic Source Routing (DSR) protocol is a simple and effective protocol designed specifically for mobile ad hoc networks. DSR uses source routing rather than hop-by-hop routing, which consists two processes: Route Discovery and Route Maintenance [3]. Route Discovery is basically the process that a node, which is ready for packet delivery, gets a path by flooding a Route Request (RREQ) message. Route Maintenance is based on the node's responsibility that it shall guarantee the successful transmission of packets to its next hop. More detail can be found in [3].

DSR protocol has a low overhead, and the route cache can reduce the cost of Route Discovery. Besides, the protocol can work very well in multi-path routing and nonsymmetrical transmit pattern. However, DSR protocol has demerits: the redundant overhead, which comes from the path information in data packets; the flood of RREQ packets and the pollution of stale links. And the overhead brought by the flood of message determines that DSR is not applicable in large scale networks.

The route cache strategy for DSR was proposed by Prof David B. Johnson in [8]: A node forwarding any packet may add the routing information in that packet to its own route cache, and this information can be used to reply any kind of packets: RREQ, RREP, et al.. Because of the existence of the route cache, the accumulated routing information can be directly used to reply a RREQ message other than forwarding the RREQ by an intermediate node. Thus the source node can get a route to the destination more quickly. However, the route caching strategy worsens the stale links flood. These results, as one would expect, can affect the performance of DSR seriously. Such that a number of proposals are proposed for tackling the route cache problem.

Three choices designed for solving the route cache problem are illustrated in [9]. They are cache structure, cache capacity and cache timeout. Actually, they are affected by each other rather than three separate choices. There are two kinds of cache structure, path cache and link cache. A link cache is more preferable because it can effectively utilize all of the obtained information that a node has learned, and it requires less storage space at the price of designing a much more complex graph search algorithm to find a path to the destination. For a link cache, there is a fixed maximum of N×N links in a MANETs with N nodes. However, for a path cache, the maximum storage space required is much larger. So they divide the caches into two segments: the primary cache (has been used before) and the secondary cache (has not been used yet), only the secondary caches can be directly deleted. Cache timeout policy gives a timeout which may be either static or adaptive to a link cache. However, there is no need to set up the timeout for a path cache because of the limit of the storage space.

In [14] it is claimed that the link cache has a better performance than the path cache, and it is important to adjust the lifetime of the links dynamically to the status of the network. When a link enters the link cache, it is assigned a predefined static lifetime T1 seconds. If the link is used during T1, the lifetime will be extended to a plus T2 seconds.

Active Packets are proposed in [10] to assist to update the route cache in DSR. An Active Packet is a packet that wanders among all nodes, aiming at recording the network's topology information. Active Packet visits each node twice. The first visit is to obtain topology information of the network, and the second visit is to update route cache based on the obtained information. This method reduces the miss rate and the overhead, and is extended in [11]: In its second visit, flood is used to accelerate the update of route cache. In [10], the Active Packets are periodically generated by a randomly-chosen node, which may cause the existence of several Active Packets in the network at the same time. So the authors of [11] choose the last node that the Active Packet visited in the first visit as the Active Packet generator for the second visit. This mechanism removes invalid cache links and speeds up the Route Discovery. Furthermore, it shows off a reasonable method to get the topology of the overall network.

In [12] four solutions are introduced to tackle the route cache problem: 1) Update Route Caching (URC), which is based on the idea that route errors should be noticed very fast to all nodes. To that end, flooding can be a good choice. 2) Negative Cache Validation (NCV), which means invalid routes should be stored by every node. 3) Temporal Cache Validation (TCV) introduces a timeout to the links in the route caches. 4) Combined Cache Validation (CCV) combines the URC and the TCV.

The authors of [13] present three main troubles with the DSR protocol that cause the route cache problem: Incomplete error notification, no expiry, and quick pollution. They develop three mechanisms to address these problems respectively: Wider Error Notification, namely the flood of RERR; Timer-based Route Expiry, similar to the link lifetime in [14] and TCV in [12]; and Negative Caches, which is the same as the NCV in [12].

In [15] the authors define a new cache structure called cache table and present a distributed cache update algorithm, through which the broken link messages are only transmitted to the nodes who have cached them other than flooding RERR. Thus it prevents the pollution of the invalid routes.

Based on the viewpoints above, we find that the four most prevalent methods used to tackle the route cache problem are: 1) cache timeout [9], [14], with the form of TCV in [12], and Timer-based Route Expiry in [13]; 2) RERR flooding, named URC in [12], Wider Error Notification in [13], and part of the global RERR flooding, the cache table strategy in [15]; 3) Negative Caches in [13], also termed NCV in [12]; and 4) Active Packets in [10] and [11].

Among the four methods, the Active Packets strategy works quite different, for the reason that Active Packets extend DSR in an energetic way: it imports a new packet structure and the corresponding forwarding algorithm rather than making mild adjustment to the route cache. Active Packets capture the topology of the overall network at the expense of increasing a little overhead. We consider that this information in Active Packets should be used more adequately. For instance, we can derive a path between any two nodes through the network by using the information, as long as designing an appropriate mechanism to update this information timely. Also we can see in [12,13,15], RERR flooding is employed to update the information stored in the route cache. Accordingly, we establish our Tiding Active Packets (TAP) protocol, a marriage of Active Packets scheme with RERR flooding mechanism, both of which are improving strategies of DSR route cache. As expected, TAP is only applicable in a relative large scale network with little mobility, and the overhead of RERR flooding maybe considerable. However, as we will see later, TAP has a good performance under a certain circumstance and outperforms its source strategies and DSR on several metrics.

3 The Tiding Active Packets (TAP) Protocol

Although TAP is composed of the two improving strategies of DSR, it has nothing in common with DSR. In fact, it is a novel protocol. There are three processes in TAP: Topology Collection; Path Calculation; and Topology Maintenance.

3.1 Topology Collection

During the topology collection phase, theoretically an Active Packet will make two visits to all the nodes. By the first visit, Active Packet will travel to each node, gathering its neighboring information. When an Active Packet finishes information collection, it starts the second visit. This time, all nodes will get the overall topology information from the Active Packet and employ this information in the Route Discovery algorithm, which is called Path Calculation in TAP.

Each node need to locally maintain the following data structures in Table 1.

The variable named 'LAST' plays two different roles during different phases: one is to store the node ID, where the Active Packet comes from, during the first visit, i.e., to remember who sends the Active Packet to it in order to make backtrack later; the other is to indicate whether it has received the Active Packet

Table 1. Data Structure of Node

Name	Storing	Data Structure
Neighborhood Table	Neighbor nodes' ID	Linked list
Topology Cache	Topology information	Two-dimensional linked list
AP Tag	Delivery state of an Active Packet	2 bits
DATA Tag	Delivery state of a DATA packet	2 bits
LAST	ID/Tag	1 byte

during the second visit. Therefore 'LAST' is initiated a value different from any node's ID or 0. More elaborate explanations will be found in the following segments.

Since our protocol relies heavily on Active Packet and its delivery, we make an introduction about an Active Packet. The data structure of an Active Packet is given in Table 2:

Table 2. Data Structure of Active Packet

Name	Storing	Data Structure
TYPE	The packet type: AP	1 byte
LAST	The node ID of last hop	1 byte
NEXT	The node ID of next hop (first visit)/0 (second visit)	1 byte
BACKDATE	0 (forward)/1 (backtracking)	1 bit
TOPO	Topology information: A node list and corresponding nodes' Neighbor-nodes Lists respectively	Two-dimensional linked list
DEST	The node ID of backtracking destination, only used for backtracking	1 byte

Each node in the network maintains a Neighbor-nodes Table, which is built by broadcasting HELLO packet periodically. Initially, an Active Packet can be generated by any node in the network. The initial node adds itself into the node list in 'TOPO' field of the Active Packet, and inserts its neighbor nodes in the corresponding Neighbor-nodes List in 'TOPO'. Then it sets 'TYPE' in the Active Packet as 'AP', 'BACKDATE' as 0, 'LAST' as its ID, 'NEXT' as one of its randomly chosen neighbors, sets the 'DEST' as 0 and broadcasts the Active Packet.

When an Active Packet travels around the network to make the first visit, it collects the whole network's topology by recording all nodes' ID and their Neighborhood Tables into 'TOPOLOGY'.

When a node N receives an Active Packet (For simplicity in notation, denote N as current node or its ID and AP as the Active Packet.):

If the field 'NEXT' in AP is not 0, it means this is the first visit of AP, under this circumstance, the value of 'LAST' in N can't be 0 because this is the first visit of AP and, N is impossible to have received a second-visiting AP anyway. An AP with a field 'NEXT' that doesn't match with N should be destroyed because N isn't its next hop on its journey. If the AP is on the forward way, that is, AP is not backtracking, which is indicated by a 0-value of field 'BACKDATE' in AP, The AP will be tackled as follows:

1) Find N in the node list in 'TOPO' in AP, and insert its neighbor nodes in the corresponding Neighbor-nodes List in 'TOPO' in AP;

2) Check the node list in 'TOPO' in AP, add its neighbor nodes, which are not included in the node list, into the node list;

3) Check whether the first visit has been finished, in a way that, for each node in the node list in 'TOPO' in AP, if its Neighbor-nodes List is filled, it is said that all nodes have been visited, such that the first visit has been finished, then save the topology information to its Topology Cache and set the 'NEXT' in AP as 0, 'LAST' in AP as N, 'LAST' in N as 0, and broadcast AP in a flooding manner; else if the first visit has not been finished, it firstly checks whether all its neighbors are visited, if not, sets the 'NEXT' in AP as a randomly chosen unvisited neighbor, sets 'LAST' in AP as N and broadcasts AP. If all its neighbors are visited, a backtracking is necessary. Then set 'NEXT' in AP as 'LAST' in N, set 'LAST' in AP as N, set 'BACKDATE' in AP as 1 and broadcast AP.

Else if the AP is backtracking, if the field 'DEST' in AP is 0, N checks whether all its neighbors are visited, if not, sets the 'NEXT' in AP as a randomly chosen unvisited neighbor, sets 'BACKDATE' in AP as 0, sets 'LAST' in AP as N and broadcasts AP. If all its neighbors are visited, a continuing backtracking is necessary. Then set 'NEXT' in AP as the value of 'LAST' in N, set 'LAST' in AP as N, set 'BACKDATE' in AP as 1 and broadcasts AP. If the field 'DEST' in AP is not 0, it is said that this node is the intermediate node on the backtracking. Then set 'NEXT' in AP as the value of 'DEST' in AP, set 'DEST' in AP as 0, set 'LAST' in AP as N, set 'BACKDATE' in AP as 1 and broadcast AP.

If the field 'NEXT' in AP is 0, this is the second visit of AP: flooding. Then the field 'BACKDATE' in AP makes no sense. If 'LAST' in N is not 0, it means that N hasn't received a second-visiting AP. Then it saves the topology information to its Topology Cache, sets 'LAST' in N as 0 and broadcasts it. If 'LAST' in N is 0, then N has received a second-visiting AP, that is, N has finished the Topology Collection and will not tackle AP any more. Destroy AP.

A presentation on 'DEST' in the Active Packet should be specified for a clearly understanding. Since a node has the responsibility of delivering Active Packets successfully, it sends an AP-ACK back to the node that the Active Packet comes from. Backtracking could be quite easy since current node locally saves the node ID from which the AP comes. If a backtracking fails (No AP-ACK is sent back), then probably this link is broken. The node holding AP will update the AP's node ID list and Neighbor-node ID list accordingly. And an unvisited node that is one-hop away will be chosen to backtrack. If no such node exists, an unvisited node that is two-hop away will be chosen. In the latter situation, the field 'NEXT' in AP will indicate the intermediate node ID for the two-hop backtracking while the field 'DEST' will be changed to the destination node ID.

Note here we use a twice-visit mechanism for Active Packets, similar to the one in [10] and [11]. However, the differences lie in: 1) In [10], [11], it does not mention the update of node ID list when the Active Packet visits each node for the first time. While in TAP, each node will simultaneously update the node ID list and Neighbor-nodes ID list in the Active Packet; 2) It is mentioned in [10] and [11] that the first visit finishes when there is no node in the list that has not been visited. We make this more concrete by arguing 'If and only if the corresponding Neighbor-node ID list for every node in the Node ID list is not empty, then the first visit has been done'. Moreover, we also take network partitions into account by setting a global timeout named first_visit_timeout. The first visit is forced to finish after the timeout. Then the half-baked topology information is broadcasted to every node through the second visit. And the half-baked topology information will be made up during the Topology Maintenance.

Consider the wireless Ad Hoc network depicted in Fig. 1 as an example.

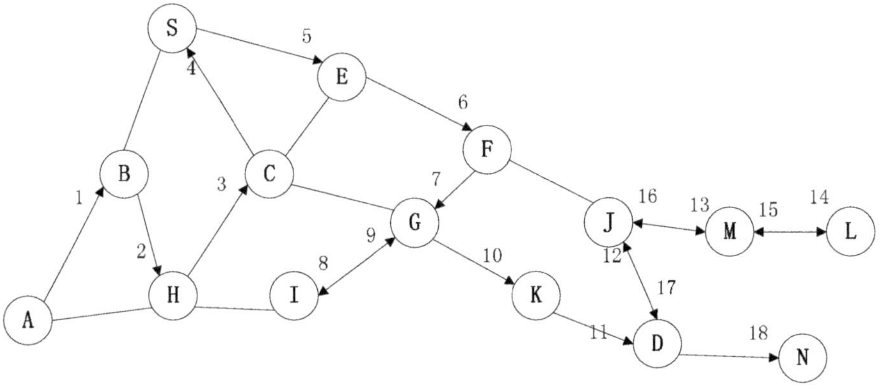

Fig. 1. Topology

The topology information in Active Packet is shown in Table 3, and the numbers in bracket indicate the sequence of the operation. These numbers are also shown in Fig. 1, with the arrows indicating the direction of AP in Table 3. For instance, in the very beginning of the operation, the whole Topology Information is NULL, therefore Table 3 is empty. Then in the first step, items with label (1) will be put into corresponding cells in the table. Similarly, in the second step, items with label (2) will occur. So on and so forth, until in the last step of the first visit, same thing happens to items with label (19). More tables shall be showed to depict the steps elaborately where the limit of space is under consideration.

Table 3. Topology Information

Node ID	Neighbor-node Table	The direction of AP
A–(1)	B H–(1)	A→B–(1)
B–(1)	A H S–(2)	B→H–(2)
H–(1)	A B C I–(3)	H→C–(3)
S–(2)	B C E–(5)	S→E–(5)
C–(3)	S H E G–(4)	C→S–(4)
I–(3)	H G–(9)	I→G(backdate)–(9)
E–(4)	S C F–(6)	E→F–(6)
G–(4)	C F I K–(8)	G→I–(8); G→K–(10)
F–(6)	E G J–(7)	F→G–(7)
J–(7)	F D M–(13)	J→M–(13); J→D(backdate)–(17)
K–(8)	G D–(11)	K→D–(11)
D–(11)	J K N–(12)	D→J–(12); D→N–(18)
N–(12)	D–(19)	The first visit is complete–(19)
M–(13)	J L–(14)	M→L–(14); M→J(backdate)–(16)
L–(14)	M–(15)	L→M(backdate)–(15)

3.2 Path Calculation

A node calculates its path to the destination before it needs to forward a data packet. The pseudocodes for this process (get a path from node S to a destination) are as follows:

```
    i= 1;
    Used_Node_Set = {all nodes that the data packet has passed by
before current node receives it & current node};
    do
    {
        Find every node X that is i-hop away from S;
        if X is the destination node
        then
            save the path;
            break;
        else if X is found in the Used_Node_Set
            then discard the path;
            else save the path;
        Insert X into the Used_Node_Set;
        i ++;
    } while (i < max_hop)
```

Note max_hop could be specified according to the node number of the whole network since the more the nodes, the more the hops that are probably needed to get to the target node. Apparently we can find a path with least hops using the algorithm above mentioned.

TAP uses hop-by-hop routing rather than source routing to transmit data. The reason is that if source routing is used, the probability of incurred broken paths will be more considerable due to the cumulated links. While for the hop-by-hop routing, each node calculates paths to the destination respectively, and only needs to forward the packet to the next hop in its path. Once the link is found broken, it can update local topology information immediately. Thus, we are able to enhance the packet delivery ratio and accelerate the update of invalid links as well.

When an intermediate node receives the data packet, it calculates its own route to the destination, sets the field 'NEXT' in the packet and transmits the packet. Note that when calculating the route to the destination, the intermediate node needs to make sure that the path doesn't contain a node that has been found in the route before. This process ends until the packet arrives at the destination.

3.3 Topology Maintenance

A local data cache is needed because a node has the responsibility to make sure the successful transmission of a data packet to its next hop. During the process of hop-by-hop routing, the node caches every packet whose acknowledgement has not been received yet and retransmits it in case of packet losing or corruption. If, in worst situation, the node cannot receive the acknowledgement for a fixed period of time (long enough), it will delete the link locally and re-calculate another route to forward the packet.

Each node maintains its Neighborhood Table in the whole process, and initiates RERR (Route Error) to notice other nodes when it detects changes of its neighbors. This certainly incurs extra overhead. But on the other hand, it can not only update the topology information in each node, but also help to make up the half-baked topology information when an Active Packet doesn't get the full topology information of the whole network. For example, when a node moves beyond the vicinity of one of its neighbors, they will both find this broken link though their next HELLO message. Subsequently, a RERR message recording the broken link will be flooded. Moreover, if a node corrupts, all its neighbors will find their corresponding broken links. Then, through flooding of RERR messages, all nodes will clear up the records corresponding to the corrupted node in their Neighbor-node Table.

4 Performance Evaluation

For the reason that TAP comes from DSR and its improving strategies, we compare our TAP protocol with several DSR-related protocols, such as the original DSR protocol without route cache or data salvation, the RC-DSR protocol that uses the link cache and the AP-DSR which uses Active Packets to tackle the route cache problem. We want to evaluate TAP in terms of influence of the route cache and its improving strategies to DSR. The simulator is OPNET. The area of the simulation is 1000×1000 meters with 100 nodes inside and a transmit radius of 150 meters. We assume nodes move following the simplest random waypoint mobility model. Node speed is randomly chosen from 0m/s to 1m/s so that we can simulate a pedestrian's speed, and the pause time is set to 0. The communication model is Constant Bit Rate (CBR) with one packet per second. The initialization is completed by the time of 150 seconds and the transmission starts right after that time, we simulate the course for 10 minutes.

The metrics we compare include packet delivery ratio, throughput, the overhead of route discovery and the overhead of route maintenance. We choose these metrics to analyze the influence of route cache and Active Packets to the protocol.

It can be seen in Fig. 2 that DSR has a good packet delivery ratio of 91.83%, while the best is 94.99%, which is achieved by TAP. It means that there are broken links during the transmission of packets. Due to the invalid links in RC-DSR, the packet delivery ratio reaches only 42.36%. AP-DSR, which is based on RC-DSR, has a better result of 60.46%. This is achieved simply by having Active Packets to tackle the route cache problem. However, compared to DSR and TAP, a packet delivery ratio of 60% cannot be regarded as good. The main reason for this is invalid links.

It can be summarized that the use of route cache incurs a lot of invalid links, which is the major cause of the low performance. The Active Packets can, to some extent, tackle the problem effectively. While TAP goes even further with proactive scheme thus has the best performance.

Figure 3 depicts the results of throughput. This is quite similar to the packet delivery ratio somewhat. The original DSR also has a rather good throughput, while RC-DSR and AP scheme perform a little worse. TAP has the best packet delivery ratio and throughput because: 1) it is quite often that TAP can finally find a path; 2) each node only need to transmit the packet to the next node in the path so that the packet can be closer and closer to the destination continuously. Things are different for DSR. It is much more difficult to find a path, though DSR has a good packet delivery ratio once Route Discovery is successfully completed.

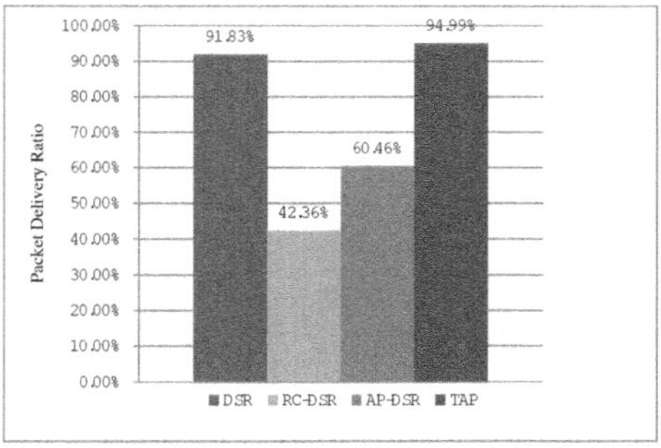

Fig. 2. Packet Delivery Ratio

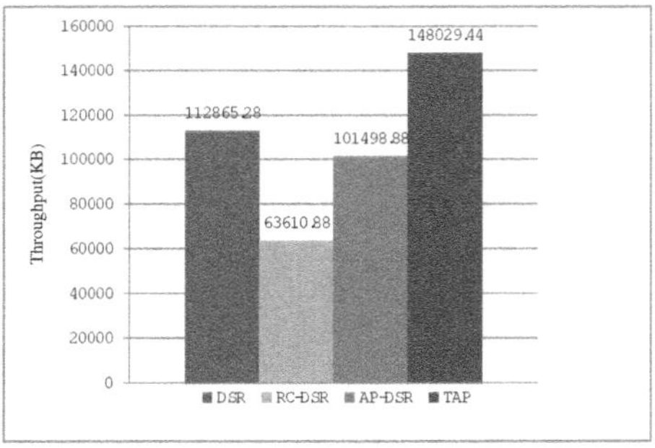

Fig. 3. Throughput

In Fig. 4, we can see that DSR has more route discovery overhead because of the lack of route cache. RC-DSR and AP-DSR use similar route discovery process except Active Packets, so they both work with low overhead. AP-DSR updates the route cache more frequently, that is why it has got more overhead than RC-DSR. The overhead of TAP comes from the initialization of TAP, so it is low too.

Figure 5 shows route maintenance overhead of different protocols. DSR has a good packet delivery ratio, so it needs less route maintenance. RC-DSR uses route cache mechanism, therefore it is very possible to have lots of invalid routes. With RERR packets generated to deal with those invalid routes, more overhead occurs. Comparatively, AP-DSR produces more overhead because of the Active Packets and HELLO packets in the network. TAP uses flood for RERR transmission and nodes initiate HELLO packets periodically. All these lead to the most overhead among the four protocols.

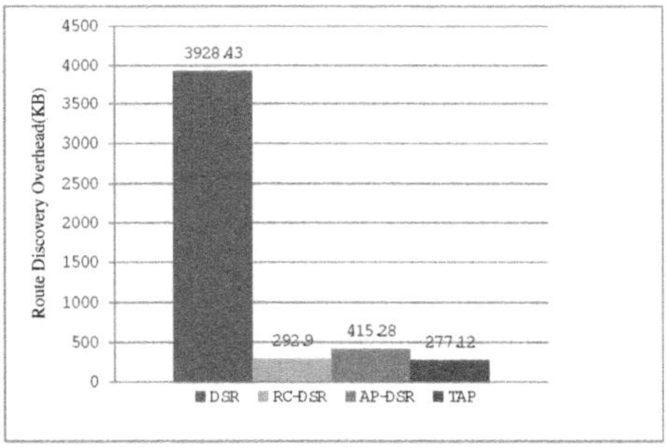

Fig. 4. Route Discovery Overhead

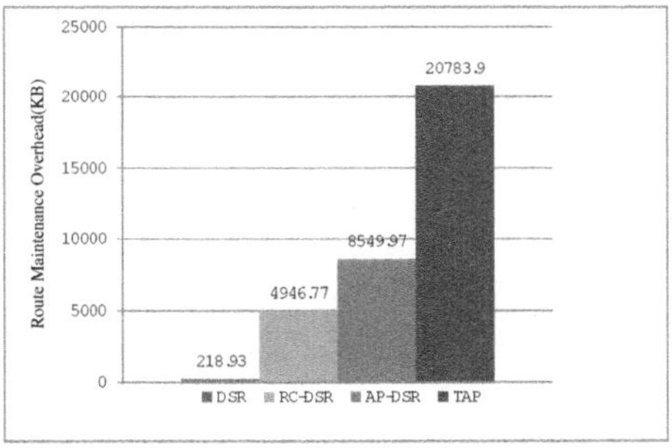

Fig. 5. Route Maintenance Overhead

The details of packet transmission for a specific node in each protocol are demonstrated in Fig. 6–Fig. 9. They work in the same environment except for the protocol in use. Thus we are able to observe the performance of a certain node in each protocol.

Figure 6 shows that DSR protocol works quite steadily. Packet lose is found occasionally because of the lack of data salvation.

RC-DSR is more susceptible to route cache. This can be seen in Fig. 7. It has a good performance when invalid routes are not used by the nodes, contrarily, once the paths that the protocol found contain some invalid links, the packet delivery ratio will decrease considerably. While the source node still gets a path to the destination, although it contains some invalid links, the source node considers it as a good path, so the forwarding is not affected.

In Fig. 8, AP-DSR conducts better than RC-DSR obviously. It forwards more packets than RC-DSR with the help of Active Packets. But the Active Packets cannot clean up all invalid routes.

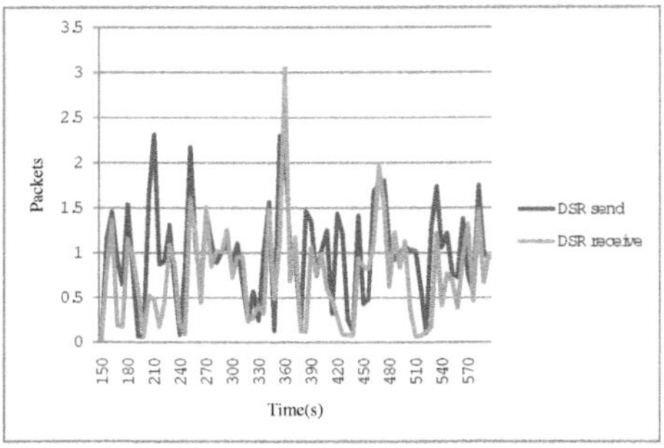

Fig. 6. DSR

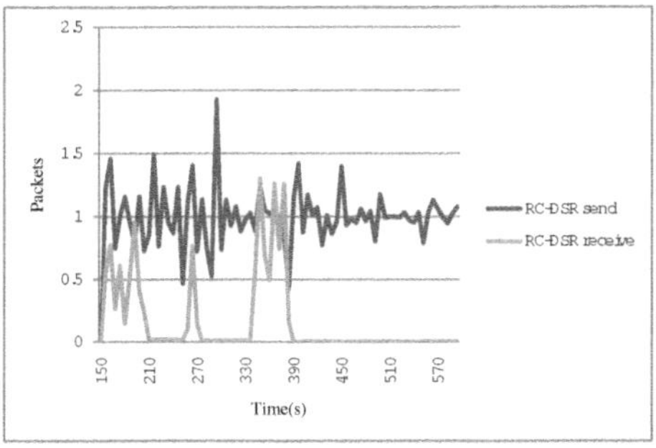

Fig. 7. RC-DSR

In Fig. 9, TAP has a pretty good performance. Few packets are lost because the topology was maintained almost at any moment, so the nodes can easily find paths to the destination.

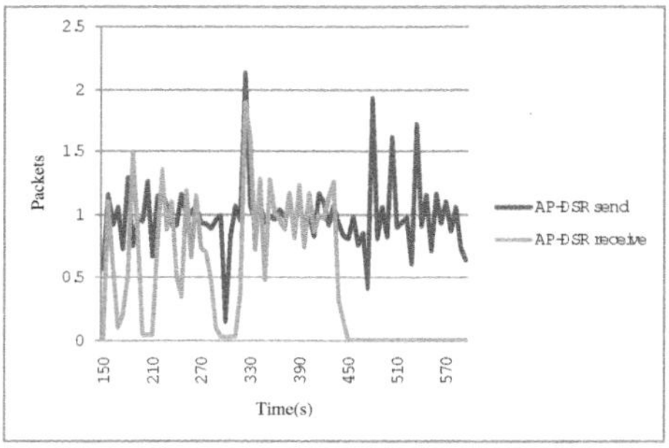

Fig. 8. AP-DSR

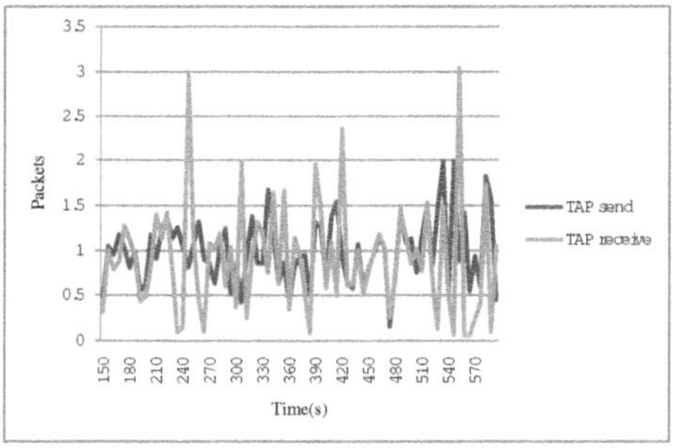

Fig. 9. TAP

It can be observed in the simulation results that DSR has a good packet delivery ratio, which means that when the source node finds a route, the transmission can be successfully completed mostly. In RC-DSR the paths often contain lots of invalid links so that it has a low packet delivery ratio and throughput, and high route maintenance overhead. AP-DSR acts much better than RC-DSR in almost every metric due to the Active Packets in the network. TAP has the best packet delivery ratio and the best throughput. Each node maintains an integrated topology so that the failure that a packet can't be transmitted is very infrequent. However, the overhead which is brought by the flood of RERR and the HELLO packets initiated periodically is also considerable, but we believe that it could be meliorated.

Considering that TAP is nearly symmetrical entirely, when the number of nodes that need to transmit packets is large, such as a P2P network, the overhead of TAP won't increase, while the other three protocols will.

5 Conclusion

Route cache mechanism in DSR protocol utilizes the information existing adequately and also brings new problem. The invalid links decrease the performance of the protocol. We propose the TAP protocol based on the method that Active Packets get the topology information through twice visits of each node, and the fact that flooding can be used to help the cache update with RERR. TAP is a semi-proactive protocol, and it uses the hop-by-hop routing. However, it breaks away the DSR protocol, uses link cache to save the storage space, and it uses RERR flooding, a replacement strategy rather than timeout to execute the cache update. The simulation indicates that TAP has a good performance in packet delivery ratio and throughput. And the considerable overhead of TAP is still to be ameliorated. Other than the protocols else, TAP embodies the equality and the distribute manner well. TAP will not incur more overhead with the increase of the number of the source node. And the route maintenance is apart from the source node, it is very convenient because it mends the route locally.

We aim at reducing the overhead of TAP in future work, and utilize the distribute manner more sufficiently, such as adding the QoS requirement, or the reliable routing. In addition, the node speed needs to be increased to tackle more dynamic networks, and node corruption should be considered more thoroughly in future work.

References

1. Perkins, C.: Mobile Ad-Hoc Networks. Addison-Wesley, Reading (2000)
2. Perkins, C., Bhagwat, P.: Highly dynamic Destination-Sequenced Distance-Vector routing (DSDV) for mobile computers. In: Proc. ACM SIGCOMM 1994 Conference on Communications Architectures, pp. 234–244 (1994)
3. Johnson, D., Maltz, D.: Dynamic source routing in ad hoc wireless networks. In: Mobile Computing, ch. 5, pp. 153–181. Kluwer Academic Publishers, Dordrecht (1996)
4. Perkins, C.: Ad Hoc On Demand Distance Vector (AODV) routing. Internet-Draft. draft-ietf-manet-aodv-00.txt (1997) (work in progress)
5. Haas, Z., Pearlman, M.: The Performance of Query Control Scheme for the Zone Routing Protocol. In: Proc. ACM SIGCOMM 1998, pp. 167–177 (1998)
6. Park, V., Corson, M.: Temporally-Ordered Routing Algorithm (TORA) version 1: Functional specification. Internet-Draft. draft-ietf-manet-tora-spec-00.txt (1997) (work in progress)
7. Murthy, S., Garcia-Luna-Aceves, J.J.: An Efficient Routing Protocol for Wireless Networks. ACM Mobile Networks and Applications Journal. Special issue on Routing in Mobile Communication Networks (1996)
8. Johnson, D., Maltz, D., Broch, J.: The dynamic source routing protocol for mobile ad hoc networks (Internet-draft). In: Mobile Adhoc Network (MANET) Working Group. IETF (1998)
9. Hu, Y., Johnson, D.: Caching strategies in on-demand routing protocols for wireless ad hoc networks. Proc. The 6th Annual IEEE/ACM International Conference on Mobile Computing and Networking, MobiCom 2000, pp. 231–242 (2000)

10. He, Y., Raghavendra, C., Berson, S., Braden, B.: Active packets improve dynamic source routing for ad-hoc networks. Proc. IEEE Conference on Open Architectures and Network Programming (OPENARCH 2002) (2002)
11. Marandin, D.: Improvement of Link Cache Performance in Dynamic Source Routing (DSR) Protocol by Using Active Packets. In: Koucheryavy, Y., Harju, J., Sayenko, A. (eds.) NEW2AN 2007. LNCS, vol. 4712, pp. 367–378. Springer, Heidelberg (2007)
12. Murugan, K., Sivasankar, S., Balaji, S., Shanmugavel, S.: Implementation and performance study of route caching mechanisms in DSR and HER routing algorithms for MANET. In: Pan, Y., Chen, D.-x., Guo, M., Cao, J., Dongarra, J. (eds.) ISPA 2005. LNCS, vol. 3758, pp. 1135–1145. Springer, Heidelberg (2005)
13. Marina, M., Das, S.: Performance of Route Caching Strategies in Dynamic Source Routing. In: Proc. Int'l Workshop on Wireless Networks and Mobile Computing (WNMC) in Conjunction with Int'l Conf. on Distributed Computing Systems (ICDCS), pp. 425–432 (2001)
14. Lou, W., Fang, Y.: Predictive caching strategy for on-demand routing protocols in ad hoc networks. Wireless Networks 8(6) (2002)
15. Yu, X., Kedem, Z.: A distributed adaptive cache update algorithm for the dynamic source routing protocol. NYU Computer Science Department Technical Report TR 2003-842 (2003)

LALO: A Link-Aware Lightweight Routing Protocol for Data Delivery in Vehicular Ad Hoc Networks

Hu Shen, Xiaodong Wang, Yanqiang Sun, Yanrong Ding, and Xingming Zhou

School of Computer
National University of Defense Technology
Changsha, China
shen.hooo@gmail.com

Abstract. This paper tailors for data delivery in large scale sparsely connected Vehicular Ad Hoc Networks (VANETs). Many classic routing protocols have demonstrated the effectiveness of their data delivery policies by making use of vehicular traffic statistics. These results are encouraging, however, all protocols adopt centralized schemes with a view to get real-time traffic statistics. In our purposed routing protocol, we firstly introduce a distributed scheme to gather local traffic statistics, and develop simple and convenient techniques to construct a criterion for path-selecting when packet carriers enter intersections. Finally we have tested our protocol with a real city-map and realistic vehicle mobile traces, and the experiments results show that the proposed LALO protocol outperforms other existing solutions, especially decreases routing protocol overhead by nearly 36.74%.

Keywords: VANETs routing protocol wireless communication.

1 Introduction

In recent years, VANETs attracts great interest of many researchers. This new type network integrates the cutting-edge wireless communication, mobile computing and advanced sensing technologies [1]. VANETs is formed by moving vehicles and becoming a common platform for a wide variety of applications, ranging from road safety notify, query and location services to advertisement and entertainment.

Due to high mobility and sparse distribution, the network topology of VANETs would change rapidly, and communication links may be frequently disrupted [2][3]. Traditional routing protocols in mobile ad hoc networks (MANETs) [4][5][6] are based on a common assumption: there are one or more persistent communication paths from source to destination. Much effort has been devoted to meet the challenge of disrupt-tolerant data delivery in VANETs but most of aforetime work [7][8][9] is limited to one hop or short range multi-hop communication while few highly effective works has been done in large scale multi-hop communication, which could be transformed into the *minimal-delay least-cost routing problem* [10] known to be NP-complete.

Vahdat et al. introduced Epidemic Routing [11], where random pair-wise exchanges of messages among mobile hosts ensure eventual message delivery. This

Z. Yu et al. (Eds.): UIC 2010, LNCS 6406, pp. 459–473, 2010.

solution exploring every possible path and bring a relative higher delivery ratio, but it generates many redundant copies and decreases the network efficiency sharply.

VADD protocol [12] proposed by Zhao and Cao choose its forwarding path by using Gaussian Elimination algorithm. By computing the expected packet delivery cost from an intersection to its neighbor intersection, they transformed the former NP-complete problem into a polynomial solvable problem. However, VADD protocol needs many assistant traffic statistics such as real-time traffic density and vehicle speed on roads. And this approach is still too computationally expensive to be applied in large city-level scenarios.

Antonios et al. proposed two routing algorithms, D-Greedy and D-MinCost [13] and they tried to satisfy bounded delays requirement in packet delivery, whist trying to minimize the utilization of the wireless medium by making use of traffic statistics in various parts of the city. This protocol chooses carry rather than forward policy except for urgent need, hence it suffers a large loss in delivery delay (the time bound is thousands of seconds).

All aforementioned work [11][12][13] could solve multi-hop data delivery *minimal-delay least-cost routing problem* in large scale of VANETs to some degree, but these work is not satisfying and more effort should be devoted in.

In this paper, we propose a link-aware lightweight routing protocol (LALO) and the main contributions of our work are summarized as follows:

- Link-aware: we adopt a distributed scheme to gather surrounding road status information rather than require it from centre servers. This mechanism could guarantee that vehicle nodes get the necessary real-time road statistics and at the same time decrease routing protocol overhead to a relative lower level.
- Lightweight: our link-aware algorithm is based on one-hop beacon probe and our path-selection algorithm is also very simple and convenient (to be solved in time $\theta(1)$), so the computing complexity is much smaller than other existing protocols.
- Realistic simulation: in our evaluation, we use realistic vehicle traces on a real city map. And we set up numbers of intersections and vehicle nodes much enough to depict the true case of data delivery in VANETs.

The rest of this paper is organized as follows. Section II introduces the classical application scenario, assumptions and the goal of our research work. Section III describes the details of the routing protocol based on a distributed information gathering scheme, and its working mechanism. In section IV, we test our routing protocol on a workbench based on a real city map and realistic vehicle traces, and compare its experimental results with other existing routing protocols'. Section V gives conclusions of this paper.

2 Model

2.1 Scenario

For the moment, wireless infrastructure is not very popular cause of the relative expensive cost. Only a few places such as big marketplaces, coffee houses and bus stations are equipped with wireless access points (APs) connecting to Local Area Network (LAN) or Internet. Due to the limitation of the number and communication coverage of APs as showed in Figure 1, it is impossible that every vehicle could connect with APs directly. But vehicles far away from APs also need to communicate with LAN or Internet, for instance, people driving in outskirts of a city want to query commodities information in marketplaces to make his or her shopping list; they want to know current roadway status of whole city and position of parking lots to make a driving plan, etc. The distance between vehicles initiating queries and their nearest APs might be miles or even tens of miles. Data delivery between query vehicles and LAN (or Internet) is supposed to use vehicular ad-hoc networks to make a bridge. In general, these query applications is not highly sensitive to delivery delay, they can tolerate time delay up to minutes.

2.2 Assumptions

We assume that vehicles are equipped with a position system device such as GPS, which is very popular now, so vehicles are able to know their real-time location. Every wireless access point (AP) connects with each other by wired links, APs are marked up in the digital map pre-loaded in vehicles and the map could show the general picture of a city's streets. This assumption is also reasonable because many mature commercial products could satisfy such requirements.

We assume that the vehicles have the capacity of computing and buffering. Vehicles communicate with each other through short range wireless channel and the range of transceiver is about 250m. Some information like source vehicle location, destination AP location, packet generated time, expiration time, etc, is contained in the head of data packet.

2.3 Research Goal

As a result of high mobility and relative spatial distribution of nodes in VANETs, communication links for data delivery would suffer frequent fragmentation, even at a high density of nodes deployment in VANETs [2]. Hence, carry-and-forward policy[16] should be introduced for the reliable delivery of data packets. However, this policy does not ensure a delay bound for data packet delivery, so data packets successfully transmitted might lose their actual effect. In this paper, we dedicate to improve the delivery ratio and decrease the delay time, in addition we want to reduce the routing protocol, computing overhead and increase the utilization of VANETs' bandwidth with our best effort.

3 LALO Design

We abstract the city map as a directed graph $G(U,V,E)$, where V is a finite set of nodes represent the intersections, and E is a set of edges represent streets connecting neighbor intersections. $\exists e_{ab} \in E$, it means that there is a edge connects intersection a and intersection b. U is a subset of V and it represents the set of wireless access points (APs).

When a packet carrier A is in intersection a demonstrated in Figure 2, data packets are supposed to be transmitted to the coffee house B. There are four forwarding paths candidate: street e_{ab}, street e_{ac}, street e_{ad} and street e_{ae}. Hence, the problem is how to select an optimal forwarding path from these streets, how to construct and calculate performance metrics of each choice, and father more how to choose a desirable vehicle as the best next forwarding node. All of this should be appropriately arranged in our routing protocol.

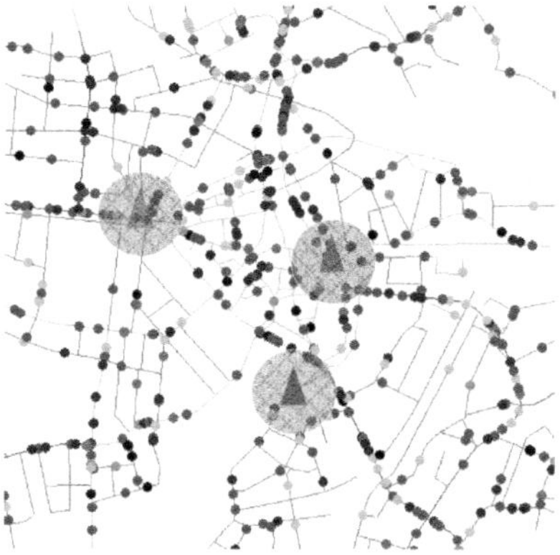

Fig. 1. Scenario of VANETs

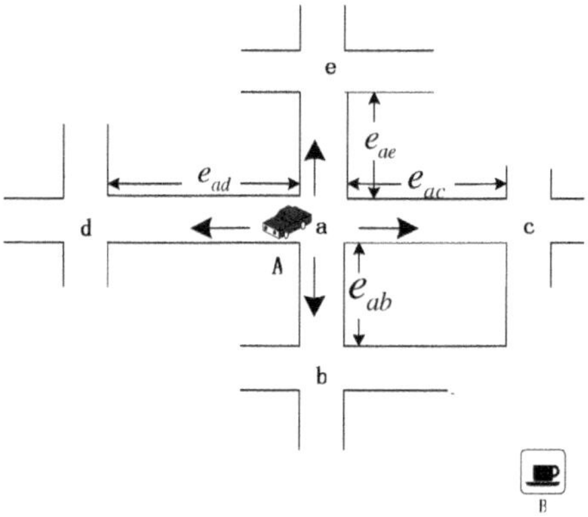

Fig. 2. Find a forwarding path

Intuitively, in Figure 2, street e_{ab} and street e_{ac} would be better choices relative to street e_{ad} and street e_{ae} in consideration of the length of routing path.

But we must notice here that the optimal forwarding path in VANETs is not the traditional shortest path [14]. This is due to the carry delay of data packet delivery is *several orders-of-magnitude* longer than the forward delay. So the length of routing path is not the only or even not the most important performance metric of data delivery. For example, a vehicle needs 36 seconds to travel along a street of 1 km at the speed of 100Km/h, while it takes only milliseconds to transmit data packet through relay vehicle nodes. Some state-of-the-art routing protocols [12][13][14] in VANETs adopt the performance metric of Expected packet Delivery Delay (EDD) as the criterion of the next optimal forwarding path. The typical solution of Gaussian Elimination algorithm solves the computation of EDD in time $\theta(n^3)$ (n is the number of intersections in the map) and it requires real-time traffic statistics such as traffic density and vehicle speed on all roads. Hence, the computing complexity and additional protocol overhead of this solution couldn't be ignored and it would be much more serious in large scale scenarios.

To solve the above-mentioned problem, we develop a distributed scheme to gather local traffic statistics, and we conveniently construct a criterion for path-selection (which is to be solved in time $\theta(1)$) based on the estimation of local traffic statistics. Our algorithm doesn't require real-time traffic statistics from centre servers and the computation complexity of the criterion for path-selection is simplified greatly.

3.1 Local Information Gathering Scheme

In this paper, other than protocols like VADD [12] and TBD [14] require real-time traffic statistics of whole map from centre servers, as illustrated in Figure 3, we develop a distributed scheme to gather the local traffic information for reducing the protocol overhead: a simple beacon probing algorithm provides packet carriers with their neighbors' current position and last history position, then packet carriers could estimate the traffic statistics using the information within their transmission range. This kind of traffic statistics estimation is effective, because generally speaking, in a city-level scenario, the average length of a street between two intersections is 500m and the classic transmission range of a vehicle transceiver is 250m.

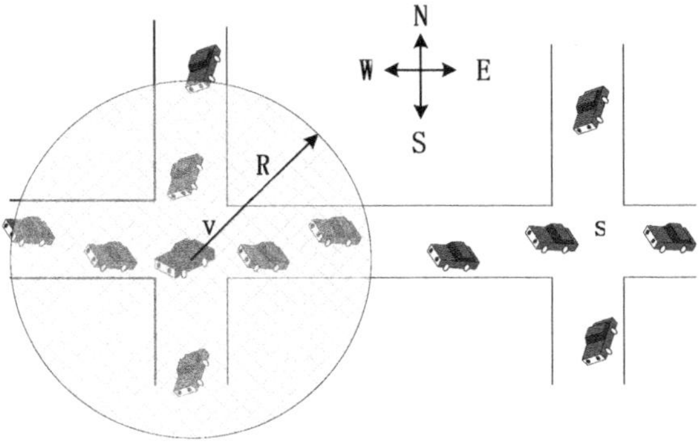

Fig. 3. Local information gathering scheme

3.1.1 Beacon Probing

Periodically, the packet carrier broadcast a beacon, which contains its own IP address and the current position. We encode IP address as four one-byte unsigned char quantities and encode position as two four-byte floating-point quantities for x and y coordinate value respectively. To avoid synchronization of neighbors' beacon, we jitter each beacon's transmission by 50% of the interval T between beacons, such that the mean inter-beacon transmission interval is T , and the inter-beacon transmission interval uniformly distributed in $[0.5T, 1.5T]$.

When neighbor vehicles receive a beacon, they stop forwarding the beacon to next-hop vehicles, hence, beacon probing is limited to one-hop transmission range and avoids beacon flooding storm. Neighbor vehicles reply the packet carrier with short packets containing their own IP addresses, the current position and the last history position. The packet carrier refreshes its neighbor table: add new neighbor vehicles to the neighbor table; refresh position information items of previous existing neighbor vehicles; delete the neighbor vehicles which fail to give a reply longer than timeout interval (the timeout interval is $4.5T$ in this work).

Beacon probing algorithm is described as follows:

```
p - the packet to forward
A - the vehicle carrying packet p
N[] - a list of all neighbor vehicles of A
Period start
  /* local maximum probing ( transmission range of A is R,
   * define a basic intervle time T ) */
  compute a inter-beacon intvel time -> wait_time
    wait_time = 0.5T + Random::uniform(T)
  wait_time expiration
  A make a beacon broadcast within its transmission range
    beacon packet <- IP address, x coordinate value
                     y coordinate value of A
  /* refresh A's neighbor table N[],
   * define a reply intervle 4.5T */
  Reply intervle start
  if A receives a reply message
    reply message <- IP address ip_address, current x coordinate value
                     current y coordinate value, last x coordinate value
                     last y coordinate value of the neighbor node
    lookfor ip_address of reply mesage in N[]
    if ip_address in N[] (the index is i)
        replace N[i]'s coordinate value
    else
        add an element to N[]
    endif
  endif
  Reply intervle end
  clear elements without reply in N[]
Period end
```

Fig. 4. Beacon probing algorithm

3.1.2 Estimation of Traffic Statistics

We estimate vehicle density, vehicle speed and traffic direction by using of information collected through local beacon probe: firstly, we count the amount of vehicles detected in every direction according to the relative location between the packet carrier and its neighbor vehicles; secondly, we calculate vehicle density of each street based on the amount of vehicles abovementioned and the coverage range of vehicles' transceiver; finally, vehicles' moving direction and speed are computed by their current location and their last history location.

3.2 Path-Selection Algorithm

In this paper, we try to make use of location information provided by position system and digital map to construct a criterion of path-selection: Each intersection is marked up with the difficulty index of forwarding data packet from the intersection to its destination AP. By comparing the difficulty index of current intersection with those of its adjacent intersections, we could find the optimal forwarding path conveniently.

Some important definitions and notations as following:

Firstly notice here the node $v \in V$, the edge $e_{vs} \in E$ and the wireless AP $u \in U$,

- v : the intersection in which the packet carrier located.
- s : an intersection adjacent to v .

- r_{vs} : the street connects v and s.
- n_{vs} : the amount of vehicles on r_{vs}.
- ρ_{vs} : the vehicle density on r_{vs} estimated.
- R : transmission range of the packet carrier.
- α : the correction factor.
- **Location value** (x_v, y_v) : the latitude and longitude value of node v respectively.
- **Forwarding difficulty index** $\varphi(v)$: the Euclidean distance between node v and its nearest wireless access point.

$$\varphi(v) = \min\{\| v-u \|\}(\forall u \in U)$$

$$\| v-u \| = \sqrt{(x_v - x_u)^2 + (y_v - y_u)^2}$$

- **Vectors** $\vec{i}$ and $\vec{j}$: basis vectors of the latitude and longitude direction respectively.
- **Node vector** $\vec{v}$: the location vector of node v.

$$\vec{v} = x_v \vec{i} + y_v \vec{j}$$

- **Moving vector** $\vec{e_{vs}}$: the vector difference from node a to node b.

$$\vec{e_{vs}} = \vec{s} - \vec{v} = (x_s - x_v)\vec{i} + (y_s - y_v)\vec{j}$$

- **Destination vector** $\vec{v_d}$: the vector difference from node v to its destination wireless access point $u \in U$.

$\vec{v_d} = (x_u - x_v)\vec{i} + (y_u - y_v)\vec{j}$, and $\| v-u \| = \varphi(v)$ expected to be satisfied.

We know that the shorter the distance between data packets and destination AP, the larger the probability of success reception of data packets. So when a packet carrier in an intersection faces to choose a forwarding path, the all-important consideration is to shorten the delivery distance with the best effort.

Theorem 1: The direction on which the node v 's difficult index decreases sharpest is the direction of node v 's destination vector.

Proof: As showed in Figure 5, we know $\varphi(v)$'s grads direction is the direction on which node v 's difficult index decreases sharpest, and we have

$$grad\varphi(v) = \frac{\partial\varphi}{\partial x_v}\vec{i} + \frac{\partial\varphi}{\partial y_v}\vec{j} = [(x_v - x_u)\vec{i} + (y_v - y_u)\vec{j}]/\varphi = -\vec{v_d}/\varphi \qquad \blacksquare$$

Our routing protocol is inspired by this idea that in order to forward data packets as quickly as possible, the packet carrier in an intersection always chooses the street whose direction is most closest to the direction of the intersection's destination vector. As mentioned before, besides the length of routing path, there are some other performance metrics would bring influence to data delivery in VANETs and they are deserved careful consideration.

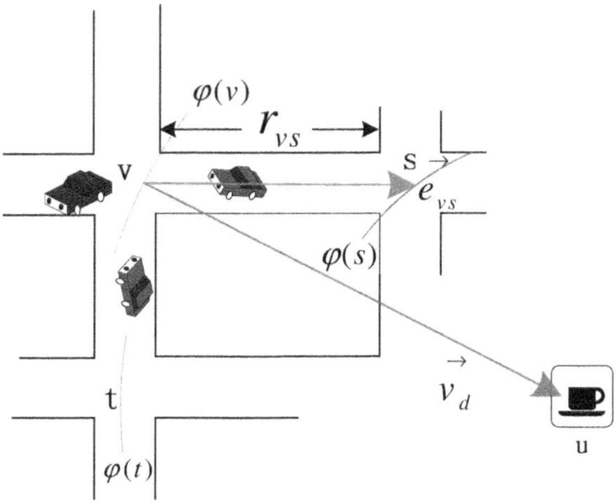

Fig. 5. Path-selection modeling

Among all the performance metrics besides the length of routing path, the most important one is the vehicle density of each street because it determines the transmission capacity of the forwarding path (we leave the other performance metrics like traffic direction and vehicle speed to future work).

Taking consideration of the performance metrics of the length of forwarding path and the vehicle density, we construct a criterion to guide the forwarding path selection. We suppose that a packet carrier enters into an intersection v, then the criterion value of forwarding data packet on road r_{vs} is:

$$Cr_{vs} = (\vec{e}_{vs} \bullet grad\varphi(v)) + \alpha * \rho_{vs} = \frac{(\vec{e}_{vs} \bullet \vec{v}_d)}{\varphi(v)} + \frac{\alpha * n_{vs}}{R}$$

3.3 Other Details of LALO

Data delivery in LALO has two transition modes: Intersection Mode and Straightway Mode, by switching between the two transition modes, data packets would find an optimal forwarding path to destination APs. In addition, the modeling and analysis above only consider the routing from vehicle nodes to destination APs. Communication of message is a bidirectional process, we must take into account the reverse routing from APs to travelling vehicle nodes.

A. Intersection Mode

When a packet carrier enters an intersection, firstly the vehicle node would detect its neighbor vehicles through beacon probing and get some location information from pre-loaded digital map, then the packet carrier compares all candidate forwarding paths and chooses the path of the largest Cr value as the next forwarding path.

B. Straightway Mode

When a data packet carrier is in a straightway, it adopts a geographic greedy carry-and-forward policy. If there are vehicle nodes available in the transmission range of the current data carrier, then data packets would transmitted to the vehicle node which is the closest to the target intersection; or else, the packet carrier keeps holding the packets, and waits for a relay vehicle usable.

C. The reverse routing

The difference between routing from a vehicle to AP and its reverse routing is that the latter's destination vehicle is moving. Our solution based on vehicle mobility tracing and prediction. By learning knowledge from destination vehicle's history location information in data packets sent by it, AP can figure out the history trajectory of the vehicle. After AP receives the query packets, it attaches prediction trajectory of the destination vehicle with the query reply. When reply packets arrive at the predicted location of receiver, the packet carrier will make a broadcast showed in Figure 6. The processing of the reverse routing is similar to the routing from the vehicle to AP, but what deserves to pay attention is we should choose the path owning the smallest Cr value as the next forwarding path in the reverse routing.

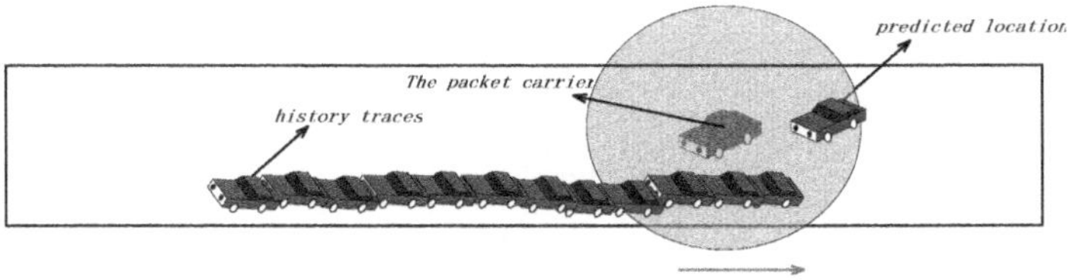

Fig. 6. Reverse routing

D. The vehicle to be next packet carrier

According to abovementioned policies like beacon probe, path-selection, carry-and-forward and converse routing, we could find next-hop vehicles available approximately but we are obligated to confirm determine which vehicle be the best next packet carrier. Different available vehicles imply different advantages and disadvantages: a vehicle with a top-grade location might be at a disadvantage of moving direction or speed, or a vehicle with the optimal moving direction is not in a good location or at a high moving speed. We ought to keep a balance among performance metrics of location, moving direction and moving speed. This procedure is complex as it involves the pattern of vehicular mobility, hence, we let it to future work. In this paper, we simply adopt the greedy forwarding policy based on location.

4 Evaluation

4.1 Simulation Setup

In order to evaluate our routing algorithm on a realistic scenario, we use a real map of Oldenburg, Germany and a group of realistic vehicle traces generated by a spatiotemporal network generator [15] as showed in Figure 7. The size of the extracted simulation area is 4km × 3km with 400 vehicles involved.

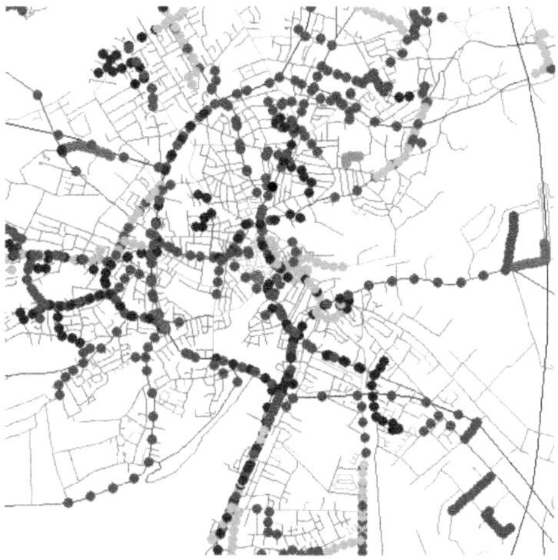

Fig. 7. A snapshot of the traces generated in the extracted map of Oldenburg, Germany

We implement and evaluate our routing algorithm LALO in NS2 with the scenario and data aforementioned and compare the performance of the LALO protocol with several existing protocols. For all protocols (except for GPSR), we give limited buffer size and manage the buffer space with simple FIFO policy.

The settings of NS2 simulation environment are listed in Table1 as following:

4.2 Results Analysis

We compare the performance of LALO with other three existing protocols: GPSR [6], the epidemic routing protocol [11], and VADD [12] as follows. We set the data sending rate of CBR flows as the variable. We must notice here that the buffer size is different between the epidemic routing protocol's evaluations and the other protocols': in GPSR, VADD and LALO protocols, the default buffer size is set to 400 and we could consider it to be unlimited buffer space for each vehicle node; while in the epidemic routing protocol's evaluation, the default buffer size is only set to 50, because larger buffer size would cause the collapse of evaluations due to our experimentation computer's limited computing and memory capacity. In addition, we implement GPSP without buffer policy according to paper [6].

Table 1. Simulation settings

Parameter	Value
Simulation area	5000m × 3200m
Num of intersections	70
Num of APs	3
Num of vehicles	400
Num of CBR flows	12
Transmission range	250m
Intersection range	50m
Vehicle velocity	0~100 miles per hour
Buffer size	400
Data packet size	1460B
CBR rate	0.1~1 packet per second
Vehicle beacon interval	0.5 sec
Simulation time	550 sec

A. Delivery Ratio

Figure 8(a) shows the result of packet delivery ratio as a function of data sending rate. We observed that GPSR(without buffer) has the lowest delivery ratio, and obviously it is unsuitable to be used as the routing protocol of VANETs. While epidemic routing explores every possible forwarding path, thereby its performance should be the best theory bound, but when we increases the data sending rate of CBR flows, the delivery ratio of epidemic routing drops sharply. We could learn the reason from Figure 10 (a) and (b). Since epidemic routing is a multicast protocol, it would generate much more network traffic, so its MAC layer collisions would increase and its packet delivery ratio reduces. In addition, Figure 9 show that the average number of forwarding hops in epidemic routing is much smaller than those of VADD and LALO and it decreases rapidly as the data sending rate increases. That means the effective delivery area in epidemic routing is much smaller than VADD and LALO, especially in the over loading VANETs. The performance of VADD doesn't perform well as it performs in the

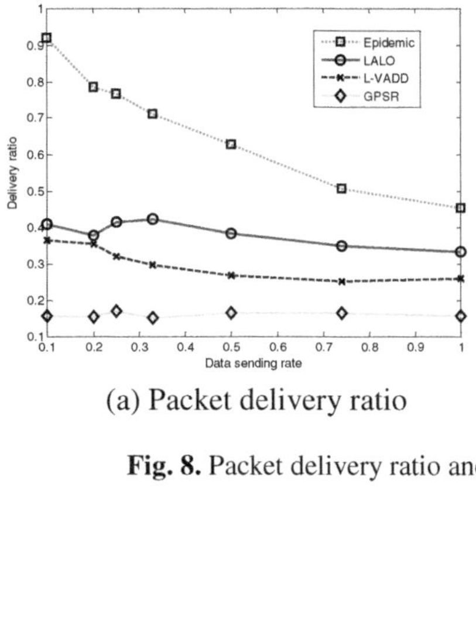

(a) Packet delivery ratio

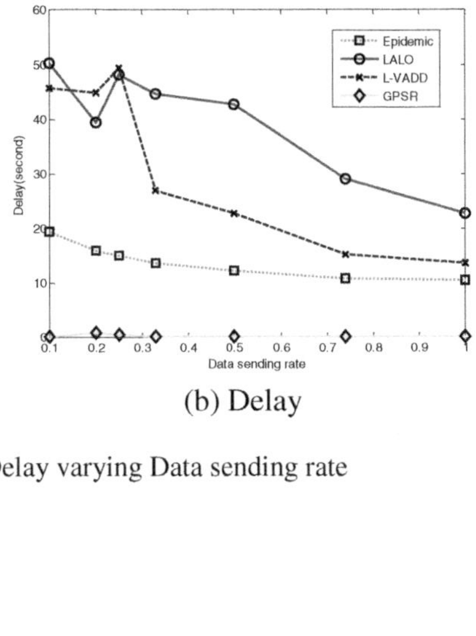

(b) Delay

Fig. 8. Packet delivery ratio and Delay varying Data sending rate

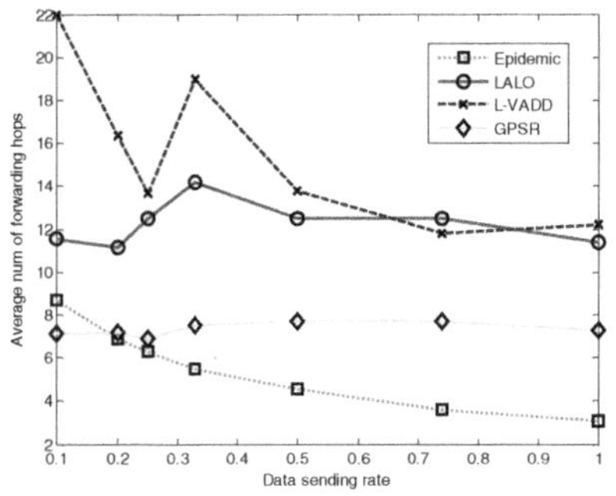

Fig. 9. The average number of forwarding hops varying Data sending rate

paper [10] shows than it doesn't suit in a city-level scenario with much more intersections and vehicle nodes. Finally our LALO routing outperforms 25% than VADD routing on average.

B. Delay

Figure 8(b) shows packet delay as a function of data sending rate. GPSR doesn't adopt carry strategy so its delay is very small. The performance of epidemic routing seems better than VADD and LALO, because it emphasizes particularly on packets neighbor to APs. Finally, we compare LALO with VADD, and on average the VADD routing outperforms 14% than LALO. We think this result is acceptable because most applications in VANETs are delay-tolerant and their time bound could up to minutes.

C. Protocol Overhead

Figure 10(a) shows the routing protocols overhead, measured in the total number of routing protocols packets generated in network-wide during the entire simulation as a function of data sending rate and Figure 10(b) shows the total packets dropped and dumped as a function of data sending rate. We observed the generated network traffic of epidemic routing is much larger than the others' and epidemic routing would bring lots of dropped packets cause of MAC layer collisions and dump packets cause of

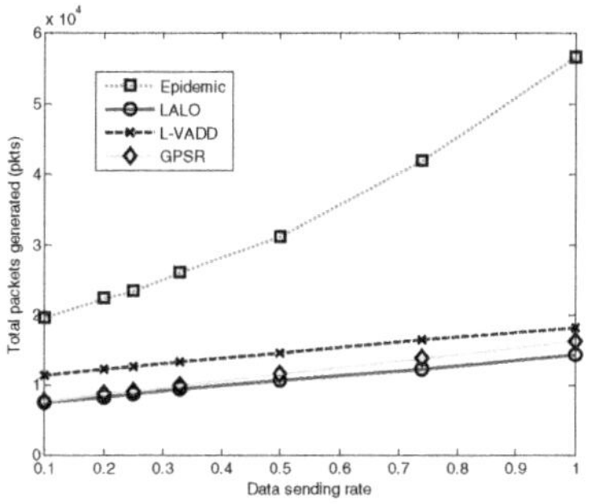

(a) Total packets generated

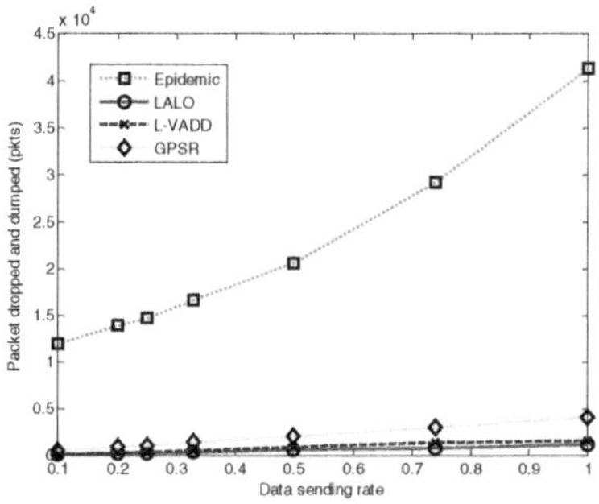

(b) Packet dropped and dumped

Fig. 10. Routing protocol overhead varying Data sending rate multicasting. So epidemic routing is very sensitive to network transmission overload and its network efficiency is the worst among all protocols evaluated. The protocol overhead of GPSR, VADD and LALO are linear functional with the variable of data sending rate approximately. And LALO performances best, it outperforms 36.74% than VADD on average in the respect of the total packets generated.

D. The Impact of Buffer Size

All the previous results (except for the results of epidemic protocol's evaluations) implicitly assume unlimited buffer size for each vehicle node. Figure 11 and Figure 12 show how routing protocols react to the different limited buffer size in terms of delivery ratio, delay, routing protocol overhead. We choose the deployment scenario with data sending rate of 0.25.

As showed in Figure 11(a), when the buffer size increases, the data delivery ratio increases. This is due to the reason that larger buffer space increases the chance for the packet carrier to find a usable vehicle to relay the data packet. By contraries, with limited buffer size, new data packets may replace the old undelivered packets, resulting in packets drops and low delivery ratio. Figure 11 and Figure 12 show that the epidemic routing protocol is highly sensitive to buffer size, when buffer size increases from 20 to 50, delivery ratio of epidemic protocol rises 28.84% while it also costs

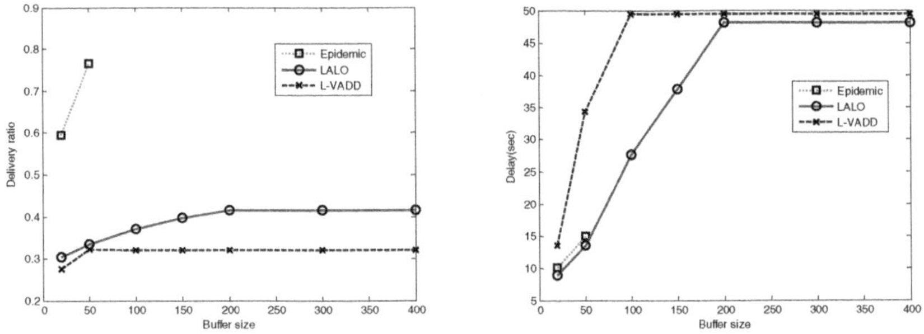

(a) Delivery ratio (b) Delay

Fig. 11. Packet delivery ratio and Delay varying Buffer size

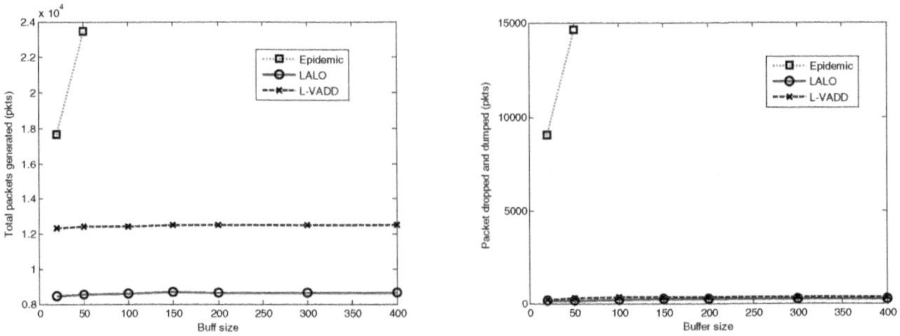

(a) Total packets generated (b) Packet dropped and dumped

Fig. 12. Routing protocol overhead varying Buffer size

much because the delay, protocol overhead and packets dropped and dumped increase 48.46%, 32.76% and 61.56% respectively. The reason is that larger buffer size leads to more data packets exchange between peers, and the chance of congestion and drop increase. Between LALO and VADD, VADD reach the steady state at a smaller buffer size than LALO, but LALO outperforms than VADD in terms of most performance metrics.

5 Conclusions

We have proposed a link-aware lightweight routing protocol (LALO) for supporting delay tolerate applications in sparsely connected Vehicular Ad hoc Networks (VANETs). Our algorithm doesn't rely on real-time traffic statistics provided by centralized servers while we firstly develop a distributed information gathering scheme and we design a lightweight routing protocol based on link-ware traffic statistics estimation. This distributed scheme is of better robust and decreases protocol overhand. In addition, our path-selection algorithm solves the problem of path selection in a constant time by using the location information and greedy policy.

We have evaluated our routing protocol in a busy urban scenario, and made comparisons with three other existing protocols: epidemic routing, GPSR and VADD. Experimental results showed that our algorithm has a better general performance than them. However there is a huge enhancement space yet.

As future work, we will consider more complex modeling of path-selection by taking consideration of vehicle speed, moving direction, etc. And we want to know other variables like the amounts of vehicle nodes and intersections how to influence the performance of routing protocols.

Acknowledgement

We thank Jing Zhao for sharing his VADD source code to us.

References

1. Chen, W., Delgrossi, L., Kosch, T., Saito, T.: Topics in Automotive Networking. Journal of IEEE Communication 47(11), 82–83 (2009)
2. Blum, J.J., Eskandarian, A., Hoffman, L.J.: Challenges of Intervehicle Ad Hoc Networks. IEEE Transactions On Intelligent Transportation Systems 5(4) (December 2004)
3. Disruption tolerant networking, DTN (2008), `http://www.darpa.mil/sto/solicitations/DTN/index.htm`
4. Johnson, D., Maltz, D.: Dynamic Source Routing in Ad Hoc Wireless Networks. In: Mobile Computing, pp. 153–181. Kluwer, Dordrecht (1996)
5. Perkins, C.E., Royer, E.M.: Ad hoc on-demand distance vector routing. In: 2nd IEEE Workshop on Mobile Computing Systems and Applications (February 1999)
6. Karp, B., Kung, H.T.: GPSR: Greedy perimeter stateless routing for wireless networks. In: Proceedings of ACM MOBICOM 2000 (August 2000)

7. Xu, Q., Mark, T., Ko, J., Sengupta, R.: Vehicle-to-Vehicle Safety Messaging in DSRC. In: Proceedings of VANET (October 2004)
8. Xu, B., Ouksel, A., Woflson, O.: "Opportunistic Resource Exchange in Inter-vehicle Ad Hoc Networks. In: IEEE International Conference on Mobile Data Management, MDM (2004)
9. Yang, X., Liu, J., Zhao, F., Vaidya, N.: A Vehicle-to-Vehicle Communication Protocol for Cooperative Collision Warning. In: Int'l Conf. on Mobile and Ubiquitous Systems: Networking and Services, MobiQuitous 2004 (August 2004)
10. Garey, M., Johnson, D.: Computers and Intractability: A Guide to the Theory of NP-Completeness, Series of Books in the Mathematical Sciences. W.H. Freeman, New York (January 1979)
11. Vahdat, A., Becker, D.: Epidemic routing for partially connected ad hoc networks. In: Technical Report CS-200006 (2000)
12. Zhao, J., Cao, G.: Vadd: Vehicle-assisted data delivery in vehicular ad hoc networks. In: Conf. on Computer Communications (INFOCOM) (2006)
13. Skordylis, A., Trigoni, N.: Delay-bounded Routing in Vehicular Ad-hoc Networks. In: MobiHoc. ACM, New York (May 2008)
14. Jeong, J., Guo, S., Gu, Y., He, T., Du, D.: TBD: Trajectory-Based Data Forwarding for Light-Traffic Vehicular Networks. In: ICDCS. IEEE, Los Alamitos (June 2009)
15. Brinkhoff, T.: A Framework for Generating Network-Based Moving Objects. GeoInformatica 6(2), 155–182 (2002)
16. Pelusi, L., Passarella, A., Conti, M.: Opportunistic Networking: Data Forwarding in Disconnected Mobile Ad Hoc Networks. IEEE Communications Magazine 44(11), 134–141 (2006)

POCOSIM: A Power Control and Scheduling Scheme in Multi-Rate Wireless Mesh Networks

Weihuang Li, Pin Lv, Yingwen Chen, and Ming Xu

Department of Network Engineering, School of Computer
National University of Defense Technology
Changsha, China 410073

Abstract. Transmission power control (TPC) is a key technique in wireless networking. There are abundant works on TPC aiming at saving the energy or improving the performance of WSNs, MANETs and WLANs. However, the research on throughput-and-fairness-oriented TPC scheme represented for multi-rate wireless mesh networks is rather limited. As routers usually have stable power supply, throughput rather than energy consumption is the most crucial factor in wireless mesh networks. Therefore POCOSIM (POwer COntrol and Scheduling scheme In Multi-rate wireless mesh networks) is introduced in this paper to improve the throughput and the fairness in the context of multi-rate WMN. Traffic patterns of the system are analyzed based on a model of conflict graph, and a differential evolution based algorithm is proposed to optimize the time allocation vector. Simulations demonstrate that POCOSIM can improve the throuhgput and also can strike a balance between throughput and fairness.

1 Introduction

In recent years, wireless mesh network (WMN) has attracted increasingly more attention in both academic and industrial circles and is highly appreciated for its convenient deployment, low cost, wide coverage, broadband networking and so on. These benefits result in the wide spread of WMN in many scenarios, such as Internet subscribing, video streaming, emergency networking and etc. It can be deployed as the infrastructure of the ubiquitous computing environment since it can integrate networks of different accessing technologies.

In WMN, nodes are comprised of mesh routers (MRs) and mesh clients (MCs) [1]. The MR usually has minimal mobility and has no strict constraints on power consumption. A number of MRs interconnected by wireless links form the communication backbone/infrastructure of WMN. A gateway (GW) bridges the WMN to external networks (e.g. the Internet). In the case of backhaul access to the Internet or video surveillance, the packets emitted by MCs will be routed to the GW through multi-hop paths in the mesh backbone and then enter the wired networks, and this is the data aggregation traffic type we consider in this paper.

Z. Yu et al. (Eds.): UIC 2010, LNCS 6406, pp. 474–488, 2010.

In order to provide a good user experience, the WMN should maximize the throughput as much as possible to meet the requirements of users or applications. Power control is a key technology to the performance of the WMN, because selecting the transmit power for each packet is of foremost importance to maximize network capacity [10][15]. The reason is as follows. Nowadays, multiple modulating and coding schemes become available as well as multi-rate function is defined by some standards and supported by much hardware. For example, IEEE 802.11b defines four different bit-rates which are 1Mbps, 2Mbps, 5.5Mbps and 11Mbps respectively, while IEEE 802.11a/g support eight various bit-rates from 6Mbps to 54Mbps. The bit-rate of a wireless link depends on the signal noise ratio (SNR) at the receiver, namely higher SNR generally means higher bit-rate. In order to elevate the bit-rate of the link, the transmitter can increase its transmission power. However, this behavior may cause more severe interference to other links, which may not benefit the throughput of the whole network. As a result, the transmission power of each MR should be scheduled carefully so that the performance of the entire WMN can be further enhanced.

Although there have been many researches on power control aiming at improving the power efficiency or prolonging the life time of the nodes in the environment of wireless sensor networks (WSN) and mobile ad-hoc networks (MANET), few works have been done to maximize the throughput and the fairness by means of power control that considering multi-rate function in the context of WMN without power constraint.

In this paper, we propose POCOSIM (POwer COntrol and Scheduling scheme In Multi-rate wireless mesh network) to meliorate the throughput and fairness of the multi-rate WMN. The system is modeled as a conflict graph and formulated as multi-object programming problem. A differential evolution algorithm is used to solve the problem and has shown its effectiveness and efficiency according to simulations results.

The remainder of the paper is organized as follows. The related works on the subject of power control are briefly surveyed in Section 2. In Section 3, the motivation of this paper is explained by an example. We describe the system model and formulate the power control problem in multi-rate WMN in Section 4. And Section 5 specifies POCOSIM in detail. Experiment results are presented in Section 6, and final conclusion as well as future works is provided in Section 7.

2 Related Works

In wireless networks, transmission power control (TPC) can save the energy of the wireless equipments and improve the capacity of the networks. Thus, efficient power control technology is highly valuable for the enhancement of the network performance. At present, abundant works on TPC have been proposed which mainly aimed at the environment of WSN [3][7], MANET [9][8] or WLAN [12]. As a research direction, joint link power control and scheduling in multi-hop wireless networks has been paid growing attention [4]. However, the goal of original solutions was to decrease and balance the power consumption of the whole network and to reduce interference among wireless nodes. Therefore, the nodes tended to select the minimal transmission power which met the requirement of connectivity. This strategy could increase the spatial reuse of channels as well as the throughput of network to some extent.

Recently, with the rapid spread of wireless networks and continued growth of performance requirements, utilizing TPC to guarantee QoS has become a notable research direction [5][15]. Literature [15] pointed out that the optimal transmission power traditional techniques selected was fixed; however, in order to satisfy various bandwidth requirements of different nodes, the optimal power should switch agilely under diverse collision patterns. A novel power selection scheme joint with random access was proposed in [15]. The scheme computed the probability of random access of every power allocation pattern after modeling the system into Markov chain and could improve the throughput effectively. [14] proposed a joint scheduling and power control schemes to increase the throughput performance and consider the trade-off between throughput and fairness. It defined the demand satisfaction factor (DSF) to characterize the fairness and the maximum throughput, and presented the SLPR heuristic to solve the problem. However, it didn't take multi-rate technology into account. Thus, its effectiveness would be limited in multi-rate context.

Furthermore, development of modulation and coding techniques as well as popularization of network equipments with multi-rate support makes the study of TPC under multi-rate condition become a new trend [2][11][16]. In IEEE 802.11 WLAN, the optimization is mainly applied to the single-hop communication between APs and stations. Literature [2] put forth two kinds of adaptive algorithms for adjusting power and bit-rate based on link state with the purposes of maximizing throughput and minimizing energy consumption respectively. The link quality, which was measured by the reception or non-reception of the ACK frames, determined the selected power and bit-rate. The method could raise throughput and save energy effectively. But when the number of nodes in the coverage area of an AP was relatively large, the collision caused by hidden terminals would be more severe and the performance would suffer obvious decline. K. Ramachandran et al. proposed Symphony [11], a greedy approach for the IEEE 802.11 WLAN with restricted power and high node density. To minimize the transmission power at the highest transmission bit-rate, the node decided its bit-rate and power after three steps: initialization, REF and OPT. Owing to its greediness, each node only focused on the maximization of its own throughput and overlooked the impact on other concurrent transmissions. Thus, it likely could not achieve the throughput optimization of the overall network. TPC under multi-rate condition represented for MANET are also limited. X. Zhang et al. [16] modeled the overall throughput of the network, analyzed the relation between power and throughput and obtained the relation graph from theoretical and simulation results. The graph showed that the optimum transmission power existed, which could make the network achieve the maximum throughput. However, [16] assumed the powers of every node are equal and did not give a further discussion about how to compute the optimum power. For the multi-hop wireless networks that the nodes distribute unevenly, the power of every node should be adjust respectively to benefit the whole network.

Traditional TPC techniques are not suitable for WMN due to its unique characteristics. To the best of our knowledge, there have been few throughput-and-fairness-oriented transmission power control and scheduling schemes proposed for the multi-rate WMN so far. We represent such a scheme based on the characteristics of the WMN intending to improve its performance.

3 Motivation Example

To illustrate how power control affects the throughput and fairness of the WMN, we take a WMN with quite simple topology for example.

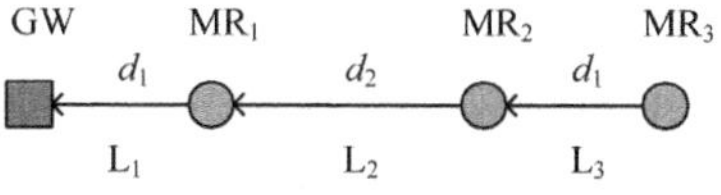

Fig. 1. An example scenario

Consider the scenario in Fig. 1. Three MRs form a chain-like 3-hop backbone and all the data are aggregated to GW. L_1 to L_3 are the links between each adjacent-node pair. The distance between MR_1 and GW, which is d_1, equals to which between MR_2 and MR_3. And the distance between MR_1 and MR_2, say d_2, is longer than d_1. Every MR has two power levels, denoted by p_1 and p_2 respectively. Without loss of generality, let p_1 be the lower one of the two, viz. $p_1 < p_2$. If MR_1 transmit data packets to GW using the power p_1, the bit-rate of the link L_1 will be r_1. Assume MR_2 does not be interfered with when MR_1 transmits at this power level. Consequently, at this time MR_3 can transmit packets to MR_2 concurrently at the power level of p_1 too. If MR_1 chooses to use the higher power level, p_2, the bit-rate of the link L_1 can be upgraded to r_2, a higher level. But now MR_2 will be within the interference range of MR_1, which causes MR_3 must keep silence and no concurrent transmission will happen. As the nearest MR to GW, MR_1 has the most data to transmit to GW, including the packets sent by the stations being associated with itself and the packets from the downstream MRs. Hence, the bit-rate of the link L_1 should be as high as possible. However, if MR_1 always choose the highest power level to transmit data, MR_3 will probably suffer starvation. In order to keep balance between throughput and fairness, the WMN should switch between the above two states.

Therefore, the WMN needs to control and schedule the power of each MR to give attention to both throughput and fairness.

4 System Model

4.1 WMN Architecture

We consider an area where a group of MRs compose a wireless mesh network. Each MR is equipped with two radio modules; one is used to connect to other

MRs to form the backbone and the other one acts as the access point to serve the stations. To maintain the connectivity of the network, the radios composing the backbone are configured to operate on the same channel. Hence, only the power control in the backbone is considered.

The MRs themselves do not generate data packets. All the data packets in the WMN are originated from stations and relayed by the MRs to route to the GW. Besides the packets from its own subnet, the MR also has to forward the data packets from its downstream MRs. The throughput of an MR can be divided into two parts: the local throughput and the foreign throughput. The local throughput means the throughput from the local subnet while the foreign throughput is the throughput from downstream MRs. Evidently, the nearer the MR is from the GW, the more bandwidth it needs. It is assumed that every MR always has data to transmit and its memory space is large enough to buffer the packets when the channel is busy. The throughput of the networks is defined to be the sum of the throughput of every link in the WMN. And the fairness is measured by the gap between the maximum and the minimum local throughput among all the links.

In this paper, we give examples and evaluate the performance using the WMN with chain-like topology as shown in Fig. 1. But our scheme can be applied to any topologies because the power control and scheduling scheme is topology-independent. The simplest situation is taken only for easy understanding.

4.2 Bit-Rates of Wireless Links

Besides power control, bit-rate control is another important issue in wireless networking and many approaches have been proposed to adapt the bit-rate with variable channel conditions. For simplicity, we assume the channel state is always stable and utilize the SNR-based bit-rate control method to choose bit-rates for wireless links. That is, the bit-rate R of the wireless link can be formulated in a subsection function with SNR as independent variable:

$$R = f(SNR) = \begin{cases} 0 & SNR < s_1 \\ r_1 & s_1 \leq SNR < s_2 \\ \vdots & \\ r_n & SNR \geq s_n \end{cases} \quad (1)$$

SNR depends on the power of the transmitter, the path loss and the accumulated noise at the receiver. To reduce the complexity of the problem, we ignore the accumulated effect of the noise and define the interference range as the transmission range of the least bit-rate (e.g. 6Mbps in IEEE 802.11a or 1Mbps in IEEE 802.11b). Actually, our scheme can fit any bit-rate control algorithm.

4.3 Conflict Graph

Before describing conflict graph, we first introduce the concept of traffic pattern. A traffic pattern is a combination of several transmission links which can be activated concurrently with specific transmission power. And in a network, there are a number of traffic patterns which are mutually different. In this section, we use conflict graph to analyze the network and find out all traffic patterns of it.

The interference relationship among the links in WMN can be abstracted into a conflict graph. In the conflict graph, a vertex represents a link with a specific bit-rate in the real network. If Link L_i in the WMN has j optional bit-rate, from r_1 to r_j, there are j corresponding vertices in the conflict graph, denoted by v_{i1} to v_{ij}. If two links with certain optional rates cannot transmit data concurrently, an edge will be added between the two vertices which indicate the interferential links with these rates. The conflict graph of the WMN in Fig. 1 is shown in Fig. 2.

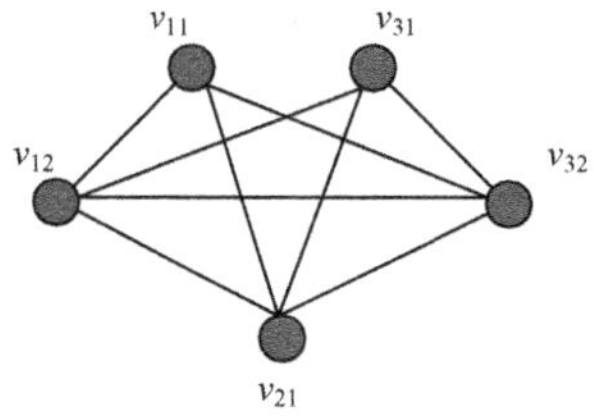

Fig. 2. The conflict graph of the example scenario

To find out all the traffic patterns, the independent sets in the conflict graph should be found out to make sure every vertex at least is included in one independent set. The independent sets indicate the possible traffic patterns. For instance, in Fig. 2, following independent sets are identified: $\{v_{11}, v_{31}\}$, $\{v_{12}\}$, $\{v_{21}\}$, $\{v_{32}\}$. The set of $\{v_{11}, v_{31}\}$ means the link L_1 and L_3 can transmit concurrently both using the bit-rate of r_1. And $\{v_{12}\}$ implies that, when L_1 raise its power to achieve the bit-rate of r_2, no concurrent transmission will happen.

Every independent set can be denoted by an $N \times 1$ vector $\boldsymbol{R}^{(m)} = [r_1^{(m)}, r_2^{(m)}, \cdots, r_N^{(m)}]$. The vector represents a traffic pattern which points out the bit-rate of every link. Consider the above example again. The set of $\{v_{11}, v_{31}\}$ can be converted to the vector of $[r_1, 0, r_1]$, and the corresponding vector of $\{v_{12}\}$ is $[r_2, 0, 0]$.

According to the relationship between the power and bit-rate, the vectors of bit-rates can be transformed to $N \times 1$ vectors of transmission powers $\boldsymbol{P} = [P_1, P_2, \cdots, P_N]$. For example, the corresponding power vector of $[r_1, 0, r_1]$ is $[p_1, 0, p_1]$ and which of $[r_2, 0, 0]$ is $[p_2, 0, 0]$.

4.4 Problem Formulation

Suppose there are M traffic patterns of the WMN, the power control and scheduling scheme is used to choose the suitable patterns and assign transmission time for them. Thus, the output of the scheme should be an $M \times 1$ time allocation vector $\boldsymbol{T} = [t^{(1)}, t^{(2)}, \cdots, t^{(M)}]$ which record the active time of each traffic pattern, e.g. the active time of the traffic pattern $\boldsymbol{R}^{(m)}$ is $t^{(m)}$. The time $t^{(m)}$ represents the proportion of the unit time, so that the following equation holds:

$$\sum_{m=1}^{M} t^{(m)} = 1 \tag{2}$$

For a traffic pattern denoted by $\boldsymbol{R}^{(m)}$, the throughput during its active time can be computed by:

$$TH^{(m)} = \sum_{i=1}^{N} t^{(m)} r_i^{(m)} \tag{3}$$

And the throughput of the whole WMN in unit time is:

$$TH = \sum_{m=1}^{M} TH^{(m)} \tag{4}$$

To facilitate the discussion, we index the MRs and the links with the hop counts to the GW. The fairness is defined to be the difference between the maximum local throughput and the minimum local throughput among all the MRs:

$$FAI = \max|_{i=1}^{N}(THL_i) - \min|_{i=1}^{N}(THL_i) \tag{5}$$

where THL_i denotes the local throughput of the i-th MR. The local throughput THL_i can be obtained by:

$$THL_i = \begin{cases} TH_i - TH_{i+1} & i < N \\ TH_i & i = N \end{cases} \tag{6}$$

where TH_i denotes the throughput of the link L_i:

$$TH_i = \sum_{m=1}^{M} t^{(m)} r_i^{(m)} \tag{7}$$

$$TH_{i+1} \leq TH_i \tag{8}$$

Finally, the optimization can be formulated into multi-object programming with constrains:

$$\max \; TH \tag{9}$$
$$\min \; FAI \tag{10}$$
$$s.t. \; THL_i \geq 0 \qquad i = 1, 2, \cdots, N \tag{11}$$
$$\sum_{m=1}^{M} t^{(m)} = 1 \tag{12}$$

5 POCOSIM

5.1 Overview

POCOSIM is implemented on both GW and MRs as shown in Fig. 3. At the GW side, there are three modules: information collecting module, DE algorithm module and information promulgate module. Two other modules exist at the MR side which are information exchange module and wireless radio configuration module. The flow of POCOSIM is described as follows:

Step 1. The information exchange module of each MR collects the link information including the power and rate levels it can use, and sends it to GW.

Step 2. The information collecting module of GW collects the link information from each MR. According to the information it obtain, GW builds up the conflict graph and find out all the independent sets.

Step 3. In the DE algorithm module, the independent sets are viewed as traffic patterns. The object of this algorithm is to calculate the optimal time allocation vector to regulate the active time of each traffic pattern.

Step 4. The information promulgate module of GW informs the MRs how (the power) and when (the time) to transmit their data packets.

Step 5. After receiving the instruction, the MRs set their transmission parameters and transmit data in the timeslot assigned to each.

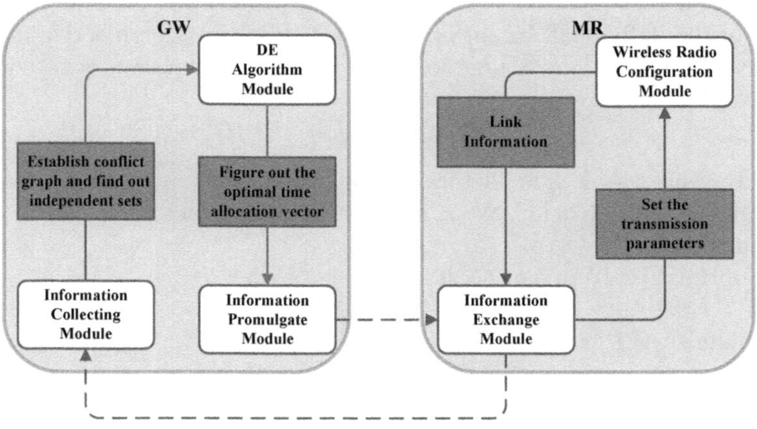

Fig. 3. The flow of POCOSIM

5.2 Differential Evolution Based Algorithm

Differential evolution (DE) is a parallel direct search method which is characterized as self-organizational, self-adaptive and parallelizable. The main idea of DE is described as follows: Firstly, DE chooses three different individuals for each one in current ES-community to generate a new one; Secondly, crossover the new and the original individual to attain a trial individual; Finally, evaluate the cost of the trial and the original individual respectively, and keep the lower one to evolve on [13]. We develop a DE-based algorithm which is the core of POCOSIM.

DE-Based Power Control and Scheduling Scheme. To leverage DE algorithm, the concepts in power control and scheduling problem need to be match the terms in DE.

Individual chromosome: We define the time allocation vector $\boldsymbol{T} = [t^{(1)}, t^{(2)}, \cdots, t^{(M)}]$ as an M-dimensional chromosome. The genes of the chromosome are the allocated time of each traffic pattern. Fig. 4 demonstrates the format of the chromosome.

$t^{(1)}$	$t^{(2)}$	$t^{(3)}$	...	$t^{(M-1)}$	$t^{(M)}$

Fig. 4. The format of the chromosome

Different time allocation decisions are mapped to different chromosomes. Evolution community is comprised of several chromosomes.

Individual evaluating objective function: The objective function, which is also can be called cost-function in a minimization problem, is used to evaluate the quality of the individual. In our optimization problem, the objective function is make up of the throughput function and the fairness function, denoted as:

$$f(\boldsymbol{T}) = \alpha \cdot FAI - \beta \cdot TH \tag{13}$$

where α, β are the weight factors of the throughput and the fairness respectively, and $\alpha + \beta = 1$ holds. We can adjust these two factors to satisfy different requirements.

The optimal problem can be described as follows:
Find $\boldsymbol{T} = [t^{(1)}, t^{(2)}, \cdots, t^{(M)}]$,
to minimize $f(\boldsymbol{T}) = \alpha \cdot FAI - \beta \cdot TH$,
subject to constrains $g_j(\boldsymbol{T}) \leq 0$, $j = 1, 2, \cdots, N$, where

$$g_j(\boldsymbol{T}) = \begin{cases} TH_{j+1} - TH_j & if\ j < N \\ -TH_N & otherwise \end{cases}$$

And subject to boundary constrains $\mathbf{0} \leq \boldsymbol{T} \leq \mathbf{1}$, where $\sum_{m=1}^{M} t^{(m)} = 1$.

Boundary constrains: According to [6], in order to ensure $t^{(m)}$ in every generation lies inside the range $[0, 1]$ and $\sum_{m=1}^{M} t^{(m)} = 1$, the parameter values which are outside the initialized range are replaced by random values generated within the feasible range.

$$t^{(m)'} = \begin{cases} random(0,1) & if\ t^{(m)} < 0\ or\ t^{(m)} > 1 \\ t^{(m)} & otherwise \end{cases} \tag{14}$$

$$t^{(m)''} = \frac{t^{(m)'}}{\sum_{m=1}^{M} t^{(m)'}} \tag{15}$$

Constraint functions:

A soft-constraint (penalty) approach is applied for handling the constraint functions [6]. The cost function is formulated as follows:

$$f_{cost}(\boldsymbol{T}) = (f(\boldsymbol{T}) + a) \prod_{j=1}^{J} c_j^{b_j} \tag{16}$$

where

$$c_j = \begin{cases} 1.0 + s_j g_j(\boldsymbol{T}) & if\ g_j(\boldsymbol{T}) > 0 \\ 1 & otherwise \end{cases} \tag{17}$$

$$s_j \geq 1 \tag{18}$$

$$b_j \geq 1 \tag{19}$$

$$\min f(\boldsymbol{T}) + a > 0 \tag{20}$$

According to [6], setting $s_j = 1$ and $b_j = 1$ works satisfactorily.

Termination conditions: When an optimal result has kept the lowest value of the cost-function for a predetermined amount of generations, the algorithm will be terminated.

Steps of solving the problem. According to the DE algorithm and above concept mappings, the flow of the solution can be divided into following five steps:

Initialization: In this step, setting the parameters which are used to the evolution. H denotes the population size of the evolution community, namely, the amount of the individuals in the community. In this paper, an individual is a time allocation scheme. Crossover probability P_c denotes the probability of the perturbation among the individuals. In order to converge quickly, we set $P_c = 0.9$, and set the crossover factor $F = 0.6$. The amount of the evolve generations is denoted as g. lb and ub denote the lower bound and upper bound of the time, which are set to 0 and 1 respectively. The vector $\boldsymbol{T(g)} = [\boldsymbol{T_1(g)}, \boldsymbol{T_2(g)}, \cdots, \boldsymbol{T_H(g)}]$, where $\boldsymbol{T_h(g)} = [t_h^{(1)}(g), t_h^{(2)}(g), \cdots, t_h^{(M)}(g)]$, and $t_h^{(m)}(g)$ denotes the time allocation of the m-th mode of the h-th individual in the g-th ES-community generation. The vector $\boldsymbol{T(0)} = [\boldsymbol{T_1(0)}, \boldsymbol{T_2(0)}, \cdots, \boldsymbol{T_H(0)}]$ denotes the initial stochastic evolution community.

Individual evaluation: In this step, formulate the value of the objective function $f_{cost}(\boldsymbol{T_h(g)})$ to evaluate the quality of $\boldsymbol{T_h(g)}$.

Mutation: For each individual $\boldsymbol{T_h(g)}$ in the community, generate a mutant vector according to

$$\boldsymbol{V_h'(g+1)} = \boldsymbol{T_{r_1}(g)} + F(\boldsymbol{T_{r_2}(g)} - \boldsymbol{T_{r_3}(g)}) \tag{21}$$

with random parameters, r_1, r_2, $r_3 \in \{1, 2, 3, \cdots, M\}$, mutually different. $\boldsymbol{V_h'(g+1)}$ is the mutant vector and $\boldsymbol{V_h'(g+1)} = [v_h^{(1)'}(g+1), v_h^{(2)'}(g+1), \cdots,$ $v_h^{(M)'}(g+1)]$. Through this mutant vector, attain the trial vector according to

$$t_h^{(m)'}(g+1) = \begin{cases} v_h^{(m)'}(g+1) & if\ (rand(m) \le P_c)\ or\ m = rnbr(h) \\ t_h^{(m)}(g) & if\ (rand(m) > P_c)\ and\ m \ne rnbr(h) \end{cases} \tag{22}$$

In Equation(22), $rand(m)$ is a random number for the m-th element of the vector to decide whether to be replaced by the mutant element or not, and $rand(m) \in (0, 1)$. $rnrb(h)$ is a randomly chosen index which guarantees that trial vector gets one element from the mutant vector $\boldsymbol{V_h'(g+1)}$.

Because of the constraint $\sum_{m=1}^{M} t^{(m)} = 1$, we introduce

$$t_h^{(m)''}(g+1) = \frac{t_h^{(m)'}(g+1)}{\sum_{m=1}^{M} t_h^{(m)'}(g+1)} \tag{23}$$

Finally, the trial vector $\boldsymbol{T_h''(g+1)}$ of M dimensions is composed of $t_h^{(m)''}(g+1)$, $(m = 1, 2, 3, \cdots, M)$.

Selection: Formulate the cost-function of the trial vector, to decide whether or not it should substitute the original one. It is described as follows:

$$\boldsymbol{T_h(g+1)} = \begin{cases} \boldsymbol{T_h''(g+1)} & if\ f_{cost}(\boldsymbol{T_h''(g+1)}) < f_{cost}(\boldsymbol{T_h(g)}) \\ \boldsymbol{T_h(g)} & otherwise \end{cases} \tag{24}$$

Termination: When the best solution of the community has kept unchanged for predefined generations, terminate the process and output the result as the optimal solution. Otherwise, turn to the step of *Individual evaluation* to move on.

6 Performance Evaluation

6.1 Simulation Setup

We have conducted simulations to demonstrate that POCOSIM can improve the throughput and the fairness of the WMN. To simplify the problem, we take two different rate levels: 12Mbps and 18Mbps and two different power levels: 20dbm and 13dBm. The clear-channel-assessment (CCA) sensitivity is set to -82dBm.

We use $P_r = P_t - L_p$, where $L_p = 46 + 10\log r^3$ as the path loss model. We assume the load of the network is high, and after emitting a packet the MR immediately has a next packet to transmit. In the simulation, several MRs (from 3 to 7) form the chain-like topology of the backbone. The MRs are immobile and the routing paths are predetermined. The distances between every adjacent MRs pair are all equal to 30m.

6.2 Simulation Results

We compare the performance of POCOSIM with the optimal fixed-rate scheme in terms of total throughput of the whole WMN. Two situations of each scheme are considered, which are throughput-oriented and fairness-oriented respectively. In throughput-oriented case, the fairness among the MRs is not taken into account. To maximize the global throughput, some MRs may suffer starvation. In fairness-oriented case, the local throughput differences among MRs are minimized at the expense of global throughput degradation. Fig. 5 shows the result of the four strategies. The throughputs are equal when the amount of MRs is 3. In this case, no concurrent transmissions happen, even though each MR uses its lowest power level to transmit data. However, with the increase of the MRs, more concurrent transmissions are active and advantages of POCOSIM are increasingly obvious.

When making a trade-off between throughput and fairness through setting the weight factor $\alpha = \beta = 0.5$, the throughputs of WMN under POCOSIM and fixed-power scheme are compared in Fig. 6. It shows that the gap of throughput performance between them is larger and larger as the number of MRs increasing.

The impact of the weight factor of throughput and fairness is also studied, which are shown in Fig. 7 and Fig. 8. β denotes the weight of the global throughput.

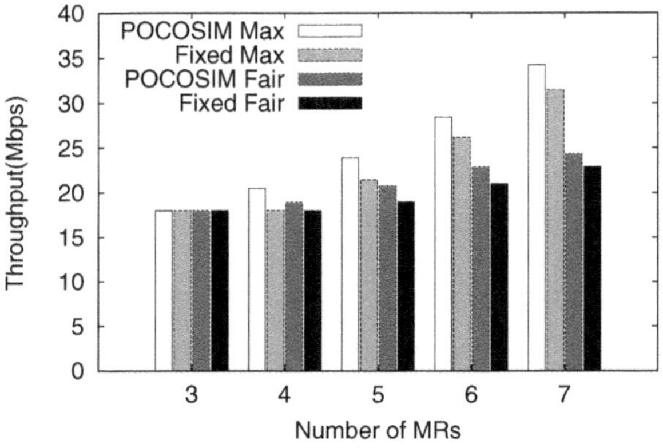

Fig. 5. The throughputs of four strategies

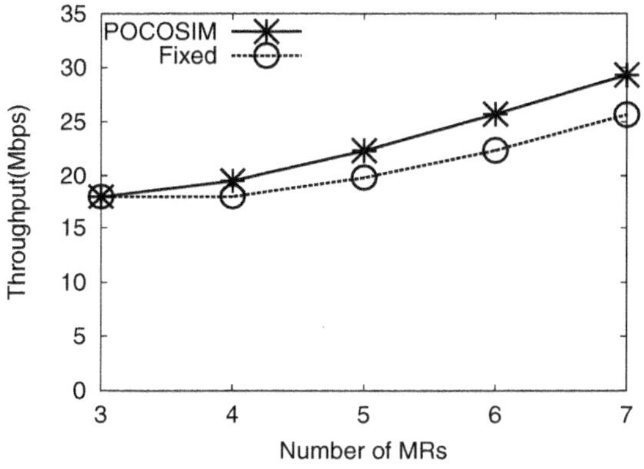

Fig. 6. Through comparison in trade-off mode

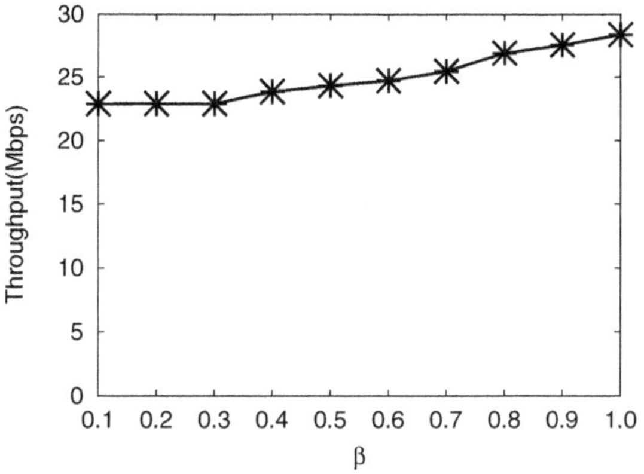

Fig. 7. The relationship between throughput and weight factor β

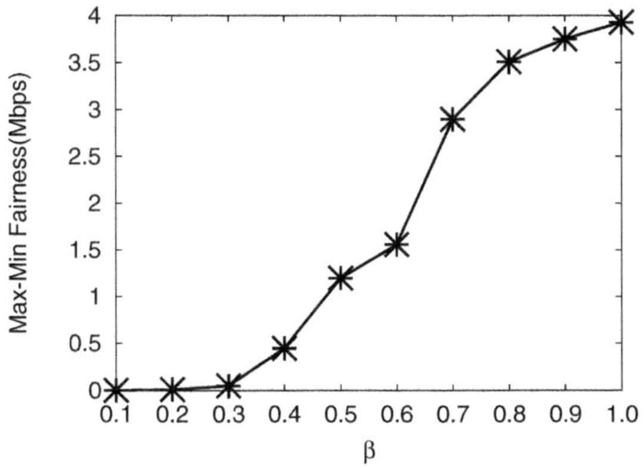

Fig. 8. The relationship between the fairness and weight factor β

Based on the observations from the simulation results, we summarize POCOSIM as follows:

When the number of MRs is large enough to permit concurrent transmissions being activated, POCOSIM can achieve up to 10% higher throughput than the fixed-power scheme. The larger β is, the higher global throughput can be achieved but the weaker the fairness among MRs is. The value of α and β can be adjusted to certain scenes according to their extra requirements.

The above results illustrate that, by controlling and scheduling the transmission power of the MRs, POCOSIM outperforms the fixed-power scheme in throughput and the fairness of the WMN. Therefore, the effectiveness of POCOSIM is proven.

7 Conclusion

Transmission power control is of vital importance in wireless networking. Based on the consideration of improving the throughput and fairness of multi-rate WMN, a POwer COntrol and Scheduling scheme In Multi-rate wireless mesh networks (POCOSIM) is introduced in this paper. Conflict graph is used to model the system, thereby transferring the problem into a multi-object programming one. A DE-based algorithm is presented to solve this problem and the effectiveness of POCOSIM is shown by simulations results. POCOSIM works in a centralized manner. Future attention will mainly focus on developing a distributed algorithm to make MRs select power self-adaptively in the dynamic environment.

Acknowledgment

The work is partially supported by grant No. 09ZZ4034 from the Hunan Provincial Natural Science Foundation of China.

References

1. Akyildiz, I., Wang, X., Wang, W.: Wireless mesh networks: a survey. Computer Networks 47(4), 445–487 (2005)
2. Chevillat, P., Jelitto, J., Truong, H.: Dynamic data rate and transmit power adjustment in IEEE 802.11 wireless LANs. International Journal of Wireless Information Networks 12(3), 123–145 (2005)
3. Correia, L., Macedo, D., dos Santos, A., Loureiro, A., Nogueira, J.: Transmission power control techniques for wireless sensor networks. Computer Networks 51(17), 4765–4779 (2007)
4. ElBatt, T., Ephremides, A.: Joint scheduling and power control for wireless ad hoc networks. IEEE Transactions on Wireless Communications 3(1), 74–85 (2004)
5. Kulkarni, G., Raghunathan, V., Srivastava, M.: Joint end-to-end scheduling, power control and rate control in multi-hop wireless networks. In: IEEE Global Telecommunications Conference, GLOBECOM 2004, vol. 5 (2004)
6. Lampinen, J., Zelinka, I.: Mixed integer-discrete-continuous optimization by differential evolution. In: Proceedings of the 5th International Conference on Soft Computing, pp. 71–76. Citeseer (1999)
7. Lin, S., Zhang, J., Zhou, G., Gu, L., Stankovic, J., He, T.: ATPC: adaptive transmission power control for wireless sensor networks. In: Proceedings of the 4th International Conference on Embedded Networked Sensor Systems, p. 236. ACM, New York (2006)
8. Monks, J., Bharghavan, V., Hwu, W.: A power controlled multiple access protocol for wireless packetnetworks. In: Proceedings of Twentieth Annual Joint Conference of the IEEE Computer and Communications Societies, IEEE INFOCOM 2001, vol. 1 (2001)
9. Muqattash, A., Krunz, M.: Power controlled dual channel (PCDC) medium access protocol for wireless ad hoc networks. In: Twenty-Second Annual Joint Conference of the IEEE Computer and Communications Societies, IEEE INFOCOM 2003, vol. 1 (2003)
10. Gupta, P., Kumar, P.R.: Thecapacity of wireless networks. IEEE Transaction 46, 388–404 (2000)
11. Ramachandran, K., Kokku, R., Zhang, H., Gruteser, M.: Symphony: synchronous two-phase rate and power control in 802.11 wlans. In: Proceeding of the 6th International Conference on Mobile Systems, Applications, and Services, pp. 132–145. ACM, New York (2008)
12. Rasti, M., Sharafat, A., Seyfe, B.: Pareto-efficient and goal-driven power control in wireless networks: a game-theoretic approach with a novel pricing scheme. IEEE/ACM Transactions on Networking (TON) 17(2), 556–569 (2009)
13. Storn, R., Price, K.: Differential evolution–a simple and efficient heuristic for global optimization over continuous spaces. Journal of global optimization 11(4), 341–359 (1997)
14. Tang, J., Xue, G., Chandler, C., Zhang, W.: Link scheduling with power control for throughput enhancement in multihop wireless networks. IEEE Transactions on Vehicular Technology 55(3), 733–742 (2006)
15. Yan, G., Zheng, Z., Kumar, P.R.: Joint random access and power selection for maximal throughput in wireless networks. In:Twenty-ninth Annual Conference on Computer Communications, IEEE INFOCOM 2010 (2010)
16. Zhang, X., Gao, Q., Zhang, J., Wang, G.: Impact of transmit power on throughput performance in wireless ad hoc networks with variable rate control. Computer Communications 31(15), 3638–3642 (2008)

Modeling Contacts and Mobility for Wireless Mobile Networks

Ye Tian[1] and Jiang Li[2]

[1] Anhui Province Key Laboratory of High Performance Computing and Application, School of Computer Science and Technology, University of Science and Technology of China, Hefei, Anhui 230026, China
yetian@ustc.edu.cn
[2] Department of Systems and Computer Science, Howard University, Washington DC 20059, USA
jli@scs.howard.edu

Abstract. The inter-contact time between mobile human-carried devices is one of the key metrics in studying the mobility-assisted routing paradigms for wireless mobile networks. Recent studies on this topic are focused on the aggregated distribution integrating all the device pairs' inter-contact times. In this work, we study real-world inter-contact times from a new aspect. By dividing the device pairs in groups and by investigating the group-wise inter-contact time distribution, we find that for the frequently contacting pairs, there are three segments on the distribution curve. We use superposition of three stochastic contact processes caused by the devices' independent movements and human intentions to explain the segments. Furthermore, we propose a mobility model, where each node uses a priority queue to schedule its movement, to emulate real-world human mobility. Theoretical analysis shows that the priority queue results in a power-law inter-contact time and we also demonstrate that our model seamlessly integrates the three contact processes. Finally, simulation study testifies that our mobility model could reproduce the contacts with their inter-contact times resembling the empirical ones, therefore is accurate in characterizing the complexity of the device contacts in wireless mobile networks.

Keywords: Inter-contact times, mobility model, wireless mobile networks.

1 Introduction

In recent years, an infrastructure-free wireless mobile network composed of human-carried mobile devices such as cell phones and PDAs has been proposed (e.g. [1] [2] [3] [4]). In such a network, as the topology is not always connected, a mobility-assisted routing paradigm (e.g. [2] [3]) is applied, where a node receiving the data which is not destinated to itself holds the data, until it encounters the destination node or another node considered as the next hop for data delivery. Clearly in such

Z. Yu et al. (Eds.): UIC 2010, LNCS 6406, pp. 489–503, 2010.

a routing scheme, contacts between the devices are the only opportunity for communication, so the interval between consecutive contacts of a device pair, which is referred to as the *inter-contact time*, is essential.

In this paper, we investigate the inter-contact times obtained from a number of real-world datasets. Unlike previous studies, we group the device pairs according to their contacting frequencies and analyze the *group-wise inter-contact time distribution*. We find that for a frequently contacting group, there are three segments on its distribution curve, which is different from the previous observations [5] [6]. Based on well-known results of human dynamics, we use *superposition* of three stochastic contact processes caused by devices' random movements and intentions of the humans carrying the devices to explain the observation.

We further present a mobility model for human-carried devices in wireless mobile network. In our model, each node uses a *priority queue* to schedule its movement. Theoretical analysis shows that power-law inter-contact times are resulted, and the model has integrated the three contact processes seamlessly. From simulation we find that the model generates contacts with their inter-contact times of the same characteristics as the ones empirically observed. As the model exhibits the same characteristics as the ones observed from real world, it is very suitable to be applied in emulating and evaluating realistic wireless mobile networks composed of human-carried devices.

The remainder part of this paper is organized as the follows: Section 2 surveys the related work; We analyze the group-wise inter-contact time distribution in Section 3; In Section 4, the three stochastic contact processes are proposed, and we explain the empirical inter-contact time distribution with superposition of the three processes; We present the mobility model in Section 5, and analyze and examine the inter-contact times produced by our model in this section; Finally, Section 6 concludes this paper.

2 Related Work

In recent years, contact patterns of human-carried devices, in particular, the inter-contact times, are widely studied. By investigating a number of real-world datasets, Chaintreau et. al. find that the inter-contact time distributions aggregating all the device pairs are power-law, with the exponents smaller than one [5]. Recently, Karagiannis et. al. observe that a dichotomy exists on the complementary cumulative distribution function (CCDF) curves of the device pairs' aggregated inter-contact times [6]. Yoneki et. al. find that the inter-meeting times among meeting groups do not follow a power-law distribution [7]. A number of mobility models are proposed to interpret these observations. For example, Karagiannis et. al prove that for a random walk (RW) on a circuit, the distribution of two nodes' inter-meeting time scales as $n^{-1/2}$, when the inter-meeting time n is sufficiently large, and there is an exponential tail [6]. Cai et. al. derive a similar result using more general random mobility models of random waypoint model (RWP) or RW on a two-dimensional area with finite boundary, and point out that the finite boundary is responsible for the exponential tail [8]. While some other general-purpose mobility models, such as the time-variant community mobility [9] and the levy walk model [10], also stick to the observations from the aggregated inter-contact times in [5] and [6]. On the other hand, although Conan et. al. address the heterogeneity in inter-contact times by studying contacts from single pairs of devices [11], however, the raw nature of pairwise contact data prohibits people to find more insights regarding device's contact pattern.

Meanwhile, it is every interesting to note that besides the inter-contact time, many recent studies [12] [13] [14] [15] reveal that in human activities, the inter-event time is power-law. Barabasi et. al. studies the time intervals between sending emails by a group of users, and reports that the distribution of the inter-email times by one user is power-law, of which the cumulative distribution function (CDF) could be modeled as $F(\tau) \sim \tau^{-2}$ [12]. In [13], [14], and [15], the intervals between human activities of visiting web sites, responding surface mails, and initializing finance transactions are examined, and it is observed that in these activities, the inter-event time distributions are all power-law, with a CDF as $F(\tau) \sim \tau^{-\alpha}$, where $\alpha \geq 2$.

3 Studying Group-Wise Inter-contact Time

We obtain and study the inter-contact times for pairs of devices in three real-world datasets, denoted as Reality [16], Dartmouth [17], and UCSD [18]. Unlike previous studies, in this work, we sort all the device pairs of a dataset in an ascending order based on their mean inter-contact times, and group the pairs in each ten percentiles. For example, by denoting the percentile group of "10-20", we mean the pairs with their mean inter-contact times between the first ten and the first twenty percents in this order.

We plot the aggregated inter-contact time distribution in CCDF for each percentile groups in $0-50\%$ of the three datasets, as pairs in these groups contribute majority of the contacts. We also plot the distributions aggregating all the inter-contact times in the datasets for comparison. From the figures one can see that the distributions cannot be simply considered as exponential or power-law, suggesting the complexity in devices' contacting behaviors. Moreover, one can see that except for the "0-10" group in Dartmouth, all the other distribution

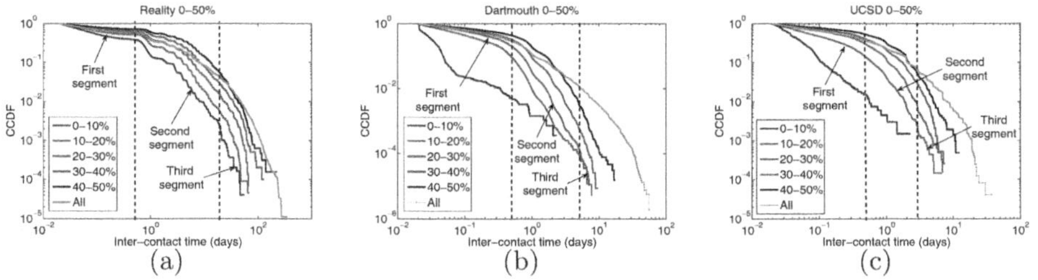

Fig. 1. Inter-contact time distribution of percentile groups in $0-50\%$ for (a) Reality, (b) Dartmouth, (c) UCSD

curves of a same dataset closely resemble each other, suggesting that the device pairs in these groups were following similar patterns in making contacts.

To further investigate the frequently contacting device pairs, we focus on the percentile group with most contacts in each dataset, that is, the "0-10" group in Reality, the "20-30" group in Dartmouth, and the "10-20" group in UCSD. By carefully examining the figures, one can see that the distribution curve could be divided into three segments, as labeled in Fig. 1(a-c). The first segment's inter-contact time is from 0 to a certain characteristic time, and the segment is almost a straight line with a slope rate less than one. The second segment's range is from the first characteristic time to another characteristic time, and the segment is also power-law, but its slope rate is no less than two, as demonstrated in the figure. The third segment is the rest of the distribution curve with inter-contact times larger than the second characteristic time. If the distributions were plotted under linear-log scale, one can see that the segments are straight lines, making them as exponential tails.

For less frequently contacting groups in $50-100\%$, we also study their inter-contact times, and find that their inter-contact times are exponentially distributed. We do not show the results here for space reason.

4 Interpreting the Inter-contact Time Distribution

4.1 Source of the Contacts

To interpret the inter-contact time distributions observed from real-world datasets, we first discuss the causes of the device contacts. Generally, the contacts between human-carried devices are the result of human movement. Simplified random mobility models such as random waypoint model (RWP) or random walk (RW) are usually used to model human movement. Studies [19] [20] prove that under these mobility models, the inter-meeting times are exponentially distributed. And people also use these simple random mobility models to explain power-law inter-contact times, as in [6] and [8]. However, we believe that these simple random mobility models are not sufficient to explain our observation in Section 3, because of the following reasons. First of all, [6] and [8] suggest that the power-law inter-contacts appear only when the inter-contact time is sufficiently large (Theorem 2 in [6] and Theorem 4 in [8]). However, from Fig. 1, one can see that the first power-law curve segment appears when the inter-contact time is less than half a day, which apparently is not very large. Moreover, [6] and [8] cannot explain the second power-law segment, which has a slope rate no less than two.

Meanwhile, recent studies show that in many human activities, the inter-event time is power-law, of which the distribution function can be modeled as $F(\tau) \sim \tau^{-\alpha}$, with $\alpha \geq 2$. These activities include sending emails [12], visiting websites [13], responding surface mails [14], and initializing finance transactions [15]. Clearly, these findings strongly suggest that power-law inter-event time distribution with a slope rate larger than two is an universal principle in many human activities including human contacts. However, we must note that human contacting is a little different from other human activities such as sending emails and visiting websites, as in these activities, events are purely intentional results, but the contacts between two human beings may be unintentional (although each one moves intentionally).

Motivated by the above discussion, we use two factors to interpret the contacts between two human-carried devices: 1) independent random movement of devices that result in exponential inter-contact times; and 2) the same principle causing power-law inter-event times in other human activities such as email sending and website visiting. We deem the contacts caused by the first factor *unintentional*, as they are a byproduct of the device's independent random movement. The contacts caused by the second factor are regarded as *intentional*. Unintentional contacts may be the result of random movement of devices within a large (or "global") area as well as of movement restricted within a small (or "local") area. Contacts due to the former type of movement are likely to have larger inter-contact times than those due to the latter. In addition, "local" movement usually leads to "bursty" contacts, while "global" movement is more likely to incur "scattered" contacts. For example, the entire campus of a university can be viewed as a global area, while a building or a lab of the university can be viewed as a local area. Any two students on the campus have chances to encounter each other, but the contacts are scattered as the two students are unlikely to meet often in such a large area. On the other hand, when the two students are in a same building of the campus, they are more likely to make frequent contacts, until any of them leaves the building. The contacts are bursty as the time that the two students stay in the building is limited, compared with the time they stay on the campus. They will have another sequence of bursty contacts when they are within a local area simultaneously again.

Formally, we define three stochastic contact processes in the following.

- The first contact process is caused by device's local independent random movement, and the contacts are bursty. When there are contacts, the inter-contact time distribution could be expressed as

$$F_1(t) = 1 - e^{-\lambda_l t}$$

  with $\lambda_l > 0$; as the contacts are in bursts, there exist long intervals without contacts between contact bursts. We refer to this process as *local contact process* (denoted as *LCP* for short).
- The second contact process is intentional. Similar to the inter-event time in other human activities, the inter-contact time is power-law. To make our analysis mathematically tractable, we use the shifted Pareto distribution to express the inter-contact time distribution as

$$F_2(t) = 1 - \left(1 + \frac{t}{t_m}\right)^{-\alpha}, \alpha \geq 2$$

  where $t_m > 0$ and $\alpha \geq 2$, and t_m is the smallest value t can take. As it is human's intention that causes the contacts, the process is refer to as the *intentional contact process* (denoted as *ICP* for short).

- The third contact process is caused by device's global independent random movement, and the inter-contact time distribution could be expressed as

$$F_3(t) = 1 - e^{-\lambda_g t}$$

with $\lambda_g > 0$. We refer to this process as the *global contact process* (denoted as *GCP* for short).

Given the three contact processes, we assume that LCP's mean inter-contact time, $1/\lambda_l$, is much smaller than that of the other two processes; while GCP's mean inter-contact time, $1/\lambda_g$, is much larger than that of the other two. For ICP, as its inter-contact time distribution is power-law, it has many very short inter-contact times as well as many inter-contact times that are very long. The underlying intuition of our assumption is that if two persons are in a small area simultaneously, they are more likely to encounter each other. In a large global area, unintentional contacts happen less frequently than intentional ones (especially those between people with certain relationship).

In the following subsections, we show that the three segments on the distribution curves observed in Section 3 could be explained by the superposition of the three stochastic contact processes aforementioned. By superposition, we mean that events from different source processes are undifferentiated. Strict definition can be found in [21].

4.2 Explaining the Knob between the Second and the Third Segments

We first explain the knob between the second the third segments on the inter-contact time distributions in Fig. 1. As the second characteristic time separating the two segments is from days to tens of days, which is sufficiently large, we ignore the first contact process which produces small inter-contact times in bursts, and focus on the second and the third contact processes. Assuming that the two processes are independent and renewal, with their inter-contact times following the distributions of $F_2(t)$ and $F_3(t)$ respectively, the inter-contact time distribution of the superposition process from ICP and GCP could be expressed as [21]

$$R_s(t) = \frac{\bar{v}_2 \bar{v}_3}{\bar{v}_2 + \bar{v}_3} (\psi_2(t) R_3(t) + \psi_3(t) R_2(t)) \tag{1}$$

where $R_i(t) = 1 - F_i(t)$, $\bar{v}_i$ is the mean contact rate, and $\psi_i(t) = \int_t^\infty R_i(u)du$, for $i = 2, 3$.

By applying Equ. (1), we can obtain expression of the inter-contact time distribution for the superposition process. Taking logarithm, we have

$$\log R_s(t) = \log\left(1 + \frac{\lambda_g t}{\lambda_g t_m + \alpha - 1}\right) - \lambda_g t_m \frac{t}{t_m} - \alpha \log\left(1 + \frac{t}{t_m}\right) \tag{2}$$

Since the mean inter-contact time of GCP is much larger than ICP, we have $(\alpha - 1) \gg \lambda_g t_m$. We consider two cases.

- Case I, the inter-contact time is moderately larger than t_m, but is much smaller than $\frac{\alpha-1}{\lambda_g}$, i.e., $t_m < t \ll \frac{\alpha-1}{\lambda_g}$. First of all we know that $\frac{t}{t_m} > \log\left(1+\frac{t}{t_m}\right)$. On the other hand, as $\alpha > (\alpha-1)$ and $(\alpha-1) \gg \lambda_g t_m$, we have $\alpha \gg \lambda_g t_m$. Mutipling α with $\log\left(1+\frac{t}{t_m}\right)$ and $\lambda_g t_m$ with $\frac{t}{t_m}$, recall that $\frac{t}{t_m}$ is only moderately larger than $\log\left(1+\frac{t}{t_m}\right)$ but $\alpha \gg \lambda_g t_m$, it should have $\alpha\log\left(1+\frac{t}{t_m}\right) \gg \lambda_g t_m \frac{t}{t_m}$. In addition, as $\lambda_g t \ll \alpha-1$, $\frac{\lambda_g t}{\lambda_g t_m+\alpha-1} \to 0$, so $\log\left(1+\frac{\lambda_g t}{\lambda_g t_m+\alpha-1}\right) \approx \frac{\lambda_g t}{\lambda_g t_m+\alpha-1} \ll \lambda_g t_m \frac{t}{t_m} \ll \alpha\log\left(1+\frac{t}{t_m}\right)$. Since $\log\left(1+\frac{\lambda_g t}{\lambda_g t_m+\alpha-1}\right)$ and $\lambda_g t_m \frac{t}{t_m}$ are much smaller than $\alpha\log\left(1+\frac{t}{t_m}\right)$, by ignoring them we can see that for this case $\log R_s(t) \approx -\alpha\log\left(1+\frac{t}{t_m}\right) \approx -\alpha\log\left(\frac{t}{t_m}\right)$. The distribution is power-law with a slope rate of α.
- Case II, the inter-contact time is much larger than $\frac{\alpha}{\lambda_g}\log(1+\frac{t}{t_m})$, i.e., $t \gg \frac{\alpha}{\lambda_g}\log(1+\frac{t}{t_m})$. Obviously, for this case $\lambda_g t_m \frac{t}{t_m} \gg \alpha\log\left(1+\frac{t}{t_m}\right)$, and since $\alpha \geq 2$, we have $\frac{t}{t_m} > \frac{\lambda_g t}{\lambda_g t_m+\alpha-1}$, so it is easy to see that $\alpha\log\left(1+\frac{t}{t_m}\right) > \alpha\log\left(1+\frac{\lambda_g t}{\lambda_g t_m+\alpha-1}\right) > \log\left(1+\frac{\lambda_g t}{\lambda_g t_m+\alpha-1}\right)$. As $\lambda_g t$ is much larger than $\alpha\log\left(1+\frac{t}{t_m}\right)$ and $\log\left(1+\frac{\lambda_g t}{\lambda_g t_m+\alpha-1}\right)$, by ignoring them, we have $\log R_s(t) \approx -\lambda_g t$, that is, the distribution has an exponential tail with a rate of λ_g.

4.3 Explaining the Knob between the First and the Second Segments

We then explain the knob between the first and the second segments observed in Fig. 1. As we are interested in the inter-contact time of the superposition process around the first characteristic time where the knob appears, which is about half a day, we ignore the process of GCP for its large mean inter-contact time, and only consider the contact processes of LCP and ICP. Unfortunately, as LCP is not renewal, we cannot apply Equ. (1) directly.

Meanwhile, as the mean inter-contact time of LCP is much less than ICP, and there are long intervals without contacts between its contact bursts, we use a two-state Markov chain for LCP to produce bursts of contacts. In this model, LCP may be in ON or OFF state: when at the ON state, with probability p a contact with a random interval to the next contact following the distribution of $F_1(t)$ is generated, and the model stays at the ON state; LCP changes to the OFF state with probability $1-p$. At the OFF state, there is no contacts for an interval of length L, and at the end of the interval, the process stays at the OFF state with a probability of q without a contact, and goes to the ON state to have a new contact with a probability $1-q$. We further assume that the influence of the contacts from LCP on the inter-contact times of ICP, especially the long inter-contact times, is neglectable. Therefore, the inter-contact times of

LCP and ICP can be considered separately. Specifically, the distribution of the inter-contact time in the superposition process can be approximated as

$$F_c(t) \approx p_1 \cdot F_1(t) + p_2 \cdot F_2(t) = \begin{cases} 1 - p_1 e^{-\lambda_l t} - p_2 \left(\frac{t}{t_m}\right)^{-\alpha}, & t > t_m \\ 1 - e^{-\lambda_l t}, & t \leq t_m \end{cases} \quad (3)$$

for $\lambda_l, t_m > 0$, and $\alpha \geq 2$

Let $R_c(t) = 1 - F_c(t)$. Since the mean inter-contact time of LCP is much less than ICP, we have $t_m \lambda_l \ll \frac{\alpha-1}{\alpha}$. Two cases are considered.

- Case I, the inter-contact time t is much smaller than t_m, i.e., $t \ll t_m$. In this case, $\log R_c(t) \approx \log e^{-\lambda_l t}$, the distribution should be exponential. However, as here we do not consider the distribution tail, we show that $R_c(t)$ can also be approximated by a power-law distribution function, as shown in the following. Let t'_m be a constant smaller than t_m, and rewrite $e^{-\lambda_l t}$ as $e^{-\lambda_l \cdot t'_m \cdot \frac{t}{t'_m}}$, since $e^{-\lambda_l \cdot t'_m \cdot \frac{t}{t'_m}} \approx \left(1 + \frac{t}{t'_m}\right)^{-\lambda_l \cdot t'_m}$ for $\frac{t}{t'_m}$ sufficiently small (note that $\log(1 + x) \approx x$ for $x \to 0$), $\log R_c(t) \approx -\lambda_l t'_m \log\left(1 + \frac{t}{t'_m}\right) \approx -\lambda_l t'_m \log\left(\frac{t}{t'_m}\right)$, which is power-law with a slope rate of $\lambda_l t'_m$. As $t_m \lambda_l \ll \frac{\alpha-1}{\alpha} < 1$ and t'_m can take any value smaller than t_m, clearly $\lambda_l t'_m < 1$. This explains the first segment.
- Case II, the inter-contact time t is larger than t_m, i.e., $t > t_m$. For this case, $R_c(t) \approx p_1 \cdot e^{-\lambda_l t} + p_2 \cdot \left(\frac{t}{t_m}\right)^{-\alpha}$. As an exponential distribution decays much faster than a power-law distribution function, when t is sufficiently large, we can ignore $p_1 e^{-\lambda_l t}$ and rewrite Equ. (3) as $\log R_c(t) = \log\left(p_2 \cdot \left(\frac{t}{t_m}\right)^{-\alpha}\right) = \log p_2 - \alpha \log\left(\frac{t}{t_m}\right)$. The distribution is power-law with a slope rate of α ($\alpha \geq 2$). This explains the second distribution curve segment.

From the above analysis, one can see than t_m actually is the first characteristic time in Section 3, thus $t_m \approx$ half a day. In addition, we believe that the first power-law curve segment observed in Fig. 1 should be the integration of a number of contact processes as LCP, as a device may be restricted in different local areas during different times. From [22], we know that synthesizing a power-law distribution with a number of exponential distributions is possible.

To validate our analysis, we simulate three contact processes of LCP, ICP and GCP with their inter-contact time distributions expressed as F_1, $F_2(t)$ and $F_3(t)$ using different parameter values of λ_l, α, t_m, and λ_g, and plot the inter-contact time distribution of the superposition process in Fig. 2. One can see from the figure that on the distribution curve there is a power-law segment with a slope rate smaller than one, followed by a power-law segment with a slope rate of approximately two, and the rest of the superposition process's distribution can be viewed as an exponential tail. Moreover, the value of t_m determines the position of the first knob. In short, the inter-contact time distribution in Equ. (2)

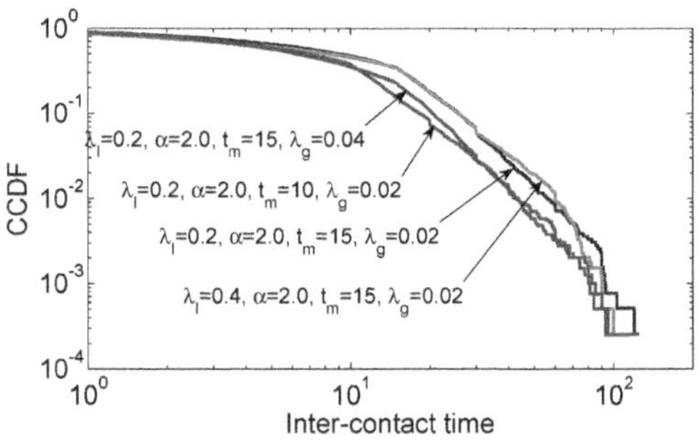

Fig. 2. Inter-contact time distribution of the superposition process of LCP, ICP, and GCP

and Equ. (3) explain the two knobs on the inter-contact time distribution curves observed in Fig. 1.

4.4 Verification by the Real-World Datasets

In the above discussions, we used the superposition of three contact processes to interpret the inter-contact time distributions observed in Section 3. In this section, we justify our explanation by analyzing the real-world datasets. Unfortunately, for all the currently available datasets, we cannot tell the source of a contact (e.g., intentional or unintentional), therefore we have to find other methods to infer the contacts in a real-world dataset.

Our approach is to consider the location where contacts took place. In UCSD, as contacts are inferred by simultaneous AP association, we recorded the location information (i.e. AP) for each contact. We found that every device stayed at one particular location for most of the time. This location is considered as its "home" location. For example, it is observed that on average a device in UCSD spent 90.9% of all its time at its home location. In our approach, we exploited

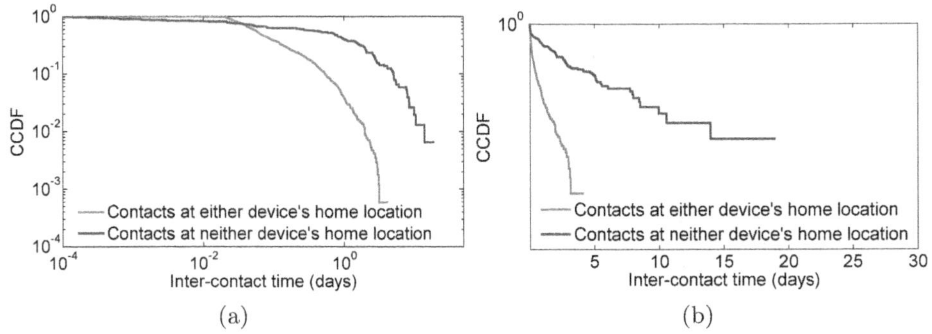

Fig. 3. Inter-contact time distribution of contacts at (a) either device's home location, and (b) neither device's home location

home locations to filter out some of the unintentional contacts caused by global device movement. Specifically, given a pair of frequently contacting devices with different home locations, we treat the contacts at either home location and the contacts at other locations separately. We collect the inter-contact times for the two types of contacts for all of the device pairs in the "10-20" percentile group in UCSD, and plot their inter-contact time distributions in Fig. 3, using a log-log scale in Fig. 3(a) and a linear-log scale in Fig. 3(b). The figures show that for the contacts at either device's home location, the power-law segments are prominent, indicating that most of the contacts at either device's home are caused by device's local independent movement and human's intention, while the inter-contact time distribution of the contacts at non-home locations is exponential, suggesting that the contacts are caused by device's global independent movement.

5 Mobility Model

In this section, we present a mobility model based on our observation and interpretation of the human-carried device contacts discussed in previous sections. Under this model, the distribution of inter-contact time between nodes closely resembles the distributions observed in the real-world datasets discussed in Section 3, with two power-law segments followed by an exponential tail. With these properties, our model can be applied for design and evaluation of mobility-assisted routing paradigms for wireless mobile networks.

5.1 Model Description

In our mobility model, we assume that nodes are equipped with omni-antennas and the disk communication model applies: a node can communicate with another if their distance is less than a communication range of r. Moreover, each node is associated with a region called its *home region*. The size of the home region is much smaller than the entire network area, but should be larger than a node's communication area (i.e., a disk of size πr^2). In our implementation, the network area is a square of $L \times L$, and the home region is a $l \times l$ square where $L > l$. Each node knows the home region of itself as well as that of all the other nodes (referred to as *foreign regions* for this node) in the network. It stays in its home region or visits another node's home region according to a two-state Markov chain. Specifically, when a node is in a region, either home or foreign, the time is divided into intervals of length T_l. At the end of each interval, if the node is in its home region, it stays at the home region during the next interval with a probability of p_H, and visits a foreign region with a probability of $1 - p_H$. Similarly, when a node is in a foreign region, it stays in the same foreign region with a probability of p_F, and returns to its home region with a probability of $1 - p_F$. When in a region, a node performs random movement. In our implementation, we uses the random waypoint mobility model without pause.

The selection of foreign region for a node to visit is critical. In our model, each node keeps a queue of *visiting plans*. A visiting plan keeps the information of the node's ID of which the home region is to be visited, as well as a priority value uniformly chosen from $[0, 1)$. When a node decides to visit a foreign region, it selects and removes the visiting plan in its queue with the highest priority, and moves to a randomly chosen position in the corresponding foreign region directly. When a node at a foreign region returns to its home region, it also moves to a randomly chosen position in its home region directly. At the same time, a new visiting plan with a randomly selected priority to the foreign region the node is currently leaving is inserted into its visiting plan queue. Clearly, the queue is a *priority queue*. In a strict priority queue, plans of low priorities may never be accessed (and removed). Therefore, we introduced randomness as follows: when selecting a visiting plan to remove, the node chooses a plan of the highest priority with a probability p_r, and if the plan of the highest priority is not chosen, the node chooses the plan with the second highest priority with probability p_r, and so on, until a plan is selected.

Finally, when a node is moving, either staying in a region or moving towards another region, the speed is randomly selected from a range of $[v_{\min}, v_{\max}]$ with a mean value as $\bar{v}$.

5.2 Analysis

In this section, we prove that power-law inter-contact times exist for node pairs under our presented model, and show that our model seamlessly integrates contact processes of LCP, ICP, and GCP between node pairs.

We first consider the interval between the executions of two consecutive visiting plans by a node. The interval includes the time for the node to move to the foreign region of the first plan, the time spent by the node to stay in the foreign region, the time for the node to return to its home region, and the time it stays in the home region of itself, until it decides to select and remove the next visiting plan. Mathematically, the expectation of the interval T could be expressed as

$$E[T] = \frac{T_l}{(1 - p_F)^2} + 2\frac{\bar{D}}{\bar{v}} + \frac{T_l}{(1 - p_H)^2}$$

where $\frac{T_l}{(1-p_H)^2}$ and $\frac{T_l}{(1-p_F)^2}$ are the expected times for a node to stay in home and foreign regions respectively, and $\bar{D}$ is the mean distance between the node's home region and a foreign region.

Given a node, we denote the time τ a visiting plan spends in queue, i.e., the period between the moment it is inserted and the moment it is removed. We assume that the visiting plan queue is a strict priority queue for simplifying our analysis. Suppose that there are M plans in the queue. Over a period sufficiently long, the probability that a plan of priority ρ gets selected is ρ^M, which is the probability that ρ is the largest value among M uniformly distributed random variables in $[0, 1)$. Assuming that the distributions of the priorities of the plans in the queue at the movements of plan selection are independent, then for a plan with priority ρ, the probability that it gets selected at the first plan selecting time after its insertion should be ρ^M; and if it is not selected, it must wait for a time of T and gets selected with the same probability ρ^M, and so on, until it is selected and removed. Therefore we could express the mean waiting time of a visiting plan with priority ρ as

$$\tau(\rho) = \sum_{i=0}^{\infty}(i+1) \times E[T] \times \rho^M \times \left(1-\rho^M\right)^i = \frac{E[T]}{\rho^M} \quad (4)$$

Consider all the plans with their priorities in a small range of $[\rho, \rho + d\rho)$. The probability that they are inserted into the queue can be expressed as $f(\rho)d\rho$, where $f(\rho)$ is the probability density function of the priority distribution, which is uniform in our model; and for all the plans with their waiting times in a small range of $[\tau(\rho), \tau(\rho) + d\tau)$, the rate of their removals is $P(\tau)d\tau$, where $P(\tau)$ is the probability density function of the waiting time. Applying Little's law, it is easy to see that

$$\frac{f(\rho)d\rho}{E[T]} = P(\tau)d\tau \Rightarrow P(\tau) = \frac{f(\rho)}{E[T]}\frac{d\rho}{d\tau}$$

From Equ. (4) we know $\frac{d\rho}{d\tau} = -\frac{1}{n}\frac{E[T]^{1/M}}{\tau^{1+1/M}}$, and since priority is uniformly distributed, $f(\rho)$ is a constant. Therefore $P(\tau) \sim \frac{1}{\tau^{1+1/M}}$, and the probability density function is power-law with an exponent of $1+\frac{1}{M}$. As priorities are randomly selected each time when a visiting plan is inserted, under our mobility model, the distribution of inter-visiting time to a specific foreign region by a node is power-law, of which the slope rate under log-log scale is $2+\frac{1}{M}$, which is larger than two.

Clearly, time between two visits of a node to another node's home region is not strictly the inter-contact time. Nonetheless, if we properly configure the model parameters, inter-visit time should be a good approximation of inter-contact time between two nodes. In other words, our mobility model contains the contact process of ICP, i.e., the contact process with power-law inter-contact times in Section 4. Moreover, as the minimum interval between two consecutive visits to a foreign region by a node is T, T actually is the characteristic time of the first knob. In other words, for the ICP's inter-contact time distribution function $F_2(t)$, $t_m = E[T]$ and $\alpha = 2 + \frac{1}{M}$.

We also show that our mobility model integrates the contact processes of LCP and GCP as well. Recall that when two nodes are in the same region, as they move independently and the region size is small, they will make frequent contacts. That corresponds to LCP where contacts are frequent and inter-contact times are exponential distributed. More specifically, at any time the probability that two devices in a same region meet with a probability of $P_l = \frac{2r\delta\bar{v}}{l^2}$, where $2r\delta\bar{v}$ is the area covered by a device in unit time when moving with the relative average speed of the device to the other device $\delta\bar{v}$. From [20], it is known that $\delta \approx 1.27$. It is well-known that when the unit time is small, the geometric distribution could be approximated as an exponential distribution, therefore for the inter-contact time distribution of the LCP contact process $F_1(t)$, $\lambda_l = \frac{2r\delta\bar{v}}{l^2}$.

The GCP process is also taken care of. As nodes are moving back and forth between its home region and a number of foreign regions, which are randomly located over the entire network area, when there are many foreign regions, traveling between them can be viewed as a global random movement. Therefore the proposed mobility model also contains the contact process of GCP with long inter-contact times exponentially distributed. Similarly, for the inter-contact time distribution of the GCP contact process $F_3(t)$, we have $\lambda_g = \frac{2r\delta\bar{v}}{L^2}$.

5.3 Validation

In this section, we show that our mobility model captures the complexity of the contact behaviors, especially the inter-contact times, of human-carried devices. We implement a simulator of wireless mobile networks, in which nodes move according to the proposed mobility model. In our simulation, we create a network containing 20 nodes that move within a global area of size 800×800, the home/foreign reign size is 50×50, the communication range is $r = 10$, the length of the interval is $T_l = 20$, the minimum and the maximum speeds are $v_{min} = 3$ and $v_{max} = 5$, and transition probabilities of the two-state Markov chain are $p_H = 0.8$ and $p_F = 0.6$, and the probability p_r is set as 0.8. Furthermore, in the simulation we divide the 20 nodes into two groups, each of 10 nodes. A node in our simulation only visits the home regions of the nodes in the same group. In this way we have two relationships between nodes: nodes in a same group and nodes in different groups.

We investigate the inter-contact time of different node pairs. In particular, three representative node pairs are studied: the pair of node 2 and node 8, the pair of node 8 and node 9, and the pair of node 2 and node 11. The nodes in the pair of pair 2-8, and 8-9, are respectively in the same group, and they visit each other's home region according to their priority queues to make contacts. While the nodes in pair 2-11 are in different groups, so they do not make such contacts. Fig. 4 plots the inter-contact time distributions of the three node pairs. From the figure one can see that for the pairs in the same group, the curves of the inter-contact time distributions closely resemble the distributions in Fig. 1, as there are two power-law segments followed by an exponential tail on the distribution curve. The inter-contact times of the node pair 2-11 are exponentially

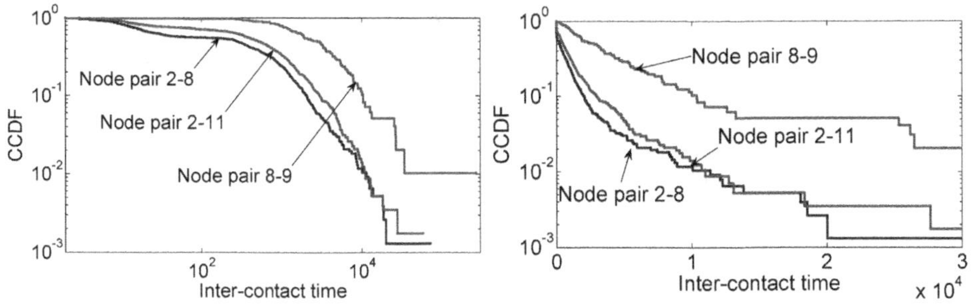

(a) (b)

Fig. 4. Inter-contact time distributions of node pairs in mobility model distributed. This observation showed that our model can reproduce the inter-contact time distributions very similar to the distributions of frequently and infrequently contacting device pairs observed in Section 3.

6 Conclusion

In this paper, we focused on examining and interpreting the inter-contact times between mobile human-carried devices. By investigating a number of real-world datasets, we found that the inter-contact time distributions of frequently-contacting percentile groups have three segments on their distribution curves. Based on existing knowledge of random movements and human activities, we conjectured that there are two reasons causing device contacts: the device's independent movement and the human's intention. We used superposition of three stochastic contact processes, i.e., the temporal local contact process, the intentional contact process, and the global contact process to explain the inter-contact time distributions observed. Based on our analysis, we proposed a mobility model for human-carried devices, and showed that the mobility model seamlessly integrates the three contact processes. Especially, we theoretically proved that the priority queue in our model generates power-law inter-visiting times. Finally, simulation experiment showed that our mobility model reproduces the contacts between node pairs with their inter-contact time distributions highly similar to the ones observed in real-world datasets, suggesting that the model could be applied in designing and evaluating realistic wireless mobile networks composed of human-carried devices.

Acknowledgement

This work was funded by the Provincial Foundation for Excellent Young Talents of Colleges and Universities of Anhui Province (No. 2010SQRL006ZD) and the Program for Innovative Research Team at University of Science and Technology of China, and was funded in part by US NSF grant CNS-0832000.

References

1. Chaintreau, A., Hui, P., Crowcroft, J., Diot, C., Gass, R., Scott, J.: Pocket switched networks: real-world mobility and its consequences for opportunistic forwarding. Technical Report UCAM-CL-TR-617, University of Cambridge (2005)
2. Hui, P., Crowcroft, J., Yoneki, E.: Bubble Rap: social-based forwarding in delay tolerant networks. In: Proc. of ACM MobiHoc 2008, Hong Kong, China (May 2008)
3. Grossglauser, M., Tse, D.N.C.: Mobility increases the capacity of ad hoc wireless networks. IEEE/ACM Trans. Networking 10(4), 477–486 (2002)
4. Jain, S., Fall, K., Patra, R.: Routing in a delay tolerant network. In: Proc. of ACM SIGCOMM 2004, Portland, OR, USA (August 2004)
5. Chaintreau, A., Hui, P., Diot, C., Gass, R., Scott, J.: Impact of human mobility on the design of opportunistic forwarding algorithms. In: Proc. of IEEE INFOCOM 2006, Barcelona, Spain (April 2006)

6. Karagiannis, T., Boudec, J.Y.L., Vojnovic, M.: Power law and exponential decay of inter contact times between mobile devices. In: Proc. of ACM MobiCom 2007, Montreal, Canada (September 2007)
7. Yoneki, E., Greenfield, D., Crowcroft, J.: Dynamics of inter-meeting time in human contact networks. In: Proc. of the International Conference on Advances in Social Networks Analysis and Mining, Athens, Greece (July 2009)
8. Cai, H., Eun, D.Y.: Crossing over the bounded domain: from exponential to power-law inter-meeting time in manet. In: Proc. of ACM MobiCom 2007, Montreal, Canada (September 2007)
9. Hsu, W., Spyropoulos, A., Psounis, K., Helmy, A.: Modeling time-variant user mobility in wireless mobile networks. In: Proc. of IEEE INFOCOM 2007, Anchorage, AK, USA (May 2007)
10. Rhee, I., Shin, M., Hong, S., Lee, K., Chong, S.: On the levy-walk nature of human mobility. In: Proc. of IEEE INFOCOM 2008, Phoenix, AZ, USA (April 2008)
11. Conan, V., Leguay, J., Friedman, T.: Characterizing pairwise inter-contact patterns in delay tolerant networks. In: Proc. of the 1st International Conference on Autonomic Computing and Communication Systems, Rome, Italy (October 2007)
12. Barabasi, A.L.: The origin of bursts and heavy tails in human dynamics. Nature 435, 207–211 (2005)
13. Dezso, Z., Almaas, E., Lukacs, A., Racz, B., Szakadat, I., Barabasi, A.L.: Dynamics of information access on the web. Phys. Rev. E 73, 66132 (2006)
14. Oliveira, J.G., Barabasi, A.L.: Human dynamics: the correspondence patterns of Darwin and Einstein. Nature 437, 1251 (2005)
15. Plerou, V., Gopikrishnan, P., Amaral, L.A.N., Gabaix, X., Stanley, H.E.: Economic fluctuations and anomalous diffusion. Phys. Rev. E 62, 3023–3026 (2000)
16. Reality: MIT Reality Mining Project, `http://reality.media.mit.edu`
17. Kotz, D., Henderson, T., Abyzov, I.: CRAWDAD trace set dartmouth/campus/movement (v. 2005-03-08) (March 2005), Downloaded from `http://crawdad.cs.dartmouth.edu/dartmouth/campus/movement`
18. UCSD: UCSD WTD project, `http://sysnet.ucsd.edu/wtd`
19. Groenevelt, R., Nain, P., Koole, G.: The message delay in mobile ad hoc networks. Perform. Eval. 62(1-4), 210–228 (2005)
20. Spyropoulos, T., Psounis, K.: Performance analysis of mobilityassisted routing. In: Proc. of ACM MobiHoc 2006, Florence, Italy (May 2006)
21. Torab, P., Kamen, E.W.: On approximate renewal models for the superposition of renewal processes. In: Proc. of IEEE ICC 2001, Helsinki, Finland (June 2001)
22. Feldmann, A., Whitt, W.: Fitting mixtures of exponentials to long-tail distributions toanalyze network performance models. In: Proc. of IEEE INFOCOM 1997 (April 1997)

A Method to Improve Adaptability of the Minstrel MAC Rate Control Algorithm

Wei Yin[1,2], Peizhao Hu[2], Jadwiga Indulska[1,2], and Konstanty Bialkowski[1,2]

[1] The University of Queensland,
School of Information Technology and Electrical Engineering
[2] National ICT Australia (NICTA)
{Firstname.Lastname}@nicta.com.au

Abstract. The MAC (Media Access Control) layer protocol in wireless networks dynamically changes its transmission rate to adapt transmission to channel conditions. Such dynamic adaptations can improve per-hop performance in wireless networks and therefore increase the network throughput. One of the best and commonly used rate control algorithms is Minstrel implemented in the MadWifi driver in Linux. In this paper we present a comprehensive evaluation of the Minstrel rate control adaptation. We show that network throughput could be further improved if the freshness level of throughput measurements currently used in Minstrel was dynamically adapted to channel conditions. This evaluation of the impact of measurement freshness on transmission rate adaptation was carried out in our platform for controllable and repeatable experiments.

1 Introduction

Wireless communication (IEEE 802.11 wireless networks in particular) has became a predominant technology for communication between Ubicomp devices. Due to the shared medium, wireless networks are prone to interference and changes of RF (Radio Frequency) signal conditions and this has impact on the network performance. There has been a large amount of research in the last decade on intelligent, ubiquitous systems that are able to evaluate computational and user context in which their operate, recognise contextual situations they are in and appropriately adapt their behaviour to the situations. This includes research on context-awareness in communication protocols in order for protocols to adapt their behaviour to the current communication situations. One example is the IEEE 802.11 MAC layer protocol that tries to recognise contextual situation of the communication channel (e.g. current signal quality) to adapt its transmission behaviour to the current situation in the channel.

The IEEE 802.11 technology supports several transmission rates and the MAC layer protocol uses rate control mechanisms to adapt to the current communication channel conditions; that is, the MAC layer rate control protocol dynamically selects a transmission rate that is most suitable for the current communication channel condition. The main research question is whether it can accurately recognise the contextual situations in which it operates, i.e. whether its sensing of the

Z. Yu et al. (Eds.): UIC 2010, LNCS 6406, pp. 504–518, 2010.

channel can be improved and therefore the protocols can better adapt (select a better transmission rate) to the current channel condition.

There are many rate control mechanisms. They reason on the situation of the communication channel based on the context information gathered through sensing/monitoring various aspects of the channel and packet transmissions. Based on what they are sensing/monitoring the rate control mechanisms can be classified into the following types: (i) ACK (Acknowledgment) based mechanisms (e.g. Minstrel [1], RRAA [8] and SampleRate [3]) - they monitor received acknowledgements and use this information to compute performance metrics (e.g., the packet delivery ratio, average transmission time and current network throughput) and appropriately adapt the transmission rate, (ii) SNR (Signal-to-Noise Ratio) based mechanisms (e.g., FARA [6] and CHARM [5]) - they monitor signal-to-noise ratio in order to select transmission rates, and (iii) BER (Bit Error Rate) based mechanisms (e.g., SoftRate [7]) - they monitor bit error rate to make decisions on adapting transmission rates. The ACK based mechanisms are the cheapest if the cost/difficulty of monitoring the channel condition is taken into account. SNR is difficult to monitor and BER based approaches require redesigning of network card interfaces.

However, the ACK based mechanisms show poor performance compared with the SNR or BER based rate control algorithms with the exception of Minstrel. Minstrel is used by the open-source Madwifi driver[1] in the Linux operating system. In addition, Minstrel has been ported to the new mac80211 wireless framework[2], which provides essential wireless networking support in new Linux kernels. In [9], we showed Minstrel's superior performance in our extensive evaluation results. In this paper, we further extend our evaluation of Minstrel's adaptability and investigate the possibility of throughput improvement in Minstrel by enhancing its adaptation mechanisms.

At the core of the Minstrel rate control algorithm is a multi-rate *retry chain*, which represents the retry preferences for the selection of next transmission rate when packet delivery fails at the current rate. Common wireless radios with Atheros 802.11a/b/g chipsets have four of these retry preferences. For most of the data packets, the retry preferences are: *best throughput*, *next best throughput*, *best probability of success*, and *lowest baserate*. Each of these preferences is associated with a specific transmission rate that is supported; for example, the *lowest baserate* for IEEE 802.11a is 6 Mbit/s.

To determine these preferences, Minstrel needs to calculates the throughput and probability of success for each supported rate. To avoid instability the calculation uses a smoothing mechanism, called Exponential Weighted Moving Average (EWMA) [1], to control the balance of influence of both the new packet delivery statistics (collected from this sampling interval) and the last probability value (calculated in the last sampling interval); the outcome of this calculation is the weighted probability of success, which is used for computing the estimated maximum throughput of a corresponding rate, and for selection of the *best probability of success* retry preference.

[1] `http://madwifi-project.org/`

[2] `http://wireless.kernel.org`

The maximum throughput of each rate is estimated using the weighted probability of success and the maximum number of packets that can be sent, while the weighted probability of success for the current interval, P_{new}, is calculated as:

$$P_{new} = (1 - \alpha) * P_{this\_interval} + \alpha * P_{previous} \quad (1)$$

- P_{new} is the weighted probability of success for this interval, which will be used by the rate selection process.
- α is a smoothing factor (or the *scaling value*) in the EWMA mechanism.
- $P_{this\_interval}$ is the probability of success of this interval before the rate selection, and it is calculated as the ratio of number of packets sent successfully to the number of packets sent:

$$P_{this\_interval} = \frac{PKT_{success}}{PKT_{sent}}$$

- $P_{previous}$ is the weighted probability of success for the last interval, which was used to select the last transmission rate.

In Eqn (1), the statistical information for computing the $P_{this\_interval}$ (i.e., the number of packets being sent successfully, $PKT_{success}$, and the number of packets being sent, PKT_{sent}) is locally available in the driver (the driver observes ACKs). However, the smoothing factor α is manually configured at program execution, and defaults to 75%. As mentioned above the α value controls the influence of current and historical measurements on the next rate selection. A value of 0% means using only the latest measurements, ignore the old results. A value of 99% means using the old results, with a tiny influence from the new measurements.

As the α value is hard-coded at run-time in Minstrel we investigate the impact of changing α, i.e. measurement freshness, on the network throughput in Minstrel in an environment where interference vary over time and strength. To create these different interference scenarios we use our controllable evaluation platform, which provides repeatable channel conditions for every experiment configuration. We compose four different evaluation scenarios, with each focusing on a different aspect of the adaptability in Minstrel. In these scenarios, we vary different properties of the interference, such as (i) *Duration* - time for which interference lasts, (ii) *Interval* - time between two adjacent interference intervals, and (iii) *Strength* - intensity of interference.

The main contributions of this paper are:

- A comprehensive evaluation of Minstrel's adaptability and impact of measurement freshness on network throughput.
- A controllable experiment setup for repeatable experiments that provides reliable and repeatable evaluation results.
- A method to improve network throughput by dynamically adjusting the α value in the EWMA mechanism.

The remainder of the paper is organised as follows. In Section 2 we briefly describe the platform for controllable and repeatable experiments, followed by a study of impact of measurement freshness on the Minstrel performance in Section 3. A mechanism which can dynamically adjust the α value is proposed in Section 4. Finally, we discuss the findings in Section 5.

2 Evaluation Platform

We perform our evaluation of Minstrel's adaptations in a controllable evaluation platform in which wireless signal is carried by coaxial cable rather than over the air by antenna [2]. Fig. 1 shows the experiment setup that we designed for the evaluation.

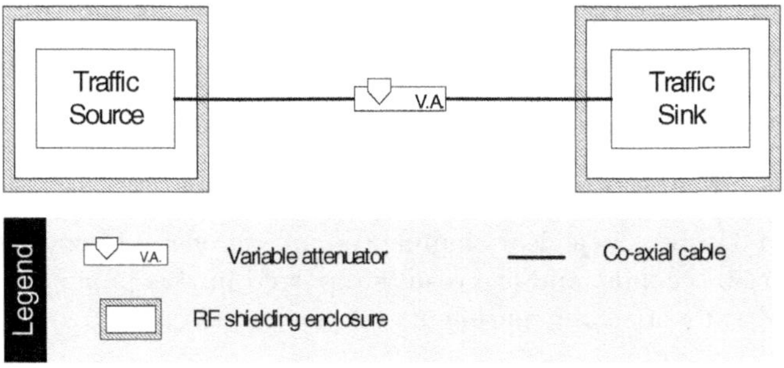

Fig. 1. Experiment setup

In this experiment setup, we emulate the changes of channel conditions, in terms of signal quality, by adjusting the value of the programmable signal attenuator attached on the wireless link. Based on the RF signal property, the ultimate effect of interference is a drop of signal quality in the channel [4]. Therefore, we can control the interference by simply increase or decrease the attenuation on a wireless link. The attenuation value is measured and referred to as the path loss (in dB). However, in this paper we use *interference strength* to represent the intensity of the interference (also in dB), which is the additional attenuation above base path loss. When the channel is set to the base path loss (i.e., no interference case), the channel is clear and is sufficient for achieving the maximum throughput, with the maximum transmission rate (i.e., 54 Mbit/s).

As shown in Fig. 1, the experiment setup includes two single board computers, each equipped with a Wistron CM9 Atheros wireless card[3]. Both computers run the Linux operating system (kernel 2.6.30) and MadWifi driver (svn version 3314). The wireless cards are connected using co-axial cables via a programmable attenuator (Vaunix LabBrick LDA-602). Using the attenuator, channel conditions are varied, by changing the level of attenuation on the wireless link. In

[3] `http://www.wneweb.com/Networking/mini-PCI.htm`

addition to the programmable attenuator, a 20 dB fixed attenuator is attached to each traffic node, and the transmission power is set to 7 dBm. This avoids the possibility of the radios being damaged, and ensures that within the operation range of the variable attenuator (0–63 dB), a full rate of link qualities is possible. That is, minimal attenuation corresponds to a full throughput link, and maximum attenuation corresponds to a fully disconnected link.

To ensure consistent results, the entire setup is enclosed within RF shielding boxes (JRE 4400), which ensures 85 dB of isolation to external sources. Further to this, all experiments are performed using IEEE 802.11a. This has two benefits, the first being that the 5 GHz frequency band is currently much less used than 2.4 GHz, and secondly it means that all transmission rates use the same family of modulation and coding rates. After configuration, each setup is confirmed manually using various tools.

The evaluation data traffic are generated using iperf[4] on each node (that is, iperf clients as the traffic sources and iperf server as the traffic sink). All transmitted data packets are captured at the receiver using a packet sniffing tool (tcpdump). Each measurement contains information regarding the achievable throughput and the number of packets that have been sent at each rate. A parser library (Banjax[5]) is used to analyse the measurement files. In the experiments, the UDP packet size is set to the iperf default size, corresponding to a maximum throughput of 34 Mbps in a clear channel (no interference). Each measurement is performed for 60 seconds, and the results reported in this paper are the average of 10 different runs of each experiment.

3 Impact of α Value in EWMA on throughput

With the experiment setup described in Section 2, we present our evaluation study on impact of the α value, in the EWMA mechanism, on network throughput. As shown in Eqn (1), the α value is a smoothing factor that the EWMA mechanism uses to control the balance of contribution of the current and historical measurements in the next rate selection. To this aim, we designed four experimental evaluation scenarios focusing on aspects of the interference characteristics (e.g., interference duration, interval, strength).

Before running the evaluation experiments, we performed a series of calibration tests, using fixed transmission rates and fixed interference strength, to identify the ideal transmission rate for each interference strength, from 0 dB to 35 dB (in 5 dB step). By ideal transmission rate, we refer to the rate that is capable of achieving the best throughput in the specific interference condition. For example, we found that the ideal transmission rate for an interference strength of 30 dB is 12 Mbit/s. These findings will be used in the following experiments to analyse the experiment results and to compute the percentage of packets sent at non-ideal transmission rates.

[4] `http://sourceforge.net/projects/iperf/`

[5] `http://code.google.com/p/banjax/`

3.1 Scenario 1 - Varying Interference Duration

The first experiment is to determine the maximum achievable throughput with different lengths of interference duration for different α values in EWMA In this experiment, we vary the interference duration from 1 ms to 101 ms, while setting the interference interval to 20 ms and interference strength to 30 dB.

The interference model that we used has a repeating pattern; such that, we create interference in a 20 ms interval and each interference lasts for a specified duration (increased from 1 ms to 101 ms for every experiment). This repeating interference model is also used in Scenarios 2 and 3. From earlier calibration tests, we identified two ideal transmission rates of 12 Mbit/s for interference strength of 30 dB and 54 Mbit/s for no interference.

During the experiment, we record not only relevant information regarding the performance of the Minstrel rate control mechanism, but also the number of packets sent at each rate. Fig. 2 shows the throughput and percentage of packets sent at non-ideal transmission rates (12Mbit/s and 54Mbit/s) with different interference durations for different α values (e.g., 25%, 45%, 75%, 85% and 95%).

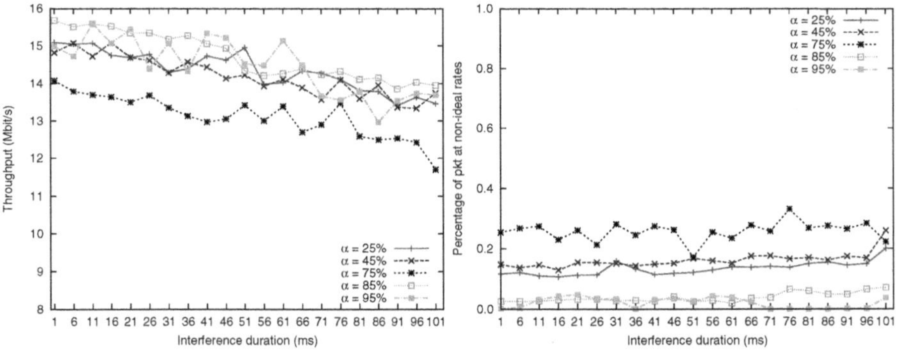

(a) Throughput for different lengths of interference duration

(b) % of Pkts at non-ideal transmission rates

Fig. 2. Impact of α value on throughput when interference duration vary

As shown in Fig. 2(a), we observe a drop in the aggregated throughput as the interference duration increases (but the throughput difference between two α values is relatively stable); the increase in interference duration meaning that the interference exists for longer time. In addition, we also find that the throughput gain of different α values vary. For example, we note an averaged difference in throughput gain of 12.3% (maximum difference is around 19.3%) between α of 75% and 85%. This suggests the 75% default α value is not an optimum for Minstrel to achieve the maximum throughput. In this case, either lower or higher α values seem to achieve better throughput.

To analyse the problem, we compute the percentage of packages sent at non-optimum transmission rates. The results are presented in Fig. 2(b). It is noted that more than 20% of the packets are sent at non-optimum rates when the α value is set to 75% (i.e., using rates other than 54 Mbit/s or 12 Mbit/s).

To summarise, based on the experiment results, Minstrel is unable to achieve its full potential with the use of default α value being set to 75%. In this scenario, it is noted that a higher α value in the EWMA allows Minstrel to achieve higher throughput.

3.2 Scenario 2 - Varying Interference Interval

The experiment settings of the second experiment is similar to Scenario 1, with the only difference in varying the interference interval rather than duration. In this experiment, we set the interference duration to 20 ms and the interference strength to 30 dB in the repeating interference model, as in Scenario 1. We vary the time between two adjacent interferences (i.e., interference interval) from 1 ms to 101 ms.

Fig. 3 shows the throughput and percentage of packets sent at non-optimum rates with different interference intervals for different α values (e.g., 25%, 45%, 75%, 85% and 95%).

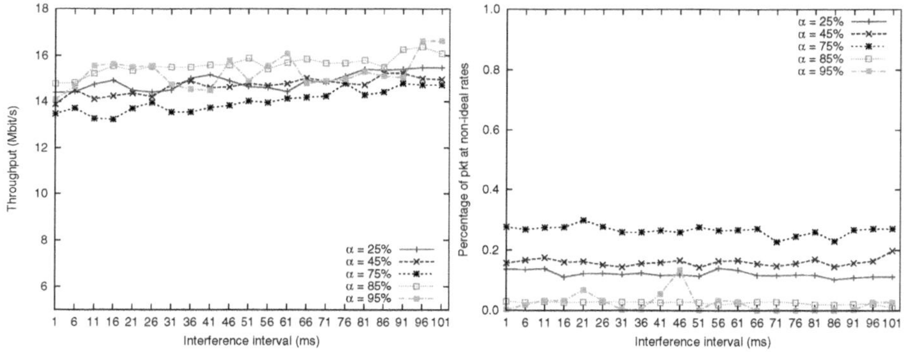

(a) Throughput for different lengths of interference interval (b) % of packets at non-ideal transmission rates

Fig. 3. Impact of α value on throughput when interference interval vary

As shown in Fig. 3(a), we observe an increase in the aggregated throughput as the interference interval increases (but the throughput difference between two α values is relatively stable). The increase of interference interval meaning that the channel is stay clear for longer time; that is, more packets can be transmitted. In addition, similar observation in throughput gain for different α values suggest that higher throughput can be achieved by using different α values other than its default value of 75% (with an averaged throughput difference of 11.4%). Fig. 3(b) also show that when the α value in EWMA is set to 75%, more than 20% of the packets are sent at non-ideal transmission rates (other than 54 Mbit/s and 12 Mbit/s). Similar to Scenario 1, it is noted that a higher α value in the EWMA allows Minstrel to achieve higher throughput.

3.3 Scenario 3 - Varying Interference Strength

In the third experiment, we then set both the interference duration and interval to 20 ms, and vary the interference strength in the repeating interference model. We vary the interference strength from 10 to 35 dB. When interference strength is greater than 35 dB, the link is disconnected when the interference is present.

Fig. 4 shows the throughput with different interference strength for different α values (e.g., 25%, 45%, 75%, 85% and 95%).

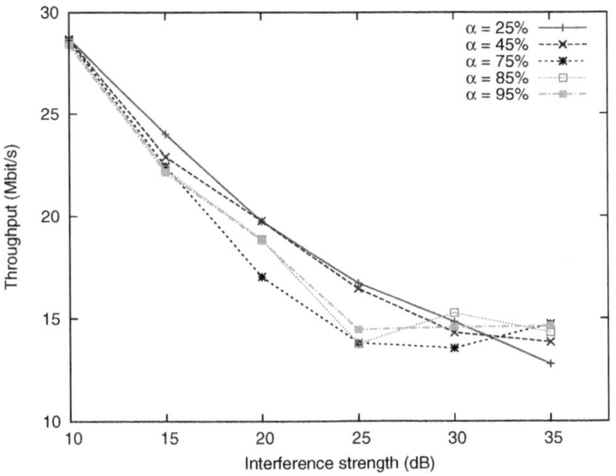

Fig. 4. Impact of α value on throughput when interference strength vary

As shown in Fig. 4, the maximum achieved throughput varies for different α values with different interference strength. However, we observe a point of interest when the interference strength is between 30 dB and 35 dB. When the strength is lower than this point, the lower α values can allow Minstrel to achieve higher throughput; when the strength is greater than that point, we observe a different behaviour in the throughput gain. Better performance is achieved by Minstrel with higher α values.

More importantly, it also shows that the default α value of 75% in EWMA is not the optimal value for achieving the maximum throughput. In addition, the experiment results suggest different throughput gains can be achieved for different α values with different interference strength.

3.4 Scenario 4 - Random Interference Model

The final experiment is conducted with a random interference model. In this model, the interference pattern is no longer repeating as in Scenarios 1, 2, and 3, but vary in the duration of each interference strength. We randomly generate 2000 samples of interference value ranging between 0 dB and 44 dB. We use these random samples as our interference model and vary the duration of the interference for every experiment. In this experiment, the duration for each of the 2000 random interference values is the same, and vary from 1 to 101 ms. This is to create the effect of continuing changes of the channel, in terms of link quality, between the sender and receiver.

Fig. 5 shows performance of different α values with different interference duration of the random model.

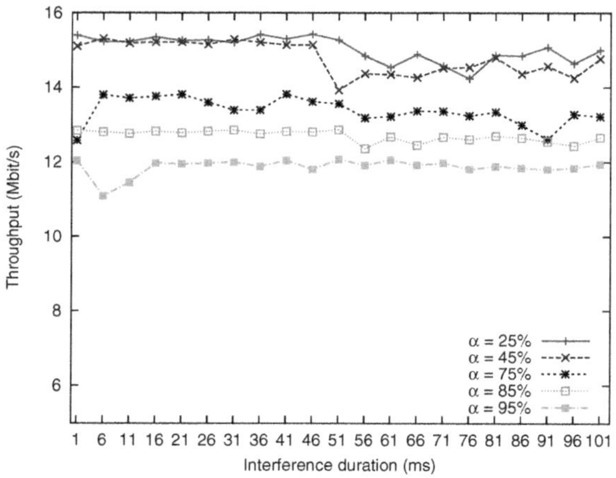

Fig. 5. Impact of α value on throughput for random interference model

The results suggest that the default α value of 75% is not optimal. In addition, there is a much clearer pattern in terms of the throughput gain; such that, the lower the α values the higher throughput Minstrel can achieve.

4 Finding the Optimal α Values in EWMA

From the experiment results presented in the last section, we conclude: (i) the default α value of 75% in the EWMA mechanism is not optimal for achieving the maximum throughput, (ii) for different α values, Minstrel can achieve different throughput (up to 19.3% throughput gain difference), and (iii) there is no single optimal α value for all scenarios.

Based on these findings, we believe that it is possible to improve the overall throughput by dynamically adapting the α value in EWMA to the changes of the channel conditions in the environment.

4.1 Experimental Study of α in EWMA

To adapt the α value appropriately, we need to understand the impact of α value on throughput, across the entire α value range (from 0% to 99%). As mentioned in Section 1, the α value balances the use of the current and historical sampling measurements for the next rate selection. A value of 0% means using only the latest measurements, while a value of 99% means using the old results, with a tiny influence from the new measurements.

To this aim, we conduct two experiments that are similar to Scenario 3 in which we vary the interference strength, as discussed in Section 3.3. The reason we use Scenario 3 for our experimental study is because the clear *change-over* behaviour happens when the interference strength increases between 30 and 35 dB, as shown in Fig. 4. This indicates that the interference strength has great impact on the maximum throughput that Minstrel can achieve and shows that an improvement in the Minstrel adaptability is needed in order to adjust the α value dynamically.

We first run experiments that show the optimal rate for particular interference levels. We run experiments with fix transmission rates for four levels of interference strength: 20 dB, 25 dB, 30 dB and 33 dB. These experiments show what would be the network throughput if there was no rate adaptation and the transmission rate was fixed at a particular rate. They also show what is the optimal rate for a particular interference strength scenario as illustrated in Fig. 6. By the optimal rate, we mean the rate which achieves the highest throughput in the varying channel condition. For example the optimal rate for varying channel of 20 dB interference strength is 36 Mbit/s.

We then run an experimental study on the impact of the α value on throughput for each α value from 0% to 99%. The study consists of separate experiments for four levels of interference strength: 20 dB, 25 dB, 30 dB and 33 dB. The interference duration and interval are both set to 20 ms.

Fig. 7 shows the impact of different α values on throughput in these four different experiment scenarios.

As shown in Fig. 7, there is a general trend of the throughput variation in these four scenarios. In particular, both Fig. 7(a) and Fig. 7(b) show that the throughput decreases as the α value increases. In these cases, smaller α values provide better opportunity for achieving higher throughput. The case when the interference strength is set to 30 dB, as shown in Fig. 7(c), shows a special circumstance in which either lower or higher α values can provide optimal throughput gains, but not the default value of 75%. In contrast, when the interference strength is increased to 33 dB as shown in Fig. 7(d), the situation changes; that is, higher α values used in Minstrel can achieve better throughput. This phenomenon can also be observed in Fig. 4. For example the throughput variation for interference of 30 dB shows the same pattern in Fig. 4 in as in Fig. 7(b). From these experiment results, we can identify two ranges for adapting Minstrel according to the changes of the channel condition, in terms of interference strength.

To further understand this phenomenon and to investigate the reason for the throughput drop when the α value is around 75%, we evaluate the contribution

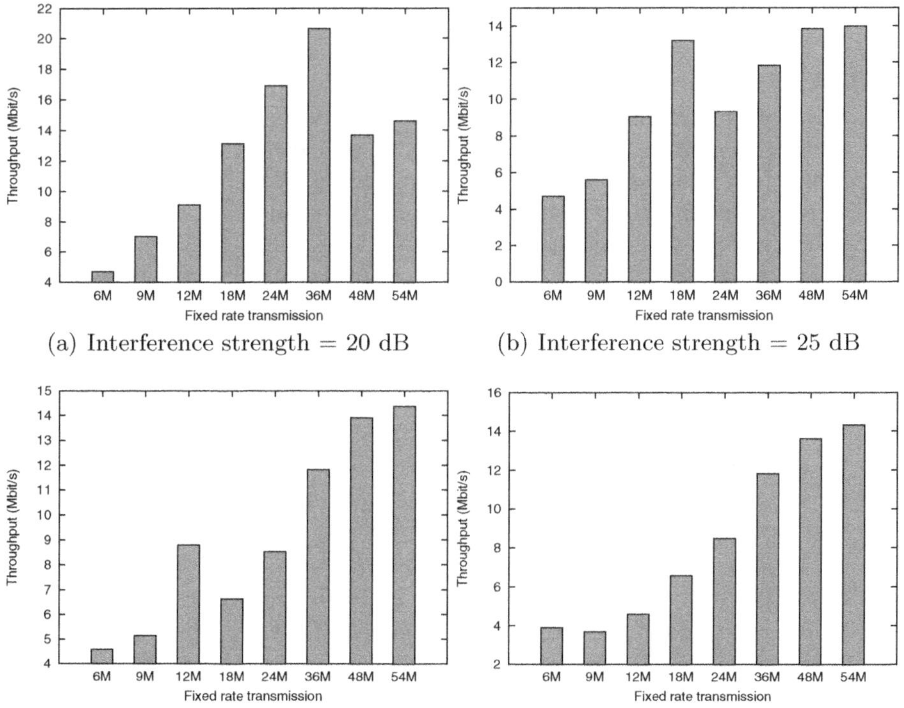

(a) Interference strength = 20 dB (b) Interference strength = 25 dB

(c) Interference strength = 30 dB (d) Interference strength = 33 dB

Fig. 6. Throughput of each supported rate for the given constant interference strength

of each transmission rate to the achieved throughput. We present the percentage of the total throughput achieved by packets sent at a particular rate in Fig. 8. It is noted that Minstrel is able to identify the two dominant rates (e.g., 54 Mbit/s and 36 Mbit/s in the case of 20 dB interference strength) when the α value is relatively low, and it prefers the optimal rate (e.g., 36 Mbit/s in the 20 dB interference case) when the α value is higher than the default value of 75%.

Based on Fig. 8, which shows how each supported rate contributes to the aggregated throughput, we can reason about the causes of a throughput drop when the α value is around 75% (as shown in Fig. 7). It is because Minstrel increases the use of sub-optimal rate. For example, with interference strength set to 25 dB, as shown in Fig. 8(b), there is an increased use of the rate of 48 Mbit/s when α is set to near 75%, rather than the optimal rate of 54 Mbit/s, as shown in Fig. 6(b). The effect of the increased use of the sub-optimal rate is the decreased use of the other rates, including the optimal rate for the given interference level. This causes the drop of the aggregated throughput.

Fig. 8 also provides an evidence for reasoning about why better throughput is achieved with either higher or lower α values. When the interference strength is relatively low, at around 20 dB as in Fig. 8(a), Minstrel has to be responsive (i.e., increase the influence of the new measurement samplings) to detect the presence

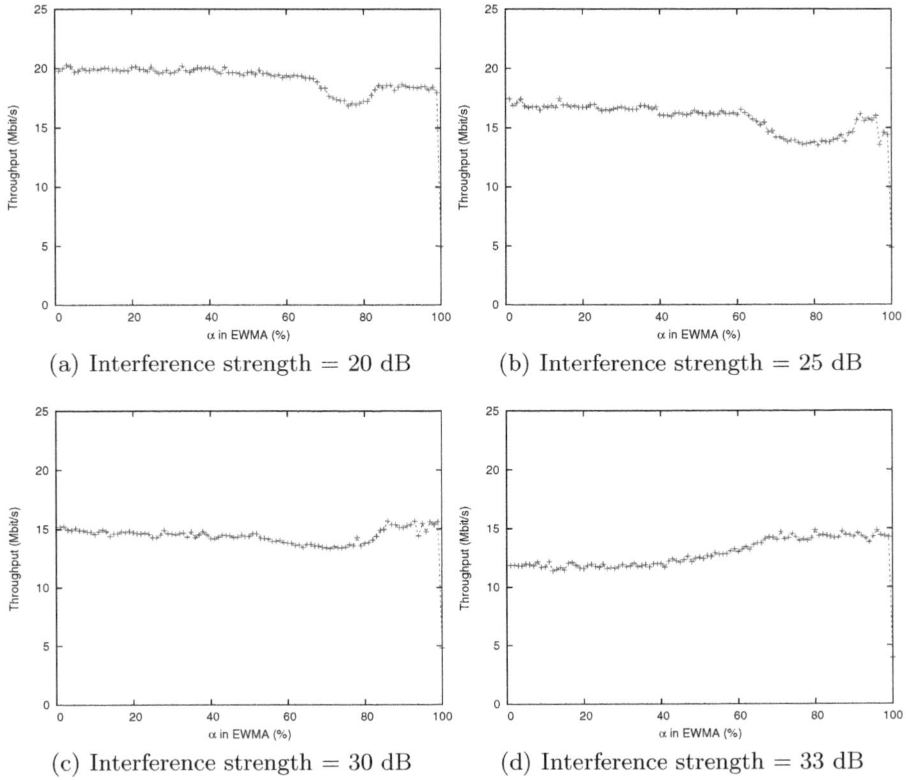

(a) Interference strength = 20 dB (b) Interference strength = 25 dB

(c) Interference strength = 30 dB (d) Interference strength = 33 dB

Fig. 7. Impact of different α values on throughput

of interference and adapt the transmission rate promptly. This is because when there is no interference the channel can support up to 54 Mbit/s, whereas up to 36 Mbit/s transmission can be supported if the interference is present. The use of an incorrect transmission rate has negative impact on the aggregated throughput. It is noted that in Fig. 8(a) Minstrel predominantly uses the optimal rate of 36 Mbit/s when the α value is greater than 80%. However, the optimal rate has poor performance if there is no interference.

In contrast, when the interference strength is relatively high, Minstrel needs to be more stable in the selection of the transmission rate (i.e., to increase the influence of the historical measurements). As shown in Fig. 8(d), when the α value is lower than 75% (i.e., Minstrel is responsive using recent sampling measurements), Minstrel tries to select rates that are other than the optimal rate (e.g., 48 Mbit/s, 36 Mbit/s) for the given interference strength. This results in lower aggregated throughput than when it is using the 54 Mbit/s transmission rate regardless of the presence of interference.

In conclusion, the aggregated throughput achieved by Minstrel depends on the α value, which controls the trade-off between responsiveness and stability of rate selection in Minstrel. The finding of this study shows that when interference

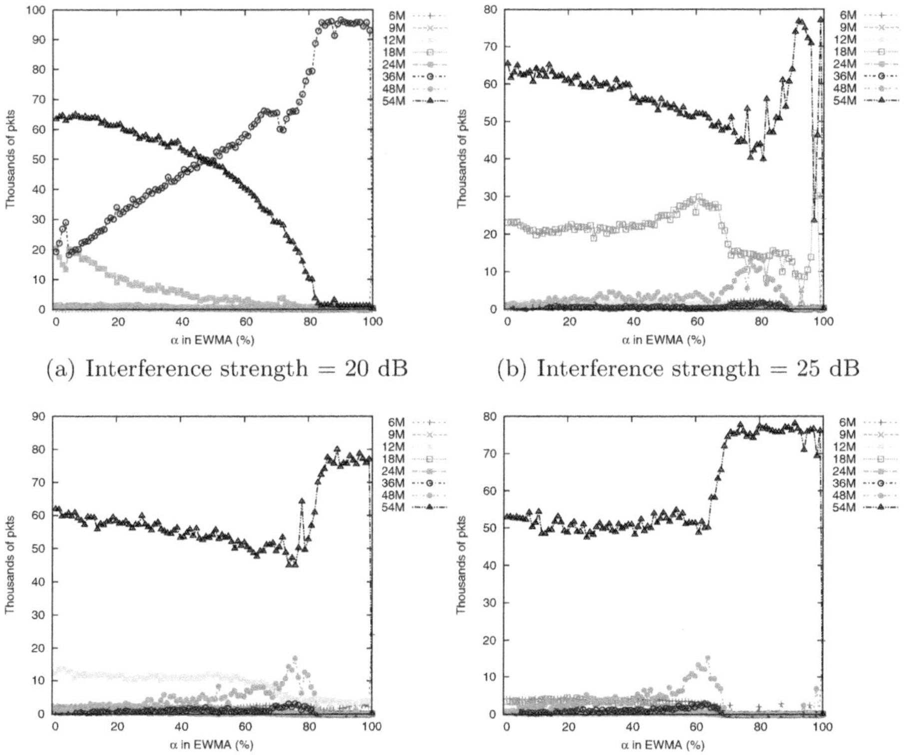

(a) Interference strength = 20 dB

(b) Interference strength = 25 dB

(c) Interference strength = 30 dB

(d) Interference strength = 33 dB

Fig. 8. Number of packets sent at each rate for different α values

strength is relatively low, Minstrel has to be more responsive; whereas in the presence of high interference strength, Minstrel has to be more stable with its selection of the transmission rate.

4.2 An Approach for Adapting α

Based on the findings from the previous experiments, we propose an approach to dynamically adapt the α value at run-time, in order to improve the aggregated throughput in the presence of various levels interferences.

In the proposed approach to Minstrel enhancement we use a sampling mechanism to probe the maximum achieved throughput for different α values. In this sampling mechanism, we use a monitor window of n rate adaptations for computing the throughput variation for two α values. Each monitor window consist of n slots, with each slot corresponding to one Minstrel rate adaptation process. In these n slots, there are $n - 1$ *MeasuringSlots* and one *SamplingSlot* at the end of the monitor window. n is a configurable parameter for adjusting the responsiveness of this adaptive solution (defaults to 10).

At the end of each rate adaptation (i.e., at the end of every slot), we compute the achieved throughput using information provided by Minstrel; that is the number of packets sent successfully at the last interval. The maximum achieved throughput is fed into a throughput statistic table, which keeps track of the maximum throughput for each selectable α value; at the beginning, these throughput values are initialised to infinity. Over time, this updated table provides information for prioritising the selection of α value, with respect to the maximum achieved throughput. A selectable α value is one of the random values chosen from either one of the two optimal α ranges. From the last experimental study, we have found that Minstrel is capable of achieving higher throughput when using either lower (towards 0%) or higher (towards 99%) α values. Therefore, we chose the two optimal α ranges around the two boundary values (about 5% range).

When the enhanced Minstrel starts, the first $n-1$ MeasuringSlots use a random α value from the two optimal ranges. When all the $n-1$ MeasuringSlots are finished, the averaged throughput is computed for the current α value. The enhanced Minstrel then uses the SamplingSlot to probe the maximum achieved throughput, with a α value (i.e., the sampling α) that has the highest throughput in the throughput statistic table. This sampling behaviour happens only if the averaged throughput of the $n-1$ MeasuringSlots is lower than the throughput of any other α value in the throughput statistic table. If that is the case, the enhanced Minstrel uses the sampling α value in the SamplingSlot and measures the throughput. If the sampled α value achieves better throughput, Minstrel uses the sampling α value. Otherwise, the current α value remains for the next $n-1$ MeasuringSlots.

5 Conclusion

The Minstrel rate control algorithm is one of the best algorithms used to estimate conditions of the communication channel at the MAC layer in order to select a transmission rate that suits the channel condition, i.e. provides the highest network throughput for the current channel condition. Minstrel calculates the throughput and probability of success for each supported transmission rate to make a decision on selecting a packet transmission rate. For this calculation it uses Exponential Weighted Moving Average that includes a smoothing factor α which controls the balance of influence between fresh and old packet delivery statistics used for the network performance evaluation. In Minstrel the α value is fixed at run-time and its default value is 75%.

In this paper we evaluated the Minstrel performance and evaluated the impact of the smoothing factor α on the network throughput. The evaluation was carried out in a platform for controllable and repeatable experiments. We evaluated the impact of measurement freshness for packet delivery statistics on the network throughput by varying interference duration, interference interval, and interference strength. Our evaluation showed that the default value of the smoothing factor α as used in Minstrel does not provide the highest possible throughput.

The network throughput can be improved if the α value is dynamically adapted to the channel condition and the throughput gain can be up to 19%. We proposed a method for Minstrel enhancement that dynamically adapts the smoothing factor α at run time to improve the network performance.

Acknowledgement

NICTA is funded by the Australian Government as represented by the Department of Broadband, Communications and the Digital Economy and the Australian Research Council through the ICT Centre of Excellence program; and the Queensland Government.

References

1. Minstrel specification, `http://madwifi-project.org/browser/madwifi/trunk/ath_rate/minstrel/minstrel.txt`
2. Bialkowski, K., Portmann, M.: Design of test-bed for wireless mesh networks. In: IEEE Antennas and Propagation International Symposium, Toronto, Canada (July 2010)
3. Bicket, J.C.: Bit-rate Selection in Wireless Networks. PhD thesis, MIT Master's Thesis (2005)
4. Bruce Carlson, A., Crilly, P.B., Rutledge, J.: Communication Systems: An Introduction to Signals and Noise in Electrical Communication, 5th edn. McGraw-Hill, New York (2010)
5. Judd, G., Wang, X., Steenkiste, P.: Low-overhead channel-aware rate adaptation. In: MobiCom 2007, Montreal, Quebec, Canada, pp. 354–357. ACM, New York (2007)
6. Rahul, H., Edalat, F., Katabi, D., Sodini, C.G.: Frequency-aware rate adaptation and mac protocols. In: MobiCom 2009, Beijing, China, pp. 193–204. ACM, New York (2009)
7. Vutukuru, M., Balakrishnan, H., Jamieson, K.: Cross-layer wireless bit rate adaptation. In: SIGCOMM 2009, Barcelona, Spain, pp. 3–14. ACM, New York (August 2009)
8. Wong, S.H.Y., Yang, H., Lu, S., Bharghavan, V.: Robust rate adaptation for 802.11 wireless networks. In: MobiCom 2006, Los Angeles, California, USA, pp. 146–157. ACM, New York (2006)
9. Yin, W., Bialkowski, K., Indulska, J., Hu, P.: Evaluation of madwifi mac layer rate control mechanisms. In: Preceeding of IEEE International Workshop on Quality of Service (IWQoS 2010), Beijing, China (June 2010)

A New Location-Aware Hierarchical Routing Protocol for MANETs

Farrukh Aslam Khan[1], Khi-Jung Ahn[2], and Wang-Cheol Song[2,*]

[1] Department of Computer Science, FAST-National University of Computer and Emerging Sciences, A. K. Brohi Road, H-11/4, Islamabad, Pakistan
farrukh.aslam@nu.edu.pk
[2] Department of Computer Engineering, Jeju National University, 66 Jejudaehakno, Jeju-si, Jeju 690-756, Korea
{kjahn,philo}@jejunu.ac.kr

Abstract. In this paper, a new hierarchical routing protocol called Location-aware Grid-based Hierarchical Routing (LGHR) is proposed for mobile ad hoc networks where the network is partitioned into non-overlapping zones and each zone is then further divided into smaller grids. Although, the protocol is a location-aware routing protocol, the routing is performed similar to link state routing i.e., the neighbor node information is needed for creating routing tables and making forwarding decisions. LGHR attempts to overcome the weaknesses of some of the existing location-aware routing protocols for mobile ad hoc networks. The performance of LGHR is compared with an existing location-aware routing protocol and the results show significant improvements of the proposed protocol over this protocol in terms of storage as well as communication overhead.

Keywords: Mobile Ad hoc Network (MANET), Hierarchical routing, Location-based routing, Non-overlapping Zones.

1 Introduction

A mobile ad hoc network is composed of a number of wireless nodes connected through radio links forming a dynamic autonomous network. Nodes communicate with one another without any centralized access points and each node acts both as a router as well as a host. Several routing protocols have been proposed by various researchers for mobile ad hoc networks which include proactive, reactive and hybrid routing [1-10]. Zone Routing Protocol (ZRP) [2] is a hybrid routing protocol in which proactive mechanism is performed for the intra-zone routing whereas reactive strategy is initiated during the inter-zone routing. Zone-based Hierarchical Link State (ZHLS) [4] is another hybrid routing protocol in which there is no central zone-head or leader and all nodes communicate in a peer-to-peer fashion. Proactive link state routing is done inside the zone and a reactive zone search mechanism is initiated when the destination node lies in a different zone than that of the source node. The problem with

---

* Corresponding author.

Z. Yu et al. (Eds.): UIC 2010, LNCS 6406, pp. 519–533, 2010.

this protocol is that every node has to keep the information of the whole zone topology which is not suitable if there are large numbers of nodes inside the zone. Since there is no central authority, every node has to keep and update routing tables even if they are not involved in forwarding packets to other nodes. Moreover, although ZHLS is a GPS-based protocol, it does not fully utilize the position information taken by the GPS receiver. For example, if a node wants to send a packet and the destination lies in the same zone, it uses its intra-zone routing table made on the basis of local link state information. And if the destination node does not lie in the same zone, it initiates a reactive zone search mechanism in order to get the zone ID of the destination. The protocol can save a lot of messages if it exploits the location information received by the GPS receiver. By knowing the location of the destination, it can easily identify the zone ID of the destination with the help of a zone map. The location of the destination can be taken from the location server as done in other location-aware protocols such as LAR, GPSR, and GRID etc.

In GRID [8], which is another location-aware reactive routing protocol, authors propose a grid-based routing mechanism in which every grid has a gateway node and routing is performed only through gateways in a grid-by-grid manner. The gateway node is elected by a gateway election procedure. One major problem with this protocol is that, since the grid size is small, the gateway nodes are likely to move out of the grid very frequently as the criterion for gateway election is only the shortest distance from the center of the grid. Hence, the nodes inside the grid have to initiate the gateway election procedure very frequently causing the network to become unstable. In GRID, there is no consideration for the speed and direction of movement of the gateway nodes. Moreover, since the routing is performed in a grid-by-grid manner and there can be several grids in a node's radio range, a packet has to travel several extra hops, which makes the protocol inefficient.

In this paper, a Location-aware Grid-based Hierarchical Routing Protocol (LGHR) is proposed for mobile ad hoc networks. Each node in the network is assumed to know its position with the help of a GPS receiver etc. The protocol attempts to overcome the problems mentioned above in both ZHLS and GRID routing protocols.

The rest of the paper is organized as follows: Sections 2 and 3 discuss the proposed protocol and its basic routing mechanism. Section 4 explains the mathematical analysis. Evaluation is done in section 5 and finally section 6 concludes the paper.

2 Location-Aware Grid-Based Hierarchical Routing Protocol

In our location-aware hierarchical routing protocol, the role of leader and gateway nodes is introduced. As stated earlier, the network is divided into non-overlapping zones. Each zone is controlled by a central node called leader. The leader is responsible for maintaining the routing information as well as making routing decisions inside a zone. A zone is further divided into smaller grids where one node is elected as a gateway node and is responsible for routing the packets to other nodes. The routing is performed in a gateway-by-gateway manner.

2.1 Network Layout and Zone Size

The network is divided into zones. Each zone is further divided into smaller equal-sided grids. Each grid can have minimum zero or maximum one gateway node. A gateway node is elected out of all the nodes present in the grid. These gateway nodes are responsible for forwarding packets in the network. Other nodes in the same grid are not involved in performing the routing operations. The layout of the network including zones, grids and gateways is shown in Fig. 1.

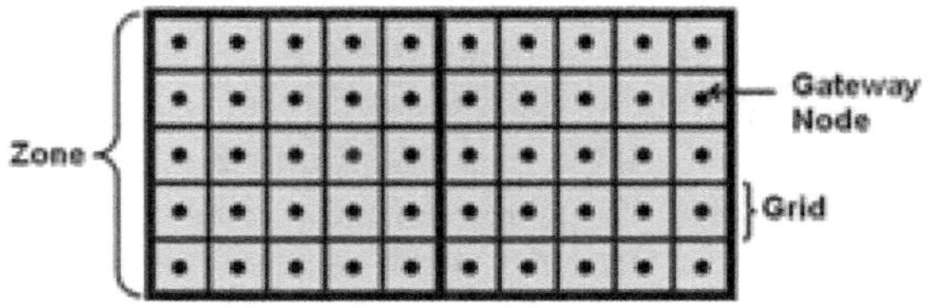

Fig. 1. The network is divided into zones and each zone is further divided into grids. Each grid can have a gateway node which is elected according to the gateway election procedure.

An important thing while dividing the network into zones is fixing the size of a zone as well as the size of each small grid. The zone size should be kept in such a way that it minimizes the communication as well as routing overhead. Hence, if the leader is in the middle of the zone, it should be able to reach any node inside the zone in less number of hops. Also, there is a need to fix the size of each small grid in a zone. In the proposed protocol, each side of a grid is kept as $r/2\sqrt{2}$ so that a node in a grid can access all nodes in its neighboring grids from anywhere in the grid. Fig. 2 (a) shows the reason why the side length of a grid is taken as $r/2\sqrt{2}$.

2.1.1 Leader Node

In LGHR, each zone in the network has a leader. The main responsibility of a leader is to lessen the routing burden on other nodes in a zone. The leader maintains two kinds of tables; a neighbor-table and a zone-table. Neighbor-table contains the neighbor node information of nodes inside a zone which is periodically sent to the leader by these nodes. Zone-table contains information about all the connected zones in the network. The leader performs two major tasks. First, it stores the neighbor information periodically sent by nodes of a zone in a neighbor-table. On the basis of this information, it constructs the intra-zone routing table for that zone. Secondly, it keeps the inter-zone connectivity information in a zone-table and performs the inter-zone routing based on this zone-table.

Leader Region. The *leader- region* is an area where the leader node can move around after becoming leader. Also, only the nodes inside a *leader-region* can compete for becoming a leader. Since all nodes are mobile, the leader can also move out of its *leader-region*. In order to make the routing process more stable, the size of the leader region is fixed in such a way that even if the leader is not at the center of the zone, it still functions as the leader. In other words, as long as it is inside the *leader-region*, it continues to perform its duties as leader. The *leader-region* is therefore taken to be $3d \times 3d$ where $d = r/2\sqrt{2}$ and 'r' is the radius of the radio range of a mobile node. The reason for fixing the value of *leader-region* is that if the value of *leader-region* changes frequently, the network may not work in a stable manner. Secondly, fixing the value to $3r/2\sqrt{2}$ is due to the fact that even if the leader is at the extreme corner of the leader region, it is still able to access the center of the zone easily. Once it moves out of the leader region, it can inform the nodes near that center of the zone that it is no more a leader now and therefore, the nodes near the center can initiate the leader election process again to elect a new leader.

Leader Election. A node nearest to the physical center of a zone is chosen as leader. Any node is considered eligible to become leader if it meets the following criteria: First, it should have enough resources e.g., storage, battery, and processing power etc. for which the values are predefined, and secondly, it should be inside the *leader-region*. A contesting node can announce itself as leader and send its position to all nodes inside the *leader-region*. Any other node nearer to the physical center of the zone can reject the announcement and declare itself as new leader. If it does not hear any other claim within a predefined interval, it becomes the leader. The node will serve as a leader even if it moves to another position inside the *leader-region*. However, if it moves out of the *leader-region*, it informs the nodes within the leader-region and these nodes do the same leader election procedure and elect a new leader.

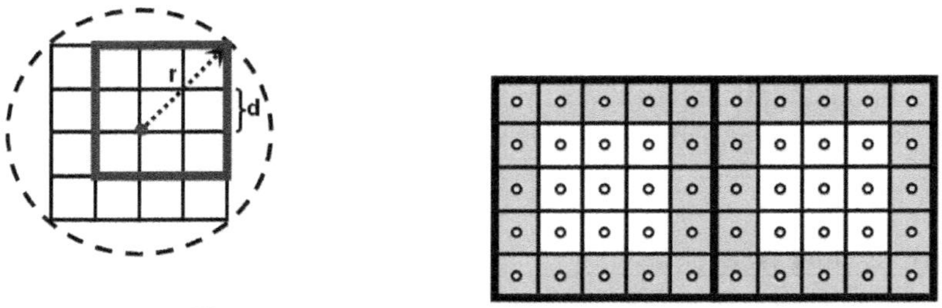

$d = r/2\sqrt{2}$

(a) (b)

Fig. 2. (a) The size 'd' of each side of a grid. (b) Two adjacent zones where the shaded grid contains the *Edge Gateway* nodes whereas the white grids have *Intermediate Gateway* nodes.

Every leader in a zone periodically broadcasts its identity to all nodes in its zone by sending the *leader-id* and its *position*. Each node in the zone pro-actively sends its position and list of neighbors to the leader node. Therefore, the leader knows the local topology inside the zone and maintains the neighbor-table. If a node is connected to a node in another zone, the *zone-id* is written in the neighbor-table instead of the *node-id*. The leader also maintains zone-table and sends it to all the leaders in other zones. This is done by using its inter-zone routing table. In case the leader fails then other nodes will stop receiving the periodic announcement packet from the leader. If the packet is not received until some predefined interval, the nodes assume that the leader is failed. Hence, the leader election process starts again and the nodes elect a new leader. If there is no node present in *leader-region*, the *leader-region* is expanded to the whole zone and leader election process is performed using all nodes in the zone.

2.1.2 Gateway Node

A node in each grid in a zone is elected as a gateway which is mainly responsible for routing packets in the network. Nodes as well as gateways in a zone send their neighbor information to the leader node. While sending their neighbor information, gateways also identify themselves in the same message so that the leader knows which nodes are gateway nodes. Based on this information, the leader constructs routing tables and periodically broadcasts them to the gateway nodes.

In our proposed protocol, there are two kinds of gateway nodes within a zone. One is called *Edge Gateway* nodes and another is called *Intermediate Gateway* nodes. *Edge Gateways* are those gateway nodes that are at the edge or boundary of a zone. All other gateways in a zone except the *Edge Gateways* are *Intermediate Gateway* nodes. The reason to classify gateways into two categories is due to their different functionalities. *Edge Gateways* are responsible for storing both intra-zone as well as inter-zone routing tables whereas the *Intermediate Gateways* are responsible for storing only the intra-zone routing tables. Hence, *Intermediate Gateways* are supposed to forward a packet within their zone and *Edge Gateways* forward packets to or from other zones. The main reason for classifying gateways into two kinds is to lessen the burden from the *Intermediate Gateway* nodes. Since the *Edge Gateways* are at the boundary of a zone, they are in a better position to maintain inter-zone routing tables. The two kinds of gateway nodes are shown in Fig. 2(b).

Gateway Election. *Only one node can be elected as gateway out of several candidate nodes. Gateway election procedure is slightly different from the leader election but it is same for both Edge and Intermediate Gateways. Any eligible node that wants to become a gateway announces itself as gateway node and broadcasts its position as well as its velocity to other nodes in the grid. The decision of making it a gateway depends on the following distance formula:*

$$dist_i = \sqrt{(X_i - X_c)^2 + (Y_i - Y_c)^2 + V_i^2} \tag{1}$$

where, X_i and Y_i are the position co-ordinates of the *ith* announcing node, X_c and Y_c are the center co-ordinates of the grid and V_i is the velocity of the *ith* node. The velocity V_i can be represented as:

$$\overrightarrow{V_i} = \overrightarrow{V_{ix}} + \overrightarrow{V_{iy}} \tag{2}$$

Based on the distance formula in eq. (1), the distance from the center of the grid is calculated. This formula incorporates both position co-ordinates as well as the velocity of the moving nodes. It will elect that node as gateway which has the minimum value of '*dist*' i.e., a node that is closer to the center of the grid as well as it has a small value of velocity would be elected as gateway. Hence, if a node that is nearest to the center and has very high velocity will not be elected as gateway. Instead, a node that is not the nearest to the center of the grid but also not the farthest having low velocity would be elected as the gateway node. If any other node has less value of *'dist'* than the announcing node, it rejects its claim and announces itself as the new gateway. Since the grid size is very small, if the only criterion for a gateway node is to be nearest to the center of the grid then there is a high probability that the gateway node would move out of the grid quite frequently and each time it moves out, a new gateway election procedure has to be started. Therefore, the network can become unstable causing the routing function to work in an undesirable manner.

One more thing to be noted is that even if the gateway elected is close to the center of the grid and its velocity is also slower than other nodes, it still can be a wrong choice to be elected as gateway. This can happen if the node is moving away from the center of the grid i.e., the direction of the moving node is opposite to the center. In this case, one has to consider the direction of velocity of the moving node.

In order to know the direction of velocity of a node, the angle θ is needed to be known with respect to the center of the grid. For this purpose, two angles are taken. The first angle θ_1 is taken with respect to the center of the grid when a node is at position (X_i, Y_i) and the second one θ_2 is taken along the X-axis with respect to the previous position $(X_i\text{-}1, Y_i\text{-}1)$ of the node currently at (X_i, Y_i). For each position, the slope m_1 and m_2 are needed. Finally the difference of both angles θ_1 and θ_2 is calculated. More details regarding this can be found in [11].

In order to know the right direction, the following two conditions must be satisfied:

1. $$\theta_{diff} \leq \frac{c}{1+e^{-\alpha dist_i}} \quad where \quad c = 45^\circ \quad and \quad \alpha > 1 \tag{3}$$

2. $$sign(m_1).sign(m_2) > 0 \tag{4}$$

Eq. (3) determines the direction of the moving node. The value of c shows the maximum value of angle for the competing nodes and it can be other than 45° depending upon the situation. This angle can be higher if there are small numbers of nodes in the grid. The parameter α is used for having transition from the maximum angle to the minimum angle of moving nodes. Larger value of α corresponds to an abrupt transition from the maximum angle to the minimum angle whereas a smaller value of α shows a slow transition of angle from the maximum value to the minimum. The condition in eq. (4) must also be satisfied i.e., the product of both the slopes m_1 and m_2 should be positive. This means that a node is moving in the same direction as it was at the previous step. Hence, for the gateway election procedure, two things are calculated: the distance and the direction of moving nodes. The distance formula is used from equation (1) and the direction of velocity is calculated from equations (3) and (4). For gateway election procedure, the three possible cases are listed below:

- If more than one nodes present in the grid and moving in different directions then *use distance formula with direction.*

- If more than one nodes present in the grid and no node is moving in the direction of the center then *use distance formula and ignore the direction.*
- If only one node present in the grid then *ignore the distance formula and ignore the direction.*

3 Zone Discovery and Basic Routing Mechanism

When a new node is activated initially, it gets its position with the help of a GPS receiver. Once it knows the position, it can easily figure out which zone it lies in using the zone map of the network.

3.1 Intra-zone Routing

Each node in a zone broadcasts a *hello* packet to its neighbors which contains its *node-id.* Also, every node in a zone sends its neighbor connectivity information to the leader node. This information includes its position and the list of its connected neighbors. From this neighbor information, the leader makes the neighbor table which contains the list of all the nodes and their neighbors. Based on the neighbor table, leader creates an intra-zone routing table for its own zone. Since only the gateway nodes forward the packet, the routing table entries include only the gateway nodes as the next hop node. Non-gateway nodes are included in the routing table only as destination nodes. After making the routing table, leader sends the individual routing tables to the respective gateway nodes. Gateway nodes use this table for making routing decisions.

The routing is mainly performed using gateway nodes. A node that wants to send a message sends it to one of the gateways in its neighborhood. Whenever a non-gateway node wants to send the packet to the destination node, it sends it to the gateway of its own grid. If there is no other node present in the grid then the source node itself is a gateway node and it already has its respective routing tables. When packet reaches a gateway node, it looks up the next hop information in the routing table and forwards packet to the next gateway node. This whole process is repeated until packet reaches the destination. The intra-zone routing process is shown in Fig. 3.

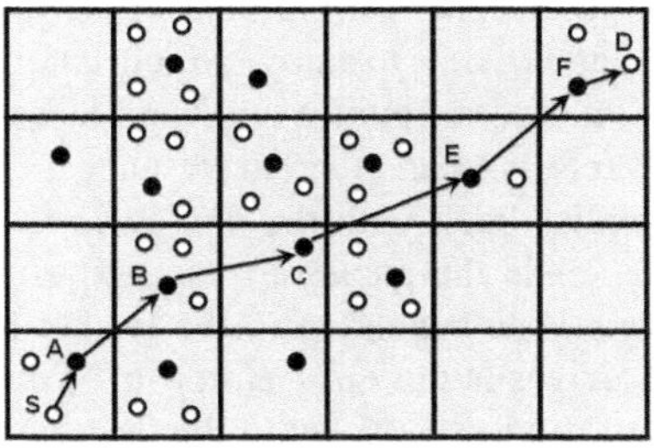

Fig. 3. Intra-zone routing mechanism; filled black circles are gateway nodes whereas unfilled circles are non-gateway nodes. Routing is performed in a gateway-by-gateway manner.

In the proposed protocol, if a gateway node is in the radio range of another gateway that does not lie in the adjacent grid, it can still forward packet to this gateway in its non-adjacent grid. This situation can be seen in Fig. 3 where node C sends a packet to node E despite the fact that there are other gateways present in C's adjacent grids. The reason is that the routing is performed in a gateway-by-gateway manner, not in a grid-by-grid manner. Since node E lies in the radio range of node C, the routing table is made in such a way that even if node E does not lie in C's adjacent grid, it is still selected as next hop gateway.

3.2 Inter-zone Routing

Every leader in the network sends the leader and zone information to all other leaders in the network. This information is forwarded using its intra-zone routing table which contains the routing information of the connected zones as well. The leader information contains the *leader-id* and the connected neighbor zones along with the cost in reaching those zones, which is mainly the distance between leader and other zones. Based on this information, leader makes the zone table. Using this information, leader then creates inter-zone routing table and sends it to all the *Edge Gateway* nodes. These gateway nodes use this table for making inter-zone routing decisions.

The reason for sending the inter-zone routing table to only the *Edge Gateways* is that these gateways are at the boundary of a zone or in other words, these *Edge Gateways* are at the intersection of two zones whereas the *Intermediate Gateways* are inside the zone and are not connected to other zones. Therefore, by doing this, a lot of extra storage overhead as well as communication overhead can be reduced by giving this responsibility to only the *Edge Gateways.*

Initially, the source node that wants to send a packet sends it to the gateway node of its own grid. The gateway checks in its routing table whether the destination node is present in the same zone it lies in. If it cannot find the destination in its intra-zone routing table, inter-zone routing is initiated. It is assumed that, like other location-based routing protocols e.g., LAR, GRID etc., a node can know the position of the destination with the help of a location server. Here, if the gateway cannot find the destination node in its intra-zone routing table, it means that the destination lies in another zone. Based on the position information, the gateway finds out the destination node's zone by mapping the position of the destination on a zone map. Here, there are two cases. If the current gateway is an *Edge Gateway*, it can forward the packet to the next gateway based on its inter-zone routing table. But, if the current gateway is an *Intermediate Gateway*, it has no way to know which gateway to forward the packet since it does not have the inter-zone routing table and keeps only the intra-zone routing table. Therefore, the *Intermediate Gateway* sends a *Next-Zone* request to the leader node. The leader replies back with the *next-zone-id*. After receiving the *next-zone-id*, the gateway node sends the packet to the next zone based on its intra-zone routing table. The *next-zone-id* is appended in the packet and forwarded to the next gateway. Once the packet arrives at the *Edge Gateway* of the next zone, if the destination lies in the same zone, it sends the packet to the destination based on its intra-zone routing table. If the destination does not lie in that zone, the *Edge Gateway* appends the *next-zone-id* in that packet and sends it to a gateway node in its zone. The next zone information is taken from the inter-zone routing table, not from the leader.

Therefore, the source gateway has to take the *next-zone-id* from the leader node only once in the beginning. Later on, the *Edge Gateway* of the next zone appends the *next-zone-id* from its own inter-zone routing table. The process is repeated at every zone until the packet reaches the destination. Here, because of the *next-zone-id* request to the leader, LGHR can be categorized as a hybrid routing protocol, where proactive neighbor connectivity information is sent by all nodes to perform intra-zone routing and a reactive *next-zone-id* request is initiated by an *Intermediate Gateway* node that wants to send a packet to a node in another zone. Inter-zone routing table is also made by using the shortest path algorithm based on number of hops from the destination.

4 Mathematical Analysis

In this section, the mathematical analysis is done for both ZHLS and LGHR. Based on this analysis, the evaluation and comparison is carried out for both protocols. The comparison of LGHR with GRID protocol cannot be fully done in all aspects as GRID is a reactive routing protocol whereas LGHR is a proactive/hybrid routing protocol.

4.1 Storage Overhead

First of all, it is assumed that the total number of nodes in the network are N and there are M zones in the network. It is also assumed that all the nodes are uniformly distributed in the whole network. Hence, the average number of nodes in one zone will be N/M. The average number of zones connected to each zone is Z.

4.1.1 For ZHLS

For each node, entries in all Node LSPs [4] are N/M and entries in all Zone LSPs are M. The entries in intra-zone routing table are $N/M - 1 + Z$ and the entries in inter-zone routing table are $M - 1$.

Hence, the total number of entries stored in one node

$= 2N/M + 2M - 2 + Z$

Total entries stored in *N/M* nodes in a zone = $N/M\ (2N/M + 2M - 2 + Z)$

Total entries stored by all nodes in *M* zones in the whole network by ZHLS are:

$$\text{Entries}_{\text{ZHLS}} = 2N^2/M + 2NM - 2N + ZN \tag{5}$$

4.1.2 For LGHR

In LGHR, *Edge Gateways* store both intra-zone and inter-zone routing tables, whereas the *Intermediate Gateways* store only the intra-zone routing tables. Since, the number of zones and grids are known at the design time, the maximum number of gateway nodes present in a zone can be determined as each grid can have a maximum of one gateway. For the purpose of generalization, it is assumed that every grid has a gateway node in a zone.

Let G be the average number of gateway nodes in a zone. Then, the total number of *Edge Gateways* in a zone is G_E and the total number of *Intermediate Gateways* in a zone is G_I. Therefore, $G = G_I + G_E$

In LGHR, the leader node makes and keeps routing tables for all the gateway nodes only, not for all the nodes in a zone.

***In case of Leader Node*:** The entries in *Node Table* are N/M and entries in *Zone Table* are M. Entries in one intra-zone routing table are $N/M - 1 + Z$ and entries in 'G' intra-zone routing tables are $G\ (N/M - 1 + Z)$. The entries in one inter-zone routing table are $M - 1$ and entries in G_E inter-zone routing tables are $G_E\ (M - 1)$.

The entries stored in a Leader Node

$$= N/M + M + G(N/M - 1 + Z) + G_E(M - 1)$$

Hence, total entries stored by *M* leaders in the network i.e., $\text{Entries}_{\text{Leader}}$ are:

$$Entries_{Leader} = N + M^2 + MG(N/M - 1 + Z) + MG_E(M - 1) \tag{6}$$

***In case of Gateway Node*:** Since *Edge Gateways* store both intra-zone routing tables and inter-zone routing tables, and *Intermediate Gateways* store only intra-zone routing tables, therefore, the entries stored in all *Edge Gateways* in the whole network are:

$$Entries_{Edge} = MG_E\ (N/M + M + Z - 2) \tag{7}$$

The entries stored in an *Intermediate Gateway* are $N/M - 1 + Z$. The entries stored in all *Intermediate Gateways* in the whole network are:

$$Entries_{Intermediate} = MG_I\ (N/M - 1 + Z) \tag{8}$$

Total entries stored by the gateway nodes i.e., $\text{Entries}_{\text{Gateway}}$ are:

$$Entries_{Gateway} = MG_E\ (N/M + M + Z - 2) + MG_I\ (N/M - 1 + Z) \tag{9}$$

Hence, total entries stored by the LGHR protocol are:

$$Entries_{LGHR} = Entries_{Leader} + Entries_{Gateway}$$

$$= \{N + M^2 + MG\ (N/M - 1 + Z) + MG_E\ (M - 1)\} + \{MG_E\ (N/M + M + Z - 2)\} + \{MG_I\ (N/M - 1 + Z)\} \tag{10}$$

4.2 Communication Overhead

The communication overhead analysis is done for both ZHLS and LGHR. For analysis, it is assumed that the nodes are uniformly distributed in the network. There are *N* nodes in the network and the average number of nodes in a zone is *N/M*.

Topology Creation Overhead

According to [4], the total communication overhead generated by the ZHLS protocol for creating the topology in one message exchange is:

$$S_{ZHLS} = N^2 / M + NM \tag{11}$$

where, N^2 / M is the message overhead due to node LSPs and NM is the overhead generated by zone LSPs.

In case of the proposed protocol LGHR,

(a) All nodes in a zone send their neighbor information to the leader node. Therefore, the amount of communication overhead generated by neighbor connectivity messages (Node LSPs in case of ZHLS) in one zone is *(N/M – 1)*. Since there are M zones in the network, therefore, the total overhead generated in the whole network due to node connectivity messages is:

$$Overhead_{node} = N - M \tag{12}$$

(b) Every leader in a zone sends the zone connectivity information (Zone LSP in case of ZHLS) to every leader in other zones. The overhead generated by these messages is:

$$Overhead_{zone} = M\ (M - 1) \tag{13}$$

(c) Every leader broadcasts the whole routing tables to the gateway nodes in its zone. Upon receiving the message, the gateway nodes store their own routing table and discard others. Non-gateway nodes just ignore the message upon receiving.

The number of routing table messages broadcasted by a leader intended for gateways in one routing table exchange in a zone = 1.

Total number of routing table messages sent by leaders in *M* zones are:

$$Overhead_{gateway} = M \tag{14}$$

Using equations (12), (13) and (14), the total communication overhead generated for topology creation by the proposed protocol is represented by:

$$Overhead_{LGHR} = Overhead_{node} + Overhead_{zone} + Overhead_{gateway} \tag{15}$$

$$Overhead_{LGHR} = M^2 - M + N$$

Overhead Generated by Zone Request

In LGHR, a source node can know the position of the destination from a location server, like any other location-based protocol. The location server sends the location of the destination to the requesting node. Once the position of the destination is known, it is very easy to know which zone the destination lies in by using zone map. Based on this information, the intra-zone and inter-zone routing decisions are made.

The overhead generated by ZHLS for zone search request is L_{ZHLS} which is:

$$L_{ZHLS} = (M - 1) \tag{16}$$

Overhead generated by LGHR for one location request to the location server is:

$$L_{LGHR} = 1 \tag{17}$$

Leader and Gateway Election Overhead

Leader nodes are elected very infrequently as the leader region in a zone is large enough for a leader to stay for longer periods of time. Therefore, the overhead generated due to leader election is not very high. The gateway nodes are elected on the basis of the lower speed and shorter distance from the center of the grid, therefore, the gateway election mechanism will not be initiated very frequently.

Periodic Hello Messages by the Leader Node

The leader node sends periodic Hello messages to all nodes inside the zone just to tell its identity. Again, the interval can be long as the leader region is large enough for the leader to stay there for quite long time. The leader sends one Hello message to *(N/M-1)* nodes in a zone, so the overhead is *(N/M-1)* for one zone. Since there are *M* zones in the network, therefore:

Total overhead for leader announcement packet is:

$$\text{Overhead}_{\text{LeaderAnnounce}} = N - M \tag{18}$$

5 Evaluation

The proposed protocol LGHR is compared with ZHLS in terms of storage overhead as well as communication overhead generated using equations in our mathematical analysis.

5.1 Storage Overhead

Based on the storage overhead analysis in the previous section, both protocols LGHR and ZHLS are compared for 9 gateways per zone for a fixed number of 9 zones. The numbers of nodes in the entire network are increased up to 1000. It is assumed that each grid in a zone has one gateway and the gateways are separated as *Edge* and *Intermediate Gateways*. Naturally, as the numbers of nodes in the network are increased, the number of entries stored by both protocols also increases. In all cases, LGHR performs better than ZHLS and stores much less entries than ZHLS. The results are shown in Fig. 4.

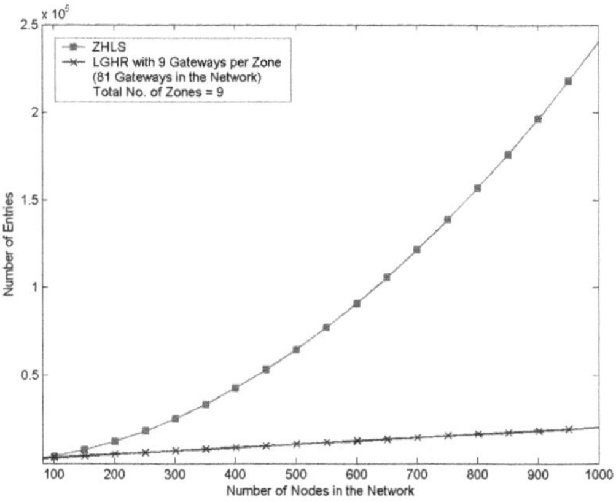

Fig. 4. Comparison of LGHR with ZHLS in terms of number of entries stored for a network of 1000 nodes having 9 zones in the network. The values are shown for 9 gateways per zone. Hence, the total number of gateways in the whole network becomes 81.

In case of 9 grids per zone with 9 zones in the network as shown in Fig. 4, there are a maximum of 81 gateways present in the whole network. In order to compare both protocols, the number of nodes must be same in both ZHLS and LGHR. As mentioned earlier, in ZHLS, every node stores all the tables whereas in LGHR, only the leader and gateway nodes store their respective tables. Therefore, by taking the maximum number of gateways mean that every grid has at least one node. In such a case, the node would be a gateway node.

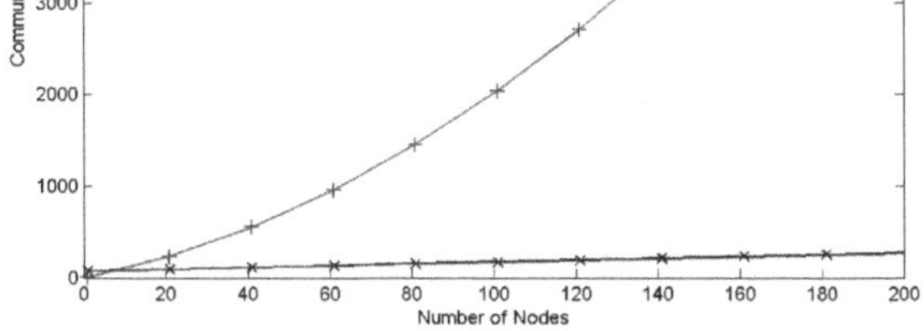

Fig. 5. Communication overhead for topology creation generated by both LGHR and ZHLS protocols in case of 9 zones in the network

The results shown are for the case of one gateway in each grid. Therefore, even if the numbers of nodes are increased in LGHR, there is a very minor increase in the number of entries stored, as the non-gateway nodes are not responsible for storing any tables; whereas in ZHLS, with increase in the number of nodes, every node has to store all the required entries and hence, there is a major increase in the storage overhead incurred by the protocol. In the figure, the effect on the storage overhead is shown from the point when the numbers of nodes in both protocols are same.

5.2 Communication Overhead

The comparison for communication overhead for topology creation for both ZHLS and LGHR protocols is shown in Fig. 5 based on our mathematical analysis. The figure shows the difference between both protocols in case of 9 zones. In all cases, the communication overhead generated by LGHR is much smaller than that of ZHLS.

6 Conclusion

In this paper, a new location-aware hierarchical routing protocol LGHR is proposed for mobile ad hoc networks for which the network is divided into non-overlapping zones and each zone is then further divided into smaller grids. The proposed protocol is compared with another location-aware routing protocol known as ZHLS. For comparison with ZHLS, the mathematical analysis is done and both ZHLS and LGHR are evaluated for storage overhead as well as communication overhead. The analysis clearly indicates that LGHR performs better than ZHLS in terms of storage overhead as well as communication overhead generated by all nodes. As a future work, the proposed protocol will be implemented in Network Simulator (NS-2) and its performance will be compared with other ad hoc routing protocols.

Acknowledgement

"This research was supported by the MKE (The Ministry of Knowledge Economy), Korea, under the ITRC (Information Technology Research Center) support program supervised by the NIPA (National IT Industry Promotion Agency)" (NIPA-2010-(C1090-1011-0009)).

References

1. Basagni, S., Chlamtac, I., Syrotiuk, V.R., Woodward, B.A.: A distance routing effect algorithm for mobility (DREAM). In: Proceedings of the 4th Annual ACM/IEEE International Conference on Mobile computing and Networking (MobiCom 1998), New York, NY, USA, pp. 76–84 (1998)
2. Haas, Z.J., Pearlman, M.R.: The performance of query control schemes for the zone routing protocol. In: Proceedings of ACM SIGCOMM Conference, pp. 167–177 (1998)
3. Jacquet, P., Muhlethaler, P., Qayyum, A.: Optimized link state routing protocol, RFC 3626 (2003)

4. Joa-Ng, M., Lu, I.-T.: A Peer-to-Peer Two-level Link State Routing Protocol for Mobile Ad hoc Networks. IEEE Journal on Selected Areas in Communication 17(8), 1415–1425 (1999)
5. Johnson, D.B., Maltz, D.A.: Dynamic Source Routing in Ad Hoc Wireless Networks. In: Mobile Computing, pp. 152–181. Kluwer Academic Publishers, Dordrecht (1996)
6. Karp, B., Kung, H.T.: GPSR: greedy perimeter stateless routing for wireless networks. In: Proceedings of the 6th Annual ACM/IEEE International Conference on Mobile Computing and Networking (MobiCom 2000), pp. 243–254 (2000)
7. Ko, Y.B., Vaidya, N.H.: Location-Aided routing (LAR) in mobile ad hoc networks. Wireless Networks 6(4), 307–321 (2000)
8. Liao, W.-H., Tseng, Y.-C., Sheu, J.-P.: Grid: A fully location-aware routing protocol for mobile ad hoc networks. Telecommunication Systems 18(1), 37–60 (2001)
9. Park, V.D., Corson, M.S.: Temporally-ordered routing algorithm (TORA), IETF Internet Draft (1999)
10. Perkins, C.E., Belding-Royer, E.M., Das, S.: Ad hoc on-demand distance vector (AODV) routing. IETF RFC 3561 (2003)
11. Khan, F.A.: Location-aware routing and geocasting in wireless ad hoc networks, PhD Thesis, Cheju National University, South Korea (2007)

Towards an Efficient and Accurate EEG Data Analysis in EEG-Based Individual Identification

Qinglin Zhao, Hong Peng*, Bin Hu, LanLan Li, YanBing Qi, QuanYing Liu, and Li Liu

School of Information Science and Engineering, Lanzhou University, Lanzhou, China
{qlzhao,pengh,bh}@lzu.edu.cn, lilanl06@lzu.cn

Abstract. Individual identification plays an important role in privacy protection and information security. Especially, with the development of brain science, individual identification based on Electroencephalograph (EEG) may be applicable. The key to realize EEG-based identification is to find the signal features with unique individual characteristics in spite of numerous signal processing algorithms and techniques. In this paper, EEG signals of 10 subjects stay in calm were collected from Cz point with eyes closed. Then EEG signal features were extracted by spectrum estimation (linear analysis) and nonlinear dynamics methods and further classified by k-Nearest-Neighbor classifier to identify each subject. Classification successful rate has reached 97.29% with linear features, while it is only 44.14% with nonlinear dynamics features. The experiment result indicates that the linear features of EEG, such as center frequency, max power, power ratio, average peak-to-peak value and coefficients of AR model may have better performance than the nonlinear dynamics parameters of EEG in individual identification.

Keywords: Individual identification, EEG, linear analysis, nonlinear dynamics method.

1 Introduction

Individual identification is crucial in real world and virtual network. Especially in the age of digitalizing and network, identity fraud is one of the most common criminal activities and is associated with large costs and serious security issues (such as leakage of important documents and the terror threats towards VIPs). Traditional identification methods, such as documents, user name and password no longer meet the demands of reality. Thus identification technology based on biometrics has emerged in nineties of the last century, such as fingerprints[1],retina[2],iris[3], voice[4], facial recognition[5], palm prints[6] and DNA identification[7], etc. However, each biometric method has its own limitations and is hard to be utilized in identifying individuals separately. For instance, fingerprints and palm prints for identification can not be applied to the hand disability. What's worse, the offender may make use of dead people's fingerprint

* Corresponding author.

Z. Yu et al. (Eds.): UIC 2010, LNCS 6406, pp. 534–547, 2010.

or palm print to attack. As to voice and face recognition, their characteristics are unstable. Voice can be changed with the physical condition and aging, and face shape can be changed with facial expression. For retina and iris, the uncertain risk of retina recognition cause signal acquisition difficulties and iris detection is limited by light, which can not be applied to dark environment. Furthermore, DNA identification can not be used in real-time system.

EEG (electroencephalogram) is a new type electo-physiological feature, compared to the biological characteristics mentioned above. Although EEG-based biometric person identification is still in its launching stage, it has its own unique advantages: 1) can't be forged or stolen; 2) EEG signal exist in all living human, and doesn't disappear because of physical disability or external damage; 3) it is harmless and easy to collect EEG signals by electrodes placed on the scalp of the subjects; 4) EEG can be integrated with other biological characteristics to identify individuals, which has great potential in automated systems with high security.

EEG signals, generated by human brain[8],will not disappear as long as life continues. Human brain contains about 10^{11} neurons and 10^{15} synapses. Different person has different brain characteristics, thus has unique EEG signal features. Therefore, EEG-based identification is feasible. According to pervious research works, comparison between the performance of linear and non-linear dynamics features in the domain of EEG-based individual identification hasn't been committed up to our knowledge. Therefore this paper is engaged in biometric identification based on EEG, especially in efforts to find effective features to describe EEG characteristics in individual identification by comparison between the performance of linear and non-linear dynamics features. Procedures included are EEG signal acquisition, feature extraction, classification, and ultimate identification.

The significance of this paper are as follows: 1) The high identification success rate of our primary experiment suggest that EEG may depict some individual characteristics and individual identification based on EEG is feasible in practice; 2) Unobtrusive to subjects: the subjects in our experiments just need to relax themselves with eyes closed and only one electrode on their scalp; 3) Comparison between linear and nonlinear methods is applied in this paper. The results of the experiment indicate that the linear features of EEG (power spectrum, center frequency, average peak-to-peak value, power ratio and coefficients of AR model) work better than the nonlinear dynamic parameters in individual identification.

2 Relevant Research

Individual identification based on biometric detects unique physical characteristics of individuals and attempts to establish the identity of given person out of a closed pool of peoples (one-to-N matching). During recent years, with the development of brain science and biometric-based identification technology, EEG-based individual identification solution has been proposed. Poulos[9],etc, used a LVQ (Learning Vector Quantizer) network to classify AR parameters describing the alpha rhythm EEG feature, with the classification performance of 72 to 84 percent, but the experiments were conducted for a relatively small number of subjects. Paranjape et al[10] proposed a method using AR model of EEG signals to identify individuals, with classification accuracy ranges from 49 to 85%. In the above methods EEG signal was recorded while the subjects were resting with eyes closed and with eyes open or closed. Palaniappan et al[11] later recorded VEP (Visual evoked potentials) while each subject perceived a single picture. However, the method need 64 electrodes to collect signal and requires that subjects focus on pictures, which makes subjects eye fatigue and may not be accessible to the blind. Graz College in Austria used 3 electrodes and collected EEG signals from C3, Cz and C4 respectively, then extracted features and finished classification with 80%-92% accuracy[12], but still demands strictly for the subjects.

The above methods presume that EEG signal is stationary and use linear methods (spectrum estimation) to extract feature, without consideration of nonstationarity of the brain system. The human brain is a dynamic system in a nature of complexity, Self-Organization and nonlinearity. Nonlinear dynamics can well describe nonstationarity of brain. On Plexus physiology point of view, the essence of EEG is cortical electrical activity of neurons. EEG signal recorded according to 10-20 international system standard is produced by lots of neurons postsynaptic potential changes and strongly nonlinear. That's to say, traditional linear analysis may not be sufficient to reflect its essential characteristics. Nonlinear dynamics methods can be used to analysis EEG and extract nonlinear dynamics parameters. Everyone may be different from others, thus different people's EEG nonlinearity of the same state may also be individual discriminate. In sum, nonlinear dynamics parameters can be applied to individual identification. Major nonlinear analysis of EEG signal includes complexity calculation and description of the levels of chaos.

In this paper, only one electrode is used to collect EEG signals with subjects' eyes closed. In order to improve the classification accuracy and explore the correlation between nonlinear dynamics parameters of EEG and person identification, we use both linear analysis and nonlinear dynamics methods to extract features, train data by KNN classification. The experiment result indicates that the linear features of EEG are better than the nonlinear dynamics parameters of EEG in individual identification.

3 Experimental Design

3.1 Experimental Procedure

Since raw EEG data is full of noise, data preprocessing is necessary. EEG data is filtered by a FIR filter of 2 and 40Hz. Further analysis is divided into two parts: the first part is using nonlinear dynamics method to extract features of EEG and linear algorithm to calculate six order AR coefficients; the second part is divided into three steps: firstly, divide alpha rhythms (8-13Hz)[13][14], theta rhythms (4-7Hz) and sensorimotor rhythm (SMR, 13-15Hz) of EEG respectively by band pass filters; secondly, in order to increase the signal-to-noise ratio, the alpha, theta and SMR rhythms filtered are extracted by ICA algorithm again to remove the artifacts; finally, linear features, center frequency, the max power and the power ratio of each rhythm, are obtained by AR models. Then the nonlinear dynamics features and the linear features are trained by classifier to identify individuals. The process of the study is illustrated by Figure 1.

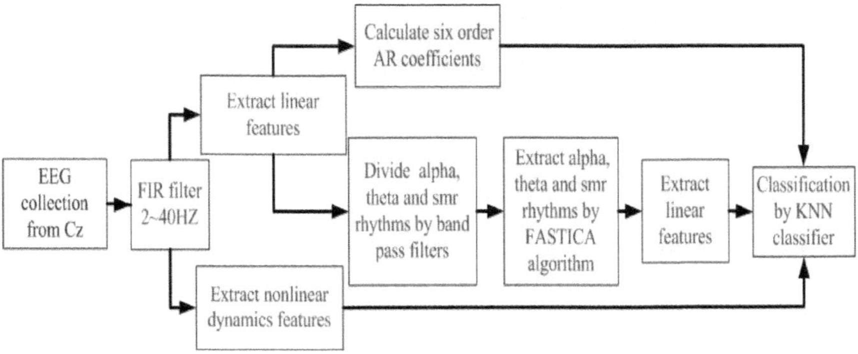

Fig. 1. The experimental procedure

3.2 Subjects and EEG Recording

In this experiment, a wireless device Nexus-4 system is used to collect subjects' EEG signals. 10 subjects (4 females and 6males) ages from 20 to 24 are arranged in a quiet and noninterference 10 m2 room. When they keep eyes closed and head still, their EEG signals are collected from Cz point in reference to A2 (the right ear lobe) according to 10-20 international system standard, illustrated in Figure 2. The data are sampled at 256HZ. Each collection time is shorted to 30s to free subjects. The EEG signal of each subject is recorded for five times at different time point distributed in a few days. Each EEG record is segmented into 2 parts with 3000 data points (samples) in length and each part is cut into three continuous 1000-point epochs. Since EEG signals can be seen as both stationary and non-stationary, signals are appropriate to be processed by linear algorithms and nonlinear dynamics methods.

4 Feature Extract

4.1 Signal Conditioning

In order to remove artifacts and obtaining better frequency characteristics, raw EEG signals needs to be filtered by FIR band pass filter with 2-40Hz cut off frequency at the first step, which can eliminate frequency interference and parts of artifact. After that, alpha rhythm (8-13Hz), theta rhythm (4-7Hz) and SMR rhythm (12-15Hz) were extracted from the conditioned signals by FIR band

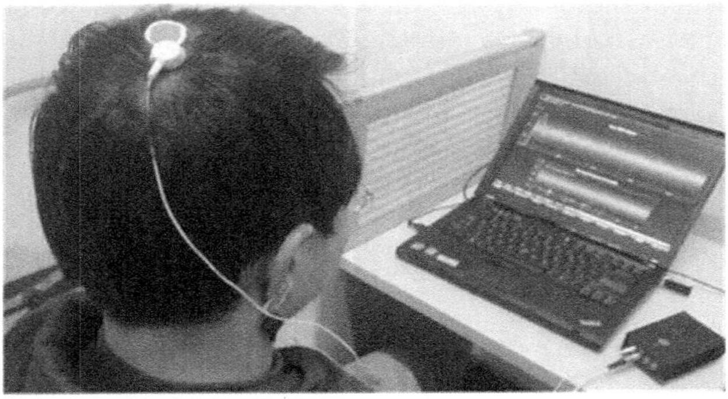

Fig. 2. A subject's EEG signals are recorded from Cz point

pass filter and FastICA[15] algorithms, which also plays a significant role in artifacts removal, such as ECG, EMG and eye-blink signals; moreover, it lays the foundation for the next step, model building and spectral analysis.

ICA aims at recovering independent sources from mixture EEGs, without knowing the mixing matrix and specific knowledge of the sources .If the sources are linearly mixed, under weak assumptions, ICA can recover the original sources. ICA is currently a popular method for blind source separation (BSS) of linear mixtures. The FastICA is the most popular algorithm for ICA at present, because FastICA[16][17] can extract the associated signals from eye-closed-EEG without knowing actual measurement of these signals and preserves other information. So FastICA was used to extract the signals, a series of sine and cosine signals were constructed as references of the extraction wave, take these series signals and EEGs to be input of FastICA mixing matrix, the FastICA algorithm is adopted to separate the signals, and then realized the corresponding waves extracting from EEG signal. It is fast and effective which is proved in this experiment.

4.2 Linear Analysis in Feature Extraction

After the removal of artifacts, the EEG signals can be considered as non-stationary random signal in short time, and obviously, parametric model is the main method to research and analyze the random signal. AR model applies to signals whose power spectrum has a peak which EEG signals fit well. EEG signals can usually be seen as being generated by a certain system which is stimulated by white noise, so we can analyze EEG signals by dealing with the relationship between the input and output of this system as long as the power of white noise and parameters of the system are known, shown in Figure.3. In other works, characteristics of EEG can be reflected by the coefficients of the model system, for example, the 6 coefficients of AR model in this paper.

The representation of AR model[18] is:

$$x(n) = -\sum_{k=1}^{p} a_k x(n-k) + u(n) \ . \tag{1}$$

in which p is the order of AR model, u(n) is white Guass noise (or the output uncorrelated errors), x(n) is input.

In building AR model[19], the order of AR model should be considered firstly. If the order is too high, power spectrum will be divisive, and it cannot guarantee the precision reversely. The prior experiments indicated that AR model in 6 8th orders can represent the EEG signal better, and we choose 6th order in this paper.

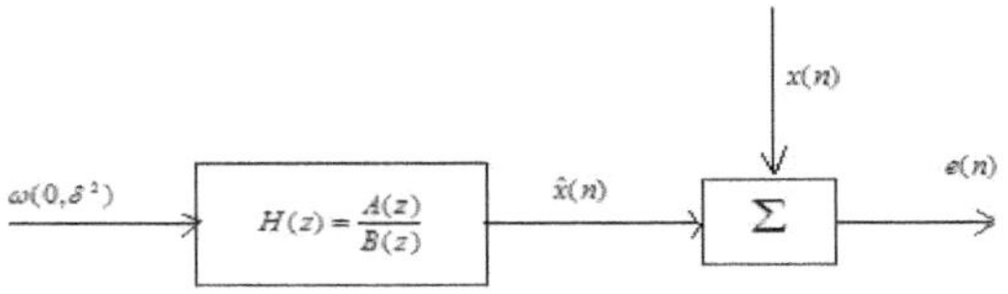

Fig. 3. AR model

Power Spectrum and Center Frequency. If the coefficients of AR model have been calculated, the power spectrum can be obtained by the following equation:

$$\Gamma_{xx}(f) = \frac{\delta_w^2}{\left|1 + \sum\limits_{k=1}^{p} a_k e^{-j2\pi fk}\right|^2} \ . \tag{2}$$

In addition, integrating the power spectrum in each rhythm can obtain the power and then obtain power ratio of each rhythm to the whole signals. The frequency which makes the power maximize is the center frequency. Power ratio, center frequency and the max power are useful features to reflect the characteristics of EEG.

4.3 Nonlinear Dynamics Method

Nonlinear analysis of EEG research are mainly calculating the complexity of EEG and describing the chaotic characteristics of brain. In this paper, C_0-complexity and ApEn are used to describe the complexity of EEG, and the correlation dimension and the largest Lyapunov exponent are used to describe the chaotic characteristics of brain.

Approximate Entropy (ApEn)[20]-[22]. ApEn is a statistical property which can be used to quantify the complexity or irregularity of a signal and ApEn measures the rate of time series producing new information. For the EEG time series, it assigns a positive value, with larger ApEn values corresponding more complexity or irregularity in the data.

The ApEn algorithm process is as follows:

1) Let the original data be X(n)= x(1), x(2),..., x(N), where N is the total number of data points. Form m-vectors X(1), X(2),..., X(N-m + 1) defined by:

$$X(i) = [x(i), x(i+1), \ldots, x(i+m-1)], i = 1, 2, \ldots, N-m+1 \; . \tag{3}$$

2) Define the distance between X(i) and X(j), d[X(i), X(j)], as the maximum absolute difference between their corresponding scalar elements.

$$d[X(i), X(j)] = \max(|x(i+k) - x(j+k)\;|) \; . \tag{4}$$

3) For a given X(i), count the number of j (j = 1, 2, . . . , N-m + 1)for j != i such that d [X (i) , X (j)] r ,denoted as N m (i). Then, for i = 1, 2, . . . , N-m + 1,

$$\mathrm{C_r^m}\,(\mathrm{i}) = \mathrm{N^m}\,(\mathrm{i})\,/(\mathrm{N} - \mathrm{m} + 1) \; . \tag{5}$$

The $\mathrm{C_r^m}$ (i) values measure, within a tolerance r, the regularity (frequency) of patterns similar to a given one of window length m.

4) Compute the natural logarithm of each $\mathrm{C_r^m}$ (i), and compute the average of it over

$$\Phi^m(r) = \frac{1}{N-m+1} \sum_{i=1}^{N-m+1} \ln C_r^m(i) \; . \tag{6}$$

Where $\Phi^m(r)$ represents the average frequency of all the m-point patterns in the sequence which is still remain close to each other.

5) Increase the dimension to m+1. Repeat steps 1) to 4) and find $\mathrm{C_r^{m+1}}$ (i) and $\Phi^{m+1}(r)$

6) The approximate entropy is defined as:

$$ApEn(m, r) = \lim_{N \to \infty} \left[\Phi^m(r) - \Phi^{m+1}(r)\right] \; . \tag{7}$$

In actual operation,the number of data point is limited when the data length is N and the result obtained through the above steps is the estimate of ApEn,which can be denoted as:

$$ApEn(m, r) = \Phi^m(r) - \Phi^{m+1}(r) \; . \tag{8}$$

Obviously, the value of the estimate depends on m and r. The two parameters must be fixed before ApEn can be calculated. As suggested by Pincus, m can be taken as 2 and r can be taken as (0.1 0.25) SDx, where SDx is the standard deviation of the original data sequence x (n). In our study we have used m = 2 and r =0.15.

C_0-complexity[23-24]. C_0-complexity is a description of time sequences randomness. The algorithm not only can get accurately results for small data sets, but also avoids time series reconstructed process. The dynamic tendency of C_0-complexity to EEG signal agrees with Approximate Entropy. Compared to Approximate Entropy, C_0-complexity is mainly calculating FFT. Do once C_0-complexity only need once FFT calculating, so it has advantage of saving a part of the computational effort.

XU Jing-Hua et al put forward C_0-complexity at practical analysis of EEG signal processing. The essence of C_0-complexity is divided time sequences into regular part and random part. C_0-complexity is defined as the ratio of square between random part and time axis to square between the whole time sequences and time axis. Recently years, the algorithm was improved and validated in mathematics by CAI Zhi-Jing et al which was given as follows:

Assuming that $\{x(t), t = 0, 1, 2, ..., N-1\}$ length of the time sequences is N,

$$f(k) = \frac{1}{N}\sum_{t=0}^{N-1} x(t)e^{-2\pi i\frac{tk}{N}}, k = 0, 1, 2..., N-1 . \tag{9}$$

In which $\{f(k), k = 0, 1, 2..., N-1\}$ are discrete Fourier Transform sequences of x(t), and i is imaginary unit. Let $W_N = e^{\frac{2\pi i}{N}}$, so f(k) is changed into

$$f(k) = \frac{1}{N}\sum_{t=0}^{N-1} x(t)W_N^{-tk}, k = 0, 1, 2..., N-1 . \tag{10}$$

The mean-square value of $\{f(k), k = 0, 1, 2..., N-1\}$ is:

$$G_N = \frac{1}{N}\sum_{k=0}^{N-1} |f(k)|^2 . \tag{11}$$

Introducing Parameter r(r is a positive integer and larger than 1), if $|f(k)|^2$ is larger than $r * G_N$,$\tilde{f}(k) = f(k)$; otherwise,$\tilde{f}(k) = 0$, in which$\tilde{f}(k)$ is reverse Fourier spectrum.

That's to say,

$$\tilde{f}(k) = \{^{f(k),|f(k)|^2 > rG_N}_{0,|f(k)|^2 \leq rG_N} . \tag{12}$$

Fourier inverse transform $\{\tilde{f}(k), k = 0, 1, 2, ..., N-1\}$:

$$\tilde{x}(t) = \sum_{k=0}^{N-1} \tilde{f}(k)W_N^{tk}, t = 0, 1, 2, ..., N-1 . \tag{13}$$

Define C_0-complexity as:

$$C_0 = \frac{\sum_{t=0}^{N-1} |x(t) - \tilde{x}(t)|^2}{\sum_{t=0}^{N-1} |x(t)|^2} . \tag{14}$$

$\tilde{x}(t)$ is regular part of time sequences, and $x(t) - \tilde{x}(t)$ is irregular part (random part) of time sequences.

If $\{x(t), t = 0, 1, 2, ..., N - 1\}$ is constant or periodic and $r > 1$, $\lim_{N \to \infty} C_0 = 0$; otherwise if $r > 1$, $0 < C_0 < 1$. In sum, the more random time sequences are, the larger the value of C_0 is.

The correlation dimension D_2 [25-26]. The correlation dimension indicates the dynamical characterize of EEG signal, the larger value of D_2, the EEG time series the more complex and tendency to chaos. The draw back of the algorithm is difficult to choose parameters, because of the results too sensitive to parameters.

The calculation steps of correlation dimension: Define EEG signal as a time sequences X(t),t=1,2,3,...T, which can reconstruct a m-dimensional vector Vm(i), i=1,2,3,,N.

N is the number of sample points, N=T-((m-1)*L); L is a time lag between samples in the time series, $L = K * \Delta t$, Δt is time sampling interval and m is called embedding dimension. Given m and L, reconstructed m-dimension vector are defined as:

$$\mathrm{V(i)} = (\mathrm{x(i)}, \mathrm{x(i + L)}, \mathrm{x(i + 2 \times L)}) . \tag{15}$$

So the correlation integral is defined as follows:

$$_m(r) = 2/(N-1) \times N \sum_{i=1}^{M-1} \sum_{j=i+1}^{M} \theta(r - (r_{ij})) . \tag{16}$$

$$r_{ij} = |V(i) - V(j)|, i \neq j . \tag{17}$$

Here, θ is the Heaviside unit function. The Heaviside function is 0 if the distance between the vectors is $> r$, and if the distance between the vectors is $< r$. Theoretically, if both m and r are sufficiently large and r is sufficiently small, the following relation is assumed to be:

$$C_m(r) \propto rD . \tag{18}$$

Here, D is the dimension of attractor. According to the relation of, the correlation dimension (D_2) is defined as:

$$D_2 = \lim_{r \to 0} \frac{\partial \log(C_m(r))}{\partial \log r} . \tag{19}$$

The dimension of attractor is estimated from the slope of a linear scaling region in the log (Cm (r))-log r plot. D_2 is close to saturation with m increasing.

The Largest Lyapunov Exponent[27]. The obvious feature of chaotic system is sensitivity to initial conditions, small disturbance will lead system trajectory exponential separation. The largest Lyapunov exponent is used to measure the exponential divergence of initially close state-space trajectories and estimate the amount of chaos in a system. If the largest lyapunov exponent $\lambda < 0$, standing for two trajectories with nearby initial conditions contract; If $\lambda > 0$, standing for two trajectories with nearby initial conditions diverge at an exponential rate and the system sensitivity to initial conditions, also indicating chaos. In this paper, Michael T.Rosenstein et al algorithm is applied in calculating The largest lyapunov exponent.

Small data sets algorithm (Michael T.Rosenstein et al algorithm):

(1) For time series x(ti) , i=1, 2, , N, calculate embedding dimension and time delay by Characteristic saturation method;
(2) Calculate the mean period set as P, of the time series by fast Fourier transform (FFT);
(3) According to time delay TAU and embedding dimension m, reconstruct phase space Yj, j=1, 2,..., M; M=N-(m-1)*TAU;
(4) Find out the nearest neighbor point $\widehat{Y_j}$ of each Yj , and limit a temporal separation;

$$d_j(0) = \min \left\| Y_j - \widehat{Y_j} \right\|, \left| j - \widehat{j} \right| > P . \quad (20)$$

(5) Calculate the distance dj(i) of each Yj, between the nearest neighbor point $\widehat{Y_j}$ and Yj with i delay;

$$d_j(0) = \min \left\| Y_j - \widehat{Y_j} \right\|, \left| j - \widehat{j} \right| > P, (i = 1, 2, ..., \min(M - j, M - \widehat{j})) . \quad (21)$$

(6) For every i, calculate the average value of lndj(i) of every j;

$$y(i) = \frac{1}{q\Delta t} \sum_{j=1}^{q} \ln dj(i) . \quad (22)$$

Here, q is the total number of nonzero dj(i), y(i) is the average divergent distance of all neighbor pairs with i steps delay.
(7) Get slope by least-squares-method (LSM);

$$y(i) = a + \lambda_1 * i . \quad (23)$$

λ_1 is the largest Lyapunov exponent.

5 Classification and Results

5.1 Classification

In our work, K-Nearest-Neighbor (KNN) Classifier[28] is applied to classify the obtained features. K-Nearest-Neighbor classifier is designed based on factual cases. Instead of being designed in advance it directly classifies the samples with unknown categories with training data. In the experiment, the total number of subjects is ten, each subject has 30 data segments. During the classification, all samples are split into three parts randomly, two of which are applied as training data and the other as test data. Thus, 200 data segments are used for training and 100 data segments used for testing.

5.2 Results

In this section, the classification results are discussed. The classification accuracy (percent) is defined based on the equation: classification accuracy(%)= (number of subjects classified correctly)/ (total number of subjects tested).

We used nonlinear dynamics methods and AR models (linear algorithm) to analysis the data between 2-40HZ, and alpha rhythms (8-13Hz), theta rhythms (4-7Hz) and SMR rhythms (13-15Hz) of EEG also used linear algorithms to analysis. The classification result of each rhythm is shown in Figure 4 and 5. Figure 4 is the classification results of linear algorithm and Figure 5 for the nonlinear dynamics classification.

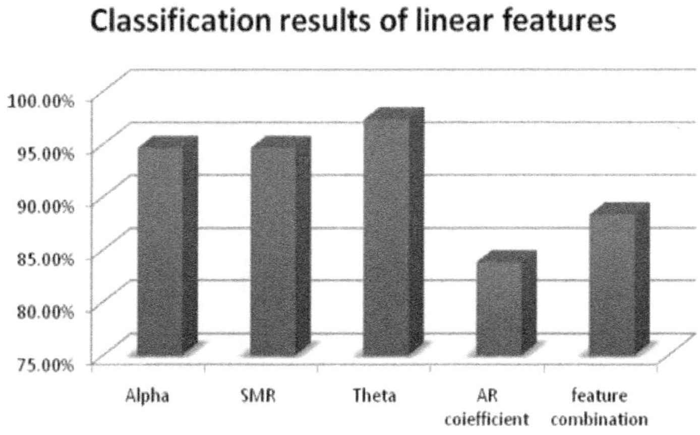

Fig. 4. Classification results of linear features

Figure 4 illustrates the results of linear features identification. The x-axis represents the linear features which are used to classify and y-axis represents the identification (or classification) accuracy. The features include the center frequency, max power, average peak-to-peak value and power ratio of alpha, theta and SMR, AR coefficients of 2-40HZ, and the combination of all linear features (features of alpha + theta + SMR + AR models).

Figure 5 illustrates the results of nonlinear dynamics parameters identification. X-axis represents the nonlinear features of classification, and y-axis represents the identification accuracy. The parameters include C_0-complexity, ApEn, the largest lyapunov exponent, D_2, and the combination of the previous four features.

In Figure 4, the classification accuracy of the center frequency, max power, average peak-to-peak value and power ratio of alpha, theta and SMR are 94.59%, 97.29% and 94.59% respectively. The identification success rate of six order AR coefficients of 2-40HZ is 83.78% and the combination of all linear features is 88.29%. In Figure 5, the identification accuracy of C0-complexity, ApEn, the

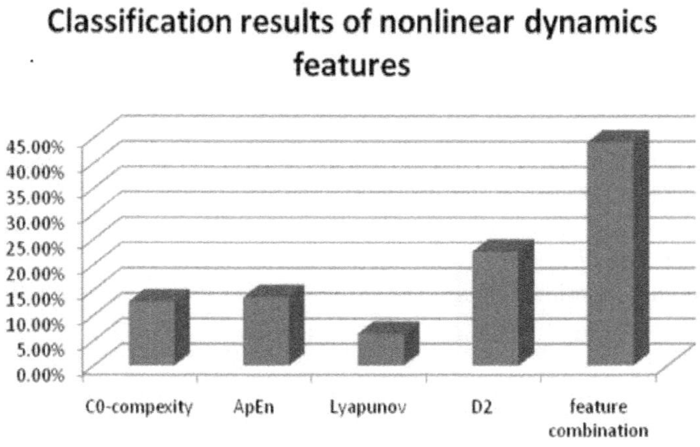

Fig. 5. Classification results of nonlinear features

largest lyapunov exponent, D2, and the combination of the previous four nonlinear features are 12.61%, 13.51%, 6.31%, 22.52% and 44.14% respectively. According to the comparison of Figure 4 and Figure 5, the linear features of EEG work obviously better than the nonlinear dynamics parameters of EEG in individual identification. In particular, the recognition rate of the center frequency, max power, average peak-to-peak value and power ratio of alpha, theta and SMR are higher than others. On the contrary, the identification accuracy of C_0-complexity, ApEn, the largest lyapunov exponent and D_2 are apparently lower. The overall high classification result indicates that the linear features, such as the center frequency, max power, average peak-to-peak value, spectral-power ratio and AR coefficients, have different properties for different subjects. It is speculated that these linear features may have a direct relation to the genetic material. Equally, the low classification result indicates that the nonlinear parameters, such as C_0-complexity, ApEn, the largest lyapunov exponent and D_2 can not describe the unique characteristic of individual. Those nonlinear features may not be the best choice to identify individual. Also, we combine all of features (all linear and nonlinear features) to identify individual and get recognition success rate 85.58% . The results suggest that nonlinear features may reduce the identification accuracy and may disturb EEG-based individual identification.

6 Conclusions

This paper presents our study on comparison between performance of linear and nonlinear dynamics parameters of EEG signal in individual identification. We measures EEG signal from Cz in reference to A2 with subjects' eyes closed, which is available to people with disabilities and other groups.

In this paper, methods of several feature vectors from recorded EEG signals are used, including linear features, center frequency, the max power, average peak-to-peak value, power ratio and six order AR coefficients, and nonlinear dynamics features, C_0-complexity, ApEn, the largest lyapunov exponent and D_2. The identification success rates of each two classes features (linear and nonlinear dynamics features) show that linear features applied may be interrelated with the unique characteristics of individuals.

Furthermore, the analysis of the experiment suggests when people are in the same state, the nonlinear dynamic parameters of them are more likely to represent general characteristics. The commonality may be considered to study some physical or mental illness.

In the future, we will test in a larger group of subjects to improve the extendibility and availability of EEG-based identification as well as investigating the influence of the changes of EEG patterns over long periods of time as it is important to identify people of different ages. Besides, we'll continue our effort to find the most effective signal features in individual identification. The application of EEG-based identification in automated systems with highly security is our ultimate goal.

Acknowledgement. This work was supported by National Natural Science Foundation of China (grant no. 60973138), the EU's Seventh Framework Programme OPTIMI (grant no. 248544), the Fundamental Research Funds for the Central Universities (grant no. lzujbky-2009-62), the Interdisciplinary Innovation Research Fund for Young Scholars of Lanzhou University (grant no. LZUJC200910).

References

1. Li, S.Z., Jain, A.K. (eds.): Handbook of Face Recognition. Springer, New York (2004)
2. Jain, A.K., Ross, A., Prabhakar, S.: An introduction to biometric recognition. IEEE Trans. Circuits Syst. Video Technology, Special Issue Image- and Video-Based Biomet. 14(1), 4–20 (2004)
3. Roizenblatt, R., Schor, P., et al.: Iris recognition as a biometric method after cataract surgery. Biomed. Eng. Online 3-2 (2004)
4. Markowitz, J.A.: Voice Biometrics. Communications of the ACM 43(9) (2000)
5. Li, S.Z., Jain, A.K. (eds.): Handbook of Face Recognition. Springer, New York (2004)
6. Duta, N., Jain, A.K., Mardia, K.V.: Matching of Palmprint. Pattern Recognition Letters 23(4) (2002)
7. Budowle, B., Bieber, F.R., Eisenberg, A.J.: Forensic aspects of mass disasters: Strategic considerations for DNA-based human identification. Legal Medicine 7 (2005)
8. Tirsch, W.S., Stude, P., Scherb, H., Keidel, M.: Temporal order of nonlinear dynamics in human brain. Brain Research Reviews 45, 79–95 (2004)
9. Poulos, M., Rangoussi, M., et al.: Person identification from the EEG using nonlinear signal classification. Methods Inf. Med. 41(1), 64–75 (2002)

10. Paranjape, R.B., Mahovsky, J., Benedicenti, L., Koles, Z.: The electroencephalogram as a biometric. On Electrical and Computer Engineering, Toronto 2, 1363–1366 (2001)
11. Palaniappan, R.: Method of identifying individuals using VEP signals and neural network. IEE Proc-Sci. Meas. Technol. 151(1) (January 2004)
12. Birbaumer, N., Hinterberger, T., Kubler, A.: The Thought Translation Device (TTD): neurobevioral mechanisims and clinical outcome[J]. IEEE Transaction on Neural Systems and Rehabilitation Engineering 11(2), 120–122 (2003)
13. Poulos, M., Rangoussi, M., et al.: On the use of EEG features towards person identification via neural networks. Med. Inform. Internet Med. 26(1), 35–48 (2001)
14. Poulos, M., Rangoussi, M., et al.: Person identification from the EEG using nonlinear signal classification. Methods Inf. Med. 41(1), 64–75 (2002)
15. Vorobyov, S., Cichocki, A., et al.: Blind noise reduction for multisensory signals using ICA and subspace filtering. With application to EEG analysis 86, 293–303 (2002)
16. Eichele, T., Calhoun, V.D., Debener, S.: Mining EEG-fMRI using independent component analysis. International Journal of Psychophysiology (2009)
17. Singh, J.: PSachin Sapatnekar Statistical timing analysis with correlated nongaussian parameters using independent component analysis. In: Proceedings of the 43rd AQnnual Conference on Design Automation (July 2006)
18. Riera, A., Soria-Frisch, A., Caparrini, M., Grau, C., Ruffini, G.: Unobtrusive Biometric System Based on Electroencephalogram Analysis. EURASIP Journal on Advances in Signal Processing, Volume 2008
19. Pardey, J., Roberts, S., et al.: A review of parametric modelling techniques for EEG analysis. Med. Eng. Phys. 18(1), 2–11 (1996)
20. Pincus, S.M., Viscarello, R.R.: Approximate Entropy: A Regularity Measure for Fetal Heart Rate Analysis
21. Pincus, S.M., Gevers, E.F., Robinson, I.C., van den Berg, G., Roelfsema, F., Hartman, M.L., et al.: Females secrete growth hormone with more process irregularity than males in both humans and rats. Am. J. Physiol. 270, E107–E115(1996)
22. Pincus, S.M., Viscarello, R.: Approximate entropy: a regularity measure for fetal heartrate analysis. Obstet. Gynecol. 79, 249–255 (1992)
23. Fang, C., Fangji, G., Jinghua, X., Zengrong, L., Ren, L.: A new measurement of complexity for studying EEG mutual information. Biophysica sinica 14(3) (1998)
24. Zhijie, C., Hao, S.: Improved C0-complexity and its applications. Journal of Fudan University 47(6) (2008)
25. Stam, C.J., van Woerkom, T.C.A.M., Pritchard, W.S.: Use of non-linear EEG measures to characterize EEG changes during mental activity. Electroencephalography and clinical Neurophysiology 99, 214–224 (1996)
26. Lee, Y.-J., Zhu, Y.-S., Xu, Y.-H., Shen, M.-F., Zhang, H.-X., Thakor, N.V.: Detection of non-linearity in the EEG of schizophrenic patients. Clinical Neurophysiology 112, 1288–1294 (2001)
27. Rosenstein, M.T., Collins, J.J., De Luca, C.J.: A practical method for calculating Largest Lyapunov exponents from small data sets, November 20 (1992)
28. Han, J., Kamber, M.: Data Mining Concepts and Techniques, 2nd edn. Elsevier Inc., Amsterdam (2006)

Activity Recognition on an Accelerometer Embedded Mobile Phone with Varying Positions and Orientations

Lin Sun[1], Daqing Zhang[1], Bin Li[1], Bin Guo[1], and Shijian Li[2]

[1] Handicom Lab, TELECOM SudParis,
9, Rue Charles Fourier, 91011, France
{Lin.Sun,Daqing.Zhang,Bin.Li,Bin.Guo}@it-sudparis.eu
[2] Department of Computer Science, Zhejiang University, Hangzhou, 310027, China
shijianli@zju.edu.cn

Abstract. This paper uses accelerometer-embedded mobile phones to monitor one's daily physical activities for sake of changing people's sedentary lifestyle. In contrast to the previous work of recognizing user's physical activities by using a single accelerometer-embedded device and placing it in a known position or fixed orientation, this paper intends to recognize the physical activities in the natural setting where the mobile phone's position and orientation are varying, depending on the position, material and size of the hosting pocket. By specifying 6 pocket positions, this paper develops a SVM based classifier to recognize 7 common physical activities. Based on 10-folder cross validation result on a 48.2 hour data set collected from 7 subjects, our solution outperforms Yang's solution and SHPF solution by 5∼6%. By introducing an orientation insensitive sensor reading dimension, we boost the overall F-score from 91.5% to 93.1%. With known pocket position, the overall F-score increases to 94.8%.

Keywords: Activity recognition, SVM, mobile phone, accelerometer.

1 Introduction

The prevailing sedentary lifestyle in modern society has lead to various physical and mental diseases, such as obesity, coronary heart diseases, type II diabetes and depression, which request enormous medical cost. According to World Health Organization, there are at least 1.9 million people die as a result of physical inactivity annually [1]. In U.S. alone, it leads to about 300, 000 preventable deaths and more than 90$ billion direct health cost annually [2]. Even though people are aware of the benefits of exercises, there is a lack of external intervention which can properly bring the busy people out of the sedentary routine, thus an automatic and personal reminder will be very helpful if it can monitor one's physical activities and persuade people to participate in physical activities regularly at the right time and place.

Activity recognition technology is a key enabling technology to tackle this problem as it's able to monitor individual's physical daily activities and the

Z. Yu et al. (Eds.): UIC 2010, LNCS 6406, pp. 548–562, 2010.

lasting duration so as to estimate the calories consumed each day. Based on the consumed calorie, the system can provide recommendation and advices when they fail to complete enough exercise and also build systems to encourage people to conduct more activities [4,5,3]. There are several ways to recognize people's daily activities. One way is using cameras to visually detect people's motion [8,7]. The drawback of this solution is that to monitor a moving person, large number of cameras need be deployed with high cost. And also the system should be designed to aggregate the information from each camera and deal with the influential factors such as lighting condition, mounting distance and angel, which make the system very complicate and impractical. Another way is using personal companion devices such as mobile phones or watches with sensing and computing power embedded to detect physical activities. The merit of this solution is that we don't need to deploy additional devices and the system is simple and easy to use. Since people carry their personal companion devices all the time and have the full control of their own devices, thus those devices won't make the users feel intrusive or cause extra money burden. Out of the two companion devices, the watches are normally placed on the wrist. Since the casual moving of arms doesn't have a direct and obvious relationship with ongoing activities, also modern watches are still not powerful enough to do data processing, therefore personal watches have a lot of constraints in detecting one's physical activities. On the contrary, mobile phones are becoming increasingly intelligent and powerful. When they are carried by people in pockets or bags, they are moving with the pace of the human body, thus they appear to be the ideal platforms for detecting people's physical activities such as sitting, walking, running and etc. Modern mobile phones like iPhone or Nokia N97 are embedded with various sensors such as the accelerometer, approximity sensor, magnetometer, GPS and etc. Of all these embedded sensors, the accelerometer is commonly used for activity recognition. Although GPS could detect one's movement in terms of location and speed, it cannot tell the user moves in an accurate manner. In particular, GPS doesn't work inside buildings where people spend most of their time in. Therefore, using the accelerometer-embedded mobile phones to recognize people's physical activities becomes the primary choice among all the solutions.

With the accelerometer-embedded mobile phone, there are two possibilities to monitor people's physical activities. One is turning the mobile phone as a pedometer, measuring the step counts and calorie consumption [9] for each user. The other is recognizing precise physical activities such as walking, running, bicycling, driving and etc. Apparently the pedometer solution is quite simple, it provides good indication for each user's calorie consumed. While it works well for the cases of walking, running, taking staircases, etc., it fails to estimate the calorie consumption correctly in the case of bicycling (helpful to the health but cannot be measured by pedometer). On the contrary, recognizing one's physical activities and the lasting duration can infer more accurate and comprehensive information about people's life style. Besides informing the calorie consumed more accurately, the activity patterns can inform users' preferences and habits, which can serve as the basis for further exercise recommendation.

[10] shows that 60% of men put their mobile phones in their pockets. With different clothes dressed each day, people are used to putting the mobile phone in different pocket (often the most convenient one). Depending on the position, material and size of the pocket, the mobile phones often have varying orientation, especially when the very pocket swings with human body. Till now, the prior work on activity recognition with accelerometer-equipped mobile devices assumes a fixed mobile phone position or certain orientation [11,12,13,14,15,16,17], this assumption usually doesn't hold for the usual case of carrying the phone in the pocket. In this work we choose to recognize seven most representative daily activities that are strongly linked to physical exercises, and we intend to investigate the activity recognition issue assuming that the mobile phone is freely placed in one of the pockets. Under this assumption, the accelerometer sensor inside the phone will take the position and orientation associated with the moving pocket.

With the varying orientation of the mobile phone, the experienced force will cause varying effect on the three components of the acceleration signal [17]. This paper attempts to propose an orientation independent sensor reading dimension which can relieve the effect of the varying orientation on the performance of the activity recognition. For the position variation of the mobile phone, besides training a single optimal SVM classifier for all seven physical activities in all the pocket positions, we would like to train an optimal classifier for each pocket location and hopefully can select the right classifier according to the mobile phone position detected in the future.

The rest of the paper is organized as follows: in Section 2, the related work about activity recognition using mobile or wearable devices is summarized. Then in Section 3, our design hypothesis is elaborated to set-up the stage for the research work. Section 4 presents the detailed design process for feature extraction and classification, aiming at developing an orientation insensitive algorithm. Section 5 describes the experimentation strategy to select the optimal size of the window as well as the optimal set of SVM parameters corresponding to different pocket position. In Section 6, the experimental results and analysis are provided to demonstrate the effectiveness of the proposed approaches for tackling the varying orientation and position issue. Finally, Section 7 gives the conclusions about the paper.

2 Related Work

Activity recognition with wearable sensors has been a hot research field in the last decade. Much research work has been done to recognize physical activities such as sitting, standing, running and so on for wellbeing management. In order to differentiate diverse activities or gestures, sensors are best placed at locations where the intrinsic characteristics of the target activities can be well captured. For example, an accelerometer placed in the ankle can measure the leg motion properly, and a barometers fixed on human body can detect the altitude change quite well. In a well cited paper by Bao et al [11], five biaxial accelerometers are placed simultaneously on the right ankle, the left thigh, the waist, the left upper arm and right wrist respectively. The work could distinguish not only the whole body movement like walking or running, but also those activities involving partial body movement such as standing still, folding laundry and brushing teeth, watching TV or reading. In [12], dozens of heterogeneous sensors are placed in various parts of the body to measure 18 different quantities, such as the acceleration of the chest and wrist, heart rate from finger, forehead and chest, temperature of the environment and skin. With the large number of sensing sources, even similar activities like Nordic walk and walk can be accurately distinguished. However, the drawbacks of all the multiple-sensor multiple-position solutions for activity recognition are high deployment cost and large deployment constraints, which lead to difficulty for real usage.

Compared to the multiple-sensor multiple-position solutions, putting multiple sensors in a single platform and one part of the human body is a preferable way for physical activity recognition. Apparently, all the sensors can only sense the information specific to the target part of the body, the ability to distinguish diverse activities decreases because the feature characteristics reflected in the attached position might be very similar. Lester [13] mounts one board embedded with eight sensors on the shoulder to classify physical activities such as sitting, standing, walking (stairs) and etc. Ravi et al [14] places an accelerometer embedded hoarder board near the pelvic region to detect similar activities, demonstrating the ability of distinguishing daily physical activities with a single accelerometer. To investigate the effect of the sensor position on the activity recognition performance, Maurer [15] deploys a multi-sensor device eWatch in locations like the left wrist, belt, necklace, right trousers pocket, shirt pocket and bag, and compares the recognition performance in those cases. The eWatch contains a dual axes accelerometer, a light sensor, a temperature sensor and a microphone, the experimental results show that with the eWatch fixed in all the locations, activities like walking, standing, sitting and running can be well detected, but ascending stairs and descending stairs are difficult to be distinguished from walking. In all the above-mentioned cases, the position of the sensor device is known and predefined, the case of unknown device position and varying orientation is not considered.

To investigate the effect of varying sensor placement on activity recognition, Lester [16] places a multi-sensor board on three representative locations, including the wrist, the waist and the shoulder. A general HMM model is built to recognize the physical activities for all three locations, in contrast to a separate HMM model for each location. The result shows that the general model performs slightly worse than separate models. However, as we can see, additional straps are usually needed to fix the device in the target location, causing fixed orientations of the platform, which is different from the common case of putting the phone in a normal pocket. To tackle the issue of varying orientations, Yang [17] proposes to compute the vertical and horizontal component of each accelerometer sensor reading for compensating the effect of gravity, based on the gravity-related estimation work of Mizell [18]. However, Yang's work doesn't show the performance improvement of using his approach, compared to the case without using the orientation-independent feature. In addition, his work doesn't consider influence of the varying positions of the sensor platforms. Baek [21] proposes to eliminate the gravity component with a second-order Butterworth highpass filter(SHPF) and extract the motion acceleration component.

Different from the prior work, we intend to address the varying position and orientation issues simultaneously in accelerometer-based physical activity recognition. The research challenges are inspired by the commonly observed phenomena that most of the people put their mobile phones in one of their pockets, and the mobile phone's position and orientation are varying, depending on the position, material and size of the hosting pocket. For the varying orientation issue, we plan to extract features that are independent or insensitive to orientation change, for the activity classification. While for the pocket position change issue, we would like to develop two solutions: One is to build a single and robust SVM classifier for all physical activities in all the pocket positions, handling the unknown phone hosting pocket problem; the other is to train a separate SVM classifier for each pocket location and hopefully the system can select the right classifier according to the mobile phone position detected using certain techniques. Experiment result shows that our proposed method outperforms Yang's work and Baek's work for over 4%. By introducing an orientation insensitive sensor reading dimension, we boost the overall F-score from 91.5% to 93.1%. With known pocket position, the overall F-score slightly increases to 94.8%, which is in consistent with the result shown in [16].

3 Our Hypothesis

In this section, we set up the hypothesis for the considered problem. We define our hypothesis space in three dimensions, i.e., pocket locations, mobile phone orientations, and physical activities. The proposed method and the experiments in the following sections are limited in the defined hypothesis space.
Generally speaking, there are six common pocket locations in people's daily costume that are frequently used to place mobile phones, including the two front pocket and two rear pockets on the trousers, and two front pockets on the coat, as shown in Fig 1(a). The size, shape and orientation of the pocket at each location may vary for different clothes such that the motion patterns of the mobile phone can be very different. For example, front pockets on casual trousers are usually looser and deeper than those on jeans. This will lead to higher vibration magnitude when walking or running. In this paper, we will investigate the influence of the six pockets locations and use location-specific classifiers to relieve such kinds of influences.

Based on the observation to a large number of people, we find that there are only a very limited number of orientations for a mobile phone to be placed into a pocket, since most people's habits and most pocket styles only fall into a few numbers of most common ones. As shown in Fig 1(b), people normally put the mobile phone into the front pocket of the trousers vertically, which can result in 4 possible orientations: upward facing out, downward facing out, upward facing in, and downward facing in. Noting that, after the mobile phone is placed inside the pocket, it may slip or rotate when the user is moving. We don't consider these uncertain cases in this paper. In the following sections, we will investigate the influences of the four mobile phone orientations and use an additional feature to relieve such kind of influences.

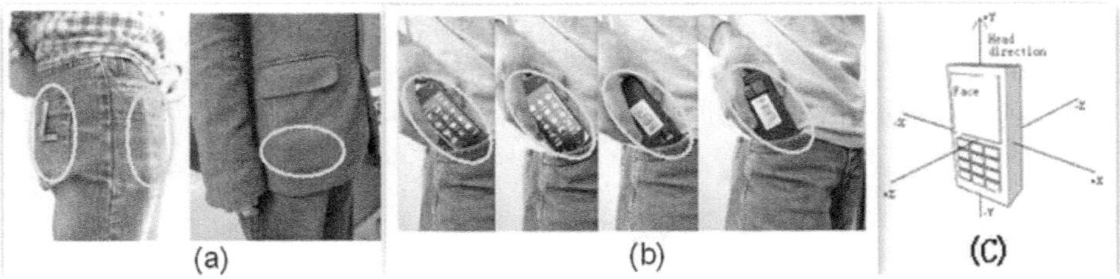

Fig. 1. (a) Pocket locations. For each pocket shown, there is a corresponding one in the left side of the body. (b) Four phone orientations when users put the mobile phone into the right front jean's pocekt. (c) Coordinate system of the accelerometer in Nokia phones.

In our real life, we observed that seven physical activities are conducted by people every day, including stationary, walking, running, bicycling, ascending stairs, descending stairs and driving. In this paper we aim to distinguish these seven physical activities with an accelerometer-embedded mobile phone. Noting that in our experimentation, some activities such as bicycling and driving require people to sit down upon something. In these cases, the mobile phone cannot be put in their rear pockets on the trousers and the experimental results for these cases are absent.

4 Activity Recognition Methodology

The proposed activity recognition method based on an accelerometer-embedded mobile phone comprises the following three steps: 1) collecting and pre-processing the sensor data from mobile phones, 2) extracting features, and 3) training classifiers. It is worth noting that in the first step, we add an additional sensor reading dimension, named acceleration magnitude, to enhance the insensitivity to the influences of the phone orientation. And in the third step, we train location-specific SVM classifiers to adapt the different pocket locations.

4.1 Sensor Data Preprocessing

The embedded triaxial accelerometer inside a mobile phone can continuously sample the experienced accelerations at each sampling interval and produce 3-D acceleration readings $A = (a_x, a_y, a_z)$, which are measures of the acceleration experienced in the three orthogonal axes: X-axis, Y-axis and Z-axis. Taking the

Nokia mobile phone for example, the coordinate system with respect to the phone body is shown in Fig 1(c). When the orientation of the phone body changes, the coordinate system will rotate accordingly and the readings at the three axes will change. Since the acceleration magnitude is a measure for the quantity of acceleration and has no directions, it is insensitive for the orientations of the mobile phones. Furthermore, we will show it is also a discriminative feature for the considered physical activities in the experimental results. As the exact orientation of the acceleration is unknown, to relieve the influences of the phone orientations, we add an additional orientation insensitive feature, i.e., the magnitude of A to the sensor readings. The sensor readings at each time slice thus becomes to be a 4-D vector $A = (A, \|A\|) = (a_x, a_y, a_z, \|a_x, a_y, a_z\|)$.

4.2 Feature Extraction

We use a half overlapping sliding window to separate the collected sensing data into a number of windows. Then, each window is further divided into multiple frames as shown in Fig 2. Instead of fixing the number of frames inside a window, we choose the frame size one second, as the collected sensing data shows that one second is long enough to comprise more than one footstep. When a window contains more footsteps, it takes information from longer time to make a classification decision, which is intuitively capable of eliminating short time noise. Various kinds of features of the accelerometer sensing data have been investigated in previous activity recognition work, including Mean, Variance, Correlation, Energy, Frequency-Domain Entropy, Cepstral Coefficients, Log FFT Frequency Bands and etc [11,12,13,14,15,16,17,19]. When the application scenarios change, the contributions of these features may change accordingly. To the best of our knowledge, little general analysis of the contributions has been reported. Applying more features may bring benefits to the recognition accuracy in the case of computing on the powerful computers. However, when we are trying to implement these features inside the resource and power limited mobile phones, we should try to avoid the features that need complex computing workload, since it consumes much of computing resources and energy, which is critical to the user experience and acceptance of such application.

Five types of features are employed in this work, including Mean, Variance, Correlation, FFT Energy and Frequency-Domain Entropy, as they have shown good performance in [19]. For each frame, there are 22 features (4 features for

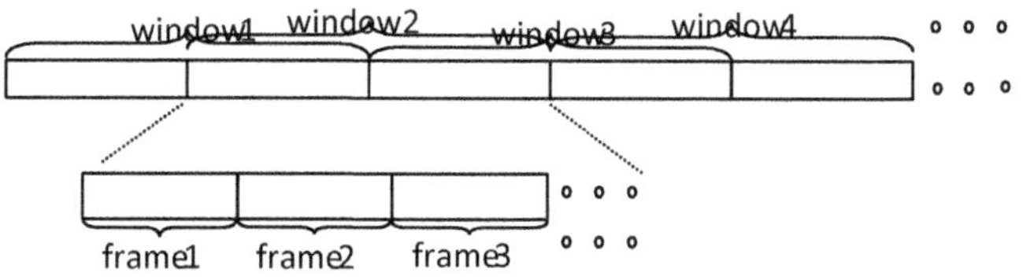

Fig. 2. Half overlapping windows and frame definitions within a window

Table 1. The extracted feature matrix for the collected sensing data

	feature vector
test cases	$\begin{matrix} t_{11} & t_{12} & \dots & t_{1n} \\ t_{21} & t_{22} & \dots & t_{2n} \\ \vdots & \vdots & \ddots & \vdots \\ t_{m1} & t_{m2} & \dots & t_{mn} \end{matrix}$

Mean, Variance, Energy, Frequency-Domain Entropy, respectively, and 6 features for Correlation). All the K frames inside a sliding window will produce a feature vector of $22 * K$ elements.

Normalization is performed on the extracted feature vectors before training. All the extracted feature vectors form an $m * n$ matrix T as shown in Table 1, where m is the number of the windows and n is the number of elements in a feature vector for a window. For the cth column $\overrightarrow{t_c}(c = 1, 2, \dots, n)$ in T, the maximum value $Max(\overrightarrow{t_c})$ and minimum value $Min(\overrightarrow{t_c})$ are selected to scale the column to [0, 1] with equation (1).

$$\overrightarrow{t_{ci}} = \frac{\overrightarrow{t_{ci}} - Min(\overrightarrow{t_c})}{Max(\overrightarrow{t_c}) - Min(\overrightarrow{t_c})}, i = 1 \dots m \tag{1}$$

4.3 SVM Classification and Evaluation Metrics

In this paper, we adopt LibSVM [20] to perform SVM training and classification within our experimentation. We use the RBF (Radial Basis Function) kernel and choose the optimal tradeoff parameter C and the bandwidth *Gamma* in RFB kernel by conducting a grid search with cross validation using the gird.py python script provided with LibSVM.

We use the balanced F-score as the performance index to evaluate the experiment results. The definition is as following:

$$\text{F-score} = 2 * \frac{precision * recall}{precision + recall}. \tag{2}$$

For the test result, the F-score is calculated for each activity and the overall F-score for the classification model is computed by averaging the F-scores for all the activities.

5 Experimentation Methodology

We program a python application to collect accelerometer information from two Nokia N97s to conduct the experimentation. The data sampling rate is reduced to 10Hz by getting the mean of the data from 0.1 seconds. In order to ease the data labeling work, we build a simple touch screen user interface to label the data when launching the application as shown in Fig 3. Before recording data, the application lables the test with user's selection of the activities, pocket locations and phone orientations. After successfully launching the application, testers put the mobile phone into the right pocket with the chosen orientation and start to conduct the selected activity.

In order to fully investigate the influences of the orientation, we asked the test subjects to test the aforementioned 4 possible orientations for each pocket and each activity. Noting that when dealing with front pockets of the coat, the mobile phone is horizontally facing the body instead of vertically facing the body, which is different with the trousers scenario.

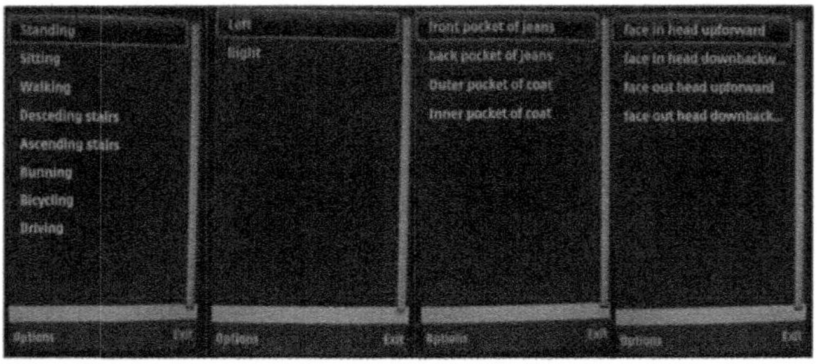

Fig. 3. Experiment interface on Nokia N97

One female and six males test subjects aged 25~46 were volunteered to conduct the experiment from Institute TELECOM SudParis during a period of three weeks. Before conducting the experiments, an introduction of how to use the application was given to the test subjects. Before each test, they were only given instructions about in which pocket and in which orientation to put the mobile phone. There were no limitations for the clothes, such as whether to wear tight or loose clothes, or whether to wear a jeans or a pant. Each time the test subject carried two mobile phones. They launched the application in the mobile phone, selected the setups, put them into the target pockets and started to do the target application. When the test was finished, the test subject took out the mobile phone and stopped the application. A log file whose name contains information about the activity type, pocket locations, phone orientation and the starting time was produced with the contents of time stamps and accelerometer readings and stored in the mobile phone memory. During the experimentation, no concerns were given to the mobile phones.

The data at the beginning and the end of the log file was cut off since people need time to put the mobile phones inside the pockets and also take it out. Observations from the experiment suggest that the dirty data is about less than 10 seconds. So we exclude 10 seconds data from the beginning and the end of the log file. Totally about 48.2 hours sampling data is collected (Table 2).

Table 2. The sampling time of the each activity during the experimentation

Activity	Time(Hour)
Stationary	10.4
Walking	9.8
Running	6.3
Bicycling	6.6
Ascending stairs	4.6
Descending stairs	4.0
Driving	6.5
Total	48.2

6 Result Analysis

We collect a data set of about 48.2 hours from the experimentation. The window size is chosen as 1 second as it's normally sufficient for more than 1 steps. In order to optimize the SVM model, a grid search is performed to choose the best *Cost* and *Gamma* paramters.

The 10-folder cross-validation is used to evaluate the SVM models. We put all the test cases in one data set and then randomly divide it into 10 equal-sized folders. Each time we choose one folder as the test data set and the rest as the training data set. We train the SVM model with the training data set, evaluate it with the test data set and get the precision, recall and the F-score for each activity. After each folder is tested, we compute the average F-score of all the folders as the overall results for the activities.

6.1 Generic SVM Model Analysis

We train a generic SVM model to recognize these activities without the consideration of the exact pocket where the phone is in. The window length represents the time duration of the accelerometer data that is needed to distinguish an activity. When the frame size is fixed, with small window size, the decision is made with the information within short time duration and the features may be insufficient to describe an activity. On the contrary, with large length, the decision is made with large amount of features over long time duration and with limited training data, it may cause over-fitting problems. So there should be a suitable window length that could achieve the best tradeoff. To choose the best window length for the generic SVM model, we evaluate the window length from 1 to 6 seconds. The mean F-scores produced by the cross-validation for each window length are shown as the blue line in Fig 4. One can see that the F-score achieves the peak 93.1% when the window length is 4 seconds. When the window length is smaller or larger, the F-score decreases.

In order to verify the classification contributions of the acceleration magnitude, we build generic SVM models without the acceleration magnitude as one element of the sensor readings for all the window lengths. The overall F-score

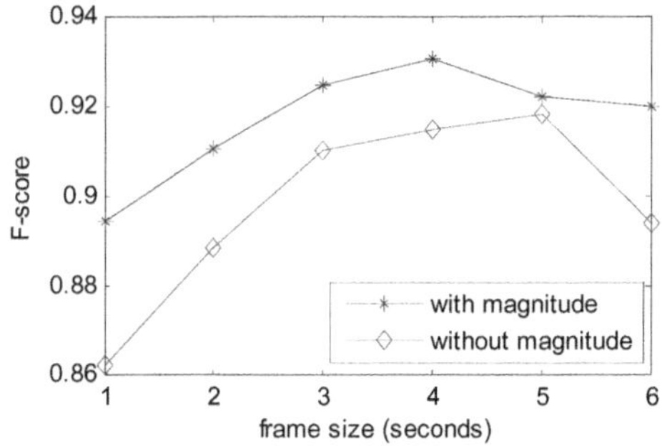

Fig. 4. The overall F-score for the generic SVM models w/ and w/o the acceleration magnitude

Table 3. Recognition result comparison

Solution	Precision	Recall	F-score
Our solution	93.2%	93.0%	93.1%
Yang's solution	87.5%	87.0%	87.2%
SHPF	88.5%	88.0%	88.1%

with respect to the window length is shown as the red line in Fig 4. One can see that the overall F-scores with acceleration magnitude outperform those without it for all the frame sizes. It is also interesting to note that the optimal window length shifts to 5 seconds, which suggests that, without the orientation insensitive features, we need more time to achieve the best performance.

The confusion matrix for the generic SVM model is shown in Table 4 and the precision, recall and F-score of each acitivity are shown in Table 5.One can see that both the precision and recall of "running" is very high compared with other activities, meaning that it is quite distinguishable than other activities.

To compare with Yang's solution, we estimate the gravity acceleration by averaging the signal in each axis during a sampling interval of 10 seconds as proposed in Yang's work and use the result to compute the vertical and horizontal accelerations. To compare with Baek's work, we also use SHPF to filter the sampling data. then use the same feature extraction and parameter optimization process for SVM to conduct the activity recogntion work. The result is shown in Table 3. We can see that our method outperforms their method about 5~6%.

6.2 Location Adaptation Analysis

We train location-specific SVM models with the experiment data from each pocket and compare the classification F-score with the generic SVM model for each activity. Fig 5 shows that the individual SVM model outperforms the generic SVM models for all the activities, meaning that with the location context of the mobile phone, we could train location-specific SVM classifiers to achieve

Table 4. Confusion matrix for the generic SVM model with window length 3 seconds

Predicted \ Actual	Sta.	Walk.	Run.	Bicy.	Asce.	Desc.	Drive.
Stationary	6450	96	139	85	41	73	376
Walking	33	6475	65	29	197	155	10
Running	15	24	6490	2	14	66	8
Bicycling	56	28	17	4256	16	36	56
Ascending	6	123	21	34	6310	222	12
Descending	18	89	99	25	260	6281	10
Driving	262	5	9	129	2	7	4088

Table 5. Precision, recall and F-score for the generic SVM model

	Sta.	Walk.	Run.	Bicy.	Asce.	Desc.	drive	overall
Precision	0.888	0.930	0.981	0.953	0.938	0.926	0.908	0.932
Recall	0.943	0.947	0.949	0.933	0.922	0.920	0.900	0.930
F-score	0.915	0.938	0.964	0.943	0.930	0.922	0.902	0.931

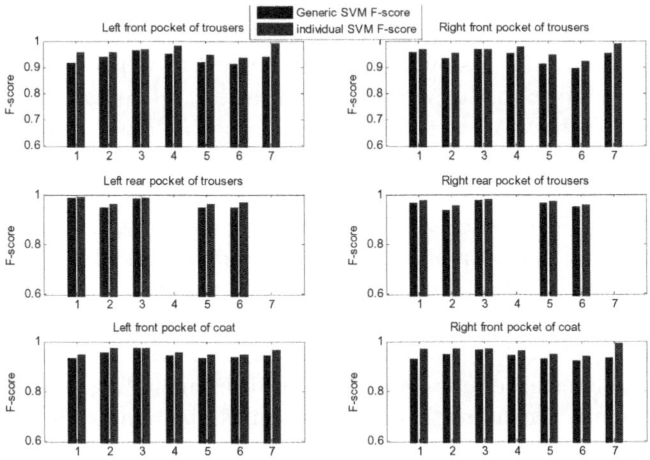

Fig. 5. F-score comparison of each activity for the generic SVM model and individual models

higher accuracy. This result also implies that, compared with the generic SVM model, location-specific models only reflect the acceleration patterns from one fixed location and should have less uncertainty.

Table 6 shows the overall Precision, Recall and F-score of the generic SVM model without acceleration magnitude, generic SVM model with acceleration magnitude and the individual SVM models. We can see that an overall F-score of 91.5% has been achieved for unknown pocket positions. By introducing an

Table 6. Precision, recall and F-score comparisons

	Overall Precision	Overall Recall	Overall F-score
Generic SVM without Magnitude	91.6%	91.4%	91.5%
Generic SVM with Magnitude	93.2%	93.0%	93.1%
Individual SVM with Magnitude	94.8%	94.8%	94.8%

orientation insensitive feature, the overall F-score is boosted to 93.1%. With known pocket position, the overall F-score increases to 94.8%.

7 Conclusion and Future Work

In this paper, we investigated the physical activity recognition issue on an accelerometer-embedded mobile phone, considering most of people's habit of putting the mobile in one of the pockets. In contrast to the previous work of assuming that the phone is placed in a known position or fixed orientation, this paper intends to recognize the physical activities in the natural setting where the mobile phone's position and orientation are varying, depending on the position, material and size of the hosting pocket.

For the varying orientation issue, we add the acceleration magnitude as a new sensor reading dimension, which can relieve the effect of the orientation change on the performance of activity classification. While for the pocket position change issue, we develop two solutions: One is building a single and robust SVM classifier for all physical activities in all the pocket positions, handling the unknown phone hosting pocket problem; the other is training a separate SVM classifier for each pocket location so that the system can select the right classifier according to the mobile phone position detected. Five features including mean, variance, correlation, energy and entropy are extracted to build the SVM classifiers with optimized cost and gamma parameters.

By specifying six pocket positions for hosting the mobile phone, this paper targets to recognize seven common physical activities, including stationary, walking, running, bicycling, ascending stairs, descending stairs and driving. Based on 48.2 hours data collected from seven subjects, our method is shown to have better perfomance than the works in [17,21]. By adding the magnitude of the acceleration as the 4th data dimension for feature extraction, we manage to boost the overall F-score of SVM classifier to 93.1%. With the magnitude of the acceleration as the 4th data dimension for feature extraction and selecting a separate SVM classifier for each pocket position, the overall F-score of the classifiers for the seven activities can increase to 94.8%.

For the future work, we plan to implement other classification algorithms and compare their performance with that of the SVM-based classifiers presented in this paper. We also plan to build the exercise reminder application on top of the activity recognition algorithms, aiming to achieve the goal of prompting the mobile user at the right time, in the right place and the right manner.

Acknowledegement

The authors would like to thank Chanaphan Prasomwong and Wei Wang for building the data collection program with python in Nokia N97 and collecting experiment data.

References

1. World Health Organization: Move for Health, `http://www.who.int/moveforhealth/en/`
2. Manson, J.E., Skerrett, P.J., Greenland, P., VanItallie, T.B.: The Escalating Pandemics of Obesity and Sedentary Lifestyle: A Call to Action for Clinicians. Arch. Intern. Med. 164(3), 249–258 (2004)
3. Consolvo, S., et al.: Activity Sensing in the Wild: A Field Trial of UbiFit Garden. In: CHI 2008 (2008)
4. Lin, J., Mamykina, L., Lindtner, S., Delajoux, G., Strub, H.: Fish'n'Steps: Encouraging Activitiy with an Interactive Computer Game. In: Dourish, P., Friday, A. (eds.) UbiComp 2006. LNCS, vol. 4206, pp. 261–278. Springer, Heidelberg (2006)
5. Anderson, I., Maitlan, J., Sherwood, S., Barkhuus, L., Chalmers, M., Hall, M., Brown, B., Muller, H.: Shakra: Tracking and Sharing Daily Activity Levels with Unaugmented Mobile Phones. Mobile Networks and Applications, 185–199 (2007)
6. Maitland, J., Sherwood, S., Barkhuus, L., Anderson, I., Hall, M., Brown, B., Chalmers, M., Muller, H.: Increasing the Awareness of Daily Activity Levels with Pervasive Computing. In: Proc. of Pervasive Health 2006 (2006)
7. Pavan, T., Chellappa, R., Subrahmanian, V.S., Udrea, O.: Machine Recognition of Human Activities: A survey. IEEE Transactions on Circuits and Systems for Video Technology 18(11) (2008)
8. Hu, W., Tan, T., Wang, L., Maybank, S.: A survey on Visual Surveillance of Object Motion and Behaviors. IEEE Transactions on Systems, Man, and Cybernetics. Part C: Applications and Reviews 34(3) (2004)
9. Fujiki, Y.: iPhone as a Physical Activity Measurement Platform. In: CHI 2010 USA (2010)
10. Ichikawa, F., Chipchase, J., Grignani, R.: Where is the Phone? A Study of Mobile Phone Location in Public Spaces. In: The Second International Conference on Mobile Technology, Application and Systems, pp. 797–804 (2005)
11. Bao, L., Intille, S.: Activity Recognition from User-Annotated Acceleration Data. In: Ferscha, A., Mattern, F. (eds.) PERVASIVE 2004. LNCS, vol. 3001, pp. 1–17. Springer, Heidelberg (2004)
12. Parkka, J., Ermes, M., Korpipaa, P., Mantyjarvi, J., Peltolla, J., Korhonen, I.: Activity Classification Using Realistic Data From Wearable Sensors. IEEE Transactions on Information Technology in Biomedicine, 119–128 (2006)
13. Lester, J., Choudhury, T., Kern, N., Borriello, G., Hannaford, B.: A hybrid discriminative /generative approach for modeling human activities. In: Proc. of the International Joint Conference on Artificial Intelligence (IJCAI), pp. 776–772 (2005)
14. Ravi, N., Dandekar, N., Mysore, P., Littman, M.L.: Activity Recognition from Accelerometer Data. In: AAAI, pp. 1541–1546 (2005)
15. Maurer, U., Smailagic, A., Siewiorek, D.P., Deisher, M.: Activity Recognition and Monitoring Using Multiple Sensors on Different Body Positions. In: Proc. Of the International Workshop on Wearable and Implantable Body Sensor Netowrks (BSN 2006), pp. 113–116 (2006)

16. Lester, J., Choudhury, T., Kern, N., Borriello, G.: A Practical Approach to Recognize Physical Activities. In: Fishkin, K.P., Schiele, B., Nixon, P., Quigley, A. (eds.) PERVASIVE 2006. LNCS, vol. 3968, pp. 1–16. Springer, Heidelberg (2006)
17. Yang, J.: Toward Physical Activity Diary: Motion Recognition Using Simple Acceleration Features with Mobile Phones. In: IMCE 2009 Beijing, China (2009)
18. Mizell, D.: Using gravity to estimate accelerometer orientation. In: ISWC 2003, Proc. Of the 7th IEEE International Symposium on Wearable Computers, USA, p. 252 (2003)
19. Wu, J., Pan, G., Zhang, D., Qi, G., Li, S.: Gesture Recognition with a 3-D Accelerometer. In: Zhang, D., Portmann, M., Tan, A.-H., Indulska, J. (eds.) UIC 2009. LNCS, vol. 5585, pp. 25–38. Springer, Heidelberg (2009)
20. Chang, C.-C., Lin, C.-J.: LIBSVM: a library for support vector machines (2001) Software available at `http://www.csie.ntu.edu.tw/~cjlin/libsvm`
21. Baek, J., Kim, S., Kim, H., Cho, J., Yun, B.: Recognition of User Activity for User Interface on a Mobile Device. In: Proc. of the 24th South East Asia Regional Computer Conference, Thailand (2007)

A Hybrid Content Delivery Approach for a Mixed Reality Web Service Platform

Yu You, Petros Belimpasakis, and Petri Selonen

Nokia Research Center
P.O. Box 1000
FI-33721 Tampere, Finland
{firstname.lastname}@nokia.com

Abstract. This paper presents the development of a Mixed Reality Web service platform (MRS-WS). The platform provides a general RESTful interface for building rich mixed reality mash-ups and 3rd party solutions for open innovation. The platform serves geo-spatially oriented content, advanced geo-data like 3D building models, street-view panoramas and terrain mesh data, and a generic service plug-in model for integrating 3rd-party services and social connections in a secure and scalable manner. Apart from the RESTful approach, this paper presents another case scenario that supports pushing data to many service consumers via a publish/subscribe (pub/sub) mechanism in favor of scalability and expressiveness. Together with the mobile clients, it supports automatic information discovery of "what matters to the user", e.g. based on the built-in mobile sensors and simple user contexts. The paper describes the design and experiments in the industrial scenario.

Keywords: Web Services, REST, Mixed Reality, Publish/Subscribe, Mobile.

1 Introduction

Mixed Reality (MR), defined by Milgram and Kishino [1], positioning itself in between Augmented Reality (AR) and Augmented Virtuality (AV), refers to the merging of physical and virtual worlds to produce brand new experiences such as visualizations where physical and digital objects co-exist, and interactions in real time. Rooted from the AR by Azuma [2], MR systems face new challenges to offer people the ability of experiencing the resulting mixed environment. Nevertheless the design of the co-existence of two physical and digital worlds may also rely on the use of other interaction modalities than the traditional visual ones such as head mounted displays (HMD). Höllerer and Feiner [3] provided an overview of mobile AR systems. A phone becomes a "magic lens" which lets users look through the mobile's display at a world that has been supplemented with information about the objects that it sees [4]. The various device built-in sensors such as GPS, accelerometer, magnetometer as well as audio and image recognition provide a solid technical infrastructure for making new mixed reality applications and services [5].

Z. Yu et al. (Eds.): UIC 2010, LNCS 6406, pp. 563–576, 2010.

Lately many mobile AR applications, such as Layar [6] and Wikitude [7], overlay location-based spatial data on top of real-time media sceneries (such as camera live-feed), instrumented by the device built-in sensors. Those applications either provide their own proprietary backend, or fetch geo-contents from public Internet services like Wikipedia or Flickr. The lack of having open application programming interfaces (APIs) for mashing-up have kept these applications isolated, resulting in limited amount of content, prohibited sharing content with other similar systems [8]. Very few mobile AR applications such as Layar and Junaio [9] have provided an API that tunnels digital content through external content providers hosting remotely. They support a limited set of media types and content typically in the form of point of interests (POIs). Essentially, every new MR application has had to re-invent the wheel by building yet another MR backend to host their content.

While mobile AR applications are gaining more attention world wide, at Nokia Research Center, an effort was started to move from stand-alone AR back-ends to a common MR Web service platform. An essential aim is to build a common backend for easily creating MR Web services and mobile AR applications for fusing digital content with real world data as well as transparently aggregating third-party content. Typical high-level requirements for such a MR web service are as follows:

- secure and scalable geo-referenced content storing, searching, and retrieving,
- portable data structure for different platforms, from desktop to mobile,
- easy to access to digital and aggregated external content and support social connections.

To avoid re-inventing the backend for every new service, we started developing a generic Web service platform for serving MR content for various types of applications and solutions. The MR platform, hence referred to as MRS-WS, has geo-spatial relations in the core of its API design, meaning that special attention is placed on searching and storing content with geographical location and spatial arrangement information. The system not only stores user-generated multimedia content with metadata, but also other static digitalized location-sensitive content like city 3D models, street-view panoramas, building models, points of interest (POIs), terrain morphology and road network data. The platform enables logically linking digital content with physical objects in situ, with dedicated mobile clients, or in an off-line mode from desktop environments (e.g. PCs).

2 A Hybrid MR Content Delivery Approach

In the domain of MR, one of key use cases is to enable interactions between digital data and physical objects, or cross-referenced in a mutual way. The MR platform, eventually, will serve digital contents, which the value of the service is in storing, retrieving and managing interlinked content that have geographic references. Like the case of real physical objects, every meaningful content should have at least one unique permanent virtual address. Nevertheless the real content of the objects may vary over the time, the semantics of the referenced data by the address should not stale. Such addressability is addressed through the use of URI (Uniform resource Identifier) in favor of the way the content is requested over the standard HTTP. The content itself is stateless in terms of the client-side software execution contexts and states. We took the approach of REST and the resource oriented architecture (ROA) [10] (see the next Section for the detailed explanation). This RESTful approach satisfied the needs for building such scalable MR content serving for almost every normal situation. In the MR domain, the RESTful approach, however, has one particular scalable issue under one situation: when a large mount of content updates happening at the same location or a very near proximity, for instance, at some hot touring cites like Paris Louvre Museum, or in front of the Forbidden City, China. Either vertical or horizontal server scaling won't help very much based on the pure RESTful design [11]. In short, the pulling type of queries is neither scalable nor the best approach for frequently updated MR content.

Data pushing has long being a live research topic for decades [12, 13]. It's usually realized as asynchronous binding operations and timely notifying the clients whenever new data is available. The client may choose whether or not to read the data at any point as long as such binding is valid. Among many implementations, the publish-subscribe (pub/sub) model is the most typical one, which fits our MR use cases very well. As we know, for instance, virtualization is not the only modality in terms of interactions in AR/MR worlds [14]. Having a pushing mechanism in place enables more variety of modalities a client could possibly support. The client could start to vibrate when it is approaching to an interesting place within the range of a pre-defined geographic geometry region (for example, the quad tree based 2-D geo-spatial partitioning technique[1]). The client could be notified by the MR content as long as such binding operation to that location is valid. Combining with other networking techniques, the total bandwidth used at the server side can be saved tremendously, which scales up the backend, naturally.

3 System Architecture and Design

The MR platform adopts the Resource-oriented architecture and provides RESTful web services [10]. Generally speaking, RESTful web services and traditional web servers are not much different in terms of the architecture. On the contrary, they share many similar or identical design elements, such as the layered architecture where different functional entities are separated into multiple tiers, from the client, representation layer, control layer (e.g. business logic) to the data persistence layer. However, the representation layer in our case mainly represents the web tier to handle the stateless resources only, rather than mixing up other kind of data, for example, the data for the user interface, or the state concerns of any client-side business logic. Apart from the value of scalable service implementation, RESTful design [16] enables mapping addressable entities (aka. resources) to the specific resource model, the domain model and finally the database schema. The resource model divides resources into three basic elements:

- Items that represent individual resources having a state that can be created, retrieved, modified and deleted;

[1] The details can be found at: `http://msdn.microsoft.com/en-us/library/bb259689.aspx`

- Containers that can be used for retrieving collections of items and creating them; and
- Projections that are specific or filtered views of containers.

Each resource is mapped respectively to a unique Web Uniform Resource Identifiers (URIs). For example, a container for photos could be /content/photos and one item of the container is /content/photos/12345. Resources can have sub-resources and references to other resources, and so on. With the term sub-resources we refer to those resources that are accessible through a root resource. For instance, the location of a photo is a sub-resource of a photo item. Sub-resources can be containers or items.

As long as the resource representation supports Web feed data formats like ATOM, clients can subscribe to container and/or item resource URIs and pull updates periodically. In addition to acting as feed channels, those URIs can be used to represent the pub/sub channels suitable for push-based content delivery. By far our main design goal is limited only to the data traffic from the platform to the clients. We implemented the resource channels as read-only. To serve our use case for having a context-aware content pushing, separating read-write pub/sub channels are needed for collecting contextual data from the clients.

Fig. 1 shows the architectural layers of the platform. The design of the architecture is to provide a uniformed REST API set (see Appendix I for an overview of the APIs) for local MR contents plus mashed-up contents from 3rd party service providers available to the service clients. According to the REST principle, each resource handler is identified by a URI and represents the unique interface for one function or dataset. For example, the clients send HTTP requests to the resource handler. The stateless requests from the client contain the method information in the header, mostly POST, GET, PUT, and DELETE, which will be mapped to corresponding operational functions of the resource implementation (in the Control tier).

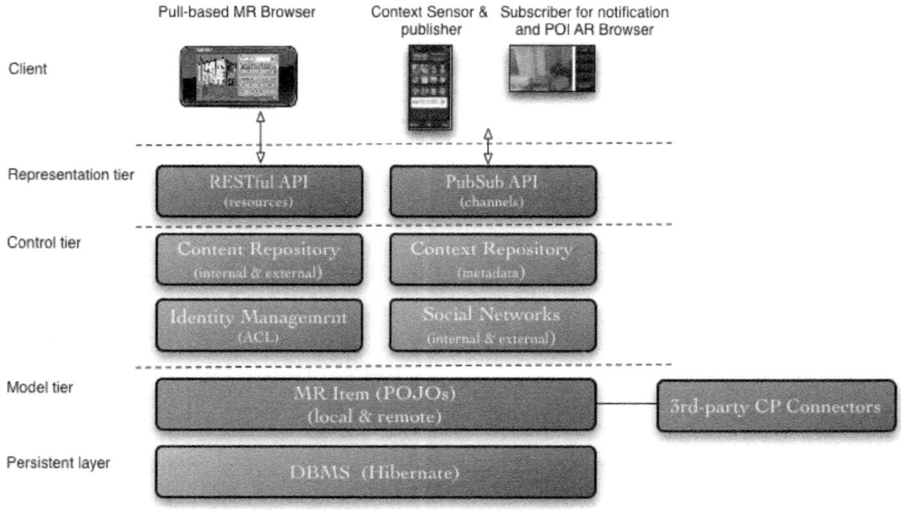

Fig. 1. MRS-WS platform in a nutshell

After the representation tier, there are four main functional modules that connect the lower model data and their representation: content repository for all geo-contents (real and reference to external content repositories); context repository for contextual data plus filers for searching mainly; identity management for user management and the access control list (ACL); and the social networks for aggregating external social sites. The model tier servers a persistent layer that uses the Active Records Pattern to build up Java persistent objects (POJOs) from the physical database clusters (DBMS).

Table 1 describes the logic resource binding of the RESTful and pub/sub APIs in terms of the different architectural tiers. Following we will take a location proximity search as an example to illustrate how the MR contents are delivered through two different content delivery approaches.

Table 1. MRS-WS resource binding

	REST API	Pub/Sub API	Representation (XML/JSON)	Model (Hibernate, Java EE)	Persistence (MySQL)
Item	MR content bound to the URI. Supported default operations are GET, PUT and DELETE.	N/A	Representation parsing/generation based on the item attributes. Subresources inlined per request basis.	A native Java object (POJO) generated for each item with a Hibernate Data Access Object and binding to RDBMS tables.	Items are rows in respective database table with columns specified by item attributes. References map to foreign keys.
Container	Collection of MR content bound to the URI. Supported default operations are GET and POST.	Channels	Representation parsing/generation delegated to item representations.	Logic item POJO collections.	Logic RDBMS table row collections.
Projection	Implemented on top of respective Containers. Same supported operations.	Channels	Representation generation delegated to Container.	Extended retrievals to database, using item mappings.	Stored procedures for more advanced database jointed queries. Tables implied by Container.

To understand the two different content delivery modes, next we introduce the two simple examples implementing the same function: search the MR content (named annotations) at a given location (longitude: 23.864365 and latitude: 61.442619) as the center of a circle proximity which radius is 1.5 kilometer. After we understand the details at the server side, we will present our experiments on the mobile client side, particularly on the usage of the pub/sub mode.

3.1 RESTful Interface for Pull-Based Content Delivery

To illustrate the RESTful calls from a developer's perspective, we take a deeper look into one particular API example, the Annotation API (See a list of REST APIs our current implementation supports in the Appendix). An Annotation is a MR content type that can comprise a title and a textual description, as well as links to other content elements like photos. Essentially an Annotation is a way of the users to annotate physical entities with digital information and share these annotations to groups of friends or to the general public at will (see a detailed analysis regarding the engineering process from MR domain model to information and finally resource model at [15]).

The default operations for annotations are: GET and POST for annotation containers, GET, PUT, POST and DELETE for individual annotation items and GET for projections. A sample representation subset for an annotation resource is given below, showing attributes inherited from Content and abstract Item classes. The simplified HTTP GET operation could be (see some MR-related headers in the Appendix):

```
GET
/mrs/rest/content/annotations/?lat=61.446129&lon=23.86436
5&radius=1.5
```

And one example response would be:

```
<annotations>
    <annotation>
    <id>4128673</id>
    <owner>test1</owner>
    <updated>2010-02-08 14:13:56</updated>
    <published>2010-02-08 14:13:56</published>
    ...
    <title>My annotation</title>
    <visibility>public</visibility>
    <alert>true</alert>
    <location>
      <lat>61.4467</lat>
      <lon>23.8575</lon>
      ...
      <bearing>1.0</bearing>
    </location>
    <building href="...">....</building>
</annotation>
```

3.2 Pub-Sub Interface for Push-Based Content Delivery

Unlike the RESTful mode where the service consumers always initializes the communication, the pub/sub mode is, however, to decouple the parties by somehow hiding the explicit communication handshakes from the clients. The data communicated is normally transferred over a commonly known and delegated entity, named an information bus, for some large scale settings. The data sender, aka. the provider, publishes data to the information bus and the receiver, aka. the consumer, can subscribes data they want to receive. This kind of interaction enables some independencies to both parties (publishers and subscribers) where they need not even know of their existence in advance.

In systems based on the publish/subscribe interaction paradigm, subscribers register their interests in an event (or pattern of events), or to the predefined logic channels, and are asynchronously[2] notified of events generated by publishers.

There are basically two types of pub/sub models to chose: event-based and topic-based. Event-based model are used often under the situation where the correlation between parties can be defined by a set of events. The topic-based model, on the other hand, is based on the predicate concerning the content, or/and the attributes of the notifications in systems. Certainly a hybrid model can also be possibly applied. Given the nature of our MR use cases, which most of our notifications are related to different types of geo location-based contents along with other situational context data on the mobile devices, we decided to use a content- or topic-based pub/sub technique and implement our pub/sub solution based on the XMPP pub/sub standard XEP 60[3].

To re-use what we have already in the RESTful API, the pub/sub channel names are formed as resource containers and projection URIs. For instance, the Annotation container resource is: *http://{your_domain_name}/mrs/rest/content/annotations/*. The correspondent pub/sub channel for annotation notification is: */mrs/content/annotations/*. The query parameters used in REST calls are converted into a form of XML payload to configure the subscription options. For example, the subscription payload looks like:

```
<pubsub>
  <options node='/mrs/content/annotations'
jid=foo@nokiaresearch.com'>
  <x type='submit'>
  <field
var='pub/sub#proximity_type'><value>circle</value></field
>
  <field
var='pub/sub#proximity_longitude'><value>23.864365</value
></field>
  <field
var='pub/sub#proximity_latitude'><value>61.446129</value>
</field>
  <field var='pub/sub#proximity_radius>
      <value>1.5</value>
  </field>
  </x>
  </options>
</pubsub>
```

There are more other common criteria like the item limit (page count) information the clients can provide to the server. The default messages from the pub/sub channel are just the notifications of the MR contents with their URIs. Clients then can pull the details by sending GET requests. However, it is also allowed to publish the contents in the payload directly, as long as the server load is allowed[4].

---

2 In comparison to the "always connected" end-to-end interaction paradigm.

3 http://xmpp.org/extensions/xep-0060.html

4 Usually publishing massive contents over pub/sub channels to a large number of subscribers is regarded as a bad design.

In our current experiment, the MR content pushing is handled based on the static channels filtering by the search parameters, almost logically the same way as pull requests. Though the implementation uses a pre-defined and fixed quad tree indexing to partition the locations for server-side content caching in terms of efficiency, when the mobile device moves and publishes its locations to the server, the server actually sends the notifications only when tree node traverse takes place in either one of four directions. The granularity level of server-side caching, i.e. the depth of the quad tree, is determined by the real size of the subscription a client is interested in, for example, the *proximity_radius* value in the above example. The actual search is based on the PostGIS, a GIS extension of PostgreSQL server.

4 Mobile Experiments

4.1 Standard Pull-Based Experiment: A Mobile MR World Browser

We developed a mobile MR client named Cityscene based on the RESTful pull approach (see Fig. 2). The client pulls points of interests (POI) near the user location. Other geo-content such as 360-degree street-view panoramas and 3D building models [17, 18] are requested as well as the POI data when the location is changed. The client renders the POI appropriately onto the panoramic street view mode; or into an AR mode through the camera viewfinder.

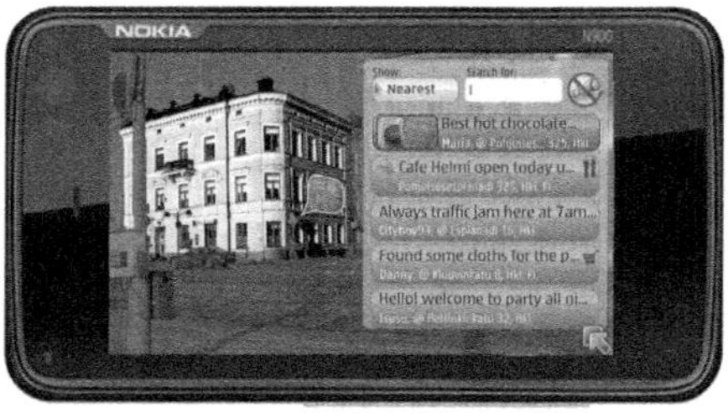

Fig. 2. Mobile MR world browser

The client runs not only on mobile devices, but also on PC environments. The same content (POI and panorama photos, etc.) can be requested both from the mobile and the desktop clients. However, the content authoring (e.g. adding new user-generated content) is more preferably done from the desktop, because of the fact that we have not found convenient ways for users to accurately position MR contents in situ on mobile devices.

4.2 Context-Based Adaptive Location Publishing and Content Discovery

Motion Detection and Adaptive Location Publishing

Unlike the pull-mode, we realize the MR scenario use case into two separate components, implemented as mobile widgets: the context publisher widget (the publisher); and the mobile launcher. The publisher is responsible of pushing all situational context data through the pub-sub channel to the MRS-WS backend. The launcher is actually a subscriber that can be configured to launch our MR viewer application (the viewer) when notifications from the pub-sub channels arrive. Unlike the standalone MR World browser (see Fig. 2), the unique feature of the launcher is that it can wake up and pass parameters to the target application. We will explain it shortly.

As we could understand, continuously collecting sensor data (e.g. GPS location) and publishing situational contextual information over the TCP network consumes a lot of energy, which would drain the battery power quickly. Based on our tests in the wild, full-charged high-end phones like Nokia N97 will operate only about half a day when the context publisher always runs. We come up with a very simple state machine implemented in the publisher, with an adaptive publishing rate, to minimize the power consumption for mobile devices.

Fig. 3 shows the state machine with four basic activity/inactivity states the publisher defines, based on the accelerometer and GPS sensors. We apply four different sampling rates respectively and publish the latest location data to the context channel, to which the platform is subscribing. The published data is signed with the user's own access secret for securing the data and identifying the sender. The signing mechanism is a variant version of Amazon S3 authentication [19], for the sake of simplicity and reliability.

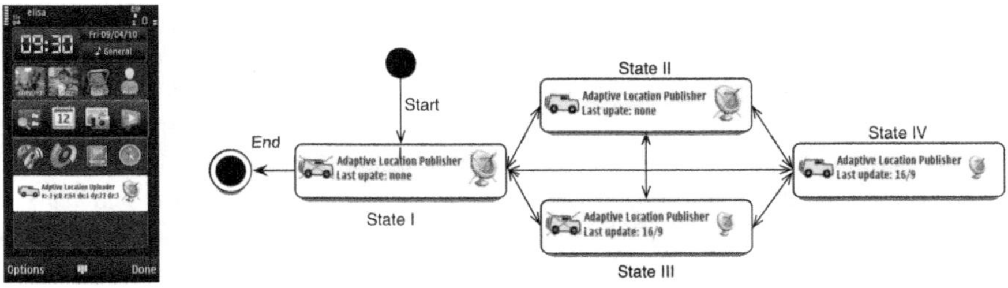

Fig. 3. Sensor S60 WRT Widget and its four motion-location states based on accelerometer and GPS sensors

In the State I, the publisher works in a stand-by mode. No location data is published to the backend. While the device starts to move, the state of the GPS sensor is checked. Based on the availability of GPS location data, two different states could happen: moving with no GPS coverage, e.g. in-door moving (State II) and moving with valid location data (State III). We apply different sampling rates respectively in favor of energy saving and bandwidth effectiveness. The sampling rate is chosen based on user preference or the one automatically generated from given concrete query parameter about the location distance of interests in kilometer in relation to current moving speed. There is another state when a device is still with a valid GPS coverage (State IV). We simply publish the location only when the change of location is big enough.

The three-axis accelerometer on the mobile device provides constant pitch, roll and bearing data with some noises. To get rid of device sensor noise and other irrelevant environmental noise like jittering, the sampling rate is experimentally defined as short as few seconds. The axis vectors then are calculated based on a simple in/activity motion detection algorithm (1), Displacement means and activity threshold for motion detection), with a given displacement threshold ($Dt = 6$). It is worth noting that this is not a proof by no means for a real physical motion detection using on mobile phones with built-in accelerometer (check Yang's experiment [20] for advanced motion detection & recognition on mobile devices).

$$Ave(d) = \frac{1}{n}\sum_{1}^{n} Di \qquad Ave(x) \geq Dt \vee Ave(y) \geq Dt \vee Ave(z) \geq Dt \tag{1}$$

To gain more advantage of the adaptive sampling, under that state III (moving and GPS), we can de-compose the state into two sub-states: 1) slow moving; and 2) fast moving, based on the statistical displacement data from the accelerometer sensor. We further tune the sampling rate of obtaining the location. For the simplicity sake, we did not use the velocity attribute from the GPS module for some more advanced adaptive sampling rate. The power saving may not be so different due to the fact that obtaining speed data from GPS module also consumes more power.

Content Notification and Wake-up Scenario

In previous section we gave a pub/sub example about a content channel to which a client can subscribe. Notifications are sent for both existing and new MR content within the deepest quad tree nodes (See Section 2) of the geographic locations in response to each mobile client's last location position. Apart from the location filtering, more criteria can be applied as well as locations, such as other metadata like tags and POI categories. As mentioned early, a mobile launcher is in charge of receiving notifications and waking up a separate AR viewer application (See Fig. 4). The user can then pick up the content and have an AR see-through layer on top of the camera viewfinder. Using the built-in mobile magnetometer sensor, the viewer application detects the camera orientation (converted to Azumith value) and the rough geo-distance (see Haversine formula [21]) and transforms the world coordinates to the relative screen coordinates. The user can turn the mobile device around to locate the MR content visually by following the visual arrow indicator. A tiny radar UI component is also used for the content right behind the user. The advantage of this experiment is that the launcher can be configured to wake up an application even when the target application is not running.

Fig. 4. Mobile AR viewer in action (Left: the target place is off-screen on the left; Right: the target place is marked on the camera view)

5 Future Work

Currently the pub/sub channels are almost identical to the pull resource URIs. Using the same container URI structure as the forms of the pub/sub channels is straightforward and consistent for different situations, for example, in terms of proximity search. Nevertheless, separate dedicated read/write channels are still needed for context data collection. They are not very extensible and most often client-specific. From the API perspective, it would be convenient to get rid of client-specific channels and use the subscription options as a hint for accepting publishing context data from the clients. Another improvement is the support of multiple subscriptions. It means that a client can subscribe to the same channel several times with different subscription options.

In our mobile experiment where adaptive context publishing is demonstrated, at the client side we used very simple state machine to mimic the complex real situation. The question is, no matter how complex the state machine the mobile client would use, how to somehow update the subscription status to adapt the contextual changes in a user-friendly way. By means of user-friendly, for example, it can be referred to stopping receiving event notifications and saving battery life after the timeout in the sleeping state. Or based on the changes of user profile on the mobile, the client can switch its states accordingly, and so on. In our current design, the lifecycle of the AR browser waked up by the launcher is pretty transient compared to other core mobile applications such as contacts and calendar. This design is exactly an example how we could improve the total usability by tremendously saving the power consumption and extending the battery life from few hours to days.

In our experiment we only used a particular piece of context information: the geo-location. There are large types of context information a high-end (even a middle e level) mobile device could possibly sensor and capture [22, 23]. Neither does our experiment define a meta-meta context model that interprets low-level context data into a more unified and portable data forms or context ontology. More intelligent server-side context-aware pushing than our current location-aware content delivering is definitely one of our future research directions.

Publishing users' locations at real-time definitely imposes a big concern on the privacy. By default, like other sensitive data such as user profile, all locations are private and used as parameters only when the correct owners can be identified and properly authenticated. The MRS-WS platform does support authentication and authorization at the MR content level. Concerning the hybrid delivery mode, the push mode requires extra security requirements into the design, particularly, in the case of one-to-many and many-to-one publishing and subscription.

From a Web services point of view, the team plans to focus more on the web services, especially focusing on context-aware services and adding more intelligence into our services, keeping also the mobile client and mixed reality aspects on board. From a Mixed Reality point of view, the focus will be more on supporting content discovery of what matters to the user; and enabling flexible and dynamic relevant information by orchestrating content and metadata coming from different sources.

6 Summary

This paper presented the experiences gained during the development of a mixed reality Web service platform. One of the main goals is to provide a common interface for building rich mixed reality mash-ups and 3rd party solutions and supporting open innovation. The platform serves geo-spatially oriented content, advanced geo-data like 3D point-cloud models, street-view panoramas and city building outlines, and social connections in a secure and scalable manner.

The convenient RESTful design was nevertheless found sufficient enough for building a scalable MR service platform, because of the nature of the large amount of location-associated content update by the clients. Apart from the pulling, we added the publication/subscription support and presented our mobile experiments based on an adaptive location-aware mobile AR scenario. This paper also provided analysis about the experiments and particularly the features such as adaptive context publishing and automatic content discovering.

Acknowledgement

The authors would like to thank Arto Nikupaavola for the database design, David Murphy for the mobile AR viewer and the rest of the Mixed Reality Program team from the Nokia Research Center for their valuable support.

References

1. Milgram, P., Kishino, F.: A Taxonomy of Mixed Reality Visual Displays. IEICE Transactions on Information Systems E77-D (12), 1321–1329 (1994)
2. Azuma, R.T., Baillot, Y., Behringer, R., Feiner, S., Julier, S., MacIntyre, B.: Recent Advances in Augmented Reality. IEEE Computer Graphics and Applications 21(6), 34–47 (2001)
3. Höllerer, T., Feiner, S.: Mobile augmented reality. In: Karimi, H., Hammad, A. (eds.) Telegeoinformatics: Location-Based Computing and Services, Taylor and Francis Books Ltd., London (2004)
4. Mobile Mixed Reality, The Vision, Nokia, http://research.nokia.com/files/NTI_MARA_June_2009.pdf
5. Kähäri, M., Murphy, D.J.: MARA - Sensor Based Augmented Reality System for Mobile Imaging. In: 5th IEEE and ACM International Symposium on Mixed and Augmented Reality (ISMAR 2006), Santa Barbara, USA (2006)
6. Layar, Augmented reality world browser, http://www.layar.com
7. Wikitude, Wikitude world browser, http://www.wikitude.org/wikitude-ein-reisefuhrer
8. Belimpasakis, P., Selonen, P., You, Y.: Bringing User-Generated Content from Internet Services to Mobile Augmented Reality Clients. In: Workshop on Cloud Mobile Convergence for Virtual Reality 2010 (CMCVR 2010), Waltham, MA, USA (2010)
9. Junaio, Mobile AR browser, http://www.junaio.com/
10. Fielding, R.T.: Architectural Styles and the Design of Network-based Software Architectures. Doctoral Thesis. University of California, Irvine (2000)
11. Henshaw-Plath, E.R., Elliott-McCrea, K.: Beyond REST? Building data services with XMPP, OSCON (2008)
12. Kendall, J.E., Kendall, K.E.: Information Delivery Systems: An Exploration of Web Pull and Push Technologies. Communications of the AIS 1(4) (1999)

13. Cheverst, K., Mitchell, K., et al.: Investigating Context-aware Informaiton Push vs. Information Pull to Tourists. In: MobileHCI 2001 Workshop on HCI with Mobile Devices, Lille, France (2001)
14. Coutrix, C., Nigay, L.: Mixed Reality: A model of Mixed Interaction. In: 8th International ACM Conference on Advanced Visual Interfaces, AVI 2006, Venezia, Italy, pp. 43–50. ACM Press, New York (2006)
15. Selonen, P., Belimpasakis, P., You, Y.: Experiences In Building a RESTful Mixed Reality Web Service Platform. In: Benatallah, B., Casati, F., Kappel, G., Rossi, G. (eds.) ICWE 2010. LNCS, vol. 6189, pp. 400–414. Springer, Heidelberg (2010)
16. Allamaraju, S., Amudsen, M.: RESTful Web Services Cookbook. O'Reilly, Sebastopol (2010)
17. Pylvanainen, T., Roimela, K., Vedantham, R., Itaranta, J., Wang, R., Grzeszczuk, R.: Automatic Alignment and Multi-View Segmentation of Street View Data using 3D Shape Priors. In: Symposium on 3D Data Processing, Visualization and Transmission (3DPVT), Paris, France (2010)
18. Belimpasakis, P., You, Y., Selonen, P.: Enabling Rapid Creation of Content for Consumption in Mobile Augmented Reality. In: The 4th IEEE Conference on Next Generation Mobile Applications, Services and Technologies (NGMAST 2010), Amman, Jordan (2010)
19. Amazon S3 authentication, `http://docs.amazonwebservices.com/AmazonS3/latest/dev/index.html?RESTAuthentication.html`
20. Yang, J.: Toward physical activity diary: motion recognition using simple acceleration features with mobile phones. In: 1st International Workshop on Interactive Multimedia For Consumer Electronics, Beijing, China (2009)
21. Haversine formula, Wikipedia (2010), `http://en.wikipedia.org/wiki/Haversine_formula`
22. Belimpasakis, P., Roimela, K., You, Y.: Experience Explorer: a Life-Logging Platform Based on Mobile Context Collection. In: 3rd IEEE Conference on Next Generation Mobile Applications, Services and Technologies (NGMAST 2009), Cardiff, Wales, UK (2009)
23. Location, Context, and Mobile Services, Nokia Technology Insights series (2009)

Appendix: MRS-WS RESTful API Overview

To all those RESTful resources and containers, user-generated content and static geodata, a uniform set of operations can be applied. Examples include:

- geo-searching for performing searches in a bounded box (e.g. /photos/?lat1=41.95&lon1=-87.7&lat2=41.96&lon2=-87.6) or in proximity (e.g. /photos /?lat=41.8&lon=-87.6&radius=1);
- pagination [x-mrs-api: page(), pagesize()] for controlling the number of objects fetched from a container per request by setting the page size and number;
- verbosity [x-mrs-api: verbosity()] for controlling the representation subset, ie.e selected attributes for the retrieved items; and
- inlining [x-mrs-deco: inline()] for selecting which sub-resources and referenced items are included per resources in the response to decide when to reduce the number of requests to the server and when to reduce the amount of data transferred.

Below is a table showing main container and item resources the platform supports currently, with correspondent HTTP operations and response status codes.

Table 2. MRS-WS RESTful API (part)

Resource URI /mrs/rest	Description	Inline elements
/panos	Panoramas	-
/panos/{pano.id}	Specific panorama item	buildings, pois, locations
/buildings	Buildings	-
/buildings/{building.id}	Building foot print outlines	obj, pois, locations
/terrain	Terrain tiles	
/terrain/{terrain.id}	Individual terrain tile	obj, locations
/pois	Points of Interest	-
/pois/{poi.id}	Individual POI	-
/users/{user.nickname}/content/	All user content	pointclouds, annotations, photos
/users/{user.nickname}/content/pointclouds	Pointclouds	-
/users/{user.nickname}/content/pointclouds /{pointcloud.id}	3D mesh	media, locations, comments, tags
/users/{user.nickname}/content/annotations	Annotations	
/users/{user.nickname}/content/annotations /{annotation.id}	Annotation	locations, comments, tags, building
/users/{user.nickname}/content/contexts	Context data	.
/users/{user.nickname}/content/photos	Photos	.
/users/{user.nickname}/content/photos/{ph oto.id}	Photo	media, locations, comments, tags
/users/{user.nickname}/comments/	Comments	.
/users/{user.nickname}/comments/{comme nt.id}	Individuel comment	-
[parent resource]/tags/	Tags	
[parent resource]/tags/{tag.name}	Individuel tag	-

Analyzing the Behavioral Structure Characteristics from Web Traffic*

Ke Yu, Xiaofei Wu, Yang Cao, and Zhijia Nian

School of Information and Communication Engineering
Beijing University of Posts and Telecommunications
100876, Beijing, China
{yuke,wuxf}@bupt.edu.cn

Abstract. Nowadays Web service becomes one of the most popular services in information society. Understanding the characteristics of Web service and traffic is critical for traffic modeling and network optimization. In this paper, based on a large sample of flow data collected from operational network of ISP, the statistical characteristics of the behavioral structure of the Web are investigated. The behavioral structure is modeled as a weighted bipartite digraph, and the degree and strength distribution of hosts, the assortativity coefficient, the community structure are analyzed. Analysis results show that the behavioral structure of the Web exhibit characteristics such as scale-free and highly clustered, which implies the heterogeneous behavior of users on the Web.

Keywords: Web service, user behavior, bipartite graph, network flow data.

1 Introduction

World-Wide Web is one of the most important applications on Internet. Recently the emergence of Web 2.0 makes Web service become the most popular service in information society. Understanding the characteristics of Web structure and traffic is critical for evaluating the performance of network protocols, for improving user's Quality of Experience (QoE), and for protecting the network from malicious attack. [1-3] have studied the graph structure of the Web. The Web graph is an unweighted directed graph, in which vertices represent Web pages and directed edges are hyperlinks. Connectivity information collected by various crawlers or Web data mining indicates that the Web graph is essentially a complex network, which presents such characteristics as small-world, scale-free and community structure [4].

Existing researches mainly focus on the link structure of the Web, which provides the connectivity information of Web pages. Based on the link structure, link-based ranking strategies such as PageRank algorithm have been developed to improve Web-search query results. However, the link structure cannot describe users' behavior on the Web. When users are browsing the Web, Web traffic constitutes an overlay on the

* The paper is supported by the Fundamental Research Funds for the Central Universities of China (2009RC0108), and is partially supported by State 863 Project (2009AA01Z246) and the 111 Project (No. B08004) of China.

Z. Yu et al. (Eds.): UIC 2010, LNCS 6406, pp. 577–589, 2010.

top of the link structure. The overlay is named *the behavioral structure* since it can reflect navigation patterns, community structure, and network congestion resulting from users' behavior. In fact, the behavioral structure provides the usage information of the Web, based on which we can further understand the dynamics of information on the Web and the evolution of Web service.

In this paper, we focus on the characteristics of behavioral structure of the Web. Based on flow data collected from operational network of ISP, the behavioral structure of the Web can be represented by a weighted directed graph. Vertices are hosts with specific IP addresses, and directed edges mean actual HTTP transfers among these hosts. Furthermore, each edge is associated with a weight which expresses the aggregate amount of data sent from one host to the other. We study the statistical properties of the behavioral structure, including the degree and strength distribution of hosts, the assortativity coefficient as well as community structure. Analysis results show the heterogeneous behavior of users on the Web.

The remainder of the paper is organized as follows. Section 2 reviews the related work. Section 3 describes the collection of network flow data and the construction of behavioral structure of the Web. In Section 4, statistical properties of the behavioral structure are analyzed. In Section 5, conclusion and future work are presented.

2 Related Work

There are mainly two kinds of data which can be used to analyze statistical patterns related to the behavior of users on the Web. One is Web usage data gathered from server/client/proxy log. The other is flow data collected from network routers or traffic monitoring systems. By analyzing Web usage data, we can understand Web usage patterns i.e. user habits in browsing information such as user access properties, association rules and sequential patterns in user sessions, user classification, and Web page clustering. The results of Web usage mining can help us to improve the system design and the accessibility of Web sites. On the other hand, by analyzing network flow data, we can investigate large-scale user behavior on the Web, such as characteristics of aggregative traffic, overlay structure, and utilization of network resource. In fact, Web flow data provides a global view of user behavior on the Web from the perspective of bearer network, which is helpful for traffic modeling, analysis of long-term trends of traffic and application, and network optimization.

In recent years there are numerous researches about Web user behavior analysis, most of which are based on Web usage data. A framework of mining Web usage patterns from Web log files was proposed in [5], through which evolving user profiles in dynamic Web sites were discovered and evaluated. [6] proposed two Web user clustering algorithms by considering not only the page preferences but also the access time, and evaluated them under real server log files. In [7], instead of using server log as main data source, client level data was taken into account. By applying graph mining method to study user navigation pattern and browsing time, user session could be reconstructed exactly and current usage of Web sites could be evaluated.

To the best of our knowledge, there are a few literatures related to user behavior analysis based on Web traffic. [8] investigated the properties of global Web traffic based on one-day network flow data gathered from the Abilene network (Internet2).

Statistical analysis showed that client-server connections and traffic flows exhibited heavy-tailed probability distributions lacking any typical scale, and proved non-trivial correlations between information flow and connectivity pattern. In [9], based on two-week flow records collected from an edge router of a local campus network, a behavioral network was constructed. Structure analysis indicated that degree as well as strength distribution of servers and clients had long tails, and clients could be divided into different interest communities.

However, due to limitations of flow data source and analysis methods, the characteristics of global behavior of Web user as well as the relation between traffic and user behavior are far from being well understood. In [8], Abilene network carried only academic and research traffic, and it was never congested. Moreover, only those flows involving TCP connections with an endpoint on port 80 were considered as Web traffic. In [9], flow data was gathered from a small local area network with about 16500 users. In our paper, based on accurate measurement by high-performance network traffic monitors deployed in an operational wide area network, flow data related to Web traffic is distilled to construct the behavioral structure of the Web. These accurate flow records allow us to more closely observe the interactions among hosts, and more accurately model the characteristics of the behavioral structure as complex network. Statistical properties of the behavioral structure are analyzed to investigate the heterogeneous behavior of users on the Web and the relation between traffic and user behavior.

3 Behavioral Structure of the Web

3.1 Flow Data Collection

In order to analysis Web user behavior on commodity Internet, flow data is collected by several high-performance network traffic monitors from an operational network. The wide area network is an access network of a province in south China, which comprises several service systems as well as Internet Data Centers (IDCs) and serves more than 10 million users. The schematic diagram of network architecture is shown in Figure 1, in which several access routers (ARs) are connected to the aggregate routers, which in turn connect to the core routers (CRs) in the national backbone of the ISP. Moreover, network traffic monitors with hardware probe are deployed at the 10Gps trunk links between the access network and the national backbone, which record information of each flow coming into or leaving from the access network.

By adopting advanced traffic identification and classification technologies, the network traffic monitors can collect and distinguish flow data from different Internet applications, such as Web, FTP, Email, VoIP, Video Stream, P2P, Instant Messaging (IM) and so on. Each flow record contains information about a single network flow, which is defined as one or more packets sent from a particular source host and port, to a particular destination host and port, using a particular protocol, over some time interval.

The network traffic monitors collected 24-hour flow data from the operational network on March 23, 2010. Due to tremendous amount of the flow data, we store flow records in about 5-minute interval, so we have more than 280 samples of flow

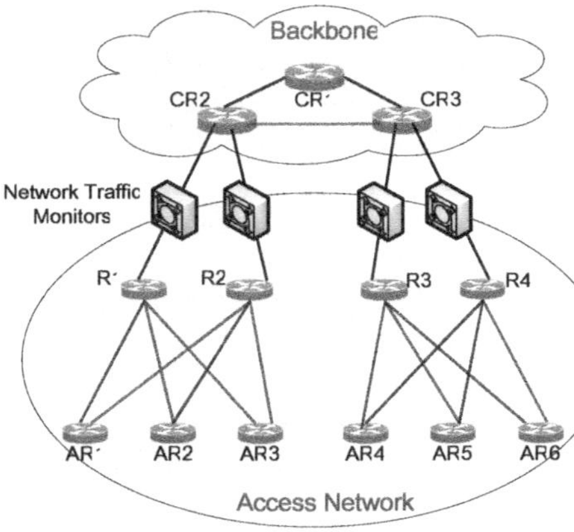

Fig. 1. Network Architecture

data. There are about 5 million to 9 million flow records in each sample file, and the entries in each flow record include occurring time, source and destination IP address and port, total number of packets and bytes in the flow, and application type. Our paper is focusing on Web traffic, which involves flows related to HTTP, HTTPS, HTTPProxy, and WAP, and constitutes 40% to 45% records of the total flow data.

3.2 Behavioral Structure Construction

Based on each sample of flow data, we can construct the behavioral structure of the Web. By considering hosts with specific IP addresses involved in flows as vertices, and actual HTTP transfers between pairs of hosts as directed edges, to which we assign weights representing the aggregate amount of data transmitted between pairs of hosts, the behavioral structure of the Web can be represented by a weighted directed graph $G=(V,E), |V|=N, |E|=M$.

Web service involves two kinds of hosts, Web servers and clients. Generally data is transferred between server and client, and a few HTTP transfers occur between two servers due to Web page redirection. So the vertex set V can be partitioned into two subsets, with $V_S=\{i_1,i_2,\cdots,i_{N_S}\}$ identifying hosts acting as servers, and $V_C=\{j_1,j_2,\cdots,j_{N_C}\}$ identifying hosts acting as clients. Note that there exit some hosts such as cache or proxy servers acting as server and client synchronously, but the number of such hosts is much smaller than the total number of hosts. We regard these hosts as servers for simplification, and thus $N=N_S+N_C$. Directed edge (i_k, j_l) and (j_l,i_k) represent server-to-client and client-to-server connection respectively. The number of edge (i_k,i_l) meaning server-to-server connection is very small (less than 0.5% of the total number of edges), so we don't consider edge (i_k,i_l) in graph G . As a result, the behavioral structure of the Web can be represented by a weighted bipartite digraph, as shown in Figure 2.

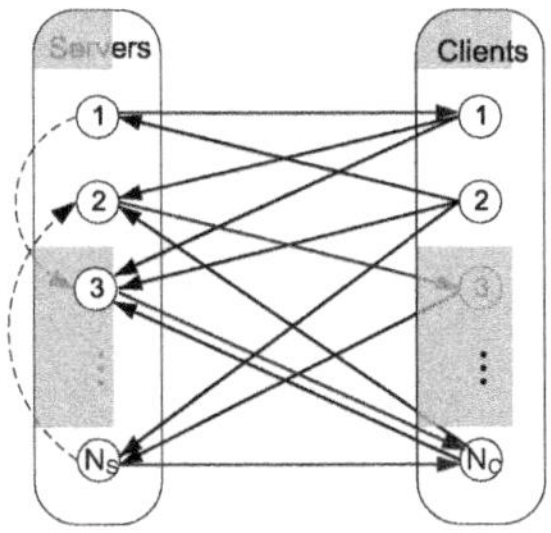

Fig. 2. Weighted Bipartite Digraph Representing the Behavioral Structure of the Web

3.3 Statistical Characteristics

Based on aforementioned weighted bipartite digraph, a number of statistical characteristic quantities can be derived, including out-degree, in-degree, degree distribution, assortativity coefficient, out-strength, in-strength, strength distribution, clustering coefficient and so on.

For a vertex $i \in V$, the in-degree k_i^{in} means the number of directed edges with i as their terminal vertex. The out-degree k_i^{out} means the number of directed edges with i as their initial vertex. The in-degree distribution $p(k^{in})$ is defined as the probability that a vertex chosen at random has in-degree k^{in}. The out-degree distribution $p(k^{out})$ has the similar definition. Note that the cumulative degree distribution function (CDDF) is frequently used, which is defined as the fraction of vertices with degree larger than or equal to k.

$$P_k = \sum_{k'=k}^{\infty} p(k') \tag{1}$$

In order to determine degree correlation, the assortativity coefficient is defined as follows [10]:

$$r = \frac{\frac{1}{M}\sum_i j_i k_i - [\frac{1}{M}\sum_i \frac{1}{2}(j_i + k_i)]^2}{\frac{1}{M}\sum_i \frac{1}{2}(j_i^2 + k_i^2) - [\frac{1}{M}\sum_i \frac{1}{2}(j_i + k_i)]^2} \tag{2}$$

where j_i and k_i are degrees at both ends of the ith edge, and M is the total number of edges. If $r > 0$ the network is assortative, which implies that vertices with high degree tend to connect with vertices with high degree; if $r < 0$ the network is disassortative, which implies that vertices with high degree tend to connect with vertices with low degree; for $r = 0$ there is no correlation between vertex degrees.

For a vertex $i \in V$, the in-strength s_i^{in} is defined as the sum of weights of directed edges with i as their terminal vertex.

$$s_i^{in} = \sum_j w_{ji} \tag{3}$$

The out-strength s_i^{out} is the sum of weights of directed edges with i as their initial vertex.

$$s_i^{out} = \sum_j w_{ij} \tag{4}$$

The in-strength distribution $p(s^{in})$ is the probability that a vertex chosen at random has in-strength s^{in}. The out-strength distribution $p(s^{out})$ has the similar definition. Note that the cumulative distribution function is also used for strength distribution.

$$P_s = \sum_{s'=s}^{\infty} p(s') \tag{5}$$

In order to analyze the clustering characteristics of graph, clustering coefficient of vertex i is defined:

$$c_i = \frac{2E_i}{k_i(k_i - 1)} \tag{6}$$

Where k_i is the number of the nearest neighbors of vertex i, and E_i denotes the number of edges practically connecting the nearest neighbors of vertex i.

The clustering coefficient of a graph C is the mean of c_i.

However, for bipartite graph, $\forall i \in V, c_i = 0$. So in our paper we use the following definition of clustering coefficient proposed by [11].

$$c_{i,mn} = \frac{q_{imn}}{k_m + k_n - q_{imn} - 2} \tag{7}$$

Where m and n are the pair of neighbors of vertex i; k_m and k_n are the degree of vertex m and n respectively; q_{imn} is the number of existent squares which include three vertices i, m and n.

To investigate the community structure of the behavioral structure of the Web, the bipartite graph is transformed to one-mode graph. We focus on the community structure of clients since the communities may represent different interest groups of users. The one-mode graph of clients is $G_C = (V_C, E_C)$, in which two vertices are connected only if the two clients communicate with at least one common server. After one-mode projection, the community structure of G_C can be investigated by analyzing the size of the largest strong connected component (SCC) and the largest weak connected component (WCC), which reflects the extent of user clustering.

4 Structural Characteristics Analysis

We analyze the characteristics of the behavioral structure constructed by a number of samples of flow data, and acquire the similar results. Due to limitation of paper space, the analysis results from two typical sample files are presented in this section. One sample file contains more than 6 million flow records in 5 minutes, from which 32603 vertices and 66826 edges are distilled to construct the weighted bipartite digraph of the Web. The other sample file contains more than 45 million records, which involves 227176 vertices and 817134 edges. The sizes of the two behavioral structures are summarized in Table 1.

Table 1. Behavioral structure size

	vertices	edges	servers	clients	server-server edges
5-minute graph	32603	66826	11553	21050	275, 0.41% of total
1-hour graph	227176	817134	88812	138364	4017, 0.49% of total

4.1 Degree Analysis

Firstly, degree and degree distribution of servers and clients are analyzed. The basic metrics related to degree are summarized in Table 2. It can be seen that for clients, max and mean out/in-degree of 1-hour graph are larger than those of 5-minute graph; but for servers, as the graph size increases with time, though max out/in degree increases, the mean out/in degree decreases.

Table 2. Basic metrics related to degree

	5-minute graph		1-houre graph	
	server	client	server	client
max out-degree	313	68	6459	89
mean out-degree	2.92	1.55	2.60	1.73
max in-degree	450	102	14819	170
mean in-degree	2.82	1.61	2.68	1.68

The out-degree and in-degree distributions of 5-minute and 1-hour graph are shown in Figure 3 and Figure 4 respectively. Note that we use the cumulative degree distribution function (CDDF) in our paper. We can see that degree distributions of servers and clients are heavy-tailed, which can be approximated to a power-law distribution $p(n) \sim n^{-r}$ over several orders of magnitude. The power exponents fitting for degree distributions of two graphs are summarized in Table 3.

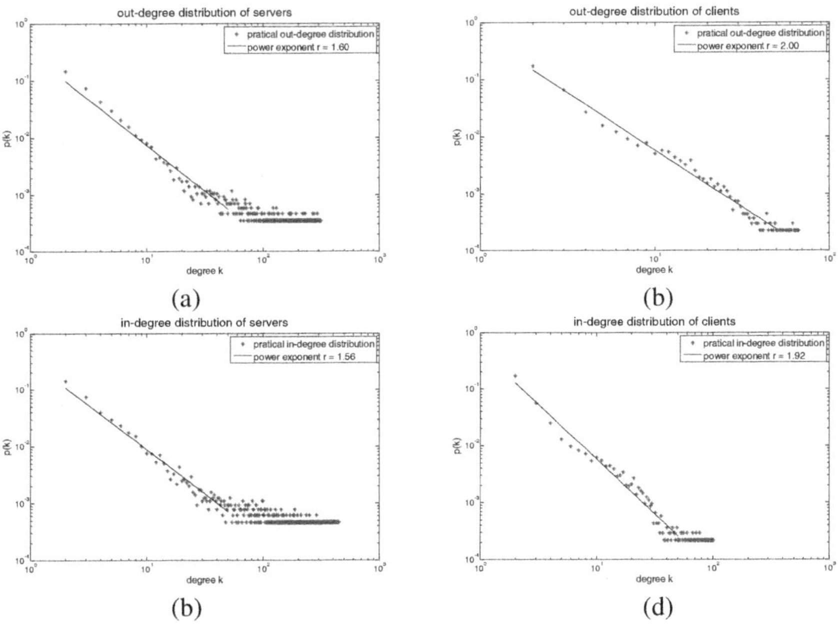

Fig. 3. Degree distribution of 5-minute graph. (a) is the out-degree distribution of servers, (b) is the out-degree of clients; (c) is the in-degree distribution of servers; (d) is the in-degree of clients.

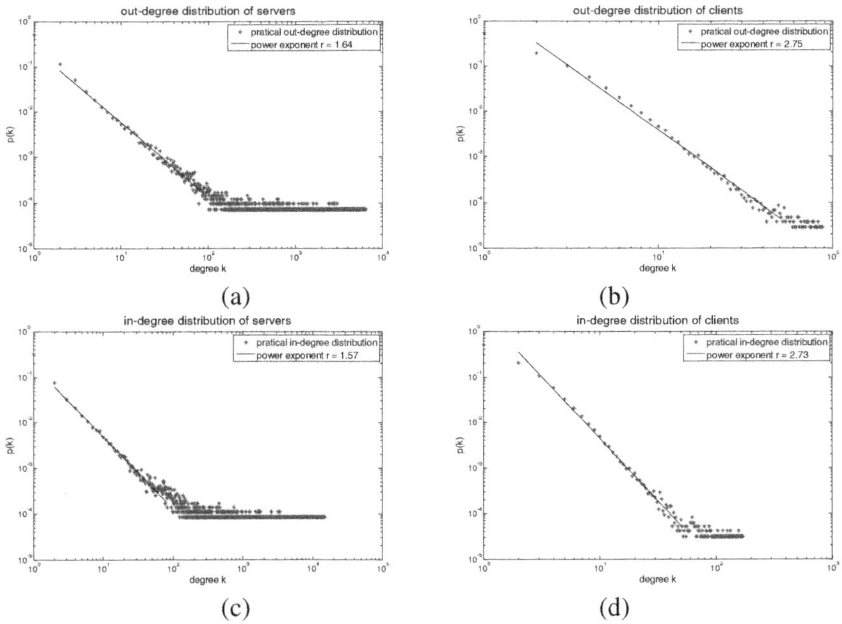

Fig. 4. Degree distribution of 1-hour graph. (a) is the out-degree distribution of servers, (b) is the out-degree of clients; (c) is the in-degree distribution of servers; (d) is the in-degree of clients.

Table 3. Power exponent fitting for out-degree and in-degree distribution

	5-minute graph		1-houre graph	
	server	client	server	client
out-degree distribution	1.60	2.00	1.64	2.75
in-degree distribution	1.56	1.92	1.57	2.73

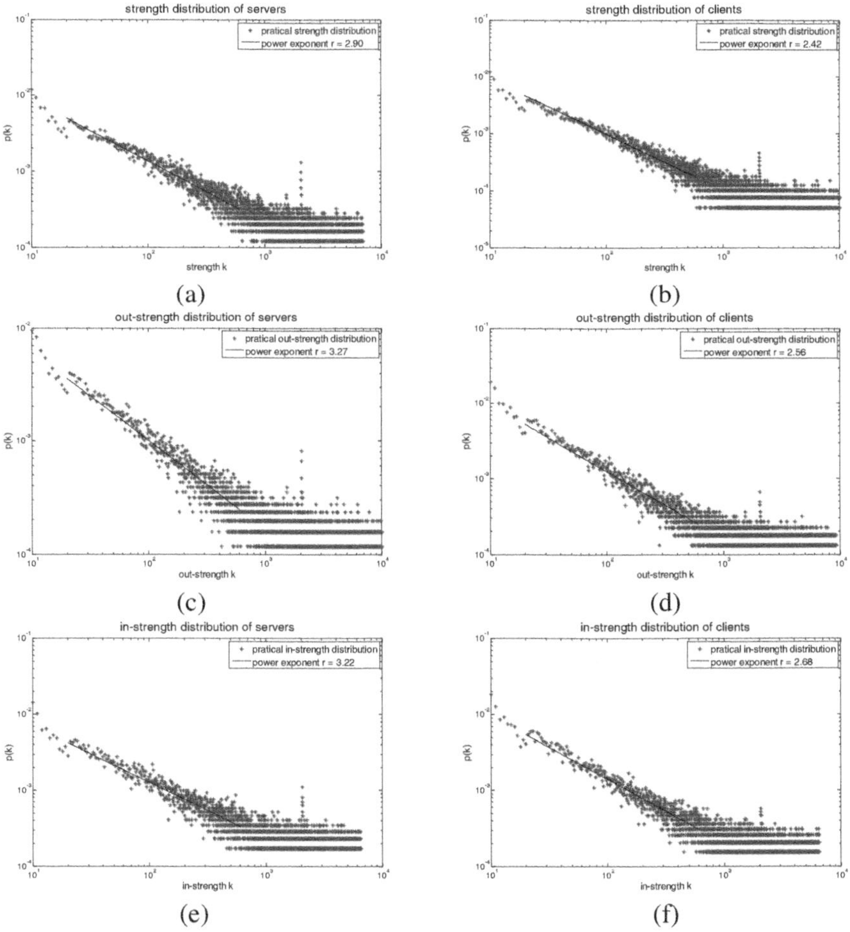

Fig. 5. Strength distribution of 5-minute graph. (a) is total strength distribution of servers, (b) is the total strength distribution of clients; (c) is the out-strength distribution of servers; (d) is the out-strength distribution of clients; (e) is the in-strength distribution of servers; (f) is the in-strength distribution of clients.

From the degree distribution results, we can see that the connections between Web servers and clients present heterogeneous behavior. There exit some "hub" servers or hot-spot Web sites which are visited by a large number of clients. The existence of "hub" clients may imply anomalous behavior of users. Another interesting observation is the impact of time scale of sample file on power exponent r. The power exponents of 1-hour graph are all larger than that of 5-minute graph, which is more obvious for client. The result implies that as the graph size increases, the degree distributions of servers and clients tend to be heavy-tailed.

In order to investigate the degree correlation, we calculate the assortative coefficients of two graphs. The assortative coefficients for 5-minute and 1-hour graph are -1.137475 and -1.000896 respectively, which implies that the behavioral structure of Web is a disassortative network, as most of the technical networks.

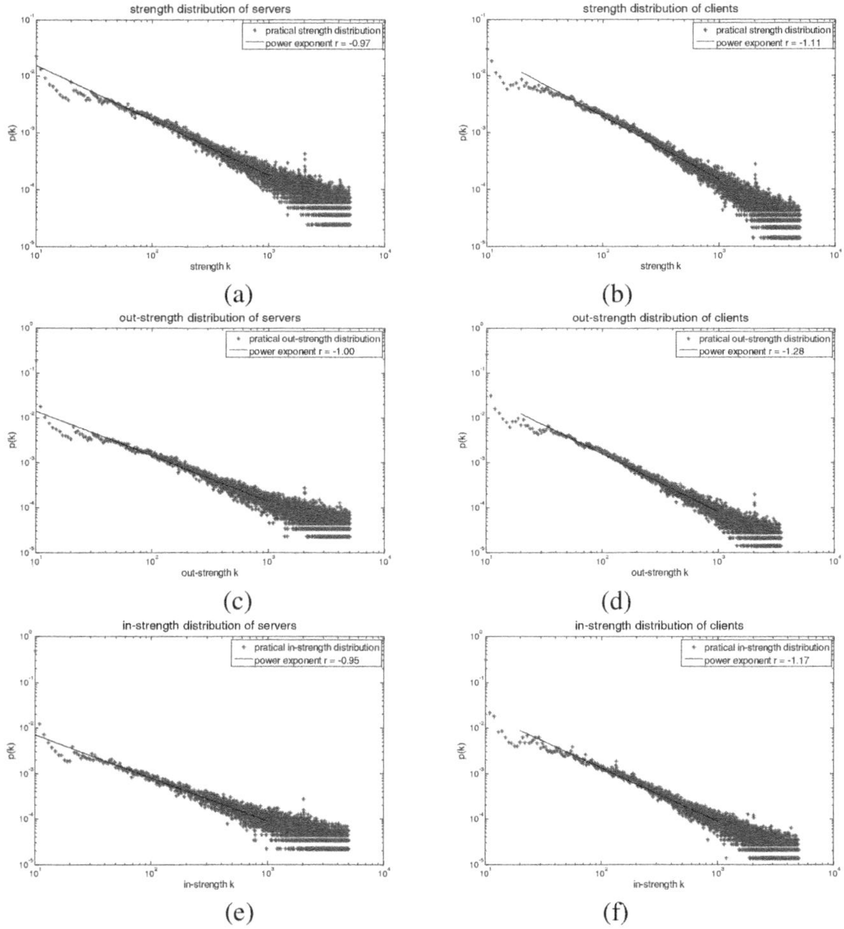

Fig. 6. Strength distribution of 1-hour graph. (a) is total strength distribution of servers, (b) is the total strength distribution of clients; (c) is the out-strength distribution of servers; (d) is the out-strength distribution of clients; (e) is the in-strength distribution of servers; (f) is the in-strength distribution of clients.

4.2 Strength Analysis

Secondly, strength and strength distribution of servers and clients are analyzed. Note that in order to simplify analysis results, we use the number of packets transmitted in flows as the weight of edge. There are similar results if the number of bytes transmitted in flows is taken as the weight of edge. Moreover, we also use the cumulative distribution function in our paper.

The strength distributions of 5-minute and 1-hour graph are shown in Figure 5 and Figure 6 respectively, which are heavy-tailed, and can be approximated to a power-law distribution over several orders of magnitude. The power exponents fitting for strength distributions are summarized in Table 4. We can conclude that traffic between servers and clients are unbalanced, which may result from heterogeneous connections on the Web.

Table 4. Power exponent fitting for strength distribution

	5-minute graph		1-houre graph	
	server	client	server	client
total strength distribution	2.90	2.42	0.97	1.11
out-strength distribution	3.27	2.56	1.00	1.28
in-strength distribution	3.22	2.68	0.95	1.17

From the strength distribution results, we can see that there still exit "hub" servers and "hub" clients from the point of view of data transmission. The impact of time scale of sample file on power exponent r can also be seen from the results. The power exponents of 1-hour graph are much smaller than that of 5-minute graph. The result implies that as the graph size increases with time, the strength distributions of servers and clients tend to be less heavy-tailed.

4.3 Clustering and Community Analysis

For the weighted bipartite digraph, we calculate clustering coefficient based on definition (7). The clustering coefficient of 5-minute and 1-hour graph are 0.146993 and 0.056294 respectively, which are both larger than those of randomly generated bipartite grpahs with the same number of vertices and edges ($C_{rand-5m} = 0.000098$, $C_{rand-1h} = 0.000134$). The result means that the behavioral structure of the Web is highly clustered.

Table 5. Community analysis

one-mode graph of clients	vertices	edges	SCC	WCC
5-minute graph	21050	109462	7515 35.7% of the total number of vertices	20713 98.4%
1-hour graph	138364	844023	45245 32.7%	135043 97.6%

After producing the one-mode graph of clients G_C, the SCC and WCC size of the graphs are analyzed, as shown in Table 5. We can see that the clustering phenomenon of clients is obvious, since the SCC and WCC accounts for the largest proportion of the total number of vertices. By identifying communities or clusters of hosts, different interest group of users can be discovered.

5 Conclusion and Future Work

In this paper, based on abundant flow data collected from operational network, the behavioral structure of the Web is modeled as a weighted bipartite digraph. By considering two graphs with different time scales, i.e. 5-minute and 1-hour graph, the statistical characteristics of the behavioral structure, including the degree and strength distribution of hosts, the assortativity coefficient, the clustering coefficient and community structure are investigated. Analysis results show that the behavioral structure of the Web exhibit characteristics such as scale-free and highly clustered, which implies the heterogeneous behavior of users on the Web.

More structural characteristics of the behavioral structure of the Web will be studied in our future work, and novel complex network models will be proposed to describe the user behavior and the dynamics of information on the Web.

References

1. Albert, R., Jeong, H., Barabasi, A.L.: Diameter of the World Wide Web. Nature 401, 130–131 (1999)
2. Broder, A., et al.: Graph structure in the web. The International Journal of Computer and Telecommunications Networking 33, 309–320 (2000)
3. Adamic, L.A.: The Small World Web. In: Abiteboul, S., Vercoustre, A.-M. (eds.) ECDL 1999. LNCS, vol. 1696, p. 443. Springer, Heidelberg (1999)
4. Newman, M.E.J.: The Structure and Function of Complex Networks. SIAM Review 45(2), 167–256 (2003)
5. Nasraoui, O., Soliman, M., Saka, E., Badia, A., Germain, R.: A Web Usage Mining Framework for Mining Evolving User Profiles in Dynamic Web Sites. IEEE Transactions on Knowledge and Data Engineering 20 (February 2008)
6. Petridou, S.G., Koutsonikola, V.A., Vakali, A.I., Papadimitriou, G.I.: Time Aware Web Users Clustering. IEEE Transactions on Knowledge and Data Engineering 20, 653–667 (2008)
7. Heydari, M., Helal, R.A., Ghauth, K.I.: A Graph-Based Web Usage Mining Method Considering Client Side Data. In: 2009 International Conference on Electrical Engineering and Informatics, IECCI 2009 (August 2009)
8. Meiss, M., Menczer, F., Vespignani, A.: On the lack of typical behavior in the global Web traffic network. In: Proceedings of the 14th International Conference on World Wide Web, pp. 510–518 (May 2005)

9. Jun, C., Shun-Zheng, Y.: The structure analysis of user behaviors for web traffic. In: Proceedings of 2009 ISECS International Colloquium on Computing, Communication, Control, and Management, vol. 4, pp. 501–506 (August 2009)
10. Newman, M.E.J.: Assortative mixing in networks. Physics Review Letters 89(20), 208701 (2002)
11. Zhang, P., et al.: Clustering coefficient and community structure of bipartite networks. Physica A 387, 6869–6875 (2008)

A Smartphone-Based Obstacle Sensor for the Visually Impaired

En Peng, Patrick Peursum, Ling Li, and Svetha Venkatesh

Department of Computing, Curtin University of Technology, Perth, Australia
{e.peng,p.peursum,l.li,s.venkatesh}@curtin.edu.au

Abstract. In this paper, we present a real-time obstacle detection system for the mobility improvement for the visually impaired using a handheld Smartphone. Though there are many existing assistants for the visually impaired, there is not a single one that is low cost, ultra-portable, non-intrusive and able to detect the low-height objects on the floor. This paper proposes a system to detect any objects attached to the floor regardless of their height. Unlike some existing systems where only histogram or edge information is used, the proposed system combines both cues and overcomes some limitations of existing systems. The obstacles on the floor in front of the user can be reliably detected in real time using the proposed system implemented on a Smartphone. The proposed system has been tested in different types of floor conditions and a field trial on five blind participants has been conducted. The experimental results demonstrate its reliability in comparison to existing systems.

Keywords: Obstacle detection; visually impaired; real-time; monocular vision.

1 Introduction

Mobility assistance is desperately needed by the visually impaired because obstacles can cause injuries. Consultation with an expert group [16] has highlighted that available mobility assistances are dissatisfactory to the blind for various reasons. Thus this research aims to fill this gap by building a low-cost, non-intrusive and simple system for blind navigation.

Several methods already exist for providing mobility assistance for the visually impaired, ranging from human helpers to modern devices. A human guide is the most intelligent assistant, but is not always readily available. On the other hand, a white cane is the most readily available mobility tool but is very intrusive and makes the blind person highly conspicuous. A guide dog[16] is a good choice because they are loyal and less intrusive but is as expensive as a car and each dog is only capable of providing assistance for a few years due to a long rigorous training process. Some blind people develop the echolocation ability to gain a measure of self-sufficiency in their mobility. Echolocation is the ability to sense objects by listening for echoes - i.e. human based sonar. However, echolocation is a difficult skill to master and is not able to detect small objects.

Z. Yu et al. (Eds.): UIC 2010, LNCS 6406, pp. 590–604, 2010.

Due to the issues with these traditional mobility solutions, a range of technological solutions have been developed, commonly referred to as electronic travel aids (ETAs). An ETA based on optical triangulation, e.g. LaserCane [1], is accurate but has a very narrow scan beam and costs more than five times the price of a typical mid-range Smartphone [19]. An ETA based on acoustic triangulation, e.g. MiniGuide [17] and GuideCane [14], can find open areas and can be as cheap as a mid-range Smartphone. However, a MiniGuide is unable to detect low-height objects on the floor and the GuideCane is very bulky. An ad-hoc ETA based on stereo vision, e.g. a Minoru 3D webcam [18] plus a notebook computer running the vOICe software, can recover full depth map but such a system is not popular due to the lack of a stereo camera in many portable devices.

Despite the existence of various mobility assistants, it is still difficult to find an assistant that is ultra-portable, low cost, non-intrusive, and able to detect on-floor obstacles. Motivated by this gap, we propose a solution embedded on a mobile phone platform since many visually impaired people already make use of Smartphones due to their many useful features (camera, optical character recognition, text-to-speech, voice command, GPS navigation, etc.) By utilizing the embedded camera on the Smartphone, it is possible to make the system non-intrusive through computer vision techniques. The main challenge here is how to detect on-floor obstacles through computational efficient computer vision techniques that can run in real time on a Smartphone. There are similar techniques for autonomous navigation employed in robots or autonomous vehicles, but they are computationally expensive [12], restricted to certain environments e.g. roads [11], and/or requiring a training phase to learn the scene's characteristics and thus not portable to different environments [10]. The proposed research seeks to effectively make use of perspective projection knowledge and fast computer vision techniques (color histograms and edge detection). By combining these techniques, the proposed system is able to detect most on-floor obstacles in real time on a Smartphone without any prior training/adapting stages. The system is compared to two other systems, the edge based approach of Taylor et al. [12] and the color histogram based approach of Tan et al.[11], which are also efficient enough to run on a Smartphone. Experiments and field trials have shown that the proposed system has better accuracy whilst being more computationally efficient.

The remainder of the paper is organized as follows: Section 2 introduces the related work. Section 3 explains the proposed on-floor obstacle detection system. In Section 4, the implementation on the Smartphone and the usage are discussed. The evaluation results of the system are presented in Section 5 before the conclusions are made in Section 6.

2 Related Work

As we have decided to utilize the embedded camera on Smartphones, we will review existing approaches that could lead to the obstacle detection using a monocular camera: three-dimensional structure reconstruction, two-dimensional motion analysis, and recognition.

Three-dimensional structure reconstruction from monocular images is probably the most geometrically intuitive way to identify obstacles: the relative distance between the camera and each object can be easily computed for each frame and thus any obstacle can be determined. This problem has been investigated by many researchers for decades. Most of the efforts have been on stationary scene reconstruction, while a few researchers are interested in the scene with moving objects. Among existing approaches, traditional structure from motion (SFM) is the most well known. SFM approach [8] first finds the correspondence between images, and then initializes the 3D scene using matches that satisfy the epipolar constraints while does not related by a homography, and finally other frames are added to refine the scene using bundle adjustment. This approach can be accurate but the computation cost is very high. Monocular simultaneous localization and mapping (MonoSLAM) [2] is a recent approach that can be classified as a real-time online SFM using a monocular camera. MonoSLAM aims to localize the camera by simultaneously recovering the 3D structure of the landmarks in the scene. This approach requires a high frame rate so that landmarks can be tracked within a small search window. The number of landmarks is also limited in this approach in order to achieve real-time performance. When there is a moving object in the scene, traditional SFM will fail to work. In such case, some researchers proposed that the correspondence between images is clustered into different groups [13], as they are related with different fundamental matrixes. However, the research in this area is in the preliminary stage. Furthermore, it is still impratical to implement these SFM algorithms (including MonoSLAM) on the mobile phone due to low computation power.

Two-dimensional motion analysis is another way to identify the obstacles, which does not involve 3D reconstruction. Instead, the 3D movements of objects or the time-to-contact may be estimated. This approach first computes the 2D optical flow motion from an input video, then analyze it using different criteria: for example, by simply comparing the sum of 2D motion field between the left and right halves of the image, obstacles can be avoided by turning to the side with smaller sum (balance strategy) [3]. When the camera is moving straight forward and smoothly in a constant speed, the time-to-contact can be estimated by utilizing the focus of expansion and the divergence from the focus of expansion [9]. If the camera is not constantly moving and its motion is unknown, it becomes very hard to determine the depth from the 2D flow, because it could be projected from different 3D flow.

Through recognition based on knowledge context [7], shape [5], or color [6], it is possible to identify the obstacles. The knowledge on the context or shape normally requires massive training efforts and would be unsuitable to reliably recognition. In contrast to the context/shape, the color information is easier to learn and recognize. The existing methods employ the color information mainly in three ways:

1. Mathematically-defined color models: the colors in the desired regions are modeled with a Gaussian or a Mixture of Gaussians (MoG) models - the training process may takes from as short as a few minutes (context-aware) to as long as several hours (manual) [10]. However, these models are based on snapshots of the scene as it is during training, and so are not applicable if the person moves to a new scene;
2. Color histograms: by sacrificing memory, color histograms represent the desired colors in the simplest form. Due to its simplicity, the computation is very efficient and so can be continuously recalculated which is ideal for application in mobile platform. Tan et al. [11] assume that the small area in front of a vehicle is always clear and the color histogram is sampled. By maintaining a set of such color histograms for the clear road and a histogram for the background determined in previous frame, it calculates the probability of a pixel belonging to road by distance measurements on histograms. After linear combination of the previous and current probability of the same pixel, it can be determined if a pixel belongs to a road or the background. In comparison to mathematical models, histograms directly represent the true (empirical) color distribution rather than fitting it to a (potentially inaccurate) model [10,11,15];
3. Edges: when the desired region is known as consisting of a uniform color, its appearance may consist of different colors due to illumination variances on that region or due to camera artifacts. In most cases, the transitions between these colors are smooth. Therefore, edges, or unsmooth color transitions, often indicate borders between objects. Taylor et al.[12] assumes that floors consist of uniform colors and a simple seeded region growing method is used based on normalized red (r), normalized green (g), hue (h) and intensity (i) channels to expand the safe region for navigation.

Among these related works, only limited approaches are possible to run on a device with low-computational power, such as mobile phones, without prior-learning: color histogram based recognition and edge based recognition. The proposed system will hence build on these approaches. The proposed system will be introduced in the next section.

3 Proposed System

Similar to the related work on recognition based color histograms and edges, the proposed system assumes that a small region of the floor in front of the user is safe. In addition, the proposed system assumes that the user is able to maintain the Smartphone at a certain tilt angle, e.g. 45° , all the time so that the floor in front of the user is always visible in the image. With these two assumptions, the idea behind the proposed system is based on the image region that is assumed to be a clear floor region and finding anything that looks different from it. We compute the distance from the user, after which the safe path is found.

The proposed system will be described in three parts: image region of interest, initial histogram for safe region, and safe path finding.

3.1 Image Region of Interest

Many existing methods process all pixels in an image or do so in the worst case[12]. In fact, not all pixels in the image need to be analyzed for the purpose of obstacle detection in our case. As a person normally walks straight ahead, a rectangular floor region in front of him/her is of most concern whether there is an obstacle. Therefore, only the projected image region of that rectangular region is of interest. While the exact depth of a pixel representing the floor can be accurately computed using perspective projection knowledge through a homography matrix, by assuming the camera is pointing forward with a tilt angle downwards and no roll angle, an input image can be simply explained as follows: the pixels at the lower region of the image represents the floor that is closer to the user, and a rectangular region in front of the user will appears like a trapezoid because the object looks smaller when it is farther under perspective projection.

Therefore, a proper trapezoid image region can be computed based on known tilt angle and focal length of the camera and can be defined on the image as the *image region of interest.* Thus, the maximum number of pixels needed to be processed can be decreased.

3.2 Initial Histogram for Safe Region

The small region of the floor in front of the user appears at the bottom of the image and is assumed safe. The knowledge of the safe floor can be learned from that image region. Similar to Tan et al.'s system, a color histogram will be employed to represent this image region.

In order to build a color histogram, the color space must be firstly chosen. Gevers and Smeulders [4] have evaluated several popular color spaces to determine invariance to viewpoint, object geometry and illumination for recognizing multicolored objects. However, there is no single color space that is most appropriate under all circumstances. If the conditions across images are controlled, the RGB color space is the most appropriate for recognizing multicolored objects although it has worse performance in terms of discriminative power due to its sensitivity to varying image conditions. As for an embedded camera on a Smartphone handheld by a human, the image changes could be frequent due to auto white balance and auto exposure of the camera affected by the environment where it is pointed to. However, different regions within a single image should have the same white balance level and have the same exposure time. Hence, we decide to build a histogram for each frame and choose the simplest RGB color space because it is the most appropriate when the imaging conditions is constant according to [4].

To build a traditional RGB histogram from a small region in a tiny image is not robust. The number of pixels in each bin could be very small and thus the color distribution could not be well represented. Bootstrapping is a way to increase the number of samples - but it will increase computational cost and may introduce incorrect samples. We therefore adopt a binary RGB histogram with

16^3 bins, which does not concern pixel counts in each bin. The corresponding bin of a pixel in the sampling region is labeled as *true*. In addition, the neighboring 9 bins of this bin are also labeled as true to accommodate small variations to the color. Thus, a binary *RGB* histogram is initially built for the safe region. Next, we will introduce the safe path finding process based on this initial histogram for the safe region in the *image region of interest*.

3.3 Safe Path Finding

We define four states of a pixel: *uninterested*, *unvisited*, *floor*, *obstacle*. Since only the *image region of interest* is of concern, we label all pixels in that region as *unvisited* and the rest as *uninterested*. As the small region at the bottom of the image is considered as the floor, we label all pixels in this small region as *floor*. Our remaining task is to process any pixel labeled *unvisited*, if that pixel is of interest.

A classifier has to be built with the prior knowledge of both classes (*floor* and *obstacle*). In Tan et al.'s system, in addition to the histogram of the road (*floor*), the histogram of the background (*obstacle*) is also built based on the pixels classified as "background" in the previous frame. The knowledge of two classes enables them to classify a pixel. After linear combination of the current frame and the previous frame on the probability of each pixel, the largest region of pixels classified as "road" is considered as road while other pixels are considered as background. However, their system could not be simply applied in our case because the background information in the previous frame is unreliable due to various factors such as lighting changes, scene changes caused by rapid hand movements.

Since a histogram for *obstacle* could not be reliably obtained, thresholding is the most appropriate approach based on the knowledge on only one class (*floor*). If the floor is known consisting of a single color, the problem becomes easy and can be solved by seeded region growing with a pre-defined threshold for finding edges, e.g. the Taylor et al.' system. However, we may have multiple colors in the histogram sampled from the safe region. We thus propose the following scheme to determine if a pixel belongs to the floor, which uses both histograms and edges:

1. The current pixel for determination should be a neighboring pixel of a pixel already identified as *floor*;
2. The histogram bin corresponding to the color of the current pixel is firstly checked - if it is *true*, the current pixel can be determined as *floor* and the determination process is complete;
3. A 3×3 Laplacian edge detector is convolved with the given pixel in *R*, *G* and *B* channels respectively. If the convolved value in any channel is above a pre-defined threshold, the current pixel is determined as *obstacle* and the determination process is complete;
4. The current pixel is then determined as *floor*, since it has a similar color with one of the known colors of the floor. The current pixel's color is used to update the histogram by labeling the corresponding bin as *true*.

With this scheme, a pixel can be identified as *floor* or *obstacle* with either histogram or edge constraints. Since the pixel to be determined needs to be a neighboring pixel of a pixel determined as *floor*, we will now discuss the image pixel scanning scheme.

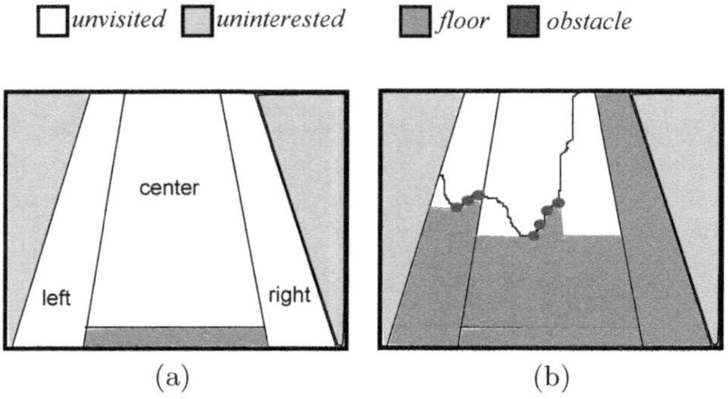

Fig. 1. Image label illustrations: (a) before scanning; (b) an example result after scanning

The *image region of interest* is subdivided into three sub-regions: center, left and right. The center sub-region represents the main path for the user, i.e. the floor area that the user would step on if walking straight ahead. The left and right sub-regions represent the areas to the side and can become alternative paths if the main path is obstructed. Figure 1(a) illustrates such sub-divisions. We propose a pixel scanning scheme that efficiently computes the safe depth in each of these three paths.

1. Considering all pixels at the bottom line of the *image region of interest* as seed points, we first process the center sub-region and then the side sub-regions;
2. For each sub-region, we initialize V_i (i=center, left or right), defined as the y coordinate of its safe depth visualized in the image, as the y coordinate of a top pixel in the *image region of interest.* After that, each seed point will be processed: starting from the seed point that is the closest from bottom center of the image and then propagating to left/right;
3. From each seed point, a set of pixels (a line segment from the seed point to a point where $y = V_i$) are of interest which represents a very narrow path that is parallel to the user's orientation.
4. For each pixel of interest, if it is labeled *unvisited,* we apply the aforementioned scheme to determine if it is *floor* or *obstacle.* After the determination (if required), if a pixel is labeled as obstacle, the rest of unexplored interested pixels from the same seed point is discarded and V_i is updated to the current y coordinate. All pixels beyond $y = V_i$ can be skipped since the obstacle has been found in this region.

After the above pixel scanning process, V_{center}, V_{left} and V_{right} can be obtained which can be converted to corresponding depths d_{center}, d_{left} and d_{right} in metric units, given the camera focal length and tilt angle of the camera. If any of these safe depths is over a pre-defined threshold, the corresponding path is considered a safe path. The safe path(s) can hence be found. Figure 1(b) illustrates an example resulted from the scanning. In this example, the solid thick line represents the border of the expected obstacle. According to the proposed scanning scheme described above, the safe depth of each path can be determined after encountering with only a small number of pixels of the obstacle, eliminating the need to process many other pixels in the *image region of interest.*

4 Implementation and Usage

The proposed system is implemented on a mid-range Smartphone - Nokia E71. The main built-in camera of this Smartphone has the maximum video frame rate of 15 fps and minimum image dimension of 128×96 pixels for video capture. It works on a single 369 MHz ARM 11 processor. With the S60 3rd Edition SDK for Symbian OS and Carbide.c++ IDE, applications can be developed and many features on the phone can be controlled, such as camera, vibration feedback, voice, etc.

Because there is no accelerometer on this particular Smartphone, we assume that the user will hold the phone at a tilt angle of about 45° , which allows the depth threshold for safe path to be similar to the height of the camera. The height of the camera is pre-defined as one meter and is adjustable by simply pushing a button. With the pre-defined camera height, the farthest detectable depth is about two meters since the embedded camera has a field of view of about 40° vertically. In addition, the input image is sub-sampled to 64×48 pixels for storage and performance considerations. In terms of feedback, like other ETAs such as the MiniGuide, the vibration feedback is provided if the main (center) path is not safe. In addition, auditory feedback can also be provided *on demand*, mainly for new users, through a button giving verbal instructions as to the safe depth on the main path. If the safe depth of the main path is under a threshold (unsafe to proceed), it further advises as to which side paths are safe.

The standard usage of the system is as follows:

1. The users may adjust the camera height based on the pose which they find most comfortable. The determination of the camera height may require assistance from another person;
2. The users hold the phone in the correct pose: put it in the center in front of the body, and point it forward with about 45° downward tilt angle;
3. The users can keep walking forward until the Smartphone is vibrating;
4. If the Smartphone is vibrating and the auditory feedback is not utilized, the user may sweep the Smartphone left or right, or point to other directions until it stops vibrating. The users should then adjust themselves to the pointing direction of the Smartphone and continue to proceed forward;

5. Whether the Smartphone is vibrating or not, if the users *want* the auditory feedback, they may push a button to obtain auditory feedback on demand. For example, if there is an obstacle, the users may hear "0.9 meters, bear left". In this case, the users should step a little bit to the left and the Smartphone should stop vibrating and thus the users can proceed forward. If there is another obstacle far from the user, the users may hear "1.9 meters", and the user is given an idea how far the obstacle is.

5 Results

The proposed system implemented on the Smartphone is evaluated in different environments before it is tested in a field trial and compared against two existing approaches. The results on the evaluation are first presented, followed by the discussion on the field trial experiment.

5.1 Quantitative Evaluation

We will compare the proposed system with Tan et al.'s color histogram based system and Taylor et al.'s edge based system. We hold the Smartphone at a tilt angle of about 45° and about one meter above the floor. Therefore the depth range for dangerous obstacles is around one meter, which means any obstacle farther than one meter is considered safe. For the purposes of evaluation, we record the input images as we navigate. The recorded input images are then processed using Taylor et al.'s system, Tan et al.'s system, and the proposed system.

In Tan et al.'s system, up to four normalized rg histograms are used to represent the road (based on the reference area) and one rg histogram is built for the background (from the previous frame). It uses a linear combination of current and previous frame to compute the probability of road at each pixel after the distance measurement. Each pixel can be determined as either road (*floor*) or background (*obstacle*). After that, our pixel scan direction is used to find obstacles in the user's path (see Section 3.3). In their original paper, the classified pixels are further fit with a road model, which is irrelevant to this paper and hence not implemented.

In Taylor et al.'s system, a basic seeded region growing method is used to find same-color regions in the images based on r, g, h and i channels. Our pixel scan direction is then used to find obstacles in user's path.

Accuracy. We conduct a set of tests to evaluate the accuracy of the three systems in three different indoor environments, where the floor is (1) un-patterned non-reflective, (2) patterned non-reflective or (3) un-patterned reflective. An example from each sequence is shown in Figure 2. In each test, we manually label the ground truths in each input image: if any obstacle is present within the bottom half (up to about one meter's distance) of central trapezoid region (the center path), the frame is labeled as positive. Otherwise, it is labeled as negative.

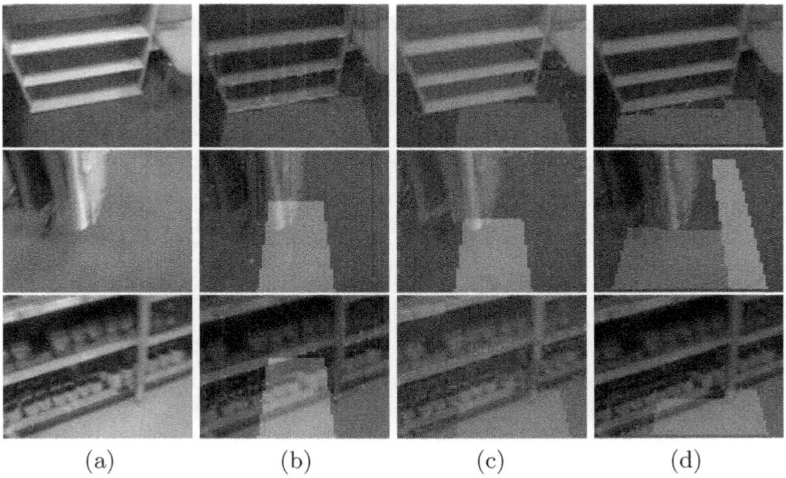

Fig. 2. Example frame from Sequence #1∼#3(Row 1∼3): (a) original input image; (b) output using Taylor's method; (c) output using Tan's method; (d) output using the proposed method

For each device, the true positives (*TP*) which represents an obstacle has been correctly identified after manual verification, the false positives (*FP*), the true negatives (*TN*) and the false negatives (*FN*) are recorded for each frame in each sequence. We compute

- *positive predictive value* (a.k.a *precision*, $TP/(TP+FP)$) indicating how much a positive feedback (e.g. vibration) can be trusted;
- *negative predictive value* ($TN/(TN+FN)$)indicating how much a negative feedback (e.g. no vibration) can be trusted;
- *sensitivity* (a.k.a *recall*, $TP/(TP+FN)$ indicating how reliable the system is to pick up all obstacles;
- *specificity* ($TN/(TN+FP)$) indicating how reliable the system is to identify a safe path;
- the overall accuracy of the system ($(TP+TN)/(TP+FP+TN+FN)$).

As Tables 1∼3 show, the proposed system outperforms other systems in every test. In general, Tan et al. and Taylor et al.'s systems are usually quite poor at avoiding false alarms. Overall, the proposed system has a overall accuracy of over 94% in all these situations, while the other two systems can only achieve about 80% in certain situation(s).

Speed. While accuracy is important in determining if an obstacle can be correctly identified, the speed of processing is also important as it controls how heavy the computation is and how quickly the user will receive a response. The performance data are listed in Table 4. In comparison between these three real-time systems, the proposed system only takes 7ms to compute which is 10% of

Table 1. Results - Quantitative - Sequence #1 (464 frames)

Measurement	Taylor et al.	Tan et al.	Proposed
Positive Predictive Value/Precision	89.58%	45.51%	96.00%
Negative Predictive Value	77.17%	83.69%	99.31%
Sensitivity/Recall	50.59%	86.47%	98.82%
Specificity	96.60%	40.14%	97.62%
Overall Accuracy	79.74%	57.11%	98.06%

Table 2. Results - Quantitative - Sequence #2 (375 frames)

Measurement	Taylor et al.	Tan et al.	Proposed
Positive Predictive Value/Precision	13.00%	64.91%	100.0%
Negative Predictive Value	77.63%	91.82%	94.26%
Sensitivity/Recall	46.03%	58.73%	69.84%
Specificity	37.82%	93.59%	100.0%
Overall Accuracy	39.20%	87.73%	94.93%

Table 3. Results - Quantitative - Sequence #3 (496 frames)

Measurement	Taylor et al.	Tan et al.	Proposed
Positive Predictive Value/Precision	34.48%	73.86%	97.50%
Negative Predictive Value	72.65%	86.70%	93.36%
Sensitivity/Recall	65.22%	70.65%	84.78%
Specificity	42.71%	88.44%	99.00%
Overall Accuracy	49.83%	82.82%	94.50%

Table 4. Results - Speed

	Taylor et al.	Tan et al.	Proposed
Computation time per frame	8∼83 ms	30 ms	7 ms
Time spent (percentage of idle time)	12%∼125%	45%	10%
Theoretical frame rate (fps)	12∼125	33	150
Actual frame rate (fps)	8∼15	15	15

the idle time and thus significantly save the battery life while Tan et al.'s system requires about 45% of the idle time and Tayler's system takes up to 100%. Taylor et al.'s system has wide variation in speed because it depends on the distance of the obstacle: it performs faster when the obstacle is close as fewer pixels need to be processed. Based on the results from accuracy and performance comparison, we then provide the proposed system to real blind people for a field trial.

5.2 Real-World Evaluation

The proposed system implemented on the Smartphone was given to several blind users for evaluation. We will discuss the goal, environment, subjects, procedures, issues, feedback and limitations of the field trial.

Goal. The goal of this experiment is to evaluate to what extent a blind user feels the differences among the three systems and how good the systems are in relation to each other from a human perspective. The reason for doing this is that it is difficult to translate quantitative accuracy numbers from Table 1~3 into human experience.

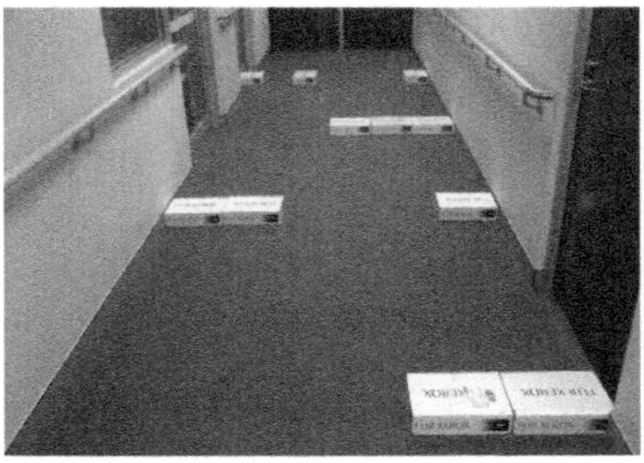

Fig. 3. Experiment setup

Environment. The experiment took place in the Association for the Blind of Western Australia. Eleven paper boxes were randomly placed in a corridor by ensuring there was no straight safe path (see Figure 3). Low height boxes are chosen due to safety concerns and the blind participant would not be able to sense the boxes even by taking advantage of echolocation. Therefore, the result obtained under such environment setup would not be affected by the skills of the participant.

Subjects. Five blind adult volunteers were invited to participate in this experiment. We identify them as P1 to P5 in this paper. To ensure that the evaluation is unbiased, we did not tell the participant which system was developed by us until after the experiment was finished. Each participant was first given a random system for testing, during which the participant can get familiar with correctly holding the Smartphone and learn how to obtain/understand feedback from the Smartphone before the evaluation process starts. The order of the systems given to the participant for evaluation was randomly defined because the number of participants does not meet the requirement of Latin square.

Procedures. During the testing and evaluation of the systems, the participants were requested to walk through the corridor with only the Smartphone, without white cane, guide dog or other ETAs. The participant was asked to point the Smartphone to the front with about 45° tilt angle and stop proceeding once the Smartphone starts vibrating. Once the Smartphone vibrates, the participant either swept the phone to find a clear path or used auditory feedback (their choice). Though detailed instructions were given, the participant was followed by a human guide to ensure safety. The human guide only provided three types of assistance: 1) reminding the participant of the correct holding posture of the Smartphone; 2) stopping the participant from proceeding when an obstacle is about to be encountered but the participant shows no sign of stopping; 3) informing the participant of the safe path to proceed when the participant could not find a clear path using the Smartphone. After the participants finished experiencing the three different systems, they were asked to rank the systems (if they could feel the differences) and give each system a score between one (worst) and ten (best). Further comments from the participant were also recorded.

Issues. One of the five participants (P3) had difficulty holding and using the phone as needed, and due to the limited training time was unable to overcome this. Hence P3 could not distinguish between the three systems. In contrast, P2 got used to the device very quickly as we were told that P2 had been using another ETA, the MiniGuide, for about 10 years. Obviously, the system presents usability barriers to its usage, but all existing ETAs also suffer from similar issues.

Feedback. The feedbacks from all participants except P3 are then consolidated and the rating for each system is shown in Table 5. Only P1 thought Tan et al.'s system was better. All others preferred the proposed system. As Table 5 shows, the proposed system is generally 50% better than Tan et al.'s system and is almost twice as good as Taylor et al.'s system according to the participants.

Table 5. Results - Real World

Subject	Taylor et al.	Tan et al.	Proposed
P1	5	10	7.5
P2	7	4	10
P3	N/A	N/A	N/A
P4	4	4	10
P5	4	7	10

Limitations. During the experiment, we observed that it is not easy for most participants to hold the Smartphone at the requested tilt angle (around 45°) all the time. Since there is no embedded accelerometer in this specific Smartphone, longer training time would be useful for the user to get accustomed to it. The problem can be addressed if a Smartphone with accelerometer is used.

6 Conclusions and Future Work

This paper presents a real-time obstacle detection system implemented on a Smartphone, which can be used by the visually impaired as a mobility tool. By combining color histograms, edge cues and pixel-depth relationship, the proposed system is able to detect on-floor obstacles and provides feedback to the user through vibration and voice-on-demand. The proposed system has been tested in different environments and provides consistent and reliable results despite the simplicity of the system. The proposed system has been evaluated by blind users and received a high ranking. There is still plenty of room to improve the proposed system, such as utilizing the embedded accelerometer in some Smartphone and dealing with more complex floor patterns, etc.

References

1. Benjamin, J.M., Ali, N.A., Schepis, A.F.: A Laser Cane for the Blind. In: Proceedings of the San Diego Biomedical Symposium, vol. 12, pp. 53–57 (1973)
2. Davison, A.J., Reid, I.D., Molton, N.D., Stasse, O.: MonoSLAM: real-time single camera SLAM. IEEE Transactions on Pattern Analysis and Machine Intelligence (PAMI) 29(6), 1052–1067 (2007)
3. Duchon, A.P., Warren, W.H., Kaelbling, L.P.: Ecological robotics. Adaptive Behavior 6(3-4), 473–507 (1998)
4. Gevers, T., Smeulders, A.W.M.: Color-based object recognition. Pattern Recognition 32(3), 453–464 (1999)
5. Liebelt, J., Schmid, C., Schertler, K.: Viewpoint-independent object class detection using 3D feature maps. In: Proceedings of IEEE Conference on Computer Vision and Pattern Recognition, CVPR (2008)
6. Plagemann, C., Endres, F., Hess, J., Stachniss, C., Burgard, W.: Monocular range sensing: a non-parametric learning approach. In: Proceedings of the IEEE International Conference on Robotics and Automation, ICRA (2008)
7. Saxena, A., Sun, M., Ng, A.Y.: Make3D: learning 3-D scene structure from a single still image. IEEE Transactions on Pattern Analysis and Machine Intelligence (PAMI) 30(5), 824–840 (2009)
8. Snavely, N., Seitz, S.M., Szeliski, R.: Modeling the world from Internet photo collections. International Journal of Computer Vision (IJCV) 80(2), 189–210 (2008)
9. Souhila, K., Karim, A.: Optical flow based robot obstacle avoidance. International Journal of Advanced Robotic Systems 4(1), 13–16 (2007)
10. Sridharan, M., Stone, P.: Color learning and illumination invariance on mobile robots: a survey. Robotics and Autonomous Systems (RAS) Journal 57(6-7), 629–644 (2009)
11. Tan, C., Hong, T., Chang, T., Shneier, M.: Color model-based real-time learning for road following. In: Proceedings of IEEE Intelligent Transportation Systems Conference, ITSC (2006)
12. Taylor, T., Geva, S., Boles, W.W.: Monocular vision as a range sensor. In: Proceedings of International Conference on Computational Intelligence for Modelling, CIMCA (2004)
13. Tola, E., Knorr, S., Imre, E., Alatan, A.A., Sikora, T.: Structure from motion in dynamic scenes with multiple motions. In: Workshop on Immersive Communication and Broadcast Systems, ICOB (2005)

14. Ulrich, I., Borenstein, J.: The GuideCane-applying mobile robot technologies to assist the visually impaired. IEEE Transactions on Systems, Man, and Cybernetics, Part A 31(2), 131–136 (2001)
15. Ulrich, I., Nourbakhsh, I.: Appearance-based obstacle detection with monocular color vision. In: Proceedings of the AAAI National Conference on Artificial Intelligence (2000)
16. The Association for the Blind of WA (2010), http://www.abwa.asn.au
17. GDP Research (2010), http://www.gdp-research.com.au
18. Minoru 3D webcam (2010), http://www.minoru3d.com
19. Currently Available Electronic Travel Aids for the Blind (2010), http://www.noogenesis.com/eta/current.html

SSP: Smart Service Provider A Smart Environment Providing Contextual Services on Android Mobile Devices

Pascal Bruegger, Benjamin Hadorn, and Béat Hirsbrunner

Pervasive and Artificial Intelligence Research Group, University of Fribourg,
Pérolles 90, 1700 Fribourg, Switzerland
{pascal.bruegger,benjamin.hadorn,beat.hirsbrunner}@unifr.ch
http://diuf.unifr.ch/pai

Abstract. Smart environments are increasingly available and support users in their daily activities in different ways. This paper presents a service-based approach for users active in a smart environment such as a building, campus or public place. The concept is illustrated through the SSP project which provides environment-specific and contextual services on mobile devices running the Android platform.

Keywords: Smart environment, context-awareness, pervasive computing, mobile computing.

1 Introduction

We are experiencing an increasing level of connectivity and automation in our environment. At lot of devices are proposed to consumers to help them in their common tasks such as driving, road navigation, accessing information, booking or buying things and providing contextual advice. In fact, since the rapid development of mobile technologies and applications, users are constantly connected to other users, infrastructures and services. There have also been important developments in the field of sensors and controllers allowing the development of smart mobile devices (e.g. iPhone, Android, GPS navigation systems). These devices have quickly become the essential companion of average users: they are their calendars, mailboxes and sources of information, allowing them to locate themselves, to communicate and so on. Environments are also benefiting from the rapid development and miniaturisation of sensors: they are becoming smart. So called "smart environments" are network-enabled devices and applications capable of adapting their behaviour in order to provide services and to make the life of users more comfortable. As proposed by Das and Cook [8], a smart environment can be defined as *one that is able to autonomously acquire and apply knowledge about the environment and adapt to its inhabitants' preferences and requirements in order*

Z. Yu et al. (Eds.): UIC 2010, LNCS 6406, pp. 605–619, 2010.

to improve their experience. They point out four main components that constitute smart environments: smart devices and embedded systems, wireless mobile communication, a computing paradigm and a middleware.

In this paper we present the SSP project which uses the four main components described by Das and Cook. SSP focuses on public spaces or buildings and intends to make them smarter by providing services based on the user's profile, activity and location. SSP provides a middleware based on two projects developed at the university of Fribourg: uMove [3] and CMP[1] for the coordination and communication [13].

The rest of the paper is organised as follows: Section 2 gives a brief overview of relevant projects treating smart environments. Section 3 describes the SSP project and our approach. Section 4 describes the concept of Kinetic User Interface (KUI) and the uMove framework. Section 5 presents the architecture of the applications and describes the inter-application communication. Section 6 presents two case studies and the prototypes implemented and tested. Finally, we draw conclusions and propose future work in section 7.

2 Related Work

In recent years, "smart environments" have become a dynamic field of research and many projects have been developed around this topic. The field is divided into several sub-topics such as "smart-homes" and "intelligent buildings" with projects such as EasyLiving from Microsoft [7] which focuses on the interaction between users and the multimedia devices in a house, "Hestia" from the University of Fribourg [6] presenting a solution to integrate user activity in the management of heating systems and the "Aware Home" from Georgia Tech [16]. Different aspects within those topics are investigated such as security, authentication [1], context-awareness [10] and monitoring of user activity [14]. Another interesting aspect is the development of context-aware architectures and middlewares for smart environments, like those proposed in HP's CoolTown[2], the Aura[3] project from Carnegie Mellon University and the Georgia Tech Context Toolkit [9]. In [19], the authors describe MoCA, a project that is close to the service provider presented in this paper except that they take the user's location into consideration and not their profile and activities. Those projects treat different aspects of the topic, propose interesting solutions and they have inspired the concept of services in smart environments as we propose in this paper.

3 SSP Project Issues and Description

There are two main issues tackled in this project which concern different aspects of context-awareness. The first issue is the extension of traditional context-aware

[1] Coordination Model for Pervasive Computing Systems.

[2] `http://www.hpl.hp.com/techreports/2001/HPL-2001-22.pdf`

[3] `http://www.cs.cmu.edu/~aura/`

middleware such as the Context Toolkit by offering 1) a complete framework including a conceptual model to help system designers to define their context-aware system and 2) a context-aware middleware also taking into account user activities and situations. The second issue is to investigate and propose a solution for providing contextualised services in a light-weight manner on a user's mobile device in different environments, in our case studies a university campus and a nursing home. By services, we mean applications providing useful information about possibilities. For instance, in the campus case, available lectures, menus from the cafeteria, classroom locations, library opening hours, a building map, administrative information and even a friend's location. The campus becomes a smart environment in the sense that it is equipped with a technological infrastructure based on a computing system which *observes*, by means of sensors, the different entities (places, rooms, users) populating the campus and *provides* contextual services (in a large sense) to users and/or other computing systems (for instance danger alarms). We propose the concept of a service for smartphones which fills the gap between web-services or web-based applications like those proposed in HP's CoolTown or downloadable applications from the Internet.

3.1 Services for Mobile Devices

In contrast to the concept of applications loadable from a centralised source, we propose a different approach where *services* are contextually available within specific environments (e.g. campus, shopping mall, train station) like in MoCA [19]. This notion comes from the concept of applications that are not loadable once and permanently installed, but available and installable at the time the user is in the environment proposing it and are automatically uninstalled when the user leaves the environment. Such service are still applications and not web services.

We have identified at least three advantages of this approach. First, a user entering an SSP environment always gets the newest version of the application. For instance, a graphical interface can evolve over time and change properties, making an older version obsolete. Second, the programmers developing services can work on extensions or maintenance without worrying about compatibility between versions. Third, we avoid overloading the mobile device with applications which are used only in given contexts and locations. Finally, this service concept favours the development of small and specialised services with a minimal memory footprint rather than heavy applications using a lot of mobile resources.

3.2 SSP General Architecture

The project is separated into two components which are managing 1) the building (server-based system) and 2) the mobile devices (client and mobile application). We propose to have an identical architecture on both sides (server and client) in order to facilitate the development and the maintenance of the systems. To do so, we used uMove [5], our context-aware framework developed at the University of Fribourg, and adapted it for the server and the mobile devices.

The campus (in our case study a building) is equipped with a server-based computing system capable of: 1) logically representing the physical entities of the building (e.g. rooms, departments, people), 2) contextually providing services assigned to the different entities, 3) automatically managing the entering and exiting users and 4) managing the relations between the different entities active in the environment.

The users carry a smart phone running Android and the small application communicating with the server-based system. This application is meant to 1) establish the communication, 2) log into the system, 3) send the current user's contexts (including the location) and the activity to the server and 4) receive the list of available services.

In the next sections, we describe the different components of our system and present the concept of Kinetic User Interfaces used in the modelling and the implementation of the prototype.

4 KUI Model: A Systemic Approach to Model a Physical World

The first step in the project was to model the environment (the "world") observed by the system in order to track and identify the different entities populating it and using the services. For this, we developed the concept of a Kinetic User Interface (KUI) and uMove, its implementation [3].

The concept of KUI is a way of grouping Weiser's Ubiquitous Computing vision [21] and Dourish's Embodied Interaction vision [11]. In the '90s, Marc Weiser predicted that computers would disappear and computing power would fade into the network infrastructure. Paul Dourish investigated how to move the interface "off the screen" and into the real world. In his model, users can interact with physical objects augmented with computational abilities. KUI-based systems are intended to enable the merging of these two visions, where the motions of users or objects in physical space are recognised and processed as meaningful events. The KUI model is a conceptual framework which can help in the design of pervasive systems including mobile applications or server-based systems integrating a user's locations, activities and other contexts.

The KUI model is based on General System Theory (GST). GST, defined by von Bertalanffy [20], gives the framework and the concepts to model specific systems studied in sciences such as biology or chemistry. We consider that any user or object moving in their environment is part of a system made up of different components such as buildings, rooms, streets, objects and other users. For Alain Bouvier[4], a system (a complex organised unit) is a set of elements or entities in dynamic interaction. In the KUI model, everything is an entity within a system. We have included two concepts which are not present in the definitions above. Usually a system (e.g. a cell in biology or a solar system) is externally observed from a certain point of view. We consider the *observer* (who/what is

[4] Management et projet - ed. Hachette, p.18.

observing the system) and the *viewer* (the observer's point of view) as part of the system because conceptually if a system is not observable, it does not exist.

We define a system as *a set of observable, interacting and interdependent entities, physical or virtual, forming an integrated whole. The system includes different types of entities: actors, observers and viewers.*

4.1 Actors

Actors are the observable entities of the system. They can be physical or virtual, living things (humans or animals), moving objects (cars or planes) or zones (rooms, floors or buildings). An actor is made of *contexts* and does *activities.*

Contexts. A. Dey et al. in [9] define a context as any information that can be used to characterise the situation of an actor. Context includes location, identity, activity and time. In our model, contexts are used to define the attributes of an entity and do not include the activity. The activity is influenced by the environment and therefore by the contexts in which it is done. We mainly use the following contexts in our model: identity, location, geometry, status (mobile or static), structure (atomic or containing other actors) and relations (spatio-temporal, interactional). Other contexts (temperature, light intensity) can be defined for an actor and would depend on the specificity of the system.

Activities. For Loke [18], activity typically refers to actions or operations undertaken by human beings such as "cooking", "running", or "reading". For Y. Li and J. Landay [17], an action like "running" is not considered as an activity because it focuses on an immediate goal. For Kuutti, in [15], an activity is the long-term transformation process of an object (e.g. a user's body) always oriented toward a motive (e.g. keeping fit), otherwise it becomes an action. In our model, we consider an activity to be made of detected motions aggregated into operations and actions, and it is an input for observers.

4.2 Observers and Viewers

Observers are the agents which collect and analyse information (activities and contexts) about actors and places and possibly react to particular situations. To illustrate this concept, let us take the example of a family house where several rooms (kitchen, living room, bedrooms) afford different activities. Observers shall be placed in each room in order to evaluate situations taking place in them. Our concept of observer is inspired by Weiser's idea of calm technology[5] which tends to limit the direct interaction with computers systems (sensor-based) and lets users concentrate on their human activities. There is no interference between

[5] The coming age of calm technology, `http://www.cs.ucsb.edu/~ebelding/courses/284/w04/papers/calm.pdf`

observers, actors and places: the observer only reports situations to applications and lets them decide what to do.

Actors are observed from certain points of view. Each point of view represents a focus on the situation. Many observers can use similar views for a different situation analysis. A view is a multi-dimensional filter placed between an observer and the actors. We have 2 dimensions in our model of view: range and level (Fig. 1 a)). The range influences the scope of the observation (e.g. the ocean or only a cruise boat) and the level gives the granularity of the observation (e.g. decks or decks and cabins or passengers).

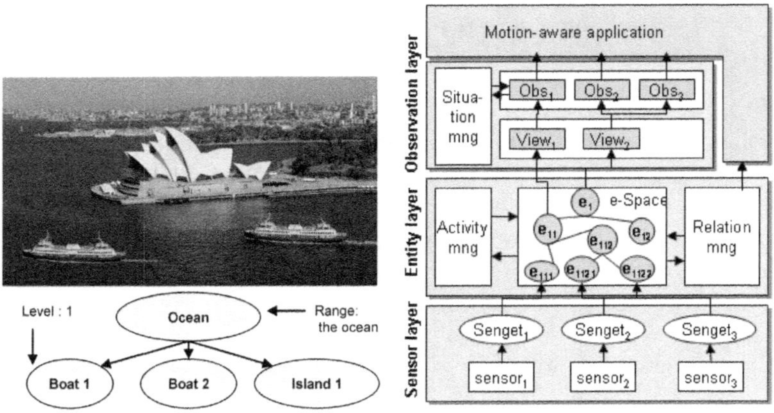

Fig. 1. a) Viewer in KUI: Range and Level parameters, b) uMove Framework

5 uMove: The Development Framework

The uMove framework ([4] sec. 3) allows to define and implement a KUI system on top of which different specific applications will be developed (e.g. user tracking, activity-based smart alert). The framework contains two specific parts: the conceptual framework and the Java API. Unlike [12] who focus only on specific applications or prototypes, uMove allows programers to easily create all entities, the relations between them and the connected sensors, and to load the activity and situation recognition modules (algorithms or classes). However, uMove does not provide, as [2] does, the activity (task) and situation recognition modules or algorithms. Instead, it allows them to be separately developed and connected to entities (actors and observers) active in the system.

5.1 Conceptual Framework

The conceptual framework is the tool used by developers to theoretically design the system that will be observed. As shown in Fig. 1 b), a KUI system has three layers responsible for the different objects interacting together.

Sensor Layer. The sensor layer contains the *sengets*[6] which are the logical abstractions of the sensors connected to the system. For instance, an application tracking the movement of users within a building may need to connect location sensors, independent of their type. The location senget connects any type of sensors (e.g. RFID, Bluetooth or wifi) and provides the entity location to the higher level.

Actor Layer. The *entity layer* contains the logical representation of the physical entities (i.e. users, places, objects) being observed. Each entity (actor, places or zones) is defined by its identity, its role, its location within the system and its current motion and activity. Entities are organised in an n-ary tree and all have a parent node except the root of the system (e.g. the world or the building). Entities get their contexts updated from the connected sengets. An entity can be attached to an activity manager object which determines the current activity.

Observation Layer. The *observation layer* analyses the current situation of the actor based on their activity and contexts. They listen for any entity changes and forward them to the situation manager in order to have the new situation analysed and if needed, inform the application (e.g. a "warning" message or a "critical situation" message).

6 Coordination and Communication in uMove

The communication in uMove is managed by a component called the Coordination manager. This component allows the different entities (actors, sengets, observers, viewers) to transparently communicate with each other and also allows different uMove systems to be connected to one another (Fig. 2). Each entity communicates together in the same way regardless of whether they are local (same uMove) or remote (on a mobile uMove).

6.1 Inter-object Communication

The communication between objects is based on the message listener concept. For instance, an observer listening to an actor automatically receives messages any time changes occur. This type of asynchronous communication allows the system to be dynamic, possibly distributed, and guarantees that all processes run in parallel. Each object (senget, actor, observer) is connected to a *port* object which is dedicated to listening to a channel established and managed by the coordination manager.

[6] Stands for *sensor gadget* similar to the concepts of widget (Windows gadget) or phidget (physical gadget).

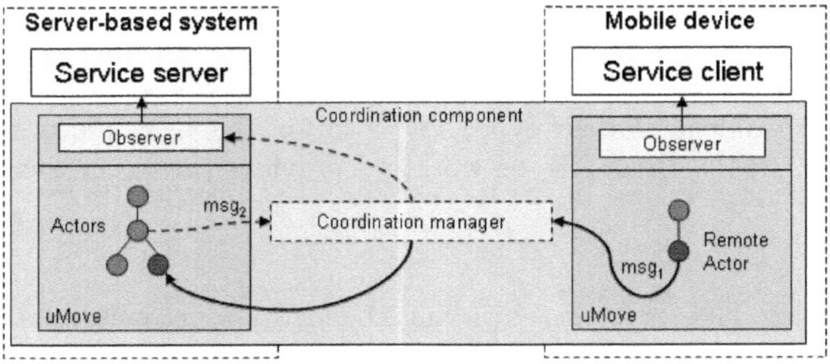

Fig. 2. Coordination: message passing between entities in local and remote uMove systems

7 Services: Definition and Monitoring

The concept of services is one key point of this project and is used at different levels. The first level concerns the identification and the "login" (KUI Service) of a mobile device running a KUI system and entering into a smart environment. The second level is the application level where services are provided to users.

7.1 Model of Service

All services are based on the same model which contains four components (Fig 3): Service Object, Service Provider, Service Session, Service Client.

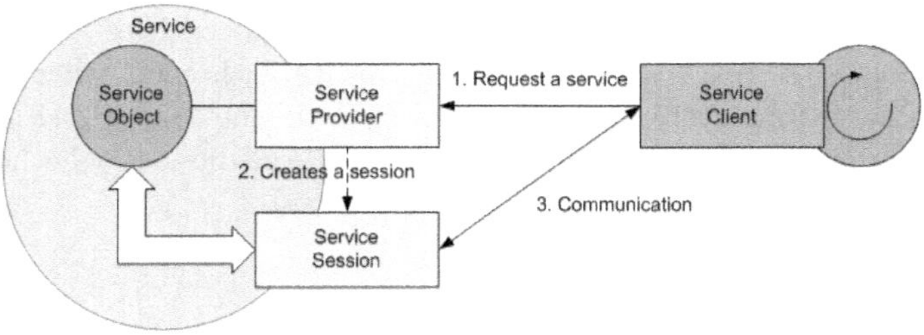

Fig. 3. Model of Service in the KUI system

The Service Object. It is the "processor" of the service. It receives, processes and sends the answer to any request coming from the client. This object (the class) is developed specifically for a service (e.g. menu service, meeting service).

The Service Provider. It is the object that connects a service client to the service object. It uses a public port that listens to any request for a connection coming from a service client.

The Service Session. It is a dedicated object created by the service provider when a connection request comes from a service client. A session is private and controls the communication between the Service Client and the Service Object. It is similar to the creation of a socket between two remote objects.

The Service Client. It is the counterpart of the Service Session. It manages the communication between the application using a service on the mobile device and the service object on the server side. The Client Service is attached to a public port declared in a port list in the mobile KUI system (attached to an actor).

Connection to a Service. When a client requests a connection to a specific service, three steps are done (Fig. 3). The first step is for the Service Client to contact the Service Provider using its public port (1). Then, the Service Provider creates a Service Session object (2) and connects the port of the Service Client to the Service Session port (3). Once the connection is complete, the Service Object and the Service Client can start to communicate. The protocol used in our project is TCP-based (using wireless communication).

7.2 Monitoring

The concept of services is now defined but we still have to answer the following question: how can services be discovered? A specific package called Monitoring has been developed in order for a KUI system (for instance, a mobile device) to 1) be detected by an other KUI System (smart environment) and 2) get the list of available services.

Monitoring Mobile Devices. Each time a mobile device running a KUI system enters in a zone covered by a smart environment, it is contacted, identified and integrated into the smart environment. A mobile KUI system entering in a WIFI zone broadcasts a ping message containing its open listening port for any echo message. If, in this network, a smart environment is active, it will answer with an echo message containing the open port address of the main service. This service is used to log the mobile device in the smart environment and creates a permanent communication channel. This channel will be used to pass all messages about public services available in the smart environment and all context changes (e.g. location, motion, temperature) from the mobile device to the server. It can happen that multiple smart environments from different building overlap and provide different services. To benefit from all of these services, our mobile KUI system allows connection to multiple smart environments at the same time.

Services List Update. Services are stored in a Service Registry in every smart environment and can always be enabled or disabled. Each time a service changes, the Coordination manager checks for all matching clients in order to send the update. The Service Registry also keeps track of which service is available for which client (meaning mobile KUI systems). This depends on the context of the user. For instance, a chat service might not be available to the user if he stands in a meeting room and his agenda has an entry "Meeting, priority 1" or the menu service is disabled if clearly the user's activity shows that he is leaving to catch his train.

7.3 Types of Service

As already mentioned in this section, there exist two types of service in a KUI system. The first type is a KUI service and the second one is all other public services.

KUI Service. The integration of a mobile device is managed by the KUI Service. At first there is the login procedure as explained in 7.2. Once the communication channel is established between the two KUI systems, the KUI service creates a KUI Session object (sec. 7.1) and an *Actor Stub* for the Actor object representing the user in the mobile KUI system (Fig. 4). The Actor Stub allows to reduce the traffic of information between the client and the server in the sense that each time the Actor object has a context change, it is transmitted once to its stub. From the server point of view, the Actor Stub represents a copy of the original Actor and can be used by the server side at anytime without generating traffic for a read of contextual information that is perhaps unchanged since last read. The KUI Service is always present and cannot be disabled. It also allows proper management of the disconnection of a mobile device by removing the Actor Stub and the KUI Session and closing the communication channel.

Public Services. They are typically specific applications developed for the smart environment consumers (users). They can be added, removed, enabled and disabled at the server level. Developers can create a service by simply implementing the `IService` interface and its method `process()` which will be called (callback mechanism) when a Service Client requests something. On the client side (mobile device) the developer implements the `IClientService` interface. This interface allows an application to connect to a Service Client port and therefore to access a Service Object on the server side.

In the next section, we present the two first prototypes which were developed in the framework of Master projects ([13], chap. 6).

8 Case Studies

Two case studies are currently running and using a KUI system and services. The first one focuses on service availability within a smart environment and the second one is a complete project that monitors the situation of an elderly person in a nursing home and alerts the most appropriate medical assistant in case of need.

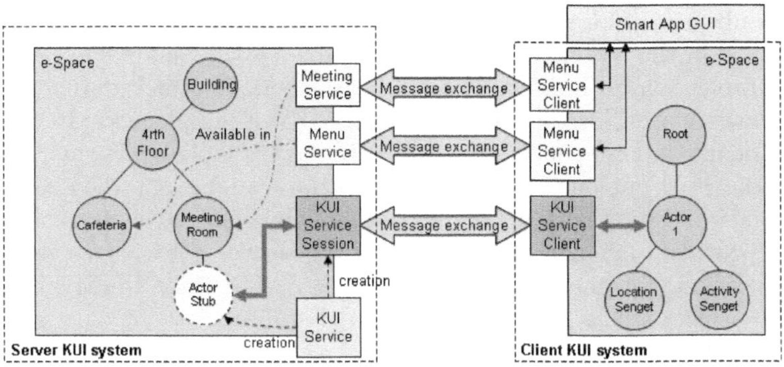

Fig. 4. Integration of a new mobile device by the KUI Session Service and service connections

8.1 Service Provider on Campus.

The smart environment is set up in our lab at the University of Fribourg and covers rooms on the 4th floor. The goal of the case study, was to test 1) the monitoring and integration of a mobile KUI system and 2) the concept of services contextually available in concrete situations. The scenario is based on user tracking in the different rooms of the 4th floor and the management of services using the user's contextual information. The idea is to have users moving around the floor carrying their Android phone running a KUI-enabled application (SmartApp). The Smart Environment detects, integrates and tracks them. It also provides services according the user's location and contexts (Fig. 4).

Setup. The project is decomposed into two applications which run respectively on a standard computer (server side) and on a Motorola MileStone[7] device running the Android 2.0 platform. Two applications were developed using the three Java libraries: uMove, Coordination, and Monitoring.

Server Application. This application contains two components: 1) the KUI System which manages the tree of entities (actors and zones) composing the floor and an application containing the logic and graphical user interface representing the map of the rooms and the user's location.

Mobile Application. The mobile application (SmartApp) for Android contains a KUI system which consists of an Actor and a couple of sengets (Location and Activity) which provide the contexts of the user (Fig. 4). This application is a standard Android application (.APK format) developed in Java and using

[7] `http://www.motorola.com/Consumers/US-EN/Consumer-Product-and-Services/Mobile-Phones/Motorola-DROID-US-EN`

the three libraries (uMove, Coordination, and Monitoring JARs). The JAR are pre-installed in the mobile device and accessible by the SmartApp.

The Graphical user interface is still relatively simple as it is only a prototype, but it allows testing of the different aspects of the implemented concept. At first, the main window proposes the login into the available smart environment by pressing the Start button (Fig. 5 a)). It starts the scanning and the identification. The second window (Fig. 5 b)) allows to manually change the user's location in order to provoke a change of context and the service that corresponds to the current location (e.g. the cafeteria and its menu). The third window lists all the available services in the smart environment (Fig. 5 c)).

The actual version of services are simple static texts sent to the client when requested. We have developed two services: the menu service showing the menu of the cafeteria and the meeting service which lists the meetings scheduled in the room. What we wanted to test with this prototype was not the implementation of complex services but more the context-sensitive aspect of the concept and for this, two different features were implemented. The first one concerns the room-dependent service. For instance, the menu service is only active when the user is in the cafeteria and the same rule also applies for the meeting service and the meeting room. The second aspect concerns the possibility to add other user contexts such as an agenda or an activity to help decide if the service must be enabled or not. In this case study, we used the tilt of the accelerometer to control the service activation. The choice was made, first to test the easiness of accessing any sensors with the Android platform and second, to show that different sensors producing contexts through the senget can be used to activate given services. To do this, we have developed the concept of rules that are applied to decide if a service must be provided or not. A simple example are the activity rules: the system decides when, for instance, the voice chat service is available. This is typically activity (as well as location) dependent. If the user is in a meeting in a given place, the voice chat service is disabled. In this case, the rule is programmed and evaluated every time 1) the service is available, 2) the location has changed and/or 3) the activity has changed. The concept of rules is not detailed here because it is ongoing research and more experiments are necessary for this promising aspect of context-awareness.

8.2 EMS - Elderly Monitoring System

The EMS project was developed in the framework of a Master level final project at the University of Applied Sciences of Bern - Switzerland. The goal of the project was to provide an application to a nursing home for monitoring of resident's activities and situations and alerting the appropriate medical staff if intervention is required.

Setup. The setup is close to the previous case study. The project is decomposed into a server-based application running a server-based service and two types of Android mobile applications and services.

Fig. 5. a) Main window, b) Menu front-end allowing to choose the location c) Available Service list window

Server Application. The server runs a KUI system modelling the environment of the nursing home (floors, rooms, residents, nurses and doctors). On top of the KUI system, the main server service is attached to an observer and receives the different situation alerts detected by the observer (ref. 5.1). This service contains the algorithm which processes any alerts and sends messages to the concerned medical staff who carry the Android mobile device. A group of important activities such as walking, falling and resting are processed in order to be sent with the resident's contexts (e.g. location or temperature) to the observer for situation analysis.

Mobile Application. On the mobile side, the KUI application uses different services depending on the user. If the mobile device belongs to a resident, the KUI application sends the contexts (e.g. location, temperature) and the recognized and current activity to the server application. There is, for now, no interaction between the resident and their mobile device. The idea is to let the resident carry out their daily activities without worrying about the mobile device (calm technology). For the medical staff, the KUI application does the same as for the resident, sending context and current activities manually selected (e.g. taking care of a person, resting, setting a room). But, an alarm service, as well as other services, are also running.

Alarm Service. The alarm service is the core service of the project in the sense that the algorithm is distributed between the server service which receives the alert and the client service which will receive the intervention request and treat it with the interaction of the user. The algorithm takes different parameters into consideration to decide who needs to be notified. First there is the assessment of the situation and the level of required competencies (nurse, doctor or both). Second, it checks the available staff around the resident according to medical staff activities. Once the message is sent, one or more staff need to confirm the intervention before the alarm is released. If no one answers the server request, the server service extends the range of people to be contacted.

State of the Project. The prototype is now running and tests are currently being done. The application will be deployed in the near future in a lab condition in order to conduct primarily user testing and evaluation, especially on the usability of the mobile application.

9 Conclusion and Future Work

In this paper, we have presented the SSP project which provides contextualized services in smart environments. The project is based on the concepts of KUI and CMP and is implemented in Java using uMove, Coordination and Monitoring APIs. Each user entering an SSP environment with an Android device running the client SmartApp is identified and integrated into the system and can benefit from the services available in this environment. We have also presented two prototypes with a server-based application that provide services and client applications running on the Android platform 2.0.

The next important step now will be to carry out user evaluations on the usefulness of the service concept and do usability testing in smart environments such as train stations, nursing homes and university campuses. We are currently working on a project that will propose a service management both on the server-side and on the client. This service manager will allow to add and remove services on servers and deal with the upload and removal of service clients (APK applications) on Android devices.

Acknowledgments

We would like to thank Agnes Lisowska Masson for her advice and corrections on this paper. This work is supported by the Swiss National Fund for Scientific Research Grant n.116355.

References

1. Abdallah, M., Fred, C., Farah, A.: An authentication architecture dedicated to dependent people in smart environments. In: Okadome, T., Yamazaki, T., Makhtari, M. (eds.) ICOST 2007. LNCS, vol. 4541, pp. 90–98. Springer, Heidelberg (2007)
2. Bannach, D., Lukowicz, P., Amft, O.: Rapid prototyping of activity recognition applications. In: Pervasive Computing, pp. 22–31 (April-June 2008)
3. Bruegger, P., Hirsbrunner, B.: Kinetic user interface: Interaction through motion for pervasive computing systems. In: Stephanidis, C. (ed.) UAHCI 2009. LNCS, vol. 5615, pp. 297–306. Springer, Heidelberg (2009)

4. Bruegger, P., Lalanne, D., Lisowska, A., Hirsbrunner, B.: Tools for designing and prototyping activity-based pervasive applications. In: MoMM 2009, Kuala Lumpur. ACM, New York (December 2009)
5. Bruegger, P., Pallotta, V., Hirsbrunner, B.: Ubiglide: a motion-aware personal flight assistant. In: Strang, T. (ed.) Adjunct Proceedings UBICOMP, Innsbruck, Austria, September 2007, pp. 155–158 (2007)
6. Brugger, P., Pallotta, V., Hirsbrunner, B.: Optimizing heating systems management using an activity-based pervasive application. JDIM - Journal of Digital Information Management (2009) ISSN 0972-7272
7. Brumitt, B., Meyers, B., Krumm, J., Kern, A., Shafer, S.A.: Easyliving: Technologies for intelligent environments. In: Thomas, P., Gellersen, H.-W. (eds.) HUC 2000. LNCS, vol. 1927, pp. 12–29. Springer, Heidelberg (2000)
8. Das, S.K., Cook, D.J.: Designing and modeling smart environments (invited paper). In: WOWMOM 2006, Washington, DC, USA, pp. 490–494. IEEE Computer Society, Los Alamitos (2006)
9. Dey, A., Abowd, E.D., Salber, G.D.: A conceptual framework and a toolkit for supporting the rapid prototyping of context-aware applications. Human Computer Interaction Journal 16, 97–166 (2001)
10. Dey, A.K., Abowd, G.D., Salber, D.: A context-based infrastructure for smart environments (1999), `http://www.cc.gatech.edu/fce/ctk/pubs/MANSE99.pdf`
11. Dourish, P.: Where the Action Is: The Foundations of Embodied Interaction. MIT Press, Cambridge (2001)
12. Ghiani, G., Patterno, F., Santoro, C., Spano, D.: A location-aware guide based on active rfids in multi-device environments. In: CADUI 2008, Spain (2008)
13. B. Hadorn. Coordination model for pervasive computing: a model to create and design applications using a pervasive middleware, Msc Thesis (March 2010), `http://diuf.unifr.ch/pai/wiki/doku.php/education:student_master_projects`
14. Hussain, S., Erdogen, S.Z., Park, J.H.: Monitoring user activities in smart home environments. Information Systems Frontiers 11(5), 539–549 (2009)
15. Kuutti, K.: Activity Theory as a Potential Framework for Human-Computer Interaction Research. MIT Press, Cambridge (1996)
16. Lesser, V., Atighetchi, M., Benyo, B., Horling, B., Xuan, P., Zhang, S.X.Q., Wagner, T.: The intelligent home testbed. In: Proceedings of the Autonomy Control Software Workshop (1999)
17. Li, Y., Landay, J.A.: Activity-based prototyping of ubicomp applications for long-lived, everyday human activities. In: CHI 2008: SIGCHI Conference, pp. 1303–1312. ACM, New York (2008)
18. Loke, S.W.: Representing and reasoning with situations for context-aware pervasive computing: a logic programming perspective. The Knowledge Engineering Review, 213–233 (2004)
19. Viterbo, J., Endler, M., Sacramento, V.: Discovering services with restricted location scope in ubiquitous environments. In: MPAC 2007, pp. 55–60. ACM, New York (2007)
20. von Bertalanffy, L.: General System Theory. Foundations, Development, applications. George Braziller (1969)
21. Weiser, M.: The computer for the 21st century. Scientific American 265 3, 94–104 (1991)

Using Cohesive Subgroups for Analyzing the Evolution of the Friend View Mobile Social Network

Alvin Chin and Hao Wang

Nokia Research Center
Building 2, No. 5 Donghuan Zhonglu, Economic and Technological Development Area
Beijing, China, 100176
{alvin.chin,ext-hao.10.wang}@nokia.com

Abstract. The mobility of users and the ubiquity of the mobile phone and Internet are leading to the development of mobile social networks. Much work has been done on modeling the evolution of online social networks using mathematical, social network analysis, and graph theoretic methods, however few using cohesive subgroups and similarity. In this paper, we present a study of the evolution of the Nokia Friend View mobile social network using network and usage statistics, and use the DISSECT method [7] for characterizing this evolution through the movement of cohesive subgroups. We discover that the friend network becomes less dense and less clustered (with fewer subgroups) over time, and the DISSECT method [7] helped to identify these cohesive subgroups and accurately predicted its most active users. We visualized these cohesive subgroups and modeled the evolution using persistence of subgroups. These results point the way towards an analytical framework for comparing mobile social networks which may help facilitate development of new recommender applications.

Keywords: Mobile social network, social network evolution, social network analysis, subgroup identification, cohesive subgroups, centrality, similarity modeling.

1 Introduction

Online social networks such as Facebook and LinkedIn are increasingly being used for sharing content and keeping in contact with friends, colleagues and family. With the ubiquity of the mobile phone and wireless technologies, location can be added as a context to localize the content such as location of photos taken and status updates, thus creating mobile social networks. Mobile social networking applications such as Foursquare and BuddyCloud use location of users to provide services such as finding people and places nearby, providing relevant content, providing search and updated points of interest, and creating specific topic channels from which other people can subscribe to.

Previous work has studied the structure and properties of online social networks [9, 17, 18, 22] and their evolution [1, 3, 17, 22, 24]. Most use social network properties over time or create models of evolution using group formation, clustering and

Z. Yu et al. (Eds.): UIC 2010, LNCS 6406, pp. 620–634, 2010.

partitioning, or mathematical modeling and graph theory, but fail to enumerate the cohesive subgroups and their persistence over time. There have been few studies of analyzing cohesive subgroups in the evolution of a mobile social network because the data is difficult to obtain. Therefore, our objective is to use cohesive subgroups as the method for describing the evolution of a mobile social network. Our research questions are the following. First, what are the cohesive subgroups of people that exist in a mobile social network over time? Second, which subgroups are ephemeral and which subgroups persist over time, and third, how do the persistent subgroups evolve and change over time?

In this paper, we analyze Friend View, a mobile social network created by Nokia Research Center, by quantifying its network properties, and then describe the evolution of Friend View in terms of its cohesive subgroups and how they change over time using the DISSECT method of Chin and Chignell [7]. Friend View is a service that allows mobile users to find others, update their status and location, add friends, and keep updates with others. We obtained the dataset of Friend View with the user names being anonymized. We discover that the DISSECT method helped to find cohesive subgroups in the interaction network, their persistence over time, and accurately predicted the most active users.

Our contributions are the following. First, we study the evolution of a mobile social network from the first day that it started to its last day. Although it can be argued that the dataset for Friend View is short (only 11 months), it provides us with the complete data for the entire network, as opposed to others who study only a subset of the entire social network. Second, we identify cohesive subgroups in different time periods during the evolution, and classify their persistence based on how the members within the subgroups move from one subgroup to another, split into several subgroups, or stay within the same subgroup.

The paper is organized as follows. Section 2 describes related work on identifying subgroups and modeling the properties and evolution of online social networks. In Section 3, we introduce and describe the user interface and usage statistics of Friend View along with the number of users and friend pairs over time. In Section 4, we analyze the comment interaction network of Friend View by using the DISSECT method of Chin and Chignell [7] to track the cohesive subgroups and their persistence and movement over time. In Section 5, we discuss the implications of the Friend View analysis and applications of our work. Finally, we conclude the paper in Section 6 and provide areas for future work.

2 Related Work

There has been much work in studying the properties and structure in online social networks such as Twitter [18], Wealink [17], Yahoo! 360 and Flickr [22], and Cyworld [9], however there have been only a few works studying the evolution of social networks by analyzing cohesive subgroups over time. In this section, we review methods for finding subgroups and modeling evolution.

2.1 Finding Subgroups

Most available methods for identifying subgroups are based on some combination of the following measures and techniques: centrality, cohesiveness, and clustering and partitioning. Centrality [16] identifies the most important active people that are well connected in the network. Centrality is a useful predictor of subgroup membership because those who are actively involved in one or more subgroups will generally score higher with respect to centrality scores within the surrounding network. Betweenness centrality has been used to find and measure subgroup and community membership [31, 38], whereas degree [14, 29, 41] and closeness centrality [23, 28] have been used for characterizing influential members.

Cohesive subgroups within social networks can indicate the most active members within a community [15, 40]. Cliques and k-plexes have been used to characterize groupings in social networks [8, 13], but are not suited to large networks because their computational complexity scales exponentially with the number of nodes in the network and their discovery is an NP-complete problem [2].

Clustering and techniques such as link analysis [4, 19] and co-citation analysis [20, 21] can be used to detect subgroups. Hierarchical clustering is often used to quantify the structure of community in web networks (e.g., [10, 12]) where the cluster orderings in the dendrogram form the subgroups. In contrast, groups formed in partitioning methods are not nested, but partitioning techniques are computationally efficient. Criteria and methods aimed at identifying optimal partitions include modularity [34], vector partitioning [39] or normalized cut metrics [24] for finding subgroups.

Hierarchical clustering has been shown to produce similar subgroupings as k-plex analysis for some data examples and is less computationally intensive [6]. Modularity has been proposed as an optimizing method for partitioning dendrograms [30]. Sometimes clustering and partitioning algorithms are combined in order to identify subgroups (e.g. [26]). However, little evaluative research has been carried out for determining which methods of unsupervised subgroup formation work well in subgroup analysis of social networks, and under what conditions.

2.2 Modeling Evolution

Online social networks evolve over time and much research has looked into the temporal aspects of social networks changing over time such as Leydesdorff et al [25] and Snijders et al [35]. Within social networks, subgroups of people may be found that vary in cohesiveness [33].

Using social network analysis, Kumar et al [22] analyzed the structure of Yahoo! 360 and Flickr networks and Barabási et al [3] analyzed scientific collaborations over time, to create a model of evolution and used simulation to test the model. Hu and Wang [17] studied the evolutions of degree, network density, clustering coefficient, number of users, modularity, and degree assortativity, in order to reveal the properties and evolutionary patterns of the Wealink online social network.

Other researchers have created models of evolution using group formation, clustering, and partitioning methods. For example, Backstrom et al [1] developed a method for measuring the movement of individuals between communities, examined the properties of membership of how groups formed, and identified which communities grew over time. Tang et al [37] adopted a spectral clustering framework using the temporal information to detect, identify and model community evolution in dynamic multi-mode networks. Cortes et al [11] proposed a bottom-up data structure to represent all small subgroups based on the "Communities of Interests" concept on each user in the dynamic network, and then updating all communities. Palla et al [32] quantified the social group evolution using cliques.

Mathematical modeling and graph theory can be used for modeling evolution of communities. Lin et al [27] detected communities using a non-matrix factorization and iterative algorithm for solving the evolutionary clustering problem in Chakrabarti et al. [5]. Sun et al [36] proposed a tool named GraphScope, based on information theory, to monitor communities and their membership changes in a stream of graphs efficiently. Leskovec et al [24] created a mathematical theoretical model for characterizing and describing the densification and shrinking diameter phenomenon in social networks over time.

For modeling evolution, few researchers have looked into the visualization and activity of the most influential members in the network over time, concentrating instead on the statistics of the network. Chin and Chignell [6, 7] proposed a similarity modeling approach to quantify changes in subgroup structure over time. In this approach cohesiveness over time is quantified in terms of the similarity of the subgroupings that are identified in different time periods. We adopt this approach for studying the evolution of a mobile social network.

3 Nokia Friend View

In this section, we introduce Nokia Friend View and its user interface. We then report on usage statistics and network properties of Friend View.

3.1 User Interface

Friend View is a location-based microblogging service from Nokia Research Center that was launched in the beginning of November 2008, and was discontinued at the end of September 2009 since it was an experimental service. It allowed users to post messages about their status and activity with other friends in their social network from GPS-enabled Nokia S60 phones or from the web.

Friend requests can be sent manually by entering the person's name or selecting the person who commented on the original status message. If the recipient accepts the friend request, the two users become friends and can see each other's message updates and threads. Users can post an optional status message with annotated GPS location. In the Friend View mobile phone interface shown in Figure 1, users can see all their friends' locations and status messages on a map in the "What's up" tab (a), and view and make comments to other conversation threads started from status messages (b).

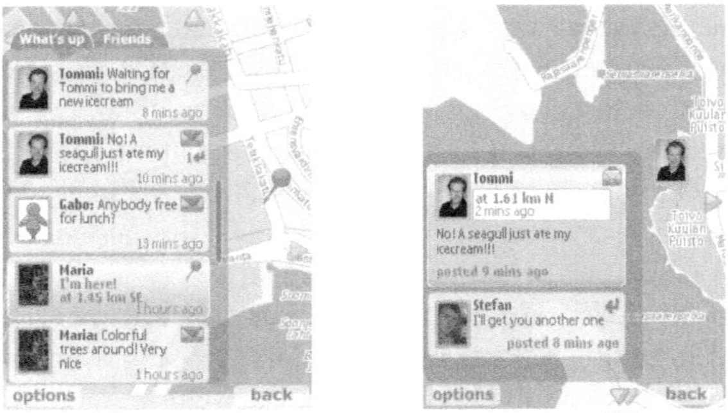

(a) (b)

Fig. 1. Mobile phone user interface of Friend View showing (a) status messages from friends showing location on a map, and (b) comments to a friend's status message

3.2 Usage Statistics

We obtained a complete dataset of Friend View interactions for the entire period of its operation that consisted of all users that posted status messages and comments. Consistent with ethics requirements, all data was anonymized prior to analysis, conformed to standard personal data protection laws, and people were labeled with unique, but not identifying, codes. The usage statistics, broken down into user and friend statistics, along with status message and comment statistics are summarized below.

A total of 62736 status messages were posted by 16176 users, providing an average of 3.88 status messages per user. Out of the 62736 status messages, 9363 status messages had associated comments that were posted by 2395 users, and 22251 comments were posted from 2283 users, producing a mean of 3.91 status messages with comments per user, and a mean of 2.38 comments per status message. Overall, users posted a small number of status messages (around 20, and generally a lot fewer), and a small number of comments (around 10 or less), but there were a few users in the long tail of the distribution that had an excessive number of status messages and comments that amounted in the hundreds and even thousands.

3.3 Network Statistics

We studied the network statistics of Friend View with the number of users and friend pairs over its entire duration. We extracted 11 snapshots of the dataset with an interval of one month from November 1, 2008 to September 30, 2009, like that in [17]. Figure 2 (a) shows the number of new users and new friend pairs for every month over the lifetime of Friend View, and Figure 2 (b) shows the total number of users and friend pairs.

The growth patterns for the number of new users and new friend pairs are similar in shape, with the highest number occurring at the beginning when many users joined Friend View and were eager to try out the service, and then decreases until the end of the service, with the exception of a few spikes like the seventh month. It is interesting that in the 7th month (June 2009), the number of new users encounters a huge spike and almost reaches the level from the beginning. We believe that this behaviour may have been caused as a result of a touch version of Friend View that was released during that time. However, the number of new pairs of friends in June 2009 decreases albeit very little. We speculate that if the huge spike of new users did not happen, then the number of new pairs of friends would decrease even more still and that value in August 2009 would not remain at the same level as the previous month. In Figure 2 (b), the number of users and friend pairs start small, rapidly accelerate, and then stabilize. In the case of the number of users, it still continues to grow while the number of friend pairs appears to plateau during the 10th and 11th months.

In the next section, we explain a method for modeling evolution by discovering cohesive subgroups over time.

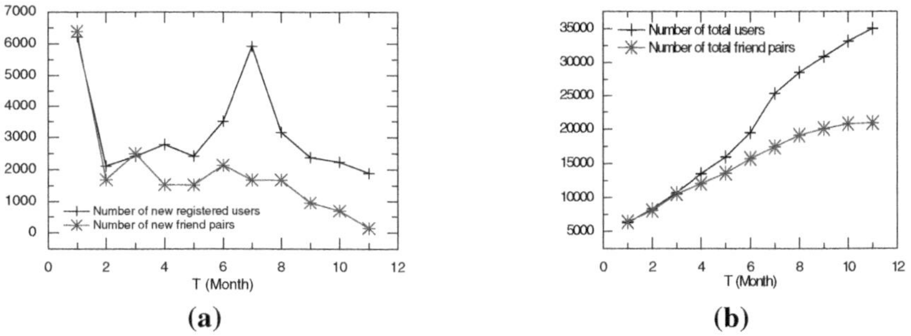

Fig. 2. Time evolution of (a) the number of new users and friend pairs and (b) the total number of users and friend pairs

4 Modeling Evolution with Cohesive Subgroups Using the DISSECT Method

To model the evolution of a social network, rather than create a simulation, theoretical, or statistical model, we seek to understand the behavior of its relevant members. We determine who are the relevant members over time, how they are grouped with other members, and how relevant members move within or between subgroups, using the DISSECT (Data-Intensive Socially Similar Evolving Community Tracker) method of Chin and Chignell [7]. For Friend View, we apply the DISSECT method to the interaction network. The interaction network consists of users with status messages and associated comments which form the conversations among users and from which relevant members can be added as friends. The detailed description about the interaction network is given in Section 3.2.

The DISSECT method tracks evolution of multiple known subgroups in terms of similarity-based cohesiveness over time, which is an improvement over the original SCAN (Social Cohesion Analysis of Networks) method also by the same authors [30].

The main steps in the framework of DISSECT consist of: 1) finding the time periods for cohesive analysis, 2) selecting the possible members of latent cohesive subgroups based on a certain network centrality cutoff, 3) performing hierarchical cluster analysis of each network snapshot in each of the time periods to discover the latent subgroups, and 4) calculating similarity of the known subgroups and finding the best network centrality that results in the largest similarity between subgroups in successive time periods. For more detailed implementation and discussion of the DISSECT and SCAN methods, please refer to [7] and [30] respectively.

4.1 Steps in the DISSECT Method

4.1.1 Find the Initial Time Periods for Analysis

The dataset is divided into time periods for tracking subgroups in the network over time. Time periods should be long enough so that there is enough data to distinguish potential subgroups, and there should be a sufficient number of them to estimate cohesion over time.

4.1.2 Select the Possible Members of Known Subgroups to Be Tracked (From Previous Step) Using Select from the SCAN Method

While betweenness centrality appears to be a useful filter for screening potential subgroup members, other centrality measures such as degree and closeness centrality may also be used [6]. Degree centrality may be a good default measure with which to screen potential subgroup members because it deals with direct interactions where the ties having stronger bonds indicate stronger cohesion, and also because it has the lowest computational complexity compared to the other centrality measures [6].

4.1.3 Perform Clustering of Snapshots in Time of Known Subgroups of People Using the Collect Step from the SCAN Method

This step is identical to the Collect step from the original SCAN method, with the provision that other cluster methods may be used in addition to, or instead of, weighted average hierarchical clustering.

4.1.4 Repeat Previous Two Steps for Different Values of Centrality

Since there is as yet no known "best" or most appropriate centrality cutoff value for selecting potential subgroup members, a search process may be used to identify particular cutoff values that lead to identification of the most cohesive groups. Different types of search strategies may be employed but they would involve repetition of steps 4.1.2 and 4.1.3 over a range of values of centrality, with the goal of maximizing the cohesiveness (self-similarity over time) of the obtained subgroupings. In this case, the similarity measures suggested by [6] are recommended, although other similarity measures may also be used.

4.1.5 Select and Characterize the Obtained Subgroupings in Terms of Their Cohesiveness and Their Behaviour over Time

The search process briefly described above may also be expanded by search over different definitions of time periods, as well as different centrality measures and centrality cutoff values. For instance, both the starting points and durations of time periods could be varied. It seems likely that strongly cohesive subgroups that remain intact over a sustained period of time should be "easy to find" with a range of time period definitions and centrality measurement and filtering strategies. In contrast, the search process envisioned above might be useful in finding more ephemeral subgroups that exist for only short periods of time and for tracking, in more detail, evolution in subgroupings.

4.2 Applying the DISSECT Method

We now apply the DISSECT method to the Friend View interaction network. The interaction network is a directed graph *G(V,E)*, where *V* represents the set of Friend View users and *E* represents the set of comments to status messages posted by users, where a directed edge exists between user A and user B if user A posted a comment in response to user B's status message and the edge weight *w* indicates the number of comments that A made in response to all of B's status messages. We then remove all nodes that have no edges.

We performed a link analysis (commenter and poster names) using the DISSECT method [7] to determine how well the method performs in the absence of content analysis (which is subjective, error prone, and time consuming). Due to the anonymized nature of the data, no labeling information was attached to the people in the network. The DISSECT method was applied as follows.

4.2.1 Define the Time Periods to Partition the Network into Time Snapshots

We define the time periods used for the evolution in Table 1 using Figure 2 to help guide us for the different phases of evolution based on the user growth.

Table 1. Time periods chosen for analysis in the evolution of Nokia Friend View

Time period	Time range	Growth phase
T1	Nov. 1 to 30, 2008	Beginning, initial growth
T2	Dec. 1 2008 to Feb. 28, 2009	Early growth
T3	Mar. 1 to May 31, 2009	Rapid growth
T4	Jun. 1 to Jul. 31, 2009	Rapid slowing of growth
T5	Aug. 1 to Sept. 30, 2009	Growth decline

In the first month of Nokia Friend View (T1), many early technology adopters tried out the service, which continued into the first couple of months in T2. At the beginning of March through June (T3), due to the adoption by internal employees, Nokia fanatics and friend recommendations, the service spread to many social networking news sites, which led to Friend View's rapid growth. The service then reached its peak during June and July (T4), as most people already were using the service. Finally, with the announcement that Friend View was going to be discontinued during the beginning of September, this naturally led to the decline in growth in T5.

4.2.2 Selecting Possible Members

For each time period, we first selected the cutoff points for normalized betweenness and degree centrality (as suggested by [7]) in order to select the possible subgroup members whose centrality was above this cutoff value. To determine the betweenness and degree centrality cutoff points, their frequency distributions were inspected for each time period. Figure 3 shows the betweenness centrality frequency distribution for the first time period T1. This tends to result in a cutoff value that focuses subsequent analysis on a relatively small set of active people. The degree centrality frequency distribution is similar, and therefore omitted in this paper.

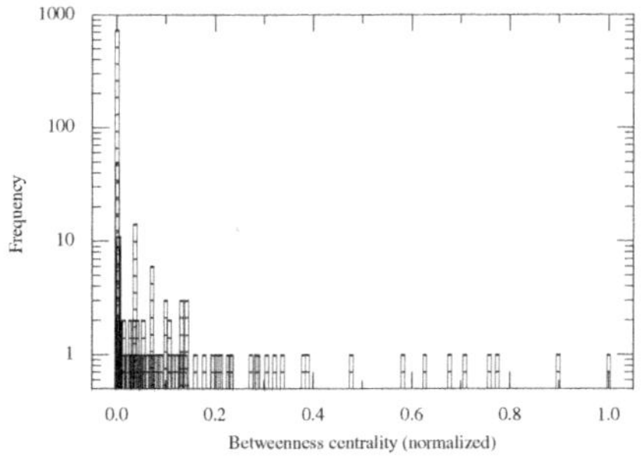

Fig. 3. Betweenness centrality distribution for the first time period (T1) in Nokia Friend View

From this distribution, the cutoff was chosen for each centrality measure to be the largest value in the distribution that separates a smaller group of higher centrality members from the larger group of people with lower centralities [7]. In this case, a betweenness centrality cutoff of 0.2 was chosen for T1. Based on inspection of the corresponding distributions for T2 through T5, a betweenness centrality cutoff of 0.2 was also chosen for those time periods. For degree centrality, the same process was also used and a cutoff of 0.005 was chosen. Other values of betweenness and degree centrality selected for the search process were a betweenness centrality cutoff of 0.1 and a degree centrality cutoff of 0.03. Higher cutoff values were not considered in this case as they would have resulted in a very small number of people being considered for possible subgroup membership.

4.2.3 Forming Possible Cohesive Subgroups

Once we selected the betweenness and degree centrality cutoff values, then for each cutoff value, all members in the network with betweenness centrality and degree centrality higher than the selected cutoff values are chosen for weighted average hierarchical clustering (from the DISSECT method), in order to find cohesive subgroups.

4.2.4 Similarity Analysis and Visualization for Evolution of Cohesive Subgroups

We use modularity [30] to select the partition to cut the dendrogram (resulting from hierarchical clustering) and find the optimum possible cohesive subgroups. Next, to determine which of these optimum possible cohesive subgroups (computed for each betweenness and degree centrality cutoff) are the actual cohesive subgroups for that time period, we perform a similarity analysis to find the most similar overlap in cohesive subgroup members using the method of Chin and Chignell [7]. The selected betweenness and degree centrality cutoff values are determined from the highest similarity as computed using the method in [7], and are summarized in Table 2.

From the visualization of optimum possible cohesive subgroups (not shown here due to space limit), subgroup members tend to be tightly connected with each other, suggesting strong cohesion. As well, the number of cohesive subgroups decreases over time as the subgroup becomes larger, indicating that people are connected to new friends and their conversations.

Table 2. Centrality cutoffs for each time period based from the DISSECT method [7]

Time period	Betweenness centrality cutoff	Degree centrality cutoff
T1	0.2	0.005
T2	0.1	0.003
T3	0.1	0.003
T4	0.2	0.005
T5	0.1	0.003

Figure 4 shows the movement of people between the Friend View subgroups based on the similarity analysis and quantifies the subgroups similar to [32]. The members have been grouped together based on the subgroups found from the DISSECT method, with each member having a shape that corresponds to the time period where that member is first found in other time periods as indicated in the legend. The arrows indicate how the member or subgroup moved from one subgroup in the previous period to the next period. From this figure, it can be seen that there are two subgroups at T1 (3, 32, 37, 7, 9, 34, 16) and (5, 21, 17, 24, 28, 11, 32, 33, 13). The second of these groups started splitting up in T2 and had completely dispersed by T3. Across the entire trial only three people stayed together across all the time periods (7, 9, and 37) and a further two people paired up in T2 and then stayed together for the remainder of the trial. Other people moved around between the time periods, sometimes moving to a different subgroup and sometimes appearing to drop out and become singletons. Since the data was anonymized, it is not possible to identify who participated in the cohesive subgroups. However, ID numbers were assigned in the order of adoption (beginning with the number 1) so the low ID numbers shown in Figure 4 (all below 50) indicated that the people who participated in subgroups were the early adopters in the trial.

The subgroups shown in Figure 4 can be characterized in terms of how persistent they are over the time periods. Persistence is based on how long a user belongs to and stays in a subgroup. The most *persistent group* (37, 7, 9) remains together through all the time periods. *Semi-persistent groups* may be defined as groups that stayed together for some portion of the trial. They include the following groupings (6, 26) that

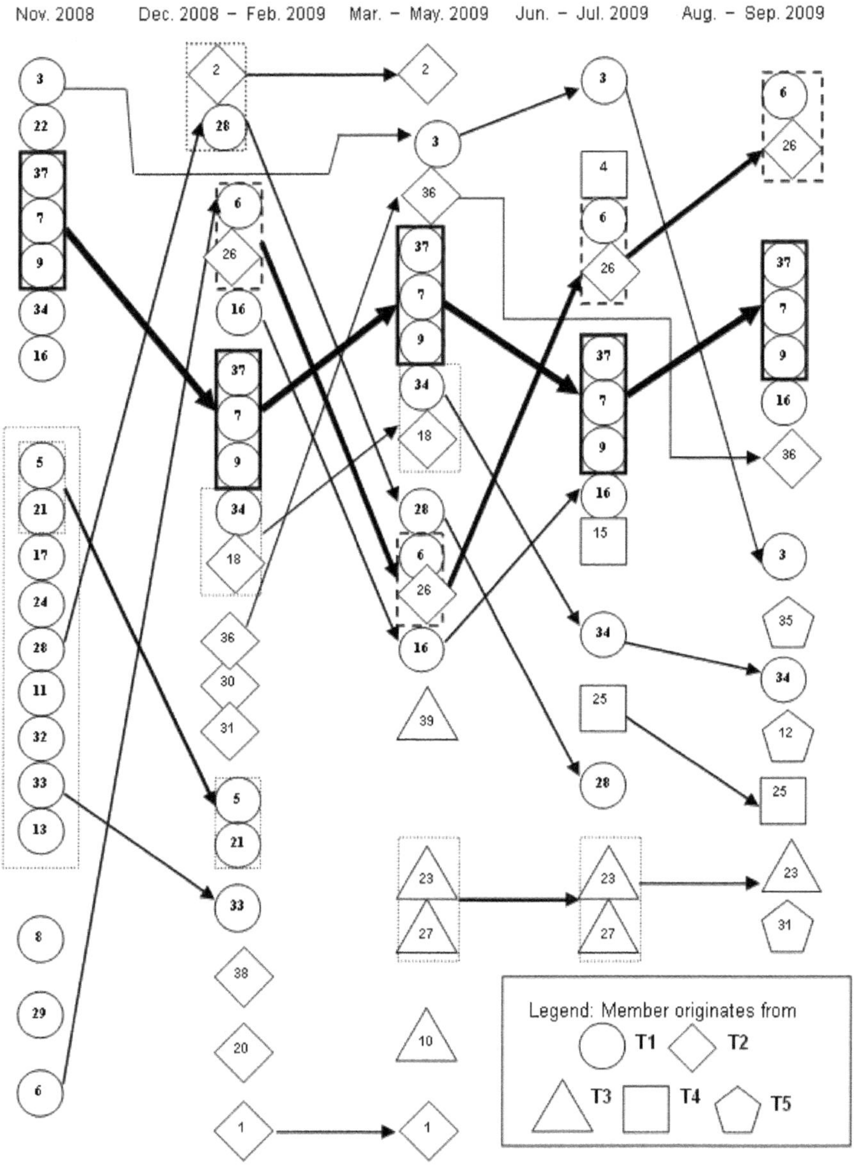

Fig. 4. Visualization of the evolution of members and subgroups in different time periods in Friend View

persist from T2 through to T5 and (5, 21) from T1 to T2. *Temporal groups* have persistent members in one period and then divide into different groups in the next time period. An example temporal group is (5, 21, 17, 24, 28, 11, 32, 33, 13) which formed in T1 but then divided into different groups in later time periods. *Ephemeral groups* may be defined as having members that are together in only one period such as (3, 22) in T1, and (30, 31) in T2. Based on this analysis, the different types of subgroups observed in the Friend View trial are listed in Table 3 according to their persistence. Note that since this analysis extends over five time periods, a particular person may participate in more than one type of subgroup at non-overlapping time durations.

We discovered very little evidence of new subgroups (involving new members) being formed after T2. Thus cohesive subgrouping activity was driven by the early adopters, and with most of the cohesive subgroup formation being done in the early part of the trial (although with some movement of members between and out of subgroups in later stages of the trial).

Table 3. Enumeration of all the different type of Friend View subgroup members discovered from the DISSECT method according to persistence

Type of subgroup	Subgroup members	Persistence
Persistent core subgroup	(37, 7, 9)	T1 to T5
Semi-persistent group	(6,26)	T2 to T5
	(5, 21)	T1 to T2
Temporal group	(5,21,17,24,28,11,32,33,13) (2,28)	T1, T2
Ephemeral group	(3,22) (30,31)	T1, T2

4.3 Cohesion and Message Activity

The DISSECT method for finding cohesive members in Friend View only takes into account the social network properties, but not the actual number of status messages posted by each member. Therefore, we wanted to see if members of cohesive subgroups tend to post more status messages, have a higher degree and betweenness centrality, and higher indegree and outdegree (with respective to unique members that make comments) than others that are non-members of cohesive subgroups. Since cohesive subgroup members tend to have more message activity and conversation than non-members [8], we expected that relationship to also hold in the Friend View data.

We discovered the number of unique people that a member makes comments to another member's status message or comment for that period, is the highest correlated with the number of status messages (posted at that period), followed by the number of unique individuals that make comments to a member's status message. Of those people selected using the centrality cutoff, people in the identified subgroups sent more messages as expected. In this sample, the correlations between betweenness centrality and message activity were of the same order as the correlations between degree centrality and message activity.

5 Discussion

Overall, Friend View had persistent core subgroups that stayed within all the time periods, as well as semi-persistent, temporal and ephemeral subgroups. Since the Friend View dataset did not contain the actual content of the status messages and the comments, we could not perform a content analysis in order to more accurately filter out Friend View users that would not be part of cohesive subgroups. Since we did not perform any analysis concerning different sized durations of time periods, future work will involve developing similarity measures that take into account variable time windows and all possible combinations of time windows (rather than pairwise consecutive time windows). Some possible methods for selecting time periods could be probabilistic stochastic models [35], sliding time windows [30], and time graphs and burst analysis [1].

We discovered relatively few subgroups in the Friend View data, therefore based on our experience, large datasets should use degree centrality instead of betweenness centrality because betweenness centrality seems to be a better indicator of activity in a relatively small and densely connected network [7]. In very large networks (such as the one formed in the Friend View trial) where there are only isolated pockets of people who know each other, degree centrality (with its emphasis on whom the people are directly connected to) may be a better reflection of activity and a better filter for selecting people who are likely to belong to subgroups that might be cohesive. In addition, the few relatively small subgroups are probably as a result of selecting a relatively stringent centrality cutoff criterion, therefore, it is recommended to have algorithmic methods of centrality cutoff selection that supplement the visual inspection of the frequency distribution used in the research reported here.

As this study primarily dealt with investigating the detailed evolution using cohesive subgroups, we did not compare our results with other work, however this is reserved for future work.

6 Conclusion

In this paper, we studied the evolution of a mobile social network called Nokia Friend View using network properties. We then identified cohesive subgroups and relevant members using the DISSECT framework [7]. We discovered that the DISSECT method found different types of cohesive subgroups based on persistence in time: persistent, semi-persistent, temporal and ephemeral groups. We compared the persistent groups with the original post and comment statistics, and discovered that the most active members were the ones who were a part of the persistent groups.

Since Nokia Friend View has been discontinued, we do not have an opportunity to obtain a larger dataset. For future work, we plan to use other social network datasets to examine the value of the DISSECT approach. Relevant research issues include the choice of time periods using various statistical and time-based models, developing other measures for similarity assessment, and using content analysis to determine semantic properties that govern or explain subgroup membership. The DISSECT framework may also be applied to other online social networks to determine whether the similar cohesive subgroups along with network and message statistics, and the social graph of the friend and interaction network, can be used to improve friend recommendations.

Acknowledgements

We would like to thank James Reilly and Matti Sillanpaa from the Nokia Friend View team for providing us with the anonymized data set from Friend View.

References

1. Backstrom, L., Huttenlocher, D., Kleinberg, J., Lan, X.: Group formation in large social networks: membership, growth, and evolution. In: ACM SIGKDD, pp. 44–54. ACM, New York (2006)
2. Balasundaram, B., Butenko, S., Hicks, I., Sachdeva, S.: Clique relaxations in social network analysis: The maximum k-plex problem. Tech. rep., Texas A and M Engineering (2008)
3. Barabasi, A., Jeong, H., Neda, Z., Ravasz, E., Schubert, A., Vicsek, T.: Evolution of the social network of scientific collaborations. Physica A: Statistical Mechanics and its Applications 311(3-4), 590–614 (2002)
4. Brin, S., Page, L.: The anatomy of a large-scale hypertextual web search engine. In: WWW 1998, pp. 107–117 (1998)
5. Chakrabarti, D., Kumar, R., Tomkins, A.: Evolutionary clustering. In: Proceedings of the 12th ACM SIGKDD, pp. 554–560 (2006)
6. Chin, A., Chignell, M.: Automatic detection of cohesive subgroups within social hypertext: A heuristic approach. New Review of Hypermedia and Multimedia 14(1), 121–143 (2008)
7. Chin, A., Chignell, M.: DISSECT: Data-Intensive Socially Similar Evolving Community Tracker. Computational Social Network Analysis, 81–105
8. Chin, A., Chignell, M.: Identifying subcommunities using cohesive subgroups in social hypertext. In: HT 2007, pp. 175–178. ACM, New York (2007)
9. Chun, H., Kwak, H., Eom, Y., Ahn, Y., Moon, S., Jeong, H.: Comparison of online social relations in volume vs interaction: a case study of cyworld. In: Proc. of the 8th ACM SIGCOMM IMC Conference, pp. 57–70. ACM, New York (2008)
10. Clauset, A.: Finding local community structure in networks. Physical review E 72(2), 26132 (2005)
11. Cortes, C., Pregibon, D., Volinsky, C.: Communities of interest. Intelligent Data Analysis 6(3), 211–219 (2002)
12. Donetti, L., Munoz, M.: Detecting network communities: a new systematic and efficient algorithm. Journal of Statistical Mechanics: Theory and Experiment, P10012 (2004)
13. Du, N., Wu, B., Pei, X., Wang, B., Xu, L.: Community detection in large-scale social networks. In: 1st SNA-KDD, pp. 16–25. ACM, New York (2007)
14. Fisher, D.: Using egocentric networks to understand communication. IEEE Internet Computing 9(5), 20–28 (2005)
15. Fortunato, S., Latora, V., Marchiori, M.: Method to find community structures based on information centrality. Physical review E 70(5), 56104 (2004)
16. Freeman, L.: Centrality in social networks conceptual clarification. Social networks 1(3), 215–239 (1979)
17. Hu, H., Wang, X.: Evolution of a large online social network. Physics Letters A 373(12-13), 1105–1110 (2009)
18. Java, A., Song, X., Finin, T., Tseng, B.: Why we twitter: understanding microblogging usage and communities. In: 1st SNA-KDD, pp. 56–65. ACM, New York (2007)
19. Kleinberg, J.: Authoritative sources in a hyperlinked environment. Journal of the ACM (JACM) 46(5), 604–632 (1999)
20. Kleinberg, J.: Bursty and hierarchical structure in streams. Data Mining and Knowledge Discovery 7(4), 373–397 (2003)
21. Kumar, R., Novak, J., Raghavan, P., Tomkins, A.: Structure and evolution of blogspace. Communications of the ACM 47(12), 35–39 (2004)
22. Kumar, R., Novak, J., Tomkins, A.: Structure and evolution of online social networks. In: Proceedings of the 12th ACM SIGKDD, pp. 611–617. ACM, New York (2006)

23. Kurdia, A., Daescu, O., Ammann, L., Kakhniashvili, D., Goodman, S.: Centrality measures for the human red blood cell interactome. In: Engineering in Medicine and Biology Workshop, pp. 98–101. IEEE, Los Alamitos (2007)
24. Leskovec, J., Kleinberg, J., Faloutsos, C.: Graph evolution: Densification and shrinking diameters. ACM Transactions on Knowledge Discovery from Data (TKDD) 1(1), 2 (2007)
25. Leydesdorff, L., Schank, T., Scharnhorst, A., De Nooy, W.: Animating the development of Social Networks over time using a dynamic extension of multidimensional scaling (2008), http://arxiv.org/pdf/0809.4655
26. Li, N., Chen, G.: Analysis of a Location-Based Social Network. In: Proceedings of the Intern. Confer. on Computational Science and Engineering, pp. 263–270. IEEE, Los Alamitos (2009)
27. Lin, Y., Chi, Y., Zhu, S., Sundaram, H., Tseng, B.: Facetnet: a framework for analyzing communities and their evolutions in dynamic networks. In: WWW 2008, pp. 685–694. ACM, New York (2008)
28. Ma, H., Zeng, A.: The connectivity structure, giant strong component and centrality of metabolic networks. Bioinformatics 19(11), 1423–1430 (2003)
29. Memon, N., Larsen, H., Hicks, D., Harkiolakis, N.: Detecting hidden hierarchy in terrorist networks: Some case studies. In: Yang, C.C., Chen, H., Chau, M., Chang, K., Lang, S.-D., Chen, P.S., Hsieh, R., Zeng, D., Wang, F.-Y., Carley, K.M., Mao, W., Zhan, J. (eds.) ISI Workshops 2008. LNCS, vol. 5075, pp. 477–489. Springer, Heidelberg (2008)
30. Moody, J., McFarland, D., Bender deMoll, S.: Dynamic network visualization1. American Journal of Sociology 110(4), 1206–1208 (2005)
31. Newman, M., Girvan, M.: Finding and evaluating community structure in networks. Physical Review E 69(2), 26113 (2004)
32. Palla, G., Barabási, A., Vicsek, T.: Quantifying social group evolution. Nature 446(7136), 664–667 (2007)
33. Piper, W., Marrache, M., Lacroix, R., Richardsen, A., Jones, B.: Cohesion as a basic bond in groups. Human Relations 36(2), 93 (1983)
34. Ruan, J., Zhang, W.: An efficient spectral algorithm for network community discovery and its applications to biological and social networks. In: Proceedings of the 2007 Seventh IEEE International Conference on Data Mining 2007, pp. 643–648 (2007)
35. Snijders, T., Steglich, C., Schweinberger, M.: Modeling the co-evolution of networks and behavior. Longitudinal Models in the Behavioral and Related Sciences, 41–71 (2007)
36. Sun, J., Faloutsos, C., Papadimitriou, S., Yu, P.: Graphscope: parameter-free mining of large time-evolving graphs. In: Proceedings of the 13th ACM SIGKDD, pp. 687–696. ACM, New York (2007)
37. Tang, L., Liu, H., Zhang, J., Nazeri, Z.: Community evolution in dynamic multi-mode networks. In: 14th ACM SIGKDD, pp. 677–685 (2008)
38. Tyler, J., Wilkinson, D., Huberman, B.: E-mail as spectroscopy: Automated discovery of community structure within organizations. The Information Society 21(2), 143–153 (2005)
39. Wang, G., Shen, Y., Ouyang, M.: A vector partitioning approach to detecting community structure in complex networks. Computers & Mathematics with Applications 55(12), 2746–2752 (2008)
40. Wellman, B.: Structural analysis: From method and metaphor to theory and substance. Contemporary Studies in Sociology 15, 19–61 (1997)
41. Welser, H., Gleave, E., Fisher, D., Smith, M.: Visualizing the signatures of social roles in online discussion groups. Journal of Social Structure 8(2) (2007), http://www.cmu.edu/joss/content/articles/volume8/Welser/

Towards Topic-Based Trust in Social Networks

Tomáš Knap and Irena Mlýnková

Faculty of Mathematics and Physics
Charles University in Prague, Czech Republic
{tomas.knap,irena.mlynkova}@mff.cuni.cz

Abstract. The vast majority of applications consider generic notion of trust of a person to others, which is not restricted to any particular context or situation. Motivated by the financial scenario consuming data from distributed sources on the Web, we argue that we (as information consumers) cannot trust the information publishers or authors in general, however, only regarding the particular topics of the consumed data sources. To enable the so-called topic-based trust between users, we (1) propose a mechanism to persist the topic-based trust in a FOAF social network, (2) survey the topic hierarchies suitable for classifying the topics used in the trust model, and (3) propose an algorithm to compute trust with respect to the particular topic.

Keywords: Trust, Trust model, Social network.

1 Introduction

Trust is a crucial concept in human's everyday life and governs the substantial amount of human's decisions. When deciding whether to trust or distrust the other *person* in the particular *context/situation*, we are influenced by many objective and subjective factors, such as by our previous experience with that person and his/her *social network* (friends, family); previous experience of our friends with that person; rumors about that person; the aspects which influence the *trust decision*, although not directly connected with the subject of the decision, such as clothing, decency, or loveliness of that person; urgent need of the subject of the trust decision; or our instantaneous psychological state of mind, unrelated to the trust decision made.

The aspects above (just to mention some of them) influence the human's trust decision and illustrate the complexity of trust as a computational concept and the consequent difficulties to model trust in applications. The application's trust decision process is always a simplification of the human's trust decision process – different simplifications are suitable for P2P networks [16], to provide trustworthy product reviews in an eShop [4], or to ensure trustworthiness of data on the Semantic Web [2].

There are semantic web (or simply web) applications, such as FilmTrust[1] or Advogato[2], where the generic notion of trust is acceptable and reasonable, because the

[1] http://trust.mindswap.org/FilmTrust/
[2] http://advogato.org

Z. Yu et al. (Eds.): UIC 2010, LNCS 6406, pp. 635–649, 2010.

notion of trust is restricted to a particular area of expertise by the intended use of the application (movies recommendation in FilmTrust and software developing in Advogato) [8]. Notwithstanding, in case of the vast majority of web applications, such as social networking applications (e.g. MySpace[3]) or applications recommending/ scoring information on the Web (e.g. the WIQA Browser[4]), the generic notion of trust is neither applicable nor reasonable.

In our financial scenario, we are motivated by the latter type of applications. A financial analyst Alice is preparing the financial report for May 2010. To achieve her goal, she is using a Linked Data[5] [6] *mashup application* consuming and aggregating information included in stock markets time series, financial reports, government data, demographics, previous analysis, and third-party qualitative and quantitative analysis, physically distributed in various *data sources*, such as RDF/XML [23] documents, database tables, and XHTML pages.

Further, let us assume that Alice (A) is part of the social network SN of her colleagues working in the financial sector as well as other friends of Alice. Alice can expresses in the social network SN her trust in colleagues Bob (B) and David (D) regarding "finance", partial trust in Cyril (C) regarding "sport", and distrust in David regarding "cooking". Similarly, Bob, Cyril, and David can express their trust relations to other people. Since it has been widely documented that social networks have the properties of small world networks, where the average distances between nodes in the network are small and connectance of nodes is high [9,10], there is a chance of close (indirect) relationship of Alice and other financial experts.

Such a social network SN (visualized in Fig. 1) can be used as the base for an algorithm (called TopicTrust) assigning the nodes B, C, D (authors of the data source S) a *trust value* based on (1) the topic T of the consumed data source S and (2) the relation of the information consumer A (Alice) and the particular author (B, C, D) of the data source S. To that end, we suppose that every data source S_i is annotated by appropriate metadata holding the *author* and the *topic* of the data source S_i, for example by utilizing Dublin Core Metadata Initiative[6]. The current activities in the area of data provenance and annotations are showing that these assumptions are being fulfilled by more and more data sources[7] [18]. The fact that B is an author of the data source S is shortened as B_S. Similarly, the topic T of S is shortened as T_S.

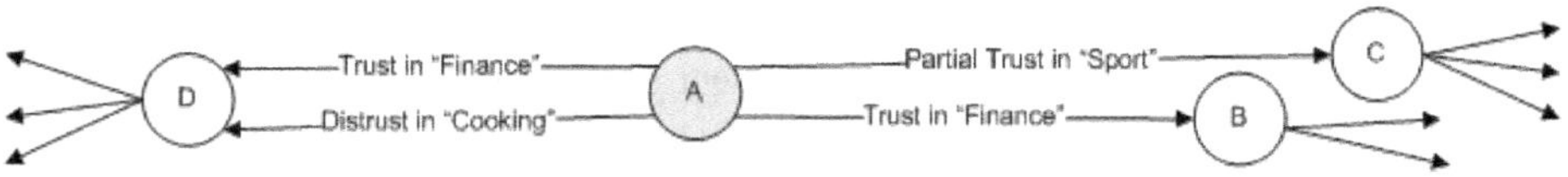

Fig. 1. Sample social network Alice is part of

The mashup application Alice is using accommodates a *ranking algorithm*, which helps Alice deciding the right data source by scoring and sorting the consumed data

[3] `http://www.myspace.com/`
[4] `http://www4.wiwiss.fu-berlin.de/bizer/wiqa/browser/index.htm`
[5] `http://www.w3.org/DesignIssues/LinkedData.html`
[6] `http://dublincore.org/`
[7] `http://twiki.ipaw.info/bin/view/Challenge`

sources according to the results of many analyses [19], such as the analysis of data provenance [18], data timeliness and popularity [15], reputation of data sources [16, 17]. The trust values assigned by the TopicTrust algorithm can be utilized by a *social topic-based trust analysis* for scoring the consumed data sources. To observe to which extent the social topic-based trust analysis can extend and improve the ranking algorithm, we assume a ranking algorithm *SRANK* sorting the data sources only according to the results of the social topic-based trust analysis.

To realize the TopicTrust algorithm (the core part of SRANK), we have to address the tasks T1–T3:

- T1 Find the way how Alice can express in her social network that she trusts the particular author regarding the particular topic of the consumed data source.
- T2 How to compute the initial trust value of Alice in her neighbors, the initial trust value of Alice's neighbors in their neighbors etc.
- T3 How to combine the initial (local) trust values to the (global) trust value between Alice and the author A_{Si} which determines the final score of the given data source S_i consumed by the mashup application w.r.t the social topic-based trust analysis.

Resulting from the tasks (T1 – T3) outlined, the goal of this paper is the TopicTrust algorithm enabling the social topic-based trust analysis. The major contributions (C1 – C3) are as follows:

- C1 Introduction of the topic-based trust model and specification of the persistence of the model in a social network (Generated by T1)
- C2 Definition of an algorithm TopicTrust for computing topic-based trust among two persons by leveraging the algorithm TidalTrust proposed in [8, 2] with the vital concepts of topics (Generated by T2 and T3)
- C3 Defining the requirements for and surveying the topic hierarchies suitable for classifying the topics used in the trust model (Generated by C1 and C2)

The rest of the paper is organized as follows. In Section 2, we introduce the topic-based trust model, discuss the persistence of the model, and elaborate topic hierarchies, suitable for classifying the topics used in the trust model. Section 3 depicts in detail the TopicTrust algorithm for computing topic-based trust. Section 4 evaluates the results of the ranking algorithm SRANK. Section 5 reviews related work. The paper is rounded off with a conclusion and discussion in Section 6.

2 Topic-Based Trust Model

Manifestations of trust are easy-to-recognize because we experience and rely on it every day, but at the same time trust is quite challenging to define because it manifests itself in many different forms and it is used with wide variety of meanings [4, 14, 17]. Nevertheless, we stick to the formalism introduced in Definition 1, because (1) it best correlates with the financial scenario, where the information consumer Alice is relying on authors of the data sources, (2) it involves the restriction of trust to the particular topic of the consumed data source, and (3) it comprehends trust as the subjective opinion of a node *A* (information consumer) about the other node *B*, not as the global reputation of the node *B* in the social network [8, 16]. Definition 1 drives the comprehension of the term trust in our topic-based trust model.

Definition 1 (Topic-based Trust). Trust is that which the *consumer* knows about the *author* of the consumed data source w.r.t the *topic* of the consumed data source and can rely upon to some extent.[8]

The "reliance to some extend" (introduced in Definition 1) is expressed in a form of a trust value. The trust value is quantified either on a discrete or continuous scale. Marsh [21], Lausen and Ziegler [22] (just to mention some of them) introduce continuous trust value ranging from -1 to 1; on the other hand, TidalTrust algorithm [2, 8] uses nine discrete trust values (*trust levels*) ranging from "absolute trust" to "absolute distrust". Since we partially utilize TidalTrust algorithm in the TopicTrust algorithm, we use in our trust model five discrete trust levels to express *trust relations*, i.e. an extent to which a person trusts/distrusts other persons regarding a particular topic – "Trust", "Partial Trust", "Neutral", "Partial Distrust", "Distrust". We decided to use fewer trust levels than Golbeck et al. in [2, 8], because the more trust levels the model has the more confusing the interpretation of their differences is (trust is a subjective concept). Table 1 depicts the proposed trust levels, their meanings, shortcuts, and the interpretation on the scale 0% – 100%, where 0% represents complete distrust, 50% neutral state, and 100% complete trust. The trust formulas in the last column of Table 1 are discussed in Section 3.

Table 1. The trust levels proposed in our topic-based trust model. The variable *d* in all trust formulas represents the distance between the topics (discussed in Section 3).

Trust Level	Meaning	Shortcut	Trust scale	Trust Formula
Trust	Person A *trusts* person B	T	100%	$5 + 4/(2^{\lvert d \rvert})$
Partial Trust	A *trusts partially* B	TP	75%	$5 + 4/(2^{\lvert d \rvert+1})$
Neutral	A *knows* B	K	50%	5
Partial Distrust	A *distrusts partially* B	DP	25%	$5 - 4/(2^{\lvert d \rvert+1})$
Distrust	A *distrusts* B	D	0%	$5 - 4/(2^{\lvert d \rvert})$

When proposing the topic-based trust model, the further problems to be solved are (1) how to persist the trust levels proposed (see Subsection 2.1), (2) which topics are allowed to be specified as topics in Definition 1 (see Subsection 2.2), and (3) how the trust values are computed (see Section 3).

2.1 Persistence of the Trust Model

Before clarifying *how* the trust model is persisted, we introduce the model of the social network [9, 10] and the implementation of the social network which *is suitable* for the trust model persistence.

A *social network* is typically modeled as a directed graph *SN* = (*V*, *E*), where the vertices *V* of the graph *SN* represent persons and the edges *E* relations between these

[8] Based on the definitions introduced at `http://safevote.com/papers/trustdef.htm`

persons [2, 8, 22]. Many social networks coexist in the Web information space[9], however, they are tightly connected with the applications utilizing them. Contrary, the *Friend of a Friend* (FOAF) project[10] is an ontology to describe people, documents, and relations between them in an open and application independent way using RDF model. The FOAF ontology contains class `foaf:Person` and the property `foaf:knows`, expressing that a person *A* knows[11] a person *B*. The instances of the class `foaf:Person` form the vertices of the social network *SN* and the instances of the property `foaf:knows` create social links between people, which are represented by edges in *SN*. To illustrate the wider acceptance of the FOAF ontology, the semantic web index Sindice[12] (indexing 117.41 millions of semantic web documents to the date 24.7.2010) points out that the property `foaf:knows` is used by 14 millions of the documents. Since there are no other open, application independent, machine readable, and widely used implementations of the social networks, we decided to choose the social network created by the class `foaf:Person` and the property `foaf:knows` as the basis for holding the trust relations between persons.

Unfortunately, no constructs in the FOAF ontology allow us to express that Alice trusts Bob regarding "finance" (as depicted in Fig. 1). In other words, FOAF ontology could persist only the trust level `K` (as the property `foaf:knows`). To that end, we propose an extension of FOAF ontology, called Topic-based Trust Module[13] having the capability to persist the rest of the trust levels (`T`, `TP`, `DP`, `D`).

The simple idea is to propose four new *binary trust properties* (defined as subproperties of `foaf:knows`) – `trusts`, `trustsPartially`, `distrusts Partially`, and `distrusts` – for persisting the trust levels `T`, `TP`, `DP`, and `D`. Nevertheless, when restricting the given binary trust property on the particular topic, we cope with the N-ary relation, which cannot be easily expressed in RDF. The W3C Note [20] elaborates several ways how to avoid N-ary relations – all of them require the introduction of an auxiliary class representing the N-ary relation, which we call `TrustContext`. Consequently, every person has a property `hasTrustContext`, which relates the given person to the `TrustContext`; the `TrustContext` itself describes (1) the other person, we express trust in (by a property `regardingPerson`), (2) the required trust level (by a property `trustLevel`), and (3) the topic to which the trust is restricted (by a property `regardingTopic`). We call this construct as an *N-ary trust property* (See Example 1). Since the person can express trust in another person regarding all topics, the Topic-based Trust Module supports both ways for expressing the trust relations – using binary or N-ary trust properties.

We conclude this section with the definition of a *social trust network*, which is a directed multigraph *STN* = (*V*, *E*), where the vertices *V* of the graph (also called *nodes*) represent `foaf:Person` instances and the edges *E* are built by `foaf:knows` properties and trust properties (binary and N-ary). If a node *N* is part of the *STN*, we say that it is a *social trust network containing N*.

---

[9] See [8] (Chapter 2) for the list of web-based social networks.

[10] `http://xmlns.com/foaf/spec/`

[11] See `http://xmlns.com/foaf/spec/#term_knows` for the precise definition

[12] `http://www.sindice.com`

[13] The full ontology can be downloaded at `http://www.ksi.mff.cuni.cz/~knap/tta/ttm.owl`

Example 1. A sample FOAF fragment in RDF/XML serialization expressing that Alice trusts Bob regarding "finance" (the namespace of the Topic-based Trust Module is the default namespace).

```
<foaf:Person rdf:about="http://.../Alice" >
  <hasTrustContext>
    <TrustContext>
      <trustLevel rdf:resource="http://.../#Trust"/>
      <regardingPerson rdf:resource="http://.../Bob"/>
      <regardingTopic rdf:resource="http://.../Finance"/>
    </TrustContext>
  </hasTrustContext>
</foaf:Person>
```

2.2 Topic Hierarchies

This subsection starts with the definition of the *topic forest* as a structure for holding hierarchies of topics. Let us denote $TH = (V, E)$ as the *topic hierarchy* with the set of vertices V representing topics and the set of edges E, s.t. every edge leading from A to B expresses that the topic A is the subtopic of the topic B. Then the set $\{TH : TH$ is a topic hierarchy$\}$ is called a *topic forest*. Every topic forest implicitly contains one special topic hierarchy having a single topic "ALL", which is used to express that a person has a trust relation with another person w.r.t all topics.

The list of the requirements on the topic hierarchies suitable for classifying the topics in the topic-based trust model is as follows (based on [3,5,7]):

- R1 The topic hierarchy is ontologically well-defined [3].
- R2 All topics at the same level (i.e. topics with the same distance from the root topic) cover approximately the same fragment of the universe and have the same level of abstraction.
- R3 The distance between a topic and its subtopics is similar for all subtopics.
- R4 The topic hierarchy has reasonable depth (i.e. the ontology is big enough).
- R5 The topics cover only useful concepts – e.g. topics like "artifact" or "physical entity" are not suitable.
- R6 Topic hierarchy has human/nearly-human accuracy of relations between topics.

Taking into account the proposed requirements, the survey of the available topic hierarchies follows and is summarized in Table 2. The Wikipedia categorization system[14] (WikiCat) serves as a source for lots of topics, however, it satisfies only R4 [3]. WordNet [12], the lexical database of English synsets (sets of cognitive synonyms), manually built at the University of Princeton, satisfies R1, R4, and R6; however, it violates R2 and R3 [7] (efforts to address these issues are pointed out in [5]) and R5 (could be meliorated by cutting of the auxiliary topics around the root topic). YAGO, Yet Another Great Ontology [3], connects together WordNet with a part of WikiCat to create richer ontology than WordNet (satisfies R4) with almost human accuracy (satisfies R6). Due to its design, YAGO still satisfies R1, however, similarly as

[14] `http://en.wikipedia.org/wiki/Wikipedia:Categorization`

WordNet, it does not satisfy R2, R3, and R5, which cannot be easily meliorated, because YAGO partially employes WikiCat. WordNet Domains (WND) [5] are language independent domains for categorization of WordNet synsets. WND is based on the Dewey Decimal Classification[15] (DDC), a general knowledge organization tool which is the most widely used taxonomy for library organization purposes. Both these hierarchies (WND and DDC) satisfy R1 – R3 and R6; however, they violate R4 (DDC has only 5 – 6 levels of topics, WND even less) and R5 (can be solved by cutting off the first level of the abstract topics of the topic hierarchy and the orphaned topic hierarchies can form our topic forest). The advantage of WND in comparison with DDC is that (1) it is not designed primarily for the classification of books and (2) it considers popular and recent topics [5].

Although the violation of R4 cannot be easily addressed by WND, we decided to use WND as our topic forest (after solving the problem with R5 as described). As soon as R2 and R3 are satisfied by WordNet (and there are ongoing efforts in this area [5]), we can start using WordNet (again after cutting off the top abstract levels of topics violating R5). Since every synset in WordNet is mapped to one of the WND topics, our trust model will stay backward compatible with the topics expressed in WND.

Table 2. The results of the satisfaction of the requirements (R1 – R6) by topic hierarchies surveyed. "++" denotes the best choice for the given requirement (if decidable), "+" denotes the suitable choice, "0" could be made suitable, "-" unsuitable.

	R1	R2	R3	R4	R5	R6
Wikipedia	-	-	-	+	-	-
WordNet	+	0	0	+	0	+
YAGO	+	-	-	++	-	+
DDC	+	+	+	-	0	+
WND	+	+	+	-	0	+

3 Algorithm for Computing Topic-Based Trust

In Section 2, we have defined the topic-based trust model, its persistence and the topic forest utilized. What is missing is the actual trust algorithm computing the trust value between two persons based on the trust relations in the social trust network. This part is covered in this section by introducing TopicTrust algorithm (TTA).

The inputs to TTA (see Alg. 1) are the information consumer A (Alice in the financial scenario), the author B_D (Bob in the financial scenario), the topic T_D, the social trust network STN containing node A, and the topic forest TF. TTA involves the execution of two main algorithms – TopicTrustLocal (TTLA) and TidalTrust (TiTA) – represented in Alg. 1 by the corresponding methods calls – `TopicTrustLocal` (Row 5) and `TidalTrust` (Row 6). Alg. 1 introduces in Row 2 a social network $SN_2 = (V, E_2, w)$ different from the social trust network $STN = (V, E)$. SN_2 is the social network required by the authors of TiTA [2, 8]; it has the same set of vertices as STN,

[15] `http://www.oclc.org/dewey/`

the edges E_2 are build iteratively in Row 4, and every edge $e \in E_2$ is weighted by a weighting function w: $E_2 \rightarrow [1..9]$[16].

In Rows 3 – 5, for every two distinct nodes $M, N \in V$, connected by at least one edge (*STN* is a multigraph), the edge (M, N) is added to E_2 (Row 4) and the weight for the edge (M,N) is equal to the value returned by TTLA (Row 5).

TTLA computes the so-called *initial trust value* (*itv*) for all edges between the given nodes M, N, the topic T_D, and the topic forest *TF*. Hence, *itv* represents the quantified summary view on all trust relations between nodes M and N, w.r.t. T_D and *TF* ($itv \in [1..9]$ by the definition of the function w). TTLA is described in more detail in Subsection 3.1; it presents one of the major contributions of the paper.

Thereafter, TiTA (defined in [8,2]) is executed for nodes A (called *source* in [8]), B_D (called *sink* in [8]), and social network SN_2 (Row 6). The output of TiTA (and the whole TTA) is the desired (global) *trust value*, computed according to the formula introduced in Subsection 3.2 and fully discussed in [8, 2]. The computed trust value can be used as the input to the algorithm SRANK of the financial scenario to sort the data sources according to the decreasing trust value.

```
(1) TrustValue TTA(Topic T_D, Node A, Node B_D,
                    SocialTrustNetwork STN(V,E), TopicForest TF) {
(2)    SocialNetwork SN_2 = (V, E_2, w); E_2 = {};
(3)     forall (M,N ∈ V & M ≠ N & ∃(M,N) ∈ E) {
(4)        E_2 = E_2 ∪ ((M,N));
(5)        w((M,N)) = TopicTrustLocal(M, N, STN, T_D, TF); }
(6)     return TidalTrust(A, B_D, SN_2); }
```

Alg. 1. TopicTrust algorithm, the execution of TTLA and TiTA is bolded

TTA supposes that the topic forest *TF* and the social trust network *STN* are available for the execution of TTLA. *STN* is built from the knowledge of the initial node's FOAF file by following and crawling the `foaf:knows` and trust properties (both binary and N-ary) using principles in [6]. Obviously, it is a time-consuming task to rebuild *STN* on-demand for every execution of TTLA, therefore, some tradeoff between performance and timeliness of trust relations is necessary. Typically, the service computing TTA should involve cache, which is holding and periodically updating the local copy of the trust relations in *STN*.

The practical implementation of TTA should integrate both algorithms – TTLA and TiTA – by computing *itv* only when it is required by TiTA (i.e. when the edges of the node M are going to be examined by TiTA, we launch TTLA on the nodes $M, N \in V$, $(M, N) \in E$, to compute *itv* for these edges).

```
TTLA(Node M, Node N, SocialTrustNetwork STN(V,E),
       Topic T_D, TopicForest TF) {
   TopicForest aTF = stepTFM(M, N, STN, T_D, TF);
   return stepITVC(T_D, aTF); }
```

Alg. 2. TopicTrustLocal algorithm, the two major steps – TFM and ITVC are bolded

[16] The interval [1..9] is utilized by the TidalTrust algorithm described in [8].

3.1 Algorithm TopicTrustLocal (TTLA) – Computing the Initial Trust Value

TTLA (see Alg. 2), which computes the initial trust value *itv*, has two major steps – *Topic Forest Marking* (*TFM*, generated by the method `stepTFM` in Row 2) and the *Initial Trust Value Computation* (*ITVC*, generated by the method `stepITVC` in Row 3). The TFM step (Alg. 3) annotates the topics in the topic forest *TF* with the appropriate trust levels found in the trust relations of the social trust network or derived by the TFM step in order to simplify the ITVC step (Alg. 4), which computes the actual *itv* returned by TTLA. The syntactical constructs of the algorithms Alg. 3 and Alg. 4 are detailed below the algorithms in their captions.

The TFM step (Alg. 3) firstly initializes the trust forest *TF*, so that no topic is annotated (Row 2). Then, for each trust relation discovered in *STN* between nodes *M*, *N* (Rows 3 – 10) with the trust level $L \neq$ K, and restricted to the topic *t*, the TFM step annotates the topic *t* in the topic forest *TF* with the trust level *L* (Row 5). In case of binary relations, the special topic "ALL" is annotated (Row 4). Consequently, if the topic *t* is annotated by the trust level T (TP), TTLA annotates all ancestor topics *s* of *t* in the topic hierarchy *TH* ($TH \in TF$ & $t,s \in TH$) with the trust level T (TP), because the author who is trustworthy regarding the particular topic *t* is automatically considered as trustworthy regarding all more general topics in the same topic hierarchy (Rows 6 – 8). If the topic *t* is annotated by the trust level D (DP), TTLA annotates the topic T_D with the trust level D (DP) as long as the topic $T_D \in TH$ is the descendant of $t \in TH$ (Rows 9 – 10). In other words, if Alice distrusts or partially distrusts Bob regarding a topic *t*, then the whole topic hierarchy with the topic *t* as the root is regarded as distrusted. The result of the TFM step (Row 11) is the annotated topic forest *aTF*, which is an input to the ITVC step.

```
(1)  TopicForest stepTFM(Node M, Node N,
         SocialTrustNetwork STN(V,E), Topic T_D, TopicForest TF) {
(2)     forall (Topic t ∈ TF) TF[t] = {};
(3)     forall (Edge e=(M,N) ∈ E) {
(4)        Topic t = TF[e.TOPIC]; if(e.isBinary()) t = TF["ALL"];
(5)        t = t ∪ e.TL;
(6)        if(e.TL == TL.T || e.TL == TL.TP ) {
(7)           while (t.hasParent()) {
(8)               t = t.parent(); t = t ∪ e.TL; }}
(9)       else if (e.TL == TL.D || e.TL == TL.DP ) {
(10)          if (t.ancestorOf(T_D)) T_D = T_D ∪ e.TL; }}
(11)    return TF; }
```

Alg. 3. The TFM step of TTLA – the expression `TF[t]` references the topic $t \in TF$, `e.TOPIC` is the topic restricting the trust relations *e*, `TL.T`, `TL.TP`, `TL.D`, `TL.DP` are shortcuts for the appropriate trust levels according to Table 1. The method `e.isBinary()` is true if and only if the examined trust relation (edge *e*) represents a binary trust property. The method `t.hasParent()` indicates whether the given topic *t* has a parent topic in the topic hierarchy $TH \in TF$, $t \in TH$. Similarly, the method `t.ancestorOf(T_D)` indicates whether the topic *t* is the ancestor of the topic T_D in the topic hierarchy $TH \in TF$, $T_D \in TH$, $t \in TH$.

The Initial Trust Value Computation step (Alg. 4) processes the annotated topic forest *aTF* in a breadth-first search (BFS) way, governed by the queue *q*, and starting from the topic T_D (Row 2). As soon as the currently examined topic t (Row 3) has some annotations in *aTF* prepared by the TFM step (Row 5), the annotations are examined in the order defined in Rows 6 – 9; *itv* is computed by choosing the appropriate trust formula in Table 1 and returned by TTLA (Rows 6 – 9). The variable d in all trust formulas in Table 1 represents the distance between the topic T_D and the topic t currently examined (i.e. the number of relations "isSubtopicOf" between two topics in the same topic hierarchy). Otherwise, if the current topic t does not contain any annotation in *aTF*, its parent and/or child topics are added to the queue q (Rows 10 – 14). The parent topic of the topic t is added to the queue q if and only if the topic t is T_D or an ancestor of the topic T_D. Similarly, the child topics of the topic t are added to the queue q if and only if the topic t is T_D or the descendant of the topic T_D. This behavior corresponds with the BFS processing of *aTF*. If the queue q is empty (Row 3), i.e. all topics in the topic hierarchy involving T_D were examined and no annotation was found, the formula `TABLE_1['K']` is returned as *itv* (Row 15).

Regarding the order in which the annotations are processed, if the topic T_D directly contains annotation `D` or `DP`, these annotations are prioritized against `T` or `TP` (Rows 6 – 9). As long as T_D does not contain any annotation, the parent topic of the topic t can contain only annotations `T` or `TP` (according to Row 10 in Alg. 3) and the children of t can contain only the trust levels `D`, `DP` (according to Rows 7 – 8 in Alg. 3). Since the parent topic of t is added to the queue earlier than all its child topics, later in the computation of the ITVC step (when the topic t $\neq T_D$ is taken from the queue q in Row 3), the annotations `T` and `TP` are prioritized against `D` and `DP`.

If the topic "ALL" contains some markers (see Row 4), the actual topic t taken from the queue q (Row 3) is unimportant, because the consumer trusts the author regarding all topics (as a result, Rows 5 – 9 are always executed).

```
(1)  TrustValue stepITVC(Topic T_D, TopicForest aTF) {
(2)     Queue<Topic> q = {T_D};
(3)     while (q is not empty) { Topic t = q.head();
(4)        if (aTF["ALL"]!= null) t = aTF["ALL"];
(5)        if (aTF[t]!=null) {
(6)           if (TL.D in aTF[t]) return TABLE_1['D'];
(7)           if (TL.DP in aTF[t]) return TABLE_1['DP'];
(8)           if (TL.T in aTF[t]) return TABLE_1['T'];
(9)           if (TL.TP in aTF[t]) return TABLE_1['TP']; }
(10)       else {
(11)          if (t == T_D // t.ancestorOf(T_D))
(12)             if (t.hasParent()) q.push(t.parent());
(13)          if (t == T_D // t.descendantOf(T_D))
(14)             if (t.hasChildren()) q.push(t.children()); }}
(15)    return TABLE_1['K']; }
```

Alg. 4. The ITVC step of TTLA – the method `q.head()` retrieves and removes the head of the queue q. `TABLE_1['X']` refers to the trust formula in Table 1 corresponding to the trust level X. The method `t.descendantOf(T_D)` indicates whether the topic t is the descendant of the topic T_D in the topic hierarchy $TH \in aTF$, $T_D \in TH$, $t \in TH$.

The trust formulas in Table 1 follow the classical distance decay model [24] – with the increasing distance d between the topic T_D and the topic t annotated by the trust level `T` or `TP` (respectively `D` or `DP`), the trust value calculated by the appropriate formula in Table 1 is getting lower (respectively higher) based on the distance *d*. To model the different trust scales (see Table 1), the formulas for the trust levels `TP` and `DP` have the corresponding distance *d* increased by one. The particular magical numbers in trust formulas in Table 1 are selected so that the resulting $itv \in [1..9]$.

3.2 Algorithm TidalTrust (TiTa) – Computing the Trust Value

TiTA is in detail described in [8], we depict here only the core formula (Formula 1) for computing the trust value between nodes *i* and *s* (denoted t_{is}) as the weighted average over distinct *trust relation paths* from *i* to *s*. The trust relation path (or simply *path*) is a progression of edges $(A_1,A_2),(A_2,A_3),\ldots,(A_{N-1},A_N)$ in SN_2, so that $(A_m,A_{m+1}) \in E_2$, $m \in [1..N-1]$, and the ending node of one edge is the starting node of the next edge in the progression of edges (except of the ending node of the last edge). In Formula 1, the expression *adj(i)* describes all nodes connected with the node *i* by the edge in SN_2.

$$t_{is} = \frac{\sum\limits_{j \in adj(i) \mid t_{ij} >= \max} t_{ij} t_{js}}{\sum\limits_{j \in adj(i) \mid t_{ij} >= \max} t_{ij}} \tag{1}$$

TiTA follows the standard rules of network capacity depicted in [2], i.e. the maximum amount of trust that the source can give to the sink is limited to be no larger than the smallest edge weight along that path. Therefore, when $t_{js} > t_{ij}$ in Formula 1 then $t_{js} = t_{ij}$ in the computation of the trust value t_{is}.

The variable *max* in Formula 1 represents the largest trust value that can be used as a minimum threshold for every node, such that a path can be found from the source to the sink which has all initial trust values higher than this threshold. After computing the variable *max*, we restrict the weighted average in Formula 1 to use only edges t_{ij} satisfying the condition $t_{ij} >= max$, which corresponds to the fact that people are more likely to connect with people they trust highly [8].

Furthermore, the shortest path length required to connect the source to the sink is the maximum considered depth of paths in TiTA [8]. Therefore, if there are more paths from the source to the sink, only the shortest paths are considered in the computation of the weighted average in Formula 1. This approach preserves the benefits of shorter path lengths without a priori limiting the length of the path between the source and the sink.

4 TopicTrust Algorithm Evaluation

Due to various ways how to interpret trust on the Web and the fact that the target user of the financial scenario is the average (non-technical) web user, we compared the results of the algorithm SRANK (incorporating TTA) with the results obtained by a panel of ten human subjects[17] not familiar with the research presented here.

[17] People with age between 18 and 27 (with different areas of expertise).

The goal of the human subjects was the same as of the algorithm SRANK – they were asked to rank (in five scenarios) data sources created by different authors and having the fixed topic *T*. Each scenario includes a social trust network *STN* with trust relations between an information consumer and authors of the incoming sources (in a similar way as in Fig. 1). The human subjects were asked to rank according to their comprehension of trust/distrust and with respect to the given impact of the scenario (emphasized criterion). The list of Scenarios 1 – 5 together with their impact and the list of algorithms they evaluate (in parentheses) is in Table 3.

Table 3. The impacts of Scenarios 1 – 5 given to the panel of human subjects and the normalized Spearman's Footrule distance measure (NSF)

The Impact of Scenario	NSF
1: Different types of trust relations in STN, all paths have length 1 (TTLA)	1.29
2: Trust relations with more specific/general topics than *T* (TTLA, TiTA)	0.84
3: The impact of (1) longer trust relation paths and (2) the count of distinct trust relation paths between two nodes (TiTA)	0.97
4: Multiple competing trust relation paths between two nodes (TTLA)	0.89
5: Less trusted first/second trust relations in the trust relation paths (TiTA)	1.52

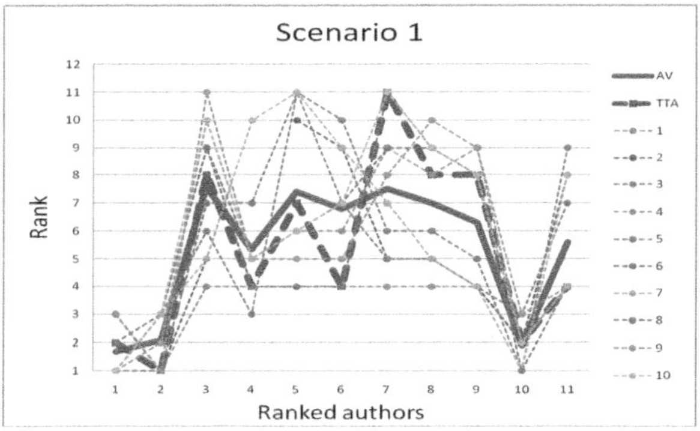

Fig. 2. Scenario 1 – The ranks of the authors according to TTA and human subjects

Fig. 2 illustrates the disagreement between human-ranked results and the results of the algorithm SRANK in Scenario 1. The *x*-axis represents the authors which are ranked; the *y*-axis represents the final rank given to the author by the algorithm SRANK and human subjects. The dotted thin lines (1-10) with circles represent the human-ranked results of the human subjects (1-10), whereas the dotted bold line (TTA) represents results of the algorithm SRANK. The solid bold line (AV) represents the average of all humans' rankings.

The Spearman's Footrule distance measure of the algorithm SRANK's results with respect to the average user's rankings, normalized according to the number of authors in *STN* of the given scenario is depicted for each scenario in Table 3 (NSF column).

Discussion of the Results.[18] Scenario 1 confirms the appropriate comprehension of the basic trust levels (`T`, `TP`, `K`, `DP`, `D`) and partially proofs the suitability of formulas in Table 1. It is surprising that an unknown node (not occurring in the social trust network *STN*) is often ranked lower than a known and distrusted node. Much more differences between the results of the algorithm SRANK and the human's rankings are in the comprehension of distrust. Scenarios 1, 2 and 4 reveal that the concept of distrust is very subjective and must be precisely defined in the guidelines for the trust model usage. Moreover, Scenario 3 shows that in the majority of human rankings, the trust value is decreasing with the increasing length of the trust relation paths between nodes. This behavior should be incorporated to the algorithm SRANK. Scenarios 3 and 5, focusing on the different properties of TidalTrust's Formula 1 in Section 3.2, does not confirm the suitability of the variable *max* in Formula 1, nor the computation of the weighted average itself.

5 Related Work

Goldbeck et al. introduce in [8] a trust algorithm TidalTrust for computing trust in web-based social networks and propose Trust module – an extension to FOAF – for expressing and persisting that "a person trusts others regarding the given topic" [8,2].

The original Trust module (OTM) supported nine trust levels from "absolute trust" to "absolute distrust", both general and topic-based trust concepts. Nevertheless, OTM is no longer available; it was replaced by a simplified version of the Trust module[19] involving just two properties `trusts` and `distrusts`, hence, lacking the support for topics. Our Topic-based Trust module is inspired by OTM, however, differently from OTM, (1) it has only five trust levels for easier interpretation of the trust levels by trust model users and (2) each trust level is expressed (in case of N-ary trust relations) as a property `trustLevel` of an auxiliary class `trustContext`, not directly as a special property of the trusting person. This approach decouples the proposed trust levels from the way of handling N-ary trust relations in RDF. To add, the Topic-based Trust module takes into account the properties of the new version of the Trust Module by making them equivalent with our binary trust properties.

The algorithm TidalTrust incorporates the topic-based trust very superficially – it computes the trust value for a data source with the initial trust values taken as they are persisted in FOAF files. Therefore, the algorithm TidalTrust does not provide any way how to use the information that "user *U* is trusted regarding the topic *T*" when considering topics which are more general or more specific than the topic *T*. Based on the very particular motivation in Section 1, we fill this gap by introducing the algorithm TopicTrustLocal for computing initial trust values (see Section 3.1).

Ziegler and Laursen [22] extensively examined the propagation of trust and distrust in social networks and present Appleseed trust metric as an improved version of the

[18] The questionnaire given to the panel of human subjects (including Scenarios 1 – 5) is available at `http://www.ksi.mff.cuni.cz/~knap/tta/scenariosQ.pdf` and all the result graphs are available at `http://www.ksi.mff.cuni.cz/~knap/tta/scenariosR.pdf`

[19] `http://www.mindswap.org/~golbeck/web/trust.owl`

Advogato[20] trust metric. In comparison with Appleseed metric, our trust metric (TTA) always computes trust between two persons – information consumer and author. On the other hand, Appleseed calculates trust for a collection of nodes at once by energizing the selected node (an information consumer) and spreading the energy to other persons connected by trust relations. The problem of this algorithm is the normalization of the trust value – the more trust relations the person is part of, the less energy (trust) each of these trust relations obtain.

In TTA, we take the trust as a subjective concept, the subjective reliance of one node on another node. The other approach is to compute global reputation of all nodes in the social network using PageRank-like algorithm [15] for `foaf:knows` relations or algorithms for finding experts in social networks [1]. Although these approaches could supplement TTA, they do not consider the individualities of the nodes (their position in the social network), hence, cannot replace TTA.

6 Conclusion and Future Work

We showed in the financial motivational scenario that the generic notion of trust is neither applicable nor reasonable. To that end, we proposed the novel topic-based trust model, and (1) introduced Topic-based Trust Module to persist the trusts model in a FOAF social network, (2) presented the TopicTrust algorithm (TTA) computing the topic-based trust among two persons in the FOAF social network by leveraging the algorithm TidalTrust with the vital concepts of topics, and (3) surveyed the topic hierarchies suitable for classifying the topics used in the trust model and suggested WordNet Domains as the topic hierarchy.

We compared the results of the algorithm SRANK (utilizing TTA) with the results of a panel of human subjects and the preliminary results showed that TTA can extend and improve the ranking algorithms with the important dimension of the topic-based trust in social networks (the Spearman's Footrule distance measure is less than 1 in Scenarios 2-4). Nevertheless, we identified several disputable aspects of the TopicTrustLocal and TidalTrust algorithms as well (see Section 4). Therefore, we plan to analyze the algorithm SRANK in more complex real-world testing scenarios in order to confirm or refute these findings and bring the comprehension of trust and distrust as close as possible to the average information consumers on the Web. In parallel, our future work involves evaluation of the ontology proposed in the Topic-based Trust Module and the research of caching strategies to speed up the processing of trust relations. After that the web service implementing the TopicTrust algorithm will be made available to the users and ranking algorithms.

Acknowledgments. We would like to thank to all volunteers participating in the TopicTrust algorithm evaluation. The work presented in this article has been funded in part by the Czech Science Foundation (GACR, grant numbers 201/09/H057 and P202/10/0573) and GAUK 3110.

[20] `http://www.advogato.org/`

References

1. Breslin, J., et al.: Finding Experts Using Internet-Based Discussions in Online Communities and Associated Social Networks. In: Proceedings of the 1st International Expert Finder Workshop at Knowledge Web General Assembly (2007)
2. Golbeck, J., Parsia, B., Hendler, J.: Trust Networks on the Semantic Web. In: Proceedings of Cooperative Information Agents, Finland (2003)
3. Suchanek, F.M., Kasneci, G., Weikum, G.: Yago – A Core of Semantic Knowledge. In: 16th International World Wide Web Conference (2007)
4. Josang, A., Ismail, R., Boyd, C.: A Survey of Trust and Reputation Systems for Online Service Provisions. Decision Support Systems 43(2), 618–644 (2007)
5. Bentivogli, L., Forner, P., Magnini, B., Pianta, E.: Revising WordNet Domains Hierarchy: Semantics, Coverage, and Balancing. In: Proceedings of COLING 2004 Workshop on Multilingual Linguistic Resources, Switzerland, pp. 101–108 (2004)
6. Bizer, C., Heath, T., Berners-Lee, T.: Linked Data – The Story So Far. International Journal on Semantic Web and Information Systems, IJSWIS (2009)
7. Boyd-Graber, J., Fellbaum, C., Osherson, D., Schapire, R.: Adding Dense, Weighted Connections to WORDNET. In: Proceedings of the Global WordNet Conference (2006)
8. Golbeck, J.: Computing and Applying Trust in Web-based Social Networks. Ph.D. Dissertation (2005)
9. Newman, M.: Models of the small world. J. Stat. Phys. 101, 819–841 (2000)
10. Milgram, S.: The small word problem. Psychology Today 2, 60–67 (1967)
11. Golbeck, J.: Trust and Nuanced Profile Similarity in Online Social Networks. ACM Transactions on the Web (2009) (in press)
12. Miller, G.A.: WordNet: A Lexical Database for English. Communications of the ACM 38(11), 39–41 (1995)
13. Watts, D.: Small Worlds: The Dynamics of Networks between Order and Randomness. Princeton University Press, Princeton (1999)
14. McKnight, D.H., Chervany, N.L.: The Meanings of Trust. Technical Report MISRC Working Paper Series 96-04, University of Minnesota (1996)
15. Page, L., Brin, S., Motwani, R., Winograd, T.: The pagerank citation ranking: Bringing order to the web. Technical report, Stanford Digital Library Technologies Project (1998)
16. Kamvar, S.D., Schlosser, M.T., Garcia-Molina, H.: The eigentrust algorithm for reputation management in P2P networks. In: WWW 2003: Proceedings of the 12th International Conference on World Wide Web, pp. 640–651 (2003)
17. Artz, D., Gil, Y.: A Survey of Trust in Computer Science and the Semantic Web. Journal of Web Semantics: Science, Services and Agents on the World Wide Web (2007)
18. Moreau, L.: The Foundation for Provenance on the Web. Submitted to Foundations and Trends in Web Science (2009)
19. Aleman-Meza, B., et al.: Ranking Complex Relationships on the Semantic Web. IEEE Internet Computing 9(3) (2005)
20. Noy, N., Rector, A. (eds.): Defining N-ary Relations on the Semantic Web. Information W3C Working Group Note (2006)
21. Marsh, C.: Formalising Trust as a Computational Concept. Ph.D. Thesis (1994)
22. Ziegler, C., Lausen, G.: Propagation Models for Trust and Distrust in Social Networks. Information Systems Frontiers 7(4-5), 337–358 (2005)
23. Backett, D. (ed.): RDF/XML Syntax Specification (Revised). W3C Recommendation (2004)
24. Nekola, J.C., White, P.S.: The distance decay of similarity in biogeography and ecology. Journal of Biogeography 26, 867–878 (1999)

Mlogger: An Automatic Blogging System by Mobile Sensing User Behaviors

Jun-Zhao Sun[1,2], Jiehan Zhou[2], and Timo Pihlajaniemi[2]

[1] Academy of Finland, Finland
[2] Department of Electrical and Information Engineering, University of Oulu
Oulu, Finland
{junzhao.sun,jiehan.zhou,tp}@ee.oulu.fi

Abstract. Context-awareness is the leading feature of pervasive computing. Blog is one of the first and key elements in social computing. In the emerging pervasive social computing paradigm, an interesting topic is how to blog with user behaviors automatically associated. In this paper, we present Mlogger, an automatic blogging system that can detect, recognize and track user behaviors and associate them with new blog entries. In the system, Sun SPOTs are used for sensing raw behavioral data. A Mlogger back-end system is designed to process those raw data and infer high-level user behavioral information such as "what the user is doing, and where, when, and with whom?". Associated with the inferred information, a new entry about user behaviors can be created and published automatically.

Keywords: Pervasive social computing, blog, user behavioral information, wireless sensor networks.

1 Introduction

Social computing is the collaborative and interactive aspect of online behavior. The term can be understood in contrast to personal computing, which describes the behavior of isolated users. Social computing represents the intersection of social behavior and computational systems. Social computing is closely related to Web 2.0, which is regarded as the framework of applications supporting the processes of social computing. Blogs, among others, is one of the most popular applications of social computing. Other applications include wikis, Twitter, RSS, instant messaging, multiplayer gaming and open source development, as well as social networking and social bookmarking sites.

Pervasive computing comes into being and penetrates everyday objects and activities. Context awareness is one important component in pervasive computing. The collection of context information relies heavily on various sensors deployed in physical environments. Recent advances in wireless communications and electronics have enabled the development of low-cost, low-power, multifunctional sensor nodes that are small in size and communicate in short distances by wireless radios. These tiny sensor nodes that consist of sensing, data processing, and communicating components, leverage the idea of sensor networks. Sensor networks represent significant

Z. Yu et al. (Eds.): UIC 2010, LNCS 6406, pp. 650–664, 2010.

improvement over traditional sensors. The concept of micro-sensing and wireless connection of sensor nodes promises many new application areas e.g. military, environment, health, home, to name a few.

Merging social computing and pervasive computing promises a new computing paradigm, *pervasive social computing*. One joint point studied in this paper is how to automatically add entries to a blog by tracking users' behaviours. Here, user behavior is the context information, the detection, recognition and tracking of which relies mostly on techniques like various sensor techniques. The relevant user behavioral information is broad, varying from time, location and route to group and activity, and even motion.

Existing research in automatic and context-associated blogging focuses on *geoblogging* [1] that attaches specific geographic location information to blog entries via geotags. *Geotagging* is the process of adding geographical identification metadata to various media such as photographs, video, websites, or RSS feeds and is a form of geospatial metadata [2]. By searching a list of tagged blogs and pictures, users can select areas of specific interest to them on interactive maps. Along with the combination of GPS Phones and GSM localization, geoblogging has led to the *moblogging*, where blog entries are tagged with exact position of the user [3].

In addition to geographic location information, there is other contextual information regarding user behaviors that could be explored for blogging. In this paper, we describe *Mlogger*, an automatic blogging system by mobile sensing the user behavioral information. In Mblogger, we use mobile sensing devices for sensing the user's daily behaviors. Mlogger analyzes and infers the raw data and automatically generates a new post to the user's blog. For the purpose of rapidly prototyping, the mobile sensing devices chosen in this paper is Sun SPOTs, an embedded hardware module that is equipped with accelerometer, temperature and light sensors as well as radio communication capacity.

The remainder of this paper is organized as follows. Section 2 briefly introduces the Sun SPOTs platform. Section 3 analyzes the requirements and proposes the architecture. Detailed design and implementation of front-end and back-end systems are presented in Section 4 and 5, respectively. Section 6 analyzes related work. Finally, Section 7 concludes the paper.

2 Mlogger Platform

The platform for developing Mlogger is Sun SPOT [4], as shown in Fig. 1. Sun SPOT (Sun Small Programmable Object Technology) is an embedded hardware modules developed by Sun Microsystems as an experimental platform for developers to build sensor-based devices and applications. The dimension is only 41x23x70 mm, of 54 grams. The device is equipped with a 180 MHz 32 bit ARM920T CPU, 512K RAM, and 4M Flash memory. It also includes three on-board sensors, accelerometer, temperature and light sensors. It has the USB interface for connecting to a PC.

SPOT communicates using 2.4 GHz IEEE 802.15.4 radio with integrated antenna, including the base-station approach for networking. In addition to the free-range Sun SPOTS, there are also basestation Sun SPOTs. The basestation connects to a development machine (e.g. a PC) and allows the developer to write programs that can run on the PC and use the basestation's radio to communicate with remote Sun SPOTs, and also to deploy and debug applications on remote Sun SPOTs. SPOT supports mesh network by using IPv6/LowPan and AODV (Ad-hoc On-demand Distance Vector) protocols for ad hoc multihop networking and routing.

(a) A Sun SPOT (b) A typical configuration

Fig. 1. Sun SPOT platform and a typical configuration of a multi-hop network

The Sun SPOT is a Java programmable embedded device designed for flexibility. It is programmed almost entirely in Java to allow regular programmers to create projects that used to require specialized embedded system development skills. It is built on the Squawk, an open-source J2ME CLDC 1.1 and MIDP 1.0 capable Java Virtual Machine. Standard Java IDEs (e.g. NetBeans) can be used to create Sun SPOT applications. The development tools also include an Emulator that is capable of running a Sun SPOT application on a PC for testing a program before deploying it to a real SPOT, or if a real SPOT is not available.

One of the major design goals of Sun SPOTs was to provide a tool for rapidly prototyping sensor-based applications. There have been a number of projects based on it. We choose it to be the platform of our project mostly because it is able to sense surroundings and easy to program.

3 Mlogger Design Requirements and Architecture

A Mlogger scenario we consider in this paper is described as follows.

A user brings a free-range Sun SPOT all the time when he is in his daily routine. The SPOT keeps recording, periodically, the surroundings by sensing the environmental data. When the free-range SPOT carried by the user is in the range of a basestation SPOT, the free-range SPOT uploads all the samples to the basestation. The computer is able to analyze the data, to infer the information like what the user was doing, and when, where, how and with whom. The inferred information will be eventually constructed into one post that can be sent to the user's blog.

To realize the above scenario, we need a Mlogger system in the support of sensing and recording raw data involved in the moments of a mobile user, and generating raw data into high-level information about who was doing what, where, when and how.

The key functionalities lie in data collection and data processing. The former relates to how the flow of sensing data is sampled, transmitted and stored, while the latter concerns how to analyze and explain the data to obtain high-level information related to user behavior. Other design requirements are on data storage, data illustration, new blog post creation and publishing, setting capacities, performance, etc.

We propose the Mlogger architecture illustrated in Fig. 2. As shown in the figure, the system consists of three parts: SPOTs, host PC, and blog server. SPOTs connect to host PC via wireless network, through basestation SPOT that is connected to the host PC by USB cable. The host PC has connection to the Internet, so that new posts can be uploaded to a particular blog site specified by the user.

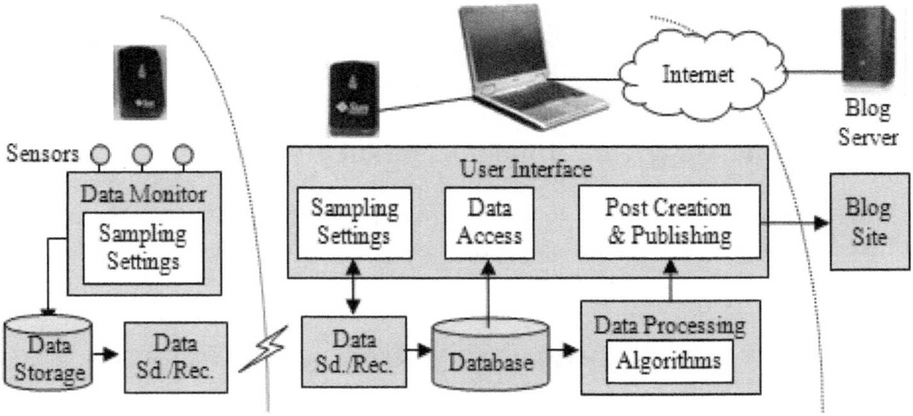

Fig. 2. Mlogger Architecture Overview

The core module inside SPOTs is the data monitor. It keeps sensing the surroundings by using the equipped sensors according to the sampling setting parameters like sample rate and duration. As the SPOT is moving with the user, the basestation SPOT is not always available in range. Therefore, data samples as well as the corresponding time stamp need to be first stored to the local Flash memory, and later sent to the host PC when the basestation is available. The architecture allows multiple SPOTs to share one host PC. In this case, each SPOTs is recognized to be one user.

Consequently, the sampling data in SPOT is transmitted to the host PC in a stream, which is organized into tables and stored into a database. The sensing parameters can be read and set by the user with a sampling settings interface. Data stored in the database can be retrieved with various conditions by the user. Two common ways of data access are snapshot query and time-based query. The snapshot query returns all the data fields for a given time point, while time-based query shows a specific attribute changing over a time interval.

Raw sensing data is not the purpose. Instead, what really of interest is the information about user's activities. The host PC is responsible for processing the raw data by using a data processing module, for analyzing the data stored in the database, detecting special events, and recognizing user's behavior. Advanced algorithms are needed for the analysis, event detection and behavior recognition. After behavior recognition, the user can interact with the blog server for updating and publishing a new post to his blog. Publishing a new post to a blog site is straightforward, since most blog service provider provides simple protocol and data API for making new posts.

The Mlogger system can be easily divided into two parts:

- The front-end software is to operate on free-range SPOTs to sample data and send to the basestations.
- The back-end software is to operate on host PC to collect and store data, show and analyze data, and create and publish new posts to user's blog.

The two parts of software communicate with each other for sending/receiving sensor data as well as new settings. The following two sections describes the software design of the two parts.

4 Front-End Design and Implementation of Mlogger

The main task of the front-end software in free-range SPOTs is to sample, in a periodical fashion, data from all the on-board sensors, and transmit data to the basestation whenever it is in the radio range. The class diagram is shown in Fig. 3.

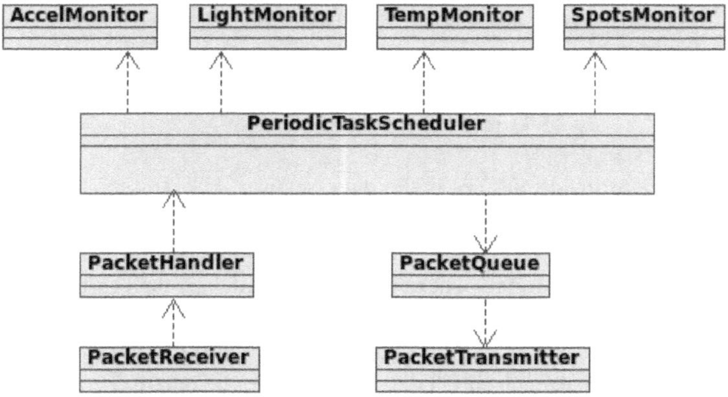

Fig. 3. Front-end class diagram

1. The core of the structure is the PeriodicTaskScheduler class, which is provided for running a task, such as taking samples, at a regular interval using the timer/counter hardware. The PeriodicTaskScheduler class also tries to establish a radio connection with the basestation SPOT and host PC, by periodically broadcasting a connection request and listen to response on a pre-defined port number. When the basestation is found and a radiogram connection has been established, the routine will setup both PacketReceiver and PacketTransmitter services to handle communications with the host PC in terms of data and settings transmissions.

2. The PacketReceiver class is used to receive commands from the host application and dispatch them to PacketHandler class to handle the command. Possible packet types include packet used to specify new settings to the sensor monitors, to request current settings of the monitors, and to request a status report. The PacketTransmitter class handles sending reply packets back to the host PC in response to the received requests. It also packages the sensor readings together with its time stamp into a radio datagram and send to the host PC. Data packets are put into a PacketQueue first, and will not be sent out until the connection is established.

3. The AccelMonitor class controls and reads data from the SPOT's accelerometer according to the local settings, and sends the host a telemetry stream of accelerometer readings via Radiogram packets. The local settings include the scale, calibration, and sample interval. Readings sent to the host PC include time stamp, current acceleration, magnitude of the current total acceleration, relative acceleration, as well as the inclination or tilt of one axis with respect to the total acceleration.

4. The TempMonitor class controls and reads data from the SPOT's temperature sensor according to the local settings, and sends the host a telemetry stream of temperature readings via Radiogram packets. Each reading is associated with the time stamp which is sent together with the data in one packet.

5. The LightMonitor class controls and reads data from the SPOT's light sensor according to the local setting on the sample interval, and sends the host a telemetry stream of light sensor readings via Radiogram packets. The return value is of integer type ranging from 0 to 740. Each light sample is associated with the time stamp which is sent together with the data in one packet.

6. The SpotsMonitor class implements the function of recording all the other free-range as well as basestation SPOTs met by the current SPOT, by periodically broadcasting a connection request and listen to response on a pre-defined port number. Once a response datagram is received, the IEEE address is extracted from the datagram and sent to the host PC together with the time stamp.

5 Back-End Design and Implementation of Mlogger

In general, the sensor data is sent to the base station SPOT that further moves the data into the host PC via USB cable. In the PC phase, the data is tabularized, saved and presented both as tables and as diagrams with time as x-axis. Furthermore, the data is processed to find out when and what happened to whom. The result of this processing is sent to a blog site. Below we first introduce the design of the database, classes and user interface. We then explain the data processing algorithms. Finally, we describe the blog entry creation and publishing.

5.1 Database, Class Structure, and User Interfaces

1. Database. The Mlogger database is the center of operations of the host PC tasks. It contains several tables for all the data and settings used in the system, including

- A Settings table containing the user preferences of the SPOT users, that can be retrieved from there when new settings are sent to the free range SPOTs.
- A Readings table containing the sensor data received from the free range SPOTs, that can be retrieved and displayed.
- A contact table containing all the met SPOTs in form of the IEEE 64-bit addresses and groups, to be used for activity recognition.
- A behavior table containing the sequence of recognized activities together with the time-location information.
- A blog entries table containing entries are not sent right away, from where the user may retrieve them and edit them.

The interface between the Java code and the MySQL code is the mysql-connector-java plugin.

2. Class structure. Fig. 4 illustrates the class structure of the host PC tasks. The listening, packet handling and receiving are performed by the DataReceiverSaver class. This class also creates an instance of the ActionSolver class, which then does the data processing as regards the deriving of the context information from raw data.

The DataReceiverSaver listens for transmissions of free range SPOTs at port number 43. If the IEEE address of a transmitting SPOT matches one in the Settings table, the new settings are sent over. The host also listens for transmissions of free range SPOTs at port 67 for the incoming sensor data to be saved into the Readings table.

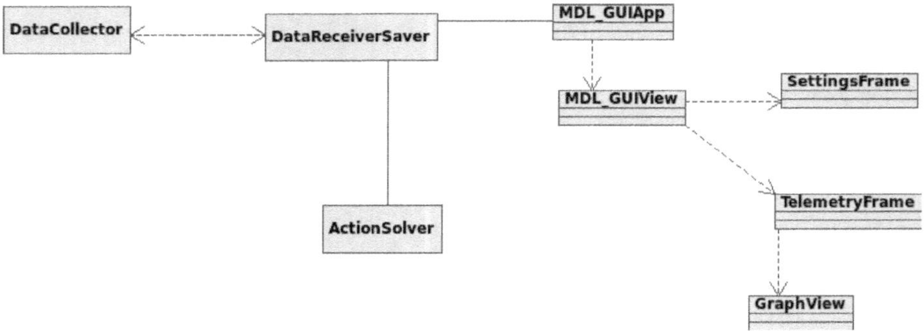

Fig. 4. Back-end class diagram

3. User interface. The user interface is handled by the MDL_GUIView class, which is an extension of the FrameView interface. Its main window's File menu has two choices: SPOTSettings and Logs. The former open the Settings GUI that lets the user enter the desired settings into the MySQL database table Settings for safekeeping, and then send them to the user's free range SPOT on the basis of the its IEEE address. The latter opens a Jdialog window with three choices: Light Sensor Log, Temp Sensor Log, and Acceleration Log. By entering the IEEE address of a SPOT, the log is rendered on the basis of the sensor data saved in the Readings database table.

5.2 Data Processing Algorithms

The algorithms are used to analyze raw readings to derive information including when, who, what, and where, as described below.

1. When. Timing information is easy to be obtained, as each sensor data is associated with a time stamp. To construct the new entry to blog, only start time of any new activity is needed.

2. Who. With the SpotsMonitor class in front-end free-range SPOT, all the other free-range as well as basestation SPOTs met by the user's SPOT will be recorded in form of the IEEE address. At the host PC, user is able to group these SPOTs into different groups. The groups include hosts, family, friends, colleagues, classmates, strangers, and so forth. This forms a Contact Table, as an example shown in Table 1, which is saved in the database.

Table 1. Example Contact Table

Address	Type	Name	Group
0014.4F01.0000.2E20	basestation	Home PC	host
0014.4F01.0000.2E21	basestation	Office PC	host
0014.4F01.0000.2E22	free-range	Juliet	family
0014.4F01.0000.2E23	free-range	Kitty	family
0014.4F01.0000.2E24	free-range	Bob	friends
0014.4F01.0000.2E25	free-range	Boss	colleagues
0014.4F01.0000.2E26	free-range	Eric	colleagues
0014.4F01.0000.2E27	free-range	Sb. 1	strangers

3. What. The user's activity can be detected and recognized by analyzing the raw sensor data, in particular the accelerometer data to classify the motions. The recognition method is based on a set of IF-THEN fuzzy rules as follows.

```
IF  SPOT's Motion is Still  THEN  Activity is Staying;
IF  SPOT's Motion is Low    THEN  Activity is Driving;
IF  SPOT's Motion is Medium THEN  Activity is Biking;
IF  SPOT's Motion is High   THEN  Activity is Walking;
IF  SPOT's Motion is Extreme THEN  Activity is Running;
```

In the rules, the feature "SPOT's Motion" is calculated by:

SPOT's Motion = AVG (abs(acceleration magnitude-1.0)),

where shifting window size is 5s (30 samples by default settings) with 50% window overlap.

As no training data set is available at the moment, there is no way to train the fuzzy classifier to learn, and thus the classifier is designed from prior knowledge and expertise based on empirical data as shown in Fig 5 [5]. Accordingly, the membership functions are defined in Fig. 6.

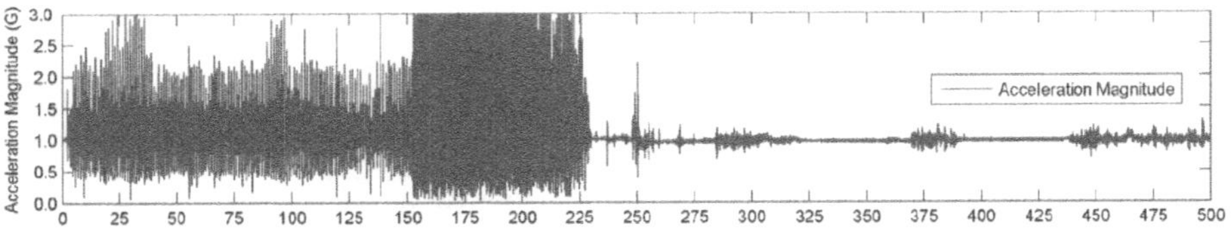

Fig. 5. The sample sensor trace with the user walking for ~150 seconds, then running until the ~225 second mark, then entering a car and driving for the remainder of the recording (with stops at the ~260 and ~325 second marks, and parking in a lot starting at the ~450 second mark). [5].

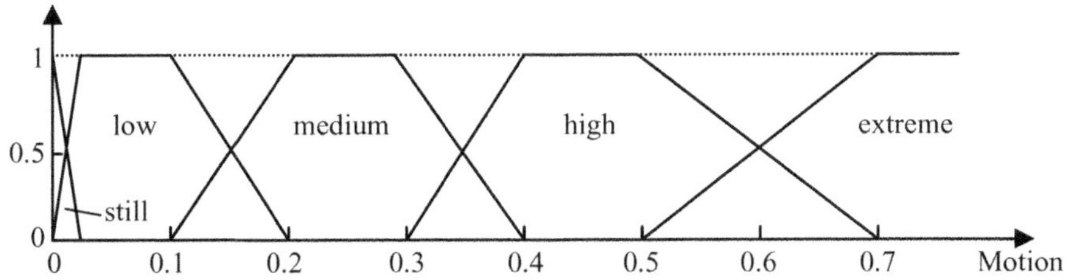

Fig. 6. Membership functions for the linguistic terms of Motion

4. Where. It is not easy to detect where the user is, without having any geographical information obtained from e.g. GPS or cellular tower. However, in this paper, in particular for the purpose of blogging, we are more interested in the places where user stays in, instead of the location where the user is at. A user's daily routine appears to be changing between different places at different time. The changes of user's locations are interleaved by movements of some ways like walking, running, biking or driving. A finite state machine (FSM) is shown in Fig. 7 to illustrate the situation. At any moment, a user is either at state "At-place", meaning a fixed place like home, office, restaurant, supermarket, or "On-road", meaning the periods of changing the places. After the "On-road", the user may move to a new place or return back to the original place.

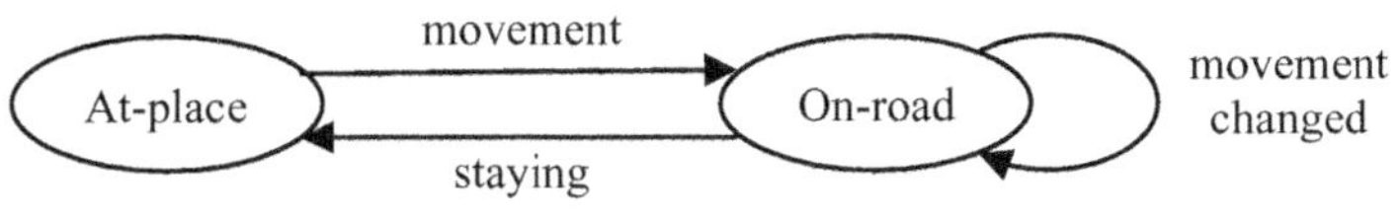

Fig. 7. State machine for modeling user behavior

As described above, user's activity at a time (i.e. status of motion: staying, walking, running, biking or driving) can be detected. In consequence, user's activity can be modeled by a sequence of moving status interleaved by staying. According to the activity information, user's current state can be determined. Fig. 8 shows an example sequence of place changing and movements over a weekday. It is worth noting here that user in movement, for example walking at home or in the office, does not necessarily means the state is On-road. Similarly, the status of staying does not directly lead to an At-place state, in considering the examples of short stop during biking and car stop because of traffic light.

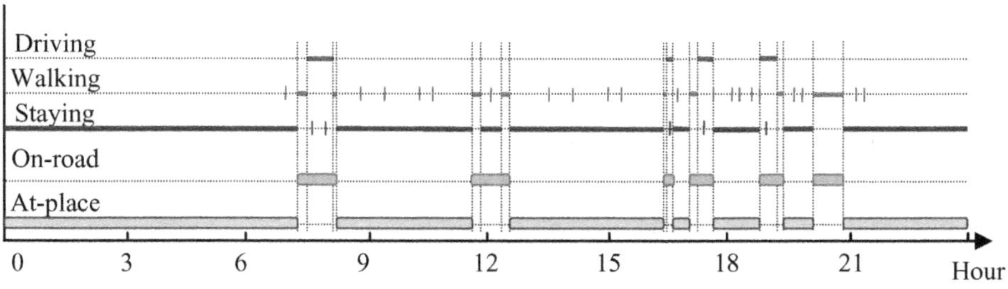

Fig. 8. State determination based on activities. The short thin vertical lines represents short period of walking and staying that have been considered as invalid and thus absorbed.

The algorithm for assigning a state to a motion is given below.

```
IF (Motion==Staying) THEN
    IF (Valid(Motion) THEN State=At-place;
    ELSE State=On-road;
          //to absorb short staying between movements
ELSE      //Motion is not Staying
    IF (Valid(Motion)) THEN State=On-road;
    ELSE State=At-place;
          //to absorb short movement between staying
```

In the algorithm, two filtering rules are defined to absorb the temporary activities. A Boolean function Valid is used to test if a motion is temporary activity or valid one. The function is defined according to prior knowledge and empirical data, as given in Table 2. Fig. 8 also shows the state transitions for the sequence of activity in the same figure.

Table 2. Valid of motions

Motion	Staying	Walking	Running	Biking	Driving
Motion period	>90s	>60s	>30s	>20s	>10s
Valid(Motion)	T	T	T	T	T

Next, when state is At-place, we need to determine at what place the user is exactly during the period. To recognize a user's current place needs to jointly consider the information of "who" and "when", i.e. which SPOTs are met during the period and at what time. In doing this, user's input on the names of the most possibly visited places is needed, as well as the association with the SPOTs in his contact list and the time in a day.

Table 3 shows a typical example. It is worth noting that the table is for weekday only. For weekend, another table can be given by using the same way. Also, in the last row of Table 3 the most possible place is given, in case nobody is met during a whole At-place state, with respect to the majority of time staying at the At-place state.

With such a table in mind, the place recognition algorithm is nothing more than to firstly determine who have been met during the At-place state duration, and next search the table to assign a appropriate place accordingly. When multiple SPOTs have been met during one At-place state, the one list first in the table is adopted. In other words, contacts in the table have different priorities. For example if the user met both the Home PC and Kitty during 9:00 to 11:00, then the user is at home instead of day-care; if the user met both Kitty and Juliet during 11:00 to 13:00, then the user is at daycare instead of cafeteria. Detailed description of the algorithm is omitted here.

Table 3. User's input on places in association with met SPOTs and time in a weekday

	21:00-7:00	7:00-9:00	9:00-11:00	11:00-13:00	13:00-17:00	17:00-19:00	19:00-21:00
Home PC	home	home	home	home	home	home	home
Kitty	home	home	daycare	daycare	daycare	home	home
Juliet	home	home	elsewhere	cafeteria	elsewhere	elsewhere	home
Bob	home	home	elsewhere	cafeteria	elsewhere	elsewhere	elsewhere
Boss	work	work	work	cafeteria	work	work	work
Strangers	home	home	work	cafeteria	work	elsewhere	home
None	home	home	work	cafeteria	work	elsewhere	home

5.3 Blogging

The user whose action has been deciphered has to have the option of editing or deleting the blog entry prior to sending. However, prior to this phase, the user needs to save his or her desired settings and preferences to the SPOT via the MySQL database or use default settings. If the mobile user has decided to apply manual blog entry editing, he or she will need to perform that function prior to the sending, or the entry is not sent

In our implementation, the user's blog is chosen to be at site blogspot, with an account named mobilelogger (URL: http://mobilelogger.blogspot.com/). In Fig. 4, the DataReceiverSaver class also takes care of the blogging of the result of the processing, using the libraries and API of com.google.gdata, provided by Google. The object instance of com.google.gdata.client.blogger.BloggerService is created in the main method of DataReceiverSaver, and given as parameter to its run()-method.

Blogging can be conducted in a periodical fashion, for example once every half an hour. This is easy and straightforward, but of less accuracy and efficiency. Our approach is to choose the time to perform the blogging to be at the moments when "situation is changed". The idea is based on the fact that, interesting events worthy of blogging usually happens during particular time interval with some changes of related observations like user's activity and temperature. Here, situation is defined to be all the information regarding the user, including the recognized information about where, who and what as well as the temperature and light information obtained from the sensors at the time. Assume one new entry is going to cover the happenings of one whole day. One line in the entry corresponds to a particular event that might be interesting to the user to enrich with his/her detailed experience, feelings, thoughts, etc. Followings are the cases that a new line is to be inserted.

- New lines need to be inserted to a new blog entry whenever the user's place is changed.
- Also, line inserting is to be done at the event when user meets a free-range or basestation SPOT) or the SPOT met before has gone.
- Similarly, events are significant and need to be put into an entry when user's movement status is changed.
- Finally, significant changes of temperature and light are to be marked in an entry. For temperature and light, a change is defined as when:

  abs (AVG (values (t to t+30s))-AVG (values (t-30s to 5)) > Threshold.

  For temperature, the threshold is set to 2 Celcius; for light, it is set to 25. In other words, the temperature is categorized into bins of width 2 Celcius, and for light the width of bins is 25.

6 Related Work

The work presented in this paper is closely related to two research areas, one is human behaviour recognition and modelling, the other is automatic and context-associated blogging.

The problem of behaviour recognition and modelling has been an active research topic for a long time, and still remains very challenging. There has been a huge number of research carried out in many communities, such as computer vision and graphics, AI and pattern recognition, context-awareness for pervasive and ubiquitous computing, smart environment, intelligent user interface, social computing, and data mining. It would not be possible and necessary to go through all the existing solutions on this direction in this paper.

Almost all the existing research aim to recognize human behaviour to the best accuracy. One the other hand, the behaviour to be recognized is expected to be as exact as possible. One difference of our work from the existing research is that its goal of successful recognition is in a coarse-grained fashion. Our work does not require very precise recognition of user's exact behavior . For example, it would be enough to know that user is at home, no matter he is seating in a sofa or lying in bed. The information provided by the recognition algorithms is to be used as a reminder to the blogger who is going to edit, change, and correct the suggestions and add more details when creating new entry to his blog.

Existing research in automatic and context-associated blogging are mainly in the area of *geoblogging* [1]. Geoblogging attaches specific geographic location information to blog entries via geotags. *Geotagging* [2] is the process of adding geographical identification metadata to various media such as photographs, video, websites, or RSS feeds and is a form of geospatial metadata. These data usually consist of latitude and longitude coordinates, though they can also include altitude, bearing, distance, accuracy data, and place names. In *Moblogging* [3], blog entries are tagged with exact position of the user.

While the basic idea of Geoblogging is the same as ours: tagging blog entries with extra metadata, we are aiming at broader context association than only geographical information. This of course depends on the rich availability of sensors in various modalities as well as corresponding data processing and information fusion algorithms for behavioral recognition.

7 Discussions

In this paper, we aim to practice the merging of the two popular computing paradigms, pervasive and social computing, by proposing Mlogger, a novel architecture and system for blogging with user behavioral information automatically associated. Using Sun SPOTs as the platform for collecting real-time data like moving, temperature, and light. Off-line data processing is employed to detect, recognize and track user behavior and associates it with new blog entries.

Regarding the proposed architecture, it is important to note that, even though the proposed architecture places the data processing algorithms into the back-end (i.e., the host PC), an alternative way is to put simple algorithms into the front-end (i.e. the free-range Sun SPOTs) which enables the activity recognition being conducted immediately over the raw readings. In this way, the time and energy for transmitting a big amount of raw data can be saved, because only the recognition results need to be sent to the host PC. This is only applicable to algorithms that do not need very much history data, or the case in which algorithms need to be adjusted or changed during the operation.

As for the front-end design, by putting data processing algorithms to front-end, only the activity recognition results need to be sent to the back-end. In our design however, all raw readings are transmitted. Between the two extreme choices, one compromised approach is that, the Sun SPOTs receive event subscriptions from the host PC applications, and notify host applications only when the events occur. In the simplest case, subscribed events are represented in the form of upper and lower thresholds to the sensor readings.

For recognizing user's activity, as the main focus of this paper is in proposing the architecture instead of the activity recognition, we use relatively simple approach here based on fuzzy-rules. More advanced methods for activity recognition based on accelerometer can be found in [6-13]. One reason is that, data needed for training advanced models is not available at the moment. Moreover, as behavioral information is just used as reminder for user blogging, the required accuracy is not as high as other context-aware applications.

It is not easy to detect the user's position without having any geographical information. Fortunately, given the output information on when, who, and what that have been recognized, plus temperature and light samples, we can recognize user's current places by fusing all the available information with suitable algorithms. Obviously, time plays a very clear role in determining user's location. Thus, models conditioned on both the hour of day as well as weekday or weekend need to be developed for clustering locations and sequence of locations, provided that training data is available.

In this paper however, since no training data is available, we use a sample approach based on empirical knowledge. When training data is available, the model can be detailed by separating each day (Monday, Tuesday, etc.) in one week, and small time interval (e.g. every 15 min) in a day.

We plan to extend our model in a number of ways. First, we are going to get the prototype fully evaluated, to be deeply aware of the field experience and to gather feedback from users, as well as to evaluate and improve the adopted algorithms.

Secondly, when enough data has been collected from long-term running of the prototype, the proposed algorithms are to be trained with parameters learned and adjusted.

Third, new advanced algorithms are to be developed and tested. On this direction, there are following things under plan: 1) to develop new advanced algorithms that take advantage of e.g. HMM, neural networks, and other AI techniques; 2) to employ more sophisticated signal processing techniques, for example to differentiate the 3-axis data, to use FFT to find out the frequency features, to explore the periodical features in walking, running and biking; 3) to elaborate user activities and locations, for example to name more places user frequently visits. Currently the information of user activity and location is too coarse. 5) to consider and fuse with other sensor data obtained from various sources, like light, temperature, etc.

Finally, we are planning to use some other platforms with more capacities in environment and user sensing. More and more advanced smart phones are released onto the market, like Apple iPhone, Nokia Nseries, Google Nexus One. These devices are equipped with a lot of sensors including 1) wireless connectivity like 2G/2.5G/3G, Wi-Fi, Bluetooth, IrDA, radio, etc.; 2) user interfaces like keyboard, touch screen, microphone, camera, etc.; 3) embedded sensors like ambient light sensor, accelerometer, compass, barometer and temperature sensor, light phototransistor, humidity sensor, etc. By using the extremely rich capacity of sensing the surroundings, a lot of data and information can be obtained, which enables more accurate and detailed recognition of user behavior as well as more fancy applications.

Acknowledgement. The financial support by the Academy of Finland (Project No. 113950) is gratefully acknowledged. The authors would like to thank the students in Software Project course, Hongwei Ge and Fang Yang for implementing the front-end part of the Mlogger system.

References

1. Geoblogging, Wikipedia, `http://en.wikipedia.org/wiki/Geotagging`
2. Geotagging, Wikipedia, `http://en.wikipedia.org/wiki/Geotagging`
3. Moblogging, Wikipedia, `http://en.wikipedia.org/wiki/Mobile_blogging`
4. SunSPOTWorld, `http://www.sunspotworld.com/`
5. Welbourne, E., Lester, J., LaMarca, A., Borriello, G.: Mobile Context Inference Using Low-Cost Sensors. In: Strang, T., Linnhoff-Popien, C. (eds.) LoCA 2005. LNCS, vol. 3479, pp. 254–263. Springer, Heidelberg (2005), doi:10.1007/11426646_24
6. Michael, K., McNamee, A., Michael, M.G., Tootell, H.: Location-Based Intelligence – Modeling Behavior in Humans using GPS. In: Proceedings of the International Symposium on Technology and Society (ISTAS 2006), New York (June 2006), doi:10.1109/ISTAS.2006.4375889

7. Ermes, M., Parkka, J., Mantyjarvi, J., Korhonen, I.: Detection of Daily Activities and Sports With Wearable Sensors in Controlled and Uncontrolled Conditions. IEEE Transactions on Information Technology in Biomedicine 12(1), 20–26 (2008), doi:10.1109/TITB.2007.899496
8. Eagle, N., Pentland, A.: Eigenbehaviors: Identifying Structure in Routine. Behavioral Ecology and Sociobiology 63(7), 1057–1066 (2009), doi:10.1007/s00265-009-0830-6
9. Baek, J., Lee, G., Park, W., Yun, B.-J.: Accelerometer Signal Processing for User Activity Detection. In: Negoita, M.G., Howlett, R.J., Jain, L.C. (eds.) KES 2004. LNCS (LNAI), vol. 3215, pp. 610–617. Springer, Heidelberg (2004)
10. Jia, N.: Detecting Human Falls with a 3-Axis Digital Accelerometer. Analog Dialogue 43 (July 2009)
11. Brezmes, T., Gorricho, J.-L., Cotrina, J.: Activity Recognition from Accelerometer Data on a Mobile Phone. In: Omatu, S., Rocha, M.P., Bravo, J., Fernández, F., Corchado, E., Bustillo, A., Corchado, J.M. (eds.) IWANN 2009. LNCS, vol. 5518, pp. 796–799. Springer, Heidelberg (2009), doi:10.1007/978-3-642-02481-8_120
12. Lee, M.-h., Kim, J., Kim, K., Lee, I., Jee, S.H., Yoo, S.K.: Physical Activity Recognition Using a Single Tri-Axis Accelerometer. In: Proceedings of the World Congress on Engineering and Computer Science (WCECS 2009), San Francisco, USA, vol. 1, pp. 14–17 (October 2009)
13. Jeong, D.-U., Do, K.-H., Chung, W.-Y.: Implementation of the Wireless Activity Monitoring System Using Accelerometer and Fuzzy Classifier. International Journal of Information Systems for Logistics and Management 3(2), 115–120 (2008)

Managing Workplace Resources in Office Environments through Ephemeral Social Networks

Lijun Zhu[1,2], Alvin Chin[1], Ke Zhang[1], Wenchang Xu[3], Hao Wang[1], and Li Zhang[2]

[1] Nokia Research Center, Beijing, 100176, China
{ext-lijun.2.zhu,alvin.chin,ke.4.zhang,hao.ui.wang}@nokia.com
[2] Department of Electronic Engineering, Tsinghua University, Beijing, 100084, China
wencxu@gmail.com
[3] Department of Computer Science and Technology, Tsinghua University, Beijing, 100084, China
chinazhangli@mail.tsinghua.edu.cn

Abstract. With the ubiquity of mobile devices, GPS and WiFi, location-based social networking services are developing rapidly. The rise of services such as Foursquare and Google Buzz, enable users to instantaneously in real-time report their activity to online social networks around the places they visit. The people that we encounter and connect with around physical resources such as meetings, provide opportunities for extending our social networks which are rarely captured. In this paper, we designed and deployed an indoor location-based resource management and social networking system called Nokia Find & Connect for managing workplace resources and enabling social networking in office environments. Central to our system is the concept of an ephemeral social network, temporary networks that are created for a specific time and event like a meeting. We carried out a trial to study the impact of our system on managing office resources and creating ephemeral social networks. Results show that Nokia Find & Connect inspired people to make new friends and provided great convenience when people book or are about to have a meeting.

Keywords: Mobile social network, workplace management, ephemeral social network, location-based services, opportunistic networking.

1 Introduction

With the ubiquity of mobile devices and network technology, online social networking sites (OSNs) have blossomed during the past few years, however they are not integrated with real life. For example, in the office, people often cannot find the meeting and do not remember if they have met the person nearby. In current OSNs, it is tedious and error prone for people to manually update their personal

Z. Yu et al. (Eds.): UIC 2010, LNCS 6406, pp. 665–679, 2010.

status when changing location or activity. Adding positioning technologies such as GPS to mobile devices that are combined with the OSN can be a feasible solution to the above problems, as have been implemented by Foursquare and Google Buzz.

According to Jyri Engestrom, "social networks consist of people who are connected by a shared object" which he calls object-centred sociality [1]. For example, in Flickr, the social objects are the photos which users tag, comment and share with others. Therefore, the problem yet to be solved is how to use the resources in the physical environment (like the office) to help facilitate social networking and vice versa. Physical resources are social objects where people connect to each other. In the office, the meeting room is the shared social object because people meet there. In addition, physical resource management is difficult because current systems assume that users will notify the system if they are not using that resource. In the office, there is commonly a shortage of meeting rooms when in actuality, many of these rooms are not used.

Our research questions are the following. First, how can positioning and social networking technologies be used to efficiently manage office resources. Second, how can ephemeral social networks be used to improve current social networking protocols, where ephemeral social networks are created based on opportunistic encounters that occur for a short time period during a specific activity. Inspired by the demands of managing office resources and the concept of object-centred sociality, we designed and developed a location-based social networking solution for workplace and office management called Nokia Find & Connect(NF&C) that uses the workplace resources such as meeting rooms and desks as social objects. Our major contributions are two-fold, first, we present NF&C as a system and user interface for efficiently managing office resources dynamically and locating rooms and people, forming the basis for social networking. Second, we conduct a real-life case study of NF&C by deploying it in our office to demonstrate its viability.

This paper is organized as follows. Section 2 describes background and related work. Section 3 explains the motivation and describes the system, functionality and user interface of NF&C. In Section 4, we analyze the data collected from our office trial to determine its usage, system efficiency and validity. Finally, Section 5 concludes the paper and discusses areas for future work.

2 Background and Related Work

2.1 Location-Based Services (LBS)

We are seeing an increasing number of commercial LBSes (eg. Foursquare and Google Buzz) as well as research LBSes (Intel's PlaceLab [2] and MIT's iFind [3]). However, most of these efforts have focused on accuracy improvement and ignored their impact on the social network. Barkhuus et al [4] discussed how the awareness of location people experienced of each other affected their self-presentation, but did not mention about the affection on the social network.

Tsai et al [5] also described their location-sharing application, but focused more on the impact of feedback. WhozThat [6] builds a system that ties together online social networks with mobile phones, but does not utilize the advantage of location awareness to bring convenience. However, many of the previous systems fail to exploit how mobile social interactions can be recorded and used to create and maintain social networks.

2.2 Indoor Positioning

Indoor positioning technology uses either sensors or wireless LAN (WLAN) for location tracking and navigation. There are many sensor-based indoor positioning systems such as infrared sensing [7, 8], ultrasonic sensing [9, 10], and radio frequency identification (RFID) [11, 12]. However, these systems are dependent on specific device and network, are limited in sensing range (usually less than 1 meter), and are complex to deploy. On the other hand, WLAN-based positioning [13, 14] has wide coverage and does not require additional hardware. WLAN-based positioning can be based on propagation model [13, 15] or machine learning [13, 16]. Considering existing techniques and our actual demand, we decided to choose the machine learning WLAN-based positioning technique to build our positioning system.

2.3 Proximity-Based Systems and Opportunistic Networking

Many applications of social proximity-sensing software are based on ephemeral social networks and proximity encounters. Eagle and Pentland [17] review some of this work which include LoveGetty, SocialNet and Jabberwocky. The proximity encounters, which can be detected by RF or Bluetooth, can be used for introducing people directly and making inferences about a user's social network like Serendipity [17] or for finding people nearby and suggesting people to add based on frequency of encounters like Aka-Aki [18]. This relates to the concept of the "familiar stranger" [19] where people often pass by or encounter others but do not know them, otherwise known as opportunistic networking [20]. Mobile social networks can use opportunistic contacts for friend recommendations [21] and for collaborative internet access [22], yet there still does not exist a killer application [23]. Ephemeral groups, related to proximity encounters and opportunistic networking, are ad-hoc and used for collaboration [24] and informal communication [25].

Considering the above systems, none take into account the social interactions that occur in the ephemeral social networks and the social context of the environment. We developed Nokia Find & Connect for combining the location of encounters and social objects and the content of social events based on meetings, for managing workplace resources and enabling social networking in the office environment.

3 Nokia Find and Connect

NF&C is a location-based mobile social networking solution for workplace management based on the problem that the inefficient use of workplace resources results in unnecessary loss of valuable work time. For example, many meeting rooms are often reserved but not actually occupied. NF&C provides a solution for updating the status of meeting rooms and reservations in real-time that reflect the room's actual occupancy and use, based on WiFi indoor positioning and allows users to create social networks from opportunistic encounters and meetings. In this section, we describe the system structure of NF&C, and then introduce the user interface and functions of the system.

3.1 System Architecture

Figure 1 shows the overall system structure of NF&C where the positioning subsystem provides the user's location and the NF&C subsystem provides location-based services, resource management, and social networking to users.

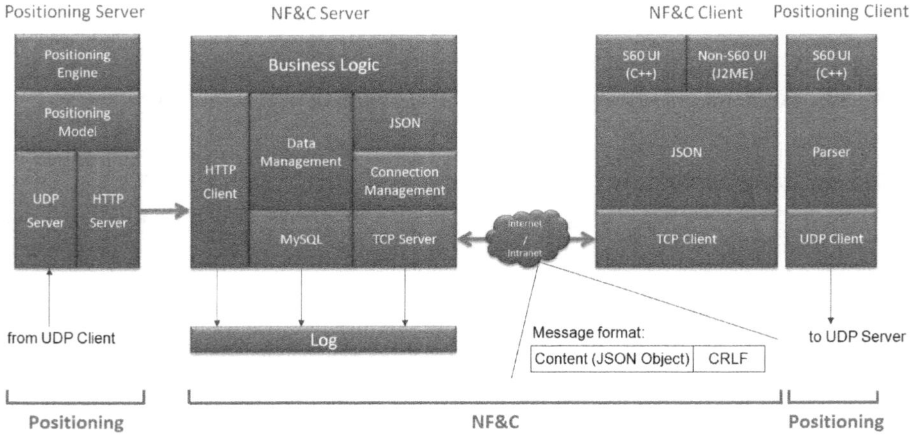

Fig. 1. System Architecture of NF&C

The positioning subsystem consists of the Positioning Client and the Positioning Server. The Positioning Client collects WiFi signal strengths from nearby WLAN access points at a user-specified interval, and sends them to the Positioning Server through UDP (User Datagram Protocol). After the Positioning Server receives the WiFi signal data, the Positioning Engine uses the Positioning Model and machine learning algorithms to approximate the positioning of the user on a floor map. The Positioning Model is created by performing a site survey that involves recording the WiFi signal strengths and access points of all floors in the building on the floor map. For our implementation, we used an off-the-shelf commercial WiFi positioning server.

The NF&C subsystem consists of the NF&C Client and NF&C Server. The NF&C Client sends requests to and receives responses from the NF&C server in JSON format through TCP. The business logic layer provides the functionality of resource management and social networking as explained in Section 3.2. The JSON message format includes two parts, the content label and the content value. The NF&C server reparses the JSON message, and sends the result back to the NF&C Client using TCP, while storing all data in a MySQL database.

3.2 Functions and User Interface

The user interface for NF&C has a main home screen and 3 functional modules: Maps, Reservations, and Contacts. All of these functions have been implemented on the Symbian C++ platform for Nokia S60 3rd and 5th edition phones. Figure 2 shows the screenshots of the functions in the NF&C user interface.

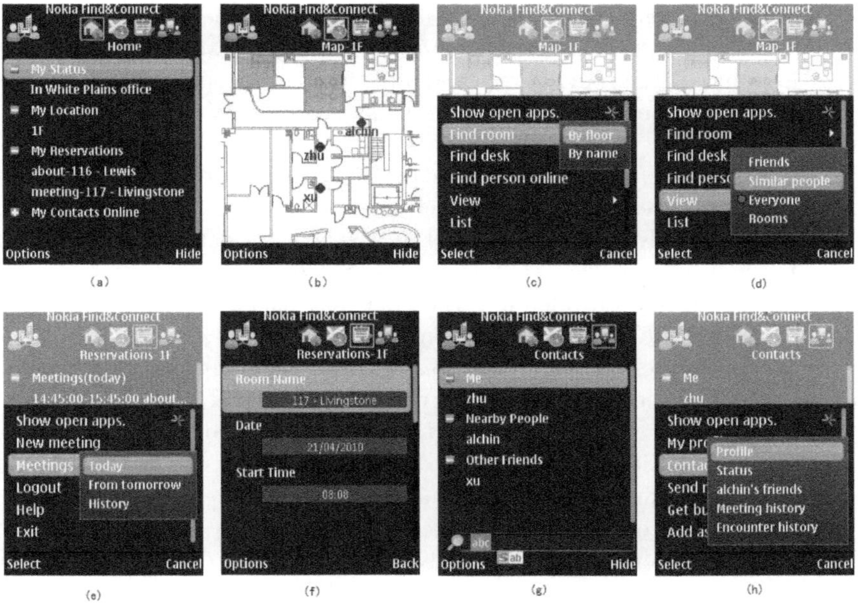

Fig. 2. Client user interface of NF&C: (a)Home screen; (b)Maps screen; (c)Maps function list; (d)View options of Maps; (e)Meetings function list; (f)New meeting reservation; (g)Contacts screen; and (h)Contact details

Home screen : The Home screen (Figure 2 (a)) provides a personalized summary of the features consisting of 4 parts: My Status, My Location, My Reservations and My Contacts Online. My Status is an automatic status message that dynamically changes according to the user's location and the user's activity or event. Currently, My Status is divided into "In Office", "In a meeting", "Online" (if logged in but not in the office) and "Offline". My Location shows the floor where the user is at or "Not in office" if outside of the office. My Reservations has a list of today's meetings where you are an organizer or participant. My Contacts Online shows all of your online friends.

Maps : The Maps module contains 5 parts: My Location, Find Room, Find Desk, Find Person Online, and View. In My Location, the user's location is shown on the floor map as in Figure 2 (b). For privacy, users can set their location sharing to private to not share their location with others. Users can search for meeting rooms and desks by floor and by name, show the resource details on the map, and reserve rooms as in Figure 2 (c). Find Person Online finds out if someone you know is online. View provides a filter as to what you want to see on the map, and is broken down into People Nearby, Similar People, Everyone, and Rooms as shown in Figure 2 (d).

Reservations : In Figure 2 (e), the reservation services include reserving a new meeting (Figure 2 (f)), editing, or deleting a meeting. Users can find today's meetings, future meetings and past meetings in this module. If the meeting is reserved but not occupied, the NF&C server will delete the meeting reservation 10 minutes after the meeting start time if no one is in the room, allowing others to use the room. If the room is reserved and there are people in the room, then the status of the room is occupied and all the participants' status is changed to "In a meeting".

Contacts : From Figure 2 (g), users can manage their profile similar to other social networking sites. Users can manage their friends by adding and removing friends, group friends together, and obtain the friend's details. When the user selects a friend or a contact that is nearby, the user can look at the contact details. These include downloading the contact's business card to the phone, finding out when the user met that contact using the meeting history, finding out the last encounter time and location, and sending questions or messages to that contact. The meeting history is an ephemeral social network (defined in the next section) because it records all the people you encountered in meetings. We use friend-of-a-friend mechanism to determine how A can know B through C where A and C are friends and B and C are friends and have met. Last encounter is useful to help in friend recommendations by finding those people you have physically encountered recently and often.

Therefore, by tracking a user's location with WiFi in meeting rooms and combining that with the meeting management system in the Reservations module, we can infer whether a user is in a meeting. Then we can use notifications, status updates, messaging, and friend management to communicate this activity to others. This addresses the first research question of how positioning and social networking technologies can be used to efficiently manage office resources.

3.3 Ephemeral Social Network in Nokia Find and Connect

Current online social networks (OSNs) are inconsistent with physical real social networks because users can randomly send and accept friend requests, therefore prompting the question: How many friends in your online social network are your true friends? [26] Also, it is popular that when you come across a person, you have a recollection but cannot remember who that person is or where you have met. There is no system to record this temporary event to remind you. The question then becomes how to capture social networks as they happen occasionally in the real world. Our solution to this is the concept of an ephemeral social network, which is related to that of ephemeral groups [24].

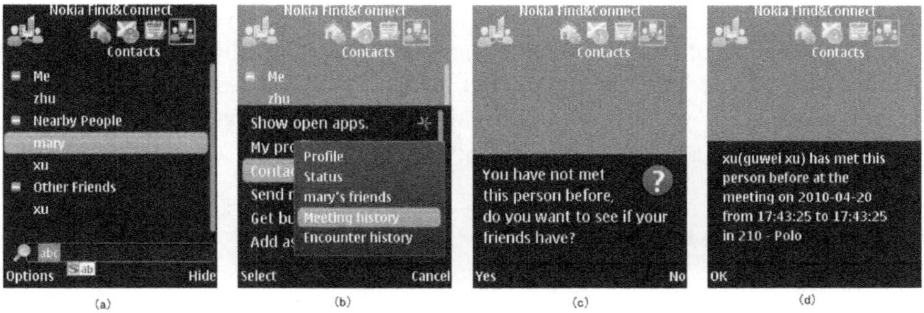

Fig. 3. Client User Interface of NF&C: (a)Nearby people with Mary selected; (b)Contact details for Mary; (c)Meeting history between you and Mary; (d)Finding out your friend Xu has met Mary before

The ephemeral social network is defined as a social network created spontaneously in an ad-hoc manner at a specific point in time for a specific purpose and lasting a short time. For example, employees have opportunities to attend a meeting for cooperation of a project. It is possible for some of them to know each other, while others may not. However, the ephemeral social network is created by the interaction among the participants during the meeting marked by meeting topic, meeting time and participants. Thus, it is probable to find out some interesting information, such as who just passed by, who are friends during the meeting and what are their common interests. Ephemeral social networks occur frequently in our daily lives where people opportunistically encounter each other or get together for a special purpose like having lunch in the canteen, attending a lecture, or attending other organized activities.

The ephemeral social networks in NF&C are based on encounters and meetings. We incorporate encounters into the NF&C framework so that users can find other people nearby using our user interface. If one user is interested in a certain person that just passed by, the user can find out who that person is by using the View People Nearby function and then view the contact details. Then, the user could get some information about that person and send an instant message to start a meaningful conversation, and add that person as a friend. Users can also find out if they or their friends have met a certain person from the meeting. Users can also download business cards from the participants of the meeting and record their contacts on the phone. Therefore, users can set up the relationships among the nearby people to provide services to help users build and strengthen the relationships, because NF&C has recorded the ephemeral social networks. This addresses the second research question of how ephemeral social networks can be used to improve current social networking protocols.

4 Analysis of Nokia Find and Connect

Nokia Find & Connect was developed and piloted in Beijing for four weeks during August 2009. We received 247 registrations, of which 234 were enrolled and 151 actually used our software. Due to time constraints, we did not implement all the features of the Contacts screen but just the Profile feature. At the end of the four week trial, participants completed an online survey about the usage, helpfulness and their evaluation of NF&C.

4.1 Data Collection

The collected data from the trial include the functions that users used, their position, friend lists, meetings, meeting history, encounter history and evaluation of NF&C using the server database, server logs and survey (with their names being anonymized). The server logs recorded every request from the clients including time, username and specific function name and parameters for further data analysis. The survey was used to evaluate the helpfulness and ease of use of NF&C.

We now analyze NF&C according to the following categories: Usage, meeting management analysis, ephemeral social network analysis and evaluation of NF&C.

4.2 Usage

During the trial, a total of 151 users used NF&C, with 125553 NF&C requests sent. This gave an average of 24 requests for each person every day.

Figure 4 shows the request distribution for all the features over the four week period. As shown in Figure 4 (a), meetings have the highest utilization which validates our hypothesis of NF&C motivation. We discover that the "Find Office" and "Find Room" features are in great demand when the user does not know the office or room location. In Figure 4(d), the number of requests for "Others Near Me" and "Find Someone" are much greater than for "Friends Near Me". This is because it is easy for users to find their friends directly but they turn to NF&C to find information of unknown people nearby or encountered people. An anomaly for meetings is that users can start and end the same meeting for several times, because due to time limitations, we did not track if users were in the meeting room at the time of the meeting. Therefore, the number of requests for "Start Meeting" are greater than for "Book a Meeting" in Figure 4 (e). Also, we find that people forget to end meetings as the number of "Start Meeting" requests are more than the number of "End Meeting" requests. This will be fixed in our next version.

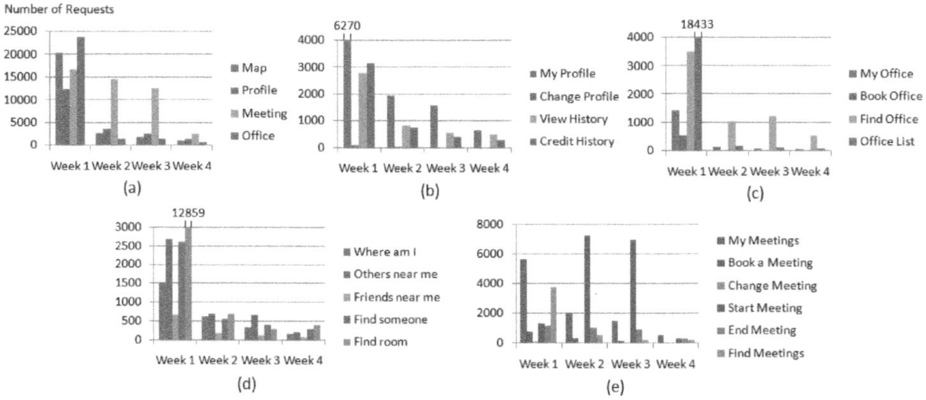

Fig. 4. Distribution of requests by week in:(a) all the features;(b)Profile;(c)Office; (d)Map;(e)Meetings

4.3 Meeting Management Analysis

According to the usage, the meeting features are the most widely used. Therefore, we analyze this module to study how our system affects users' behaviors and how it enables social networking around meetings. We implemented a credit system to encourage users to start and end meetings on time. We add 5 credits if the user starts or ends a meeting more than 10 minutes earlier than the reserved time, and deduct 5 credits if the user starts or ends a meeting more than 10 minutes later than the reserved time.

At the end of the trial, there are a total of 3536 meeting reservations with more than one person, of which 88.94% are started on time and 88.21% are ended on time, and an average of 2.07 participants per meeting. There are a total of 6130 credit records stored in our database, of which 92.68% are add credits and 3.96% are deduct credits. This high percentage of add credits is a result of the side effect of the credit system because users can repeatedly start and end meetings at any time.

For social networking around meetings, of all 512 one-to-one relationships, 182 pairs participated in at least one same meeting and 211 meetings were among friends. It is important to note that many of the meetings did not actually occur. Nonetheless, these results preliminary show that relationships around meetings are an important component of a user's social network in office environments, helped users form a good meeting habit, and helped make better use of workplace resources. The effect on the maintenance and extension of such relationships will be discussed in the next section on ephemeral social network analysis.

4.4 Ephemeral Social Network Analysis

In this section, we analyze the different types of ephemeral social networks that arise from the encounters and the meetings.

Encounters: As mentioned above, our analysis of the ephemeral social network is based on the encounters. The locations of users are updated every 1 minute while the encounters are calculated every 5 minutes. The algorithm of the encounters is as follows. STEP 1: Calculate the distance of two persons on the same floor. STEP 2: If the distance is within 5 meters, find out the last 2 distances of these two persons, else go to STEP 1. STEP 3: If there is at least 1 record of the last 2 distances that is within 5 meters, this is assumed to be the same encounter, else this is a new encounter.

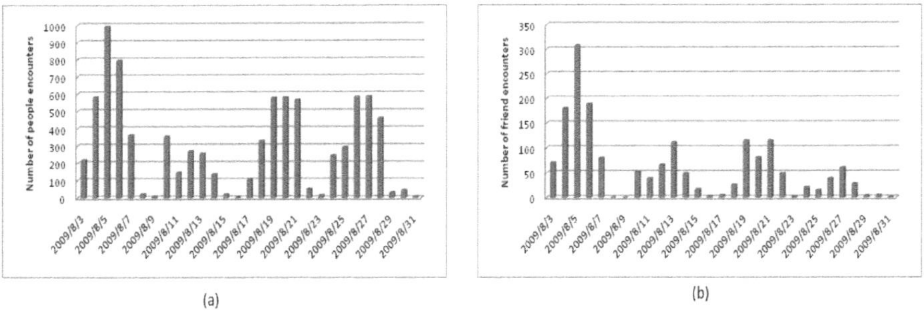

Fig. 5. Encounters:(a)Distribution of people encounters;(b)Distribution of friend encounters

The observation of Figure 5 is that the first week involved the most number of people encounters as well as friend encounters. The spikes in the graph include the games that we arranged on those days to encourage people to use NF&C. Comparing all the people in the trial with those that had meetings, we discover that a user encountered an average of 107.45 people, had an average of 21.52 friend encounters, and an average of 4.94 friends. The users who attended meetings had higher statistics, that is, they had an average of 140.75 encounters, an average of 28.29 friend encounters, and an average of 5.39 friends. This shows how ephemeral social networks formed from meetings have contributed to greater social networking.

Social Networks: In NF&C, we have three types of independent social interactions (friends, encounters and meetings), which define and construct the different types of social networks. Suppose we have two users A and B. A and B are considered as friends if A adds B as a friend and B confirms this friend request. A and B are considered as encounters if the location of both users satisfies the definition of an encounter as described in the encounter algorithm in the previous subsection. Finally, A and B are considered as having met if both have attended at least one meeting together. This results in a total of 5 types of social networks that are undirected and unweighted, and considered valid, which we describe below.

Friend network(FN): An edge between two users means that the two people are friends, regardless if they have encountered each other or not. People encounter network(PEN): An edge between two users means that both have encountered before. Friend encounter network(FEN): An edge between two users means that both are friends and have encountered before. Meeting participants network(MPN): An edge between two users means that both have attended the same meeting at least once regardless if they are friends. Meeting friend participants network(MFPN): An edge means that the two people are friends and have attended the same meeting at least once.

As is shown in Figure 6(a), 47.2% of nodes in MPN have friends while 87.1% of nodes in PEN do. From Figure 6 (b), about 24.3% of unique edges in MPN and only about 9.3% of unique edges in PEN become friends in our system. Therefore, it seems more helpful and efficient to get more friends from meetings than from encounters. Another observation is that the number of nodes and edges of FEN are similar to that of MFPN. From Figure 6, there are 59 nodes and 91 unique edges in MFPN while there are 70 nodes and 129 unique edges in FEN. Therefore, ephemeral social networks from meetings have greatly contributed to building the friend network.

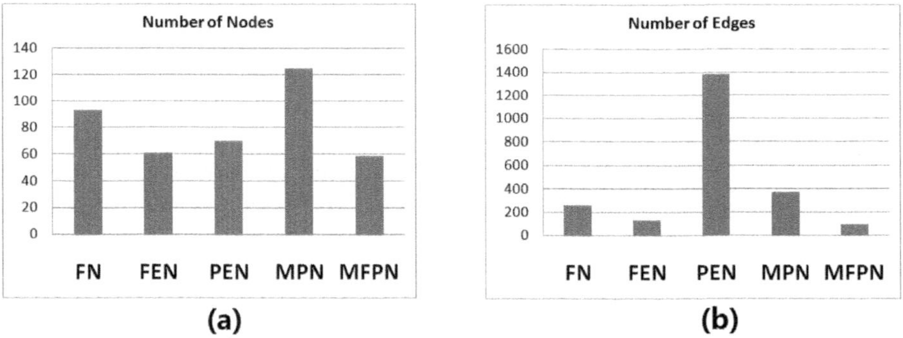

Fig. 6. The attributes of the 5 networks:(a)Number of nodes;(b)Number of unique edges

Properties of Social Networks: We examine the properties for each of the 5 social networks (that are fully connected) in NF&C using the following common social network properties [27]. Density is the proportion of ties in a network relative to the total number possible (sparse versus dense networks). Average shortest path(ASP) is defined as the average number of steps along the shortest paths for all possible pairs of network nodes. Diameter is the maximum length of all shortest paths between any two connected nodes. Average clustering coefficient(ACC) is a measure of degree to which nodes in a graph tend to cluster together, which relate to a subgroup's group betweenness centralization(GBC range: $0 < GBC < 1$) where $GBC = 0$, when all the nodes have exactly the same betweeness index and $GBC = 1$, when one node falls on all other geodesics between all the remaining (N-1) nodes. This is exactly the situation realized by a star graph.

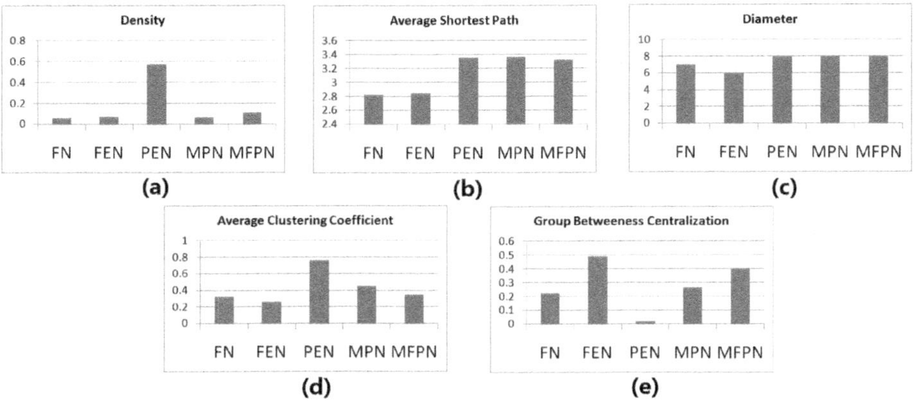

Fig. 7. The attributes of the 5 Networks:(a)Density; (b)Average shortest path; (c)Diameter; (d)Average clustering coefficient; (e)Group betweenness centralization

Figure 7(b) obviously shows that the average shortest path of PEN and MPN are 17.9% higher than that of FN, FEN and MFPN, which implies that becoming a friend of each other helps a lot in terms of communication efficiency, especially in the office environment when we try to connect and communicate with others. This is also supported in Figure 7(c), where the diameter of PEN and MPN is higher than other networks. Average clustering coefficient of PEN and MPN is higher than that of FN, FEN and MFPN, as shown in Figure 7(d). Higher average clustering coefficient of PEN can be explained in that encounters in PEN mainly happened within several well-connected subgroups, which is true for example in that people encounter each other a lot during lunch and at the office building entrance. The spike in density in Figure 7(a) supports this explanation. In MPN, people attending meetings together are mainly on the same team and connect a lot whenever a meeting starts, while the possibility of people from different teams attending a meeting together is relatively small. These two reasons result in a high average clustering coefficient in MPN. However, average clustering coefficient of FN, FEN and MFPN is small, showing that people in these networks are connected more uniformly.

Therefore these results show that social networks that involve friends (FN, FEN, and MFPN) have small and uniform subgroups compared to those that do not involve friends (PEN and MPN) where they are large, dense, and have well-connected subgroups.

4.5 Evaluation of Nokia Find and Connect

In this section, we evaluate the usability of our system. We conducted a survey to collect users' evaluations on NF&C by rating the helpfulness and convenience levels of each feature using a Likert scale from 1 (low) to 5 (high). We received 76 valid feedbacks, 29 from females and 45 from males with 2 hiding their gender. Table 1 shows the usage and usability statistics for each of the NF&C features. The Meeting feature overall was the most helpful as it received the highest evaluation (3.85) followed by the Map, which is in line with our statistical results above. The Map feature was the most easy to use (3.80) followed by the Profile (3.70) and Meeting (3.68). When asked whether they thought NF&C was useful, 81.6% of the responders said yes while only 14.5% of the responders said no. The features that users were willing to use if NF&C was provided again in the future, were Map (90.4%) and Meeting (92.6%) as expected.

Therefore, the results from the data analysis prove that NF&C appears to be useful and is generally well accepted by users.

Table 1. Usage and Usability Evaluation of NF&C

Feature	Helpful	Easy to use	Willingness to use
Profile	3.10	3.70	75.3%
Map	3.73	3.80	90.4%
Meeting	3.85	3.68	92.6%
Office	3.13	3.56	66.1%

5 Conclusion and Future Work

In this paper, we designed and developed an indoor location and proximity-based social networking solution for workplace and office management on mobile devices called NF&C. We described NF&C as a system and user interface to efficiently manage office resources dynamically and locate rooms and people, forming the basis for social networking. To address the gap between physical and online social networks, we proposed the concept of ephemeral social network and implemented some applications of encounters and meetings, how it affected meeting behaviors, and how it utilized ephemeral social network relationships to extend the social network in the workplace. We conducted a user study of NF&C by deploying it in our office environment to demonstrate its viability as described in the user evaluation of the system.

Our conclusions are as follows. First, meeting features have the highest utilization ratio in the office-based environment which validates our hypothesis of NF&C motivation. Second, NF&C helped users form a good meeting habit to start and end meetings on time and make better use of workplace resources. Third, ephemeral social networks based on meetings and encounters contributed to an increase in friend social networking.

Our future work involves the following. First, we have started to improve the NF&C UI and build a better robust system to give users a better user experience and secure their privacy. Second, we would like to perform user studies in other office locations to determine if culture and location has an affect on the use of NF&C and ephemeral social networks, as well as gather more data for our research. Third, we would like to explore the efficiency of meeting management using ephemeral social networks and location, by using actual location to determine the status of the meeting rooms and synchronizing with our office meeting room reservation system. Fourth, we would like to investigate how encounters and ephemeral social networks can be used to improve friend recommendations. Finally, we would like to deploy NF&C to other indoor environments like a conference and analyze the results in order to prove the viability of ephemeral social networking.

References

1. Engestrom, J.: Why some social network services work and others don't- or: the case for object-centered sociality (2005)
2. Hightower, J., LaMarca, A., Smith, I.: Practical lessons from place lab. IEEE Pervasive Computing 5, 32–39 (2006)
3. Huang, S., Proul, F., Ratti, C.: ifind: a peer-to-peer application for real-time location monitoring on the mit campus. In: CUPUM 2007 - 10th International Conference on Computers in Urban Planning and Urban Management (2007)
4. Barkhuus, L., Brown, B., Bell, M., Sherwood, S., Hall, M., Chalmers, M.: From awareness to repartee: sharing location within social groups. In: CHI 2008: Proceeding of the Twenty-Sixth Annual SIGCHI Conference on Human factors in Computing Systems, pp. 497–506. ACM, New York (2008)
5. Tsai, J., Kelley, P., Drielsma, P.H., Cranor, L., Hong, J., Sadeh, N.: Who's viewed you?: the impact of feedback in a mobile location-sharing application. In: SOUPS 2009: Proceedings of the 5th Symposium on Usable Privacy and Security, pp. 1–1. ACM, New York (2009)
6. Beach, A., Gartrell, M., Akkala, S., Elston, J., Kelley, J., Nishimoto, K., Ray, B., Razgulin, S., Sundaresan, K., Surendar, B., Terada, M., Han, R.: Whozthat? evolving an ecosystem for context-aware mobile social networks. IEEE Network 22, 50–55 (2008)
7. Want, R., Hopper, A., Falcao, V., Gibbons, J.: The active badge location system. ACM Trans. Inf. Syst. 10, 91–102 (1992)
8. Ward, A., Jones, A., Hopper, A.: A new location technique for the active office. IEEE Personal Communications 4, 42–47 (1997)
9. Harter, A., Steggles, P., Ward, A., Webster, P.: The anatomy of a context-aware application. In: Mobile Computing and Networking, pp. 59–68 (1999)
10. Priyantha, N.B., Chakraborty, A., Balakrishnan, H.: The cricket location-support system. In: MobiCom 2000: Proceedings of the 6th Annual International Conference on Mobile Computing and Networking, pp. 32–43. ACM, New York (2000)
11. Hightower, J., Want, R., Borriello, G.: SpotON: An indoor 3d location sensing technology based on RF signal strength. UW CSE 00-02-02, University of Washington, Department of Computer Science and Engineering, Seattle, WA (2000)

12. Ni, L.M., Liu, Y., Lau, Y.C., Patil, A.P.: Landmarc: indoor location sensing using active rfid. Wirel. Netw. 10, 701–710 (2004)
13. Bahl, P., Padmanabhan, V.: Radar: an in-building rf-based user location and tracking system. In: INFOCOM 2000. Nineteenth Annual Joint Conference of the IEEE Computer and Communications Societies, Proceedings, vol. 2, pp. 775–784. IEEE, Los Alamitos (2000)
14. de Moraes, L.F.M., Nunes, B.A.A.: Calibration-free wlan location system based on dynamic mapping of signal strength. In: MobiWac 2006: Proceedings of the 4th ACM International Workshop on Mobility Management and Wireless Access, pp. 92–99. ACM, New York (2006)
15. Barsocchi, P., Lenzi, S., Chessa, S., Giunta, G.: A novel approach to indoor rssi localization by automatic calibration of the wireless propagation model. In: IEEE 69 Vehicular Technology Conference, VTC Spring 2009, pp. 1–5 (2009)
16. Ladd, A.M., Berkis, K.E., Rudys, A., Kavraki, L.E., Wallach, D.S.: Robotics-based location sensing using wireless ethernet. Wirel. Netw. 11, 189–204 (2005)
17. Eagle, N., Pentland, A.: Social serendipity: mobilizing social software. IEEE Pervasive Computing 4, 28–34 (2005)
18. aka-aki networks GmbH: aka-aki (2007-2010), `http://www.aka-aki.com/`
19. Paulos, E., Goodman, E.: The familiar stranger: anxiety, comfort, and play in public places. In: CHI 2004: Proceedings of the SIGCHI Conference on Human Factors in Computing Systems, pp. 223–230. ACM, New York (2004)
20. Su, J., Chin, A., Popivanova, A., Goel, A., de Lara, E.: User mobility for opportunistic ad-hoc networking. In: WMCSA 2004: Proceedings of the Sixth IEEE Workshop on Mobile Computing Systems and Applications, Washington, DC, USA, pp. 41–50. IEEE Computer Society, Los Alamitos (2004)
21. Chaintreau, A., Fraigniaud, P., Lebhar, E.: Opportunistic spatial gossip over mobile social networks. In: WOSP 2008: Proceedings of the First Workshop on Online Social Networks, pp. 73–78. ACM, New York (2008)
22. Chen, L.J., Huang, T.K., Chiou, C.L.: Poster abstract: scalable and collaborative internet access for opportunistic people networks. In: MobiHoc 2008: Proceedings of the 9th ACM International Symposium on Mobile ad Hoc Networking and Computing, pp. 459–460. ACM, New York (2008)
23. Lindgren, A., Hui, P.: The quest for a killer app for opportunistic and delay tolerant networks (invited paper). In: CHANTS 2009: Proceedings of the 4th ACM Workshop on Challenged Networks, pp. 59–66. ACM, New York (2009)
24. Wang, B., Bodily, J., Gupta, S.K.S.: Supporting persistent social groups in ubiquitous computing environments using context-aware ephemeral group service. In: PERCOM 2004: Proceedings of the Second IEEE International Conference on Pervasive Computing and Communications (PerCom 2004), Washington, DC, USA, p. 287. IEEE Computer Society, Los Alamitos (2004)
25. Brothers, L., Hollan, J., Nielsen, J., Stornetta, S., Abney, S., Furnas, G., Littman, M.: Supporting informal communication via ephemeral interest groups. In: CSCW 1992: Proceedings of the 1992 ACM Conference on Computer-Supported Cooperative Work, pp. 84–90. ACM, New York (1992)
26. Miller, V.L.: Are your facebook friends really your friends ? (2009)
27. Wasserman, S., Faust, K.: Social Network Analysis: Methods and Applications. Cambridge University Press, Cambridge (1994)

Contextual Biometric-Based Authentication for Ubiquitous Services

Ileana Buhan[1], Gabriele Lenzini[2], and Saša Radomirović[3]

[1] Philips Research
5656 AE Eindhoven, The Netherlands
ileana.buhan@philips.nl

[2] Interdisciplinary Centre for Security, Reliability and Trust
University of Luxembourg
L-1359 Luxembourg, Luxembourg
gabriele.lenzini@uni.lu

[3] Faculty of Science, Technology and Communication
University of Luxembourg
L-1359 Luxembourg, Luxembourg
sasa.radomirovic@uni.lu

Abstract. We introduce and comment on the concept of contextual pseudo identity. A contextual pseudo identity is a soft identity token that is built from both a user's biometric and the context. When it comes to ubiquitous authentication, a contextual pseudo identity promises better security than that offered by traditional biometrics-based identity tokens: the use of context improves the tokens' disposability and renewability, which are two essential properties in the protection of a user's real identity. Our algorithm for generating contextual pseudo identities extends a Fuzzy Embedder so that it accepts both biometric and context-dependent input. We prove that our way of processing the context preserves the security and reliability properties of the Fuzzy Embedder used in our extension. An example shows how a user can utilize contextual pseudo identity to authenticate to and access ubiquitous services.

Keywords: Context-aware Authentication, Ubiquitous Services, Biometrics, Fuzzy Embedder.

1 Introduction

Nowadays, thanks to the wide diffusion of wireless networks, an increasing number of services are offered ubiquitously to mobile users. Users have to authenticate themselves in order to get access to ubiquitous services: authenticated users can have customized functionalities and, at the same time, they are discouraged from abusing the service.

Typical authentication procedures verify a user's identity on the basis of the following three paradigms: "what a user knows", "who a user is", "what a user has". The first paradigm is related to secrets of any kind (e.g., PIN, passwords),

Z. Yu et al. (Eds.): UIC 2010, LNCS 6406, pp. 680–693, 2010.

the second to the use of biometric data (e.g., fingerprints, palm vein pattern), and the third to the possession of physical tokens (e.g., smart cards, RFID tags).

In practice, login and password (i.e., "what a user knows") is still the most frequently adopted authentication mechanism [1]. In particular, mobile users authenticate themselves to their device by means of a secret code or a gesture performed on the device's keyboard or screen. If the mobile device acts as a gateway to a remote service, the latter can, in turn, ask for another login/password authentication, which is again inserted using the device's input interface. Despite its widespread use, the use of secrets such as PINs or login/password pairs is largely recognized as being insecure.

Concerning "who the user is", we observe an increasing diffusion of devices with biometric readers such as, for instance, fingerprint scanners on laptops. However, biometrics is mainly used to authenticate the user to the device, and not yet to authenticate the user to an external service accessible from the device. (We will comment on this in Sect. 2.) At the current state of security engineering, biometrics-based service authentication is limited due to the risk that theft of biometric information can cause enormous damage to its victims because biometric identifiers are usually non-renewable. Moreover, non-renewability together with the possibility of linking users across different databases carries serious threats against privacy.

The use of hard ID-tokens (i.e., "what the user has") for authenticating mobile users to ubiquitous services, only scarcely practiced until recently, is actually enjoying a moment of glory: personalized smart cards, NFC or RFID badges are offered as a means to obtain access to e.g., commercial promotions, public transportation, and governmental services.

However, in order to avoid that the loss of a card leads to (more serious) identity theft, the link between users and their ID-tokens must be carefully secured in *all phases* of the authentication process. We observe that many service providers accept the mobile phone as an ID-token. This means, that the service providers generally trust the procedures adopted by the mobile operators for identity registration and authentication. Despite this, the use of a mobile device as an identity token has a few evident drawbacks, among which the risk of having it stolen. Even though a PIN or a pattern is required to unlock the phone, getting control of a phone is quite easy: secrets can be easily eavesdropped on by shoulder surfing, or obtained with a bit of engineering once in possession of the phone or the SIM card. Unsurprisingly, the number of mobile phones forgotten, lost, or stolen is higher than the number of stolen credit cards (here, we mean physical cards, not credit card numbers.

The observations above suggest that a stronger tie is needed between a user and his mobile device. In this context the use of biometrics for the purpose of authentication would make it difficult for anybody else but the owner of the device to unlock the device. When using biometrics to authenticate a user to his mobile device, the latter can act as a reliable ID-token on behalf of its owner.

Outline. In this paper we suggest an even stronger binding between users and mobile devices based on a combination of biometric features of the user and contextual information. In Sect. 2 we review the current state of the art in biometrics-based authentication, with particular focus on a scheme called *Fuzzy Embedder*, which roots in biometric encryption. In Sect. 3 we introduce the concept of contextual pseudo identity, and we show how to extend a Fuzzy Embedder to generate contextual pseudo identities. We also comment on the nature of contextual data. In Sect. 4 we explain how to implement our extension of Fuzzy Embedder and we discuss its reliability and security properties. Finally, in Sect. 5 we introduce and comment on a series of concepts that root on contextual pseudo identities and that we propose to be the building block for a design of contextual service with strong authentication. Finally, Sect. 6 and Sect. 7 comment, respectively, the related work and the future work.

2 On Biometric Authentication

The use of biometrics for identification and authentication of individuals has been subject to extensive research during the last decades. A wide variety of biometric modalities have been investigated (e.g., iris, fingerprint, voice, gait, face, and alike). Aspects such as the recognition performance, robustness, and persistence are well documented and the limitations of specific modalities and applications have been described in various publications (e.g., [5]). The current maturity level of biometrics as authentication means has facilitated the use of biometrics in a range of applications.

An important security issue for biometric systems concerns the renewability and revocability of biometric references. Individuals have a limited number of irises and fingers. Thus, a biometric reference that is compromised once is compromised forever.

The risk of compromised biometric references is mitigated by the use of *biometric encryption*, which allow the construction of renewable biometric references. Biometric encryption aims to protect the stored biometric identity of a user from abuse in two ways:

1. By revealing nothing about the underlying biometrics.
2. By allowing revocation and renovation (also called restoration or renewance) whenever intrusion is detected.

Biometric Encryption. The main challenge in protecting biometric references using cryptographic techniques is coping with the noise introduced into biometric samples during data acquisition and processing. Biometric encryption schemes can transform a noisy, biometric measurement represented as a sequence of non-uniformly distributed real numbers into a reproducible, uniformly-distributed binary string. There are many parameters that control this transformation, for example the length of the output binary sequence, the probability that two measurements coming from the same users will be mapped to the same binary sequence, etc.

Two abstractions, *secure sketches* and *fuzzy extractors* were proposed by Dodis *et al.* [14] to describe the process of transforming a biometric characteristic into a reproducible, uniform binary sequence. A secure sketch can correct the noise between two biometric measurements coming from the same user by using some public information called a *sketch*. The result of a secure sketch is a reproducible sequence, which is not necessarily uniformly distributed. Fuzzy extractors can be used to extract randomness from biometric data to make the output of a secure sketch suitable for use as cryptographic keys. Both constructions work only on biometric data represented as discrete variables. The process of transforming a continuous variable into a discrete variable influences the performance of fuzzy extractors and secure sketches.

Fuzzy Embedders. Fuzzy Embedders were proposed by Buhan *et al.* [8] as an extension to the fuzzy extractor idea. A Fuzzy Embedder can transform a noisy, non-uniform continuous variable, into a reproducible, uniformly random string, which is suitable to be used as a cryptographic key. A Fuzzy Embedder is a pair of procedures. The first, Embed, is used once to generated an identity token from biometric data The second, Reproduce, is used to authenticate the user. We now recall the formal definition of a Fuzzy Embedder Scheme [8]. In the following $P = \{0,1\}^*$ is a discrete space and $\mathcal{U}$ is an n-dimensional continuous metric space with distance function d. $\mathcal{U}$ is the sample space of all possible biometric inputs. $X : \mathcal{U} \to \mathbb{R}^n$ is a continuous random variable representing the possible biometric fingerprints of a particular user.

Definition 1 (Fuzzy Embedder Scheme). *A* $(U, \ell, \rho, \epsilon, \delta)$-Fuzzy Embedder Scheme *is a pair of polynomial-time algorithms,* Embed *and* Reproduce, *which are defined as follows:*

- $\mathsf{Embed} : \mathcal{U} \times \{0,1\}^\ell \to P$. *This algorithm takes* $x \in \mathcal{U}$ *and* $r \in \{0,1\}^\ell$ *as input, and returns a string* $p \in P$.
- $\mathsf{Reproduce} : \mathcal{U} \times P \to \{0,1\}^\ell \cup \{\perp\}$. *This algorithm takes* $x' \in \mathcal{U}$ *and* $p \in P$ *as input, and returns a string in* $\{0,1\}^\ell$ *or an error* $\perp$.

Given any random variable X *over* $\mathcal{U}$ *and a random variable* R *over* $\{0,1\}^\ell$, *the parameters* ρ, ϵ, *and* δ *are defined as follows:*

$$\rho = \min_{r \in \{0,1\}^\ell} \max_{x \in \mathcal{U}} \{\Pr(\mathsf{Reproduce}(X, \mathsf{Embed}(x, r)) = r\}$$

Here, $\max_{x \in \mathcal{U}}$ *assures the choice of the best possible representative for* X.

$$\epsilon = I(R; \mathsf{Embed}(X, R))$$
$$\delta = I(X; \mathsf{Embed}(X, R))$$

Here, $I(X;Y)$ *is the Shannon mutual information between* X *and* Y.

Informally, ρ is the (worst case) probability that the Fuzzy Embedder can successfully reproduce the embedded key: it measures the *reliability* of a Fuzzy Embedder. The quantities ϵ and δ are security parameters; ϵ measures the amount of information that Embed reveals about R and δ measures the amount of information that Embed reveals about X.

3 Contextual Pseudo Identities

We now extend the Fuzzy Embedder so that it can accept context among its input. As a consequence, we obtain a process to generate what we call a *contextual pseudo identity*. We start recalling what a pseudo identity is.

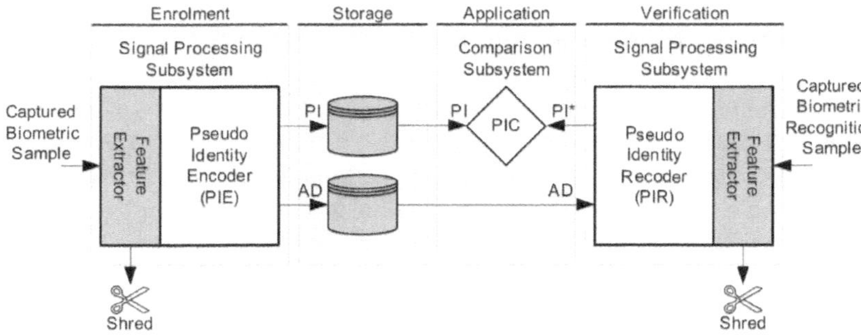

Fig. 1. Pictorial description of the phases Enrollment and Verification

Pseudo Identities. A pseudo identity (PI) [7] is a biometric reference which is anonymous and renewable. PIs have been proposed as part of the standard ISO/IEC WD 24745, which describes how PIs are created and managed. According to the standard, PIs are created together with some auxiliary data during a process called *Biometric Enrollment*, which requires the capture of one or more biometric samples. After the enrollment the used biometric samples are destroyed and the PI and auxiliary data safely stored for later use. In the *Biometric Verification* process, the user provides again a biometric sample of his. Together with the provision of the auxiliary data, the present sample is used to generate PI*, an actual pseudo identity. The user is authenticated if and only if (the hash of) PI* and PI coincide. The two phases are summarized in Fig. 1.

Contextual Pseudo Identities. A contextual pseudo identity (CPI) is a pseudo identity that also depends on contextual data. A contextual datum can describe, for example, the environment (e.g., the identity's location) or a situation (e.g., the fact that the identity is traveling). Generally speaking, the use of contextual data allows to link a pseudo identity to a specific situation. A contextual piece of information can be automatically evinced from the environment or from the user: as such, it can be used to contextualize a pseudo identity to a circumstantial state e.g., the location of the user, its state of mind, etc.

3.1 Contextual Information

Context is any information that can be used to characterize the situation of a person, a place, or an object that is relevant to the interaction between a user and an application, including the user and the application [13].

In pervasive environments, where users carry or wear devices with embedded networking and communication abilities, data referring to the user can be composed from what he gathers about phenomena that occur in the surroundings or in nearby objects (e.g., RFID tags, WiFi access points, Bluetooth sources). By accessing the Internet, the users' current situation can be linked with information available on the web, such as local weather conditions or daily news. Moreover, devices can retrieve geo-located information concerning specific geographical sites and information related to them. Devices with GPS are able to retrieve the current location of users, so that they can contribute to the specification of context where interaction between user and service takes place. (Bluetooth, RFID, WiFi, or NFC can also be used to compose location information, mainly indoors.) Because mobile phones frequently have embedded cameras, a picture of a place can also be part of the context. Finally any sequence of digits, or set of gestures that the user enters into the device can describe the user's mood, attitude, or state of mind.

An example of a contextual datum is described by the "W4 model" [11]. Here, a contextual datum depicts a situation where someone, or something, does some activity, in a certain place and at a certain time. In fact, the context is represented in terms of the four following items: Who, What, Where, and When. *Who* refers to subject of the situation (e.g., the user or its mobile device), *What* is the activity that the subject is performing, *Where* is the location where the interaction takes place (e.g., it can be represented with geographic coordinates, regions, or it can be the name of place like e.g., "Schiphol airport"). Finally, *When* is a time information: it can be a range, a concise description, or a high level value such as "Easter week".

The technology to acquire contextual information is becoming widely available and commercially affordable. Although there is no general infrastructure for contextual information yet, nor has a standard for contextual model been established, an increasing number of applications are offering contextualized services by relying on ad-hoc solutions for context management. Proposals for widespread context-aware architectures are discussed in literature (e.g., see [10]). For example, IYOUIT [3] is a mobile application that allows users to automatically collect context information centered in places they visit and the people they meet. It aggregates information from the Internet and from other mobile clients. From this (low level) data, the IYOUIT framework is able to evince high level contextual data concerning the social relationships with buddies (e.g., "colleague", "family member"), qualitative location information like "@home" and "@office", weather in Beufort scale (e.g., "light air", "gentle breeze"), abstract situations like "business meeting", and events like e.g., "going from home to work" or "returning from vacation". The context is so efficiently managed that changes in context be processed to automatically write a user's blog [4].

In the remainder of this paper we abstract away from any detail concerning context modeling, implementation and management; instead we refer to context as a vector of discrete data. Without loss of generality, an instance of a context is represented as a vector $\mathbf{c} = (c_1, \ldots, c_k)$ where $c_i \in \mathbb{N}$ encodes an atomic unit of context information (called *knowledge atom* in [11]).

3.2 Contextual Biometric Enrollment and Verification

Let *Bob* be a user, and b and $\mathbf{c}$ the user's biometrics and a contextual information, respectively. We assume that m is a trusted hardware with a biometric input interface and with computational and storage capabilities.

In the Biometric Enrollment phase, *Bob* generates a contextual pseudo identity, cpi, that depends on his biometrics and on the context. The trusted hardware will destroy the input just after it produces cpi, while $h(cpi)$ and the additional data ad are safely stored in m. They will be used later in the verification phase. The enrollment phase is so formalized:

Protocol 1 (Enrollment (b,c)). *Creation of the contextual pseudo identity, of the additional data and their storage into the trusted hardware m.*

$$\begin{array}{ll} \textit{Encode.} & (cpi, ad) := \texttt{Encode}(b, \mathbf{c}) \\ \textit{Store.} & (h(cpi), ad) \rightarrow m \end{array}$$

Here $\texttt{Encode}(\_)$ is the function that realizes the Pseudo Identity Encoding in Fig. 1 but modified so that it takes also the context as an input parameter. The function $h(\_)$ is a hash function. The symbol $\rightarrow$ stands for store in (resp. $\leftarrow$ stands for load from) while $:=$ denotes a value assignment.

Security & Privacy Issues. The Enrollment procedure must possess at least the following security features. First, it must preserve *irreversibility*, that is no non-negligible information about the user's biometrics may be recovered from the knowledge of the output of the Encode procedure and from the knowledge of the context. The context is, generally, public information. Second, Enrollment must be *collision resistant*, which means that it is highly improbable to obtain the same pair of *cpi* and *ad* starting from different biometric samples or from different contexts, or both. For what concerns user privacy, the Enrollment procedure should preserve *unlikability*. This property, which was formalized in [19], requires that it is impossible to determine whether two different biometric templates are generated from the same biometric sample. In our case this property can be reformulated to require that it is infeasible to decide whether two different CPIs are generated from the same biometrics in the same context. Unlinkability is extremely important in a setting, where users may register to services using different contextual pseudo identities. An implementation of Encode must satisfy certain conditions in order to satisfy the preceding properties. We discuss this issue in Sect. 4.

In the Biometric Verification phase, the user reproduces his contextual pseudo identity, by providing an actual biometric sample and additional data. The "reproduced" contextual pseudo identity, cpi^*, is verified against the one stored in m. The user is authenticated if and only if there is a match.

Protocol 2 (Verification (b',$\mathbf{c}'$)). *Loading of the stored data, decoding of the contextual pseudo identity given an actual biometric sample and context, and final authentication check.*

Load.	$(h(cpi), ad) \leftarrow m$
Decode.	$cpi^* := \texttt{Decode}(b', \mathbf{c}', ad)$
Authenticate.	$\texttt{if}\ h(cpi^*) = h(cpi)\ \texttt{then}\ 1,\ \texttt{else}\ 0$

Here $\texttt{Decode}(\_)$ is the function that realizes the decoding (see Fig. 1).The operator $=$ means equality.

Security Issues. The verification of a contextual biometric pseudo identity has to be security compliant. This means that an implementation of Verification must be *correct*, in the sense that given two biometrics of the same user and in the same context, it should be guaranteed that the correct CPI is retrieved. Moreover, Verification must also be *sound*, i.e., the combination of additional data with the wrong biometric sample or with the right biometrics in the wrong context, should not produce a valid CPI. We will discuss reliability and security of our implementation in Sect. 4.

4 Implementation Using Fuzzy Embedder

We now show how to implement the two functions $\texttt{Encode}(\_)$ and $\texttt{Decode}(\_)$ by using a Fuzzy Embedder (see Definition 1). The result of this effort is an effective implementation of the contextual pseudo identity that is compliant with the $ISO/IECWD$24745.

We start with the implementation of $\texttt{Encode}(b, \mathbf{c})$, where $b \in \mathcal{U}$ and $\mathbf{c} \in \mathbb{N}^k$. For the implementation (see Algorithm 1) we make use of the function $\mathsf{Embed} : \mathcal{U} \times \{0,1\}^\ell \rightarrow P$ of the Fuzzy Embedder. The operator $\langle \_, \_, \_ \rangle : \mathcal{U} \times \{0,1\}^\ell \times \mathbb{N}^k \rightarrow P$ is used to combine the biometric data and randomness with the context input. We call $\langle b, r, \mathbf{c} \rangle$ an *enhanced biometric identifier.*

Several different ways of implementing this operator are conceivable. In our implementation, a hash of the context is added to the output of the Fuzzy Embedder. In this manner the security and reliability properties of the Fuzzy Embedder are preserved as shown below.

Thus, we define $\langle \_, \_, \_ \rangle$ as follows. Recall from Sect. 3.1 that $\mathbf{c}$ is a vector $(c_1, \ldots, c_k) \in \mathbb{N}^k$. Let $h(\_)$ be a cryptographic hash function which, by abuse of notation, we assume to map $\mathbb{N}^k$ to P, and let $\oplus$ be the XOR operator on P. Then $\langle b, r, \mathbf{c} \rangle = \mathsf{Embed}(b, r) \oplus h(c)$. The formal code of our implementation of $\texttt{Encode}(b, \mathbf{c})$ is given in Algorithm 1.

Algorithm 1. Calculate $\texttt{Encode}(b, \mathbf{c})$

1. **let** r be a random element in R
2. $ad := \langle b, r, \mathbf{c} \rangle = \mathsf{Embed}(b, r) \oplus h(\mathbf{c})$
3. **return** (r, ad)

To implement $\texttt{Decode}(b', \mathbf{c}', ad)$ we use the function $\mathsf{Reproduce} : \mathcal{U} \times P \rightarrow \{0,1\}^\ell \cup \bot$. Its parameters are $b \in \mathcal{U}$, $\mathbf{c} \in \mathbb{N}^k$, and $ad \in P$ (i.e., a biometric sample, contextual information and additional data). Assuming $\langle \_, \_, \_ \rangle$ being defined as above we apply the function straightforwardly (see Algorithm 2).

Algorithm 2. Calculate $\texttt{Decode}(b', \mathbf{c}', ad)$

1. $r' := \mathsf{Reproduce}(b', ad \oplus h(\mathbf{c}'))$
2. **return** r'

4.1 Reliability and Security Discussion

In this paragraph we prove that the use of context does not change the reliability and security parameters of the Fuzzy Embedder in our extension. We assume independence between context and biometrics.

Theorem 1 (Reliability). *Algorithms 1 and 2 give an implementation that within the correct context is as reliable as the reliability of the $(\mathcal{U}, \ell, \rho, \epsilon, \delta)$-Fuzzy Embedded Scheme used in the implementation.*

Proof. Let $\langle x, r, \mathbf{c} \rangle$ be an enhanced biometric. The Embed and $\mathsf{Reproduce}$ functions as well as x and r are independent of $\mathbf{c}$. Thus the reliability of encoding and decoding is by definition equal to the reliability ρ of the Embed and Reproduce functions. Formally, the reliability of encoding and decoding in the correct context is

$$\rho' = \min_{r \in \{0,1\}^\ell} \max_{x \in \mathcal{U}} \{\Pr(\texttt{Decode}(X, \mathbf{c}, \langle x, r, \mathbf{c} \rangle) = r\}.$$

Within the correct context, we have

$$\begin{aligned} \texttt{Decode}(X, \mathbf{c}, \langle x, r, \mathbf{c} \rangle) &= \mathsf{Reproduce}(X, \langle x, r, \mathbf{c} \rangle \oplus h(\mathbf{c})) \\ &= \mathsf{Reproduce}(X, \mathsf{Embed}(x, r)). \end{aligned}$$

The first equality follows by Algorithms 1 and 2, the second follows by definition of the enhanced biometric: $\langle x, r, \mathbf{c} \rangle = \mathsf{Embed}(x, r) \oplus h(c)$. Therefore,

$$\begin{aligned} \rho' &= \min_{r \in \{0,1\}^\ell} \max_{x \in \mathcal{U}} \{\Pr(\texttt{Decode}(X, \mathbf{c}, \langle x, r, \mathbf{c} \rangle) = r\} \\ &= \min_{r \in \{0,1\}^\ell} \max_{x \in \mathcal{U}} \{\Pr(\mathsf{Reproduce}(X, \mathsf{Embed}(x, r)) = r\} \\ &= \rho \end{aligned}$$

□

Observe that by the preceding theorem, correctness of our implementation of the verification protocol follows from a sufficiently reliable Fuzzy Embedder. Similarly, soundness of the protocol follows from corresponding properties of the Fuzzy Embedder and the collision resistance of the hash function applied to the context. The following theorem concerns the security of the data generated by the enrollment protocol.

Theorem 2 (Security). *Algorithms 1 and 2 reveal as much information about a user's biometrics and random seed as the $(\mathcal{U}, \ell, \rho, \epsilon, \delta)$-Fuzzy Embedder Scheme used in the implementation.*

Proof. The amount of information revealed by the Fuzzy Embedder Scheme is measured by the parameters ϵ and δ defined in Sect. 2. We have to prove that for any choice of the context $\mathbf{c}$, it holds that:

$$\epsilon = I(R; \mathsf{Embed}(X, R)) = I(R; \langle X, R, \mathbf{c}\rangle) \text{ and}$$
$$\delta = I(X; \mathsf{Embed}(X, R)) = I(X; \langle X, R, \mathbf{c}\rangle)$$

For convenience we will write $N = \langle X, R, \mathbf{c}\rangle$ and $M = \mathsf{Embed}(X, R)$. The proof follows by applying the data processing inequality twice to obtain $I(R; N) \geq I(R; M)$ as well as $I(R; M) \geq I(R; N)$, since $\mathbf{c}$ is independent of X and R and $\langle X, R, \mathbf{c}\rangle = \mathsf{Embed}(X, R) \oplus h(\mathbf{c}))$.

More explicitly, for two discrete random variables, U, V, we have, $I(U; V) = H(U) - H(U|V)$, where $H(U)$ is the Shannon entropy of U, $H(U|V)$ is the conditional entropy of U given V. Since $\mathbf{c}$ is fixed public information, independent of X and R and $\langle X, R, \mathbf{c}\rangle = \mathsf{Embed}(X, R) \oplus h(\mathbf{c})$, we have $H(N) = H(M)$ and in particular $H(N|R) = H(M|R)$. Thus,

$$\begin{aligned} I(R; N) &= I(N; R) \\ &= H(N) - H(N|R) \\ &= H(M) - H(M|R) \\ &= I(R; M) \end{aligned}$$

Similarly, we can prove $I(X; \mathsf{Embed}(X, R)) = I(X; \langle X, R, \mathbf{c}\rangle)$. However, since X is a continuous random variable, the argument is slightly more delicate. □

5 Discussion

In this section we discuss the use of context in biometric authentication and on how to use a contextual pseudo identity in ubiquitous authentication.

On Context in Biometric Encryption. The combination of biometrics with context information can be seen as an enhanced identifier that offers clear advantages. The addition of contextual information can enhance security by limiting the scope within which certain transactions can be authorized. In particular, this is a step forward towards preventing *relay attacks* or *Mafia fraud attacks* [6,12]. These attacks abuse an authenticated session between the victim and a malicious service provider to access an out-of-context service. The context information can furthermore act as salt for a biometric Finally, the solution is user-friendly. On the one hand, the context information is derived automatically by the device and thus no effort is required from the user. On the other hand, it is widely acknowledged that entering biometric information is more user-friendly than entering a password or PIN especially for devices like mobile phones or personal assistants. In the next section we classify the encoded enhanced identifiers namely the context-pseudo identities in three classes, each class having a well-defined scope and role.

On the Use of Contextual Pseudo Identities. We now discuss the use of Contextual Pseudo Identity (CPI) in the design of authentication protocols for ubiquitous services. We assume that there are at least three entities being involved: a user, his mobile device, and a service provider. We aim at achieving a protocol where the user first authenticates to his mobile phone and then uses the mobile phone to authenticate himself to the service provider. We distinguish between three types of CPI.

- Disposable CPIs are created for a specific purpose and never used thereafter.
- Recurring CPIs are meaninful only in certain contexts and only in them.
- Master CPIs are adopted to manage disposable and recurring CPIs.

Disposable CPIs provide identity tokens which are valid only for one session of use of an ubiquitous service (temporary context). The context used in the enrollment and verification phases, can be a time interval with a defined expiration date. Disposable CPIs also help to preserve the privacy of the position of people accessing the service in a fashion similar to the use of disposable MAC addresses [16], which avoids that a malicious person accessing the network could trace the MAC address of an individual and thus locate his or her position.

Recurring CPIs provide tokens which identify the user in certain situations that reoccur with regularity (recurrent context). The context used in the enrollment and verification phases can be a recourring event, a location, a situation or a combination of them ("when", "where", and "what").

Master CPIs are introduced to allow *Bob* to enroll disposable and recurring CPIs on his mobile phone. Here a contextual seed for the enrollment and verification phases can a datum linked to the user ("who").

Example. Figure 2 depicts an example of how to use CPIs. A user, say *Bob*, wants to access a ubiquitous service. He has already enrolled his Master CPI (MCPI in the figure) into his mobile device. He subscribes to a new service by running a new Enrollment session. First he authenticates himself to his mobile device by proving possession of the Master CPI (*Bob* has to explicitly declare e.g., by pressing a button that he is going for a verification based on Master CPI) then he generates a Disposable or a Recurring CPI. The hash of this CPI is both registered in the mobile phone and it is given to the service as ID-token. (Here we assume a secure channel between the service provider and the user.) When *Bob* is willing to use the service, he has to prove possession of the Disposable or Recurring CPI to the server. *Bob*'s biometric, the context, and the additional data (which is stored in the mobile device) are the keys for *Bob* to have access to his phone. After this authentication ends successfully, *Bob*'s pseudo identity is sent to the service provider for a second verification phase, this time to authenticate *Bob* before providing the service.

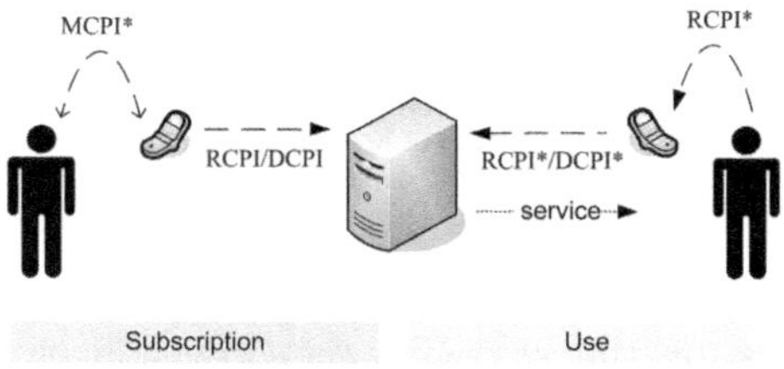

Fig. 2. Main roles and phases in authentication to an ubiquitous service, using contextual pseudo identities

6 Related Work

Context-aware (or when context is mainly location, location-aware) authentication has been introduced to facilitate access to many personal computing devices. The shift from a 'one-to-one to a 'many-to-many mapping between users and computers has set up new usability challenges for user authentication. Bardram *et al.* [2] introduced the concept of proximity-based login, where users access a computer by simply approaching it physically. They also proposed several authentication protocols, analyzed possible security attacks to them, and tested the advantages and disadvantages of their solutions in a (dynamic) hospital set-up.

Another relevant work reporting on experiments in location-based authentication is [17]; Here a service provider evaluates the identity of an approaching user by processing contextual information such as the presence and the position of devices that are linked to the user's identity. The level of authentication in a certain place is calculated on the basis of the paradigm "what the user has, when and where" in terms of number of ID-tokens related to an identity that confirm that the identity stands in that place according to what has been measured in the environment.

There are several constructions known in the literature that can achieve anonymous biometric authentication. *Fuzzy sketches* and *fuzzy extractors* [15] are strategies to reconstruct, during the authentication phase, the biometric signal that was recorded during enrollment. A fuzzy extractor transforms a noisy, non-uniform biometric measurement into a uniform and reproducible sequence. A *Fuzzy Embedder* [9] links the biometric data with a binary string k, generated externally. When using *cancelable biometrics* [18] a distance-preserving one-way transformation is applied on the biometric data and the comparison between the enrollment sample and the authentication is performed in the encrypted domain. Breebaart, et al. [7] define security and privacy in the context of anonymous biometric authentication with the help of an ideal trusted biometric system. Simoens, et al.[20] formalize the concept of irreversibility and indistinguishability as privacy attributes for anonymous biometric systems.

7 Conclusion and Future Work

We have proposed and discussed an extension of Fuzzy Embbeder, that accepts contextual information as well as biometric input. A Fuzzy Embedder is a process used to obtain a stable digital encryption key from biometric data. This key can be used to authenticate the user afterwards. Usually the user authenticates himself, by re-generating the key with the provision of a new sample of his biometric. In our extension, the key depends also on the context; we call it contextual pseudo identity. To reproduce a contextual pseudo identity a user has to provide a new sample of the original biometric in the same context. We argue that the context can be modeled as a vector of natural numbers, which a mobile device can evince from the environment before starting the process of generating the user's pseudo identity. We study a way of combining biometrics and contextual information which preserve the reliability and security of the original Fuzzy Embedder. In this way, we prove that any context can be added to biometrics-based authentication.

The work presented here is a first step towards the goal to prove that the use of contextual pseudo identities plays a role in improving the socio-aspect of security at the level of authentication protocols. Intuitively, an attacker has to put in more effort if he wants to copy a contextual pseudo identity with respect to the effort required to reproduce an identity token generated from a PIN or a biometric only. Proving this intuition right, against a certain threat model, is left for future work. Another problem to be considered in future work is to prove that contextual pseudo-identities provide protection against the traceability of a user when he is authenticating himself to different ubiquitous services.

References

1. Anderson, R.: Security Engineering, 2nd edn. Wiley, Chichester (2007)
2. Bardram, J., Kjær, R.E., Pedersen, M.Ø.: Context-aware user authentication - supporting proximity-based login in pervasive computing. In: Dey, A.K., Schmidt, A., McCarthy, J.F. (eds.) UbiComp 2003. LNCS, vol. 2864, pp. 107–123. Springer, Heidelberg (2003)
3. Böhm, S., Koolwaaij, J., Souville, M.L., Wagner, B., Wibbels, M.: Introducing IYOUIT. In: Sheth, A.P., Staab, S., Dean, M., Paolucci, M., Maynard, D., Finin, T., Thirunarayan, K. (eds.) ISWC 2008. LNCS, vol. 5318, pp. 804–817. Springer, Heidelberg (2008)
4. Böhm, S., Koolwaaij, J., Luther, M.: Share whatever you like. In: Proc. of the 1st Int. DisCoTec Workshop on Context-aware Adaptation Mechanisms for Pervasive and Ubiquitous Services (CAMPUS 2008), Oslo, Norway, June 3, vol. 11. EASS (2008)
5. Bolle, R., Connell, J., Pankanti, S., Ratha, N., Senior, A.: Guide to Biometrics. Springer, Heidelberg (2003)
6. Brands, S., Chaum, D.: Distance-bounding protocols (extended abstract). In: Helleseth, T. (ed.) EUROCRYPT 1993. LNCS, vol. 765, pp. 344–359. Springer, Heidelberg (1994)

7. Breebaart, H., Yang, B., Buhan-Dulman, I., Busch, C.: Biometric Template Protection: The need of open standard. Datenschutz und Datensicherheit - DuD 33(5), 299–304 (2008)
8. Buhan, I., Doumen, J., Hartel, P., Tang, Q., Veldhuis, R.: Embedding renewable cryptographic keys into continuous noisy data. In: Chen, L., Ryan, M.D., Wang, G. (eds.) ICICS 2008. LNCS, vol. 5308, pp. 294–310. Springer, Heidelberg (2008)
9. Buhan, I., Doumen, J., Hartel, P., Tang, Q., Veldhuis, R.: Embedding renewable cryptographic keys into continuous noisy data. In: Chen, L., Ryan, M.D., Wang, G. (eds.) ICICS 2008. LNCS, vol. 5308, pp. 296–310. Springer, Heidelberg (2008)
10. Castelli, G., Mamei, M., Zambonelli, F.: Enginnering contextual information for pervasive multiagent systems. In: Weyns, D., Brueckner, S.A., Demazeau, Y. (eds.) EEMMAS 2007. LNCS (LNAI), vol. 5049, pp. 223–239. Springer, Heidelberg (2008)
11. Castelli, G., Rosi, A., Mamei, M., Zambonelli, F.: A simple model and infrastructure for context-aware browsing of the world. In: Proc. of the 5th Annual IEEE Conf. on Pervasive Computing and Communication (PERCOM 2007), White Plains, NY, USA, March 19-23, pp. 229–238. IEEE Computer Society, Los Alamitos (2007)
12. Desmedt, Y.: Major security problems with the "unforgeable" (Feige-)Fiat-Shamir proofs of identity and how to overcome them. In: Securicom 1988, 6th Worldwide Congress on Computer and Communications Security and Protection, pp. 147–159 (1988)
13. Dey, A.K.: Understanding and Using Context. Personal and Ubiquitous Conputating Journal 5(16), 4–7 (2001)
14. Dodis, Y., Reyzin, L., Smith, A.: Fuzzy extractors: How to generate strong keys from biometrics and other noisy data. In: Cachin, C., Camenisch, J.L. (eds.) EUROCRYPT 2004. LNCS, vol. 3027, pp. 523–540. Springer, Heidelberg (2004)
15. Dodis, Y., Reyzin, L., Smith, A.: Fuzzy extractors: How to generate strong keys from biometrics and other noisy data. In: Cachin, C., Camenisch, J.L. (eds.) EUROCRYPT 2004. LNCS, vol. 3027, pp. 523–540. Springer, Heidelberg (2004)
16. Gruteser, M., Grunwald, D.: Enhancing location privacy in wireless lan through disposable interface identifiers: a quantitative analysis. Mob. Netw. Appl. 10(3), 315–325 (2005)
17. Lenzini, G.: Design of architectures for proximity-aware services: Experiments in context-based authentication with subjective logic. Architecting Dependable Systems 5835, 284–307 (2009)
18. Ratha, N., Chikkerur, S., Connell, J.H., Bolle, R.: Generating cancelable fingerprint templates. IEEE Transactions on Pattern Analysis and Machine Intellingence 29(4) (April 2007)
19. Simoen, K., Tuyls, P., Preneel, B.: Privacy Weakenesses in Biometric Sketches. In: Proc. of the IEEE Symposium on Security and Privacy (S&P 2009), Oakland, California, USA, May 7-20, pp. 188–203. IEEE Computer Society, Los Alamitos (2009)
20. Simoens, K., Tuyls, P., Preneel, B.: Privacy weakness in biometric sketches. In: IEEE Symposium on Security and Privacy, Oakland, California, USA, pp. 188–203 (May 2009)

Author Index

GPSR Compliance

The European Union's (EU) General Product Safety Regulation (GPSR) is a set of rules that requires consumer products to be safe and our obligations to ensure this.

If you have any concerns about our products, you can contact us on ProductSafety@springernature.com

In case Publisher is established outside the EU, the EU authorized representative is:

Springer Nature Customer Service Center GmbH
Europaplatz 3
69115 Heidelberg, Germany

Batch number: 10712242

Printed by Printforce, the Netherlands